# AMERICA

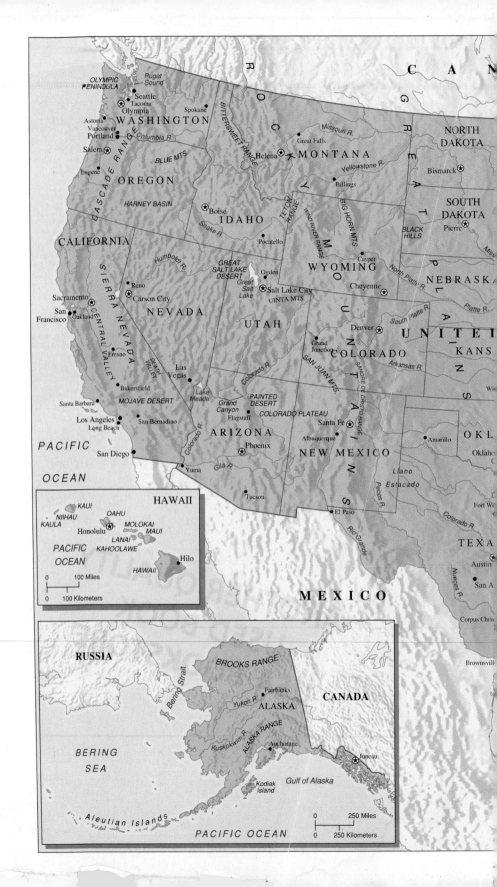

OLYMPIC PENINSULA
Puget Sound
Seattle
Tacoma
Olympia
Astoria
Vancouver
Portland
Salem
Eugene

WASHINGTON
Spokane
BITTERSWEET RANGE
CASCADE RANGE
Columbia R.
BLUE MTS.
OREGON
HARNEY BASIN

CALIFORNIA

Humboldt R.
SIERRA NEVADA
Reno
Carson City
Sacramento
San Francisco
Oakland
CENTRAL VALLEY
Fresno
DEATH VALLEY
NEVADA

Bakersfield
Santa Barbara
MOJAVE DESERT
Los Angeles
Long Beach
San Bernardino
San Diego
PACIFIC
OCEAN

ROC
K
C A N
GREAT

Great Falls
Missouri R.
Helena
MONTANA
Yellowstone R.
Billings

NORTH DAKOTA
Bismarck

SOUTH DAKOTA
Pierre
BLACK HILLS

Boise
Snake R.
IDAHO
Pocatello
TETON RANGE
WIND RIVER RANGE
BIG HORN MTS.

M
O
U
N
T
A
I
N
S

GREAT SALT LAKE DESERT
Ogden
Great Salt Lake
Salt Lake City
UINTA MTS.

Casper
WYOMING
Cheyenne
North Platte R.

GREAT
P L A I N S
NEBRASKA

UTAH

Las Vegas
Lake Meade
Grand Canyon
PAINTED DESERT
Flagstaff
COLORADO PLATEAU
ARIZONA
Phoenix
Colorado R.
Yuma
Gila R.

Colorado R.
Grand Junction
SAN JUAN MTS.
SANGRE DE CRISTO RANGE

COLORADO
Denver
South Platte R.
Platte R.
Arkansas R.

UNITED
KANSAS
W

Santa Fe
Albuquerque
NEW MEXICO
Amarillo
Llano Estacado
Pecos R.

OKLA
Oklaho
Fort W
Colorado R.

PACIFIC
OCEAN

HAWAII

KAUI
NIIHAU
KAULA
OAHU
Honolulu
MOLOKAI
LANAI
MAUI
KAHOOLAWE
PACIFIC
OCEAN
HAWAII
Hilo

0    100 Miles
0    100 Kilometers

El Paso
Rio Grande

TEXA
Austin
San A

Tucson

MEXICO

Corpus Chris

RUSSIA

BROOKS RANGE
Bering Strait
Fairbanks
Yukon R.
ALASKA
Kuskokwim R.
ALASKA RANGE
Anchorage
Juneau

CANADA
Brownsvill

BERING
SEA

Kodiak Island
Gulf of Alaska

Aleutian Islands

0    250 Miles
0    250 Kilometers

PACIFIC OCEAN

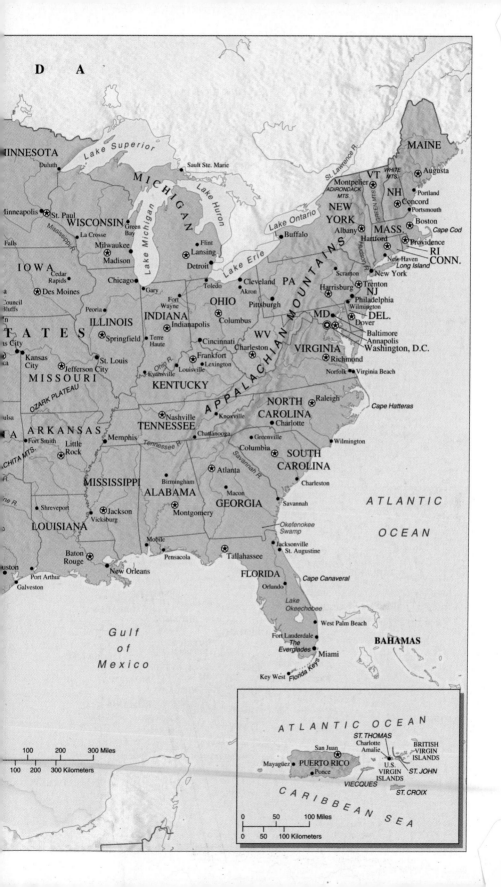

D A

MINNESOTA

Duluth

Lake Superior

Sault Ste. Marie

MICHIGAN

Lake Huron

MAINE

Augusta

WHITE MTS.

VT

Montpelier

ADIRONDACK MTS.

NH

Portland

Concord

Portsmouth

Minneapolis

St. Paul

WISCONSIN

Green Bay

Lake Michigan

NEW YORK

Albany

Boston

MASS.

Cape Cod

La Crosse

Milwaukee

Buffalo

Lake Ontario

Hartford

Providence

RI

Falls

Mississippi R.

Madison

Flint

Lansing

Lake Erie

CONN.

New Haven

Long Island

IOWA

Cedar Rapids

Chicago

Detroit

Cleveland

PA

Scranton

New York

Des Moines

Gary

Toledo

Akron

Harrisburg

Trenton

NJ

Council Bluffs

Peoria

Fort Wayne

OHIO

Pittsburgh

Philadelphia

Wilmington

ILLINOIS

INDIANA

Columbus

MD

DEL.

Dover

Springfield

Terre Haute

Indianapolis

Cincinnati

WV

Baltimore

Annapolis

Kansas City

Jefferson City

St. Louis

Frankfort

Lexington

Charleston

VIRGINIA

Washington, D.C.

MISSOURI

Evansville

Louisville

Ohio R.

Richmond

KENTUCKY

Norfolk

Virginia Beach

OZARK PLATEAU

Nashville

Knoxville

NORTH CAROLINA

Raleigh

Cape Hatteras

Tulsa

ARKANSAS

TENNESSEE

Chattanooga

Charlotte

Fort Smith

Little Rock

Memphis

Tennessee R.

Greenville

Wilmington

OUACHITA MTS.

Columbia

SOUTH CAROLINA

MISSISSIPPI

Birmingham

Atlanta

Charleston

ALABAMA

Macon

GEORGIA

Savannah

ATLANTIC

Shreveport

Jackson

Vicksburg

Montgomery

OCEAN

LOUISIANA

Mobile

Okefenokee Swamp

ine R.

Baton Rouge

Pensacola

Tallahassee

Jacksonville

St. Augustine

ouston

New Orleans

FLORIDA

Cape Canaveral

Port Arthur

Galveston

Orlando

Lake Okeechobee

Gulf

of

Mexico

West Palm Beach

BAHAMAS

Fort Lauderdale

The Everglades

Miami

Key West

Florida Keys

100   200   300 Miles

100   200   300 Kilometers

ATLANTIC OCEAN

ST. THOMAS

Charlotte Amalie

BRITISH VIRGIN ISLANDS

San Juan

Mayagüez

PUERTO RICO

U.S. VIRGIN ISLANDS

ST. JOHN

Ponce

VIECQUES

ST. CROIX

CARIBBEAN SEA

0   50   100 Miles

0   50   100 Kilometers

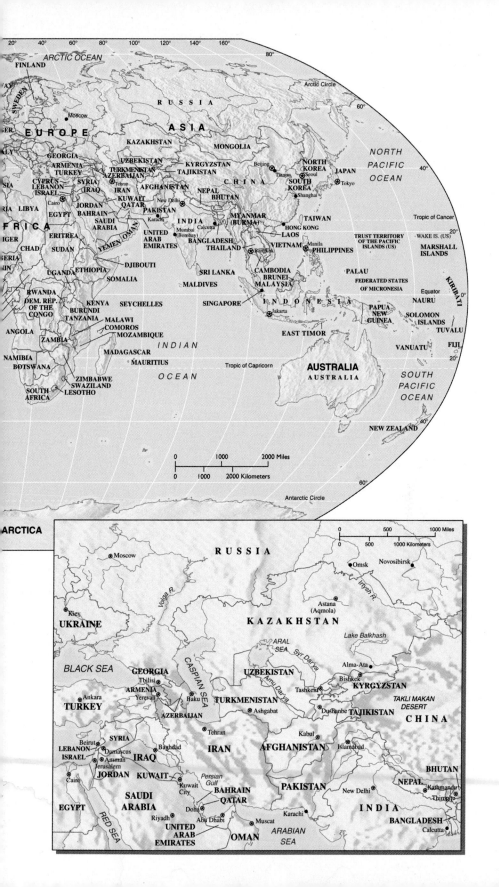

# AMERICA

## A NARRATIVE HISTORY

*Ninth Edition*

### VOLUME 2

GEORGE BROWN TINDALL

DAVID EMORY SHI

W · W · NORTON & COMPANY · NEW YORK · LONDON

W. W. Norton & Company has been independent since its founding in 1923,
when William Warder Norton and Mary D. Herter Norton first published
lectures delivered at the People's Institute, the adult education division of
New York City's Cooper Union. The firm soon expanded its program beyond
the Institute, publishing books by celebrated academics from America
and abroad. By mid-century, the two major pillars of Norton's publishing
program—trade books and college texts—were firmly established. In the 1950s,
the Norton family transferred control of the company to its employees, and
today—with a staff of four hundred and a comparable number of trade, college, and professional titles published each year—W. W. Norton & Company
stands as the largest and oldest publishing house owned wholly by its employees.

Editor: Jon Durbin
Project editors: Kate Feighery and Melissa Atkin
Electronic media editor: Steve Hoge
Associate media editor: Lorraine Klimowich
Assistant editor: Justin Cahill
Editorial assistant, media: Stefani Wallace
Marketing manager, History: Heather Arteaga
Production manager: Ashley Horna
Photo editor: Stephanie Romeo
Composition: Jouve International-Brattleboro, VT
Manufacturing: Quad/Graphics-Taunton, MA

Library of Congress Cataloging-in-Publication Data

Tindall, George Brown.
    America : a narrative history / George Brown Tindall,
David Emory Shi.—9th ed.
        p.    cm.
    Includes bibliographical references and index.
    ISBN 978-0-393-91262-3 (hardcover)
    1. United States—History—Textbooks.    I. Shi, David E.    II. Title.

E178.1.T55 2013                                         2012034504
973—dc23

ISBN This Edition: 978-0-393-91264-7

W. W. Norton & Company, Inc., 500 Fifth Avenue, New York, NY 10110-0017
wwnorton.com

W. W. Norton & Company Ltd., Castle House, 75/76 Wells Street, London W1T 3QT

1 2 3 4 5 6 7 8 9 0

FOR BRUCE AND SUSAN
AND FOR BLAIR

---

FOR
JASON AND JESSICA

**GEORGE B. TINDALL** recently of the University of North Carolina, Chapel Hill, was an award-winning historian of the South with a number of major books to his credit, including *The Emergence of the New South, 1913–1945* and *The Disruption of the Solid South.*

**DAVID E. SHI** is a professor of history and the president emeritus of Furman University. He is the author of several books on American cultural history, including the award-winning *The Simple Life: Plain Living and High Thinking in American Culture* and *Facing Facts: Realism in American Thought and Culture, 1850–1920.*

# CONTENTS

# *Part Six* / MODERN AMERICA

# *Part Seven* / THE AMERICAN AGE

# MAPS

# PREFACE

This edition of *America: A Narrative History* includes the most substantial changes since I partnered with George Tindall in 1984, but I have been diligent to sustain his steadfast commitment to a textbook grounded in a compelling narrative history of the American experience. From the start of our collaboration, we strove to write a book animated by colorful characters, informed by balanced analysis and social texture, and guided by the unfolding of key events. Those classic principles, combined with a handy format and low price, have helped make *America: A Narrative History* one of the most popular and well-respected American history textbooks.

This Ninth Edition of *America* features a number of important changes designed to make the text more teachable and classroom-friendly. Chief among them are major structural changes, including the joining of several chapters to reduce the overall number from thirty-seven to thirty-four, as well as the re-sequencing of several chapters to make the narrative flow more smoothly for students. Major organizational changes include:

- New Chapter 4, *From Colonies to States*, combines *The Imperial Perspective* and *From Empire to Independence* from previous editions to better integrate the events leading up to the American Revolution.
- New Chapter 9, *The Dynamics of Growth*, now leads off Part III, *An Expansive Nation*, to first introduce the industrial revolution and the growth of the market economy before turning to major political, social, and cultural developments.
- New Chapter 12, *The Old South*, has been moved up, now appearing between the chapters on the Jacksonian era and the American Renaissance, in order to foreground the importance of slavery as a major issue during this period.

- *From Isolation to Global War*, a chapter from previous editions, has been broken up, and its parts redistributed to new Chapter 26, *Republican Resurgence and Decline*, and new Chapter 28, *The Second World War*, in order to better integrate the coverage of domestic politics and international relations during this period.
- New Chapter 30, *The 1950s: Affluence and Anxiety in an Atomic Age*, combines *Through the Picture Window* and *Conflict and Deadlock: The Eisenhower Years* from the previous editions to better show the relationship between political, social, and cultural developments during the 1950s.

In terms of content changes, the overarching theme of the new edition is the importance of African-American history. While African-American history has always been a central part of the book's narrative, this Ninth Edition features enhanced and fully up-to-date treatment based on the best recent scholarship in African-American history, including African slavery, slavery in America during the colonial era and revolutionary war, the slave trade in the South, slave rebellions, the practical challenges faced by slaves liberated during the Civil War, the Wilmington Riot of 1898, in which an elected city government made up of blacks was ousted by armed violence, President Woodrow Wilson's segregationist views and policies, the Harlem Renaissance, the Double V Campaign during World War II, and the Freedom Summer of 1964.

Of course, as in every new edition, there is new material related to contemporary America—the first term of the Barack Obama administration, the killing of al Qaeda leader Osama bin Laden, and the emergence of the Tea Party and the Occupy Wall Street movements—as well as the stagnant economy in the aftermath of the Great Recession. In addition, I have incorporated fresh insights from important new scholarly works dealing with many significant topics throughout this new edition.

*America*'s **New Student Resources** are designed to make students better readers. New, carefully crafted pedagogical features have been added to the Ninth Edition to further guide students through the narrative.

- **Focus questions, chapter summaries**, and new **bold-face key terms** work together seamlessly to highlight core content. The chapters are enhanced with easy-to-read full-color maps and chapter chronologies.
- New **Author Videos** feature David Shi explaining major developments in American history. Each of the 42 video segments includes additional media, such as illustrations and maps, to enhance the learning experience.

- New "**Critical Reading Exercises**," tied directly to the Ninth Edition, help students learn how to read the textbook. Students are guided through a series of exercises to identify the most important information from select passages in each chapter.

- New **Cross-Chapter Quizzes** in the Norton Coursepacks are designed to help students prepare for midterm and final examinations by challenging them to think across periods, to trace longer-term developments, and to make connections and comparisons.

- A new edition of ***For the Record: A Documentary History of America***, by David E. Shi and Holly A. Mayer (Duquesne University), is the perfect companion reader for *America: A Narrative History*. The new Fifth Edition has been brought into closer alignment with the main text. *For the Record* now has 250 primary-source readings from diaries, journals, newspaper articles, speeches, government documents, and novels, including a number of readings that highlight the substantially updated theme of African-American history in this new edition of *America*. If you haven't looked at *For the Record* in a while, now would be a good time to take a look.

- New **Norton Mix: American History** enables instructors to build their own custom reader from a database of nearly 300 primary and secondary source selections. The custom readings can be packaged as a standalone reader or integrated with chapters from *America* into a custom textbook.

- *America: A Narrative History* **StudySpace** (wwnorton.com/web /america9) provides a proven assignment-driven plan for each chapter. In addition to the new "Critical Reading Exercises" and new "Author Videos," highlights include focus questions, learning objectives, chapter outlines, quizzes, iMaps and new iMap quizzes, map worksheets, flashcards, interactive timelines, and "U.S. History Tours" powered by Google Earth map technology. There are also several hundred multimedia primary-source selections—including documents, images, and audio and video clips—grouped by topic to aid research and writing.

*America's* **New Instructor Resources** are designed to provide additional resources that will enable more dynamic classroom lectures:

- New **Norton American History Digital Archive** disks on African-American history are the eighth and ninth disks in this extraordinary collection of digital resources for classroom lecture. The 2 new disks come with nearly

400 selections from African-American history, including illustrations, photographs and audio and video clips.

- New **PowerPoint Lectures with dynamic Author Videos**. Replete with every image and map from the textbook, the *America* Ninth Edition **PowerPoints** now also feature the new **Author Videos**. These classroom-ready presentations can be used as lecture launchers or as video summaries of major issues and developments in American history.

- New enhanced **Coursepack** integrates all **StudySpace** content with these handy features and materials: 1) *Forum Questions* designed for online and hybrid courses; 2) *Critical Reading Exercises* that report to your LMS Gradebook; 3) *Cross-Chapter Quizzes* for each half of the survey course.

- The **Instructor's Manual and Test Bank**, by Mark Goldman (Tallahassee Community College), Michael Krysko (Kansas State University), and Brian McKnight (UVA, Wise), includes a test bank of multiple-choice, short-answer, and essay questions, as well as detailed chapter outlines, lecture suggestions, and bibliographies.

It's clear why *America* continues to set the standard when it comes to providing a low-cost book with high-value content. Your students will buy it because it's so affordable, and they'll read it because the narrative is so engaging!

# ACKNOWLEDGMENTS

In preparing the Ninth Edition, I have benefited from the insights and suggestions of many people. Some of those insights have come from student readers of the text, and I encourage such feedback. I'd particularly like to thank Eirlys Barker, who has worked on much of the new StudySpace content, Laura Farkas (Wake Technical College), who has created the wonderful new "Critical Reading Exercises," and I'd like to give special thanks to Brandon Franke (Blinn College, Bryan) for his work on the new PowerPoint lectures. Finally, many thanks to Mark Goldman, Michael Krysko, and Brian McKnight for their efforts on the Instructor's Manual and Test Bank.

Numerous scholars and survey instructors advised me on the new edition: Eirlys Barker (Thomas Nelson Community College), Blanche Bricke (Blinn College), Michael Collins (Midwestern State University), Scott Cook (Motlow State Community College), Carl Creasman, Jr. (Valencia College), Stephen Davis (Lone Star College), Susan Dollar (Northwestern State University of Louisiana), Alicia Duffy (University of Central Florida), Laura Farkas (Wake Technical Community College), Jane Flaherty (Texas A&M University), Brandon Franke (Blinn College), Mark Goldman (Tallahassee Community College), James Good (Lone Star College), Barbara Green (Wright State University), D. Harland Hagler (University of North Texas), Michael Harkins (Harper College), Carolyn Hoffman (Prince George's Community College), Marc Horger (Ohio State University), Michael Krivdo (Texas A&M University), Margaret Lambert (Lone Star College), Pat Ledbetter (North Central Texas College), Stephen Lopez (San Jacinto College), Barry Malone (Wake Technical Community College), Dee Mckinney (East Georgia College), Lisa Morales (North Central Texas College), Robert Outland III (Louisiana State University), Catherine Parzynski (Montgomery County Community College), Robert Lynn Rainard (Tidewater Community College), Edward Duke Richey (University of North Texas), Stuart Smith III

(Germanna Community College), Roger Tate (Somerset Community College), Kyle Volk (University of Montana), Vernon Volpe (University of Nebraska), Heidi Weber (SUNY Orange), Cecil Edward Weller, Jr. (San Jacinto College), and Margarita Youngo (Pima Community College).

Once again, I thank my friends at W. W. Norton for their consummate professionalism and good cheer, especially Jon Durbin, Justin Cahill, Steve Hoge, Melissa Atkin, Kate Feighery, Lorraine Klimowich, Stephanie Romeo, Debra Morton-Hoyt, Ashley Horna, Heather Arteaga, Julie Sindel, and Tamara McNeill.

# AMERICA

# 17

# RECONSTRUCTION: NORTH AND SOUTH

## FOCUS QUESTIONS

Ⓢ  wwnorton.com/studyspace

- What were the different approaches to the Reconstruction of the Confederate states?
- How did white southerners respond to the end of the old order in the South?
- To what extent did blacks function as citizens in the reconstructed South?
- What were the main issues in national politics in the 1870s?
- Why did Reconstruction end in 1877?

In the spring of 1865, the Civil War was finally over. At a frightful cost of 620,000 lives and the destruction of the southern economy and much of its landscape, the Union had emerged triumphant, and some 4 million enslaved Americans had seized their freedom. The ratification of the Thirteenth Amendment in December 1865 abolished slavery everywhere. Now the nation faced the daunting task of reuniting. A civil war fought by the North to save the Union had become a transforming social force. The abolition of slavery, the war-related disruptions to the economy, and the horrifying human losses suffered during the war had destroyed the plantation system and upended racial relations in the South. The defeated Confederacy now had to come to terms with a new order as the United States set about "reconstructing" a ravaged and often resentful South. The era of Reconstruction, from 1865 to 1877, was a period of political complexity and social turbulence that generated far-reaching implications for American life. It witnessed a prolonged debate about issues of enduring significance, questions about the nature of freedom, equality, and opportunity. By far the most important of those questions was the fate of African Americans.

The Union could not have been saved without the help of the blacks, but what would be their status in the postwar era?

## THE WAR'S AFTERMATH

In the war's aftermath the victors confronted difficult questions: How should the United States be reunited? What was the status of the states that had seceded? Should the Confederate leaders be tried for treason? Should former Confederates automatically have their U.S. citizenship restored? How should new governments be formed in the South? How and at whose expense was the South's economy to be rebuilt? Should debts incurred by the Confederate state governments be honored? Who should pay to rebuild the South's railroads and public buildings, dredge the clogged southern harbors, and restore damaged levees? What was to be done for the freed slaves? Were they to be given land? social equality? education? voting rights?

Such complex questions required sober reflection and careful planning, but policy makers did not have the luxury of time or the benefit of consensus. Some northerners wanted the former Confederate states returned to the Union with little or no changes in the region's social, political, and economic life. Others wanted southern society punished and transformed. The editors of the nation's foremost magazine, *Harper's Weekly*, expressed this vengeful attitude when they declared at the end of 1865 that "the forgive-and-forget policy . . . is mere political insanity and suicide."

**DEVELOPMENT IN THE NORTH**   To some Americans the Civil War had been more truly a social revolution than the War of Independence, for it reduced the once-dominant influence of the South's planter elite in national politics and elevated the power of the northern "captains of industry." During and after the Civil War, the U.S. government grew increasingly aligned with the interests of corporate leaders. The wartime Republican Congress had delivered on the party's major platform promises of 1860. In the absence of southern members, the wartime Congress had centralized national power and enacted the Republican economic agenda. It passed the Morrill Tariff, which doubled the average level of import duties. The National Banking Act created a uniform system of banking and banknote currency and helped finance the war. Congress also decided that the first transcontinental railroad would run along a north-central route, from Omaha, Nebraska, to Sacramento, California, and it donated public land and sold bonds to ensure its financing. In the Homestead Act of 1862, moreover, Congress provided free federal homesteads of 160 acres to settlers, who had only to occupy the land for five years to gain title. No cash was needed. The Morrill Land Grant Act of the same year conveyed to each state 30,000 acres of federal land per member of Congress from the state. The sale of some of the land provided funds to create colleges of "agriculture and mechanic arts." Such measures helped stimulate the North's economy in the years after the Civil War.

**DEVASTATION IN THE SOUTH**   The postwar South offered a sharp contrast to the victorious North. Along the path of General William Tecumseh Sherman's Union army, one observer reported in 1866, the countryside "looked for many miles like a broad black streak of ruin and desolation." Burned-out Columbia, South Carolina, said another witness, was "a wilderness of ruins"; Charleston, a place of "vacant houses, of widowed women, of rotting wharves, of deserted warehouses, of weed-wild gardens, of miles of grass-grown streets, of acres of pitiful and voiceless barrenness."

Throughout the South, property values had collapsed. Confederate bonds and paper money were worthless; most railroads were damaged or destroyed. Cotton that had escaped destruction was seized by federal troops. Emancipation

**A street in the "burned district"**

Ruins of Richmond, Virginia, in the spring of 1865.

wiped out $4 billion invested in human flesh and left the labor system in disarray. The great age of expansion in the cotton market was over. Not until 1879 would the cotton crop again equal the record harvest of 1860; tobacco production did not regain its prewar level until 1880; the sugar crop of Louisiana did not recover until 1893; and the old rice industry along the coast of South Carolina and Georgia never regained its prewar levels of production or profit.

For many southerners, the emotional devastation caused by the war was worse than the physical destruction. Many families had lost sons and husbands; other war veterans returned with one or more limbs missing. Few families were untouched by the war, and most Confederates resented the humiliation of military occupation. The scars felt by a war-damaged, land-proud South would take time to heal, a very long time.

**A TRANSFORMED SOUTH**    The defeat of the Confederacy transformed much of southern society. The freeing of slaves, the destruction of property, and the collapse of land values left many planters destitute and homeless. Amanda Worthington, a planter's wife from Mississippi, saw her whole world destroyed. In the fall of 1865, she assessed the damage: "None of us can realize that we are no longer wealthy—yet thanks to the Yankees, the cause of all unhappiness, such is the case." Union soldiers who fanned out across the defeated South to impose order were cursed and spat upon. A Virginia woman expressed a spirited defiance common among her circle of friends: "Every day, every hour, that I live increases my hatred and detestation, and loathing of that race. They [Yankees] disgrace our common humanity. As a people I consider them vastly inferior to the better classes of our slaves." Fervent southern nationalists, both men and women, implanted in their children a similar hatred of Yankees and a defiance of northern rule. One mother said that she trained her children to "fear God, love the South, and live to avenge her."

**LEGALLY FREE, SOCIALLY BOUND**    In the former Confederate states, the newly freed slaves often suffered most of all. They were no longer slaves, but were they citizens? After all, the U.S. Supreme Court in the *Dred Scott* decision (1858) had declared that enslaved Africans and their descendants were not eligible for citizenship. Abraham Lincoln's Emancipation Proclamation of 1863 implied that former slaves would become U.S. citizens, but citizenship was then defined and protected by *state* law, and the southern states in 1865 did not have state governments. The process of forming new state governments required first deciding the official status of the seceded states: Were they now conquered territories? If so, then the Congress had the authority to recreate their state governments. But what if it were decided, as Lincoln argued, that the former Confederate states had never officially left the Union because the act of secession was itself illegal? In that circumstance, the process of re-forming state governments would fall within the jurisdiction of the executive branch and the citizens of the states.

Adding to the political confusion was the need to help the former slaves, most of whom had no land, no home, and no food. A few northerners argued that what the ex-slaves needed most was their own land. A New Englander traveling in the postwar South noted that the "sole ambition of the freedman" was ". . . to become the owner of a little piece of land, there to erect a humble home, and to dwell in peace and security at his own free will and pleasure." In coastal South Carolina and in Mississippi, former slaves had been "given" land by Union armies after they had taken control of Confederate areas during the war. But such transfers of white-owned property to former slaves were reversed during 1865. Even northern abolitionists balked at proposals to confiscate white-owned land and distribute it to the freed slaves. Citizenship and legal rights were one thing, wholesale confiscation of property and land redistribution quite another. Nonetheless, discussions of land distribution fueled false rumors that freed slaves would get "forty acres and a mule," a slogan that swept across the South at the end of the war. Instead of land or material help, the freed slaves more often got advice about proper behavior.

In July 1865, hundreds of freed blacks gathered near an old church on St. Helena Island off the South Carolina coast. There, Martin Delaney, a major in the 104th U.S. Colored Troops, addressed them. Before the Civil War, he had been a free black and a prominent abolitionist in the North. Now he was speaking to former slaves about their future. He began by assuring the gathering that slavery had indeed been "absolutely abolished." But abolition, he stressed, was less the result of Abraham Lincoln's leadership than it was the outcome of former slaves and free blacks like him deciding to resist and undermine the Confederacy. "We would not have become free," Delaney insisted, "had we not armed ourselves and fought for our independence." He then turned to the economic plight of the freed slaves, noting that many of the white planters were claiming that former slaves were lazy and "have not the intelligence to get on for yourselves without being guided and driven to the work by overseers." Delaney dismissed such assumptions as lies intended to restore a system of forced labor. He then told the freed slaves that their best hope was to become self-sustaining farmers: "Get a community and get all the lands you can—if you cannot get any singly." Then "grow as much vegetables etc., as you want for your families; on the other part of land you cultivate rice and cotton." Doing so would free the former slaves from continuing dependence on whites. If they could not find enough money to buy land, he suggested, then they should work out an arrangement to cultivate land owned by others in exchange for a share of the crop. Whatever method they chose, Delaney stressed, they must find ways to become economically self-reliant. Otherwise, they would find themselves slaves again.

**Major Martin Delaney**

Delaney exhorted former slaves to achieve self-sufficiency.

When Major Delaney concluded his remarks, the crowd's "excitement was immense," said an observer. The former slaves cheered his emphasis on their gaining economic independence. One of them said that Delaney "was the only man who ever told [us] the truth." Another freedman pledged that he and the others were determined to "get rid of the Yankee employer"—men who were being paid by the federal government to cultivate cotton on abandoned plantations during the Civil War. Most of the former slaves at the gathering shared the determination of another freedman who declared that the white planters would "have to work themselves or starve or leave the country—we will not work for them anymore." Several white planters were in the audience when Major Delaney spoke, and an army officer at the scene reported that they "listened with horror depicted in their faces" when Delaney urged the former slaves to rid themselves of their dependence on their former white owners. The planters predicted that such speeches would incite "open rebellion" among the southern blacks. Equally concerned were two white federal army officers sent to monitor Major Delaney's remarks. One of them observed that Delaney struck him as "a thorough hater of the White race" who urged the former slaves "not to work for any man, but for themselves." According to the officer's report, Delaney's message contradicted the federal government's official policy that "all the [freed]men should be employed by their former masters as far as possible." Even more worrisome was that Delaney seemed to encourage the possible use of force by African Americans in the postwar South. His "mention of having two hundred thousands [of black] men [in the federal army] well drilled in arms—does he not hint to them what to do? If they should be compelled to work for [white] employers?"

THE FREEDMEN'S BUREAU   The gathering at St. Helena Island revealed the complexity and volatility of the uncertain situation facing former slaves. Would the freed blacks work for white planters? What would happen to the cotton economy if the former slaves focused on subsistence farming, growing corn and beans for food rather than cotton for profit? How would the former slaves gain access to any cash if they could hardly grow enough food to subsist on? It fell to the federal government to provide answers to such thorny questions.

On March 3, 1865, while the war was still raging, Congress created within the War Department the Bureau of Refugees, Freedmen, and Abandoned Lands to provide "such issues of provisions, clothing, and fuel" as might be needed to relieve "destitute and suffering refugees and freedmen and their wives and children." It was the first federal experiment in social welfare, albeit temporary. In May 1865, General Oliver O. Howard, commissioner of what came to be called the **Freedmen's Bureau**, declared that freed slaves "must be free to choose their own employers, and be paid for their labor." He sent Freedmen's Bureau agents to the South to negotiate labor contracts (something new for both blacks and white planters), provide medical care, distribute food, and set up schools. The bureau organized its own courts to deal with labor disputes and land titles, and its agents were authorized to supervise trials involving blacks in other courts.

The intensity of racial prejudice in the South often thwarted the efforts of Freedmen's Bureau agents—as well as federal troops—to protect and assist the former slaves. In late June 1865, for example, a white planter in the low country of South Carolina, near Charleston, signed a contract with sixty-five of his former slaves calling for them to "attend & cultivate" his fields "according to the usual system of planting rice & provision lands, and to conform to all reasonable rules & regulations as may be prescribed" by the white owner. In exchange, the workers would receive "half of the crop raised after having deducted the seed of rice, corn, peas & potatoes." Any workers who violated the terms of the contract could be evicted from the plantation, leaving them jobless and homeless. A federal army officer who witnessed the contract reported that he expected "more trouble on this place than any other on the river." Another officer objected to the contract's provision that the owner could require workers to cut wood or dig ditches without compensation. But most worrisome was that the contract essentially enslaved the

**Freedmen's school in Virginia**

Throughout the former Confederate states, the Freedmen's Bureau set up schools for former slaves, such as this one.

workers because no matter "how much they are abused, they cannot leave without permission of the owner." If they chose to leave, they would forfeit any right to a portion of the crop. Across the former Confederacy at the end of the war, it was evident that the former white economic elite was determined to continue to control and constrain African Americans.

## THE BATTLE OVER POLITICAL RECONSTRUCTION

The question of how to reconstruct the South's political structure centered on deciding which governments would constitute authority in the defeated states. As Union forces advanced into the Confederacy during the Civil War, President Lincoln in 1862 had named military governors for conquered Tennessee, Arkansas, and Louisiana. By the end of the following year, he had formulated a plan for regular governments in those states and any others that might be liberated from Confederate rule.

LINCOLN'S PLAN AND CONGRESS'S RESPONSE    In late 1863, President Lincoln had issued a Proclamation of Amnesty and Reconstruction, under which any former Rebel state could form a Union government whenever a number equal to 10 percent of those who had voted in 1860 took an oath of allegiance to the Constitution and the Union and had received a presidential pardon. Participants also had to swear support for laws and proclamations dealing with emancipation. Certain groups, however, were excluded from the pardon: Confederate officials; senior officers of the Confederate army and navy; judges, congressmen, and military officers of the United States who had left their federal posts to aid the rebellion; and those accused of failure to treat captured African American soldiers and their officers as prisoners of war.

Under this plan, governments loyal to the Union appeared in Tennessee, Arkansas, and Louisiana during the war, but Congress recognized neither their representatives nor their electoral votes in the 1864 presidential election. In the absence of specific provisions for Reconstruction in the Constitution, politicians disagreed as to where authority to restore Rebel states properly rested. Lincoln claimed the right to direct Reconstruction under the clause that set forth the presidential power to grant pardons and under the constitutional obligation of the United States to guarantee each state a republican form of government. Many Republican congressmen, however, argued that this obligation implied that Congress, not the president, should supervise Reconstruction.

A few conservative and most moderate Republicans supported Lincoln's program of immediate restoration. The small but influential group of Radical Republicans, however, favored a sweeping transformation of southern society based upon granting freed slaves full-fledged citizenship. The Radicals hoped to reconstruct southern society so as to dismantle the planter elite and the Democratic party.

The Radical Republicans were talented, earnest legislators who insisted that Congress control the Reconstruction program. To this end, in 1864 they helped pass the Wade-Davis Bill, sponsored by Senator Benjamin Franklin Wade of Ohio and Representative Henry Winter Davis of Maryland. In contrast to Lincoln's 10 percent plan, the Wade-Davis Bill would have required that a majority of white male citizens declare their allegiance and that only those who could take an "ironclad" oath (required of federal officials since 1862) attesting to their *past* loyalty could vote or serve in the state constitutional conventions. The conventions, moreover, would have to abolish slavery, exclude from political rights high-ranking civil and military officers of the Confederacy, and repudiate debts incurred during the conflict.

Passed during the closing day of the session, the Wade-Davis Bill never became law: Lincoln vetoed it. In retaliation, furious Republicans penned the Wade-Davis Manifesto, which accused the president of exceeding his constitutional authority. Lincoln offered his last view of Reconstruction in his final public address, on April 11, 1865. Speaking from the White House balcony, he pronounced that the Confederate states had never left the Union. Those states were simply "out of their proper practical relation with the Union," and the object was to get them back "into their proper practical relation." At a cabinet meeting, Lincoln proposed the creation of new southern state governments before Congress met in December. He shunned the vindictiveness of the Radicals. He wanted "no persecution, no bloody work," no radical restructuring of southern social and economic life.

## THE ASSASSINATION OF LINCOLN

On the evening of April 14, 1865, less than a week after Robert E. Lee surrendered his Confederate army, Abraham Lincoln and his wife Mary went to see a play at Ford's Theatre in Washington, D.C. With his trusted bodyguard called away to Richmond and the policeman assigned to his theater box away from his post, Lincoln was defenseless as **John Wilkes Booth** slipped into the unguarded presidential box. Booth, a prominent actor and Confederate sympathizer, fired his pistol point-blank at the back of the president's head. As the president slumped forward, Booth pulled out a knife, stabbed Lincoln's aide, and jumped from the box to the stage, breaking his leg in the process. He then mounted a waiting horse and fled the city. The president died the following morning. Accomplices of Booth had simultaneously targeted Vice President **Andrew Johnson** and Secretary of State William H. Seward. Seward and four others, including his son, were victims of severe knife wounds. Johnson escaped injury, however, because his would-be assassin got cold feet and wound up tipsy in the barroom of the vice president's hotel. Booth was pursued into Virginia and killed in a burning barn. Three of his collaborators were convicted by a military court and hanged, along with Mary Surratt, at whose boardinghouse they had plotted.

Lincoln's death stunned the nation. The outpouring of grief was overwhelming. General Ulysses S. Grant observed that Lincoln "was incontestably the greatest man I ever knew." Lincoln's body lay in state for several days in Washington, D.C., before being transported by train on April 21 for burial in Springfield, Illinois. Along the way, the coffin was made available for people to view. In Philadelphia, three hundred thousand mourners paid their last respects. In New York City, the coffin was placed in the City Hall

**Paying respect**

The only photograph of the late Lincoln in his coffin, displayed here in New York's City Hall rotunda.

rotunda, visited by five hundred thousand people. The coffin was then paraded through Manhattan to the Hudson River Railway Terminal. One of the spectators was six-year-old Theodore Roosevelt. On May 4, Lincoln was laid to rest in Springfield.

JOHNSON'S PLAN    Lincoln's death elevated to the White House Andrew Johnson of Tennessee, a combative man who lacked most presidential virtues. Johnson was provincial and bigoted—he harbored fierce prejudices. He was also short-tempered and impetuous. At the inaugural ceremonies in early 1865, he had delivered his vice-presidential address in a state of slurring drunkenness that embarrassed Lincoln and the nation. Johnson was a war (pro-Union) Democrat who had been put on the National Union ticket in 1864 as a gesture of unity. Of origins as humble as Lincoln's, Johnson was an orphan who had moved as a youth from his birthplace in Raleigh, North Carolina, to Greeneville, Tennessee, where he became the proprietor of a tailor shop. Self-educated with the help of his wife, he had served as mayor, congressman, governor, and senator, then as the Unionist military governor of Tennessee before he became vice president. In the process, he had become an advocate of the small farmers in opposition to the privileges of the large planters—"a bloated, corrupted aristocracy." He also shared the racist attitudes of most white yeomen. "Damn the negroes," he exclaimed to a friend during the war, "I am fighting those traitorous aristocrats, their masters."

Some Radicals at first thought Johnson, unlike Lincoln, to be one of them. Johnson had, for example, once asserted that treason "must be made infamous and traitors must be impoverished." Senator Benjamin Wade loved such vengeful language. "Johnson, we have faith in you," he promised. "By the gods, there will be no trouble now in running this government." But Wade would soon find Johnson as unsympathetic as Lincoln, if for different reasons.

Johnson's loyalty to the Union sprang from a strict adherence to the Constitution and a fervent belief in limited government. When discussing what to do with the former Confederate states, Johnson preferred the term *restoration* to *reconstruction*. In 1865, he declared that "there is no such thing as reconstruction. Those States have not gone out of the Union. Therefore reconstruction is unnecessary." Like many other whites, he also opposed the growing Radical sentiment to grant the vote to African Americans.

**Andrew Johnson**

A pro-Union Democrat from Tennessee.

Johnson's plan to restore the Union thus closely resembled Lincoln's. A new Proclamation of Amnesty, issued in May 1865, excluded not only those Lincoln had barred from pardon but also everybody with taxable property worth more than $20,000. Those wealthy planters, bankers, and merchants were the people Johnson believed had led the South to secede. They were allowed to make special applications for pardon directly to the president, and before the year was out Johnson had issued some thirteen thousand pardons.

Johnson followed up his amnesty proclamation with his own plan for readmitting the former Confederate states. In each state, a native Unionist became provisional governor, with authority to call a convention of men elected by loyal voters. Lincoln's 10 percent requirement was omitted. Johnson called upon the state conventions to invalidate the secession ordinances, abolish slavery, and repudiate all debts incurred to aid the Confederacy. Each state, moreover, had to ratify the Thirteenth Amendment ending slavery. In his final public address, Lincoln had endorsed a limited black suffrage. Johnson repeated Lincoln's advice. He reminded the provisional governor of Mississippi, for example, that the state conventions might "with perfect safety" extend suffrage to African Americans with education or with military service so as to "disarm the adversary," the adversary being "radicals who are wild upon" giving all African Americans the right to vote.

The state conventions for the most part met Johnson's requirements. But Carl Schurz, a German immigrant and war hero who became a prominent Missouri politician, found during a visit to the South "an *utter absence of national feeling* . . . and a desire to preserve slavery . . . as much and as long as possible." Southern whites had accepted the situation because they thought so little had changed after all. Emboldened by Johnson's indulgence, they ignored his pleas for moderation and conciliation. Suggestions of black suffrage were scarcely raised in the state conventions and promptly squelched when they were.

SOUTHERN INTRANSIGENCE    When Congress met in December 1865, for the first time since the end of the war it faced the fact that the new state governments in the postwar South were remarkably like the old Confederate ones. Southern voters had acted with extreme disregard for northern feelings. Among the new members presenting themselves to Congress were Georgia's Alexander Stephens, former vice president of the Confederacy, now claiming a seat in the Senate; four Confederate generals; eight colonels; and six cabinet members. Congress forthwith denied seats to all such officials. It was too much to expect, after four bloody years, that the Unionists in Congress would welcome back ex-Confederate leaders.

Furthermore, the new all-white southern state legislatures, in passing repressive "**black codes**" designed to restrict the freedom of African Americans, demonstrated that they intended to preserve slavery as nearly as possible. As one white southerner stressed, "The ex-slave was not a free man; he was a free Negro," and the black codes were intended to highlight the distinction.

The black codes varied from state to state, but some provisions were common in many of them. Existing marriages, including common-law marriages, were recognized (although interracial marriages were prohibited), and testimony of blacks was accepted in legal cases involving blacks—and in six states in all cases. Blacks could own property. They could sue and be sued in the courts. On the other hand, they could not own farmland in Mississippi or city lots in South Carolina; they were required to buy special licenses to practice certain trades in Mississippi. Only a few states allowed blacks to serve on juries. Blacks who worked for whites were required to enter into labor contracts with their employers, to be renewed annually. Unemployed ("vagrant") blacks were often arrested and punished with severe fines, and if unable to pay they were forced to labor in the fields of those who paid the courts for this source of cheap labor. In other words, aspects of slavery were simply being restored in another guise. When a freedman in South Carolina told a white employer that he wanted to get a federal army officer to review his labor contract, the employer killed him.

Faced with such blatant evidence of southern intransigence, moderate Republicans in Congress drifted toward the Radicals' views. The new Con-

**(?) "Slavery Is Dead" (?)**

Thomas Nast's cartoon suggests that slavery was not dead in the postwar south.

gress set up a Joint Committee on Reconstruction, with nine members from the House and six from the Senate, to gather evidence of southern efforts to thwart Reconstruction. Initiative fell to determined Radical Republicans who knew what they wanted: Benjamin Wade of Ohio, George Washington Julian of Indiana, and—most conspicuously of all—**Thaddeus Stevens** of Pennsylvania and Charles Sumner of Massachusetts.

**THE RADICAL REPUBLICANS**   Most Radical Republicans had been connected with the anti-slavery cause for decades. In addition, few could escape the bitterness bred by the long war or remain unaware of the partisan advantage that would come to the Republican party from black suffrage. The Republicans needed African American votes to maintain their control of Congress and the White House. They also needed to disenfranchise former Confederates to keep them from helping to elect Democrats eager to restore the old southern ruling class to power. In public, however, the Radical Republicans rarely disclosed such partisan self-interest. Instead, they asserted that the Republicans, the party of Union and freedom, could best guarantee the fruits of victory and that extending voting rights to African Americans would be the best way to promote their welfare.

The growing conflict of opinion over Reconstruction policy brought about an inversion in constitutional reasoning. Secessionists—and Andrew Johnson—were now arguing that the Rebel states had in fact remained in the Union, and some Radical Republicans were contriving arguments that they had left the Union after all. Thaddeus Stevens argued that the Confederate states should be viewed as conquered provinces, subject to the absolute will of the victors, and that the "whole fabric of southern society must be changed." Most Republicans, however, held that the Confederate states continued to exist as entities, but by the acts of secession and war they had forfeited "all civil and political rights under the Constitution." And Congress, not the president, was the proper authority to determine how and when such rights might be restored.

JOHNSON'S BATTLE WITH CONGRESS    A long year of political battling remained, however, before this idea triumphed. By the end of 1865, the Radical Republicans' views had gained a majority in Congress, if one not yet large enough to override presidential vetoes. But the critical year of 1866 saw the gradual waning of Andrew Johnson's power and influence, much of which was self-induced. Johnson first challenged Congress in 1866, when he vetoed a bill to extend the life of the Freedmen's Bureau. The measure, he said, violated the Constitution in several ways: it made the federal government responsible for the care of poor blacks, it was passed by a Congress in which eleven ex-Confederate states had been denied seats, and it used vague language in defining the "civil rights and immunities" of African Americans. For the time being, Johnson's prestige remained sufficiently intact that the Senate upheld his veto.

Three days after the veto, however, during an impromptu speech, Johnson undermined his already weakening authority with a fiery assault upon the Radical Republican leaders. From that point forward, moderate Republicans deserted a president who had opened himself to counterattack. The Radical Republicans took the offensive. Johnson was "an alien enemy of a foreign state," Stevens declared. Sumner called him "an insolent drunken brute," a charge Johnson was open to because of his behavior at the 1865 inauguration.

In mid-March 1866 the Radical-led Congress passed the Civil Rights Act, written by Illinois senator Lyman Trumbull (who also drafted the Thirteenth Amendment). A response to the black codes and the neo-slavery system created by unrepentant southern state legislatures, it declared that "all persons born in the United States and not subject to any foreign power, excluding Indians not taxed," were citizens entitled to "full and equal benefit of all laws." The granting of citizenship to native-born blacks, Johnson fumed, exceeded the scope of federal power. It would, moreover, "foment discord among the races." Johnson vetoed the bill, but this time, on April 9, Congress overrode the presidential veto. On July 16, it enacted a revised Freedmen's Bureau Bill, again overriding a veto. From that point on, Johnson steadily lost both public and political support.

THE FOURTEENTH AMENDMENT    To remove all doubt about the legality of the new Civil Rights Act, the joint committee recommended a new constitutional amendment, which passed Congress on June 16, 1866, and was ratified by the states two years later, on July 28, 1868. The **Fourteenth Amendment** went far beyond the Civil Rights Act, however. It established a constitutional guarantee of basic citizenship for all Americans, including African Americans. The amendment reaffirms the state and federal citizenship of persons born or naturalized in the United States, and it forbids any state (the word *state* would be important in later litigation) to "abridge the privileges or immunities of citizens," to deprive any *person* (again an important term) "of life, liberty, or property, without due process of law," or to "deny any person . . . the equal protection of the laws." These three clauses have been the subject of many lawsuits, resulting in applications not widely, if at all, foreseen at the time. The "due-process clause" has come to mean that state as well as federal power is subject to the Bill of Rights, and it has been used to protect corporations, as legal "persons," from "unreasonable" regulation by the states. Other provisions of the amendment have had less far-reaching effects. One section specified that the debt of the United States "shall not be questioned" by the former Confederate states and declared "illegal and void" all debts contracted in aid of the rebellion. The Fourteenth Amendment also prohibited the president from granting pardons to former Confederate leaders.

President Andrew Johnson's home state was among the first to ratify the Fourteenth Amendment. In Tennessee, which had more Unionists than any other Confederate state, the government had fallen under Radical Republican control. The state's governor, in reporting the results to the secretary of the Senate, added, "Give my respects to the dead dog of the White House." His words illustrate the growing acrimony on both sides of the Reconstruction debates. In May and July, race riots in Memphis and New Orleans added fuel to the flames. Both incidents involved indiscriminate massacres of blacks by local police and white mobs. The carnage, Radical Republicans argued, was the natural fruit of Andrew Johnson's lenient policy toward white supremacists. "Witness Memphis, witness New Orleans," Massachusetts senator Charles Sumner cried. "Who can doubt that the President is the author of these tragedies?"

## RECONSTRUCTING THE SOUTH

THE TRIUMPH OF CONGRESSIONAL RECONSTRUCTION    As 1866 drew to an end, the congressional elections promised to be a referendum on the growing split between President Andrew Johnson and the Radical Republicans. To win votes, Johnson went on a speaking tour of the Midwest. But his efforts backfired when several of his speeches turned into undignified shouting contests between him and his critics. In Cleveland, Johnson described the Radical Republicans as "factious, domineering, tyrannical" men, and he foolishly exchanged hot-tempered insults with a heckler. At another stop, while Johnson was speaking from the back of a railway car, the engineer mistakenly pulled the train out of the station, making the president appear quite the fool. Such incidents tended to confirm Johnson's image as a "ludicrous boor" and a "drunken imbecile," an image that Radical Republicans promoted. The 1866 congressional elections were a devastating defeat for Johnson; Republicans won more than a two-thirds majority in each house, a comfortable margin with which to override presidential vetoes.

The Republican-controlled Congress in fact enacted several important provisions even before the new members took office. Two acts passed in 1867 extended voting rights to African Americans in the District of Columbia and the territories. Another law provided that the new Congress would convene on March 4 instead of the following December, depriving Johnson of a breathing spell. On March 2, 1867, two days before the old Congress expired, it passed, over Johnson's vetoes, three crucial laws promoting what came to be called "Congressional Reconstruction": the Military Reconstruction Act, the Command of the Army Act (an amendment to an army appropriation), and the Tenure of Office Act.

Congressional Reconstruction was designed to prevent white southerners from manipulating the reconstruction process. The Command of the Army Act required that all orders from the commander in chief go through the headquarters of the general of the army, a post then held by Ulysses S. Grant. The Radical Republicans distrusted President Johnson and trusted General Grant, who was already leaning their way. The Tenure of Office Act required Senate permission for the president to remove any federal officeholder whose appointment the Senate had confirmed. The purpose of at least some congressmen was to retain Secretary of War Edwin Stanton, the one Radical Republican sympathizer in Johnson's cabinet.

The Military Reconstruction Act was hailed—or denounced—as the triumphant victory of Radical Reconstruction, for it set a precedent among former slave societies in providing voting rights to freed slaves almost immediately after emancipation. It also represented the nation's first effort in military-enforced nation building. The North's effort to "reconstruct" the South by force after the Civil War set a precedent for future American military occupations and attempted social transformations. The act declared that "no legal state governments or adequate protection for life and property now exists in the rebel States." One state, Tennessee, was exempted from the application of the new act because it had already ratified the Fourteenth Amendment. The other ten southern states were divided into five military districts, and the commanding officer of each was authorized to keep order and protect the "rights of persons and property." The Military Reconstruction Act then stipulated that new constitutions in each of the former Confederate states were to be framed by conventions elected by male citizens aged twenty-one and older "of whatever race, color, or previous condition." Each state constitution had to guarantee the right of African American males to vote. Once the constitution was ratified by a majority of voters and accepted by Congress, other criteria had to be met. The new state legislature had to ratify the Fourteenth Amendment, and once the amendment became part of the Constitution, any given state would be entitled to representation in Congress.

Several hundred African American delegates participated in the statewide political conventions. Most had been selected by local political meetings or churches, fraternal societies, Union Leagues, or black army units from the North, although a few simply appointed themselves. The African American delegates "ranged [across] all colors and apparently all conditions," but free mulattoes from the cities played the most prominent roles. At Louisiana's Republican state convention, for instance, nineteen of the twenty black delegates had been born free.

President Johnson reluctantly appointed military commanders under the new Military Reconstruction Act, but the situation remained uncertain for a time. Some people expected the Supreme Court to strike down the act, and no process existed for the new elections. Congress quickly remedied that on March 23, 1867, with the Second Reconstruction Act, which directed the army commanders to register all adult men who swore they were qualified. Before the end of 1867, new elections had been held in all the states but Texas, and blacks participated in high numbers, giving virtually all of their votes to Republican candidates.

Having clipped the president's wings, the Republican Congress moved a year later to safeguard its Reconstruction program from possible interference by the Supreme Court. On March 27, 1868, Congress simply removed the power of the Supreme Court to review cases arising under the Military Reconstruction Act, which Congress clearly had the right to do under its power to define the Court's jurisdiction. The Court accepted this curtailment of its authority on the same day it affirmed the principle of an "indestructible Union" in *Texas v. White* (1869). In that case the Court also asserted the right of Congress to reframe state governments, thus endorsing the Radical Republican point of view.

THE IMPEACHMENT AND TRIAL OF JOHNSON     By 1868, Radical Republicans had decided that Andrew Johnson must be removed from office. The Republicans had unsuccessfully tried to impeach Johnson early in 1867, alleging a variety of flimsy charges, none of which represented an indictable crime. Then Johnson himself provided the occasion for impeachment when he deliberately violated the Tenure of Office Act in order to test its constitutionality. Secretary of War Edwin Stanton had become a thorn in Johnson's side, refusing to resign despite his disagreements with the president's Reconstruction policy. On August 12, 1867, during a congressional recess, Johnson suspended Stanton and named General Ulysses S. Grant in his place. When the Senate refused to confirm Johnson's action, however, Grant returned the office to Stanton.

The Radical Republicans now saw their chance to remove the president. On February 24, 1868, the Republican-dominated House passed eleven articles of impeachment by a party-line vote of 126 to 47. Most of the articles

**The trial of Andrew Johnson**

House of Representatives managers of the impeachment proceedings. Among them were Benjamin Franklin Butler (Republican of Massachusetts, seated left) and Thaddeus Stevens (Republican of Pennsylvania, seated with cane).

focused on the charge that Johnson had unlawfully removed Secretary of War Stanton.

The Senate trial began on March 5, 1868, and continued until May 26, with Chief Justice Salmon P. Chase presiding. It was a great spectacle before a packed gallery. The five-week trial ended in May 1868, and the Senate voted 35 to 19 for conviction, only one vote short of the two thirds needed for removal from office. Although the Senate failed to remove Johnson, the trial crippled his already weakened presidency. During the remaining ten months of his term, he initiated no other clashes with Congress. In 1868, Johnson sought the Democratic presidential nomination but lost to New York governor Horatio Seymour, who then lost to the Republican, Ulysses S. Grant, in the general election. The impeachment of Johnson was in the end a great political mistake, for the failure to remove the president damaged Radical Republican morale and support. Nevertheless, the Radical cause did gain something: to stave off impeachment, Johnson agreed not to obstruct the process of Congressional-led Reconstruction.

REPUBLICAN RULE IN THE SOUTH   In June 1868, Congress agreed that eight southern states—all but Virginia, Mississippi, and Texas—had met the more stringent conditions for readmission. Congress rescinded Georgia's admission, however, when the state legislature expelled twenty-eight African American members and seated former Confederate leaders. The federal military commander in Georgia then forced the legislature to reseat the black members and remove the Confederates, and the state was compelled to ratify the **Fifteenth Amendment** before being admitted in July 1870. Mississippi, Texas, and Virginia had returned earlier in 1870, under the added requirement that they, too, ratify the Fifteenth Amendment. That amendment, submitted to the states in 1869 and ratified in 1870, forbids the states to deny any person the vote on grounds of "race, color, or previous condition of servitude." Kentucky, the birthplace of Abraham Lincoln, was the only state in the nation that failed to ratify all three of the constitutional amendments related to ending slavery—the Thirteenth, Fourteenth, and Fifteenth.

Long before the new governments were established, groups promoting the Republican party had begun to spring up in the South, chiefly sponsored by the Union League, founded in Philadelphia in 1862 to support the Union. League recruiters in the South enrolled African Americans and loyal whites, initiated them into the secrets and rituals of the order, and instructed them "in their rights and duties." Their recruiting efforts were so successful that in 1867, on the eve of South Carolina's choice of convention delegates, the league reported eighty-eight chapters, which claimed to have enrolled almost every adult black male in the state.

## THE RECONSTRUCTED SOUTH

THE FREED SLAVES    African Americans in the postwar South were active agents in affecting the course of Reconstruction, though it was not an easy process. During the era of Reconstruction, whites, both northern and southern, harbored racist views of blacks. A northern journalist traveling in the South after the war reported that the "whites seem wholly unable to comprehend that freedom for the negro means the same thing as freedom for them." Many whites presumed that the freed slaves would not be willing to work. Federal troops often tried to convince—or force—freedmen to return to plantations to work as wage laborers. Local planters conspired together to control the wages paid to freedmen. White southerners also used terror, intimidation, and violence to suppress black efforts to gain social and economic equality. In Texas, a white farmer told a former slave that his freedom would do him "damned little good . . . as I intend to shoot you"— and he did. In July 1866, a black woman in Clinch County, Georgia, was arrested and whipped sixty-five times for "using abusive language" during an encounter with a white woman. The Civil War had brought freedom to enslaved African Americans, but it did not bring them protection against exploitation or abuse.

After emancipation, Union soldiers and northern observers in the South often commented that freed slaves did not go far away from where they had been enslaved. But why would they leave what they knew so well? As a group of African Americans explained, they did not want to abandon "land they had laid their fathers' bones upon." A Union officer noted that southern blacks seemed "more attached to familiar places" than any other group in the nation.

Participation in the Union army or navy had provided many freedmen with training in leadership. Black military veterans would form the core of the first generation of African American political leaders in the postwar South. Military service gave many former slaves their first opportunities to learn to read and write. Army life also alerted them to new opportunities for economic advancement, social respectability, and civic leadership. Fighting for the Union cause also instilled a fervent sense of nationalism. A Virginia freedman explained that the United States was "now *our* country—made emphatically so by the blood of our brethren."

Former slaves established churches after the war, which quickly formed the foundation of African American community life. Many blacks preferred the Baptist denomination, in part because its decentralized structure allowed each congregation to worship in its own way. By 1890, over 1.3 million African Americans in the South had become Baptists, nearly three times as many as had joined any other black denomination. In addition to forming viable new congregations, freed African Americans organized thousands of fraternal, benevolent, and mutual-aid societies, as well as clubs, lodges, and associations. Memphis, for example, had over two hundred such organizations; Richmond boasted twice that number.

Freed blacks also hastened to reestablish their families. Marriages that had been prohibited during slavery were now legitimized through the assistance of the Freedmen's Bureau. By 1870, a preponderant majority of former slaves were living in two-parent households. With little money or technical training, freed blacks faced the prospect of becoming wage laborers. Because there were so few banks left in the South, it was virtually impossible for former slaves to get loans to buy farmland. For many freed blacks (and poor whites) the primary vocational option after the war was sharecropping, in which the crop produced was divided between the tenant farmer and the landowner. Sharecropping enabled mothers and wives to contribute directly to the family's income.

African American communities in the postwar South also sought to establish schools. Planters had denied education to blacks in part because

**The First African Church**

On the eve of its move to a new building, the First African Church of Richmond, Virginia, was featured in a short article, including illustrations such as the one above, in *Harper's Weekly*, in June 1874.

they feared that literate slaves would read abolitionist literature and organize uprisings. After the war, the white elite worried that formal education would encourage poor whites and poor blacks to leave the South in search of better social and economic opportunities. Economic leaders wanted to protect the competitive advantage afforded by the region's low-wage labor market. "They didn't want us to learn nothin'," one former slave recalled. "The only thing we had to learn was how to work." White opposition to education for blacks made education all the more important to African Americans. South Carolina's Mary McLeod Bethune, the fifteenth child of former slaves, reveled in the opportunity to gain an education: "The whole world opened to me when I learned to read." She walked five miles to school as a child, earned a scholarship to college, and went on to become the first black woman to found a school that became a four-year college, Bethune-Cookman, in Daytona Beach, Florida. African American churches and individuals helped raise the money and often built the schools and paid the teachers. Soldiers who had acquired some literacy skills often served as the teachers, and the students included adults as well as children.

AFRICAN AMERICANS IN SOUTHERN POLITICS    In the postwar South, the new role of African Americans in politics caused the most controversy. If largely uneducated and inexperienced in the rudiments of politics, southern blacks were little different from the millions of newly enfranchised propertyless whites in the age of Andrew Jackson's political reforms or immigrants in postwar cities. Some freedmen frankly confessed their disadvantages. Beverly Nash, an African American delegate to the South Carolina convention of 1868, told his colleagues: "I believe, my friends and fellow-citizens, we are not prepared for this suffrage. But we can learn. Give a man tools and let him commence to use them, and in time he will learn a trade. So it is with voting."

By 1867, however, former slaves had begun to gain political influence and vote in large numbers, and this development revealed emerging tensions within the African American community. Some southern blacks resented the presence of northern brethren who moved south after the war, while others complained that few ex-slaves were represented in leadership positions. There developed real tensions in the black community between the few who owned property and the many who did not. In North Carolina by 1870, for example, less than 7 percent of blacks owned land, and most of them owned only a few acres; half of black property owners had less than twenty acres. Northern blacks and the southern free black elite, most of whom were urban dwellers and many of whom were mulattoes, often opposed efforts to redistribute land to the freedmen, and many insisted that political equality did

**Freedmen voting in New Orleans**

The Fifteenth Amendment, ratified in 1870, guaranteed at the federal level the right of citizens to vote regardless of "race, color, or previous condition of servitude." But former slaves had been registering to vote—and voting in large numbers—in state elections since 1867, as in this scene.

not mean social equality. As a black Alabama leader stressed, "We do not ask that the ignorant and degraded shall be put on a social equality with the refined and intelligent." In general, however, unity rather than dissension prevailed, and African Americans focused on common concerns such as full equality under the law.

Brought suddenly into politics in times that tried the most skilled of statesmen, many African Americans served with distinction. Nonetheless, the derisive label "black Reconstruction," used by later critics, exaggerates African American political influence, which was limited mainly to voting. Such criticism also overlooks the political clout of the large number of white Republicans, especially in the mountain areas of the Upper South, who also favored the Radical plan for Reconstruction. Only one of the new state conventions, South Carolina's, had a black majority, seventy-six to forty-one. Louisiana's was evenly divided racially, and in only two other conventions were more than 20 percent of the members black: Florida's, with 40 percent, and Virginia's, with 24 percent. The Texas convention was only 10 percent black, and North Carolina's was 11 percent—but that did not stop a white newspaper from calling it a body consisting of "baboons, monkeys, mules . . . and other jackasses."

**African American political figures of Reconstruction**

Blanche K. Bruce (left) and Hiram Revels (right) served in the U.S. Senate.
Frederick Douglass (center) was a major figure in the abolitionist movement.

In the new state governments any African American participation was a
novelty. Although some six hundred blacks—most of them former slaves—
served as state legislators, no black man was ever elected governor, and only
a few served as judges. In Louisiana, however, Pinckney Pinchback, a northern black and former Union soldier, won the office of lieutenant governor
and served as acting governor when the white governor was indicted for corruption. Several African Americans were elected lieutenant governor, state
treasurer, or secretary of state. There were two black senators in Congress,
Hiram Revels and Blanche K. Bruce, both Mississippi natives who had been
educated in the North, and fourteen black members of the House of Representatives during Reconstruction.

"CARPETBAGGERS" AND "SCALAWAGS"    The top positions in
postwar southern state governments went for the most part to white Republicans, whom the opposition whites labeled "**carpetbaggers**" and "**scalawags**,"
depending upon their place of birth. Northerners who allegedly rushed
South with all their belongings in carpetbags to grab the political spoils were
more often than not Union veterans who had arrived as early as 1865 or 1866,
drawn South by the hope of economic opportunity and other attractions that

many of them had seen in their Union service. Many other so-called carpet-baggers were teachers, social workers, or preachers animated by a sincere missionary impulse.

The scalawags, or native white Republicans, were even more reviled and misrepresented. A Nashville newspaper editor called them the "merest trash." Most scalawags had opposed secession, forming a Unionist majority in many mountain counties as far south as Georgia and Alabama and especially in the hills of eastern Tennessee. Among the scalawags were several distinguished figures, including the former Confederate general James Longstreet, who decided after Appomattox that the Old South must change its ways. He became a successful cotton broker in New Orleans, joined the Republican party, and supported the Radical Reconstruction program. Other so-called scalawags were former Whigs attracted by the Republican party's economic program of industrial and commercial expansion.

THE RADICAL REPUBLICAN RECORD   Former Confederates resented the new state constitutions because of their provisions allowing for black voting and civil rights. Yet most of those constitutions remained in effect for some years after the end of Radical Republican control, and later constitutions incorporated many of their features. Conspicuous among the Radical innovations were such steps toward greater democracy as requiring universal manhood suffrage, reapportioning legislatures more nearly according to population, and making more state offices elective. In South Carolina, former Confederate leaders opposed the Radical state legislature not simply because of its black members but also because lower-class whites were enjoying unprecedented political power too.

Given the hostile circumstances under which the Radical governments operated, their achievements were remarkable. They constructed an extensive railroad network and established state-supported public school systems. Some six hundred thousand black pupils were enrolled in southern schools by 1877. State governments under the Radicals also gave more attention to the poor and to orphanages, asylums, and institutions for the deaf and the blind of both races. Public roads, bridges, and buildings were repaired or rebuilt. African Americans achieved rights and opportunities that would never again be taken away, at least in principle: equality before the law and the rights to own property, carry on business, enter professions, attend schools, and learn to read and write.

Yet several of these Republican state regimes also engaged in corrupt practices. Bids for state government contracts were accepted at absurdly high prices, and public officials took their cut. Public money and public credit were often awarded to privately owned corporations, notably rail-

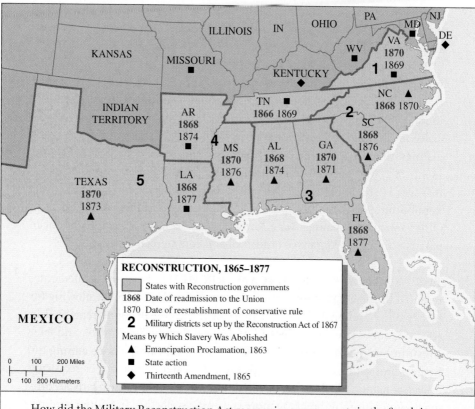

**RECONSTRUCTION, 1865–1877**

States with Reconstruction governments
**1868** Date of readmission to the Union
**1870** Date of reestablishment of conservative rule
**2** Military districts set up by the Reconstruction Act of 1867
Means by Which Slavery Was Abolished
▲ Emancipation Proclamation, 1863
■ State action
◆ Thirteenth Amendment, 1865

How did the Military Reconstruction Act reorganize governments in the South in the late 1860s and 1870s? What did the former Confederate states have to do to be readmitted to the Union? Why did "Conservative" parties gradually regain control of the South from the Republicans in the 1870s?

roads, under conditions that invited influence peddling. Corruption was not invented by the Radical Republican regimes, nor did it die with them. Louisiana's "carpetbag" governor recognized as much. "Why," he said, "down here everybody is demoralized. Corruption is the fashion."

RELIGION AND RECONSTRUCTION The religious community played a critical role in the implementation and ultimate failure of Radical Reconstruction, and religious commentators offered quite different interpretations of what should be done with the defeated South. Thaddeus Stevens and many other Radical Republican leaders who had spent their careers promoting the abolition of slavery and racial equality were motivated primarily by religious ideals and moral fervor. They wanted no compromise with racism. Likewise, most of the Christian missionaries who headed south after the Civil War brought with them a progressive vision of a biracial "beloved community" emerging in the reconstructed South, and they strove to promote social and political equality for freed slaves. For these crusaders, civil rights was a sacred cause. They used Christian principles to challenge the prevailing theological and "scientific" justifications for racial inferiority. They also promoted Christian solidarity across racial and regional lines.

At the same time, the Protestant denominations, all of which had split into northern and southern branches over the issues of slavery and secession, struggled to reunite after the war. A growing number of northern ministers promoted reconciliation between the warring regions after the Civil War. These "apostles of forgiveness" prized white unity over racial equality. For example, the Reverend Henry Ward Beecher, the powerful New York minister whose sister Harriet Beecher Stowe wrote *Uncle Tom's Cabin*, wanted white southern planters—rather than federal officials or African Americans themselves—to oversee Reconstruction. Not surprisingly, Beecher's views gained widespread support among evangelical ministers in the South.

The collapse of the Confederacy did not prompt southern whites to abandon their belief that God was on their side. In the wake of defeat and emancipation, white southern ministers reassured their congregations that they had no reason to question the moral foundations of their region or their defense of white racial superiority. For African Americans, however, the Civil War and emancipation demonstrated that God was on *their* side. Emancipation was in their view a redemptive act through which God wrought national regeneration. African American ministers were convinced that the United States was indeed a divinely inspired nation and that blacks had a providential role to play in its future. Yet neither black nor idealistic white northern ministers could stem the growing chorus of whites who were willing to abandon goals of racial equality in exchange for national religious reconciliation. By the end of the nineteenth century, mainstream American Protestantism promoted the image of a "white republic" that conflated whiteness, godliness, and nationalism.

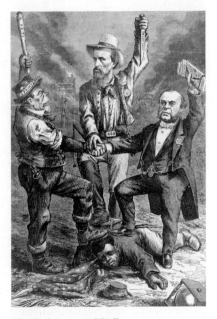

**The "white republic"**

This cartoon illustrates white unity against racial equality.

## THE GRANT YEARS

Ulysses S. Grant, who served as president during the collapse of Republican rule in the South, brought to the White House little political experience. But in 1868 northern voters supported the "Lion of Vicksburg" because of his record as the Union army commander. He was the most popular man in the nation. Both parties wooed him, but his falling-out with President Andrew Johnson had pushed him toward the Republicans. They were, as Thaddeus Stevens said, ready to "let him into the church."

THE ELECTION OF 1868    The Republican party platform of 1868 endorsed congressional Reconstruction. One plank cautiously defended black suffrage as a necessity in the South but a matter each northern state should settle for itself. Another urged payment of the national debt "in the utmost good faith to all creditors," which meant in gold. More important than the platform were the great expectations of a heroic soldier-president and his slogan, "Let us have peace."

**"The Working-Man's Banner"**

This campaign banner makes reference to the working-class origins of Ulysses S. Grant and his vice-presidential candidate, Henry Wilson, by depicting Grant as a tanner of hides and Wilson as a shoemaker.

The Democrats took opposite positions on both Reconstruction and the debt. The Republican Congress, the Democratic party platform charged, instead of restoring the Union had "so far as in its power, dissolved it, and subjected ten states, in the time of profound peace, to military despotism and Negro supremacy." As for the federal debt, the party endorsed Representative George H. Pendleton's "Ohio idea" that, since most war bonds had been bought with depreciated **greenbacks**, they should be paid off in greenbacks rather than in gold. With no conspicuously available candidate in sight, the Democratic Convention turned to Horatio Seymour, wartime governor of

New York. Seymour neither sought nor embraced the nomination, leading opponents to call him the Great Decliner. Yet the Democrats made a closer race of it than the electoral vote revealed. While Grant swept the Electoral College by 214 to 80, his popular majority was only 307,000 out of a total of over 5.7 million votes. More than 500,000 African American voters accounted for Grant's margin of victory.

Grant had proved himself a great military leader, but as the youngest president ever (forty-six years old at the time of his inauguration), he was often blind to the political forces and influence peddlers around him. He was awestruck by men of wealth and unaccountably loyal to some who betrayed his trust, and he passively followed the lead of Congress. This approach at first endeared him to Republican party leaders, but at last it left him ineffective and others grew disillusioned with his leadership.

At the outset, Grant consulted nobody on his seven cabinet appointments. Some of his choices indulged personal whims; others simply displayed bad judgment. In some cases, appointees learned of their nomination from the newspapers. As time went by, Grant betrayed a fatal gift for losing men of talent and integrity from his cabinet. Secretary of State Hamilton Fish of New York turned out to be a happy exception; he guided foreign policy throughout the Grant presidency. Other than Fish, however, the Grant cabinet overflowed with incompetents.

THE GOVERNMENT DEBT     Financial issues dominated Grant's presidency. After the war, the Treasury had assumed that the $432 million worth of greenbacks issued during the conflict would be retired from circulation and that the nation would revert to a "hard-money" currency—gold coins. But many agrarian and debtor groups resisted any contraction of the money supply resulting from the elimination of greenbacks, believing that it would mean lower prices for their crops and more difficulty repaying long-term debts. They were joined by a large number of Radical Republicans who thought that a combination of high tariffs and inflation would generate more rapid economic growth. As Senator John Sherman explained, "I prefer gold to paper money. But there is no other resort. We must have money or a fractured government." In 1868 congressional supporters of such a "soft-money" policy halted the withdrawal of greenbacks from circulation. There matters stood when Grant took office.

The "sound-money" (or hard-money) advocates, mostly bankers and merchants, claimed that Grant's election was a mandate to save the country from the Democrats' "Ohio idea" of using greenbacks to repay government bonds. Quite influential in Republican circles, the hard-money advocates also reflected the deeply ingrained popular assumption that gold coins were morally preferable to paper currency. Grant agreed as well. On March 18, 1869, the Public Credit Act, which said that the federal debt must be paid in gold, became the first act of Congress that Grant signed.

SCANDALS   The complexities of the "money question" exasperated Grant, but that was the least of his worries, for his administration soon fell into a cesspool of scandal. In the summer of 1869, two unscrupulous financial buccaneers, Jay Gould and James Fisk, connived with the president's brother-in-law to corner the nation's gold market. That is, they would create a public craze for gold by purchasing massive quantities of the precious yellow metal. As more buyers joined the frenzy, the value of gold would soar. The only danger to the scheme lay in the possibility that the federal Treasury would burst the bubble by selling large amounts of gold, which would deflate its value.

Grant apparently smelled a rat from the start, but he was seen in public with the speculators, leading people to think that he supported the run on gold. As the rumor spread on Wall Street that the president was pro-gold, the value of gold rose from $132 to $163 an ounce. Finally, on Black Friday, September 24, 1869, Grant ordered the Treasury to sell a large quantity of gold, and the bubble burst. Fisk got out by repudiating his agreements and hiring thugs to intimidate his creditors. "Nothing is lost save honor," he said.

The plot to corner the gold market was only the first of several scandals that rocked the Grant administration. During the presidential campaign of 1872, the public learned about the financial crookery of the **Crédit Mobilier** of America, a sham construction company run by of directors of the Union Pacific Railroad who had milked the Union Pacific for exorbitant fees in order to line the pockets of the insiders who controlled both firms. Union Pacific shareholders were left holding the bag. The schemers bought political support by giving congressmen shares of stock in the enterprise. This chicanery had transpired before Grant's election in 1868, but it now touched a number of prominent Republicans. The beneficiaries of the scheme included Speaker of the House Schuyler Colfax, later vice president, and Representative James A. Garfield, later president. Of the thirteen members of Congress involved, only two were censured.

Even more odious disclosures soon followed, some involving the president's cabinet. The secretary of war, it turned out, had accepted bribes from merchants who traded with Indians at army posts in the West. He was impeached, but he resigned in time to elude a Senate trial. At the same time, post-office contracts, it was revealed, went to carriers who offered the highest kickbacks. The secretary of the Treasury had awarded a political friend a commission of 50 percent for the collection of overdue taxes. In St. Louis, a "whiskey ring" bribed tax collectors to bilk the government out of millions of dollars in revenue. Grant's private secretary was enmeshed in that scheme, taking large sums of money and other valuables in return for inside information. There is no evidence that Grant himself was ever involved in, or personally profited from, any of the fraud, but his poor choice of associates and his gullibility earned him widespread criticism. Democrats castigated Republicans for their "monstrous corruption and extravagance."

WHITE TERROR    President Grant initially fought hard to enforce the federal efforts to reconstruct the postwar South. But southern resistance to "Radical rule" increased and turned violent. In Grayson County, Texas, three whites murdered three former slaves because they felt the need to "thin the niggers out and drive them to their holes."

The prototype of all the terrorist groups was the Ku Klux Klan (KKK), organized in 1866 by some young men of Pulaski, Tennessee, as a social club, with the costumes and secret rituals common to fraternal groups. At first a group of pranksters, its members soon turned to intimidation of blacks and white Republicans. The KKK and its imitators, like Louisiana's Knights of the White Camelia and Mississippi's White Line, spread rapidly across the South in answer to the Republican party's. Klansmen rode about the countryside, hiding behind masks and under robes, spreading horrendous rumors, issuing threats, harassing African Americans, and wreaking violence and destruction. "We are going to kill all the Negroes," a white supremacist declared during one massacre.

Klansmen focused their terror on prominent Republicans, black and white. In Mississippi they killed a black Republican leader in front of his family. Three white "scalawag" Republicans were murdered in Georgia in 1870. That same year an armed mob of whites assaulted a Republican political rally in Alabama, killing four blacks and wounding fifty-four. In South Carolina white supremacists were especially active—and violent. Virtually the entire white male population of York County joined the KKK, and they were

**"Worse Than Slavery"**

This Thomas Nast cartoon chides the Ku Klux Klan for promoting conditions "worse than slavery" for southern blacks after the Civil War.

responsible for eleven murders and hundreds of whippings. In 1871, some five hundred masked men laid siege to the Union County jail and eventually lynched eight black prisoners.

At the urging of President Grant, who showed true moral courage in trying to protect southern blacks, the Republican-dominated Congress struck back with three Enforcement Acts (1870–1871) to protect black voters. The first of these measures levied penalties on anyone who interfered with any citizen's right to vote. A second placed the election of congressmen under surveillance by federal election supervisors and marshals. The third (the Ku Klux Klan Act) outlawed the characteristic activities of the KKK—forming conspiracies, wearing disguises, resisting officers, and intimidating officials—and authorized the president to suspend habeas corpus where necessary to suppress "armed combinations."

In 1871, the federal government singled out nine counties in upcountry South Carolina as an example, suspended habeas corpus, and pursued mass prosecutions. In general, however, the Enforcement Acts suffered from weak and inconsistent execution. As time passed, President Grant vacillated between clamping down on the Klan and capitulating to racial intimidation. The strong tradition of states' rights and local autonomy in the South, as well as pervasive racial prejudice, resisted federal force. The unrelenting efforts of whites to use violence to thwart Reconstruction continued into the 1870s. On Easter Sunday in 1873 in Colfax, Louisiana, a mob of white vigilantes disappointed by local election results attacked a group of black Republicans, slaughtering eighty-one. It was the bloodiest racial incident during the Reconstruction period. White southerners had lost the war, but during the 1870s they won the peace with their reactionary violence. In the process, the goals of racial justice and civil rights were blunted. In 1876, the U.S. Supreme Court gave implied sanction to the Colfax Massacre when it ruled in *United States v. Cruikshank* (1876) that states' rights trumped federal authority when it came to protecting freed blacks from white terrorists.

REFORM AND THE ELECTION OF 1872    Long before President Grant's first term ended, a reaction against Radical Reconstruction and incompetence and corruption in the administration had incited mutiny within the Republican ranks. A new faction, called Liberal Republicans, favored free trade rather than tariffs, the redemption of greenbacks with gold, a stable currency, an end to federal Reconstruction efforts in the South, the restoration of the rights of former Confederates, and civil service reform. In 1872 the Liberal Republicans held their own national convention, in which they produced a compromise platform condemning the Republi-

### "What I Know about Raising the Devil"

With the tail and cloven hoof of the devil, Horace Greeley (center) leads a small band of Liberal Republicans in pursuit of incumbent president Ulysses S. Grant and his supporters in this 1872 cartoon.

cans' Radical Reconstruction policy as well as government corruption, but they remained silent on the protective tariff. The delegates embraced a quixotic presidential candidate: **Horace Greeley**, the prominent editor of the *New York Tribune* and a longtime champion of just about every reform available. Greeley had promoted vegetarianism, socialism, and spiritualism. His image as an eccentric was complemented by his record of hostility to the Democrats, whose support the Liberals needed. The Democrats nevertheless swallowed the pill and gave their nomination to Greeley as the only hope of beating Grant.

The result was a foregone conclusion. Republican regulars duly endorsed Grant, Radical Reconstruction, and the protective tariff. Greeley carried only six southern and border states and none in the North. Grant won by 3,598,235 votes to Greeley's 2,834,761.

CONSERVATIVE RESURGENCE   The KKK's impact on southern politics varied from state to state. In the Upper South, it played only a modest role in facilitating a Democratic resurgence in local elections. But in the Deep South, Klan violence and intimidation had more substantial effects. In overwhelmingly black Yazoo County, Mississippi, vengeful whites used terrorism to reverse the political balance of power. In the 1873 elections the Republicans cast 2,449 votes and the Democrats 638; two years later the Democrats polled 4,049 votes, the Republicans 7. Throughout the

South the activities of the Klan and other white supremacists weakened black and Republican morale, and in the North they encouraged a growing weariness with efforts to reconstruct the South and protect civil rights. "The plain truth is," noted *The New York Herald*, "the North has got tired of the Negro."

The erosion of northern interest in civil rights resulted from more than weariness, however. Western expansion, Indian wars, new economic opportunities, and political controversy over the tariff and the currency distracted attention from southern outrages against Republican rule and black rights. Given the violent efforts of reactionary whites to resist Reconstruction, it would have required far more patience and conviction to protect the civil rights of blacks than the North possessed, and far more resources than the pro-Reconstruction southerners could employ. In addition, after a devastating business panic that occurred in 1873 followed by a prolonged depression, desperate economic circumstances in the North and the South created new racial tensions that helped undermine federal efforts to promote racial justice in the former Confederacy. Republican control in the South gradually loosened as "Conservative" parties—a name used by Democrats to mollify former Whigs—mobilized the white vote. Prewar political leaders reemerged to promote the antebellum Democratic goals of limited government, states' rights, and free trade. They politicized the race issue to excite the white electorate and intimidate black voters. The Republicans in the South became increasingly an organization limited to African Americans and federal officials. Many "scalawags" and "carpetbaggers" drifted away from the Radical Republican ranks under pressure from their white neighbors. Few of them had joined the Republicans out of concern for black rights in the first place. And where persuasion failed to work, Democrats were willing to use chicanery. As one enthusiastic Democrat boasted, "The white and black Republicans may outvote us, but we can outcount them."

The diminishing commitment of the North to the ideals of Reconstruction reached a crisis when federal troops occupied the Louisiana legislature in January 1875 to quell a riot occasioned by the appearance of several white Democrats who tried to claim seats despite their not being officially elected. The incident backfired. Many northern Republicans were aghast at the idea of soldiers taking control of a state legislative session. Although President Grant defended the army's action, the widespread newspaper coverage of the incident helped accelerate the decline in public support for Reconstruction. Later that year, when the Mississippi governor appealed to Grant to provide federal troops to ensure an honest state election, Grant refused.

Republican political control collapsed in Virginia and Tennessee as early as 1869; in Georgia and North Carolina it collapsed in 1870, although North

Carolina had a Republican governor until 1876. Reconstruction lasted longest in the Deep South states with the largest black population, where whites abandoned Klan masks for barefaced intimidation in paramilitary groups such as the Mississippi Rifle Club and the South Carolina Red Shirts. By 1876, Radical Republican regimes survived only in Louisiana, South Carolina, and Florida, and those collapsed after the elections of that year.

PANIC AND REDEMPTION    Economic distress followed close upon the public scandals besetting the Grant administration. Such developments help explain why northerners lost interest in Reconstruction. A contraction of the nation's money supply resulting from the withdrawal of greenbacks and investments in new railroads helped precipitate a financial crisis. In 1873, the market for railroad bonds turned sour as some twenty-five railroads defaulted on their interest payments. The prestigious investment bank of Jay Cooke and Company went bankrupt on September 18, 1873, and the ensuing stampede of investors eager to exchange securities for cash forced the stock market to close for ten days. The panic of 1873 set off a depression that lasted six years, the longest and most severe that Americans had yet suffered. Thousands of businesses went bankrupt, millions of people lost their jobs, and as usually occurs, voters blamed the party in power for their economic woes.

Hard times and political scandals hurt Republicans in the midterm elections of 1874. The Democrats won control of the House of Representatives and gained seats in the Senate. The new Democratic House launched inquiries into the scandals and unearthed further evidence of corruption in high places. The financial panic, meanwhile, focused attention once more on greenback currency.

Since the value of greenbacks was lower than that of gold, greenbacks had become the chief circulating medium. Most people spent greenbacks first and held their gold or used it to settle foreign accounts, thereby draining much gold out of the country. The postwar reduction of greenbacks in circulation, from $432 million to $356 million, had made for tight money. To relieve the currency shortage and stimulate business expansion, the Treasury issued more greenbacks. As usually happened during economic hard times in the nineteenth century, debtors, the people hurt most by depression, called upon the federal government to inflate the money supply so as to make it easier for them to pay their obligations.

For a time the advocates of paper money were riding high. But in 1874, Grant vetoed a bill to issue more greenbacks. Then, in his annual message, he called for the redemption of greenbacks in gold, making greenbacks "good as gold" and raising their value to a par with that of the gold dollar. Congress obliged by passing the Specie Resumption Act of 1875. The payment in gold

THE NATIONALISTS AND THEIR PAPER JACKASS.

**Anti-Greenback cartoon**

This cartoon features a "paper jackass" to criticize "countrymen" for fueling inflation through the printing of paper money.

to people who turned in their paper money began on January 1, 1879, after the Treasury had built a gold reserve for that purpose and reduced the value of the greenbacks in circulation. This act infuriated those promoting an inflationary monetary policy and prompted the formation of the Greenback party, which elected fourteen congressmen in 1878. The much-debated and very complex "money question" was destined to remain one of the most divisive issues in American politics.

THE COMPROMISE OF 1877    President Grant, despite the controversies swirling around him, wanted to run again in 1876, but many Republicans balked at the prospect of the nation's first three-term president. After all, the Democrats had devastated the Republicans in the 1874 congressional elections: the decisive Republican majority in the House had evaporated, and the Democrats had taken control. In the summer of 1875, Grant acknowledged the growing opposition to his renomination and announced his retirement. James Gillespie Blaine of Maine, former Speaker of the House and one of the nation's favorite orators, emerged as the Republican front-runner, but he, too, bore the taint of scandal. Letters in the possession of James Mulligan of Boston linked Blaine to dubious railroad dealings, and the "Mulligan letters" found their way into print.

The Republican Convention therefore eliminated Blaine and several other hopefuls in favor of Ohio's favorite son, Rutherford B. Hayes. Elected governor of Ohio three times, most recently as an advocate of gold rather than greenbacks, Hayes had also made a name for himself as a civil service reformer. But his chief virtue was that he offended neither Radicals nor reformers. As a journalist put it, he was "a third rate nonentity, whose only recommendation is that he is obnoxious to no one."

The Democratic Convention was abnormally harmonious from the start. The nomination went on the second ballot to Samuel J. Tilden, a wealthy corporation lawyer and reform governor of New York who had directed a campaign to overthrow the notorious Tweed ring controlling New York City politics.

The 1876 campaign raised no burning issues. Both candidates favored the trend toward relaxing federal authority and restoring white conservative rule

### The Compromise of 1877

This illustration represents the compromise between Republicans and southern Democrats that ended Radical Reconstruction.

in the South. In the absence of strong differences, Democrats aired the Republicans' dirty linen. In response, Republicans waved "the bloody shirt," which is to say that they linked the Democratic party to secession, civil war, and the outrages committed against Republicans in the South. As one Republican speaker insisted, "The man that assassinated Abraham Lincoln was a Democrat.... Soldiers, every scar you have on your heroic bodies was given you by a Democrat!"

Despite the lack of major issues, the 1876 election generated the most votes in American history up to that point. Early election returns pointed to a Tilden victory. Tilden enjoyed a 254,000-vote edge in the balloting and had won 184 electoral votes, just one short of a majority. Hayes had only 165 electoral votes, but the Republicans also claimed 19 doubtful votes from Florida,

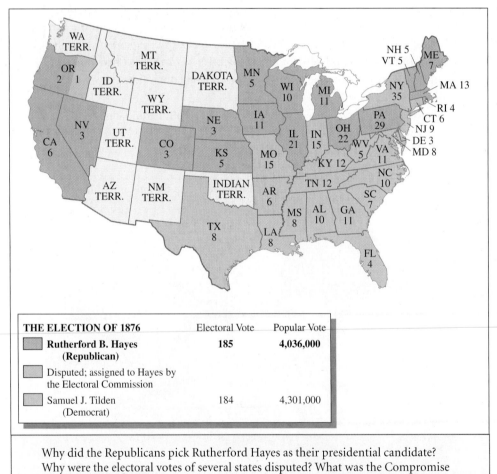

| THE ELECTION OF 1876 | Electoral Vote | Popular Vote |
|---|---|---|
| **Rutherford B. Hayes** (Republican) | **185** | **4,036,000** |
| Disputed; assigned to Hayes by the Electoral Commission | | |
| Samuel J. Tilden (Democrat) | 184 | 4,301,000 |

Why did the Republicans pick Rutherford Hayes as their presidential candidate? Why were the electoral votes of several states disputed? What was the Compromise of 1877?

Louisiana, and South Carolina. The Democrats laid a counterclaim to 1 of Oregon's 3 electoral votes, but the Republicans had clearly carried that state. In the South, the outcome was less certain, and given the fraud and intimidation perpetrated on both sides, nobody will ever know what might have happened if, to use a slogan of the day, "a free ballot and a fair count" had prevailed.

In all three of the disputed southern states, rival election boards sent in different returns. The Constitution offered no guidance in this unprecedented situation. Finally, on January 29, 1877, the Congress decided to set up a special Electoral Commission with fifteen members, five each from the House, the Senate, and the Supreme Court. The commission's decision went by a vote of 8 to 7 along party lines, in favor of Hayes. After much bluster and the threat of a filibuster by the Democrats, the House voted on March 2 to accept the report and declared Hayes elected by an electoral vote of 185 to 184.

Critical to this outcome was the defection of southern Democrats, who had made several informal agreements with the Republicans. On February 26, 1877, prominent Ohio Republicans (including future president James A. Garfield) and powerful southern Democrats struck a secret bargain at Wormley's Hotel in Washington, D.C. The Republicans promised that if Hayes were elected, he would withdraw the last federal troops from Louisiana and South Carolina, letting the Republican governments there collapse. In return, the Democrats promised to withdraw their opposition to Hayes, accept in good faith the Reconstruction amendments (including civil rights for blacks), and refrain from partisan reprisals against Republicans in the South.

THE END OF RECONSTRUCTION   In 1877, new president Hayes withdrew federal troops from Louisiana and South Carolina, and those states' Republican governments collapsed soon thereafter. Over the next three decades, the protection of black civil rights crumbled under the pressure of restored white rule in the South and the force of Supreme Court decisions narrowing the scope of the Reconstruction amendments to the Constitution. As a former slave observed in 1877, "The whole South—every state in the South—has got [back] into the hands of the very men that held us as slaves."

Radical Reconstruction never offered more than an uncertain commitment to black civil rights and social equality. Yet it left an enduring legacy— the Thirteenth, Fourteenth, and Fifteenth Amendments—not dead but dormant, waiting to be reawakened. If Reconstruction did not provide social equality or substantial economic opportunities for African Americans, it did create the foundation for future advances. It was a revolution, sighed former governor of North Carolina Jonathan Worth, and "nobody can anticipate the action of revolutions."

## CHAPTER SUMMARY

• **Reconstruction** Abraham Lincoln and his successor, southerner Andrew John-son, wanted a lenient and quick plan for Reconstruction. Lincoln's assassination made many northerners favor the Radical Republicans, who wanted to end the grasp of the old planter class on the South's society and economy. Congressional Reconstruction included the stipulation that to reenter the Union, former Confederate states had to ratify the Fourteenth and Fifteenth Amendments. Congress also passed the Military Reconstruction Act, which attempted to protect the voting rights and civil rights of African Americans.

• **Southern Violence** Many white southerners blamed their poverty on freed slaves and Yankees. White mobs attacked blacks in 1866 in Memphis and New Orleans. That year, the Ku Klux Klan was formed as a social club; its members soon began to intimidate freedmen and white Republicans. Despite government action, violence continued and even escalated in the South.

• **Freed Slaves** Newly freed slaves suffered economically. Most did not have the resources to succeed in the aftermath of the war's devastation. There was no redistribution of land; former slaves were given their freedom but nothing else. The Freedmen's Bureau attempted to educate and aid freed slaves and reunite families. Many former slaves found comfort in their families and the indepen-dent churches they established. Some took part in state and local government under the last, radical phase of Reconstruction.

• **Grant Administration** During Ulysses S. Grant's administration, fiscal issues dominated politics. Paper money (greenbacks) was regarded as inflationary; and agrarian and debtor groups opposed its withdrawal from circulation. Many members of Grant's administration were corrupt; scandals involved an attempt to corner the gold market, construction of the intercontinental railroad, and the whiskey ring's plan to steal millions of dollars in tax revenue.

• **End of Reconstruction** Most southern states had completed the requirements of Reconstruction by 1876. The presidential election returns of that year were so close that a special commission was established to count contested electoral votes. A decision hammered out at a secret meeting gave the presidency to the Republican, Rutherford B. Hayes; in return, the Democrats were promised that the last federal troops would be withdrawn from Louisiana and South Carolina, putting an end to the Radical Republican administrations in the southern states.

## CHRONOLOGY

| | |
|---|---|
| 1862 | Congress passes the Morrill Land Grant Act |
| | Congress guarantees the construction of a transcontinental railroad |
| | Congress passes the Homestead Act |
| 1864 | Lincoln refuses to sign the Wade-Davis Bill |
| 1865 | Congress sets up the Freedmen's Bureau |
| April 14, 1865 | Lincoln is assassinated |
| 1866 | Ku Klux Klan is organized |
| | Congress passes the Civil Rights Act |
| 1867 | Congress passes the Military Reconstruction Act |
| | Congress passes the Tenure of Office Act |
| 1868 | Fourteenth Amendment is ratified |
| | Congress impeaches President Andrew Johnson; the Senate fails to convict him |
| 1877 | Compromise of 1877 ends Reconstruction |

## KEY TERMS & NAMES

Freedmen's Bureau  p. 710

John Wilkes Booth  p. 713

Andrew Johnson  p. 713

black codes  p. 716

Thaddeus Stevens  p. 717

Fourteenth Amendment p. 719

Fifteenth Amendment p. 723

carpetbaggers  p. 728

scalawags  p. 728

greenbacks  p. 732

Crédit Mobilier scandal p. 734

Horace Greeley  p. 737

Compromise of 1877 p. 740

# Part Five

# GROWING

# PAINS

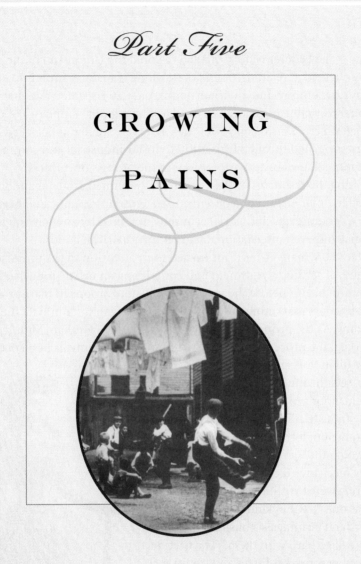

The Federal victory in 1865 restored the Union and in the process helped accelerate America's stunning transformation into an agricultural empire and an urban-industrial nation-state. A distinctly national consciousness began to displace the regional emphases of the antebellum era. During and after the Civil War, the Republican-led Congress pushed through legislation to foster industrial and commercial development and western expansion. In the process of ruthlessly exploiting the resources of the continent, the United States abandoned the Jeffersonian dream of a decentralized agrarian republic and began to forge a dynamic new industrial economy nurtured by an increasingly national and even international market for American goods.

After 1865, many Americans turned their attention to the unfinished business of settling a continent and completing an urban-industrial revolution begun before the war. Fueled by innovations in mass production and mass marketing, huge corporations began to dominate the economy. As the prominent social theorist William Graham Sumner remarked, the process of industrial development "controls us all because we are all in it. It creates the conditions of our own existence, sets the limits of our social activity, and regulates the bonds of our social relations."

The Industrial Revolution was not only an urban phenomenon; it transformed rural life as well. Those who got in the way of the new emphasis on large-scale, highly mechanized commercial agriculture and ranching were brusquely pushed aside. Farm folk, as one New Englander stressed, "must understand farming as a business; if they do not it will go hard with them." The friction between new market forces and traditional folkways generated political revolts and social unrest during the last quarter of the nineteenth century. Fault lines appeared throughout the social order, and they unleashed tremors that exerted what one writer called "a seismic shock, a cyclonic violence" upon the political culture.

The clash between tradition and modernity peaked during the 1890s, one of the most strife-ridden decades in American history. A deep depression, agrarian unrest, and labor violence unleashed fears of class warfare. This turbulent situation transformed the presidential-election campaign of 1896 into a clash between rival visions of America's future. The Republican candidate, William McKinley, campaigned on behalf of modern urban-industrial values. By contrast, William Jennings Bryan, the nominee of the Democratic and Populist parties, was an eloquent defender of America's rural past. McKinley's victory proved to be a watershed in American political and social history. By 1900, the United States would emerge as one of the world's greatest industrial powers, and it would thereafter assume a new leadership role in world affairs—for good and for ill.

# 18

## BIG BUSINESS AND ORGANIZED LABOR

FOCUS QUESTIONS    Ⓢ   wwnorton.com/studyspace

- What fueled the growth of the post–Civil War economy?
- What roles were played by leading entrepreneurs like John D. Rockefeller, Andrew Carnegie, and J. Pierpont Morgan?
- Who composed the labor force of the period, and what were labor's main grievances?
- What led to the rise of labor unions?

America emerged as an industrial and agricultural giant in the late nineteenth century. Blessed with vast natural resources, impressive technological advances, relentless population growth and entrepreneurial energy, and little government regulation, the economy grew more rapidly and changed more dramatically than ever before. Between 1869 and 1899, the nation's population nearly tripled, farm production more than doubled, and the value of manufactured goods grew sixfold. Within three generations after the Civil War, the predominantly rural nation burst forth as the world's preeminent commercial, agricultural, and industrial power. By 1900, the United States dominated global markets in steel and oil, wheat and cotton. Corporations grew enormously in size and power, and social tensions and political corruption worsened with the rising scale of business enterprise.

## THE RISE OF BIG BUSINESS

In the decades after the Civil War, huge corporations came to dominate the economy—as well as political and social life. As businesses grew, their owners sought to integrate all the processes of production and distribution of goods into single companies, thus creating even larger firms. Others grew by mergers, joining forces with their competitors in an effort to dominate entire industries. This process of industrial development transformed the nation's economy and social life. It also sparked widespread dissent and the emergence of an organized labor movement representing wage workers.

Many factors converged to help accelerate economic growth after the Civil War. The nation's unparalleled natural resources—forests, mineral wealth, rivers—along with a rapidly expanding population, were crucial ingredients. At the same time, inventors and business owners developed more efficient, labor-saving machinery and mass-production techniques that spurred dramatic advances in productivity and efficiency. As the volume and efficiency of production increased, the larger businesses and industries expanded their operations across the country and in the process developed standardized machinery and parts, which became available nationwide. Innovative, bold leadership was another crucial factor spurring economic transformation. A group of shrewd, determined, and energetic entrepreneurs took advantage of fertile business opportunities to create huge new enterprises. Federal and state politicians after the Civil War actively encouraged the growth of business by imposing high tariffs on foreign imports as a means of blunting competition and by providing land and cash to finance railroads and other transportation improvements. At the same time that the federal government was issuing massive land grants to railroads and land speculators, it was also distributing 160-acre homesteads to citizens, including single women and freed slaves, through the important Homestead Act of 1862.

Equally important in propelling the post–Civil War economic boom was what government did not do in the decades after the Civil War: it did not regulate the activities of big businesses, nor did it provide any oversight of business operations or working conditions. The so-called Gilded Age was dominated by unfettered capitalism operating within a turbulent, anarchic environment free of income tax, meddling regulators, and other curbs on the behavior of freewheeling entrepreneurs.

Business leaders spent a lot of time—and money—ensuring that government stayed out of their businesses. In fact, political corruption was so rampant that it was routine. Business leaders usually got what they wanted from Congress and state legislators—even if they had to pay for it. The collaboration between elected officials and business executives was so commonplace that in 1868 the New York state legislature legalized the bribery of politicians.

At the same time that the industrial sector was witnessing an ever-increasing concentration of large companies, the agricultural sector by 1870 was also experiencing such rapid growth that it had become the world's leader, fueling the rest of the economy by providing wheat and corn to be milled into flour and meal. With the advent of the commercial cattle industry, the processes of slaughtering and packing meat themselves became major industries. So the farm sector directly stimulated the industrial sector of the economy. A national government-subsidized network of railroads connecting the East and West Coasts played a crucial role in the development of related industries and in the evolution of an interconnected national market for goods and services. The industrial transformation also benefited from an abundance of power sources—water, wood, coal, oil, and electricity—that were inexpensive compared with those of the other nations of the world.

THE SECOND INDUSTRIAL REVOLUTION   The Industrial Revolution "controls us all," said Yale sociologist William Graham Sumner, "because we are all in it." Sumner and other Americans living during the second half of the nineteenth century experienced what economic historians have termed the Second Industrial Revolution. The First Industrial Revolution began in Britain during the late eighteenth century. It was propelled by the convergence of three new technologies: the coal-powered steam engine, textile machines for spinning thread and weaving cloth, and blast furnaces to produce iron. The Second Industrial Revolution began in the mid–nineteenth century and was centered in the United States and Germany. It was spurred by three related developments. The first was the creation of interconnected transportation and communication networks, which facilitated the emergence of a national and even an international market for American goods and services. Contributing to this development were the completion of the national telegraph and railroad networks; the emergence of steamships, which were much larger and faster than sailing ships; and the laying of the undersea telegraph cable, which spanned the Atlantic Ocean and connected the United States with Europe.

During the 1880s a second major breakthrough—the widespread application of electrical power—accelerated the pace of industrial change. Electricity created dramatic advances in the power and efficiency of industrial machinery. It also spurred urban growth through the addition of electric trolleys and subways, and it greatly enhanced the production of steel and chemicals.

The third major catalyst for the Second Industrial Revolution was the systematic application of scientific research to industrial processes. Laboratories staffed by graduates of new research universities sprouted up across the country, and scientists and engineers discovered dramatic new ways to improve industrial processes. Researchers figured out, for example, how to refine kerosene and gasoline from crude oil and how to improve steel production. Inventors developed new products—telephones, typewriters, adding machines, sewing machines, cameras, elevators, and farm machinery—that resulted in lower prices for an array of consumer items. These advances in turn expanded the scope and scale of industrial organizations. Capital-intensive industries such as steel and oil, as well as processed food and tobacco, took advantage of new technologies to gain economies of scale that emphasized maximum production and national as well as international marketing and distribution.

RAILROADS    More than any other technological innovation, the railroads symbolized the urban-industrial revolution. No other form of transportation exercised as much influence in the development of post–Civil War America. Railroads shrunk time and distance. They moved masses of people and goods faster and farther than any other form of transportation. The advent of the nation's railroad network prompted the creation of uniform national and international time zones and spurred the use of wristwatches, for the trains were scheduled to run on time. A British traveler in America in the 1860s said that a town's connection to a railroad was "the first necessity of life, and gives the only hope of wealth." Although the first great wave of railroad building occurred in the 1850s, the most spectacular growth took place during the quarter century after the Civil War. From about thirty-five thousand miles of track in 1865, the national rail network grew to nearly two hundred thousand miles by 1897. The transcontinental rail lines led the way, and they helped populate the Great Plains and the Far West. Such a sprawling railroad system was expensive, and the long-term debt required to finance it would become a major cause of the financial panic of 1893 and the ensuing depression.

Railroads were America's first big business, the first magnet for the great financial market known as Wall Street in New York City, and the first industry to develop a large-scale management bureaucracy. Railroads were much larger enterprises than textile mills and iron foundries, the other large industries in the 1860s and 1870s. They required more capital and more complex management. The railroads opened the western half of the nation to economic development, enabled federal troops to suppress Indian resistance, ferried millions of European and Asian immigrants across the country, provided the catalyst for transforming commercial agriculture into a major international industry, and transported raw materials to factories and finished goods to retailers. In so doing, they created an interconnected national market. At the same time, the railroads were themselves the largest consumers of the iron, steel, lumber, and other capital goods that freight cars carried. Railway stations became a dominant new public space in towns and cities. At one point, New York City's massive Penn Station employed three thousand people. The hotel built adjacent to the station and owned by the railroad employed hundreds more. From the 1860s through the 1950s, most people entered or left a city through its railroad stations.

But the railroads created problems as well as blessings. Too many were built, often in the wrong places, at a time when they were not truly needed. In their race to build new rail lines, companies allowed for dangerous working conditions that caused thousands of laborers to be killed or injured. Shoddy construction caused tragic accidents and required rickety bridges and trestles to be rebuilt. Numerous railroads were poorly or even criminally managed and went bankrupt. The lure of enormous profits helped to corrupt the political system as the votes of politicians were "bought" with cash or shares of stock in the railroad companies. Railroad executives essentially created the modern practice of political "lobbying," and they came to exercise a dangerous degree of influence over both the economy and the political system. As Charles Francis Adams Jr., the head of the Union Pacific Railroad, acknowledged, "Our method of doing business is founded upon lying, cheating, and stealing—all bad things."

BUILDING THE TRANSCONTINENTALS    The renewal of railroad building after the Civil War filled out the rail network east of the Mississippi River. Gradually, tracks in the South that had been destroyed during the war were rebuilt, and a web of new trunk lines was added throughout the country. But the most spectacular achievements were the monumental transcontinental lines built west of the Mississippi River across desolate plains, over roaring rivers and deep canyons, and around as well as through the nation's tallest mountains.

Before the Civil War, differences between the North and South over the choice of routes had held up the start of a transcontinental line. Secession and the departure of southern congressmen for the Confederacy in 1861 finally permitted Republicans in Congress to pass the Pacific Railway Act in 1862, which authorized the construction of a rail line along a north-central route, to be built by the Union Pacific Railroad westward from Omaha, Nebraska, and by the Central Pacific Railroad eastward from Sacramento, California. Both companies began construction during the war, but most of the work was done after 1865. The first transcontinental railroads were utterly dependent on government support. They received huge loans, massive grants of "public" land taken from the Indians, and lavish cash subsidies from the federal government. The Union Pacific pushed west across the plains at a rapid pace, avoiding the Rocky Mountains by going through Evans Pass in Wyoming. Construction of the 2,000-mile rail line and hundreds of

**Transcontinental railroads**

Using picks, shovels, wheelbarrows, and horse-drawn carts, Chinese laborers largely helped to construct the Central Pacific track.

trestles and bridges was hasty, and much of it had to be redone later. The executives and financiers directing the transcontinental railroads often cut corners, bribed legislators, and manipulated accounts to line their own pockets. They also ruthlessly used federal troops to suppress the Plains Indians.

But the shenanigans of the railroad barons do not diminish the fact that the transcontinental railroads were, in the words, of General William Tecumseh Sherman, the "work of giants." Building rail lines across the West involved heroic feats of daring by workers and engineers who laid the rails, erected the bridges and trestles, and gouged out the tunnels under dangerous working conditions and harsh weather. The transcontinental railroads tied the nation together, changed the economic and political landscape, and enabled the United States to emerge as a world power.

It took armies of laborers to build the railroads. Some ten thousand men worked on the two railroads as they raced to connect with one another. The Union Pacific work crews, composed of former Union and Confederate soldiers, former slaves, and Irish and German immigrants, coped with bad roads, water shortages, extreme weather conditions, Indian attacks, and frequent accidents and injuries. The Central Pacific crews were mainly Chinese workers lured to America first by the California gold rush and then by railroad jobs. Most of these "coolie" laborers were single men intent upon accumulating money and returning to their homeland, where they could then afford to marry and buy a parcel of land. Their temporary status and dream of a good life back in China apparently made them more willing than American laborers to endure the low pay of railroad work and the dangerous working conditions. Many railroad construction workers died on the job.

All sorts of issues delayed the effort to finish the transcontinental line. Iron prices spiked. Broken treaties prompted Indian raids. Blizzards shut down work for weeks. Fifty-seven miles east of Sacramento, construction crews encountered the towering Sierra Nevada Mountains, which they had to cross before reaching more level terrain in Nevada. The Union Pacific had built 1,086 miles compared with the Central Pacific's 689 when the race ended on the salt flats at Promontory, Utah. There, on May 10, 1869, former California governor Leland Stanford drove a gold spike symbolizing the railroad's completion.

The next transcontinental line, completed in 1881, linked the Atchison, Topeka, and Santa Fe Railroad with the Southern Pacific Railroad at Needles

**The Union Pacific meets the Central Pacific**

The celebration of the completion of the first transcontinental railroad, Promontory, Utah, May 10, 1869.

in southern California. The Southern Pacific, which had absorbed the Central Pacific, pushed through Arizona to Texas in 1882, where it made connections to St. Louis and New Orleans. To the north the Northern Pacific had connected Lake Superior with Oregon by 1883, and ten years later the Great Northern, which had slowly and carefully been building westward from St. Paul, Minnesota, thrust its way to Tacoma, Washington. Thus, before the turn of the century, five major trunk lines existed, supplemented by connections that enabled the construction of other transcontinental routes.

FINANCING THE RAILROADS   The shady financial practices of railroad executives earned them the label of "robber barons," an epithet soon extended to other "captains of industry" as well. These were shrewd, deter-

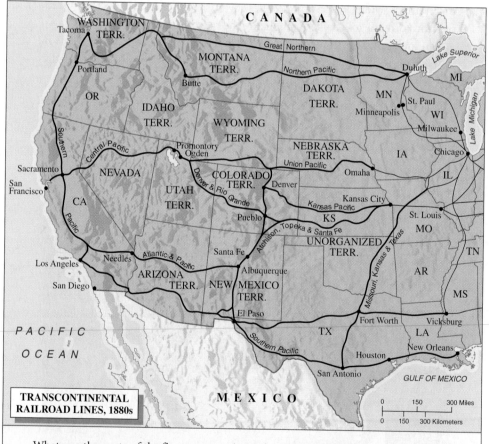

TRANSCONTINENTAL
RAILROAD LINES, 1880s

What was the route of the first transcontinental railroad, and why was it not in the South? Who built the railroads? How were they financed?

mined, and often ruthless and dishonest men. "What do I care about law?" asked the railroad tycoon Cornelius Vanderbilt. "Hain't I got the power?" The building of the Union Pacific and the Central Pacific—as well as other transcontinental rail lines—involved shameless profiteering by construction companies controlled by insiders who overcharged the railroad companies. One such company, Crédit Mobilier of America, according to congressional investigators, bribed congressmen and charged the Union Pacific $94 million for a construction project that cost at most $44 million.

The prince of the railroad robber barons was **Jay Gould**, a secretive trickster who mastered the fine art of buying rundown railroads, making cosmetic improvements, and selling out at a profit, all the while using corporate funds for personal investments and the payment of judicious bribes for politicians and judges. Nearly every enterprise he touched was compromised or ruined; Gould, meanwhile, was building a fortune that amounted to $100 million upon his death, at age fifty-six.

Few railroad fortunes were amassed in those freewheeling times by purely honest methods, but compared with opportunistic rogues such as Gould, most railroad owners were saints. They at least took some interest in the welfare of their companies, if not always in that of the public. **Cornelius Vanderbilt**, called "the Commodore" by virtue of his early exploits in steamboating, stands out among the railroad barons. Already rich before the Civil War, he decided to give up the hazards of wartime shipping in favor of land transport. Under his direction the first of the major eastern railroad consolidations took form.

In 1869, the clever, daring, ruthless, relentless, revered, and hated Vanderbilt merged separate rail lines connecting Albany and Buffalo, New York, into a single powerful rail network led by the New York Central. This accomplished, he forged connections to New York City and Chicago, all the while amassing one of the greatest personal fortunes America has ever seen. After the Commodore's death, in 1877, his son William Henry extended the Vanderbilt railroads to include more than thirteen thousand miles in the Northeast. The consolidation

**Jay Gould**
Prince of the railroad buccaneers.

**"Commodore" Cornelius Vanderbilt**

Vanderbilt consolidated control of the vast New York Central Railroad in the 1860s.

trend was nationwide: about two thirds of the nation's railroad mileage were under the control of only seven companies by 1900.

INVENTIONS SPUR MANU- FACTURING The story of manufacturing after the Civil War shows much the same pattern of expansion and merger in old and new industries. Technological innovations spurred phenomenal increases in industrial productivity. The U.S. Patent Office, which had recorded only 276 inventions during its first decade of existence, the 1790s, registered almost 235,000 new patents in the 1890s. New processes in steelmaking and oil refining enabled those industries to flourish. The invention of the refrigerated railcar allowed the beef, mutton, and pork of the West to reach national markets in the East, giving rise to great packinghouse enterprises in the Midwest. Corrugated rollers that could crack the hard, spicy wheat of the Great Plains provided impetus to the flour milling industry that centered in Minneapolis under the control of the Pillsbury Company and others.

The list of commercial innovations after the Civil War was lengthy: barbed wire, farm implements, the air brake for trains (1868), steam turbines, electrical devices, typewriters (1867), vacuum cleaners (1869), and countless others. Before the end of the century, the internal-combustion engine and the motion picture were stimulating new industries that would emerge in the twentieth century.

These technological advances transformed daily life. Few if any inventions of the time could rival the importance of the telephone, which twenty-nine-year-old inventor Alexander Graham Bell patented in 1876. To promote the new device transmitting voices over wires, the inventor and his supporters formed the Bell Telephone Company, which was eventually surpassed by the American Telephone and Telegraph Company.

In the development of electrical industries, the name Thomas Alva Edison stands above those of other inventors. In his laboratory in Menlo Park, New Jersey, Edison invented the phonograph in 1877 and the first light bulb in 1879. Altogether he created or perfected hundreds of new devices and processes, including the storage battery, Dictaphone, mimeograph, electric motor, electric transmission, and the motion picture camera and projector.

Until 1880 or so, the world was lit by flickering oil and gas lamps. In 1882 the Edison Electric Illuminating Company supplied electrical current to eighty-five customers in New York City, beginning the great electric utility industry. A number of companies making lightbulbs merged into the Edison General Electric Company in 1888. But the use of direct current limited Edison's lighting system to a radius of about two miles. To cover greater distances required an alternating current, which could be transmitted at high voltage and then stepped down by transformers. George Westinghouse, inventor of the air brake for railroads,

**New technologies**

Alexander Graham Bell being observed by businessmen at the New York end of the first long-distance telephone call to Chicago, 1892.

developed the first alternating-current electric system in 1886 and set up the Westinghouse Electric Company to manufacture the equipment. Edison resisted the new method as too risky, but the Westinghouse system won the "battle of the currents," and the Edison companies had to switch over. After the invention in 1887 of the alternating-current motor by a Croatian immigrant named Nikola Tesla, Westinghouse improved upon it. The invention of electric motors enabled factories to locate wherever they wished; they no longer had to cluster around waterfalls and coal deposits for a ready supply of energy. The electric motor also led to the development of elevators and streetcars. Buildings could go higher with electric elevators, and cities could spawn suburbs because of electric streetcars providing transportation.

## ENTREPRENEURS

Thomas Alva Edison and George Westinghouse were rare examples of inventors with the luck and foresight to get rich from the industries they created. The great captains of commerce during the Gilded Age were more

**John D. Rockefeller**

His Standard Oil Company dominated the oil industry.

often pure entrepreneurs rather than inventors, outsized men who were ruthless competitors adept at increasing production, lowering prices, and garnering efficiencies. Several post–Civil War entrepreneurs stand out for both their achievements and their special contributions: John D. Rockefeller and Andrew Carnegie for their innovations in organization, J. Pierpont Morgan for his development of investment banking, and Richard Sears and Alvah Roebuck for their creation of mail-order retailing. In their different ways, each of these titans dealt a mortal blow to the small-scale economy of the early republic, fostering vast industries that forever altered the size and scope of business and industry.

ROCKEFELLER AND THE OIL TRUST    Born in New York, **John D. Rockefeller** moved as a youth to Cleveland, Ohio. Soon thereafter his father abandoned the family. Raised by his mother, a devout Baptist, Rockefeller developed a passion for systematic organization and self-discipline. Scrupulously honest but fiercely ambitious, he was obsessed with precision, order, and tidiness, and early on he decided to bring order and rationality to the chaotic oil industry.

The railroad and shipping connections around Cleveland made it a strategic location for servicing the booming oil fields of western Pennsylvania. The first oil well in the United States began producing in 1859 in Titusville, Pennsylvania, and led to the Pennsylvania oil rush of the 1860s. Because oil could be refined into kerosene, which was widely used in lighting, heating, and cooking, the economic importance of the oil rush soon outstripped that of the California gold rush of just ten years before. Well before the end of the Civil War, drilling derricks checkered western Pennsylvania, and refineries sprang up in Pittsburgh and Cleveland. Of the two cities, Cleveland had the edge in rail service, so Rockefeller focused his energies there.

Rockefeller recognized the potential profits in refining oil, and in 1870 he incorporated his various interests, naming the enterprise the **Standard Oil Company of Ohio**. Although Rockefeller was the largest refiner, he wanted to weed out the competition in order to raise prices. He bought out most of his Cleveland competitors; those who resisted were forced out. By

**The rise of oil**

Wooden derricks crowd the farm of John Benninghoff in Oil Creek, Pennsylvania, in the 1860s.

1879, Standard Oil controlled over 90 percent of the oil refining in the country.

Much of Rockefeller's success was based upon his determination to reduce expenses and eliminate waste as well as "pay nobody a profit." Instead of depending upon the products or services of other firms, known as middlemen, Standard Oil produced its own oil, barrels, and whatever else it needed—in economic terms, this is called vertical integration. The company also kept large amounts of cash reserves to make it independent of banks in case of a crisis. Furthermore, Rockefeller gained control of his transportation needs. With Standard Oil owning most of the pipelines leading to railroads, plus the rail-road tank cars and the oil-storage facilities, it was able to dissuade the railroads from serving its eastern competitors. Those rivals that had insisted upon hold-ing out rather than selling their enterprise to Rockefeller then faced a giant marketing organization capable of driving them to the wall with price wars.

To consolidate their scattered business interests under more efficient con-trol, Rockefeller and his advisers resorted to a new legal device: in 1882 they organized the Standard Oil Trust. All thirty-seven stockholders in various Standard Oil enterprises conveyed their stock to nine trustees, receiving "trust certificates" in return, which paid them annual dividends from the company's earnings. The nine trustees thereby controlled all the varied Standard Oil companies.

But the trust device, widely copied by other companies in the 1880s, proved vulnerable to prosecution under state laws against monopoly or restraint of trade. In 1892, Ohio's supreme court ordered the Standard Oil Trust dissolved. Gradually, however, Rockefeller perfected the idea of the holding company: a company that controlled other companies by holding all or at least a majority of their stock. He was convinced that such big business was a natural result of capitalism at work. "It is too late," he declared in 1899, "to argue about the advantages of [huge] industrial combinations. They are a necessity." That year, Rockefeller brought his empire under the direction of the Standard Oil Company of New Jersey, a gigantic holding company. Though less vulnerable to prosecution under state law, some holding companies were broken up by the Sherman Anti-Trust Act of 1890.

Rockefeller not only made a colossal fortune, but he also gave much of it away, mostly to support education and medicine. A man of simple tastes who opposed the use of tobacco and alcohol and believed his fortune was a public trust awarded by God, he became the world's leading philanthropist. He donated more than $500 million during his ninety-eight-year lifetime. "I have always regarded it as a religious duty," Rockefeller said late in life, "to get all I could honorably and to give all I could."

CARNEGIE AND THE STEEL INDUSTRY   Like Rockefeller, **Andrew Carnegie** experienced an uncommon rise from poverty to riches. Born in Scotland, he migrated in 1848 with his family to Allegheny County, Pennsylvania. Then thirteen, he started work as a bobbin boy in a textile mill. In 1853 he became personal secretary and telegrapher to Thomas Scott, then district superintendent of the Pennsylvania Railroad and later its president. When Scott moved up, Carnegie took his place as superintendent. During the Civil War, when Scott became assistant secretary of war in charge of transportation, Carnegie went with him and developed a military telegraph system.

Carnegie kept on moving—from telegraphy to railroading to bridge building and then to steelmaking and investments. Intelligent, energetic, practical, and ferociously ambitious,

**Andrew Carnegie**
Steel magnate and business icon.

he wanted not simply to compete in an industry; he wanted to dominate it. To do so he was willing to abuse his power and become a compulsive liar.

Until the mid–nineteenth century, steel could be made only from wrought iron—itself expensive—and only in small quantities. Then, in 1855, Briton Sir Henry Bessemer invented what became known as the Bessemer converter, a process by which steel could be produced directly and quickly from pig iron (crude iron made in a blast furnace). In 1873, Carnegie resolved to concentrate on steel. Steel was the miracle material of the post–Civil War era, not because it was new but because Bessemer's process had made it suddenly cheap. As more steel was produced, its price dropped and uses soared. In 1860 the United States had produced only 13,000 tons of steel. By 1880, production had reached 1.4 million tons.

Andrew Carnegie was never a technical expert on steel. He was a promoter, salesman, and organizer with a gift for hiring men of expert ability. He insisted upon up-to-date machinery and equipment and used times of recession to expand cheaply by purchasing struggling companies. He also preached to his employees a philosophy of continual innovation in order to reduce operating costs.

## Carnegie's empire

The huge Carnegie steel plant at Homestead, Pennsylvania.

Carnegie believed that he and other captains of industry, however harsh their methods, were public benefactors. In his best-remembered essay, "The Gospel of Wealth" (1889), he argued that, "Not evil, but good, has come to the race from the accumulation of wealth by those who have the ability and energy that produces it." He applied Charles Darwin's concept of evolution to society, arguing that the law of human competition is "best for the trade, because it insures the survival of the fittest in every department."

Not only did Carnegie make an incredible amount of money; like Rockefeller, he also gave much of it away. After retiring from business at age sixty-five, he devoted himself to dispensing his fortune for the public good. He called himself a "distributor" of wealth (he disliked the term *philanthropy*). He gave money to many universities, built 1,700 public libraries, and helped fund numerous hospitals, parks, halls for meetings and concerts, swimming pools, and church buildings. He also donated eight hundred organs to churches around the world.

**J. PIERPONT MORGAN, FINANCIER**  Unlike Rockefeller and Carnegie, **J. Pierpont Morgan** didn't build industries; he financed them. He also was not a "rags-to-riches" story; he was born to wealth. His father was a partner in a London bank. After attending boarding school in Switzerland and university in Germany, the younger Morgan was sent in 1857 to work in a New York firm representing his father's interests and in 1860 set himself up as its New York agent under the name J. Pierpont Morgan and Company. That firm, under various names, channeled European capital into the United States and grew into a financial power in its own right.

**J. Pierpont Morgan**

Morgan is shown here in a famous 1903 portrait by Edward Steichen.

Morgan was an investment banker, which meant that he would buy corporate stocks and bonds wholesale and sell them at a profit. The growth of large corporations put investment firms such as Morgan's in an increasingly strategic position in the economy. Since the investment business depended upon the general good health of client companies, investment bankers became involved in the operation of their clients' firms, demanding seats on the boards of directors so as to influence company policies.

Like John D. Rockefeller, J. P. Morgan sought to consolidate rival firms into giant trusts. Morgan realized early on that railroads were the key modern industry, and he acquired and reorganized one line after another. By the 1890s, he alone controlled a sixth of the nation's railway system. To Morgan, an imperious, domineering man, the stability brought by his operations helped the economy and the public. His crowning triumph was consolidation of the steel industry. After a rapid series of mergers in the iron and steel industry, he bought out Andrew Carnegie's huge steel and iron holdings in 1901. In rapid succession, Morgan added other steel interests as well as the Rockefeller iron ore holdings in Minnesota's Mesabi Range and a Great Lakes shipping fleet. The new United States Steel Corporation, a holding company for these varied interests, was a marvel of the new century, the first billion-dollar corporation, the climactic event in the age of relentless business consolidation.

SEARS AND ROEBUCK    American inventors helped manufacturers after the Civil War produce a vast number of new products, but the most important economic challenge was extending the reach of national commerce to the millions of people who lived on isolated farms and in small towns. In the aftermath of the Civil War, a traveling salesman from Chicago named Aaron Montgomery Ward decided that he could reach more people by mail than on foot and in the process could eliminate the middlemen whose services increased

**The rise of business**

A lavish dinner celebrated the merger of the Carnegie and Morgan interests in 1901. The shape of the table is meant to symbolize a rail.

**Cover of the 1897 Sears, Roebuck and Company catalog**

Sears, Roebuck's extensive mail-order business and discounted prices allowed its many products to reach customers in cities and in the backcountry.

the retail price of goods. Beginning in the early 1870s, Montgomery Ward and Company began selling goods at a 40-percent discount through mail-order catalogs.

By the end of the century, a new retailer had come to dominate the mail-order industry: **Sears, Roebuck and Company**, founded by two young midwestern entrepreneurs, Richard Sears and Alvah Roebuck, who began offering a cornucopia of goods by mail in the early 1890s. The Sears, Roebuck catalog in 1897 was 786 pages long. It featured groceries, drugs, tools, bells, furniture, iceboxes, stoves, household utensils, musical instruments, farm implements, boots and shoes, clothes, books, and sporting goods. The company's ability to buy goods in high volume from wholesalers enabled it to sell items at prices below those offered in rural general stores. By 1907, Sears, Roebuck and Company had become one of the largest business enterprises in the nation.

The Sears catalog helped create a truly national market and in the process transformed the lives of millions of people. With the advent of free rural mail delivery in 1898 and the widespread distribution of Sears catalogs, families on farms and in small towns and villages could purchase by mail the products that heretofore were either prohibitively expensive or available only to city dwellers. By the turn of the century, 6 million Sears catalogs were being distributed each year, and the catalog had become the single most widely read book in the nation after the Bible.

## THE WORKING CLASS

The captains of industry and finance dominated economic life during the so-called Gilded Age. Their innovations and their businesses provided a rapidly growing American population with jobs. But it was the laboring classes who actually produced the iron and steel, coal and oil, beef and pork, and the array of new consumer items filling city department stores and the shelves of "general" stores.

SOCIAL TRENDS    Accompanying the spread of huge corporations after the Civil War was a rising standard of living for most people. If the rich were getting richer, a lot of other people were at least getting better off. But disparities in the distribution of wealth grew wider during the second half of the nineteenth century. In both 1860 and 1900, the richest 2 percent of American families owned more than a third of the nation's wealth, while the top 10 percent owned almost three fourths of it.

The continuing demand for unskilled or semiskilled workers, meanwhile, attracted new groups entering the workforce at the bottom: immigrants above all, but also growing numbers of women and children. Because of a long-term decline in prices and the cost of living, real wages and earnings in manufacturing went up about 50 percent between 1860 and 1890 and another 37 percent from 1890 to 1914. By modern-day standards, however, working conditions were dreary and often dangerous. The average work-week was fifty-nine hours, or nearly six ten-hour days, but that was only an average. Most steelworkers put in a twelve-hour day, and as late as the 1920s a great many worked a seven-day, eighty-four-hour week.

Although wage levels were rising overall, working and living conditions remained precarious. In the crowded tenements of major cities, the death rate was much higher than that in the countryside. Factories often maintained poor health and safety conditions. American industry had the highest accident rate in the world. In 1913, for instance, there were some twenty-five thousand workplace fatalities and seven hundred thousand serious job-related injuries. The United States was the only industrial nation in the world that had no workmen's compensation program to provide financial support for workers injured on the job. The new industrial culture after the Civil War was also increasingly impersonal. Ever-larger numbers of people were dependent upon the machinery and factories of owners whom they seldom if ever saw. In the simpler world of small shops, workers and employers could enter into close relationships; the new large factories and corporations, on the other hand, were governed by a bureaucracy in which ownership was separate from management. Much of the social history of the modern world in fact turns upon the transition from a world of personal relationships to one of impersonal, contractual relationships.

CHILD LABOR    A growing number of wage laborers after the Civil War were children—boys and girls who worked full-time for meager wages under unhealthy conditions. Young people had of course always worked in America: farms required everyone to pitch in. After the Civil War, however, millions of children took up work outside the home, operating machines, sorting coal, stitching clothes, shucking oysters, peeling shrimp, canning food, blowing glass, and tending looms. Parents desperate for income believed they had no choice but to put their children to work. By 1880, one out of every six children in the nation was working full-time; by 1900, there were almost 2 million child laborers in the United States. In southern cotton mills, where few African Americans were hired, a fourth of the employees were below the age of fifteen, with half of the children younger than twelve. Children as young as eight were laboring alongside adults twelve hours a day, six days a week. This meant they received little or no education and had little time for play or parental nurturance.

Factories, mills, mines, and canneries were dangerous places, especially for children. Few machines had safety devices, and few factories or mills had ventilating fans or fire escapes. Throughout Appalachia, soot-smeared boys worked deep in the coal mines. In New England and the South, thousands of young girls worked in dusty textile mills, brushing away lint from the clacking machines and retying broken threads. Children suffered three times as

**Children in industry**

Four young boys who did the dangerous work of mine helpers in West Virginia in 1900.

many accidents as adult workers, and respiratory diseases were common in the unventilated buildings. A child working in a textile mill was only half as likely to reach the age of twenty as a child outside a mill. Although some states passed laws limiting the number of hours children could work and establishing minimum-age requirements, they were rarely enforced and often ignored. By 1881 only seven states, mostly in New England, had laws requiring children to be at least twelve before they worked for wages. Yet the only proof required by employers in such states was a statement from a child's parents. Working-class and immigrant parents were often so desperate for income that they forged work permits for their children or taught them to lie about their age to keep a job.

DISORGANIZED PROTEST    Under these circumstances it was very difficult for workers to organize unions. Most civic leaders respected property rights more than the rights of labor; they readily deferred to the wishes of business leaders. Many business executives believed that a "labor supply" was simply another commodity to be procured at the lowest possible price. Among factory workers and miners recently removed from an agrarian world of independent farmers, the idea of labor unions was slow to take hold. And much of the workforce was made up of immigrant workers from a variety of cultures. They spoke different languages and harbored ethnic animosities. Nonetheless, with or without unions, workers staged impromptu strikes in response to wage cuts and other grievances. Such action often led to violence, however, and three incidents of the 1870s colored much of the public's view of labor unions thereafter.

THE MOLLY MAGUIRES    The decade's early years saw a reign of terror in the Pennsylvania coalfields, attributed to an Irish group called the **Molly Maguires**. The Mollies took their name from an Irish patriot who had led violent resistance against the British. They were outraged by the dangerous working conditions in the mines and the owners' brutal efforts to suppress union activity. Convinced of the justness of their cause, the Mollies used intimidation, beatings, and killings to right perceived wrongs against Irish workers. Later investigations have shown that agents of the mine operators themselves stirred up some of the trouble. The terrorism reached its peak in 1874–1875, when mine owners hired Pinkerton detectives to stop the movement. One of the agents who infiltrated the Mollies produced enough evidence to have the leaders indicted. At trials in 1876, twenty-four of the Molly Maguires were convicted; ten were hanged. The trials also resulted in a wage reduction in the mines and the final destruction of the Miners' National Association, a weak union the Mollies had dominated.

THE GREAT RAILROAD STRIKE OF 1877   A far more widespread labor incident was the Great Railroad Strike of 1877, the first major interstate strike in American history. After the financial panic of 1873 and the ensuing depression, the major rail lines in the East had cut wages. In 1877, they announced another 10 percent wage cut, which led most of the railroad workers at Martinsburg, West Virginia, to walk off the job and block the tracks. Walkouts and sympathy demonstrations spread spontaneously from Maryland to California. The railroad strike soon engulfed hundreds of cities and towns, leaving in its wake over a hundred people dead and millions of dollars in property destroyed. In Pittsburgh thousands of striking workers burned thirty-nine buildings and destroyed over a thousand rail cars and locomotives. Nonstriking rail workers were harassed and assaulted. In San Francisco, the strikers took out their wrath on Chinese immigrants. Such racist populism was commonplace across the Far West. Militiamen called in from Philadelphia managed to disperse one crowd at the cost of twenty-six lives but then found themselves besieged in the railroad's roundhouse, where they disbanded and shot their way out.

Federal troops finally quelled the widespread violence. Looting, rioting, and burning went on for another day until the frenzy wore itself out. A reporter described the scene as "the most horrible ever witnessed, except in the carnage of war. There were fifty miles of hot rails, ten tracks side by side, with as many miles of ties turned into glowing coals and tons on tons of iron car skeletons and wheels almost at white heat." Eventually the disgruntled workers, lacking organized bargaining power, had no choice but to drift back to work. The strike failed.

For many Americans, the railroad strike raised the specter of a worker-based social revolution. As a Pittsburgh newspaper warned, "This may be the beginning of a great civil war in this country between labor and capital." Equally disturbing to those in positions of corporate and political power was the presence of many women among the protesters. A Baltimore journalist noted that the "singular part of the disturbances is the very active part taken by the women, who are the wives and mothers of the [railroad] firemen." From the point of view of organized labor, however, the Great Railroad Strike demonstrated potential union strength and the need for tighter organization.

THE SAND-LOT INCIDENT   In California the railroad strike indirectly gave rise to a working-class political movement. In 1877, a meeting in a San Francisco sand lot intended to express sympathy for the railroad strikers ended with attacks on some passing Chinese. Within a few days, sporadic anti-Chinese riots had led to a mob attack on Chinatown. The depression of the 1870s had hit the West Coast especially hard, and the Chinese were handy scapegoats for frustrated white laborers who believed the Asians had taken their jobs.

Soon an Irish immigrant, Denis Kearney, organized the Workingmen's Party of California, whose platform called for the United States to stop Chinese immigration. A gifted agitator who had only recently become a naturalized American, Kearney harangued the "sand lotters" about the "foreign peril" and assaulted the rich railroad barons for exploiting the poor. The Workingmen's movement peaked in 1879, when it elected members to the state legislature and the mayor of San Francisco. Kearney lacked the gift for building a durable movement, but as his infant party fragmented, his anti-Chinese theme became a national issue—in 1882, Congress voted to prohibit Chinese immigration for ten years.

**ANTI-CHINESE AGITATION**    The growing tensions between labor and management over wages and working conditions took an ugly turn when white workers on the West Coast vented their anger about terrible living and working conditions and frustration with the loss of jobs by lashing out against Chinese immigrants. In dozens of cities, thousands of Chinese were threatened, abused, expelled, beaten, and killed. In 1876 white vigilantes

**Denis Kearney**

This cartoon shows support for Denis Kearney, who organized the Workingmen's Party of California, and his Chinese labor exclusion policy.

near Truckee, California, set on fire two cabins filled with terrified Chinese, and shot them as they fled. The harassment and persecution of Chinese peaked during the 1880s after Congress passed the bill restricting further immigration from China. During the 1880s, seven thousand lawsuits were filed on behalf of dispossessed Chinese immigrants, demanding that the United States enforce its own laws. But the anti-Chinese prejudice continued. In 1892, Congress passed a law written by California Congressman Thomas J. Geary. The Geary Act renewed the exclusion of new Chinese immigrants and required all Chinese residents of the United States to carry a resident permit, a sort of internal passport. Failure to carry the permit was punishable by deportation or a year of hard labor. In addition, Chinese were not allowed to testify in court and could not receive bail in habeas corpus proceedings. Chinese Americans refused to comply with what they called the Dog Tag Law (only 3,169 of the estimated 110,000 Chinese in the country registered by the April 1893 deadline). Their doing so constituted the largest act of civil disobedience in American history to that point.

TOWARD PERMANENT UNIONS    Efforts to build a national labor union movement gained momentum during the second half of the nineteenth century. Earlier efforts, in the 1830s and 1840s, had largely been dominated by reformers with schemes that ranged from free homesteads to utopian socialism. But the 1850s had seen the beginning of "job-conscious" unions in selected skilled trades. By 1860, there were about twenty such craft unions. During the Civil War, because of the demand for skilled labor, those unions grew in strength and number.

Yet there was no overall federation of such groups until 1866, when the National Labor Union (NLU) convened in Baltimore. The NLU comprised delegates from labor and reform groups more interested in political and social reform than in bargaining with employers. The groups espoused ideas such as the eight-hour workday, workers' cooperatives, greenbackism (the printing of paper money to inflate the currency and thereby relieve debtors), and equal rights for women and African Americans. After the head of the union died suddenly, its support fell away quickly, and by 1872 the NLU had disbanded. The NLU was not a total failure, however. It was influential in persuading Congress to enact an eight-hour workday for federal employees and to repeal the 1864 Contract Labor Act, passed during the Civil War to encourage the importation of laborers by allowing employers to pay for their passage to America. Employers had taken advantage of the Contract Labor Act to recruit foreign laborers willing to work for lower wages than their American counterparts.

THE KNIGHTS OF LABOR    Before the NLU collapsed, another labor group of national standing had emerged: the Noble Order of the **Knights of Labor**, a name that evoked the aura of medieval guilds. The founder of the Knights of Labor, Uriah S. Stephens, a Philadelphia tailor, was a habitual joiner involved with several secret orders, including the Masons. His early training for the Baptist ministry also affected his outlook. Secrecy, he felt, along with a semireligious ritual, would protect members from retaliation by employers and create a sense of solidarity.

The Knights of Labor, started in 1869, grew slowly, but during the depression of the 1870s, as other unions collapsed, it spread more rapidly. In 1878, its first general assembly established it as a national organization. Its preamble and platform endorsed the reforms advanced by previous workingmen's groups, including the creation of bureaus of labor statistics and mechanics' lien laws (to ensure payment of salaries), elimination of convict-labor competition, establishment of the eight-hour day, and use of paper currency. One plank in the platform, far ahead of the times, called for equal pay for equal work by men and women. Throughout its existence the Knights of Labor emphasized reform measures and preferred boycotts to strikes as a way to put pressure on employers. The Knights of Labor also proposed to organize worker cooperatives that would enable members, collectively, to own their own large-scale manufacturing and mining operations. The Knights allowed

**Members of the Knights of Labor**

This national union was more egalitarian than most of its contemporaries.

as members all who had ever worked for wages, except lawyers, doctors, bankers, and those who sold liquor. Theoretically it was one big union of all workers, skilled and unskilled, regardless of race, color, creed, or sex.

In 1879, Terence V. Powderly, the thirty-year-old mayor of Scranton, Pennsylvania, succeeded Stephens as head of the Knights of Labor. Born of Irish immigrant parents, Powderly had started working for a railroad at age sixteen. In many ways he was unsuited to his new job as head of the Knights of Labor. He was frail, sensitive to criticism, and indecisive at critical moments. He was temperamentally opposed to strikes, and when they did occur, he did not always support the local groups involved. Yet the Knights owed their greatest growth to strikes that occurred under his leadership. In the 1880s the Knights increased their membership from about one hundred thousand to more than seven hundred thousand. In 1886, however, the organization peaked and went into rapid decline after the failure of a railroad strike.

ANARCHISM   The increasingly violent tensions between labor and management during the late nineteenth century in the United States and Europe helped generate the doctrine of anarchism. Anarchists believed that government—any government—was in itself an abusive device used by the rich and powerful to oppress and exploit the working poor. Anarchists dreamed of the eventual disappearance of government altogether, and many of them believed that the transition to such a stateless society could be hurried along by promoting revolutionary action among the masses. One favored tactic was the use of dramatic acts of violence against representatives of the government. Many European anarchists emigrated to the United States during the last quarter of the nineteenth century, bringing with them their belief in the impact of "propaganda of the deed."

THE HAYMARKET AFFAIR   Labor-related violence increased during the 1880s as the gap between the rich and working poor widened. Between 1880 and 1900, 6.6 million hourly workers participated in more than twenty-three thousand strikes nationwide. Chicago, the fastest growing city in the nation, was a hotbed of labor unrest and a magnet for immigrants, especially German and Irish laborers, some of whom were socialists or anarchists who endorsed violence as a means of transforming the capitalist system. Their foremost demand was for an eight-hour working day.

What came to be called the Haymarket affair grew indirectly out of prolonged agitation for an eight-hour workday. In 1884, Knights of Labor organizers set May 1, 1886, as the deadline for adopting the eight-hour workday. When the deadline passed, forty thousand Chicago workers went on strike.

On May 3, 1886, violence erupted at the McCormick Reaper Works plant, where farm equipment was made. Striking union workers and "scabs" (nonunion workers who defied the strike) clashed outside the plant. The police arrived, shots rang out, and two strikers were killed.

Evidence of police brutality infuriated the leaders of the minuscule anarchist movement in Chicago, which included many women. They printed leaflets demanding "Revenge!" and "Workingmen, to Arms!" Calls went out for a mass demonstration the following night at Haymarket Square to protest the killings. On the evening of May 4, after listening to long speeches complaining about low wages and long working hours and promoting anarchism, the crowd was beginning to break up when a group of policemen arrived and told the militants to disperse. At that point, someone threw a bomb at the police; seven were killed and sixty wounded. People screamed and ran in every direction. Amid the chaos of America's first terrorist bombing, the police fired into the crowd, killing and wounding an unknown number of people, including other policemen. Throughout the night, rampaging police arbitrarily arrested scores of people without evidence and subjected them to harsh questioning. All labor meetings were banned across the city. Newspapers across the nation printed lurid headlines about anarchy erupting in Chicago. One New York newspaper demanded stern punishment for "the few long-haired, wild-eyed, bad-smelling, atheistic, reckless foreign wretches" who promoted such anarchistic labor unrest.

At trials during the summer of 1886, seven anarchist leaders were sentenced to death despite the lack of any evidence linking them to the bomb thrower, whose identity was never established. All but one of the convicted

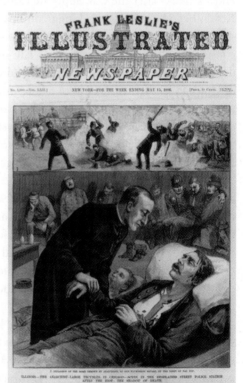

**The Haymarket Affair**

A priest gives last rites to a policeman after anarchist-labor violence erupts in Haymarket Square, Chicago.

were German speaking, and that one held a membership card in the Knights of Labor. The facts of the case were lost amid the emotions of the moment. In a statement to the court after being sentenced to hang, Louis Lingg declared that he was innocent of the bombing but was proud to be an anarchist who was "in favor of using force" to attack the abuses of the capitalist system.

Lawyers for the anarchists appealed the convictions to the Illinois Supreme Court. Meanwhile, petitions from around the world arrived at the governor's office appealing for clemency for the seven convicted men. One of the petitioners was **Samuel Gompers**, the founding president of the American Federation of Labor (AFL), a new organization that would soon supplant the faltering Knights of Labor as the nation's leading union. "I abhor anarchy," Gompers stressed, "but I also abhor injustice when meted out even to the most despicable being on earth."

On September 14, 1887, the state supreme court upheld the convictions, and six weeks later the U.S. Supreme Court refused to consider the case. On November 10, 1887, Louis Lingg committed suicide in his cell. That same day, the Illinois governor commuted the sentences of two of the convicted conspirators to life imprisonment. The next day the four remaining condemned men were hanged. Two hundred thousand people lined the streets of Chicago as their caskets were taken for burial. To labor militants around the world, the executed anarchists were working-class martyrs; to the police and the economic elite in Chicago, they were demonic assassins.

The violent incident at Haymarket Square triggered widespread revulsion at the Knights of Labor and labor groups in general. Despite his best efforts, Terence Powderly could never dissociate in the public mind the Knights from the anarchists. He clung to leadership until 1893, but after that the union evaporated. By the turn of the century, it was but a memory. Besides fear of their supposed radicalism, several factors accounted for the Knights' decline: a leadership devoted more to reform than to the nuts and bolts of organization, the failure of the Knights' cooperative worker-owned enterprises, and a preoccupation with politics that led the Knights to sponsor labor candidates in hundreds of local elections.

The Knights nevertheless attained some lasting achievements, among them the creation of the federal Bureau of Labor Statistics in 1884 as well as several state labor bureaus; the Foran Act of 1885, which, though weakly enforced, penalized employers who imported contract labor (an arrangement similar to the indentured servitude of colonial times, in which workers were committed to a term of labor in exchange for transportation to America); and an 1880 federal law providing for the arbitration of labor disputes. The Knights by example also spread the idea of unionism and initiated a new type of union organization: the industrial union, an industry-wide union of skilled and unskilled workers.

GOMPERS AND THE AFL   The craft unions (skilled workers) generally opposed efforts to unite with industrial unionism. Leaders of the craft unions feared that joining with unskilled laborers would mean a loss of their craft's identity and a loss of the skilled workers' greater bargaining power. Thus in 1886, delegates from twenty-five craft unions organized the **American Federation of Labor (AFL)**. Its structure differed from that of the Knights of Labor in that it was a federation of national organizations, each of which retained a large degree of autonomy and exercised greater leverage against management.

Samuel Gompers served as president of the AFL from its start until his death, in 1924, with only one year's interruption. Born in England of Dutch Jewish ancestry, Gompers came to the United States as a teenager, joined the Cigarmakers' Union in 1864, and became president of his New York City local union in 1877. Unlike Terence Powderly and the Knights of Labor, Gompers focused on concrete economic gains—higher wages, shorter hours, better working conditions—and avoided involvement with utopian ideas or politics.

Gompers was temperamentally more suited than Powderly to the rough-and-tumble world of unionism. He had a thick hide, liked to talk and drink with workers in the back room, and willingly used strikes to achieve favorable trade agreements, including provisos for union recognition in the form of closed shops (which could hire only union members) or union-preference shops (which could hire others only if no union members were available).

The AFL at first grew slowly, but by 1890 it had surpassed the Knights of Labor in membership. By the turn of the century, it claimed 500,000 members in affiliated unions; in 1914, on the eve of World War I, it had 2 million; and in 1920 it reached a peak of

**Samuel Gompers**

Head of the American Federation of Labor striking an assertive pose.

4 million. But even then the AFL embraced less than 15 percent of the nation's nonagricultural workers. All unions, including the unaffiliated railroad brotherhoods, accounted for little more than 18 percent of those workers. Organized labor's strongholds were in transportation and the building trades. Most of the larger manufacturing industries—including steel, textiles, tobacco, and packinghouses—remained almost untouched. Gompers never frowned upon industrial unions, and several became important affiliates of the AFL: the United Mine Workers, the International Ladies Garment Workers, and the Amalgamated Clothing Workers. But the AFL had its greatest success in organizing skilled workers.

THE HOMESTEAD STRIKE   Two violent incidents in the 1890s stalled the emerging industrial-union movement and set it back for the next forty years: the **Homestead steel strike** of 1892 and the **Pullman strike** of 1894. These two dramatic labor conflicts in several respects represented the culminating events of the Gilded Age, an era of riotous economic growth during which huge corporations came to exercise overweening influence over American life. Both events pitted organized labor in a bitter contest against two of the nation's largest and most influential corporations. In both cases the stakes were enormous. The two strikes not only represented a test of strength for the organized labor movement but also served to reshape the political landscape at the end of the nineteenth century.

The Amalgamated Association of Iron and Steel Workers, founded in 1876, was the largest craft union at the time. By 1891, it boasted 24,000 members. But it excluded unskilled steelworkers and had failed to organize the larger steel plants. The massive Homestead Works near Pittsburgh was an important exception. There the union, which included about a fourth of Homestead's 3,800 workers, had enjoyed friendly relations with Andrew Carnegie's company until Henry Clay Frick became its president in 1889. A showdown was delayed until 1892, however, when the union contract came up for renewal. Carnegie, who had expressed sympathy for unions in the past, had gone hunting in his native Scotland and left matters in Frick's hands. Yet Carnegie knew what was afoot: a cost-cutting reduction in the number of highly paid skilled workers through the use of labor-saving machinery and a deliberate attempt to smash the union. "Am with you to the end," he wrote to Frick.

As negotiations dragged on, the company announced on June 25 that it would treat workers as individuals unless an agreement with the union was reached by June 29. A strike—or, more properly, a lockout of unionists—began on that date. In no mood to negotiate, Frick built a twelve-foot-high fence around the entire plant, equipped it with watchtowers, searchlights, and barbed wire, and hired three hundred union-busting men from the Pinkerton Detective Agency to protect what was soon dubbed Fort Frick. On the morning of July 6, 1892, when the untrained Pinkertons floated up the Monongahela River on barges, unionists were waiting behind breastworks on shore. Who fired the first shot remains unknown, but a fourteen-hour battle broke out in which seven workers and three Pinkertons died. In the end, the Pinkertons surrendered and were marched away, subjected to taunts and beatings from crowds in the street. Six days later, Pennsylvania's governor dispatched 8,500 state militia to protect the strikebreakers, whom Frick hired to restore production.

The strike dragged on until November, but by then the union was dead at Homestead, its leaders charged with murder and treason. Its cause was not helped when an anarchist, a Lithuanian immigrant named Alexander Berkman, tried to assassinate Frick on July 23, shooting him twice in the neck and stabbing him three times. Despite his wounds, Frick fought back fiercely and, with the help of staff members, subdued Berkman. Much of the local sympathy for the strikers evaporated. As a union leader explained, Berkman's bullets "went straight through the heart of the Homestead strike." Penniless and demoralized, the defeated workers ended their walkout on November 20 and accepted the company's terms. Only a fifth of the strikers were hired back. Carnegie and Frick, with the support of local, state, and national government officials, had eliminated the union. Across the nation in 1892, state militias intervened to quash twenty-three labor disputes. In the ongoing struggles between workers and owners, big business held sway—in the workplace and in state governments.

The Homestead strike was symptomatic of the overweening power of industrial capitalism. By 1899, Andrew Carnegie could report to a friend: "Ashamed to tell you [of my] profits these days. Prodigious!" None of Carnegie's steel plants after the Homestead strike employed unionized workers. Frick split with Carnegie after he learned that his boss had been telling lies about him. Frick told Carnegie that he had grown "tired of your business methods, your absurd newspaper interviews and personal remarks and unwarranted interference in matters you know nothing about." When Carnegie sought to reconcile with his former lieutenant, Frick told the messenger: "You can say to Andrew Carnegie that I will meet him in hell (where we are both going) but not before."

**THE PULLMAN STRIKE** Even more than the confrontation at the Homestead steel plant, the Pullman strike of 1894 was a notable walkout in American history, for it paralyzed the economies of the twenty-seven states and territories making up the western half of the nation. It involved a dispute at Pullman, Illinois, a model industrial town built on four thousand acres outside Chicago, where workers of the Pullman Palace Car Company were housed. Employees who built rail cars were required to live in the company town, pay rents and utility costs that were higher than those in nearby towns, and buy goods from company stores. During the depression of 1893, George Pullman laid off 3,000 of his 5,800 employees and cut wages 25 to 40 percent, but not rents and other charges. After Pullman fired three members of a workers' grievance committee, a strike began on May 11, 1894.

During this tense period, Pullman workers had been joining the new American Railway Union, founded the previous year by **Eugene V. Debs**. The tall, gangly Debs was a man of towering influence and charismatic appeal. A child of working-class immigrants, he quit school at age fourteen and began working for an Indiana railroad. By the early 1890s, Debs had become a tireless spokesman for labor radicalism, and he strove to organize *all* railway workers—skilled or unskilled—into the American Railway Union, which soon became a powerful new labor organization. Debs quickly turned his attention to the controversy in Pullman, Illinois.

In June 1894, after George Pullman refused Debs's plea for a negotiated settlement of the strike, the union workers stopped handling Pullman railcars. By the end of July, they had shut down most of the railroads in the Midwest. Railroad executives then hired strikebreakers to connect mail cars to Pullman cars so that interference with Pullman cars would entail interference with the federal mail. The U.S. attorney general, a former attorney for railroad companies, swore in 3,400 special deputies to keep the trains running. When clashes occurred between those deputies and some of the strik-

**The Pullman strike**

Troops guarding the railroads, 1894.

ers, angry workers ignored Debs's plea for an orderly boycott. They assaulted strikebreakers ("scabs") and destroyed property.

Finally, on July 3, 1894, President Grover Cleveland sent federal troops into the Chicago area, where the strike was centered. The Illinois governor insisted that the state could keep order, but President Cleveland claimed authority and stressed his duty to ensure delivery of the mail. Meanwhile, the attorney general won an injunction forbidding any interference with the mail or any effort to restrain interstate commerce. On July 13, the union called off the strike. A few days later, the district court cited Debs for violating the injunction, and he served six months in jail. The Supreme Court upheld the decree in the case of *In re Debs* (1895) on broad grounds of national sovereignty: "The strong arm of the national government may be put forth to brush away all obstructions to the freedom of interstate commerce or the transportation of the mails." Debs served his jail term, during which he read deeply in socialist literature, and emerged to devote the rest of his life to socialism.

MOTHER JONES    One of the most colorful and beloved labor agitators at the end of the nineteenth century was a remarkable woman known simply as Mother Jones. White haired, pink cheeked, and dressed in matronly black dresses and hats, she was a tireless champion of the working poor who used fiery rhetoric to excite crowds and attract media attention. She led marches, dodged bullets, served jail terms, and confronted business titans and police with disarming courage. In 1913, a district attorney called her the "most dangerous woman in America."

Born in Cork, Ireland, in 1837, Mary Harris was the second of five children in a poor Catholic family that fled the Irish potato famine at midcentury and settled in Toronto. In 1861, she moved to Memphis and began teaching. There, as the Civil War was erupting, she met and married George Jones, an iron molder and staunch union member. They had four children, and then disaster struck. In 1867 a yellow fever epidemic devastated Memphis, killing Mary Jones's husband and four children. The grief-stricken thirty-seven-year-old widow moved to Chicago and took up dressmaking, only to see her shop, home, and belongings destroyed in the great fire of 1871. Having lost her family and her finances and angry at the social inequality and injustices she saw around her, Mary Jones drifted into the labor movement and soon emerged as its most passionate advocate. Chicago was then the seedbed of labor radicalism, and the union culture nurtured in Mary Jones a lifelong dedication to the cause of wage workers and their families.

The gritty woman who had lost her family now declared herself the "mother" of the fledgling labor movement. She joined the Knights of Labor as an organizer and public speaker. In the late 1880s she became an ardent traveling

**Mother Jones**

A pioneer of the labor movement.

speaker for the United Mine Workers (UMW), various other unions, and the Socialist party. For the next thirty years, she crisscrossed the nation, recruiting union members, supporting strikers (her "boys"), raising funds, walking picket lines, defying court injunctions, berating politicians, and spending time in prison.

Wherever Mother Jones went, she promoted higher wages, shorter hours, safer workplaces, and restrictions on child labor. Coal miners, said the UMW president, "have had no more staunch supporter, no more able defender than the one we all love to call Mother." During a miners' strike in West Virginia, Jones was arrested, convicted of "conspiracy that resulted in murder," and sentenced to twenty years in prison. The outcry over her plight helped spur a Senate committee to investigate conditions in the coal mines; the governor set her free.

Mother Jones was especially determined to end the exploitation of children in the workplace. In 1903, she organized a highly publicized weeklong march of child workers from Pennsylvania to the New York home of President Theodore Roosevelt. The children were physically stunted and mutilated, most of them missing fingers or hands from machinery accidents. President Roosevelt refused to see the ragtag children, but as Mother Jones explained, "Our march had done its work. We had drawn the attention of the nation to the crime of child labor." Soon the Pennsylvania state legislature increased the legal working age to fourteen.

Mother Jones lost most of the strikes she participated in, but over the course of her long life she saw average wages increase, working conditions improve, and child labor diminish. Her commitment to the cause of social justice never wavered. At age eighty-three, she was arrested after joining a miners' strike in Colorado and jailed in solitary confinement. At her funeral, in 1930, one speaker urged people to remember her famous rallying cry: "Pray for the dead and fight like hell for the living."

SOCIALISM AND THE UNIONS  The major unions for the most part never allied themselves with socialists, as many European labor movements did. But socialist ideas had been circulating in the United States at least since the 1820s. Marxism, one strain of socialism, was imported mainly by German immigrants. Karl Marx's International Workingmen's Association, founded in England in 1864 and later called the First International, inspired only a few affiliates in the United States. In 1872, at Marx's urging, the headquarters was moved from London to New York. In 1877, Marxists in America organized the Socialist Labor party, a group so dominated by immigrants that German was initially its official language.

The movement gained little notice before the rise of Daniel De Leon in the 1890s. As editor of a Marxist newspaper, the *People,* he became the dominant figure in the Socialist Labor party. He strove to organize socialist industrial unions and to build a political party that would abolish the government once it gained power, after which the unions of the Socialist Trade and Labor Alliance, formed under his supervision, would become the units of control. De Leon preached revolution at the ballot box, not by violence.

Eugene V. Debs was more successful than De Leon at building a socialist movement in America, however. In 1897, Debs announced that he was a socialist and organized the Social Democratic party from the remnants of the American Railway Union; he won over 96,000 votes as its candidate for president in 1900. The next year his followers joined a number of secessionists from De Leon's party to set up the Socialist Party of America. Debs polled over 400,000 votes as the party's candidate for president in 1904 and more than doubled that,

**Eugene V. Debs**

Founder of the American Railway Union and later candidate for president as head of the Socialist Party of America.

to more than 900,000 votes, or 6 percent of the popular vote, in 1912. In 1910, Milwaukee, Wisconsin, elected a socialist mayor and congressman.

By 1912, the Socialist party seemed well on the way to becoming a permanent fixture in American politics. Thirty-three cities had socialist mayors. The party sponsored five English-language daily newspapers, eight foreign-language dailies, and a number of weeklies and monthlies. In the Southwest the party built a sizable grassroots following among farmers and tenants. Oklahoma, for instance, had more paid-up party members in 1910 than any other state except New York and in 1912 gave 16.5 percent of its popular vote to Debs, a greater proportion than any other state ever gave him. But the Socialist party reached its peak in 1912. It would be racked by disagreements over America's participation in World War I and was split thereafter by desertions to the new Communist party.

THE WOBBLIES    During the years of Socialist party growth, a parallel effort to revive industrial unionism emerged, led by the **Industrial Workers of the World (IWW)**. The chief base for this group was the Western Federation of Miners, organized at Butte, Montana, in 1893. Over the next decade, the Western Federation was the storm center of violent confrontations with unyielding mine operators who mobilized private armies against it in Colorado, Idaho, and elsewhere. In 1905 the founding convention of the IWW drew a variety of delegates who opposed the AFL's philosophy of organizing unions made up only of skilled workers. Eugene V. Debs participated, although many of his comrades preferred to work within the AFL. Daniel De Leon seized this chance to strike back at craft unionism. He argued that the IWW "must be founded on the class struggle" and "the irrepressible conflict between the capitalist class and the working class."

But the IWW waged class war better than it articulated class ideology. Like the Knights of Labor, it was designed to be "one big union," including all workers, skilled or unskilled. Its roots were in the mining and lumber camps of the West, where the unstable seasonal conditions of employment created a large number of nomadic workers, to whom neither the AFL's pragmatic approach nor the socialists' political appeal held much attraction. The revolutionary goal of the Wobblies, as they came to be called, was an idea labeled syndicalism by its French supporters: the ultimate destruction of the government and its replacement by one big union. But just how that union would govern remained vague.

Like other radical groups, the IWW was split by sectarian disputes. Because of policy disagreements all the major founders withdrew, first the Western Federation of Miners, then Debs, then De Leon. William D. "Big Bill" Haywood of the Western Federation remained, however, and as its leader he held the group together. Haywood was an imposing figure. Well over six feet tall, handsome and muscular, he commanded the attention and respect of his listeners. This hard-rock miner, union organizer, and socialist from Salt Lake City despised the AFL and its conservative labor philosophy. He called Samuel Gompers "a squat specimen of humanity" who was "conceited, petulant, and vindictive." Instead of following Gompers's advice to organize only skilled workers, Haywood promoted the concept of one all-inclusive union dedicated to a socialism "with its working clothes on."

Haywood and the Wobblies, however, were reaching out to the fringe elements of the labor force with the least power and influence, chiefly the migratory workers of the West and the ethnic groups of the East. Always ambivalent about diluting their revolutionary principles, Wobblies scorned the usual labor agreements even when they participated in them. As a consequence, they engaged in spectacular battles with employers but scored few victories. The largest was a textile strike at Lawrence, Massachusetts, in 1912 that garnered wage raises, overtime pay, and other benefits. But the next year a strike of silk workers at Paterson, New Jersey, ended in disaster, and the IWW entered a rapid decline.

The Wobblies' fading was accelerated by the hysterical opposition they aroused. Its members were branded anarchists, bums, and criminals. The IWW was effectively destroyed during World War I, when most of its leaders were jailed for conspiracy because of their militant opposition to American entry into the war. Big Bill Haywood fled to the Soviet Union, where he married a Russian woman, died in 1928, and was honored by burial in the Kremlin wall. The short-lived Wobblies left behind a rich folklore of nomadic workingmen and a gallery of heroic agitators, such as Elizabeth Gurley Flynn, a dark-haired Irishwoman who at age eighteen chained herself to a lamppost to impede her arrest during a strike. The movement also bequeathed martyrs such as the Swedish American singer and labor organizer Joe Hill, framed (so the faithful assumed) for murder and executed by a Utah firing squad. His last words were written to Haywood: "Goodbye, Bill. I die like a true blue rebel. Don't waste any time mourning. Organize." The intensity of conviction and devotion to a cause shown by Hill, Flynn, and others ensured that the IWW's ideal of a classless society did not die.

THE STRESSES OF SUCCESS  The phenomenal industrial empires created by the Gilded Age captains of industry and finance generated enormous fortunes and marked improvements in the quality of everyday life. But the Industrial Revolution also created profound inequalities and fermenting social tensions. As often happens, unregulated capitalism led to excesses that bred instability and unrest. By the end of the nineteenth century, as the labor unions and farmers' organizations argued, an unregulated economy had become recklessly out of balance—and only state and federal government intervention could restore economic legitimacy and social stability.

## CHAPTER SUMMARY

- **Second Industrial Revolution**  The postwar economy was characterized by large-scale industrial development and a burgeoning agriculture sector. The Second Industrial Revolution was fueled by the creation of national transportation and communications systems, the use of electric power, and the application of scientific research to industrial processes. The federal government encouraged growth by imposing high tariffs on imported products and granting the railroad companies public land.

- **Rising Big Business**  The leading entrepreneurs were extraordinarily skilled at organizing and controlling industry. John D. Rockefeller eventually controlled nearly every facet of the oil industry, consolidating that control through trusts and holding companies. Andrew Carnegie, who believed that competition benefited both society and business, came to dominate the steel industry by buying struggling companies. J. Pierpont Morgan, an investment banker, not only controlled most of the nation's railroads but also bought Carnegie's steel interests in 1901, thereby creating the nation's first billion-dollar corporation.

- **Labor Conditions and Organizations**  The labor force was largely composed of unskilled workers, including recent immigrants and growing numbers of women and children. Children as young as eight years of age worked twelve hours a day in coal mines and southern mills. In hard times, business owners cut wages without discounting the rents they charged for company housing or the prices they charged in company stores.

- **Rising Labor Unions**  It was difficult for unskilled workers to organize effectively. Strikebreakers were plentiful because new immigrants were desperate for work. Business owners often had recourse to state and local militias, which would be mobilized against strikers in the face of perceived anarchy. Craft unions made up of skilled workers became more successful at organizing as the American Federation of Labor focused on concrete economic gains and better working conditions and avoided involvement in politics.

## CHRONOLOGY

| | |
|---|---|
| 1855 | Bessemer converter process allows steel to be made quickly and inexpensively |
| 1859 | First oil well is struck in Titusville, Pennsylvania |
| 1869 | First transcontinental railroad is completed at Promontory, Utah |
| 1876 | Alexander Graham Bell patents his telephone |
| 1876 | Thomas A. Edison makes the first successful incandescent lightbulb |
| 1877 | Great Railroad Strike |
| 1882 | John D. Rockefeller organizes the Standard Oil Trust |
| 1886 | In the Haymarket incident, a bomb set off at a Chicago labor rally kills and wounds police officers |
| 1886 | American Federation of Labor is organized |
| 1892 | Homestead Strike |
| 1894 | Pullman Strike |
| 1901 | J. Pierpont Morgan creates the U.S. Steel Corporation |

## KEY TERMS & NAMES

# 19

## THE SOUTH AND THE WEST TRANSFORMED

FOCUS QUESTIONS          wwnorton.com/studyspace

- How did life in the South change politically, economically, and socially after the Civil War?
- What happened to Native Americans as whites settled the West?
- What were the experiences of farmers, cowboys, and miners in the West?
- How did mining affect the development of the West?
- How important was the concept of the frontier to America's political and diplomatic development?

After the Civil War, the devastated South and the untamed West provided enticing opportunities for American inventiveness and entrepreneurship. The two distinctive regions were ripe for development, and each in its own way became like a colonial appendage of the more prosperous Midwest and Northeast. The war-devastated South had to be rebuilt; the sparsely settled trans-Mississippi West beckoned agricultural and commercial development. Entrepreneurs in the North eagerly sought to exploit both regions by providing the capital for urbanization and industrialization. This was particularly true of the West, where before 1860 most Americans had viewed the region between the Mississippi River and California as a barren landscape unfit for human habitation or cultivation, an uninviting land suitable only for Indians and animals. Half the state of Texas, for instance, was still not settled at the end of the Civil War. After 1865, however, the federal government encouraged western settlement and economic development. The construction of transcontinental railroads, the military conquest of the Indians, and a generous policy of distributing government-owned lands combined to help lure thousands of pioneers and enterprising capitalists westward. Charles Goodnight, a Texas cattle rancher, recalled that "we were adventurers in a great land as fresh and full of the zest of darers." By 1900, the South and the West had been transformed in ways—for good and for ill—that few could have predicted, and twelve new states were created out of the western territories.

## THE MYTH OF THE NEW SOUTH

A FRESH VISION    During the 1880s, the major prophet of the so-called **New South** was Henry W. Grady, editor of the *Atlanta Constitution*. "The Old South," he said, "rested everything on slavery and agriculture, unconscious that these could neither give nor maintain healthy growth." The New South, on the other hand, "presents a perfect democracy" of small farms and diversifying industries. The postwar South, Grady believed, held the promise of a real democracy, one no longer run by the planter aristocracy and no longer dependent upon slave labor.

Henry Grady's compelling vision of a New South modeled after the North attracted many supporters who fervently preached the gospel of industrial development. South Carolinian Benjamin F. Perry urged business leaders to "educate the masses, industralize, work hard, and seek Northern capital [investments] to develop Southern resources." The Confederacy, he and others reasoned, had lost the war because it had relied too much upon King Cotton—and slavery. In the future, the South must follow the North's example and diversify its economy by developing an industrial sector to go along with its agricultural emphasis. From that central belief flowed certain corollaries: that a more efficient agriculture would be a foundation for economic growth, that more widespread education, especially vocational training, would promote regional prosperity, and that sectional peace and racial harmony would provide a stable social environment for economic growth.

ECONOMIC GROWTH    The New South vision of a more diversified economy made a lot of sense, but it was only partially fulfilled. The chief accomplishment of the New South movement was a dramatic expansion of the region's textile industry, which produced cotton-based bedding and clothing. From 1880 to 1900, the number of cotton mills in the South grew from 161 to 400, the number of mostly white mill workers (among whom women and children outnumbered men) increased fivefold, and the demand for cotton went up eightfold. By 1900, the South had surpassed New England as the largest producer of cotton fabric in the nation.

Tobacco growing and cigarette production also increased significantly. Essential to the rise of the tobacco industry was the Duke family of Durham, North Carolina. At the end of the Civil War, the story goes, Washington Duke took a barnful of tobacco and, with the help of his two sons, beat it out with hickory sticks, stuffed it into bags, hitched two mules to his wagon, and set out across the state, selling tobacco in small pouches as he went. By 1872, the Dukes had a factory producing 125,000 pounds of tobacco annually, and Washington Duke prepared to settle down and enjoy success.

His son James Buchanan "Buck" Duke wanted even greater success, however. He recognized that the tobacco industry was "half smoke and half ballyhoo," so he poured large sums into advertising schemes and perfected the mechanized mass production of cigarettes. Duke also undersold competitors in their own markets and cornered the supply of ingredients needed to make cigarettes. Eventually his competitors agreed to join forces, and in 1890 Duke brought most of them into the American Tobacco Company, which controlled nine tenths of the nation's cigarette production and, by 1904, about three fourths of all tobacco production. In 1911 the Supreme Court ruled that the massive company was in violation of the Sherman Anti-Trust Act and ordered it broken up, but by then Duke had found new worlds to conquer, in hydroelectric power and aluminum.

Systematic use of other natural resources helped revitalize the region along the Appalachian Mountain chain from West Virginia to Alabama. Coal production in the South (including West Virginia) grew from 5 million tons in 1875 to 49 million tons by 1900. At the southern end of the mountains, Birmingham, Alabama, sprang up during the 1870s in the shadow of Red Mountain, so named for its iron ore, and boosters soon tagged the steelmaking city the Pittsburgh of the South.

Urban and industrial growth spawned a need for housing, and after 1870 lumbering became a thriving industry in the South. Northern investors bought up vast pine forests throughout the region. By the turn of the century, lumber had surpassed textiles in value. Tree cutting seemed to know no bounds, despite the resulting ecological devastation. In time the cutover southern forests would be saved only by the warm climate, which fostered quick growth of planted trees.

AGRICULTURE OLD AND NEW   By the end of the nineteenth century, however, the South fell far short of the diversified economy and racial harmony that Henry Grady and other proponents of the New South had envisioned in the mid-1880s. The South in 1900 remained the least urban, least industrial, least educated, and least prosperous region. The typical southerner was less apt to be tending a textile loom or iron forge than, as the saying went, facing the eastern end of a westbound mule or risking his life in an Appalachian coal mine. The traditional overplanting of cotton and tobacco fields continued after the Civil War and expanded over new acreage even as its export markets leveled off.

The majority of southern farmers were not flourishing. A prolonged deflation in crop prices affected the entire economy during the last third of the nineteenth century. Sagging prices for farm crops made it more difficult than ever to own land. By 1890, low rates of farm ownership in the Deep South belied Henry Grady's dream of a southern democracy of small landowners: South Carolina, 39 percent; Georgia, 40 percent; Alabama, 42 percent; Mississippi, 38 percent; and Louisiana, 42 percent.

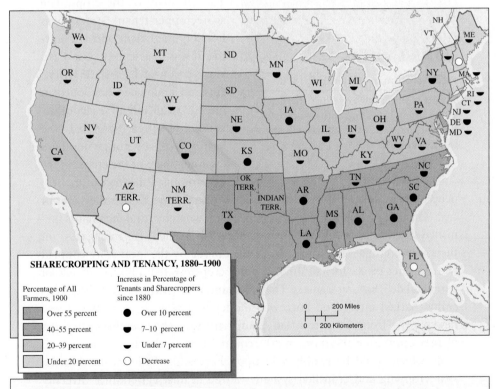

SHARECROPPING AND TENANCY, 1880–1900

Percentage of All Farmers, 1900

Over 55 percent
40–55 percent
20–39 percent
Under 20 percent

Increase in Percentage of Tenants and Sharecroppers since 1880

● Over 10 percent
◗ 7–10 percent
◔ Under 7 percent
○ Decrease

Why was there a dramatic increase in sharecropping and tenancy in the late nineteenth century? Why did the South have more sharecroppers than other parts of the country? Why, in your opinion, was the rate of sharecropping low in the western territories of New Mexico and Arizona?

**Picking cotton in Mississippi, 1870**

Tenant farming was extremely inefficient, as the tenant lacked incentive to care for the land and the owner was largely unable to supervise the work.

Poverty forced most southern farm workers to give up their hopes of owning land and become sharecroppers or tenants. **Sharecroppers**, who had nothing to offer the landowner but their labor, worked the owner's land in return for seed, fertilizer, and supplies and a share of the crop, generally about half. Tenant farmers, hardly better off, might have their own mule, plow, and line of credit with the country store. They were entitled to claim a larger share of the crops. The sharecropper-tenant system was horribly inefficient and corrupting. It was in essence a post–Civil War version of land slavery. Tenants and landowners developed an intense suspicion of each other. Landlords often swindled the farm workers by not giving them their fair share of the crops.

The postwar South suffered from an acute, prolonged shortage of money; people in the former Confederacy had to devise ways to operate without cash. One innovation was the crop-lien system whereby rural merchants furnished supplies to small farm owners in return for liens (or mortgages) on their future crops. Over time, the credit offered by the local store coupled with sagging prices for cotton and other crops created a hopeless cycle of perennial debt among farmers. The merchant, who assumed great risks, generally charged interest on borrowed money that ranged, according to one newspaper, "from 24 percent to grand larceny." The merchant, like the planter (and often the same man), required farmer clients to grow a cash crop, which could be readily sold upon harvesting. This meant that the sharecropping and crop-lien systems warred against agricultural diversity and placed a premium on growing a staple "cash" crop, usually cotton or tobacco. It was a vicious cycle. The more cotton that was grown, the lower the price. If a farmer borrowed $1000 when the price of cotton was 10¢ cents a pound, he had to grow more than 10,000 pounds of cotton to pay back his debt plus interest. If the price of cotton dropped to 5¢, he had to grow more than 20,000 pounds just to break even.

Tenant farming and sharecropping unwittingly caused profound environmental damage. Growing commercial row crops like cotton on the same land year after year leached the nutrients from the soil. Tenants had no incentive to take care of farm soil by manuring or rotating crops because the land was not their own. They used fertilizers to accelerate the growing cycle, but the extensive use of phosphate only accelerated long-term soil depletion by enabling multiple plantings each year. Fertilizer, said an observer, seduced southern farmers into believing that there was a "short cut to prosperity, a royal road to good crops of cotton year after year. The result has been that their lands have been cultivated clean year after year, and their fertility has been exhausted." Once the soil had lost its fertility, the tenants moved on to another farm, leaving behind rutted fields whose topsoil washed away with each rain. The silt and mud flowed into creeks and rivers, swamping many lowland fields and filling millponds and lakes. By the early twentieth century, much of the rural South resembled a ravaged land: deep gullies sliced through eroded hillsides, and streams and deep lakes were clogged with silt. As far as the eye could see, red clay devoid of nutrients dominated the landscape.

The stagnation of rural life thus held millions, white and black, in bondage to privation and ignorance. Eleven percent of whites in the South were illiterate at the end of the nineteenth century, twice the national average. Then as now, poverty accompanied a lack of education. The average annual income of white southerners in 1900 was about half of that of Americans outside the South. Yet the poorest people in the poorest region were the 9 million former slaves and their descendants. Per capita black income was a third of that of southern whites. African Americans also remained the least educated people in the region. The black illiteracy rate in the South in 1900 was nearly 50 percent, almost five times higher than that of whites.

THE REDEEMERS (BOURBONS)   In post–Civil War southern politics, centuries-old habits of social deference and political elitism still prevailed. "Every community," one U.S. Army officer noted in postwar South Carolina, "had its great man, or its little great man, around whom his fellow citizens gather when they want information, and to whose monologues they listen with a respect akin to humility." After Reconstruction, such "great" men dominated local southern politics, usually because of their ownership of land or their wealth. The supporters of these postwar Democratic leaders referred to them as "**redeemers**" because they supposedly saved the South from Yankee domination, as well as from the straitjacket of a purely rural economy. The redeemers included a rising class of lawyers, merchants, and entrepreneurs who were eager to promote a more diversified economy based upon industrial development and railroad expansion. The opponents of the redeemers labeled them "**Bourbons**" in an effort to depict them as reactionaries. Like the French royal family of the same name, which Napoléon had said forgot nothing and learned nothing in the ordeal of the French revolution, the ruling white Bourbons of the postwar South were said to have forgotten nothing and to have learned nothing in the ordeal of the Confederacy and the Civil War.

During and after the late 1870s, the Bourbon governors and legislators of the New South slashed state expenditures, including those for the public-school systems started during the Reconstruction era immediately after the war. The urge to reduce state expenditures created one of the darkest blots on the Bourbon record: convict leasing. During the Civil War, many southern prisons and jails were destroyed. After the war, state and local governments were so strapped for cash that they looked for ways to reduce the expense of jailing people convicted of crimes. At the same time, white land owners whose slaves had been freed were desperate for farm workers. State governments therefore began "leasing" convicts, most of them African Americans, to white farmers as a way for southern states to avoid penitentiary expenses and generate revenue. White leaders often used a racist argument to rationalize the leasing of convicts, most of whom were African Americans: an "inferior" and "shiftless" race, they claimed, benefited from the discipline of working for others.

Perhaps the ultimate paradox of the Bourbons' rule was that these champions of white supremacy tolerated a lingering black voice in politics and showed no haste to raise the barriers of racial segregation in public places. In the 1880s, southern politics remained surprisingly open and democratic, with 64 percent of eligible voters, blacks and whites, participating in elections. African Americans sat in the state legislature of South Carolina until 1900 and in the state legislature of Georgia until 1908; some of them were Democrats. The South sent African American congressmen to Washington, D.C., in every election except one until 1900, though they always represented gerrymandered districts in which most of the state's African American voters had been placed. Under the Bourbons, the disenfranchisement of African American voters remained inconsistent, a local matter brought about mainly by fraud and intimidation, but it occurred often enough to ensure white control of the southern states.

A like flexibility applied to other aspects of race relations. The color line was drawn less strictly immediately after the Civil War than it would be in

**The effects of Radical and Bourbon rule in the South**

This 1880 cartoon shows the South staggering under the oppressive weight of military Reconstruction (left) and flourishing under the "Let 'Em Alone Policy" of President Rutherford B. Hayes and the Bourbons (right).

the twentieth century. In some places, to be sure, racial segregation appeared before the end of Reconstruction, especially in schools, churches, hotels, and rooming houses and in private social relations. In places of public accommodation such as trains, depots, theaters, and diners, discrimination was more sporadic.

The ultimate achievement of the New South promoters and their allies, the Bourbons, was that they reconciled tradition with innovation. By promoting the growth of industry, the Bourbons led the South into a new economic era, but without sacrificing a mythic reverence for the Old South. Bourbon rule left a permanent mark on the South's politics, economics, and race relations.

## THE NEW WEST

Like the South, the West is a region wrapped in myths and stereotypes. The vast land west of the Mississippi River contains remarkable geographic extremes: majestic mountains, roaring rivers, searing deserts, sprawling grasslands, and dense forests. For vast reaches of western America, the great epics of the Civil War and Reconstruction were remote events hardly touching the lives of the Indians, Mexicans, Asians, trappers, miners, and Mormons scattered through the plains and mountains. There the march of settlement and exploitation continued, propelled by a lust for land and a passion for profit. Between 1870 and 1900, Americans settled more land in the West than had been occupied by all Americans up to 1870. On one level, western settlement beyond the Mississippi River constitutes a colorful drama of determined pioneers and two-fisted gunslingers overcoming all obstacles to secure their vision of freedom and opportunity amid the region's awesome vastness. The post–Civil War West offered the promise of democratic individualism, economic opportunity, and personal freedom that had long before come to define the American dream. On another level, however, the colonization of the Far West was a tragedy of shortsighted greed and irresponsible behavior, a story of reckless exploitation that scarred the land, decimated its wildlife, and nearly exterminated Native American culture.

In the second tier of trans-Mississippi states—Iowa, Kansas, Nebraska—and in western Minnesota, farmers began spreading across the Great Plains after mid-century. From California, miners moved east through the mountains, drawn by one new strike after another. From Texas, nomadic cowboys migrated northward onto the plains and across the Rocky Mountains, into the Great Basin of Utah. The settlers encountered climates and landscapes markedly different from those they had left behind. The Great Plains were arid, and the scarcity of water and timber rendered useless the familiar trappings of the pioneer: the ax, the log cabin, the rail fence, and the accustomed methods of tilling the soil. For a long time the region had been called the Great American Desert, unfit for human habitation and therefore, to white Americans, the perfect refuge for Indians. But that view changed in the last half of the nineteenth century as a result of newly discovered deposits of gold, silver, and other minerals, the completion of the transcontinental railroads, the destruction of the buffalo, the collapse of Indian resistance, the rise of the range-cattle industry, and the dawning realization that the arid region need not be a sterile desert. With the use of what water was available, new techniques of dry farming and irrigation could make the land fruitful after all.

THE MIGRATORY STREAM   During the second half of the nineteenth century, an unrelenting stream of migrants flowed into the largely Indian and Hispanic West. Millions of Anglo-Americans, African Americans, Mexicans, and European and Chinese immigrants transformed the patterns of western society and culture. Most of the settlers were relatively prosperous white, native-born farm folk. Because of the expense of transportation, land, and supplies, the very poor could not afford to relocate. Three quarters of the western migrants were men.

The largest number of foreign immigrants came from northern Europe and Canada. In the northern plains, Germans, Scandinavians, and Irish were especially numerous. In the new state of Nebraska in 1870, a quarter of the 123,000 residents were foreign-born. In North Dakota in 1890, 45 percent of the residents were immigrants. Compared with European immigrants, those from China and Mexico were much less numerous but nonetheless significant. More than 200,000 Chinese arrived in California between 1876 and 1890.

AFRICAN AMERICAN MIGRATION    In the aftermath of the collapse of Radical Republican rule in the South, thousands of African Americans began migrating west from Kentucky, Tennessee, Louisiana, Arkansas, Mississippi, and Texas. Some six thousand southern blacks arrived in Kansas in 1879, and as many as twenty thousand followed the following year. These African American migrants came to be known as Exodusters because they were making their exodus from the South—in search of a haven from racism and poverty.

The foremost promoter of black migration to the West was Benjamin "Pap" Singleton. Born a slave in Tennessee in 1809, he escaped and made his way to Michigan. After the Civil War, he returned to Tennessee, convinced

**Nicodemus, Kansas**

A colony founded by southern blacks in the 1860s.

that God was calling him to rescue his brethren. When Singleton learned that land in Kansas could be had for $1.25 an acre, he led his first party of two hundred colonists to Kansas in 1878, bought 7,500 acres that had been an Indian reservation, and established the Dunlop community. Over the next several years, thousands of African Americans followed Singleton into Kansas, leading many southern leaders to worry about the loss of black laborers in the region. In 1879, whites closed access to the Mississippi River and threatened to sink all boats carrying black colonists from the South to the West. An army officer reported to President Rutherford B. Hayes that "every river landing is blockaded by white enemies of the colored exodus; some of whom are mounted and armed, as if we are at war."

The exodus of black southerners to the West died out by the early 1880s. Many of the settlers were unprepared for the living conditions on the plains. Their Kansas homesteads were not large enough to be self-sustaining, and most of the black farmers were forced to supplement their income by hiring themselves out to white ranchers. Drought, grasshoppers, prairie fires, and dust storms led to crop failures. The sudden influx of so many people taxed resources and patience. Many of the African American pioneers in Kansas soon abandoned their land and moved to the few cities in the state. Life on the frontier was not the "promised land" that settlers had been led to expect. Nonetheless, by 1890 some 520,000 African Americans lived west of the Mississippi River. As many as 25 percent of the cowboys who participated in the Texas cattle drives were African Americans.

In 1866, Congress passed legislation establishing two "colored" cavalry units and dispatched them to the western frontier. Nicknamed "buffalo soldiers" by the Indians, the men were mostly Civil War veterans from Louisiana and Kentucky. They built and maintained forts, mapped vast areas of the Southwest, strung hundreds of miles of telegraph lines, protected railroad construction crews, subdued hostile Indians, and captured outlaws and rustlers. Eighteen of the buffalo soldiers won Congressional Medals of Honor for their service.

MINING THE WEST  Valuable mineral deposits continued to lure people to the West after the Civil War. The California miners of 1849 (forty-niners) set the typical pattern, in which the sudden, disorderly rush of prospectors to a new find was quickly joined by camp followers—a motley crew of peddlers, saloon keepers, prostitutes, cardsharps, hustlers, and assorted desperadoes eager to mine the miners. If a new field panned out, the forces of respectability and more subtle forms of exploitation slowly worked their way in. Lawlessness gave way to vigilante rule and, finally, to a stable community.

The drama of the 1849 gold rush was reenacted time and again in the following three decades. Along the South Platte River, not far from Pikes Peak in Colorado, a prospecting party found gold in 1858, and stories of success brought perhaps one hundred thousand "fifty-niners" into the country by the next year. New discoveries in Colorado kept occurring: near Central City in 1859, at Leadville in the 1870s, and the last important strikes in the West, again gold and silver, at Cripple Creek in 1891 and 1894. During those years, farming and grazing

**Deadwood, Dakota Territory**

A gold-rush town in 1876, before the Dakotas became states.

had given the economy a stable base, and Colorado, the Centennial State, entered the union in 1876.

While the early miners were crowding around Pikes Peak, the Comstock Lode was discovered near Gold Hill, Nevada. H. T. P. Comstock, a Canadian-born fur trapper, had drifted to the Carson River diggings, which opened in 1856. He talked his way into a share in a new discovery made by two other prospectors in 1859 and gave it his own name. The lode produced gold and silver. Within twenty years, it had yielded more than $300 million from shafts that reached hundreds of feet into the mountainside. In 1861, largely on account of the settlers attracted to the Comstock Lode, Nevada became a territory, and in 1864 the state of Nevada was admitted to the Union in time to give two electoral votes to Abraham Lincoln (the new state's third electoral voter got caught in a snowstorm).

The growing demand for orderly government in the West led to the hasty creation of new territories and eventually the admission of a host of new states. After Colorado's admission in 1876, however, there was a long hiatus because of party divisions in Congress: Democrats were reluctant to create states out of territories that were heavily Republican. After the sweeping Republican victory in the 1888 legislative races, however, Congress admitted

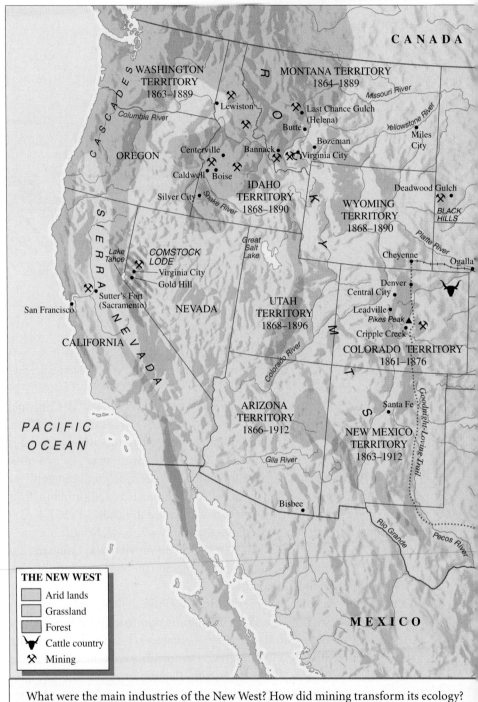

THE NEW WEST

- Arid lands
- Grassland
- Forest
- Cattle country
- Mining

What were the main industries of the New West? How did mining transform its ecology?

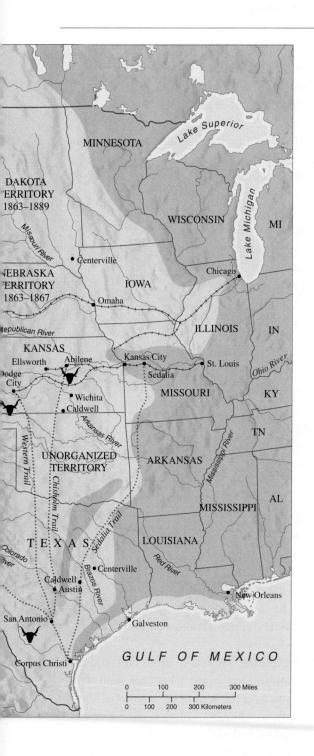

the Dakotas, Montana, and Washington in 1889 and Idaho and Wyoming in 1890. Utah entered the Union in 1896 (after the Mormons abandoned the practice of polygamy) and Oklahoma in 1907, and in 1912 Arizona and New Mexico rounded out the forty-eight contiguous states.

MINING AND THE ENVIRONMENT    During the second half of the nineteenth century, the nature of mining changed drastically. It became a mass-production industry as individual prospectors gave way to large companies. The first wave of miners who rushed to California in 1849 sifted gold dust and nuggets out of riverbeds by means of "placer" mining, or "**panning**." But once the placer deposits were exhausted, efficient mining required large-scale operations and huge investments. Companies shifted from surface digging to hydraulic mining, dredging, or deep-shaft "hard-rock" mining.

Hydraulicking, dredging, and shaft mining transformed vast areas of vegetation and landscape. Huge hydraulic cannons shot an enormous stream of water under high pressure, stripping the topsoil and gravel from the bedrock and creating steep-sloped barren canyons that could not sustain plant life. The tons of dirt and debris unearthed by the water cannons covered rich farmland downstream and created sandbars that clogged rivers and killed fish. All told, some 12 billion tons of earth were blasted out of the Sierra Nevada Mountains and washed into local rivers.

Irate California farmers in the fertile Central Valley bitterly protested the damage done downstream by the industrial mining operations. In 1878, they formed the Anti-Debris Association, with its own militia, to challenge the powerful mining companies. Efforts to pass state legislation restricting hydraulic mining repeatedly failed because mining companies controlled the votes. The Anti-Debris Association then turned to the courts. On January 7, 1884, the farmers won their case when federal judge Lorenzo Sawyer, a former miner, outlawed the dumping of mining debris where it could reach farmland or navigable rivers. Thus *Woodruff v. North Bloomfield Gravel Mining Company* became the first major environmental ruling in the nation. As a result of the ruling, hydraulic mining dried up, leaving a legacy of abandoned equipment, ugly ravines, ditches, gullies, and mountains of discarded rock and gravel.

THE INDIAN WARS    As the frontier pressed in from east and west, some 250,000 Native Americans were forced into what was supposed to be their last refuge, the Great Plains and the mountain regions of the Far West. The 1851 Fort Laramie Treaty, in which the chiefs of the Plains tribes agreed to accept definite tribal borders and allow white emigrants to travel on their trails unmolested, worked for a while, with wagon trains passing safely through Indian lands and the army building roads and forts without resistance. Fighting resumed, however, as the emigrants began to encroach upon Indian lands on the plains rather than merely pass through them.

From the early 1860s until the late 1870s, the frontier raged with Indian wars. In 1864, Colorado's governor persuaded most of the warring Indians in his territory to gather at Fort Lyon, on Sand Creek, where they were promised protection. Despite that promise, Colonel John M. Chivington's untrained militia attacked an Indian camp flying a white flag of truce, slaughtering two hundred peaceful Indians—men, women, and children—in what one general called the "foulest and most unjustifiable crime in the annals of America."

With other scattered battles erupting, a congressional committee in 1865 gathered evidence on the grisly Indian wars and massacres. Its 1867 "Report on the Condition of the Indian Tribes" led to the creation of an Indian Peace Commission charged with removing the causes of the Indian wars. Congress decided that this would be best accomplished at the expense of the Indians, by persuading them to take up life on out-of-the-way reservations. Yet the persistent encroachment of whites on Indian hunting grounds continued. In 1870, Indians outnumbered whites in the Dakota Territory by two to one; in 1880, whites outnumbered Indians by more than six to one.

In 1867 a conference at Medicine Lodge, Kansas, ended with the Kiowas, Comanches, Arapahos, and Cheyennes reluctantly accepting land in western Oklahoma. The following spring the Sioux agreed to settle within the Black Hills Reservation in Dakota Territory. But Indian resistance in the southern plains continued until the Red River War of 1874–1875, when General Philip Sheridan forced the Indians to disband in the spring of 1875. Seventy-two Indian chiefs were imprisoned for three years.

Meanwhile, trouble was brewing again in the north. In 1874, Lieutenant Colonel **George A. Custer**, a reckless, glory-seeking officer, led an exploratory expedition into the Black Hills. Miners were soon filtering onto the Sioux hunting grounds despite promises that the army would keep them out. The army had done little to protect Indian land, but when ordered to move against wandering bands of Sioux hunting on the range according to their treaty rights, it moved vigorously.

What became the **Great Sioux War** was the largest military event since the end of the Civil War and one of the largest campaigns against Indians in American history. The war lasted fifteen months and entailed fifteen battles in present-day Wyoming, Montana, South Dakota, and Nebraska. The heroic Chief Sitting Bull ably led the Sioux. In 1876, after several indecisive encounters, Custer found the main encampment of Sioux and their Northern Cheyenne allies on the Little Bighorn River. Separated from the main

What was the Great Sioux War? What happened at Little Bighorn, and what were the consequences? Why were hundreds of Indians killed at Wounded Knee?

body of soldiers and surrounded by 2,500 warriors, Custer's detachment of 210 men was annihilated.

Instead of following up their victory, the Indians celebrated and renewed their hunting. The army quickly regained the offensive and compelled the Sioux to give up their hunting grounds and goldfields in return for payments. Forced onto reservations situated on the least valuable land in the region, the Indians soon found themselves struggling to subsist under harsh conditions. Many of them died of starvation or disease. When a peace commission imposed a settlement, Chief Spotted Tail said: "Tell your people that since the Great Father promised that we should never be removed, we have been moved five times. . . . I think you had better put the Indians on wheels and you can run them about wherever you wish."

In the Rocky Mountains and to the west, the same story of hopeless resistance was repeated. Indians were the last obstacle to white western expansion, and they suffered as a result. The Blackfeet and Crows had to leave their homes in Montana. In a war along the California-Oregon boundary, the Modocs held out for six months in 1871–1872 before they were overwhelmed. In 1879 the Utes were forced to give up their vast territories in western Colorado. In Idaho the peaceful Nez Percé bands, many of which had converted to Christianity and embraced white culture, refused to surrender land along the Salmon River, and prolonged fighting erupted there and in eastern Oregon. Joseph, one of several Nez Percé chiefs, delivered an eloquent surrender speech that served as an epitaph to the Indians' efforts to withstand the march of American empire: "I am tired of fighting. Our chiefs are killed. . . . The old men are all dead. . . . I want to have time to look for my children, and see how many of them I can find. . . . Hear me, my chiefs! I am tired. My heart is sick and sad. From where the sun now stands I will fight no more forever."

A generation of Indian wars virtually ended in 1886 with the capture of Geronimo, a chief of the Chiricahua Apaches, who had fought white settlers in the Southwest for fifteen years. But there would be a tragic epilogue. Late in 1888, Wovoka (or Jack Wilson), a Paiute in western Nevada, fell ill and in a delirium imagined he had visited the spirit world, where he learned of a deliverer coming to rescue the Indians and restore their lands. To hasten their

**The Battle of Little Bighorn, 1876**

A painting by Amos Bad Heart Bull, an Oglala Sioux.

**Indian wars**

Chief Joseph of the Nez Perce.

deliverance, he said, the Indians must take up a ceremonial dance at each new moon. The **Ghost Dance** craze fed upon old legends of a coming messiah and spread rapidly. In 1890, the Lakota Sioux adopted it with such fervor that it alarmed white authorities. They banned the Ghost Dance on Lakota reservations, but the Indians defied the order and a crisis erupted. On December 29, 1890, a bloodbath occurred at Wounded Knee, South Dakota. An accidental rifle discharge led nervous soldiers to fire into a group of Indians who had come to surrender. Nearly two hundred Indians and twenty-five soldiers died in the Battle of Wounded Knee. The Indian wars had ended with characteristic brutality and misunderstanding. General Philip Sheridan was acidly candid in summarizing how whites had treated the Indians: "We took away their country and their means of support, broke up their mode of living, their habits of life, introduced disease and decay and among them, and it was for this and against this that they made war. Could anyone expect less?"

THE DEMISE OF THE BUFFALO   Over the long run, the collapse of Indian resistance in the face of white settlement on the Great Plains resulted as much from the decimation of the buffalo herds as from the actions of federal troops. In 1750, there were an estimated 30 million buffalo; by 1850 there were less than 10 million; by 1900, only a few hundred were left. What happened to them? The conventional story focuses on intensive harvesting of buffalo by white hunters after the Civil War. Americans east of the Mississippi River developed a voracious demand for buffalo robes and buffalo leather. The average white commercial hunter killed one hundred animals a day, and the hides and bones (to be ground into fertilizer) were shipped east on railroad cars. Some army officers encouraged the slaughter. "Kill every buffalo you can!" Colonel Richard Dodge told a sport hunter in 1867. "Every buffalo dead is an Indian gone."

This conventional explanation tells only part of a more complicated story, however. The buffalo disappeared from the western plains for a variety of environmental reasons, including a significant change in climate; competition for forage with horses, sheep, and cattle; and cattle-borne disease. A prolonged drought on the Great Plains during the late 1880s and 1890s—the same drought that would help spur the agrarian political revolt and the rise of populism—also devastated the buffalo herds by reducing the grasslands upon which the animals depended. At the same time, the buffalo had to compete for forage with other grazing animals. By the 1880s over 2 million horses were roaming buffalo lands. In addition, the Plains Indians themselves, empowered by horses and guns and spurred by the profits reaped from selling hides and meat to white traders, accounted for much of the devastation of the buffalo herds after 1840. White hunters who killed buffalo by the millions in the 1870s and 1880s played a major role in the animals' demise, but only as the final catalyst. If there had been no white hunters, the buffalo would probably have lasted only another thirty years, because their numbers had been so greatly reduced by other factors.

INDIAN POLICY    The slaughter of buffalo and Indians ignited widespread criticism. Politicians and religious leaders castigated the persistent mistreatment of Indians. In his annual message of 1877, President Rutherford B. Hayes joined the protest: "Many, if not most, of our Indian wars have had their origin in broken promises and acts of injustice on our part." Helen Hunt Jackson, a novelist and poet, focused attention on the Indian cause in *A Century of Dishonor* (1881). Its impact on American attitudes toward the Indians was comparable to the effect that Harriet Beecher Stowe's *Uncle Tom's Cabin* (1852) had on the abolitionist movement before the Civil War. U.S. policies regarding Indians gradually became more benevolent, but this change did little to ease the plight of the Indians and actually helped destroy the remnants of their culture. The reservation policy inaugurated by the Peace Commission in 1867 did little more than extend a practice that dated from colonial Virginia. Partly humanitarian in motive, it also saved money: housing and feeding Indians on reservations cost less than fighting them.

Well-intentioned reformers sought to "Americanize" Indians by dealing with them as individuals rather than tribes. The fruition of such reform efforts came with the Dawes Severalty Act of 1887. Sponsored by Senator Henry L. Dawes of Massachusetts, the act divided tribal lands, granting 160 acres to each head of a family and lesser amounts to others. But the more it changed, the more Indian policy remained the same. Despite the best of intentions, the Dawes Act created opportunities for increased white plundering of Indian land and disrupted what remained of the traditional culture. Between 1887 and 1934, Indians lost an estimated 86 million of their 130 million acres. Most of what remained was unsuited for agriculture.

CATTLE AND COWBOYS   While the West was being taken from the Indians, cattle entered the grasslands where the buffalo had roamed. Much of the romance of the open-range cattle industry derived from its Mexican roots. The Texas longhorns and the cowboys' horses had in large part descended from stock brought to the New World by the Spaniards, and many of the industry's trappings had been worked out in Mexico first: the cowboy's saddle, chaps (*chaparreras*) to protect the legs, spurs, and lariat.

For many years, wild cattle competed with the buffalo in the Spanish borderlands. Natural selection and contact with Anglo-American cattle produced the Texas longhorns: lean and rangy, they were noted more for speed and endurance than for yielding a choice steak. They had little value, moreover, because the largest markets for beef were too far away. At the end of the Civil War, as many as 5 million cattle roamed the grasslands of Texas, still neglected—but not for long. In the upper Mississippi Valley, where herds had been depleted by the war, cattle were in great demand, and the Texas cattle could be had just for the effort of rounding them up.

New opportunities arose as railroads pushed farther west, where cattle could be driven through relatively vacant lands. Joseph G. McCoy, an Illinois livestock dealer, recognized the possibilities of moving the cattle trade west. In 1867 in Abilene, Kansas, he bought 250 acres for a stockyard; he then built a barn, an office building, livestock scales, a hotel, and a bank. He then sent an agent into Indian-owned areas to recruit owners of herds bound north to go through Abilene. Over the next few years, Abilene flourished as the first successful Kansas cowtown. The ability to ship huge numbers of western cattle by rail transformed ranching into a major industry. As the railroads moved west, so did the cowtowns—Ellsworth, Wichita, Caldwell, and Dodge City in Kansas; farther north to Ogallala, Nebraska; Cheyenne, Wyoming; and Miles City, Montana.

During the twenty years after the Civil War, some forty thousand cowboys roamed the Great Plains. They were young—the average age was twenty-four—and from diverse backgrounds. Some 30 percent were Mexican or African American, and hundreds were Indians. Many others were Civil War veterans from the North and the South, and still others were immigrants from Europe. The life of a cowboy, for the most part, was rarely as exciting as has been depicted by movies and television shows. Working as a ranch hand involved grueling, dirty wage labor interspersed with drudgery and boredom, often amid terrible weather conditions.

The thriving cattle industry spurred rapid growth in the region, however. The population of Kansas increased from 107,000 in 1860 to 365,000 ten years later and reached almost 1 million by 1880. Nebraska witnessed similar increases. During the 1860s, cattle would be delivered to rail depots, loaded

**The cowboy era**

Cowboys herd cattle near Cimarron, Colorado, 1905.

onto freight cars, and shipped east. By the time the animals arrived in New York or Massachusetts, some would be dead or dying, and all would have lost significant weight. The secret to higher profits in the cattle industry was to devise a way to slaughter the cattle in the Midwest and ship the dressed carcasses east and west. That process required refrigeration to keep the meat from spoiling. In 1869, G. H. Hammond, a Chicago meat packer, shipped the first refrigerated beef in an air-cooled railroad car from Chicago to Boston. Eight years later, Gustavus Swift developed a more efficient system of mechanical refrigeration, an innovation that earned him a fortune and provided the cattle industry with a major stimulus.

In the absence of laws governing the open range, cattle ranchers at first worked out a code of behavior largely dictated by circumstances. As cattle often wandered onto other ranchers' claims, cowboys would "ride the line" to keep the animals off the adjoining ranches. In the spring they would "round up" the herds, which invariably got mixed up, and sort out ownership by identifying the distinctive ranch symbols "branded," or burned, into the cattle. All that changed in 1873, when Joseph Glidden, an Illinois farmer, invented the first effective barbed wire, which ranchers used to fence off their claims at relatively low cost. Ranchers rushed to buy the new wire fencing, and soon the open range was no more. Cattle raising, like mining, evolved from a romantic adventure into a big business dominated by giant enterprises.

THE END OF THE OPEN RANGE  The flush times of the cowtown soon passed, however, and the long cattle drives played out too, because they were economically unsound. A combination of factors put an end to the open range. Farmers kept crowding in and laying out homesteads and waging "barbed-wire wars" with ranchers by cutting the ranchers' fences or policing their own. The boundless range was being overrun with cattle by 1883, and expenses mounted as stock breeders formed associations to keep intruders off overstocked ranges, establish and protect land titles, deal with railroads and buyers, fight prairie fires, and cope with rustlers as well as wolves and cougars. The rise of sheepherding by 1880 caused still another conflict with the cattle ranchers. A final blow to the open-range industry came with two unusually severe winters, in 1886 and 1887, followed by ten long years of drought.

The dangers of the trail, the wear and tear on men and cattle, the charges levied on drives across Indian territory, and the advance of farms across the trails combined to persuade cattlemen that they could function best near railroads. As railroads spread out into Texas and across the plains, the cattle business spread with them over the High Plains as far north as Montana and on into Canada.

**Langtry, Texas, 1900**

Judge Roy Bean's courthouse and saloon.

Surviving the hazards of the range required ranchers to establish legal title and fence in the land, limit the herds to a reasonable size, and provide shelter and hay during the rigors of winter. Moreover, as the long cattle drives gave way to more rail lines and refrigerated railcars, the cowboy settled into a more sedentary existence. Within merely two decades, from 1866 to 1886, the era of the cowboy had come and gone.

RANGE WARS   Conflicting claims over land and water rights triggered **range wars**, violent disputes between ranchers and farmers. Ranchers often tried to drive off neighboring farmers, and farmers in turn tried to sabotage the cattle barons, cutting their fences and spooking their herds. The cattle ranchers also clashed with sheepherders over access to grassland. A strain of ethnic and religious prejudice heightened the tension between ranchers and herders. In the Southwest, shepherds were typically Mexican Americans; in Idaho and Nevada they were from the Basque region of Spain, or they were Mormons. Many Anglo-American cattle ranchers and cowboys viewed those ethnic and religious groups as un-American and inferior, adopting a racist attitude that helped them rationalize the use of violence against sheepherders. Warfare gradually faded, however, as the sheep for the most part found refuge in the high pastures of the mountains, leaving the grasslands of the plains to the cattle ranchers.

Yet there also developed a perennial tension between large and small cattle ranchers. The large ranchers fenced in huge tracts of public land, leaving the smaller ranchers with too little pasture. To survive, the smaller ranchers cut the fences. In central Texas this practice sparked the Fence-Cutters' War of 1883–1884. Several ranchers were killed and dozens wounded before the state ended the conflict by passing legislation outlawing fence cutting.

FARMERS AND THE LAND   Farming has always been a hard life, and it was made more so on the Great Plains by the region's unforgiving environment and mercurial weather. After 1865, on paper at least, the federal land laws offered farmers favorable terms. Under the Homestead Act of 1862, a settler ("homesteader") could gain title to federal land simply by staking out a claim and living on it for five years, or he could buy land at $1.25 an acre after six months. But such land legislation was predicated upon the tradition of farming the fertile lands east of the Mississippi River, and the laws were never adjusted to the fact that much of the prairie was suited only for cattle raising. Cattle ranchers were forced to obtain land by gradual acquisition from homesteaders or land-grant railroads.

As so often happens, environmental forces influenced development. The arid climate, rather than new land laws, shaped institutions in the West after the Civil War. Where farming was impossible, ranchers simply established dominance by control of the water, regardless of the law. Belated legislative efforts to develop irrigable land finally achieved a major success when the 1902 Newlands Reclamation Act (after the aptly named Senator Francis G. Newlands of Nevada) set up the Bureau of Reclamation. The proceeds of public land sales in sixteen states created a fund for irrigation projects, and the Reclamation Bureau set about building such major projects as the Boulder (later the Hoover) Dam on the Nevada-Arizona line, the Roosevelt Dam in Arizona, the Elephant Butte Dam in New Mexico, and the Arrowrock Dam in Idaho.

The lands of the New West, like those on previous frontiers, passed to their ultimate owners more often from private hands than directly from the government. Many of the 274 million acres claimed under the Homestead Act passed quickly to ranchers or speculators and thence to settlers. The land-grant railroads got some 200 million acres of land owned by the federal government between 1851 and 1871. Over time, the railroads sold much of

**The construction of Hoover Dam**

When completed in 1936, Hoover Dam was the world's largest concrete structure.

the land to create towns and ranches along the rail lines. The West of ranchers and farmers was in fact largely the product of the railroads; they were the lifeblood of the western economy.

The first arrivals on the sod-house frontier faced a grim struggle against danger, adversity, and monotony. Though land was relatively cheap, horses, livestock, wagons, wells, lumber, fencing, seed, and fertilizer were not. Freight rates and interest rates on loans seemed criminally high. As in the South, declining crop prices produced chronic indebtedness, leading strapped western farmers to promote the inflation of the money supply. The virgin land itself, although fertile, resisted planting; the heavy sod broke many a plow. Since wood was almost nonexistent on the prairie, pioneer families used buffalo chips (dried dung) for fuel.

Farmers and their families also fought a constant battle with the elements: tornadoes, hailstorms, droughts, prairie fires, blizzards, and pests. Swarms of locusts often clouded the horizon, occasionally covering the ground six inches deep. A Wichita newspaper reported in 1878 that the grasshoppers devoured "everything green, stripping the foliage off the bark and from the tender twigs of the fruit trees, destroying every plant that is good for food or pleasant to the eyes, that man has planted."

As the railroads brought piles of lumber from the East, farmers could leave their sod houses (homes built of sod) to build more comfortable frame dwellings. New machinery helped provide fresh opportunities. In 1868, James Oliver, a Scottish immigrant living in Indiana, made a successful chilled-iron plow. This "sodbuster" plow greatly eased the task of breaking the tough grass roots of the plains. Improvements and new inventions in threshing machines, hay mowers, planters, manure spreaders, cream separators, and other devices lightened the burden of farm labor but added to the farmers' capital outlay. In Minnesota, the Dakotas, and central California the gigantic "bonanza farms," with machinery for mass production, became the marvels of the age. On one farm in North Dakota, 13,000 acres of wheat made a single field. Another bonanza farm employed over 1,000 migrant workers to tend 34,000 acres.

While the overall value of farmland and farm products increased in the late nineteenth century, small farmers did not keep up with the march of progress. Their numbers grew in size but decreased in proportion to the population at large. Wheat in the western states, like cotton in the antebellum South, was the great export crop that spurred economic growth. For a variety of reasons, however, few small farmers prospered. By the 1890s, they were in open revolt against the "system" of corrupt processors (middlemen) and "greedy" bankers who they believed conspired against them.

PIONEER WOMEN    The West remained a largely male society throughout the nineteenth century. Women were not only a numerical minority;
they also continued to face traditional legal barriers and social prejudice.
A wife could not sell property without her husband's approval, for example.
Texas women could not sue except for divorce, nor could they serve on
juries, act as lawyers, or witness a will.

But the fight for survival in the trans-Mississippi West made men and
women more equal partners than in the East. Many women who lost their
mates to the deadly toil of sod busting thereafter assumed complete responsibility for their farms. In general, women on the prairie became more independent than women leading domestic lives back East. A Kansas woman
explained "that the environment was such as to bring out and develop the
dominant qualities of individual character. Kansas women of that day
learned at an early age to depend on themselves—to do whatever work there
was to be done, and to face danger when it must be faced, as calmly as they
were able."

THE END OF THE FRONTIER    American life reached an important
juncture at the end of the nineteenth century. The 1890 national census
reported that the frontier era in American development was over; people by
then had spread across the entire continent. This fact inspired the historian
**Frederick Jackson Turner** to develop his influential frontier thesis, first outlined in "The Significance of the Frontier in American History," a paper

**Women of the frontier**

A woman and her family in front of their sod house. The difficult life on the prairie
led to more egalitarian marriages than were found in other regions of the country.

delivered to the American Historical Association in 1893. "The existence of an area of free land," Turner wrote, "its continuous recession, and the advance of American settlement westward, explain American development." The frontier, he added, had shaped the national character in fundamental ways. It was

> to the frontier [that] the American intellect owes its striking characteristics. That coarseness and strength combined with acuteness and acquisitiveness; that practical, inventive turn of mind, quick to find expedients; that masterful grasp of material things, lacking in the artistic but powerful to effect great ends; that restless, nervous energy; that dominant individualism, working for good and for evil, and withal that buoyancy and exuberance which comes with freedom—these are traits of the frontier, or traits called out elsewhere because of the existence of the frontier.

In 1893, Turner concluded, "four centuries from the discovery of America, at the end of a hundred years under the Constitution, the frontier has gone and with its going has closed the first period of American history."

Turner's "frontier thesis" guided several generations of scholars and students in their understanding of the distinctive characteristics of American history. His view of the frontier as the westward-moving source of the nation's democratic politics, open society, unfettered economy, and rugged individualism, far removed from the corruptions of urban life, gripped the popular imagination as well. But it left out much of the story. The frontier experience Turner described exaggerated the homogenizing effect of the frontier environment and virtually ignored the role of women, African Americans, Native Americans, Mormons, Hispanics, and Asians in shaping the diverse human geography of the western United States. Turner also implied that the West would be fundamentally different after 1890 because the frontier experience was essentially over. But in many respects that region has retained the qualities associated with the rush for land, gold, timber, and water rights during the post–Civil War decades. The mining frontier, as one historian has recently written, "set a mood that has never disappeared from the West: the attitude of extractive industry—get in, get rich, get out."

## CHAPTER SUMMARY

- **Indian Wars and Policies**   By 1900, Native Americans in the West were no longer free to roam the plains. Disease and the influx of farmers and miners reduced their numbers and curtailed their way of life. Instances of resistance, such as the Great Sioux War, were crushed. Initially, Indian tribes were forced to sign treaties and were confined to reservations. Beginning in 1887, the American government's Indian policy was aimed at forcing Indians to relinquish their traditional culture and adopt individual land ownership, settled agriculture, and Christianity.

- **Life in the West**   Life in the West was harsh and violent, but the promise of cheap land or wealth from mining drew settlers from the East. Most cowboys and miners did not acquire wealth, however, because raising cattle and mining became large-scale enterprises that enriched only a few. Although most westerners were white Protestant Americans or northern European immigrants, Mexicans, African Americans, and Chinese contributed to the West's diversity. As a consequence of the region's rugged isolation, women achieved greater equality in everyday life than did most women elsewhere in the country.

- **Growth of Mining**   Mining lured settlers to largely uninhabited regions, thereby hastening the creation of new territories and the admission of new states into the Union. By the 1880s, when mining became a big business employing large-scale equipment, its environmental impact could be seen in the blighted landscape.

- **The American Frontier**   The historian Frederick Jackson Turner believed that the enduring presence of the frontier was responsible for making Americans individualistic, materialistic, practical, democratic, and energetic. In 1893 he declared that the closing of the frontier had ended the first stage of America's history.

## CHRONOLOGY

| | |
|---|---|
| 1859 | Comstock Lode is discovered |
| 1862 | Congress passes the Homestead Act |
| 1864 | Sand Creek Massacre |
| 1873 | Joseph Glidden invents barbed wire |
| 1876 | Battle of Little Bighorn |
| 1877 | With the Compromise of 1877, Rutherford B. Hayes becomes president and Reconstruction comes to an end |
| 1886 | Surrender of Geronimo marks the end of the Indian wars |
| 1887 | Congress passes the Severalty Act |
| 1890 | Battle of Wounded Knee |
| 1893 | Frederick J. Turner's "frontier thesis" |

## KEY TERMS & NAMES

# 20

# THE EMERGENCE OF
# URBAN AMERICA

FOCUS QUESTIONS          (S) wwnorton.com/studyspace

- What accounted for the rise of cities in America?
- How did the "new immigration" change America at the end of the nineteenth century?
- What new forms of mass entertainment had emerged by 1900?
- What was the impact of Darwinian thought on social sciences?

ithin three decades after the Civil War, a stunning transformation had occurred in American life. A society long rooted in the soil and focused on domestic issues became an urban-industrial nation inextricably involved in world markets and global politics. Cities are one of humanity's greatest creations, and in the United States during the second half of the nineteenth century, cities grew at a rate unparalleled in world history. The late nineteenth century, declared an economist in 1899, was "not only the age of cities, but the age of great cities." Between 1860 and 1910, the urban population mushroomed from 6 million to 44 million. By 1920, more than half the nation's population lived in urban areas. This rise of big cities created a distinctive urban culture. People from different ethnic and religious backgrounds and every walk of life poured into the high-rise apartment buildings and ramshackle tenements springing up in every major city. They came in search of jobs, wealth, and excitement.

Not surprisingly, the rise of metropolitan America created an array of new social problems. Rapid urban development produced widespread poverty and political corruption. How to feed, clothe, shelter, and educate the new arrivals taxed the imagination—and the patience—of urban leaders. Further complicating efforts to improve the quality of life in the nation's cities was increasing residential segregation according to racial and ethnic background and social class.

## AMERICA'S MOVE TO TOWN

The prospect of good jobs and social excitement in the cities lured workers by the millions from the countryside and overseas. City people became distinctively urban in demeanor and outlook, and the contrasts between farm and city life grew more vivid with each passing year.

EXPLOSIVE URBAN GROWTH    The frontier was a societal safety valve, the historian Frederick Jackson Turner said in his influential thesis on American development. Its cheap lands afforded a release for the population pressures mounting in the cities. If there was such a thing as a safety valve in the nineteenth century, however, Turner had it exactly backward. The flow of population toward the cities was greater than the flow toward the West. Much of the westward movement, in fact, was itself an urban movement, spawning new towns near the mining digs or at the railheads. On the Pacific coast, a greater portion of the population was urbanized than anywhere else; its major concentrations were around San Francisco Bay at first and then in Los Angeles, which became a boomtown after the arrival of the Southern Pacific and Santa Fe Railroads in the 1880s. In the Northwest, Seattle grew quickly, first as the terminus of three transcontinental railroad lines and, by the end of the century, as the staging area for the Yukon gold rush. Minneapolis, St. Paul, Omaha, Kansas City, and Denver experienced rapid growth as well. The South, too, produced new cities: Durham, North Carolina, and Birmingham, Alabama, which were centers of tobacco and iron production, and Houston, Texas, which handled cotton and cattle and, later, oil.

While the Far West had the greatest proportion of urban dwellers, the Northeast had far more people in its teeming cities. These city dwellers were increasingly landless and homeless: they had nothing but their labor to sell. By 1900, more than 90 percent of the residents in New York City's Manhattan lived in rented houses or congested multi-story apartment buildings, called tenements.

Several technological innovations allowed city buildings to expand vertically to accommodate their surging populations. In the 1870s, developments in heating, such as steam circulating through radiators, enabled the construction

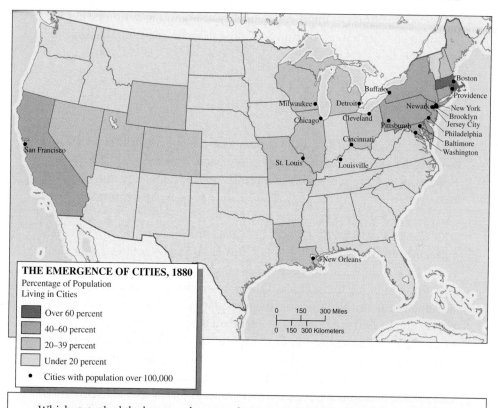

**THE EMERGENCE OF CITIES, 1880**
Percentage of Population
Living in Cities

Over 60 percent

40–60 percent

20–39 percent

Under 20 percent

• Cities with population over 100,000

Which states had the largest urban population in 1880? What drove the growth of western cities? How were western cities different from eastern cities?

of large apartment buildings, since fireplaces were no longer needed. In 1889, the Otis Elevator Company installed the first electric elevator, which made possible the erection of taller buildings—before the 1860s few structures had risen beyond three or four stories. And during the 1880s, engineers developed cast-iron and steel-frame construction techniques. Because such materials were stronger than brick, they allowed developers to erect high-rise buildings, called skyscrapers.

Cities also expanded horizontally after the introduction of important transportation innovations. Before the 1890s, the chief power sources of urban transport were either animals or steam. Horse- and mule-drawn streetcars had appeared in antebellum cities, but they were slow and cumbersome, and cleaning up after the animals added to the cost. In 1873, San Francisco became the first city to use cable cars that clamped onto a moving underground cable driven by a central power source. Some cities used

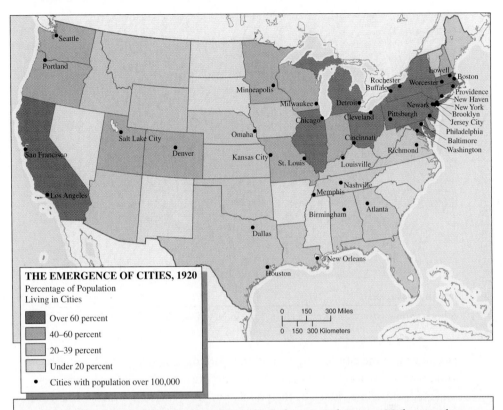

**THE EMERGENCE OF CITIES, 1920**

Percentage of Population
Living in Cities

- Over 60 percent
- 40–60 percent
- 20–39 percent
- Under 20 percent
- • Cities with population over 100,000

How did technology change urban life in the early twentieth century? What was the role of mass transit in expanding the urban population? How did the demographics of the new cities change between 1880 and 1920?

steam-powered trains on elevated tracks, but by the 1890s electric trolleys were preferred. Mass transit received an added boost when subways were built in Boston, New York City, and Philadelphia.

The spread of mass transit allowed large numbers of people to become commuters, and a growing middle class retreated from downtown to live in quieter tree-lined "streetcar suburbs," whence they could travel into the central city for business or entertainment (though working folk generally stayed put, unable to afford even the nickel fare). Urban growth often became a sprawl, since it usually took place without plan, in the interest of a fast buck, and without thought to the need for parks and public services.

The use of horse-drawn railways, cable cars, and electric trolleys helped transform the social character of cities. After the Civil War, the emergence of suburbs began to segregate people according to their wealth. The more affluent

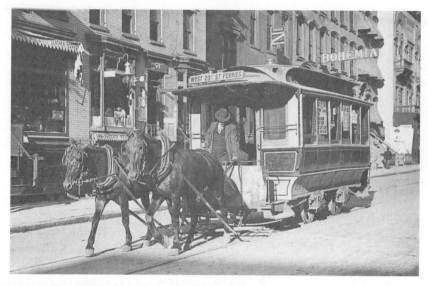

**Urban mass transit**

A horse-drawn streetcar moving along rails in New York City.

moved outside the city, leaving behind the working folk, many of whom were immigrants or African Americans. The poorer districts of a city became more congested and crime ridden as the population grew, fueled by waves of newcomers from abroad.

THE ALLURE AND PROBLEMS OF THE CITIES    The wonders of the cities—their glittering new electric lights, their streetcars, telephones, department stores, vaudeville shows and other amusements, newspapers and magazines, and a thousand other attractions—cast a magnetic lure on rural youth. In times of rural depression, thousands left farms for the cities in search of opportunity and personal freedom. The exodus from the countryside was especially evident in the East, where the census documented the shift in population from country to city. Yet those who moved to the city often traded one set of problems for another. Workers in the big cities often had no choice but to live in crowded apartments, most of which were poorly designed. In 1900, Manhattan's 42,700 tenements housed almost 1.6 million people. Such unregulated urban growth created immense problems of sanitation, health, and morale.

During the last quarter of the nineteenth century, cities became so cramped and land so scarce that designers were forced to build upward. In New York City this resulted in tenement houses, shared buildings with multiple housing units. These structures were usually six to eight stories tall, lacked elevators, and were jammed tightly against one another. Twenty-four to thirty-two families would cram into each building. Some city blocks housed almost four thousand people. Shoehorned into their quarters, families living in tenements had no privacy, free space, or sunshine; children had few places to play except in the streets; infectious diseases and noxious odors were rampant. Not surprisingly, the mortality rate among the urban poor was much higher than that of the general population. In one poor Chicago district at the end of the century, three out of five babies died before their first birthday.

CITIES AND THE ENVIRONMENT    Nineteenth-century cities were filthy and disease ridden, noisy and smelly. They overflowed with garbage, contaminated water, horse urine and manure, roaming pigs, and untreated sewage. Providing clean water was a chronic problem, and raw sewage was dumped into streets and waterways. Epidemics of water-related diseases such as cholera, typhoid fever, and yellow fever ravaged urban populations. Animal waste was pervasive. In 1900, for example, there were over 3.5 million horses in American cities, each of which generated 20 pounds of manure and several gallons of urine daily. In Chicago alone, 82,000 horses produced 300,000 tons of manure each year. The life expectancy of urban draft horses was only two years, which meant that thousands of horse carcasses had to be disposed of each year. In New York City, 15,000 dead horses were removed annually.

During the late nineteenth century, municipal reformers organized to clean up the cities. The "sanitary reformers"—public health officials and municipal engineers—persuaded city governments to banish hogs and cattle within the city limits, mount cleanup campaigns, build water and sewage systems, institute trash collection, and replace horses with electric streetcars. By 1900, 94 percent of American cities had developed regular trash-collection services.

Yet such improvements in public health involved important social and ecological trade-offs and caused unanticipated problems. Waste that once had been put into the land was now dumped into waterways. Similarly, solving the horse-manure problem involved trade-offs. The manure dropped on city streets caused stench and bred countless flies, many of which carried diseases such as typhoid fever. But urban horse manure also had benefits. Farmers living on the outskirts of cities used it to fertilize hay and vegetable crops. City-generated manure was the agricultural lifeblood of the vegetable farms outside New York, Baltimore, Philadelphia, and Boston.

Ultimately, however, the development of public water and sewer systems and flush toilets separated urban dwellers and their waste from the agricultural

**Urbanization and the environment**

A garbage cart retrieves trash in New York City, ca. 1890.

cycle at the same time that the emergence of refrigerated railcars and massive meatpacking plants separated most people from their sources of food. While the advances provided great benefits, a flush-and-forget-it mentality emerged. Well into the twentieth century, people presumed that running water purified itself, so they dumped massive amounts of untreated waste into rivers and bays. What they failed to calculate was the carrying capacity of the waterways. The high phosphorous content of bodily waste dumped into streams led to algae blooms that sucked the oxygen out of the water and unleashed a string of environmental reactions that suffocated fish and affected marine ecology. In sum, city growth had unintended consequences.

## THE NEW IMMIGRATION

The Industrial Revolution brought to American shores waves of new immigrants from every part of the globe. Between 1860 and 1920, about one in seven Americans was foreign-born. Immigrants were even more numerous in cities. By 1900, nearly 30 percent of the residents of major cities were foreign-born. These newcomers provided much-needed labor, but their arrival sparked ugly racial and ethnic tensions.

AMERICA'S PULL    The migration of foreigners to the United States has been one of the most powerful forces shaping American history, and this was especially true between 1860 and 1920. In steadily rising numbers, immigrants moved from the agricultural areas of eastern and southern Europe directly to the largest cities of America. Once in the United States, they wanted to live with others who shared their language, customs, and religion. Ethnic neighborhoods in American cities preserved familiar folkways and shielded newcomers from the shocks of a strange culture. In 1890, four out of five New Yorkers were foreign-born, a higher proportion than in any other city in the world. New York had twice as many Irish as Dublin, as many Germans as Hamburg, and half as many Italians as Naples. In 1893, Chicago claimed the largest Bohemian (Czech) community in the world, and by 1910, the size of its Polish population ranked behind only the populations of Warsaw and Lodz.

This nation of immigrants continued to draw new inhabitants for much the same reasons as before and from much the same segments of society. Immigrants took flight from famine or the dispiriting lack of opportunity in their native lands. They fled racial, religious, and political persecution and

**Steerage deck of the S.S. *Pennland*, 1893**

These immigrants are about to arrive at Ellis Island in New York Harbor. Many newcomers to America settled in cities because they lacked the means to take up farming.

compulsory military service. Yet more immigrants were probably pulled by America's promise than were pushed out by conditions at home. American industries, seeking cheap labor, sent recruiting agents abroad. Railroads, eager to sell land and build up the traffic on their lines, distributed tempting propaganda in Europe in a medley of languages. Under the Contract Labor Act of 1864, the federal government helped pay an immigrant's passage. The law was repealed in 1868, but not until 1885 did the government forbid companies to import contract labor, a practice that put immigrant workers under the control of their employers.

After the Civil War, the tide of immigration rose from just under 3 million in the 1870s to more than 5 million in the 1880s, then fell to a little over 3.5 million in the depression decade of the 1890s and rose to its high-water mark of nearly 9 million in the first decade of the twentieth century. The numbers declined to 6 million from 1910 to 1920 and to 4 million in the 1920s, after which official restrictions nearly cut the flow of immigrants.

Before 1880, immigrants were mainly from northern and western Europe. By the 1870s, however, that pattern had begun to change. The proportion of Slavs and Jews from southern and eastern Europe rose sharply. After 1890, these groups made up a majority of the newcomers, and by the first decade of the new century they formed 70 percent of the immigrants to this country. Among the new immigrants were Italians, Hungarians, Czechs, Slovaks, Poles, Serbs, Croats, Slovenes, Russians, Romanians, and Greeks—all people whose culture and language were markedly different from those of western Europe and whose religion for the most part was Judaism, Eastern Orthodox, or Roman Catholicism.

ELLIS ISLAND    As the number of immigrants passing through the port of New York soared during the late nineteenth century, the state-run receiving center, called Castle Garden, overflowed with corruption. Money changers cheated new arrivals, railroad agents overcharged them for tickets, and baggage handlers engaged in blackmail. With reports of such abuses filling the newspapers, Congress ordered an investigation, which resulted in the closure of Castle Garden in 1890. Thereafter the federal government's new Bureau of Immigration took over the business of admitting newcomers to New York City.

To launch this effort, Congress funded the construction of a new reception center on a tiny island off the New Jersey coast, a mile south of Manhattan, near the Statue of Liberty. In 1892, **Ellis Island** opened its doors to the "huddled masses" of the world. In 1907, the reception center's busiest year, more than 1 million new arrivals passed through the receiving center, an

**The Registry Room at Ellis Island**

Inspectors asked arriving passengers twenty-nine probing questions, including "Are you a polygamist?"

average of about 5,000 per day; in one day alone, immigration officials processed some 11,750. These were the immigrants who crammed into the steerage compartments deep in the ships' hulls. Those refugees who could afford first- and second-class cabins did not have to visit Ellis Island; they were examined on board, and most of them simply walked down the gangway onto the docks in lower Manhattan.

STRANGERS IN A NEW LAND  Once on American soil, immigrants felt exhilaration, exhaustion, and usually a desperate need for work. Many were greeted by family and friends who had come over before them, others by representatives of immigrant-aid societies or by hiring agents offering jobs in mines, mills, or sweatshops. Since most immigrants knew little if any English and nothing about American employment practices, they were easy subjects for exploitation. In exchange for a bit of whiskey and a job, obliging hiring agents claimed a healthy percentage of their wages. Among Italians and Greeks these agents were known as *padrones*, and they dominated the labor market in New York. Other contractors provided train tickets to inland cities such as Buffalo, Pittsburgh, Cleveland, Chicago, Milwaukee, Cincinnati, and St. Louis.

As strangers in a new land, most of the immigrants naturally gravitated to neighborhoods populated by their own kind. The immigrant enclaves—nicknamed Little Italy, Little Hungary, Chinatown, and so on—served as crucial transitional communities between the newcomers' Old World past and their New World future. By 1920, Chicago had some seventeen separate Little Italy colonies scattered across the city, representing various home provinces. In such kinship communities, immigrants practiced their native religion, clung to their native customs, and conversed in their native tongue. But they paid a price for such community solidarity. When the "new immigrants" moved into an area, older residents typically moved out, taking with them whatever social prestige and political influence they had achieved. The quality of living conditions quickly deteriorated as housing and sanitation codes went unenforced.

**THE NATIVIST RESPONSE**   Then, as now, many native-born Americans saw the wave of new immigrants as a threat to their way of life and their jobs. "Immigrants work for almost nothing," groused one laborer. Other "**nativists**" felt that the newcomers threatened traditional American culture. A Stanford University professor called Africans "illiterate, docile, lacking in self-reliance and initiative, and not possessing the Anglo-Teutonic conceptions of law, order, and government." Cultural differences confirmed in the minds of nativists the assumption that the Nordic peoples of the old immigration were superior to the Slavic, Italian, Greek, and Jewish peoples of the new immigration. Many of the new immigrants were illiterate, and more appeared so because they could not speak English. Some resorted to crime, encouraging suspicions that criminals were being quietly helped out of Europe just as they had once been transported from England to the colonies.

Religious prejudice, mainly anti-Catholic, anti-Buddhist, and anti-Semitic sentiments, also underlay hostility toward the latest newcomers. During the 1880s, nativist groups emerged to stop the flow of immigrants. The most successful of the nativist groups, the American Protective Association (APA), operated mainly in Protestant strongholds of the upper Mississippi Valley. Its organizer harbored paranoid fantasies of Catholic conspiracies and was especially eager to keep public schools free from Jesuit control. The association grew slowly from its start in 1887 until 1893, when leaders took advantage of a severe depression to draw large numbers of the frustrated to its ranks. The APA promoted government restrictions on immigration, more stringent naturalization requirements, workplaces that refused to employ aliens or Catholics, and the teaching of the "American" language in the schools.

IMMIGRATION RESTRICTION    Throughout American history, Congress has passed inconsistent laws regulating immigration, laws that frequently have been rooted in racial and ethnic prejudice. During the late nineteenth century, such prejudice took an ugly turn. The Chinese were victims of every act of discrimination the European immigrants suffered and more. They were not white; they were not Christian; many were not literate. By 1880, there were some seventy-five thousand Chinese in California, about a ninth of the state's population. Many white workers resented the Chinese for accepting lower wages, but their greatest sin, the editor of the *New York Nation* opined with tongue-in-cheek irony, was perpetuating "those disgusting habits of thrift, industry, and self-denial."

In 1882, Congress overturned President Chester A. Arthur's veto of the **Chinese Exclusion Act**. It thus became the first federal law to restrict immigration on the basis of race and class, shutting the door to Chinese immigrants for ten years. The discriminatory legislation received overwhelming support. One congressman explained that because the "industrial army of Asiatic laborers" was increasing the tension between workers and management, "the gate must be closed." The Chinese Exclusion Act was periodically renewed before being extended indefinitely in 1902. Not until 1943 were barriers to Chinese immigration finally removed.

The 1882 Chinese Exclusion Act was the first federal law to restrict immigration explicitly on the basis of racial and class criteria. It was not the last. In 1891, the prominent politician Henry Cabot Lodge of Massachusetts took up the cause of excluding illiterate foreigners, a measure that would have affected much of the new wave of immigrants even though literacy in English was not required. Lodge and other prominent New Englanders organized the Immigrations Restriction League, an organization dedicated to saving the Anglo-Saxon "race" in America from being "contaminated" by alien immigrants. Three presidents vetoed bills embodying the restriction of illiterate immigrants on the grounds that they penalized people for lack of opportunity: Grover Cleveland in 1897, William H. Taft in 1913, and Woodrow Wilson in 1915 and 1917. The last time, however, Congress overrode the veto.

Although these legislative efforts sharply reduced the flow of Chinese immigrants, they did not stop the influx completely. In 1910, the West Coast counterpart of Ellis Island opened on rugged Angel Island, six miles off-shore from San Francisco, to process tens of thousands of Asian immigrants, most of them Chinese. Those arrivals from China who could claim a Chinese American parent were allowed to enter, as were certain officials, teachers, merchants, and students. The powerful prejudice that the Chinese immigrants encountered helps explain why over 30 percent of the arrivals at Angel Island were denied entry.

**Anti-Chinese protest, California, 1880**

Widespread racism and prejudice against the Chinese resulted in the Chinese Exclusion Act (1882), which banned Chinese immigration.

## POPULAR CULTURE

The flood of people into large towns and cities created new patterns of recreation and leisure. Traditionally, people in rural areas were tied to the rituals of the harvest season and intimately connected to their neighbors and extended families. By contrast, most middle-class urban whites had enough money to be more mobile; they were primarily connected to the other members of their nuclear family (made up only of parents and children), and their affluence enabled them to enjoy greater leisure time and an increasing discretionary income. Middle- and upper-class urban families spent much of their leisure time together at home, usually in the parlor, singing around a piano, reading novels, or playing cards, dominoes, backgammon, chess, and checkers.

In the congested metropolitan areas, politics became as much a form of public entertainment as it was a means of providing civic representation and public services. People flocked to hear visiting candidates speak. Impassioned oratory, whether delivered by elected officials or ministers, was the primary medium of civic culture. In cities such as New York, Philadelphia, Boston, and Chicago, membership in a political party was akin to belonging to a social club. In addition, labor unions provided activities that were more social than economic in nature, and members often visited the union hall as much to socialize as to discuss working conditions. The sheer number of city dwellers also helped generate new forms of mass entertainment, such as traveling Wild West shows, vaudeville shows, and spectator sports.

A READING PUBLIC  In the half century after the Civil War, newspapers were the primary means of communication. They were not only the source of local and national news, but also were the primary medium for political life. Many of them also published poetry and fiction. Between 1870 and 1900, the number of daily newspapers—in English as well as numerous foreign languages—grew twice as fast as the population, and the number of subscribers grew even faster. Most of the newspapers were openly partisan, identifying with one of the major national political parties.

VAUDEVILLE  Growing family incomes and innovations in urban transportation—cable cars, subways, as well as electric streetcars and streetlights—enabled more people to take advantage of urban cultural life. Attendance at theaters, operas, and dance halls soared after the Civil War. But by far the

**Vaudeville**

For as little as one cent, vaudeville offered customers entertainment.

most popular—and most diverse—form of theatrical entertainment in the late nineteenth century was vaudeville. The term derives from a French word for a play accompanied by music.

Vaudeville "variety" shows featured comedians, singers, musicians, blackface minstrels, farcical plays, animal acts, jugglers, gymnasts, dancers, mimes, and magicians. Vaudeville houses attracted all social classes and types—men, women, and children. The shows included something to please every taste and, as such, reflected the diversity of city life. To commemorate the opening of a palatial new Boston theater in 1894, an actress read a dedicatory poem in which she announced that "all are equals here"; the vaudeville house was the people's theater: it knew "no favorites, no class." She promised the spectators that the producers would "ever seek the new" in providing entertainers who epitomized "the spice of life, Variety," with its motto "ever to please—and never to offend."

SALOON CULTURE   The most popular destinations for the urban working class were saloons and dance halls. The saloon was the poor man's social club during the late nineteenth century. By 1900, there were more saloons in the United States (over 325,000) than there were grocery stores and meat markets. Immigrants owned most saloons, many of which were financed by the huge, often German American–owned breweries such as Adolphus Busch's Budweiser. New York City alone had ten thousand saloons, or one for every five hundred residents. Often sponsored by beer brewers and frequented by local politicians, saloons offered a free lunch to encourage patrons to visit and buy 5¢ beer or 15¢ whiskey.

Saloons provided much more than food and drink, however; they were in effect public homes, offering haven and fellowship to people who often worked ten hours a day, six days a week. Saloons were especially popular among male immigrants seeking companionship in a new land. Saloons served as busy social hubs and were often aligned with local political machines. In New York City in the 1880s, most of the primary elections and local political caucuses were conducted in saloons.

Men went to saloons to learn about jobs, engage in labor union activities, cash paychecks, mail letters, read newspapers, and gossip about neighborhood affairs. Because saloons were heated and offered public restrooms, they also served as places of refuge for poor people whose own slum tenements or cramped lodging houses were not as accommodating. Many saloons included gymnasiums. Patrons could play handball, chess, billiards, darts, cards, or dice.

Saloons were defiantly male enclaves. Although women and children occasionally entered a saloon—through a side door—in order to carry home a pail of beer (called "rushing the growler") or to drink at a backroom party, the main bar at the front was for men only. Some saloons provided "snugs," small separate rooms for female patrons.

Saloons aroused intense criticism. Anti-liquor societies such as the Women's Christian Temperance Union and the Anti-Saloon League charged that saloons contributed to alcoholism, divorce, crime, and absenteeism from work. Reformers such as the colorful Carry Nation demanded that saloons be closed down. Yet drunkenness in saloons was the exception rather than the rule. Most patrons of working-class saloons had little money to waste, and recent studies have revealed that the average amount of money spent on liquor was no more than 5 percent of a man's annual income. Saloons were the primary locus of the workingman's leisure time and political activity. As a journalist observed, "The saloon is, in short, the social and intellectual center of the neighborhood."

OUTDOOR RECREATION The congestion and disease associated with city life led many people to participate in forms of outdoor recreation to restore their vitality and improve their health. A movement to create urban parks flourished after the construction of New York's Central Park in 1858. Its planner, **Frederick Law Olmsted**, went on to design parks for Boston, Brooklyn, Chicago, Philadelphia, San Francisco, and many other cities. Although originally intended as places where people could walk and commune with nature, parks soon offered more vigorous forms of exercise and recreation—for men and women.

Croquet and tennis courts were among the first additions to city parks because they took up little space and required little maintenance. Lawn tennis was invented by an Englishman in 1873 and arrived in the United States a year later. By 1885, New York's Central Park had thirty courts. Even more popular than croquet or tennis was cycling, or "wheeling." In the 1870s, bicycles began to be manufactured in the United States, and by the end of the century a bicycle craze had swept the country. Bicycles were especially popular with women who chafed at the restricting conventions of the Victorian era. The new vehicles offered exercise, freedom, and access to the countryside.

The urban working poor could not afford to acquire a bicycle or join a croquet club, however. Nor did they have as much free time as the affluent. At the end of their long days and on Sundays, they sought recreation and fellowship on street corners or on the front stoops of their apartment buildings. Organ grinders and other musicians would perform on the sidewalks among the food vendors. Many ethnic groups, especially the Germans and the Irish, formed male singing, drinking, or gymnastic clubs. Working folk also attended bare-knuckle boxing matches or baseball games and on Sundays would gather for picnics. By the end of the century, large-scale amusement

**Tandem tricycle**

In spite of the danger and discomfort of early bicycles, "wheeling" became a popular form of recreation and mode of transportation.

parks such as the one at Brooklyn's Coney Island provided entertainment for the entire family. Yet many inner-city youth could not afford the trolley fare, so the crowded streets and dangerous alleys remained their playgrounds.

WORKING WOMEN AND LEISURE   In contrast to the male public culture centered in saloons, the leisure activities of working-class women, many of them immigrants, were more limited at the end of the nineteenth century. Married women were so encumbered by housework and maternal responsibilities that they had little free time. As a social worker noted, "The men have the saloons, political clubs, trade-unions or [fraternal] lodges for their recreation . . . while the mothers have almost no recreation, only a dreary round of work, day after day, with occasionally doorstep gossip to vary the monotony of their lives." Married working-class women often used the streets as their public space. Washing clothes, supervising children, or shopping at the local market provided opportunities for fellowship with other women.

Single women had more time for leisure and recreation than did working mothers. They flocked to dance halls, theaters, amusement parks, and picnic grounds. On hot summer days, many working-class folk went to public beaches. With the advent of movie theaters during the second decade of the twentieth century, the cinema became the most popular form of entertainment for women.

Young single women participated in urban amusements for a variety of reasons: escape, pleasure, adventure, companionship, and autonomy. As a promotional flyer for a movie theater promised, "If you are tired of life, go to the movies. If you are sick of troubles rife, go to the picture show. You will forget your unpaid bills, rheumatism and other ills, if you stow your pills and go to the picture show." Urban recreational and entertainment activities also allowed opportunities for romance and sexual relationships. Not surprisingly, young women eager for such recreation encountered far more obstacles than did young men. Just as reformers sought to shut down saloons, parents and authorities tried to restrict the freedom of young women to engage in "cheap amusements." Yet many young women followed their own wishes and in so doing helped carve out their own social sphere.

SPECTATOR SPORTS  In the last quarter of the nineteenth century, new spectator sports such as college football and basketball and professional

**Steeplechase Park, Coney Island, Brooklyn, New York**

Members of the working class could afford the inexpensive rides at this popular amusement park.

baseball gained mass appeal, reflecting the growing urbanization of life. People could gather easily for sporting events in the large cities. Spectator sports became urban extravaganzas, unifying the diverse ethnic groups in the large cities and attracting people with the leisure time and cash to spend on watching others perform—or bet on the outcome.

Football emerged as a modified form of soccer and rugby. The College of New Jersey (Princeton) and Rutgers played the first college football game in 1869. Basketball was invented in 1891, when Dr. James Naismith, a physical education instructor, nailed two peach baskets to the walls of the Young Men's Christian Association (YMCA) training school in Springfield, Massachusetts. Naismith wanted to create an indoor winter game that could be played between the fall football and spring baseball seasons. Basketball quickly grew in popularity among boys and girls. Vassar and Smith Colleges added the sport in 1892. In 1893, Vanderbilt University, in Nashville, became the first college to field a men's team.

Baseball laid claim to being America's national pastime at mid-century. Contrary to popular opinion, Abner Doubleday did not invent the game. Instead, Alexander Cartwright, a New York bank clerk and sportsman, is recognized as the father of organized baseball. In 1845, he gathered a group of merchants, stockbrokers, and physicians to form the Knickerbocker Base Ball Club of New York.

The first professional baseball team was the Cincinnati Red Stockings, which made its appearance in 1869. In 1900 the American League was organized, and two years later the first World Series was held. Baseball became the national pastime and the most democratic sport in America. People from all social classes (mostly men) attended the games, and recent immigrants were

**Baseball card, 1887**

The excitement of rooting for the home team united all classes.

among the most faithful fans. The *St. Louis Post-Dispatch* reported in 1883 that "a glance at the audience on any fine day at the ball park will reveal . . . telegraph operators, printers who work at night, travelling [sales]men . . . men of leisure . . . men of capital, bank clerks who get away at 3 P.M., real estate men . . . barkeepers . . . hotel clerks, actors and employees of the theater, policemen and firemen on their day off . . . butchers and bakers." Cheering for a city baseball team gave rootless people a common loyalty and a sense of belonging.

Only white players were allowed in the major leagues. African Americans played on "minor league" teams or in all-black Negro leagues. In 1887, the Cuban Giants, an exhibition team made up of black players, traveled the country. A few major league white teams agreed to play them. An African American–owned newspaper announced in early 1888 that the Cuban Giants "have defeated the New Yorks, 4 games out of 5, and are now virtually champions of the world." But, it added, "the St. Louis Browns, Detroits and Chicagos, afflicted by Negrophobia and unable to bear the odium of being beaten by colored men, refused to accept their challenge."

By the end of the nineteenth century, sports of all kinds had become a major cultural phenomenon in the United States. A writer for *Harper's Weekly* announced in 1895 that "ball matches, football games, tennis tournaments, bicycle races, [and] regattas, have become part of our national life." They "are watched with eagerness and discussed with enthusiasm and understanding by all manner of people, from the day-laborer to the millionaire." One reporter in the 1890s referred to the "athletic craze" that was sweeping the American imagination. Moreover, it was in 1892 that a Frenchman, Pierre de Coubertin, called for the revival of the ancient Olympic Games, and the first modern Olympiad was held four years later.

## EDUCATION AND SOCIAL THOUGHT

THE SPREAD OF PUBLIC EDUCATION   Efforts to expand access to public education, spurred partly by the determination to "Americanize" immigrant children, helped quicken the emergence of a new urban culture. In 1870, there were 7 million pupils in public schools; by 1920, the number had risen to 22 million. The percentage of school-age children in attendance went from 57 to 78 during those years.

The spread of secondary schools accounted for much of the increased enrollment in public schools. In antebellum America, private academies had prepared those who intended to enter college. At the beginning of the Civil

War, there were only about a hundred public high schools in the whole nation, but their number grew to about eight hundred in 1880 and to six thousand at the turn of the century. Their curricula at first copied the academies' emphasis on higher mathematics and classical languages, but the public schools gradually adapted their programs to those students not going on to college, devising vocational training in such arts as bookkeeping, typing, drafting, and the use of tools.

VOCATIONAL TRAINING    Vocational training was most intensely promoted after the Civil War by missionary schools for African Americans in the South, such as the Hampton Institute in Virginia. Congress had supported vocational training at the college level for many years. The Morrill Act of 1862 granted each state thirty thousand acres per representative and senator, the income from which was to be applied to teaching agriculture and the mechanic arts in what came to be known as the land-grant colleges. Among the new land-grant institutions were Clemson University, Pennsylvania State University, and Iowa State University. In 1890 a second Morrill Act provided federal grants to these colleges.

**Vocational education**

Students in a current-events class at Virginia's Hampton Institute, 1899.

HIGHER EDUCATION   The demand for higher learning after the Civil War led to a dramatic increase in the college-student population, from 52,000 in 1870 to 157,000 in 1890 and 600,000 in 1920. To accommodate the diverse needs of these growing numbers, colleges moved from rigidly prescribed courses toward an elective system. The new approach allowed students to favor their strong points in selecting their classes. But as Henry Cabot Lodge complained, it also allowed students to "escape without learning anything at all by a judicious selection of unrelated subjects taken up only because they were easy or because the burden imposed by those who taught them was light."

Colleges remained largely male bastions, but women's access to higher education improved markedly in the late nineteenth century. Before the Civil War, a few men's colleges had admitted women, though most state universities in the West were open to women from the start. Colleges in the South and the East fell in line very slowly. Vassar, opened in New York in 1865, was the first women's college to teach by the same standards as the best of the men's colleges. In the 1870s, two additional excellent women's schools appeared in Massachusetts: Wellesley and Smith, the latter being the first to set the same admission requirements as men's colleges. By the end of the century, women made up more than a third of all college students.

INTELLECTUAL LIFE   Much as popular culture was transformed as a result of the urban-industrial revolution, intellectual life also adapted to new social realities. The new urban culture relished new knowledge and immediate experience. A growing number of writers, artists, and intellectuals were not interested in romantic themes and idealized life. They focused their efforts on the emerging realities of scientific research and technology, factories and railroads, cities and immigrants, wage labor and social tensions.

The prestige and premises of modern science increased enormously during the second half of the nineteenth century. Researchers explored electromagnetic induction, the conservation of matter, the laws of thermodynamics, and the relationship between heat and energy. Breakthroughs in chemistry led to new understandings about the formation of compounds and the nature of chemical reactions. Discoveries of fossils opened up new horizons in geology and paleontology, and greatly improved microscopes enabled zoologists to decipher cell structures.

Virtually every field of thought in the post–Civil War years felt the impact of Charles Darwin's controversial book *On the Origin of Species* (1859). Darwin used extensive observations and cast-iron logic to argue that most organisms produce many more offspring than can survive. Those offspring with advantageous characteristics tend to live while others die—from disease or

**Women as students**

An astronomy class at Vassar College, 1880.

predators. This random process of "natural selection" over millions of years led to the evolution of species from less complex forms of life: those species that survived by reason of quickness, shrewdness, or other advantages reproduced their kind, while others fell by the wayside. As Darwin wrote, "the vigorous, the healthy, and the happy survive and multiply."

The idea of species evolution shocked people who embraced a literal interpretation of the biblical creation stories. Darwin's findings suggested that there was no providential God controlling the cosmos. Life was the result of the blind natural process of selection. And people were no different from plants and animals; like everything else, they too evolved by trial and error rather than by God's purposeful hand. The fossil record revealed a natural history of conflict, pain, and species extinction. What kind of benevolent God would be so cruel as to create a world of such waste, strife, and sorrow? Darwin showed that there could be no proof for the existence of God.

Darwin's findings—as well as the implications that people drew from them—generated heated arguments between scientists and clergymen. Some Christians rejected Darwin's secular doctrine, while others found their faith severely shaken not only by evolutionary theory but also by the urging of professional scientists to apply the critical standards of scholarship to the Bible itself. Most of the faithful, however, came to reconcile science and religion.

They viewed evolution as the divine will, one of the secondary causes through which God worked.

**SOCIAL DARWINISM** Although Charles Darwin's theory of evolution applied only to biological phenomena, others drew broader inferences from it. The temptation to apply evolutionary theory to the social (human) world proved irresistible. Darwin's fellow Englishman **Herbert Spencer**, a social philosopher, became the first major prophet of what came to be called **social Darwinism**, a cluster of ideas that exercised an important influence on American thought.

**Charles Darwin**

Darwin's theories influenced more than a century of political debate.

Spencer argued that human society and institutions, like the organisms studied by Darwin, evolved through the same process of natural selection. The result, in Spencer's chilling phrase, was the "survival of the fittest." For Spencer, such social evolution was the engine of progress, ending "only in the establishment of the greatest perfection and the most complete happiness." Darwin dismissed Spencer's theories as poppycock. Spencer's arguments, he said, "could never convince me." Darwin especially objected to Spencer's assumption that the evolutionary process in the natural world had any relevance to the human realm.

Others, however, eagerly endorsed Spencer's notion of social Darwinism. If, as Spencer believed, society naturally evolved for the better, then government interference with the process of social evolution was a serious mistake because it would keep unsound people from being weeded out. Social Darwinism implied a hands-off government policy; it decried the regulation of business, the graduated income tax, and sanitation and housing regulations. Such intervention, Spencer charged, would help the "unfit" survive and thereby impede progress. (Ironically, Spencer himself was notoriously frail and would not have been among the surviving "fittest.") The only acceptable charity to Spencer was voluntary, and even that was of dubious value. Spencer warned that "fostering the good-for-nothing [people] at the expense of the good, is an extreme cruelty."

For Spencer and his many American supporters, successful businessmen and corporations provided living proof of the concept of the "survival of the fittest." If small businesses were crowded out by huge corporate trusts and monopolies, that too was part of the evolutionary process. The oil tycoon John D. Rockefeller told his Baptist Sunday-school class that the "growth of a large business is merely a survival of the fittest.... This is not an evil tendency in business. It is merely the working-out of a law of nature and a law of God."

The ideas of Charles Darwin and Herbert Spencer spread quickly. *Popular Science Monthly*, founded in 1872, became the chief medium for popularizing Darwinism. That year, Spencer's chief academic disciple, William Graham Sumner, began teaching at Yale University, where he preached the gospel of natural selection. Sumner's most lasting contribution, made in his book *Folkways* (1907), was to argue that it would be a mistake for government to interfere with established customs in the name of ideals of equality or natural rights.

PRAGMATISM   Early in the twentieth century, Darwin's concept of evolutionary development found expression in **pragmatism**, a philosophical principle set forth by the Harvard psychologist and philosopher **William James** in his book *Pragmatism: A New Name for Some Old Ways of Thinking* (1907). Pragmatists, said James, believed that ideas gain their validity not from their inherent truth but from their social consequences and practical applications, just as scientists test the validity of their ideas in the laboratory and judge their import by their applications. Pragmatism reflected a commonsensical quality often looked upon as genuinely American: the inventive, experimental spirit that judged ideas on their results (what James called their "cash value") and their ability to adapt to changing social needs and environments. James essentially said that philosophical ideas that were only discussed in classrooms were lifeless. Many philosophers, he declared, philosophize for the sake of philosophizing; he wanted to philosophize in order to help people live better.

**William James**

The conceptual founder of pragmatism.

John Dewey, who would become the chief philosopher of pragmatism after James, preferred the term *instrumentalism*, by which he meant that ideas should be instruments for action, especially social reform. Dewey, unlike James, threw himself into progressive social movements promoting the rights of labor and women, the promotion of peace, and the reform of education. He believed that education was not just book learning; it was the process through which society would gradually progress toward the goal of economic and social democracy. Pragmatic ideas, Dewey, with William James, insisted, were instruments for social action, not simply abstractions to generate philosophical discussion.

**Lester Frank Ward**

Proponent of reform Darwinism.

REFORM DARWINISM Pragmatism was but one example of many efforts to interpret Darwinist evolutionary theory as justifying efforts at social reform. So-called **reform Darwinism** found its major advocate in an obscure Washington, D.C. civil servant, Lester Frank Ward, who fought his way up from poverty and never lost his empathy for the underdog. Ward's book *Dynamic Sociology* (1883) singled out one product of evolution that Chales Darwin and Herbert Spencer had neglected: the human brain. Yes, people, like animals, compete, as William Graham Sumner stressed, but they also collaborate; they have minds that can shape social evolution. Humans also show compassion for others. Far from being the helpless subject of evolution, Ward argued, humanity could control and shape the process of evolutionary social development. Ward's progressive reform Darwinism challenged Sumner's conservative social Darwinism by arguing that cooperation, not competition, would better promote social progress. According to Ward, Sumner's "irrational distrust of government" might have been justified in an earlier day of monarchy and tyranny but was not applicable under a representative system of government. Democratic government could become the agency of progress by pursuing two main goals: reducing poverty, which impeded the development of the mind, and promoting the education of all classes. "Intelligence, far more than necessity," Ward wrote, "is the mother of invention," and "the influence of knowledge as a social factor, like that of wealth, is proportional to the extent of its distribution." Intellect, rightly informed by science, could foster societal improvement. This intellectual justification for social reform would become one of the pillars of the "progressive" movement that would transform urban America during the late nineteenth century and after.

## CHAPTER SUMMARY

- **Rise of Cities** America's cities grew in all directions after the Civil War. Electric elevators and new steel-frame construction allowed architects to extend buildings upward. Mass transit enabled the middle class to retreat to suburbs. Crowded tenements bred disease and crime and created an opportunity for urban political bosses to accrue power, in part by distributing to the poor the only relief that existed.

- **New Immigration** By 1900, 30 percent of Americans were foreign-born, with many immigrants coming from eastern and southern Europe rather than western and northern Europe, like most immigrants of generations past. Thus their languages and culture were vastly different from those of native-born Americans. They tended to be Catholic, Eastern Orthodox, or Jewish rather than Protestant. Beginning in the 1880s, nativists advocated immigration laws to exclude the Chinese and the poor and demanded that immigrants pass a literacy test. A federal immigration station on Ellis Island, in New York Harbor, opened in 1892 to process immigrants arriving by ship from across the Atlantic.

- **Mass Entertainment** Cities began to create urban parks, like New York's Central Park, as places for all citizens to stroll, ride bicycles, or play games such as tennis. Vaudeville shows emerged as a popular form of entertainment. Saloons served as local social and political clubs for men. It was in this era that football, baseball, and basketball emerged as spectator sports.

- **Social Darwinism** Charles Darwin's *On the Origin of Species* shocked people who believed in a literal interpretation of the Bible's account of creation. Herbert Spencer and William Graham Sumner, who equated economic and social success with the "survival of the fittest" and advanced the idea that government should not interfere to promote equality, applied Darwin's scientific theory to human society and social institutions.

## CHRONOLOGY

| | |
|---|---|
| **1858** | Construction of New York's Central Park begins |
| **1859** | Darwin's *On the Origin of Species* is published |
| **1882** | Congress passes the Chinese Exclusion Act |
| **1889** | Otis Elevator Company installs the first electric elevator |
| **1891** | Basketball is invented |
| **1892** | Ellis Island, a federal center for processing immigrants, opens |
| **1900** | Baseball's National League is formed |

## KEY TERMS & NAMES

# 21

# GILDED AGE POLITICS AND AGRARIAN REVOLT

FOCUS QUESTIONS     Ⓢ   wwnorton.com/studyspace

- What were the major features of American politics during the Gilded Age?
- What were the major issues in politics during this period?
- What were the main problems facing farmers in the South and the Midwest after the Civil War?
- How and why did farmers become politicized?
- What was significant about the election of 1896?
- How did African American leaders respond to the spread of segregation in the South?

In 1873, the writers Mark Twain and Charles Dudley Warner created an enduring label for the post–Civil War era when they collaborated on a novel titled *The Gilded Age*, a colorful depiction of the widespread political corruption and corporate greed that characterized the period. Generations of political scientists and historians have since reinforced the two novelists' judgment. As a young college graduate in 1879, future president Woodrow Wilson described the state of the political system after the Civil War: "No leaders, no principles; no principles, no parties." Indeed, the real movers and shakers of the Gilded Age were not the men who sat in the White House or Congress but the captains of industry who crisscrossed the continent with railroads and adorned its cities with plumed smokestacks and gaudy mansions.

## PARADOXICAL POLITICS

Political life in the **Gilded Age**, the thirty-five years between the end of the Civil War and the end of the nineteenth century, had several distinctive elements. Perhaps the most important feature of Gilded Age politics was its localism. Unlike today, the federal government in the nineteenth century was an insignificant force in the lives of Americans, in part because it was so small. In 1871, the entire federal workforce totaled 51,000 civilians (most of them postal workers), and only 6,000 of them actually worked in Washington, D.C. Not until the twentieth century did the federal government begin to overshadow the importance of local and state governments. By 1914, for example, there would be 401,000 federal civilian employees.

Most Americans were far more engaged in local politics. In cities crowded with waves of new immigrants, the political scene was usually controlled by "rings"—small groups of powerful political insiders who managed the nomination and election of candidates, conducted primaries, and influenced policy. Each ring typically had a powerful "boss" who ran things, using his **political "machine"**—a network of neighborhood activists and officials—to govern the town or city. Throughout most of the nineteenth century, almost every governmental job—local, state, and federal—was subject to the latest election results. So for hundreds of thousands of citizens, an election was not simply a contest between candidates, but also a referendum on a single, urgent question: "Will I keep my government job?" This meant that whichever political party was in power expected government employees to become campaign workers doing the bidding of the party bosses during important elections.

CITY POLITICS    After the Civil War, the sheer size of the rapidly growing cities helped create a new form of politics. Because local government was often fragmented and beset by parochial rivalries, a need grew for a central organization to coordinate citywide services such as public transportation, street lighting, sewers, police and fire protection, paved roads, bridges, harbor facilities, garbage collection, schools, housing, parks, and hospitals. Urban political machines consisting of local committeemen and district captains led by a political boss thus became even more powerful. While the city bosses engaged in graft, buying and selling votes, taking kickbacks and payoffs, they also provided needed services. Political bosses organized loyal neighborhood voters into wards or precincts, and staged torchlight election parades, fireworks displays, and free banquets and alcoholic beverages for voters. They also mediated neighborhood disputes, helped the needy, and distributed "patronage"

THE "BRAINS"

**William "Boss" Tweed**

Tweed is represented here as having a moneybag face and a $15,500 diamond stickpin.

(municipal jobs and contracts) to loyal followers and corporate contributors. They gave food, coal, and money to the poor; found jobs for those who were out of work; sponsored English-language classes for immigrants; organized sports teams, social clubs, and neighborhood gatherings; and generally helped newcomers adjust to their new life. In return, the political professionals felt entitled to some reward for having done the grubby work of the local organization.

Colorful, larger-than-life figures such as New York City's William "Boss" Tweed shamelessly ruled, plundered, and occasionally improved municipal government, often through dishonest means and frequent bribes. Until his arrest in 1871 and his conviction in 1873, Tweed used the Tammany Hall ring to dominate the nation's largest city. The Tammany Hall machine doled out contracts to business allies and jobs to political supporters. In the late, 1870s one of every twelve New York men worked for the city government. The various city rings and bosses were often corrupt, but they did bring structure, stability, and services to rapidly growing inner-city communities, many of them composed of immigrants newly arrived from Ireland, Germany, and, increasingly, from southern and eastern Europe.

NATIONAL POLITICS  Several factors gave national politics during the Gilded Age its distinctive texture. First, like the urban political machines, the national political parties during the Gilded Age were much more dominant forces than they are today. Party loyalty was intense, often extending over several generations in Irish and Italian families in cities such as Boston, Providence, Rhode Island, New York City, Newark, New Jersey, and Philadelphia.

A second distinctive element of Gilded Age politics was the close division between Republicans and Democrats in Congress, which created the sense of a stalemated political system. Both parties avoided controversial issues or bold initiatives because neither gained dominant power. Voters of the time nonetheless thought politics was very important, making widespread political participation the third distinctive element of post–Civil War politics. Voter turnout during the Gilded Age was commonly about 70 to 80 percent, even in the South, where the disenfranchisement of African Americans was not yet complete. (By contrast, the turnout for the 2008 presidential election was almost 57 percent.)

The paradox of such a high rate of voter participation in the face of the inertia at the national political level raises an obvious question: How was it that elected officials who failed to address the "real issues" of the day presided over the most highly organized and politically active electorate in U.S. history? The answer is partly that the politicians and the voters believed that they *were* dealing with crucial issues: tariff rates, the regulation of corporations, monetary policy, Indian disputes, civil service reform, and immigration. But the answer also reflects the extreme partisanship of the times and the essentially local nature of political culture during the Gilded Age. Politics was then the most popular form of local entertainment.

PARTISAN POLITICS Most Americans after the Civil War were intensely loyal to one of the two major parties, Democratic or Republican. Most voters cast their ballots for the same party, year after year, generation after generation. Loyalty to a party was often an emotional choice, as parties openly appealed to particular regional, ethnic, and religious ties. During the 1870s and 1880s, for example, people continued to fight the Civil War using highly charged political rhetoric as their weapon. Republicans regularly "waved the bloody shirt" in election campaigns, meaning that they reminded voters that the Democratic Party was the party of "secession and civil war," while their party, the party of Lincoln and Grant, had abolished slavery and saved the Union. Democrats, especially in the South, responded by reminding voters that they were the party of white supremacy and states' rights. Blacks in the South, by contrast, voted Republican (before they were disenfranchised) because it was the "party of Lincoln," the "Great Emancipator." Third parties, such as the Greenbackers, Populists, and Prohibitionists, appealed to particular interests and issues, such as currency inflation or temperance legislation.

Political parties also gave people an organizational anchor in an unstable world. Local party officials took care of those who voted their way and distributed appointive public offices and other favors to party loyalists. The city political machines used patronage and favoritism to keep the loyalty of business supporters while providing jobs or food or fuel to working-class voters who had fallen on hard times. Politics was also a form of popular entertainment. The party faithful eagerly took part in rallies and picnics and avidly read newspaper coverage of political issues. Members of political parties developed an intense camaraderie.

Party loyalties and voter turnout in the late nineteenth century reflected religious and ethnic divisions as well as geographic differences. The Republican party attracted mainly Protestants of British descent. The party was dominant in New England, New York, and the upper Midwest. The Republicans, the party of Abraham Lincoln, could also rely upon the votes of Union veterans of the Civil War.

The Democrats, by contrast, tended to be a heterogeneous, often unruly coalition embracing southern whites, northern immigrants, Roman Catholics living in the northern states, Jews, freethinkers, and all those repelled by the "party of morality." As one Chicago Democrat explained, "A Republican is a man who wants you t' go t' church every Sunday. A Democrat says if a man wants to have a glass of beer on Sunday he can have it."

Republicans also promoted what were called nativist policies, which imposed restrictions on immigration and the employment of foreigners. Efforts to prohibit the sale of alcoholic beverages revived along with nativism in the 1880s. Among the immigrants who crowded into the growing cities were many Irish, Germans, and Italians, all of whom tended to enjoy wine and beer on a daily basis. The mostly rural Republican Protestant moralists increasingly saw saloons as the central social evil around which all others revolved, including vice, crime, political corruption, and neglect of families, and they associated these problems with the ethnic groups that frequented saloons. The feisty Carry Nation, a militant member of the Women's Christian Temperance Union (WCTU) who was known for attacking saloons with a hatchet, charged that saloons stripped women of everything by seducing working men: "Her husband is torn from her, she is robbed of her sons, her home, her food, and her virtue."

POLITICAL STALEMATE    Between 1869 and 1913, from the presidency of Ulysses S. Grant through that of William Howard Taft, Republicans monopolized the White House except for the two nonconsecutive terms of the conservative New York Democrat Grover Cleveland, but otherwise national politics was remarkably balanced between the two major parties. Between 1872 and 1896, no president won a majority of the popular vote. In each of those presidential elections, sixteen states invariably voted Republican and fourteen voted Democratic, leaving a pivotal six states whose results determined the outcome. The important swing-vote role played by two of those states, New York and Ohio, helps explain the election of eight presidents from those states from 1872 to 1908.

No chief executive between Abraham Lincoln and Theodore Roosevelt could be described as a "strong" president. None challenged the prevailing view that Congress, not the White House, should formulate policy. Senator John Sherman of Ohio expressed the widely held notion that the legislative branch should predominate in a republic: "The President should merely obey and enforce the law."

Republicans controlled the Senate and Democrats controlled the House during the Gilded Age. Only during 1881 to 1883 and 1889 to 1891 did a Republican president coincide with a Republican Congress, and only between 1893 and 1895 did a Democratic president enjoy a Democratic majority in Congress. On the important questions of the currency, regulation of big business, farm problems, civil service reform, and immigration, the parties differed very little. As a result, they primarily became vehicles for seeking office and dispensing "patronage" in the form of government jobs and contracts.

STATE AND LOCAL INITIATIVES    Americans during the Gilded Age expected little direct support from the federal government; most significant political activity occurred at the state and local levels. Only 40 percent of government spending and taxing occurred at the federal level. Then, unlike today, the large cities spent far more on local services than did the federal government, and three fourths of all public employees worked for state and local governments. Local issues generated far more excitement than complex national debates over tariffs and monetary policies. It was the state and local governments that first sought to curb the power and restrain the abuses of corporate interests.

## CORRUPTION AND REFORM: HAYES TO HARRISON

After the Civil War, a close alliance developed between business and political leaders at every level. As a leading congressman, for example, James Gillespie Blaine of Maine saw nothing wrong in his accepting gifts of stock from an Arkansas railroad after helping it win a land grant from Congress. Free railroad tickets, free entertainment, and a host of other favors were regularly provided to politicians, newspaper editors, and other leaders in positions to influence public opinion or affect legislation.

Both Republican and Democratic leaders also squabbled over the "spoils" of office, the appointive political positions at the local and the national levels. After each election, it was expected that the victorious party would replace the defeated party's government appointees with its own. The patronage system of awarding government jobs to supporters invited corruption. It also was so time-consuming that it distracted elected officials from more

**"The Bosses of the Senate"**

This 1889 cartoon bitingly portrays the period's corrupt alliance between big business and politics.

important issues. Yet George Washington Plunkitt, a Democratic boss in New York City, spoke for many Gilded Age politicians when he explained that "you can't keep an organization together without patronage. Men ain't in politics for nothin'. They want to get somethin' out of it." Each party had its share of corrupt officials willing to buy and sell government appointments or congressional votes, yet each also witnessed the emergence of factions promoting honesty in government. The struggle for "cleaner" government soon became one of the foremost issues of the day.

HAYES AND CIVIL SERVICE REFORM    President Rutherford B. Hayes brought to the White House in 1877 a new style of uprightness, in sharp contrast to the graft and corruption practiced by members of the Grant administration. The son of an Ohio farmer, Hayes was wounded four times in the Civil War and was promoted to the rank of major general. Elected governor of Ohio in 1867, he served three terms.

Hayes's own party, the Republicans, was split between so-called **Stalwarts** and Half-Breeds, led respectively by Senators Roscoe Conkling of New York and James Gillespie Blaine of Maine. The Stalwarts had been "stalwart" in their support of President Grant during the furor over the misbehavior of his cabinet members. They also had promoted Radical Reconstruction of the defeated South and benefited from the "spoils system" of distributing federal political jobs to party loyalists. The Half-Breeds acquired their name because they were only half-loyal to Grant and half-committed to reform of the spoils system. For the most part, the two Republican factions were loose alliances designed to advance the careers of Conkling and Blaine.

To his credit, Hayes aligned himself with the growing public discontent over political corruption. American leaders were just learning about the "merit system" for hiring government employees, which was long estab-lished in the bureaucracies of France and Germany, and the new British practice in which civil service jobs were filled by competitive written tests rather than awarded as political favors.

Hayes irritated Republican leaders by making political appointments based on merit: he pledged that those already in office would be dismissed only for the good of the government and not for political reasons; party members would have no more influence in appointments than other qual-ified citizens; government employees would not be forced to make political contributions; and no officeholder could manage election campaigns for political organizations, although all could vote and express their opinions.

On the economic issues of the day, Hayes held to a conservative line that would guide his successors for the rest of the century. His solution to labor troubles, demonstrated in his response to the Great Railroad Strike of 1877, was to send in federal troops to break the strike. His answer to demands for an expansion of the currency was to veto the 1878 Bland-Allison Act, which provided for a limited increase in the supply of silver coins. The act passed anyway when Congress overrode Hayes's veto. A bruised president confided in his diary that he had lost the support of his own party. In 1879, with a year still left in his term, Hayes was ready to leave the White House. "I am now in my last year of the Presidency," he wrote a friend, "and look forward to its close as a schoolboy longs for the coming vacation."

THE 1880 ELECTION   With President Hayes out of the running for a second term, the Republicans nominated the dark-horse Ohio candidate, James A. Garfield. A native of Ohio and an early foe of slavery, Garfield, like Hayes and Grant, had distinguished himself during the Civil War and retired from the army as a major general before being elected to Congress in 1863, where he had become one of the outstanding leaders in the House. Now he was the Republican nominee for president. The convention named

Chester A. Arthur, the deposed head of the New York Customhouse, as the candidate for vice president.

The Democrats selected retired Union general Winfield Scott Hancock to counterbalance the Republicans' "bloody-shirt" attacks on Democrats as the party of secessionism and the Confederacy. Former Confederates nevertheless advised their constituents to "vote as you shot"—that is, against the Republicans. In an election characterized by widespread bribery, Garfield eked out a plurality of only 39,000 votes, or 48.5 percent of the vote, but with a comfortable margin of 214 to 155 in the Electoral College. In his inaugural address, President Garfield confirmed that the Republicans had ended efforts to reconstruct the former Confederacy and stamp out its racist heritage. He declared that southern blacks had been "surrendered to their own guardianship."

Garfield showed great potential as a new president, but never had a chance to prove it. On July 2, 1881, after only four months in office, he was walking through the Washington, D.C., railroad station when Charles Guiteau, a deranged man who had been turned down for a federal job, shot the president twice. As a policeman wrestled the assassin to the ground, Guiteau shouted: "Yes! I have killed Garfield! [Chester] Arthur is President of the United States. I am a Stalwart!"—a statement that would greatly embarrass the Stalwart Republicans. A seriously wounded Garfield was taken upstairs and given brandy. The attending physician concluded that he would probably survive, but the president murmured: "Thank you, doctor, but I am a dead man." Garfield lingered near death for two months. On September 19, he died of complications resulting from his inept medical care. At his sensational ten-week-long trial, Charles Guiteau explained that God had ordered him to kill the president. The jury refused to believe that he was insane and pronounced him guilty of murder. On June 30, 1882, Guiteau was hanged; an autopsy revealed that his brain was diseased.

Chester Arthur proved to be a surprisingly competent president. He distanced himself from the Stalwarts and established a genuine independence, even becoming a civil service and tariff reformer. The assassin Guiteau had unwittingly stimulated widespread public support for reforming the distribution of government jobs. In 1883, a reform bill sponsored by "Gentleman George" H. Pendleton, a Democratic senator from Ohio, set up a three-member federal Civil Service Commission, the first federal regulatory agency established on a permanent basis. A growing percentage of all federal jobs would now be filled on the basis of competitive examinations rather than political favoritism. The Pendleton Civil Service Reform Act was thus the vital step in a new approach to government administration that valued merit over partisanship.

The high protective tariff, a heritage of the Civil War designed to deter foreign imports by taxing them, had by the early 1880s raised federal revenues to a point where the government was enjoying an embarrassment of riches, an annual budget surplus that drew money into the Treasury and out of daily circulation, thus constricting economic growth. Some argued that lower tariff rates would reduce consumer prices by enabling foreign competition with American producers and at the same time leave more money in circulation to fuel economic growth. In 1882, a special presidential commission recommended a substantial reduction in tariff rates. The proposal gained President Arthur's support, but then ran up against swarms of lobbyists representing different industries determined to keep the rate on their particular commodity high. The resulting "mongrel tariff" of 1883, so called because of its different rates for different commodities, provided for a slight overall rate reduction, but was more indicative of the growing power of special interest groups influencing Congress.

THE CAMPAIGN OF 1884    Chester Arthur's presidential record might have attracted voters, but it did not please leaders of his party. So in 1884 the Republicans dumped Arthur and turned to the glamorous senator **James Gillespie Blaine** of Maine, longtime leader of the Republican Half-Breeds. Blaine was the consummate politician. He inspired the party faithful with his oratory, and at the same time he knew how to wheel and deal in the backrooms, sometimes evading the law in the process. Newspapers turned up evidence of his corruption. Based on references in the "Mulligan letters,"

they revealed that Blaine was in the pocket of the railroad barons. While serving as Speaker of the House, he had sold his votes on measures favorable to their interests. Nobody ever proved that Blaine had committed any crimes, but the circumstantial evidence was powerful: his mansion in Washington, D.C., could not have been built on his senatorial salary alone, nor could his palatial home in Augusta, Maine (which has since become the state's governor's mansion).

During the campaign, more letters surfaced with disclosures embarrassing to Blaine. For the reform element of the

**Senator James Gillespie Blaine of Maine**

The Republican candidate in 1884.

Republican party, this was too much, and prominent leaders and supporters of the party refused to endorse Blaine's candidacy. Party regulars scorned them as "goo-goos"—the good-government crowd, who ignored partisan realities. The editor of the *New York Sun* jokingly called the anti-Blaine Republicans **Mugwumps**, after an Algonquian Indian word for a self-important chieftain. The Mugwumps were a self-conscious political elite dedicated to promoting the public welfare. They were centered in the large cities and major universities of the northeast. Mostly educators, writers, or editors, they included the most famous American of all, Mark Twain. The Mugwumps generally opposed tariffs and championed free trade. They opposed the regulation of railroads as well as efforts to inflate the money supply by coining more silver. Their foremost goal was to expand civil service reform by making all federal jobs nonpartisan. Their break with the Republican party, the party of Lincoln, testified to the depth of their convictions.

The rise of the Mugwumps influenced the Democrats to nominate the New Yorker Grover Cleveland, a minister's son, as a reform candidate. He had first attracted national attention when, in 1881, he was elected as the anti-corruption mayor of Buffalo. In 1882 he was elected governor of New York, and he continued to build a reform record by fighting New York City's corrupt Tammany Hall ring. As mayor and as governor, he repeatedly vetoed bills serving selfish interests. He supported civil-service reform, opposed expanding the money supply, and preferred free trade rather than high tariffs.

A stocky 270-pound man, Cleveland provided a sharp contrast to the Republican Blaine. He possessed little charisma but impressed the public with his stubborn integrity. A juicy scandal erupted when the *Buffalo Evening Telegraph* revealed that as a bachelor, Cleveland had befriended an attractive Buffalo widow who later named him the father of a baby born to her in 1874. Cleveland had since provided financial support for the child. The respective escapades of Blaine and Cleveland provided some of the most colorful battle cries in political history: "Blaine, Blaine, James G. Blaine, the continental liar from the state of Maine," Democrats chanted; Republicans countered with "Ma, ma, where's my pa? Gone to the White House, ha, ha, ha!"

Near the end of the toxic campaign, Blaine and his supporters committed two fateful blunders. The first occurred at New York City's fashionable Delmonico's restaurant, where Blaine went to a private dinner with several millionaire bigwigs to discuss campaign finances. Accounts of the event appeared in the opposition press for days. The second fiasco occurred when one member of a delegation of Protestant ministers visiting Republican headquarters in New York referred to the Democrats as the party of "rum, Romanism, and rebellion." Blaine, who was present, let pass the implied

**"Another Voice for Cleveland"**

This 1884 cartoon attacks "Grover the Good" for fathering an illegitimate child.

insult to Catholics—a fatal oversight, since he had always cultivated Irish American support with his anti-English talk and public reminders that his mother was Catholic. Democrats spread the word that Blaine was at heart anti-Irish and anti-Catholic. The two incidents may have tipped the 1884 presidential election. The electoral vote, in Cleveland's favor, stood at 219 to 182, but the popular vote ran far closer: Cleveland's plurality was fewer than 30,000 votes. Cleveland won the key state of New York by the razor-thin margin of 1,149 votes out of the 1,167,169 cast.

CLEVELAND AND THE SPECIAL INTERESTS President Cleveland was an unusual president in that he opposed any federal government favors to big business. "A public office is a public trust" was one of his favorite mottoes. He held to a strictly limited view of government's role in both economic and social matters, a rigid philosophy illustrated by his 1887 veto of a congressional effort to provide desperate Texas farmers with seeds in the aftermath of a devastating drought that had parched the western states, summer after summer, for five years between 1887 and 1892. "Though the

**Grover Cleveland**

As president, Cleveland made the issue of tariff reform central to the politics of the late 1880s.

people support the government, the government should not support the people," Cleveland asserted.

Cleveland urged Congress to adopt an important new policy: federal regulation of interstate railroads. Since the late 1860s, states had adopted laws regulating railroads, but in 1886 a Supreme Court decision in the case of *Wabash, St. Louis, and Pacific Railroad Company v. Illinois*, the justices denied the right of any state to regulate rates charged by railroads engaged in interstate traffic. Cleveland thereupon urged Congress to take the lead in regulating the rail industry.

Congress followed through, and in 1887 Cleveland signed into law an act creating the Interstate Commerce Commission (ICC). The law empowered the ICC's five members to ensure that freight rates were "reasonable and just." The commission's actual powers proved to be weak, however, when tested in the courts, in large part because of the vagueness of the phrase "reasonable and just."

TENSIONS OVER THE TARIFF   President Cleveland's most dramatic challenge to the power of Big Business focused on tariff reform. During the late nineteenth century, critics charged that government tariff policies had fostered big business at the expense of small producers and retailers by effectively shutting out foreign imports, thereby enabling U.S. corporations to dominate their American markets and charge higher prices for their products. Cleveland agreed that tariff rates were too high and often inequitable. Congress, Cleveland argued, should reduce the tariff rates. The stage was set for the election of 1888 to highlight a difference between the major parties on an issue of substance.

THE ELECTION OF 1888   Cleveland was the obvious nominee of his party for reelection. The Republicans, now calling themselves the GOP (Grand Old Party) to emphasize their party's longevity, turned to the obscure Benjamin Harrison, whose greatest attribute was his availability. The grandson of President William Henry Harrison, he resided in Indiana, a pivotal state, and had a good war record. There was little in his political record to offend any voter. He had lost a race for governor and served one term in the Senate (1881–1887). The Republican platform accepted Cleveland's challenge to make the tariff the chief issue.

The Republicans enjoyed a huge advantage over the Democrats in funding and organization. To fend off Cleveland's efforts to reduce the tariff, business executives contributed over $3 million to the Republican campaign. On the eve of the election, Cleveland suffered a more devastating blow. A California Republican had written the British ambassador to the United States, Sir Lionel Sackville-West, using

**A billion-dollar hole**

In an attack on Benjamin Harrison's spending policies, Harrison is shown pouring Cleveland's huge surplus down a hole.

the false name Charles F. Murchison. Posing as an English immigrant in America, he asked advice on how to vote in the presidential election. Sackville-West, engaged at the time in sensitive negotiations over British and U.S. access to Canadian fisheries, hinted that the man should vote for Cleveland. The letter aroused a storm of protest against foreign intervention in American elections. The Democrats' explanations never caught up with the public's sense of outrage. Still, the outcome was incredibly close. Cleveland won the popular vote by 5,538,000 to 5,447,000, but Harrison carried the Electoral College by 233 to 168.

REPUBLICAN REFORM UNDER HARRISON    As president, Benjamin Harrison was a competent figurehead overshadowed by his flamboyant secretary of state, James Gillespie Blaine. Harrison owed a heavy debt to Union Civil War veterans, which he discharged by signing the Dependent Pension Act, substantially the same measure that Cleveland had vetoed. The number of veterans receiving federal pensions almost doubled between 1889 and 1893.

During the first two years of Harrison's term, the Republicans controlled the presidency and both houses of Congress for only the second time since 1875. In 1890, they passed a cluster of significant legislation. In addition to

**"King of the World"**

Reformers targeted the growing power of monopolies, such as that of John D. Rockefeller's Standard Oil.

the Dependent Pension Act, Congress and the president approved the Sherman Anti-Trust Act, the Sherman Silver Purchase Act, the McKinley Tariff Act, and the admission of Idaho and Wyoming as new states, which followed the admission of the Dakotas, Montana, and Washington in 1889.

Both parties had pledged to do something about the growing power of big businesses to fix prices and control markets. The Sherman Anti-Trust Act, named for Ohio senator John Sherman, prohibited companies from conspiring to establish monopolies. Its passage turned out to be largely symbolic, however. During the next decade, successive administrations rarely enforced the new law. From 1890 to 1901, only eighteen lawsuits were instituted, and four of those were against labor unions rather than corporations.

INADEQUATE CURRENCY    Complex monetary issues dominated the political arena during the Gilded Age. The fact that several farm organizations organized the Greenback party in 1876, which nominated presidential candidates in three national elections, illustrated the issue's significance to voters. The nation's money supply in the late nineteenth century lacked the flexibility to grow along with the expanding economy. From 1865 to 1890, the amount of currency in circulation decreased about 10 percent, while the population and the economy were rapidly growing. Such currency deflation raised the cost of borrowing money, as a shrinking money supply caused bankers to hike interest rates on loans. The American emphasis on metallic money dated from the Mint Act of 1792, which authorized the coinage of silver and gold at a ratio of 15 to 1. This meant that the amount of silver in a dollar coin weighed fifteen times as much as that in a gold dollar, a reflection of the relative value of gold and silver at the time.

In 1873, the Republican-controlled Congress declared that silver could no longer be used for coins, only gold. This gold-only decision occurred just when new mines in the western states had begun to increase the supply of silver. Debt-ridden farmers and laborers who advocated currency inflation through the unlimited coinage of silver denounced the "crime of '73," arguing that eastern bankers and merchants had conspired to stop coining silver so as to ensure a nationwide scarcity of money. The Bland-Allison Act of 1878 and the Sherman Silver Purchase Act of 1890 provided for some silver coinage, but too little in each case to offset the overall contraction of the currency as the population and the economy grew.

By the 1880s, hard-pressed farmers in the West and South demanded increased coinage of silver to inflate the currency and thereby raise commodity prices, making it easier for them to earn the money they needed to pay their mortgages and other debts. The farmers found allies among legislators representing the new western states where the silver mines were located. All six of the states admitted to the Union in 1889 and 1890 had substantial silver mines, and their new congressional delegations—largely Republican—wanted the federal government to mint more silver. The "silver delegates" shifted the balance in Congress enough to pass the Sherman Silver Purchase Act (1890), which required the Treasury to purchase 4.5 million ounces of silver each month with new paper money. Yet eastern business and financial groups viewed the inflationary act as a threat, setting the stage for the currency issue to eclipse all others during the financial panic that would sweep the country three years later.

Republicans viewed their victory over Grover Cleveland and the Democrats in 1888 as a mandate not just to maintain the high tariffs insulating companies from foreign competition but to raise them even higher. Piloted through Congress by Ohio representative William McKinley, the McKinley Tariff Act of 1890 raised duties on manufactured goods to their highest level ever, so high that the threat of foreign competition diminished, encouraging many businesses to charge higher prices. Voters rebelled. In the 1890 midterm elections, citizens repudiated the McKinley Tariff with a landslide of Democratic votes. In the new House, Democrats outnumbered Republicans by almost three to one; in the Senate the Republican majority was reduced to eight. One of the election casualties was Congressman McKinley himself.

The Democratic victory in the 1890 Congressional elections may also have been a reaction to Republican efforts at the state level to legislate against alcoholic beverages. Between 1880 and 1890 sixteen out of twenty-one states outside the South held referenda on a constitutional ban of alcoholic beverages, although only six states passed prohibition statutes. Republican moralists were playing a losing game, arousing wets (anti-prohibitionists) on the Democratic side. Another issue that served to mobilize Democratic resistance was the Republican attempt to eliminate funding for state-supported

Catholic (parochial) schools. In 1889, Wisconsin Republicans pushed through a law that required schools to teach only in English. Such efforts turned large numbers of outraged immigrants into Democratic activists. In 1889 and 1890, the Democrats swept state after state.

## THE FARM PROBLEM AND AGRARIAN PROTEST MOVEMENTS

The 1890 congressional elections also revealed a deep-seated unrest in the farming communities of the South and on the plains of Kansas and Nebraska, as well as in the mining towns of the Rocky Mountain region. People used the term "revolution" to describe the swelling grassroots support for the Populists, a new third party focused on addressing the needs of small farmers, many of whom did not own the land they worked. In

**"I Feed You All!"**

This 1875 poster shows the farmer at the center of society.

drought-devastated Kansas, Populists took over five Republican congressional seats. On a national level, the newly elected Populists and Democrats took control of Congress just as an acute economic crisis appeared on the horizon: farmers' debts were mounting as crop prices plummeted.

ECONOMIC CONDITIONS    Since the end of the Civil War, farmers in the South and the plains states suffered from worsening economic and social conditions. The source of their problems was a long decline in commodity prices, from 1870 to 1898, caused by overproduction and growing international competition in world markets. From 1870 to the mid-1890s, corn prices plunged by a third, wheat by more than half, and cotton by two thirds. The vast new land brought under cultivation in the West poured an ever-increasing supply of agricultural commodities into the market, driving prices down. Capitalism is supposed to work that way, but considerations of abstract economic forces puzzled many farmers. How could one speak of overproduction when so many remained in need? Instead, they reasoned, there must be a screw loose somewhere in the system.

Struggling farmers targeted the railroads and the food processors who handled the farmers' and ranchers' products as the prime villains. Farmers resented the high railroad freight rates that prevailed in farm regions with no alternative forms of transportation. High tariffs on imported goods also operated to farmers' disadvantage because the tariffs deterred foreign competition, allowing U.S. companies to raise the prices of manufactured goods upon which farmers depended. Farmers, however, had to sell their wheat, cotton, and other staples in foreign markets, where competition lowered prices.

Debt, too, had been a perennial problem of agriculture. After the Civil War, farmers had become ever more enmeshed in debts owed to local banks or merchants. As commodity prices dropped, the burden of debt grew because farmers had to cultivate more wheat or cotton to raise the same amount of money; and by growing more, they furthered the vicious cycle of commodity surpluses and price declines.

THE GRANGER MOVEMENT    When the U.S. Department of Agriculture sent Oliver H. Kelley on a tour of the South in 1866, he was disheartened by the isolation of people living on farms. To address the problem, Kelley and some government clerks in 1867 founded the National Grange of the Patrons of Husbandry, better known as the Grange (an old word for granary), as each chapter was called. In the next few years, the Grange mushroomed, reaching a membership as high as 1.5 million by 1874. The Grange started as a social and educational response to the farmers' isolation, but as it grew, it began to promote farmer-owned cooperatives for the buying and selling of crops. The farmers who joined the Grange wanted to free themselves from the high fees charged by grain-elevator operators and food processors by banding together to buy their own warehouses and storage elevators.

The Grange soon became indirectly involved in politics, through independent third parties, especially in the Midwest during the early 1870s. The Grange's chief political goal was to regulate the rates charged by railroads and warehouses. In five states, Grangers brought about the passage of "Granger laws," which at first proved relatively ineffective but laid a foundation for stronger legislation. Warehouse owners challenged the laws in the "Granger cases" that soon advanced to the Supreme Court, where they claimed to have been deprived of property without due process of law. In a key case involving warehouse regulation, *Munn v. Illinois* (1877), the Supreme Court ruled that the state, according to its "police powers," had the right to regulate property that affected the public welfare. If regulatory power were abused, the ruling said, "the people must resort to the polls, not the courts." Later, however, the courts would severely restrict state regulatory powers.

The **Granger movement** gradually declined as members directed their energies into farm cooperatives, many of which failed, and political action. In 1875, insurgent farmers formed the Independent National party, more commonly known as the Greenback party because of its emphasis on the virtues of paper money. In the 1878 congressional elections, the Greenback party polled over 1 million votes and elected fifteen congressmen. But in 1880, the party's fortunes declined, and it disintegrated after 1884.

FARMERS' ALLIANCES    As the Grange lost energy, other agricultural organizations, known as **Farmers' Alliances**, grew in size and significance. Like the Grange, the Farmers' Alliances (Northern and Southern) organized social and recreational activities, but they also emphasized political action. Struggling farmers throughout the South and Midwest, where tenancy rates were highest, rushed to join the Alliance movement as a means of addressing the hardships created by chronic indebtedness, declining crop prices, and devastating droughts. Yet unlike the Grange, which was a national organization that tended to attract more prosperous farmers, the Alliances were grassroots organizations that would become the largest and most dynamic farmers' movement in history.

The Alliance movement swept across the cotton belt in the South and established strong support in Kansas and the Dakotas. In 1886, a white minister in Texas responded to the appeals of African American farmers by organizing the Colored Farmers' National Alliance. The white leadership of the

Alliance movement in Texas endorsed this development because the Colored Alliance stressed that its objective was economic justice, not social equality. By 1890, the Alliance movement had members from New York to California, numbering about 1.5 million, and the Colored Farmers' National Alliance claimed over 1 million members.

The Alliance movement welcomed rural women and men over sixteen years of age who displayed a "good moral character," believed in God, and demonstrated "industrious habits." The slogan of the Southern Alliance was "equal rights to all, special privileges to none." A North Carolina woman relished the "grand opportunities" the Alliance provided women, allowing them to emerge from household drudgeries. "Drudgery, fashion, and gossip," she declared, "are no longer the bounds of woman's sphere." One Alliance publication made the point explicitly: "The Alliance has come to redeem woman from her enslaved condition, and place her in her proper sphere." The number of women in the movement grew rapidly, and many assumed key leadership roles in the "grand army of reform."

The Alliance movement sponsored some one thousand rural newspapers to spread the word about the farm problem. It also recruited forty thousand lecturers, who fanned out across the countryside to help people understand

**Members of the Texas Farmers' Alliance, 1880s**

Alliances united local farmers, fostered a sense of community, and influenced political policies.

the "tyrannical" forces arrayed against the farm sector: bankers and creditors, Wall Street financiers, railroads, and corporate giants who controlled both the commodities markets and the political process. Unlike the Grange, however, the Alliance proposed an elaborate economic reform program centered on the creation of farm cooperatives.

In 1887, Charles W. Macune, the Alliance president, proposed that Texas farmers create their own Alliance Exchange in an effort to free themselves from their dependence upon commercial warehouses and grain elevators, food processors, and banks. Members of the exchange would act collectively, pooling their resources to borrow money from banks and purchase their goods and supplies from a new corporation created by the Alliance in Dallas. The exchange would also build its own warehouses to store and market members' crops. While their crops were being stored, member farmers would be able to obtain cash loans to buy household goods and agricultural supplies. Once the stored crop was sold, the farmers would pay back the credit provided by the Alliance warehouse.

This grand cooperative scheme collapsed when Texas banks refused to accept the paper money from Alliance members. Macune and others then focused their energies on what Macune called a "subtreasury plan," whereby farmers would be able to store their harvested crops in new government warehouses and obtain cash in the form of government loans for up to 80 percent of the value of their crops at 1 percent interest. Besides providing immediate cash, the plan would allow farmers the leeway to store a crop in hopes of getting a better price later. The plan would also promote inflation because the loans to farmers would be made in new legal-tender notes. Monetary inflation was a popular idea with farmers because so many farmers were debtors, and debtors like inflation because it allows them to repay their long-term debts with cheaper money.

The subtreasury plan was immensely popular with distressed farmers, but it never became law. In 1890, Congress nixed the proposal. Its defeat, as well as setbacks to other Alliance proposals, convinced many farm leaders that they needed more political power in order to secure the reforms necessary to save the agricultural sector: railroad regulation, currency inflation, state departments of agriculture, anti-trust laws, and more accessible farm-based credit (loans).

FARM POLITICS    In the farm states west of the Mississippi River, hard times had descended after the terrible blizzards of 1887, which killed most of the cattle and hogs across the northern plains. Two years later, a prolonged drought destroyed millions of acres of corn, wheat, and oats. Distressed farmers lashed out against what they considered to be a powerful conspiracy of eastern financial and industrial interests, which they variously called "monopolies," "the money power," "Wall Street," or "organized wealth." Desperate for assistance, they agitated for third-party political action to address their economic concerns. In Colorado in 1890, farm radicals joined with miners and railroad workers to form the Independent party. That same year, Nebraska farmers formed the People's Independent party. Across the South, however, white Alliance members hesitated to bolt the Democratic party, seeking instead to influence or control it. Both approaches gained startling success. New third parties under various names upset the political balance in western states, almost electing a governor under the banner of the new **People's party** (also known as the **Populist** party) in Kansas (where a Populist was elected governor in 1892) and taking control of one house of the state legislature there and both houses in Nebraska. In South Dakota and Minnesota, Populists gained a balance of power in the state legislatures, and Kansas sent a Populist to the U.S. Senate. The Populist party claimed to represent small farmers and wage laborers, blacks and poor whites, in their fight against greedy banks and railroads, corporate monopolies, and corrupt politics. The Populists called for more rather than less government intervention in the economy, for only government was capable of expanding the money supply, counterbalancing the power of big business, and providing efficient national transportation networks to support the needs of agribusiness.

The farm protest movement produced colorful leaders, especially in Kansas, where **Mary Elizabeth Lease** emerged as a fiery speaker. Born in Pennsylvania, Lease migrated to Kansas, taught school, raised a family, and failed at farming in the mid-1880s. She then studied law, "pinning sheets of notes above her wash tub," and became one of the state's first female attorneys. At the same time, she took up public speaking on behalf of various causes, including freedom for her ancestral Ireland, temperance, and women's suffrage. By the end of the 1880s, Lease had joined the Alliance as well as the Knights of Labor, and she soon applied her considerable

**Mary Elizabeth Lease, 1890**

A charismatic leader in the farm protest movement.

oratorical gifts to the cause of currency inflation, arguing for the coining of massive amounts of silver. A tall, proud, and imposing woman, Lease drew attentive audiences. "The people are at bay," she warned in 1894; "let the bloodhounds of money beware." She urged angry farmers to obtain their goals "with the ballot if possible, but if not that way then with the bayonet." Like so many of the Populists, Lease viewed the urban-industrial East as the enemy of the working classes. "The great common people of this country," she shouted, "are slaves, and monopoly is the master. The West and South are bound and prostrate before the manufacturing East."

Jeremiah "Sockless Jerry" Simpson was an equally charismatic agrarian radical. Born in Canada, he served as a seaman on Great Lakes steamships before buying a farm in northern Kansas. A shrewd man with huge, callused hands, he reduced the complex economic and political issues of the day to a simple formula: "Man must have access to the land," he maintained, "or he is a slave." He warned Republicans that Populism was the wave of the future: "You can't put this movement down by sneers or by ridicule, for its foundation was laid as far back as the foundation of the world. It is a struggle between the robbers and the robbed." Simpson dismissed his Republican opponent, a wealthy railroad lawyer, as an indulgent pawn of the corporations whose "soft white hands" and "silk hosiery" betrayed his true priorities. His outraged opponent thereupon shouted that it was better to have silk socks than none at all, unwittingly providing Simpson with his folksy nickname. Sockless Jerry won a seat in Congress, and so, too, did many other friends of "the people" in the Midwest.

In the South, the Alliance forced Democrats to nominate candidates pledged to their program. The southern states elected four pro-Alliance governors, seven pro-Alliance legislatures, forty-four pro-Alliance congressmen, and several senators. Among the most respected of the southern Alliance leaders was Thomas E. Watson of Georgia. The son of prosperous slaveholders who had lost everything after the Civil War, Watson became a successful lawyer and orator on behalf of the Alliance cause. He took the lead in urging African American tenant farmers and sharecroppers to join with their white counterparts in ousting the white political elite. "You are kept apart," he told black and white farmers, "that you may be separately fleeced of your earnings."

THE POPULIST PARTY AND THE ELECTION OF 1892 The success of the Alliances led to the formation of a third political party on the national level. In 1892, a gathering of Alliance leaders in St. Louis called for a national convention of the People's Party at Omaha, Nebraska, to adopt a platform and choose candidates. The Populist Convention opened on July 4,

**The Populist party**

A Populist gathering in Callaway, Nebraska, 1892.

1892. Delegates drafted a platform that included the subtreasury plan, unlimited coinage of silver, a progressive income tax whose rates would rise with personal income levels, and federal control of the railroads. The Populists also called for the government to reclaim from railroads and other corporations lands "in excess of their actual needs" and to forbid land ownership by immigrants who had not gained citizenship. Finally, the platform endorsed the eight-hour workday (rather than ten or twelve hours) and restriction of immigration. The party took these last positions in an effort to win support from urban factory workers, whom Populists looked upon as fellow "producers." The party's platform turned out to be more exciting than its candidate. Iowa's James B. Weaver, an able, prudent man, carried the stigma of his defeat on the Greenback ticket twelve years before. To attract southern voters who might be put off by Weaver's service in the Civil War as a Union general, the party named a former Confederate general for vice president.

The Populist party was the startling new feature of the 1892 campaign. The major parties renominated the same candidates who had run in 1888: Democrat Grover Cleveland and Republican Benjamin Harrison. The tariff issue monopolized their attention. Both major candidates polled over 5 million votes, but Cleveland carried a plurality of the popular votes and a majority of the Electoral College. The Populist Weaver polled over 1 million votes and carried Colorado, Kansas, Nevada, and Idaho, for a total of twenty-two electoral votes. Alabama was the banner Populist state of the South, with 37 percent of its vote going to Weaver.

## THE ECONOMY AND THE SILVER SOLUTION

**THE DEPRESSION OF 1893**   While the farmers were funneling their discontent into politics during the fall of 1892, a fundamental weakness in the economy was about to cause a major collapse and a social rebellion. Just ten days before Grover Cleveland started his second term, in the winter of 1893, the Philadelphia and Reading Railroad declared bankruptcy, setting off a national financial panic that mushroomed into the worst depression the nation had ever experienced. Other overextended railroads collapsed, taking many banks with them. A quarter of unskilled urban workers lost their jobs, and by the fall of 1893 over six hundred banks had closed and fifteen thousand businesses had failed. Entire farm regions in the South and West were devastated by the spreading depression that brought unprecedented suffering. Farm foreclosures soared. Between 1890 and 1894, more than eleven thousand farm mortgages were foreclosed in Kansas alone. In fifteen rural Kansas counties, three quarters of the people lost their farms. Residents grimly said: "In God we trusted, in Kansas we busted." By 1900, a third of all farmers were tenants rather than landowners. As the agricultural sector struggled, so too did county governments dependent on farm taxes.

**National panic**

The New York Stock Exchange on the morning of Friday, May 5, 1893.

By 1894, the nation's economy had reached bottom. The catastrophic depression lasted another four years, with unemployment hovering at 20 percent and hunger stalking the streets of many cities. In New York City, some 35 percent were unemployed, and twenty thousand homeless people camped out at police stations and other makeshift shelters. President Cleveland's response to the economic catastrophe was recklessly conservative: he sought to convince Congress to return the nation's money supply to a gold standard by repealing the Sherman Silver Purchase Act of 1890, a move that worsened rather than improved the financial situation.

The economy needed more money in circulation, not less. Unemployment and labor unrest only increased as investors rushed to exchange their silver for gold, thus further constricting the money supply. Violent labor strikes at Pullman, Illinois, and at the Homestead Works outside Pittsburgh symbolized the fracturing of the social order. In 1894 some 750,000 workers went on strike; railroad construction workers, laid off in the West, began tramping east and talked of marching on Washington, D.C. The devastating depression of the 1890s was reshaping America's economic and political landscape.

One protest group that reached Washington, D.C., was called Coxey's Army, led by Jacob S. Coxey, a wealthy Ohio quarry owner turned Populist who demanded that the federal government provide the unemployed with meaningful work. Coxey, his wife, and their son, Legal Tender Coxey, rode in a carriage ahead of some four hundred hardy protesters who marched hundreds of miles to the nation's capital. Police arrested Coxey for walking on the grass. Although his ragtag army dispersed peacefully, the march on Washington, as well as the growing political strength of Populism, struck fear into the hearts of many American conservatives. Critics portrayed Populists as "hayseed socialists" whose election would endanger the capitalist system.

The 1894 congressional elections, taking place amid this climate of mushrooming anxiety, produced a severe setback for the Democrats, who paid politically for the economic downturn. The Republicans were the chief beneficiaries. The Republicans gained 121 seats in the House, the largest increase ever. Only in the "Solid South" did the Democrats retain their advantage. The third-party Populists emerged with six senators and seven representatives. They polled 1.5 million votes for their congressional candidates and expected the festering discontent in rural areas to carry them to national power in 1896.

SILVERITES VERSUS GOLDBUGS    The course of events would dash that hope, however. In the mid-1890s, radical efforts to address the ravages of the depression focused on the currency issue. President Cleveland's success in convincing Congress to repeal the Sherman Silver Purchase Act created an irreparable division in his own party. One embittered pro-silver Democrat labeled the president a traitor.

The western states with large silver deposits now escalated their demands for the "unlimited" coinage of silver, presenting a strategic dilemma for Populists: Should the party promote the long list of varied reforms it had originally advocated, or should it try to ride the silver issue into power? The latter seemed the practical choice. Although the coinage of silver would not have

provided the economic panacea its advocates claimed, the "free silver" crusade took on powerful symbolic overtones. The Populist leaders decided,
over the protests of more radical members, to hold their 1896 nominating
convention *after* the two major party conventions, confident that the Republicans and Democrats would at best straddle the silver issue, enabling the
Populists to lure away silverite Republicans and Democrats.

THE REMARKABLE ELECTION OF 1896    Contrary to those expectations, the major parties took opposite positions on the currency issue.
The Republicans, as expected, nominated **William McKinley** on a gold
standard–only platform. McKinley, a former congressman and governor of
Ohio, symbolized the mainstream Republican values that had served the
party well during the Gilded Age. After the convention, a friend told McKinley that the "money question" would determine the election. The Republican
candidate dismissed that notion, insisting that the tariff would continue to
govern national political campaigns. But one of McKinley's advisers disagreed. "In my opinion," said Judge William Day of Ohio, "in thirty days you
won't hear of anything else" but the money question. He was right.

The Democratic nominating convention in the Chicago Coliseum, the
largest building in the world, was one of the great turning points in American political history. The pro-silver delegates, mostly from rural areas,
surprised the party leadership and the "Gold Democrats" by capturing the
convention for their inflationary crusade. Thirty-six-year-old **William
Jennings Bryan** from Nebraska gave the convention's final speech before
the balloting began for the party's presidential nominee.

And what a speech it was. A fervent evangelical moralist, Bryan was a two-
term congressman who had been defeated in the Senate race in 1894, when
Democrats were swept out of office by the dozens. In the months before the
1896 Democratic convention, he had traveled throughout the South and the
West, speaking passionately for the unlimited coinage of silver and against
President Cleveland's "do-nothing" response to the depression. Bryan championed the poor, the discontented, and the oppressed against the financial
and industrial titans. He was the first leader of a major party to call for the
expansion of the federal government to promote the welfare of the working
and middle classes by providing subsidies for farmers, legalizing labor
strikes, regulating railroads, taxing the rich, and breaking up "trusts" (financial and industrial monopolies). Bryan spoke for the evangelical Protestant
tradition, for the rural America that was losing ground to urban America,
for the South and West regions that remained dependent on the financial
and corporate interests of the East.

Bryan was a magnetic public speaker with a booming voice, a crusading minister in the role of a politician, self-infatuated and self-dramatizing. At the 1896 Democratic Convention, Bryan was a "dark horse" candidate in a field of more prominent competitors for the presidential nomination. So he had to take a calculated risk: he would be intentionally provocative and even disruptive. In his famous speech to the convention, his carefully rehearsed phrases and gestures were designed to arouse passions and seize control of the convention from the party leaders. Bryan claimed to speak for the "producing masses of this nation" against the eastern "financial magnates" who enslaved them by constricting the money supply. As his melodramatic twenty-minute speech reached a crescendo, Bryan fused Christian imagery with Populist anger:

**William Jennings Bryan**

His "cross of gold" speech at the 1896 Democratic Convention roused the delegates and secured him the party's presidential nomination.

> I come to speak to you in defense of a cause as holy as the cause of liberty— the cause of humanity. . . . We have petitioned, and our petitions have been scorned. We have entreated, and our entreaties have been disregarded. We have begged, and they have mocked when our calamity came. We beg no longer; we entreat no more; we petition no more. We defy them!

The messianic Bryan then stretched his fingers across his forehead and shouted his dramatic conclusion: "You shall not press down upon the brow of labor this crown of thorns. You shall not crucify mankind upon a cross of gold!" He then extended his arms straight out from his sides, posing as if being crucified. It was a riveting performance.

As Bryan strode triumphantly off the stage, the delegates erupted in a frenzy of wild applause and adulation. "Everybody seemed to go mad at once," reported the *New York World*. It was pure theater, but it worked better than even Bryan had anticipated. Republicans were not impressed, however. A partisan newspaper observed that no political movement had "ever before spawned such hideous and repulsive vipers" as the populist Democrats had done.

The day after his riveting speech, Bryan won the presidential nomination on the fifth ballot, but in the process the Democratic party was fractured. Disappointed pro-gold, pro-Cleveland Democrats dismissed Bryan as a socialist fanatic. They were so alienated by Bryan's inflationary crusade and populist rhetoric that they walked out of the convention and nominated their own candidate, Senator John M. Palmer of Illinois. "Fellow Democrats," Palmer announced, "I will not consider it any great fault if you decide to cast your vote for [the Republican] William McKinley."

Two weeks later, when the Populists gathered in St. Louis for their own presidential nominating convention, they faced an impossible choice. They could name their own candidate and divide the pro-silver vote with the Democrats, or they could endorse the Democratic Bryan and probably lose their identity as an independent party. In the end they backed Bryan, the "matchless champion of the people," but chose their own vice-presidential candidate, former congressman Thomas E. Watson of Georgia, and invited the Democrats to drop their vice-presidential nominee. Bryan refused the request.

The election of 1896 was one of the most dramatic in history, in part because of the striking contrast between the candidates, and in part because the severity of the economic depression made the stakes so high. Bryan, the nominee of both the Democrats and the Populists, crisscrossed the country like a man on a mission, delivering impassioned speeches on behalf of "the struggling masses" of workers, farmers, and small-business owners. At every stop he promised that the unlimited coinage of silver would solve the nation's economic problems. He said that strikes by labor unions should be legalized, farmers should be given federal subsidies, the rich should be taxed, corporate campaign contributions should be banned, and liquor should be outlawed. Bryan's populist crusade was for whites only, however. Like so many otherwise progressive Democratic leaders, he never challenged the pattern of racial segregation and violence against blacks in the solid Democratic South. In fact, he believed in white racial superiority.

McKinley, meanwhile, stayed at home during the campaign. He knew he could not compete with Bryan as an orator, so he conducted a traditional "front-porch campaign," receiving select delegations of Republican supporters at his home in Canton, Ohio, and giving only prepared statements to the press. McKinley's brilliant campaign manager, Marcus "Mark" Hanna, a wealthy business executive, shrewdly portrayed Bryan as a "Popocrat," a radical whose "communistic spirit" would ruin the capitalist system and create a

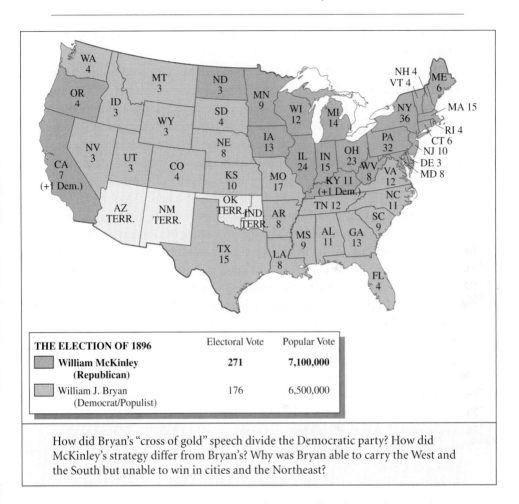

| THE ELECTION OF 1896 | Electoral Vote | Popular Vote |
|---|---|---|
| William McKinley (Republican) | 271 | 7,100,000 |
| William J. Bryan (Democrat/Populist) | 176 | 6,500,000 |

How did Bryan's "cross of gold" speech divide the Democratic party? How did McKinley's strategy differ from Bryan's? Why was Bryan able to carry the West and the South but unable to win in cities and the Northeast?

class war. Hanna convinced the Republican party to proclaim that it was "unreservedly for sound money." Theodore Roosevelt, a rising star among the Republicans, was aghast at the thought of Bryan becoming president. "The silver craze surpasses belief," he wrote a friend. "Bryan's election would be a great calamity."

By preying upon such fears, the McKinley campaign raised vast sums of money from corporations and wealthy donors to finance an army of 1,400 Republican speakers who traveled the country in his support. It was the most sophisticated—and expensive—presidential campaign up to that point in history. McKinley promoted himself as the "advance agent of prosperity" who would provide workers with a "full dinner pail." In the end, Bryan and the Democratic-Populist-silverite candidates were overwhelmed by the better-organized Republican campaign. McKinley won the popular vote by

7.1 million to 6.5 million and the Electoral College vote by 271 to 176. Two million more voters cast their ballot than in 1892.

Bryan carried most of the West and the South but found little support in the metropolitan centers east of the Mississippi River and north of the Ohio and Potomac Rivers. In the critical Midwest, from Minnesota and Iowa eastward to Ohio, Bryan carried not a single state. Bryan's evangelical Protestantism repelled many Roman Catholic voters, who were normally drawn to the Democrats. Farmers in the Northeast, moreover, were less attracted to agrarian radicalism than were farmers in the wheat and cotton belts of the West and South, where there were higher rates of tenancy. Among factory workers in the cities, Bryan aroused little support. Wage laborers found it easier to identify with McKinley's pledge to restore the industrial economy than with Bryan's free-silver evangelism. Some workers, moreover, may have been intimidated by owners' threats to close their businesses if Bryan won. Whatever the factors, Bryan, the supposed "communist," accepted defeat with magnanimity. He telegraphed McKinley that "We have submitted the issue to the American people and their will is law." Although Bryan had lost, his candidacy had begun the process of transforming the Democratic party from being a bulwark of pro-business conservatism and fiscal restraint to the twentieth-century party of liberal reform. The Populist party virtually disintegrated. Having garnered a million votes in 1896, it collected only fifty thousand votes in 1900. Conversely, McKinley's victory climaxed a generation-long struggle for the political control of industrializing America. The Republicans were dominant.

## RACE RELATIONS DURING THE 1890s

The turbulence in American life during the 1890s also affected race relations—for the worse. The civil rights fought for in the Civil War and codified in the Thirteenth, Fourteenth, and Fifteenth Amendments afterward fell victim to the complex social, economic, political, and cultural forces unleashed by America's rapid growth. Even the supposedly radical William Jennings Bryan was not willing to support the human rights of African Americans.

DISENFRANCHISING AFRICAN AMERICANS  Race relations were in part a victim of the terrible depression of the 1890s. At the end of the nineteenth century, a violent "Negrophobia" swept across the South and much of the nation. In part, the new wave of racism was spurred by the revival in the

United States and Europe of the old idea that the Anglo-Saxon "race" was genetically and culturally superior to other races. Another reason for the intensification of racism was that many whites had come to resent any signs of African American economic success and political influence in the midst of the decade's economic downturn. An Alabama newspaper editor declared that "our blood boils when the educated Negro asserts himself politically." By the 1890s, a new generation of African Americans born and educated since the end of the Civil War was determined to gain true equality. This younger generation was more assertive and less patient than their parents. "We are not the Negro from whom the chains of slavery fell a quarter century ago, most assuredly not," a black editor announced. A growing number of young white adults, however, were equally determined to keep "Negroes in their place."

Racial violence and repression escalated dramatically during the last decade of the nineteenth century and the first two decades of the twentieth. Ruling whites ruthlessly exercised their will over all areas of black life, imposing racial subjugation and segregation by preventing blacks from voting and by enacting **"Jim Crow" laws** mandating separation of the races in various public places. The phrase "Jim Crow" derived from "Jump Jim Crow," an old song-and-dance caricature of African Americans performed by white actor Thomas D. Rice in blackface during the 1830s. Thereafter, "Jim Crow" had become a pejorative expression meaning "Negro." The renewal of statutory racial segregation resulted from a calculated campaign by white elites and racist thugs to limit African American political, economic, and social participation at the end of the nineteenth century.

The political dynamics of the 1890s exacerbated the rise of racial tensions. The Populist revolt in the rural South divided the white vote (which had become all-Democratic) to such an extent that in some southern states the black vote determined election outcomes. Some white Populist leaders courted black votes and brought African Americans prominently into their leadership councils. In response, race-baiting white politicians argued that the black vote should be eliminated from southern elections. Because the Fifteenth Amendment made it impossible simply to deny African Americans the right to vote, white officials pursued disenfranchisement indirectly, through such "legal" devices as poll taxes (also called head taxes) and literacy tests designed to impede often-illiterate black voters—and many poor whites as well. And where such "legal" means were insufficient, insurgent white candidates were willing to use fraud and violence to overthrow the white ruling elite by eliminating the black vote.

Benjamin Tillman, the white supremacist governor of South Carolina (1890–1894), was a good example of the transformation in southern politics at the end of the nineteenth century. He and other political rebels ousted the Bourbon elite ("aristocrats") that had long governed in the former Confederate states. Tillman claimed that "I organized the majority [of voters] and put the old families out of business, and we became and are the rulers of the state." He also boasted about defeating the Bourbons by eliminating the black vote. "We have done our level best [to prevent blacks from voting] . . . we have scratched our heads to find out how we could eliminate the last one of them. We stuffed ballot boxes. We shot them. We are not ashamed of it."

Mississippi led the way to the near-total disenfranchisement of blacks and many poor whites as well. The state called a constitutional convention in 1890 to change the suffrage provisions included in the Radical Republican constitution of 1868. The so-called **Mississippi Plan** set the pattern that seven more states would follow over the next twenty years. First, a residence requirement—two years in the state, one year in an election district—struck at those African American tenant farmers who were in the habit of moving yearly in search of better economic opportunities. Second, voters were disqualified if convicted of certain crimes disproportionately involving blacks. Third, all taxes, including a poll tax, had to be paid before a person could vote. This proviso fell most heavily on poor whites and blacks. Fourth and finally, all voters had to be literate, and white registrars determined who was literate.

Other states added variations on the Mississippi Plan for eliminating black voting. In 1898, Louisiana invented the "grandfather clause," which allowed illiterate whites to vote if their fathers or grandfathers had been eligible to vote on January 1, 1867, when African Americans were still disenfranchised. By 1910, Georgia, North Carolina, Virginia, Alabama, and Oklahoma had adopted the grandfather clause. Every southern state, moreover, adopted a statewide Democratic primary between 1896 and 1915, which became the only meaningful election outside isolated areas of Republican strength. With minor exceptions, the Democratic primaries excluded African American voters altogether. The effectiveness of these measures can be seen in a few sample figures. Louisiana in 1896 had 130,000 registered black voters. By 1900, the number was only 5,320. In Alabama in 1900, 121,159 black men over twenty-one were literate, according to the census; only 3,742, however, were registered to vote.

**THE SPREAD OF RACIAL SEGREGATION**  At the same time that southern blacks were being shoved out of the political arena, they were being segregated in the social sphere. The symbolic first target was the railroad passenger car. In 1885, the novelist George Washington Cable noted that in South Carolina, blacks "ride in first class [rail] cars as a right" and "their presence excites no comment." From 1875 to 1883, in fact, any local or state government-mandated racial segregation violated the federal Civil Rights Act (1875), which forbade racial discrimination in public places such as hotels, restaurants, and trains. By 1883, however, many northern whites endorsed the resegregation of southern life. In that year the U.S. Supreme Court ruled jointly on five separate civil rights cases involving discrimination against blacks by businesses or individuals. The Court held, with only one dissenting vote, that the Civil Rights Act of 1875 was unconstitutional. The judges explained that private *individuals* and *organizations* could engage in acts of racial discrimination because the Fourteenth Amendment specified only that "no State" could deny citizens equal protection of the law.

The Court's interpretation in what came to be called the *Civil Rights Cases* (1883) left as an open question the validity of various state laws *requiring* racially separate public facilities under the principle of "separate but equal," a slogan popular in the South in the late nineteenth century. In the 1880s, Tennessee and Mississippi required railroad passengers to occupy the car set aside for their race. When Louisiana followed suit in 1890, dissidents challenged the law in the case of *Plessy v. Ferguson*, which the Supreme Court decided in 1896.

The test case originated in New Orleans when Homer Plessy, an octoroon (a person having one-eighth African ancestry), refused to leave a whites-only railroad car when told to do so and was later convicted of violating the law. The Supreme Court ruled in 1896 that states had a right to create laws segregating public places such as schools, hotels, and restaurants. Justice John Marshall Harlan, a Kentuckian who had once owned slaves, was the only member of the Court to dissent from the ruling. He stressed that the Constitution is "color-blind, and neither knows nor tolerates classes among citizens. In respect of civil rights, all citizens are equal before the law." He feared that the Court's ruling would plant the "seeds of race hate" under "the sanction of law."

That is precisely what happened. The shameful ruling in the *Plessy* case legitimized the practice of racially **"separate but equal"** facilities in virtually every area of southern life, including streetcars, hotels, restaurants, hospitals, parks, sports stadiums, and places of employment. In 1900, the editor of the *Richmond Times* expressed the prevailing view throughout the South:

> It is necessary that this principle be applied in every relation of Southern life. God Almighty drew the color line and it cannot be obliterated. The negro must stay on his side of the line and the white man must stay on his side, and the sooner both races recognize this fact and accept it, the better it will be for both.

**"Separate but equal"**

Students exercising during the school day at an all-black elementary school in Washington, D.C.

Widespread violence accompanied the creation of Jim Crow laws. From 1890 to 1899, lynchings in the United States averaged 188 per year, 82 percent of which occurred in the South; from 1900 to 1909, they averaged 93 per year, with 92 percent in the South. Whites were 32 percent of the victims during the former period but only 11 percent in the latter. Lynchings usually involved a black man (or men) accused of a crime, often rape of a white woman. White mobs would seize the accused, torture, and kill him, often by hanging but always in ghastly ways. Lynchings became so common as a grisly method of keeping blacks "in their place" that participating whites viewed them as forms of outdoor recreation. Crowds, including women and children, would watch the grisly event amid a carnival-like atmosphere.

By the end of the nineteenth century, legalized racial discrimination—segregation of public facilities, political disenfranchisement, and vigilante justice—had elevated government-sanctioned bigotry to an official way of life in the South. South Carolina governor Benjamin Tillman murderously declared in 1892 that blacks "must remain subordinate or be exterminated."

MOB RULE IN NORTH CAROLINA   The widespread efforts of white southerners to strip blacks on their civil rights was violently illustrated in the thriving coastal port of Wilmington, North Carolina, then the largest city in the state, with about twenty thousand residents. In 1894 and 1896, black voters, by then a majority in the city, elected a coalition of Republicans and Populists to various municipal offices. That blacks had come to control the electoral process infuriated the city's white elite. "We will never surrender to a ragged raffle of Negroes," warned a former congressman and Confederate colonel named Alfred Waddell, "even if we have to choke the Cape Fear River with [black] carcasses." It was not an idle threat.

On the morning of November 10, 1898, some two thousand well-armed white men and boys rampaged through the streets of Wilmington. They first destroyed the offices of *The Daily Record*, the city's black-owned newspaper. The vigilantes then moved into the black neighborhoods, indiscriminately shooting African Americans and destroying homes and businesses. Scores, perhaps a hundred, all black, were killed. The white mob then stormed the city hall, forced the white mayor and his board of black and white aldermen to resign, and declared that Colonel Waddell was the new mayor. The racist mob next forced the African American business leaders and elected officials to board northbound trains, taking them out of the state. The new

**The Wilmington Insurrection**

A mob of armed white supremacists destroyed the printing press of the *The Daily Record*, a black-owned newspaper in Wilmington, North Carolina.

self-appointed, all-white city government issued their own "Declaration of White Independence" that stripped blacks of their voting rights and their jobs. Desperate black residents appealed for help to the governor as well as to President William McKinley, but they did nothing.

The Wilmington Insurrection marked the first time in history that a lawfully elected municipal government had been overthrown in the United States. Two years later, in the 1900 statewide elections, white supremacist Democrats vowed to cement their control of the political process. The night before the election, Colonel Waddell urged supporters to use any means necessary to suppress black voting: "You are Anglo-Saxons. You are armed and prepared and you will do your duty. . . . Go to the polls tomorrow, and if you find the negro out voting, tell him to leave the polls and if he refuses, kill him, shoot him down in his tracks. We shall win tomorrow if we have to do it with guns." The Democratic party won by a landslide.

THE BLACK RESPONSE   African Americans responded to the resurgence of racism and statutory segregation in various ways. Some left the South in search of greater equality, security, and opportunity, but the vast majority stayed in their native region. In the face of overwhelming force and prejudicial justice, most accommodated themselves to the realities of white supremacy and segregation. "Had to walk a quiet life," explained James Plunkett, a Virginia African American. "The least little thing you would do, they [whites] would kill ya."

Yet accommodation to the realities of white power did not mean submission. Excluded from the dominant white world and eager to avoid confrontations, black southerners after the 1890s adapted to the reality of segregation by nurturing their own culture and racial pride. A young white visitor to Mississippi in 1910 noticed that nearly every black person he met had "two distinct social selves, the one he reveals to his own people, the other he assumes among the whites."

African American churches continued to serve as the hub for black community life. Churches were used not only for worship but also for activities that had nothing to do with religion: social gatherings, club meetings, political rallies. For men especially, churches offered leadership roles and political status. Serving as a deacon was often one of the most prestigious positions an African American man could achieve. Churches enabled African Americans of all classes to interact and exercise roles denied them in the larger society.

One irony of mandated racial segregation was that it opened up economic opportunities for blacks. A new class of African American entrepreneurs emerged to provide services—insurance, banking, mortuaries, barbering—

to the black community in the segregated South. At the same time, African Americans formed their own social and fraternal clubs and organizations, all of which helped bolster black pride and provided both fellowship and opportunities for service.

Middle-class black women formed thousands of racial-uplift organizations across the South and around the nation. The women's clubs were engines of social service in their communities. Members cared for the aged and the infirm, the orphaned and the abandoned. They created homes for single mothers and provided nurseries for working mothers. They sponsored health clinics and classes in home economics for women. In 1896, the leaders of such women's clubs from around the country converged to form the National Association of Colored Women, an organization created to combat racism and segregation. Its first president, Mary Church Terrell, told members that they had an obligation to serve the "lowly, the illiterate, and even the vicious to whom we are bound by the ties of race and sex, and put forth every effort to uplift and reclaim them."

LONELY WARRIOR—IDA B. WELLS  One of the most outspoken African American activists of the time was **Ida B. Wells**. Born into slavery in 1862 in Mississippi, she attended a school staffed by white missionaries. In 1878, an epidemic of yellow fever killed her parents as well as an infant brother. At age sixteen, Wells assumed responsibility for her five younger siblings and secured a job as a rural schoolteacher. In about 1880, she moved to nearby Memphis, Tennessee, along the Mississippi River, where she taught in segregated schools and gained entrance to the social life of the city's striving African American middle class.

In 1883, Wells confronted the reality and power of white supremacy. After being denied a seat on a railroad car because she was black, she became the first African American to file suit against such discrimination. The circuit court decided in her favor and fined the railroad, but the Tennessee Supreme Court overturned the ruling. Wells thereafter

**Ida B. Wells**
While raising four children, Wells sustained her commitment to ending racial and gender discrimination.

discovered "[my] first and [It] might be said, my only love"—journalism—and, through it, a weapon with which to wage her crusade for justice. Writing under the pen name Iola, she became a prominent editor of *Memphis Free Speech*, a newspaper focusing on African American issues.

In 1892, when three of her friends were murdered by a white mob, Wells launched a lifelong crusade against lynching. Angry whites responded to the efforts of the "lonely warrior" by destroying her office and threatening to lynch her. The undaunted, tireless Wells moved to New York City and continued to use her fiery journalistic talent to criticize Jim Crow laws and demand that blacks have their voting rights restored. In the spring of 1898, the lynching of an African American postmaster in South Carolina so incensed Wells that she spent five weeks in Washington, D.C., fruitlessly trying to persuade the federal government to intervene. Wells remained resolute and resilient. Eleven years later, in 1909, she helped found the National Association for the Advancement of Colored People (NAACP). She also endorsed women's suffrage. In promoting full equality, Wells often found herself in direct opposition to Booker T. Washington, the most prominent black leader in the late nineteenth century.

WASHINGTON AND DU BOIS    By the 1890s **Booker T. Washington**, born in Virginia of a slave mother and a white father, had become the foremost black educator in the nation. He argued that blacks should not focus on

**Booker T. Washington**

Founder of the Tuskegee Institute.

fighting racial segregation. Instead, they should first establish an economic base for their advancement before striving for social equality and political rights. In a famous speech at the Cotton States and International Exposition in Atlanta in 1895, Washington advised fellow African Americans: "Cast down your bucket where you are—cast it down in making friends ... of the people of all races by whom we are surrounded. Cast it down in agriculture, mechanics, in commerce, in domestic service, and in the professions." He conspicuously omitted politics from that list and offered an indirect endorsement of segregation: "In all things that are purely social we can be as separate as the five fingers, yet one as the hand in all things essential to mutual progress." In sum, Washington wanted first to build a prosperous black community; civil rights and social integration could wait.

By the turn of the century, Booker T. Washington had become the most influential African American leader in the nation. Some people, however, bitterly criticized him for making a bad bargain: the sacrifice of broad educational and civil rights for increased economic opportunities. **W.E.B. Du Bois** led this criticism. A native of

**W.E.B. Du Bois**

A fierce advocate for black education.

Massachusetts, Du Bois first experienced southern racial prejudice as a student at Fisk University in Nashville, Tennessee. Later he was the first African American to earn degrees from Harvard (in history and sociology) and briefly attended the University of Berlin. In addition to an active career promoting civil rights, he left a distinguished record as a scholar, authoring over twenty books. Trim and dapper, sporting a goatee, carrying a cane, and often wearing gloves, Du Bois had a flamboyant personality and a combative spirit. Not long after he began his teaching career at Atlanta University in 1897, he began a very public assault on Booker T. Washington's strategy for improving the quality of life for African Americans.

Du Bois called Washington's 1895 speech "the Atlanta Compromise" and said that he would not "surrender the leadership of this race to cowards." Washington, Du Bois argued, preached "a gospel of Work and Money to such an extent as . . . to overshadow the higher aims of life." Washington was asking blacks to give up aspirations for political power, civil rights, and higher education so as to "concentrate all their energies on industrial education, the accumulation of wealth, and the conciliation of the South." Du Bois stressed that the priorities should be reversed. African American leaders should adopt a strategy of "ceaseless agitation" directed at ensuring the right to vote and winning civil equality. The education of blacks, Du Bois maintained, should not be merely vocational but should develop bold leaders willing to challenge segregation and discrimination through political action.

He demanded that disenfranchisement and legalized segregation cease immediately and that the laws of the land be enforced. The dispute between Washington and Du Bois came to define the tensions that would divide the twentieth-century civil rights movement: militancy versus conciliation, separatism versus assimilation, social justice versus economic opportunities.

A NEW ERA  The dispute between W.E.B. Dubois and Booker T. Washington over the best strategy for blacks to regain their civil rights occurred at the same time that William Jennings Bryan and William McKinley were disputing the best way to end the terrible economic depression that had come to define the decade of the 1890s. The presidential election of 1896 was a climactic political struggle between the forces representing urban-industrial America and rural-agrarian America. Over 79 percent of eligible voters participated. McKinley's victory demonstrated that urban-industrial values had indeed taken firm hold of the political system. President McKinley's first important act was to call a special session of Congress to raise the tariff again. The Dingley Tariff of 1897 was the highest ever. By 1897, economic prosperity was returning, helped along by inflation of the currency, which confirmed the arguments of the Greenbackers and silverites that the money supply was inadequate. But the inflation came, in one of history's many ironies, not from the federal government printing more greenbacks or coining more silver dollars but from a flood of new gold discovered in South Africa, northwest Canada, and Alaska. In 1900, Congress passed and President McKinley signed a bill affirming that the United States money supply would be based only on gold.

The decade of the 1890s marked the end of one era and the beginning of a new one. At the close of the nineteenth century, the longstanding issues of tariff and currency policy gave way to global concerns: the outbreak of the War of 1898 and the U.S. acquisition of territories outside the Western Hemisphere. At the same time, the advent of a new century brought new social and political developments. The most disturbing of those new developments was ever-deepening racial segregation and racial violence. The most positive was the emergence of progressivism, a diverse new national movement promoting social and political reform. Even though the Populist movement faded with William Jennings Bryan's defeat, most of the progressive agenda promoted by Bryan Democrats and Populists, dismissed as too radical and controversial in 1896, would be implemented by "progressive" political forces over the next two decades. Bryan's impassioned candidacy helped transform the Democratic party into a vigorous instrument of "progressive" reform during the early twentieth century. As the United States entered the twentieth century, it began to place more emphasis on the role of the national government in society and the economy. Bigness in government began to counteract bigness in business.

## CHAPTER SUMMARY

- **Gilded Age Politics**  Americans were intensely loyal to the two major parties, which operated on a local level by distributing favors. "City machines" also provided working-class men with jobs and gave relief (money or necessities) to the poor, thereby winning votes. The major political parties shared power nearly equally during the Gilded Age; such parity made neither party willing to embrace bold initiatives.

- **National Politics**  Politicians focused on tariff reform, the regulation of corporations, Indian wars and Indian policy, civil service reform, and immigration. In the 1884 presidential election, Republicans favoring reform, dubbed Mugwumps, bolted their party to support Democrat Grover Cleveland, a reformer.

- **Farm Problems**  Farmers had serious grievances at the end of the nineteenth century. Commodity prices were falling because of domestic overproduction and international competition, and many farmers had gone into debt buying new machinery on credit and paying the railroads exorbitant rates to ship their goods to market. In addition, high tariffs allowed manufacturers to raise the price of goods that farmers needed.

- **Farm Movements**  Despite farmers' traditional reluctance to organize, many reacted to their difficulties by joining the Granger movement, which promoted farmer-owned cooperatives and, subsequently, Farmers' Alliances, grassroots social organizations that also promoted political action. Influenced by their success, delegates from farm, labor, and reform organizations in 1892 established the People's party, also known as the Populist party. Populists sought greater regulation of business by the federal government and the free coinage of silver (because they hoped that the ensuing inflation of the money supply would make it easier for them to repay their debts).

- **Rise of Populism**  The Populists did well in 1892 and, with the depression of 1893, had high hopes for the next presidential election. But the Democrat, William Jennings Bryan, stole the silver issue from the Populists. The Populists thus fused with the Democrats, but Bryan lost the election to the Republicans. The People's party did not recover from the blow.

- **Southern Segregation**  By 1900 elite southern whites had regained control of state governments; prominent black Republicans had been squeezed out of political positions; and black men were being kept from exercising their right to vote. Segregation became the social norm. Some African American leaders, most prominently Booker T. Washington, believed that by showing deference to whites, blacks could avoid violence while quietly acquiring an education and property. Others, like Ida B. Wells and W. E. B. Du Bois, wanted to fight segregation and lynching through the courts and the political system.

## CHRONOLOGY

| | |
|---|---|
| **1877** | Rutherford B. Hayes is inaugurated president |
| **1877** | Supreme Court issues *Munn v. Illinois* decision |
| **1881** | James A. Garfield is assassinated |
| **1883** | Congress passes the Pendleton Civil Service Reform Act |
| **1886** | Supreme Court issues *Wabash, St. Louis, and Pacific Railroad Company v. Illinois* decision |
| **1887** | Interstate Commerce Commission is created |
| **1890** | Congress passes the Sherman Anti-Trust Act, the Sherman Silver Purchase Act, and the McKinley Tariff |
| **1892** | People's party drafts its Omaha platform |
| **1893** | Economic depression affects a substantial proportion of the population |
| **1890** | Mississippi Plan resegregates public facilities by race |
| **1895** | Booker T. Washington delivers his Atlanta Compromise speech |
| **1896** | Supreme Court issues *Plessy v. Ferguson* decision |
| **1909** | National Association for the Advancement of Colored People (NAACP) is created |

## KEY TERMS & NAMES

# Part Six

# MODERN AMERICA

he United States entered the twentieth century on a wave of unrelenting change, not all of it beneficial. In 1800, the nation was a rural, agrarian society largely detached from the concerns of international affairs. By 1900, the United States had become a highly industrialized urban society with a growing involvement in world politics and international commerce. In other words, the nation was on the threshold of modernity.

The prospect of modernity both excited and scared Americans. Old truths and beliefs clashed with unsettling scientific discoveries and social practices. People debated the legitimacy of Darwinism, the existence of God, the dangers of jazz, and proposals to prohibit the sale of alcoholic beverages. The advent of automobiles and airplanes helped shrink distance, and such communications innovations as radio and film helped strengthen a sense of national consciousness. In the process, the United States began to emerge from its isolationist shell. Throughout most of the nineteenth century, policy makers had sought to isolate America from the intrigues and conflicts of the great European powers. As early as 1780, John Adams had warned Congress against involving the United States in the affairs of Europe. "Our business with them, and theirs with us," he wrote, "is commerce, not politics, much less war."

With only a few exceptions, statesmen during the nineteenth century followed such advice. Noninvolvement in foreign wars and nonintervention in the internal affairs of foreign governments formed the pillars of American foreign policy until the end of the century. During the 1890s, however, expanding commercial interests around the world led Americans to broaden the horizons of their concerns. Imperialism was the grand imperative among the great European powers, and a growing number of American expansionists demanded that the United States also adopt a global ambition and join in the hunt for new territories and markets. Such mixed motives helped spark the War of 1898 and helped to justify the resulting acquisition of colonies outside the continental United States. Entangling alliances with European powers soon followed.

The outbreak of the Great War in Europe in 1914 posed an even greater challenge to the tradition of isolation and nonintervention. The prospect of a German victory over the French and the British threatened the European balance of power, which had long ensured the security of the United States. By 1917 it appeared that Germany might emerge triumphant and begin to menace the Western Hemisphere. Woodrow Wilson's crusade to transform international affairs in accordance with his idealistic principles during the First World War severed American foreign policy from its isolationist moorings. It also spawned a prolonged debate about the role of the United States in world affairs, a debate that World War II would resolve for a time on the side of internationalism.

While the United States was entering the world stage as a formidable military power, it was also settling into its role as a great industrial power. Cities and factories sprouted across the landscape. An abundance of new jobs and affordable farmland served as a magnet attracting millions of immigrants from nearly every landmass on the globe. They were not always welcomed, nor were they readily assimilated. Ethnic and racial strife, as well as labor agitation, increased at the turn of the century. In the midst of such social turmoil and unparalleled economic development, reformers made their first sustained attempt to adapt political and social institutions to the realities of the industrial age. The worst excesses and injustices of urban-industrial development—corporate monopolies, child labor, political corruption, hazardous working conditions, urban ghettos—were finally addressed in a comprehensive way. During the Progressive Era (1890–1917), local, state, and federal governments sought to rein in the excesses of industrial capitalism and develop a more rational and efficient public policy.

A conservative Republican resurgence challenged the notion of the new regulatory state during the 1920s. Free enterprise and corporate capitalism witnessed a dramatic revival. But the stock market crash of 1929 helped propel the United States and the world into the worst economic downturn in history. The unprecedented severity of the Great Depression renewed  public demands for federal programs to protect the general welfare. "This nation asks for action," declared President Franklin Delano Roosevelt in his 1933 inaugural address. The many New Deal initiatives and agencies instituted by Roosevelt and his Democratic administration created the framework for a welfare state that has since served as the basis for public policy.

The New Deal helped revive public confidence and put people back to work, but it did not end the Great Depression. It took a world war to restore full employment. The necessity of mobilizing the nation in support of the Second World War also accelerated the growth of the federal government. And the unparalleled scope of the war helped catapult the United States into a leadership role in world politics. The use of atomic bombs to end the war against Japan ushered in a new era of nuclear diplomacy that held the fate of the world in the balance. For all of the new creature comforts associated with modern life, Americans in 1945 found themselves living amid an array of new anxieties.

# 22

## SEIZING AN AMERICAN EMPIRE

FOCUS QUESTIONS          (S)   wwnorton.com/studyspace

- What motivated America's "new imperialism"?
- What was the role of religion as a motive for American territorial expansion?
- What were the causes of the War of 1898?
- What did America gain from the War of 1898?
- What were the main achievements of President Roosevelt's foreign policy?

Throughout the nineteenth century Americans displayed what one senator called "only a languid interest" in foreign affairs. The overriding priorities were at home: industrial development, western settlement, and domestic politics. Foreign relations simply were not important to the vast majority of Americans. After the Civil War, an isolationist mood swept across the United States as the country basked in its geographic advantages: wide oceans as buffers, the powerful British navy situated between America and the powers of Europe, and militarily weak neighbors in the Western Hemisphere.

Yet the notion of the United States having been ordained by God to expand its territory and its democratic values remained alive in the decades after the Civil War. Several prominent political and business leaders argued that sustaining rapid industrial development required the acquisition—or conquest—of foreign territories in order to gain easier access to vital raw materials. In addition, as their exports grew, American manufacturers and commercial farmers became increasingly intertwined in the world economy. This growing involvement in international commerce, in turn, required an expanded naval force to protect the shipping lanes from hostile action. And a modern steam-powered navy needed bases where its ships could replenish their supplies of coal and water.

For these and other reasons, the United States during the last quarter of the nineteenth century expanded its military presence and territorial possessions beyond the Western Hemisphere. Its motives for doing so were a mixture of moral and religious idealism (spreading the benefits of democratic capitalism and Christianity to "backward peoples"), popular assumptions of racial superiority, and naked greed. Such confusion over ideals and purposes ensured that the results of America's imperialist adventures would be decidedly mixed. Within the span of a few months in 1898 the United States, which was born in a revolution against British colonial rule, would itself become an imperial power whose expanding overseas commitments would have unforeseen—and tragic—consequences.

## Toward the New Imperialism

By the late nineteenth century, the major European nations had unleashed a new surge of imperialism in Africa and Asia, where they had seized territory, established colonies, and promoted economic exploitation, racial superiority, and Christian evangelism. Writing in 1902, the British economist J. A. Hobson declared that imperialism was "the most powerful factor in the current politics of the Western world."

IMPERIALISM IN A GLOBAL CONTEXT    Western imperialism and industrial growth generated a quest for new markets, new sources of raw materials, and new opportunities for investment. The result was a widespread process of aggressive imperial expansion into Africa and Asia. Beginning in the 1880s, the British, French, Belgians, Italians, Dutch, Spanish, and Germans used military force and political guile to conquer those continents. Each of the imperial nations, including the United States, dispatched missionaries to convert conquered peoples to Christianity. By 1900, some 18,000 missionaries were scattered around the world. Often the conversion to Christianity was the first step in the loss of a culture's indigenous traditions. Western religious efforts also influenced the colonial power structure. A British expansionist explained the global ambitions of the imperialist nations: "Today, power and domination rather than freedom and independence are the ideas that appeal to the imagination of the masses—and the national ideal has given way to the imperial." This imperial outlook triggered clashes among the Western powers that would lead to unprecedented conflict in the twentieth century.

AMERICAN IMPERIALISTS    As the European nations expanded their control over much of the rest of the world, the United States also began to acquire new territories. A small yet vocal and influential group of public officials aggressively promoted the idea of acquiring overseas possessions. The expansionists included Senators Albert J. Beveridge of Indiana and Henry Cabot Lodge of Massachusetts, as well as Theodore Roosevelt and naval captain Alfred Thayer Mahan.

During the 1880s, Captain Mahan had become a leading advocate of sea power and Western imperialism. In 1890 he published ***The Influence of Sea Power upon History, 1660–1783***, in which he argued that national greatness and prosperity flowed from maritime power. Mahan insisted that modern economic development required a powerful navy, a strong merchant marine, foreign commerce, colonies, and naval bases. A self-described imperialist, Mahan championed America's "destiny" to control the Caribbean, build an isthmian canal to connect the Pacific and the Caribbean, and spread Western civilization in the Pacific. His ideas were widely circulated in popular journals and within political and military circles. **Theodore Roosevelt**, the war-loving assistant secretary of the navy, ordered a copy of Mahan's book for every American warship. Yet even before Mahan's writings became influential, a gradual expansion of the navy had begun. In 1880, the nation had fewer than a hundred seagoing vessels, many of them rusting or rotting at the docks. By 1896, eleven powerful new steel battleships had been built or authorized.

IMPERIALIST THEORY    Claims of racial superiority bolstered the new imperialist spirit. Spokesmen in each industrial nation, including the United States, used the arguments of social Darwinism to justify economic exploitation and territorial conquest. Among nations as among individuals, expansionists claimed, the fittest survive and prevail. John Fiske, a historian and popular lecturer on Darwinism, developed racial corollaries from Charles Darwin's ideas. In *American Political Ideas Viewed from the Standpoint of Universal History* (1885), he stressed the superior character of "Anglo-Saxon" institutions and peoples. The English-speaking "race," he argued, was destined to dominate the globe and transform the institutions, traditions, language— even the blood—of the world's peoples. Josiah Strong added the sanction of religion to theories of racial and national superiority. In his best-selling book *Our Country: Its Possible Future and Its Present Crisis* (1885), Strong asserted that the "Anglo-Saxon" embodied two great ideas: civil liberty and "a pure spiritual Christianity." The Anglo-Saxon was "divinely commissioned to be, in a peculiar sense, his brother's keeper."

## Expansion in the Pacific

For Josiah Strong and other expansionists, Asia offered an especially alluring target for American imperialism. In 1866, the secretary of state, William H. Seward, had predicted that the United States must inevitably exercise commercial domination "on the Pacific Ocean, and its islands and continents." Eager for American manufacturers to exploit Asian markets, Seward believed the United States first had to remove all foreign interests from the northern Pacific coast and gain access to that region's valuable ports. To that end, he cast covetous eyes on the British colony of British Columbia, sandwiched between Russian America (Alaska) and the Washington Territory.

Late in 1866, while encouraging British Columbians to consider making their colony a U.S. territory, Seward learned of Russia's desire to sell Alaska. He leaped at the opportunity, in part because its acquisition might influence British Columbia to join the union. In 1867, the United States bought Alaska for $7.2 million, thus removing Russia, the most recent colonial power, from North America. Critics scoffed at "Seward's folly" of buying the Alaskan "icebox," but it proved to be the biggest bargain since the Louisiana Purchase. Seward's successors at the State Department sustained his expansionist vision. Acquiring key ports on islands in the Pacific Ocean was the major focus of overseas activity throughout the rest of the nineteenth century. Two island groups occupied especially strategic positions: Samoa and Hawaii (the Sandwich Islands). Both had major harbors, Pago Pago and Pearl Harbor, respectively. In the years after the Civil War, American interest in those islands deepened.

SAMOA   In 1878, the Samoans signed a treaty with the United States that granted a naval base at Pago Pago and extraterritoriality for Americans (meaning that in Samoa, Americans remained subject only to U.S. law), exchanged trade concessions, and called for the United States to help resolve any disputes with other nations. The Senate ratified this accord, and in the following year the German and British governments worked out similar arrangements with other islands in the Samoan group. There matters rested

**American expansion**

In a critical comment on William H. Seward's 1867 purchase of Alaska, this cartoon represents the territory as a block of ice labeled "Russian America."

until civil war broke out in Samoa in 1887. A peace conference in Berlin in 1889 established a protectorate over Samoa, with Germany, Great Britain, and the United States in an uneasy partnership.

HAWAII   In Hawaii, the Americans had a clearer field to exploit. The islands, a united kingdom since 1795, had a sizable population of American missionaries and sugar planters and were strategically more important to the United States than Samoa. In 1875, the kingdom had signed a reciprocal trade agreement, according to which Hawaiian sugar would enter the United States duty-free, and Hawaii promised that none of its territory would be leased or granted to a third power. This agreement resulted in a boom in sugar production, and American planters in Hawaii soon formed an economic elite that built its fortunes on cheap immigrant labor, mainly Chinese and Japanese. By the 1890s, the native Hawaiian population had been reduced to a minority by smallpox and other foreign diseases, and Asians quickly became the most numerous group.

In 1885, President Grover Cleveland called the Hawaiian Islands "the stepping-stone to the growing trade of the Pacific." Two years later, Americans in Hawaii forced the king to convert the monarchy to a constitutional government, which they dominated. In 1890, however, the McKinley Tariff

**Cutting sugar cane**

Heightened demand for cheap labor in the sugar cane fields dramatically affected the demographic and political conditions of the Hawaiian islands.

destroyed Hawaii's favored position in the sugar trade by putting the sugar of all countries on the duty-free list and granting growers in the continental United States a 2¢ subsidy per pound of sugar. This change led to an economic crisis in Hawaii and brought political turmoil as well.

In 1891, when **Liliuokalani**, the king's sister, ascended the throne, she tried to eliminate the political power exercised by American planters. Two years later, Hawaii's white population revolted and seized power. The U.S. ambassador brought in marines to support the coup. As he cheerfully reported to the secretary of state, "The Hawaiian pear is now fully ripe, and this is the golden hour for the United States to pluck it." Within a month a committee of the new government in Hawaii turned up in Washington, D. C. with a treaty calling for the island nation to be annexed to the United States.

President Cleveland then sent a special commissioner to investigate the situation in Hawaii. The commissioner removed the marines and reported that the Americans in Hawaii had acted improperly. Most Hawaiians opposed annexation to the United States, the commissioner found. He concluded that the revolution had been engineered mainly by the American planters hoping to take advantage of the subsidy for sugar grown in the

United States. Cleveland proposed to restore the queen to power in return for amnesty to the revolutionists. The provisional government controlled by the sugar planters refused to give up power, however, and on July 4, 1894, it created the Republic of Hawaii, which included in its constitution a standing provision for American annexation. In 1897, when William McKinley became president, he was looking for an excuse to annex the islands. "We need Hawaii," he claimed, "just as much and a good deal more than we did California. It is manifest destiny." When the Japanese, also hoping to take over the islands, sent a naval flotilla to Hawaii, McKinley responded by sending U.S. warships and asked the Sen-

**Queen Liliuokalani**

The Hawaiian queen sought to preserve her nation's independence.

ate to approve a treaty to annex the islands. When the Senate could not muster the two-thirds majority needed to approve the treaty, McKinley used a joint resolution of the House and the Senate to achieve his aims. The resolution passed by simple majorities in both houses, and Hawaii was annexed by the United States in the summer of 1898.

## THE WAR OF 1898

Until the 1890s, reservations about acquiring overseas possessions had checked America's drive to expand. Suddenly, in 1898 and 1899, such inhibitions collapsed, and the United States aggressively thrust its way to the far reaches of the Pacific. The spark for this explosion of imperialism lay not in Asia but in Cuba, a Spanish colony ninety miles southwest of the southern tip of Florida. Ironically, the chief motive was a sense of outrage at another country's imperialism. Americans wanted the Cubans to gain their independence from Spain.

"CUBA LIBRE" Throughout the second half of the nineteenth century, Cubans had repeatedly revolted against centuries-old Spanish rule, only to be ruthlessly suppressed. As one of Spain's oldest colonies, Cuba was a major export market for the mother country. Yet American sugar and mining companies had also invested heavily in Cuba. The United States in fact traded more with Cuba than Spain did.

On February 24, 1895, insurrection again broke out as Cubans waged guerrilla warfare against Spanish troops. In 1896 the Spanish commanding general, Valeriano Weyler, adopted a controversial policy whereby his troops herded Cubans behind Spanish lines, housing them in detention (*reconcentrado*) centers so that no one could join the insurrections by night and appear peaceful by day. In some of the centers, a combination of tropical climate, poor food, and unsanitary conditions quickly produced a heavy toll of disease and starvation. Tens of thousands of Cuban peasants died in the primitive camps.

Events in Cuba supplied dramatic headlines for newspapers and magazines. **William Randolph Hearst's *New York Journal*** and **Joseph Pulitzer's *New York World*** were at the time locked in a monumental competition for readers, striving to outdo each other with sensational headlines about every Spanish atrocity in Cuba, real or invented. "It was a battle of gigantic proportions," one journalist later wrote, "in which the sufferings of Cuba merely chanced to furnish some of the most convenient ammunition." Hearst, for example, christened the Spanish commander "Butcher Weyler." The newspapers' sensationalism as well as their intentional efforts to manipulate public opinion came to be called **yellow journalism**. Hearst wanted a war against Spain to catapult the United States into global significance. Once war was declared against Spain, Hearst took credit for it. One of his newspaper headlines blared: "HOW DO YOU LIKE THE JOURNAL'S WAR?"

PRESSURE FOR WAR    At the outset of the Cuban rebellion in 1895, President Grover Cleveland tried to protect U.S. business interests in Cuba while avoiding military involvement. Mounting public sympathy for the rebel cause prompted acute concern in Congress, however. By concurrent resolutions on April 6, 1896, the House and Senate endorsed the granting of official recognition to the Cuban rebels. After his inauguration in March 1897, President William McKinley continued the posture of sympathetic neutrality, but with each passing month Americans called for greater assistance to the Cuban insurgents. In 1897, Spain offered Cubans autonomy (self-government without formal independence) in return for ending the rebellion. The Cubans rejected the offer. Spain was impaled on the horns of a dilemma, unable to end the insurrection and unready to give up Cuba.

Early in 1898, events pushed the two nations into a war that neither government wanted. On January 25, the U.S. battleship *Maine* docked in Havana harbor, ostensibly on a courtesy call. On February 9, the *New York*

**The sinking of the *Maine* in Havana Harbor**

The uproar created by the incident and its coverage in the "yellow press" helped to push President William McKinley to declare war.

*Journal* released the text of a letter from the Spanish ambassador Depuy de Lôme to a friend in Havana. In the so-called **de Lôme letter**, which had been stolen from the post office by a Cuban spy, de Lôme called President McKinley "weak and a bidder for the admiration of the crowd, besides being a would-be politician who tries to leave a door open behind himself while keeping on good terms with the jingoes of his party." De Lôme resigned to prevent further embarrassment to his government.

Six days later, during the night of February 15, 1898, the *Maine* exploded and sank in Havana harbor, with a horrible loss of 260 men. The ship's captain, one of only 84 survivors, scribbled a telegram to Washington: "*Maine* blown up in Havana Harbor at nine forty tonight and destroyed. Many wounded and doubtless more killed or drowned. . . . Public opinion should be suspended until further report."

Although years later the sinking was ruled an accident caused by a coal explosion, those eager for a war with Spain in 1898 saw no need to withhold judgment. Upon learning about the loss of the *Maine*, the thirty-nine-year-old assistant secretary of the navy, Theodore Roosevelt, told a friend that he "would give anything if President McKinley would order the fleet to Havana tomorrow." He called the sinking "an act of dirty treachery on the part of the Spaniards." The United States, he claimed, "needs a war." The outcry against Spain rose in a crescendo with the words "Remember the *Maine*!" The weight of outraged public opinion and the influence of Republican militants such as Roosevelt and the president's closest friend, Senator Henry Cabot Lodge, eroded McKinley's neutrality. On March 9, the president asked Congress for a $50 million appropriation for defense. Still McKinley sought to avoid war, as did many business leaders. Their caution infuriated Roosevelt. "We will have this war for the freedom of Cuba," he fumed on March 26, "in spite of the timidity of the commercial interests." Roosevelt grumbled to a friend that McKinley "has no more backbone than a chocolate éclair." The president grew so frustrated by the jingoistic Roo-

**News announcements, 1898**

A crowd watches men post news announcements outside the *New York Tribune* building during the War of 1898.

sevelt that he refused to see him. "He is too pugnacious," McKinley objected. "I want peace."

In March 1898 McKinley demanded that Spain declare a cease-fire in Cuba by April 1. The Spanish government grudgingly complied. On April 10, the Spanish agreed that the Cubans could form an autonomous government, but the message came too late. The following day, McKinley asked Congress for authority to use armed forces in Cuba. On April 20, Congress declared Cuba independent and demanded the withdrawal of Spanish forces. The **Teller Amendment**, added on the Senate floor to the war resolution, disclaimed any intention of the U.S. eventually taking control of Cuba. McKinley signed the war resolution, and a copy went off to the Spanish government. Never has an American war, so casually begun and so enthusiastically supported, generated such unexpected and far-reaching consequences.

Why such a rush to war after the American ambassador had predicted that Spain would cave in before the summer was out? Chiefly because public pressure demanded war. Leaders of the business community wanted a quick resolution of the problem. Still, it is fair to ask why McKinley did not take a stronger and more patient stand for peace. He might have defied Congress and public opinion, but in the end he decided that the political risk was too high. The ultimate blame for war, if blame must be levied, belongs to the American people for letting themselves be whipped into such a hostile frenzy.

McKinley called for 125,000 volunteers to supplement the 28,000 men in the U.S. Army. Among the first to enlist was the man who most lusted for war against Spain: Theodore Roosevelt. His wife and friends in the Congress urged him to remain at his post with the navy. Even President McKinley told Roosevelt to stay put, but the militant New Yorker felt he had "to live up to the doctrines I have tried to preach." Roosevelt viewed war as a means of testing his own masculinity and fulfilling the nation's destiny to be a great power.

MANILA   The war with Spain lasted only 114 days. The conflict was barely under way before the U.S. Navy produced a spectacular victory in an unexpected location in the Pacific Ocean: Manila Bay in the Philippines, an archipelago of seven thousand islands some seven thousand miles away. Just before war had been declared, Theodore Roosevelt, still serving as the assistant secretary of the navy, had ordered (without getting the permission of his superiors) Commodore **George Dewey**, commander of the small U.S. fleet in Asia, to engage Spanish forces in the Philippines in case of war in Cuba. President McKinley had approved the orders.

Commodore Dewey arrived late on April 30 with four cruisers and two gunboats, and they quickly destroyed or captured all the outdated Spanish warships in Manila Bay without suffering any major damage themselves. Dewey was now in awkward possession of the bay without any ground forces to go onshore. Promised reinforcements, he stayed while German and British warships cruised offshore like watchful vultures, ready to take control of the Philippines if the United States did not do so. In the meantime, **Emilio Aguinaldo**, the leader of the Filipino nationalist movement, declared the Philippines independent on June 12. With Aguinaldo's help, Dewey's forces entered Manila on August 13. The Spanish garrison preferred to surrender to the Americans rather than to the vengeful Filipinos. News of the American victory sent President McKinley scurrying to find a map of Asia to locate "these darned islands" now occupied by U.S. soldiers and sailors.

THE CUBAN CAMPAIGN    While these events transpired halfway around the world, the fighting in Cuba reached a surprisingly quick climax. The U.S. Navy blockaded the Spanish navy inside Santiago harbor while some 17,000 American troops hastily assembled at Tampa, Florida. One prominent unit was the First Volunteer Cavalry, better known as the **Rough Riders**, a regiment with "special qualifications" made up of former Ivy League athletes, ex-convicts, Cherokee, Choctaw, Chickasaw, Pawnee, and Creek Indians, and southwestern sharpshooters. Of course, the Rough Riders are best remembered because Lieutenant Colonel Theodore Roosevelt was second in command. Roosevelt did not care about the sordid backgrounds of some of the Rough Riders: "Wherever they came from, and whatever their social position," he wrote, they "possessed in common the traits of hardihood and a thirst for adventure" that he himself displayed. One of the Rough Riders said that Lieutenant Colonel Roosevelt was "nervous, energetic, virile. He may wear out some day, but he will never rust out." Roosevelt wrote President McKinley that he hoped "we will be put in Cuba with the very first troops, the sooner the better." When the 578 Rough Riders, accompanied by a gaggle of reporters and photographers, landed in oppressive heat on June 22, 1898, at the undefended southeastern tip of Cuba, they were the first American troops ever sent overseas. But chaos ensued upon their arrival, as their horses and mules were mistakenly sent elsewhere, leaving the Rough Riders to become the "Weary Walkers." Only Roosevelt ended up with his horse, Little Texas.

Land and sea battles around Santiago quickly broke Spanish resistance. On July 1, about seven thousand U.S. soldiers took the fortified village of

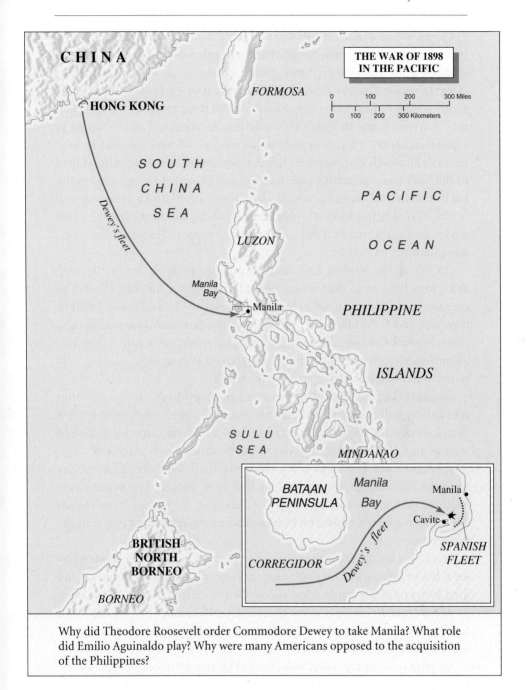

Why did Theodore Roosevelt order Commodore Dewey to take Manila? What role did Emilio Aguinaldo play? Why were many Americans opposed to the acquisition of the Philippines?

El Caney. While a much larger force attacked San Juan Hill, a smaller unit, including the dismounted Rough Riders together with African American soldiers from two cavalry units, with Roosevelt at their head yelling "Charge!", seized nearby Kettle Hill. Roosevelt later claimed that he "would rather have led that charge than [have] served three terms in the U.S. Senate." A friend wrote to Roosevelt's wife that her husband was "reveling in victory and gore." Thanks to widespread media coverage, much of it exaggerated, Roosevelt had become a home-front legend, the most beloved hero of the brief war. Roosevelt's oversized ego and penchant for self-promotion led him to lobby Congress—unsuccessfully—to award him a Congressional Medal of Honor for his much-publicized headlong gallop at the head of his troops in Cuba. (President Bill Clinton finally awarded Roosevelt the medal posthumously in 2001.)

On July 3, the Spanish navy made a gallant run for it, but its decrepit ships were little more than sitting ducks for the newer American fleet. The casualties were as one-sided as those at Manila: 474 Spanish were killed or wounded and 1,750 taken prisoner, while only one American was killed and one wounded. Spanish officials in Santiago surrendered on July 17. On July 25 an American force moved into Spanish-held Puerto Rico, meeting only minor resistance as it took control of the island.

The next day, the Spanish government in Madrid sued for peace. After discussions lasting two weeks, an armistice was signed on August 12, less than four months after the war's start and the day before Americans entered Manila. In Cuba, the Spanish forces formally surrendered to the U.S. commander, boarded ships, and sailed for Spain. Excluded from the ceremony were the Cubans, for whom the war had been fought. The peace treaty specified that Spain should give up Cuba and that the United States should annex Puerto Rico and occupy Manila pending the transfer of power in the Philippines.

In all, over 60,000 Spanish soldiers died of disease or wounds in the four-month war. Among the 274,000 Americans who served during the war, 5,462 died, but only 379 in battle. Most succumbed to malaria, typhoid, dysentery, or yellow fever. At such a cost the United States was launched onto the world scene as a great power, with all the benefits—and burdens—of a new colonial empire of its own.

America's role in the world was changed forever by the campaign, for the United States emerged as an imperial power. Halfway through the brief conflict in Cuba, John Hay, soon to be secretary of state, wrote a letter to his close friend, Theodore Roosevelt. In acknowledging Roosevelt's trial by fire, Hay called it "a splendid little war, begun with the highest motives, carried

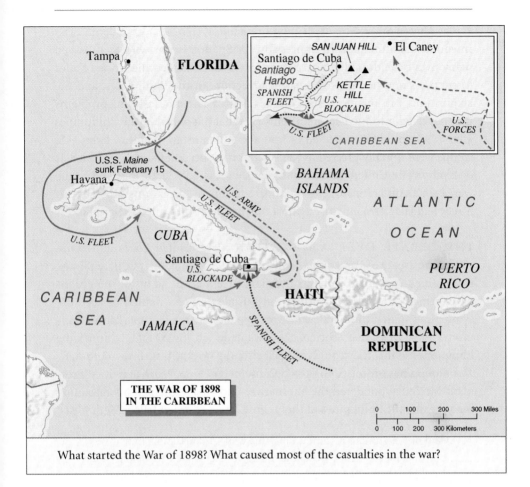

THE WAR OF 1898
IN THE CARIBBEAN

What started the War of 1898? What caused most of the casualties in the war?

on with magnificent intelligence and spirit, favored by that fortune that loves the brave."

The end of the "splendid little war" was also the pathetic end of Spain's once-great New World empire. Fighting backward Spain, said the young writer Sherwood Anderson, was "like robbing an old gypsy woman in a vacant lot at night after the fair." Victory in the War of 1898 boosted American self-confidence and reinforced the self-serving American belief, tinged with racism, that the nation had a "manifest destiny" to reshape the world in its own image. Josiah Strong had boasted in 1895 that Americans "are a race of unequaled energy" who represent "the largest liberty, the purest Christianity, the highest civilization" in the world. "Can anyone doubt that this race . . . is destined to dispossess many weaker races, assimilate others, and mold the remainder until . . . it has Anglo-Saxonized mankind?"

The United States liberated Spain's remaining colonies, yet in some cases it would substitute its own oppression for Spain's. If war with Spain saved many lives by ending the insurrection in Cuba, it also led the United States to suppress another anti-colonial insurrection, in the Philippines, and the acquisition of its own imperial colonies created a host of festering problems that persisted into the twentieth century. What happened in the Philippines after 1898 would be replicated in Iraq and Afghanistan a century later: U.S. troops were initially greeted as saviors but then became quickly despised as occupiers. The United States triumphantly declared a victorious end to the war, even as bitter "insurgent" fighting continued. Allegations of American forces regularly using torture against the insurgents horrified the public.

**THE DEBATE OVER ANNEXATION**  The United States and Spain signed the Treaty of Paris on December 10, 1898, ending the war between the two nations. It granted Cuba its independence, but the status of the Philippines remained unresolved. American business leaders wanted to keep the Philippines so that they could more easily penetrate the vast markets of populous China. Missionary societies also wanted the United States to annex the Philippines so that they could bring Christianity to "the little brown brother." The Philippines promised to provide a useful base for all such activities. President McKinley pondered the alternatives and later explained his reasoning for annexing the Philippines (a "holy cause") to a group of fellow Methodists:

> And one night late it came to me this way—I don't know how it was, but it came: (1) that we could not give them back to Spain—that would be cowardly and dishonorable; (2) that we could not turn them over to France or Germany—our commercial rivals in the Orient— that would be bad business and discreditable; (3) that we could not leave them to themselves—they were unfit for self-government—and they would soon have anarchy and misrule over there worse than Spain's was; and (4) that there was nothing left for us to do but to take them all, and to educate the Filipinos, and uplift and civilize and Christianize them, and by God's grace do the very best we could by them, as our fellowmen for whom Christ also died. And then I went to bed, and went to sleep and slept soundly.

In one brief statement, McKinley had summarized the motivating ideas of American imperialism: (1) national glory, (2) commerce, (3) racial superiority, and (4) evangelism. American negotiators in Paris finally offered the Spanish $20 million for the Philippines, Puerto Rico, and Guam, a Spanish-controlled island in the Pacific with a valuable harbor.

Meanwhile, Americans had taken other giant steps in the Pacific. Congress had annexed Hawaii in the midst of the War of 1898. In 1898, the United States had also claimed Wake Island, located between Guam and the Hawaiian Islands, which would become a vital link in a future transpacific telegraph cable. Then, in 1899, Germany and the United States agreed to partition the Samoa Islands. The United States annexed the easternmost islands; Germany took the rest.

By early 1899, the Treaty of Paris, ending the War of 1898, had yet to be ratified in the Senate, where most Democrats and Populists and some Republicans opposed it. Anti-imperialists argued that acquisition of the Philippines would corrupt the American principle, dating back to the Revolution, that people should be self-governing rather than colonial subjects. Opponents also noted the inconsistency of liberating Cuba and annexing the Philippines, as well as the danger that the Philippines would become impossible to defend if a foreign power such as Japan attacked. The opposition might have been strong enough to kill the treaty had not the Democrat William Jennings Bryan influenced the vote for approval. Ending the war, he argued, would open the way for the future independence of the Philippines. His support convinced enough Democrats to enable passage of the peace treaty in the Senate on February 6, 1899, by the narrowest of margins: only one vote more than the necessary two thirds. Senator Henry Cabot Lodge of Massachusetts described his efforts to gain approval of the treaty as "the closest, hardest fight" he had witnessed in the Senate. He also admitted that if U.S. troops had not provoked a clash with Filipino insurgents the weekend before, the treaty would have been rejected and the Philippines would have been set free.

But McKinley had no intention of granting the Philippines independence. He insisted that the United States take control of the islands as an act of "benevolent assimilation" and launch America's first exercise in nation building. In February 1899, in the incident Senator Lodge referred to, an American soldier outside Manila fired on soldiers in the Filipino Army of Liberation, and two of them were killed. Suddenly, the United States found itself in a new war, this time a crusade to suppress the Filipino independence movement. Since Aguinaldo's forces, called *insurrectos*, were more or less in control of the islands outside Manila, what followed was largely a brutal American war of conquest.

THE PHILIPPINE-AMERICAN WAR   The American effort to quash Filipino nationalism lasted three years, eventually involved some 126,000 U.S. troops, and took the lives of hundreds of thousands of Filipinos (most of them civilians) and 4,234 American soldiers. The nature of the war also cost

**Turmoil in the Philippines**

Emilio Aguinaldo (seated third from right) and other leaders of the Filipino insurgence.

the United States much of its professed benevolence. It was a sordid conflict, with grisly massacres committed by both sides. It did not help matters that many American soldiers referred to their Filipino opponents as "niggers."

Within the first year of the war in the Philippines, American newspapers had begun to report an array of atrocities committed by U.S. troops— villages burned, prisoners tortured and executed. A favorite means of torture was the "water cure," an old technique developed in the Spanish Inquisition during the sixteenth century whereby a captured Filipino insurgent would be placed on his back on the ground. While soldiers stood on his out-stretched arms and feet, they pried his mouth open, holding it in place with a stick. They then poured salt water into the captive's mouth and nose until his stomach was bloated, whereupon the soldiers would stomp on the pris-oner's abdomen, forcing out of his mouth and nose all of the water, now mixed with gastric juices. This process would be repeated until the captive told the soldiers what they wanted to know—or he died. A Senate investiga-tion revealed the scope of such atrocities, but the senators did nothing. Their attitude resembled that of President Theodore Roosevelt, who was con-vinced that "nobody was seriously damaged" by the "water cure," whereas "Filipinos had inflicted terrible tortures upon our own people." The "dark abuses" stained American claims of solely noble intentions in the Philip-pines. Thus did the United States alienate and destroy a Filipino independence movement modeled after America's own struggle for independence from Great Britain. Organized Filipino resistance had collapsed by the end of 1899, but even after the American capture of Aguinaldo in 1901, sporadic guerrilla action lasted until mid-1902.

Against the backdrop of this nasty guerrilla war, the great debate over imperialism continued in the United States. In 1899 several anti-imperialist groups combined to form the American Anti-Imperialist League. The league attracted members representing many shades of opinion. Former presidents Grover Cleveland and Benjamin Harrison urged President McKinley to withdraw U.S. forces from the Philippines. Andrew Carnegie footed the bills for the League; and on imperialism, at least, the union leader Samuel Gompers agreed with the steel king. Presidents Charles Eliot of Harvard and David Starr Jordan of Stanford University supported the group, along with the social reformer Jane Addams. The drive for imperialism, said the philosopher William James, had caused the nation to "puke up its ancient soul."

RELIGION AND EMPIRE   Many religious leaders energetically supported the war against Spain and the imperial conquest of Spain's colonies around the globe. In Boston, for example, the *Herald* reported that Protestant ministers were the most rabid advocates of the new imperialism because

**"The water cure"**

A prisoner of war being tortured during the Philippine-American War.

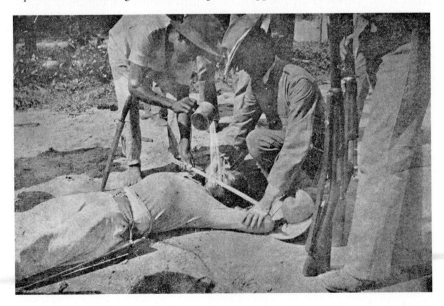

it afforded them opportunities for "evangelization of the world." Global missionary activity had soared after the Civil War as religious organizations asserted that Christianity was the "highest and purest form of religion in the world." Evangelicals eagerly spread the blessings of Christianity around the globe.

Protestant missionaries and their supporting organizations unabashedly promoted the global superiority of the Anglo-Saxon "race" and the Christian religion, and they were often virulently anti-Catholic. The *California Christian Advocate*, for example, cheered the declaration of war with Catholic Spain in 1898: "The war is the Kingdom of God coming!" Another Protestant magazine, the *Pacific Advocate*, announced that "the cross will follow the flag" as "righteous" American soldiers prepared to liberate Cuba from Spanish control. Another evangelical declared that missionary activity was itself "a war of conquest." For Catholic Americans, however, the war against Spain, one of the oldest and most intensely Catholic nations in the world, was more problematic. They objected to Protestant plans to evangelize the Catholic Cubans. A Catholic official warned that efforts to convert the Catholics of Cuba, Puerto Rico, and the Philippines "would be the speediest and most effective way to make the inhabitants of those islands discontented and opposed to America."

In the debate over America's annexing the Spanish colonies, religious arguments held sway. Senator Albert J. Beveridge, an ardent imperialist, declared that "we are God's chosen people." The United States, he added, had a "sacred duty" to bring the blessings of American Christianity to the lands acquired from Spain. Others shared this notion of providential responsibility for the "backward" peoples of the world. Lyman Abbott, a prominent Protestant clergyman and editor, said that America was a divine instrument of Christian imperialism. It was, he said, "the function of the Anglo-Saxon race to confer these gifts of civilization, through law, commerce, and education, on the uncivilized people of the world." Abbott lambasted the anti-imperialists:

> It is said that we have no right to go to a land occupied by barbaric people and interfere with their life. It is said that if they prefer barbarism they have a right to be barbarians. I deny the right of a barbaric people to retain possession of any quarter of the globe. What I have already said I reaffirm: barbarism has no rights which civilization is bound to respect. Barbarians have rights which civilized people are bound to respect, but they have no right to their barbarism.

Abbott and others insisted that the United States could not shirk its providential duty to "save" the former Spanish colonies from degenerating into chaos.

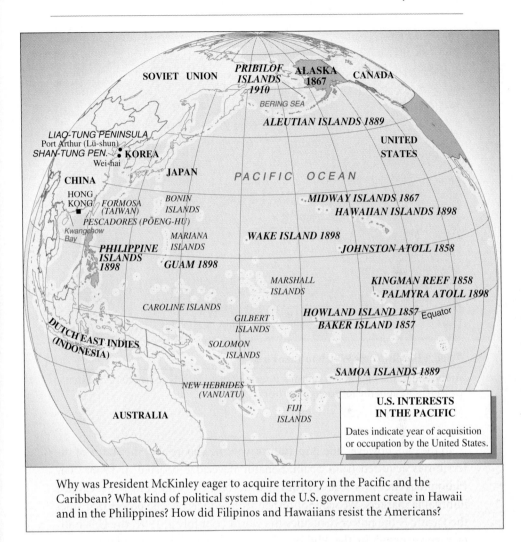

SOVIET UNION

PRIBILOF
ISLANDS
1910

ALASKA
1867

CANADA

BERING SEA

ALEUTIAN ISLANDS 1889

UNITED
STATES

LIAO-TUNG PENINSULA
Port Arthur (Lü-shun)
SHAN-TUNG PEN.
Wei-hai

KOREA

JAPAN

PACIFIC OCEAN

CHINA

HONG
KONG
FORMOSA
(TAIWAN)
PESCADORES (PŌENG-HU)

BONIN
ISLANDS

MIDWAY ISLANDS 1867
HAWAIIAN ISLANDS 1898

Kwangchow
Bay

PHILIPPINE
ISLANDS
1898

MARIANA
ISLANDS

GUAM 1898

WAKE ISLAND 1898

JOHNSTON ATOLL 1858

MARSHALL
ISLANDS

KINGMAN REEF 1858
PALMYRA ATOLL 1898

CAROLINE ISLANDS

GILBERT
ISLANDS

HOWLAND ISLAND 1857
BAKER ISLAND 1857

Equator

DUTCH EAST INDIES
(INDONESIA)

SOLOMON
ISLANDS

SAMOA ISLANDS 1889

NEW HEBRIDES
(VANUATU)

AUSTRALIA

FIJI
ISLANDS

**U.S. INTERESTS
IN THE PACIFIC**

Dates indicate year of acquisition
or occupation by the United States.

Why was President McKinley eager to acquire territory in the Pacific and the Caribbean? What kind of political system did the U.S. government create in Hawaii and in the Philippines? How did Filipinos and Hawaiians resist the Americans?

ORGANIZING THE ACQUISITIONS   The debate in the United States over the future of the Philippines was intense. In the U.S. Senate, George Frisbie Hoar of Massachusetts, a Republican, was the most vocal of the anti-imperialists. He infuriated President Roosevelt when he claimed on the Senate floor that the war-loving president had "wasted $600 millions of treasure. You have sacrificed nearly 10,000 American lives—the flower of our youth. You have devastated provinces. You have slain uncounted thousands of the people you desire to benefit. Your practical statesmanship has succeeded in converting a people who three years ago were ready to kiss the hem of the garment of the American and to welcome him as liberator . . . into sullen and irreconcilable enemies, possessed of a hatred which centuries cannot eradicate."

**"Well, I Hardly Know Which to Take First!"**

At the end of the nineteenth century, it seemed that Uncle Sam had developed a considerable appetite for foreign territory.

In the end, however, the imperialists won the debate over the status of the territories acquired from Spain. Senator Beveridge boasted in 1900: "The Philippines are ours forever. And just beyond the Philippines are China's illimitable markets. We will not retreat from either. . . . The power that rules the Pacific is the power that rules the world." On July 4, 1901, the U.S. military government in the Philippines came to an end, and Judge William Howard Taft became the civil governor. The Philippine Government Act, passed by Congress in 1902, declared the Philippine Islands an "unorganized territory" and made the inhabitants citizens of the Philippines. In 1917, the Jones Act affirmed America's intention to grant the Philippines independence on an unspecified date. Finally, the Tydings-McDuffie Act of 1934 offered independence after ten more years. The Philippines would finally become independent on July 4, 1946.

Closer to home, Puerto Rico had been acquired in part to serve as a U.S. outpost guarding the approach to the Caribbean Sea and any future isthmian canal in Central America. On April 12, 1900, the Foraker Act established a government on the island. The president appointed a governor and eleven members of an executive council, and an elected House of Delegates made up the lower house of the legislature. Residents of the island were declared citizens of Puerto Rico; they were not made citizens of the United States until 1917, when the Jones Act granted them U.S. citizenship and made both houses of the legislature elective. In 1947 the governor also became elective, and in 1952 Puerto Rico became a commonwealth with its own constitution and elected officials, a unique status. Like a state, Puerto Rico is free to change its constitution insofar as it does not conflict with the U.S. Constitution.

Finally, there was Cuba. Having liberated the Cubans from Spanish rule, the Americans found themselves propping up a shaky new government whose economy was in shambles. Technically, Cuba had not gained its independence in 1898. Instead, it remained a protectorate of the United States. American troops remained in control of Cuba for four years, after which they left, but on the condition that the United States could intervene again if the political conditions in Cuba did not satisfy American expectations. Clashes between U.S. soldiers and Cubans erupted almost immediately. When President McKinley set up a military government for the island late in 1898, it was at odds with rebel leaders from the start. The United States finally fulfilled the promise of independence after the military regime had restored order, organized schools, and improved sanitary conditions. The problem of disease in Cuba prompted the work of **Dr. Walter Reed**, who made an outstanding contribution to health in tropical regions around the world. Named head of the Army Yellow Fever Commission in 1900, he proved that mosquitoes carried yellow fever. The commission's experiments led the way to effective control of the disease worldwide.

In 1900, on President McKinley's order, Cubans drafted a constitution modeled on that of the United States. The Platt Amendment, added to an army appropriations bill passed by Congress in 1901, sharply restricted the new Cuban government's independence, however. The amendment required that Cuba never impair its independence by signing a treaty with a third power, that it keep its debt within the government's power to repay it out of ordinary revenues, and that it acknowledge the right of the United States to intervene in Cuba whenever it saw fit. Finally, Cuba had to sell or lease to the United States lands to be used for coaling or naval stations, a proviso that led to a U.S. naval base at Guantánamo Bay, which still exists today.

Under pressure, the Cuban delegates added the Platt Amendment to their constitution. But resentments against America festered. As early as 1906, an insurrection arose against the new government, and President Theodore Roosevelt responded by sending now Secretary of War William Howard Taft to suppress the rebels. Backed by U.S. armed forces, Taft assumed full government authority, as he had in the Philippines, and the American army stayed until 1909, when a new Cuban president was peacefully elected. Sporadic interventions by U.S. troops would follow for more than two decades.

## Imperial Rivalries in East Asia

During the 1890s, the United States was not the only nation to emerge as a world power. Japan defeated China in the First Sino-Japanese War (1894–1895). China's weakness enabled European powers to exploit it. Russia, Germany, France, and Great Britain established spheres of influence in China by the end of the century. In early 1898 and again in 1899, the British asked the American government to join them in preserving the territorial integrity of China against further imperialist actions. Both times the Senate rejected the request because it risked an entangling alliance in a region—Asia—where the United States as yet had no strategic investment.

**"The Open Door"**

Cartoon depicting Uncle Sam propping open a door for China with a brick labeled "U.S. Army and Navy Prestige," as colonial powers look on.

THE "OPEN DOOR" The American outlook toward Asia changed with the defeat of Spain and the acquisition of the Philippines. Instead of acting jointly with Great Britain, however, the U.S. government decided to act alone. What came to be known as the **Open Door policy** was outlined in Secretary of State John Hay's Open Door Note, dispatched in 1899 to his counterparts in London, Berlin, and St. Petersburg (Russia) and a little later to Tokyo, Rome, and Paris. It proposed to keep China open to trade with all countries on an equal basis. More specifically, it called upon foreign powers, within their spheres of influence, (1) to refrain from interfering with any treaty port (a port open to all by treaty) or any vested interest, (2) to permit Chinese authorities to collect tariffs on an equal basis, and (3) to show no favors to their own nationals in the matter of harbor dues or railroad charges. As it turned out, none of the European powers except Britain accepted Hay's principles, but none rejected them either. So Hay simply announced that all the major powers involved in China had accepted the policy.

The Open Door policy was rooted in desire of American businesses to exploit Chinese markets. However, it also tapped the deep-seated sympathies of those who opposed imperialism, especially as the policy pledged to protect China's territorial integrity. But the much-trumpeted Open Door policy had little legal standing. When the Japanese, concerned about Russian pressure in Manchuria, asked how the United States intended to enforce the policy, Hay replied that America was "not prepared . . . to enforce these views." So it would remain for forty years, until continued Japanese expansion in China would bring America to war in 1941.

**THE BOXER REBELLION**   A new Asian crisis arose in 1900 when a group of Chinese nationalists known to the Western world as Boxers (Fists of Righteous Harmony) rebelled against foreign encroachments on China,

**Trade with China**

U.S. troops marching in Beijing after quelling the Boxer Rebellion.

especially Christian missionary efforts, and laid siege to foreign embassies in Peking. An international expedition of British, German, Russian, Japanese, and American forces mobilized to relieve the embassy compound. Hay, fearful that the intervention might become an excuse to dismember China, took the opportunity to further refine the Open Door policy. The United States, he said in a letter of July 3, 1900, sought a solution that would "preserve Chinese territorial and administrative integrity" as well as "equal and impartial trade with all parts of the Chinese Empire." Six weeks later the expedition reached Peking and quelled the Boxer Rebellion.

## BIG-STICK DIPLOMACY

More than any other American of his time, Theodore Roosevelt transformed the role of the United States in world affairs. The nation had emerged from the War of 1898 a world power with major new responsibilities. To ensure that the United States accepted its international obligations, Roosevelt stretched both the Constitution and executive power to the limit. In the process, he pushed a reluctant nation onto the center stage of world affairs.

ROOSEVELT'S RISE    Born in 1858, Roosevelt had grown up in Manhattan in cultured comfort, had visited Europe as a child, spoke German fluently, and had graduated from Harvard with honors in 1880. A sickly, scrawny boy with poor eyesight and chronic asthma, he built himself up into a physical and intellectual athlete, a man of almost superhuman energies who became a lifelong practitioner of the "strenuous life." Roosevelt loved rigorous exercise and outdoor activities. A boxer, wrestler, mountain climber, hunter, and outdoorsman, he also displayed extraordinary intellectual curiosity. He became a voracious reader, a learned natural scientist, dedicated bird-watcher, a renowned historian and essayist, and a zealous moralist. He wrote thirty-eight books on a wide variety of subjects. His boundless energy and fierce competitive spirit were infectious, and he was ever willing to express an opinion on any subject. Within two years of graduating from Harvard, Roosevelt won election to the New York legislature. "I rose like a rocket," he later observed.

But with the world seemingly at his feet, disaster struck. In 1884, Roosevelt's beloved mother Mittie, only forty-eight years old, died. Eleven hours later, in the same house, his twenty-two-year-old wife Alice died in his arms of kidney failure, having recently given birth to their only child. The double funeral was so wrenching that the officiating minister wept throughout his prayer. In an attempt to recover from this "strange and terrible fate," a distraught Roosevelt turned his baby daughter Alice over to his sister, quit his political career, sold the family house, and moved west to take up cattle ranching in the Dakota Territory. The blue-blooded New Yorker escaped his grief by plunging himself into virile western activities: he relished hunting big game, leading cattle roundups, capturing outlaws, fighting Indians (whom he termed a "lesser race")—and reading novels by the campfire. When a drunken cowboy, a gun in each hand, tried to bully the tinhorn Roosevelt, teasing him about his glasses, the feisty Harvard dude laid him out with one punch. Although his western career lasted only two years, he never got over being a cowboy.

Back in New York City, Roosevelt remarried and ran unsuccessfully for mayor in 1886; he later served six years as civil service commissioner and two years as New York City's police commissioner. In 1896, Roosevelt campaigned hard for William McKinley, and the new president was asked to reward him with the position of assistant secretary of the navy. McKinley initially balked, saying that young Roosevelt was too "hotheaded," but he eventually relented and appointed the war-loving aristocrat. Roosevelt took full advantage of his celebrity with the Rough Riders during the war in Cuba to win the governorship of New York in November 1898. By then he had become the most prominent Republican in the nation.

In the 1900 presidential contest, the Democrats turned once again to William Jennings Bryan, who sought to make American imperialism the "paramount issue" of the campaign. The Democratic platform condemned the Philippine conflict as "an unnecessary war" that had placed the United States "in the false and un-American position of crushing with military force the efforts of our former allies to achieve liberty and self-government."

The Republicans welcomed the chance to disagree. They renominated McKinley and named Theodore Roosevelt, now virtually Mr. Imperialism, his running mate. Marcus "Mark" Hanna, now a senator from Ohio but still a powerful Republican strategist, had strenuously opposed Roosevelt's nomination at a party caucus: "Don't any of you realize that there's only one life between this madman and the White House?" Yet Hanna's concerns went unheeded because Roosevelt's much-publicized combat exploits in Cuba had made him a national celebrity. Colonel Roosevelt was named "Man of the Year" in 1898. Elected governor of New York that year, Roosevelt nevertheless leapt at the chance to be vice president in part because he despised Bryan as a dangerous "radical" who called for the federal government to take ownership of railroads. Roosevelt was more than a match for Bryan as a

**Mr. Imperialism**

This 1900 cartoon shows the Republican vice-presidential candidate, Theodore Roosevelt, overshadowing his running mate, President William McKinley.

campaign speaker, and he criss-crossed the nation on behalf of McKinley, speaking in opposition to Bryan's "communistic and socialistic doctrines" promoting higher taxes and the free coinage of silver. McKinley outpolled Bryan by 7.2 million to 6.4 million popular votes and 292 to 155 electoral votes. Bryan even lost his own state of Nebraska.

Less than a year after McKinley's victory, however, his second term ended tragically. On September 6, 1901, at a reception at the Pan-American Exposition in Buffalo, an unemployed anarchist named Leon Czolgosz (pronounced chole-gosh) approached the fifty-eight-year-old president with a gun concealed in a bandaged hand and fired at point-blank range. McKinley died eight days later, and Theodore Roosevelt was elevated to the White House. "Now look," erupted Mark Hanna, the Ohio businessman and politico, "that damned cowboy is President of the United States!"

Six weeks short of his forty-third birthday, Roosevelt was the youngest man ever to reach the White House, but he had more experience in public affairs than most and perhaps more vitality than any. One observer compared him to Niagara Falls, "both great wonders of nature." Even Woodrow Wilson, Roosevelt's main political opponent, said that the former "Rough Rider" was "a great big boy" at heart. "You can't resist the man." Roosevelt's glittering spectacles, glistening teeth, and overflowing gusto were a godsend to the cartoonists, who added another trademark when he pronounced the adage "Speak softly, and carry a big stick."

Along with Roosevelt's boundless energy went a sense of unshakable self-righteousness, which led him to cast nearly every issue in moral and patriotic terms. He was the first truly activist president. He considered the presidency his "bully pulpit," and he delivered fist-pumping speeches on the virtues of righteousness, honesty, civic duty, and strenuosity. Nowhere was President Roosevelt's forceful will more evident than in his conduct of foreign affairs.

THE PANAMA CANAL   After the War of 1898, the United States became more deeply involved in the Caribbean. One issue overshadowed every other in the region: the Panama Canal. The narrow isthmus of Panama had first become a major concern of Americans in the late 1840s, when it became an important overland route to the California goldfields. Two treaties dating from that period loomed years later as obstacles to the construction of a canal. The Bidlack Treaty (1846) with Colombia (then New Granada) guaranteed both Colombia's sovereignty over Panama and the neutrality of the isthmus. In the Clayton-Bulwer Treaty (1850) the British agreed to acquire no more Central American territory, and the United States joined them in agreeing to build or fortify a canal only by mutual consent.

After the War of 1898, Secretary of State John Hay asked the British ambassador for such consent. The outcome was the Hay-Pauncefote Treaty of 1901. Other obstacles remained, however. From 1881 to 1887, a French company under Ferdinand de Lesseps, who had engineered the Suez Canal in Egypt between 1859 and 1869, had spent nearly $300 million and some twenty thousand lives to dig less than a third of a canal across Panama, still under the control of Colombia. The company asked that the United States purchase its holdings, which it did.

Meanwhile, Secretary Hay had opened negotiations with Ambassador Tomás Herrán of Colombia. In return for acquiring a canal zone six miles wide, the United States agreed to pay $10 million in cash and a rental fee of $250,000 a year. The U.S. Senate ratified the Hay-Herrán Treaty in 1903, but the Colombian senate held out for $25 million in cash. In response to this act by those "foolish and homicidal corruptionists in Bogotá," Theodore Roosevelt, by then president, flew into a rage. Meanwhile the Panamanians revolted against Colombian rule. Philippe Bunau-Varilla, an employee of the French canal company, assisted them, and reported, after visiting Roosevelt

**Digging the canal**

President Theodore Roosevelt operating a steam shovel during his 1906 visit to the Panama Canal.

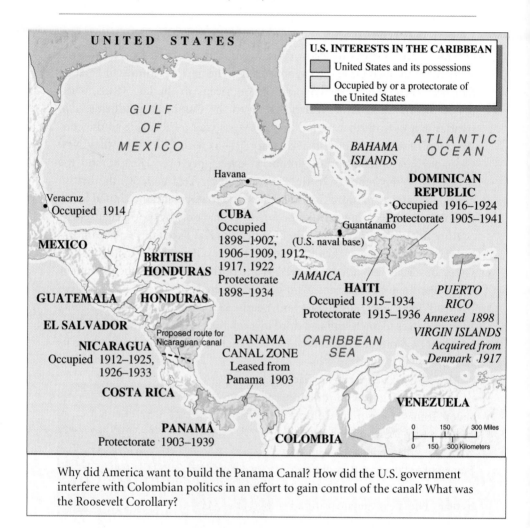

UNITED STATES

**U.S. INTERESTS IN THE CARIBBEAN**

United States and its possessions

Occupied by or a protectorate of the United States

GULF OF MEXICO

ATLANTIC OCEAN

BAHAMA ISLANDS

Havana

DOMINICAN REPUBLIC
Occupied 1916–1924
Protectorate 1905–1941

Veracruz
Occupied 1914

CUBA
Occupied
1898–1902,
1906–1909, 1912,
1917, 1922
Protectorate
1898–1934

Guantánamo
(U.S. naval base)

MEXICO

BRITISH HONDURAS

GUATEMALA    HONDURAS

JAMAICA

HAITI
Occupied 1915–1934
Protectorate 1915–1936

PUERTO RICO
Annexed 1898

EL SALVADOR

NICARAGUA
Occupied 1912–1925,
1926–1933

Proposed route for
Nicaraguan canal

PANAMA
CANAL ZONE
Leased from
Panama 1903

CARIBBEAN SEA

VIRGIN ISLANDS
Acquired from
Denmark 1917

COSTA RICA

VENEZUELA

PANAMA
Protectorate 1903–1939

COLOMBIA

0    150    300 Miles
0    150    300 Kilometers

Why did America want to build the Panama Canal? How did the U.S. government interfere with Colombian politics in an effort to gain control of the canal? What was the Roosevelt Corollary?

and Hay in Washington, D.C., that American warships would arrive at Colón, Panama, on November 2.

The Panamanians revolted the next day. Colombian troops, who could not penetrate the overland jungle, found U.S. ships blocking the sea-lanes. On November 13, the Roosevelt administration received its first ambassador from Panama, who happened to be Philippe Bunau-Varilla; he eagerly signed a treaty that extended the Canal Zone from six to ten miles in width. For $10 million down and $250,000 a year, the United States received "in perpetuity the use, occupation and control" of the Canal Zone. The U.S. attorney general, asked to supply a legal opinion upholding Roosevelt's actions, responded wryly, "No, Mr. President, if I were you I would not have any taint of legality about it." Roosevelt later explained that "I took the Canal Zone and let Congress debate; and while the debate goes on the [construction of the] Canal does also." The strategic canal opened on August 15, 1914, two weeks after the outbreak of World War I in Europe.

**The world's policeman**

President Theodore Roosevelt wields "the big stick," symbolizing his aggressive diplomacy.

THE ROOSEVELT COROL-LARY The behavior of the United States in gaining control of the Panama Canal created ill will throughout Latin America that would last for generations. Equally galling to Latin American sensibilities was the United States' constant meddling in the internal affairs of various nations. A prime excuse for intervention in those days was to force the collection of debts owed to foreign corporations. In 1904, a crisis over the debts of the Dominican Republic prompted Roosevelt to formulate U.S. policy in the Caribbean. In his annual address to Congress in 1904, he outlined what came to be known as the **Roosevelt Corollary to the Monroe Doctrine**: the principle, in short, that since the Monroe Doctrine prohibited intervention in the region by Europeans, the United States was justified in intervening first to forestall involvement by outsiders.

THE RUSSO-JAPANESE WAR    In east Asia, meanwhile, the principle of equal trading rights embodied in the Open Door policy was tested when rivalry between Russia and Japan flared into warfare. By 1904, the Japanese had decided that the Russians threatened their ambitions in China and Korea. On February 8, Japanese warships devastated the Russian fleet. The Japanese then occupied the Korean peninsula and drove the Russians back into Manchuria. But neither side could score a knockout blow, and neither relished a prolonged war. Roosevelt offered to mediate their conflict. When the Japanese signaled that they would welcome a negotiated settlement, Roosevelt sponsored a peace conference in Portsmouth, New Hampshire. With the Treaty of Portsmouth, signed on September 5, 1905, the concessions all went to the Japanese. Russia acknowledged Japan's "predominant political, military, and economic interests in Korea" (Japan would annex the kingdom in 1910), and both powers agreed to evacuate Manchuria.

RELATIONS WITH JAPAN   Japan's show of strength against Russia raised doubts among American leaders about the security of the Philippines. During the Portsmouth talks, Roosevelt sent William Howard Taft to meet with the Japanese foreign minister in Tokyo. The two men negotiated the Taft-Katsura Agreement of July 29, 1905, in which the United States accepted Japanese control of Korea, and Japan disavowed any designs on the Philippines. Three years later the Root-Takahira Agreement, negotiated by Secretary of State Elihu Root and the Japanese ambassador, endorsed the status quo and reinforced the Open Door policy by supporting "the independence and integrity of China" and "the principle of equal opportunity for commerce and industry in China."

Behind the diplomatic facade of goodwill, however, lay mutual distrust. For many Americans the Russian threat in east Asia now gave way to concerns about the "yellow peril" (a term apparently coined by Kaiser Wilhelm II of Germany). Racial animosities on the West Coast helped sour relations with Japan. In 1906, San Francisco's school board ordered students of Asian descent to attend a separate public school. The Japanese government sharply protested such prejudice, and President Roosevelt persuaded the school board to change its policy, but only after making sure that Japanese authorities would not issue "visas" to "laborers," except former residents of the United States; the parents, wives, or children of residents; or those who already possessed an interest in an American farming enterprise. This "Gentlemen's Agreement" of 1907, the precise terms of which have never been revealed, halted the influx of Japanese immigrants and brought some respite to racial agitation in California.

THE UNITED STATES AND EUROPE   At the same time that the United States was expanding into Asia and the Caribbean, tensions in Europe were boiling over. While Roosevelt was moving toward mediation of the Russo-Japanese War in 1905, a dangerous crisis was brewing in Morocco. There, on March 31, 1905, the German kaiser, Wilhelm II, stepped ashore at Tangier and gave a saber-rattling speech criticizing French and British interests in North Africa. The kaiser's speech aroused a diplomatic firestorm. Roosevelt felt that the United States had a huge stake in preventing the outbreak of a major war. At the kaiser's behest, he talked the French and the British into attending an international conference at Algeciras, Spain, with

U.S. delegates present. Roosevelt then maneuvered the Germans into accepting his compromise proposal.

The Act of Algeciras, signed in 1906, affirmed the independence of Morocco and guaranteed an open door for trade there but provided for the training and control of Moroccan police by France and Spain. The U.S. Senate ratified the agreement, but stipulated that America remain committed to neutrality in European affairs. Roosevelt received the Nobel Peace Prize in 1906 for his diplomacy at Portsmouth and Algeciras. Despite his bellicosity on other occasions, he had earned it.

Before Roosevelt left the White House, he celebrated America's rise to the status of a world power with one great flourish. In 1907, he sent the entire U.S. Navy, by then second in strength only to the British fleet, on a grand tour around the world, announcing that he was ready for "a feast, a frolic, or a fight." He got mostly the first two and none of the last. At every port of call down the Atlantic coast of South America, up the west coast, out to Hawaii, and down to New Zealand and Australia, the "Great White Fleet" received rousing welcomes. The triumphal procession continued home by way of the Mediterranean and steamed back into American waters in early 1909, just in time to close out Roosevelt's presidency on a note of success.

Yet it was a success that would have mixed consequences. Roosevelt's effort to deploy American power abroad was accompanied by a racist ideology shared by many prominent political figures of the time. He once told the graduates of the Naval War College that all "the great masterful races have been fighting races, and the minute that a race loses the hard fighting virtues . . . it has lost the right to stand as equal to the best." On another occasion he called warfare the best way to promote "the clear instinct for race selfishness" and insisted that "the most ultimately righteous of all wars is a war with savages." Such a belligerent, self-righteous bigotry defied America's egalitarian ideals and would come back to haunt the United States in world affairs—and at home.

## CHAPTER SUMMARY

- **New Imperialism**  By the beginning of the twentieth century, the idea of a manifest destiny and American industrialists' need for new markets for their goods fueled America's "new imperialism." The ideology of social Darwinism was used to justify the colonization of less developed nations as white Americans held that their own industrial superiority proved their racial superiority and, therefore, the theory of the survival of the fittest. White Americans rationalized further that they had a duty to Christianize and uplift "backward" peoples.

- **Religion and Imperialism**  Protestant missionaries felt impelled to take Christianity to native peoples throughout the world. An indigenous people's acceptance of Christianity was the first step toward the loss of their own culture.

- **War of 1898**  Spain still had an extensive empire, and Cuba was one of its oldest colonies. When Cubans revolted against Spain in 1895, many Americans were sympathetic to their demand for independence. The insurrection was harshly suppressed, and sensational coverage in certain New York newspapers further aroused Americans' sympathy. Early in 1898, the publication of a letter by Spain's minister to the United States, Depuy de Lôme, which criticized President McKinley, and then the explosion of the U.S. battleship *Maine* in Havana Harbor, propelled America into a war with Spain despite the reluctance of President McKinley and many business interests.

- **Results of the War of 1898**  Although the Teller Amendment declared that the United States had no intention of annexing Cuba, America curtailed Cuba's freedom and annexed other territories taken from Spain in the War of 1898. Insurrection followed in the Philippines when insurgents saw that the islands would be administered by the United States. In the treaty that ended the war, the United States gained Puerto Rico as well as Guam and other islands in the Pacific. Meanwhile, Hawaii had been annexed during the war.

- **Big-Stick Diplomacy**  As president, Theodore Roosevelt actively pursued an imperialist foreign policy, confirming the United States' new role as a world power. With his Big-Stick Diplomacy, he arbitrated the treaty that ended the Russo-Japanese War, proclaimed the Open Door policy with China, allowed his administration to engage in dealings that made possible American control over the Panama Canal, and sent the navy's entire fleet around the world as a symbol of American might. He articulated an extension of the Monroe Doctrine whereby the United States might intervene in disputes between North and South America and other world powers.

## CHRONOLOGY

| | |
|---|---|
| 1894 | Republic of Hawaii is proclaimed |
| 1895 | Cuban insurrection breaks out against Spanish rule |
| 1898 | U.S. battleship *Maine* explodes in Havana Harbor |
| 1898 | War of 1898 |
| 1898 | United States annexes Hawaii |
| 1899 | U.S. Senate ratifies the Treaty of Paris, ending the War of 1898 |
| 1899–1902 | Filipino insurgents resist U.S. domination |
| 1900 | Army Yellow Fever Commission confirms the cause of yellow fever |
| 1900 | International alliance quells the Boxer Rebellion |
| 1903 | Panamanians revolt against Colombia |
| 1905 | Russo-Japanese War |
| 1907 | Great White Fleet circumnavigates the globe in a demonstration of America's rise to world-power status |
| 1914 | Panama Canal opens |

## KEY TERMS & NAMES

# 23

## "MAKING THE WORLD OVER": THE PROGRESSIVE ERA

FOCUS QUESTIONS    (S)   wwnorton.com/studyspace

- Who were the progressives, and what were their major causes?
- Who were the muckrakers, and what impact did they have?
- What were Theodore Roosevelt's and William Howard Taft's progressive programs, and what were those programs' goals?
- Why was the election of 1912 significant?
- How was Woodrow Wilson's progressivism different from Roosevelt's?

Theodore Roosevelt's emergence as a national political leader coincided with the onset of what historians have labeled the Progressive Era (1890–1920), a period of dramatic political reform and social activism. During those thirty years, governments—local, state, and federal—grew in scope, power, and activism. Progressive reformers attacked corruption and inefficiency in government and used government authority to regulate businesses and workplaces through regular on-site inspections, regulatory commissions, and antitrust laws. The Progressive Era also witnessed the passage of a graduated ("progressive") federal income tax, the creation of a new national banking system, and the first governmental attempts to conserve natural resources and environmental treasures. In addition, the Progressive Era saw an explosion of grassroots reform efforts across the United States, including the prohibition of alcoholic beverages and the awarding of voting rights for women.

Progressivism was a wide-ranging impulse rather than a single organized movement, a multifaceted, often fragmented, and at times contradictory response to the urgent problems created by unregulated industrialization, unplanned urbanization, unrelenting immigration, and the unequal distribution of wealth and power. Progressives believed that America was in a serious crisis by the late nineteenth century, and the crisis would not resolve itself. It required action—by governments, by churches, by experts, and by volunteers. As Jane Addams, the nation's leading social reformer, who would become the first woman to win the Nobel Peace Prize, stressed, "Action is indeed the sole medium of expression for ethics."

Beginning in the late nineteenth century, progressives emerged in every area of life: neighborhood churches, organized labor, local political life, social service organizations, higher education, and the professions. The progressives were optimistic that society could be improved through creative initiatives and concerted action, moral idealism and social scientific research. They were reformers but not radicals; they opposed violence and only a few flirted with socialism. By working together in a spirit of community, individuals, organizations, and "good" governments could ensure social "progress."

Progressives came in all stripes: men and women; Democrats, Republicans, and Populists; labor unionists and business executives; teachers and professors; social workers and municipal workers; ardent religionists as well as atheists and agnostics. Whatever their motives and methods, they were earnest, well-intentioned, good-hearted people who greatly improved the quality of life and the effectiveness and integrity of government. By the 1920s, progressives had implemented significant changes at all levels of government and across all levels of society.

Yet progressivism had flaws too. The progressives were mostly middle-class urban reformers armed with Christian moralism as well as the latest research from the new social sciences, but their "do-good" perspective was often limited by class biases and racial prejudices. Progressivism had blind spots, especially concerning the volatile issues of race relations and immigration policy. Some reform efforts were in fact intended as middle-class tools to exercise paternalistic oversight of "common" people.

By the start of the twentieth century, so many activists were trying to improve social conditions that people began to speak of a Progressive Era, a time of fermenting idealism and sweeping social, economic, and political changes. The scope of the social crisis was so vast and complex that new remedies were needed. As the inventive genius Thomas Edison said, "We've stumbled along for a while, trying to run a new civilization in old ways, but we've got to start to make this world over."

## Elements of Reform

During the last quarter of the nineteenth century, political progressives at the local and state levels crusaded against the abuses of urban political bosses and corporate barons. Their goals were greater democracy, honest and efficient government, more effective regulation of business, and greater social justice for working people. Only by expanding the scope of local, state, and federal government involvement in society, they believed, could these goals be accomplished. The "real heart of the movement," declared one reformer, was "to use the government as an agency of human welfare."

Progressivism also contained an element of conservatism, however. In some cases the regulation of business was proposed *by* business leaders who preferred regulated stability in their marketplace to the chaos and uncertainty of unrestrained competition. In addition, many reformers were motivated by conservative religious beliefs that led them to focus their energies on moral regulations such as the prohibition of alcoholic beverages and Sunday closing laws, whereby businesses were not allowed to be open on the Christian Sabbath.

In sum, progressivism was diverse in both its motives and its agenda. Few people embraced all of the progressive causes. What reformers shared was a common assumption that the complex social ills and tensions generated by the urban-industrial revolution required new responses and better, more honest, more efficient, and expanded governments. Progressives asked local, state, and federal governments to provide a broad range of direct public services: public schools, good roads (a movement propelled first by cyclists and then by automobilists), environmental conservation and preservation, workplace regulations, limitations on the use of child labor, public health and welfare, care of the disabled, and farm loans and technical expertise, among others. Such initiatives represented the first steps toward what would become known during the 1930s and thereafter as the welfare state.

THE VARIED SOURCES OF PROGRESSIVISM   The progressive impulse arose in response to many societal changes, the most powerful of which were the growing tensions between labor and management in the 1880s, the chronic corruption in political life, the abusive power of big business, the hazards of the industrial workplace, especially for women and children, and the social miseries created by the devastating depression of the 1890s. The depression brought hard times to the cities, worsened already dreadful working conditions in factories, mines, and mills, deepened distress in rural areas, and aroused both the fears and the conscience of the rapidly growing middle class. Although the United States boasted the highest per capita income in the world, it also harbored some of the poorest people. In 1900, an estimated 10 million of the 82 million Americans lived in desperate poverty. Most of the destitute were among the record number of arriving immigrants, many of whom lived in city slums.

Populism was one of the primary catalysts of progressivism. The Populist platform of 1892 outlined many political reforms that would be accomplished during the Progressive Era. After the collapse of the farmers' movement and the revival of the agricultural economy at the turn of the century, the reform spirit shifted to the cities, where middle-class activists had for years attacked the problems of political corruption and urban development.

The Mugwumps, those gentlemen reformers who had fought the spoils system and insisted that government jobs be awarded on the basis of merit, supplied progressivism with an important element of its thinking: the honest-government ideal. Over the years the honest-government movement had been broadened to include efforts to address festering urban problems such as crime, vice, and the efficient provision of gas, electricity, water, sewers, mass transit, and garbage collection.

Another significant force in fostering the most radical wing of progressivism was the influence of socialist doctrines. The small Socialist party served as the left wing of progressivism. Most progressives balked at the radicalism of socialist remedies and labor violence. In fact, the progressive impulse arose in part from a desire to counter the growing influence of militant socialism by promoting more mainstream reforms. As Theodore Roosevelt explained, "In the interest of the working man himself, we need to set our faces like flint against mob violence just as against corporate greed." The prominent role played by religious activists and women reformers was also an important source of progressive energy.

## THE SOCIAL GOSPEL

During the late nineteenth century, more and more people took action to address the complex social problems generated by rapid urban and industrial growth. Some reformers focused on legislative solutions to social problems; others stressed direct assistance to the laboring poor in their neighborhoods or organized charity. Whatever the method or approach, however, social reformers were on the march at the turn of the century, and their activities gave to American life a new urgency and energy.

CHRISTIAN CRUSADERS FOR REFORM    Churches responded slowly to the mounting social concerns of urban America, for American Protestantism had become one of the main props of the established social order. The Reverend Henry Ward Beecher, pastor of the fashionable Plymouth Congregational Church in Brooklyn, preached the virtues of unregulated capitalism, social Darwinism, and the unworthiness of the poor. As the middle classes moved out to the new suburbs made possible by streetcar lines, their churches followed, leaving inner-city neighborhoods churchless. From 1868 to 1888, for instance, seventeen Protestant churches abandoned the area below Fourteenth Street in Manhattan. As ministers catered to the wealthy, they used their sermons to reinforce the economic and social inequalities that grew ever wider during the second half of the nineteenth century.

By the 1870s, however, a younger generation of Protestant and Catholic religious leaders had grown concerned that Christianity had turned its back on the poor and voiceless, the very people that Jesus had focused on. During the last quarter of the nineteenth century, a growing number of churches and synagogues began devoting their resources to community service and care of the unfortunate. The Young Men's Christian Association (YMCA) entered the United States from England in the 1850s and grew rapidly after 1870; the Salvation Army, founded in London in 1878, came to the United States a year later.

RELIGIOUS REFORMERS    Church reformers who feared that Christianity was losing its relevance among the masses began to preach what came to be called the **social gospel**. In 1875, Washington Gladden, a widely respected Congregational pastor in Springfield, Massachusetts, invited striking workers at a shoe factory to attend his church. They refused because the factory owners and managers were members of the church. Gladden decided that there was something wrong when churches were divided along class lines, so he wrote a pathbreaking book titled *Working People and Their Employers* (1876). Gladden argued that true Christianity lies not in rituals, dogmas, or even the mystical experience of God but in the principle that "thou shalt love thy neighbor as thyself." He rejected the notion put forth by social Darwinists that the poor deserved their destitute fate and should not be helped. Christian values and virtues should govern the workplace, with worker and employer united in serving each other's interests. Gladden endorsed labor's right to organize unions and complained that class distinctions should not split congregations.

Gladden's efforts helped launch a new era in the development of American religious life. He and other like-minded ministers during the 1870s and 1880s reached out to the working poor who worked long hours for low wages, had inadequate housing, lacked insurance coverage for on-the-job accidents, and had no legal right to form unions. By the start of the twentieth century, the acknowledged intellectual leader of the social gospel movement was the Baptist Walter Rauschenbusch, a seminary professor in New York who spent a decade ministering to the destitute poor in New York City's "Hell's Kitchen" neighborhood. In an influential book, *Christianity and the Social Crisis* (1907), as well as other writings, Rauschenbusch developed a theological basis for the social gospel movement. "If society continues to disintegrate and decay," he warned, "the Church will be carried down with it." But if the religious community "can rally such moral forces that injustice will be oversome . . . it will itself rise to higher liberty and life." The Church was indispensable to religion, he insisted, but "the greatest future awaits religion in the public life of humanity." One young minister who was transformed by Rauschenbusch's compelling case for a "holistic social gospel" said that his efforts "ushered in a new era in Christian thought and action."

## EARLY EFFORTS AT URBAN REFORM

THE SETTLEMENT HOUSE MOVEMENT   While preachers of the social gospel dispensed inspiration, other dedicated reformers attacked the problems of the slums from residential community centers called **settlement houses**. By 1900, perhaps a hundred settlement houses existed in the United States, some of the best known being Jane Addams and Ellen Gates Starr's Hull-House in Chicago (1889), Robert A. Woods's South End House in Boston (1891), and Lillian Wald's Henry Street Settlement (1893) in New York City.

The settlement houses were designed to bring together prosperous men and women with the working poor, often immigrants. The houses were in rundown neighborhoods. They usually were segregated by gender and staffed mainly by young middle-class idealists, a majority of them college-trained women who had few other outlets for meaningful work outside the home. Settlement workers sought to broaden the horizons of the upper-middle-class volunteers and improve the lives of slum dwellers in diverse ways. At Hull-House, for instance, **Jane Addams** rejected the "do-goodism" spirit of religious reformers. Her approach used pragmatism rather than preaching, focusing on the practical needs of the working poor and newly arrived immigrants— as well as the benefits of affluent volunteers being exposed to the realities of underclass life. As Addams insisted, citizens in a democracy "cannot

**Jane Addams**

By the end of the century, religious groups were taking up the settlement house movement.

cooperate so long as one group sets itself up as superior [to another]." She and her staff helped enroll neighborhood children in clubs and kindergartens and set up a nursery to care for the infant children of working mothers. The program gradually expanded as Hull-House sponsored health clinics, lectures, music and art studios, an employment bureau, men's clubs, training in skills such as bookbinding, a gymnasium, and a savings bank. Florence Kelley, who joined the Hull-House settlement in 1891 and eight years later moved to the Henry Street Settlement in the Lower East Side of New York City, played a powerful role in getting an array of legislation passed that addressed horrible housing and working conditions.

Settlement house leaders realized, however, that the spreading slums made their work as effective as bailing out the ocean with a teaspoon. They therefore organized political support for local and state laws that would ensure sanitary housing codes and create public playgrounds, juvenile courts, mothers' pensions, workers' compensation laws, and legislation prohibiting child labor and monitoring the working conditions in factory "sweatshops." Lillian Wald promoted the establishment of the federal Children's Bureau in 1912, and Jane Addams, for her work in the peace movement, received the Nobel Peace Prize for 1931. When Addams died, in 1935, she was the most venerated woman in America. The settlement houses provided portals of opportunity for women to participate and even lead many progressive efforts to improve living and working conditions for newly arrived immigrants as well as American citizens.

WOMEN'S EMPLOYMENT AND ACTIVISM Settlement house workers, insofar as they were paid, made up but a fraction of all gainfully employed women. With the rapid growth of the general population, the number of employed women steadily increased, as did the percentage of women in the labor force. The greatest leaps forward came in the 1880s and the first decade of the new century, which were also peak decades of immi-

**Elizabeth Cady Stanton**

In this 1870s engraving, Stanton speaks at a meeting of the National Woman Suffrage Association.

gration, a correlation that can be explained by the immigrants' need for income. The number of employed women went from over 2.6 million in 1880 to 4 million in 1890, then from 5.1 million in 1900 to 7.8 million in 1910. The employment of women in large numbers was the most significant event in women's history. Through all those years domestic work remained the largest category of employment for women; teaching and nursing also remained among the leading fields. The main change was that clerical work (bookkeeping, stenography, and the like), and sales jobs became increasingly available to women.

These changes in occupational status had little connection to the women's rights movement, which increasingly focused on the issue of suffrage. Immediately after the Civil War, Susan B. Anthony and Elizabeth Cady Stanton, seasoned leaders of the suffrage movement, demanded that the Fifteenth Amendment give the vote to women as well as to black men. They refused to support the amendment without such a change, and they stooped to using racist arguments to promote their cause. In 1868, New Yorker Stanton appealed to the pervasive racism across America when she wrote in her suffragist newspaper, *The Revolution*, that women deserved the vote more than African American and immigrant men. "Think of Patrick and Sambo,

and Hans and Yung Tung," she advised readers. In her view, illiterate, ignorant men had no right to help elect politicians and help make laws affecting
educated women. Such arguments, however, made little impression on the
defenders of a man's prerogative, who insisted that women belonged in the
domestic sphere.

Although denied voting rights, women became increasingly involved in the
public sphere outside the home. Women's organizations grew exponentially
during the Gilded Age. Church groups, book clubs, women's clubs, mothers'
clubs, and temperance societies provided active outlets outside the home. The
largest and most influential women's organization was the Women's Christian
Temperance Union (WCTU). Founded in 1874, it expanded throughout the
nation during the 1880s. By 1890, the WCTU counted some 150,000 members, most of whom were white, urban, middle class Protestants. Led by
Frances Willard, the WCTU focused on stopping alcohol abuse but also agitated for prison reforms, aid for homeless children, pre-school education
(kindergartens), sex education, aid to working women, and women's suffrage.
The WCTU did more than any other organization to mobilize women in support of progressive social reforms.

In 1869, a divisive issue broke the unity of the women's movement: whether
the movement should concentrate on gaining the vote at the expense of promoting other women's issues. Susan B. Anthony and Elizabeth Cady Stanton
founded the National Woman Suffrage Association (NWSA) to promote a
women's suffrage amendment to the Constitution, but they considered gaining
the right to vote as but one among many feminist causes to be promoted. Later
that year, activists formed the American Woman Suffrage Association (AWSA),
which focused single-mindedly on the suffrage as the first and basic reform.

It would be another half century before the battle would be won, and the
long struggle focused the women's cause ever more on the primary objective
of the vote. In 1890, after three years of negotiation, the rival groups united
as the National American Woman Suffrage Association (NAWSA), with Elizabeth Cady Stanton as president for two years, to be followed by Susan B.
Anthony until 1900. The work thereafter was carried on by a new generation
of activists, led by Anna Howard Shaw and Carrie Chapman Catt.

The suffrage movement remained in the doldrums until the cause of voting rights at the state level easily won a Washington state referendum in 1910
and then carried California by a close majority in 1911. The following year
three more western states—Arizona, Kansas, and Oregon—joined in to make
a total of nine western states with full suffrage. In 1913, Illinois granted
women suffrage in presidential and municipal elections. Yet not until New
York acted in 1917 did a state east of the Mississippi adopt universal suffrage.

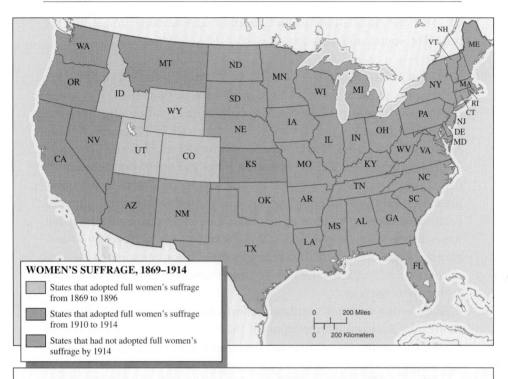

**WOMEN'S SUFFRAGE, 1869–1914**

☐ States that adopted full women's suffrage from 1869 to 1896

■ States that adopted full women's suffrage from 1910 to 1914

■ States that had not adopted full women's suffrage by 1914

0    200 Miles

0    200 Kilometers

Which states first gave women the right to vote? Why did it take fifty-one years, from Wyoming's grant of full suffrage to women until ratification of the Nineteenth Amendment, for women to receive the right to vote? How was suffrage part of a larger women's reform movement?

Despite the focus on the vote, women did not confine their public work to that issue. In 1866 the Young Women's Christian Association (YWCA), a parallel to the YMCA, appeared in Boston and spread elsewhere. The New England Women's Club, started in 1868 by Julia Ward Howe and others, was an early example of the women's clubs that proliferated to such an extent that a General Federation of Women's Clubs was established in 1890 to tie them all together. Many women's clubs focused solely on "literary" and social activities, but others became deeply involved in charities and reform. The New York Consumers' League, formed in 1890, and the National Consumers' League, formed nine years later, sought to make the buying public, chiefly women, aware of unfair labor conditions. One of its devices was the "White List" of firms that met its minimum standards. The National Women's Trade Union League, founded in 1903, performed a similar function of bringing educated and middle-class women together with working women for the benefit of women unionists.

STATE REFORMS AND LEGAL BACKLASH    Even without the support of voting women in most places, many states during the late nineteenth century started regulating big business and working conditions in the public interest. By the end of the century, nearly every state had begun to regulate railroads, if not always effectively, and had moved to supervise banks and insurance companies. By one count, the states and territories passed more than 1,600 laws between 1887 and 1897 relating to conditions in the workplace: limiting the number of hours required of workers, providing special protection for women, limiting or forbidding child labor, requiring that wages be paid regularly and in cash, and calling for factory inspections. Nearly all states had boards or commissioners of labor, and some had boards of conciliation and arbitration. Still, conservative judges limited the practical impact of the laws.

In thwarting such new regulatory efforts, the conservative U.S. Supreme Court used a revised interpretation of the Fourteenth Amendment clauses forbidding the states to "deprive any person of life, liberty, or property, without due process of law" or to deny any person "the equal protection of the laws." Two significant steps of legal reasoning turned the due-process clause into a bulwark of private property. First, the judges reasoned that the word *person* in the clause included corporations. Second, the courts moved away from the old view that "due process" referred only to correct procedures, adopting instead the doctrine of "substantive due process," which allowed courts to review the substance of a legislative action. The principle of substantive due process enabled judges to overturn laws that deprived persons (and corporations) of property to an unreasonable degree and thereby violated due process.

THE MUCKRAKERS    Chronic urban poverty, unsafe working conditions, and worrisome child labor in mills, mines, and factories were complex social issues; remedying them required raising public awareness and political action. The "**muckrakers**," investigative journalists who thrived on exposing social ills and corporate and political corruption, got their name from Theodore Roosevelt, who acknowledged that crusading journalists were "often indispensable to . . . society, but only if they know when to stop raking the muck." By writing exposés of social ills in newspapers and magazines, the muckrakers gave journalism a new social purpose, a political voice beyond simply endorsing one party or another.

The golden age of muckraking is sometimes dated from 1902, when Sam McClure, the owner of best-selling *McClure's Magazine*, decided to use the publication to expose the rampant corruption in politics and corporations. "Capitalists, working-men, politicians, citizens—all break-ing the law or letting it be broken. Who is left to uphold" American democracy, McClure asked. His answer was investigative journalism. *McClure's* bravely took on corporate monopolies and crooked political machines while revealing the awful living and working conditions expe-rienced by masses of Americans. *McClure's* published articles by Lin-coln Steffens on municipal corrup-tion, later collected into a book, *The Shame of the Cities* (1904). *McClure's* also published Ray Stannard Baker's account of the strike by coal miners

**Cover of *McClure's Magazine*, 1902**

This cover features Ida Tarbell's muckracking series on the Standard Oil Company.

in West Virginia and Ida M. Tarbell's devastating *History of the Standard Oil Company* (1904). Tarbell's revelations helped convince the Supreme Court in 1911 to rule that John D. Rockefeller's Standard Oil Company must be dismantled. Other reform-minded books that began as magazine articles exposed corruption in the stock market, the meat-processing industry, the life-insurance business, and the political world. Many of the muckrakers were animated by their own version of the Social Gospel. Steffens, for exam-ple, stressed that "the doctrine of Jesus is the most revolutionary propaganda that I have ever encountered."

Without the muckrakers, the far-flung reform efforts of progressivism would never have achieved widespread popular support. In feeding the pub-lic's appetite for sordid social facts, the muckrakers demonstrated one of the salient features of the Progressive movement, and one of its central failures: the progressives were stronger on diagnosis than on remedy. They professed a naive faith in the power of democracy. Give the people the facts, expose corruption, and bring government close to the people, reformers believed, and the correction of evils would follow automatically. The cure for the ills of democracy, it seemed, was a more informed and a more active democracy. What they failed to acknowledge was that no reform would change the essentially flawed nature of human beings.

## FEATURES OF PROGRESSIVISM

DEMOCRACY    Progressives at the local and state levels focused on cleaning up governments. Too many elected officials, they believed, did the bidding of corporations rather than served the interests of all the people. The most important reform that political progressives promoted to democratize government and encourage greater political participation was the direct primary, whereby all party members would participate in the election of candidates, rather than the traditional practice in which an inner circle of party activists chose the nominee. Under the traditional convention system, only a small proportion of voters attended the local caucuses or precinct meetings that sent delegates to party nominating conventions. While this traditional method allowed seasoned leaders to sift the candidates, it also lent itself to domination by political professionals. Direct primaries at the local level had been held sporadically since the 1870s, but after South Carolina adopted the first statewide primary in 1896, the movement spread within two decades to nearly every state.

The party primary was but one expression of a broad progressive movement for greater public participation in the political process. In 1898, South Dakota became the first state to adopt the initiative and referendum, procedures that allow voters to enact laws directly rather than having to wait for legislative action. If a designated number of voters petitioned to have a measure put on the ballot (the initiative), the electorate could then vote it up or down (the referendum). Oregon adopted a spectrum of reform measures, including a voter-registration law (1899), the initiative and referendum (1902), the direct primary (1904), a sweeping corrupt-practices act (1908), and the recall (1910), whereby corrupt or incompetent public officials could be removed by a public petition and vote. Within a decade, nearly twenty states had adopted the initiative and referendum, and nearly a dozen had accepted the recall.

Most states adopted the party primary even in the choice of U.S. senators, heretofore selected by state legislatures. Nevada was first, in 1899, to let voters express a choice that state legislators of their party were expected to follow in choosing senators. The popular election of U.S. senators required a constitutional amendment, and the House of Representatives, beginning in 1894, four times adopted such an amendment, only to see it defeated in the

Senate, which came under increasing attack as a "millionaires' club." In 1912 the Senate finally accepted the inevitable and agreed to the Seventeenth Amendment, authorizing popular election of senators. The amendment was ratified in 1913.

EFFICIENCY    A second major theme of progressivism was the "gospel of efficiency." In the business world during the early twentieth century, Frederick W. Taylor, the original "efficiency expert," was developing the techniques he summed up in his book *The Principles of Scientific Management* (1911). **Taylorism**, as scientific industrial management came to be known, promised to reduce waste and inefficiency in the workplace through the scientific analysis of labor processes. By breaking down the production of goods into sequential steps and meticulously studying the time it took each worker to perform a task, Taylor prescribed the optimum technique for the average worker and established detailed performance standards for each job classification. The promise of higher wages for higher productivity, he believed, would motivate workers to exceed "average" expectations.

Instead, many workers resented Taylor's innovations. They saw in scientific management a tool for employers to make people work faster than was healthy, sustainable, or fair. Yet Taylor's controversial system brought concrete improvements in productivity, especially among those industries whose production processes were highly standardized and whose jobs were rigidly defined. "In the future," Taylor predicted in 1911, "the system [rather than the individual workers] will be first."

In government, the efficiency movement demanded the reorganization of agencies to eliminate redundancy, to establish clear lines of authority, and to assign responsibility and accountability to specific officials. Two progressive ideas for making municipal government more efficient gained headway in the first decade of the new century. One, the commission system, was first adopted by Galveston, Texas, in 1901, when local government there collapsed in the aftermath of a devastating hurricane and tidal wave. The system placed ultimate authority in a board composed of elected administrative heads of city departments—commissioners of sanitation, police, utilities, and so on. The more durable idea, however, was the city-manager plan, under which a professional administrator ran the municipal government in accordance with policies set by the elected council and mayor. Staunton, Virginia, first adopted the plan in 1908. By 1914 the National Association of City Managers had heralded the arrival of a new profession.

By the early twentieth century, many complex functions of government and business had come to require specialists with technical expertise. As

**Robert M. La Follette**

A progressive proponent of expertise in government.

Woodrow Wilson wrote, progressive ideals could be achieved only if government at all levels—local, state, and national—was "informed and administered by experts." This principle of government by nonpartisan experts was promoted by progressive Governor Robert M. La Follette of Wisconsin, who established a Legislative Reference Bureau to provide elected officials with research, advice, and help in the drafting of legislation. The "Wisconsin idea" of efficient and more scientific government was widely publicized and copied. La Follette also pushed for such reforms as the direct primary, stronger railroad regulation, the conservation of natural resources, and workmen's compensation programs to support laborers injured on the job.

ANTI-TRUST REGULATION  Of all the problems facing American society at the turn of the century, one engaged a greater diversity of progressive reformers and elicited more solutions than any other: the regulation of giant corporations, which became a third major theme of progressivism. Bipartisan concern over the concentration of economic power had brought passage of the Sherman Anti-Trust Act in 1890, but the act had turned out to be more symbolic than effective.

The problem of concentrated economic power and its abuse offered a dilemma for progressives. Four broad solutions were available, but of these, two were extremes that had limited support: letting the capitalist system operate without regulation (laissez-faire) or, at the other extreme, adopting a socialist program mandating government ownership of big businesses. At the municipal level, however, the socialist alternative was rather widely adopted for public utilities and transportation—so-called gas and water socialism; otherwise, it was not seriously considered as a general policy. The other choices were either to adopt a policy of trust-busting in the belief that restoring old-fashioned competition would best prevent economic abuses or to accept big business in the belief that it brought economies of scale but to regulate it to prevent abuses.

Efforts to restore the competition of small firms proved unworkable, however, partly because breaking up large corporations was a complicated process. To some extent, regulation and "stabilization" won acceptance among business leaders; whatever respect they paid to competition in the abstract, they preferred not to face it in practice. As time passed, however, regulatory agencies often came under the influence or control of those they were supposed to regulate. Railroad executives, for instance, generally had more intimate knowledge of the intricate details involved in their business, giving them the advantage over the outsiders who might be appointed to the Interstate Commerce Commission (ICC).

SOCIAL JUSTICE    A fourth important feature of the Progressive movement was the effort to promote greater social justice through the creation of nonprofit charitable service organizations; efforts by reformers to clean up cities through personal hygiene, municipal sewers, and public-awareness campaigns; and reforms aimed at regulating child labor and the consumption of alcohol.

Middle-class women were the driving force behind the grassroots **social justice** movement. In massive numbers they fanned out to address social ills. The Women's Christian Temperance Union (WCTU), founded in 1874, was the largest women's group in the nation at the end of the nineteenth century, boasting three hundred thousand members. Frances Willard, the dynamic president of the WCTU between 1879 and 1898, believed that all social problems were interconnected and that most of them resulted from alcohol abuse. Members of the WCTU strove to close saloons, improve prison conditions, shelter prostitutes and abused women and children, support female labor unions, and champion women's suffrage. The WCTU also lobbied for the eight-hour workday, the regulation of child labor, better nutrition, the federal inspection of food

**Frances Elizabeth Willard**

Willard founded the WCTU and lobbied for women's suffrage.

processors and drug manufacturers, free kindergartens and public play-grounds, and uniform marriage and divorce laws across the states.

With time it became apparent that social evils extended beyond the reach of private charities and grassroots organizations and demanded government intervention. In 1890, almost half of American workers toiled up to twelve hours a day—sometimes seven days a week—in unsafe, unsanitary, and unregulated conditions for bare subsistence wages. Labor legislation was per-haps the most significant reform to emerge from the drive for progressive social justice. It emerged first at the state level. The National Child Labor Committee, organized in 1904, led a movement for laws prohibiting the employment of young children. Within ten years, through the organization of state and local committees and a graphic documentation of the evils of child labor by the photographer Lewis W. Hine, the committee pushed through legislation in most states banning the labor of underage children (the minimum age varying from twelve to sixteen) and limiting the hours older children might work.

Closely linked to the child-labor reform movement was a concerted effort to regulate the hours of work for women. Spearheaded by **Florence Kelley**, the head of the National Consumers' League, this progressive crusade promoted state laws to regulate the long working hours imposed on women who were wives and mothers. Many states also outlawed night work and labor in dangerous occupations for both women and children. But numerous exemp-tions and inadequate enforcement often nullified the intent of those laws.

**Child labor was commonplace**

A young girl working as a spinner in a cotton mill in Vermont, 1910.

The Supreme Court pursued a curiously erratic course in ruling on state labor laws. In *Lochner v. New York* (1905), the Court voided a ten-hour-workday law because it violated workers' "liberty of contract" to accept any jobs they wanted, no matter how bad the working conditions or pay. But in *Muller v. Oregon* (1908), the high court upheld a ten-hour-workday law for women largely on the basis of socio-logical data regarding the effects of long hours on the health and morals of women. In *Bunting v. Oregon* (1917), the Court accepted a maximum ten-hour day for both men and women but for twenty more years held out against state minimum-wage laws.

Legislation to protect workers against avoidable accidents gained impetus from disasters such as the March 25, 1911, fire at the Triangle Shirtwaist fac-tory (called a "sweatshop") in New York City, in which 146 of the 850 workers died, mostly women in their teens, almost all of whom were Jewish and Ital-ian immigrants. Escape routes were limited because the owner kept the stair-way door locked to prevent theft. Workers trapped on the three upper floors of the ten-story building died in the fire or leaped to their death. The work-ers had wanted to form a union to negotiate safer working conditions, better pay, and shorter hours, but the owner had refused. The tragic fire served as the catalyst for progressive reforms. A state commission investigated the fire, and thirty-six new city and state laws and regulations were implemented, many of which were copied by other states around the nation. One of the most important advances along these lines was the series of workers' compensation laws enacted after Maryland led the way in 1902. Accident-insurance systems replaced the old common-law principle that an injured worker was entitled to compensation only if employer negligence could be proved, a costly and capricious procedure from which the worker was likely to win nothing or be granted excessive awards from an overly sympathetic jury.

PROGRESSIVISM AND RELIGION    Religion was a crucial source of energy for progressive reformers. Many Christians and Jews embraced the social gospel, seeking to express their faith through aid to the less fortunate. Jane Addams called the impulse to found settlement houses for the waves of immigrants arriving in American cities "Christian humanitarianism." She and others often used the phrase "social righteousness" to explain the con-nection between progressive social activism and religious belief. Protestants, Catholics, and Jews worked closely together to promote state laws providing for minimum-wage levels and shorter workdays. Some of the reformers applied their crusade for social justice to organized religion itself. Frances Willard, who spent time as a traveling evangelist, lobbied church organiza-tions to allow women to become ministers. As she said, "If women can orga-nize missionary societies, temperance societies, and every kind of charitable organization . . . why not permit them to be ordained to preach the Gospel and administer the sacraments of the Church?"

PROHIBITION   Opposition to alcohol abuse was an ideal cause in which to merge the older religious-based ethics with the new social ethics promoting reforms. Given the importance of saloons as arenas for often-corrupt local political machines, prohibitionists could equate the "liquor traffic" with progressive suspicion of bossism and "special interests." By eliminating booze and closing saloons, reformers hoped to remove one of the tools used by political bosses to win over converts. The battle against alcoholic beverages had begun in earnest during the nineteenth century. The WCTU had promoted the cause since 1874, and a Prohibition party had entered the national elections in 1876. But the most successful political action followed the formation in 1893 of the Anti-Saloon League, an organization that pioneered the strategy of the single-issue pressure group. Through its singleness of purpose, it forced the prohibition issue into the forefront of state and local elections. At its "Jubilee Convention" in 1913, the bipartisan Anti-Saloon League endorsed a prohibition amendment to the Constitution, adopted by Congress in 1917. By the time it was ratified, two years later, state and local action had already dried up areas occupied by nearly three fourths of the nation's population.

## Roosevelt's Progressivism

While most progressive initiatives originated at the state and local levels during the late nineteenth century, federal reform efforts coalesced around 1900 with the emergence of Theodore Roosevelt as a national political leader. He brought to the White House in 1901 perhaps the most complex personality in American political history: he was a political reformer, an environmentalist, an obsessive hunter, a racist, and a militaristic liberal. Roosevelt developed an expansive vision of the presidency that well suited the cause of progressive reform. In one of his first addresses to Congress, he stressed the need for a new political approach. When the Constitution was drafted in 1787, he explained, the nation's social and economic conditions were quite unlike those at the dawn of the twentieth century. "The conditions are now wholly different and wholly different action is called for." More than any other president since Abraham Lincoln, Roosevelt possessed an activist bent. A skilled political maneuverer, he greatly expanded the role and visibility of the presidency by his use of the "bully pulpit," as well as the authority and scope of the federal government. He cultivated party leaders in Congress and steered away from such divisive issues as the tariff and regulation of the banks. And when he did approach the explosive issue of regulating the trusts, he took care to reassure the business community of his intentions. For him, politics was the art of the possible. Unlike the more radical progressives and the doctrinaire "lunatic fringe," as he called it, he would take half a loaf rather than none at all.

EXECUTIVE ACTION    Roosevelt accomplished more by vigorous executive action than by passing legislation. He argued that as president he might do anything not expressly forbidden by the Constitution. The humorist Mark Twain said that Roosevelt was ready "to kick the Constitution into the backyard whenever it gets in the way." In 1902, Roosevelt endorsed a "Square Deal" for all, calling for more rigorous enforcement of existing anti-trust laws and stricter controls on big business. From the outset, however, Roosevelt avoided wholesale trust-busting. Effective regulation of corporate giants was better than a futile effort to dismantle large corporations. Because Congress balked at regulatory legislation, Roosevelt sought to force the issue by a more vigorous prosecution of the 1890 Sherman Anti-Trust Act. In 1902, Roosevelt ordered the U.S. attorney general to break up the Northern Securities Company, a giant conglomerate of interconnected railroads. In 1904, the Supreme Court ordered the railroad combination dissolved.

THE 1902 COAL STRIKE    Roosevelt also used the "big stick" against corporations in the coal strike of 1902. On May 12, some 150,000 members of the United Mine Workers (UMW) walked off the job in Pennsylvania and West Virginia. They were seeking a 20 percent wage increase, a reduction in daily working hours from ten to nine, and official recognition of the union by the mine owners. The mine operators refused to negotiate. Instead, they shut down the mines to starve out the miners, many of whom were immigrants from eastern Europe. One mine owner expressed the prejudices of many other owners when he proclaimed, "The miners don't suffer—why, they can't even speak English."

By October 1902, the prolonged shutdown had caused the price of coal to soar, and hospitals and schools reported empty coal bins. President Roosevelt decided upon a bold move: he invited leaders of both sides to a conference in Washington, D.C., where he appealed to their "patriotism, to the spirit that sinks personal considerations and makes individual sacrifices for the public good." The mine owners attended the conference but arrogantly refused even to speak to the UMW leaders. The "extraordinary stupidity and temper" of the "wooden-headed" owners infuriated Roosevelt. The president wanted to grab the spokesman for the mine owners "by the seat of his breeches" and "chuck him out" a window. Roosevelt threatened to take over

**Roosevelt's duality**

Theodore Roosevelt as an "apostle of prosperity" (top) and as a Roman tyrant (bottom). Roosevelt's energy, self-righteousness, and impulsiveness elicited sharp reactions.

the mines and send in the army to run them. When a congressman questioned the constitutionality of such a move, an exasperated Roosevelt roared, "To hell with the Constitution when the people want coal!" The threat to militarize the mines worked. The coal strike ended on October 23. The miners won a reduction to a nine-hour workday but only a 10 percent wage increase, and no union recognition by the owners. Roosevelt had become the first president to use his authority to arbitrate a dispute between management and labor.

**EXPANDING FEDERAL POWER**  Roosevelt continued to use unprecedented executive powers to enforce the Sherman Anti-Trust Act (1890). Altogether, his administration initiated about twenty-five anti-trust suits against oversized corporations. In 1903, Congress passed the Elkins Act, which made it illegal for railroads to take, as well as to give, secret rebates on freight charges to their favorite customers. All shippers would pay the same price. That same year, Congress created a new Bureau of Corporations to monitor the activities of interstate corporations. When Standard Oil refused to turn over its records, the government brought an anti-trust suit that resulted in the breakup of the huge company in 1911. The Supreme Court also ordered the American Tobacco Company to divide its enterprises because it had come to monopolize the cigarette industry.

## ROOSEVELT'S SECOND TERM

Roosevelt's aggressive leadership built a coalition of progressives and conservatives who assured his election in his own right in 1904. The Republican Convention chose him by acclamation. The Democrats, having lost with William Jennings Bryan twice, turned to the more conservative Alton B. Parker, chief justice of the New York Supreme Court. Roosevelt's invincible popularity plus the sheer force of his personality swept the president to an impressive victory by a popular vote of 7.6 million to 5.1 million. With 336 electoral votes for the president and 140 for Parker, Roosevelt savored his lopsided victory. The president told his wife that he was "no longer a political accident." He now had a popular mandate. On the eve of his inauguration in March 1905, Roosevelt announced: "Tomorrow I shall come into office in my own right. Then watch out for me!"

**LEGISLATIVE LEADERSHIP**  Elected in his own right, Roosevelt approached his second term with heightened confidence and an even

**"The Lion-Tamer"**

Theodore Roosevelt confronts the beasts of the steel trust, the oil trust, the beef trust, and others in the arena of Wall Street.

stronger commitment to progressive reform. In 1905, he devoted most of his annual message to the needed regulation of big business. His comments irked many of his corporate contributors and congressional Republican leaders. Said steel baron Henry Clay Frick, "We bought the son of a bitch and then he did not stay bought."

The independent-minded Roosevelt took aim at the railroads first. The Elkins Act of 1903, finally outlawing rebates, had been a minor step. Railroad executives themselves welcomed it as an escape from shippers clamoring for special favors. But a new proposal for railroad regulation endorsed by Roosevelt was something else again. Enacted in 1906, the Hepburn Act for the first time gave the ICC the power to set maximum freight rates for the railroad industry.

Regulating railroads was Roosevelt's first priority, but he also embraced the regulation of meat packers, food processors, and makers of drugs and patent medicines. Muckraking journalists revealed that companies were engaged in all sorts of unsanitary and dangerous activities in the preparation of food products. Perhaps the most telling blow against such abuses was struck by Upton Sinclair's novel *The Jungle* (1906). Sinclair wrote the book to promote socialism, but its main impact came from its portrayal of filthy conditions in Chicago's meatpacking industry:

> It was too dark in these storage places to see well, but a man could run his hand over these piles of meat and sweep off handfuls of the dried dung of rats. These rats were nuisances, and the packers would put poisoned bread out for them, they would die, and then rats, bread, and meat would go into the hoppers together.

Roosevelt read *The Jungle*—and reacted quickly. He sent two agents to Chicago, and their report confirmed all that Sinclair had said about the unsanitary conditions in the packing plants. Congress and Roosevelt responded by creating the Meat Inspection Act of 1906. It required federal inspection of meats destined for interstate commerce and empowered officials in the Agriculture Department to impose sanitation standards in processing plants. The Pure Food and Drug Act, enacted the same day, placed restrictions on the makers of prepared foods and patent medicines and forbade the manufacture, sale, or transportation of adulterated, misbranded, or harmful foods, drugs, and liquors.

**The meat industry**

Pigs strung up along the hog-scraping rail at Armour's packing plant in Chicago, ca. 1909.

ENVIRONMENTAL CONSERVATION One of the most enduring legacies of Roosevelt's leadership was his energetic support for the emerging environmental conservation movement. Roosevelt was the first president to challenge the long-standing myth of America's having inexhaustible natural resources. In fact, Roosevelt declared that conservation was the "great material question of the day." Just as reformers promoted the regulation of business and industry for the public welfare, conservationists championed efforts to manage and preserve the natural environment for the benefit of future generations.

The first promoters of resource conservation were ardent sportsmen among the social elite (including Theodore Roosevelt), who worried that unregulated commercial hunters and trappers were wantonly killing game animals to the point of extermination. In 1886, for example, the sportsman-naturalist George Bird Grinnell, editor of *Forest and Stream*, founded the Audubon Society to protect wild birds from being killed for their plumage. Two years later Grinnell, Roosevelt, and a dozen other recreational hunters formed the Boone and Crockett Club, named in honor of Daniel Boone and David (Davy) Crockett, the legendary frontiersmen. The club's goal was to ensure that big-game animals were protected for posterity. By 1900 most states had enacted laws regulating game hunting and had created game

**Nathaniel Pitt Langford**

The first superintendent of Yellowstone National Park, on Jupiter Terrace at Mammoth Hot Springs, ca. 1875.

refuges and wardens to enforce the new rules, much to the chagrin of local hunters, including Native Americans, who now were forced to abide by state laws designed to protect the interests of wealthy recreational hunters.

Roosevelt and the sportsmen conservationists formed a powerful coalition promoting rational government management of natural resources: rivers and streams, forests, minerals, and natural wonders. Those concerns, as well as the desire of railroad companies to transport tourists to destinations featuring majestic scenery, led the federal government to displace Indians in order to establish the 2-million-acre Yellowstone National Park in 1872 at the junction of the Montana, Wyoming, and Idaho Territories (the National Park Service would be created in 1916 after other parks had been established). In 1881, Congress created a Division of Forestry (now the U.S. Forest Service) within the Department of the Interior. As president, Theodore Roosevelt created fifty federal wildlife refuges, approved five new national parks, fifty-one federal bird sanctuaries, and designated eighteen national monuments, including the Grand Canyon. Roosevelt's brash style of getting things done was no better illustrated than when he was at his desk in the White House and asked an aide, "Is there any law that prevents me from declaring Pelican Island a National Bird Sanctuary?" Not waiting for an answer, he replied, "Very well, then," reaching for his pen, "I declare it."

In 1898, while serving as vice president, Roosevelt had endorsed the appointment of **Gifford Pinchot**, a close friend and the nation's first professional forester, as the head of the U.S. Division of Forestry. Pinchot and Roosevelt were pragmatic conservationists; they believed in economic growth as well as environmental preservation. To them, conservation entailed the scientific ("progressive") management of natural resources to serve the public interest. Pinchot explained that the conservation movement sought to promote the "greatest good for the greatest number for the longest time."

Roosevelt and Pinchot were especially concerned about the millions of acres still owned by the federal government. Over the years, vast tracts of public land had been given away or sold at discount prices to large business enterprises. Roosevelt and Pinchot were determined to end such

**Gifford Pinchot**

Pinchot is seen here with two children at the edge of a larch grove.

careless exploitation. Roosevelt as president used the Forest Reserve Act (1891) to protect some 172 million acres of timberland. Lumber companies were furious, but Roosevelt held firm. As he bristled, "I hate a man who skins the land."

Theodore Roosevelt's far-flung conservation efforts also encompassed reclamation and irrigation projects. In 1902 the president signed the Reclamation Act (also known as the Newlands Act, after its sponsor, Nevada senator Francis G. Newlands). The Reclamation Act established a new federal agency within the Interior Department, called the Reclamation Service (renamed the Bureau of Reclamation in 1923), to administer a massive new program designed to bring water to arid western states. Using funds from the sale of federal lands in sixteen states in the West, the Reclamation Service constructed dams and irrigation systems to transform barren desert acreage into farmland.

Roosevelt also came to view spectacular environmental areas as natural wonders worthy of human reverence and perpetual preservation. Overall, Roosevelt's conservation efforts helped curb the unregulated exploitation of natural resources for private gain. He had set aside over 234 million acres of federal land for conservation purposes, including the creation of forty-five national forests in eleven western states. As Pinchot recalled late in life, "Launching the conservation movement was the most significant achievement of the T. R. Administration, as he himself believed."

## FROM ROOSEVELT TO TAFT

Toward the end of his second term, Roosevelt declared, "I have had a great time as president." Although eligible to run again, he opted for retirement. Once out of office, the fifty-year-old Roosevelt set off in 1909 on a prolonged safari in Africa, prompting his old foe J. Pierpont Morgan to mutter, "Let every lion do his duty."

Roosevelt decided that his successor should be his secretary of war, William Howard Taft, and the Republican Convention ratified the choice on its first ballot in 1908. The Democrats gave William Jennings Bryan one more chance at the highest office. Still vigorous at forty-eight, Bryan retained a faithful following but struggled to attract national support. Roosevelt advised Taft: "Do not answer Bryan; *attack* him. Don't let him make the issues." Taft followed Roosevelt's advice, declaring that Bryan's election would result in a "paralysis of business."

**William Howard Taft**

Speaking at Manassas, Virginia, in 1911.

The Republican platform endorsed Roosevelt's progressive policies. The Democratic platform hardly differed on the need for regulation of business, but it called for a lower tariff and opposed court injunctions against labor unions that organized strikes. In the end, voters opted for Roosevelt's chosen successor: Taft swept the Electoral College, 321 to 162. The real surprise of the election, however, was the strong showing of the Socialist party candidate, labor hero Eugene V. Debs. His 421,000 votes revealed again the depth of working-class resentment in the United States.

William Howard Taft had superb qualifications to be president. Born in Cincinnati in 1857, he had graduated second in his class at Yale and had become a preeminent legal scholar, serving on the Ohio Supreme Court and as U.S. solicitor general. In 1900, President William McKinley had appointed Taft as the first governor-general of the Philippines, and three years later Roosevelt named him secretary of war. Taft would become the only person to serve both as president and as chief justice of the Supreme Court. He was a progressive conservative who vowed to protect "the right of property" and the "right of liberty." In practice, this meant that the new president was even more determined than Roosevelt to preserve "the spirit of commercial freedom" against monopolistic trusts. However, Taft was a very different president than Roosevelt. He detested the give-and-take of backroom politics and never felt comfortable in the White House. He once observed that whenever someone said "Mr. President," he looked around for Roosevelt.

TARIFF REFORM    Taft's domestic policies generated a storm of controversy within his own party. Contrary to longstanding Republican tradition, Taft preferred a lower tariff, and he made this the first important issue of his presidency. But Taft proved less skillful than Roosevelt in dealing with Congress. The resulting tariff was a hodgepodge that on the whole changed very little. Temperamentally conservative, inhibited by scruples about interfering too much with the legislative process, Taft drifted into the orbit of the Republican Old Guard and quickly alienated the progressive wing of his party, whom he tagged "assistant Democrats."

BALLINGER AND PINCHOT    In 1910, President Taft's policies drove the wedge deeper between the conservative and progressive Republican factions. What came to be called the Ballinger-Pinchot controversy made Taft appear to be abandoning Roosevelt's conservation policies. The strongest conservation leaders, such as Roosevelt and Gifford Pinchot, a Pennsylvanian, were often easterners, and Taft's secretary of the interior, Richard A. Ballinger of Seattle, was well aware that many westerners opposed conservation programs on the grounds that they held back full economic development of the Far West. Ballinger therefore threw open to commercial use millions acres of federal lands that Roosevelt had ordered conserved. As chief of forestry, Pinchot reported to Taft his concerns about the land "giveaway," but the president refused to intervene. When Pinchot went public with the controversy early in 1910, Taft fired him. In doing so, he set in motion a feud with Roosevelt that would eventually cost him his reelection.

**TAFT AND ROOSEVELT**   Taft's dismissal of Pinchot infuriated Roosevelt, who eventually decided that Taft had fallen under the spell of the Republican Old Guard leadership. During the fall of 1910, Roosevelt made several speeches promoting "sane and progressive" Republican candidates in the congressional elections. In a speech at Osawatomie, a small town in eastern Kansas, he gave a catchy name to his latest progressive principles, the "**New Nationalism**," which greatly resembled the populist progressivism of William Jennings Bryan. Roosevelt issued a stirring call for more stringent federal regulation of huge corporations, a progressive income tax, laws limiting child labor, and a "Square Deal for the poor man." He also proposed the first efforts at campaign finance reform. "There can be no effective control of corporations while their political activity remains," Roosevelt said. "To put an end to it will be neither a short nor an easy task, but it can be done." His purpose was not to revolutionize the political system but to save it from the threat of revolution. "What I have advocated," he explained a few days later, "is not wild radicalism. It is the highest and wisest kind of conservatism."

On February 24, 1912, Roosevelt challenged Taft's leadership by entering the race for the presidency. He had decided that Taft had "sold the Square Deal down the river," and he now dismissed Taft as a "hopeless fathead." Taft was both stunned and hurt. A reporter who approached President Taft on a train found him slumped over, his head in his hands. Taft looked up and said, "Roosevelt was my closest friend." Then he started weeping.

Roosevelt's rebuke of Taft was in many ways undeserved. During Taft's first year in office, one political tempest after another had left his image irreparably damaged. The three years of solid achievement that followed came too late to restore its luster or reunite his divided party. Taft had at least attempted tariff reform, which Roosevelt had never dared. He replaced Roosevelt's friend Gifford Pinchot with men with impeccable credentials as conservationists. In the end his administration preserved more public land in four years than Roosevelt's had in nearly eight. Taft's administration also filed more anti-trust suits against big corporations, by a score of eighty to twenty-five.

**Political giants**

A cartoon showing Roosevelt charging through the air at Taft, who is seated on a mountaintop.

In 1910, with Taft's support, Congress passed the Mann-Elkins Act, which for the first time empowered the ICC to initiate changes in railroad freight rates, extended its regulatory powers to telephone and telegraph companies, and set up the Commerce Court to expedite appeals of ICC rulings. Taft also established the Bureau of Mines and the federal Children's Bureau (1912), and he called for statehood for Arizona and New Mexico and territorial government for Alaska (1912). The **Sixteenth Amendment** (1913), authorizing a federal income tax, was ratified with Taft's support before he left office, and the Seventeenth Amendment (1913), providing for the popular election of senators, was ratified soon after he left office.

But Taft's progressive record did not prevent Roosevelt from turning on him. Roosevelt won all but two of the thirteen states that held presidential primaries, even Taft's home state of Ohio. But the groundswell of popular support for Roosevelt was no match for Taft's decisive position as sitting president and party leader. In state nominating conventions the Taft forces prevailed. So Roosevelt entered the Republican National Convention about a hundred votes short of victory. The Taft delegates proceeded to nominate their man by the same steamroller tactics that had nominated Roosevelt in 1904.

Roosevelt was outraged at what he called Taft's "successful fraud" in getting the nomination. The angry Roosevelt delegates—mostly social workers,

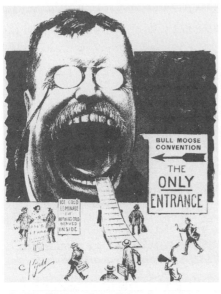

**The "Bull Moose" candidate in 1912**

A skeptical view of Theodore Roosevelt.

reformers, intellectuals, and executives who favored Roosevelt's leadership—assembled in a rump convention to create a third political party. "If you wish me to make the fight I will make it," Roosevelt told the delegates, who then organized a Progressive party convention, which assembled in Chicago on August 5. Roosevelt appeared before the delegates, feeling "fit as a bull moose." He was "stripped to the buff and ready for the fight," he said in a fiery speech that was interrupted 145 times by applause. "We stand at Armageddon, and we battle for the Lord." Many of the most prominent progressives endorsed Roosevelt's bid to be the first president representing a third party, the **"Bull Moose" progressive party**. In her speech seconding Roosevelt's nomination, Jane Addams took particular pride in the party's commitment to give women the vote through a constitutional amendment. But few professional politicians turned up. Progressive Republicans decided to preserve their party credentials and fight another day. The disruption of the Republican party caused by the rift between Taft and Roosevelt gave hope to the Democrats, whose leader, Virginia-born New Jersey governor **Woodrow Wilson**, had enjoyed remarkable success in his brief political career.

## Woodrow Wilson's Progressivism

WILSON'S RISE   The emergence of Thomas Woodrow Wilson as the Democratic nominee in 1912 climaxed a political rise that was surprisingly rapid. In 1910, before his nomination and election as governor of New Jersey, Wilson had been president of Princeton University, but he had never run for public office. Yet he had extraordinary abilities: a keen intellect and an analytical temperament, superb educational training, a fertile imagination, and a penchant for boldness. Born in Staunton, Virginia, in 1856, the son of a "noble-saintly mother" and a stern Presbyterian minister, Wilson had grown up in

Georgia and the Carolinas during the Civil War and Reconstruction. Young Wilson, tall and slender with a lean, long face, inherited his father's unquestioning piety. He once declared that "so far as religion is concerned, argument is adjourned." Wilson also developed a consuming ambition to "serve" humankind. Driven by a sense of providential destiny, he nurtured an obstinate righteousness and habitual intransigence that would prove to be his undoing.

Wilson graduated from Princeton in 1879. After finishing "terribly boring" law school at the University of Virginia he had a brief, unfulfilling legal practice in Atlanta. From there he went to the new Johns Hopkins University in Baltimore, where he found his calling in the study of history and political science. After a seventeen-year stint as a popular college professor, he was unanimously elected president of Princeton University in 1902. Eight years later, in 1910, Democratic party leaders in New Jersey offered Wilson their support for the 1910 gubernatorial nomination. The party leaders sought a respectable conservative to help them ward off progressive challengers, and Wilson fit the bill: he was conservative in his background and temperament, a southern Democrat who had displayed a profound distrust of radical ideas such as those professed by William Jennings Bryan and other populists. Like Roosevelt, however, Wilson began to view progressive reform as a necessary expedient in order to stave off more radical social change. Elected as a reform candidate, Governor Wilson turned the tables on the state's Democratic party bosses who had put him on the ticket by persuading the state legislature to adopt an array of progressive reforms: a workers' compensation law, a corrupt-practices law, measures to regulate public utilities, and ballot reforms.

Such strong leadership brought Wilson to the attention of national Democratic party leaders. At the 1912 Democratic nominating convention, Wilson faced stiff competition from several party regulars, but with the support of William Jennings Bryan, he prevailed on the forty-sixth ballot. Wilson justifiably called his nomination a "political miracle."

THE ELECTION OF 1912  The 1912 presidential campaign involved four candidates: Wilson and Taft represented the two major parties, while Eugene V. Debs of Indiana ran as a Socialist ("This is our year!" he declared), and Roosevelt headed the Progressive party ticket. They all shared a basic progressive assumption that the old notion of do-nothing government was bankrupt; modern conditions required active measures to promote the general welfare. The rise of big business, in other words, required a bigger role for government. But they differed in the nature and extent of their activism.

No sooner did the formal campaign open than Roosevelt's candidacy almost ended. While entering a car on his way to deliver a speech in Milwaukee, he was shot by John Schrank, a mentally disturbed New Yorker who believed any president seeking a third term should be shot. The bullet went through Roosevelt's overcoat, spectacles case, and fifty-page speech, then fractured a rib before lodging just below his right lung, an inch from his heart. "Stand back, don't hurt the man," he yelled at the crowd as they mobbed the attacker. Roosevelt demanded that he be driven to the auditorium to deliver his speech. In a dramatic gesture he showed the audience his bloodstained shirt and punctured text and vowed, "It takes more than this to kill a bull moose."

As the campaign developed, Taft quickly lost ground. "There are so many people in the country who don't like me," he lamented. The contest settled down to a running debate over the competing programs touted by the two front-runners: Roosevelt's New Nationalism and Wilson's New Freedom. The miscellany of ideas that Roosevelt fashioned into his New Nationalism had first been outlined in *The Promise of American Life* (1909) by Herbert Croly, a then-obscure New York journalist. Croly stressed that progressives were not romantic idealists; they were pragmatists and realists who believed that "good" governments were needed to protect democratic ideals. Through long-range planning, expert management, modern efficiencies, and organized discipline and integrity, progressive governance could ensure that compassionate capitalism flourished. Herbert Croly's central thesis about progressivism was that government needed to expand its scope and powers to match the growing size and power of corporate America.

Roosevelt viewed Croly's book as the guide to his version of progressivism. His New Nationalism would use government authority to promote social justice by enacting overdue reforms such as workers' compensation programs for on-the-job injuries, regulations to protect women and children in the workplace, and a stronger Bureau of Corporations. These ideas and more went into the platform of the Progressive party, which called for a federal trade commission with sweeping authority over business and a tariff commission to set rates on a "scientific basis."

**Wilson's reforms**

Woodrow Wilson campaigning from a railroad car.

Before the end of his administration, Woodrow Wilson would be swept into the current of the New Nationalism, too. But initially he adhered to the decentralizing anti-trust traditions of his party. At the start of the 1912 campaign, Wilson conferred with Louis D. Brandeis, a progressive lawyer from Boston who focused Wilson's thought much as Croly had focused Roosevelt's. Brandeis's design for Wilson's **New Freedom** program differed from Roosevelt's New Nationalism in its insistence that the federal government should restore competition in the economy rather than focus on regulating huge monopolies. Whereas Roosevelt admired the power and efficiency of law-abiding corporations, even if they were virtual monopolies, Brandeis and Wilson were convinced that all huge industries needed to be broken up, not regulated. Wilson's approach to progressivism required a vigorous anti-trust policy, lower tariffs to allow more foreign goods to compete in American markets, and dissolution of the concentration of financial power in Wall Street. Unlike Roosevelt, Brandeis and Wilson saw the expansion of federal power as only a temporary necessity, not a permanent condition. Government intervention was needed to ensure that "fair play" occurred in the marketplace. Roosevelt, who was convinced that both giant corporations and an expanding federal government were permanent developments, dismissed the New Freedom as mere fantasy. For his part, Taft attacked his two progressive opponents by reminding them that the federal government "cannot create good times. It cannot make the rain to fall, the sun to shine or the crops to grow," but too many "meddlesome" regulations could deny the nation the prosperity it deserved.

On election day, the Republican schism between Taft and Roosevelt opened the way for Woodrow Wilson to win handily in the Electoral College, garnering 435 votes to 88 for Roosevelt and 8 for Taft. But in popular votes, Wilson had only 42 percent of the total. Roosevelt received 27 percent, and Taft 23 percent. After learning of his election, Wilson told the chairman of the Democratic party that "God ordained that I should be the next president of the United States." Perhaps. But had the Republican party not been split in two, Wilson would have been trounced. His was the victory of a minority candidate over a divided opposition. A majority of voters had endorsed progressivism, but only a minority preferred Wilson's program of reform, the New Freedom.

The **election of 1912** was significant in several ways. First, it was a high-water mark for progressivism, with all the candidates claiming to be progressives of one sort or another. The election was also the first to feature party primaries. The two leading candidates debated the basic issues of progressivism in a campaign unique in its focus on vital alternatives and in its highly philosophical tone. This was an election with real choices. The Socialist party, the left wing of progressivism, polled over nine hundred thousand votes for Eugene V. Debs, its highest proportion ever. Debs, the son of immigrant shopkeepers, was a fabled union organizer who had run for president twice before but had never garnered so many votes.

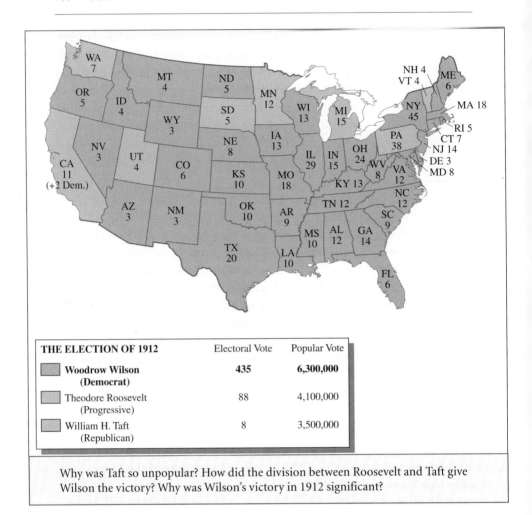

| THE ELECTION OF 1912 | Electoral Vote | Popular Vote |
|---|---|---|
| **Woodrow Wilson** (Democrat) | **435** | **6,300,000** |
| Theodore Roosevelt (Progressive) | 88 | 4,100,000 |
| William H. Taft (Republican) | 8 | 3,500,000 |

Why was Taft so unpopular? How did the division between Roosevelt and Taft give Wilson the victory? Why was Wilson's victory in 1912 significant?

Second, the election gave Democrats effective national power for the first time since the Civil War. For two years during the second administration of Grover Cleveland, from 1893 to 1895, they had held the White House and majorities in both houses of Congress, but they had fallen quickly out of power during the severe economic depression of the 1890s. Now, under Wilson, they again held the presidency and were the majority in both the House of Representatives and the Senate.

Third, the election of Wilson brought southerners back into the orbit of national and international affairs in a significant way for the first time since the Civil War. Five of Wilson's ten cabinet members were born in the South, three still resided there, and William Jennings Bryan, the secretary of state, was an idol of the southern masses. At the president's right hand, and one of the most influential members of the Wilson circle, at least until 1919, was "Colonel" Edward M. House of Texas. Wilson described House as "my second personality. He is my independent self." House was responsible for getting Wilson's proposals through Congress. Southern Congressmen, by virtue of their seniority, held the lion's share of committee chairmanships. As a result, much of the progressive legislation of the Wilson era would bear the names of the southern Democrats who guided it through Congress.

Fourth and finally, the election of 1912 altered the character of the Republican party. The defection of the Bull Moose Progressives had weakened the party's progressive wing. The leaders of the Republican party that would return to power in the 1920s would be more conservative in tone and temperament.

WILSONIAN REFORM  On March 4, 1913, a huge crowd surrounded the Capitol in Washington, D.C., to witness Woodrow Wilson's inauguration as the first Democratic president since Grover Cleveland. The new president's eloquent speech championed the ideals of social justice that animated many progressives. "We have been proud of our industrial achievements," he said, "but we have not hitherto stopped thoughtfully enough to count the human cost . . . the fearful physical and spiritual cost to the men and women and children upon whom the dead weight and burden of it all has fallen pitilessly the years through." He promised specifically a lower tariff and a new nationally regulated banking system.

If Roosevelt had been a strong president by force of personality, Wilson became a strong president by force of conviction. He was an expert on managing legislation through the Congress. The American president, he had written in *Congressional Government,* "is . . . the political leader of the nation, or has it in his choice to be. The nation as a whole has chosen him, and is conscious that it has no other political spokesman. His is the only national voice in affairs." Wilson relished public support, but, like Roosevelt, he also courted members of Congress through personal contacts, invitations to the White House, and speeches in the Capitol. He was a remarkably savvy legislative leader. During his first two years, Wilson pushed through more new bills than any previous president.

THE TARIFF  Wilson's leadership faced its first big test on the issue of tariff reform. He believed that corporations were misusing tariffs to suppress foreign competition and keep prices artificially high. He often claimed that the "tariff made the trusts," believing that tariffs had encouraged the growth of industrial monopolies and degraded the political process by producing armies of paid lobbyists who invaded Congress each year. In attacking high tariffs, Wilson sought to strike a blow for consumers and honest government. He acted quickly and boldly, summoning Congress to a special session (which lasted eighteen months—the longest in history) and addressing the legislators in person—the first president to do so since John Adams. Congress acted vigorously on tariff reductions; the new bill passed the House easily. The crunch came in the Senate, the traditional graveyard of tariff reform. Swarms of industry lobbyists got so thick in Washington, Wilson said, that "a brick couldn't be thrown without hitting one of them." The president turned the tables with a public statement that focused the spotlight on the "industrious and insidious" tariff lobby.

The Underwood-Simmons Tariff became law in 1913. It was the first time the tariff had been lowered since the Civil War. To compensate for the reduced tariff revenue, the bill created the first graduated income tax levied under the newly ratified Sixteenth Amendment: 1 percent on income over $3,000 ($4,000 for married couples) up to a top rate of 7 percent on annual income of $500,000 or more.

THE FEDERAL RESERVE ACT   Before the new tariff had cleared the Senate, the administration proposed the first major banking and currency reform since the Civil War. Ever since Andrew Jackson had killed the Second Bank of the United States in the 1830s, the nation had been without a central bank. Instead, the money supply was administered in a decentralized fashion by hundreds of private banks. Such a decentralized system fostered instability and inefficiency. By 1913, virtually everyone had agreed that the banking system needed restructuring. Wilson told Congress that a federal banking system was needed to ensure that "the banks may be the instruments, not the masters, of business and of individual enterprise and initiative."

**"Reading the Death Warrant"**

Woodrow Wilson's plan for banking and currency reform spells the death of the "money trust," according to this cartoon.

The Federal Reserve Act of 1913 created a new national banking system, with regional reserve banks supervised by a central board of directors. There would be twelve Federal Reserve banks, each owned by member banks in its district, which could issue Federal Reserve notes (currency) to member banks. All national banks became members; state banks and trust companies could join if they wished. Each member bank had to transfer 6 percent of its capital to the Federal Reserve bank and deposit a portion of its reserves there. This arrangement made it possible to expand both the money supply and bank credit in times of high business activity or as the level of borrowing increased.

The new system corrected three great defects in the previous arrangement: now bank reserves could be pooled, affording greater security; both the nation's currency supply and bank credit became more elastic to respond to economic growth; and the concentration of the nation's monetary reserves in New York City was decreased. The new national banking system represented a dramatic new step in active government intervention and control in one of the most sensitive segments of the economy. It was the most significant domestic initiative of Wilson's presidency.

ANTI-TRUST LAWS   While promoting banking and tariff reforms, Wilson made trust-busting the central focus of the New Freedom. Giant corporations had continued to grow despite the Sherman Anti-Trust Act and the federal watchdog agency, the Bureau of Corporations. Wilson's solution to the problem was a revision of the Sherman Act to define more explicitly what counted as restraint of trade. He decided to make a strong Federal Trade Commission (FTC) the cornerstone of his anti-trust program. Created in 1914, the five-member commission replaced Roosevelt's Bureau of Corporations and assumed new powers to define "unfair trade practices" and issue "cease-and-desist" orders when it found evidence of unfair competition.

Henry D. Clayton, a Democrat from Alabama on the House Judiciary Committee, drafted an anti-trust bill in 1914 that outlawed practices such as price discrimination (charging different customers different prices for the same goods); "tying" agreements, which limited the right of dealers to handle the products of competing manufacturers; and corporations' acquisition of stock in competing corporations. In every case, however, conservative forces in the Senate qualified these provisions by tacking on the weakening phrase "where the effect may be to substantially lessen competition" or words of similar effect. And conservative southern Democrats and northern Republicans amended the Clayton Anti-Trust Act to allow for broad judicial review of the FTC's decisions, thus further weakening its freedom of action. In accordance with the president's recommendation, however, corporate officials were made individually responsible for any violations.

Agrarian activists in alliance with organized labor won a stipulation that declared farm-labor organizations were not unlawful combinations in restraint of trade. Injunctions in labor disputes, moreover, were not to be handed down by federal courts unless "necessary to prevent irreparable injury to property." Though hailed by union leaders as labor's Magna Carta, these provisions were later neutralized by court decisions. Wilson himself remarked that the act did little more than affirm the right of unions to exist by forbidding their dissolution for acting in restraint of trade.

Administration of the anti-trust laws generally proved disappointing to the more vehement progressives under Wilson. The president reassured business leaders that his purposes were friendly. As his secretary of commerce put it later, Wilson hoped to "create in the Federal Trade Commission a counselor and friend to the business world." But its first chairman lacked forcefulness, and under its next head, a Chicago industrialist, the FTC practically abandoned its function as watchdog of big business activities. The Justice Department, meanwhile, offered help and advice to businessmen interested in arranging matters so as to avoid anti-trust prosecutions. The appointment of conservative men to the ICC and the Federal Reserve won plaudits from the business world and profoundly disappointed progressives.

SOCIAL JUSTICE    In November 1914, President Wilson announced that progressivism had accomplished its major goals. He had fulfilled his promises to lower the tariff, reorganize the banking system, and strengthen the anti-trust laws. The New Freedom was now complete, he wrote late in 1914; the future would be "a time of healing because [it would be] a time of just dealing." Wilson's announcement that the New Freedom was finished bewildered many progressives, especially those who had long advocated "social-justice" legislation. Although Wilson endorsed states allowing women to vote, he declined to support a federal suffrage amendment because his party platform had not done so. He also withheld support from federal child-labor legislation because he regarded it as a state matter. He opposed a bill providing low-interest loans to farmers on the grounds that it was "unwise and unjustifiable to extend the credit of the government to a single class of the community." Herbert Croly, the editor of *The New Republic*, who had written *The Promise of the American Life* and was widely regarded as the leading progressive theorist, was dumbfounded by Wilson's conservative turn. He wondered how Wilson could assert "that the fundamental wrongs of a modern society can be easily and quickly righted as a consequence of [passing] a few laws." Wilson's about-face, he concluded, "casts suspicion upon his own sincerity or upon his grasp of the realities of modern social and industrial life."

PROGRESSIVISM FOR WHITES ONLY   African American leaders were also perplexed and disappointed by Wilson's resurgent conservatism. Like many other progressives, Woodrow Wilson showed little interest in the plight of African Americans. In fact, he shared many of the racist attitudes prevalent at the time. Although Wilson denounced the Ku Klux Klan's "reign of terror," he sympathized with its motives of restoring white rule in the postwar South and relieving whites of what he called the "ignorant and hostile" power of the black vote. As a student at Princeton, Wilson had detested the enfranchisement of blacks, arguing that Americans of Anglo-Saxon origin would always resist domination by "an ignorant and inferior race." In the late nineteenth century, Professor Wilson had written that the suppression of black political rights in the post–Civil War South reflected "the natural, inevitable ascendancy of the whites."

Later, as a politician, Wilson courted African American voters, but he rarely consulted black leaders and repeatedly avoided opportunities to associate with them in public or express support for African Americans. That he refused to create a National Race Commission was a great disappointment to the black community, as was Wilson's appointment to his cabinet of

**The privileged elite**

President Wilson and the First Lady ride in a carriage.

southerners who were uncompromising racists. Josephus Daniels, a North Carolina newspaper editor who became Wilson's secretary of the navy, wrote that "the subjection of the negro, politically, and the separation of the negro, socially, are paramount to all other considerations in the South." Daniels, as well as other cabinet members, set about racially segregating the employees in their agencies. Secretary of State William Jennings Bryan, who had changed his residency from Nebraska to Florida, thanked God that he was "a member of the greatest of all the races, the Caucasian race." As a three-time presidential candidate, he had studiously ignored the "race problem." Now, as secretary of state, he supported efforts to segregate federal employees by race—separate offices, dining facilities, restrooms, and water fountains.

In November 1914 a delegation of national black leaders visited Wilson in the White House to complain about a self-proclaimed "progressive" president adopting such a "regressive" racial policy. Wilson initially claimed ignorance of the efforts to segregate federal offices, but he eventually argued that both races benefited from the new segregation policies because they eliminated "the possibility of friction." William Trotter, a Harvard-educated African-American newspaper editor who helped found the National Association for the Advancement of Colored People (NAACP) and the Equal Rights League, scolded the first-year president: "Have you a 'new freedom' for white Americans, and a new slavery for 'your Afro-American fellow citizens?' God forbid." A furious Wilson then told the black visitors to leave. The segregationist policies of the administration blatantly contradicted the "progressive" commitment of Bryan and Wilson to social equality. Their progressivism was for whites only.

THE WOMEN'S MOVEMENT    The suffrage movement had garnered little support during Theodore Roosevelt's presidency. He explained that he personally supported voting rights for women but "I am not an enthusiastic advocate of it because I do not regard it as a very important matter." He believed that women should continue to focus their energies on motherhood, "which is more important than any man's work." By 1912, however, Roosevelt had changed his mind. During the presidential campaign, he admitted that "I am rather in favor of the suffrage, but very tepidly." For his part, Woodrow Wilson, despite having two daughters who were suffragists, insisted that the issue of women's voting rights should be left to the states. He also believed that women should "supplement a man's life" rather than seek equality in every sphere. A Mississippi Democrat was more blunt in his opposition: "I would rather die and go to hell," he claimed, "than vote for woman's suffrage."

The lack of support from the progressive presidents led some leaders of the suffrage movement to revise their tactics in the second decade of the new century. In 1910, **Alice Paul**, a Quaker social worker who had earned a doctoral degree in political science from the University of Pennsylvania, returned from an apprenticeship with the militant suffragists of England, who had developed effective forms of civil disobedience as a way of generating attention and support. The courageously militant Paul became head of the National American Woman Suffrage Association (NAWSA). She instructed female activists to picket state legislatures, target and "punish" politicians who failed to endorse suffrage, chain themselves to public buildings, incite police to arrest them, and undertake hunger strikes. In 1913, Paul organized five thousand suffragists to march in protest at Woodrow Wilson's presidential inauguration. Four years later, Paul helped form the National Woman's Party. By 1917, she had decided that suffragists must do something even more dramatic to force President Wilson to support their cause: picket the White House. On January 11, 1917, Paul and her followers took up positions around the White House. They took turns carrying their signs on the sidewalks all day, five days a week, for six months, whereupon the president ordered their arrest. Some sixty suffragists were jailed. For her role, Alice Paul was sentenced to seven months in prison. She then went on a hunger strike, leading prison officials to force feed her through a tube inserted in her nose. Under an avalanche of press coverage and public criticism, President Wilson pardoned her and the other jailed activists.

The courageous proponents of women's suffrage put forth several arguments in favor of voting rights. Many assumed that the right to vote and hold office was a matter of simple justice: women were just as capable as men in exercising the rights and responsibilities of citizenship. Others insisted that women were morally superior to men and therefore would raise the quality of the political process by their participation in it. They also would be less prone to use warfare as a solution to international disputes and national differences. Women voters, advocates argued, would also promote the welfare of society rather than partisan or selfish gains. Allowing women to vote would create a great engine for progressive social change. One activist explicitly linked women's suffrage with the social gospel, declaring that women embraced Christ more readily than men; if they were elected to public office, they would "far more effectively guard the morals of society and the sanitary conditions of cities."

Yet the women's suffrage movement was not immune from the prevailing social, ethnic, and racial prejudices of the day. **Carrie Chapman Catt** echoed the fears of many middle- and upper-class women when she warned of the danger that "lies in the votes possessed by the males in the slums of the cities, and the ignorant foreign [immigrant] vote." She added that the nation, with "ill-advised haste" had enfranchised "the foreigner, the Negro and the Indian" but still balked at women voting. In the South, suffragists catered to generations of deeply embedded racism. One of them declared that giving white women the vote "would insure immediate and durable white supremacy." Most of the suffrage organizations excluded African American women.

Whatever the motives, a grudging President Wilson finally endorsed what journalists called the Susan B. Anthony Amendment in early 1918, explaining to the Senate that he saw it as a reward for the role women had played in supporting the war effort. After six months of delay, debate, and failed votes, the Congress passed the **Nineteenth Amendment** in the spring of 1919 and sent it to the states for ratification. Tennessee's legislature was the last of thirty-six state assemblies to approve the amendment, and it did so in dramatic fashion. The initial vote was deadlocked 48–48. Then a twenty-four-year-old legislator named Harry Burn changed his vote to yes at the insistence of his mother. The Nineteenth Amendment was ratified on August 18, 1920, making the United States the twenty-second nation in the world to allow women's suffrage. It was the climactic achievement of the Progressive Era. Suddenly 9.5 million women were eligible to vote; in the 1920 presidential election they would make up 40 percent of the electorate.

### Alice Paul

Alice Paul's strategies of civil disobedience became increasingly militant. Here she sews a suffrage flag, which she often brandished at strikes and protests.

MARGARET SANGER AND BIRTH CONTROL    Perhaps the most controversial women's issue of the Progressive Era involved birth control. In 1916, the first birth-control clinic in the nation opened in Brooklyn, New York. One of the staff members was a feisty woman named **Margaret Sanger**, a nurse and midwife. Sanger had grown up with ten siblings, one of whom she helped deliver when she was eight years old. While working in the tenements of Manhattan, Sanger saw many poor, young mothers struggling to provide for their growing families. She also witnessed the consequences of unwanted pregnancies, tragic miscarriages, and amateur abortions. The young women she encountered were desperate for information about how to avoid pregnancy. Sanger insisted that women ("doomed people") could never "be on equal footing with men until they have complete control over their reproductive functions." So Sanger began to distribute birth-control information to working-class women in 1912 and resolved to spend the rest of her life helping women gain control of their bodies. Two years later, she began publishing the *Woman Rebel*, a monthly feminist newspaper which authorities declared obscene. In 1921, Sanger organized the American Birth Control League, which later changed its name to Planned Parenthood. The Birth Control League distributed birth-control information to doctors, social workers, women's clubs, and the scientific community, as well as to thousands of women. Such efforts aroused intense opposition, but Sanger and others persisted in their efforts to enable women to control whether they became pregnant. Sanger was viewed as a hero by many progressive reformers. In the 1920s, however, she alienated supporters of birth control by endorsing what was called eugenics: the effort to reduce the number of genetically "unfit" people in society by sterilizing the mentally incompetent and other people with certain unwanted hereditary conditions. Birth control, she stressed in a chilling justification of eugenics, was "the most constructive and necessary of the means to racial health."

PROGRESSIVE RESURGENCE    The need to weld a winning political coalition in 1916 pushed Woodrow Wilson back onto the road of reform. Progressive Democrats were growing restless with his conservative stance, and after war broke out in Europe in August 1914, further divisions arose over defense preparedness and foreign policy issues. At the same time, the Republicans were repairing their own rift, as the "Bull Moose" Progressive party showed little staying power in the midterm elections and Theodore Roosevelt showed little will to preserve it. Wilson could gain reelection only by courting progressives of all parties. In 1916, the president scored points with them when he nominated Louis D. Brandeis to the Supreme Court. Conservatives waged a vigorous battle against Brandeis, but Senate progressives rallied to win confirmation of the social-justice champion, the first Jewish member of the Court.

Meanwhile, Wilson announced a broad new program of farm and labor reforms. The agricultural sector continued to suffer from a shortage of capital. To address the problem, Wilson supported a proposal to set up special rural banks to provide long-term farm loans. The Federal Farm Loan Act became law in 1916. Under the control of the Federal Farm Loan Board, twelve Federal Land banks paralleled the regional Federal Reserve banks and offered farmers loans of five to forty years' duration at low interest rates.

Thus the dream of federal loans to farmers, long advocated by Populists, finally came to fruition when Congress passed the Warehouse Act of 1916, which enabled farmers who stored their harvest in designated warehouses to receive federal receipts that could be used as collateral for short-term bank loans. Farmers were also pleased by the passage of the Smith-Lever Act of 1914 and the Smith-Hughes Act of 1917. The first provided federal financing for farm-demonstration agents who fanned out to educate farmers about new equipment and new ideas related to agricultural efficiency. The second measure extended agricultural and mechanical education to high schools. Farmers with the newfangled automobiles had more than a passing interest as well in the Federal Highways Act of 1916, which helped finance new highways. The progressive resurgence of 1916 broke the logjam on workplace reforms as well.

LABOR LEGISLATION   One of the longstanding goals of many progressive Democrats was a federal child labor law. When Congress passed the Keating-Owen Act, Wilson expressed doubts about its constitutionality, but he eventually signed the landmark legislation, which excluded from interstate commerce any goods manufactured by children under the age of fourteen. The Keating-Owen Act was later ruled unconstitutional by the Supreme Court on the grounds that regulating child labor was outside the bounds of regulating interstate commerce. Effective action against child labor abuses had to await the New Deal of the 1930s.

Another important accomplishment was the eight-hour workday for railroad workers, a measure that the Supreme Court upheld. The Adamson Act of 1916 resulted from a threatened strike of railroad unions demanding an eight-hour workday and other concessions. Wilson, who objected to some of the demands, nevertheless went before Congress to request action on the hours limitation. The Adamson Act required an eight-hour workday, with time and a half for overtime, and appointed a commission to study the problem of working conditions in the railroad industry.

## LIMITS OF PROGRESSIVISM

During Wilson's two terms as president, progressivism reached its zenith. After two decades of political ferment (three if the Populist years are counted), the great contribution of progressive politics was the firm establishment and general acceptance of the public-service concept of government. The Progressive Era was an optimistic age in which all sorts of reformers assumed that no problem lay beyond solution. But like all great historic movements, progressivism displayed elements of paradox and irony. Despite all of the talk of greater democracy, progressivism had a blind spot when it came to racial equality. The Progressive Era was the age of disenfranchisement for southern blacks. The first two decades of the twentieth century also witnessed a new round of anti-immigrant prejudice. The initiative and referendum, supposedly democratic reforms, proved subject to manipulation by corporations and political machines that could mount well-financed publicity campaigns. And much of the public policy of the time came to be formulated by elites—technical experts and members of appointed boards—rather than by representative segments of the population. There is a fine irony in the fact that the drive to increase the political role of ordinary people paralleled efforts to strengthen executive leadership and exalt government technical expertise. This "progressive" age of efficiency and bureaucracy, in business as well as government, brought into being a society in which more and more of the decisions affecting people's lives were made by unelected bureaucrats.

Progressivism was largely a middle-class movement in which the destitute poor and unorganized had little influence. The supreme irony was that a movement so dedicated to the rhetoric of democracy should experience so steady a decline in voter participation. In 1912, the year of Roosevelt's Bull Moose campaign, with four presidential candidates, voting dropped off by between 6 and 7 percent. The new politics of issues and charismatic leaders proved to be less effective in turning out voters than traditional party organizations and party bosses had been. And by 1916, the optimism of an age that presumed social progress was already confronted by a vast slaughter. In 1914, Europe had stumbled into a horrific world war, and the United States would soon be drawn into its destruction. The twentieth century, which dawned with such bright hopes for social progress, held in store episodes of unparalleled brutality and holocaust.

*End of Chapter Review*

## CHAPTER SUMMARY

- **Progressivism**  Progressives believed that industrialization and urbanization were negatively affecting American life. They were middle-class idealists in both political parties who sought reform and regulation in order to ensure social justice. Many progressives wished to curb the powers of local political machines and establish honest and efficient government. They also called for an end to child labor, laws promoting safety in the workplace, a ban on the sale of alcoholic beverages, legislation curbing trusts, and women's suffrage.

- **Muckrakers**  Theodore Roosevelt named the journalists whose works exposed social ills "muckrakers." New, inexpensive popular magazines, such as *McClure's*, published articles about municipal corruption, horrendous conditions in meatpacking plants and urban slums, and predatory business practices. By raising public awareness of these issues, muckrakers contributed to major changes in the workplace and in governance.

- **Square Deal Program**  President Roosevelt used his executive position to promote his progressive Square Deal program, which included regulating trusts, arbitrating the 1902 coal strike, regulating the railroads, and cleaning up the meat and drug industries. President Taft continued to bust trusts and reform the tariff, but Republican party bosses, reflecting their big business interests, ensured that the tariff reductions were too few to satisfy the progressives in the party. Roosevelt decided to seek the Republican presidential nomination in 1912 because of progressives' disillusionment with Taft.

- **Presidential Election of 1912**  In 1912, after the Republicans renominated Taft, Roosevelt's supporters bolted the convention, formed the Progressive party, and nominated Roosevelt. Although some Democratic progressives supported Roosevelt, the split in the Republican party led to Woodrow Wilson's success. Having won a majority in both houses of Congress as well as the presidential election, the Democrats effectively held national power for the first time since the Civil War.

- **Wilsonian Progressivism**  Although Woodrow Wilson was a progressive, his approach was different from Roosevelt's. His New Freedom program promised less federal intervention in business and a return to such traditional Democratic policies as a low tariff. Wilson began a rigorous anti-trust program and oversaw the establishment of the Federal Reserve System. He opposed federal programs promoting social justice and initially withheld support for federal regulation of child labor and a constitutional amendment guaranteeing women's suffrage. A southerner, he believed blacks were inferior and supported segregation.

## CHRONOLOGY

| | |
|---|---|
| 1889 | Hull-House, a settlement house, opens in Chicago |
| 1902 | Theodore Roosevelt attempts to arbitrate the coal strike |
| 1902 | Justice Department breaks up Northern Securities Company |
| 1903 | Congress passes the Elkins Act |
| 1906 | Upton Sinclair's *The Jungle* is published |
| 1906 | Congress passes the Meat Inspection Act and the Pure Food and Drug Act |
| 1908 | Supreme Court issues *Muller v. Oregon* decision |
| 1909 | William Taft is inaugurated president |
| 1910 | Congress passes the Mann-Elkins Act |
| 1911 | Triangle Shirtwaist Company fire |
| 1913 | Congress passes the Federal Reserve Act |
| 1914 | Congress passes the Clayton Anti-Trust Act |
| 1916 | Louis Brandeis is nominated to fill a seat on the Supreme Court |
| 1920 | Nineteenth Amendment, guaranteeing women's suffrage, is ratified |

## KEY TERMS & NAMES

social gospel  p. 936

settlement houses  p. 937

Jane Addams  p. 937

muckrakers  p. 942

Taylorism  p. 945

social justice  p. 947

Florence Kelley  p. 948

Gifford Pinchot  p. 956

New Nationalism  p. 960

Sixteenth Amendment  p. 961

"Bull Moose" progressive party  p. 962

Woodrow Wilson  p. 962

New Freedom  p. 965

Election of 1912  p. 965

Alice Paul  p. 973

Carrie Chapman Catt p. 973

Nineteenth Amendment p. 974

Margaret Sanger  p. 975

# 24

# AMERICA AND
# THE GREAT WAR

FOCUS QUESTIONS

Ⓢ wwnorton.com/studyspace

- Why did Woodrow Wilson involve the United States in Mexico's revolutionary turmoil?
- Why did the United States enter the Great War in Europe?
- How did Wilson promote his peace plan?
- Why did the Senate refuse to ratify the Treaty of Versailles?
- What were the consequences of the war at home and abroad?

Throughout the nineteenth century, the United States reaped the benefits of its distance from the frequent wars that plagued Europe. The Atlantic Ocean provided a welcome buffer. During the early twentieth century, however, the nation's comfortable isolation ended. Ever-expanding world trade entwined American interests with the fate of Europe. In addition, the development of steam-powered ships and submarines meant that foreign navies could threaten American security. At the same time, the election of Woodrow Wilson in 1912 brought to the White House a self-righteous moralist determined to impose his standards for proper conduct on renegade nations. This combination of circumstances made the outbreak of the "Great War" in Europe in 1914 a profound crisis for the United States, a crisis that would transform the nation's role in international affairs.

## WILSON AND FOREIGN AFFAIRS

Woodrow Wilson had no experience or expertise in international relations. The former college professor admitted before taking office that "it would be an irony of fate if my administration had to deal chiefly with foreign affairs." But events in Latin America and Europe were to make the irony all too real. From the summer of 1914, when a catastrophic world war erupted in Europe, foreign relations increasingly overshadowed all else, including Wilson's ambitious domestic program of progressive reforms. Wilson began his presidency as a pacifist, but by the end of his second term he had ordered more U.S. military interventions abroad than any president before or since.

IDEALISTIC DIPLOMACY   Although devoid of international experience, Wilson did not lack ideas or convictions about global issues. He saw himself as a man of providential destiny who would help create a new world order governed by morality and idealism rather than selfish national interests. Both Wilson and Secretary of State William Jennings Bryan believed that America had a religious duty to advance democracy and Christianity around the world. As Wilson had declared a few years before becoming president, "Every nation of the world needs to be drawn into the tutelage of America." Wilson and Bryan developed a diplomatic policy based on this pious idealism. During 1913 and 1914, the pacifist Bryan negotiated some thirty "cooling-off" treaties, under which participating nations pledged not to go to war over any disagreement for a period of twelve months pending mediation by an international arbitration panel. The treaties were of little consequence, however. They were soon forgotten in the revolutionary sweep of world events that would make the twentieth century the bloodiest in recorded history.

INTERVENTION IN MEXICO   Mexico, which had been in the throes of revolutions for nearly three years, presented a thorny problem for Woodrow Wilson soon after he took office early in 1913. In 1910, popular resentment against the long-standing Mexican dictatorship had boiled over into revolt. Revolutionary armies occupied Mexico City, and then the victorious rebels began squabbling among themselves. The leader of the rebellion, a progressive reformer named Francisco Madero, was himself overthrown by his chief of staff, General Victoriano Huerta, who assumed power in 1913 and had Madero murdered.

President Wilson refused to recognize any government that used force to gain power. Instead, he stationed U.S. warships off Veracruz, on the Gulf of Mexico, to halt arms shipments to Huerta's regime. "I am going to teach the South American republics to elect good men," Wilson vowed to a British diplomat. On April 9, 1914, several American sailors gathering supplies in Tampico, Mexico, strayed into a restricted area and were arrested. Mexican officials quickly released them and apologized to the U.S. naval commander. There the incident might have ended, but the pompous naval officer demanded that the Mexicans salute the American flag. Wilson backed him up by sending some six thousand U.S. marines and sailors ashore at Veracruz on April 21, 1914. They occupied the city at a cost of nineteen American lives; at least two hundred Mexicans were killed.

The use of U.S. military force in Mexico played out like many previous American interventions in the Caribbean and Central America. The public and the Congress readily endorsed the decision to send troops because American honor was presumed to be at stake, but the complex realities of U.S. troops fighting in a foreign country eventually led to prolonged involvement and public disillusionment. Wilson assumed the Mexican people would welcome the American troops as liberators. Instead, the U.S. occupation of Veracruz aroused the opposition of all factions against the "Yankee imperialists." The American troops finally left Veracruz in late 1914. A year later, the United States and several Latin American governments recognized a new government in Mexico.

Still the troubles south of the border continued. Bickering among various Mexican factions erupted in chaotic civil war. The prolonged upheaval spawned rival revolutionary armies, the largest of which was led by **Francisco Pancho Villa**. Woodrow Wilson vowed to stay out of the turmoil. "The country is theirs," he concluded. "The government is theirs. Their liberty, if they can get it, is theirs, and so far as my influence goes while I am president, nobody shall interfere with them."

In 1916, the charismatic Villa and his men seized a train and murdered sixteen American mining engineers in a deliberate attempt to trigger U.S. intervention and to build up Villa as a popular opponent of the "gringos." That failing, he crossed the border on raids into Texas and New Mexico. On March 9, he and his men went on a rampage in Columbus, New Mexico, burned the town, and killed seventeen Americans, men and women. A furious Woodrow Wilson abandoned his policy of "watchful waiting." He sent General **John J. Pershing** across the Mexican border with a force of eleven thousand U.S. soldiers. For nearly a year, Pershing's troops chased Villa through northern Mexico. They had no luck and were ordered home in 1917.

OTHER PROBLEMS IN LATIN AMERICA   In the Caribbean, Wilson found it as hard to act on his democratic ideals as it was in Mexico. The "**dollar diplomacy**" practiced by the Taft administration had encouraged U.S. bankers to aid debt-plagued governments in Haiti, Guatemala, Honduras, and Nicaragua. Despite Wilson's public stand against using military force to back up American investments, he kept U.S. marines in Nicaragua, where they had been sent by President Taft in 1912 to prevent renewed civil war.

**Pancho Villa**

Villa (center) and his followers rebelled against the president of Mexico and antagonized the United States with attacks against "gringos."

Then, in 1915, he dispatched more marines to Haiti after that country experienced two chaotic revolutions. The U.S. troops stayed in Nicaragua until 1933 and in Haiti until 1934. Disorders in the Dominican Republic brought U.S. Marines to that country in 1916; they remained until 1924. The repeated use of military force only exacerbated the hatred many Latin Americans felt toward the United States, then and since. As the *New York Times* charged, Wilson's frequent interventions made Taft's dollar diplomacy look like "ten cent diplomacy."

## AN UNEASY NEUTRALITY

During the summer of 1914, problems in Latin America and the Caribbean, as well as family tragedy, loomed larger in President Wilson's thinking than the gathering storm in Europe. During his first year as president, his wife, Ellen, had contracted kidney disease, and she died on August 6, 1914. President Wilson was devastated. "Oh, my God! What am I to do?" he exclaimed. Yet six months later the president fell in love with Edith Bolling Galt, a Washington widow, and in December 1915 they were married.

Ellen Wilson had died just as another tragedy was erupting overseas. When the thunderbolt of war struck Europe in the summer of 1914, most Americans saw it "as lightning out of a clear sky," as one North Carolinian wrote. Whatever the troubles in Mexico, whatever disorders and interventions agitated other nations, it seemed unreal that Europe could descend into an orgy of mutual destruction. At the beginning of the twentieth century, Europe had been peaceful and prosperous. No one imagined the scale of a new industrialized form of warfare; it would assume horrible proportions and involve unprecedented ruthlessness. Between 1914 and 1921, the First World War was directly responsible for the deaths of over 9 million combatants and the horrible wounding of 15 million more; it would produce at least 3 million widows and 6 million orphans. The war's sheer horror and destructiveness, its obscene butchery and ravaged landscapes, defied belief.

The First World War resulted from festering imperial rivalries and ethnic conflicts in central Europe that set in motion a series of disastrous events and decisions. The Austro-Hungarian Empire had grown determined to suppress the aggressive expansionism of Serbia, a small, independent kingdom. Germany was equally eager to sustain its dominant standing in central Europe against a resurgent Russia and its ally France. War erupted when an Austrian citizen of Serbian descent assassinated the Austrian ruler, Archduke Franz Ferdinand, in the Bosnian town of Sarajevo. Austria-Hungary's furious determination to punish Serbia for the murder led Russia to mobilize its army in sympathy with its Slavic friends in Serbia. That in turn triggered reactions by a complex system of European alliances: the Triple Alliance, or Central Powers (Germany, Austria-Hungary, and Italy), and the Triple Entente, or Allied Powers (France, Great Britain, and Russia). When Russia refused to stop its army's mobilization, Germany, which backed Austria-Hungary, declared war on Russia on August 1, 1914, and on France two days later. Germany then activated a long-planned invasion plan of France that went through neutral Belgium, an action that brought Great Britain reluctantly into the rapidly widening war on August 4. Japan, eager to seize German colonies in the Pacific, declared war on August 23, and Turkey entered on the side of the Central Powers in October. Although allied with the Central Powers, Italy initially stayed out of the war and then struck a bargain under which it joined the Allied Powers in 1915. The early weeks of the war involved fast-moving assaults and enormous casualties. On one day, August 22, 1914, 27,000 French soldiers were killed. By 1915, almost twenty thousand square miles in Belgium and France were in German hands.

The real surprise in 1914 was not the outbreak of war but the nature of the war that unfolded. The First World War was unlike any previous conflict in its scale, scope, and carnage. Machine guns, high-velocity rifles, aerial bombing, poison gas delivered by wind and artillery shells, flame throwers, land mines, long-range artillery, and armored tanks changed the nature of warfare and produced horrific casualties and widespread destruction. Total war among industrialized nations meant that everyone was considered a combatant, including civilians. Each side tried to starve the other into submission by sealing off foreign trade, often by sinking commercial vessels and passenger liners. Intentional destruction extended well beyond the battlefields. Occupied cities saw their cultural monuments—cathedrals, museums, historic buildings—systematically destroyed. In the first month of the war, for example, German forces overran Louvain, Belgium, where they not only murdered 248 civilians but also burned the city's ancient library to the ground. The brutal war on the "eastern front" in Russia was intended to be a war of racial annihilation. Russia used the pretext of the war to expel 500,000 Jews and 743,000 Poles. Each nation engaged in the war talked regularly about God, duty, sacrifice, patriotism, and honor, but the arbitrary horrors and wastefulness of World War I involved dishonorable actions and decisions that we have yet to understand but cannot forget.

## Verdun

A landscape image from Verdun, taken immediately after the battle, shows how the firepower ravaged the land.

What began as a war of quick movement in August 1914 bogged down after 1915 into a stalemated war of senseless attrition punctuated by massive battles that contributed little except more obscene slaughter. During the devastating Battle of Verdun, in northeast France, which lasted from February to December 1916, some 32 million artillery shells were fired—1,500 shells for every square meter of the battlefield. Such unprecedented massed firepower ravaged the landscape, shattering villages and turning farmland and forests into cratered wasteland. The casualties were staggering. Some 162,000 French soldiers died at Verdun; German losses were 143,000. Charles de Gaulle, a young French lieutenant who would become the nation's prime minister, said the conflict had become a "war of extermination."

Trench warfare gave the First World War its lasting character. Most battles were won not by skillful maneuvers or by superior generalship but by brute force. The object of what came to be called "**industrial war**" was not so much to gain ground but simply to decimate the other army in a prolonged war of attrition until their manpower and resources were exhausted. The war on the western front usually involved hundreds of thousands of men crawling out of their muddy dugouts and rat-infested, corpse-crammed trenches after hours of being pummeled by enemy artillery bombardments (shrapnel

### Trench warfare

American troops eat amidst the reek of death and threat of enemy fire in a front-line trench in France.

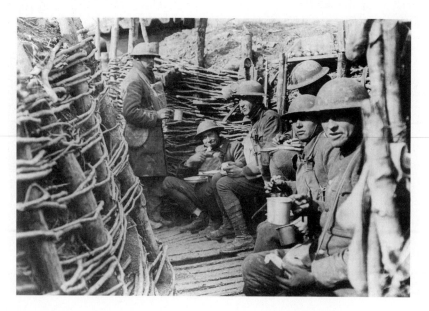

from long-distance artillery caused 60 percent of the war's casualties). They then had to cross a blood-soaked "no-man's-land," stitched with barbed wire and sown with mines, to engage in suicidal assaults on well-defended enemy machine-gun emplacements. In one attack at Ypres in Belgium, the British lost thirteen thousand men in only three hours of fighting, which gained them only one hundred yards of meaningless acreage. Life in the war zone was especially miserable. In addition to the dangers of enemy fire, soldiers on both sides were forced to deal with flooded trenches and terrible diseases such as trench fever and trench foot, which could lead to amputation. Lice and rats were constant companions. The stench was unbearable. Soldiers on both sides ate, slept, and fought among the dead and amid the reek of death.

INITIAL REACTIONS   As the trench war along the western front in Belgium and France stalemated, casualties soared and pressure for American intervention increased. Shock in the United States over the bloodbath in Europe gave way to gratitude that a wide ocean stood between America and the killing fields. "Our isolated position and freedom from entangling alliances," said the *Literary Digest,* ensure that "we are in no peril of being drawn into the European quarrel." President Wilson repeatedly urged Americans to remain "neutral in thought as well as in action." That was more easily said than done. More than a third of the nation's citizens were "hyphenated Americans," first- or second-generation immigrants who retained strong ties to their native country. Among the 13 million immigrants from the countries at war living in the United States, German Americans were by far the largest group, numbering 8 million. And the 4 million Irish Americans harbored a deep-rooted enmity toward England, which over the centuries had conquered and subjugated the Irish. These groups instinctively leaned toward

The Samson-like "War" pulls down the temple of "Civilization"

Most Americans tended to support the Allied Powers, but everyone was shocked by the carnage of the Great War.

the Central Powers. But old-line Americans, largely of British origin, sup-ported the Allied Powers. American leaders were pro-British from the outset of the war. Robert Lansing, first counselor of the State Department; Walter Hines Page, ambassador to London; and "Colonel" Edward House, Wilson's closest adviser—all saw in German militarism a potential danger to the United States.

A STRAINED NEUTRALITY    At first, the war in Europe brought a slump in American exports and the threat of a depression, but by the spring of 1915 the Allies' demand for food and war supplies generated an incredible economic boom for American businesses, bankers, and farmers. To finance their purchases of American supplies, the Allies, especially Britain and France, needed loans. Early in the war, Secretary of State William Jennings Bryan, a strict pacifist, declared that loans to any warring nation were "inconsistent with the true spirit of neutrality." Yet Wilson quietly began approving short-term loans to sustain trade with the desperate Allies. By the fall of 1915, Wilson had removed all restrictions on loans. American investors would eventually advance over $2 billion to the Allies before the United States entered the war, and only $27 million to Germany.

The administration nevertheless clung to its official stance of neutrality through two and a half years of warfare in Europe. Wilson tried valiantly to uphold the "freedom of the seas," which had guided U.S. policy since the Napoleonic Wars of the early nineteenth century. On August 6, 1914, Secretary of State Bryan called upon the warring nations ("belligerents") to respect the rights of neutral nations like the United States to continue its commerce with them by shipping goods across the Atlantic. The Central Powers promptly accepted, but the British refused because they would lose some of their advantage in sea power. In November 1914 the British declared the whole North Sea a war zone, sowed it with mines, and ordered neutral ships to submit to searches. In March 1915, they announced that they would seize ships carrying goods to Germany. American protests were ignored.

NEUTRAL RIGHTS AND SUBMARINES    With the German fleet bottled up by the British blockade, the German government proclaimed a war zone around the British Isles. Enemy merchant ships in those waters would be attacked by submarines, the Germans declared, and "it may not always be possible to save crews and passengers." As the chief advantage of U-boat (*Unterseeboot*) warfare was in surprise, the German decision violated the long-established procedure of stopping an enemy vessel and providing for the safety of passengers and crew before sinking it. Since the British some-

**WORLD WAR I IN EUROPE, 1914**
- Central Powers (Triple Alliance)
- Allied Powers (Triple Entente)
- Neutral countries

How did the European system of alliances spread conflict across all of Europe? How was World War I different from previous wars? How did the war in Europe lead to ethnic tensions in the United States?

times flew neutral flags as a ruse, neutral ships in this war zone would also be in danger.

The United States pronounced the new German submarine policy "an indefensible violation of neutral rights." Wilson warned that Germany would be held to "strict accountability" for any destruction of American lives and property. Then, on May 7, 1915, a German submarine sank a huge ocean liner moving slowly through the Irish Sea. Only as it tipped into the waves was the German commander able to make out the name *Lusitania* on

The *Lusitania*

Americans were outraged when a German torpedo sank the *Lusitania* on May 7, 1915.

the stern. Before the much-celebrated new British passenger liner had left New York City, bound for England, the German embassy had published warnings in American newspapers against travel to the war zone, but 128 Americans were nonetheless among the 1,198 persons lost.

Americans were outraged. The sinking of the *Lusitania* was an act of piracy, Theodore Roosevelt declared. To quiet the uproar, Wilson urged patience: "There is such a thing as a man being too proud to fight. There is such a thing as a nation being so right that it does not need to convince others by force that it is right." Critics lambasted his lame response to the deaths of 128 Americans. Roosevelt castigated Wilson's "unmanly" stance, calling him a "jackass" and threatening to "skin him alive if he doesn't go to war" over the *Lusitania* tragedy. Wilson acknowledged that he had misspoken. "I have a bad habit of thinking out loud," he confessed to a friend the day after his "too proud to fight" speech. The meek language, he admitted, had "occurred to me while I was speaking, and I let it out. I should have kept it in." His previous demand for "strict accountability" now forced him to make a stronger response. On May 13, Secretary of State Bryan reluctantly signed a note demanding that the Germans abandon unrestricted submarine warfare and pay reparations for the sinking of the *Lusitania*. The Germans responded that the ship was armed (which it was not) and secretly carried a cargo of rifles and ammunition (which it did). A second note, on June 9, repeated American demands in stronger terms. The United States, Wilson asserted, was "contending for nothing less high and sacred than the rights of humanity." Bryan, unwilling to risk war over the issue, resigned in protest. He groused to Wilson that Colonel House "has been [acting as] secretary of state, not I, and I have never had your full confidence." Edith Galt, not yet Wilson's wife, took great delight in Bryan's resignation. "Hurrah! Old Bryan is out!" she told the president. "I could shout and sing that at last the world will *know* just what he is." Bryan's successor, Robert Lansing, signed the controversial "*Lusitania* Note" to the Germans.

**Stand by the president**

In this 1915 cartoon, Woodrow Wilson holds to the middle course between the pacifism of Bryan (whose sign reads, "Let Us Avoid Unnecessary Risks") and the belligerence of Roosevelt (whose sign reads, "Let Us Act without Unnecessary Delay").

In response to the uproar over the sinking of the *Lusitania*, the German government had secretly ordered U-boat captains to avoid sinking any more passenger vessels. When, despite the order, two American lives were lost in the sinking of the New York–bound British liner *Arabic*, the Germans paid a cash penalty to the families of the deceased and offered a public assurance on September 1, 1915: "Liners will not be sunk by our submarines without warning and without safety of the lives of non-combatants, provided that the liners do not try to escape or offer resistance." With this so-called *Arabic* Pledge, Wilson's resolute stand seemed to have resulted in a victory for his neutrality policy.

During early 1916, Wilson's trusted adviser Colonel House visited London, Paris, and Berlin in an effort to negotiate an end to the war but found neither side ready to begin serious negotiations. On March 24, 1916, a U-boat torpedoed the French steamer *Sussex,* injuring two Americans. When President Wilson threatened to break off relations, Germany renewed its pledge that U-boats would not torpedo merchant and passenger ships. This *Sussex* Pledge was far stronger than the earlier German promise after the *Arabic* sinking the year before. The *Sussex* Pledge implied the virtual abandonment of submarine warfare.

**THE DEBATE OVER PREPAREDNESS** The *Lusitania* incident and, more generally, the quarrels over neutral commerce contributed to a growing demand in the United States for a stronger army and navy. On December 1, 1914, champions of "preparedness" organized the National Security League to promote their cause. After the *Lusitania* sinking, Wilson asked the War and Navy Departments to develop plans for military expansion.

Pacifists, however, as well as many isolationists in the rural South and West, were opposed to a defense buildup. The new Democratic leader in the House spoke for many Americans when he declared his opposition to "the big Navy and big Army program of the jingoes and war traffickers." During the fall of 1915, the administration's plan to enlarge the army and create a national reserve force of 400,000 ran into such stubborn opposition in Congress that Wilson was forced to accept a compromise between advocates of an expanded force under federal control and advocates of a traditional citizen army. The National Defense Act of 1916 expanded the regular federal army from 90,000 to 175,000 and permitted gradual enlargement to 223,000. It also increased the National Guard to 440,000. Pacifist progressives heaped scorn on Wilson for supporting the military buildup. Jane Addams, the nation's leading social reformer, and Carrie Chapman Catt, one of the most prominent proponents of women's suffrage, asserted that the president was "selling out" to "militarism." Former secretary of state Bryan complained in early 1916 that Wilson wanted to "drag this nation into war."

Opponents of the military buildup insisted that the financial burden should rest upon the wealthy people they held responsible for promoting the military expansion and profiting from trade with the Allies. The income tax became their weapon. Supported by a groundswell of popular support, legislators wrote into the Revenue Act of 1916 changes that doubled the basic income tax rate from 1 to 2 percent, lifted the surtax to a maximum of 13 percent (for a total of 15 percent) on income over $2 million, added an estate tax, levied a 12.5 percent tax on munitions makers, and added a new tax on excess corporate profits. The new taxes amounted to the most clear-cut victory for radical progressives in the entire Progressive Era, a victory further consolidated and advanced after America entered the war. It was the capstone to the progressive legislation that Wilson supported in preparation for the upcoming presidential election.

**THE ELECTION OF 1916** As the 1916 election approached, Republicans hoped to regain their normal electoral majority, and Theodore Roosevelt hoped to be their leader again. But he had committed the deadly political sin of bolting his party in 1912. His eagerness for the United States to enter the war also scared many voters. Needing a candidate who would draw Bull Moose Progressives back into the fold, the Republican leaders turned to Supreme Court Justice Charles Evans Hughes, who had a progressive record as governor of New York from 1907 to 1910.

The Democrats, as expected, chose Woodrow Wilson again. Their platform endorsed a program of social-welfare legislation and prudent military preparedness in case the nation were drawn into the European war. The party referred the idea of women's suffrage to the states and pledged support for a postwar league of nations to enforce peace. The Democrats' most popular issue, however, was an insistent pledge to keep the nation out of the war in Europe. The peace theme, refined in the slogan "He kept us out of war," became the rallying cry of the Wilson campaign.

The candidates in the 1916 presidential election were remarkably similar. Both Wilson and Hughes were the sons of preachers; both were attorneys and former professors; both had been progressive governors; both were known for their pristine integrity. Theodore Roosevelt highlighted the similarities between them when he called the bearded Hughes a "whiskered Wilson." Wilson, however, proved to be the better campaigner. In the end, his twin pledges to keep America out of war and to expand his progressive social agenda brought a narrow victory. The final vote showed a Democratic sweep

**Peace with honor**

Woodrow Wilson's policies of neutrality proved popular in the 1916 campaign.

of the Far West and the South, enough for narrow victories in the Electoral College, by 277 to 254, and in the popular vote, by 9 million to 8.5 million. Despite the victory, the closeness of the election did not bode well for the Democrats.

LAST EFFORTS FOR PEACE    Immediately after the election, Wilson again offered to mediate an end to the war in Europe, but neither side was willing to abandon its major war aims. Wilson then made one more appeal for peace, in the hope that public opinion would force the hands of the warring governments. Speaking before the Senate on January 22, 1917, he asserted the right of the United States to propose a lasting peace settlement, which would have to be a "peace without victory," for only a "peace among equals" could endure. Although Wilson did not know it, he was already too late. Exactly two weeks before he spoke, impatient German military leaders had decided to wage unrestricted submarine warfare on Allied shipping. They took the calculated risk of arousing American anger in the hope of scoring a quick knockout on the battlefields of Europe before U.S. troops could join the war. On January 31, the new policy was announced, effective the next day. All vessels would be sunk without warning. "Freedom of the seas," said the *Brooklyn Eagle,* "will now be enjoyed [only] by icebergs and fish."

On February 3, 1917, Wilson told a joint session of Congress that the United States had broken diplomatic relations with the German government. Three weeks later he asked for authority to arm U.S. merchant ships and "to employ any other instrumentalities or methods" necessary and "to protect our ships and our people." There was little quarrel with arming merchant ships, but there was bitter opposition to Wilson's vague reference to "any other instrumentalities or methods." A dozen die-hard noninterventionists in Congress filibustered the measure until the legislative session expired on March 4. A furious Wilson decided to outflank Congress. On March 12, the State Department announced that a forgotten law of 1792 allowed the arming of merchant ships regardless of congressional inaction.

World events then took another unexpected turn—and another. On February 25, Wilson learned that the British had intercepted an important message from the German foreign minister, Arthur Zimmermann, to the Mexican government. The note urged the Mexicans to invade the United States. In exchange for their making war on America, Germany guaranteed that Mexico would recover its "lost territory in Texas, New Mexico, and Arizona." On March 1, news of the Zimmermann telegram broke in the American press and infuriated the public. Then, later in March 1917, on the other side of the world, a revolution overthrew Russia's czarist government and established the provisional government of a Russian republic. The fall of the czarist autocracy gave Americans the illusion that all the major Allied powers were now fighting for constitutional democracy—an illusion that was shattered in November 1917, when Vladimir Lenin and the Bolsheviks, a determined group of revolutionaries, seized power in war-weakened Russia and established a Communist dictatorship. The bookish Lenin transformed communism into an all-embracing ideology mercilessly imposed on an entire society, eliminating civil liberties, religious life, and the free press, and killing or imprisoning opposition leaders. Communism would become the most significant new political movement of the twentieth century.

## AMERICA'S ENTRY INTO THE WAR

In March 1917, German submarines sank five U.S. merchant vessels in the North Atlantic. That was the last straw for a frustrated President Wilson, who on April 2 asked Congress to recognize that imperial Germany and the United States were at war. In his message to Congress, Wilson transformed the war in Europe from being a conventional struggle for power among historic European rivals to a righteous conflict between democratic ideals and autocratic tyranny. America's effort to maintain a principled neutrality had become in Wilson's mind an unprecedented "great crusade" to end wars forever. He insisted that "the world must be made safe for democracy," or, more accurately, that victory by the democratic nations would make the world safer. The war resolution passed the Senate by a vote of 82 to 6 on April 4. The House concurred, 373 to 50, and Wilson signed the measure on April 6, 1917.

How had matters come to this less than three years after Wilson's proclamation of neutrality? The most prominent causes for America's entrance into the war were the effects of British propaganda in the United States and America's deep involvement in trade with the Allies, which some observers credited to the intrigues of war profiteers and munitions makers. Some proponents of war thought an Allied defeat and German domination of Europe would threaten U.S. security, especially if it meant the destruction of the British navy. Such factors, however, would not have been decisive without the issue of Germany's unrestricted submarine warfare on the Atlantic. Once Wilson had taken a principled stand for the traditional rights of neutral nations and noncombatants on the high seas, he was to some extent at the mercy of ill-considered decisions by the German military leadership.

AMERICA'S EARLY ROLE   War had been declared, but now it needed to be fought. Despite Congress's earlier military preparedness measures, the army remained small and untested. The navy also was largely undeveloped. Now the Wilson administration needed quickly to build and train an army of millions and transport them across an Atlantic Ocean infested with German submarines. The call to arms generated some unusual responses. The old political warhorse William Jennings Bryan, who had resigned as secretary of state over Wilson's policies, now abandoned his pacifism and wired President Wilson that he was willing to serve in the army. Another volunteer was the sixty-year-old former president, Theodore Roosevelt, in ill health and blind in one eye. He visited Wilson in the White House and offered to raise a regiment of army volunteers, just as he had done with the Rough Riders in 1898. Though charmed by his longtime critic, Wilson refused Roosevelt's offer to fight again. Rebuffed but not fazed, Roosevelt kept trying to enlist and resolved to run against Woodrow Wilson in 1920. In the meantime, Roosevelt's four sons joined the army. Two of them would be badly wounded in France, while a third, Quentin, a pilot, was shot down and killed. Their father died in 1919.

**The thrill of American liberty**

This Liberty Loan poster urges immigrants to do their duty for their new country by buying government bonds to help pay for the war.

The formidable challenge of mobilizing the entire nation for war led to an unprecedented expansion of federal government authority. Woodrow Wilson's administration did not invite Americans to support the war effort; it ordered them to do so. Power became increasingly centralized in Washington, as the government conscripted millions of men, directed the conversion of industries and farms to wartime needs, took over the railroads, mediated labor disputes, and in many other respects assumed control of national life. On June 26, 1917, just three months after the declaration of war, the first contingent of the American Expeditionary Force, about 14,500 soldiers commanded by General John J. Pershing, disembarked on the French coast.

When the United States entered the war, the combined strength of the regular army and National Guard was only 379,000; at the end it would be 3.7 million. The need for such large numbers of troops forced Wilson to implement a military draft. Under the Selective Service Act of 1917, all men aged twenty-one to thirty (later, eighteen to forty-five) could be drafted for military service. All told, about 2 million mostly under-trained American troops crossed the Atlantic, and about 1.4 million saw at least some combat, including 42,000 African Americans.

MOBILIZING A NATION   Complete economic mobilization on the home front was necessary to conduct the war efficiently. The Army Appropriation Act of 1916 had created a Council of National Defense, which in turn led to the creation of other wartime agencies. The **Food Administration**, headed by Herbert Hoover, a future president, sought to raise agricultural production while reducing civilian consumption of foodstuffs. "Food will win the war" was the slogan. Hoover directed a national conservation campaign promoting "meatless Tuesdays," "wheatless Wednesdays," "porkless Saturdays," the planting of "victory gardens," and the creative use of leftovers.

The War Industries Board (WIB), established in 1917, soon became the most important of all the federal mobilization agencies. Bernard Baruch, a brilliant financier who exercised a virtual dictatorship over the economy, headed the WIB. Under Baruch, the purchasing bureaus of the United States and Allied governments submitted their needs to the board, which set priorities and issued production quotas to industries. The board could allocate raw materials, order construction of new plants, and with the approval of the president, fix prices. Despite such efforts, however, the unprecedented mobilization effort was often chaotic. Anything that could go wrong did go wrong. Men were drafted only to discover there were no uniforms, weapons, or housing for them. Most of the artillery used by the American army in France had to be acquired from the Allies.

A NEW LABOR FORCE   The closing off of foreign immigration and the movement of 4 million men from the workforce into the armed services created an acute labor shortage across the wartime United States. To meet it, women, African Americans, and other ethnic minorities were encouraged to enter industries and take on jobs heretofore dominated by white men. Northern businesses sent recruiting agents into the southern states to find workers for their factories and mills. Over four hundred thousand southern blacks (and a significant number of whites) began a Great Migration north-ward during the war years, a mass movement that continued unabated through the 1920s and changed the political and social dynamics of north-ern cities. Recruiting agents and newspaper editors portrayed the North as the "land of promise" for southern blacks suffering from their region's depressed agricultural economy and rising racial intimidation and violence. The African American *Chicago Defender* exclaimed: "To die from the bite of frost is far more glorious than at the hands of a mob." By 1930 the number of African Americans living in the North was triple that of 1910. Mexican Americans followed the same migratory pattern in Texas and the Far West.

But the newcomers were not always welcomed. Many white workers in northern cities resented the new arrivals, and racial tensions sparked clashes across the country. In 1917 over forty African Americans and nine whites were killed during a riot over employment in a defense plant in East St. Louis, Illinois. Two years later the toll of a Chicago race riot was nearly as high, with twenty-three African Americans and fifteen whites left dead. In these and other incidents of racial violence, the pattern was the same: whites angered by the influx of southern blacks into their communities would seize upon an incident as an excuse to rampage through black neighborhoods, killing, burning, and looting while white policemen looked the other way or even encouraged the hooliganism.

**Women aid the war effort**

Women working at the Bloomfield International Fuse Company, New Jersey, 1918.

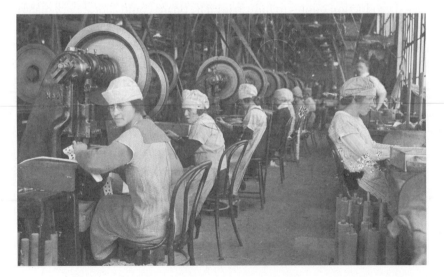

For many women, black and white, intervention in World War I also generated dramatic changes. Initially women supported the war effort in traditional ways. They helped organize fundraising drives, conserved foodstuffs and war-related materials, supported the Red Cross, and joined the army nurse corps. But as the scope of the war widened, both government and industry recruited women to work on farms, loading docks, and railway crews, as well as in the armaments industry, machine shops, steel and lumber mills, and chemical plants. Many women leaders saw such opportunities as a breakthrough. "At last, after centuries of disabilities and discrimination," said a speaker at a Women's Trade Union League meeting in 1917, "women are coming into the labor [force] and festival of life on equal terms with men."

In fact, however, war-generated changes in female employment were limited and brief. About 1 million women participated in "war work," but most of them were young and single and already working outside the home. Most returned to their previous jobs once the war ended. In fact, male-dominated unions encouraged women to revert to their stereotypical domestic roles after the war ended. The Central Federated Union of New York insisted that "the same patriotism which induced women to enter industry during the war should induce them to vacate their positions after the war." The anticipated gains of women in the workforce failed to materialize. In 1920, the 8.5 million working women made up a smaller percentage of the labor force than had working women in 1910. Still, one lasting result of women's contributions to the war effort was Woodrow Wilson's grudging decision to endorse women's suffrage. In the fall of 1918, he told the Senate that giving women the vote was "vital to the winning of the war."

WAR PROPAGANDA   The war effort led the government to mobilize more than economic life: the progressive gospel of efficiency suggested mobilizing public opinion as well. On April 14, 1917, eight days after the declaration of war, President Wilson established the **Committee on Public Information**, composed of the secretaries of state, war, and the navy. Its executive head, **George Creel**, a Denver newsman, sold Wilson on the idea that the best approach to influencing public opinion was propaganda instead of censorship. Creel organized a propaganda machine to explain the Allies' war aims to the people and, above all, to the enemy, where it might help sap their morale. To generate support for the war effort, Creel gathered a remarkable group of journalists, photographers, artists, entertainers, and others useful to his purpose. A film division produced feature movies such as *The Beast of Berlin*. Hardly any public group escaped a harangue by one of

**The Beast of Berlin**

A scene from the movie *The Beast of Berlin*, which gave audiences a propagandistic view of World War I.

the 75,000 "four-minute men" organized to give short speeches on liberty bonds, the need to conserve food and fuel, and other timely topics.

CIVIL LIBERTIES   By arousing public opinion to such a frenzy, the war effort spawned grotesque campaigns of "Americanism" and witch-hunting. Popular prejudice equated anything German with disloyalty. Symphonies refused to perform classical music written by Bach and Beethoven, schools dropped German language classes, and patriots translated *sauerkraut* into "liberty cabbage," *German measles* into "liberty measles," and *dachshunds* into "liberty pups." President Wilson had foreseen these consequences. "Once lead this people into war," he said, "and they'll forget there ever was such a thing as tolerance." What Wilson did not say was that he would lead the effort to suppress civil liberties during and after the war.

Under the Espionage and Sedition Acts, Congress suppressed criticism of government leaders and war policies. The Espionage Act of 1917 imposed penalties of up to $10,000 and twenty years in prison for anyone who gave aid to the enemy; who tried to incite insubordination, disloyalty, or refusal of duty in the armed services; or who sought to interfere with the war effort. President Wilson had also wanted the bill to allow the government to censor newspapers, but Congress refused. The Sedition Act of 1918 extended the penalties to those who did or said anything to obstruct the government sale of war bonds or to advocate cutbacks in production, and—just in case something had been overlooked—for saying, writing, or printing anything "disloyal, profane, scurrilous, or abusive" about the American form of government, the Constitution, or the army and navy.

The Espionage and Sedition Acts generated more than a thousand convictions. Socialists and other radicals were the primary targets. Victor Berger, a Socialist congressman from Milwaukee, received a twenty-year sentence for editorials in the Milwaukee *Leader* that called the war a capitalist conspiracy. Eugene V. Debs, who had polled over 900,000 votes for president in 1912, repeatedly urged men to refuse to serve in the military, even though he knew he could be prosecuted for such remarks under the Espionage Act. "I would a thousand times rather be a free soul in jail than a sycophant and a coward in the streets," he told a Socialist gathering in 1918. He received his wish. Debs was arrested and given a ten-year prison sentence for encouraging draft resistance. In 1920, still in jail, he polled nearly 1 million votes for president. Woodrow Wilson, the self-styled "progressive" president, nevertheless refused to pardon the progressive socialist Debs.

In two important decisions just after the war, the Supreme Court upheld the Espionage and Sedition Acts. *Schenck v. United States* (1919) reaffirmed the conviction of a man for circulating anti-draft leaflets among members of the armed forces. In this case, Justice Oliver Wendell Holmes said, "Free speech would not protect a man in falsely shouting fire in a theater, and causing a panic." The government was allowed to suppress speech where there was "a clear and present danger." In *Abrams v. United States* (1919), the Court upheld the conviction of a man who circulated pamphlets opposing American intervention in Russia to oust the Bolsheviks. Here, Holmes and Louis Brandeis dissented from the majority view. The "surreptitious publishing of a silly leaflet by an unknown man," they argued, posed no danger to government policy.

## AMERICA AT WAR

American troops played little more than a token role in the European fighting until early 1918. Before that they were parceled out in quiet sectors mainly for training purposes. All through 1917, the Allied armies remained

**The Meuse-Argonne offensive**

U.S. soldiers fire an artillery gun in Argonne, France.

on the defensive, and late in the year their situation turned desperate. In October the Italian lines collapsed and were overrun by Austrian forces. With the help of troops from France, the Italians finally held their ground. In November the Bolshevik Revolution overthrew the infant Russian republic, and the Communist leaders dropped out of the war. With the Central Powers victorious over Russia, they were free to concentrate their forces on the western front. The American war effort thus became a "race for the defense of France." The French premier Georges Clemenceau appealed to the Americans to accelerate their mobilization. "A terrible blow is imminent," he predicted to a journalist. "Tell your Americans to come quickly."

THE WESTERN FRONT    On March 21, 1918, Clemenceau's prediction came true when the Germans began the first of several spring offensives in France and Belgium to try to end the war before the Americans arrived in force. By May 1918, there were 1 million fresh but untested and undertrained U.S. troops in Europe, and for the first time they made a difference. During the first week in June, a marine brigade blocked the Germans at Belleau Wood, and army troops took Vaux and opposed the Germans at Château-Thierry. Though these relatively modest actions had limited mili-

ENGLAND

NORTH
SEA

Rotterdam

NETHERLANDS

Oostende

Antwerp

Dieppe

Ghent

Scheldte River

Brussels

Calais

Ypres

Boulogne

Armentières

Lille

BELGIUM

Mons

Meuse River

Cologne

GERMANY

Koblenz

Rhine River

Arras

Cambrai

Oise River

Somme River

Amiens
Cantigny

Sedan

LUXEMBOURG

Compiègne

Aisne River

ARGONNE FOREST

Étain

BELLEAU WOOD

Soissons

Reims

Vesle R.

Verdun

Château-Thierry

Épernay

Metz

Seine River

Paris

Marne River

FRANCE

St.-Mihiel

Nancy

Strasbourg

Versailles

Moselle River

**WORLD WAR I,
THE WESTERN FRONT, 1918**

--- Western front, March 1918
— German offensive, spring 1918
→ Allied counteroffensive
— Western front, November 1918

0        50 Miles
0    50 Kilometers

SWITZERLAND

Why was the war on the western front a stalemate for most of World War I? What was the effect of the arrival of the American troops? Why was the Second Battle of the Marne the turning point of the war?

tary significance, their effect on Allied morale was significant. The British and the French armies continued to bear the brunt of the fighting.

The turning point in France came on July 15, 1918, in the Second Battle of the Marne. On both sides of the French town of Reims, the German assault was repelled, and soon the British, French, and Americans began to push the Germans back into Belgium. Then, on August 10, the U.S. First Army attacked the Germans at St.-Mihiel, southeast of Verdun. There, on September 12, an army of more than 500,000 staged the first strictly American

**American casualties**

A Salvation Army worker writing a letter home for a wounded soldier.

offensive of the war. Within three days the outnumbered Germans had pulled back. The climactic American role in the fighting occurred in the great Meuse-Argonne offensive, begun on September 26, 1918. American divisions joined British and French armies in a drive toward Sedan and its railroad, which supplied the entire German front. It was the largest American action of the war, involving 1.2 million U.S. troops and resulting in 117,000 American casualties, including 26,000 dead. But along the entire front from Sedan to Flanders, the Germans were defeated and in retreat. "America," wrote German general Erich Ludendorff, "thus became the decisive power in the war."

THE BOLSHEVIKS   When the war broke out in 1914, Russia was one of the Allied Powers. Over the next three years the Russians suffered some 6.6 million casualties. By 1917, there were shortages of ammunition for the Russian troops and food for the Russian people. The czarist government fell into such disarray that it was forced to transfer power to a new provisional republican government that itself succumbed, in November 1917, to a revolution led by Vladimir Lenin and his Bolshevik party, who promised war-weary Russians "peace, land, and bread."

The **Bolsheviks** were a small but determined sect of ruthless ideologues, convinced that they were in the irresistible vanguard of historical change as described by Karl Marx in the mid-nineteenth century. They found themselves in the right place at the right time—a backward country devastated by prolonged war, besieged by invading armies, and burdened by a mediocre government. As Lenin observed, power was lying in the streets, waiting to be picked up. Both Marx and Lenin believed that communism would be an international movement. Once in control of the Russian government, however, Lenin and the Bolsheviks unilaterally stopped fighting in World

War I. Instead of launching an international revolution, Lenin withdrew Russia from European affairs. With German troops deep in Russian territory and armies of "White" Russians (anti-Bolsheviks) organizing resistance to their power, the Bolsheviks concluded a separate peace with Germany, the Treaty of Brest-Litovsk, on March 3, 1918. To prevent military supplies from falling into German hands and encourage anti-Bolshevik forces in the developing Russian Civil War, President Wilson sent American forces into Russia's Arctic ports. Troops were also sent to eastern Siberia, where they remained until April 1920 in an effort to curb growing Japanese ambitions there. The Allied intervention in Russia failed because the Bolsheviks were able to consolidate their power. Russia took no further part in World War I and did not participate in the peace settlement. The failed Allied intervention largely served to generate among Soviets a long-lasting suspicion of the West.

THE FOURTEEN POINTS   As the conflict in Europe was ending, neither the Allies nor the Central Powers, despite Wilson's prodding, had stated openly what they hoped to gain from the fighting. Wilson repeated that the Americans had no selfish war aims: "We desire no conquest, no dominion," he stressed in his war message of 1917. "We are but one of the champions of the rights of mankind." The idealistic minister-president was convinced that the European war was a reactionary event, the result of the outdated rivalries between the social and political dynasties of the Old World. But he was wrong. The First World War had become so horrific because the forces of nationalism and democracy had been unleashed. It was no longer simply a war between armies but a war between entire nations determined to fight to the bitter end. Wilson believed that the United States had a special mission to lead the world out of conflict and chaos. People everywhere, he assumed, "are looking to us for direction and leadership." Unfortunately for Wilson's idealistic purposes, after the Bolsheviks seized power in Russia in 1917, they published copies of secret treaties in which the British and French had promised territorial gains in order to win Italy, Romania, and Greece to their side. When an Interallied Conference in Paris late in 1917 failed to agree on a statement of war aims, Colonel House advised Wilson to formulate his own plans to restructure postwar Europe and remake the world in the American image.

During 1917 a group of American experts, called the Inquiry, began drafting a peace plan. With advice from these experts, Wilson himself developed what would come to be called the **Fourteen Points**, which he presented to a joint session of Congress on January 8, 1918, "as the only possible program" for peace. The first five points called for diplomacy to be conducted openly rather than hidden in secret treaties, the recognition of neutral nations to continue oceangoing commerce in time of war ("freedom of the seas"), removal of international trade barriers, reduction of armaments, and an impartial reconfiguration of the victors' colonial empires based upon the desires of the populations involved. Most of the remaining points dealt with territorial claims: they called on the Central Powers to evacuate occupied lands and to allow the various overlapping nationalities and ethnic groups to develop their own new nation-states (the difficult concept of "self-determination"), a crucial principle for Wilson. Point 13 called for the creation of an independent nation for the Poles, a people long dominated by the Russians on the east and the Germans on the west. Point 14, the capstone of Wilson's postwar scheme, called for the creation of a "league" of nations to protect global peace. When the Fourteen Points were made public, African American leaders asked the president to add a fifteenth point: an end to racial discrimination. Wilson did not respond.

The Fourteen Points embodied Wilson's sincere ideals, but they also served the purpose of psychological warfare. One of the reasons for issuing the Fourteen Points was to keep Russia in the war by stating the principles by which the peace would be arranged— a vain hope, as it turned out. Another was to reassure the citizens of the Allied Powers that they were involved in a noble cause. A third was to drive a wedge between the governments of the Central Powers and their people by offering a reasonable peace.

On October 3, 1918, a new German chancellor asked for an end to the fighting on the basis of the Fourteen Points. The Allies accepted the Fourteen Points as a basis of negotiations, but with two significant reservations: the British insisted on the right to discuss limiting freedom of the seas, and the French demanded reparations (payments by the vanquished to the victors) from Germany and Austria for war damages.

**Allied victory**

Celebration of the armistice ending World War I, New York City, November 1918.

The French insisted on harsh provisions in the peace treaty to weaken
So did the British prime minister David Lloyd George. Vittorio

Meanwhile, the German home front was being torn apart by a loss of morale, culminating in a naval mutiny at Kiel. Germany's allies dropped out of the war: Bulgaria on September 29, 1918, Turkey on October 30, and Austria-Hungary on November 3. On November 9 the kaiser abdicated, and a German republic was proclaimed. Then, on November 11 at 5 A.M., an armistice was signed. Six hours later, at the eleventh hour of the eleventh day of the eleventh month, and after 1,563 days of warfare, the guns fell silent. Under the armistice agreement the Germans had to evacuate occupied territories, pull their troops back behind the Rhine River, and surrender their naval fleet and railroad equipment. The Germans were assured that Woodrow Wilson's Fourteen Points would be the basis for the peace conference.

During its nineteen months of participation in the Great War, the United States saw 126,000 of its servicemen killed. Germany's war dead totaled over 2 million, including civilians; France lost nearly 1.4 million combatants, Great Britain lost 703,000 soldiers, and Russia lost 1.7 million. The new Europe emerging from the carnage would be much different: much poorer, more violent, more polarized, more cynical, less sure of itself, and less capable of decisive action. The United States, for good or ill, would be sucked into the vacuum of power created by the destructiveness of the Great War. For the moment, however, the news of peace led to wild celebrations throughout the world. The madness had ended, and fear and grief gave way to hope. "The nightmare is over," wrote the African American activist W.E.B. Du Bois. "The world awakes. The long, horrible years of dreadful night are passed. Behold the sun!"

## The Fight for the Peace

The gruesome combat and destruction had ended, but Europe's postwar future was a muddle. Woodrow Wilson had promised a "great crusade" that would "make the world safe for democracy." For a glorious moment, the American president was humanity's self-appointed prophet of peace. He felt guided "by the hand of God." His messianic vision of creating a universal "community of power," a peacekeeping "league of nations" to replace the old war-breeding power politics of Europe promised a bright future for the world. If the diplomats failed to follow his plans, he warned, "there will be another world war" within a generation.

DOMESTIC UNREST   Woodrow Wilson made several fateful decisions at the war's end that would come back to haunt him. First, he decided to attend the peace conference that convened in Paris on January 18, 1919. Never before had an American president left the nation for such a prolonged period. Wilson's decision to spend months in Europe dramatized all the more his crusading vision for a lasting peace. From one viewpoint, it was shrewd, for his prestige and determination made a difference at the Paris peace talks. But during his prolonged trip abroad (six months) he lost touch with political developments at home. His progressive political coalition was already unraveling under the pressures of wartime discontent. Western farmers complained about the government's control of wheat prices. Eastern businessmen chafed at federal revenue policies designed, according to the *New York Sun*, "to pay for the war out of taxes raised north of the Mason and Dixon Line." Leaders of labor unions, despite real gains in wages and working conditions during the war, were unhappy with inflation and the problems of reconversion to a peacetime economy.

Second, in the midterm elections of 1918, Wilson defied his advisers and urged voters to elect a Democratic Congress to support his foreign policies. Republicans, who for the most part had supported Wilson's war measures, now took affront. In elections held on November 5, a week before the armistice, the Democrats lost control of both houses of Congress. With an opposition majority in the new Congress, Wilson further weakened his standing by making a third mistake: he failed to appoint a prominent Republican to the staff of peace commissioners. Former president Taft groused that Wilson's real intention in going to Paris was "to hog the whole show."

When Wilson reached Paris in December 1918, he was greeted as a hero, even a savior. The cheering millions in war-torn Europe saw in the American idealist a prophet of peace and a spokesman for humanity who had promised that the great crusade would be the "war to end wars." Their heartfelt support no doubt strengthened his hand at the conference, but Wilson had to deal with some tough-minded statesmen who did not share his utopian zeal. They would force him to abandon many of his principles and ideals.

The Paris Peace Conference lasted from January to June 1919 and included delegates from all countries that had declared war or broken diplomatic relations with Germany. The conference was controlled by the Big Four: the prime ministers of Britain, France, and Italy and the president of the United States. Japan restricted its interests to Asia and the Pacific. French premier Georges Clemenceau was a stern realist who had little patience with Wilson's utopianism. "God gave us the Ten Commandments and we broke them," Clemenceau sneered. "Wilson gave us the Fourteen Points—we shall see." The French insisted on harsh provisions in the peace treaty to weaken Germany. So did the British prime minister David Lloyd George. Vittorio

**The Paris Peace Conference**

Woodrow Wilson (second from left) with Georges Clemenceau of France (center) and Arthur Balfour of Great Britain (second from right) during the Paris Peace Conference in 1919.

Orlando, prime minister of Italy, focused his efforts on getting territories from defeated Austria.

THE LEAGUE OF NATIONS   As the tense, complex negotiations began, Woodrow Wilson made another controversial decision: he insisted that his cherished **League of Nations** be the top priority in the treaty making. Whatever compromises he might have to make regarding territorial boundaries and financial claims, whatever mistakes might result, Wilson believed that a league of nations committed to collective security would ensure international stability. Wilson presided over the commission set up to draft its charter. Article X of the charter, which Wilson called "the heart of the League," pledged member nations to impose military and economic sanctions against aggressors. The use of armed force would be a last (and an improbable) resort. The League, it was assumed, would exercise enormous moral influence, making military action unnecessary. Its structure would allow each member an equal voice in the Assembly; the Big Five (Britain, France, Italy, Japan, and the United States) and four other nations would make up the

**"The League of Nations Argument in a Nutshell"**

Jay N. "Ding" Darling's summation of the League controversy.

executive Council, the administrative staff, with headquarters in Geneva, Switzerland, would make up the Secretariat; and a Permanent Court of International Justice (set up in 1921 and usually called the World Court) could "hear and determine any dispute of an international character."

On February 14, 1919, Wilson presented the finished draft of the League covenant to the Allies and departed Paris for a visit home. Already he faced opposition among Republicans. Wilson's proposed League of Nations, Theodore Roosevelt grumbled, would revive German militarism and undermine American morale. "To substitute internationalism for nationalism," the former president argued, "means to do away with patriotism." Roosevelt's close friend and fellow Republican, **Henry Cabot Lodge**, the powerful chairman of the Senate Foreign Relations Committee, also scorned Wilson's naive idealism. He announced that the League's structure was unacceptable because it would allow an international organization to usurp the Senate's constitutional authority to declare war. Lodge's statement bore the signatures of thirty-nine Republican senators or senators-elect, more than enough to block ratification.

**TERRITORY AND REPARATIONS**   Back in Paris in the spring of 1919, Wilson gave in to French demands for territorial concessions and **reparations** payments by Germany that would keep it dangerously weak, impoverished, and eager for revenge during the 1920s. Even after making major concessions, Wilson clashed sharply with the French premier Clemenceau over how to treat defeated Germany, but after the American president threatened to leave the conference, they decided that the Rhineland region along the border between France and Germany would be a "demilitarized" zone for fifteen years. France could also exploit Germany's Saar Valley coal mines for fifteen years, after which the region's residents would vote to determine their national allegiance.

In other territorial matters, Wilson had to abandon his lofty principle of national self-determination whereby every ethnic group would be allowed to form its own nation. Wonderful in theory, it proved disastrous in reality. As Robert Lansing, who succeeded William Jennings Bryan as Wilson's secretary of state, correctly predicted, trying to allow every ethnic group in Europe—Poles, Czechs, Slovaks, Slovenes, Serbs, Latvians, Lithuanians, Estonians, Hungarians, Romanians, Bulgarians, Italians, Turks, Armenians, and others—to determine its own fate "will raise hopes which can never be realized." In the end, Wilson's commitment to self-determination would be "discredited" as the "dream of an idealist who failed to realize the danger until it was too late." As a result of the Great War, four long-standing multinational empires had disintegrated: the Russian, Austro-Hungarian, German, and Ottoman (Turkish). Hundreds of millions of people had to be reorganized into new nations. There was in fact no way to make Europe's boundaries correspond to its tangled ethnic groupings. The folk wanderings of centuries had left ethnically mixed populations scattered throughout Central Europe. In some areas, moreover, national self-determination yielded to other interests: the Polish Corridor, for instance, gave newly independent Poland its much-needed outlet to the sea through German territory. One part of the Austro-Hungarian Empire became Czechoslovakia, which included the German-speaking Sudetenland, an area favored with good natural defenses. Another part united with Serbia to create the kingdom of Yugoslavia. Still other substantial parts of the former empire passed to Poland (Galicia), Romania (Transylvania), and Italy (Trentino–Alto Adige and Trieste). All in all, the new boundaries more nearly followed the ethnic divisions of Europe than had the prewar lines.

The discussion of reparations triggered bitter exchanges at the conference. The British and the French wanted Germany to pay for the entire financial cost of the war, including the payment of veterans' pensions. On this point, Wilson made perhaps his most fateful concessions. He accepted a clause in the treaty in which Germany confessed responsibility for the war and thus took responsibility for its entire expense. The "war guilt" clause offended Germans and made for persistent bitterness that Adolf Hitler would later seize upon to launch his Nazi party movement. Wilson himself privately admitted that if he were a German he would refuse to sign the treaty.

On May 7, 1919, the victorious powers presented the treaty to the German delegates, who returned three weeks later with 443 pages of criticism. A few changes were made, but when the Germans still refused to sign, the French threatened to move their army across the Rhine River. Finally, on June 28, 1919, the Germans gave up and signed the treaty in the glittering Hall of Mirrors at Versailles. When Adolph Hitler, a young German corporal, learned of the Versailles Treaty's provisions imposed upon Germany, he seethed with anger and vowed revenge. "It cannot be that two million Germans have fallen in vain," he screamed. ". . . we demand vengeance!"

WILSON'S LOSS AT HOME   On July 8, 1919, having been in Paris for months, Woodrow Wilson returned home with the Versailles Treaty amid a great clamor of popular support. A third of the state legislatures had already endorsed the League of Nations, as had thirty-three of the nation's forty-eight governors. Two days later, on July 10, Wilson called upon the Senate to accept "this great duty" and ratify the treaty that had been guided "by the hand of God." "The stage is set, the destiny disclosed," he said. Wilson then grew needlessly confrontational. He dismissed critics of his beloved League of Nations as "blind and little provincial people." The whole world, Wilson claimed, was relying on the United States to sign the Versailles Treaty: "Dare we reject it and break the heart of the world?"

Congressional leaders were ready to break the world's heart. Senator Henry Cabot Lodge, a staunch Republican with an intense dislike for Wilson, sharpened his partisan knives. He denounced the Versailles Treaty's foolish "scheme of making mankind suddenly virtuous by a statute or a written constitution." Lodge and Wilson detested each other. Wilson, thought Lodge, was too filled with prophetic certitude, too prone to promise more than he could deliver when great principles entailed great sacrifices. Lodge was keenly aware of the undercurrents already stirring up opposition to the treaty in Congress: the resentment against the treaty felt by German American, Italian American, and Irish American ethnic groups within the United States, the disappointment of liberals with Wilson's compromises on reparations and territories, the distractions of demobilization and the resulting domestic problems of converting quickly to a peacetime economy, and the revival of isolationism. Some Republicans claimed that Wilson's preoccupation with his cherished League of Nations revealed that he really wanted to be president of the world.

In the Senate, a group of "irreconcilables," fourteen Republicans and two Democrats, refused to support American membership in the League of Nations on any terms. They were mainly western and midwestern progressives who feared that such sweeping foreign commitments threatened domestic reforms. The irreconcilables would be useful to Lodge's purpose, but he belonged to a larger group called the "reservationists," men who insisted upon limiting American participation in the League. Lodge proposed a set of amendments that addressed his reservations. The only way to get Senate approval of the treaty was for Wilson to meet with Lodge and others and agree to revisions. Republican senator James Watson of Indiana told Wilson he had no choice: "Mr. Presi-

**EUROPE AFTER THE TREATY OF VERSAILLES, 1918**

········ 1914 boundaries

New nations

Plebiscite areas

Occupied area

Why was self-determination difficult for states in Central Europe? How did territorial concessions weaken Germany? Why might territorial changes like the creation of the Polish Corridor or the concession of the Sudetenland to Czechoslovakia have created problems that would surface in the future?

dent, you are licked. There is only one way you can take the United States into the League of Nations." The president lashed back: "Lodge reservations? Never!" Wilson was temperamentally incapable of compromising with Lodge and the Republicans. He especially opposed weakening Article X of the League covenant, which provided for collective action against aggression. Wilson would not retreat, nor would he compromise. He refused to negotiate with Lodge. As the months passed, he eventually sought to make the debate over the

Versailles Treaty a partisan question by promising that the coming 1920 presidential election would become a "great solemn referendum" on the issue.

By September 1919, with momentum for ratification of the Versailles Treaty slackening, Wilson decided to outflank his Senate opponents by taking the treaty issue directly to the people (although a Republican pointed out that the people could not vote on the issue; the Senate would). His doctor, family, and friends urged Wilson not to go because of his poor health and chronic hypertension. But Wilson said, "I cannot turn back now. I cannot put my personal safety, my health, in the balance against my duty. I must go." On the evening of September 2, 1919, Wilson set forth on a grueling railroad tour through the Midwest to the West Coast. In all he traveled ten thousand miles in twenty-two days, giving thirty-two major speeches. For a while, Wilson seemed to be regaining public support, but after delivering a speech on September 25, 1919, in Pueblo, Colorado, he experienced blinding headaches and numbness that prompted his wife and doctor to urge the president to return to Washington. He initially refused to go, arguing that Lodge and other opponents "will say that I am a quitter . . . and the treaty will be lost." But those around him won the argument, and the train was redirected to Washington, D.C. Then, on October 2, 1919, the president suffered a severe stroke (cerebral hemorrhage) that almost killed him. The episode left the president paralyzed on his left side and an invalid for the rest of his life. Even more devastating was the effect of the stroke on his personality. Wilson after 1919 became emotionally unstable and even delusional (he would die in 1924). For seventeen months his protective wife, Edith, along with aides and trusted Cabinet members, kept him isolated from all but the most essential business. Wilson's disability intensified his stubbornness. In the face of formidable opposition in the Senate to the League of Nations section in the Versailles Treaty, he refused to compromise and was needlessly confrontational. As he scoffed to an aide, "Let Lodge compromise." The president's hardened arteries hardened his political judgment as well.

For his part, Senator Lodge pushed through the Senate fourteen changes in the draft of the Versailles Treaty, most of them having to do with the League of Nations. Wilson scoffed at the proposed changes, arguing that Lodge's revisions did not "provide for ratification but, rather, for the nullification of the treaty." As a result, Wilson's supporters in the Senate found themselves thrown into an unlikely combination with the irreconcilables, who opposed the treaty under any circumstances. The Senate vote on Lodge's revised treaty was 39 for and 55 against. On the question of approving the original treaty without reservations, irreconcilables and the so-called reservationists, led by Lodge, combined to defeat ratification again, with 38 for and 53 against.

So Woodrow Wilson's grand effort at global peacemaking had failed. Because of his refusal to compromise on the details of the proposed League of Nations, the Senate refused to ratify the entire Versailles Treaty. As a consequence, Congress was forced to declare an official end to American involvement in the First World War by a joint resolution on May 20, 1920, which Wilson vetoed in a fit of vengefulness. It was not until July 2, 1921, after the president had left office, that a joint congressional resolution officially ended the state of war with Germany and Austria-Hungary, almost eighteen months since the fighting had stopped. Separate peace treaties with Germany, Austria, and Hungary were ratified on October 18, 1921, but by then Warren G. Harding was president of the United States.

The treaties ending the First World War did little to ensure postwar peace. The Great War had destroyed old Europe, but peace did not bring stability. Most Germans and Austrians felt that they were the victims of a harsh, vindictive peace forced upon them by the victors. The new nations created at Versailles out of the defeated empires—Estonia, Latvia, Lithuania, Czechoslovakia, Finland, and Poland—were poor, unstable, insecure, and resentful of their neighbors. There was no real stability in Europe after the war, just an interlude born of exhaustion. The war wreaked havoc on trade relationships and bankrupted national treasuries. Such festering vengefulness among the vanquished would interact with widespread economic, social, and political instability throughout Europe to help spawn fascism in Italy, Austria, and Germany during the 1920s.

## LURCHING FROM WAR TO PEACE

The Versailles Treaty, for all the time it spent in the Senate, was but one issue clamoring for public attention in the turbulent period after the war. The year 1919 began with ecstatic victory parades that soon gave way to widespread labor unrest, race riots, domestic terror, and government tyranny. Demobilization of the armed forces and war industries proceeded in haphazard fashion. The end of the war brought the sudden cancellation of war-related contracts that left workers and business leaders to cope with the chaotic conversion to a peacetime economy on their own. Wilson's leadership was missing. Preoccupied by the war and the League, and then bedridden by the stroke, he became grim and peevish. His administration stumbled through its last two years.

**THE SPANISH FLU**  Amid the confusion of postwar life, many Americans confronted a virulent menace that produced far more casualties than the war itself. It became known as the **Spanish flu** (although its origins were probably in a U.S. Army camp in Kansas), and its contagion spread around the globe, transformed modern medicine, and altered the course of world history. The pandemic erupted in the spring of 1918 and lasted a year, killing as many as 100 million people worldwide, twice as many as died in the First World War. In the United States alone it accounted for 675,000 deaths, nearly seven times the number of American combat deaths in France. No disease in human history had killed so many people. Mortuaries ran out of coffins; morgues ran out of space. The chief of staff of the German army claimed that the flu epidemic among his troops caused the failure of the 1918 spring offensive, thereby hastening the end of the war. At the Paris Peace Conference, during the most intense week of negotiations, Woodrow Wilson himself fell ill with the flu and a prolonged high temperature. Observers said when he returned to the bargaining table he was not the same man who had left it.

American soldiers returning from France brought the flu with them, and it raced through the crowded army camps and naval bases. Some 43,000 servicemen died of influenza in 1918. By September the epidemic had spread to the civilian population. In that month alone 10,000 Americans died from the disease. "Nobody seemed to know what the disease was, where it came from or how to stop it," observed the editors of *Science* magazine in 1919. In Philadelphia, 528 people were buried in a single day. Life-insurance companies nearly went bankrupt, hospitals were besieged, and cemeteries ran out of burial space.

By the spring of 1919, the pandemic had finally run its course. It ended as suddenly—and as inexplicably—as it had begun. Although another out-

**Influenza epidemic**

Office workers wearing gauze masks during the Spanish flu epidemic of 1918.

break occurred in the winter of 1920, the population had grown more resistant to its assaults. No plague, war, famine, or natural catastrophe in world history killed so many people in such a short time.

THE ECONOMIC TRANSITION   Disease was only one of many challenges confronting postwar America. Consumer prices continued to rise after the war, and discontented workers, released from wartime constraints, were more willing to go out on strike for their demands. In 1919, more than 4 million workers participated in 3,600 strikes against management. Most of the workers sought nothing more than higher wages and shorter workweeks, but their critics linked them with the worldwide Communist revolution being fomented in the Soviet Union. Some workers in the East won their demands early in the year, but after a general strike in Seattle, public opinion began to turn against labor's demands. Seattle's mayor denounced the walkout of sixty thousand workers as evidence of Bolshevik influence. The strike lasted only five days, but public alarm over the affair damaged the cause of unions across the country.

An American Federation of Labor campaign to organize steelworkers suffered from charges of radicalism against its leader, William Z. Foster, who had joined the Socialists in 1900 and later emerged as a Communist. The focus on Foster's radicalism obscured the squalid conditions and long hours that had marked the steel industry since the Homestead strike of 1892: the twelve-hour day, often combined with a seven-day week, was common. On September 22, 1919, after U.S. Steel refused to talk, some 340,000 workers walked out. When information about working conditions became widely known, public opinion turned in favor of the steelworkers, but too late: the strike had ended after four months. Steelworkers remained unorganized until the 1930s.

The most celebrated postwar labor dispute was the Boston police strike. Though less significant than the steel strike in the numbers involved, it inadvertently launched a presidential career. On September 9, 1919, most of Boston's police force went out on strike. Massachusetts governor Calvin Coolidge was furious. He mobilized the National Guard to keep order, and after four days the police strikers offered to return, but the commissioner refused to take them back. When labor leader Samuel Gompers appealed for their reinstatement, Coolidge responded in words that suddenly turned him into a national figure: "There is no right to strike against the public safety by anybody, anywhere, any time."

RACIAL FRICTION   The summer of 1919 also sparked a season of deadly race riots across the nation. As more and more African Americans, 367,000 of whom were war veterans, moved to different parts of the nation,

**Domestic unrest**

A victim of racial rioting in Chicago, July 1919.

developed successful careers, and asserted their rights in the face of deeply embedded segregationist practices, resentful whites began to display an almost hysterical racism. What the African American leader James Weldon Johnson called the Red Summer (*red* here signifying blood) began in July, when a vengeful mob of whites invaded the black section of Longview, Texas, angry over rumors of interracial dating. They burned shops and houses and ran several African Americans out of town. A week later in Washington, D.C., often false or exaggerated reports of black assaults on white women aroused white mobs, and for four days gangs of white and black rioters waged a race war in the streets until soldiers and driving rains ended the fighting. These were but preliminaries to the Chicago riot of late July, in which 38 people were killed and 537 injured. The climactic disorders of the summer occurred in the rural area around Elaine, Arkansas, where African American tenant farmers tried to organize a union. According to official reports, 5 whites and 25 blacks died in the rioting, but the death toll may have actually included more than 100 blacks. Altogether, twenty-five race riots erupted in 1919, and there were eighty racial lynchings.

THE RED SCARE   Reactions to the wave of labor strikes and race riots reflected the impact of the Bolshevik Revolution in Russia. Some radicals thought America's domestic turbulence was the first scene in a drama of world revolution. Many Americans decided that they might be right. After all, a tiny faction in Russia, the Bolsheviks, had exploited confusion to impose its totalitarian will over a huge nation. In 1919, left-wing members of the Socialist party formed the Communist party (U.S.A.) and the short-lived Communist Labor party. Wartime hysteria against all things German was readily transformed into a postwar Red Scare against all Communists.

Fears of revolution in America were fueled by the actions of scattered militants. In April 1919, the post office intercepted nearly forty homemade mail bombs addressed to prominent citizens. One slipped through and blew off the hands of a Georgia senator's maid. In June, another bomb destroyed the front of Attorney General **A. Mitchell Palmer**'s house in Washington, D.C. The explosion killed the terrorist and almost killed Palmer. Although the bombings were probably the work of a small group of Italian anarchists, the attorney general and many other Americans concluded that a Communist "blaze of revolution" was "sweeping over every American institution of law and order."

Soon, federal government agencies organized witch hunts trying to ferret out anarchists and Communists. In August 1919, Attorney General Palmer appointed a twenty-four-year-old attorney named J. Edgar Hoover to lead a new government division created to collect files on radicals. On November 7, 1919, while President Wilson lay incapacitated in the White House, federal agents rounded up 450 alien "radicals," most of whom were simply recent Russian immigrants looking for work. All were deported to Russia without a court hearing. On January 2, 1920, police raids in dozens of cities swept up 5,000 more suspects, many taken from their homes without arrest warrants. What came to be called the **First Red Scare** (followed by a similar outbreak of anti-communist hysteria during the 1950s) represented the largest violation of civil liberties in American history.

Attorney General Palmer, eager to win the Democratic nomination for president in 1920, continued to exaggerate the Red menace, but the panic subsided within a few months. By the summer of 1920, the Red Scare had begun to evaporate. Bombings in the United States tapered off; the wave of strikes and race riots receded. By September 1920, when a bomb explosion at the corner of Broad and Wall Streets in New York City killed thirty-eight people, Americans were ready to take it for what it was: the work of a crazed mind and not the start of a revolution. The Red Scare nonetheless left a lasting mark on American life and bolstered the continuing crusade for "100 percent Americanism" and restrictions on immigration.

Despite the extraordinary turbulence in the immediate aftermath of the First World War, there was little doubt that the conflict had changed the trajectory of modern history. Germany and Austria were devastated. The Bolshevik Revolution caused Russia to abandon its western European allies and drop out of the war. Thereafter, Soviet communism would be one of the most powerful new forces shaping twentieth century. At the same time, the United States had emerged from the war not simply a great power, but the most powerful nation in the world. For the first time in its history, the United States had decisively intervened in a major European war. And now, in the war's aftermath, the United States had emerged largely unscathed physically, and American capitalists were eager to fill the vacuum created by the wartime destruction of the European economies. What came to be called the "American Century" was at hand—for better or worse.

## CHAPTER SUMMARY

- **Wilson and Mexico**  Woodrow Wilson wanted to foster democratic governments in Latin America; he got the United States involved in Mexican politics after Mexico experienced several military coups. The popular Francisco Pancho Villa tried to gain power in Mexico by promoting an anti-American program, even making raids across the border into New Mexico.

- **Causes of WWI**  Europe had developed a system of alliances that divided the continent in two. Democratic Britain and France, along with the Russian Empire, had formed the Triple Entente. Central Powers were comprised of the new German Empire, Austria-Hungary, and Italy. The assassination of the heir to the Austro-Hungarian throne by a Serbian nationalist triggered the world war in August 1914.

- **U.S. Enters WWI**  Most Americans supported the Triple Entente, or Allied Powers, at the outbreak of World War I. The Wilson administration declared the nation neutral but allowed businesses to extend credit to the Allies to purchase food and military supplies. Americans were outraged by the Germans' use of unlimited submarine warfare, especially after the 1915 sinking of the British liner *Lusitania*. In 1917 unrestricted submarine activity and the revelation of the Zimmermann telegram, in which the Germans sought to incite the Mexicans to wage war against the United States, led the United States to enter the Great War.

- **Wilson's Peace Plan**  Wilson insisted that the United States wanted no selfish gains from the war, only a new, democratic Europe to emerge from the old empires. His famous Fourteen Points speech outlined his ideas for the establishment of continent-wide democratic nation-states and a league of nations.

- **Treaty of Versailles**  The United States did not ratify the Treaty of Versailles because Wilson had alienated the Republican senators whose support he needed for ratification. A coalition of "irreconcilables" formed in the Senate: midwestern and western progressives who feared that involvement in a league of nations would stifle domestic reforms and that ratification would necessitate involvement in future wars. The irreconcilables were joined by "reservationists," who would accept the treaty with certain limitations on America's involvement in the League of Nations. Wilson's illness and his refusal to compromise ensured failure of ratification.

- **Consequences of WWI**  As a result of the war, four European empires were dismantled, replaced by smaller nation-states. The reparations imposed on Germany and the "war guilt" clause laid the foundations for German bitterness. The presence of a Communist regime in the old Russian Empire had major consequences in America.

## CHRONOLOGY

| | |
|---|---|
| 1914 | United States intervenes in Mexico |
| 1914 | World War I begins in Europe |
| 1915 | British liner *Lusitania*, with Americans aboard, is torpedoed without warning by a German submarine |
| 1916 | Congress passes the National Defense Act |
| March 1917 | Zimmermann telegram reveals that Germany is attempting to incite Mexico to enter the war against the United States |
| April 1917 | United States enters the Great War |
| January 1918 | Woodrow Wilson delivers his Fourteen Points speech |
| November 11, 1918 | Representatives of warring nations sign armistice |
| 1919 | Supreme Court issues *Schenck v. United States* decision |
| May 1919 | Treaty of Versailles is presented to the Germans |
| 1919 | Race riots break out in Chicago |
| 1919 | U.S. attorney general launches Red Scare |
| July 1921 | Joint resolution of Congress officially ends the war among the United States, Germany, and Austria-Hungary |

## KEY TERMS & NAMES

# 25

## THE MODERN TEMPER

### FOCUS QUESTIONS    Ⓢ   wwnorton.com/studyspace

- What accounted for the nativism of the 1920s?
- What was meant by the Jazz Age?
- How did the new social trends of the 1920s challenge traditional attitudes?
- What was modernism, and how did it influence American culture?

All historical eras exhibit contradictions, but the 1920s were a decade of especially sharp extremes. The ten years between 1919 and the onset the Great Depression at the end of 1929 encompassed a period of unprecedented economic prosperity and cultural experimentation as well as political conservatism and religious fundamentalism. Having experienced the constraints of wartime, many Americans feverishly pursued personal pleasures. The new and unusual clashed openly with the conventional and the commonplace. Modernists and traditionalists waged cultural warfare with one another, one group looking to the future for inspiration and the other looking to the past for guidance. Terrorist attacks increased, as did labor and racial violence. In 1920, a horse-drawn wagon laden with dynamite exploded at the corner of Wall and Broad streets in New York City, killing thirty-eight people and wounding hundreds. That the bombers were never found fueled public concern that the United States was on the brink of chaos and revolution. Benton MacKaye, a leading environmentalist, said that America during the 1920s was the most "volcanic of any area on earth." The nation was roiling with change and conflict, and he predicted a period of "deep domestic strife."

The scope and pace of societal changes were bewildering. At long last, women were allowed to vote; meanwhile, beer and liquor were outlawed. Innovations such as national radio networks, talking motion pictures, mass ownership of automobiles, the emergence of national chain stores, the soaring popularity of spectator sports, and the rise of mass marketing and advertising transformed America into the world's leading consumer society. The culture of mass consumption fueled the explosive growth of middle-class urban life. The 1920 census revealed that for the first time more Americans lived in cities than in rural areas. The popularity of the consumer culture also assaulted traditional virtues such as frugality, prudence, and religiosity.

In the political arena reactionaries and rebels battled for control of a postwar society riven by conflict. The brutal fight between Woodrow Wilson and the Republican-led Senate over the Versailles Treaty, coupled with the administration's savage crackdown on dissenters and socialists, had weakened an already fragmented and disillusioned progressivism. As the tireless reformer Amos Pinchot bitterly observed, President Wilson had "put his enemies in office and his friends in jail." By 1920, many alienated progressives had grown skeptical of any politician claiming to be a reformer or an idealist. The prominent social reformer Jane Addams sighed that the 1920s were "a period of political and social sag."

At the same time, the postwar wave of strikes, bombings, anti-Communist hysteria, and race riots symbolized a frightening new era of turmoil that led many people to cling to old ideas and ways of life. Traditionalists, many of them from rural areas, were especially disturbed by urban political radicalism and carefree urbane ways of life. Those who believed in the "old-time religion" were dismayed by the inroads of secular materialism. It was just such a reversion to traditional values that led voters to elect Republican Warren G. Harding president in 1920. He promised to return America to "normalcy."

Mainstream Americans were also shocked by the new "modernist" forms of artistic expression and sexual liberation. Mabel Dodge, a leading promoter of modern art and literature, said that the generation of young literary and artistic rebels emerging during the war years and after were determined to overthrow "the old order of things." Novelist F. Scott Fitzgerald wrote in *This Side of Paradise* (1920) that the younger generation of Americans, the "sad young men" who had fought in Europe to "make the world safe for democracy" had "grown up to find all Gods dead, all wars fought, all faiths in man shaken." Cynicism had displaced idealism for those alienated by the horrible war and the failed peace. As Fitzgerald asserted, "There's only one lesson to be learned from life anyway. . . . That there's no lesson to be learned from life." Fitzgerald and other self-conscious modernists were labeled a "lost generation" in the sense that many of them had lost faith in many of the values and institutions of Western civilization and were frantically looking for new gods. As Frederic Henry, a character in Ernest Hemingway's novel *A Farewell to Arms* (1929) declares, "Abstract words such as glory, honor, courage, or hallow were obscene" in the context of the colossal casualties caused by the war. Many of the modernists celebrated emotion over reason, change and "newness" over stability and tradition, youthful liberation and excesses over maturity, responsibility, and sobriety.

In sum, postwar life in America and Europe was fraught with turbulent changes, contradictory impulses, superficial frivolity, and seething tensions. As the French painter Paul Gauguin acknowledged, the upheavals of cultural modernism and the aftermath of the war produced "an epoch of confusion," a riotous clash of irreverent new ideas and enthusiasms with traditional manners and morals.

## THE REACTIONARY TWENTIES

Many traditionalists were aghast at the social turmoil of 1919. They located the germs of dangerous radicalism in the multiethnic cities teeming with immigrants and foreign ideas such as socialism, communism, and anarchism. The reactionary conservatism of the 1920s fed on the growing popularity of nativism, Anglo-Saxon racism, and militant Protestantism.

NATIVISM    The Red Scare of 1919 helped generate a surge of anti-immigrant hysteria called **nativism**. The foreign connections of so many political radicals convinced many people that the troublemakers in the post-war era were foreign-born. The flow of immigrants, slowed by the war, rose again at its end. From June 1920 to June 1921, more than eight hundred thousand people emigrated to the United States, 65 percent of them from southern and eastern Europe. Many more were on the way. In the early 1920s over half of the white men and a third of the white women working in industry were immigrants, most of them from central or eastern Europe. That socialism and anarchism were popular in those regions made immigrant workers especially suspect in the eyes of many Americans concerned about the "foreign invasion."

SACCO AND VANZETTI    The most celebrated criminal case of the 1920s seemed to prove the connection between immigrants and radicalism.

**Sacco and Vanzetti**

The trial and conviction of these working-class Italian immigrants became a public spectacle due in part to a growing mood of nativism.

It involved two working-class Italian immigrants who described themselves as revolutionary anarchists: shoemaker **Nicola Sacco** and fish peddler **Bartolomeo Vanzetti**. On May 5, 1920, they were arrested outside Boston, Massachusetts, for stealing $16,000 from a shoe factory and killing the paymaster and a guard. Both were armed when arrested, both lied to police about their activities, and both were identified by eyewitnesses. But the stolen money was never found. The Sacco and Vanzetti case occurred at the height of Italian immigration to the United States and against the backdrop of numerous terror attacks by anarchists. It was amid such a charged atmosphere that the criminal case became a huge public spectacle. The judge who presided over the 1921 trial was openly prejudicial, referring to the defendants as "anarchist bastards." Sacco and Vanzetti were convicted and ordered executed, but appeals of the verdict lasted seven years. People then and since claimed that Sacco and Vanzetti were sentenced for their political ideas and ethnic origin rather than for any crime they had committed. But despite public demonstrations around the world on behalf of the two men, the evidence convicting them was compelling; after seven years of legal wrangling, political battles, and international protests, they were executed on August 23, 1927. After thanking the warden for his kindness, Vanzetti said, "I wish to forgive some people for what they are now doing to me."

IMMIGRATION RESTRICTION   Concerns about foreign radicals invading the United States generated new efforts to restrict immigration. An alarmed Congress passed the Emergency Immigration Act of 1921, which restricted European arrivals each year to 3 percent of the total number of each nationality represented in the 1910 census. The Immigration Act of 1924 reduced the number to 2 percent based on the 1890 census, which included fewer of the "new" immigrants from southern and eastern Europe. This law set a permanent limitation, which became effective in 1929, of slightly over 150,000 new arrivals per year based on the "national origins" of the U.S. population as of 1920. The purpose of the new quotas was clear: to tilt the balance in favor of immigrants from northern and western Europe, who were assigned about 85 percent of the total. The law completely excluded people from east Asia—a gratuitous insult to the Japanese, who were already kept out of the United States by their Gentlemen's Agreement with Theodore Roosevelt.

On the other hand, the Immigration Act of 1924 left the gate open to new arrivals from countries in the Western Hemisphere, so that an ironic consequence of the new law was a substantial increase in the Hispanic Catholic population of the United States. Legal arrivals from Mexico peaked at 89,000 in 1924. Lower figures after that date reflect the Mexican government's policies of clamping down on the outflow. Waves of illegal immigrants continued to flow across the border, however, in response to southwestern agriculture's demand for "stoop" labor. People of Latin American descent (chiefly Mexicans, Puerto Ricans, and Cubans) became the fastest-growing ethnic minority in the country.

THE KLAN   During the postwar years nativist prejudice against "foreigners" took on a new form: a revived, nationwide **Ku Klux Klan** modeled on the white vigilante group founded to oppose Reconstruction in the post–Civil War South. The new Klan was devoted to "100 percent Americanism" and restricted its membership to militant white Protestants born in the United States. It was determined to protect its warped notion of the American way of life not only from African Americans but also from Roman Catholics, Jews, and immigrants. The United States was no melting pot, the twentieth-century Klan's founder, William J. Simmons, warned: "It is a garbage can! . . . When the hordes of aliens walk to the ballot box and their votes outnumber yours, then that alien horde has got you by the throat." Simmons, a habitual joiner and promoter of fraternal orders, had gathered a hooded group of bigots near Atlanta on Thanksgiving night 1915. There, "bathed in the sacred glow of the fiery cross, the invisible empire was called from its slumber of half a century to take up a new task."

The revived Klan's appeal to bigotry extended well beyond the states of the former Confederacy: it thrived in small towns and cities in the North and especially in the Midwest, with major strongholds in Oregon and on Long Island, New York. In 1924, there were 35,000 Klansmen in Detroit, 55,000 in Chicago, 200,000 in Ohio, and 240,000 in Indiana. In Oregon, Indiana, Colorado, Texas, and Arkansas, Klan-endorsed candidates won

**Klan rally**

In 1925 the Ku Klux Klan staged a huge parade down Pennsylvania Avenue in Washington, D.C.

the governorships. Texas elected a Klansman as its U.S. Senator. The robes, the flaming crosses, the eerie processionals, the kneeling recruits, the occult liturgies—all tapped a deep urge toward mystery and brought drama into the dreary routine of a thousand communities. The Klan was a vicious reaction to shifting moral standards and social status, the declining influence of churches, and the broad-mindedness of city dwellers and college students. As a prominent southern journalist observed, the new Klan attracted "respectable" members of communities. The South "swarmed with little businessmen . . . the rural clergy belonged to it [the Klan] or had traffic with it *en masse*." The Klan was "anti-Negro, anti-alien, anti-red, anti-Catholic, anti-Jew, anti-Darwin, anti-Modern, anti-Liberal, Fundamentalist, vastly Moral, militantly Protestant." Although the Klan raised lots of money and elected Klan-backed politicians, it rarely succeeded in its goal of coercing African Americans and immigrants to leave their communities. In the mid-1920s the Klan's peak membership may have been as high as 4 million, but its influence evaporated after passage of the punitive 1924 immigration law. The Klan also suffered from recurrent factional quarrels and schisms, and its flagrant acts of violence tarnished its moral pretensions. A controversial 1925 court case eroded the appeal of the Klan when a Klan leader in Indiana was convicted of raping and murdering a twenty-one-year-old Sunday school teacher. By 1930, Klan membership had dwindled to 100,000, mostly southerners. Yet the deep strain of bigotry and intolerance underlying the Klan lived on, fed by primal fears and hatreds that have yet to disappear.

FUNDAMENTALISM    While the Klan saw a threat mainly in the "alien menace," many adherents of the old-time religion saw secular threats emerging in many churches: new "liberal" ideas held that the Bible should be studied in the light of modern scholarship (the "higher criticism") or that it could be reconciled with biological theories of evolution. Such "modern" notions surfaced in schools and even pulpits. In resisting the inroads of secularism, orthodox Christians embraced a militant new **fundamentalism**, which was distinguished less by a faith that many others shared than by a posture of hostility toward any other belief.

Among rural fundamentalist leaders only former secretary of state and three-time presidential candidate William Jennings Bryan had the following, prestige, and eloquence to make the movement a popular crusade. The aging Bryan continued to espouse a colorful blend of progressive populism and religious fundamentalism. In 1921, he promoted state laws to prohibit the teaching of evolution in the public schools. He denounced the evolutionary theory of Charles Darwin with the same zeal he had once used in opposing Republican William McKinley. "Evolution," he said, "by denying the need or possibility of spiritual regeneration, discourages all reforms, for reform is always based upon the regeneration of the individual." Anti-evolution bills emerged in legislatures, but the only victories came in the South—and there were few of those. Some officials took direct action without legislation. Governor Miriam "Ma" Ferguson of Texas outlawed textbooks upholding Darwinism. "I am a Christian mother," she declared, "and I am not going to let that kind of rot go into Texas schoolbooks."

DARWINISM ON TRIAL    The climax came in Tennessee, where in 1925 the state legislature passed a bill outlawing the teaching of evolution in public schools and colleges. The governor signed the bill with the hope that it would never be applied. He was wrong. In the tiny foothills town of Dayton, in eastern Tennessee, citizens eager to benefit from a burst of publicity persuaded a twenty-four-year-old high-school science teacher and part-time football coach, John T. Scopes, to accept an offer from the American Civil Liberties Union (ACLU) to defend a test case. They succeeded beyond their wildest hopes: the publicity was worldwide and enduring—but not all flattering.

Before the opening of the twelve-day "monkey trial" on July 10, 1925, the streets of Dayton swarmed with publicity hounds, curiosity seekers, evangelists, atheists, hot-dog and soda-pop hucksters, hundreds of reporters, and national radio coverage. The carnival-like atmosphere was infectious. Main Street merchants festooned their shop windows with pictures of apes and monkeys lampooning Darwinian evolution. The sheriff's motorcycle carried a sign reading "Monkeyville Police." The nation's most prominent journalist, the savagely witty H. L. Mencken of Baltimore, said in his first story about the "trial of the century" that he had been greatly surprised by the town of Dayton: "I expected to find a squalid southern village, with darkies snoozing on the houseblocks [porch], pigs rooting under the houses and the inhabitants full of hookworm and malaria. What I found was a country town full of charm and even beauty."

The two stars of the show were both showmen who loved a big payday: William Jennings Bryan, who had offered his services to the prosecution, and Chicagoan Clarence Darrow, the nation's most famous trial lawyer. Darrow, who had supported Bryan's 1896 presidential candidacy, was a fierce defender of the rights of the working class and organized labor, leading one journalist to call him the "attorney for the damned." When Darrow learned that Bryan would be aiding the state attorneys, he volunteered his services— for free—to the ACLU attorneys defending John T. Scopes. Darrow had spent much of his career attacking religious intolerance. Bryan, however, was not intimidated by Darrow's arrival in Dayton. "Darrow is an atheist," he charged, while "I'm an upholder of Christianity. That's the difference between us." Bryan told the media that the trial was not about Scopes but about a state's right to determine what was taught in the public schools. He also raised the stakes when he announced that the "contest between evolution and Christianity is a duel to the death." Darrow countered: "Scopes is not on trial. Civilization is on trial. Nothing will satisfy us but broad victory." Darrow was determined to prove "that America is founded on liberty and not on narrow, mean, intolerable and brainless prejudice of soulless religio-maniacs."

Ironies abounded as the "trial of the century" opened in Dayton. Both Bryan and Darrow had spent their careers promoting the interests of working people and worked together on many common causes. They also shared a desire to make the trial of John T. Scopes an exercise in public education— but from two very different perspectives. When the judge ruled out Darrow's effort to call scientists to testify about biblical accuracy, the defense on July 20 called Bryan as an "expert" witness on biblical interpretation (Mencken

**Courtroom scene during the Scopes trial**

The media, food vendors, and others flocked to Dayton, Tennessee, for the case against John T. Scopes, the teacher who taught evolution.

described him as a "fundamentalist pope"). Darrow treated Bryan as a hostile witness, barraging him with sharp questions about inconsistencies and fables in the Bible. In a heated exchange with Darrow, Bryan repeatedly trapped himself in literal-minded interpretations (Jonah was swallowed by a whale, Joshua made the sun stand still, the earth was created in six days, etc.) and revealed his ignorance of biblical history and scholarship. Bryan gradually conceded that he had never thought through the possibility that many of the Bible's stories conflicted with common sense and basic scientific truths. At one point, the agnostic Darrow, who had spent much of his career ridiculing religious fundamentalists, declared that Bryan was "not competent." Bryan lashed back, charging that Darrow was putting "revealed religion" on trial. "I am here to defend it." He claimed that Darrow was insulting Christians. Darrow, his thumbs clasping his colorful suspenders, shot back: "You insult every man of science and learning in the world because he does not believe in your fool religion." It was a bitter scene. At one point, Darrow and Bryan, their patience exhausted in the broiling summer heat, lunged at each other, shaking their fists, prompting the judge to adjourn court. Darrow claimed victory. His goal was to "show the country what an ignoramus Bryan was, and I succeeded."

The next day, as the trial ended, the judge ruled that the only issue before the jury was whether Scopes had taught evolution, and no one had denied that he had. He was found guilty, but the Tennessee Supreme Court, while upholding the state's anti-evolution statute, overruled the $100 fine on a technicality. H. L. Mencken's newspaper, the *Baltimore Evening Sun*, immediately offered to pay the fine for Scopes. The chief prosecutor accepted the higher court's advice against "prolonging the life of this bizarre case" and dropped the issue. Both sides were justified in claiming victory. With more accuracy than he intended, Bryan described the trial as a "duel to the death." Five days after it closed, he died of a heart condition aggravated by heat and fatigue. During the next two years, Mississippi, Texas, and other mostly southern states followed the lead of Tennessee in passing laws barring the teaching of evolution. The Scopes trial did not end the uncivil war between evolutionists and fundamentalists. It continues to this day.

PROHIBITION   William Jennings Bryan died knowing that one of his other crusades had succeeded: alcoholic beverages had been outlawed. The movement to prohibit beer, wine, and liquor offered another example of reforming zeal channeled into a drive for moral righteousness and social conformity. Around 1900, the leading temperance organizations, the Women's Christian Temperance Union (WCTU) and the Anti-Saloon League, had launched a campaign for a national prohibition law. By the 1910s, the Anti-Saloon League had become one of the most effective pressure groups in history, mobilizing Protestant churches behind its single-minded battle to elect "dry" candidates to local, state, and national offices. Those advocating the prohibition of alcoholic beverages often displayed blatant ethnic and social prejudices. The head of the Anti-Saloon League, for example, castigated German Americans because they "eat like gluttons and drink like swine." For many anti-alcohol crusaders, the primary goal of eliminating alcoholic beverages seemed to be policing the behavior of the poor, the foreign-born, and the working class. One prohibitionist referred to Italian immigrants as "Dagos, who drink excessively [and] live in a state of filth."

At its Jubilee Convention in 1913, the league endorsed a prohibition amendment to the Constitution. The 1916 elections finally produced enough members in both houses of Congress to pass legislation outlawing alcoholic beverages. Soon the wartime spirit of sacrifice, the need to use grain for food rather than for booze, and wartime hostility to German American brewers transformed the cause of prohibition into a virtual test of patriotism. On December 18, 1917, the wartime Congress sent to the states the Eighteenth Amendment, which on January 16, 1920, one year after ratification, banned the manufacture, sale, and transportation of intoxicating liquors. The popular evangelist Billy Sunday, who described himself as a "temperance Republican down to my toes," told the ten thousand people gathered at his tabernacle to celebrate the outlawing of strong drink that the age of righteousness was at hand: "Men will walk upright now; women will smile and the children will laugh."

Prohibition was the most ambitious social reform ever attempted in the United States. But it proved to be a colossal failure. The new amendment did not suddenly persuade people to stop drinking. Instead, it motivated millions of people to use ingenious—and illegal—ways to satisfy their thirst for alcohol. The Volstead Act (1919), which outlined the actual rules and regulations triggered by the Eighteenth Amendment, had so many loopholes that it virtually guaranteed failure. Individuals and organizations were allowed to keep and drink any liquor owned on January 16, 1919. Not surprisingly, people stocked up before then. The Yale Club in Manhattan, for example, stored enough liquor to subsist for the fourteen years that Prohibition was enforced. Farmers were still allowed to "preserve" their fruits through the process of fermenting them, which resulted in barns stockpiled with "hard cider" and homemade wine. So-called medicinal liquor was also still allowed, which meant that physicians (and even veterinarians) grew tired writing numerous prescriptions for "medicinal" brands such as Old Grand-Dad and Jim Beam whiskies.

An even greater weakness of the new Prohibition law was that Congress never supplied adequate funding to enforce it. In 1920 there were only 1,520 Prohibition agents spread across the United States. Given the perennial public thirst for booze, the spotty support for Prohibition among local officials, and the profits to be made in making illegal booze, called bootlegging, it would have taken armies of enforcement agents to police the nation. Nor did the Republican presidents during the 1920s embrace the "fanaticism" over temperance. Warren G. Harding, who regularly consumed bootleg liquor in the White House, said he was "unable to see this as a great moral issue." In working-class and ethnic-rich Detroit the bootleg liquor industry during the Prohibition era was second in size only to the auto industry. New York City's police commissioner estimated that there were 32,000 illegal bars ("speakeasies") in the city during Prohibition. In Washington, D.C., the largest bootlegger reported that "a majority of both houses" of Congress were regular customers of his products. As the popular humorist Will Rogers

**Prohibition**

A 1926 police raid on a speakeasy, where illegal "bootleg" liquor was sold.

quipped, "Prohibition is better than no liquor at all." What Congress did not count on was the staggering amount of liquor tax revenue that the federal treasury lost by outlawing alcohol.

It would be too much to say that Prohibition gave rise to organized crime, but it supplied criminals with a source of enormous new income while the automobile and the submachine gun provided criminals greater mobility and firepower. Organized crime leaders showed remarkable gifts for exploiting loopholes in the law when they did not simply bribe policemen and politicians. Well-organized crime syndicates behaved like giant corporations; they controlled the entire stream of liquor's production, pricing, and distribution. The result: Prohibition witnessed a fourteen-year-orgy of criminal activity unparalleled in history.

The most celebrated Prohibition-era gangster was **"Scarface" Al Capone**. Born in 1899 and raised in New York City, where he was connected to two murders before he reached the age of twenty, he left for Chicago in 1920. There he thuggishly seized control of the huge illegal liquor business in the city. In 1927 his Chicago-based bootlegging, prostitution, and gambling empire brought him an income of $60 million, which he flaunted with expensive suits and silk pajamas, a custom-upholstered bulletproof Cadillac, a platoon of bodyguards, and lavish support for city charities. Capone insisted that he was merely providing the public with the goods and services it demanded: "They say I violate the prohibition law. Who doesn't?" He neglected to say that he had also bludgeoned to death several police lieutenants and ordered the execution of dozens of rival criminals. Dedicated law-enforcement officials led by Federal Bureau of Investigation agent Eliot Ness began to smash his bootlegging operations in 1929, but they were unable to pin anything on Capone until a Treasury agent infiltrated his gang and uncovered evidence that nailed him for federal tax evasion. Tried in 1931, Capone was sentenced to eleven years in prison.

## THE "JAZZ AGE" DURING THE "ROARING TWENTIES"

In many ways, the reactionary temper of the 1920s and the repressive movements it spawned arose as reactions to a much publicized social and intellectual revolution that threatened to rip America from its old moorings. As described by various labels given to the times, most of them exaggerations, it was an era of excess, the Jazz Age, and the **Roaring Twenties**. During those years a cosmopolitan urban America confronted a provincial, rural America, and cultural conflict reached new levels of tension. F. Scott Fitzgerald dubbed the postwar era the Jazz Age in 1922 not because he himself liked jazz music but because his circle of daring young people in the cities was, like a jazz musician, intoxicated with nervous energy. Unlike so many Americans of his age and wealth, Fitzgerald celebrated the era's spontaneity and sensual vitality.

THE NEW WOMAN AND THE NEW MORALITY    Much of the shock to old-timers during the Jazz Age came from the revolution in manners and morals, evidenced first among young people, and especially on college campuses. In *This Side of Paradise* (1920), a novel of student life at Princeton University, F. Scott Fitzgerald wrote of "the great current American phenomenon, the 'petting party.'" Prudish mothers, he said, had no "idea how casually their daughters were accustomed to be kissed." From such novels and from scores of magazine articles, the heartland learned about the wild parties, bathtub gin, promiscuity, speakeasies, "shimmy dancers," and new uses to which automobiles were put on secluded lovers' lanes.

Sex came to be discussed with a new frankness during the 1920s. Much of the talk derived from a spreading awareness of Dr. **Sigmund Freud**, the Viennese father of psychoanalysis. When in 1909 Freud visited Clark University in Massachusetts, he was surprised to find himself so well known "even in prudish America." By the 1920s, his ideas had begun to percolate among the public, and books and magazines discussed libido, inhibitions, Oedipus complexes, and repression. Some of the decade's most popular magazines were those that focused on romance and sex: *True Confessions, Telling Tales,* and *True Story.* Their story titles revealed their themes: "The Primitive Lover" ("She wanted a caveman husband"), "Indolent Kisses," and "Innocents Astray." Likewise, the most popular female movie stars—Madge Bellamy, Clara Bow, and Joan Crawford—projected an image of sensual freedom, energy, and independence. Advertisements for new movies reinforced the self-indulgent images of the Jazz Age: "brilliant men, beautiful jazz babies, champagne baths, midnight revels, petting parties in the purple dawn, all ending in one terrific climax that makes you gasp." Traditionalists were shocked at the behavior of rebellious young women. "One hears it said," lamented a Baptist magazine, "that the girls are actually tempting the boys more than the boys do the girls, by their dress and conversation."

Fashion also reflected the rebellion against prudishness and a loosening of inhibitions. The emancipated "new woman" in the 1920s was supposedly "independent, bright-eyed, alert, and alive," a young woman eager to gain new freedoms. This "new woman" eagerly discarded the constraining fashions of the nineteenth century—pinched-in corsets, confining petticoats, and floor-length dresses. In 1919 women's skirts were typically six inches above the ground; by 1927 they were at the knee, and the "flapper" was providing a shocking model of the new feminism. The name derived from the way fashionable young women allowed their unbuckled galoshes to "flap" around their ankles. Flapper fashion featured bobbed hair, minimal undergarments, gauzy fabrics, and sheer stockings. Cigarettes, booze, makeup, and jazz dancing were necessary accessories.

F. Scott Fitzgerald said the ideal flapper was "lovely and expensive and about nineteen."

**The "new woman" of the 1920s**

Two flappers dance atop the Hotel Sherman in Chicago, 1926.

Conservative moralists saw the flappers as just another sign of a degenerating society. A Catholic priest in Brooklyn lamented that the feminism emerging in the 1920s had provoked a "pandemonium of powder, a riot of rouge, and a moral anarchy of dress." Others saw in the "new women" an expression of American individualism. "By sheer force of violence," explained the *New York Times* in 1929, the flapper has "established the feminine right to equal representation in such hitherto masculine fields of endeavor as smoking and drinking, swearing, petting, and upsetting the community peace." For the most part, the college-educated "flappers" were indifferent to the legacy of progressive social reform or women's rights. Their priorities were courtship, marriage, and consumerism. Older social reformers regretted the changed priorities. Charlotte Perkins Gilman, a prominent writer and feminist, lamented in 1923 the "lowering in the standards in sex relations" among young Americans. Their cavalier use of birth control devices struck her as "selfish and fruitless indulgence." The emphasis on premarital sex, she said, illustrated the "lamentable behavior of our times." Jane Addams agreed, noting that the younger generation of Americans seemed self-absorbed. They lacked "reforming energy."

Most women in the 1920s were not flappers, however. Although many women were recruited during the war to take jobs vacated by men serving in the military, most of them were forced to give up those jobs once the war ended. True, more middle-class women attended college in the 1920s than ever before, but a higher percentage of them married after graduation than had been the case in the nineteenth century. Only 4 percent of working women in the 1920s were salaried professionals; the vast majority worked for wages. A student at all-female Smith College expressed frustration at the prevailing view that college-educated women were still expected to pursue marriage and motherhood: "We cannot believe that it is fixed in the nature of things that a woman must choose between a home and her work, when a man may have both. There must be a way out, and it is the problem of our generation to find the way."

Some women moved into new vocations created by the burgeoning consumer culture (two thirds of purchases each year were made by women shoppers) such as accounting assistants and department store clerks. The sales of cosmetics and the number of beauty shops soared from five thousand in 1920 to forty thousand in 1930, thereby creating new jobs for hair stylists, manicurists, and cosmeticians. But the majority of women remained anchored in the domestic sphere, either as full-time wives and mothers or as household servants. African American and Mexican American women faced the greatest challenges. As a New York City newspaper observed, they were forced to do "work which white women will not do." Women of color usually worked as maids, laundresses, and seamstresses or on farms.

In addition to sexism, racism also continued to limit the freedom of women during the twenties. For example, in 1919, an interracial couple from Ayer, Massachusetts, Mabel Puffer, a wealthy college graduate, and Arthur Hazzard, a handyman and leader within the local black community, decided to get married in Concord, New Hampshire. They checked into separate rooms in a hotel, then met in the lobby and walked three blocks to the courthouse to apply for a marriage license, only to be told that there was a five-day waiting period. So they waited and made preparations for the wedding. The mayor of Concord agreed to perform the service, and Hazzard's siblings and mother made plans to attend. Others were not as supportive, however. News of the interracial couple strolling the streets of Concord reached the Boston newspapers. The first story's headline, in the *Boston Traveller*, read: "Will Marry Negro in 'Perfect Union': Rich Ayer Society Woman Determined to Wed Servant Although Hometown is Aflame with Protest." The news had outraged many residents of Ayer. The next day, the *Boston Evening Globe* ran the now-provocative story on its front page. The headline was sensational: "Hope to Prevent White Woman Wedding Negro: Two Friends of Mabel E. Puffer Have Gone to Concord, N.H." Puffer's friends and relatives rushed to Concord and began exerting pressure on her and the townspeople. Suddenly, the mayor reversed himself and announced he could not perform the wedding, claiming he was called out of town on important business. The betrothed couple, after being turned down several times, finally found a minister willing to marry them. The night before the wedding was to occur, however, the Ayer police chief arrived, arrested Hazzard on charge of "enticement," and took Puffer into custody because she had been deemed "insane" for having decided to marry a working-class African American. In reporting the dramatic story, the Concord newspaper concluded that the community "gazed after their departing dust with no regrets." The nation that Woodrow Wilson had led into World War I to "make the world safe for democracy" remained a very unsafe place for those crossing the color line.

THE "NEW NEGRO" The most significant development in African American life during the early twentieth century was the **Great Migration** northward from the South. The movement of blacks to the North began in 1915–1916, when rapidly expanding war industries and restrictions on immigration together created a labor shortage; legal restrictions on immigration continued the movement in the 1920s. Altogether between 1910 and 1920 the Southeast lost some 323,000 African Americans, or 5 percent of the native black population, and by 1930 it had lost another 615,000, or 8 percent of the native black population in 1920. With the migration, a slow but steady growth in black political influence in northern cities set in. African Americans were freer to speak and act in a northern setting; they also gained political leverage by settling in large cities in states with many electoral votes.

Along with political activity came a bristling spirit of protest, a spirit that received cultural expression in what came to be called the **Harlem Renaissance**, the nation's first self-conscious black literary and artistic movement. The Harlem Renaissance grew out of the fast-growing African-American community in New York City. In 1890, one in seventy people in Manhattan was African American; by 1930 it was one in nine. The "great, dark city" of Harlem, in poet Langston Hughes's phrase, contained more blacks per square mile than any other community in the nation. The dense concentration of urban blacks generated a sense of common identity, growing power, and cultural self-expression. Writer James Weldon Johnson described a "Black Manhattan" emerging in Harlem during the 1920s. Harlem, he wrote, was a "typically Negro" community of 175,000 in that it featured "movement, color, gaiety, singing, dancing, boisterous laughter, and loud talk."

**"A Negro Family Just Arrived in Chicago from the Rural South," 1922**

Between 1910 and 1930 almost 1 million African Americans left the South.

The Harlem Renaissance was the self-conscious effort in the New York black community to cultivate racial equality by promoting African American cultural achievements. In 1924, blacks organized a banquet in Harlem to introduce the white-dominated publishing industry to African American writers. Howard University professor Alain Locke, a Harvard graduate and the nation's first black Rhodes Scholar, was the event's emcee, and he became the leader of the **New Negro** movement, an effort to promote racial equality by celebrating the cultural contributions of African Americans. In 1925, at Locke's behest, *Survey Graphic* magazine devoted its March issue ("Harlem: Mecca of the New Negro") to showcasing promising young black writers. In this sense, the writers of the Harlem Renaissance intentionally differentiated themselves from the alienated white writers making up what was called the "lost generation." They were the "found generation." James Weldon Johnson predicted that Harlem would become the "intellectual, cultural, and financial center for Negroes of the United States, and will exert a vital influence upon all Negro peoples." Johnson noted that "a people that has produced great art and literature has never been looked upon as inferior."

The writers associated with the Harlem Renaissance audaciously celebrated themselves, their black heritage, and their contemporary contributions to American culture, including jazz and the blues. As the poet Langston Hughes wrote, "I am a Negro—and beautiful. . . . The night is beautiful. So the faces of my people." His African American friends were "black like that old mule, / Black, and don't give a damn!" Perhaps the greatest single literary creation of the time was Jean Toomer's novel *Cane* (1923), which pictured the lives both of simple rural folk in Georgia's black belt and the sophisticated African American middle class in Washington, D.C. Other writers making up the Harlem Renaissance included Zora Neale Hurston, Countee Cullen, Nella Larsen, and Claude McKay. The Harlem group also promoted a racially integrated society. James Weldon Johnson coined the term "Aframerican" to combine "African American." He did so in order to emphasize that blacks were no longer divided by their heritage; they were Americans who happened to have an African ancestry. Blacks were not interlopers or "foundlings," in Locke's term, but "conscious collaborators" in the creation of American society and culture.

Alain Locke spoke for other leaders of the Harlem Renaissance by urging his literary and artistic friends to celebrate their African heritage and draw upon African art for their inspiration. Others disagreed. Langston Hughes stressed that he was an "American Negro." He "loved the surface of Africa and the rhythms of Africa—but I was not Africa. I was Chicago and Kansas City and Broadway and Harlem." The black sculptor Augusta Savage agreed. She explained that African Americans for three centuries had shared the

**Into Bondage**

This painting by Aaron Douglas exemplifies how black artists in the Harlem Renaissance used their African roots and collective history as artistic inspiration.

"same cultural background, the same system, the same standard of beauty as white Americans. . . . It is impossible to go back to primitive [African] art for our models."

THE BIRTH OF JAZZ    F. Scott Fitzgerald fastened upon the **"Jazz Age"** as a label for the broad spirit of rebellion and spontaneity he saw welling up among young Americans during the 1920s. The new jazz music had first emerged in New Orleans as an ingenious synthesis of black rural folk traditions and urban dance entertainment. During the 1920s it spread to Kansas City, Memphis, the Harlem neighborhood of New York City, and Chicago's South Side. African American Louis Armstrong, an inspired trumpeter, was the Pied Piper of jazz. Born in a New Orleans shack in 1900, he grew up drenched in jazz music. In 1922, Armstrong moved to Chicago with King Oliver's Creole Jazz Band. Thereafter, he delighted audiences with his passionate performances. "The guys never heard anything like it," recalled the black composer and bandleader Duke Ellington. The syncopated rhythms of jazz were immensely popular among rebellious young adults—both black and white—and helped create carefree new dances such as the Charleston and the Black Bottom, whose sexual gyrations shocked guardians of morality. Through the vehicle of jazz, African American performers not only shaped American culture during the twenties but also European taste as well. The controversial European modernist painters Henri Matisse and Pablo Picasso were infatuated with the improvisational inventiveness of jazz music.

GARVEYISM   The spirit of jazz and the "New Negro" also found expression in what came to be called Negro nationalism, which exalted blackness, black cultural expression, and black separatism. The leading spokesman for such views was the flamboyant **Marcus Garvey**. In 1916, Garvey brought to the all-black Harlem neighborhood in New York City the headquarters of the Universal Negro Improvement Association (UNIA), which he had started in his native Jamaica two years before. Garvey had grown convinced that racial oppression and exploitation were prevalent in most societies around the world. Traditional efforts to use civil rights legislation and court rulings to end such oppression were not working. Garvey insisted that blacks

**Frankie "Half Pint" Jackson and his band at the Sunset Cafe, Chicago, in the 1920s**

Jazz emerged in the 1920s as an especially American expression of the modernist spirit. African American artists bent musical conventions to give fuller rein to improvisation and sensuality.

had nothing in common with whites—and that was a good thing. He therefore called for the cultivation of black racial pride and promoted racial separation rather than integration. He was the first major black leader to champion what later came to be called "black power." In passionate speeches and in his newspaper, the *Negro World,* Garvey exhorted African Americans to liberate themselves from the surrounding white culture. He saw every white person as a "potential Klansman" and therefore endorsed the "social and political separation of all peoples to the extent that they promote their own ideals and civilization."

The UNIA grew rapidly amid the racial tensions of the postwar years. Garvey quickly enlisted half a million members in the UNIA and claimed as many as 6 million served by 800 offices by 1923. It became the largest black political organization in the twentieth century. In 1920, Garvey hosted in New York City UNIA's first international convention. Thousands of delegates from forty-eight states and more than twenty nations attended. In his keynote address to 25,000 delegates Garvey proclaimed that the long-suffering black peoples of the world would "suffer no longer. We shall now organize the 400,000,000 Negroes around the world into a vast organization to plant the banner of freedom on the great continent of Africa." In 1920, Garvey declared that the only lasting hope for blacks living in the United States was to flee America and build their own republic in Africa.

**Marcus Garvey**

Garvey was the founder of the Universal Negro Improvement Association and a leading spokesman for "Negro nationalism" in the 1920s.

Garvey's simple message of black nationalism and racial solidarity appealed to many struggling African Americans living in slums in northern cities. Garvey and his aides created their own black version of Christianity, organized their own fraternal lodges and community cultural centers, started their own black businesses, and published their own newspaper. Such a separatist message appalled other black leaders, however. W.E.B. Du Bois, for example, labeled Garvey "the most dangerous enemy of the Negro race. . . . He is either a lunatic or a traitor." An African American newspaper pledged to help "drive Garvey and Garveyism in all its sinister viciousness from the American soil."

Garvey's black-only crusade came to a screeching halt in May 1923 when he and several associates were put on trial for fraud related to the sale of stock in one of his struggling for-profit enterprises, the Black Star Line, a steamship corporation intended to transport American blacks to Africa. The jury acquitted everyone but Garvey. The judge sentenced him to the maximum five-year prison term. In 1927 President Calvin Coolidge pardoned Garvey on the condition that he be deported to Jamaica. One of the largest crowds in Jamaican history greeted him upon his return to his native country. Garvey died in obscurity in 1940, but the memory of his movement kept alive an undercurrent of racial nationalism that would reemerge in the 1960s under the slogan "black power."

A more lasting force for racial equality was the National Association for the Advancement of Colored People (NAACP), founded in 1910 by white progressives and black activists. Black participants in the NAACP came mainly from the Niagara Movement, a group associated with W.E.B. Du Bois that had met each year since 1905 at places associated with the anti-slavery movement (Niagara Falls; Oberlin, Ohio; Boston; Harpers Ferry) and issued defiant statements against discrimination. Within a few years, the NAACP had become a broad-based national organization. The NAACP embraced the progressive idea that the solution to social problems begins with education, by informing the people of social ills. Du Bois became the new organization's director of publicity and research and editor of its journal, *Crisis,* from 1910 to 1934. The NAACP's main strategy focused on legal action to bring the Fourteenth and Fifteenth Amendments back to life. One early victory came with *Guinn v. United States* (1915), in which the Supreme Court struck down Oklahoma's grandfather clause, used to deprive African Americans of the vote. In *Buchanan v. Worley* (1917) the Court invalidated a residential segregation ordinance in Louisville, Kentucky.

### The Crisis

This national journal of the NAACP carried the subtitle "A Record of the Darker Races."

In 1919, the NAACP launched a national campaign against lynching, then a still-common form of vigilante racism. An anti-lynching bill to make mob murder a federal offense passed the House in 1922 but lost to a fili-buster by southerners in the Senate. NAACP field secretary James Weldon Johnson believed the continued agitation on the issue did more than the bill's passage would have to reduce lynchings, which decreased to a third of what they had been in the previous decade. But even one lynching was too many for a so-called progressive society.

## MASS CULTURE

After 1920, changes in the economy, science, and social thought were more dramatic than those generated by Prohibition, the Klan, and funda-mentalism. The large, growing middle class of Americans who had formed an important segment of the progressive political coalition were now absorbed instead into the prosperous "New Era" created by advances in communications, transportation, business organization, and the spread of mass consumerism.

**THE GROWING CONSUMER CULTURE**  Economic and social life was transformed during the 1920s. The nation's total wealth almost doubled between 1920 and 1930, while workers enjoyed a 26 percent increase in income, the sharpest increase in history to that point. More people than ever before had the money and time to indulge their consumer fancies, and a growing advertis-ing industry fueled the appetites of the rapidly expanding middle and upper middle class. By the mid-1920s advertising had become a huge enterprise using sophisticated psychological research with powerful social significance. Old-time values of thrift and saving gave way to a new ethic of consumption that made spending a virtue. The innovation of installment buying enabled people to buy more by extending their payments over months rather than paying in cash. A newspaper editorial insisted that the American's "first importance to his country is no longer that of citizen but that of consumer. Consumption is a new necessity in response to dramatic increases in productivity."

Consumer-goods industries fueled much of the economic boom from 1922 to 1929. Perhaps no decade in American history witnessed such dramatic changes in everyday life. In 1920 only 35 percent of homes had electricity; by 1930 the number was 68 percent. At the same time, the number of homes with indoor plumbing doubled. Similar increases occurred in the number of households with washing machines and automobiles. Moderately priced crea-ture comforts, including items such as flush toilets, handheld cameras, wrist-watches, cigarette lighters, vacuum cleaners, washing machines, and linoleum floors, became more widely available. Inventions in communications and transportation, such as motion pictures, radio, telephones, airplanes, and automobiles, fueled the transformation in everyday life.

In 1896, a New York audience viewed the first moving-picture show. By 1908, there were nearly ten thousand movie theaters scattered across the nation; by 1924, there were twenty thousand theaters showing seven hundred new films a year. Hollywood, California, became the international center of movie production, grinding out cowboy Westerns and the timeless comedies of Mack Sennett's Keystone Company, where a raft of slapstick comedians, most notably Charlie Chaplin, perfected their art, transforming it into a form of social

**Motion pictures**

A dispirited Charlie Chaplin in a still image from his classic 1921 film *The Kid*.

criticism. By the mid-1930s, every city and most small towns had movie theaters, and movies became the nation's chief form of mass entertainment. Movie attendance during the 1920s averaged 80 million people a week. Americans spent ten times as much on movies as they did on tickets to baseball and football games.

Radio broadcasting had an even more spectacular growth. Except for experimental broadcasts, radio served only for basic communication until 1920. In that year, station WWJ in Detroit began transmitting news bulletins from the *Detroit Daily News,* and KDKA in Pittsburgh, owned by the Westinghouse Electric and Manufacturing Company, began broadcasting regularly scheduled programs. The first radio commercial aired in New York in 1922. By the end of that year, there were 508 stations and some 3 million receivers in use. In 1926, the National Broadcasting Company (NBC), a subsidiary of the Radio Corporation of America (RCA), began linking stations into a national network; the Columbia Broadcasting System (CBS) entered the field the next year. In 1927, a Federal Radio Commission was established to regulate the industry; in 1934 it became the Federal Communications Commission (FCC), with authority over other forms of communication as well. Calvin Coolidge was the first president to address the nation by radio, and he did so monthly, paving the way for Franklin Delano Roosevelt's influential "fireside chats."

**The rise of radio**

The radio brought this farm family together and connected them to the outside world. By the end of the 1930s, millions would tune in to newscasts, soap operas, sports events, and church services.

AIRPLANES, AUTOMOBILES, AND THE ECONOMY    Advances in transportation were equally significant. Wilbur and Orville Wright, owners of a bicycle shop in Dayton, Ohio, built and flew the first airplane over the beach at Kitty Hawk, North Carolina, in 1903. But the use of planes advanced slowly until the outbreak of war in 1914, after which the Europeans rapidly developed the airplane as a military weapon. When the United States entered the war, it had no combat planes—American pilots flew British or French planes. An American aircraft industry developed during the war but foundered in the postwar demobilization. Under the Kelly Act of 1925, however, the federal government began to subsidize the industry through airmail contracts. The Air Commerce Act of 1926 provided federal funds to aid in the advancement of air transportation and navigation; among the projects it supported was the construction of airports.

The infant aviation industry received a huge psychological boost in 1927 when twenty-six-year-old Charles A. Lindbergh Jr., a St. Louis–based mail pilot, made the first *solo* transatlantic flight, traveling from New York to

Paris in thirty-three and a half hours. The heroic deed, which won him $25,000 and a Congressional Medal of Honor, was truly dramatic. The night before he took off, he could not sleep, so he was already exhausted when he began the grueling flight. He flew through severe storms as well as a dense fog for part of the way that forced him to descend to within ten feet of the ocean's surface before sighting the Irish coast and regaining his bearings. When he landed in France, there were one hundred thousand people greeting him with thunderous cheers. The New York City parade celebrating Lindbergh's accomplishment surpassed even the celebration of the armistice ending World War I. Flappers developed a new dance step in Lindbergh's honor, called the Lindy Hop.

Five years later, New York honored another pioneering aviator—Amelia Earhart, who in 1932 became the first woman to fly solo across the Atlantic Ocean. Born in Kansas in 1897, she made her first solo flight in 1921 and began working as a stunt pilot at air shows across the country. Earhart's popularity soared after her transatlantic solo flight. The fifteen-hour feat led Congress to award her the Distinguished Flying Cross, and she was named Outstanding American Woman of the Year in 1932. In 1937 Earhart and a navigator left Miami, Florida, heading east on a round-the-world flight. The voyage went smoothly until they attempted the most difficult leg: from New Guinea to a tiny Pacific island 2,556 miles away. The plane disappeared, and despite extensive searches, no trace of it or the aviators was ever found. It remains the most intriguing mystery in aviation history. The accomplishments of Lindbergh and Earhart helped catapult the aviation industry to prominence. By 1930, there were forty-three airline companies in operation in the United States.

Nonetheless, by far the most significant economic and social development of the early twentieth century was the automobile. The first motorcar had been manufactured for sale in 1895, but the founding of the Ford Motor Company in 1903 revolutionized the infant industry. Henry Ford vowed "to democratize the automobile. When I'm through everybody will be able to afford one, and about everyone will have one." Ford's reliable **Model T** (the celebrated Tin Lizzie) came out in 1908 at a price of $850 (in 1924 it would sell for $290). The Model T changed little from year to year, and it came in only one color: black.

In 1916, the total number of cars manufactured passed 1 million; by 1920 more than 8 million were registered, and in 1929 there were more than 23 million. The automobile revolution gave rise to a gigantic market for oil products just as the Spindletop gusher (drilled in 1901 in Texas) heralded the opening of vast southwestern oil fields. It quickened the movement for good roads, financed in large part from a gasoline tax; speeded transportation; encouraged suburban sprawl; and sparked real estate booms in California and Florida.

**Ford Motor Company's Highland Park plant, 1913**

Gravity slides and chain conveyors contributed to the mass production of automobiles.

The automobile industry also became the leading example of modern mass-production techniques and efficiency. Ford's Highland Park plant outside Detroit was designed to increase output dramatically by creating a moving assembly line with conveyors pulling the parts along feeder lines and the chassis down an assembly line rather than making each car in place. Each worker performed a particular task, such as installing a fender or a wheel. The moving assembly line could produce a new car in ninety-three minutes. Such efficiency enabled Ford to lower the price of his cars, thereby increasing the number of people who could afford to buy them.

Just as the railroad helped transform the pace and scale of American life in the second half of the nineteenth century, the mass production of automobiles changed social life during the twentieth century. Cars enabled people to live farther away from their workplaces, thus fostering the suburban revolution. They also helped fuel the economic boom of the 1920s. Producing cars created tens of thousands of new jobs and provided "backward linkages" throughout the economy by generating a huge demand for steel, rubber, leather, oil, and gasoline. The burgeoning car culture spurred road construction, dotting the landscape with gasoline stations, traffic lights, billboards, and motor hotels ("motels"). By 1929, the federal government was constructing ten thousand miles of paved national highways each year.

SPECTATOR SPORTS  The widespread ownership of automobiles as well as rising incomes changed the way people spent their leisure time. People living in cities could drive into the countryside or visit friends and relatives in neighboring towns. On weekends, they went to the ballparks, stadiums, or boxing rinks to see prizefights and baseball or football games. During the 1920s, the mania for spectator sports emerged as a primary form of mass entertainment—and big business. Baseball became the national pastime in the 1920s. Having been created in the 1870s in rural areas, by the 1920s baseball had gone urban. With larger-than-life heroes such as New York Yankee stars George Herman "Babe" Ruth Jr. and Henry Louis "Lou" Gehrig, professional baseball teams attracted intense loyalties and huge crowds. In 1920, more than a million spectators attended Ruth's games with the New York Yankees. Two years later, the Yankees built a new stadium, called the "house that Ruth built." The Yankees dominated baseball, winning world championships in 1923, 1927, and 1928. More than 20 million people attended professional baseball games in 1927, the year that Ruth, the "Sultan of Swat," set a record by hitting sixty home runs in a season. Because baseball remained a segregated sport in the 1920s, "Negro Leagues"—amateur, semi-professional, and professional—were organized to provide opportunities for African Americans to play in and watch athletic contests.

Football, especially at the college level, also attracted huge crowds. Unlike baseball, football tended to attract more affluent spectators. It, too, benefited from outsized heroes such as Harold Edward "Red" Grange, the phenomenal running back for the University of Illinois. Grange, not Babe Ruth, was the first athlete to appear on the cover of *Time* magazine. Nicknamed the "Galloping Ghost," he was a phenomenal athlete. In a game against the University of Michigan, he scored a touchdown the first four times he carried the ball. After the victorious game, celebrating students carried Grange on their shoulders for two miles across the campus. When Grange signed a contract with the Chicago Bears in 1926, he single-handedly made professional football competitive with baseball as a spectator sport.

What Ruth and Grange were to their sports, William Harrison "Jack" Dempsey was to boxing. In 1919, he won the world heavyweight title from Jess Willard, a giant of a man weighing three hundred pounds and standing six and a half feet tall. Dempsey knocked him down seven times in the first round. By the fourth round, Willard, his face bruised and bloodied, threw in the towel. Dempsey thereafter became a dominant force in boxing, a national celebrity, and a wealthy man. Like Babe Ruth, the brawling Dempsey was especially popular with working-class men, for he too had been born poor, raised rough, and worked with his hands for wages. In 1927 when James Joseph "Gene" Tunney defeated Dempsey, over one hundred thousand people attended the dramatic fight, including a thousand reporters, ten state governors, and countless Hollywood celebrities. Some 60 million people listened to the fight over the radio. During the 1920s, spectator sports became a primary form of entertainment.

## THE MODERNIST REVOLT

The dramatic changes in society and the economy during the 1920s were accompanied by continuing transformations in science and the arts that spurred the onset of a "modernist" sensibility. Rebellious modernists came to believe that the twentieth century marked a watershed in human development. Notions of reality and human nature were called into question by sophisticated scientific discoveries and radical new forms of artistic expression. As the prominent English writer and feminist Virginia Woolf declared, "On or about December 1910, human character changed. I am not saying that one went out, as one might into a garden, and there saw that a rose had flowered, or that a hen had laid an egg. The change was not sudden and definite like that. But a change there was, nevertheless; and, since one must be arbitrary, let us date it about the year 1910."

SCIENCE AND SOCIAL THOUGHT  Physicists during the early twentieth century altered the image of the cosmos in bewildering ways. Since the eighteenth century, conventional wisdom had held that the universe was governed by laws that the scientific method could ultimately uncover. This rational world of order and certainty disintegrated at the beginning of the new century when Albert Einstein, a young German physicist with an irreverent attitude toward established truths, announced his theory of relativity, which maintained that space, time, and mass were not absolutes but instead were relative to the location and motion of the observer. Sir Isaac Newton's eighteenth-century laws of mechanics, according to Einstein's relativity theories, worked well enough at relatively slow speeds, but the more nearly one approached the velocity of light (about 186,000 miles per second), the more all measuring devices would change accordingly, so that yardsticks would become shorter, clocks and heartbeats would slow down, even the aging process would ebb.

The farther one reached out into the universe and the farther one reached inside the minute world of the atom, the more certainty dissolved. The discovery of radioactivity in the 1890s showed that atoms were not irreducible units of matter and that some of them emitted particles of energy. This meant, Einstein noted, that mass and energy were not separate phenomena but interchangeable. By 1921, when Einstein was awarded the Nobel Prize, his abstract concept of relativity had become internationally recognized—and popularized. Hundreds of books about relativity had been published. His theories also had consequences that Einstein had not foreseen. Younger physicists built upon Einstein's concepts to further transform notions of reality and the universe.

**Albert Einstein**

Widely regarded as one of the most influential scientists of the twentieth century, Einstein was awarded a Nobel Prize in 1921.

The pace of theoretical physics quickened as the twentieth century unfolded. The German physicist Max Planck suggested that electromagnetic emissions of energy, whether as electricity or light, come in little bundles that he called quanta. Einstein said much the same when he suggested that light was made up of particles, later called photons. The development of quantum theory suggested that atoms were far more complex than once believed and, as stated in 1927 in the "uncertainty principle" of the precocious twenty-five-year-old German physicist Werner Heisenberg, ultimately indescribable. One could never know both the position and the velocity of an electron, Heisenberg concluded, because the very process of observation would inevitably affect the behavior of the particle, altering its position or its velocity. The presence of the observer, in other words, changes what is being observed. Heisenberg's "uncertainty principle," which earned him a Nobel Prize, had profound philosophical and cultural implications. It posed a direct challenge to conventional notions of objectivity by declaring that observation is necessarily subjective—and therefore biased and imprecise.

Heisenberg's "uncertainty principle" constituted the most revolutionary scientific theory in 150 years, for it meant that there is no such thing as absolute truth; human knowledge has inherent limits (and biases). "The physicist thus finds himself in a world from which the bottom has dropped clean out," a Harvard mathematician wrote in 1929. The scientist had to "give up his most cherished convictions and faith. The world is not a world of reason...."

MODERNIST ART AND LITERATURE    The cluster of scientific ideas associated with Sigmund Freud and Albert Einstein helped to inspire a "modernist" revolution in the arts in Europe and America. **Modernism** is a slippery term, hard to grasp and even harder to define. At once a rebellious mood and a sensational movement, full of contradictions, modernism was an anarchical cultural revolt against conventional tastes in art, literature, drama, music, dance, and architecture. With astonishing energy and panache, modernism during the decades clustering around the turn of the twentieth century emphasized the freedom of individual writers and artists to be innovative and even scandalous in the face of traditional notions of beauty and good taste. As the American poet Ezra Pound exclaimed, "Make it New!" Modernism trumpeted an unsettling premise: reality was no longer what it had seemed. The modernist world was one in which, as Karl Marx said, "all that is solid melts into air."

Until the twentieth century, most writers and artists took for granted an accessible "real" world that could be readily observed and accurately represented. On the contrary, the young generation of self-willed modernists viewed reality as a subjective realm, something to be created as much in their minds as copied from life, something to be imagined and expressed rather than simply observed and reproduced. They thus found the subconscious regions of the psyche more interesting and more potent than the traditional focus on reason, common sense, and logic. The American artist Marsden Hartley reported from Paris in 1912 that his reading of Sigmund Freud and the "new psychologists" had prompted him to abandon his emphasis on painting objects from "real life" in favor of expressing on canvas his "intuitive abstractions." He noted that he was now painting "very exceptional things of a most abstract psychic nature." The painter Georgia O'Keeffe agreed that expressing subjectivity was one of the pillars of cultural modernism. Like Hartley, she abandoned the "realistic" emphasis on representing scenes from life; instead, she concentrated on images "I see in my head" with a "woman's feeling."

The modernists were at times deliberately obscure and difficult to access, but their youthful energies as well as their interest in the ugly and crude elements of life helped transform the dynamics of twentieth-century culture and the very meaning of beauty in art. The culture wars of the early twentieth century were almost as violent as the combat during the First World War. Rebels felt an urgent need to attack the guardians of tradition and "good taste."

The horrors of World War I accelerated the insurgency of modernism in the arts by delivering a shattering blow to the widespread belief that Western civilization was progressing. The editors of *Presbyterian* magazine announced in 1919 that "every field of thought and action has been disturbed" by the terrible war and its aftermath. The war's colossal carnage disillusioned many young intellectuals and spurred a new "modernist" sensibility among some of the most talented artists and writers, many of whom had already been shorn of conventional religious belief.

Modernism appeared first in Europe at the end of the nineteenth century and had become a pervasive international force by 1920. It arose out of a widespread recognition that Western civilization had entered an era of bewildering change and disorienting upheavals. New technologies, new modes of transportation and communication, and new scientific discoveries such as quantum mechanics, relativity theory, and Freudian psychology combined to rupture traditional perceptions of reality, liberate new ways of understanding human behavior and consciousness, and generate new forms of artistic expression. "One must never forget," declared Gertrude Stein, the experimentalist poet, "that the reality of the twentieth century is not the reality of the nineteenth century, not at all." Modern artists were preoccupied with exploring the nature of consciousness and with experimenting with new artistic forms. The result was a bewildering array of avant-garde intellectual and artistic movements: impressionism, futurism, Dadaism, surrealism. Modernists ferociously violated conventional expectations. Their writings and paintings were often ambiguous and even opaque, even impenetrable. Clarity was less important than authenticity. Modernists also showed little interest in political life or social reform. As F. Scott Fitzgerald explained, he and the other Jazz Age rebels "had no interest in politics at all." Many of them turned their backs on mainstream American life (the bourgeoisie), dominated as it was by political conservatism, money-getting, and consumerism.

**The Fitzgeralds celebrate Christmas**

F. Scott Fitzgerald and his wife, Zelda, lived in and wrote about the "greatest, gaudiest spree in history."

THE ARMORY SHOW   The modernist impulse in America appeared first in major artistic bohemias in Chicago and New York City, especially in the area of lower Manhattan known as Greenwich Village. In 1913 European modernism made its formal debut in the United States at the Armory Show, a much-discussed international art exhibition that opened in a National Guard armory in New York City and later went on to Chicago, Philadelphia, and Boston. The exhibit shocked most Americans with its display of the latest works by rebellious artists: postimpressionists, expressionists, primitives, and cubists. Pablo Picasso's work made its American debut at the Armory Show. The *New York Times* warned visitors who shared the "old belief in reality" that they would enter "a stark region of abstractions" at the Armory Show that would be "hideous to our unaccustomed eyes." The artists on display were "in love with science but not with objective reality," leading them to produce baffling paintings that were "revolting in their inhumanity." The riotous energies and courageous experiments on display at the Armory Show generated shock, indignation, and ridicule, but the exhibition was a huge success. Over 250,000 people paid to view the traveling exhibit, which dominated newspaper headlines for weeks. Mabel Dodge, the wealthy patron of radical art, announced that the Armory Show was the most important event in American life since the Revolutionary War. Nearly "every thinking person nowadays is in revolt against something," she claimed.

A chance encounter between the acclaimed poets Robert Frost and Wallace Stevens illustrated the changing cultural landscape in the early twentieth century. Stevens said that the "trouble with your poems, Frost, is that they have subjects and they make the visible world easy to see." Stevens insisted that the *modern* poet should "escape from facts" and become the "priest of the invisible." What was most "real" to Stevens was not "a collection of solid, static objects" but the intangible realm "within or beneath the surface of reality." Modernism, in other words, was less interested in promoting social change or pleasing popular taste than it was in expressing the subjective world of complex emotions and abstract concepts.

POUND, ELIOT, AND STEIN   The chief American prophets of modern art and literature were neither in Chicago nor in New York but in England and Europe: Idaho-born Ezra Pound and St. Louis-born T. S. Eliot in London and Californian Gertrude Stein in Paris. Working separately and spreading their influence together, they were all self-conscious revolutionaries deeply concerned with creating strange, new, and often beautifully difficult forms of modernist expression. They found more inspiration and more receptive audiences in Europe than in the United States. In a letter to his father seeking assistance in promoting his first book of poems, Ezra Pound wrote what could have served as a manifesto for his disruptive modernist approach to art: "WHANG—Boom—Boom—cast delicacy to the winds." Pound abhorred respectability and "public stupidity." As the foreign editor of the Chicago-based *Poetry* magazine, he became the cultural impresario of modernism, the conduit through which many American poets achieved publication. In bitter poems and earnest essays denouncing war and commercialism, Pound displayed an incessant, uncompromising urgency in his efforts to transform the literary landscape. An English poet called him a "solitary volcano." T. S. Eliot claimed that Pound was single-handedly responsible for the modernist movement in poetry. Pound recruited, edited, published, and reviewed the best among the new generation of modernist writers, improving their writing, bolstering their courage, and propelling their careers. In his own poetry he expressed the feeling of many that the war had wasted a whole generation of young men who died in defense of a "botched civilization."

Pound conquered literary London in the years before and during World War I. One of the young American writers he took under his wing was T. S. Eliot, who had recently graduated from Harvard. Within a few years, the younger Eliot had greatly surpassed Pound both as a poet and a critic to become the leading American modernist. Eliot declared that traditional poetry "was stagnant to a degree difficult for any young poet to imagine." Eliot's epic 433-line poem *The Waste Land* (1922), which Pound edited, has become a monument of modernism. It expressed a deep sense of postwar disillusionment and melancholy that had a powerful effect on other disillusioned writers during the decade. As a poet and critic writing for the *Criterion*, which he founded in 1922, Eliot became the arbiter of modernist taste in Anglo-American literature.

Gertrude Stein was the self-appointed champion of the American modernists who, like her, chose to live in Paris rather than London or the United States. In 1903, she, along with her brother, Leo, an art collector, moved to Paris, where she lived the rest of her life. Long regarded as no more than the literary eccentric who wrote, "Rose is a rose is a rose is a rose," Stein was in fact one of the chief promoters of the triumphant subjectivity undergirding modernist expression. She sought to capture in words the equivalent of abstract painting. Even more important, she hosted a cultural salon in Paris that became a regular gathering place for American and European modernists.

**Gertrude Stein**

Pablo Picasso's 1906 portrait of the writer.

THE "LOST GENERA-TION" It was Gertrude Stein who in Paris in 1921 told young Ernest Hemingway that he and his friends who had served in the war "are a lost generation." When Hemingway objected, she held her ground. "You are [lost]. You have no respect for anything. You drink yourselves to death." When Hemingway published his first novel, *The Sun Also Rises* (1926), he used the phrase "lost genera-tion" as the book's epigraph, drawing inspiration from both Stein and Pound. The bleak but captivating novel centers on Jake Barnes, a young American jour-nalist castrated by a war injury. His despairing impotence leads him and his unhappy friends to wander the cafes and nightclubs of postwar Europe, acknowledging that they were all wounded and sterile in their own way: they had lost their innocence, their illusions, and their motivation. In Hemingway's next novel, *A Farewell to Arms* (1929), he adopted a similar focus, depicting the desperate search of the "lost generation" for "real" life punctuated by the doomed, war-tainted love affairs of young Americans. These novels feature the frenetic, hard-drinking lifestyle and the cult of robust masculinity that Hemingway himself epitomized. Hundreds of writers tried to imitate Heming-way's distinctively terse, tough but sensitive style of writing, but few had his exceptional gift, which lay less in what he had to say than in the way he said it.

The earliest chronicler of the "lost generation," F. Scott Fitzgerald, blazed up brilliantly and then quickly flickered out like all the tinseled, sad young characters who people his novels. Famous at age twenty-four, having pub-lished the spectacularly successful novel *This Side of Paradise* in 1920, Fitzgerald, along with his wife, Zelda, lived in and wrote about the "greatest, gaudiest spree in history." Fitzgerald's stories during the 1920s were painfully autobiographical. They centered on self-indulgent people during the Jazz Age—glamorous, brassy, and cynical young men and women who oscillate between parties and romances with carefree ease. What gave depth to the best of Fitzgerald's work was what a character in *The Great Gatsby* (1925), Fitzgerald's finest novel, called "a sense of the fundamental decencies" amid all the surface gaiety—and almost always a sense of impending doom in a world that had "lost" its meaning amid the revelations of modern science and the horrors of world war.

Societies do not readily surrender old values and attitudes for new. The great majority of Americans did not identify with the alienation and rebelliousness associated with Fitzgerald, Hemingway, and others claiming to represent the "lost generation." Most Americans—including most writers and artists—did not share their sense of rebellious despair or their disdain for the "booboisie" dominating middle-class life. Instead, most Americans were attracted to more traditional values and conventional forms of expression. They celebrated America's widespread prosperity and traditional pieties. Far more people read the uplifting poetry of Carl Sandburg than the despairing verse of T. S. Eliot. The best-selling novelist of the 1920s was not Ernest Hemingway or F. Scott Fitzgerald; it was Zane Grey, a former Ohio dentist who wrote dozens of popular western novels featuring violence and heroism on the frontier. "We turn to him," said one literary critic, "not for insight into human nature and human problems, nor for refinements of art, but simply for crude epic stories."

The sharp contrast between the fiction of Zane Grey and Ernest Hemingway—and their readers—showed yet again how conflicted and contradictory cultural life had become during the 1920s. For all of the attention given to modernism and cultural radicalism, then and since, the prevailing tone of life between the end of World War I and the onset of the Great Depression was not disillusionment or despair but optimism. During the 1920s, what one writer called the "ballyhoo years," political conservatism, economic growth, mass consumerism, and an often zany frivolity were the prevailing forces shaping the national mood—and anchoring a contradictory "epoch of confusion."

## CHAPTER SUMMARY

- **Nativism**  With the end of the Great War, race riots and the fear of communism ushered in a wave of virulent nativism. With many "old stock" Americans fearing that many immigrants were socialists, Communists, or anarchists, Congress passed laws to restrict immigration. The revived Ku Klux Klan was devoted to "100 percent Americanism" and regarded Catholics, Jews, immigrants, and African Americans as threats to America.

- **Jazz Age**  The carefree fads and attitudes of the 1920s, perhaps best represented by the frantic rhythms of jazz music and the fast-paced, sexy movies from Hollywood, led F. Scott Fitzgerald to dub the decade the Jazz Age. The hemlines of women's dresses rose, and sex was openly discussed. The Harlem Renaissance gave voice to black literature and music, and African Americans in northern cities felt freer to speak out against racial injustice and express pride in their race.

- **Reactionary Mood**  Many white Americans felt that their religion and way of life were under attack by modern trends. They feared that women's newly earned right to vote might destabilize the family and that scientific scholarship would undermine biblical truth. These modern and traditional forces openly clashed at the Scopes trial in Dayton, Tennessee, in 1925, where the right to teach evolution in public schools was tested in court.

- **Modernism**  The carnage of the Great War shattered Americans' belief in the progress of Western civilization. In the movement known as modernism, young artists and intellectuals reflected this disillusionment. For modernists, the world could no longer be easily observed through reason, common sense, and logic; instead, reality was something to be created and expressed through new artistic and literary forms, like abstract painting, atonal music, free verse in poetry, and stream-of-conscious narrative and interior monologues in stories and novels.

## CHRONOLOGY

| 1903 | Wright Brothers fly the first airplane |
| 1903 | Ford Motor Company is founded |
| 1905 | First movie house opens |
| 1910 | National Association for the Advancement of Colored People is founded |
| 1916 | Marcus Garvey brings to New York the Universal Negro Improvement Association |
| 1920 | Prohibition begins |
| 1920 | F. Scott Fitzgerald's *This Side of Paradise* is published |
| 1921 | Albert Einstein receives the Nobel Prize in physics |
| 1921 | Congress passes the Emergency Immigration Act |
| 1922 | T. S. Eliot's *The Waste Land* is published |
|  | First radio commercial is aired |
| 1924 | Congress passes the Immigration Act |
| 1925 | Scopes "monkey trial" tests the teaching of evolution in Tennessee public schools |
| 1927 | Charles Lindbergh Jr. makes first solo transatlantic flight |

## KEY TERMS & NAMES

# 26

# REPUBLICAN
# RESURGENCE
# AND DECLINE

**FOCUS QUESTIONS**                                    Ⓢ   wwnorton.com/studyspace

- To what extent were the policies of the 1920s a rejection of progressivism?
- What was the effect of isolationism and the peace movement on American politics between the two world wars?
- Why were the 1920s an era of conservatism?
- What drove the growth of the American economy in the 1920s?
- What were the causes of the stock market crash and the Great Depression?

**B**y 1920, the progressive political coalition that elected Theodore Roosevelt in 1904 and reelected Woodrow Wilson in 1916 had fragmented. It unraveled for several reasons. For one thing, its leaders were no more. Roosevelt died in 1919 at the age of sixty, just as he was beginning to campaign for the 1920 Republican presidential nomination. Wilson, too, had envisioned an unprecedented third term, but a stroke forced him to finish out his second term broken physically and mentally. Many Americans preferred other candidates anyway. Organized labor resented the Wilson administration's crackdown on striking workers in 1919–1920. Farmers in the Great Plains and the West thought that wartime price controls on commodities had discriminated against them. Liberal intellectuals became disillusioned with grassroots democracy because of popular support for Prohibition, the Ku Klux Klan, and religious fundamentalism. By 1920, the middle class had become preoccupied with restoring a "new era" of prosperity based on mass production

## CHRONOLOGY

| | |
|---|---|
| 1903 | Wright Brothers fly the first airplane |
| 1903 | Ford Motor Company is founded |
| 1905 | First movie house opens |
| 1910 | National Association for the Advancement of Colored People is founded |
| 1916 | Marcus Garvey brings to New York the Universal Negro Improvement Association |
| 1920 | Prohibition begins |
| 1920 | F. Scott Fitzgerald's *This Side of Paradise* is published |
| 1921 | Albert Einstein receives the Nobel Prize in physics |
| 1921 | Congress passes the Emergency Immigration Act |
| 1922 | T. S. Eliot's *The Waste Land* is published |
| | First radio commercial is aired |
| 1924 | Congress passes the Immigration Act |
| 1925 | Scopes "monkey trial" tests the teaching of evolution in Tennessee public schools |
| 1927 | Charles Lindbergh Jr. makes first solo transatlantic flight |

## KEY TERMS & NAMES

# 26

## REPUBLICAN
## RESURGENCE
## AND DECLINE

FOCUS QUESTIONS          Ⓢ  wwnorton.com/studyspace

• To what extent were the policies of the 1920s a rejection of progressivism?

• What was the effect of isolationism and the peace movement on
  American politics between the two world wars?

• Why were the 1920s an era of conservatism?

• What drove the growth of the American economy in the 1920s?

• What were the causes of the stock market crash and the Great
  Depression?

By 1920, the progressive political coalition that elected
Theodore Roosevelt in 1904 and reelected Woodrow
Wilson in 1916 had fragmented. It unraveled for several
reasons. For one thing, its leaders were no more. Roosevelt died in 1919 at
the age of sixty, just as he was beginning to campaign for the 1920 Republican presidential nomination. Wilson, too, had envisioned an unprecedented
third term, but a stroke forced him to finish out his second term broken
physically and mentally. Many Americans preferred other candidates anyway. Organized labor resented the Wilson administration's crackdown on
striking workers in 1919–1920. Farmers in the Great Plains and the West
thought that wartime price controls on commodities had discriminated
against them. Liberal intellectuals became disillusioned with grassroots
democracy because of popular support for Prohibition, the Ku Klux Klan,
and religious fundamentalism. By 1920, the middle class had become preoccupied with restoring a "new era" of prosperity based on mass production

and mass consumption. Finally, the public turned away from Progressivism in part because it had accomplished its major goals: the Eighteenth Amendment (1919), which outlawed alcoholic beverages, and the Nineteenth Amendment (1920), which allowed women nationwide to vote.

Progressivism did not disappear in the 1920s, however. Progressive Republicans and Democrats dominated key leadership positions in Congress during much of the decade even while conservative Republicans occupied the White House. The progressive impulse for honest, efficient government and regulation of business remained strong, especially at the state and local levels, where efforts to improve public education, public health, and social-welfare programs gained momentum during the decade. At the national level, however, conservative Republicans returned to power.

## "Normalcy"

THE ELECTION OF 1920   After World War I, most Americans had grown weary of Woodrow Wilson's crusading idealism. Wilson himself recognized the shifting public mood. "It is only once in a generation," he remarked, "that a people can be lifted above material things. That is why conservative government is in the saddle two thirds of the time."

In 1920, Republican party leaders eager to regain control of the White House turned to a stunning mediocrity: the affable, dapper, silver-haired Ohio senator **Warren G. Harding**. He set the conservative tone of his presidential campaign when he told a Boston audience that it was time to end Wilsonian progressivism: "America's present need is not heroics, but healing; not nostrums, but normalcy; not revolution, but restoration; not agitation, but adjustment; not surgery, but serenity; not the dramatic, but the dispassionate." In contrast to Wilson's grandiose internationalism, Harding promised to "safeguard America first . . . to exalt America first, to live for and revere America first."

Harding's vanilla promise of a "**return to normalcy**" reflected both his own conservative values and voters' desire for stability and order. The son of an Ohio farmer, he was neither a prophet nor a crusader. He described himself as "just a plain fellow" who was "old-fashioned and even reactionary in matters of faith and morals." But far from being an old-fashioned moralist in his personal life, Harding drank bootleg liquor in the midst of Prohibition, smoked and chewed tobacco, relished weekly poker games, and had numerous affairs and several children with women other than his austere wife, whom he called "the Duchess." The general public, however, remained unaware of Harding's escapades. Instead, voters saw him as a handsome, charming, lovable politician. Harding acknowledged his limitations in vision, leadership, and intellectual power, once admitting that "I cannot hope to be one of the great presidents, but perhaps I may be remembered as one of the best loved."

The Democrats in 1920 hoped that Harding would not be president at all. James Cox, a former newspaper publisher and former governor of Ohio, won the presidential nomination of an increasingly fragmented Democratic party on the forty-fourth ballot. For vice president the convention named New Yorker Franklin Delano Roosevelt, who as assistant secretary of the navy occupied the same position his Republican cousin Theodore Roosevelt had once held.

The Democrats suffered from the breakup of the Wilsonian coalition and the conservative postwar mood. In the words of the progressive journalist William Allen White, Americans in 1920 were "tired of issues, sick at heart of ideals, and weary of being noble." The country voted overwhelmingly for Harding's promised "return to normalcy." Harding polled 16 million votes to 9 million for Cox, who won no state outside the still solidly Democratic South. The Republican domination in both houses of Congress increased. As a disconsolate Wilson supporter said, "an age had ended."

EARLY APPOINTMENTS AND POLICY Harding in office had much in common with Ulysses S. Grant. His cabinet, like Grant's, mixed some of the "best minds" in the party, whom he had promised to seek out, with a few of the worst. Charles Evans Hughes, like Grant's Hamilton Fish, became a distinguished secretary of state. Herbert Hoover in the Commerce Department, **Andrew W. Mellon** in the Treasury Department, and Henry C. Wallace in the Agriculture Department functioned efficiently and made policy on their own. Other cabinet members and administrative appointees, however, were not so conscientious. The secretary of the interior landed in prison, and the attorney general narrowly escaped serving time. Many lesser offices went to members of the "Ohio gang," a group of Harding's drinking buddies who met in a house on K Street near the White House to help the president relieve the pressures of his high office.

Until he became president, Harding had loved politics. He was the party hack par excellence, "bloviating" (a favorite verb of his, which means "speaking with gaseous eloquence") at public events, jollying it up in the clubhouse and cloakroom, hobnobbing with the great and near great in Washington, D.C. As president, however, Harding was simply in over his head, and self-doubt overwhelmed him. "I don't think I'm big enough for the Presidency,"

**The Ohio gang**

President Warren Harding surrounded himself with a network of friends, often appointing them to public office despite inferior credentials.

he confided to a friend. Harding much preferred to relax with the Ohio gang, who shared his taste for whiskey, poker, and women.

Still, Harding and his friends had a political agenda. They set about dismantling or neutralizing many of the social and economic components of progressivism. The president's four Supreme Court appointments were all conservatives, including Chief Justice William Howard Taft, the former president, who announced that he had been "appointed to reverse a few decisions." During the 1920s, the Taft court struck down a federal child-labor law and a minimum-wage law for women, issued numerous injunctions against striking labor unions, and passed rulings limiting the powers of federal regulatory agencies.

The Harding administration inherited a slumping economy burdened by high wartime taxes and a national debt that had ballooned from $1 billion in 1914 to $24 billion in 1920. To address such challenges, the new president established a pro-business tone reminiscent of the McKinley White House in the 1890s. Harding vetoed a bill to provide war veterans with a cash bonus, arguing that it would increase the federal budget deficit.

To deal with the postwar recession and generate economic growth, Secretary of the Treasury Mellon reduced government spending and lowered taxes. He persuaded Congress to pass the landmark Budget and Accounting Act of 1921, which created a new Bureau of the Budget to streamline the process of preparing an annual federal budget to be presented for approval by the Congress. The bill also created a General Accounting Office to audit spending by federal agencies. This act realized a long-held desire of progressives to bring greater efficiency and nonpartisanship to the budget preparation process. Mellon also initiated a series of general tax reductions, insisting that the reductions should go mainly to the rich, on the "trickle down" principle that wealth in the hands of the few would spur economic growth through increased capital investment.

In Congress, a group of western Republicans and southern Democrats fought a dogged battle to preserve the "progressive" approach to income taxes (a graduated scale of higher rates on higher income levels) built into wartime taxes, but Mellon, in office through the 1920s, eventually won out. At his behest, Congress in 1921 repealed the wartime excess-profits tax and lowered the maximum rate on personal income from 65 to 50 percent. Subsequent revenue acts lowered the maximum tax rate to 40 percent in 1924 and to 20 percent in 1926. The Revenue Act of 1926 extended further benefits to high-income groups by lowering estate taxes and repealing the gift tax. Unfortunately, much of the tax money released to the wealthy helped fuel the speculative excess of the late 1920s as much as it fostered gainful enterprise. Mellon, however, did balance the federal budget for a time. Government expenditures fell, as did the national debt. Mellon's admirers tagged him the greatest secretary of the Treasury since Alexander Hamilton in the late eighteenth century.

In addition to tax cuts, Mellon—the third-richest man in the United States, after John D. Rockefeller and Henry Ford—favored the time-honored Republican policy of high tariffs on imported goods. The Fordney-McCumber Tariff of 1922 increased rates on imports of chemical and metal products to help prevent the revival of German corporations that had dominated those industries before the First World War. To please commercial farmers, who historically benefited little from tariffs, the new act further extended the duties on agricultural imports.

Rounding out the Republican economic program of the 1920s was a more lenient attitude toward government regulation of corporations. Neither Harding nor his successor, Calvin Coolidge, could dissolve the regulatory agencies created during the Progressive Era, but they named commissioners who promoted regulation "friendly" to business interests. Harding appointed conservatives to the Interstate Commerce Commission, the Federal Reserve Board, and the Federal Trade Commission. Progressive Republican senator

George W. Norris characterized the new appointments as "the nullification of federal law by a process of boring from within." Senator Henry Cabot Lodge agreed, boasting that "we have torn up Wilsonism by the roots."

In one area, however, Warren G. Harding proved to be more progressive than Woodrow Wilson. He reversed the Wilson administration's segregationist policy of excluding African Americans from federal government jobs. He also spoke out against the vigilante racism that had flared up across the country during and after the war. In his first speech to a joint session of Congress in 1921, Harding insisted that the nation must deal with the festering "race question." The horrific racial incidents during and after World War I were a stain on America's democratic ideals. The new president, unlike his Democratic predecessor, attacked the Ku Klux Klan for fomenting "hatred and prejudice and violence," and he urged Congress "to wipe the stain of barbaric lynching from the banners of a free and orderly, representative democracy." The Senate, however, failed to pass the bill Harding promoted.

## ISOLATIONISM IN FOREIGN AFFAIRS

In 1920, the Americans who elected Warren G. Harding were weary of war and Woodrow Wilson's crusading internationalism. They wanted their new president to revive the tradition of isolationism, whereby the United States had sought to remain aloof from the squabbles among European nations. To that end, Harding said good riddance to Wilson's desire for America to play a leading role in the new League of Nations. As he said in his 1920 victory speech, "You just didn't want a surrender of the United States. That's why you didn't care for the League [of Nations], which is now deceased." The postwar spirit of isolation found other expressions as well: the higher tariff rates on foreign imports, the Red Scare, and the restrictive immigration laws with which the nation all but shut the door to newcomers.

Yet the desire to stay out of foreign wars did not mean that the United States could ignore its own expanding global interests. American businesses now had worldwide connections. The United States was the world's chief banker. American investments and loans abroad put in circulation the dollars that enabled foreigners to purchase U.S. exports. Moreover, America's overseas possessions, especially the Philippines, directly involved the country in world affairs.

WAR DEBTS AND REPARATIONS    Probably nothing did more to heighten American isolationism from foreign affairs—or anti-American feeling in Europe—than the complex issue of paying off huge war debts during the 1920s. In 1917, when France and Great Britain ran out of money to pay for military supplies during the First World War, the U.S. government had advanced them massive loans, first for the war effort and then for post-war reconstruction projects. Most Americans, including Andrew W. Mellon, expected the war-related debts to be paid back, but Europeans had a different perception. The European Allies had held off the German army at great cost while the United States was raising an army in 1917. The British also noted that after the American Revolution, the newly independent United States had repudiated old debts to British investors; the French likewise pointed out that they had never been repaid for helping the Americans win the Revolution and gain their independence.

But the most difficult challenges in the 1920s were the practical problems of repayment. To get U.S. dollars to use to pay their war-related debts, European nations had to sell their goods to the United States. However, soaring American tariff rates during the 1920s made imported European goods more expensive and the war-related debts incurred by Britain and France harder to pay. The French and the British insisted that they could repay their debts to the United States only as they unrealistically sought to collect $33 billion in reparations from defeated Germany, whose economy was in a shambles during the 1920s, ravaged by runaway inflation. Twice during the 1920s the financial strain on Germany brought the structure of international payments to the verge of collapse, and both times the international Reparations Commission called in private American bankers to work out rescue plans. Loans provided by U.S. banks thus propped up the German economy so that Germany could pay its reparations to Britain and France, thereby enabling them to pay their debts to the United States.

ATTEMPTS AT DISARMAMENT    After the First World War, many Americans decided that excessive armaments were responsible for causing the terrible conflict. The best way to keep the peace, they argued, was to limit the size of armies and navies. The United States had no intention of maintaining a large army after 1920, but under the shipbuilding program begun in 1916, it had constructed a powerful navy second only to that of Great Britain. Neither the British nor the Americans wanted a naval armaments race, but both were worried about the alarming growth of Japanese power.

To address the problem, President Harding in 1921 invited diplomats from eight nations to a naval-armaments conference in Washington, D.C. U.S. secretary of state Charles Evans Hughes welcomed the delegates by making a blockbuster proposal. The only way out of an expensive armaments race, he declared, "is to end it now" by eliminating scores of existing warships and pro-

**The Washington Conference, 1921**

The Big Five at the conference were (from left) Iyesato Tokugawa (Japan), Arthur Balfour (Great Britain), Charles Evans Hughes (United States), Aristide Briand (France), and Carlo Schanzer (Italy).

hibiting the construction of new battleships. It was one of the most dramatic moments in diplomatic history. In less than fifteen minutes, one journalist reported, Hughes had destroyed more warships "than all the admirals of the world have sunk in a cycle of centuries." His audacious proposal to end the naval arms race was greeted by a "tornado of cheering" among the delegates.

Following Hughes's lead, delegates from the United States, Britain, Japan, France, and Italy signed the Five-Power Treaty (1922), which limited the size of their navies. It was the first disarmament treaty in history. The five major powers also agreed to refrain from further fortification of their Pacific possessions. In particular, the United States and Great Britain promised not to build any new naval bases north of Singapore or west of Hawaii. The agreement in effect partitioned the world: U.S. naval power became supreme in the Western Hemisphere, Japanese power in the western Pacific, and British power dominated from the North Sea to Singapore.

With these agreements in hand, President Harding could boast of what seemed to be a brilliant diplomatic coup that relieved citizens of the need to pay for an enlarged navy and warded off potential conflicts in the Pacific. Yet the agreements were without obligation and without teeth. The naval-disarmament treaty set limits only on "capital" ships (battleships and aircraft carriers); the race to build cruisers, destroyers, submarines, and other smaller craft continued. Expansionist Japan withdrew from the agreement in 1934, and the Soviet Union and Germany had been excluded from the conference. Thus, twelve years after the Washington Conference, the dream of naval disarmament died.

THE KELLOGG-BRIAND PACT    During and after the First World War, many Americans embraced the fanciful ideal of simply abolishing war with a stroke of a pen. In 1921, a wealthy Chicagoan founded the American Committee for the Outlawry of War. "We can outlaw this war system just as we outlawed slavery and the saloon," said one of the more enthusiastic converts.

The seductive notion of simply abolishing war culminated in the signing of the Kellogg-Briand Pact. This unique treaty started with an initiative by the French foreign minister Aristide Briand, who in 1927 proposed to Secretary of State Frank B. Kellogg that the two countries agree never go to war against each other. This innocent-seeming proposal was actually a clever ploy to draw the United States into the French security system by the back door. In any future war, for instance, such a pact would inhibit the United States from seeking reprisals in response to any French intrusions on neutral rights. Kellogg was outraged to discover that Briand had urged leaders of the American peace movement to put pressure on the government to sign the accord.

Kellogg then turned the tables on Briand. He countered with a plan to have all nations sign the pact. Caught in a trap of his own making, the French foreign minister finally agreed. The Pact of Paris (its official name), signed on August 27, 1928, declared that the signatories "renounce it [war] as an instrument of national policy." Eventually sixty-two nations signed the pact, but all reserved the right of "self-defense" as an escape hatch. The U.S. Senate ratified the agreement by a vote of 85 to 1. One senator who voted for "this worthless, but perfectly harmless peace treaty" wrote a friend later that he feared it would "confuse the minds of many good people who think that peace may be secured by polite professions of neighborly and brotherly love."

THE WORLD COURT    The isolationist mood in the United States was no better illustrated than in the repeated refusal by the Senate during the 1920s to approve American membership in the World Court, formally called the Permanent Court of International Justice, at The Hague in the Netherlands. Created in 1921 by the League of Nations, the World Court, composed of fifteen international judges, was intended to arbitrate disputes between nations. Presidents Harding, Coolidge, and Hoover all asked the Senate during the 1920s to approve American membership in the World Court, but the legislative body refused, for the same reasons that the Senate had refused to sign the Versailles Treaty: they did not want the United States to be bound in any way by an international organization.

IMPROVING RELATIONS IN LATIN AMERICA   The isolationist attitude during the 1920s led the decade's Republican presidents—Harding, Calvin Coolidge, and Herbert Hoover—to soothe tensions with America's neighbors to the south, most of which harbored long-festering resentments against "Yankee imperialism." The Harding administration agreed in 1921 to pay the republic of Colombia the $25 million it had demanded for America's rights to the Panama Canal. In 1924, American troops left the Dominican Republic after eight years of intervention. U.S. Marines left Nicaragua in 1925 but returned a year later at the outbreak of disorder and civil war. There, in 1927, the Coolidge administration brought both parties into an agreement for U.S.-supervised elections, but one rebel leader, César Augusto Sandino, held out, and the marines stayed until 1933.

The troubles in Nicaragua increased strains between the United States and Mexico. Relations had already been soured by repeated Mexican threats to expropriate American oil properties in Mexico. In 1928, however, the U.S. ambassador negotiated an agreement protecting rights for American businesses acquired before 1917. Expropriation did in fact occur in 1938, but the Mexican government agreed to reimburse American owners.

## The Harding Scandals

ADMINISTRATIVE CORRUPTION   Republican conservatives such as Henry Cabot Lodge, Andrew W. Mellon, Calvin Coolidge, and Herbert Hoover operated out of a philosophical conviction that was intended to benefit the nation. Members of President Harding's "**Ohio Gang**," however, used White House connections to line their own pockets. Early in 1923, for example, Harding learned that the head of the Veterans Bureau was systematically looting medical and hospital supplies. A few weeks later, the legal adviser to the Veterans Bureau committed suicide. More questionable incidents occurred in quick succession. Not long afterward a close friend of Attorney General Harry M. Daugherty, who had set up an office in the Justice Department from which he peddled influence for a fee, shot himself. Finally, the attorney general himself was implicated in the fraudulent handling of German assets seized after the war. When discovered, he refused to testify on the grounds that he might incriminate himself. These were but the most visible among the many scandals that touched the Justice Department, the Prohibition Bureau, and other federal agencies under Harding.

One major scandal rose above all the others, however. **Teapot Dome**, like the Watergate break-in fifty years later, became the catchphrase for the climate of corruption surrounding the Harding administration. The Teapot Dome was a government-owned oil field in Wyoming. It had been set aside as an oil reserve for ensuring fuel for warships. Harding decided to move administrative control of Teapot Dome from the Department of Navy to the Department of Interior. Thereafter, his secretary of interior, Albert B. Fall, a former Republican senator from New Mexico, began signing sweetheart contracts with close friends who were executives of petroleum companies that wanted access to the oil field. It turned out that he had taken bribes of about $400,000 (which came in "a little black bag") from an oil tycoon. Fall was convicted of conspiracy and bribery and sentenced to a year in prison, the first former cabinet official ever to serve time as a result of misconduct in office.

### "Juggernaut" of corruption

This 1924 cartoon alludes to the dimensions of the Teapot Dome scandal.

How much Harding himself knew of the scandals swirling about him is unclear, but he knew enough to be troubled. "My God, this is a hell of a job!" he confided to a journalist. "I have no trouble with my enemies; I can take care of my enemies all right. But my damn friends, my God-damn friends. . . . They're the ones that keep me walking the floor nights!" In 1923, Harding left on what would be his last journey, a speaking tour to the West Coast and a trip to the Alaska Territory. In Seattle, he suffered an attack of food poisoning, recovered briefly, then died in a San Francisco hotel.

The nation was heartbroken. Not since the death of Abraham Lincoln had there been such an outpouring of grief for a "beloved president," for the kindly, ordinary man who found it in his heart (as Woodrow Wilson had not) to pardon Eugene V. Debs, the Socialist who had been jailed for opposing U.S. entry into World War I. As the funeral train carrying Harding's body crossed the continent to Washington, D.C., then back to Ohio, millions stood by the tracks to honor their lost leader. Eventually, however, grief yielded to scorn and contempt. For nearly a decade, the revelations of scandals within the Harding administration were paraded before investigating committees and then the courts. In 1927 an Ohio woman named Nan Britton published a sensational book that claimed that she had had numerous trysts with Harding in the White House and that he was the father of her daughter. Harding's love letters to another man's wife also surfaced.

As a result of Harding's amorous detours and corrupt associates, his foreshortened administration came to be viewed as one of the worst in history. More recent assessments suggest, however, that the scandals obscured accomplishments. Some historians credit Harding with leading the nation out of the turmoil of the postwar years and creating the foundation for the decade's remarkable economic boom. These revisionists also stress that Harding was a hardworking president who played a far more forceful role than previously assumed in shaping his administration's economic and foreign policies and in shepherding legislation through Congress. Harding also promoted diversity and civil rights. He appointed Jews to key federal positions, and he became the first president to criticize racial segregation in a speech before a white audience in the South. No previous president had promoted women's rights as forcefully as he did. But even Harding's foremost scholarly defender admits that he lacked good judgment and "probably should never have been president."

"SILENT CAL" The news of Harding's death found Vice President Calvin Coolidge visiting his father in the isolated mountain village of Plymouth, Vermont, his birthplace. There, at 2:47 A.M. on August 3, 1923, by the

**Conservatives in the White House**

Warren G. Harding (left) and Calvin Coolidge (right).

light of a kerosene lamp, Colonel John Coolidge administered the presidential oath of office to his son. The rustic simplicity of Plymouth, the very name itself, evoked just the image of traditional roots and solid integrity that the country would long for amid the coming disclosures of corruption and carousing in the Harding administration.

Coolidge brought to the White House a clear conviction that the presidency should revert to its Gilded Age stance of passive deference to Congress. "Four fifths of our troubles," Coolidge predicted, "would disappear if we would sit down and keep still." He abided by this rule, insisting on twelve hours of sleep and an afternoon nap. The satirist H. L. Mencken asserted that Coolidge "slept more than any other president, whether by day or by night."

PRO-BUSINESS CONSERVATISM    Americans embraced the unflappability and unstained integrity of **Silent Cal**. He was simple and direct, a self-righteous man of strong principles, intense patriotism, pinched frugality, and few words. After being reelected president of the Massachusetts State Senate, his four-sentence inaugural address was the shortest ever: "Conserve the foundations of our institutions. Do your work with the spirit of a soldier in the public service. Be loyal to the Commonwealth, and to yourselves. And be brief—above all things, be brief." President Coolidge, said a critic, "can be silent in five languages." Although a man of few words, he was not as bland or as dry as critics claimed. He promoted his regressive conservatism with a ruthless consistency. Even more than Harding, Coolidge identified the nation's welfare with the success of big business. "The chief business of the American people is business," he preached. "The man who builds a factory builds a temple. The man who works there worships there." Where Harding had sought to balance the interests of labor, agriculture, and industry, Coolidge focused on promoting industrial development. He strove to end federal regulation of business and industry and reduce taxes as well as the national debt. The nation had too many laws, Coolidge insisted, and "we would be better off if we did not have any more." His fiscal frugality and pro-business stance led the *Wall Street Journal* to exult: "Never before, here or anywhere else, has a government been so completely fused with business."

THE ELECTION OF 1924  In filling out Harding's unexpired term, Calvin Coolidge distanced himself from the scandals of the administration by putting in charge of the prosecutions two lawyers of undoubted integrity. A man of honesty and ability, a good administrator who delegated well and managed Republican factions adroitly, Coolidge quietly took control of the party machinery and seized the initiative in the 1924 campaign for the presidential nomination, which he won with only token opposition.

Meanwhile, the Democrats again fell victim to dissension, prompting the humorist Will Rogers's classic statement that "I am a member of no organized political party. I am a Democrat." The Democratic party's fractiousness illustrated the deep divisions between urban and rural America during the 1920s. It took the Democrats 103 ballots to decide on a presidential candidate: John W. Davis, a corporate lawyer from West Virginia who could nearly outdo Coolidge in his conservatism.

While the Democrats bickered, rural populists and urban progressives again decided to desert both national parties. Meeting in Cleveland, Ohio, on July 4, 1924, activists reorganized the old 1912 Progressive party and nominated Robert M. "Fighting Bob" La Follette for president. The sixty-nine-year-old Wisconsin progressive senator had voted against the 1917 war resolution against Germany. Now, he won the support of the Socialist party and the American Federation of Labor.

In the 1924 campaign, the voters preferred to "keep cool with Coolidge," who swept both the popular and the electoral votes by decisive majorities. Davis took only the solidly Democratic South, and La Follette carried only his native Wisconsin. The popular vote went 15.7 million for Coolidge, 8.4 million for Davis, and 4.8 million for La Follette—the largest popular vote ever polled by a third-party candidate.

## THE NEW ERA

Coolidge's landslide victory represented the pinnacle of postwar conservatism. The Democratic party was in disarray, and the Republicans were triumphant. Business executives interpreted the Republican victory in 1924 as a vindication of their leadership, and Coolidge saw the economy's surging prosperity as a confirmation of his support of big business. In fact, the prosperity and technological achievements of the time known as the New Era had much to do with Coolidge's victory over the Democrats and Progressives.

STABILIZING THE ECONOMY   During the 1920s, the drive for efficiency, which had been a prominent feature of the progressive impulse, powered the tandem wheels of mass production and consumption and became a cardinal belief of Republican leaders. **Herbert Hoover**, who served as secretary of commerce in the Harding and Coolidge cabinets, was himself a remarkable success story. Born into an Iowa farm family in 1874, he had lost both of his parents by age ten. As an orphan he was raised by Quaker family members in Iowa and Oregon. The shy but industrious "loner" majored in geology at Stanford University and became a world-renowned mining engineer and multimillionaire before the age of forty.

President Woodrow Wilson called upon Hoover to head up the Food Administration during World War I, and he served with Wilson among the U.S. delegation at the Versailles peace conference. Hoover idolized Wilson and supported American membership in the League of Nations. A young Franklin Delano Roosevelt, then serving as assistant secretary of the navy, was dazzled by Hoover, the man he would later defeat in the presidential election of 1932. He was "certainly a wonder, and I wish we could make him President of the United States." But Hoover later declared himself a Republican who promoted a progressive conservativism. In a book titled *American Individualism* (1922), he prescribed an "ideal of *service*" that went beyond "rugged individualism" to promote the greater good. He wanted government officials to encourage business leaders to forego "cutthroat competition" by engaging in "voluntary cooperation" through the formation of trade associations that would share information and promote standardization and efficiency.

As secretary of commerce during the 1920s, Hoover transformed the trifling Commerce Department into the government's most dynamic agency. He sought out new markets for business, promoted more efficient design, production, and distribution, created a Bureau of Aviation, and the next year established the Federal Radio Commission.

Hoover's priority was the burgeoning trade-association movement. Through trade associations, business leaders competing in a given industry shared information on every aspect of the industry: sales, purchases, shipments, production, and prices. That information allowed them to operate more efficiently by more accurately predicting costs, setting prices, and assessing markets while maintaining a more stable workforce and paying steadier wages. Sometimes abuses crept in as associations engaged in price-fixing and other monopolistic practices, but the Supreme Court in 1925 held the practice of sharing information as such to be within the law.

THE BUSINESS OF FARMING    During the 1920s, agriculture remained the weakest sector in the economy. Briefly after the war, farmers' hopes soared on wings of prosperity. The wartime boom fed by sales abroad lasted into 1920, and then commodity prices collapsed as European agricultural production returned to prewar levels. Overproduction brought lower prices for crops. Wheat prices went in eighteen months from $2.50 a bushel to less than $1; cotton from 35¢ per pound to 13¢. Low crop prices persisted into 1923, especially in the wheat and corn belts, and after that improvement was spotty. A bumper cotton crop in 1926 resulted only in a price collapse and an early taste of depression in much of the South, where foreclosures and bankruptcies spread.

Yet the most successful farms, like the most successful corporations, were getting larger, more efficient, and more mechanized. By 1930, about 13 percent of all farmers had tractors, and the proportion was even higher on the western plains. Better plows, harvesters, combines, and other machines were part of the mechanization process that accompanied improved crop yields, fertilizers, and methods of animal breeding.

Most farmers in the 1920s were simply struggling to survive. And like their predecessors, they sought political help for their plight. In 1924, Senator Charles L. McNary of Oregon and Representative Gilbert N. Haugen of Iowa introduced the first **McNary-Haugen bill**, which sought to secure "equality for agriculture in the benefits of the protective tariff." The proposed bill called for surplus American crops to be sold on the world market in order to raise prices in the home market. The goal was to achieve "parity"—that is, to raise domestic farm prices to a point where they would have the same purchasing power relative to other prices that they had enjoyed between 1909 and 1914, a time viewed in retrospect as a golden age of American agriculture.

The McNary-Haugen bill passed both houses of Congress in 1927, only to be vetoed by President Coolidge, who dismissed the bill as unsound. The

**Farming technology**

Mechanization became increasingly important in early twentieth-century agriculture. Here, a silo leader, or grain pump, stands at the center of this Wisconsin farm.

process was repeated in 1928, when Coolidge criticized the measure's price-fixing as un-American and unconstitutional to boot. In a broader sense, however, McNary-Haugenism did not fail. The debates over the bill made the "farm problem" a national policy issue and defined it as a problem of finding foreign markets for crop surpluses. Moreover, the evolution of the McNary-Haugen plan revived the idea of a political alliance between the rural South and the West, a coalition that in the next decade became a dominant influence on national farm policy.

SETBACKS FOR UNIONS   Urban workers more than farmers shared in the affluence of the 1920s. "A workman is far better paid in America than anywhere else in the world," a French visitor wrote in 1927, "and his standard of living is enormously higher." Nonfarm workers gained about 20 percent in real wages between 1921 and 1928 while farm income rose only 10 percent.

Organized labor, however, did no better than organized agriculture in the 1920s. Although President Harding had endorsed collective bargaining and tried to reduce the twelve-hour workday and the six-day workweek so that the working class "may have time for leisure and family life," he ran into stiff opposition in Congress. Overall, unions suffered a setback after the growth years during the war. The Red Scare and strikes of 1919 created concerns that unions practiced subversion, an idea that the enemies of unions promoted. The brief postwar depression of 1921 further weakened the unions, and they felt the severe impact of open-shop associations designed to prevent unions that proliferated across the country after the war, led by chambers of commerce and other business groups. In 1921, business groups in Chicago designated the open shop the "American plan" of employment. Although the open shop in theory implied only an employer's right to hire anyone, in practice it meant discrimination against unionists and a refusal to recognize unions even in shops where most of the workers belonged to one.

To suppress unions, employers often required "yellow-dog" contracts, which forced workers to agree to stay out of a union. Owners also used labor spies, blacklists, intimidation, and coercion. Some employers tried to kill the unions with kindness. They introduced programs of "industrial democracy" guided by company unions or various schemes of "welfare capitalism," such

### The Gastonia strike

These female textile workers pit their strength against that of a National Guardsman during a strike at the Loray Mill in Gastonia, North Carolina, in 1929.

as profit sharing, bonuses, pensions, health programs, recreational activities, and the like. The benefits of such programs were often considerable.

Prosperity, propaganda, and active hostility combined to cause union membership to drop from about 5 million in 1920 to 3.5 million in 1929. Samuel Gompers, founder and longtime president of the American Federation of Labor (AFL), died in 1924; William Green of the United Mine Workers (UMW), who took his place, embodied the conservative, even timid, attitude of unions during the period. The outstanding exception to the anti-union policies of the decade was the passage of the Railway Labor Act in 1926, which abolished the federal Railway Labor Board and substituted a new Board of Mediation. The act also provided for the formation of railroad unions "without interference, influence, or coercion," a statement of policy not extended to other workers until the 1930s.

## PRESIDENT HOOVER, THE ENGINEER

HOOVER VERSUS SMITH    On August 2, 1927, while on vacation in the Black Hills of South Dakota, President Coolidge suddenly announced that he would not "run for President in 1928." His retirement message surprised the nation and cleared the way for Herbert Hoover to win the Republican nomination in 1928. The Republican platform took credit for the nation's rampant prosperity, cost cutting, debt and tax reduction, and the protective tariff ("as vital to American agriculture as it is to manufacturing"). It rejected the McNary-Haugen farm program but promised to create a federal farm board to manage crop surpluses more efficiently.

The Democratic nomination went to four-term New York Governor **Alfred E. Smith**. The party's farm plank pledged "economic equality of agriculture with other industries." Like the Republicans, the Democrats promised to enforce the Volstead Act (1919), which had defined as "intoxicating" any drink having has much as 0.5 percent alcohol, even though Al Smith was himself a vocal opponent of Prohibition.

The two candidates' sharply different images obscured the essential similarities of their programs. Hoover was a child of a rural Quaker family, the successful engineer and businessman, the architect of Republican prosperity, while Smith was the prototype of those things that rural and small-town America distrusted: the son of Irish immigrants, Roman Catholic, and anti-Prohibition (in direct opposition to his party's platform). Outside the large cities those attributes were handicaps that Smith could scarcely surmount, for all his affability and wit. Militant Protestants launched a furious assault

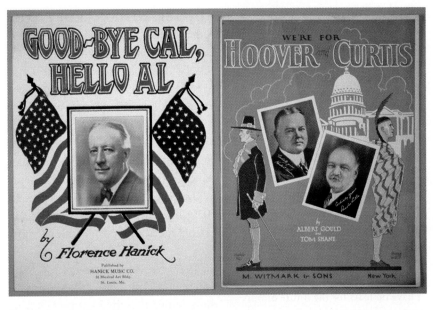

**Campaign sheet music**

The sheet music for the Democratic nominee, Alfred E. Smith (left) and the Republican nominee, Herbert Hoover (right) drew on popular tunes and motifs of the time.

on him, especially in the Democratic-controlled South. The Ku Klux Klan, for example, mailed thousands of postcards proclaiming that the Catholic New Yorker was the Antichrist.

In the election of 1928, more people voted than ever before. Hoover won in the third consecutive Republican landslide, with 21 million popular votes to Smith's 15 million and an even more top-heavy electoral-vote majority of 444 to 87. Hoover even cracked the Democrats' Solid South, leaving Smith only six Deep South states plus Massachusetts and Rhode Island. The election was above all a vindication of Republican prosperity, although Calvin Coolidge was skeptical that his successor could sustain the good times. He derisively called Hoover the Wonder Boy, and had quipped in 1928 that the new president had "offered me unsolicited advice for six years, all of it bad."

The shattering defeat of the Democrats concealed a major political realignment in the making. Al Smith had nearly doubled the vote for John W. Davis, the Democratic candidate of four years before. Smith's urban image, though a handicap in the hinterlands, swung big cities back into the Democratic column. In the farm states of the West, there were signs that some disgruntled farmers had switched over to the Democrats. A coalition of urban workers and unhappy farmers was in the making, that would later rally behind Franklin D. Roosevelt.

**Herbert Hoover**

"I have no fears for the future of our country," Hoover told the nation at his inauguration in 1929.

HOOVER IN CONTROL At the end of 1928, President-elect Herbert Hoover sought to demonstrate his activist bent by touring ten Latin American nations. Once in office a few weeks later, he reversed Woodrow Wilson's policy of refusing to recognize "bad" regimes in the Western Hemisphere and reverted to the older policy of recognizing governments in power regardless of their actions. In 1930, he generated more goodwill in Latin America by permitting publication of a memorandum drawn up in 1928 by Undersecretary of State J. Reuben Clark. The Clark Memorandum denied that the Monroe Doctrine justified U.S. military intervention in Latin America. Although Hoover never endorsed the memorandum, he never intervened in the region. Before he left office, steps had been taken to withdraw American forces from Nicaragua and Haiti.

The milestone year 1929 dawned with high hopes. The economy seemed sound, per capita income was rising, and the chief architect of Republican prosperity was about to enter the White House. "I have no fears for the future of our country," Hoover told the audience at his inauguration. "It is bright with hope." No nation, he declared, was more secure in its accomplishments. Although four years later, Hoover would be savaged for such rosy pronouncements, at the time his upbeat pronouncements seemed justified. In 1929, more Americans were working than ever before, and they were earning record levels of income.

Hoover's programs to stabilize business growth carried over into his plans for agriculture, the weakest sector of the economy. To treat the malady of glutted commodities markets, he called Congress into special session and convinced the legislators to approve the Agricultural Marketing Act of 1929. It created a Federal Farm Board to help support voluntary farm "cooperatives"—an old idea first promoted by the Populists whereby farmers joined together to reduce their expenses and also moderate the sometimes dramatic fluctuations in commodity prices. Alas, before the new programs had a chance to prove themselves, the farm sector was devastated by the onset of the **Great Depression.**

Farmers gained even less from another prolonged Congressional debate over raising tariffs on imports. What Hoover won after fourteen months of struggle with lobbyists in Congress was in fact a disastrous hike in tariff duties on imported manufactured items as well as farm goods. The Tariff of 1930, authored by two leading Republican "protectionists," Willis C. Hawley and Reed Owen Smoot, was intended to help the farm sector by reducing imports of farm products into the United States. But lobbyists in Washington, D.C., convinced Congress to raise duties on hundreds of imported items to an all-time high. The result was a global disaster. Some 1,028 economists petitioned Hoover to veto the short-sighted bill because its logic was flawed: by trying to "protect" American farmers from foreign competition, the bill would actually raise prices on most raw materials and consumer products. The new Hawley-Smoot Tariff created an economic fiasco. It prompted other countries to retaliate, often by shipping their goods away from the United States and by putting tariffs on American goods coming into their ports, thereby making it more difficult for American farms and businesses to ship their products abroad. As a result, U.S. exports plummeted after the passage of the infamous Hawley-Smoot Tariff.

THE ECONOMY OUT OF CONTROL    The new tariff did nothing to check a deepening economic crisis. After the postwar slump of 1921, the naïve idea grew that the economy had entered a new era of *perpetual* growth. Greed then propelled a growing contagion of get-rich-quick schemes. Such speculative mania fueled the Florida real estate boom. Thousands of people invested in Florida real estate, usually at long distance, eager for quick profits in the nation's fastest-growing state. In mid-1926, however, the Florida real estate bubble burst.

For the losers it was a sobering lesson, but it proved to be but an audition for the great bull market in stocks. Until 1927 stock values had gone up with corporate profits, but then they began to soar on wings of pure speculation. Treasury Secretary Andrew W. Mellon's tax reductions had given affluent people more money to spend, much of which found its way to the stock market. Instead of speculating in real estate, one could **buy stock "on margin"**—that is, make a small down payment (the "margin") and borrow the rest from a broker, who held the stock as security in case the stock price plummeted. If the stock declined, and the buyer failed to meet a "margin call" for more funds, the broker could sell the stock to cover his loan. Brokers' loans to stock purchasers more than doubled from 1927 to 1929.

Stock market investors ignored warning signs. By 1927, residential construction and automobile sales were slowing and the rate of consumer spending had also slowed. By mid-1929, production, employment, and other measures of economic activity were declining. Still, the stock market rose. By 1929, the stock market had become a fantasy world, driven more by hope and greed than by actual business performance. The few financiers and brokers who counseled caution were ignored. President Hoover also voiced concern about the "orgy of mad speculation," and he tried to discourage the irrational faith in the stock markets, but to no avail. On October 22, a leading bank president assured reporters that there was "nothing fundamentally wrong with the stock market or with the underlying business and credit structure."

**THE CRASH AND ITS CAUSES**    The next day, stock values tumbled and triggered a wild scramble by panicking people to unload stocks. On Tuesday, October 29, the most devastating single day in the stock market's history to that point, widespread panic had set in. By the end of the month, stocks on the New York Stock Exchange had fallen in value by an average of 37 percent. Business and government leaders initially expressed confidence that the markets would rebound. According to President Hoover, "the fundamental business of the country" was sound. But the hysteria continued. The *New York Times* stock average, which stood at 452 in September 1929, bottomed at 52 in July 1932. The collapse of the stock market revealed that the much-trumpeted economic prosperity of the 1920s had been built on weak foundations. By 1932, the nation's economy had experienced a broad collapse that brought prolonged, record levels of unemployment and widespread human suffering. From 1929 to 1933, U.S. economic output (called gross domestic product or GDP) dropped almost 27 percent. The unemployment rate by 1932 was 23 percent.

The stock market crash did not cause the Great Depression, but it did shake public confidence in the nation's financial system, and it revealed major structural flaws in the economy and in government policies. Too many businesses had maintained high retail prices and taken large profits while holding down wage increases. As a result, about a third of personal income went to only the top 5 percent of the population. By plowing most profits back into expansion rather than wage increases, the business sector brought on a growing imbalance between rising industrial productivity and declining consumer purchasing power. As consumer spending declined because wage increases were not keeping up with price increases, the rate of investment in new factories and businesses

**Stock market crash**

Apprehensive crowds gather on the steps of the Subtreasury Building, opposite the New York Stock Exchange, as news of a stock collapse spreads on October 29, 1929.

also plummeted. For a time the erosion of consumer purchasing power had been concealed by an increase in installment buying, and the volume of foreign loans and investments, which supported foreign demand for American goods, had concealed the deflationary effects of the high tariffs. But the flow of American capital abroad began to dry up when the stock market began to look more attractive. Swollen corporate profits, together with Treasury Secretary Mellon's business-friendly tax policies, enticed the rich into more frenzied stock market speculation. When trouble came, the bloated corporate structure collapsed.

Government policies also contributed to the financial debacle. Mellon's tax reductions led to oversaving by the general public, which helped diminish the demand for consumer goods. Hostility toward labor unions impeded efforts to ensure that wage levels kept pace with corporate profits. High tariffs discouraged foreign trade. Lax enforcement of anti-trust laws also encouraged high retail prices.

Another culprit was the gold standard, whereby nations pegged the value of their paper currency to the size of their gold reserves so as to avoid hyperinflation. Gold had long been thought to be the foundation of a sound money supply. When gold drained out of a nation, the amount of paper money shrunk; when a nation accumulated gold, the money supply expanded. When economic output, prices, and savings began dropping in 1929, policy makers—certain that they had to keep their currencies tied to the gold supply at all costs—tightened access to money at the very moment that economies needed an expanding money supply to keep growing. The only way to restore economic stability within the constraints of the gold standard was to let prices and wages continue to fall, allowing the downturn, in Mellon's words, to "purge the rottenness out of the system." Instead, the lack of innovative engagement among government and financial leaders turned a recession into the world's worst depression as nations followed Mellon's contractionist philosophy. From 1929 to 1933, 40 percent of American banks disappeared, taking with them the savings accounts of millions of people. Unlike today, nothing was done by the Federal Reserve system to shore up the banking sector. As a result, defaults and bankruptcies fed deflation. The nation's money supply shrank by a third, which in turn drove prices and production down. By 1936, the horrible effects of such a deflationary spiral would lead more than two dozen nations, including the United States, to abandon the gold standard, thereby enabling the expansion of the money supply which in turn led to economic growth.

THE HUMAN TOLL OF THE DEPRESSION    The devastating collapse of the economy caused immense social hardships. By 1933, 13 million people were out of work. Millions more who kept their jobs saw their hours and wages reduced. The contraction of the economy squeezed debtors, especially farmers and laborers who had made installment purchases or mortgages. By 1933, a thousand Americans per day were losing their homes to foreclosure. The home construction industry went dormant. Factories shut down, banks closed, farms went bankrupt, and millions of people found themselves not only jobless but also homeless and penniless. Hungry people lined up at soup kitchens; others rummaged through trash cans behind restaurants. Many slept on park benches or in alleys. Others congregated in makeshift shelters in vacant lots. Thousands of desperate men in search of jobs rode the rails. These hobos, or tramps, as they were derisively called, sneaked onto empty railway cars and rode from town to town, looking for work. During the winter, homeless people wrapped themselves in newspapers to keep warm, sarcastically referring to their coverings as Hoover blankets. Some died from exposure. Others grew so weary of their grim fate that they ended their lives. The suicide rate soared during the 1930s. Americans had never before, and have never since, experienced social distress on such a scale.

HOOVER'S EFFORTS AT RECOVERY   Although the policies of government officials helped to bring on the economic collapse, few politicians even acknowledged that there was an unprecedented crisis: all that was needed, they claimed, was a slight correction of the market. Those who held to the dogma of limited government thought the economy would cure itself. Nothing should be done; the depression should be allowed to run its course until the economy had purged itself of its excesses. The best policy, Treasury Secretary Mellon advised, would be to "liquidate labor, liquidate stocks, liquidate the farmers, liquidate real estate." Initially, this "liquidationist" philosophy prevailed in government. Wages, stock prices, and property values were allowed to keep falling on the assumption that eventually they would reach a point where people would start buying again. But it did not work. Falling wages and land values made it harder for farmers, businesses, and households to pay their debts. As people defaulted on loans and mortgages and more people lost jobs, wages and property values kept dropping, worsening the slump. With so many people losing jobs and income, consumers and businesses simply could not buy enough goods and services to get the economy growing again.

President Hoover was less willing than Mellon to sit by and let events take their course. He in fact did more than any president had ever done before in such dire economic circumstances. Still, his own political philosophy, now hardened into dogma, set firm limits on government action, and he was unwilling to set that philosophy aside even to meet an unprecedented national emergency. "You know," Hoover told a journalist, "the only trouble with capitalism is capitalists; they're too damn greedy."

As the economy floundered, Hoover believed that the nation's fundamental business structure was sound and that the people simply needed their confidence restored. So he invited business, financial, and labor leaders to the White House and urged them to keep their mills and shops open, maintain wage rates, and spread out the work to avoid layoffs—in short, to let the first shock of depression fall on corporate profits rather than on wage earners. In return, union leaders, who had little choice, agreed to refrain from demanding higher wages and going on strike. In speech after speech, Hoover exhorted people to keep up hope and reassured business leaders that the economy would rebound. To help steady the nation's nerves, the president intentionally described the economic downturn not as a "panic," or as a "crisis," but as a "depression," thinking that it was a less inflammatory word. By 1931 Hoover was calling the economic calamity "a great depression," an unfortunate choice of words that would come back to haunt him. In early May 1930, he told the U.S. Chamber of Commerce that he was "convinced we have passed the worst and with continued effort we shall rapidly recover." As it happened, however, uplifting words were not enough.

So Hoover did more than enlist the support of the business community and reassure the public. He accelerated the start of government construction projects in order to provide jobs, but cutbacks by state and local governments in their projects more than offset the new federal spending. At Hoover's demand, the Federal Reserve Board returned to an easier monetary policy, and Congress passed a modest tax reduction to put more cash into people's pockets. The Federal Farm Board stepped up its loans and its purchases of farm surpluses, only to face bumper crops in 1930 despite droughts in the Midwest and Southwest.

Hoover's efforts to address the burgeoning economic crisis were not enough, however. Because he never understood or acknowledged the seriousness of the economic problems, he and his administration never did enough to stop the Depression from worsening. Vice President Charles Curtis claimed that "prosperity was "just around the corner." Hoover shared the assumption that the nation was simply experiencing a short-term shock, not a prolonged malaise, so drastic action was not warranted. In June 1930, Hoover told a delegation of bankers that the "depression is over." But more and more people kept losing their jobs, and disappointment in the president deepened. By the fall of 1930, more than 25,000 businesses had failed, there were five million people unemployed, and many city governments were buckling under the strain of lost revenue and growing human distress. Hoover dismissed the concerns of "calamity mongers and weeping men." He balked at giving uplifting speeches, admitting that he was no Theodore Roosevelt.

## GLOBAL CONCERNS

JAPAN INVADES CHINA  At the same time that Herbert Hoover was wrestling with the onset of an economic depression at home, he was also confronting a growing crisis in Asia. In 1931–1932, some ten thousand Japanese troops occupied Manchuria, a vast province in northeast China blessed with valuable deposits of iron ore and coal. The Japanese renamed Manchuria "The Republic of Manchukuo" and proclaimed its independence from China. It was the first major step in the effort to control all of China.

The Japanese takeover of Manchuria challenged the will of the Western democracies to enforce world peace, and they failed the test. Hoover's secretary of state, Henry L. Stimson, wanted to use the threat of force to deter the

**Japan and China**

Japan's seizure of Manchuria in 1931 prompted this American condemnation.

Japanese advance in China but worried that the president "being a Quaker and an engineer did not understand the psychology of combat. . . ." In January 1932, Hoover and Stimson announced that the United States would not recognize any territorial changes in China that violated previous treaties. In revealing that the United States was unwilling to use even the threat of force to stop Japanese aggression, the so-called Hoover-Stimson Doctrine foreshadowed the timid nature of American diplomacy during the 1930s and revealed the hollowness of the Kellogg-Briand Treaty outlawing war. But Hoover's stance also reflected American public opinion. "The American people don't give a hoot in a rain barrel who controls North China," said a Philadelphia newspaper. When the League of Nations condemned Japanese aggression in China, Japan simply withdrew from the League in 1933. An uneasy peace settled upon east Asia for four years, during which time aggressive Japanese military leaders increased their political sway in Tokyo.

**STRESSES AND STRAINS**   One reason that Americans were so indifferent about Japanese aggression in China is that the problems at home were so severe—and getting worse. As always, a depressed economy hurt the party in power, and the Democrats shrewdly exploited Hoover's predicament. The squalid shantytowns that sprouted across the country to house the destitute and homeless became known as Hoovervilles; a Hoover flag was an empty pocket turned inside out. In November 1930 the Democrats gained their first national victory since 1916, winning a majority in the House and a near majority in the Senate. Hoover refused to see the elections as a warning signal. Instead he grew more resistant to calls for dramatic measures.

In the first half of 1931, economic indicators rose, renewing hope for an upswing. Then, as recovery beckoned, another shock occurred. In May 1931, the failure of Austria's largest bank triggered a financial panic in central Europe. To ease concerns, President Hoover negotiated in June a one-year moratorium on both payments of war reparations and war debts by the

**Impact of the Depression**

Two children set up shop in a Hooverville in Washington, D.C.

European nations. Hoover's moratorium was perhaps the most decisive, popular initiative of his presidency, but it did little to stop the collapsing world economy. The global shortage of monetary exchange drove Europeans to withdraw their gold from American banks and dump their American securities (stocks and bonds). One European country after another abandoned the gold standard and devalued its currency. Even the Bank of England went off the gold standard.

At the end of 1932, after Hoover's debt moratorium ended, most European countries defaulted on their war debts to the United States. In retaliation, Congress passed the Johnson Debt Default Act of 1934, which prohibited even private loans to any government that had defaulted on its debts to the United States. Foreign withdrawals of money from U.S. banks helped spread a sense of panic. Using conventional wisdom, the Federal Reserve system sought to protect the value of the nation's gold reserves by raising interest rates. But what the American banks needed most was not tighter access to money but easier money to ease the *liquidity* crisis: banks desperately needed cash to meet the demands of panicky depositors who wanted to cash in their checking and savings accounts. By the end of 1931, over six hundred U.S. banks had gone bankrupt. Almost 25 percent of the workforce—15 million people—were unemployed. The resulting societal misery was unprecedented. Some jobless, homeless people grew desperate. Men started forest fires in hopes of being hired to put them out. Others committed petty crimes in order to be arrested; at least jails provided them with food and shelter.

CONGRESSIONAL INITIATIVES   With a new Congress in session in 1932, demands for federal action impelled Hoover to stretch his individualistic philosophy to its limits. He was now ready to use government resources to shore up the financial institutions of the country. That year, the new Congress set up the **Reconstruction Finance Corporation** (RFC) with $500 million (and authority to borrow $2 billion more) for emergency loans to struggling banks, life-insurance companies, and railroads. Under Charles G. Dawes, Calvin Coolidge's vice president, the RFC had authorized $1.2 billion in loans within six months. It staved off several bankruptcies, but Hoover's critics called it favoritism to big businesses, the most damaging instance of which was a $90 million loan to Dawes's own Chicago bank, made soon after he left the RFC in 1932. The RFC nonetheless remained a key federal agency through the mid-1940s.

Further help to the financial structure came with the Glass-Steagall Act of 1932, which broadened the definition of commercial loans that the Federal

Reserve would support. The new arrangement also released about $750 million in gold formerly used to back Federal Reserve notes, countering the effect of foreign withdrawals and domestic hoarding of gold at the same time that it enlarged the supply of credit. For homeowners, the Federal Home Loan Bank Act of 1932 created with Hoover's blessing a series of discount banks for home mortgages. They provided to savings-and-loan and other mortgage agencies a service much like the one that the Federal Reserve system provided to commercial banks.

Hoover's critics said all these "unprecedented" measures reflected a dubious "trickle-down" theory. If government could help huge banks and railroads, asked New York Democratic senator Robert F. Wagner, "is there any reason why we should not likewise extend a helping hand to that forlorn American, in every village and every city of the United States, who has been without wages since 1929?" The contraction of the nation's money supply devastated debtors such as farmers and those who made purchases on the installment plan or held balloon-style mortgages, whose monthly payments increased over time.

By 1932, members of Congress, mostly Democrats, were filling the hoppers with bills for federal measures to provide relief to the people hit hardest by the economic collapse. At that point, Hoover might have pleaded "dire necessity" and taken the leadership of the relief movement and salvaged his political fortunes. Instead, he held back and only grudgingly edged toward addressing the widespread human distress. On July 21, 1932, he signed the Emergency Relief Act, which avoided a direct federal dole (cash payment) to individuals but gave the RFC $300 million for relief loans to the states, authorized loans of up to $1.5 billion for state and local public construction projects, and appropriated $322 million for federal public works.

FARMERS AND VETERANS IN PROTEST   Government expenditures to provide relief for farmers had long since dried up. In mid-1931 the federal government quit buying crop surpluses and helplessly watched prices for commodities slide. Faced with the loss of everything, desperate farmers defied the law. Angry mobs stopped foreclosures and threatened to lynch the judges sanctioning them. In Nebraska, farmers burned corn to keep warm. Iowans formed the militant Farmers' Holiday Association, which called a farmers' strike.

The economic crisis spawned desperate talk of revolution. "Folks are restless," Mississippi governor Theodore Bilbo told reporters in 1931. "Communism is gaining a foothold. . . . In fact, I'm getting a little pink myself." Across the country the once-obscure Communist party began to draw crowds to its rallies. Yet for all the sound and fury, few Americans embraced communism during the 1930s. Party membership in the United States never rose much above one hundred thousand.

Fears of organized revolt arose when unemployed veterans converged on the nation's capital in the spring of 1932. The "**Bonus Expeditionary Force**" grew quickly to more than twenty thousand. Their purpose was to get immediate payment of the cash bonus to nearly 4 million World War I veterans that Congress had approved in 1924. The House passed a bonus bill, but when the Senate voted it down, most of the veterans went home. The rest, along with their wives and children, having no place to go, camped in vacant federal buildings and in a shantytown at Anacostia Flats, within sight of the Capitol.

Eager to disperse the homeless veterans, Hoover persuaded Congress to pay for their tickets home. More left, but others stayed even after Congress adjourned, hoping at least to meet with the president. Late in July, the administration ordered the government buildings cleared. In the ensuing melee, a policeman panicked, fired into the crowd, and killed two veterans. The secretary of war then dispatched about seven hundred soldiers under overeager General Douglas MacArthur, who was aided by junior officers Dwight D. Eisenhower and George S. Patton. MacArthur, who dismissed the veterans as "communists," ordered his soldiers to use horses, tanks, tear gas, and bayonets to rout the unarmed veterans and their families and burn their makeshift camp. Dozens of protesters were injured in the melee, and an eleven-week-old boy born at Anacostia died from exposure to tear gas. Eisenhower, who had opposed the use of force, said it was "a pitiful scene." Franklin D. Roosevelt, then serving as governor of New York, concluded after learning of the army's action that General MacArthur was one of the most dangerous men in America.

In response to outrage across the nation, MacArthur hysterically claimed that the "mob" of military veterans and their families was about to seize control of the government. The administration insisted that the Bonus Army consisted mainly of communists and criminals, but neither a grand jury nor the Veterans Administration could find evidence to support the charge. One observer wrote that the unemployed war veterans revealed "an atmosphere of hopelessness, of utter despair, though not of desperation. . . . They have no enthusiasm whatever and no stomach for fighting."

Their disheartened mood, and the mood of the country, echoed that of the beleaguered Hoover himself. He worked hard, seven days a week, but the stress had sapped his health and morale. "I am so tired," he said, "that

**Anger and frustration**

Unemployed military veterans, members of the Bonus Expeditionary Force, clash with Washington, D.C., police at Anacostia Flats in July 1932.

every bone in my body aches." Presidential news conferences became more strained and less frequent. While traveling with a group of Cabinet officers, Hoover asked the secretary of the Treasury for a nickel to phone a friend; the secretary said, "Here are two nickels—call them both." When aides urged Hoover to seize the reins of leadership, he said "I have no Wilsonian qualities." The president's deepening sense of futility became increasingly evident to the country. In a mood more despairing than rebellious, Americans in 1932 eagerly anticipated what the next presidential campaign would produce.

## FROM HOOVERISM TO THE NEW DEAL

THE ELECTION OF 1932  On June 14, 1932, while the ragtag Bonus Army was still encamped in Washington, D.C., glum Republicans gathered in Chicago to renominate Herbert Hoover. The delegates went through the motions in a mood of defeat. By contrast, the Democrats converged on

Chicago later in June confident that they would nominate the next president. The fifty-year-old New York governor Franklin D. Roosevelt was already the front-runner, with most of the delegates lined up, and he went over the top on the fourth ballot.

Born in 1882, the adored only child of wealthy parents, educated by tutors at Hyde Park, his father's Hudson River estate in New York, young Roosevelt led a cosmopolitan life. His parents arranged for a private railroad car to deliver him to Groton, an elite Massachusetts boarding school. He later attended Harvard College and Columbia University Law School. While a law student, he married his distant cousin, Anna Eleanor Roosevelt, a niece of his fifth cousin, Theodore Roosevelt, then president of the United States.

In 1910, Franklin Roosevelt won a Democratic seat in the New York State Senate. As a freshman legislator, he displayed the contradictory qualities that would characterize his political career: he was an aristocrat with empathy for common folk, a traditionalist with a penchant for experimentation, an affable charmer with a buoyant smile and upturned chin who harbored enormous self-confidence and optimism as well as profound convictions, and a skilled political tactician with a shrewd sense of timing and a distinctive willingness to listen to and learn from others.

Tall, handsome, and athletic, Roosevelt seemed destined for greatness. In 1912, he backed Woodrow Wilson for president, and for both of Wilson's terms he served as assistant secretary of the navy. Then, in 1920, largely on the strength of his name, he became James Cox's running mate on the Democratic ticket. The following year, at age thirty-nine, his career was cut short by the onset of polio that left him permanently disabled, unable to stand or walk without braces. But the battle for recovery transformed the young aristocrat. He became less arrogant, less superficial, more focused, and more interesting. A friend recalled that Roosevelt emerged from his struggle with polio "completely warm-hearted, with a new humility of spirit" that led him to identify with the poor and the suffering. Justice Oliver Wendell Holmes later summed up his qualities this way: "a second-class intellect—but a first-class temperament."

For seven years, aided by his talented wife, Eleanor, Roosevelt strengthened his body to compensate for his disability, and in 1928 he won the governorship of New York. Reelected by a whopping majority of 700,000 in 1930, Roosevelt became the Democrats' favorite for president in 1932. In a bold, unprecedented gesture during the summer of 1932, Roosevelt flew for nine hours to Chicago to accept the Democratic presidential nomination instead of awaiting formal notification. He had intentionally broken with

**The "New Deal" candidate**

Governor Franklin Delano Roosevelt, the Democratic nominee for president in 1932, campaigning in Topeka, Kansas. Roosevelt's confidence inspired voters.

tradition, he told the delegates, because the stakes were so high. "Republican leaders not only have failed in material things, they have failed in national vision, because in disaster they have held out no hope. . . . I pledge you, I pledge myself to a new deal for the American people" that would "break foolish traditions." Roosevelt's acceptance speech was a bundle of contradictions, promising "to cut taxes and balance the budget" as well as to launch numerous expensive innovations to provide the people with "work and security." What his New Deal "crusade" would be in practice Roosevelt had little idea as yet, but he was much more willing to experiment than Hoover. What was more, his upbeat personality communicated joy, energy, and hope. Roosevelt's campaign song was "Happy Days Are Here Again."

Partly to dispel doubts about his health, the Democratic nominee set forth on a grueling campaign tour in 1932. He blamed the Depression on the Republicans, attacked Hoover for his "extravagant government spending," and he repeatedly promised Americans a New Deal. Like Hoover, Roosevelt pledged to balance the budget, but he was willing to incur short-term deficits

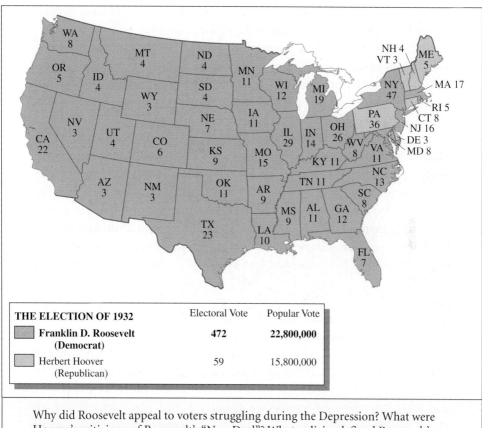

| THE ELECTION OF 1932 | Electoral Vote | Popular Vote |
|---|---|---|
| ▨ Franklin D. Roosevelt (Democrat) | 472 | 22,800,000 |
| ▨ Herbert Hoover (Republican) | 59 | 15,800,000 |

Why did Roosevelt appeal to voters struggling during the Depression? What were Hoover's criticisms of Roosevelt's "New Deal"? What policies defined Roosevelt's New Deal during the presidential campaign?

to prevent starvation and revive the economy. On the tariff he was evasive. On farm policy, he offered several options pleasing to farmers and ambiguous enough not to alarm city dwellers. He called for strict regulation of utilities and for at least some government development of electricity, and he consistently stood by his party's pledge to repeal the Prohibition amendment. Perhaps most important, he recognized that a revitalized economy would require national planning and new ideas. "The country needs, and, unless I mistake its temper, the country demands bold, persistent experimentation," he said. "Above all, try something."

What came across to voters, however, was less the content of Roosevelt's speeches than his uplifting confidence and his commitment to change. By contrast, Hoover lacked vitality and vision. Democrats, Hoover argued, ignored the international causes of the Depression. They were also taking a reckless course. Roosevelt's proposals, he warned, "would destroy the very foundations of our American system." Pursue them, he warned, and "grass will grow in the streets of a hundred cities, a thousand towns." But few were listening. Mired in the persistent Depression, the country wanted a new course, a new leadership, a new deal.

Some disillusioned voters took a dim view of both major candidates. Those who believed that only a radical departure would suffice supported the Socialist party candidate, Norman Thomas, who polled 882,000 votes, and a few preferred the Communist party candidate, who won 103,000. The wonder is that a desperate people did not turn in greater numbers to radical candidates. Instead, they swept Roosevelt into office with 23 million votes to Hoover's 16 million. Hoover carried only four states in New England, plus Pennsylvania and Delaware, and lost decisively in the Electoral College by 472 to 59.

THE 1933 INAUGURATION    For the last time the nation waited four months, from early November until March 4, for a newly elected president and Congress to take office. The Twentieth Amendment, ratified on January 23, 1933, provided that presidents would thereafter take office on January 20 and the newly elected Congress on January 3. Just two weeks before his March inauguration, Roosevelt survived an attempted assassination while speaking in Miami, Florida. The gunman, an unemployed bricklayer and Italian-born anarchist, fired five shots at the president-elect. Roosevelt was not hit, but the mayor of Chicago was killed.

The bleak winter of 1932–1933 witnessed spreading destitution and misery. Unemployment increased, and panic struck the banking system. As bank after bank collapsed, people rushed to their own banks to remove their deposits. Many discovered that they, too, were caught short of cash. When the Hoover administration ended in early 1933, four fifths of the nation's banks were closed, and the country teetered on the brink of economic paralysis.

The profound crisis of confidence that greeted Roosevelt when he took the oath of office on March 4, 1933, soon gave way to a mood of expectancy and hope. The charismatic new president displayed monumental self-assurance when he declared "that the only thing we have to fear is fear itself—nameless, unreasoning, unjustified terror which paralyzes needed efforts to convert retreat into advance." If need be, he said, "I shall ask the Congress for . . . broad executive power to wage a war against the emergency as great as the power that would be given me if we were in fact invaded by a foreign foe." It was a measure of the country's mood that Roosevelt's call for unprecedented presidential power received the loudest applause.

*End of Chapter Review*

## CHAPTER SUMMARY

- **"Return to Normalcy"**  Although progressivism lost its appeal after the Great War, the Eighteenth Amendment (paving the way for Prohibition) and the Nineteenth Amendment (guaranteeing women's suffrage) marked the culmination of that movement at the national level. Reformers still actively worked for good and efficient government at the local level, but overall the drive was for a "return to normalcy"—conformity and moral righteousness.

- **Isolationism**  America distanced itself from global affairs—a stance reflected in the Red Scare, laws limiting immigration, and high tariffs. Yet America could not ignore international events because its business interests were becoming increasingly global. Although the United States never joined the League of Nations, it sent unofficial observers to Geneva. The widespread belief that arms limitations would reduce the chance of future wars led America to participate in the Washington Naval Conference of 1921 and the Kellogg-Briand Pact of 1928.

- **Era of Conservatism**  Many Americans, particularly people in rural areas and members of the middle class, wanted a return to a quieter, more conservative way of life after World War I, and Warren G. Harding's landslide Republican victory allowed just that. The policies of Harding's pro-business cabinet were reminiscent of those of the McKinley White House more than two decades earlier. Union membership declined in the 1920s as workers' rights were rolled back by a conservative Supreme Court and in response to fears of Communist subversion. Workers, however, shared in the affluence of the 1920s, thereby contributing to the rise of a mass culture.

- **Growth of Economy**  The budget was balanced through reductions in spending and taxes, while tariffs were raised to protect domestic industries, setting the tone for a prosperous decade. Harding's successor, Calvin Coolidge, actively promoted the interests of big business. The public responded enthusiastically to the mass marketing of new consumer goods such as radios and affordable automobiles. Agricultural production, however, lagged after the wartime boom evaporated.

- **The Great Depression**  The stock market crash revealed the structural flaws in the economy, but it did not cause the Great Depression. Government policies throughout the twenties—high tariffs, lax enforcement of anti-trust laws, an absence of checks on speculation in real estate and the stock market, and adherence to the gold standard—contributed to the onset of the Depression. Hoover's attempts to remedy the problems were too few and too late. Banks failed, businesses closed, homes and jobs were lost.

## CHRONOLOGY

| | |
|---|---|
| 1921 | Representatives of the United States, Great Britain, France, Italy, and Japan attend the Washington Naval Conference |
| 1922 | United States begins sending observers to the League of Nations |
| | Benito Mussolini comes to power in Italy |
| 1923 | President Warren G. Harding dies in office |
| 1928 | Herbert Hoover is elected president |
| | More than sixty nations sign the Kellogg-Briand Pact pledging not to go to war with one another, except in matters of self-defense |
| October 29, 1929 | Stock market crashes |
| 1930 | Congress passes the Hawley-Smoot Tariff |
| 1932 | Congress sets up the Reconstruction Finance Corporation |
| 1932 | Congress passes the Glass-Steagall Act |
| 1933 | Bonus Expeditionary Force converges on Washington to demand payment of bonuses promised to war veterans |

## KEY TERMS & NAMES

# 27

## NEW DEAL AMERICA

FOCUS QUESTIONS                    ⑤ wwnorton.com/studyspace

- What were the immediate challenges facing Franklin Delano
  Roosevelt in March 1933?
- What were the lasting effects of the New Deal legislation?
- Why did the New Deal draw criticism from conservatives and
  liberals?
- How did the New Deal expand the federal government's authority?
- What were the major cultural changes of the 1930s?

Franklin Delano Roosevelt was elected in 1932 to lead an anxious nation mired in the third year of an unprecedented depression. No other business slump had been so deep, so long, or so painful. One out of every four Americans in 1932 was unemployed; in many large cities, nearly half of the adults were out of work. Some five hundred thousand people had lost homes or farms because they could not pay their mortgages. Thousands of banks had failed; millions of depositors had lost their life savings. The suffering was global. The worldwide depression helped accelerate the rise of fascism and communism; totalitarianism was on the march in Europe and Asia. "The situation is critical," the prominent political analyst Walter Lippmann warned President-elect Roosevelt. "You may have to assume dictatorial powers." Roosevelt did not become a dictator, but he did take decisive action that transformed the scope and role of the federal government. He and a supportive Congress immediately adopted bold measures intended to relieve the human suffering and promote economic recovery. Although the New Deal initiatives produced mixed results, they halted the economic downturn and provided the foundation for a system of federal social welfare programs.

COMPETING PROPOSALS     In 1933, the relentlessly optimistic **President Roosevelt** confronted three major challenges: reviving the economy, relieving the widespread human misery, and rescuing the farm sector and its desperate families. To address these daunting challenges, Roosevelt assembled a "brain trust" of talented advisers who feverishly set to work developing ideas to address the nation's compelling problems. More than any previous president, Roosevelt made effective use of his advisers, constantly learning from them as well as refereeing their disputes with one another. The diverse group of professors, planners, policy makers, and administrators making up the brain trust were brilliant and opinionated: they offered conflicting opinions about how best to rescue the economy from depression. Some promoted vigorous enforcement of the anti-trust laws as a means of restoring business competition; others argued for the opposite, saying that anti-trust laws should be suspended so as to enable the largest corporations to collaborate with the federal government and thereby better manage the overall economy. Still others called for a massive expansion of social welfare programs and a prolonged infusion of increased government spending to address the profound human crisis and revive the economy.

Roosevelt was willing to try some elements of each approach without ever embracing any one of them completely. In part, his flexible outlook reflected a stern political reality: seasoned conservative southern Democrats controlled the Congress, and the new president could not risk alienating these powerful proponents of balanced budgets and limited government. Roosevelt's inconsistencies also reflected his own outlook. He did not have a comprehensive philosophy of government. When asked what his philosophy was, he replied, "I am a Christian and a Democrat—that's all." Roosevelt was a pragmatist rather than an ideologue, a tinkerer more than a dogmatist. As he once explained, "Take a method and try it. If it fails, admit it frankly and try another." Roosevelt's elastic New Deal would therefore take the form of a series of trial-and-error actions, some of which were well-intentioned failures.

Roosevelt and his advisers initially settled on a three-pronged strategy to revive the economy. First, they sought to remedy the immediate banking crisis and to provide short-term emergency relief for the jobless. Second, the New Dealers tried to promote industrial recovery by increasing federal spending and by facilitating cooperative agreements between management and organized labor. Third, they attempted to raise depressed commodity prices by paying farmers to reduce the size of their crops and herds. When the overall supply of agricultural products was reduced, prices for grain and meat would rise over time and thereby increase farm income. None of these initiatives worked perfectly, but their combined effect was to restore hope and energy to a nation paralyzed by fear and uncertainty.

STRENGTHENING THE MONETARY SYSTEM    Money is the lubricant of capitalism, and money was fast disappearing from circulation by 1933. Panicky depositors withdrew their savings from banks and hoarded their currency. By taking money out of circulation, however, people unwittingly exacerbated the Depression. On his second day in office, Roosevelt called upon Congress to meet in a special session on March 9, and together they declared a four-day bank holiday to allow the financial panic to subside. It took Congress only seven hours to pass the Emergency Banking Relief Act, which permitted sound banks to reopen and appointed managers for those that remained in trouble. On March 12, in the first of his radio-broadcast "fireside chats," the president assured the 60 million Americans listening that it was safer to "keep your money in a reopened bank than under the mattress." His reassurances soothed a nervous nation. The following day, deposits in reopened banks exceeded withdrawals. "Capitalism was saved in eight days," said one of Roosevelt's advisers. The banking crisis had ended, and the new administration was ready to get on with its broader program of economic recovery.

Roosevelt next followed through on two campaign pledges. At his behest, Congress passed an Economy Act, granting the executive branch the power to cut government workers' salaries, reduce payments to military veterans for non-service-connected disabilities, and reorganize federal agencies in the interest of reducing expenses. Second, Roosevelt ended Prohibition. The Beer-Wine Revenue Act amended the Volstead Act to permit the sale of beverages with an alcohol content of 3.2 percent or less. The **Twenty-first Amendment**, already submitted by Congress to the states, would be declared ratified on December 5, thus ending the "noble experiment" of Prohibition.

The measures of March were but the beginning of an avalanche of New Deal legislation. From March 9 to June 16, the so-called Hundred Days, a cooperative Congress endorsed fifteen major pieces of legislation proposed by the president that collectively transformed the role of the federal government in social and economic life. Journalist Walter Lippmann said that during the Hundred Days the United States "became an organized nation confident of our power to provide for our own [economic] security and to control our own destiny."

Several of the programs comprising what came to be called the **First New Deal** (1933–1935) addressed the acute debt problem faced by farmers and homeowners. During 1933, a thousand homes or farms were being foreclosed upon each day. Desperate farmers across the country used violence and intimidation to halt the eviction of their friends and neighbors. In 1933, farmers in Le Mars, Iowa, attacked a judge in his courtroom because he refused to stop signing farm foreclosure orders. Scores of angry men surrounded the judge, hitting and choking him until they slipped a noose around his

**The galloping snail**

A vigorous Roosevelt drives Congress to action in this *Detroit News* cartoon from March 1933.

neck—though they stopped short of hanging him. Iowa's governor declared martial law and sent 250 National Guardsmen to keep the peace.

By executive decree, Roosevelt reorganized all federal farm credit agencies into the Farm Credit Administration. By the Emergency Farm Mortgage Act and the Farm Credit Act, Congress authorized the extensive refinancing of farm mortgages at lower interest rates to stem the tide of foreclosures. The Home Owners' Loan Act provided a similar service to city dwellers through the Home Owners' Loan Corporation, which refinanced mortgage loans at lower monthly payments for strapped homeowners, again helping to slow the rate of foreclosures. In 1934, Roosevelt created the Federal Housing Administration (FHA), which offered Americans much longer home mortgages (twenty years) to reduce their monthly payments. The Banking Act further shored up confidence in the banking system. Its Federal Deposit Insurance Corporation (FDIC) guaranteed personal bank deposits up to $5,000. To prevent speculative abuses, the Banking Act separated investment and commercial banking corporations and extended the Federal Reserve Board's regulatory power. The Federal Securities Act required the full disclosure of information about new stock and bond issues, at first by registration with the Federal Trade Commission (FTC) and later with the Securities and Exchange Commission (SEC), which was created to regulate the chaotic stock and bond markets.

RELIEF MEASURES    Another urgent priority in 1933 was relieving the widespread human distress caused by the Great Depression. Herbert Hoover had stubbornly refused to provide direct assistance to the unemployed and homeless. Roosevelt was more flexible. For example, he convinced Congress to create the Civilian Conservation Corps (CCC) to provide jobs to unemployed, unmarried young men aged eighteen to twenty-five. Nearly 3 million men were hired to work at a variety of CCC jobs in national forests, parks, and recreational areas and on soil-conservation projects. CCC workers built roads, bridges, campgrounds, and fish hatcheries; planted trees; taught farmers how to control soil erosion; and fought fires. They were paid a nominal sum of $30 a month, of which $25 went home to their families. The enrollees could also earn high-school diplomas.

The Federal Emergency Relief Administration (FERA) addressed the broader problems of human distress. Harry L. Hopkins, a tough-talking, big-hearted social worker who had directed then-Governor Roosevelt's relief

**Federal relief programs**

Civilian Conservation Corps enrollees in 1933, on a break from work. Directed by army officers and foresters, the CCC adhered to a semi-military discipline.

efforts in New York State, was appointed director of the FERA. The agency expanded federal assistance to the unemployed. Federal money flowed to the states in outright grants rather than "loans." Hopkins pushed an "immediate work instead of dole" approach on state and local officials, but they preferred the dole (direct cash payments to individuals) as a quicker way to reach the needy.

The first large-scale experiment with *federal* work relief, which put people directly on the government payroll at competitive wages, came with the formation of the Civil Works Administration (CWA). Created in November 1933, after the state-sponsored programs funded by the FERA proved inadequate, the CWA provided federal jobs to those unable to find work that winter. It was hastily conceived and implemented, but during its four-month existence the CWA put to work over 4 million people. The agency organized a variety of useful projects: making highway repairs and laying sewer lines, constructing or improving more than a thousand airports and forty thousand schools, and providing fifty thousand teaching jobs that helped keep rural schools open. As the number of people employed by the CWA soared, however, the program's costs skyrocketed to over $1 billion. Roosevelt balked at such expenditures and worried that people would become dependent upon federal jobs. So in the spring of 1934, he ordered the CWA dissolved. By April, some 4 million workers were again unemployed.

## REGULATORY EFFORTS

In addition to rescuing the banks and providing immediate relief to the unemployed, Roosevelt and his advisers promoted the long-term recovery of agriculture and industry during the Hundred Days in the spring of 1933. The languishing economy needed a boost—a big one. There were 13 million people without jobs.

AGRICULTURAL ASSISTANCE The sharp decline in commodity prices after 1929 meant that many farmers could not afford to plant or harvest their devalued crops. Farm income had plummeted from $6 billion in 1929 to $2 billion in 1932. The **Agricultural Adjustment Act** of 1933 created a new federal agency, the Agricultural Adjustment Administration (AAA), which sought to raise prices for crops and herds by paying farmers to reduce production. The money for such payments came from a tax levied on the processors of certain basic commodities—cotton gins, for example, and flour mills.

By the time Congress acted, however, the spring growing season was already under way. The prospect of another bumper cotton crop forced the AAA to sponsor a plow-under program. To destroy a growing crop was a "shocking commentary on our civilization," Agriculture Secretary Henry A. Wallace lamented. "I could tolerate it only as a cleaning up of the wreckage from the old days of unbalanced production." Moreover, given the oversupply of hogs, some 6 million pigs were slaughtered and buried. It could be justified, Wallace said, only as a means of helping farmers do with pigs what steelmakers did with pig iron—cut production to raise prices.

For a while these farm measures worked. By the end of 1934, Wallace could report significant declines in wheat, cotton, and corn production and a simultaneous increase in commodity prices. Farm income increased by 58 percent between 1932 and 1935. The AAA was only partially responsible for the gains, however. A devastating drought that settled over the plains states between 1932 and 1935 played a major role in reducing production and creating the epic "**dust bowl**" migrations so poignantly evoked in John Steinbeck's famous novel, *The Grapes of Wrath* (1939). Many migrant families had actually been driven off the land by AAA benefit programs that encouraged large farmers to take land worked by tenants and sharecroppers out of cultivation.

Although it created unexpected problems, the AAA achieved successes in boosting the overall farm economy. Conservatives castigated its sweeping powers, however. On January 6, 1936, in *United States v. Butler,* the Supreme Court declared the AAA's tax on food processors unconstitutional because the Constitution does not delegate to the federal government the power to control agricultural production. The administration hastily devised a new plan in the Soil Conservation and Domestic Allotment Act, which it pushed through Congress in six weeks. The new act omitted processing taxes and acreage quotas but provided benefit payments for soil-conservation practices that reduced the planting of soil-depleting crops, thus indirectly achieving crop reduction.

The act was an almost unqualified success as an engineering and educational project because it helped heal the scars of erosion and the plague of dust storms. But soil conservation nevertheless failed as a device for limiting production. With their worst lands taken out of production, farmers cultivated their fertile acres more intensively. In response, Congress passed the Agricultural Adjustment Act of 1938, which reestablished the earlier programs but left out the processing taxes. Benefit payments would come from federal funds. By the time the second AAA was tested in the Supreme Court, new justices had altered its outlook. This time the law was upheld as a legitimate exercise of federal power to regulate interstate commerce.

REVIVING INDUSTRIAL GROWTH   The industrial counterpart to the AAA was the **National Industrial Recovery Act** (NIRA), the two major parts of which dealt with economic recovery and public-works projects. The latter part created the Public Works Administration (PWA), granting $3.3 billion for new government buildings, highway construction, flood control projects, and other transportation improvements. Under the direction of Interior Secretary Harold L. Ickes, the PWA indirectly served the purpose of relief for the unemployed. Ickes focused it on well-planned permanent improvements, and he used private contractors rather than workers on the government payroll. PWA workers built Virginia's Skyline Drive, New York's Triborough Bridge, the Overseas Highway from Miami to Key West, and Chicago's subway system.

The more controversial part of the NIRA created the **National Recovery Administration** (NRA), headed by Hugh S. Johnson, a chain-smoking retired army general. Its purpose was twofold: (1) to stabilize the economy by reducing chaotic competition through the implementation of industry-wide codes that set wages and prices and (2) to generate more purchasing power for consumers by providing jobs, defining workplace standards, and raising wages. In each major industry, committees representing management, labor, and government drew up the fair practices codes. The labor standards featured in every code set a forty-hour workweek and minimum weekly wages of $13 ($12 in the South, where living costs were lower), which more than doubled earnings in some cases. Announcement of a proviso prohibiting the employment of children under the age of sixteen did "in a few minutes what neither law nor constitutional amendment had been able to do in forty years," Johnson said.

Labor unions, already hard-pressed by the economic downturn and a loss of members, were understandably concerned about the NRA's efforts to reduce competition by allowing competing businesses to cooperate by fixing wages and prices. To gain union support, the NRA included a provision (Section 7a) that guaranteed the right of workers to organize unions. But while prohibiting employers from interfering with union-organizing efforts, the NRA did not create adequate enforcement measures, nor did it require employers to bargain in good faith with labor representatives.

For a time the NRA worked, and the downward spiral of wages and prices subsided. But as soon as economic recovery began, business owners complained that the larger corporations dominated the code-making activities and that price-fixing robbed small producers of the chance to compete. In 1934, an investigating committee substantiated some of the charges. Moreover, allowing manufacturers to limit production had discouraged capital

**"The Spirit of the New Deal"**

In this cartoon, employer and employee agree to cooperate in the spirit of unity that inspired the National Recovery Administration.

investment. And because the NRA wage codes excluded agricultural and domestic workers, three out of every four employed African Americans derived no direct benefit from the program. By 1935, the NRA had developed more critics than friends. When it effectively died, in May 1935, struck down by the Supreme Court as unconstitutional, few paused to mourn.

Yet the NRA experiment left an enduring mark. With dramatic suddenness the industry-wide codes had set new workplace standards, such as the forty-hour work week, a minimum wage, and the abolition of child labor. The NRA's endorsement of collective bargaining spurred the growth of unions. Moreover, the codes advanced trends toward stabilization and rationalization that were becoming the standard practice of business at large and that, despite misgivings about the concentration of power, would be further promoted by trade associations. Yet as 1934 ended, economic recovery was nowhere in sight.

REGIONAL PLANNING   One of the most innovative New Deal programs was the creation of the Tennessee Valley Authority (TVA), a bold venture designed to bring electrical power, flood control, and jobs to one of the poorest regions in the nation. In May 1933, Congress created the TVA as a multipurpose public corporation serving seven states: Alabama, Georgia, Illinois, Kentucky, Mississippi, North Carolina, and Tennessee. By 1936, it had six dams completed or under way and a master plan to build nine high dams on the Tennessee River, which would create the "Great Lakes of the South," and other dams on the tributaries. The agency, moreover, opened the rivers to boats and barges, fostered soil conservation and forestry, experimented with fertilizers, drew new industries to the region, encouraged the formation of labor unions, improved schools and libraries, and sent cheap electric power pulsating through the valley for the first time. But the construction of dams and the creation of huge power-generating lakes also meant the destruction of homes, farms, and communities. "I don't want to move," said an elderly East Tennessee woman. "I want to sit here and look out over these hills where I was born." Inexpensive electricity became more and more the TVA's reason for being—a purpose that would become all the more important during World War II. The TVA transported farm families of the valley from the age of kerosene to the age of electricity.

**Norris Dam**

The massive dam in Tennessee, completed in 1936, was essential to the TVA's effort to expand power production.

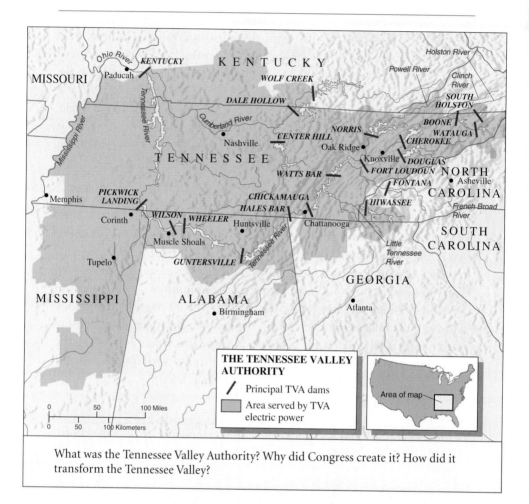

THE TENNESSEE VALLEY
AUTHORITY

/ Principal TVA dams

▢ Area served by TVA
electric power

Area of map

What was the Tennessee Valley Authority? Why did Congress create it? How did it transform the Tennessee Valley?

## THE SOCIAL COST OF THE DEPRESSION

Although programs of the so-called First New Deal helped ease the devastation wrought by the Depression, they did not restore prosperity or end the widespread human suffering. By 1935 the Depression continued to take a toll on Americans as the shattered economy slowly worked its way back to health.

CONTINUING HARDSHIPS   As late as 1939, some 9.5 million workers (17 percent of the labor force) remained unemployed. Prolonged economic hardship continued to create personal tragedies and tremendous social strains. Poverty led desperate people to do desperate things. Petty theft soared during the 1930s, as did street-corner begging, homelessness, and prostitution. Although the divorce rate dropped during the decade, in part because couples could not afford to live separately or pay the legal fees to obtain a divorce, all too often husbands down on their luck simply deserted their wives and children. A 1940 survey revealed that 1.5 million husbands had left home. With their future uncertain, married couples often decided not to have children; the birthrate plummeted. Parents sometimes could not support their children. In 1933, the Children's Bureau reported that one out of every five children was not getting enough to eat. Struggling parents sent their children to live with relatives or friends. Some nine hundred thousand children simply left home and joined the army of homeless "tramps."

DUST BOWL MIGRANTS   In the southern plains of the Midwest and the Mississippi Valley, a decade-long drought during the 1930s spawned an environmental and human catastrophe known as the dust bowl. Colorado, New Mexico, Kansas, Nebraska, Texas, and Oklahoma were the states hardest hit. In the scorching heat, crops withered and income plummeted. Relentless winds swept across the treeless plains, scooping up millions of tons of

**Dust storm approaching, 1930s**

When a dust storm blew in, it brought utter darkness, as well as the sand and grit that soon covered every surface, both indoors and out.

**A sharecropper's family affected by the Oklahoma dust bowl**

When the drought and dust storms showed no signs of relenting, many people headed west toward California.

parched topsoil into billowing dark clouds that floated east across entire states, engulfing farms and towns in what were called black blizzards. A massive dust storm in May 1934 darkened skies from Colorado to the Atlantic seaboard, depositing silt on porches and rooftops as well as on ships in the Atlantic Ocean. In 1937 there were seventy-two such major dust storms. The worst of them killed livestock and people and caused railroads to derail and automobiles to career off roads. By 1938, over 25 million acres of prairie land had lost most of its topsoil.

What made the dust storms worse than normal was the transition during the early twentieth century from scattered subsistence farming to widespread commercial agriculture. Huge "factory farms" used dry-farming techniques to plant vast acres of wheat, corn, and cotton. The advent of powerful tractors, deep-furrow plows, and mechanical harvesters greatly increased the scale and intensity of farming—and the indebtedness of farmers. The mercurial cycle of falling crop prices and rising indebtedness led farmers to plant as much and as often as they could. Overfarming and overgrazing disrupted the fragile ecology of the plains by decimating the native prairie grasses that stabilized the nutrient-rich topsoil. Constant plowing loosened vast amounts of dirt, which were easily swept up by powerful winds. Hordes of grasshoppers followed the gigantic dust storms and devoured what meager crops were left standing.

Human misery paralleled the environmental devastation. Parched farmers could not pay mortgages, and banks foreclosed on their property. Suicides soared. With each year, millions of people abandoned their farms. Uprooted farmers and their families formed a migratory stream of hardship flowing westward from the South and the Midwest toward California, buoyed by currents of hope and desperation. The West Coast was rumored to have plenty of jobs. So off they went on a cross-country trek in pursuit of new opportunities. Frequently lumped together as "Okies" or "Arkies," most of the dust bowl refugees were from cotton belt communities in Arkansas, Texas, and Missouri, as well as Oklahoma. During the 1930s and 1940s, some eight hundred thousand people left those four states and headed to the Far West. Not all were farmers; many were white-collar workers and retailers whose jobs had been tied to the health of the agriculture sector. Most of the dust bowl migrants were white, and most were adults in their twenties and thirties who relocated with spouses and children. Some traveled on trains or buses; others hopped a freight train or hitched a ride; most rode in their own cars, the trip taking four to five days on average.

Most people uprooted by the dust bowl gravitated to California's urban areas—Los Angeles, San Diego, or San Francisco. Others moved into the San Joaquin Valley, the agricultural heartland of California. There they discovered that rural California was no paradise. Only a few of the Midwestern migrants, mostly whites, could afford to buy land. Most found themselves competing with local Hispanics and Asians for seasonal work as pickers in the cotton fields or orchards of large corporate farms. Living in tents or crude cabins and frequently on the move, they suffered from exposure and poor sanitation.

They also felt the sting of social prejudice. The novelist John Steinbeck explained that "Okie us'ta mean you was from Oklahoma. Now it means you're a dirty son-of-a-bitch. Okie means you're scum." Such hostility toward the migrants drove a third of them to return to their home states. Most of the farm workers who stayed tended to fall back upon their old folkways rather than assimilate into their new surroundings. These gritty "plain folk" had brought with them their own prejudices against blacks and ethnic minorities, as well as a potent tradition of evangelical Protestantism and a distinctive style of music variously labeled country, hillbilly, or cowboy. This "Okie" subculture remains a vivid part of California society.

MINORITIES AND THE NEW DEAL   The Great Depression was especially traumatic for the most disadvantaged groups. However progressive Franklin Delano Roosevelt was on social issues, he failed to assault long-standing patterns of racism and segregation for fear of alienating conservative southern Democrats in Congress. As a result, many of the New Deal programs discriminated against blacks. The FHA, for example, refused to guarantee mortgages on houses purchased by blacks in white neighborhoods. In addition, both the CCC and the TVA practiced racial segregation.

The efforts of the Roosevelt administration to raise crop prices by reducing production proved especially devastating for African Americans and Mexican Americans. To earn the federal payments for reducing crops as provided by the AAA and other New Deal agriculture programs, many farm owners would first take out of cultivation the marginal lands worked by tenants and sharecroppers. The effect was to drive the landless off farms and eliminate the jobs of many migrant workers. Over two hundred thousand black tenant farmers nationwide were displaced by the AAA.

Mexican Americans suffered as well. Thousands of Mexicans had migrated to the United States during the 1920s, most of them settling in California, New Mexico, Arizona, Colorado, Texas, and the midwestern states. But because many of them were unable to prove their citizenship, either because they were ignorant of the regulations or because their migratory work hampered their ability to meet residency requirements, they were denied access to the new federal relief programs under the New Deal. As economic conditions worsened, government officials called for the deportation of Mexican-born Americans to avoid the cost of providing them with public services. By 1935, over 500,000 Mexican Americans and their American-born children had returned to Mexico. The state of Texas alone returned over 250,000 people.

Deportation became a popular solution in part because of the rising level of involvement of Mexican American workers in union activities. In 1933, Mexican American women in El Paso, Texas, formed the Society of Female Manufacturing Workers to protest wages as low as 75¢ a day. In the same year some 18,000 Mexican cotton pickers went on strike in California's San Joaquin Valley. Police crushed the strike by burning the workers' camps.

**Migratory Mexican field worker at home**

On the edge of a frozen pea field in Imperial Valley, California, this home to a migratory Mexican family reflects both poverty and impermanence.

The Great Depression also devastated Native Americans. They initially were encouraged by Roosevelt's appointment of John Collier as the commissioner of the Bureau of Indian Affairs (BIA). Collier steadily increased the number of Native Americans employed by the BIA and strove to ensure that Native Americans gained access to the various relief programs. Collier's primary objective, however, was passage of the Indian Reorganization Act. He wanted the new legislation to replace the provisions of the General Allotment Act (1887), known as the Dawes Act, which had sought to "Americanize" the indigenous peoples by breaking up their tribal land and allocating it to individuals. Collier insisted that the Dawes Act had produced only widespread poverty and demoralization. He hoped to reinvigorate Native American cultural traditions by restoring land to tribes, granting them the right to charter business enterprises and establish self-governing constitutions, and providing federal funds for vocational training and economic development. The act that Congress finally passed was a much-diluted version of Collier's original proposal, however, and the "Indian New Deal" brought only a partial improvement to the lives of Native Americans. But it did spur the various tribes to revise their constitutions so as to give women the right to vote and hold office.

COURT DECISIONS AND CIVIL RIGHTS    Although the National Association for the Advancement of Colored People (NAACP) waged a legal campaign against racial prejudice that gathered momentum during the 1930s, a major setback occurred in the Supreme Court decision *Grovey v. Townsend* (1935), which upheld the Texas Democrats' whites-only election primary. But the *Grovey* decision held for only nine years and marked the end of the major decisions that for half a century had narrowed application of the civil rights amendments ratified after the Civil War. A reversal had already set in.

Two important precedents arose from the celebrated Scottsboro case in Alabama in 1931, in which an all-white jury, on flimsy evidence, hastily convicted nine black youths, ranging in age from thirteen to twenty-one, of raping two white women while riding a freight train headed to Memphis. Eight of the youths were sentenced to death before cheering white audiences. The injustice of the Scottsboro case aroused protests throughout the nation and

**The Scottsboro case**

Heywood Patterson (center), one of the defendants in the case, is seen here with his attorney, Samuel Liebowitz (left) in Decatur, Alabama, in 1933.

around the world. The two girls, it turned out, had been selling sex to white and black boys on the train. One of the girls eventually recanted the charges. Several groups, including the International Labor Defense (a Communist organization) and the NAACP, offered legal assistance in efforts to appeal the decision. No case in American legal history produced as many trials, appeals, reversals, and retrials. The Supreme Court, in *Powell v. Alabama* (1932), overturned the original conviction because the judge had not ensured that the accused were provided adequate defense attorneys. It ordered new trials. In *Norris v. Alabama* (1935), the Court ruled that the systematic exclusion of African Americans from Alabama juries had denied the Scottsboro defendants equal protection of the law—a principle that had widespread impact on state courts by opening up juries to blacks. Eventually, the state of Alabama dropped the charges against the four youngest of the "Scottsboro boys" and granted paroles to the others; the last one was released in 1950.

Like Woodrow Wilson, Franklin Delano Roosevelt did not give a high priority to racial issues, in part because of the power exerted by southern Democratic legislators. Nevertheless, Roosevelt included in his administration people who did care deeply about racial issues. As his first term drew to a close, Roosevelt found that there was a de facto "black cabinet" of some thirty to forty advisers in government departments and agencies, people who were very concerned about racial issues and the plight of African Americans. Moreover, by 1936 many black voters were fast transferring their political loyalty from the Republicans (the "party of Lincoln") to the Democrats and would vote accordingly in the coming presidential election. But few southern blacks were able to vote during the 1930s. The preponderant majority of African Americans still lived in the eleven southern states of the former Confederacy, the most rural region in the nation, where blacks remained disenfranchised, segregated, and largely limited to farm work. As late as 1940, fewer than 5 percent of eligible African Americans were registered to vote.

## CULTURE IN THE THIRTIES

In view of the celebrated—if exaggerated—alienation felt by the "lost generation" of writers, artists, and intellectuals during the 1920s, one might have expected the onset of the Great Depression to have deepened their despair. Instead, it brought a renewed sense of militancy and affirmation, as if society could no longer afford the art-for-art's-sake outlook of the 1920s. Said one writer early in 1932: "I enjoy the period thoroughly. The breakdown of our cult of business success and optimism, the miraculous disappearance of our famous American complacency, all this is having a tonic effect." In the early 1930s, the "tonic effect" of commitment sometimes sparked revolutionary political activities. By the summer of 1932, even the "golden boy" of the "lost generation," the writer F. Scott Fitzgerald, had declared that "to bring on the revolution, it may be necessary to work within the Communist party." But few Americans remained Communists for long. Being a notoriously independent lot, most writers rebelled at demands to hew to a shifting party line. And many abandoned communism upon learning that the Soviet leader Joseph Stalin practiced a tyranny more horrible than anything under the czars.

LITERATURE AND THE DEPRESSION    Among the writers who addressed themes of immediate social significance during the 1930s, two novelists deserve special notice: John Steinbeck and Richard Wright. The single piece of fiction that best captured the ordeal of the Depression, Steinbeck's *The Grapes of Wrath* (1939), treats workers as people rather than just a variable in a political formula. Steinbeck had traveled with displaced "Okies" driven from the Oklahoma dust bowl to pursue the illusion of good jobs in the fields of California's Central Valley. This firsthand experience allowed him to create a vivid tale of the Joad family's painful journey west from Oklahoma.

Among the most talented of the young novelists emerging in the 1930s was Richard Wright, an African American born near Natchez, Mississippi. The grandson of former slaves and the son of a Mississippi sharecropper who deserted his family, Wright ended his formal schooling with the ninth grade (as valedictorian of his class). He then worked in Memphis and devoured books he borrowed on a white friend's library card, all the while saving up to go north to escape the racism of the segregated South. In Chicago, the Federal Writers' Project gave him a chance to develop his talent. His period as a Communist, from 1934 to 1944, gave him an intellectual framework that did not overpower his fierce independence. *Native Son* (1940), Wright's masterpiece, is the story of Bigger Thomas, a product of the ghetto, a man hemmed in, and finally impelled to murder, by forces beyond his control.

POPULAR CULTURE    While many writers and artists dealt directly with the human suffering and social tensions aroused by the Great Depression, the more popular cultural outlets, such as radio programs and movies, provided patrons with a welcome escape from the decade's grim realities. By the 1930s, radio had become a major source of family entertainment. In 1930, more than 10 million families owned a radio, and by the end of the decade the number had tripled. "There is radio music in the air, every night, everywhere," reported a San Francisco newspaper. "Anybody can hear it at home on a receiving set which any boy can put up in an hour." Franklin Delano Roosevelt was the first president to take full advantage of the popularity of radio broadcasting. He hosted sixteen "fireside chats" to generate public support for his New Deal initiatives.

In the late 1920s, what had been silent films were transformed by the introduction of sound. The "talkies" made movies by far the most popular form of entertainment during the 1930s—much more popular than they are today. The introduction of double features in 1931 and the construction of outdoor drive-in theaters in 1933 boosted interest and attendance. More than 60 percent of the population—70 million people—saw at least one movie each week.

The movies of the 1930s rarely dealt directly with hard times. Exceptions were the film version of *The Grapes of Wrath* (1940) and the classic documentaries of Pare Lorentz, *The Plow That Broke the Plains* (1936) and *The River* (1937). Much more popular were feature films intended for pure entertainment; they transported viewers from the daily deprivations of the

**The Marx Brothers**

In addition to their vaudeville antics, the Marx Brothers satirized social issues such as Prohibition.

Great Depression into the escapist realm of adventure, spectacle, and fantasy. People relished shoot-'em-up gangster films, animated cartoons, spectacular musicals (especially those starring dancers Fred Astaire and Ginger Rogers), "screwball" comedies, and horror films such as *Dracula* (1931), *Frankenstein* (1931), *The Mummy* (1932), *King Kong* (1933), *The Invisible Man* (1933), and *Werewolf of London* (1935).

But the best way to escape the daily troubles of the Depression was to watch one of the zany comedies of the Marx Brothers, former vaudeville performers turned movie stars. As one Hollywood official explained, the movies of the 1930s were intended to "laugh the big bad wolf of the depression out of the public mind." *The Cocoanuts* (1929), *Animal Crackers* (1930), and *Monkey Business* (1931) introduced moviegoers to the anarchic antics of Chico, Groucho, Harpo, and Zeppo Marx, who combined slapstick humor with verbal wit to create plotless masterpieces of irreverent satire.

## THE NEW DEAL MATURES

During Roosevelt's first year in office, his programs and his personal charm generated massive support. The president's travels and speeches, his twice-weekly press conferences, and his radio-broadcast fireside chats brought vitality and warmth in contrast to the aloofness of the Hoover White House. In the congressional elections of 1934, the Democrats increased their strength in both the House and the Senate, an almost unprecedented midterm victory for a party in power. Only seven Republican governors remained in office throughout the country. Yet while Democrats remained dominant, critics of various aspects of the New Deal began to emerge in both parties as well as within the Supreme Court. Roosevelt's opponents stressed that the economy, while stabilized, remained mired in the Depression. In 1935 Roosevelt responded to the situation by launching a second wave of New Deal legislation.

ELEANOR ROOSEVELT    One of the reasons for Roosevelt's unprecedented popularity was his wife, **Eleanor Roosevelt**, who had become an enormous political asset and would prove to be one of the most influential and revered leaders of the time. Born in 1884 in New York City, the niece of Theodore Roosevelt, Eleanor was barely eight years old when her mother died. Within two more years, her younger brother and her father, a chronic alcoholic, also died. Lonely and shy, she attended school in London before marrying Franklin, a distant cousin, in 1905. During the 1920s, Eleanor Roosevelt taught school and began a lifelong crusade on behalf of women, blacks, and youth. Her compassion resulted in part from the loneliness she had experienced as she was growing up and in part from the sense of betrayal she felt upon learning in 1918 that her husband was engaged in an extramarital affair with Lucy Mercer, her personal secretary. "The bottom dropped out of my own particular world," she recalled. Eleanor and Franklin resolved to maintain their marriage, but as their son James said, it became an "armed truce." In the face of personal setbacks, Eleanor Roosevelt forged an independent life. She "lived to be kind." Compassionate without being maudlin, more stoical than sentimental, she

**The First Lady**

An intelligent, principled, and candid woman, Eleanor Roosevelt became a political figure in her own right. Here she is serving as guest host for a radio program, ca. 1935.

exuded warmth and sincerity, and she challenged the complacency of the comfortable and the affluent. "No woman," observed a friend, "has ever so comforted the distressed or so distressed the comfortable."

Eleanor Roosevelt redefined the role of the First Lady. She was an outspoken activist: the first woman to address a national political convention, to write a nationally syndicated column, and to hold regular press conferences. A tireless advocate and agitator, Eleanor crisscrossed the nation, representing the president and the New Deal, defying local segregation ordinances to meet with African American leaders, supporting women's causes and organized labor, highlighting the plight of unemployed youth, and imploring people to live up to their egalitarian and humanitarian ideals. Eleanor Roosevelt also became her husband's most visible and effective liaison with many liberal groups, bringing labor organizers, women's rights activists, and African American leaders to the White House after hours and serving to deflect criticism of the president by taking progressive stands and running political risks he himself dared not attempt. He was the politician, she once remarked, and she was the agitator.

CRITICS    By the mid-1930s, the New Deal had stopped the economy's downward slide, but prosperity remained elusive. "We have been patient and long suffering," said a farm leader. "We were promised a New Deal. . . . Instead we have the same old stacked deck." Even more unsettling to conservatives was the dramatic growth of executive power and the emergence of welfare programs that led some people to develop a sense of entitlement to federal support programs. In 1934 a group of conservative businessmen and politicians, including Alfred E. Smith and John W. Davis, two former Democratic presidential candidates, formed the American Liberty League to oppose New Deal measures as violations of personal and property rights.

More potent threats to Roosevelt came from the hucksters of social panaceas. The most flamboyant of the group was Louisiana's "Kingfish," Senator **Huey P. Long**. A short, strutting man, cunning and ruthless, Long grew up within the rural revivalism of central Louisiana and fashioned himself into a theatrical political preacher (demagogue). He sported pink suits and pastel shirts, red ties, and two-toned shoes. Long was a brilliant but unscrupulous reformer driven by a compulsive urge for power and attention. First as Louisiana's governor, then as Louisiana's political boss and senator, Long viewed the state as his political fiefdom. True, he delivered to his constituents tax favors, roads, schools, free textbooks, charity hospitals, and better public services. But in the process, he became a bullying dictator who used bribery, intimidation, and blackmail to achieve his goals.

In 1933, Long arrived in Washington as a Democratic senator. He initially supported Roosevelt and the New Deal but quickly grew suspicious of the NRA's collusion with big business. Having developed his own presidential aspirations, he had also grown jealous of "Prince Franklin" Roosevelt's mushrooming popularity. To facilitate his presidential candidacy, Long devised his own populist plan for dealing with the Great Depression, which he called the **Share-the-Wealth** Society.

**"The Kingfish"**

Huey Long, governor of Louisiana. Although he often led people to believe he was a country bumpkin, Long was a shrewd lawyer and consummate politician.

Long proposed to confiscate large personal fortunes so as to guarantee every poor family a cash grant of $5,000 and every worker an annual income of $2,500, provide pensions to the aged, reduce working hours, pay veterans' bonuses, and ensure a college education for every qualified student. It did not matter to him that his projected budgets failed to add up or that his program offered little to stimulate an economic recovery. As he told a group of distressed Iowa farmers, "Maybe somebody says I don't understand it. Well, you don't have to. Just shut your damn eyes and believe it. That's all." Whether he had a workable plan or not, by early 1935 the charismatic Long was claiming that there were twenty-seven thousand Share-the-Wealth clubs scattered across the nation with 8 million supporters. Long was convinced that he could unseat Roosevelt. "I can take him," Long bragged. "He's a phony. . . . He's scared of me. I can outpromise him, and he knows it. People will believe me and they won't believe him."

Another popular social scheme critical of Roosevelt was hatched by a tall, gray-haired, mild-mannered California doctor, Francis E. Townsend. Outraged by the sight of three elderly women raking through garbage cans for scraps of food, Townsend called for government pensions for the aged. In 1934 he began promoting the Townsend Recovery Plan, which would pay $200 a month to every citizen over sixty who retired from employment and promised to spend the money within each month. The plan had the lure of providing financial security for the aged and stimulating economic growth by freeing up jobs for younger people. Critics noted that the cost of his program, which would serve 9 percent of the population, would be more than half the national income. Yet Townsend, like Long, was indifferent to details and balanced budgets. "I'm not in the least interested in the cost of the plan," he blandly told a House committee.

A third huckster of panaceas, Father Charles E. Coughlin, the Roman Catholic "radio priest," founded the National Union for Social Justice in 1935. In passionate broadcasts over the CBS radio network, he dismissed the New Deal as a Communist conspiracy and revived the old Populist scheme of coining vast amounts of silver to increase the money supply. His remarks grew more intemperate and anti-Semitic during 1936. Like Huey Long, Coughlin appealed to people who had lost the most during the Great Depression and were receiving the least benefits from the early New Deal programs.

Coughlin, Townsend, and Long were Roosevelt's most prominent critics. Of the three, Long had the widest following. A 1935 survey showed that he could draw over 5 million votes as a third-party candidate for president in 1936, perhaps enough to undermine Roosevelt's chances of reelection. Beset by pressures from both ends of the political spectrum, Roosevelt hesitated for months before deciding to "steal the thunder" from the left by instituting an array of new programs. "I'm fighting Communism, Huey Longism, Coughlinism, Townsendism," Roosevelt told a reporter in early 1935. He

**Promoters of welfare capitalism**

Dr. Francis E. Townsend, Rev. Gerald L. K. Smith, and Rev. Charles E. Coughlin (left to right) attended the Townsend Recovery Plan convention in Cleveland, Ohio.

needed "to save our system, the capitalist system," from such "crackpot ideas." Political pressures impelled Roosevelt to move to the left, but so did the growing influence within the administration of jurists Louis D. Brandeis and Felix Frankfurter. These powerful advisers urged Roosevelt to be less cozy with big business and to push for restored competition in the marketplace and heavy taxes on large corporations.

OPPOSITION FROM THE COURT   A series of Supreme Court decisions finally galvanized the president to act. On May 27, 1935, the Court killed the National Industrial Recovery Act (NIRA) by a unanimous vote. The defendants in *Schechter Poultry Corporation v. United States*, quickly tagged the "sick-chicken" case, had been convicted of selling an "unfit chicken" and violating other NIRA code provisions. The high court ruled that Congress had delegated too much power to the executive branch when it granted the code-making authority to the NRA. In addition, Congress had exceeded its power under the commerce clause by regulating intrastate commerce. The poultry in question, the Court decided, had "come to permanent rest within the state," although earlier it had been moved across state lines. In a press conference soon afterward, Roosevelt fumed: "We have been relegated to the horse-and-buggy definition of interstate commerce." The same line of conservative judicial reasoning, he warned, might endanger other New Deal programs—if he did not act swiftly.

THE SECOND NEW DEAL (1935–1936)　To rescue his legislative program from such judicial and political challenges, Roosevelt in January 1935 launched the second phase of the New Deal, explaining that "social justice, no longer a distant ideal, has become a definite goal" of his administration. No longer was the New Deal to be focused on generating economic recovery. It would also provide stability and security for the most vulnerable Americans. The president called on Congress to pass "must" legislation that included a new public works program to employ the jobless, banking reform, increased taxes on high incomes and inheritances, and programs to protect workers against the hazards of unemployment, old age, and illness. Roosevelt's aide Harry L. Hopkins told the cabinet: "Boys—this is our hour. We've got to get everything we want—a [public] works program, social security, wages and hours, everything—now or never."

Over the next three months, dubbed the Second Hundred Days, Roosevelt used all of his considerable charm and skills to convince the Congress to pass most of the **Second New Deal**'s "must" legislation. The results changed the face of American life. The first major initiative, the $4.8-billion Emergency Relief Appropriation Act, sailed through the new Congress. Roosevelt called it the "Big Bill" because it was the largest peacetime spending bill in history. It included an array of new federal job programs managed by a new agency, the Works Progress Administration (WPA), headed by Harry L. Hopkins, which replaced the FERA. Hopkins was told to create millions of jobs quickly, and as a result some of the new jobs appeared to be make-work or mere "leaning on shovels." Money was wasted, but by the time the WPA died, during World War II, it had left permanent monuments in the form of buildings, bridges, hard-surfaced roads, airports, and schools.

The WPA also employed a wide range of talented people in the Federal Theatre Project, the Federal Art Project, the Federal Music Project, and the **Federal Writers' Project**. Writers such as Ralph Ellison, John Cheever, and Saul Bellow found work writing travel guides to the United States, and Orson Welles directed the Federal Theatre Project's productions. Critics charged that these programs were frivolous, but Hopkins replied that writers and artists needed

### City Life

This mural, painted by WPA artist Victor Arnautoff, depicts a bustling New Deal–era street scene.

"to eat just like other people." The National Youth Administration (NYA), also under the WPA, provided part-time employment to students, set up technical training programs, and aided jobless youths. Twenty-seven-year-old Lyndon B. Johnson was director of an NYA program in Texas, and Richard M. Nixon, a penniless Duke University law student, found work through the NYA at 35¢ an hour. Although the WPA took care of only about 3 million out of some 10 million jobless at any one time, in all it helped some 9 million clients weather desperate times before it expired in 1943.

THE WAGNER ACT    Another major element of the Second New Deal was the National Labor Relations Act, often called the Wagner Act in honor of the New York senator, Robert F. Wagner, who drafted it and convinced a reluctant Roosevelt to support it. The Wagner Act was one of the most important pieces of labor legislation in history. It aggressively supported the rights of working-class Americans, guaranteeing workers the right to organize unions and bargain with management. It also prohibited employers from interfering with union activities. The Wagner Act also created a National Labor Relations Board of five members to certify unions as bargaining agents where a majority of the workers approved. The board could also investigate the actions of employers and issue "cease-and-desist" orders against specified unfair practices. Emboldened by the Wagner Act, unions organized more workers across the nation during the late 1930s. More than 70 percent of Americans surveyed in a 1937 Gallup poll said they favored unions. Yet many companies continued to thwart union activities in defiance of the Wagner Act.

SOCIAL SECURITY     As Francis E. Townsend stressed, the Great Depression hit older Americans and those with disabilities especially hard. To address the peculiar problems faced by the old, infirm, blind, and disabled, Roosevelt proposed the Social Security Act of 1935. It was, he announced, the Second New Deal's "cornerstone" and "supreme achievement." Indeed, it has proved to be the most significant and far-reaching of all the New Deal initiatives. The basic concept was not new. Progressives during the early 1900s had proposed a federal system of social security for the aged, indigent, disabled, and unemployed. Other nations had already enacted such programs, but the United States had remained steadfast in its tradition of individual self-reliance. The hardships caused by the Great Depression revived the idea of a social security program, however, and Roosevelt masterfully guided the legislation through Congress.

**Social Security**

A poster distributed by the government to educate the public about the new Social Security Act.

The Social Security Act, designed by Secretary of Labor Frances Perkins, included three major provisions. Its centerpiece was a self-financed "old age" pension fund for retired people over the age of sixty-five and their survivors. Beginning in 1937, workers and employers contributed payroll taxes to establish the fund. Roosevelt stressed that the pension program was not intended to guarantee a comfortable retirement; it was designed to supplement other sources of income and protect the elderly from some of the "hazards and vicissitudes of life." Only later did voters and politicians come to view Social Security as the *primary* source of retirement income for most of the aged.

The Social Security Act also set up a shared federal-state unemployment-insurance program, financed by a payroll tax on employers. In addition, the new legislation committed the national government to a broad range of social-welfare activities based upon the assumption that "unemployables"—people who were unable to work—would remain a state responsibility while the national government would provide work relief for the able-bodied. To that end, the law inaugurated federal grants-in-aid for three state-administered public-assistance programs—old-age assistance, aid to dependent children, and aid for the blind—and further aid for maternal, child-welfare, and public health services.

When compared with similar programs in Europe, the new Social Security system was conservative. It was the only government pension program in the world financed by taxes on the earnings of workers: most other countries funded such programs out of general revenues. The Social Security payroll tax was also a regressive tax: it entailed a single fixed rate for all, regardless of income level. It thus pinched the poor more than the rich, and it also impeded Roosevelt's efforts to revive the economy because it removed from circulation a significant amount of money: the new Social Security tax took money out of workers' pockets and placed it into a retirement trust fund, exacerbating the shrinking money supply that was one of the main causes of the Depression. By taking discretionary income away from workers, the government blunted the sharp increase in consumer spending needed to restore the health of the economy. In addition, the Social Security system initially excluded 9.5 million workers who most needed the new program: farm laborers, domestic workers, and the self-employed, a disproportionate percentage of whom were African Americans.

Roosevelt regretted the limitations of the Social Security Act, but he knew that they were necessary compromises in order to see the legislation through Congress and enable it to withstand court challenges. As he replied to an aide who criticized funding the pension program out of employee contributions:

> I guess you're right on the economics, but those taxes were never a
> problem of economics. They are politics all the way through. We put
> those payroll contributions there so as to give the contributors a

moral, legal, and political right to collect their pensions and their unemployment benefits. With those taxes in there, no damn politician can ever scrap my Social Security program.

Conservatives lambasted the Social Security Act as tyrannical. Herbert Hoover was among several Americans who initially refused to apply for a Social Security card because of his opposition to the federal government creating such a program. He was issued a number anyway.

SOAKING THE RICH    Another major bill making up the second phase of the New Deal was the Revenue Act of 1935, sometimes called the Wealth-Tax Act but popularly known as the soak-the-rich tax. The Revenue Act raised tax rates on annual income above $50,000. Estate and gift taxes also rose, as did the corporate tax rate. Business leaders fumed over Roosevelt's tax and spending policies. They railed against the New Deal and Roosevelt, whom they called a traitor to his own class. Conservatives charged that Roosevelt had moved in a dangerously radical direction. The newspaper editor William Randolph Hearst growled that the wealth tax was "essentially communism." Roosevelt countered by stressing that he had no love for socialism: "I am fighting communism. . . . I want to save our system, the capitalistic system." Yet he added that to save it from revolutionary turmoil required a more equal "distribution of wealth."

## ROOSEVELT'S SECOND TERM

THE ELECTION OF 1936    On June 27, 1936, Franklin Delano Roosevelt accepted the Democratic party's nomination for a second term. The Republicans chose Governor Alfred M. Landon of Kansas, a progressive Republican who had endorsed many New Deal programs. He was probably more liberal than most of his backers and clearly more so than the party's platform, which lambasted the New Deal for overextending federal power. The Republicans hoped that the followers of Long, Coughlin, Townsend, and other dissidents would combine to draw enough Democratic votes away from Roosevelt to throw the election to them. But that possibility faded when an assassin, the son-in-law of a Louisiana judge whom Huey Long had sought to remove, shot and killed the forty-two-year-old senator in 1935. In the 1936 election, Coughlin, Townsend, and a remnant of the Long movement supported Representative William Lemke of North Dakota on a Union party ticket, but it was a forlorn effort, polling only 882,000 votes.

**Campaigning for a second term**

Roosevelt campaigning with labor leader John L. Lewis (to the right of Roosevelt) and Marvin McIntyre (far right) in Wilkes-Barre, Pennsylvania.

In the 1936 election, Roosevelt carried every state except Maine and Vermont, with a popular vote of 27.7 million to Landon's 16.7 million, the largest margin of victory in history. Democrats would also dominate Republicans in the new Congress, by 77 to 19 in the Senate and 328 to 107 in the House.

In winning another landslide election, Roosevelt forged a new electoral coalition that would affect national politics for years to come. While holding the support of most traditional Democrats, North and South, the president made strong gains in the West among beneficiaries of New Deal agricultural programs. In the northern cities he held on to the ethnic groups helped by New Deal welfare measures. Many middle-class voters whose property had been saved by New Deal measures flocked to support Roosevelt, as did intellectuals stirred by the ferment of new ideas coming from the government. The revived labor union movement threw its support to Roosevelt. And in the most profound departure of all, African American voters for the first time cast the majority of their ballots for a Democratic president. "My friends, go home and turn Lincoln's picture to the wall," a Pittsburgh journalist told black voters. "That debt has been paid in full." The final tally in the 1936 election revealed that 81 percent of those with an income under $1,000 a year opted for Roosevelt, as did 79 percent of those earning between $1,000 and $2,000. By contrast, only 46 percent of those earning over $5,000 voted for Roosevelt. He later claimed that never before had wealthy business leaders been "so united against one candidate." They were "unanimous in their hate for me—and I welcome their hatred."

THE COURT-PACKING PLAN   Roosevelt's second inaugural address, delivered on January 20, 1937, promised even greater reforms. The challenge to democracy, he maintained, was that millions of citizens "at this very moment are denied the greater part of what the very lowest standards of today call the necessities of life. . . . I see one-third of a nation ill-housed, ill-clad, ill-nourished." Roosevelt argued that the election of 1936 had been a mandate for even more extensive government action. The overwhelming three-to-one Democratic majorities in Congress ensured the passage of new legislation to buttress the Second New Deal. But one major roadblock stood in the way: the conservative Supreme Court.

By the end of its 1936 term, the Supreme Court had ruled against New Deal programs in seven of the nine major cases it reviewed. Suits challenging the constitutionality of the Social Security and Wagner acts were pending. Given the conservative tenor of the Court, the Second New Deal seemed in danger of being nullified, just as much of the original New Deal had been.

For that reason, Roosevelt devised an ill-conceived and impolitic plan to change the Court's conservative stance by enlarging it. Congress, not the Constitution, determines the size of the Supreme Court, which at different times has numbered six, seven, eight, nine, and ten justices. In 1937, the number was nine. On February 5, 1937, Roosevelt sent his controversial plan to Congress, without having consulted congressional leaders. He wanted to create up to six new Supreme Court justices.

But the "Court-packing" maneuver, as opponents quickly tagged the president's scheme, backfired. It was a shade too contrived, much too brazen, and far too political. The normally pro-Roosevelt *New York World-Telegram* dismissed it as "too clever, too damned clever." A leading journalist said Roosevelt had become "drunk with power." Roosevelt's plan angered Republicans, but it also ran headlong into a deep-rooted public veneration of the courts and aroused fears among Democrats that a future president might use the precedent for quite different purposes.

As it turned out, unforeseen events blunted Roosevelt's clumsy effort to change the Court. A sequence of Court decisions during the spring of 1937

**Court packing**

An editorial cartoon commenting on Roosevelt's grandiose plan to enlarge the Supreme Court. He is speaking to Harold Ickes, director of the Public Works Administration.

reversed previous judgments in order to uphold disputed provisions of the Wagner and Social Security acts. In addition, a conservative justice resigned, and Roosevelt named to the vacancy one of the most consistent New Dealers, Senator Hugo Black of Alabama. But Roosevelt insisted on forcing his Court-packing bill through the Congress. On July 22, 1937, the Senate overwhelmingly voted it down. It was the biggest political blunder of Roosevelt's career. He later claimed he had lost the battle but won the war. The Court had reversed itself on important New Deal legislation, and the president was able to appoint justices in harmony with the New Deal. But the episode fractured the Democratic party and blighted Roosevelt's prestige. For the first time, Democrats in large numbers, especially southerners, opposed the president, and the Republican opposition found a powerful new issue to use against the administration. During the first eight months of 1937, the momentum of Roosevelt's 1936 landslide victory evaporated. As Secretary of Agriculture Henry A. Wallace later remarked, "The whole New Deal really went up in smoke as a result of the Supreme Court fight."

A NEW DIRECTION FOR UNIONS    Rebellions erupted on other fronts even while the Court-packing bill pended. Under the impetus of the New Deal, the dormant labor union movement stirred anew. When the National Industrial Recovery Act (NIRA) demanded that every industry code affirm the workers' right to organize a union, alert unionists quickly translated it to mean "the president wants you to join the union." John L. Lewis, head of the United Mine Workers (UMW), was among the first to exploit the pro-union spirit of the NIRA. He rebuilt the UMW from 150,000 members to 500,000 within a year. Spurred by Lewis's success, Sidney Hillman of the Amalgamated Clothing Workers and David Dubinsky of the International Ladies Garment Workers organized workers in the clothing industry. As leaders of industrial unions (composed of all types of workers in a particular industry), which were in the minority by far, they found the smaller, more restrictive craft unions (composed of skilled male workers only, with each union serving just one trade) to be obstacles to organizing workers in the country's basic industries.

In 1935, with the passage of the Wagner Act, the industrial unionists formed a Committee for Industrial Organization (CIO), and craft unionists began to fear submergence by the mass unions made up of unskilled workers. Jurisdictional disputes divided them, and in 1936 the American Federation of Labor (AFL) expelled the CIO unions, which then formed a permanent structure, called after 1938 the Congress of Industrial Organizations (also known by the initials CIO). The rivalry spurred both groups to greater efforts.

The CIO's major organizing drives in the automobile and steel industries began in 1936, but until the Supreme Court upheld the Wagner Act in 1937, companies failed to cooperate with its pro-unionist provisions. Employers used various forms of intimidation to fight the infant unions. Early in 1937 automobile workers spontaneously adopted a new technique, the "sit-down strike," in which workers refused to leave a workplace until employers had granted collective-bargaining rights to their union.

Led by the fiery young autoworker and union organizer Walter Reuther, thousands of employees at the General Motors assembly plants in Flint, Michigan, occupied the factories and stopped all production. Female workers supported their male counterparts by picketing at the plant entrances. Company

**Organized labor**

CIO picketers jeer as nonstriking workers enter a mill, 1941.

officials called in police to harass the strikers, sent spies to union meetings, and threatened to fire the workers. They also pleaded with President Roosevelt to dispatch federal troops. He refused, while expressing his displeasure with the sit-down strike, which the courts later declared illegal. The standoff lasted over a month. Then, on February 11, 1937, the company relented and signed a contract recognizing the fledgling United Automobile Workers (UAW) as a legitimate union. Other automobile manufacturers soon followed suit. And the following month, U.S. Steel capitulated to the Steel Workers Organizing Committee (later the United Steelworkers of America), granting the union recognition and its members a 10 percent wage hike and a forty-hour workweek.

The Wagner Act put the power of the federal government behind the principle of unionization. Roosevelt himself, however, had come late to the support of unions and sometimes took exception to their behavior. In the fall of 1937, he became so irritated with the warfare between the mercurial John L. Lewis and the Republic Steel Corporation that he pronounced "a plague on both your houses." In 1940, an angry Lewis would back the Republican presidential candidate, but he could not carry the labor vote with him. As more wage workers became organized, they more closely identified with the Democratic party. By August 1937 the CIO claimed over 3.4 million members, more than the AFL. The unions made a difference in the lives of workers and in the political scene. Through their efforts, wages rose and working conditions improved, and Roosevelt and the Democratic party were the beneficiaries of the labor movement. But unions made little headway in the South, where conservative Democrats and mill owners stubbornly opposed efforts to organize workers.

A SLUMPING ECONOMY  During the years 1935 and 1936, the depressed economy finally showed signs of revival. By the spring of 1937, industrial output had moved above the 1929 level. The prosperity of early 1937 was achieved largely through federal spending. But in 1937, Roosevelt, worried about federal budget deficits and rising inflation, ordered sharp cuts in government spending. The result was that the economy suddenly stalled and then slid into a business slump deeper than that of 1929. The Dow Jones stock average fell some 40 percent between August and October of 1937. By the end of the year, 4 million more people had been thrown out of work. When the spring of 1938 failed to bring economic recovery, Roosevelt asked Congress to adopt a new large-scale federal spending program, and Congress voted almost $3.3 billion in new expenditures. In a short time, the increase in spending reversed the economy's decline, but only during World War II would employment reach pre-1929 levels.

The Court-packing fight, the sit-down strikes, and the 1937 recession all undercut Roosevelt's prestige and power. When the 1937 congressional session ended, the only major new bills were the Wagner-Steagall National Housing Act and the Bankhead-Jones Farm Tenant Act. The Housing Act, developed by Senator Robert F. Wagner, set up the Housing Authority, which extended long-term loans to cities for public housing projects in blighted low-income neighborhoods. The agency also subsidized rents for poor people. Later, during World War II, it financed housing for workers in new defense plants.

The Farm Tenant Act addressed the epidemic of rural poverty. It created a new agency, the Farm Security Administration (FSA), that provided loans to shore up farm owners and prevent them from sinking into tenancy. It also made loans to tenant farmers to enable them to purchase their own farms. In the end, however, the FSA proved to be little more than another relief operation that tided a few farmers over during difficult times. A more effective answer to the problem eventually arrived in the form of national mobilization for war, which landed many struggling tenant farmers in military service or the defense industry, broadened their horizons, and taught them new skills.

In 1938, the Democratic Congress also enacted the Fair Labor Standards Act. For the first time in American history, the federal government established a minimum wage of 40¢ an hour and a maximum workweek of forty hours. The act, which applied only to businesses engaged in *interstate* commerce, also prohibited the employment of children under the age of sixteen.

## THE LEGACY OF THE NEW DEAL

SETBACKS FOR THE PRESIDENT    During the late 1930s, the Democratic party fragmented. Many southern Democrats balked at the national party's growing dependence on the votes of northern labor unions and African Americans. Profane, tobacco-chewing Ellison "Cotton Ed" Smith of South Carolina, the powerful chair of the Committee on Agriculture, and several other southern delegates walked out of the 1936 Democratic party convention, with Smith declaring that he would not support any party that views "the Negro as a political and social equal." Other critics believed that Roosevelt was exercising too much power and spending too much money. Some disgruntled southern Democrats drifted toward a coalition with conservative Republicans. By the end of 1937, a bipartisan conservative bloc had coalesced against the New Deal.

In 1938, the conservative opposition stymied an attempt by Roosevelt to reorganize the executive branch of the federal government, claiming that it would lead to dictatorship. Members of the opposition also secured drastic cuts in the undistributed-profits and capital-gains taxes to help restore business "confidence." That year the House of Representatives set up a Committee on Un-American Activities, chaired by Martin Dies of Texas, who took to the warpath against Communists. Soon he began to brand New Dealers as Communists. "Stalin baited his hook with a 'progressive' worm," Dies wrote in 1940, "and New Deal suckers swallowed the bait, hook, line, and sinker." As the political season of 1938 advanced, Roosevelt unfolded a new idea as momentous as the Court-packing plan: a proposal to reshape the Democratic party in the image of the New Deal. He announced his plan to intervene in state Democratic primaries as the party's national leader to ensure that his supporters were nominated in the state primaries. The effort backfired, however, and broke the spell of Roosevelt's invincibility, or what was left of it. As in the Court-packing fight, the president had risked his prestige while handing his adversaries a combustible issue to use against him. His opponents tagged his intervention in the primaries an attempt to "purge" the Democratic party of its southern conservatives; the word evoked visions of Adolf

Hitler and Joseph Stalin, tyrants who had purged their Nazi and Communist parties with blood.

The elections of November 1938 handed the administration another setback, partly a result of the friction among the Democrats. Roosevelt had failed in his efforts to liberalize the party by ousting southern conservatives. The Democrats lost seats in both the House and the Senate, and the president now headed a divided party. In his State of the Union message in 1939, Roosevelt for the first time proposed no new reforms but spoke of the need "to invigorate the process of [economic] recovery, in order to *preserve* our reforms." The conservative coalition of Republicans and southern Democrats had stalemated the Roosevelt juggernaut. As one observer noted, the New Deal "has been reduced to a movement with no program, with no effective political organization, with no vast popular party strength behind it."

A HALFWAY REVOLUTION    The New Deal had petered out in 1939 just as war was erupting in Europe and Asia, but it had wrought several enduring changes. By the end of the 1930s, the power of the national government was vastly larger than it had been in 1932, and hope had been restored to many people who had grown disconsolate. But the New Deal entailed more than just bigger government and revived public confidence; it also constituted a significant change from the older liberalism embodied in the progressivism of Theodore Roosevelt and Woodrow Wilson. Those reformers, despite their sharp differences, had assumed that the function of progressive government was to use aggressive *regulation* of industry and business to ensure that people had an equal opportunity to pursue their notions of happiness.

Franklin Delano Roosevelt and the New Dealers went beyond this concept of regulated capitalism by insisting that the government not simply *respond* to social crises but also take positive steps to *avoid* them and their social effects. To this end, the New Deal's various benefit programs sought to ensure a minimum level of well-being for all Americans. The New Deal had established basic qualitative standards for labor conditions and public welfare and helped middle-class Americans hold on to their savings, their homes, and their farms. The protection afforded by bank-deposit insurance, unemployment pay, and Social Security pensions would come to be universally accepted as a safeguard against future depressions.

In implementing his domestic program, Roosevelt steered a zigzag course between the extremes of unregulated capitalism and socialism. The first New Deal experimented for a time with a managed economy under the NRA but abandoned that experiment for a turn toward enforcing competition and increasing government spending. The greatest failure of the New Deal was its inability to restore economic prosperity and end record levels of unemployment. In 1939, 10 million Americans—nearly 17 percent of the workforce—remained jobless. Only the prolonged crisis of World War II would finally produce full employment.

Roosevelt's pragmatism was his greatest strength—and weakness. Impatient with political theory and at heart a fiscal conservative, he was flexible in developing policy: he kept what worked and discarded what did not. The result was, paradoxically, both profoundly revolutionary and profoundly conservative. Roosevelt sharply increased the regulatory powers of the federal government and laid the foundation for what would become an expanding welfare system. New Deal initiatives left a legacy of unprecedented social welfare innovations: a joint federal-state system of unemployment insurance; a compulsory, federally administered retirement system; financial support for families with dependent children, maternal and child-care programs, and several public health programs. The New Deal also improved working condi-

### Meeting of the anti–New Dealers

Senator Ellison D. "Cotton Ed" Smith of South Carolina cringes at the thought of a fourth term for Roosevelt, while meeting with fellow anti–New Dealers at the Mayflower Hotel in Washington.

tions and raised wage levels for millions of laborers. Despite what his critics charged, however, Roosevelt was no socialist; he sought to preserve the basic capitalist structure. In the process of such bold experimentation and dynamic preservation, the New Deal represented a "halfway revolution" that permanently altered the nation's social and political landscape.

# End of Chapter Review

## CHAPTER SUMMARY

- **Stabilizing the Economy** In March 1933, the economy, including the farm sector, was shattered, and millions of Americans were without jobs and the most basic necessities of life. Franklin Delano Roosevelt and his "brain trust" of advisers set out to restore confidence in the economy by propping up the banking industry and providing short-term emergency relief for the unemployed, promoting industrial recovery, and raising commodity prices by encouraging farmers to cut back on production.

- **The New Deal** Initially, most of the New Deal programs were conceived as temporary relief and recovery efforts. They eased hardships but did not restore prosperity. It was during the Second New Deal that major reform measures, such as Social Security and the Wagner Act, reshaped the nation's social structure.

- **New Deal Criticisms** Some conservatives criticized the New Deal for violating personal and property rights and for steering the nation toward socialism. Some liberals believed that the measures did not tax the wealthy enough to provide the aged and disadvantaged with adequate financial security.

- **Federal Expansion** The New Deal expanded the powers of the national government by establishing regulatory bodies and laying the foundation of a social welfare system. The federal government would in the future regulate business and provide social welfare programs to avoid social and economic problems.

- **Culture of the 1930s** The literature of the 1930s turned away from the alienation from materialism that characterized the literary works of the previous decade's "lost generation." John Steinbeck and Richard Wright, for example, realistically depicted ordinary people living in, and suffering through, extraordinary times. Radio comedies and the new "talking" movies allowed people to escape their daily troubles.

## CHRONOLOGY

| | |
|---|---|
| March 1933 | Congress passes the Emergency Banking Relief Act |
| March 1933 | Congress passes the Beer-Wine Revenue Act |
| March 1933 | Congress establishes the Civilian Conservation Corps |
| May 1933 | Congress creates the Tennessee Valley Authority |
| June 1933 | Congress establishes the Federal Deposit Insurance Corporation |
| November 1933 | Congress creates the Civil Works Administration |
| 1935 | President Roosevelt creates the Works Progress Administration |
| 1935 | Congress passes the Wagner Act |
| 1937 | Social Security goes into effect |
| 1939 | John Steinbeck's *Grapes of Wrath* is published |
| 1940 | Richard Wright's *Native Son* is published |

## KEY TERMS & NAMES

Franklin Delano Roosevelt p. 1101

Twenty-first Amendment p. 1102

First New Deal p. 1103

Agricultural Adjustment Act p. 1105

Dust Bowl p. 1106

National Industrial Recovery Act p. 1107

National Recovery Administration p. 1107

Eleanor Roosevelt p. 1120

Huey P. Long p. 1122

Share-the-Wealth program p. 1122

Second New Deal p. 1125

Federal Writers' Project p. 1125

# 28

## THE SECOND WORLD WAR

FOCUS QUESTIONS      Ⓢ    wwnorton.com/studyspace

- What were the major events leading up to the outbreak of war in Europe and in Asia?
- What effect did the Second World War have on American society?
- How did the Allied forces win the war in Europe?
- How did the United States gain the upper hand in the Pacific sphere?
- What efforts did the Allies make to shape the postwar world?

The unprecedented efforts of Franklin Delano Roosevelt and the New Dealers to end the Great Depression did not restore prosperity or return the economy to full employment. In 1940, over 14 percent of Americans remained jobless. That changed dramatically with American involvement in the Second World War. Within months after the surprise Japanese attack on Pearl Harbor in December 1941, Roosevelt mobilized all of the nation's resources to win the battle against fascism and imperialism. Of course, the horrible war did much more than revive the economy. It changed the direction and shape of world history and transformed America's role in international affairs.

### FROM ISOLATIONISM TO INTERVENTION

Like Woodrow Wilson, Roosevelt had little experience or interest in international affairs when first elected president. In his 1933 inaugural address, he allocated only a sentence to foreign relations. The United States remained comfortable with its isolationism from international political turmoil. However, an important initiative occurred in November 1933 when Roosevelt broke precedent with his Republican predecessors and officially recognized the Soviet Union in hopes of stimulating trade with the communist nation. That he did so in the face of a scolding from his mother testified to his courage. Overall, however, the prolonged Depression forced Roosevelt to adopt a low-profile foreign policy limited to the promotion of trade and disarmament agreements. As had happened with Woodrow Wilson, the course of world events would eventually force him to shift from isolationism to intervention.

THE GOOD NEIGHBOR POLICY    Roosevelt announced in his 1933 inaugural address that he would continue the efforts of Herbert Hoover to promote what he called "the **policy of the good neighbor**" in the Western Hemisphere. That same year, at the Seventh Pan-American Conference, the United States supported a resolution declaring that no nation "has the right to intervene in the internal or external affairs of another." True to this noninterventionist commitment, the Roosevelt administration oversaw the final withdrawal of U.S. troops from Nicaragua and Haiti, and in 1934 the president negotiated with Cuba a treaty that dissolved the Platt Amendment and thus ended the last formal American claim to a right to intervene in Latin America. By refusing to intervene in Latin American countries, however, Roosevelt indirectly gave legitimacy and support to several dictators in the unstable region. In referring to the authoritarian rule of Anastasio Somoza García in Nicaragua, Roosevelt revealed a pragmatism tinged with cynicism: "He may be a son of a bitch, but he's *our* son of a bitch."

## FOREIGN CRISES

While the Roosevelt administration was grappling with the economic depression and its social effects, ominous foreign crises began to engage American attention and concern. Germany and Italy emerged during the 1930s as fascist nations bent on foreign conquest. At the same time, halfway around the world, in Asia, Japan increasingly fell under the control of militarists who were convinced that the entire continent should be governed by their "ruling race."

ITALY AND GERMANY    The rise of the Japanese militarists paralleled the rise of totalitarian dictators in Italy and Germany. Despotism thrives during periods of economic distress and political unrest, and during the 1920s and 1930s mass movements led by demagogues appeared throughout Europe. In 1922, the bombastic journalist **Benito Mussolini** had seized power in Italy. Fascism, both in Italy and in Germany, was driven by a determined minority willing to use violence as a political tool. By 1925, Mussolini was wielding dictatorial power as "Il Duce" (the Leader). All opposition political parties were eliminated. "Mussolini is always right," screamed propaganda posters.

There was always something ludicrous about the strutting, chest-thumping Mussolini. Italy, after all, was a declining industrial power whose performance in World War I was a national embarrassment. Germany was another matter, however, and there was nothing amusing about Mussolini's German counterpart, **Adolf Hitler**. His strange transformation during the 1920s from failed artist and social misfit to head of the **National Socialist German Workers' (Nazi) party** startled the world. The global Depression offered Hitler the opportunity to portray himself as the nation's messianic savior. He was a fanatical ideologue, ruthless racist, and magnetic speaker who believed that leadership required exciting the masses through intense emotional speeches. He would lie, he explained, and make his lies big "because in the big lie there is always a certain force of credibility." It was a barbaric strategy, but Hitler believed it was necessary to overthrow the old order and create a new German empire. As he proclaimed, "We want to be barbarians! It is an honorable title. We shall rejuvenate the world."

Made chancellor on January 30, 1933, five weeks before Franklin Delano Roosevelt was first inaugurated, Hitler banned all political parties except for the Nazis. He then took the title "der Führer" (the sole and supreme national leader), assumed absolute power in 1934, and demanded "unconditional obedience" from the army and the people. There would be no more elections, no more political parties, no more labor unions, no strikes. A young German soldier attended one of Hitler's "spectacle" speeches and reported that he had never heard a more "brilliant orator." Hitler's "magnetic personality is irresistible." Throughout the 1930s, Hitler's brutal Nazi police state cranked up the engines of tyranny and terrorism, propaganda and censorship. Brown-shirted "storm troopers" fanned out across the nation, burning books, sterilizing or euthanizing the disabled, and persecuting Communists and Jews, whom Hitler blamed for Germany's troubles. In 1933, Hitler pulled Germany out of the League of Nations and threatened to extend control over all the German-speaking peoples in central Europe.

**THE EXPANDING AXIS**   As the 1930s unfolded, a catastrophic chain of events in Asia and Europe sent the world hurtling toward disaster. In

**Axis leaders**

Mussolini and Hitler in Munich, June 1940.

1934, Japan renounced the Five-Power Treaty and began an aggressive military build-up in anticipation of expanding its control in Asia. The next year, Mussolini launched Italy's conquest of Ethiopia in eastern Africa. In 1935 Hitler, in explicit violation of the Versailles Treaty, announced he was revitalizing Germany's armed forces. The next year, he again brazenly violated the Versailles Treaty by sending thirty-five thousand troops, with drums beating and flags flying, into the Rhineland, the demilitarized buffer zone between France and Germany. The French failed to summon the courage to oust the German force. Although the Nazi action violated America's separate peace treaty with Germany of 1921, no one in the Roosevelt administration condemned the Nazi incursion. Roosevelt, in fact, went fishing. The failure of France, Great Britain, and the United States to enforce the provisions of the Versailles Treaty convinced Hitler that the western democracies were unwilling to thwart his aggressive plans. Hitler admitted that his show of force was a theatrical bluff: "If the French had marched into the Rhineland, we would have had to withdraw with our tail between our legs."

The year 1936 also witnessed the outbreak of the Spanish Civil War, which began when Spanish troops loyal to General Francisco Franco and other right-wing officers, with the support of the Roman Catholic Church, revolted against the new democratically elected government. Hitler and Mussolini rushed troops ("volunteers"), warplanes, and massive amounts of military and financial aid to support Franco's fascist insurgency.

At the same time that fascism was on the march across Europe, Japanese imperialists were on the move again in China. On July 7, 1937, Japanese and Chinese troops clashed at the Marco Polo Bridge, west of Beijing. The incident quickly developed into a full-scale war. By December, the Imperial

Keeping in mind the terms of the Treaty of Versailles, explain why Hitler began his campaign of expansion by invading the Rhineland and the Sudetenland. Why would Hitler have wanted to retake the Polish Corridor? Why did the attack on Poland begin World War II, whereas Hitler's previous invasions of his European neighbors did not?

**July 1937**

Japanese troops enter Beijing after the clash at the Marco Polo Bridge.

Japanese Army had captured the Nationalist Chinese capital of Nanjing, whereupon the undisciplined soldiers ran amok in a predatory frenzy, looting the city and murdering and raping large numbers of Chinese. Tens of thousands (perhaps as many as three hundred thousand) civilians were murdered in what came to be called the Rape of Nanjing.

Meanwhile, the peace of Europe was unraveling. In 1937, Italy joined Germany and Japan in establishing the Rome-Berlin-Tokyo "Axis." Having rebuilt German military power, the Austrian-born Hitler forced the *Anschluss* (union) of Austria with Germany in March 1938. Paralyzed with fear of another world war, British and French leaders sought to "appease" Hitler by signing the notorious Munich Pact on September 30, 1938. Without the consent of the Czech government, the British and French transferred the Sudeten territory in Czechoslovakia to Germany. The mountainous Sudetenland along the German border hosted over 3 million ethnic Germans. However, it also contained seven hundred thousand Czechs and was vital to the defense of Czechoslovakia.

Having promised that the Sudetenland was his last territorial demand, Hitler violated his pledge on March 15, 1939, when he sent German tanks and soldiers to conquer the remainder of Czechoslovakia. Hitler triumphantly paraded through a sullen Prague in triumph. Yet despite such provocative actions, the European democracies cowered in the face of Hitler's ruthless behavior. **Winston Churchill**, who would become the British prime minister in 1940, described the Munich Pact as "a defeat without a war." It marked the "culminating failure of British and French foreign policy and diplomacy over several years." The Munich Pact, he predicted, would not end Hitler's aggressions. "This is only the beginning of the reckoning."

DEGREES OF NEUTRALITY   Most Americans during the 1930s, including both Republicans and Democrats, responded to the mounting global crises by deepening their commitment to isolationism. As a Minnesota senator declared in 1935, "To hell with Europe and the rest of those nations!" The isolationist mood was reinforced by a Senate inquiry into the role of bankers and munitions makers in the American decision to enter World War I. Chaired by Senator Gerald P. Nye of North Dakota, the committee concluded in 1937 that bankers and munitions makers had made scandalous profits from the war. The implication was that arms traders and bankers (the "merchants of death") had spurred American intervention in the European conflict and were still at work promoting wars for profit.

During the 1930s, the United States moved toward complete isolation from the quarrels of Europe. In 1935, President Roosevelt signed the first of several neutrality laws intended to prevent the kind of entanglements that had drawn the United States into World War I. The Neutrality Act of 1935 prohibited Americans from traveling on ships owned by nations at war. It also forbade the sale of arms and munitions to any "belligerent" nation whenever the president proclaimed that a state of war existed abroad.

On October 3, 1935, when Italy invaded Ethiopia, Roosevelt invoked the Neutrality Act. One shortcoming in the law became apparent right away: the law did not cover trade in war-related materials. For example, Italy did not need to buy weapons abroad, but it did need to buy crucial supplies, such as oil, steel, and copper, which the Neutrality Act did not cover. So the sanctions imposed under the Neutrality Act had no deterrent effect on Mussolini's war machine. In the summer of 1936, Italy conquered mineral-rich Ethiopia. "At last," a gloating Mussolini exclaimed, "Italy has her empire."

When Congress reconvened in 1936, it revised the Neutrality Act by forbidding loans to nations at war. Although the Spanish Civil War involved a fascist military uprising against an elected government, Roosevelt accepted the French and British position that the western democracies should not intervene. The strong bloc of pro-Franco Catholics in America, who worried that the left-wing Spanish republic was a secular threat to the Church, also influenced Roosevelt's decision. Indeed, during the brutal civil war, Spanish anarchists and Communists ran amok ("the

Red Terror"), burning churches and killing thousands of priests, nuns, and monks. Several thousand Americans volunteered to fight on the side of the Spanish republic in what came to be called the Abraham Lincoln Brigade. That the conflict in Spain was technically not a "foreign war" led Roosevelt to ask Congress in January 1937 to revise the neutrality laws to apply to *civil* wars (he later called his action a "grave mistake"). The United States and the other western democracies then stood by as Hitler and Mussolini sent combat planes, tanks, and soldiers to Spain in support of General Franco's overthrow of democracy, which was completed in 1939, leaving almost a million Spaniards dead.

In the spring of 1937, the Congress passed another neutrality law. The Neutrality Act of 1937 allowed the president to require that goods other than arms or munitions exported to warring nations be sold on a cash-and-carry basis (that is, a nation would have to pay cash and then carry the U.S. goods away in its own ships). This was intended to preserve a profitable trade with combatants without running the risk of war.

The new law faced its first test in July 1937, when Japanese and Chinese forces clashed in China. Since neither Japan nor China officially declared war, Roosevelt was able to avoid invoking the neutrality law because its net effect would have favored the Japanese and penalized the supply-dependent Nationalist Chinese. Then, on December 12, 1937, Japanese planes sank the U.S. gunboat *Panay*, which had been lying at anchor in China, on the Yangtze River, prominently flying the American flag. The sinking of the *Panay* generated few calls for retaliation in the United States. In fact, a Texas Congressman said the incident should lead to the withdrawal of U.S. forces from Asia. "We should learn that it is about time to mind our own business."

Roosevelt, however, was not so sure that the United States could keep its back turned on an increasingly turbulent world. In October 1937, he delivered a speech in Chicago, the heartland of isolationism, in which he called for international cooperation to "quarantine the aggressors" disturbing world peace. But his appeal for a broader American role in world affairs fell flat in the Congress and across the nation. A survey revealed that 70 percent of Americans wanted all U.S. citizens to be removed from China in order to prevent a possible incident from triggering warfare.

The isolationist mood in the United States peaked in 1938 when Indiana Congressman Louis Ludlow proposed a constitutional amendment that would have required a public referendum for a declaration of war except in the case of an attack on U.S. territory. After intense lobbying from the White House against the proposal, the Ludlow Amendment barely failed to pass by

**Neutrality**

A 1938 cartoon shows U.S. foreign policy entangled by the serpent of isolationism.

a vote of 209 to 188. The close vote revealed how deeply isolationist senti- ment was ingrained in American thought during the Great Depression. That the proposed amendment was defeated also revealed that Roosevelt was growing increasingly concerned about the need to contain the aggressive militarism displayed by Japan and Germany.

## WAR CLOUDS

During the late 1930s, war clouds thickened over Asia and Europe. After Adolf Hitler's troops brazenly occupied Czechoslovakia in 1939, Franklin Delano Roosevelt abandoned his neutral stance. Hitler and Mus- solini could no longer be ignored. They were "madmen" who "respect force and force alone." Throughout late 1938 and 1939, Roosevelt sought to edu- cate Americans about the growing menace of fascism. He also convinced Congress to increase military spending in anticipation of a possible war.

THE CONQUEST OF POLAND  Meanwhile, the insatiable Hitler had set his sights on Poland, Germany's eastern neighbor. Hitler had long dreamed of Germany acquiring *Lebensraum,* or living space—territory in eastern Europe that would enable Germany to expand its empire. Modern Poland had existed only for twenty years; it had been created by the Treaty of Versailles that ended the First World War. Now it was about to be gobbled up again by predatory neighbors. To ensure that the Soviet Union did not interfere with his plans to conquer Poland, Hitler, on August 23, 1939, contradicted his frequent denunciations of communism and signed a Nazi-Soviet Non-Aggression Pact with Soviet premier **Joseph Stalin**, in which the two totalitarian tyrants secretly and cynically agreed to divide up northern and eastern Europe between them. It was perhaps the most astonishing event of an astonishing decade. A few days later, on the evening of August 31, 1939, the German secret police (*Gestapo*) entered a German concentration camp, grabbed an unsuspecting prisoner, and took him to a radio station near the Polish border. There they dressed him in a Polish army uniform and shot him. The *Gestapo* then concocted a propaganda story claiming that Poles had attacked Germany, thereby giving Hitler his pretext for attacking. At dawn on September 1, 1939, 1.5 million German troops with thousands of tanks and armored vehicles invaded Poland from the north, south, and west. Hitler ordered his armies "to kill without mercy men, women, and children of the Polish race or language."

This was the final straw. Having allowed Czechoslovakia to be gobbled up by Hitler's war machine, Britain and France now did an about-face and honored their commitment to go to war if Poland were invaded. On September 3, 1939, Europe, the world's smallest continent, again lapsed into widespread warfare. But it would take weeks for the British and French to mobilize large armies, in part because they were not eager for an offensive war, hoping against hope that the mere declaration of war would cause Hitler to pull back. They were wrong; the Germans massacred the Poles. Sixteen days after German troops moved across the Polish border, the Soviet Union invaded Poland from the east. Pressed from all sides, the large but poorly equipped Polish army (many of them fought on horseback) surrendered, having suffered seventy thousand deaths. On October 6, 1939, the Nazis and Soviets divided Poland between them. Thereafter, both the Nazis and the Soviets arrested, deported, enslaved, or murdered over 2 million Poles.

**U.S. NEUTRALITY**  President Roosevelt responded to the outbreak of war in Europe by proclaiming U.S. neutrality. However, the president would not, like Woodrow Wilson had done in 1914, ask Americans to remain neutral in thought because "even a neutral has a right to take account of the facts." In September, Roosevelt summoned Congress into special session to revise the Neutrality Act. "I regret the Congress passed the Act," the president said. "I regret equally that I signed the Act." Under the Neutrality Act of 1939, Britain and France were allowed to send their own freighters to the United States and buy military supplies.

American public opinion supported such measures. "What the majority of the American people want," wrote the editors of the *Nation*, "is to be as un-neutral as possible without getting into war." After the quick German conquest of Poland, the war in Europe settled into a stalemate during early 1940 that began to be called "the phony war." What lay ahead, it seemed, was a long war of attrition in which Britain and France would have the resources to outlast Hitler. That illusion lasted through the winter before being shattered by new German assaults.

## THE STORM IN EUROPE

*BLITZKRIEG*   In the spring of 1940, the winter's long *Sitzkrieg* (sitting war) suddenly erupted into **Blitzkrieg** (lightning war) featuring carefully coordinated columns of fast-moving German tanks, motorized artillery, and truck-borne infantry, all supported by warplanes. At dawn on April 9, without warning, Nazi armies occupied Denmark and landed along the Norwegian coast. Denmark fell in a day, Norway within a few weeks. On May 10, German forces invaded neutral Belgium, Luxembourg, and the Netherlands (Holland). A British army sent to help the Belgians and the French was forced to make a frantic retreat to the coast. The Germans then missed an opportunity to inflict a crushing defeat on the beleaguered Allies. On May 21, Hitler inexplicably ordered the fast-moving German armored units to stop, rest, and refuel. Furious German generals complied, thereby enabling the British to organize a desperate evacuation of British and French soldiers from the beaches at Dunkirk, on the northern French coast near the border with Belgium. The British government enlisted every available boat, from warship to tug to yacht. Amid the chaos, some 338,000 desperate soldiers escaped to England on over a thousand ships and small boats, barges, and ferries, leaving behind vast stockpiles of vehicles, weaponry, and ammunition. Winston Churchill called the rescue effort a "miracle of deliverance." Allowing the Allied forces to escape proved to be the first of many strategic errors that would cost Germany a victory in the Second World War.

Meanwhile, German forces cut the French armies to pieces and spread panic throughout the civilian population. On June 14, 1940, the German swastika flag flew over Paris. Eight days later, French leaders surrendered to Hitler in the same railroad car in which Germans had been forced to surrender in 1918. It was the greatest military victory in German history. The Germans established a puppet French government in Vichy to manage the vanquished nation and implement its own anti-Jewish policies. "The war is won," Hitler told Mussolini. "The rest [conquest of Great Britain and the Soviet Union] is only a matter of time."

THE DEBATE OVER AMERICA'S ROLE   The rapid collapse of France stunned everyone, including the Germans. Great Britain now stood alone facing Hitler's triumphant war machine, but in Parliament the pugnacious new prime minister, Winston Churchill, breathed defiance. He vowed that the British people would confront Hitler's menace with "blood, toil, tears, and sweat." The British would "go on to the end," he said; "we shall never surrender." Instead, "we shall fight on and on forever and ever and ever." If the independence of Great Britain were to end, Churchill growled, "let it end only when each one of us lies choking in his own blood on the ground."

As Hitler prepared to unleash his air force against Britain, the United States seemed suddenly vulnerable, and it was in no condition to wage world war if attacked. After World War I, the U.S. Army had been reduced to a small force; by 1939 it numbered only 175,000 and ranked sixteenth in the world in size, just behind Romania. It would take time to create a viable military force to stop fascism. President Roosevelt called for a precautionary military build-up and the production of 50,000 combat planes a year. In response to Churchill's desperate appeal for military supplies, Roosevelt promised to provide all possible "aid to the Allies short of war."

The world crisis transformed Roosevelt. Having been stalemated for much of his second term by growing congressional opposition, he was revitalized by the urgent need to stop Nazism in Europe. In June 1940 the president set up the National Defense Research Committee to coordinate military research, including a top-secret effort to develop an atomic bomb. The famous physicist Albert Einstein, a Jewish Austrian refugee from Nazism, had alerted Roosevelt in the fall of 1939 that the Germans were trying to create atomic bombs, leading the president to take action. The Manhattan Project launched an alliance between scientific research and the U.S. military that would blossom into what Dwight D. Eisenhower would call the "military-industrial complex." The effort to develop an atomic bomb was so secretive that few members of Congress or the Roosevelt administration knew about it.

The fall of France in late June 1940 was a devastating blow that left Great Britain standing alone against the Nazi onslaught, just as the British had stood alone against the menace of Napoleon in 1805. Late summer of 1940

**The Blitz**

In London, St. Paul's Cathedral looms above the destruction wrought by German bombs during the Blitz. Winston Churchill's response: "We shall never surrender."

brought the desperate Battle of Britain. During August the Germans gained control of all of western Europe, and Hitler began preparations for an invasion of Britain. His first priority was to destroy the British air force, just as the Germans had done to the Polish, Dutch, Belgian, and French air forces. In July and August, the numerically superior German Air Force (*Luftwaffe*) launched daily bombing raids against military targets—ships and naval bases, warplanes and airfields—across southeast England in preparation for an invasion across the English Channel from Nazi-controlled France.

The British Royal Air Force (RAF), with the benefit of radar, a new technology, surprised the world by fending off the German air assault. Hitler then ordered the German bombers to change tactics and target factories, civilians, and cities (especially London) in massive nighttime raids designed to break British morale. His decision backfired. In what came to be called "the Blitz," during September and October of 1940, the Germans caused massive destruction in Britain's major cities. Waves of German bombers, escorted by hordes of fighter planes, crossed the English Channel. On some days, a thousand German and British planes were locked in combat over British cities. The raids killed some forty-three thousand British civilians. But the Blitz enraged rather than deflated the British people at the same time that British warplanes were destroying large numbers of German fighters and bombers (1,300 between July and October). The British success in the air proved to be a decisive turning point in the war. In October 1940, Hitler was forced to postpone his planned invasion of the British Isles. If the Germans had destroyed the RAF, they could have invaded and conquered Great Britain. Instead, Great Britain, with growing assistance from the United States, became an increasingly powerful threat to Germany's western flank.

German submarine attacks on British ships, meanwhile, strained the resources of the battered Royal Navy. To address the challenge, Churchill and Roosevelt negotiated an executive agreement by which fifty "overaged" U.S. destroyers went to the British in return for allowing the U.S. to build naval and air bases on British islands in the Caribbean. Roosevelt explained the bold action as necessary for defense of the "American hemisphere." The stakes rose considerably when, on September 16, Roosevelt signed the first peacetime conscription in American history, requiring the registration of all 16 million men aged twenty-one to thirty-five.

**"The Only Way We Can Save Her [Democracy]"**

Political cartoon suggesting the U.S. not intervene in European wars.

The rapidly shifting state of global affairs prompted vigorous debate between "internationalists," who believed America's security demanded aid to Britain, and isolationists, who charged that Roosevelt was drawing the United States into another European war. In 1940, internationalists organized the nonpartisan Committee to Defend America by Aiding the Allies. On the other hand, isolationists, mostly Republicans, formed the America First Committee. The isolationists argued that the war involved, in Idaho Senator William E. Borah's words, "nothing more than another chapter in the bloody volume of European power politics." Borah and others predicted that a Nazi victory over Great Britain, while distasteful, would pose no threat to America's security.

ROOSEVELT'S THIRD TERM    In the midst of the terrible news from Europe, the 1940 presidential campaign dominated public attention. In June, just as France was falling to Germany, the Republicans nominated a dark-horse candidate, Wendell L. Willkie of Indiana, a plain-spoken corporate lawyer who as a former Democrat had voted for Roosevelt in 1932 and had remained registered as a Democrat until 1938. At the July Democratic convention in Chicago, Roosevelt easily won the nomination for a third term.

Through the summer of 1940, Roosevelt focused on urgent matters of defense and diplomacy rather than making campaign trips. Willkie warned that

Roosevelt was a "warmonger," predicting that "if you re-elect him you may expect war in April, 1941." To this Roosevelt responded, "I have said this before, but I shall say it again and again and again: Your boys are not going to be sent into any foreign wars." In November Roosevelt, buoyed by near universal support among labor unionists and northern blacks, won an unprecedented third term by a comfortable margin of 27 million votes to Willkie's 22 million and by a more decisive margin, of 449 to 82, in the Electoral College.

THE "ARSENAL OF DEMOCRACY"   A reelected Roosevelt moved quickly to provide even more military aid to Britain, whose cash was running out. Since direct American loans to the British government were prohibited by the Johnson Debt Default Act of 1934, the president created an ingenious device to supply British needs: the lend-lease program. The **lend-lease bill**, introduced in Congress on January 10, 1941, authorized the president to lend or lease military equipment to "any country whose defense the President deems vital to the defense of the United States." After the war ended, the loaned equipment would be returned to the United States. Roo-

### Lend-lease

Members of the "Mother's Crusade," urging defeat of the lend-lease program, kneel in prayer in front of the Capitol. They feared the program would bring the United States into the European war.

sevelt explained to Congress that the lend-lease program was "like lending your neighbor a garden hose when his house is on fire." But isolationists were furious. Senator Robert A. Taft of Ohio, an ardent isolationist, argued that "lending war equipment is a good deal like lending chewing gum; you wouldn't want it back when it was through." For two months, a bitter debate over the lend-lease bill raged in Congress and across the country. Isolationists saw it eventually forcing the nation into the European conflict. But the president had his way in Congress. Lend-lease became law in March, prompting Roosevelt to announce that it represented "the end of any attempts at appeasement. . . ." Most of the dissenting votes in Congress were Republicans from the staunchly isolationist Midwest.

While the nation debated neutrality, the European war expanded. Italy had officially entered the war in June 1940 as Germany's ally. In the spring of 1941, German troops joined Italian forces in Libya, forcing the British army in North Africa to withdraw to Egypt. In April 1941, Nazi forces overwhelmed Yugoslavia and Greece. With Hungary, Romania, and Bulgaria forced into the Axis fold, Hitler controlled nearly all of Europe. But his ambition was unbounded.

At 3:15 A.M. on June 22, 1941, without warning, massive German armies suddenly invaded the Soviet Union, their supposed ally. Despite numerous warnings from Soviet officials, Stalin had willfully refused to prepare for such an event. A supremely confident Hitler planned to destroy communism, enslave the vast population of the Soviet Union, and exploit its considerable natural resources. As a German officer explained, the invasion of Russia was a renewal of the "old fight of German against Slav, the defense of European culture against the Muscovite-Asiatic flood, and the repulse of Jewish Bolshevism." The war "must have as its goal the destruction of today's Russia—and for this reason it must be conducted with unprecedented harshness." The goal of Hitler's "Operation Barbarossa" was to "annihilate the enemy completely and utterly." Hitler also assumed that once Russia was conquered, Great Britain would sue for peace.

Hitler's decision to attack the Soviet Union was the defining event of the European war. For years, he had gambled on the indecision and weakness of his enemies, and repeatedly he had been proven right. Attacking the Soviet Union, however, would prove to be Hitler's greatest mistake. Initially, however, his surprise attack succeeded. Joined by Romanian and Finnish allies, the Nazis massed 3.6 million troops and thousands of tanks and planes along the 1,800-mile front from the Arctic Ocean to the Black Sea. It was the largest invasion force in European history. The German armies raced across western Russia; entire Soviet armies were surrounded and destroyed. The

German army commander claimed that "the Russian campaign has been won in the space of two weeks." He spoke too soon.

For four months the Soviets retreated in the face of the German blitzkrieg. In those four months, German forces occupied six hundred thousand square miles of Russian territory and captured 3 million Soviet troops, besieging Leningrad (formerly St. Petersburg) and threatening Moscow. The German invaders had conquered an area three times the size of France. The scale and brutality of the war on the Eastern Front were mind-boggling. When the Germans conquered the city of Kiev, some six hundred thousand Soviet troops surrendered. Stalin flirted with the idea of surrender before deciding that the Soviets would make a desperate last stand at Moscow, Leningrad, and Sevastopol. The siege of Leningrad lasted for nine hundred days and killed seven hundred and fifty thousand civilians, many of whom starved to death after the Germans surrounded the city. During the Battle of Moscow, Russian defenders executed eight thousand civilians because of "cowardice". Gradually, the Russians slowed the Nazi advance. Then, during the winter of 1941–1942, Hitler's lightly clad legions began to learn the bitter lesson the Russians had taught Napoleon and the French army in 1812. Invading armies must contend with the brutal Russian winter (temperatures of -20 degrees Fahrenheit) and Russian tenacity. Over one hundred thousand German soldiers died of frostbite.

Prime Minister Winston Churchill had already decided to offer British support to the Soviet Union in case of such an attack, for the Russians, so long as they held out against the Nazis, helped to ensure the survival of Britain. Roosevelt adopted the same pragmatic policy, offering U.S. aid to the Soviet Union. American supplies were now indispensable to Europe's defense. To deliver massive aid to Britain and the Soviet Union, convoys of supply ships had to maneuver through German submarine "wolf packs" in the North Atlantic. In April 1941, Roosevelt informed Churchill that the U.S. Navy would extend its patrols in the North Atlantic nearly all the way to Iceland in an effort to deter German submarine attacks.

In August 1941, Roosevelt and Churchill held a secret meeting off Newfoundland, where they drew up a joint statement of "common principles" known as the **Atlantic Charter**. It pledged that after the "final destruction of the Nazi tyranny" the victors would promote the self-determination of all peoples, economic cooperation, freedom of the seas, and a new system of international security. By September, eleven anti-Axis nations, including the Soviet Union, had endorsed the charter.

Thus Roosevelt had led the United States into a joint statement of war aims with the anti-Axis powers. It was not long before shooting incidents involved American ships in the North Atlantic. On October 17, 1941, while the destroyer *Kearny* was attacking German submarines, it was hit by a German torpedo, and eleven lives were lost. Two weeks later, a German submarine sank the destroyer *Reuben James,* with a loss of 115 seamen. The sinking spurred Congress to change the 1939 Neutrality Act by repealing the bans on arming merchant vessels and allowing them to enter combat zones and the ports of nations at war. Step by step, the United States had given up neutrality and embarked on naval warfare against Nazi Germany. Still, Americans hoped to avoid taking the final step into all-out war. The decision to go to war would be made in response to aggression in an unexpected quarter—Hawaii.

## THE STORM IN THE PACIFIC

JAPANESE AGGRESSION   After the Nazi victories in Europe during the spring of 1940, U.S. relations with Japan took a turn for the worse. In 1940, Japan and the United States began a series of moves, each of which aggravated the other and pushed the two nations closer to war. During the summer, Japan forced the helpless Vichy French government, now under German control, to permit the construction of Japanese airfields in French-controlled northern Indochina and to cut off the railroad into south China. The United States responded with the Export Control Act of July 2, 1940, which authorized the president to restrict the export of munitions and other strategic materials to Japan. Gradually, Roosevelt extended embargoes on aviation gas, scrap iron, and other supplies.

On September 27, 1940, the Tokyo government signed a Tripartite Pact with Nazi Germany and Fascist Italy, by which each pledged to declare war on any nation that attacked any of them. On April 13, 1941, Japan signed a non-aggression pact with the Soviet Union. When Germany invaded the Soviet Union in June, the Japanese were freed of any threat from the north—at least for a while.

In July 1941, Japan announced that it was taking control of French Indochina. Roosevelt took three steps in response: he froze all Japanese assets in the United States, he restricted oil exports to Japan (the United States was then producing half of the world's oil), and he merged the armed forces of the Philippines with the U.S. Army and put their commander, General Douglas MacArthur, in charge of all U.S. forces in east Asia. Forced by the American embargo to secure other oil supplies, the Japanese army and navy began planning attacks on the Dutch and British colonies in the South Pacific.

Actions by both sides put the United States and Japan on a collision course leading to a war that neither wanted. In his talks with the Japanese ambassador in Washington, Secretary of State Cordell Hull demanded that Japan withdraw its forces from French Indochina and China as the price of renewed trade with the United States. Prime Minister Fumimaro Konoe, while known as a man of democratic principles who preferred peace, caved in to pressures from the militarists. Perhaps he had no choice. Whatever the case, the Japanese warlords seriously misjudged the United States when they decided that the U.S. Navy was a threat to their expansionist ambitions and must be destroyed.

Why did the Japanese want to control French Indochina and the Dutch East Indies? Why did Japan sign the Tripartite Pact with Germany and Italy?

THE ATTACK ON PEARL HARBOR   Late in August 1941, Japanese Prime Minister Konoe proposed a meeting with President Roosevelt. Soon afterward, on September 6, Japanese military leaders secretly approved a surprise attack on U.S. bases in Hawaii and gave Konoe six weeks in which to reach a settlement. In October, Konoe urged War Minister Hideki Tōjō to consider withdrawal of Japanese forces in China while saving face by keeping some troops in north China. General Tōjō refused. Konoe resigned on October 15; Tōjō became prime minister the next day. The war party had now assumed control of the Japanese government, and Tōjō viewed war with the United States as inevitable.

On November 20, a Japanese official presented Secretary of State Cordell Hull with Tōjō's final proposal: Japan promised to occupy no more territory in Asia if the United States would cut off aid to China and restore trade with Japan. On November 26, Hull insisted that Japan withdraw from China altogether. Tōjō, who had expected the United States to refuse the demands, ordered a powerful fleet of Japanese warships to begin steaming secretly toward Hawaii, crowded with U.S. military installations, including Pearl Harbor, the massive naval base. The naval commander, Admiral Isoroku Yamamoto, said his audacious plan was an all-or-nothing gamble "conceived in desperation" to destroy the U.S. Pacific fleet, while Japanese armies invaded British Malaya and the Dutch East Indies, both of which were rich in supplies of rubber and oil. He knew that the Japanese could not defeat the United States in a long war; their only hope was "to decide the fate of the war on the very first day."

Officials in Washington, believing that war was imminent, sent warnings to U.S. commanders in the Pacific that the Japanese might attack somewhere in the southwest Pacific. But no one expected that Japan would launch a surprise attack five thousand miles away, at Hawaii's Pearl Harbor on the island of Oahu. In the early morning of December 7, 1941, low-flying Japanese planes began bombing the unsuspecting American fleet at Pearl Harbor. Of the eight American battleships, all were sunk or disabled, along with eleven other ships. At airfields on the island, the Japanese bombers destroyed 180 American planes. The raid, which lasted less than two hours, killed more than 2,400 American servicemen and civilians and wounded nearly 1,200 more.

The surprise attack fulfilled the dreams of its planners, but it fell short of success in two ways. The Japanese bombers ignored the onshore maintenance facilities and oil tanks in Hawaii that supported the U.S. fleet, without which the surviving ships might have been forced back to the West Coast, and they missed the American aircraft carriers that had left port a few days earlier. In the naval war to come, aircraft carriers would prove to be the decisive weapon.

**The attack on Pearl Harbor**

This view from an army airfield shows the destruction brought on by the surprise attack.

In a larger sense, the Japanese attack on Pearl Harbor was a spectacular miscalculation. It aroused the Americans to wage total war until a devastated Japan surrendered.

   With one stroke at Pearl Harbor on December 7, the Japanese had silenced America's debate on neutrality. People boiled over in vengeful fury as the United States was yanked into the Second World War. The next day, President Roosevelt, calm, composed, and determined, delivered his war message to Congress: "Yesterday, December 7, 1941—a date which will live in infamy—the United States of America was suddenly and deliberately attacked by naval and air forces of the Empire of Japan." Congress voted for the war resolution with near unanimity, the sole exception being Representative Jeannette Rankin, a Montana pacifist who refused to vote for war in 1917 or 1941. On December 11, Germany and Italy declared war on what Hitler called the "half Judaized and the other half Negrified" United States, a nation that he insisted "was not dangerous to us." The separate wars that were being waged by armies in Asia, Europe, and Africa had become one global conflict, shattering American isolationism.

# A WORLD WAR

The Japanese attack on Pearl Harbor embroiled the United States in a global conflict that would transform the nation's social and economic life, as well as its position in international affairs. The Second World War would become the most destructive conflict in history; over 50 million deaths resulted from the war, two thirds of them civilians. The fighting was so terrible in its intensity and obscene in its cruelties that it altered the nature of war itself. The warring nations developed powerful new weapons—plastic explosives, rockets, napalm, jet airplanes, and atomic bombs—and systematic genocide emerged as an explicit war aim of the Nazis. The scorching passions of such an all-out war encouraged horrific excesses. The Nazis murdered up to 6 million Jewish civilians and many others. Racist propaganda flourished on both sides, and seething hatred of the enemy led to the torture and execution of many military and civilian prisoners. The physical destruction was unprecedented, leveling whole cities, dismembering nations, and transforming societies. Many decades later, the world is still coping with the war's consequences.

SETBACKS IN THE PACIFIC   The United States had declared war on December 8, but the nation was woefully unprepared to wage a world war against what Roosevelt called the "forces of savagery and barbarism." The army and navy were understaffed and underequipped. And it would take months for the economy to make the transition to full-scale military production. Yet time was of the essence. Japanese and German forces were on the move. For months after the attack on Pearl Harbor, the news from the Pacific was "all bad," as President Roosevelt confessed. In quick sequence, the Japanese captured numerous Allied outposts before the end of December 1941: Guam and Wake Islands, the Gilbert Islands, and Hong Kong. "Everywhere in the Pacific," said Winston Churchill, "we were weak and naked."

In the Philippines, U.S. forces and their Filipino allies, outmanned, outgunned, and malnourished, surrendered in the early spring of 1942. On April 10, the Japanese gathered some twelve thousand captured American troops along with sixty-six thousand Filipinos and forced them to march sixty-five miles in six days up the Bataan peninsula. Already underfed, ravaged by tropical diseases, and provided with little food and water, the prisoners of war were brutalized in what came to be known as the Bataan Death March. Those who fell out of line were bayoneted or shot. Others were beaten, stabbed, or shot for no reason. Over ten thousand of the prisoners of war died along the way. News of the Bataan Death March outraged Americans and helps explain the Pacific war's ferocious emotional intensity.

**Early defeats**

U.S. prisoners of war, captured by the Japanese in the Philippines, 1942.

By the summer of 1942, Japan had seized control of a vast new Asian empire and was on the verge of assaulting Australia when Japanese naval leaders succumbed to what one admiral called "victory disease." Intoxicated with easy victories and lusting for more conquests, they pushed on into the South Pacific, intending to isolate Australia, and strike again at Hawaii. A Japanese mistake and a stroke of American luck enabled the U.S. Navy to frustrate the plan, however. The U.S. aircraft carriers that were luckily at sea during the Japanese attack on Pearl Harbor spent several months harassing Japanese outposts. Their most spectacular exploit, an air raid on Tokyo itself, was launched on April 18, 1942. B-25 bombers took off from the carrier *Hornet* and, unable to land on its deck, proceeded to China after dropping their bombs over Tokyo. The raid caused only token damage but did much to lift American morale amid a series of defeats elsewhere.

CORAL SEA AND MIDWAY   During the spring of 1942, U.S. forces finally halted the Japanese advance toward Australia in two key naval battles. The Battle of the Coral Sea (May 7–8, 1942) stopped a Japanese fleet convoying troops toward New Guinea. Planes from the *Lexington* and the *Yorktown* sank one Japanese carrier, damaged another, and destroyed smaller ships. American losses were greater, but the Japanese threat against Australia was repulsed.

Less than a month after the Coral Sea engagement, Admiral Yamamoto steered his armada for Midway, the westernmost of Hawaii's inhabited islands, from which he hoped to render Pearl Harbor helpless. This time it was the Japanese who were the victims of surprise. Working night and day deciphering some fifty thousand five-digit numerical groups, American cryptanalysts ("codebreakers") had broken the Japanese military communications code. This breakthrough reshaped the balance of power in the Pacific war. Admiral Chester Nimitz, commander of the U.S. central Pacific fleet, now learned from intercepted Japanese messages where Yamamoto's fleet was heading. He reinforced the American base at tiny Midway Island with planes and aircraft carriers.

The first Japanese foray against Midway, on June 4, 1942, severely damaged the island's defenses, but at the cost of about a third of the Japanese planes. American bombers struck back, sinking three aircraft carriers, and badly damaging a fourth that was later sunk by a torpedo; it was the first defeat for the Japanese navy in 350 years and the turning point of the Pacific war. It blunted Japan's military momentum, eliminated the threat to Hawaii, demonstrated that aircraft carriers, not battleships, were the decisive elements of modern naval warfare, and bought time for the United States to mobilize its massive industrial productivity for a wider war. Japanese hopes for a short, decisive war were dashed at the crucial Battle of Midway.

## MOBILIZATION AT HOME

A NATION AT WAR   American entry into the war ended not only the long public debate on isolation and intervention but also the long economic Depression. The Japanese attack on Pearl Harbor triggered an unprecedented mobilization of America's human, physical, and financial resources as the entire economy was harnessed to the war effort. Winning the war against Germany and Japan would require all of the nation's immense industrial capacity and full employment of the workforce. On December 18, 1941, Congress passed the War Powers Act, which gave the president far-reaching authority to reorganize and create government agencies, regulate business and industry, and even censor mail and other forms of communication. With the declaration of war, men between the ages of eighteen and forty-five were drafted. At one time or another between 1941–1945, some 16 million men and several hundred thousand women were in the military. The average soldier or sailor who served in the war was 26 years old, stood five feet eight, and weighed 144 pounds, an inch taller and eight pounds heavier than the typical recruit in World War I.

ECONOMIC CONVERSION   The War Production Board, created in 1942, directed the conversion of industrial manufacturing to war production. In 1941, more than 3 million automobiles were manufactured in the

United States; only 139 were built during the next four years. Instead of cars, the automobile plants began making tanks and airplanes. President Roosevelt wanted to confront the enemy with a "crushing superiority of equipment." To do so, he established staggering military production goals: sixty thousand warplanes in 1942 and twice as many the following year, fifty-five thousand anti-aircraft guns, and tens of thousands of tanks. Military-related production skyrocketed from 2 percent of the nation's economic production in 1939 to 40 percent in 1943. "Something is happening that Hitler doesn't understand," announced *Time* magazine in 1942. ". . . . It is the miracle of production."

FINANCING THE WAR    To cover the war's huge cost, Congress passed the Revenue Act of 1942 (also called the Victory Tax). It raised tax rates and increased the number of taxpayers. Whereas in 1939 only about 4 million people (about 5 percent of the workforce) filed tax returns, the new act made virtually everyone (75 percent) a taxpayer. By the end of war, 90 percent of workers were paying income tax. Tax revenues covered about 45 percent of military costs from 1939 to 1946; the government borrowed the rest. In all, by the end of the war the national debt was six times what it had been at the start of the war.

The size of the federal government soared along with its budget during the war. The number of federal workers grew from one million to four million. Throughout the economy, jobs were suddenly plentiful. The nation's unemployment rate plummeted from 14 percent in 1940 to 2 percent in 1943. Millions of people who had lived on the margins of the economic system, especially women, were now brought fully into the economy. Stubborn pockets of poverty did not disappear, but for most civilians, especially those who had earlier lost their jobs and homes to the Depression, the war spelled a better life than ever before, despite the rationing of various consumer items.

ECONOMIC CONTROLS    The war raised fears of inflation as consumer goods grew scarce. In 1942, Congress authorized the Office of Price Administration to set price ceilings. With prices frozen, basic goods had to be allocated through rationing, with coupons doled out for sugar, coffee, gasoline, automobile tires, and meat. The government promoted patriotic frugality with a massive public relations campaign that circulated posters with slogans such as "Use it up, wear it out, make it do, or do without." Businesses and workers chafed at the wage and price controls. On occasion the government seized industries threatened by strikes. Despite these problems the government effort to stabilize wages and prices succeeded. By the end of the war, consumer prices had risen about 31 percent, a record far better than the World War I rise of 62 percent.

DOMESTIC       CONSERVATISM
Despite government efforts to promote
patriotic sacrifice among civilians, discontent with price controls, labor shortages, rationing, and other petty grievances
spread. In the 1942 congressional elections, Republicans gained forty-six seats
in the House and nine in the Senate.
Democratic losses outside the "Solid
South" strengthened the conservative
southern delegation's position within the
party. During the 1940s, a bipartisan
coalition of conservatives dismantled
"nonessential" New Deal agencies such as
the Work Projects Administration (originally the Works Progress Administration), the National Youth Administration,
the Civilian Conservation Corps, and the
National Resources Planning Board.

**War-effort advertisement**

The Office of War Information
created the ad's slogan in 1943.

   Organized labor, despite substantial gains during the war, felt the impact
of the conservative trend. In the spring of 1943, when John L. Lewis led the
coal miners out on strike, Congress passed the Smith-Connally War Labor
Disputes Act, which authorized the government to seize plants and mines
useful to the war effort. In 1943 a dozen states adopted laws restricting picketing and other union activities, and in 1944 Arkansas and Florida set in
motion a wave of "right-to-work" legislation that outlawed the closed shop
(requiring that all employees be union members).

## SOCIAL EFFECTS OF THE WAR

   In making the United States the "great arsenal of democracy," the Roosevelt administration transformed the economy into the world's most efficient military machine. By 1945, the year the war ended, the United States
would be manufacturing fully half of the goods produced in the world. Such
an economic miracle transformed American society.

MOBILIZATION IN THE WEST AND SOUTH   The dramatic expan-
sion of military production after 1940 and the recruitment of millions of people into the armed forces and defense industries triggered rapid growth in the

western states. The Far West experienced the fastest rate of urban growth in the country. Nearly 8 million people moved into the states west of the Mississippi River between 1940 and 1950. The migration of workers to new defense jobs in the West had significant demographic effects. Lured by news of job openings and higher wages, African Americans from Texas, Oklahoma, Arkansas, and Louisiana headed west. During the war years, Seattle's African American population jumped from four thousand to forty thousand, Portland's from two thousand to fifteen thousand.

The South also experienced dramatic social changes as a result of the war effort. Sixty of the one hundred new army camps created during the war were in southern states. The construction of military bases and the influx of new personnel transformed the local economies. The demand for military uniforms provided a boon to southern textile mills. Manufacturing jobs led tens of thou-

**Changing focus**

With mobilization for war as the nation's priority, many New Deal programs were allowed to expire.

sands of "dirt poor" sharecroppers and tenant farmers, many of them African Americans, to leave the land and gain a steady wage working in mills and factories. Throughout the United States during the Second World War, the rural population decreased by 20 percent.

CHANGING ROLES FOR WOMEN    The war marked an important watershed in the status of women. With millions of men going into military service, the demand for civilian workers shook up old prejudices about sex roles in the workplace—and in the military. Nearly two hundred thousand women served in the **Women's Army Corps** (WAC) and the navy's equivalent, Women Accepted for Volunteer Emergency Service (WAVES). Others joined the Marine Corps, the Coast Guard, and the Army Air Force. Over 6 million women entered the workforce during the war, an increase of more than 50 percent overall and in manufacturing alone an increase of some 110 percent. One striking feature of the new labor scene was the proportion of older, married women in the workforce. In 1940 about 15 percent of married women were gainfully employed; by 1945 about 24 percent were. Many men opposed the trend. A disgruntled male legislator asked what would happen to traditional domestic tasks if women flocked to factories: "Who will do the cooking, the washing, the mending, the humble homey tasks to which every woman has devoted herself; who will rear and nurture the children?" Many women, however, were eager to get away from the grinding routine of domestic life. A female welder remembered that her wartime job "was the first time I had a chance to get out of the kitchen and work in industry and make a few bucks. This was something I had never dreamed would happen."

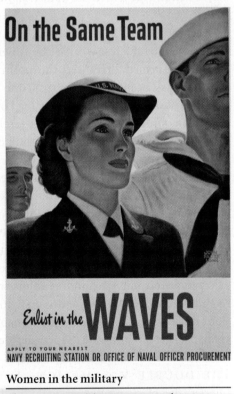

**Women in the military**

This navy-recruiting poster urged women to join the WAVES (Women Accepted for Volunteer Emergency Service).

AFRICAN AMERICANS IN THE SECOND WORLD WAR
Although Americans found themselves fighting against the explicit racial
and ethnic bigotry promoted by fascism and Nazism, racism in the United
States did not end during the war. The Red Cross, for example, initially
refused to accept blood donated by blacks, and the president of North American
Aviation announced that "we will not employ Negroes." Blacks who
were hired often were limited to the lowest-paid, lowest-skilled jobs.

Some courageous black leaders refused to accept such racist practices. In
1941, A. Philip Randolph, the head of the Brotherhood of Sleeping Car
Porters, planned a march on Washington, D.C., to demand an end to racial
discrimination in defense industries. To fend off the march, the Roosevelt
administration struck a bargain. The Randolph group called off its demonstration
in return for a presidential order that forbade discrimination in
defense industries. More than a half million African Americans left the
South for better opportunities during the war years, and more than a million
blacks nationwide joined the industrial workforce for the first time.

AFRICAN AMERICANS IN UNIFORM   The most volatile social
issue ignited by the war was African American participation in the military.
In 1941, the armed forces were the most racially polarized institution in the
nation. But African Americans rushed to enlist after the Japanese attack on
Pearl Harbor. As African American Joe Louis, the world heavyweight boxing
champion, stressed, "Lots of things [are] wrong with America, but Hitler
ain't going to fix them." About a million African Americans—men and
women—served in the armed forces during the war, but in racially segregated
units. Black soldiers and sailors were initially excluded from combat
units and relegated to menial tasks. Black officers also could not command
white soldiers or sailors. Henry L. Stimson, the secretary of war, cavalierly
claimed that "leadership is not embedded in the negro race." Every army
camp and navy base had segregated facilities—and frequent and sometimes
bloody racial "incidents." Among the most famous African American servicemen
were some six hundred pilots trained in Tuskegee, Alabama. The
so-called **Tuskegee Airmen** ended up flying more than fifteen thousand missions
during the war. Their unquestionable excellence spurred military and
civilian leaders to integrate the armed forces after the war.

THE DOUBLE V CAMPAIGN   In 1942, the editors of the *Pittsburgh
Courier,* the black newspaper with the largest national circulation, urged
African Americans to promote civil rights while also supporting the war effort.
It was called the Double V campaign because the newspaper published two

**Tuskegee Airmen, 1942**

One of the last segregated military training schools, the flight school at Tuskegee trained African American men for air combat during the Second World War.

interlocking Vs with the theme "Democracy: Victory at Home, Victory Abroad." The campaign encouraged blacks to support the war effort while fighting for civil rights and racial equality at home. The Double V campaign also demanded that African Americans who were risking their lives abroad receive full citizenship rights at home. As the newspaper explained, the Double V campaign represented a "two-pronged attack" against those who would enslave "us at home and those who abroad would enslave us. WE HAVE A STAKE IN THIS FIGHT. . . . WE ARE AMERICANS TOO!" The editors stressed that no one should interpret their "militant" efforts on behalf back civil rights "as a plot to impede the war effort. Negroes recognize that the first factor in the survival of this nation is the winning of the war. But they feel integration of Negroes into the whole scheme of things 'revitalizes' the U.S. war program." The response among the nation's black community to the *Courier*'s Double V campaign was "overwhelming." The *Courier* was swamped with telegrams and letters of support supporting the public relations campaign. Double V clubs sprouted across the nation. Other black newspapers across the nation joined the effort to promote the values at home that American forces were defending abroad.

Throughout the war, African Americans highlighted the irony of the United States fighting against racism abroad while tolerating racism at home. "The army is about to take me to fight for democracy," a Detroit draftee said,

**Victory at Home, Victory Abroad**

The *Pittsburgh Courier* sparked a national "Double V" campaign to fight for democracy abroad, in the war effort, and for democracy at home, in civil rights and racial equality.

"but I would [rather] fight for democracy right here." During the summer of 1943 alone there were 274 race-related incidents in almost 50 cities. In Detroit, growing racial tensions on a hot afternoon sparked incidents at a park that escalated into a full-fledged riot. Fighting raged through June 20 and 21, until federal troops arrived on the second evening. By then, twenty-five blacks and nine whites had been killed, and more than seven hundred people had been injured.

MEXICANS AND MEXICAN AMERICANS    As rural dwellers moved to the western cities during the war, many farm counties experienced a labor shortage. In an ironic about-face, local and federal government authorities who before the war had forced undocumented Mexican laborers back across the border now recruited them to harvest crops on American farms. Before it would provide the needed workers, however, the Mexican government insisted that the United States ensure minimum working and living conditions for the migrant farm workers. The result was the creation of the *bracero* program in 1942, whereby the Mexican government, eager to gain favor in the United States, agreed to provide seasonal farm workers to the southwestern states in exchange for a series of promises by the U.S. government: the bracero workers would not be used as strike breakers or as a pretext for lowering wages, and they would not be drafted into military service. The workers were hired on yearlong contracts, and American officials provided transportation from the border to their job sites. The United States also pledged to set aside ten percent of the wages to enable bracero workers to buy farm equipment upon their return to Mexico. Under the bracero program, some two hundred thousand Mexican farm workers entered the western United States. They provided much needed labor, but the United States rarely fulfilled its promises to them.

The rising tide of Mexican Americans in Los Angeles prompted a growing stream of anti-Mexican editorials and ugly racial incidents. Even though some three hundred thousand Mexican Americans served in the war with great valor, earning a higher percentage of Congressional Medals of Honor than any other minority group, racial prejudices still prevailed. There was constant conflict between Anglo servicemen and Mexican American gang members or teenage "zoot-suiters" in southern California. (Zoot suits were the flamboyant attire popular in the 1940s and worn by some young Mexican American men.) In 1943, several thousand off-duty sailors and soldiers, joined by hundreds of local whites, rampaged through downtown Los Angeles streets, assaulting Hispanics, African Americans, and Filipinos. The weeklong violence came to be called the zoot-suit riots.

NATIVE AMERICANS    Indians supported the war effort more fully than any other group in American society. Almost a third of eligible Native American men served in the armed forces. Many others worked in defense-related industries. Thousands of Indian women volunteered as nurses or joined the WAVES. As was the case with African Americans, Indians benefited from the experiences afforded by the war. Those who left reservations to work in defense plants or to join the military gained new vocational skills as well as a greater awareness of mainstream society and how to succeed within it.

Why did so many Native Americans fight for a nation that had stripped them of their land and decimated their heritage? Some felt that they had no choice. Mobilization for the war effort ended many New Deal programs that had provided Indians with jobs. Reservation Indians thus faced the necessity of finding new jobs elsewhere. Many viewed the Nazis and the Japanese warlords as threats to their own homeland. The most common sentiment, however, seems to have been a genuine sense of patriotism. Whatever the reasons, Indians distinguished themselves in the military. Unlike their African

**Marine Navajo "code talkers"**

The Japanese were never able to break the Native Americans' codes used by signalmen, such as those shown here during the Battle of Bougainville in 1943.

American counterparts, Indian servicemen were integrated into regular units. Perhaps the most distinctive activity performed by Indians was their service as "code talkers": every military branch used Indians, especially Navajos, to quickly encode and decipher messages using ancient Indian languages unknown to the Germans and Japanese.

DISCRIMINATION AGAINST JAPANESE AMERICANS    The attack on Pearl Harbor ignited vengeful anger toward people of Japanese descent living in the United States, known as Nisei. As Idaho's governor declared, "A good solution to the Jap problem would be to send them all back to Japan, then sink the island." Such extreme hostility helps explain why the U.S. government sponsored the worst violation of civil liberties during the twentieth century when more than 112,000 Nisei were forcibly removed from their homes on the West Coast and transported to "war relocation camps" in the interior. President Roosevelt initiated the removal of Japanese Americans (he called them "Japs") when he issued Executive Order 9066 on February 19, 1942. More than 60 percent of the internees were U.S. citizens; a third were under the age of nineteen. Forced to sell their farms and businesses at great losses, the internees lost not only their property but also their liberty. Few if any were disloyal, but all were victims of fear and racial prejudice. Not until 1983 did the government acknowledge the injustice of the internment policy. Five years later it granted those Nisei still living $20,000 each in compensation, a tiny amount relative to what they had lost during four years of confinement.

**Internment**

This young Japanese American and her parents were forced to relocate from Los Angeles to an internment camp in eastern California in 1942.

## THE ALLIED DRIVE TOWARD BERLIN

By mid-1942, the home front was hearing good news from the war fronts. Japanese naval losses at the Battles of Coral Sea and Midway had secured Australia and Hawaii. U.S. naval forces had also been increasingly successful at destroying German U-boats off the Atlantic coast. This was all the more important because the Grand Alliance—Great Britain, United States, and the Soviet Union—called for the defeat of Germany first.

WAR AIMS AND STRATEGY  A major factor affecting Allied strategy was the fighting on the vast Eastern Front in the Soviet Union, where, in fact, the outcome of the war against Hitler was largely decided. In eastern Europe during 1941–1942, two totalitarian regimes—the Nazis and the Soviets—waged colossal battles while murdering millions of civilians in horrifying slave labor/extermination camps (Nazis) and forced labor concentration camps (Soviets). Among the combatant nations, the Soviets—by far—bore the brunt of the war against the Nazis, leading Joseph Stalin, the Soviet premier, to insist that the Americans and British relieve the pressure on them by attacking the Germans in western Europe.

Roosevelt and Churchill agreed that they needed to create a second front, but they could not agree on the location of their first attack against Hitler's armies. U.S. military planners were willing to take extraordinary, indeed foolhardy, risks by striking directly across the English Channel before the end of 1942. They wanted to secure a beachhead in German-occupied France, and then move briskly against Germany itself in 1943. "We've got to go to Europe and fight," General Dwight D. Eisenhower stressed. The British, however, were wary of moving too fast. An Allied defeat on the French coast, Churchill warned, was "the only way in which we could possibly lose this

What was the Atlantic Charter? Compare and contrast the alliances in the First World War with those in the Second World War. How were the Germans able to seize most of the Allied territory so quickly?

war." Roosevelt, concerned about upcoming Congressional elections, told the U.S. military planners to accept Churchill's compromise proposal for a joint Anglo-American invasion of French North Africa, which had been captured by German and Italian armies.

THE NORTH AFRICA CAMPAIGN    On November 8, 1942, British and American forces commanded by U.S. general **Dwight D. Eisenhower** landed in Morocco and Algeria on the North African coast. Farther east, British armies were pushing the Germans back across Libya, and untested American forces were confronting seasoned German units pouring into Tunisia. Before spring, however, the British forces had taken Libya, and the Germans were caught in a gigantic pair of pincers. Hammered from all sides, unable to retreat across the Mediterranean, an army of some 250,000 Germans and Italians surrendered on May 12, 1943, leaving all of North Africa in Allied hands.

Five months earlier, in January 1943, Roosevelt, Churchill, and the Combined Chiefs of Staff met at Casablanca, the largest city in Morocco. It was a historic occasion. No U.S. president had ever flown abroad while in office, and none had ever visited Africa. Stalin declined to leave besieged Russia for the meeting, however, although he continued to press for a second front in western Europe to relieve the pressure on the Soviet Union. The British and American engagements with German forces in North Africa were minuscule in comparison with the scope and fury of the fighting in Russia. Throughout 1943, for example, while some sixty thousand British and American servicemen were killed by German forces, the Soviet Union lost *2 million* combatants.

At the Casablanca Conference, Churchill and Roosevelt spent eight days hammering out key strategic decisions. The British convinced the Americans that they should follow up a victory in North Africa with an assault on German and Italian forces on the Italian island of Sicily and in Italy itself. Roosevelt and Churchill also decided to step up the bombing of Germany and to increase shipments of military supplies to the Soviet Union and the Nationalist Chinese forces fighting the Japanese. American military-industrial productivity proved to be the most strategic asset in the war. Many of the Soviet troops who would advance west toward Berlin during the latter phase of the war rode in American trucks, ate American rations, and wore American boots. Yet, as Stalin often complained, the Americans were far more generous with supplies than they were committing large numbers of soldiers on the battlefield.

Before leaving Casablanca, Roosevelt announced, with Churchill's endorsement, that the war would end only with the "unconditional surrender" of all enemies. This decision was designed to quiet Soviet suspicions that the Western Allies might negotiate separately with the various enemy nations making

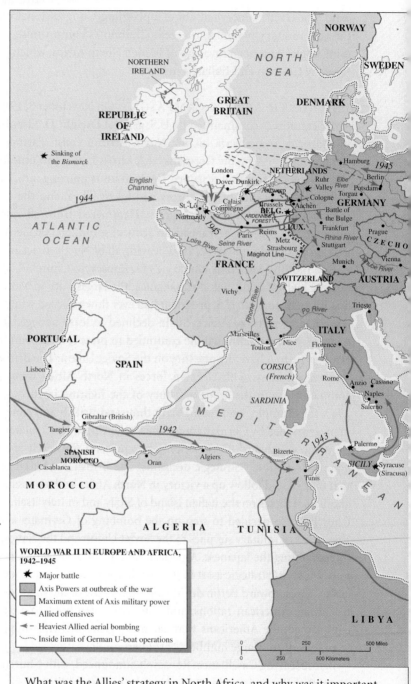

NORWAY

NORTH
SEA

SWEDEN

NORTHERN
IRELAND

GREAT
BRITAIN

DENMARK

REPUBLIC
OF
IRELAND

Hamburg  1945

★ Sinking of
the *Bismarck*

London

Berlin

English
Channel

Dover Dunkirk

NETHERLANDS

Ruhr
Valley

*Elbe
River*

Potsdam

Antwerp

Torgau

1944

Calais
St-Lô  Compiègne

Brussels
BELG.

Cologne

GERMANY

Aachen

ATLANTIC
OCEAN

Normandy

*ARDENNES
FOREST*

Battle of
the Bulge

1945

Paris

Reims

LUX.

Frankfurt

Prague

*Loire River*

*Seine River*

Metz

*Rhine River*

CZECHO

Strasbourg

Stuttgart

Maginot Line

FRANCE

SWITZERLAND

Munich

Vienna

AUSTRIA

*Danube River*

Vichy

*Rhône River*

Trieste

*Po River*

PORTUGAL

SPAIN

1944

Marseilles

Nice

ITALY

Toulon

Florence

Lisbon

*MEDITE*

CORSICA
(French)

Rome

Anzio  Cassino

Naples

SARDINIA

Salerno

Gibraltar (British)

Tangier

1942

*R R A*

1943

Palermo

SPANISH
MOROCCO

Oran

Algiers

Bizerte

*N E A N*

SICILY

Syracuse
(Siracusa)

Casablanca

Tunis

MOROCCO

ALGERIA

TUNISIA

*S E A*

**WORLD WAR II IN EUROPE AND AFRICA,
1942–1945**

★ Major battle

Axis Powers at outbreak of the war

Maximum extent of Axis military power

◄— Allied offensives

◄ - Heaviest Allied aerial bombing

········· Inside limit of German U-boat operations

LIBYA

0          250          500 Miles

0     250     500 Kilometers

What was the Allies' strategy in North Africa, and why was it important
for the invasion of Italy? Why did Eisenhower's plan on D-day succeed?
What was the Battle of the Bulge? What was the role of strategic bombing
in the war? Was it effective?

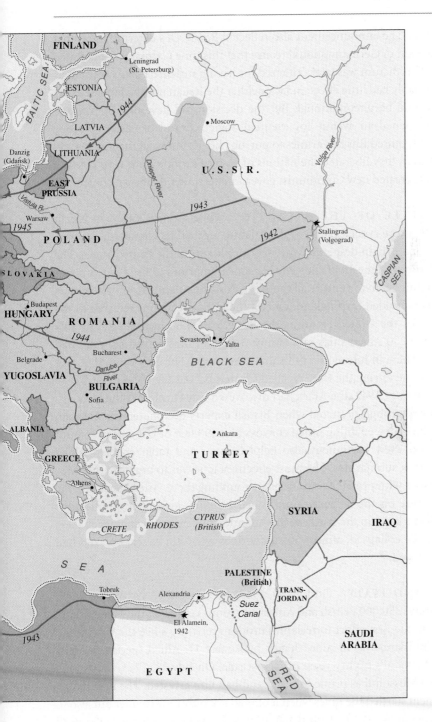

up the Axis. The announcement also reflected Roosevelt's determination that "every person in Germany should realize that this time Germany is a defeated nation." This dictum was later criticized for having stiffened enemy resistance, but it probably had little effect; in fact, neither the Italian nor the Japanese surrender would be unconditional. But the decision did have one unexpected result: it opened an avenue for eventual Soviet control of eastern Europe because it required Russian armies to pursue Hitler's forces all the way to Germany. And as they liberated the nations of eastern Europe from Nazi control, the Soviets created new Communist governments under their own control.

THE BATTLE OF THE ATLANTIC   While fighting raged in North Africa, the more crucial Battle of the Atlantic reached its climax on the high seas. Isolated Britain desperately needed supplies from the United States. The fall of France in June 1940 allowed German submarines to use French ports, thus enabling them to venture all the way across the Atlantic to sink freighters and tankers headed for England. One of the U-boat captains referred to the east coast of the United States as the "American shooting gallery." By July 1942, some 230 Allied ships and almost 5 million tons of war supplies had been lost. Then, in July alone, 143 ships were sunk. "The only thing that ever frightened me during the war," recalled Churchill, "was the U-boat peril."

By the end of 1942, the Allies had discovered ways to thwart the U-boats. A key breakthrough occurred when British experts deciphered the German naval radio codes, enabling Allied convoys to steer clear of U-boats or to hunt them down. New technology also helped: sonar and radar enabled Allied ships to track submarines. The most effective tactic was to organize the ships into convoys with protective warships surrounding them. After May 1943, the U-boats were on the defensive, and Allied shipping losses fell significantly. The U-boats kept up the Battle of the Atlantic until the war's end; when Germany finally collapsed, almost 50 submarines were still at sea, but 783 had been destroyed.

SICILY AND ITALY   On July 10, 1943, after the Allied victory in North Africa, about 250,000 British and American troops landed on the Italian island of Sicily in the first effort to reclaim European territory since the war began. The entire island was in Allied hands by August 17. Allied success in Sicily ended Mussolini's twenty years of Fascist rule. On July 25, 1943, Italy's king dismissed Mussolini as prime minister and had him arrested. The new Italian government startled the Allies when it offered not only to surrender but also to switch sides in the war. Unfortunately, mutual suspicions prolonged talks until September 3, during which time the Germans poured reinforcements into Italy. Mussolini, plucked from imprisonment by a daring German airborne

**Major General George S. Patton**

Patton commanded the U.S. invasion of Sicily, the largest amphibious action in the war up to that point. He believed that war "brings out all that is best in men."

raid, became head of a puppet Fascist government in northern Italy. On June 4, 1944, the U.S. Fifth Army entered Rome. The capture of Rome received only a brief moment of glory, however, for the long-awaited cross-Channel Allied landing in German-occupied France came two days later. Italy, always a secondary front, faded from the world's attention.

THE TEHRAN MEETING    Late in the fall of 1943, Churchill and Roosevelt had their first joint meeting with Joseph Stalin in Tehran, Iran. Although as much competitors as collaborators, they were able to forge several key agreements. Their chief subject was the planned invasion of France and a Russian offensive across eastern Europe timed to coincide with it. Stalin repeated his promise to enter the war against Japan, and the three leaders agreed to create an international organization (the United Nations) to maintain peace after the war. Upon arriving back in the United States, Roosevelt confided to Churchill his distrust of Stalin, stressing that it was a "ticklish" business keeping the "Russians cozy with us." Indeed it was.

THE STRATEGIC BOMBING OF EUROPE Behind the long-postponed Allied invasion of German-controlled France lay months of preparation. While waiting for D-day, the U.S. Army Air Force and the British Royal Air Force (RAF) had sought to pound Germany into submission. The Allied air campaign killed perhaps six hundred thousand German civilians. Yet while causing widespread damage, the strategic air offensive failed to devastate German morale or industrial production. But with air supremacy over Europe assured by 1944, the Allies were free to provide cover for the much-anticipated invasion of Hitler's "Fortress Europa." On April 14, 1944, General Eisenhower assumed control of the strategic air forces for the invasion of German-controlled France. On D-day, June 6, 1944, he told the troops, "If you see fighting aircraft over you, they will be ours."

D-DAY AND AFTER In early 1944, General Dwight D. Eisenhower arrived in London to take command of the Allied forces. Battle-tested in North Africa and the Mediterranean, he now faced the daunting task of

**Operation Overlord**

General Dwight D. Eisenhower instructing paratroopers before they boarded their airplanes to launch the D-day assault.

planning **Operation Overlord**, the daring assault on Hitler's "Atlantic Wall," a formidable series of fortifications and mines along the French coastline.

The prospect of an amphibious assault against such defenses unnerved some Allied planners. As D-day approached in June, Eisenhower's chief of staff predicted only a fifty-fifty chance of success. Operation Overlord succeeded largely because it was meticulously planned and because it surprised the Germans. The Allies fooled the Nazis into believing that the invasion would come at Pas-de-Calais, on the French-Belgian border, where the English Channel was narrowest. Instead, the landings occurred in Normandy, almost two hundred miles south. In April and May 1944, while the vast invasion forces made final preparations, the Allied air forces disrupted the transportation network of northern France, smashing railroads and bridges. By early June all was ready, and D-day fell on June 6, 1944.

On the evening of June 5, Eisenhower visited some of the sixteen thousand American paratroopers preparing to land at night behind the German lines in France to seize key bridges and roads. The men noticed his look of grave concern and tried to lift his spirits. "Now quit worrying, General," one of them said, "we'll take care of this thing for you." After the planes took off, Eisenhower returned to his car with tears in his eyes. "Well," he said quietly to his driver, "it's on." He knew that many of his troops would die within a few hours.

At dawn on June 6, the invasion fleet of some 5,300 Allied vessels carrying 370,000 soldiers and sailors filled the horizon off the Normandy coast. Sleepy German soldiers awoke to see the vast armada arrayed before them. For several hours the local German commanders misinterpreted the Normandy landings as merely a diversion for the "real" attack at Pas-de-Calais. When Hitler learned of the Allied landings, he boasted that "the news couldn't be better. As long as they were in Britain, we couldn't get at them. Now we have them where we can destroy them." In the United States, word that the long-anticipated Allied invasion of Nazi Europe had begun captured the attention of the nation. Businesses closed, church bells tolled, and traffic was stopped so that people could pray in the streets.

Despite Eisenhower's intensive planning and the imposing array of Allied troops and firepower, the D-day invasion almost failed. Thick clouds and German anti-aircraft fire caused many of the paratroopers and glider pilots to miss their landing zones. Oceangoing landing craft delivered their troops to the wrong locations. Low clouds led the Allied planes to drop their bombs too far inland—and often on Allied troops. The naval bombardment was equally ineffective. Rough seas caused injuries and nausea and capsized dozens of troop-filled landing craft. Radios were waterlogged. Over a thousand men drowned. The first units ashore lost over 90 percent of their troops to German

**The landing at Normandy**

D-day, June 6, 1944. Before they could huddle under a seawall and begin to root out the region's Nazi defenders, soldiers on Omaha Beach had to cross a fifty-yard stretch that exposed them to bullets fired from machine guns housed in concrete bunkers.

machine guns. In one company, 197 of the 205 men were killed or wounded within ten minutes. By nightfall the bodies of some five thousand killed or wounded Allied soldiers were strewn across the sand and surf of Normandy.

German losses were much higher; entire units were decimated or captured. Operation Overlord was the greatest amphibious invasion in the annals of warfare, but it was small when compared with the offensive launched by the Russians a few weeks after D-Day. Between June and August 1944, the Soviet Army killed, wounded, or captured more German soldiers (350,000) than were stationed in all of western Europe. Still, the Normandy invasion was a turning point in the war—and a pivotal point in America's rise to global power. With the beachhead secured, the Allied leaders knew that victory was in their grasp. "What a plan!" Churchill exclaimed to the British Parliament. Within two weeks of the Normandy assault, the Allies had landed 1 million troops, 556,000 tons of supplies, and 170,000 vehicles in France. On July 25, 1944, American armies in Normandy broke out westward into Brittany and eastward toward Paris. On August 15, a joint American-French invasion force landed on the French Mediterranean coast and raced up the Rhone Valley in central France. German resistance in France collapsed. A division of the Free French Resistance, aided by American forces, had the honor of liberating Paris on August 25. By mid-September, most of France and Belgium had been cleared of German troops.

## LEAPFROGGING TO TOKYO

MACARTHUR IN NEW GUINEA    Meanwhile, in Asia, the Allies began to strike back against the Japanese after the crucial Battle of Midway in June 1942. American and Australian forces under General Douglas MacArthur's command had begun to dislodge the Japanese from islands they had conquered in the southwest Pacific. In the summer, American and British troops pushed the Japanese back in New Guinea. Then, on August 7, 1942, U.S. Marines landed on Guadalcanal Island and seized the Japanese airstrip. The savage fighting on Guadalcanal lasted through February 1943, but the result was the first defeat of the Japanese army in the war.

ISLAND HOPPING    The Japanese were skilled defensive fighters. It was their suicidal fanaticism in New Guinea and on Guadalcanal that led American military strategists to adopt a "leapfrogging" strategy whereby they used airpower and seapower to neutralize Japanese strongholds on Pacific islands rather than assault them with ground troops. U.S. warplanes, for example, destroyed the Japanese airfield at Rabaul in eastern New Guinea, leaving 135,000 Japanese troops stranded on the island to sit out the war, cut off from re-supply by air and sea. What the Allies did to the Japanese garrison on Rabaul set the pattern for the remainder of the war in the Pacific.

BATTLES IN THE CENTRAL PACIFIC    On June 15, 1944, just days after the D-day invasion, U.S. forces liberated Tinian, Guam, and Saipan, three Japanese-controlled islands in the Mariana Islands. Saipan was strategically important because it allowed the new American B-29 "Superfortress" bombers to strike Japan itself. With New Guinea and the Mariana Islands all but liberated, General MacArthur's forces invaded the Japanese-held Philippines on October 20, landing first on the island of Leyte. The Japanese, knowing that the loss of the Philippines would cut them off from the essential raw materials of the East Indies, brought in warships from three directions. The three encounters that resulted on October 25, 1944, came to be known collectively as the Battle of Leyte Gulf, the largest naval engagement in history. It was a strategic victory for the Allies. The Japanese lost most of

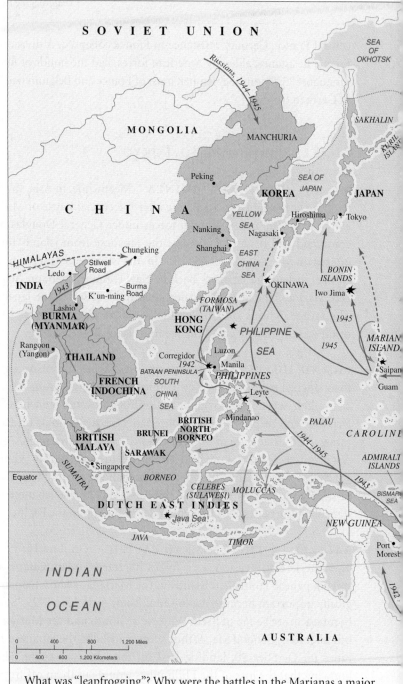

SOVIET UNION

SEA
OF
OKHOTSK

MONGOLIA

MANCHURIA

SAKHALIN

KURIL
ISLAND

Peking

KOREA

SEA OF
JAPAN

JAPAN

Russians 1944–1945

C H I N A

YELLOW
SEA

Hiroshima

Tokyo

HIMALAYAS

Chungking

Stilwell
Road

Nanking

Nagasaki

Ledo

INDIA

1943

Burma
Road

K'un-ming

Shanghai

EAST
CHINA
SEA

OKINAWA

BONIN
ISLANDS

Iwo Jima

1945

MARIAN
ISLAND

Lashio

BURMA
(MYANMAR)

FORMOSA
(TAIWAN)

HONG
KONG

PHILIPPINE

Rangoon
(Yangon)

THAILAND

Corregidor
1942

Luzon

SEA

1945

BATAAN PENINSULA

Manila

Saipan

FRENCH
INDOCHINA

SOUTH
CHINA
SEA

PHILIPPINES

Guam

Leyte

BRITISH
NORTH
BORNEO

Mindanao

PALAU

CAROLINI

BRITISH
MALAYA

BRUNEI

1944–1945

SARAWAK

ADMIRALT
ISLANDS

Equator

SUMATRA

Singapore

BORNEO

CELEBES
(SULAWESI)

MOLUCCAS

1943

BISMAR
SEA

DUTCH EAST INDIES

Java Sea

NEW GUINEA

JAVA

TIMOR

Port
Moresb

INDIAN

1942

OCEAN

AUSTRALIA

| 0 | 400 | 800 | 1,200 Miles |

| 0 | 400 | 800 | 1,200 Kilometers |

What was "leapfrogging"? Why were the battles in the Marianas a major turning point in the war? What was the significance of the Battle of Leyte Gulf? How did the battle at Okinawa affect the way both sides proceeded in the war? Why did President Truman decide to drop atomic bombs on Hiroshima and Nagasaki?

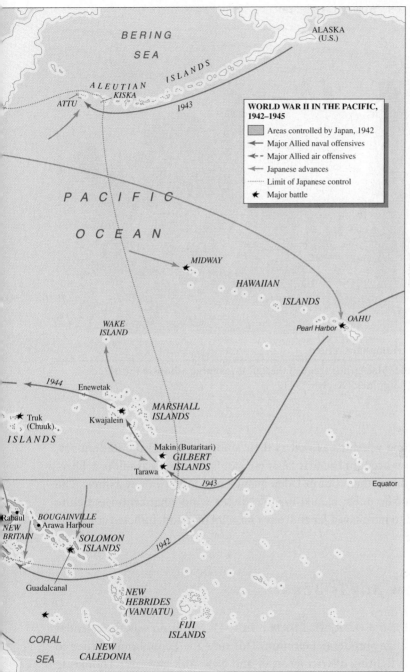

BERING

SEA

ALASKA
(U.S.)

ALEUTIAN   ISLANDS
KISKA
ATTU
1943

PACIFIC

OCEAN

MIDWAY

HAWAIIAN

ISLANDS

OAHU
Pearl Harbor

WAKE
ISLAND

1944   Enewetak

Truk
(Chuuk)
ISLANDS

Kwajalein

MARSHALL
ISLANDS

Makin (Butaritari)
GILBERT
Tarawa   ISLANDS

1943

Equator

Rabaul
NEW
BRITAIN

BOUGAINVILLE
Arawa Harbour

SOLOMON
ISLANDS

1942

Guadalcanal

NEW
HEBRIDES
(VANUATU)

FIJI
ISLANDS

CORAL

SEA

NEW
CALEDONIA

**WORLD WAR II IN THE PACIFIC,
1942–1945**

Areas controlled by Japan, 1942

Major Allied naval offensives

Major Allied air offensives

Japanese advances

Limit of Japanese control

Major battle

**MacArthur's triumphant return**

General Douglas MacArthur (center) theatrically coming ashore at the island of Leyte in the Philippines, October 1944.

their remaining warships as well as their ability to defend the Philippines. The battle also brought the first Japanese kamikaze attacks as pilots deliberately crash-dived their bomb-laden planes into American warships. The kamikaze suicide units, named for the "divine wind" that centuries before was believed to have saved Japan from a Mongol invasion, inflicted considerable damage.

## A NEW AGE IS BORN

ROOSEVELT'S FOURTH TERM   In 1944, war or no war, the calendar dictated another presidential election. This time the Republicans turned to former crime fighting district attorney and New York governor Thomas E. Dewey as their candidate. No Democrat challenged Roosevelt, but a fight did develop over the vice-presidential nomination. Vice President Henry A. Wallace had angered both southern conservatives and northern city bosses, who feared his ties to labor unions. Roosevelt finally fastened on the compromise choice of little-known Missouri senator Harry S. Truman. Dewey ran under the same handicap as Landon and Willkie had before him. He did not propose to dismantle Roosevelt's popular New Deal programs but argued that it was time for younger men to replace the "tired" old Democratic leaders. An aging Roosevelt did show signs of illness and exhaustion; nevertheless, on November 7, 1944, he was once again elected, this time by a popular vote of 25.6 million to 22 million and an electoral vote of 432 to 99.

CONVERGING MILITARY FRONTS    After their quick sweep eastward across France after the Normandy invasion, the Allied armies lost momentum in the fall of 1944 as they neared Germany. The Germans sprang a surprise in the rugged Ardennes Forest, where the Allied line was thinnest. Attacking on December 16, 1944, the Germans advanced along a fifty-mile "bulge" in the Allies' lines in Belgium and Luxembourg—hence the Battle of the Bulge. The climactic event occurred at the Belgian town of Bastogne, where German forces trapped American forces. Reinforced by the Allies just before it was surrounded, the outnumbered American units at Bastogne held for six days against relentless German attacks. On December 22, the U.S. general, Tony McAuliffe, gave his memorable answer to the Nazi demand for surrender: "Nuts." When a German major asked what the term meant, an American officer said, "It's the same as 'Go to Hell.' And I will tell you something else—if you continue to attack, we will kill every goddamn German that tries to break into this city." The American situation remained desperate until the next day, when the clouds lifted, allowing Allied airpower to halt the German advance and drop in supplies. On December 26, U.S. forces broke through to relieve besieged Bastogne. The Battle of the Bulge upset Eisenhower's timetable for ending the war, but the failure of the desperate Nazi effort at Bastogne had weakened German resources and left open the door to Germany's heartland from the west. By early March, the Allies had crossed the Rhine River, on the western German border. In April, they encircled the Ruhr Valley, center of Germany's heavy industry. Meanwhile, the Soviet offensive in eastern Europe had reached the eastern border of Germany, after taking Warsaw, Poland, on January 17 and Vienna, Austria, on April 13.

With the British and American armies racing across western Germany and the Soviets moving in from the east, the Allied war planners turned their attention to Berlin, the German capital. Prime Minister Churchill worried that if the Red Army arrived in Berlin first, Stalin would control the postwar map of Europe. He urged Eisenhower to get his troops to Berlin ahead of the Soviets. General Eisenhower, however, was convinced the Soviets would get to Berlin first no matter what the Allies decided. Berlin, he determined, was no longer of military significance; his focus remained the destruction of German

**The war's end**

U.S. soldiers corralling German prisoners of war in 1945.

ground forces. Churchill disagreed and appealed to Roosevelt, who in the end left the decision to Eisenhower. When analysts predicted that it would cost one hundred thousand Americans killed or wounded to liberate Berlin before the Soviets did, Eisenhower decided it was too high a price for what an aide called a "prestige objective," so he left Berlin to the Soviets.

YALTA AND THE POSTWAR WORLD   As the final offensives against Nazi Germany got under way, the **Yalta Conference** (February 4–11, 1945), hosted by the Soviets, brought the "Big Three" Allied leaders together in a czar's former palace at Yalta, a seaside resort on the north coast of the Black Sea. While the focus at the Tehran Conference in 1943 had been on wartime strategy, the three veteran Allied leaders now discussed the shape of the postwar world. Two aims loomed large in Roosevelt's thinking. One was the need to ensure that the Soviet Union would join the ongoing war against Japan. The other was based upon the lessons he had drawn from the First World War. Chief among the mistakes to be remedied this time were the failure of the United States to join the League of Nations and the failure of the Allies to maintain a united front against Germany after the war. Roosevelt was determined to replace the "outdated" isolationism of the 1920s and 1930s with an engaged internationalism.

The seventy-year-old Churchill arrived at Yalta focused on restoring independent, democratic France and Poland and limiting efforts by the victors to extract punitive reparations on defeated Germany, lest Europe recreate the problems caused by the Versailles Treaty ending World War I. Stalin's goals were defensive and imperialistic: he wanted to retrieve former Russian territory given to Poland after World War I and to impose Soviet control over the newly liberated countries of eastern Europe. The U.S. ambassador in Moscow felt that Stalin was "the most inscrutable and contradictory character I have ever known," a baffling man of "high intelligence [and] fantastic grasp of detail," a leader "better informed than Roosevelt, more realistic than Churchill. . . . At the same he was, of course, a murderous tyrant." At Yalta, Stalin was confident he would have his way. That the Soviet Army already controlled key areas in eastern Europe would ensure that his demands were met. As he confided to a Communist leader, "whoever occupies a territory also imposes his own social system."

### The Yalta Conference

Churchill, Roosevelt, and Stalin confer on the shape of the postwar world in February 1945.

The Yalta meeting began with the U.S. delegation calling for a conference to create a new world security organization, which Roosevelt termed the United Nations, to be held in the United States beginning on April 25, 1945. The next major topic was how a defeated Germany would be governed. The war map dictated the basic pattern of occupation zones: the Soviets would control eastern Germany, and the Americans and British would control the rich industrial areas of the west. Berlin, the German capital isolated within the Soviet zone, would be subject to joint occupation. Similar arrangements were made for Austria, with Vienna, like Berlin, under joint occupation within the Soviet zone. At the behest of Churchill and Roosevelt, Stalin agreed to the French being given an occupation zone along its border with Germany and in Berlin.

With respect to eastern Europe, Poland became the main focus of Allied concern at Yalta. Britain and France had gone to war in 1939 to defend Poland, and now, six years later, the course of the war had left Poland's fate in the hands of the Soviets. When Soviet forces reentered Poland in 1944, they had created a puppet Communist regime in Lublin. As Soviet troops reached the gates of Warsaw, the historic Polish capital, courageous Poles rose up against the Nazi occupiers. Instead of working with the Polish resistance, however, Stalin cynically ordered the Soviet army to stop its offensive for two months so as to enable the besieged Germans to kill thousands of poorly armed Poles. Stalin viewed the members of the Polish Home Army as potential rivals of the Soviets' Lublin puppet government.

The belief that postwar cooperation among the Allies could survive tragic events such as the Warsaw massacre was a triumph of hope over experience. Churchill admitted after the Yalta meetings that the only thing binding the three allies together was their common interest in defeating Nazi Germany. The Western Allies could do no more than acquiesce to Soviet demands or stall; Stalin controlled the situation on the ground in Poland. Having suffered almost 30 million deaths during the war, the Soviets were determined to dictate the postwar situation in eastern Europe. At Yalta, the Big Three promised to sponsor free elections, democratic governments, and constitutional safeguards of freedom throughout liberated Europe. The Yalta Declaration of Liberated Europe reaffirmed the principles of the Atlantic Charter, but in the end it made little difference. The Yalta Accords only postponed Soviet takeovers in eastern Europe for a few years. Russia, twice invaded by Germany in the twentieth century, was determined to create compliant buffer states between it and the Germans. Seven weeks after the Yalta meetings, Roosevelt could only lamely protest to Stalin the "discouraging lack of progress made in carrying out" his promises to organize free elections in Poland.

YALTA'S LEGACY    The Yalta Conference ended on an upbeat note. Roosevelt compared the feelings among the "Big Three" to "that of a family." Churchill and Roosevelt agreed that they had achieved the best results possible. Critics, mostly Republicans, later attacked Roosevelt for "giving" eastern Europe over to Soviet domination. But the course of the war shaped the actions at Yalta, not Roosevelt's diplomacy. Although Roosevelt was naïve in thinking that Stalin and the Soviets would allow democratic processes to shape eastern Europe, the United States had no real leverage to exert in the region. As a U.S. diplomat admitted, "Stalin held all the cards" at Yalta. The Americans and British could not have done anything to alter these facts. Allied forces in Europe would have been hopelessly outmanned and outgunned by the Red Army. By suppressing opposition in the eastern European countries liberated by the Red Army, the Soviets were acting not under the Yalta Accords but in violation of them. And geography as well as Soviet military power precluded the Americans from forcing the issue in Poland and eastern Europe.

Perhaps the most bitterly criticized of the Yalta accords was a secret agreement about the Far East, not made public until after the war. As the Big Three met at Yalta, fighting still raged against the Japanese in the Philippines and Burma. Military analysts estimated that Japan could hold out for eighteen months after the defeat of Germany. Roosevelt, eager to gain Soviet participation in the war against Japan, therefore accepted Stalin's demands on postwar arrangements in the Far East. Stalin demanded continued Soviet control of Outer Mongolia through its puppet People's Republic, acquisition of the Kuril Islands from Japan, and recovery of territory lost after the Russo-Japanese War of 1905. Stalin in return promised to enter the war against Japan two or three months after the German defeat, recognize Chinese sovereignty over Manchuria, and conclude a treaty of friendship and alliance with the Chinese Nationalists. Roosevelt's concessions would later appear in a different light, but given their geographic advantages in Asia, as in eastern Europe, the Soviets were in a position to get what they wanted in any case.

THE COLLAPSE OF NAZI GERMANY    By 1945, the collapse of Nazi Germany was imminent, but President Roosevelt did not live to join the victory celebrations. In the spring of 1945, he went to his second home, in Warm Springs, Georgia, to rest up for the conference creating the United Nations. On April 12, 1945, he died from a cerebral hemorrhage. A desperate Adolf Hitler saw in Roosevelt's death a "great miracle" for the besieged Germans. "The war is not lost," he told an aide. "Read it. Roosevelt is dead!"

Hitler's Nazi empire collapsed less than a month later. The Allied armies met advance detachments of Soviet soldiers on April 25 along the Elbe River,

**May 8, 1945**

The celebration in New York City's Times Square on V-E day.

near the German town of Torgau. Three days later, Italian partisans killed Mussolini as he tried to flee. In Berlin, which was under siege by the Soviets, Hitler married his mistress, Eva Braun, in an underground bunker on the last day of April. He then killed her and himself. On May 2, Berlin fell to the Soviets. Finally, on May 7, in the Allied headquarters at Reims, France, the chief of staff of the German armed forces signed a treaty agreeing to an unconditional surrender. So ended Nazi domination of Europe, little more than twelve years after the monomaniacal Hitler had come to power.

Allied victory in Europe generated massive celebrations on V-E day, May 8, 1945, but the elation was tempered by the tragedies that had engulfed the world: the death of Franklin Roosevelt and the deaths of untold millions over the course of the war. The Allied armies, chiefly the Americans, British, and Soviets, were unprepared for the challenges of reconstructing defeated Germany. The German economy had to be revived, a new democratic government had to be formed, and many of the German people had to be clothed, housed, and fed. There were also some 11 million foreigners left stranded in Germany, people from all over Europe who had been captured and put to work in labor camps, concentration camps, or death camps. Now the Allies were responsible for feeding, housing, and repatriating those "displaced persons."

Most shocking was the extent of the Holocaust, scarcely believable until the Allied armies liberated the Nazi death camps in eastern Europe where the Germans had enacted their **"final solution"** to what Hitler called the "Jewish problem": the wholesale extermination of some 6 million Jews along with more than 1 million other captured peoples. Reports of the Nazis' systematic genocide against the Jews had appeared as early as 1942, but such ghastly stories seemed beyond belief. The Allied troops were horrified at what they discovered in the concentration camps. Bodies were piled as high as buildings; survivors were virtually skeletons. General Eisenhower reported from one of the camps that the evidence of "starvation, cruelty, and bestiality were so overpowering as to leave me a bit sick." At Dachau, the first Nazi concentration camp in Germany, the American troops were so enraged by the sight of murdered civilians that they (and some inmates), in horrific violation of the Geneva Convention, executed the 550 Nazi guards who had surrendered.

**Holocaust survivors**

U.S. troops encounter survivors of the Nazis' Wöbbelin concentration camp in Germany, May 1945.

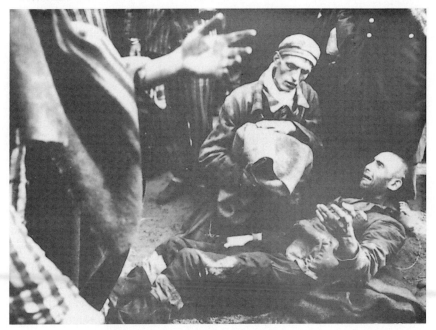

American officials, even some Jewish leaders, had dragged their feet in acknowledging the Holocaust for fear that relief efforts for Jewish refugees might stir up latent anti-Semitism at home. Under pressure, President Roosevelt had set up a War Refugee Board early in 1944. It managed to rescue about two hundred thousand European Jews and some twenty thousand others. More might have been done by broadcasts warning people in Europe that Nazi "labor camps" were in fact death traps. The Allies rejected a plan to bomb the rail lines into Auschwitz, the largest concentration camp, in Poland, although bombers hit industries five miles away. And few refugees were accepted by the United States. The Allied handling of the Holocaust was inept at best and disgraceful at worst. In 1944, Churchill called the Nazi extermination of the Jews the "most horrible crime ever committed in the history of the world."

A GRINDING WAR AGAINST JAPAN   Victory in Europe enabled Allied war planners to focus their attention on the pressing need to defeat Japan. Yet the closer the Allies got to Japan, the fiercer the resistance they encountered and the higher the casualties. While fighting continued in the Philippines, U.S. Marines landed on Japanese-controlled Iwo Jima Island on February 19, 1945, a speck of volcanic rock 760 miles from Tokyo that was needed as a base for fighter planes escorting bombers over Japan. It took nearly six weeks to secure the tiny island at a cost of nearly seven thousand American lives. The Japanese defenders on Iwo Jima and other islands fought to the death rather than surrender, often attacking in mass suicide assaults.

The fight for Okinawa Island, beginning on Easter Sunday, April 1, was even bloodier. Okinawa was strategically important because it would serve as the staging area for the planned invasion of Japan. The conquest of Japanese-controlled Okinawa was the largest amphibious operation of the Pacific war, involving some 300,000 troops, and it took almost three months to secure the island. An estimated 140,000 Japanese died in the intense fighting.

The Allied commanders then began planning for an invasion of Japan. To soften up the Japanese defenses, degrade their industrial capacity, and erode the morale of the civilian populace, the Allied command launched massive bombing raids over Japan in the summer of 1944. In early 1945, General Curtis Lemay, head of the U.S. Bomber Command, ordered devastating firebomb raids over Japanese cities. On March 9, for example, some three hundred B-29 bombers dropped napalm bombs on Tokyo, incinerating sixteen square miles of the city and killing eighty-five thousand people in the process. Firebomb raids then targeted other major cities—Kobe, Nagoya, Osaka,

Yokohama, and others—destroying 40 percent of their communities and causing 672,000 casualties.

THE ATOMIC BOMB   In early 1945, new president Harry S. Truman learned of the first successful test explosion of an atomic bomb in New Mexico. The dramatic event resulted from intensive research and development, begun in 1940, when President Roosevelt set up the secret Manhattan Project to develop atomic weaponry before Nazi Germany did. Ironically, Hitler's anti-Semitism forced many of Germany's leading scientists out of the country, and they became essential participants in the American research efforts. Gigantic secret plants to develop and test atomic bombs sprang up at Oak Ridge, Tennessee; Hanford, Washington; and Los Alamos, New Mexico; meanwhile, a group of brilliant physicists and chemists, many of them German Jewish émigrés working under J. Robert Oppenheimer, solved the scientific and technical problems of bomb design and construction. On July 16, 1945, the first "test" atomic bomb was exploded in the New Mexico desert. Oppenheimer said later that in the observation bunker "a few people laughed, a few people cried, most people were silent."

Now that the bomb had been shown to work, military planners selected two Japanese cities as targets. The first was Hiroshima, a port city of four hundred thousand people in southern Japan that was a major assembly point for Japanese naval convoys, a center of war-related industries, and headquarters of a Japanese army. On July 25, 1945, President Truman ordered that the atomic bomb be used if Japan did not surrender before August 3. Although an intense debate has emerged over the decision to drop the atomic bomb, Truman said that he "never had any doubt that it should be used." He was convinced that the new weapon would save lives by avoiding a costly invasion of Japan against its "ruthless, merciless, and fanatic" defenders.

Military planners had estimated that an invasion of Japan could cost as many as 250,000 Allied casualties and even more Japanese losses. Moreover, some 100,000 Allied prisoners of war being held in Japan would probably be executed when an invasion began. By that time, the firebombing of cities and the widespread killing of civilians had become accepted military practice. The use of atomic bombs on Japanese cities was thus seen as a logical next step to end the war. As it turned out, scientists greatly underestimated the physical effects of the atomic bomb. They predicted that 20,000 people would be killed, an estimate much too low.

In mid-July the Allied leaders met in Potsdam, Germany, near Berlin, to discuss the fate of defeated Germany and the ongoing war against Japan.

**The American Chemical Society exhibit on atomic energy**

Physicist J. Robert Oppenheimer points to a photograph of the huge column of smoke and flame caused by the bomb upon Hiroshima.

While there, they issued the Potsdam Declaration, demanding that Japan surrender or face "prompt and utter destruction." The deadline passed, and on August 6, 1945, a B-29 bomber named the *Enola Gay* took off at 2 A.M. from the island of Tinian and headed for Hiroshima. At 8:15 A.M., flying at 31,600 feet, the *Enola Gay* released the five-ton, ten-foot-long uranium bomb nicknamed Little Boy. Forty-three seconds later, as the *Enola Gay* turned sharply to avoid the blast, the bomb tumbled to an altitude of 1,900 feet, where it exploded, creating a blinding flash of light followed by a fire-ball towering to 40,000 feet. The tail gunner on the *Enola Gay* described the scene: "It's like bubbling molasses down there . . . the mushroom is spreading out . . . fires are springing up everywhere . . . it's like a peep into hell."

The bomb's shock wave and firestorm killed some seventy-eight thousand people, including thousands of Japanese soldiers and twenty-three American prisoners of war housed in the city. By the end of the year, the death toll had reached one hundred and forty thousand as the effects of radiation burns and infection took their toll. In addition, seventy thousand buildings were destroyed, and four square miles of the city turned to rubble.

President Truman was aboard the battleship *Augusta* returning from the Potsdam Conference when news arrived that the bomb had been dropped. "This is the greatest thing in history!" he exclaimed. In the United States, Americans greeted the news with similar elation. To them, the atomic bomb promised a quick end to the long nightmare of war. "No tears of sympathy will be shed in America for the Japanese people," the *Omaha World-Herald* predicted. "Had they possessed a comparable weapon at Pearl Harbor, would they have hesitated to use it?" Others were more sobering about the implications of atomic warfare. "Yesterday," the journalist Hanson Baldwin wrote in the *New York Times*, "we clinched victory in the Pacific, but we sowed the whirlwind."

Two days after the Hiroshima bombing an opportunistic Soviet Union hastened to enter the war against Japan in order to share in the spoils of victory. Truman and his aides, frustrated by the stubborn refusal of Japanese leaders to

**The aftermath of Little Boy**

This image shows the wasteland that remained after the atomic bomb Little Boy decimated Hiroshima in 1945.

surrender and fearful that the Soviet Union's entry into the war would complicate negotiations, ordered the second atomic bomb ("Fat Man") dropped. On August 9, the city of Nagasaki, a shipbuilding center, experienced the same nuclear devastation that had destroyed Hiroshima. That night, the Japanese emperor urged his cabinet to surrender. Frantic exchanges between leaders in Washington, D.C., and Tokyo ended with Japanese acceptance of the surrender terms on August 14, 1945.

## THE FINAL LEDGER

Thus ended the largest and costliest military event in human history. Between 50 and 60 million people were killed in the war between 1939 and 1945—perhaps 60 percent of them civilians, including Jews and other ethnic minorities murdered in Nazi death camps and Soviet concentration camps. An average of 27,000 people died each day during the six years of warfare. The Second World War was more costly for the United States than any other foreign war: 292,000 battle deaths and 114,000 other deaths. A million Americans were wounded; half of them were seriously disabled. But in proportion to its population, the United States suffered a far smaller loss than that of any of the other major Allies or their enemies, and American territory escaped the devastation visited on so many other parts of the world. The Soviet Union, for example, suffered 20 million deaths, China 10 million, Germany 5.6 million, and Japan 2.3 million.

The Second World War was the pivotal event of the twentieth century; it reshaped the world order. Until 1941, European colonial empires still dominated the globe, and world affairs were still determined by decisions made in European capitals. In 1941, when Japan, the Soviet Union, and the United States entered the war, the old imperial world order led by France, Germany, and the United Kingdom, dating back to the eighteenth century, came to an end. German and Italian fascism as well as Japanese militarism were destroyed. And the United States had emerged by 1945 as the acknowledged "leader of the free world." With the dropping of the atomic bombs on Japan, Winston Churchill told the House of Commons, "America stands at this moment at the summit of the world."

Of course, the Second World War also transformed American life. The war finally brought an end to the Great Depression and laid the foundation for an era of unprecedented prosperity. Big businesses were transformed into gigantic corporations as a result of huge government contracts for military production, and the size of the federal government bureaucracy mushroomed. The number of government employees increased fourfold during the war. New technologies and products developed for military purposes—radar, computers, electronics, plastics and synthetics, jet engines, rockets, atomic energy—began to transform the private sector as well. And new opportunities for women as well as for African Americans, Mexican Americans, and other minorities set in motion major social changes that would culminate in the civil rights movement of the 1960s and the feminist movement of the 1970s.

The dramatic war-related expansion of the federal government continued after 1945. Presidential authority increased enormously at the expense of congressional and state power. At the same time, the isolationist sentiment in foreign relations that had been so powerful in the 1920s and 1930s evaporated as the United States emerged from the war with new global political and military responsibilities and expanded economic interests.

The war opened a new era for the United States in the world arena. It accelerated the growth of American power and prestige while devastating all other world powers. As President Truman told the nation in a radio address in August 1945, the United States had "emerged from this war the most powerful nation in this world—the most powerful nation, perhaps, in all history." But the Soviet Union, despite its profound human and material losses during the war, emerged with much new territory and enhanced influence, making it the greatest power in Europe and Asia. Just a little over a century after the Frenchman Alexis de Tocqueville had predicted that western Europe would be overshadowed by the power of the United States and Russia, his prophecy had come to pass.

## CHAPTER SUMMARY

- **Totalitarianism**   In Italy, Benito Mussolini assumed control by promising law and order. Adolf Hitler rearmed Germany in defiance of the Treaty of Versailles and aimed to unite all German speakers. Civil war in Spain and the growth of the Soviet Union under Joseph Stalin contributed to a precarious balance of power in Europe.

- **American Neutrality**   By March 1939, Hitler had annexed Austria and seized Czechoslovakia. He sent troops to invade Poland in September of 1939, after signing a nonaggression pact with the Soviet Union. At last, the British and French governments declared war. The United States issued declarations of neutrality, but with the fall of France, accelerated aid to France and Britain.

- **Japanese Threat**   After Japan allied with Germany and Italy and announced its intention to take control of French Indochina, President Roosevelt froze Japanese assets in the United States and restricted oil exports to Japan. The Japanese bombed the Pacific Fleet in a surprise attack at Pearl Harbor, Hawaii.

- **World War II and American Society**   Americans migrated west to take jobs in defense factories; unemployment was soon a thing of the past. Farmers, too, recovered from hard times. Many women took nontraditional jobs, some in the military. About 1 million African Americans served in the military, in segregated units. Japanese Americans, however, were interned in "war relocation camps."

- **Road to Allied Victory**   By 1943, the Allies controlled all of North Africa. From there they launched attacks on Sicily and then Italy. Joseph Stalin, meanwhile, demanded a full-scale Allied attack on the Atlantic coast to ease pressure on the Eastern Front, but D-day was delayed until June 6, 1944.

- **The Pacific War**   The Japanese advance was halted as early as June 1942 with the Battle of Midway. The Americans fought slow, costly battles in New Guinea, then, in 1943, headed toward the Philippines. Fierce resistance at Iwo Jima and Okinawa and Japan's refusal to surrender after the firebombing of Tokyo led the new president, Harry S. Truman, to order the use of the atomic bomb.

- **Postwar World**   In January 1942, the Allied nations signed the Declaration of the United Nations. The Big Three—Roosevelt, Churchill, and Stalin—meeting in Yalta in February 1945, decided that Europe would be divided into occupation zones.

## CHRONOLOGY

| | |
|---|---|
| 1933 | Adolf Hitler becomes chancellor of Germany |
| 1937 | *Panay* incident |
| 1938 | Hitler forces the *Anschluss* (union) of Austria and Germany |
| 1939 | Soviet Union agrees to a nonaggression pact with Germany |
| September 1939 | German troops invade Poland |
| 1940 | Battle of Britain |
| September 1940 | Germany, Italy, and Japan sign the Tripartite Pact |
| December 7, 1941 | Japanese launch surprise attack at Pearl Harbor, Hawaii |
| June 1942 | Battle of Midway |
| January 1943 | Roosevelt, Churchill, and the Combined Chiefs of Staff meet at Casablanca |
| July 1943 | Allied forces land on Sicily |
| 1943 | Roosevelt and Churchill meet Stalin, in Tehran |
| June 6, 1944 | D-day |
| February 1945 | Yalta Conference |
| April 1945 | Franklin Delano Roosevelt dies; Hitler commits suicide |
| May 8, 1945 | V-E day |
| August 1945 | Atomic bombs dropped on Hiroshima and Nagasaki |
| September 2, 1945 | Japanese surrender |

## KEY TERMS & NAMES

"good neighbor" policy p. 1143

Benito Mussolini, "Il Duce" p. 1144

Adolf Hitler, "Führer" p. 1144

National Socialist German Workers' (Nazi) party p. 1144

Winston Churchill p. 1148

Joseph Stalin p. 1151

*Blitzkrieg* (the Blitz) p. 1152

Lend-Lease Act p. 1156

Atlantic Charter p. 1158

Women's Army Corps (WAC) p. 1169

Tuskegee Airmen p. 1170

Dwight D. Eisenhower p. 1177

Operation Overlord p. 1183

Yalta Conference p. 1190

"final solution" p. 1195

# Part Seven

# THE
# AMERICAN
# AGE

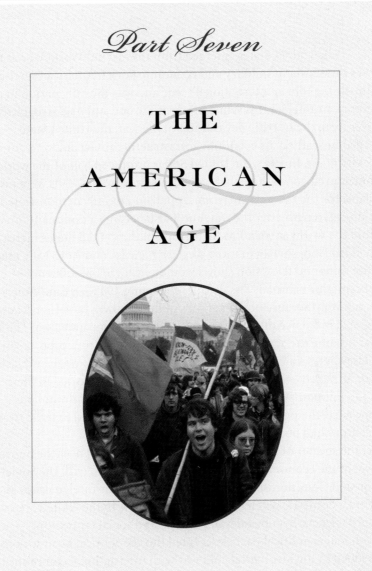

he United States emerged from the Second World War as the world's pre-eminent military and economic power. America exercised a commanding role in international trade and was the only nation in possession of atomic bombs. While much of Europe and Asia struggled to recover from the horrific devastation of the war, the United States emerged unscathed, its economic infrastructure intact and operating at peak efficiency. In 1945, the United States produced half of the world's manufactured goods. Jobs that had been scarce in the 1930s were now available for the taking. American capitalism not only demonstrated its economic strength after the war, but it also became a dominant force around the world as well. Products made in the United States increasingly filled store shelves in most Western nations, and American-made feature films and television shows would reinforce the influence of cultural capitalism abroad. The decades following 1945 were an "American Age" not only because of the nation's military power but also because of the global influence of American capitalism and consumerism. The U.S. dollar became the accepted international currency. In Europe, Japan, and elsewhere, American products, forms of entertainment, and fashion trends attracted excited attention. Many Americans gloried in their nation's military power, economic strength, and global dominance. Henry Luce, the publisher of *Life* magazine, proclaimed that the twentieth century had become the "American century."

Yet the specter of a deepening "cold war" cast a pall over the buoyant revival of the economy. The tense ideological contest with the Soviet Union and Communist China produced numerous foreign crises and sparked a domestic witch hunt for Communists in the United States that far surpassed earlier episodes of political and social repression.

Both major political parties accepted the geopolitical assumptions embedded in the ideological cold war with international communism. Both Republican and Democratic presidents affirmed the need to "contain" the spread of Communist influence around the world. This bedrock assumption eventually embroiled the United States in a costly war in Southeast Asia that destroyed Lyndon B. Johnson's presidency. The Vietnam War was also a catalyst for a countercultural movement in which young idealists among the "baby boom" generation demanded many overdue social reforms that spawned the civil rights, gay rights, feminist, and environmental movements. The social upheavals of the

1960s and early 1970s provoked a conservative backlash as well. Richard M. Nixon's paranoid reaction to his critics led to the Watergate affair and the destruction of his presidency.

Through all of this turmoil, however, the basic premises of welfare-state capitalism that Franklin Delano Roosevelt had instituted with his New Deal programs during the 1930s remained essentially intact. With only a few exceptions, Republicans and Democrats after 1945 accepted the notion that the federal government must assume greater responsibility for the welfare of individuals. Even President Ronald Reagan, a sharp critic of federal social-welfare programs, recognized the need during the 1980s for the government to provide a "safety net" for those who could not help themselves.

Yet this fragile consensus on public policy began to disintegrate in the late 1980s amid stunning international developments and less visible domestic events. The surprising collapse of the Soviet Union and the disintegration of European communism forced policy makers to respond to a post–cold war world in which the United States remained the only legitimate superpower. After forty-five years, U.S. foreign policy was no longer focused on a single adversary, and world politics lost its bipolar quality. During the early 1990s East and West Germany reunited, apartheid in South Africa ended, and Israel and the Palestinians signed a previously unimaginable treaty ending hostilities—for a while.

At the same time, U.S. foreign policy began to focus less on military power and more on economic competition and technological development. In those arenas, Japan, a reunited Germany, and Communist China challenged the United States for preeminence. By reducing the public's fear of nuclear annihilation, the end of the cold war also reduced public interest in foreign affairs. The presidential election of 1992 was the first since 1936 in which foreign-policy issues played virtually no role. Yet world affairs remained volatile and dangerous. The implosion of Soviet communism after 1989 unleashed a series of ethnic, nationalist, and separatist conflicts. During the 1990s and since, the United States found itself being drawn into crises in faraway lands such as Bosnia, Somalia, Afghanistan, and Iraq.

As the new multipolar world careened toward the end of the twentieth century and the start of a new millennium, fault lines began to appear in the social and economic landscape. A gargantuan federal debt and rising annual deficits threatened to bankrupt a nation that was becoming top-heavy with retirees. Without fully realizing it, much less appreciating its cascading consequences, the American population was becoming dis-proportionately old. The number of people aged ninety-five to ninety-nine doubled between 1980 and 1990, and the number of centenarians increased 77 percent. The proportion of the population aged sixty-five and older rose steadily during the 1990s. By the year 2010, over half of the elderly population was over seventy-five. This positive demographic fact had profound social and political implications. It made the tone of political debate more conservative and exerted increasing stress on health-care costs, nursing-home facilities, and the very survival of the Social Security system.

At the same time that the gap between young and old was increasing, so, too, was the disparity between rich and poor. This trend threatened to stratify a society already experiencing rising levels of racial and ethnic tension. Between 1960 and 2010, the gap between the richest 20 percent of the population and the poorest 20 percent more than doubled. Over 20 percent of all American children in 2012 lived in poverty compared to 15 percent in 2000, and the infant-mortality rate rose. Despite the much-ballyhooed "war-on-poverty" programs initiated by President Lyndon B. Johnson during the mid-1960s and continued in one form or another by his successors, the chronically poor at the start of the twenty-first century were more numerous than in 1964.

# 29

## THE FAIR DEAL AND CONTAINMENT

### FOCUS QUESTIONS

Ⓢ  wwnorton.com/studyspace

- How did the cold war emerge?
- How did Harry Truman respond to the Soviet occupation of eastern Europe?
- What was Truman's Fair Deal?
- What was the background of the Korean War, and how did the United States become involved?
- What were the roots of McCarthyism?

o sooner did the Second World War end than a "cold war" began. The awkward wartime alliance between the United States and the Soviet Union had collapsed by the fall of 1945. The two strongest nations to emerge from the war's carnage could not bridge their ideological differences over basic issues such as human rights, individual liberties, economic philosophy, and religious freedom. Mutual suspicion and a race to gain influence and control over the so-called non-aligned or "third world" nations further polarized the two nations. The defeat of Japan and Germany had created power vacuums that sucked the Soviet Union and the United States into an unrelenting war of words fed by clashing strategic interests and economic rivalry. During the next forty-five years of the cold war, not a single nation in western Europe would become Communist while every nation in eastern Europe (except Greece) would be controlled by Soviet communism. At the same time, the devastation wrought by the war in western Europe and the exhaustion of its peoples ignited anti-colonial uprisings in Asia and Africa that would strip Britain, France, and Holland of their empires and created fragile new nation states.

The emergence of Communist China (the People's Republic) after 1949 further complicated global politics. The postwar world was thus an unstable one in which international tensions shaped the contours of domestic politics and culture as well as foreign relations. Fueling the rivalry between East and West was a nuclear arms race that threatened to annihilate entire societies. Only too late would the two superpowers come to realize that the power to destroy does not necessarily provide the power to control world affairs.

## DEMOBILIZATION UNDER TRUMAN

TRUMAN'S UNEASY START    "Who the hell is Harry Truman?" Roosevelt's chief of staff asked the president in the summer of 1944. The question was on more lips when, after less than twelve weeks as vice president, Harry S. Truman took the presidential oath on April 12, 1945. Clearly Truman was not Franklin Delano Roosevelt, and that was one of the burdens he would bear. Roosevelt and Truman came from starkly different backgrounds. For Truman there had been no inherited wealth, no European travel, no Harvard—indeed, no college at all. Born in 1884 in western Missouri, Truman grew up in Independence, near Kansas City. Bookish and withdrawn, he moved to his grandmother's farm after high school, spent a few years working in Kansas City banks, and grew into an outgoing young man.

During the First World War, Truman served in France as captain of an artillery battery. Afterward, he and a partner started a clothing business, but it failed miserably in the recession of 1922, and Truman then became a professional politician under the tutelage of Kansas City's Democratic machine. In 1934, Missouri sent him to the U.S. Senate, where he remained obscure until he chaired a committee investigating fraud in the war mobilization effort.

Truman was a plain, decent man who lacked Roosevelt's dash and charm, his brilliance and creativity. He was terribly nearsighted and a clumsy public speaker. Yet he had virtues of his own. Some aspects of Truman's personality evoked the spirit of Andrew Jackson: his decisiveness, bluntness, feistiness, loyalty, and folksy manner. On his first full day as president, Truman was awestruck. "Boys, if you ever pray, pray for me now," he told a group of reporters. "I don't know whether you fellows ever had a load of hay fall on you, but when they told me yesterday what had happened, I felt like the moon, the stars and all the planets had fallen on me." Truman was up to the challenge, however. Despite his lack of executive experience, he was confident and self-assured—and he needed to be. Managing the transition from war to peace was a monumental task fraught with dangers. For instance, the wartime economy had ended the Great Depression and brought about full employment, but what would happen as the federal government cut back on military spending and industries transitioned from building tanks and warplanes to automobiles and washing machines? Would the peacetime economy be able to absorb the millions of men and women who had served in the armed forces? These and related issues greatly complicated Truman's efforts to lead America out of combat and into a postwar era complicated by a cold war against Communism and the need to rebuild a devastated Europe and Asia.

On September 6, 1945, Truman sent Congress a comprehensive domestic program that proposed to enlarge the New Deal. Its twenty-one points included expansion of unemployment insurance to cover more workers, a higher minimum wage, the construction of low-cost public housing, regional hydroelectric development of the nation's river valleys, and a public-works program. "Not even President Roosevelt asked for so much at one sitting," said the House Republican leader. "It's just a plain case of out-dealing the New Deal." But Truman soon saw his new domestic proposals mired in disputes over the transition to a peacetime economy.

### The Eldridge General Store, Fayette County, Illinois

Postwar America quickly demobilized, turning its attention to the pursuit of abundance.

CONVERTING TO PEACE   The raucous celebrations that greeted the news of Japan's surrender in the summer of 1945 signaled what would become the most rapid military demobilization in world history. President Truman had naively become convinced that a large air force with atomic bombs would eliminate the need for large conventional military forces. So he gutted the Marine Corps, mothballed warships, and slashed army divisions. By 1947, the total armed forces had shrunk from 12 million to 1.5 million. In just the four years between 1947 and 1951, President Truman went through four secretaries of defense because of their opposition to his efforts to shrink the military. The outbreak of the Korean War in the summer of 1950, however, awakened the president to the reality that robust conventional military forces would still be needed in a nuclear age.

After the Second World War ended, 15 million military veterans eagerly returned to schools, jobs, and families. Population growth, which had dropped off sharply in the 1930s, now soared. The "baby boom generation," those Americans born during this postwar period (roughly 1946–1964) composed a disproportionately large generation of Americans that would become a dominant force shaping the nation's social and cultural life throughout the second half of the twentieth century and after.

The end of the war, with its sudden demobilization and conversion to a peacetime economy, caused short-term problems but not the postwar depression that many had feared. Several shock absorbers cushioned the economic impact of demobilization: federal unemployment insurance and other Social Security benefits; the Servicemen's Readjustment Act of 1944, known as the GI Bill of Rights, under which the federal government spent $13 billion on military veterans for education, vocational training, medical treatment, unemployment insurance, and loans for building houses and going into business; and most important, the pent-up postwar demand for consumer goods that was fueled by wartime deprivation.

CONTROLLING INFLATION   The most acute economic problem Truman faced was not depression but inflation. During the war, America was essentially fully employed. After the war, millions of military veterans had to find jobs as civilians in a peacetime economy. The Roosevelt administration had also frozen wages and prices during the war—and prohibited labor union strikes. When wartime economic controls were removed, prices for consumer items shot up. Prices of farm commodities soared 14 percent in one month and by the end of 1945 were 30 percent higher than they had been in August. As prices rose, so, too, did corporate profits. The gap between soaring consumer prices and stagnant hourly wages prompted growing demands by labor unions for pay increases. When such raises were not forthcoming, unions launched a series of strikes. By January 1946, more workers were on strike than ever before.

Major disputes developed in the coal and railroad industries, both of which were necessary to ensure public health and safety. Like Theodore Roosevelt before him, Truman grew frustrated with the stubbornness of both management and labor. He took the drastic step of taking control of the coal mines, whereupon the mine owners agreed to union demands. Truman also seized control of the railroads and won a five-day postponement of a strike. But when the union leaders refused to make further concessions, the feisty president lashed out against their "obstinate arrogance" and threatened to draft striking workers into the armed forces. The strike ended a few weeks later.

PARTISAN COOPERATION AND CONFLICT   As congressional elections approached in the fall of 1946, public discontent ran high, with most of it focusing on the Truman administration. Both Democrats and Republicans held the president responsible for the prolonged labor turbulence. A speaker at the national convention of the Congress of Industrial Organizations (CIO), normally a pro-Democratic group, had tagged Truman "the No. 1 strikebreaker," while much of the public, angry at the striking unions, also blamed the strikes on the White House. Earlier in the year, Truman had fired ultraliberal Henry A. Wallace as secretary of commerce in a disagreement over foreign policy, thus offending the left-wing of the Democratic party. At the same time, Republicans charged that Communists had infiltrated the government and that Truman had bungled the transition to a peacetime economy. Republicans had a field day coining partisan slogans. In the elections, Republican partisans shouted "To err is Truman," and they won majorities in both houses of Congress for the first time since 1928. "The New Deal is kaput," one newspaper editor crowed—prematurely, as it turned out, for the gutsy Truman thereafter launched a ferocious defense of his administration and its policies.

The new Republican Congress, in an effort to curb the power of the unions, passed the Taft-Hartley Labor Act of 1947, which prohibited what was called a closed shop (in which nonunion workers could not be hired) but permitted a "union shop" (in which workers newly hired were required to join the union) unless banned by state law. It included provisions forbidding "unfair" union practices such as staging secondary boycotts or jurisdictional strikes (by one union to exclude another from a given company or industry), "featherbedding" (paying for work not done), refusing to bargain

**Taft-Hartley Act cartoons**

Organized labor is pulled under by the Taft-Hartley Act (left); while in the other cartoon, Taft and Hartley look for John Lewis, the head of the Mine Workers Union.

in good faith, and contributing to political campaigns. Furthermore, union leaders had to take oaths declaring that they were not members of the Communist party. The act also forbade strikes by federal employees and imposed a "cooling-off" period of eighty days on any strike that the president found to be dangerous to national health or safety.

Truman's veto of the "shocking" Taft-Hartley bill, which unions called "the slave-labor act," restored his credibility with working-class Democrats. Many blue-collar unionists who had gone over to the Republicans in 1946 returned to the Democrats. The Taft-Hartley bill passed over Truman's veto, however. By 1954, fifteen states, mainly in the South, had used the Taft-Hartley Act's authority to enact "right-to-work" laws forbidding union shops.

Truman clashed with the Republicans on other domestic issues. He vetoed a tax cut on the principle that in times of high production and high employment the federal debt should be reduced before taxes should be lowered. Yet the conflicts between Truman and Congress obscured the high degree of bipartisan cooperation in matters of government reorganization and foreign policy. In 1947, Congress passed the National Security Act, which created a National Military Establishment, headed by the secretary of defense with subcabinet Departments of the Army, the Navy, and the Air Force, as well as the National Security Council. The act also established the Central Intelligence Agency (CIA) to coordinate global intelligence-gathering activities in the cold war against communism.

## The Cold War

BUILDING THE UNITED NATIONS    The wartime military alliance against Nazism disintegrated after 1945. Franklin Roosevelt had expected that the Allied Powers in the postwar world would have separate spheres of influence around the globe but, like Woodrow Wilson before him, he focused his efforts on creating a collective security organization, the United Nations. On April 25, 1945, two weeks after Roosevelt's death and two weeks before the German surrender, delegates from fifty nations at war with Germany and Japan met in San Francisco to organize the United Nations. The General Assembly included delegates from all member nations and would meet annually. The **Security Council**, essentially an executive body, would remain in permanent session and would have "primary responsibility for the maintenance of international peace and security." Its eleven members (fifteen after 1965) included five permanent members: the United States, the Soviet Union (replaced by the Russian Federation in 1991), Great Britain, France, and the Republic of China (replaced by the People's Republic of China in 1971). Each permanent member can veto any major proposal.

DIFFERENCES WITH THE SOVIETS    Since the end of the Second World War, historians have debated the tempting but unanswerable question: Was the United States or the Soviet Union more responsible for the onset of the cold war? The conventional, or "orthodox," view argues that the Soviets, led by Joseph Stalin, a paranoid Communist dictator ruling a traditionally insecure nation, set out to dominate the globe after 1945. The United States had no choice but to stand firm in defense of democratic capitalist values. By contrast, "revisionist" scholars insist that Truman was the culprit. Instead of continuing Roosevelt's efforts to collaborate with Stalin and the Soviets, revisionists assert, Truman adopted a confrontational foreign policy designed to create American spheres of influence around the world. In this view, Truman's provocative policies aggravated the tensions between the two superpowers. Yet such an interpretation fails to recognize that both sides engaged in superheated ideological rhetoric. East and West in the postwar world were captives of a nuclear nightmare of fear, suspicion, and posturing. Scholars eager to choose sides also at times fail to acknowledge that President Truman inherited a deteriorating relationship with the Soviets. Events during 1945 made compromise and conciliation more difficult, whether for Roosevelt or for Truman.

There were signs of trouble in the Grand Alliance of Britain, the Soviet Union, and the United States as early as the spring of 1945 when the Soviet

Union installed compliant governments in eastern Europe, violating the promises of democratic elections made at the Yalta Conference. On February 1, the Polish Committee of National Liberation, a puppet group already claiming the status of provisional government, moved from Lublin to Warsaw. In March, the Soviets installed a puppet prime minister in Romania. Protests against such actions led to Soviet counter protests that the British and Americans were negotiating a German surrender in Italy "behind the back of the Soviet Union" and that German forces were being concentrated against the Soviet Union.

Such was the charged atmosphere when Truman entered the White House near the end of the war in Europe. A few days before the San Francisco conference to organize the United Nations, Truman gave Soviet foreign minister Vyacheslav Molotov a tongue-lashing in Washington on the Polish situation. "I have never been talked to like that in my life," Molotov said. "Carry out your agreements," Truman snapped, "and you won't get talked to like that."

On May 12, 1945, four days after victory in Europe, the outspoken British prime minister, Winston Churchill, sent a worried telegram to Truman: "What is to happen about Europe? An **iron curtain** is drawn down upon [the Russian] front. We do not know what is going on behind [it]." Churchill wanted to lift the iron curtain created by Soviet military occupation and install democratic governments in eastern Europe. Instead, as a gesture of goodwill to the Soviets, and over Churchill's protest, U.S. forces withdrew from the German occupation zone that had been assigned to the Soviet Union at the Yalta Conference. American diplomats still hoped that the Yalta agreements would be carried out and that the Soviet Union would help defeat Japan. There was little the Western powers could have done to prevent Soviet control of eastern Europe even if they had not let their military forces dwindle. The presence of Soviet armed forces frustrated the efforts of non-Communists to gain political influence in eastern European countries. The leaders of those opposed to Soviet influence were exiled, silenced, executed, or imprisoned.

Secretary of State James F. Byrnes, who took office in 1945, struggled through 1946 with the problems of postwar treaties. In early 1947, the Council of Foreign Ministers finally produced treaties for Italy, Hungary, Romania, Bulgaria, and Finland. In effect these treaties confirmed Soviet control over eastern Europe, which in Russian eyes seemed but a parallel to American control over Japan and Western control over most of Germany and all of Italy. The Yalta guarantees of democracy in eastern Europe had turned out much like the Open Door policy in China: little more than pious rhetoric sugar coating the realities of raw power and national interest. The Soviets controlled eastern Europe and refused to budge.

Byrnes's impulse to pressure Soviet diplomats by brandishing the atomic bomb only added to the irritations, intimidating no one. As early as April 1945, he had suggested to Truman that possession of nuclear weapons "might well put us in position to dictate our own terms at the end of the war." After becoming secretary of state, he had threatened Soviet diplomats with America's growing arsenal of nuclear weapons. But they paid little notice, in part because they were developing their own atomic bombs.

CONTAINMENT   By the beginning of 1947, relations with the Soviet Union had become even more troubled. A year before, in February 1946, Stalin had pronounced international peace impossible "under the present capitalist development of the world economy." His provocative statement impelled the State Department to send an urgent request for an interpretation of Stalin's speech to forty-two-year-old **George F. Kennan**, a brilliant diplomat and political analyst stationed at the U.S. embassy in Moscow. Kennan responded on February 22, 1946, with a "Long Telegram" in which he sketched the roots of Russian history and Soviet policy. In his extensive analysis, Kennan insisted that Roosevelt's assumptions that the Soviets would cooperate with the United States and the United Nations after the war ("peaceful coexistence") were dangerously naive. Stalin would not be swayed by good-will gestures or democratic ideals. The Soviet Union was founded on an ideology (Leninism) that presumed a fundamental conflict between the communist and capitalist worlds. The Soviets were a new kind of enemy "committed fanatically to the belief that . . . [capitalism] be destroyed." Yet Kennan noted that "the problem is within our power to solve—and that without recourse to any general military conflict." In the immediate aftermath of the war, he explained, the Soviet Union was relatively weak; it was more opportunistic than aggressive; it did not want another war; it was preoccupied with rebuilding its war-devastated infrastructure. The best way to deal with such an ideological foe was to employ patient, persistent, and prolonged efforts ("resolve") to "contain" Soviet expansionism over the long term. Kennan stressed that

**George F. Kennan**

Kennan developed the doctrine of containment.

countering the historic and ideological tendencies of the Soviet Union to exercise control over its neighbors would be the "greatest task our diplomacy has ever faced."

Secretary of State George C. Marshall was so impressed by Kennan's analysis that he summoned him to a new position in the State Department in charge of policy planning. As Kennan remembered, "My reputation was made. My voice now carried." In 1947, Kennan solidified his reputation as the nation's foremost Soviet expert when he wrote an essay titled "The Sources of Soviet Conduct," published anonymously in *Foreign Affairs* and signed by "X." Kennan provided a brilliant psychological analysis of Russian/ Soviet insecurity and intentions. Soviet foreign policy had consistently exerted "a cautious, persistent pressure toward the disruption and weakening of all rival influence and rival power." He predicted that the Soviets would try to fill "every nook and cranny available . . . in the basin of world power." Yet their almost paranoid insecurity also meant that they would usually act cautiously to reduce their risks. Therefore, he insisted, a third world war with the Soviets was unlikely as long as America adopted policies to keep them contained. As he wrote, "the main element of any United States policy toward the Soviet Union must be that of a long-term, patient but firm and vigilant *containment* of Russian expansive tendencies."

What made Kennan's pathbreaking article in *Foreign Affairs* strategically significant was his insistence that by containing Soviet expansionism the United States would eventually force the implosion of the Soviet communist system. He predicted "that Soviet power, like the capitalist world of its conception, bears within it the seeds of its own decay, and that the sprouting of those seeds is well advanced." And he insisted that the United States could accelerate the self-destruction of Soviet communism by adopting shrewd political and economic counter-pressures.

No other American diplomat at the time forecast so accurately what would in fact happen to the Soviet Union some forty years later. In its broadest dimensions, Kennan's "**containment**" concept dovetailed with the outlook of Truman and his advisers, most of whom mistakenly viewed containment primarily in military terms. But Kennan's analysis remained vague on several key issues: How exactly were the United States and its allies to "contain" the Soviet Union? How should the United States respond to specific acts of Soviet aggression around the world?

Kennan was an analyst, not a policymaker. He left the task of converting the concept of "containment" into action to President Truman and his inner circle of advisers, most of whom viewed containment as a military doctrine. They harbored a growing fear that the Soviet lust for power reached beyond eastern Europe, posing dangers in the eastern Mediterranean, the Middle East, and western Europe itself. Indeed, the Soviet Union sought to gain access to the Mediterranean Sea, long important to Russia for purposes of trade and defense. After the war, the Soviet Union pressed Turkey for territorial concessions and the right to build naval bases on the Bosporus, an important gateway between the Black Sea and the Mediterranean. In 1946, civil war broke out in Greece between a government backed by the British and a Communist-led faction that held the northern part of the country and drew supplies from Soviet-dominated Yugoslavia, Bulgaria, and Albania. On February 21, 1947, the British ambassador informed the U.S. government that the British could no longer bear the economic and military burden of aiding Greece; they would withdraw in five weeks. The American reaction was immediate. Within days, Truman conferred with congressional leaders, whereupon the chairman of the Senate Foreign Relations Committee recommended a strong presidential appeal to the nation. The president needed to "scare the hell out of the American people" about the menace of communism. Truman complied.

THE TRUMAN DOCTRINE    On March 12, 1947, President Truman gave a speech, broadcast over national radio, in which he asked Congress for $400 million in economic aid to Greece and Turkey. In his speech, the president enunciated what quickly came to be known as the **Truman Doctrine**. "I believe," Truman declared, "that it must be the policy of the United States to support free peoples who are resisting attempted subjugation by armed minorities or by outside pressures." Otherwise, the Soviet Union would come to dominate Europe, the Middle East, and Asia. George F. Kennan cringed at Truman's open-ended, indiscriminate commitment to "contain" communism everywhere; he had always insisted that American counter-pressure needed to be exercised selectively. All crises were not equally significant; American power was limited. The United States could not intervene in every "hot spot" around the world. Kennan said that Truman's concept of containment was "more grandiose and more sweeping than anything that I . . . had ever envisioned." But other presidential advisers had come to see the world as being in a permanent crisis because of the Communist menace, and they—as well as Truman—were determined to create a militarized containment policy.

In 1947, Congress passed a Greek-Turkish aid bill that helped Turkey achieve economic stability and enabled Greece to defeat a Communist insurrection in 1949. But the principles embedded in the Truman Doctrine committed the United States to intervene throughout the world in order to "contain" the spread of communism, a global commitment that would produce failures as well as successes in the years to come.

The Truman Doctrine marked the beginning, or at least the open acknowledgment, of a contest that the former government official Bernard Baruch named in a 1947 speech to the legislature of South Carolina: "Let us not be deceived—today we are in the midst of a *cold war*." Greece and Turkey were but the front lines in an ideological struggle that was spreading to western Europe, where inflation soared and wartime damage and dislocation had devastated cities, factories, mines, bridges, railroads, and farms, creating opportunities for Communist insurgents to take political advantage of the chaotic situation. Then, during 1946–1947, Europe experienced catastrophic weather—severe droughts in the summers of 1946 and 1947 that destroyed crops, followed by brutal winter temperatures and blizzards that froze rivers, shut down railroads, power plants, and coal mines. Coal shortages in London, where the temperature plunged to sixteen below zero, left only enough fuel to heat and light homes for a few hours each day. In Germany, millions died of exposure and starvation. Amid the chaos, the Communist parties of France and Italy garnered growing support for their promised solutions to the difficulties. Aid from the United Nations and imports of food from abroad had staved off mass starvation but provided little basis for economic recovery.

THE MARSHALL PLAN     In the spring of 1947, former general **George C. Marshall**, who had replaced James F. Byrnes as secretary of state in January, called for massive American aid to rescue Europe from disaster. A retired U.S. Army chief of staff, who had been the highest-ranking general during the Second World War, Marshall used the occasion of the 1947 Harvard graduation ceremonies to outline his ingenious plan for the reconstruction of Europe, which came to be known as the **Marshall Plan**. "Our policy," he said, "is directed not against country or doctrine, but against hunger, poverty, desperation, and chaos." Marshall offered U.S. aid to all European countries, including the Soviet Union. On June 27, the foreign ministers of France, Britain, and the Soviet Union met in London to discuss Marshall's overture. Soviet foreign minister Molotov arrived with eighty advisers, but during the talks he got word from Moscow to withdraw from the "imperialist" scheme. Some among the American delegation did not regret his departure. "He could have killed the Marshall Plan by joining it," said one U.S. official, who feared the Soviets might sabotage the recovery effort.

In December 1947, Truman submitted Marshall's proposal for the European Recovery Program to a special session of Congress. Two months later, a Communist-led coup in Czechoslovakia orchestrated by the Soviet Union ensured congressional passage of the Marshall Plan. It seemed to confirm the threat to western Europe. President Truman signed the unique legislation on April 3, 1948. He insisted that it be called the Marshall Plan rather than the Truman Plan because the former general was the "greatest living American," and naming it for Marshall would do "a whole hell of a lot better in Congress." From 1948 until 1951, the newly created Economic Cooperation Administration, which managed the Marshall Plan, poured $13 billion into economic recovery efforts in Europe. Most of the aid went to Great Britain, France, Italy, and West Germany. And it worked as planned.

**"It's the Same Thing"**

The Marshall Plan, which distributed aid throughout Europe, is represented in this 1949 cartoon as a modern tractor driven by a prosperous farmer. In the foreground a poor, overworked man is yoked to an old-fashioned "Soviet" plow, forced to go over the ground of the "Marshal Stalin Plan," while Stalin himself tries to persuade others that "it's the same thing without mechanical problems."

DIVIDING GERMANY  The Marshall Plan drew the nations of western Europe closer together, but it increased tensions with the Soviet Union, for Stalin correctly viewed the massive American effort to rebuild the European economy as a way to diminish Soviet influence in the region. The breakdown of the wartime alliance between the United States and the Soviet Union also left the problem of postwar Germany unsettled. Berlin had been divided into four sectors or occupation zones, each governed by one of the four allied nations: the United States, Great Britain, France, and the Soviet Union. The war-devastated German economy languished, requiring the U.S. Army to provide food and basic necessities to civilians. Slowly, the Allied occupation zones evolved into functioning governments. In 1948, the British, French, and Americans consolidated their three zones into one and developed a common currency to be used in West Germany as well as West Berlin. The West Germans set about organizing state governments and elected delegates to a federal constitutional convention.

The political unification of West Germany infuriated Stalin, who wanted to keep Germany weak and decentralized. The status of West Berlin, sitting deep inside the Soviet occupation zone (East Germany), had also become an explosive powder keg. By 1948, there were only ninety thousand U.S. troops left in western Germany and Berlin; the Soviets had a million soldiers in their much smaller eastern occupation zone. In March 1948, Stalin decided to force the issue of Berlin's future by trying to prevent the new West German currency from being delivered into the city. The Soviets began to restrict road and rail traffic into West Berlin; on June 23, 1945, they stopped all traffic into the beleaguered city. The next day, Stalin cut all electrical service to West Berlin. The Soviets hoped the blockade would force the Allies to give up the city. This warfare by starvation and intimidation placed the United States on the horns of a dilemma: risk a third world war by using force to break the blockade, or begin a humiliating retreat from West Berlin, leaving the residents to be swallowed up by the Soviet bloc. But General Lucius D. Clay, the iron-willed U.S. army commander in Germany, proposed to stand firm and even use force to break the blockade. Truman agreed, saying, "We [are going to] stay in Berlin—period."

After considering the use of armed convoys to supply the 2.5 million people living in West Berlin, the president decided—against the advice of his cabinet and General Clay—to organize a massive, sustained airlift to provide needed food and supplies to West Berliners. At the time, it seemed like an impossible task, but by October 1948 the U.S. and British air forces were flying in up to thirteen thousand tons of food, medicine, coal, and equipment a day. The massive Berlin airlift went on for eleven months, transporting 2.32 million tons of cargo. Pilots and crews risked—and at times gave—their lives on 14,036 flights, often in foul, foggy weather, to save the city.

Finally, on May 12, 1949, after extended talks, the Soviets lifted the blockade of West Berlin, in part because bad Russian harvests made them desperate for food grown in West Germany. Before the end of the year, the Federal Republic of Germany had a government functioning under Chancellor Konrad Adenauer. At the end of May 1949, an independent German Democratic Republic arose in the Soviet-controlled eastern zone, formalizing the division of Germany into eastern and western nations. West Germany gradually acquired more authority, until the Western powers recognized its full sovereignty in 1955. The Berlin airlift was the first explicit "victory" for the West in the Cold War. Its success transformed West Berliners from defeated adversaries to ardent American allies. The elected mayor of divided Berlin correctly predicted that "the magnetic pull of the West will someday pull Berlin and the Eastern zone [East Germany] back into a united Germany."

BUILDING ALLIANCES   The blockade of West Berlin convinced the allied nations that they needed to act collectively to thwart Soviet efforts at expansion into western Europe. As relations between the Soviets and western Europe chilled, transatlantic unity ripened into a formal military alliance. On April 4, 1949, the North Atlantic Treaty was signed by representatives of twelve nations: the United States, Britain, France, Belgium, the Netherlands, Luxembourg, Canada, Denmark, Iceland, Italy, Norway, and Portugal. Greece and Turkey joined the alliance in 1952, West Germany in 1955, and Spain in 1982. Senate ratification of the North Atlantic Treaty by a vote of 82 to 13 demonstrated that the isolationism of the prewar period had disappeared in the face of Soviet communism. The treaty pledged that an attack against any one of the members would be considered an attack against all and provided for a council of the **North Atlantic Treaty Organization (NATO)**.

The eventful year of 1948 produced another foreign-policy decision with long-term consequences along the east coast of the Mediterranean Sea. Palestine, as the biblical Holy Land had come to be known, had been under Turkish rule until the League of Nations made it a British protectorate after the First World War. During the early years of the twentieth century, many Zionists, who advocated a Jewish nation in the region, had migrated there. More arrived after the British gained control in 1919, and many more arrived during the Nazi persecution of European Jews in the 1930s and just after the Second World War ended. Having been promised a national home-land by the British, the Jews of Palestine demanded their own nation after the war, and they received energetic support from American Jews and worldwide Jewish organizations.

Late in 1947, the United Nations voted to partition Palestine into Jewish and Arab states, but this plan met fierce Arab opposition. No action was taken until the British control of Palestine expired on May 14, 1948, at which time Jewish leaders in

**NATO**

NATO is depicted as a symbol of renewed strength for a battered Europe.

NORTH SEA

DENMARK

SWEDEN

BALTIC SEA

U.S.S.R.

To U.S.S.R.

EAST PRUSSIA

Danzig (Gdansk)

To Poland

NETHERLANDS

Hamburg

Bremen

Access corridor

Annexed by Poland

WEST GERMANY

Berlin

Oder River

Warsaw

POLAND

EAST

Joint occupation by four powers

Neisse R.

Bonn

GERMANY

Lublin

BELGIUM

Frankfurt

Iron Curtain

SAAR

LUXEMBOURG

FRANCE

Rhine River

Danube River

CZECHOSLOVAKIA

Munich

Vienna

SWITZERLAND

AUSTRIA

HUNGARY

ROMANIA

ITALY

0    50    100 Miles

0    50    100 Kilometers

**THE OCCUPATION OF GERMANY AND AUSTRIA**

☐ French zone     ☐ U.S. zone

☐ British zone     ☐ Soviet zone

YUGOSLAVIA

How did the Allies divide Germany and Austria at the Yalta Conference? What was the "iron curtain"? Why did the Allies airlift supplies to Berlin?

Palestine, most of them immigrants from Europe, proclaimed the independence of Israel. President Truman, who had been in close touch with American Jewish leaders, officially recognized the new Israeli state within minutes; the United States became the first nation to act. Truman's decision in the face of opposition from Great Britain and the U.S. State Department made his bold action all the more remarkable. He acted in part because of his own strong biblical belief that the Jews belonged in Israel. The president had also been appalled by the revelations of the Nazi efforts to exterminate the Jews as well as the scandalously poor treatment the displaced Jews had received in the postwar years.

The creation of a Jewish state in Palestine prompted neighboring Arab nations to attack Israel, which held its own, largely through weaponry provided by the Soviet Union. UN mediators gradually worked out a truce agreement, restoring an uneasy peace by May 11, 1949, when Israel joined the United Nations. But the hard feelings and intermittent warfare between Israel and the Arab states have festered ever since, complicating U.S. foreign policy, which has tried to maintain friendship with both sides but has tilted toward Israel.

## CIVIL RIGHTS DURING THE 1940S

The social tremors triggered by the Second World War and the onset of the cold war transformed America's racial landscape. The government-sponsored racism of the German Nazis, the Italian Fascists, and the Japanese imperialists focused attention on the need for the United States to improve its own race relations and to provide for equal rights under the law. As a *New York Times* editorial explained in early 1946, "This is a particularly good time to campaign against the evils of bigotry, prejudice, and race hatred because we have witnessed the defeat of enemies who tried to found a mastery of the world upon such cruel and fallacious policy." The postwar confrontation with the Soviet Union gave American leaders an added incentive to improve race relations at home. But in the ideological contest with communism for influence in post-colonial Africa, U.S. diplomats were at a disadvantage as long as racial segregation continued in the United States; the Soviets often compared racism in the South to the Nazis' treatment of the Jews.

In the postwar South, many African American military veterans were eager to change their region's racist tradition that made a mockery of their efforts to defend the principles of liberty and democracy against fascism. The Georgia Veterans League, for example, launched an energetic effort to register black voters after the war. Some white veterans balked at such efforts, however. Many members of the Ku Klux Klan, the all-white Citizens' Councils, and other southern organizations created to promote white racial superiority had served in the military during the Second World War. As the head of one such organization declared, "Our heroes didn't die in Europe to give Negroes the right to marry our wives." One black veteran arrived home in a uniform festooned with combat medals, only to be welcomed by a white neighbor who said: "Don't you forget . . . that you're still a nigger." Those black veterans who spoke out against such racial bigotry risked their lives—literally. In 1946, four African Americans were gunned down by a white mob in rural Georgia. One of the murderers explained that George Dorsey, one of the victims, was "a good nigger" until he went in the army. "But when he came out, he thought he was as good as any white people."

Harry S. Truman was horrified by such incidents and grew ever more determined to promote civil rights. For most of his political career, Truman had shown little concern for the plight of African Americans. He had grown up in western Missouri assuming that blacks and whites preferred to be segregated from one another. As president, however, he began to reassess his convictions. In the fall of 1946, a delegation of civil rights activists urged Truman to issue a public statement condemning the resurgence of the Ku Klux Klan and the lynching of African Americans. The delegation graphically described incidents of torture and intimidation against blacks in the South. Truman was aghast. He soon appointed a Committee on Civil Rights to investigate violence against African Americans and to recommend preventive measures.

On July 26, 1948, President Truman banned racial discrimination in the hiring of federal employees. Four days later, he issued an executive order ending racial segregation in the armed forces. The air force and navy quickly complied, but the army dragged its feet until the early 1950s. By 1960, the armed forces were the most racially integrated of all national organizations. Desegregating the military was, Truman claimed, "the greatest thing that ever happened to America."

JACKIE ROBINSON    In July 1944, in the middle of the war, a bus driver at Fort Hood, Texas, directed an African American army lieutenant to "get to the back of the bus where the colored people belong." The young officer refused, explaining that the army had recently ordered its buses integrated. The bus driver said he had never heard such a thing and called upon MPs (military police) to arrest the black lieutenant, who was subsequently charged with insubordination. But a military court made up of nine white officers acquitted him. The lieutenant was Georgia-born **Jackie Robinson**, and the incident reflected his determination to defy the racist traditions in American life.

Three years later, as the professional baseball season opened in the spring, the National League's Brooklyn Dodgers included on its roster a talented player named Jackie Robinson, the first African American player to cross the color line. During Robinson's first season with the Dodgers, teammates and opposing players viciously baited him, pitchers threw at him, base runners spiked him, and spectators booed him in every city. Hotels refused him rooms, restaurants denied him service, and hate mail arrived by the bucket load. On the other hand, black spectators were electrified by Robinson's courageous example; they turned

**Jackie Robinson**

Racial discrimination remained widespread throughout the postwar period. In 1947, Jackie Robinson of the Brooklyn Dodgers became the first black player in major league baseball.

out in droves to watch him play. As time passed, Robinson won over many fans and players with his quiet courage, self-deprecating wit, and determined performance. He was named the Rookie of the Year in 1947 and later selected to six straight All-Star teams. He played in five World Series championships. Robinson's courageous performance led other teams to sign black players. Baseball's pathbreaking efforts promoting racial integration stimulated other professional sports teams to do the same. Jackie Robinson vividly demonstrated that racism, not inferiority, impeded African American advancement in the postwar era and that segregation need not be a permanent condition of American life.

SHAPING THE FAIR DEAL   By early 1948, after three years in the White House, President Truman had yet to shake the impression that he was not up to the job. The Democratic party seemed about to fragment: southern conservatives resented Truman's outspoken support of civil rights. By 1948, most political analysts assumed that Truman would lose the November election. Such gloomy predictions did not faze the combative president, however. He mounted a furious reelection campaign. His first step was to

**"I Stand Pat!"**

Truman's support of civil rights for African Americans had its political costs, as this 1948 cartoon suggests.

shore up the major elements of the New Deal coalition: farmers, unionists, and African Americans. In his 1948 State of the Union message, Truman offered something to nearly every group the Democrats hoped to attract. The first goal, Truman said, was to ensure civil rights. He added proposals to increase federal aid to education, expand unemployment and retirement benefits, create a comprehensive system of health insurance, enhance federal support for public housing projects, enable more rural dwellers to connect to electricity, and increase the minimum wage.

THE ELECTION OF 1948 The Republican-controlled Congress for the most part spurned the Truman program, an action it would later regret. At the Republican Convention, New York governor Thomas E. Dewey won the presidential nomination on the third ballot. The platform endorsed most of the New Deal reforms and approved the administration's bipartisan foreign policy; Dewey promised to run things more efficiently, however. In July, a glum Democratic Convention gathered in Philadelphia. But delegates who expected to do little more than go through the motions were doubly surprised: first by the battle over the civil rights plank, and then by Truman's acceptance speech. To keep from stirring southern hostility, the administration sought a platform plank that opposed racial discrimination only in general terms. Liberal Democrats, however, sponsored a bold resolution that called on Congress to take specific action and commended Truman "for his courageous stand on the issue of civil rights." Thirty-seven-year-old Minneapolis mayor Hubert H. Humphrey electrified the delegates and set off a ten-minute demonstration when he declared, "The time has arrived for the

Democratic party to get out of the shadow of states' rights and walk forthrightly into the bright sunshine of human rights." White segregationist delegates from Alabama and Mississippi instead walked out of the convention. The solidly Democratic South had fractured for the first time since the end of the Civil War.

On July 17, a group of rebellious southern Democrats met in Birmingham, Alabama. While waving Confederate flags and singing "Dixie," the dissident Democrats nominated South Carolina governor Strom Thurmond on a States' Rights Democratic ticket, quickly dubbed the Dixiecrat party. The **Dixiecrats** denounced Truman's "infamous" civil rights initiatives and championed states' rights. They hoped to draw enough electoral votes to preclude a majority for either major party, throwing the election into the House of Representatives, where they might strike a sectional bargain. A few days later, on July 23, the left wing of the Democratic party gathered in Philadelphia to form a new Progressive party and nominate for president Henry A. Wallace, Roosevelt's former secretary of agriculture and vice president. These splits in the Democratic ranks seemed to spell the final blow to Truman, but the

**Picketing in Philadelphia**

The opening of the 1948 Democratic National Convention was marked by demonstrations against racial segregation, led by A. Philip Randolph (left).

**The Dixiecrats nominate Strom Thurmond**

The Dixiecrats nominated South Carolina governor Strom Thurmond (center) to lead their ticket in the 1948 election.

courageous president was undaunted. He pledged to "win this election and make the Republicans like it!" He then set out on a 31,000-mile "whistle-stop" train tour, during which he castigated the "do-nothing" Eightieth Congress. Friendly audiences shouted, "Pour it on, Harry!" and "Give 'em hell, Harry." Truman responded: "I don't give 'em hell. I just tell the truth and they think it's hell."

The polls and the pundits predicted a sure win for the Republican Dewey, but on election day Truman won the biggest upset in history, taking 24.2 million votes (49.5 percent) to Dewey's 22 million (45.1 percent) and winning a thumping margin of 303 to 189 in the Electoral College. Thurmond and Wallace each got more than 1 million votes, but the revolt of right and left had worked to Truman's advantage. The Dixiecrat rebellion backfired by angering black voters, who turned out in droves to support Truman, while the Progressive party's radicalism made it hard to tag Truman as soft on communism. Thurmond carried four Deep South states (South Carolina, Mississippi, Alabama, and Louisiana) with 39 electoral votes, including one from a Tennessee elector who repudiated his state's decision for Truman. Thurmond's success hastened a momentous disruption of the Democratic Solid South that would begin a long transition in the region to Republicanism.

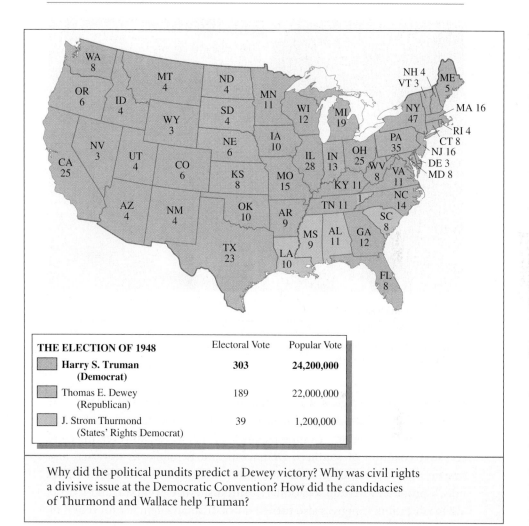

| THE ELECTION OF 1948 | Electoral Vote | Popular Vote |
|---|---|---|
| Harry S. Truman (Democrat) | 303 | 24,200,000 |
| Thomas E. Dewey (Republican) | 189 | 22,000,000 |
| J. Strom Thurmond (States' Rights Democrat) | 39 | 1,200,000 |

Why did the political pundits predict a Dewey victory? Why was civil rights a divisive issue at the Democratic Convention? How did the candidacies of Thurmond and Wallace help Truman?

Truman viewed his victory as a vindication for the New Deal and a mandate for moderate liberalism. "We have rejected the discredited theory that the fortunes of the nation should be in the hands of a privileged few," he said. His State of the Union message repeated the agenda he had set forth the year before. "Every segment of our population and every individual," he declared, "has a right to expect from his government a fair deal." Whether deliberately or not, he had invented a catchy label, the Fair Deal, to distinguish his program from the New Deal.

Most of Truman's Fair Deal proposals were extensions or enlargements of New Deal programs already in place: a higher minimum wage, expansion of

**"Dewey Defeats Truman"**

Truman's victory in 1948 was a huge upset, so much so that even the early edition of the *Chicago Daily Tribune* was caught off guard, running this presumptuous headline.

Social Security coverage to workers not included in the original bill in 1935, increased federal subsidies paid to farmers, and a sizable slum-clearance and public-housing program. Despite Democratic majorities, however, the conservative coalition of southern Democrats and Republicans thwarted any drastic new departures in domestic policy. Congress rejected civil rights bills, a proposal to create a national health insurance program, and federal aid to education. Congress also turned down Truman's demand for repeal of the Taft-Hartley Act.

## THE COLD WAR HEATS UP

As was true during Truman's first term, global concerns repeatedly distracted the president's attention from domestic issues. In his 1949 inaugural address, Truman called for a vigilant anti-Communist foreign policy resting on four pillars: the United Nations, the Marshall Plan, NATO, and a "bold new plan" for providing financial and technical assistance to underdeveloped parts of the world, which came to be known simply as Point Four. But other issues kept the Point Four program from ever reaching its potential as a means of increasing American influence abroad at the expense of communism.

"LOSING" CHINA AND THE BOMB   One of the most intractable postwar problems, a prolonged civil war in China, was fast unraveling in 1949. The Chinese Nationalists, led by Chiang Kai-shek, had been fighting Mao Zedong and the Communists since the 1920s. The outbreak of war with Japan in 1937 had halted this civil war, and both Franklin Delano Roosevelt and Stalin believed that the Nationalists would control China after the war. But the commanders of U.S. forces in China during the Second World War concluded that Chiang's government was hopelessly corrupt, tyrannical, and inefficient. After the war, American forces nevertheless ferried Nationalist Chinese armies back into the eastern and northern provinces of China as the Japanese withdrew. Civil war between the Nationalists and the Communists erupted in late 1945.

It soon became a losing fight for the Nationalists as the Communists won over the land-hungry peasantry. By the end of 1949, the Nationalist government had fled to the island of Formosa, which it renamed Taiwan. Truman's critics—mostly Republicans—now asked bitterly, "Who lost China?" But it is hard to imagine how the U.S. government could have prevented a Communist victory short of a massive military intervention, which would have been risky, unpopular, and expensive. The United States continued to recognize the Nationalist government on Taiwan as the rightful government of China, delaying formal relations with Communist China (the People's Republic of China) for thirty years.

As the Communists were gaining control of China, the Soviets were successfully testing an atomic bomb. The American nuclear monopoly had lasted just four years. The discovery of the Soviet bomb in 1949 triggered an intense reappraisal of the strategic balance of power in the world, causing Truman in 1950 to order the construction of a hydrogen bomb, a weapon far more powerful than the atomic bombs dropped on Japan, lest the Soviets make one first. Over the next forty years, the two cold war adversaries would manufacture over one hundred thousand nuclear weapons ready to be launched on land, under the sea, and in the air. Both sides were prepared to use such horrific weapons. The concept of nuclear deterrence during the cold war depended upon convincing the "other side" that a nuclear war was possible. As an American expert on nuclear weaponry explained, the nation's leaders needed to "have the balls to push the button."

The growing threat of atomic warfare with the Soviet Union led the National Security Council in April 1950 to unveil a top-secret document, known as NSC-68. It called for rebuilding America's conventional armed forces to provide military options other than nuclear war. Such a plan represented a major departure from the nation's time-honored aversion to maintaining large armies in peacetime. It was also an expensive proposition. But the public was growing more receptive to the nation's new role as world leader amid the cold war, and an invasion of South Korea in 1950 by Communist forces from the north clinched the issue for most Americans.

WAR IN KOREA    The Japanese had occupied the Korean Peninsula since 1910. After the defeat and withdrawal of the Japanese in 1945, the victorious Allies faced the difficult task of creating a new Korean nation. Soviet troops had advanced into northern Korea and accepted the surrender of Japanese forces above the 38th parallel, while U.S. forces had done the same south of that line. Rival Korean regimes then emerged. The opportunistic Soviets quickly organized a Korean government in the North along Stalinist lines, while the Americans set up a western-style regime in the South.

The division of Korea at the end of the Second World War, like the division of Germany, was a temporary necessity that became permanent. In the hectic days of August 1945, the Soviets accepted an American proposal to divide desperately poor Korea at the 38th parallel until steps could be taken to unify the war-torn country. With the onset of the cold war, however, the two sides could not agree on unification. By the end of 1948, separate regimes had appeared in the two sectors and occupation forces had withdrawn. The weakened state of the U.S. military contributed to the impression that South Korea was vulnerable to a Communist assault. Evidence later gleaned from Soviet archives reveals that Stalin as well as Mao encouraged the North Koreans to unify their country and oust the Americans from the peninsula. The Soviet-designed war plan called for North Korean forces to seize South Korea within a week. Stalin apparently assumed that the United States would not intervene.

On June 25, 1950, over eighty thousand North Korean soldiers crossed the boundary into South Korea and drove the South Korean army down the peninsula in a headlong retreat. Seoul, the South Korean capital, was captured in three days. President Truman responded decisively. He and his advisers assumed that the North Korean attack was directed by Moscow and was a brazen indication of the aggressive designs of Soviet communism. "The attack upon Korea makes it plain beyond all doubt," Truman told Congress, "that communism has passed beyond the use of subversion to conquer independent nations and will now use armed invasion and war." Truman then made a critical decision: he decided to wage war under the auspices of the United Nations rather than seeking a declaration of war from Congress.

An emergency meeting of the UN Security Council quickly censured the North Korean "breach of peace." The Soviet delegate, who held a veto power, was at the time boycotting the council because it would not seat Communist China in place of Nationalist China. On June 27, the Security Council took advantage of his absence to call on UN members to "furnish such assistance

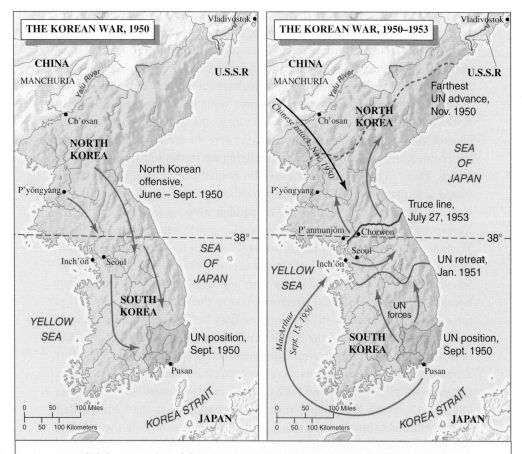

How did the surrender of the Japanese in Korea set up the conflict between Soviet-influenced North Korea and U.S.-influenced South Korea? What was General MacArthur's strategy for retaking Korea? Why did President Truman remove MacArthur from command?

to the Republic of Korea as may be necessary to repel the armed attack and to restore international peace and security in the area." Truman thereupon ordered American air, naval, and ground forces into action. In all, some fourteen other nations contributed token military units, but the United States carried the burden of the fighting. **General Douglas MacArthur** was put in command. The American defense of South Korea set a precedent of profound consequence: war by order of a president rather than by vote of Congress.

Truman's assumption that Stalin and the Soviets were behind the invasion of South Korea prompted two other decisions that had far-reaching consequences. First, Truman mistakenly viewed the Korean conflict as a diversion for a Soviet invasion of western Europe, so he ordered a major expansion of U.S. military forces in Europe. Second, he increased assistance to French troops fighting a Communist independence movement in Indochina (Vietnam), creating the Military Assistance Advisory Group for Indochina—the start of America's deepening military involvement in Southeast Asia.

For three months, the fighting in Korea went badly for the Republic of Korea and the UN forces. By September, the North Korean forces had taken control of 90 percent of the peninsula and were on the verge of decimating the South Koreans, who were barely hanging on to the southeast corner of Korea. Then, in a brilliant maneuver on September 15, 1950, MacArthur staged a surprise amphibious landing behind the North Korean lines at Inch'ŏn, the port city for Seoul. The sudden blow stampeded the North Korean forces back across the border. At that point, MacArthur persuaded Truman to allow him to push north and seek to reunify Korea. By then, however, the Soviet delegate was back in the Security Council, wielding his veto. So on October 7, the United States won approval for pushing into North Korea from the UN General Assembly, where the veto did not apply. U.S. forces had crossed the North Korean boundary by October 1 and were continuing northward toward the border with Communist China. The political objective of the war had moved from containment to liberation. President Truman, concerned about intervention by Communist China, flew seven thousand miles to Wake Island for a conference with General MacArthur on October 15. There the general discounted chances that the Chinese Red Army would act, but if it did, he predicted, "there would be the greatest slaughter."

That same day, the Communist government in Beijing announced that China "cannot stand idly by." On October 20, UN forces had entered

**September 1950**

American soldiers engaged in the recapture of Seoul from the North Koreans.

P'yŏngyang, the North Korean capital, and on October 26, advance units had reached Ch'osan, on the Yalu River, Korea's northern border with China. MacArthur predicted total victory by Christmas. On the night of November 25, however, some 260,000 Chinese "volunteers" counterattacked, and massive "human-wave" attacks, with the support of tanks and warplanes, turned the tables on the UN troops, sending them into a desperate retreat just at the onset of winter. It had become "an entirely new war," MacArthur said. He asked for thirty-four atomic bombs and proposed air raids on China's "privileged sanctuary" in Manchuria, a naval blockade of China, and an invasion of the Chinese mainland by the Taiwan Nationalists.

Truman opposed leading the United States into the "gigantic booby trap" of war with Communist China, and the UN forces soon rallied. By January 1951, over nine hundred thousand UN troops under General Matthew B. Ridgway launched a counterattack that in some places carried them back across the 38th parallel. When Truman offered negotiations to restore the prewar boundary, General MacArthur undermined the move by issuing an ultimatum for China to make peace or suffer an attack on their own country.

On April 5, on the floor of Congress, the Republican minority leader read a letter in which General MacArthur criticized the president and said that "there is no substitute for victory." Such an act of open insubordination left Truman, as the commander in chief, no choice but to accept MacArthur's aggressive demands or fire him. Civilian control of the military was at stake, Truman later said, and he acted swiftly. On April 11, 1951, the president removed the popular MacArthur (Truman called him "Mr. Prima Donna") from his command and replaced him with the more prudent Ridgway.

Truman's action ignited an uproar across the country, and a tumultuous reception greeted MacArthur upon his first return home since 1937. MacArthur's emotional departing speech to a joint session of Congress provided the climactic event. He recalled a barracks ballad of his youth "which proclaimed most proudly that old soldiers never die, they just fade away." And like the old soldiers of that ballad, he said, "I now close my military career and just fade away, an old soldier who tried to do his duty as God gave him the light to see that duty." A Senate investigation brought out the administration's arguments, best summarized by General Omar Bradley, chairman of the Joint Chiefs of Staff. "Taking on Red China," he explained, would lead only "to a larger deadlock at greater expense." The MacArthur strategy "would involve us in the wrong war at the wrong place at the wrong time and with the wrong enemy." Most Americans found General Bradley's logic persuasive.

On June 24, 1951, the Soviet representative at the United Nations proposed a cease-fire in Korea along the 38th parallel, the original dividing line between North and South; U.S. Secretary of State Dean Acheson accepted the cease-fire a few days later with the consent of the United Nations. China and North Korea responded favorably—at the time, General Ridgway's "meat-grinder" offensive was inflicting severe losses—and truce talks started on July 10, 1951, at P'anmunjŏm, only to drag on for two years while the fighting continued. The chief snags were exchanges of military prisoners and the South Korean president's insistence on unification. By the time a truce was reached, on July 27, 1953, Truman had relinquished the White House to Republican Dwight D. Eisenhower. The truce line followed the war front at that time, mostly a little north of the 38th parallel, with a demilitarized zone of two and a half miles separating the forces; repatriation of prisoners would be voluntary, supervised by a neutral commission. No peace conference ever took place, and Korea, like Germany, remained divided. The war had cost the United States more than 33,000 battle deaths and 103,000 wounded or missing. South Korean casualties, all told, were about 1 million, and North

Korean and Chinese casualties an estimated 1.5 million.

ANOTHER RED SCARE The Korean War excited a second Red Scare as people grew increasingly fearful that Communists were infiltrating American society. Since 1938 the **House Committee on Un-American Activities** (known as **HUAC**) had kept up a drumbeat of accusations about supposed Communist subversives in the federal government. On March 21, 1947, just nine days after he announced the Truman Doctrine, the president signed an executive order creating a loyalty program in the federal government. Every person entering federal service would be subject to a background investigation. By early 1951,

**Alger Hiss**

Accused of leading a Soviet spy ring, Hiss testifies before the House Un-American Activities Committee (HUAC) in August 1948.

the Civil Service Commission had cleared over 3 million people, while over 2,000 had resigned and 212 had been dismissed for doubtful loyalty.

Perhaps the case most damaging to the administration involved **Alger Hiss**, president of the Carnegie Endowment for International Peace, who had earlier served in several government agencies, including the State Department. Whittaker Chambers, a former Soviet agent and later an editor of *Time* magazine, told the HUAC in 1948 that Hiss had given him secret documents ten years earlier, when Chambers was spying for the Soviets and Hiss was working in the State Department. Hiss sued for libel, and Chambers produced microfilms of the State Department documents that he said Hiss had passed to him. Hiss denied the accusation, whereupon he was indicted and, after one mistrial, convicted in 1950. The charge was perjury, but he was convicted of lying about espionage, for which he could not be tried because the statute of limitations on that crime had expired.

Most damaging to the administration was that President Truman, taking at face value the many testimonials to Hiss's integrity, had called the charges against him a "red herring." The Hiss affair had another political consequence: it raised to national prominence a young California congressman, Richard M. Nixon, who doggedly insisted on pursuing the case and then exploited his anti-Communist rhetoric to win election to the Senate in 1950.

More cases of Communist infiltration surfaced. In 1949, eleven top leaders of the Communist party in the United States were convicted under the Smith Act of 1940, which outlawed any conspiracy to advocate the overthrow of the government. The Supreme Court upheld the law under the doctrine of a "clear and present danger," which overrode the right to free speech. What was more, in 1950 the government unearthed the existence of a British-American spy network that had fed information about the development of the atomic bomb to the Soviet Union. These disclosures led to the arrest of, among others, Klaus Fuchs in Britain and Julius and Ethel Rosenberg in the United States.

MCCARTHY'S WITCH HUNT  Revelations of Soviet spying in the United States encouraged politicians to exploit the public's fears of the Communist menace at home. If a man of such respectability as Alger Hiss was guilty, many wondered, who could be trusted? Early in 1950, a little-known Republican senator, **Joseph R. McCarthy** of Wisconsin, suddenly surfaced as the most ruthless exploiter of the nation's anxieties. He took up the cause of anti-communism with an incendiary speech at Wheeling, West

**Joseph McCarthy**

Senator McCarthy (left) and his aide Roy Cohn (right) exchange comments during testimony.

Virginia, on February 9, 1950, in which he charged that the State Department was infested with Communists—and he claimed to have their names, although he never provided them. McCarthy's headline-grabbing tactic was to unleash a barrage of general accusations in an effort to deflect attention from his lack of evidence. Concerns about the truth or fair play did not faze him. He refused to answer critics or provide evidence; his focus was on fearmongering.

And for a time it worked. McCarthy provided an anxious public genuinely worried about Communist subversion with a simple scapegoat: the Democrats were traitors. "Like a man busily shooting off firecrackers in a legislative hall," said a reporter, "McCarthy may not be persuasive, but he must be dealt with before any debate at all can progress." Despite his outlandish claims and boorish bullying, McCarthy never uncovered a single Communist agent in the government. But with the United States at war with Korean Communists in mid-1950, it was easy for him to arouse public fears. During the summer of 1951, he had outrageously called General George C. Marshall a traitor. His smear campaign went unchallenged until the end of the Korean War and helped fuel widespread concerns about communist subversion in the United States. Magazines, novels, and movies played upon fears of Communist agents infiltrating American society. The film *I Married a Communist* (1949) exemplified Hollywood's effort to capitalize on the almost hysterical concerns about Soviet efforts to infiltrate American neighborhoods and organizations.

Fears of Communist espionage led Congress in 1950 to pass the McCarran Internal Security Act over President Truman's veto, making it unlawful "to combine, conspire, or agree with any other person to perform any act which would substantially contribute to . . . the establishment of a totalitarian dictatorship." Communist and Communist-front organizations had to register with the attorney general. Immigrants who had belonged to totalitarian parties in their home countries were barred from admission to the United States. The McCarran Internal Security Act, Truman said in his veto message, would "put the Government into the business of thought control." He might in fact have said as much about the Smith Act of 1940 or even his own program of loyalty investigations. Yet documents recently uncovered in Russian archives and U.S. security agencies reveal that the Soviets did indeed operate an extensive espionage ring in the United States. Russian agents recruited hundreds of American spies to ferret out secrets regarding atomic weapons, defense systems, and military intelligence. The United States did the same in Eastern Europe and the Soviet Union.

ASSESSING THE COLD WAR   In retrospect the onset of the cold war after the end of the Second World War takes on an appearance of terrible inevitability. America's traditional commitment to democratic capitalism, political self-determination, and religious freedom conflicted with the Soviet Union's preference for spheres of influence on its periphery, totalitarianism at home, and state-mandated atheism. Insecurity, more than ideology, drove much of Soviet behavior during and after the Second World War. Russia, after all, had been invaded by Germany twice in the first half of the twentieth century, and Soviet leaders wanted tame buffer states on their borders for protection. The people of eastern Europe were again caught in the middle.

If international conditions set the stage for the cold war, the actions of political leaders and thinkers set events in motion. Hindsight is always clearer than foresight, and President Truman may have erred in 1947 when he pledged to "contain" communism everywhere. The government loyalty program he launched may also have helped aggravate the anti-Communist hysteria. Containment itself proved hard to contain amid the ideological posturing. Its theorist, George F. Kennan, later confessed that he was to blame in part because he had failed at the outset to stress that the United States needed to prioritize its response to Soviet adventurism and not focus on military responses to every trouble spot around the globe.

The years after the Second World War were unlike any other postwar period in American history. Having taken on global burdens, the nation had become committed to a permanent national military establishment, along with the attendant creation of shadowy new bureaucracies such as the National Security Council (NSC), the National Security Agency (NSA), and the Central Intelligence Agency (CIA). The federal government—and the presidency—continued to grow during the Cold War, fueled by the actions of both major political parties as well as by the intense lobbying efforts of what Dwight D. Eisenhower would call the "military-industrial complex." In 1952, President Truman created the enormous National Security Agency, entrusted with monitoring all media and communications for foreign intelligence and exempt from laws protecting privacy and civil liberties. The advent of nuclear weapons and the authority given solely to the president to order a nuclear attack further expanded executive authority.

The policy initiatives of the Truman years abandoned the nation's long-standing aversion to peacetime alliances. It was a far cry from the world of 1796, when George Washington in his farewell address warned his countrymen against "those overgrown military establishments which . . . are inauspicious to liberty" and advised his country "to steer clear of permanent alliances with any portion of the foreign world." But then Washington had warned only against participation in the "ordinary" combinations and collusions of Europe. The postwar years had seen extraordinary events as well as unprecedented new military alliances and weaponry. Times had changed dramatically, and so too had America's role in world affairs.

## CHAPTER SUMMARY

- **The Cold War**  The cold war was an ideological contest between the Western democracies (especially the United States) and the Communist countries that emerged after the Second World War. Immediately after the war, the Soviet Union established satellite governments in eastern Europe, violating promises made at the Yalta Conference. The United States and the Soviet Union, former allies, differed on issues of human rights, individual liberties, and self-determination.

- **Containment**  President Truman responded to the Soviet occupation of eastern Europe with the policy of containment, the aim of which was to halt the spread of communism. Truman proposed giving economic aid to countries in danger of Communist control, such as Greece and Turkey; and, with the Marshall Plan, he offered such aid to all European nations. In a defensive move, the United States in 1949 became a founding member of the North Atlantic Treaty Organization (NATO), a military alliance of Western democracies.

- **Truman's Fair Deal**  Truman proposed not only to preserve the New Deal but also to expand it. He vetoed a Republican attempt to curb labor unions. He oversaw the expansion of Social Security and through executive orders ended segregation in the military and banned racial discrimination in the hiring of federal employees.

- **The Korean War**  After a Communist government came to power in China in 1949, Korea became a "hot spot." The peninsula had been divided at the 38th parallel after the Second World War, with a Communist regime in the North and a Western-style regime in the South. After North Korean troops crossed the dividing line in June 1950, Truman decided to go to war under the auspices of the United Nations and without asking Congress to declare war. The war was thus waged by the United States with the participation of more than a dozen member nations of the United Nations. A truce, concluded in July 1953, established a demilitarized zone on either side of the 38th parallel.

- **McCarthyism**  The onset of the cold war inflamed another Red Scare. During the Korean War, investigations by the House Committee on Un-American Activities (known as HUAC) sought to find "subversives" within the federal government. Senator Joseph R. McCarthy of Wisconsin exploited Americans' fears of Soviet spies' infiltrating the highest levels of the U.S. government. McCarthy was successful in the short term because, with most eastern European nations being held as buffer states by the Soviet Union and the war in Korea being indirectly fought against Communist China, the threat of a world dominated by Communist governments seemed real to many Americans.

## CHRONOLOGY

| | |
|---|---|
| 1944 | Congress passes the Servicemen's Readjustment Act (GI Bill of Rights) |
| April 1945 | Fifty nations at war with the Axis Powers sign the United Nations Charter |
| 1947 | Congress passes the Taft-Hartley Labor Act |
| 1947 | National Security Council (NSC) is established |
| May 1948 | Israel is proclaimed an independent nation |
| July 1948 | Truman issues an executive order ending segregation in the U.S. armed forces |
| October 1948 | Allied forces begin airlifting supplies to West Berlin |
| November 1948 | Truman defeats Dewey in the presidential election |
| 1949 | North Atlantic Treaty Organization (NATO) is created |
| 1949 | China "falls" to communism |
| 1950 | United States and other UN members go to war in Korea |

## KEY TERMS & NAMES

# 30

# THE 1950s: AFFLUENCE AND ANXIETY IN AN ATOMIC AGE

**FOCUS QUESTIONS**                      wwnorton.com/studyspace

- Why did the U.S. economy grow rapidly in the period after the Second World War?

- To what extent was conformity the main characteristic of society in the 1950s?

- What was the image of the family in this period, and what was the reality?

- What were the main characteristics of Dwight D. Eisenhower's "dynamic conservatism"?

- How did the civil rights movement come to emerge in the 1950s?

- What shaped American foreign policy in the 1950s?

In the summer of 1959, a newlywed couple spent their honeymoon in an underground bomb shelter in the back yard of their home. *Life* magazine showed the couple in their twenty-two-ton steel and concrete bunker stocked with enough food and water to survive an atomic attack. The image of the newlyweds seeking sheltered security in a new nuclear age symbolized how America in the 1950s was awash in contrasting emotions.

A fog of fear and worry shrouded the 1950s. For all of the decade's prosperity and pleasures, the deepening cold war spawned what commentators called "an age of anxiety." The confrontation between two global superpowers—the United States and the Soviet Union—generated chronic international tensions and provoked daily anxieties about the terrible possibility of nuclear warfare. In 1949, Billy Graham, a charismatic young Protestant evangelist, told a Los Angeles audience that an atomic "arms race unprecedented in the history of the world is driving us madly toward destruction! . . . Time is desperately short. . . . Prepare to meet thy God!" Ten years later, in 1959, two out of three Americans listed the possibility of atomic war as the nation's most urgent problem.

However, a very different social outlook accompanied the terrifying expectation of nuclear holocaust in the aftermath of the Allied victory in the Second World War. The nation had emerged from the war elated, proud of its military strength, international stature, and industrial might. Having experienced years of deprivation during the Depression and the war, Americans were eager to indulge themselves in peacetime prosperity. As the editors of *Fortune* magazine proclaimed in 1946, "This is a dream era, this is what everyone was waiting through the blackouts for. The Great American Boom is on."

So it was, at least for the growing number of middle-class Americans. The postwar era witnessed a manic burst of inventive materialism. During the late 1940s and throughout the 1950s, the United States generated unprecedented economic growth that created a dazzling array of new consumer products. A broadening new middle class, constituting 60 percent of families, emerged in the 1950s (public opinion surveys revealed that three in every four Americans thought of themselves as middle class). Amid the insecurities spawned by the cold war, most Americans were remarkably content in the 1950s. Marriage rates set an all-time high, divorce and homicide rates fell, the birth rate soared, and people lived longer on average, thanks in part to medical breakthroughs such as new antibiotics and the "miraculous" polio vaccine. In 1957, the editors of *U.S. News and World Report* proclaimed that "never have so many people anywhere, been so well off."

America's stunning prosperity during the 1950s served as a powerful propaganda weapon in the cold war with the Soviet Union. In 1959, the bombastic Soviet premier Nikita Khrushchev hosted U.S. vice president Richard M. Nixon at a gaudy display of American consumer products at an exhibition in Moscow, the Soviet capital. As they toured the exhibit, Nixon boasted to his Soviet hosts of the "extraordinarily high standards of living" in the capitalistic United States, with its 56 million automobiles, 50 million television sets, appliance-laden houses, and array of leisure-time equipment. In response, Khrushchev reminded Nixon that many of the desperately poor people in the United States were homeless, whereas everyone in the Soviet Union enjoyed guaranteed housing.

## A PEOPLE OF PLENTY

POSTWAR PROSPERITY The widely publicized "kitchen debate" between Nixon and Khrushchev symbolized the two dominant themes of American life after the Second World War: unprecedented prosperity and international tension. After a surprisingly brief postwar recession in 1945–1946, the economy shifted from wartime production to the peacetime manufacture of an array of consumer goods. The economy soared to record heights. By 1970, the gap between the living standard in the United States and that in the rest of the world had become a chasm: with 6 percent of the world's population, America produced and consumed two thirds of its goods. During the 1950s, government officials assured the citizenry that they should not fear another economic collapse. "Never again shall we allow a depression in the United States," President Dwight D. Eisenhower promised.

African Americans and other minority groups did not share equally in America's bounty, however. True, by 1950, blacks were earning on average more than four times their 1940 wages. And over the two decades after 1940, life expectancy for nonwhites rose ten years and black wage earnings increased fourfold. But African Americans and members of other minority groups lagged well behind whites in their *rate* of improvement. The gap between the average yearly income of whites and minorities such as African Americans and Hispanics widened during the decade of the 1950s. At least 40 million people remained "poor" during the 1950s, but their plight was largely ignored amid the wave of middle-class consumerism.

Several factors fueled the nation's unprecedented economic strength. First, the huge federal expenditures during the Second World War and the Korean War had catapulted the economy out of the Great Depression. Government assistance to the economy continued after 1945. No sooner was the war over than the federal government turned over to civilian owners many of its war-related plants, thus giving them a boost as they retooled for peacetime manufacturing. High government spending at all levels—federal, state, and local—continued in the 1950s, thanks to the arms race generated by the cold war as well as the massive construction of new highways, bridges, airports, and ports. The military budget after 1945 represented the single most important stimulant to the economy. Military-related research also helped spawn the new glamour industries of the 1950s: chemicals (including plastics), electronics, and aviation. By 1957, the aircraft industry was the nation's largest employer.

A second major factor stimulating economic growth was the extraordinary increase in productivity stimulated by new technologies, including computers. Factories and industries became increasingly "automated." Still another reason for the surge in economic growth was the lack of foreign competition in the aftermath of the Second World War. Most of the other major industrial nations of the world—England, France, Germany, Japan, the Soviet Union—had been physically devastated during the war, leaving American manufacturers with a virtual monopoly on international trade.

The major catalyst in promoting economic expansion after 1945 was the unleashing of pent-up consumer demand. Postwar America witnessed a new phase of economic development centered on carefree consumption. The new shopping malls dotting the suburban landscape epitomized the emphasis on spending as a new form of leisure recreation. In 1955, a marketing consultant stressed that America's "enormously productive economy demands that we make consumption a way of life, that we convert the buying and use of goods into rituals, that we seek our spiritual satisfaction, our ego satisfaction, in consumption." The consumer culture, he explained, demands that things be "consumed, burned up, worn out, replaced, and discarded at an ever-increasing rate."

Americans after the Second World War engaged in a prolonged buying spree, in part because of demand from the war years and in part because of new ways to buy things. In 1949, the first credit card was issued; by the end of the decade there were tens of millions of them. "Buying with plastic" became the new form of currency, enabling people to spend more than they had in cash. The new "consumer culture" reshaped the contours of American life: the nature of work, where people lived, how they interacted with others, and what they valued. It also affected the class structure, race relations, and gender dynamics. In 1956, *BusinessWeek* magazine trumpeted that "all of our business forces are bent on getting everyone to Borrow. Spend. Buy. Waste. Want." Such uncritical praise for the "throwaway" culture of consumption during the 1950s masked the chronic poverty amid America's mythic plenty. In 1959, a quarter of the population had no assets; over half the population had no savings accounts. Poverty afflicted nearly half of the African American population compared to a quarter of whites.

A CONSUMER CULTURE   What most Americans wanted to buy after the Second World War was a new house. In 1945, only 40 percent of Americans owned homes; by 1960, the proportion increased to 60 percent. And those new homes featured the latest electrical appliances—refrigerators, washing machines, vacuum cleaners, electric mixers, carving knives, shoe polishers. During the 1950s, consumer use of electricity tripled.

**Postwar consumerism**

This Minnesota shopping mall offered a carefree outlet for the pent-up consumerism of postwar America.

By far the most popular new household product was the television. In 1946, there were 7,000 primitive black-and-white TVs in the nation; by 1960 there were 50 million, and people were watching TV almost six hours a day on average. Nine out of ten homes had a television, and by 1970, 38 percent of homes had a new color set. Watching television quickly displaced listening to the radio or going to the movies as an essential daily activity for millions of people. In 1954, grocery stores began selling "TV dinners," heated and consumed while the family watched popular shows such as *Father Knows Best*, *I Love Lucy*, *Leave It to Beaver*, and *The General Electric Theater*, hosted by Ronald Reagan.

What differentiated the affluence of the post–World War II era from earlier periods of prosperity was its ever-widening dispersion among workers as well as executives. Between 1947 and 1960, the average real income for the working class increased by as much as it had in the previous fifty years. When George Meany was sworn in as head of the American Federation of Labor–Congress of Industrial Organizations (AFL-CIO) in 1955, he proclaimed that "American labor never had it so good."

To perpetuate the growth of consumerism during the 1950s, marketing specialists and advertising agencies sought to heighten consumers' desires by appealing to their sense of social envy. Expenditures for TV advertising increased tenfold during the 1950s. Such startling growth rates led the president of NBC to claim that the primary reason for the prosperity of the 1950s was that "advertising has created an American frame of mind that makes people want more things, better things, and newer things."

Paying for such "things" was no problem. Between 1945 and 1960, consumer credit and borrowing soared 1100 percent. Personal indebtedness became a virtue rather than a vice. Frugality had become unpatriotic as consumer indebtedness grew faster than personal incomes. Low mortgage rates, tax incentives, installment buying, and credit cards helped fuel the consumer culture. While families in other industrialized nations were typically saving 10 to 20 percent of their income, American families by the 1960s were saving only 5 percent. "Never before have so many owed so much to so many," *Newsweek* announced in 1953. "Time has swept away the Puritan conception of immorality in debt and godliness in thrift."

THE GI BILL OF RIGHTS    Fears that a sharp drop in military spending and the sudden influx of veterans into the workforce would disrupt the economy and produce widespread unemployment led Congress to pass the Servicemen's Readjustment Act of 1944, the most lavish assistance program for veterans in history. Popularly known as the GI Bill of Rights (GI meaning "government issue," a phrase that was stamped on military uniforms and became slang for "serviceman"), it created a new government agency, the Veterans Administration (VA), and included provisions for unemployment pay for veterans for one year, preference for veterans applying for government jobs, low-interest loans for veterans to buy homes, access to government hospitals, and generous subsidies for on-the-job training programs and postsecondary education.

**GI Bill of Rights supplement**

This booklet informed servicemen about the new legislation.

Between 1944 and 1956, almost 8 million veterans took advantage of $14.5 billion in GI Bill subsidies to attend college or job-training programs. Some 5 million veterans bought new homes with VA-backed mortgage loans, which required no down payment and provided up to twenty years for repayment. Before the Second World War, approximately 160,000 Americans graduated from college each year. By 1950, the figure had risen to 500,000. In 1949, veterans accounted for 40 percent of all college enrollments, and the United States could boast the world's best-educated workforce.

For the first time in the nation's history, a significant number of working-class Americans (mostly men) had the opportunity to attend some form of postsecondary school. A college education or advanced vocational training served as a portal into the middle class. But while the GI Bill helped erode class barriers, it was less successful in dismantling racial barriers. Many African American veterans could not take equal advantage of the education benefits. Most colleges and universities after the war remained racially segregated, either by regulation or by practice. Of the nine thousand students enrolled at the University of Pennsylvania in 1946, for example, only forty-six were African Americans. Those blacks who were admitted to white colleges or universities were barred from playing on athletic teams, attending dances and other social events, and joining fraternities or sororities. In 1946, only a fifth of the one hundred thousand African Americans who had applied for education benefits had enrolled in a program.

THE BABY BOOM    The return of some 16 million veterans to private life also helped generate the postwar "**baby boom**." Many young married couples who had delayed having children during the Depression or the Second World War were intent on making up for lost time. Between 1946 and 1964, 76 million Americans were born, reversing a century-long decline in the nation's birth rate and creating a demographic upheaval whose repercussions are still being felt. The baby boom peaked in 1957, when a record 4.3 million births occurred, one every seven seconds. The unusually large baby boom generation has shaped much of America's social history and economic development since the 1940s. The postwar baby boom created a surge in demand for diapers, baby food, toys, medicine, schools, automobiles, books, teachers, furniture, and housing.

THE SUBURBAN FRONTIER    The second half of the twentieth century witnessed a mass migration to a new frontier—the suburbs. The acute housing shortage in the late 1940s (98 percent of cities reported shortages of houses and apartments in 1945) spurred the suburban revolution. Almost the

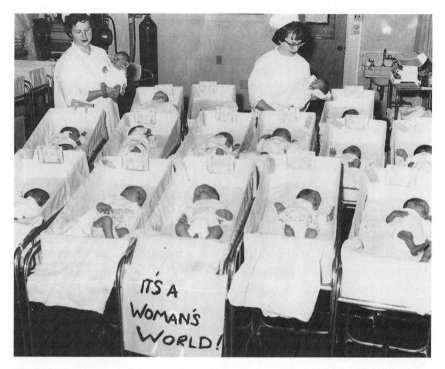

**The baby boom**

Much of America's social history since the 1940s has been the story of the baby boom generation.

entire population increase of the 1950s and 1960s (97 percent) was an urban or suburban phenomenon. Rural America continued to lose population as many among the exploding middle-class white population during the 1950s—and after—moved to what were called the sunbelt states—California, Arizona, Florida, Texas, and the southeast region. Air conditioning, developed by Willis Haviland Carrier in the first decade of the century, became a common household fixture in the 1950s and enhanced the appeal of living in warmer climates.

Suburbia met an acute need—affordable housing—and fulfilled a conventional dream—personal freedom and familial security within commuting distance of cities. During the 1950s, suburbs grew six times as fast as cities did. By 1970, more people lived in suburbs than in central cities. "Suburbia," proclaimed a journalist in 1955, "is now a dominant social group in American life." Governments encouraged and even subsidized the suburban revolution. Federal and state tax codes favored homeowners over renters, and local governments paid for the infrastructure required by new subdivisions: roads, water and sewer lines, fire and police protection. City dwellers frustrated by the urban housing shortage, inadequate public services, and mediocre inner-city schools eagerly populated the new subdivisions carved out of forests and farms.

William Levitt, a brassy New York developer, led the suburban revolution. Between 1947 and 1951, on 6,000 acres of Long Island farmland near New York City, he built 17,447 lookalike small homes (essentially identical in design) to house more than 82,000 people, mostly adults under thirty-five and their children. The planned community, called **Levittown**, included schools, swimming pools, shopping centers, and playing fields. Levittown encouraged and even enforced uniformity. The houses all sold for the same price—$6,900, with no down payments for veterans—and featured the same floor plan and accessories. Each had a picture window, a living room, bathroom, kitchen, and two bedrooms. Trees were planted every twenty-eight feet. Homeowners were required to cut their grass once a week, fences were prohibited, and laundry could not be hung outside on weekends. Levittown

**Levittown**

Identical mass-produced houses in Levittown, New York, and other suburbs across the country provided veterans and their families with affordable homes.

and other suburban neighborhoods benefited greatly from government assistance. By insuring loans for up to 95 percent of the value of a house, the Federal Housing Administration made it easy for builders to construct low-cost homes.

Other developers across the country soon mimicked Levitt's efforts, building suburban communities with rustic names such as Lakewood, Streamwood, Elmwood, Cedar Hill, Park Forest, and Deer Park. By 1955, *House and Garden* magazine declared that suburbia had become the "national way of life."

Those engaged in "white flight" from urban areas sought to maintain residential segregation in their new suburban communities. As Levitt explained, "We can solve a housing problem or we can try to solve a racial problem. But we can't combine the two." Initially, the contracts for houses in Levittown specifically excluded "members of other than the Caucasian race." A year later, however, the Supreme Court in *Shelley v. Kraemer* (1948) ruled that such racial restrictions were illegal. But the court ruling did not end segregated housing practices. In 1953, when Levittown's population reached seventy thousand, it was the largest community in the nation without a single African American resident.

During the half century after the Second World War, the suburban good life was presumed to include a big home with a big yard on a big lot accessed by a big car—or two. Cars were the ultimate status symbol. As a South Carolina real estate agent said, "We've always liked big cars. For most people, it's a status thing." Car production soared during the 1950s, and the cars grew larger and more powerful. In 1955 Americans bought nearly eight million automobiles. Car sales that year accounted for one-fifth of the nation's entire economic output. Nine out of ten suburban families owned a car, as compared to six of ten urban households. During the fifties, automobiles provided much more than transportation. They offered social status, provided freedom and mobility, and served as markers of personal identity. The "car culture" soon transformed social behavior and spawned "convenience stores," drive-in theaters, motels (motor hotels), and a new form of dining out: the fast-food restaurant. In 1954, a visionary high-school dropout-turned-entrepreneur named Ray Kroc bought a popular hamburger restaurant from the McDonald brothers in San Bernardino, California. He renamed the restaurant McDonald's and soon the golden arches alerting motorists to fast food dining were visible across the nation.

MINORITIES ON THE MOVE   African Americans were not part of the initial wave of suburban development, but they began moving in large numbers after 1945. The mass migration of rural southern blacks to the urban North and Midwest after the Second World War was much larger than that after the First World War, and its social consequences were more dramatic. After 1945, more than 5 million African Americans formed a new "great migration" northward in search of better jobs, higher wages, decent housing, and greater social equality. Most of them were southerners headed to low-income neighborhoods in cities such as Chicago, Detroit, Philadelphia, and New York City. During the 1950s, for example, the African American population of Chicago more than doubled. Blacks living in the rural South also migrated to southern cities. By 1960, for the first time in history, more blacks were living in urban areas than in rural areas. As African Americans moved into northern cities, many white residents moved to the suburbs, leaving behind proliferating racial ghettos. Detroit between 1950 and 1960, for example, gained 185,000 African Americans and lost 361,000 whites. Nine of the nation's ten largest cities lost population to the suburbs during the 1950s.

The "promised land" in the North sought by African Americans was not perfect, however. Because they were often undereducated, poor, and black, the migrants were regularly denied access to good jobs, good schools, and good housing. Although states in the North, Midwest, and the Far West did not have the most blatant forms of statutory racial discrimination common

**Family on relief**

Many black families who migrated from the South became a part of a marginalized population in Chicago, dependent on public housing.

in the South, African Americans still found themselves subject to racial prejudice in the every aspect of life: discrimination in hiring, in treatment in the workplace, in housing, in schools, and in social life. In cities outside the South, blacks and whites typically lived in separate neighborhoods and led unequal lives. Few elected officials acknowledged the problem of hostile employers and prejudiced landlords; most of them simply viewed racial segregation and discrimination as a fact of life, a natural response to difference. People everywhere, the logic went, preferred to live and mingle with their own kind. Whatever the reasons, housing in regions outside the South was virtually as segregated. When a black family tried to move into Levittown, Pennsylvania, the white residents greeted them by throwing rocks. Between 1945 and 1954, Chicago witnessed nine large race riots.

Such deeply entrenched racial attitudes forced blacks outside the South to organize their own efforts to assault the hostility and complacency they confronted. Through organizations such as the NAACP, the Congress of Racial Equality, and the National Urban League, they sought to change the hearts and minds of their white neighbors. Animated by anger, hope, and solidarity, local black leaders by the late 1950s had convinced most northern states to adopt some form of anti-discrimination legislation. Segregation of schools on the basis of race ended.

For all of the forms of racism that black migrants to the North and West encountered, however, most of them found their new lives preferable to the official segregation and often violent racism that they had left behind in the South. Southern blacks still faced voting discrimination and segregation in theaters, parks, schools, colleges, hospitals, buses, cinemas, libraries, restrooms, beaches, bars, and prisons.

By 1960, housing in the United States was more racially segregated than ever; as late as the 1990s, the nation's suburban population was 90 percent white. The United States, African Americans complained, had become a nation of "chocolate cities and vanilla suburbs." By 1960, for example, half of the population of Washington, D.C., was black, as whites migrated to the new suburbs ringing the nation's capital.

Just as African Americans were on the move, so, too, were Mexicans and Puerto Ricans. Congress renewed the bracero program, begun during the Second World War, that enabled Mexicans to work as contract laborers in the United States. Mexicans streamed across the southwest border of the United States in growing numbers. By 1960, Los Angeles had the largest concentration of Mexican Americans in the nation. Like African Americans who served in the military during the war, Mexican Americans, Puerto Ricans, and other Latino minorities benefited from the GI Bill, expanding economic opportunities, and prolonged national prosperity to join the growing middle class. Between 1940 and 1960, nearly a million Puerto Ricans, mostly small farmers and agricultural workers, moved into mainland American cities, mostly New York City. By the late 1960s, more Puerto Ricans lived in New York City than in the capital of Puerto Rico, San Juan.

## A Conformist Culture

As evidenced in many of the new look-alike suburbs sprouting up across the land, much of white middle-class social life during the 1950s exhibited an increasingly homogenized character. Suburban life encouraged uniformity. "There is no need to rub elbows with fellow Americans who are of a different class," explained one analyst of the suburban revolution. Changes in corporate life as well as the influence of the consumer culture and the cold war also played an important socializing role. "Conformity," predicted a journalist in 1954, "may very well become the central social problem of this age."

CORPORATE LIFE    The composition of the workforce and the very nature of work itself changed dramatically during the 1950s. Fewer people were self-employed, and manual labor was rapidly giving way to mental labor. The high-performing American economy began shifting from its traditional emphasis on manufacturing to service industries: telecommunications (including the new-fangled computer), sales, financial services, advertising, marketing, public relations, entertainment, clerical, and government. By the mid-1950s, white-collar (salaried) employees outnumbered blue-collar (hourly wage) workers for the first time in history. During the Second World War, big business had grown bigger—and the process continued during the 1950s. The government relaxed its anti-trust activity, and huge defense contracts promoted corporate concentration and consolidation. After the war, a wave of mergers occurred, and dominant corporate giants—including General Motors, IBM, General Electric, Westinghouse, AT&T, Xerox, DuPont, and Boeing—appeared in every major industry, providing the primary source of new jobs. Most people in the 1950s worked for giant corporations. In such huge companies, as well as similarly large government agencies and universities, the working atmosphere promoted conformity rather than individualism.

WOMEN'S "PLACE"    Increasing conformity in the workplace was mirrored in middle-class homes. A special issue of *Life* magazine in 1956 fea-

**Office in a Small City**

Edward Hopper's 1953 painting suggests the alienation associated with white-collar work and the corporate atmosphere of the 1950s.

tured the "ideal" middle-class woman, a thirty-two-year-old "pretty and popular" white suburban housewife, mother of four, who had married at age sixteen. She was described as an excellent wife, mother, volunteer, and "home manager" who preferred marriage and childrearing to a career outside the home. She made her own clothes, hosted dozens of dinner parties each year, sang in her church choir, and was devoted to her husband. "In her daily round," *Life* reported, "she attends club or charity meetings, drives the children to school, does the weekly grocery shopping, makes ceramics, and is planning to study French." The soaring birth rate reinforced the deeply embedded notion that a woman's place was in the home. "Of all the accomplishments of the American woman," the *Life* cover story proclaimed, "the one she brings off with the most spectacular success is having babies."

During the Second World War, millions of women had responded to patriotic appeals and joined the traditionally male workforce. After the war ended, however, most middle-class women turned their wartime jobs over to the returning male veterans and resumed their full-time commitment to home and family. A 1945 article in *House Beautiful* lectured women on their

**The new household**

A Tupperware party in a middle-class suburban home.

domestic responsibilities. The returning veteran, it said, was "head man again . . . Your part in the remaking of this man is to fit his home to him, understanding why he wants it this way, forgetting your own preferences." Women were also urged to dismiss wartime-generated thoughts of their own career in the workplace. *Newsweek* magazine discouraged women from even attending college when it proclaimed that "books and babies don't mix." In 1956, one fourth of all white women in college married while still enrolled in school, and most dropped out before receiving a degree. Marriage was the primary goal. Only 9 percent of young adults in the 1950s believed that a single person could be happy.

A RELIGIOUS NATION    After the Second World War, Americans joined churches and synagogues in record numbers. In 1940, less than half the adult population belonged to a church; by 1960, over 65 percent were official communicants. Sales of Bibles soared, as did the demand for books, movies, and songs with religious themes. The cold war provided a direct stimulant to Christian evangelism. Communism, explained Billy Graham, was "a great sinister anti-Christian movement masterminded by Satan" that needed to be countered wherever it emerged.

President Eisenhower, although he joined a church only after being nomi-nate for the presidency, promoted a patriotic religious crusade during the fifties. "Recognition of the Supreme Being," he declared, "is the first, the most basic, expression of Americanism. Without God, there could be no American form of government, nor an American way of life." In 1954, Congress added the phrase "under God" to the Pledge of Allegiance and in 1956 made the statement "In God We Trust" mandatory on all coins and currency. In 1956, Congress made "In God We Trust" the national motto. A godly nation, it was widely assumed, would better withstand the march of "godless" communism.

The prevailing tone of the popular religious revival of the 1950s was upbeat and soothing. As the Protestant Council of New York City explained to its corps of radio and television speakers, their addresses "should project love, joy, courage, hope, faith, trust in God, goodwill. Generally avoid con-demnation, criticism, controversy. In a very real sense we are 'selling' reli-gion, the good news of the Gospel."

The best salesman of this gospel of reassuring "good news" was the Rev-erend Norman Vincent Peale, champion of feel-good theology. No speaker was more in demand during the 1950s, and no writer was more widely read. Peale's book *The Power of Positive Thinking* (1952) was a phenomenal best seller throughout the decade—and for good reason. It offered a simple how-to course in personal happiness. "Flush out all depressing, negative, and tired thoughts," Peale advised. "Start thinking faith, enthusiasm, and joy." By following this simple formula for success, he pledged, each American could become "a more popular, esteemed, and well-liked individual."

## CRACKS IN THE PICTURE WINDOW

Amid the surging affluence of the supposed "happy days" decade, there was also growing anxiety, dissent, and diversity. Many social critics, writers, and artists expressed a growing sense of unease with the superficiality of the much-celebrated consumer culture. One of the most striking aspects of the decade was the sharp contrast between the buoyant public mood and the increasingly bitter social criticism coming from intellectuals, theolo-gians, novelists, playwrights, poets, and artists. Writer Norman Mailer, for instance, said the 1950s was "one of the worst decades in the history of man."

**THE PERILS OF CONFORMITY** Norman Mailer was one of many social critics who challenged what they viewed as the postwar era's moral complacency and bland conformity. In *The Affluent Society* (1958), for example, the prominent economist John Kenneth Galbraith attacked the prevailing notion that sustained economic growth was solving chronic social problems. He reminded readers that for all of America's vaunted prosperity, the nation had yet to eradicate poverty, especially among minorities in inner cities, female-headed households, Mexican American migrant farm workers in the Southwest, Native Americans, and rural southerners, both black and white.

Critics also questioned the supposed bliss of middle-class suburban life. John Keats, in *The Crack in the Picture Window* (1956), ridiculed the two Levittowns, in New York and Pennsylvania, as well as other mass-produced suburban communities as having been "conceived in error, nurtured in greed, corroding everything they touch." Locked into a monotonous routine, preoccupied with materialism, and engulfed by mass mediocrity, suburbanites, he concluded, were living in a "homogeneous, postwar Hell."

However, Levittown was in many ways distinctive rather than representative. There were thousands of suburbs by the mid-1950s, and few were as regimented or as unvarying as critics implied. Keats failed to recognize the benefits that the suburbs offered those who otherwise would have remained in crowded urban apartments. A 1967 analysis of the evolution of Levittown over the previous twenty years concluded that the first mass-produced suburb "permits most of its residents to be what they want to be, to center their

**Suburban life**

A woman vacuums her living room in Queens, New York, 1953, illustrating the 1950s ideal of domestic perfection enabled by electrical appliances.

lives around the home and to participate in organizations that provide sociability and the opportunity to be of service to others. . . . Whatever its imperfections, Levittown is a good place to live."

## ALIENATION AND LIBERATION

LITERATURE    During the 1950s, a growing number of writers and artists called into question the prevailing complacency about the goodness and superiority of the American way of life. As novelist John Updike observed, he and other writers felt estranged "from a government that extolled business and mediocrity." The most enduring novels of the postwar period featured the individual's struggle for survival amid the smothering forces of mass society. The characters in novels such as James Jones's *From Here to Eternity* (1951), Saul Bellow's *Seize the Day* (1956), J. D. Salinger's *Catcher in the Rye* (1951), William Styron's *Lie Down in Darkness* (1951), and Updike's *Rabbit, Run* (1961), among many others, are restless, tormented souls who can find neither contentment nor respect in an overpowering or uninterested world.

The immensely talented African American writer Ralph Ellison explored the theme of the lonely individual imprisoned in privacy in his kaleidoscopic novel *Invisible Man* (1952). By using a black narrator struggling to find and liberate himself in the midst of an oppressive white society, Ellison forcefully exposed the problem of alienation amid affluence. The narrator opens by confessing: "All my life I had been looking for something, and everywhere I turned someone tried to tell me what it was. I accepted their answers too, though they were often in contradiction and even self-contradictory. I was naive. I was looking for myself and asking everyone except myself questions which I, and only I, could answer."

**Ralph Ellison**

Ellison is best remembered for his 1952 novel *Invisible Man.*

PAINTING    After the Second World War, a group of young painters in New York City decided that the modern atomic era demanded something different from literal representation of recognizable scenes. During the late 1940s and 1950s, abstract painters dominated the international art scene.

Jackson Pollock explained that "the modern painter cannot express this age—the airplane, the atomic bomb, the radio—in the old form of the Renaissance or of any past culture. Each age finds its own technique." The spontaneous artistic technique that Pollock mastered came to be called abstract expressionism. For Pollock and others engaged in what was called "action painting," a canvas was not simply a flat surface on which to paint a recognizable scene; it was instead a dynamic arena for expressing the artist's subjective inner world. The gestural *act* of painting was more important than the painting itself. Pollock, nicknamed "Jack the Dripper," put his canvases on the floor and walked around attacking them, throwing, pouring, splashing, flicking, and dribbling paint in random patterns. Such anarchic spontaneity created mystifying canvases adorned only with splashes, drips, swaths, lines, bands, and slashes. The idiosyncratic intensity of abstract expressionism perplexed the general public but intrigued the art world.

### "Jack the Dripper"

Artist Jackson Pollock became famous for his unique painting style; here he dribbles house paint and sand on a canvas in his studio barn in Springs, NY.

THE BEATS   The desire expressed by the abstract expressionists to liber-ate self-expression and discard traditional artistic conventions was also the central concern of a small but highly visible and controversial group of young writers, poets, painters, and musicians known as the **Beats**, a term with mul-tiple meanings: "upbeat," "beatific," and the concept of being "on the beat" in "real cool" jazz music. Jack Kerouac, Allen Ginsberg, and other Beats rebelled against middle-class life and conventional literary expression.

The self-described Beat hipsters grew out of the bohemian underground in New York City's Greenwich Village. Undisciplined and unkempt, they were essentially apolitical throughout the 1950s, more interested in transforming themselves than in reforming the world. They sought personal rather than social solutions to their anxieties; they wanted their art and literature to change consciousness rather than reform social ills. As Kerouac insisted, his friends were not beat in the sense of beaten down; they were "mad to live, mad to talk, mad to be saved." They nursed an ecstatic urge to "go, go, go" and not stop until they get there, wherever "there" might be. Their road to salvation lay in hallucinogenic drugs and alcohol, casual sex, a penchant for jazz, fast cars, the street life of urban ghettos, an affinity for Buddhism, and a restless, vagabond spirit that took them speeding back and forth across the country between San Francisco and New York during the 1950s. The rebel-lious gaiety of the Beats played an important role in preparing for the more widespread youth revolt of the 1960s.

YOUTH CULTURE AND DELINQUENCY   The millions of children making up the baby boom became adolescents during the 1950s, and in the process a distinctive teen subculture began to emerge. A vast new teen mar-ket arose for items ranging from transistor radios, Hula-Hoops, Barbie dolls, and rock-and-roll records to Polaroid cameras, surfboards, *Seventeen* maga-zine, and Pat Boone movies. Teenagers in the postwar era knew nothing of economic depressions or wartime rationing; immersed in abundance from an early age, the children of prospering parents took the notion of carefree consumption for granted.

Most young people during the 1950s embraced the values of their parents and the capitalist system. One critic labeled the white college students of the postwar era "the silent generation," content to cavort at fraternity parties and "sock hops" before landing a job with a large corporation, marrying, and settling down to the routine of middle-class suburban life. Yet such general descriptions masked a great deal of turbulence. During the 1950s, a wave of juvenile delinquency swept across middle-class society. By 1956, over a million teens were being arrested each year. One contributing factor was the

**Youth culture**

A drugstore soda fountain, a popular outlet for teenagers' consumerism in the 1950s.

unprecedented mobility of young people. Access to automobiles enabled teens to escape parental control, and in the words of one journalist, cars provided "a private lounge for drinking and for petting or sex episodes."

ROCK AND ROLL    Many concerned observers blamed teen delinquency on a new form of music that emerged during the 1950s: rock and roll. Alan Freed, a Cleveland disc jockey, coined the term *rock and roll* in 1951. He had noticed white teenagers buying rhythm and blues (R&B) records that had heretofore been purchased only by African Americans and Hispanic Americans. Freed began playing R&B records on his radio show but labeled the music "rock and roll" (a phrase used in African American communities to refer to dancing and sex). Freed's popular radio program helped bridge the gap between "white" and "black" music. African American singers such as Chuck Berry, Little Richard, and Ray Charles as well as Hispanic American performers such as Ritchie Valens (Richard Valenzuela) captivated young white middle-class audiences eager to claim their own cultural style.

At the same time, Elvis Presley, the lanky son of a poor Mississippi farm family who moved to a public housing project in Memphis, Tennessee, when he was fourteen, began experimenting with "rockabilly" music, a unique blend of gospel, country-and-western, and R&B rhythms and lyrics. In 1956, the twenty-one-year-old Presley released his smash hit "Heartbreak Hotel." Over the next two years, he emerged as the most popular musician in American history. Presley's long hair and sideburns, his swiveling hips and smirking self-confidence, his leather jacket and tight blue jeans—all shouted defiance of adult conventions. His gyrating, sensual stage performances and his incomparably rich and raw baritone voice drove teenagers wild and garnered him fans across the social spectrum and around the world.

**Elvis Presley, 1956**

The teenage children of middle-class America made rock and roll a thriving industry in the 1950s and Elvis its first star. The strong beat of the music combined with the electric guitar, its signature instrument, produced a distinctive new sound.

Cultural conservatives were outraged. Critics urged parents to destroy Presley's records because they promoted "a pagan concept of life." A Catholic cardinal denounced Presley as a vile symptom of a teenage "creed of dishonesty, violence, lust and degeneration." Patriotic groups claimed that rock-and-roll music was a tool of Communist insurgents designed to corrupt youth. Yet rock and roll survived amid the criticism, and in the process it gave adolescents a self-conscious sense of belonging to a unique social group with distinctive characteristics. More important, the rock music phenomenon brought together on equal terms musicians (and their audiences) of varied races and backgrounds. In doing so, it helped dispel the long-prevailing racial prejudices that conflicted with the American egalitarian ideal.

The "unfocused rebelliousness" displayed by a growing number of young people at the end of the fifties would blossom into a true "counter culture" within a few years. As writer Nat Hentoff noted, the youthful rebels "protest segregation and [atomic bomb] testing and the hollowness of their parents, but they cannot yet say what they are for, what new society they desire. They are only *against*, but that is a beginning." By the mid-1960s, the alienated members of the baby boom generation would become the leaders of the 1960s rebellion against corporate conformity and consumerism.

## MODERATE REPUBLICANISM— THE EISENHOWER YEARS

The carefree prosperity of the 1950s was encouraged by the decade's political culture. Dwight David Eisenhower dominated the political landscape during the 1950s. The authentic military hero with an infectious grin was a model of moderation, stability, and optimism. Eisenhower's commitment to a "moderate Republicanism" promised to restore the authority of state and local governments and restrain the federal government from political and social "engineering." In the process, the former general sought to renew traditional virtues and inspire Americans with a vision of a brighter future amid a continuing cold war.

"TIME FOR A CHANGE"  By 1952, the Truman administration had piled up a heavy burden of political liabilities. Its bold stand in Korea had brought a bloody stalemate in the war, renewed wage and price controls at home, and the embarrassing exposure of corrupt lobbyists and influence peddlers who rigged defense-related federal contracts. The disclosure of corruption led Truman to fire nearly 250 employees of the Internal Revenue Service, but doubts lingered that the president would ever finish the housecleaning.

It was, Republicans claimed, "time for a change," and they saw public sentiment turning their way as the 1952 election approached. Beginning in the late 1940s, both Republican and Democratic leaders, including President Truman, recruited the nonpartisan General Eisenhower to be their presidential candidate. The affable Eisenhower, whose friends called him "Ike," had displayed remarkable organizational and diplomatic abilities in coordinating the Allied invasion of Nazi-controlled Europe. Born in Texas in 1890 and raised in Kansas, Eisenhower had graduated from the U.S. military academy at West Point before setting out on a distinguished military career. In 1952, after serving as the president of Columbia University, he had moved to Paris to become the supreme commander of NATO forces in Europe, only to be recruited as a presidential candidate. Eisenhower's decision to seek the Republican presidential nomination was wildly popular. Bumper stickers announced simply, "I Like Ike."

Eisenhower won the Republican nomination on the first ballot. He then tried to reassure the conservative wing of the party by balancing the ticket with a youthful Californian, the thirty-nine-year-old senator Richard M. Nixon, who had built a career by exposing supposed left-wing "subversives" holding government posts in the Truman administration. Yet while Eisenhower himself was intentionally vague about his presidential agenda, the Republican platform was quite specific. It insisted that there "are no Communists in the Republican Party" in contrast to the Democrats, who supposedly "shielded traitors . . . in high places." The platform added that the Democratic emphasis on "containing" communism was a "negative, futile, and misguided" form of appeasement. The Republican platform vowed that the Eisenhower administration, if elected, would roll back the communist menace by bringing "genuine independence" to the "captive peoples" of Eastern Europe.

**THE ELECTION OF 1952**   The 1952 presidential campaign matched two contrasting personalities. Eisenhower, though a political novice, had been in the public eye for a decade. Illinois governor Adlai Stevenson, the Democratic candidate, was hardly known outside Illinois. Eisenhower's campaign pledged to clean up "the mess in Washington." To this he added a promise, late in the campaign, that he would secure "an early and honorable" peace in Korea. Stevenson was outmatched. Although a brilliant man who gave witty speeches that charmed liberals, he came across to most voters as a tad too aloof, a shade too intellectual. The Republicans labeled him an "egghead" (a recently coined term describing balding professors who had more intellect than common sense).

On election night, the war hero triumphed in a landslide, gathering nearly 34 million votes to Stevenson's 27 million. The electoral vote was much more lopsided: 442 to Stevenson's 89. The hapless Stevenson failed to win his home state of Illinois. More important, the election marked a turning point in Republican fortunes in the South: for the first time in over a century, the Democratic "Solid South" was moving toward a two-party system. Stevenson carried only eight southern

**Good first impression**

In the 1952 election the Republican party won significant support in the South for the first time.

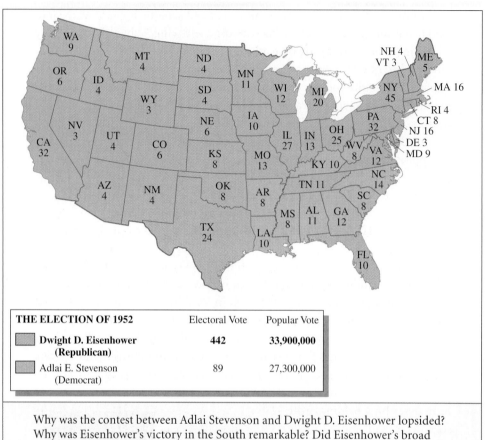

| THE ELECTION OF 1952 | Electoral Vote | Popular Vote |
|---|---|---|
| Dwight D. Eisenhower (Republican) | 442 | 33,900,000 |
| Adlai E. Stevenson (Democrat) | 89 | 27,300,000 |

Why was the contest between Adlai Stevenson and Dwight D. Eisenhower lopsided? Why was Eisenhower's victory in the South remarkable? Did Eisenhower's broad appeal help congressional Republicans win more seats?

states plus West Virginia. Eisenhower had made it respectable, even fashionable, to vote for a Republican presidential candidate in the South. Many Roman Catholics, especially those from eastern Europe, also switched from the Democrats to the Republicans, as did farmers and blue-collar workers. Eisenhower had fragmented the New Deal coalition developed by Franklin D. Roosevelt.

The voters liked Eisenhower's folksy charm and battle-tested poise better than they liked his political party. In the 1952 election, Democrats retained most of the governorships, lost control of the House by only eight seats, and broke even in the Senate, where only the vote of the vice president ensured Republican control. The congressional elections two years later would weaken the Republican grip on Congress, and Eisenhower would have to work with a Democratic Congress throughout his second term.

A "MIDDLE WAY" PRESIDENCY   Eisenhower was the first profes-sional soldier elected president since Ulysses S. Grant in 1868, and the last president born in the nineteenth century. His goal was to pursue a "middle way between untrammelled freedom of the individual and the demands of the welfare of the whole nation." He said the best path for America was "down the middle of the road." He did not intend to dismantle all of the New Deal and Fair Deal programs. Instead, he wanted to rectify the "excesses" resulting from the Democratic control of the White House for the previous twenty years. He pledged to reduce the concentration of power in the federal government and restore the balance between the executive and congressional branches. Eisen-hower's cautious personality and genial leadership style aligned perfectly with the prevailing mood of most voters. He was a conciliator rather than an ideo-logue; he sought consensus and compromise; he avoided confrontation. Eisenhower reverted to the nineteenth-century view that Congress should make policy and the president should carry it out. A journalist noted in 1959 that "the public loves Ike. The less he does, the more they love him."

Critics then and since misread Eisenhower's relaxed style and his habit of deflecting rather than answering questions as a sign that he was a lazy and even incompetent president. Not so. Far from being a "do-nothing" presi-dent, Eisenhower was a quietly effective leader who fulfilled his pledge to shun conflict and controversy by straddling the middle of the road "where the traction is best and where you can bring the most people along with you." Unlike Franklin Delano Roosevelt, Eisenhower did not believe in using power to "impose his will" on public policy. He instead preferred to use "per-suasion and cooperation."

"DYNAMIC CONSERVATISM AT HOME"   Eisenhower called his domestic program dynamic conservatism, by which he meant being "conser-vative when it comes to money and liberal when it comes to human beings." The new administration set out to reduce defense spending after the Korean War, lower tax rates, weaken government regulation of business, and restore power to the states and corporate interests. Eisenhower warned repeatedly against the dangers of "creeping socialism," "huge bureaucracies," and peren-nial budget deficits. To curb government spending, he abolished the Recon-struction Finance Corporation (created in 1932 to deal with the depression) and reduced federal subsidies to farmers.

In the end, however, Eisenhower kept intact the basic structure and premises of the New Deal, much to the chagrin of conservative Republicans. A self-described pragmatist, Eisenhower told his more conservative brother Edgar in 1954 that if the "stupid" right-wing of the Republican party tried "to abolish Social Security and eliminate labor laws and farm programs, you would not hear of that party again in our political history." In some ways, the Eisenhower administration actually expanded New Deal programs, especially after 1954, when it had the help of Democratic majorities in Congress. Amendments to the Social Security Act in 1954 and 1956 expanded coverage to millions of workers formerly excluded: white-collar professionals, domestic and clerical workers, farm workers, and members of the armed forces. Eisenhower also approved increases in the minimum wage and additional public housing projects for low-income occupants.

President Eisenhower launched two massive federal construction projects that served national needs: the St. Lawrence Seaway and the interstate highway system. The St. Lawrence Seaway project (in partnership with Canada) opened the Great Lakes to oceangoing freighters and tankers. Even more important, the Federal-Aid Highway Act (1956) created a national network of interstate highways to serve the needs of commerce and defense, as well as the convenience of citizens. The interstate highway system, funded by gasoline taxes, took twenty-five years to construct and was the largest federal construction project in history. It stretches for 47,000 miles, and contains 55,512 bridges and 14,800 interchanges. The vast project created jobs, stimulated the economy, spurred the tourism, motor hotel ("motel"), and long-haul trucking industries, and transformed the way people traveled and lived by reinforcing America's car-centered culture. At the same time, the interstate highways also hastened the decay of the passenger railroad system, deflected attention from the need for mass transit systems, and helped foster the automobile culture that over time created a national dependency on imported oil.

**THE RED SCARE**   The Republicans thought their presidential victory in 1952 would curb the often-unscrupulous efforts of Wisconsin senator Joseph R. McCarthy to find Communist spies in the federal government. But the paranoid, publicity-seeking senator grew more outlandish in his charges. Eisenhower despised the unprincipled McCarthy, but the president refused to criticize him in public, explaining that he did not want to "get into a pissing contest with that skunk." In March 1954, the president indirectly chastised McCarthy when he told a press conference that "we are defeating ourselves if we use methods [in opposing communism] that do not conform to the American sense of justice."

The cynical, bullying McCarthy finally overreached himself when he made the absurd charge that the U.S. Army itself was "soft" on communism. On December 2, 1954, the Senate voted 67 to 22 to "condemn" McCarthy for his reckless tactics. Soon thereafter, McCarthy's political influence collapsed. In 1957, at the age of forty-eight, he died of a liver inflammation brought on by years of alcohol abuse (he frequently bragged about drinking a fifth of whiskey a day). His savage crusade against communists in government had catapulted him into the limelight and captured the nation's attention for several years, but the former marine trampled upon civil liberties. McCarthy's political demise played a role in the fall elections in 1954, helping the Democrats capture control of both houses of Congress.

INTERNAL SECURITY   The anti-Communist crusade survived the downfall of Senator McCarthy, however. The Red Scare continued to excite public passions and garner bipartisan political support. In 1954, the liberal Democratic senator Hubert H. Humphrey of Minnesota sponsored the Communist Control Act, which outlawed the Communist party in the United States. On a local level, public libraries removed books deemed controversial; public school boards and university trustees fired "leftist" teachers and professors; corporations "blacklisted" people suspected of communist sympathies; and city councils ordered communists to leave their communities within forty-eight hours. Eisenhower stiffened the government security program that Truman had set up in 1947, by issuing an executive order in 1953 that that led to the firing of thousands of federal workers deemed security risks. In an even more controversial decision, Eisenhower denied clemency to Julius and Ethel Rosenberg, who were convicted of transmitting classified information about atomic bombs to the Soviets, on the grounds that they "may have condemned to death tens of millions of innocent people." Despite passionate pleas for clemency and lingering issues related to the evidence against Ethel, the Rosenbergs were electrocuted on June 19, 1953. They were the first native-born Americans to be executed for espionage by order of a civilian court.

# THE EARLY YEARS OF THE CIVIL RIGHTS MOVEMENT

Soon after the cold war began, Soviet diplomats began to use America's continuing racial discrimination against African Americans as a propaganda tool. During the mid-1950s, race relations in the United States threatened to explode the domestic tranquility masking years of social injustice. The volatile issue of ending racial segregation in the South offered Eisenhower an opportunity to exercise transformational leadership. That he balked at remedying the nation's gravest injustice constituted his greatest failure as president.

EISENHOWER AND RACE   Eisenhower had grown up in an all-white Kansas town and had spent his military career in a racially segregated army

**Chief Justice Earl Warren**

One of the most influential Supreme Court justices of the twentieth century.

in which black soldiers were assigned to noncombat units. In 1948, he had opposed Truman's decision to integrate the armed forces. Eisenhower was not a racial bigot, however. He simply feared the backlash against integration efforts. He entered the White House committed to civil rights in principle, and he pushed the issue in some areas of federal authority. During his first three years as president, for example, public facilities in Washington, D.C., were desegregated. Eisenhower also intervened to end discrimination at several military bases in Virginia and South Carolina. The president also appointed the first African American to an executive office: E. Frederic Morrow, who was named Administrative Officer for Special Projects. Beyond that, however, Eisenhower refused to push the issue of civil rights.

Two aspects of Eisenhower's philosophy limited his commitment to racial equality: his preference for state or local action over federal involvement and his doubt that laws could change traditional racist attitudes. "I don't believe you can change the hearts of men with laws or decisions," he said. Eisenhower's tepid stance meant that governmental leadership in the civil rights field would come from the judiciary more than from the executive or legislative branch.

In 1953, Eisenhower appointed former three-term Republican governor Earl Warren of California as chief justice of the Supreme Court, a decision he later pronounced the "biggest damn fool mistake I ever made." Warren, who had seemed safely conservative while active in elected politics, displayed a social conscience and a streak of libertarianism that was shared by another Eisenhower appointee to the Supreme Court, William J. Brennan Jr. The Warren Court (1953–1969), under the chief justice's influence, became a powerful force for social and political change through the 1960s.

WE SHALL OVERCOME    However, the most important leadership related to the civil rights movement came not from government officials but from the long-suffering people whose rights were most suppressed: African

Americans, Hispanic Americans, Asian Americans, and other minorities. Rural and urban, young and old, male and female, courageous blacks formed the vanguard of what would become the most important social movement in American history. With brilliance, bravery, and dignity, they fought on all fronts—in the courts, at the ballot box, and in the streets— against deeply entrenched patterns of racial segregation and discrimination. Although many African Americans moved to the North and West during and after the Second World War, a majority remained in the eleven former Confederate states. There they were forced to attend segregated public schools, accept the least desirable jobs, and operate within an explicitly seg- regated society that systematically restricted their civil rights. In the 1952 presidential election, for example, only 20 percent of eligible African Ameri- cans were registered to vote.

In the mid-1930s the National Association for the Advancement of Col- ored People (NAACP) had resolved to test the separate-but-equal judicial doctrine that had upheld racial segregation since the *Plessy* decision in 1896. Charles H. Houston, a dean at the Howard University Law School, laid the plans, and his former student Thurgood Marshall served as the NAACP's chief attorney. They focused first on higher education. But it would take almost fifteen years to convince the courts that racial segregation must end. In *Sweatt v. Painter* (1950), the Supreme Court ruled that a separate black law

**Civil rights stirrings**

In the late 1930s the NAACP began to test the constitutionality of racial segregation.

school in Texas was not equal in quality to the state's whites-only schools. The Court ordered the state to remedy the situation. It was the first step of many that would be required to dismantle America's segregated tradition.

THE *BROWN* DECISION    By the early 1950s, challenges to state laws mandating racial segregation in the public schools were rising through the appellate courts. Five such cases, from Kansas, Delaware, South Carolina, Virginia, and the District of Columbia—usually cited by reference to the first, **Brown v. Board of Education of Topeka, Kansas**—came to the Supreme Court for joint argument by NAACP attorneys in 1952. The landmark case provided an opportunity for courageous presidential leadership. President Eisenhower, however, let the opportunity slip through his fingers. He told the attorney general that he hoped the justices would defer dealing with the case "until the next Administration took over." When it became obvious that the Court was moving forward, Eisenhower invited Earl Warren to a White House dinner where he urged the chief justice to side with segregationists. Warren responded: "You mind your business and I'll mind mine."

On May 17, 1954, Chief Justice Warren wrote the opinion, handed down on May 17, 1954, in which a unanimous Court declared that "in the field of public education the doctrine of 'separate but equal' has no place." In support of its opinion, the Court cited sociological and psychological findings demonstrating that even if racially separate facilities were equal in quality, the mere fact of separating students by race engendered feelings of inferiority. A year later, after further argument, the Court directed that the process of racial integration should move "with all deliberate speed."

In the greatest mistake of his presidency, Eisenhower refused to endorse or enforce the Court's ruling. Privately, he maintained "that the Supreme Court decision set back progress in the South at least fifteen years. The fellow who tries to tell me you can do these things by force is just plain nuts." While token integration began as early as 1954 in the border states of Kentucky and Missouri, hostility mounted in the Deep South and Virginia. The Alabama senate passed a resolution "nullifying" the Supreme Court's decision; Virginia's legislature asserted the state's right to "interpose its sovereignty" against the Court's ruling. The grassroots opposition among southern whites to the Brown case was led by the newly formed Citizens' Councils, middle-class versions of the Ku Klux Klan that spread quickly across the South and eventually enrolled 250,000 members. Instead of physical violence, the Councils used economic coercion against blacks who crossed racial boundaries. The Citizens' Councils grew so powerful in many communities that membership became almost a prerequisite for an aspiring white politician. Opponents of court-ordered integration shouted defiance. Virginia senator

Harry F. Byrd supplied a rallying cry: "**Massive Resistance**." In 1956, 101 members of Congress signed a "Southern Manifesto" denouncing the Supreme Court's decision in the Brown case as "a clear abuse of judicial power." In six southern states at the end of 1956, not a single black child attended school with whites.

THE MONTGOMERY BUS BOYCOTT    The essential role played by the NAACP and the courts in providing a legal lever for the civil rights movement often overshadows the courageous contributions of individual African Americans who took great personal risks to challenge segregation. For example, in Montgomery, Alabama, on December 1, 1955, Mrs. **Rosa Parks**, a forty-two-year-old black seamstress and department store worker who was a long-time critic of segregation and secretary of the local NAACP chapter, boldly refused to give up her seat on a city bus to a white man. Like many southern communities, Montgomery, the "Cradle of the Confederacy," required blacks to give up their bus or train seat to a white when asked. Parks, however, was "tired of giving in" to the system of white racism. When

**Rosa Parks**

A Montgomery, Alabama, policeman fingerprints Parks after she was arrested for organizing a boycott of the city's buses in February 1956.

the bus driver told her that "niggers must move back" and that he would have her arrested if she did not move, she replied with quiet courage and gentle dignity, saying, "You may do that." Police then arrested her. The next night, black community leaders, including the Women's Political Council, a group of middle-class black women, met in the Dexter Avenue Baptist Church, near the State Capitol, to organize a long-planned boycott of the city's bus system, seventy-five percent of whose riders were black. Student and faculty volunteers from Alabama State University stayed up all night to distribute thirty-five thousand flyers denouncing the arrest of Rosa Parks and urging support for the boycott.

In the Dexter Avenue church's twenty-six-year-old pastor, **Martin Luther King Jr.**, the boycott movement found a brave and charismatic leader whose singular voice became a trumpet for an entire community. Born in Atlanta, the grandson of a slave and the son of a prominent minister, King was intelligent and courageous. He also was a speaker of celestial eloquence and passion. After graduating from Morehouse College in Atlanta, he attended divinity school, earned a doctorate in philosophy from Boston University, and accepted a call to preach in Montgomery. King inspired the civil rights movement with a compelling plea for nonviolent disobedience derived from his reading of the Gospels, the writings of Henry David Thoreau, and the heroic example of the pacifist leader Mahatma Gandhi in India. "We must use the weapon of love," King told his supporters. "We must realize so many people are taught to hate us that they are not totally responsible for their hate." The minister-activist shared the frustration at being "intimidated, humiliated, and oppressed because of the sheer fact that we are Negroes." But there comes a time "when people get tired of being trampled over by the iron feet of oppression." To his antagonists, the self-controlled King said, "We will soon wear you down by our capacity to suffer, and in winning our freedom we will so appeal to your heart and conscience that we will win you in the process."

The Montgomery bus boycott achieved remarkable solidarity. For 381 days, African Americans, women and men, used car pools, black-owned taxis, hitchhiked, or simply walked. White supporters provided rides. A few boycotters rode horses or mules to work. Such an unprecedented mass protest infuriated many whites. Civic leaders staunchly opposed the bus boycott. Police harassed and ticketed black car pools, and white thugs attacked walkers. Ku Klux Klan members bombed houses owned by King and other boycott leaders; they also burned black churches. King was arrested twice. In trying to calm an angry crowd of blacks eager for revenge against their white tormentors, King urged restraint: "Don't get panicky. Don't get your weapons. We want to love our enemies."

**Montgomery, Alabama**

Martin Luther King Jr., here facing arrest for leading a civil rights march, advocated nonviolent resistance to racial segregation.

On December 20, 1956, the Montgomery boycotters finally won a federal case they had initiated against racial segregation on public buses. The Supreme Court affirmed that "the separate but equal doctrine can no longer be safely followed as a correct statement of the law." The next day, King and other African Americans boarded the buses. The success of the staunchly pacifist bus boycott revealed that well-coordinated, nonviolent black activism could trigger major changes in public policy. The successful bus boycott led thousands of African Americans to replace resignation with hope; action supplanted passivity. The boycott also catapulted King into the national spotlight.

To keep alive the spirit of the boycott and spread the civil rights movement beyond Alabama, King and a group of associates met in Atlanta in 1957 to organize the Southern Christian Leadership Conference (SCLC). Several days later, King found an unexploded dynamite bomb on his front porch. Two hours later he addressed his congregation: "I'm not afraid of anybody this morning. Tell Montgomery they can keep shooting and I'm going to stand up to them; tell Montgomery they can keep bombing and I'm going to stand up to them. If I had to die tomorrow morning I would die happy because I've been to the mountain top and I've seen the promised land and it's going to be here in Montgomery."

**THE CIVIL RIGHTS ACTS OF 1957 AND 1960** President Eisenhower's timidity in the field of race relations appeared again when he was asked to protect the right of African Americans to vote. In 1956, hoping to exploit divisions between northern and southern Democrats and to reclaim some of the black vote for the Republicans, congressional leaders agreed to support what became the Civil Rights Act of 1957. The first civil rights law passed since 1875, it finally got through the Senate, after a year's delay, with the help of majority leader Lyndon B. Johnson, a Texas Democrat who won southern acceptance by watering down the proposed legislation. Eisenhower reassured Johnson that the final version represented "the mildest civil rights bill possible." The Civil Rights Act established the Civil Rights Commission and a new Civil Rights Division in the Justice Department intended to prevent interference with the right to vote. Yet by 1959 the Civil Rights Act had not added a single southern black to the voting rolls. Neither did the Civil Rights Act of 1960, which provided for federal courts to register African Americans to vote in districts where there was a "pattern and practice" of discrimination. This bill, too, lacked teeth and depended upon vigorous presidential enforcement to achieve any tangible results.

**DESEGREGATION IN LITTLE ROCK** A few weeks after the Civil Rights Act of 1957 was passed, Arkansas governor Orval Faubus called out the National Guard to prevent nine black students (six females and three males) from entering Little Rock's Central High School under a federal court order. The National Guard commander's orders were explicit: "No niggers in the building." A federal judge ordered Governor Faubus to withdraw the National Guard. When Elizabeth Eckford, a fifteen-year-old African American student, tried to enter the school, just a few blocks from the state capitol, jeering white students shrieked, "Lynch her! Lynch her!" Local authorities removed the students from the school in an effort to protect them from harm. The mayor frantically called the White House asking for federal troops to quell the violence. At that point, President Eisenhower reluctantly dispatched a thousand paratroopers to Little Rock to protect the black students as they entered the school. "For the first time in my life," said 15-year-old Minnijean Brown, "I feel like an American citizen." The soldiers stayed in Little Rock through the school year. "Sending in the troops was the hardest decision I had had to make since D-Day," Eisenhower recalled. Diehard southern segregationists lashed out at the president's actions. Senator Richard Russell of Georgia said the paratroopers were behaving like "Hitler's

**"Lynch her!"**

Fifteen-year-old Elizabeth Eckford endures the hostile screams of future classmates as she enters Central High School.

storm troops." Eisenhower was quick to explain that his use of federal troops had little to do with "the integration or segregation question" and everything to do with maintaining law and order. It was the first time since the 1870s that federal troops were sent to the South to protect the rights of African Americans. Martin Luther King, Jr., who had earlier criticized Eisenhower's tepid support of civil rights, now told the president that the "overwhelming majority of southerners, Negro and white, stand behind your resolute action to restore law and order in Little Rock."

In the summer of 1958, Govenor Faubus decided to close the Little Rock high schools rather than allow racial integration, and court proceedings dragged on into 1959 before the schools could be reopened. In that year, resistance to integration in Virginia collapsed when both state and federal courts struck down state laws that had cut off funds to integrated public schools. Thereafter, massive resistance to racial integration was confined mostly to the Deep South, where five states—from South Carolina west through Louisiana—still opposed even token integration. The demagogic Orval Faubus went on to serve six terms as governor of Arkansas.

## FOREIGN POLICY IN THE 1950S

The commitment of the Truman administration to "contain" communism was focused on the Soviet threat to western Europe. During the 1950s, the Eisenhower administration expanded America's objective from protecting a divided Europe to combating Communist tyranny around the globe. "Freedom," Eisenhower said in his 1953 inaugural address, "is pitted against slavery; lightness against dark." To the Eisenhower administration, merely "containing" communism was no longer enough: the explicit objective became a "policy of boldness" designed to "roll back" communism around the world. Unfortunately, the confrontational rhetoric about "rolling back" communism forced U.S. policy into an ever-widening global commitment to resist all Soviet initiatives, no matter how localized, in regions where the communists enjoyed geopolitical advantages. Privately, Eisenhower acknowledged that world communism was not a monolithic force always directed by the Soviets, but in public he talked tough, in part because of the expectations of right-wing Republicans whose support he needed. The result was often an incoherent diplomacy made up of bellicose rhetoric and cautious action. The Eisenhower administration discovered that the complexities of world affairs and the realities of Soviet and Communist Chinese power made the commitment to manage the destiny of the world unrealistic—and costly.

CONCLUDING AN ARMISTICE    To break the stalemate in the Korean peace talks, Eisenhower took the bold step in mid-May 1953 of intensifying the aerial bombardment of North Korea. Then the president let it be known that he would use nuclear weapons if a truce were not forthcoming. Whether for that reason or others, negotiations moved quickly toward an armistice agreement on July 26, 1953, affirming the established border between the two Koreas just above the 38th parallel. Other factors bringing about the Korean armistice were China's rising military losses in the conflict and the spirit of uncertainty and caution felt by the Soviet Communists after the death of Joseph Stalin on March 5, 1953, six weeks after Eisenhower's inauguration. After the war ended, North Korea became one of the world's weirdest dictatorships, while South Korea became a success story of democratic capitalism. Almost 34,000 U.S. troops had been killed in the Korean fighting. Yet once the Korean War ended, no more American soldiers would die in combat during the remainder of Eisenhower's two presidential terms, a record unmatched by any of his successors.

DULLES AND MASSIVE RETALIATION    The architect of the Eisenhower administration's efforts to "roll back" communism was Secretary of State **John Foster Dulles**. The son of a minister, Dulles, in the words of the

British ambassador, resembled the sixteenth-century zealots of the wars of religion who "saw the world as an arena in which the forces of good and evil were continuously at war." Like Woodrow Wilson before him, Dulles was a pompous, self-righteous, confrontational, and humorless statesman, a man of immense energy and intelligence who believed that the United States was "born with a sense of destiny and mission" to lead the world. His British counterparts, however, were not impressed with Dulles's sermonizing speeches. They liked to say, "Dull, duller, Dulles."

The foreign-policy planks of the 1952 Republican platform, which Dulles wrote, showed both the moralist and the tactician at work. The Democratic policy of "containing" communism was both "immoral" and passive, Dulles insisted. Americans should instead work toward the "liberation" of the "captive peoples" of Eastern Europe and China from atheistic communism. George F. Kennan, the leading Soviet analyst in the State Department, dismissed such rhetoric as lunacy, whereupon Dulles fired him. Eisenhower was quick to explain that the new "liberation" doctrine would not involve military force. He would promote the removal of Communist control "by every peaceful means, but only by peaceful means." Eisenhower repeatedly insisted that "there is no alternative to peace." His disavowal of force led critics to question whether the new "liberation" policy was truly any different from Truman's containment doctrine. As the editors of *The Economist* noted, "Unhappily, 'liberation' applied to eastern Europe—and Asia—means either the risk of war or it means nothing."

Dulles and Eisenhower knew that the United States could not win a ground war against the Soviet Union or Communist China, both of whose "Red" armies had millions more soldiers than did the United States. Nor could the administration afford—politically or financially—to sustain military expenditures at the levels required by the Korean War. So in an effort to get "more bang for the buck," as the secretary of defense bluntly admitted, Dulles and Eisenhower crafted a new diplomatic/military strategy that would enable them to reduce military spending. They were as committed to balancing the budget as they were determined to "roll back" communism. And the only way to balance the budget was to make drastic cuts to the Department of Defense. The "New Look" strategy centered on the risky concept of "**massive retaliation**," using the threat of nuclear warfare ("massive retaliatory power") to prevent Communist aggression. As Dulles told an army general, why have an atomic bomb if you don't plan "to use it." The massive retaliation strategy, Eisenhower, Dulles, and the military chiefs argued, would provide a "maximum deterrent at bearable cost." Vice President Richard Nixon explained the new strategy as a means of focusing resources on the primary threat—the Soviet Union. "Rather than let the Communists nibble us to death all over the world

**"Don't Be Afraid—I Can Always Pull You Back."**

Secretary of State John Foster Dulles pushes a reluctant America to the brink of war.

in little wars, we would rely in the future primarily on our massive mobile retaliatory power . . . against the major source of aggression." During the mid-1950s, the Department of Defense enacted significant troop cuts coupled with increased expenditures on nuclear weapon delivery systems—long-range bombers and missiles. The new strategy, however, only prompted the Soviets to mimic the emphasis on stockpiling more nuclear weapons, pursuing what they called "more rubble for the ruble." Both nations embarked upon a nuclear arms race that proved costly and incendiary.

Dulles's pledge to liberate the nations of eastern Europe under Soviet control had unfortunate consequences—for the "captive peoples." In 1953, when East Germans rebelled against Soviet control, and in 1956, when Hungarians rose up against Soviet occupation troops, they painfully discovered that the United States would do nothing to assist them. Soviet troops and tanks crushed the brave but outmanned rebels.

The notion of "massive retaliation" also had ominous weaknesses. As leading army generals complained, it locked the United States into an all-or-nothing response to world crises. By the mid-1950s, both the United States and the Soviet Union had developed hydrogen bombs, which were 750 times as powerful as the two atomic bombs dropped on Japan in 1945. A single hydrogen bomb would have a devastating global ecological impact, yet war planners envisioned using hundreds of them. "The necessary art," Dulles explained, was "the ability to get to the verge without getting into war. . . . If you are scared to go to the brink, you are lost." Dulles's new policy of nuclear **brinksmanship** frightened America's allies as much as it did the Communist nations. The British prime minister Winston Churchill said that the confrontational Dulles was a bull who carried "his china closet with him." Over time, the notion that the United States would risk a nuclear disaster in response to localized regional conflicts had little credibility.

## FOREIGN INTERVENTIONS

At the same time that Eisenhower and Dulles were promoting "liberation" and "massive retaliation" in their public statements, they were using covert operations orchestrated by the Central Intelligence Agency (CIA), created in 1947 and headed by Dulles's younger brother Allen Welsh Dulles, to influence the political dynamics of countries around the world.

THE CIA AND THE COLD WAR   The anti-colonial movements unleashed by the Second World War placed the United States in the awkward position of watching independence movements around the globe rebel against British and French rule. In Iran in 1951, a newly elected prime minister, European-educated Mohammed Mossadegh, organized a nationalist movement that won overwhelming control of the Iranian parliament and then, in October 1952, severed all diplomatic relations with Great Britain. The British, concerned about the loss of their oil-related investments in a nation that then possessed the world's largest known oil reserves, asked the Eisenhower administration to help undermine the Mossadegh regime. The president was receptive, stressing that "we cannot ignore the tremendous importance of 675,000 barrels of oil a day" coming from Iran.

At the behest of the British, Eisenhower approved a CIA-plan called Operation Ajax. It was designed, in the words of Allen Dulles, to "bring about the fall of Mossadegh." To create unrest in Iran, the CIA bribed Iranian army officers, paid Iranians to riot in the streets, issued anti-Mossadegh propaganda, and hired mercenaries to arrest Mossadegh, who was then convicted of high treason, imprisoned for three years, and then put under house arrest until his death in 1967. In return for access to Iranian oil, the American government thereafter provided massive support for the Shah of Iran's authoritarian regime, thereby creating a legacy of hatred among Iranians that would cause major problems later.

The success of the CIA-engineered coup in Iran emboldened Eisenhower to authorize other covert operations to undermine "unfriendly" government regimes in other parts of the world. In 1954, the target was Guatemala, a desperately poor Central American country led by Colonel Jacobo Arbenz Guzman, the former defense minister. Arbenz's decision to take over U.S.-owned property and industries in Guatemala convinced Secretary of State John Foster Dulles that Guatemala was falling victim to "international communism." Dulles persuaded Eisenhower to approve a covert CIA operation to organize a ragtag Guatemalan army in Honduras. On June 18, 1954, aided by CIA-piloted warplanes, the 150 paid "liberators" crossed the border into

Guatemala and forced Arbenz Guzman into exile in Mexico. The United States then installed a new ruler in Guatemala who created a police state and eliminated all political opposition.

The CIA operations in Iran and Guatemala revealed that the United States had become so enmeshed in cold war ideological warfare that it was secretly overthrowing elected governments around the world to ensure that they did not join the Soviet bloc. A classified report assessing the CIA's covert operations concluded in 1954 that "There are no rules" in the cold war. "Hitherto acceptable norms of human conduct do not apply." The illegal CIA operations in Iran and Guatemala succeeded in toppling rulers, but in doing so they destabilized the two countries, creating long-term problems in the Middle East and Central America.

INDOCHINA: THE BACKGROUND TO WAR    It was during the Eisenhower administration that the United States became enmeshed in the complex geopolitics of Southeast Asia. Indochina, created by French imperialists in the nineteenth century out of the old kingdoms of Cambodia, Laos, and Vietnam, offered a distinctive case of anti-colonial nationalism. During the Second World War, after Japanese troops occupied the region, they continued to use French bureaucrats and opposed the Vietnamese nationalists. Chief among the nationalists were members of the Viet Minh (League for the Independence of Vietnam), the resistance movement which fell under the influence of Communists led by wispy **Ho Chi Minh** ("bringer of light"), a seasoned revolutionary and passionate nationalist. Thin and ascetic, a chain-smoking, mild-mannered, and soft-spoken leader of genius, he was obsessed by a single goal: independence for his country. At the end of the war against Japan, the Viet Minh controlled part of northern Vietnam, and, on September 2, 1945, Ho Chi Minh proclaimed a Democratic Republic of Vietnam, with its capital in Hanoi.

**Ho Chi Minh**

A seasoned revolutionary, Ho Chi Minh cultivated a humble, proletarian image of himself as Uncle Ho, a man of the people.

The French, like the Americans later, underestimated the determination of

Vietnamese nationalists to gain their independence. In 1946, the First Indochina War began when Ho's followers forcibly resisted French efforts to restore their colonial regime. French forces quickly regained control of the cities while the Viet Minh controlled the countryside. In 1949, having set up puppet rulers in Laos and Cambodia, the French reinstated former emperor Bao Dai as the head of quasi-independent Vietnam. The Viet Minh movement thereafter became more dependent upon Communist China and the Soviet Union for financial support and military supplies.

In 1950, with the outbreak of fighting in Korea, the struggle in Vietnam became a major battleground in the cold war. When the Korean War ended, the United States continued its efforts to bolster French control of Vietnam. By the end of 1953, the Eisenhower administration was paying nearly 80 percent of the cost of the French military effort in Indochina; the United States had found itself at the "brink" of military intervention. In December 1953, some twelve thousand French soldiers parachuted into **Dien Bien Phu**, a cluster of villages in a valley ringed by mountains in northern Vietnam near the Laotian border. The French plan, which Eisenhower deemed foolish, was to use the well-fortified base to lure Viet Minh guerrillas into the open and overwhelm them with superior firepower. But the plan backfired in March 1954 when the French found themselves surrounded by fifty thousand Viet Minh fighters.

As the weeks passed, the French government pleaded with the United States to launch an air strike to relieve the pressure on Dien Bien Phu, which a French journalist called "Hell in a very small place." The National Security Council—Dulles, Nixon, and the chairman of the Joint Chiefs of Staff—urged Eisenhower to use atomic bombs to aid the trapped French force. Eisenhower snapped back: "You boys must be crazy. We can't use those awful things against Asians for the second time in less than ten years. My God!" The president opposed U.S. intervention unless the British joined the effort. When they refused, Eisenhower told the French that U.S. military action in Vietnam was "politically impossible." As Eisenhower stressed, "No one could be more bitterly opposed to ever getting the U.S. involved in a hot war in that region than I am." On May 7, 1954, the Viet Minh fighters overwhelmed the last French resistance at Dien Bien Phu. The catastrophic defeat at Dien Bien Phu signaled the end of French colonial rule in Asia.

Six weeks later, a new French government promised to negotiate a complete withdrawal from Indochina after nearly a hundred years of interrupted colonial control. On July 20, representatives of France, Britain, the Soviet Union, the People's Republic of China, and the Viet Minh signed the Geneva Accords. The complex agreement gave Laos and Cambodia their independence and divided Vietnam in two at the 17th parallel. The accords gave the Viet Minh Communists control in the North, where they imposed a totalitarian

**Dien Bien Phu**

Captured French soldiers march through the battlefield after their surrender.

communist system at a cost of one hundred thousand executions; the French would remain south of the line until nationwide elections in 1956 would reunify all of Vietnam. American and South Vietnamese representatives refused to sign the Geneva Accords, arguing that the treaties legitimized the Communist victory.

In South Vietnam, power gravitated to a new premier imposed by the French at American urging: Ngo Dinh Diem, a Catholic nationalist who had opposed both the French and the Viet Minh. In 1954, Eisenhower offered to assist Diem "in developing and maintaining a strong, viable state, capable of resisting attempted subversion or aggression through military means." In return, the United States expected Diem to enact democratic reforms and distribute land to peasants. American aid took the form of training the South Vietnamese armed forces and police. Eisenhower remained opposed to the use of U.S. combat troops, believing that military intervention would bog down into a costly stalemate—as it eventually did.

Instead of instituting the promised political and economic reforms, however, the authoritarian Diem appointed his relatives to senior government positions and suppressed his political opponents, offering little or no land distribution and permitting widespread corruption. In 1956, he refused to join in the elections to reunify Vietnam. Diem's autocratic efforts to elimi-

**POSTWAR ALLIANCES: THE FAR EAST**

- Nations having bilateral treaties with the U.S.
- Members of SEATO
- Communist bloc

How did the United States become increasingly involved in Vietnam? Why did the installation of Ngo Dinh Diem by the French and the Americans backfire and generate more conflict in Vietnam? Why was the protection of Taiwan important to the United States?

nate all opposition played into the hands of the communists, who found eager recruits among the discontented South Vietnamese. By 1957, guerrilla forces known as the **Viet Cong** were launching attacks on the Diem government, and in 1960 the resistance groups coalesced as the National Liberation Front. As guerrilla warfare intensified in South Vietnam, the Eisenhower administration viewed its only option was to "sink or swim with Diem."

By the mid-1950s, cold war ideology had led American officials to presume that the United States must thwart every act of Communist insurgency or aggression around the world. In 1954, Eisenhower used what he called the "falling domino" theory to explain why the United States needed to repulse Vietnamese communism: "You have a row of dominos set up, you knock over the first one, and what will happen to the last one is the certainty that it will go over very quickly." If South Vietnam were to succumb to Communist insurgency, he predicted, the rest of Southeast Asia would soon follow.

However, the domino analogy, used later by presidents Kennedy, Johnson, and Nixon, was too simplistic, because it assumed that communism was a monolithic global movement directed from Moscow that operated with the chain-reaction properties of chemical reactions. Yet anti-colonial insurgencies such as those in Southeast Asia might be animated by nationalist rather than ideological motives. The domino analogy also meant that the United States was coming to assume that it must police the world to ensure that the dominoes, no matter how small, did not begin falling. As a consequence, every worldwide insurgency mushroomed into strategic crises. But in Vietnam, Dulles's tactic of brinksmanship had failed.

## REELECTION AND FOREIGN CRISES

As Secretary of State John Foster Dulles tried to intimidate Communist governments by practicing nuclear brinksmanship, a new presidential campaign unfolded. Eisenhower retained widespread public support, although the Democrats controlled Congress. Meanwhile, new crises in foreign and domestic affairs required him to take more decisive action than he initially deemed prudent in order to "wage peace."

A TURBULENT ELECTION YEAR In 1956, the Republicans eagerly renominated Eisenhower and Nixon. The party platform endorsed what Eisenhower called "modern Republicanism," meaning balanced budgets, reduced government intervention in the economy, and an internationalist rather than an isolationist foreign policy. The Republicans promised "peace, progress, and prosperity," crowing that "everything's booming but the guns." The Democrats turned again to Adlai Stevenson. During the last week of the campaign, fighting erupted along the Suez Canal in Egypt and in the streets of Budapest, Hungary. These two unrelated but simultaneous world events caused a profound international crisis.

REPRESSION IN HUNGARY  During the 1950s, eastern Europeans tried to take advantage of changes in Soviet leadership to seek greater independence from Moscow. On October 23, 1956, fighting between Hungarian nationalists and Communist troops erupted in Budapest, after which Imre Nagy, a moderate Communist, was installed as head of the government. But Nagy's announcement three days later that Hungary would withdraw from the Warsaw Pact (a military alliance linking the eastern European countries under Soviet control) brought two hundred thousand Soviet troops and four thousand tanks into Budapest. Although Soviet premier Nikita Khrushchev, a coarse bully, was willing to relax relations with the Soviet-controlled eastern European countries, he refused to allow them to break with the Soviet Union or abandon their mutual defense obligations. The Soviets killed some forty thousand Hungarian "freedom fighters" before installing a more compliant leader in Hungary. They then hauled Nagy off to Moscow, where a firing squad executed him in 1958. It was a tragic ending to an independence movement that pleaded for the United States to back up its promise of "liberation" with force.

THE SUEZ WAR  The most fateful developments in the Middle East turned on the rise of the Egyptian army officer Gamal Abdel Nasser after the overthrow of King Farouk in 1952. Once in power, Nasser set out to become the acknowledged leader of the entire Arab world. To do so, he promised to destroy the new Israeli nation. Nasser, with Soviet support, also sought control of the Suez Canal, the crucial international waterway in Egypt connecting the Mediterranean and Red Seas. The canal had opened in 1869 as a joint French-Egyptian venture, and from 1882 on, British troops posted along the canal protected the British Empire's maritime "lifeline" to India and other colonies. The canal remained an essential artery of Western trade. When Nasser's nationalist regime pressed for the withdrawal of British forces from the Canal Zone, Eisenhower and Dulles supported the demand; in 1954, an Anglo-Egyptian treaty provided for British withdrawal within twenty months.

In 1955, Nasser, adept at playing both sides in the cold war, announced a huge arms deal with the Soviet Union. The United States countered by offering to help Egypt finance a massive hydroelectric dam at Aswān on the Nile River. In 1956, when Nasser increased trade with the Soviet bloc and recognized the People's Republic of China, Dulles abruptly canceled the offer to fund the Aswān Dam. Unable to retaliate against the United States, Nasser seized control of the Suez Canal Company and denied access to Israeli-bound ships. The British and the French were furious. On October 29, 1956, Israeli, British, and French forces invaded Egypt. Nasser responded by sinking all forty international ships then in the Suez Canal. A few days later, Anglo-French commandos and paratroopers took control of the canal.

The attack on Egypt by Britain, France, and Israel almost destroyed the NATO alliance. Eisenhower saw the military action by the three American allies as a revival of the "old-fashioned gunboat diplomacy" associated with colonial imperialism: "How could we possibly support Britain and France," he demanded, "if in doing so we lose the whole Arab world." Eisenhower adopted a

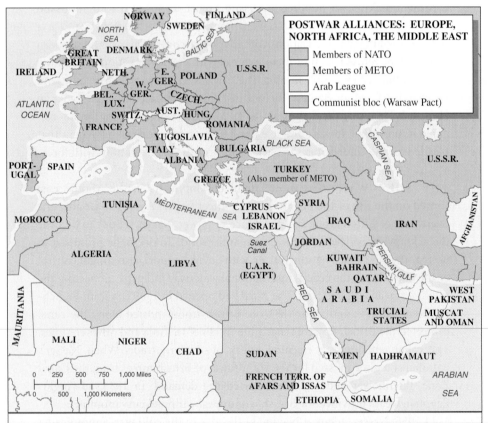

POSTWAR ALLIANCES: EUROPE, NORTH AFRICA, THE MIDDLE EAST

Members of NATO

Members of METO

Arab League

Communist bloc (Warsaw Pact)

How did General Nasser try to play the United States and the Soviet Union against each other? Why did the Israelis, French, and British attack Egypt? How was the Suez War resolved?

bold stance. He demanded that the British and French forces withdraw from the Suez Canal and that the Israelis evacuate the Sinai Peninsula—or face severe economic sanctions. That the three aggressor nations grudgingly complied with a cease-fire agreement on November 7 testified to Eisenhower's strength, influence, and savvy. Eisenhower's superb handling of the Suez Crisis greatly heightened American prestige abroad. At the United Nations, U.S. ambassador Henry Cabot Lodge reported, "Never has there been such a tremendous acclaim for the President's policy. It has been absolutely spectacular."

The two international crises in the fall of 1956—the Hungarian revolt and the Suez War—led Adlai Stevenson to declare the administration's foreign policy "bankrupt." Most voters, however, reasoned that the foreign turmoil spelled a poor time to switch leaders, and they handed Eisenhower a landslide victory over Stevenson even more lopsided than the one in 1952. In carrying Louisiana, Eisenhower became the first Republican to win a Deep South state since Reconstruction; nationally, he carried all but seven states and won the electoral vote by 457 to 73. Eisenhower's decisive victory, however, failed to swing a congressional majority for his party in either house, the first time events had transpired that way since the election of Zachary Taylor in 1848.

REACTIONS TO SPUTNIK
On October 4, 1957, the Soviets launched the first earth-orbiting communications satellite, called *Sputnik 1*. NBC News reported that it was "the most important story of the century." Americans panicked at the news. The Soviet success in space dealt a severe blow to the prestige of American science and technology. It also changed the military balance of power. If the Soviets were so advanced in rocketry, many people reasoned, then perhaps they could hit U.S. cities with armed missiles. Democrats charged that the Soviet feat had "humiliated" the United States; they launched a congressional

**By the rocket's red glare**

The Soviet success in space shocked Americans and created concerns about a "missile gap."

investigation to assess the new Soviet threat to the nation's security. "*Sputnik* mania" led the United States to increase defense spending and establish a crash program to enhance science education and military research. In 1958, Congress created the National Aeronautics and Space Administration (NASA) to coordinate research and development related to outer space. Finally, in 1958, Congress, with Eisenhower's endorsement, enacted the National Defense Education Act (NDEA), which authorized massive federal grants to colleges and universities to enhance education and research in mathematics, science, and modern languages, as well as for student loans and fellowships. The NDEA provided more financial aid to higher education than any other previous legislation.

## FESTERING PROBLEMS ABROAD

**THE EISENHOWER DOCTRINE**   In the aftermath of the Suez Crisis, Eisenhower decided that the United States must replace Great Britain and France as the guarantor of Western interests in the Middle East. In 1958, Congress approved what came to be called the Eisenhower Doctrine, a resolution that promised to extend economic and military aid to Arab nations and to use armed force if necessary to assist any such nation against Communist aggression. When Lebanon's government appealed to the United States to help fend off an insurgency, Eisenhower ordered five thousand marines into Lebanon. In October 1958, once the situation had stabilized, U.S. forces (up to fifteen thousand at one point) withdrew.

**CRISIS IN BERLIN**   The unique problem of West Berlin, an island of Western capitalism deep in Soviet-controlled East Germany, boiled over in the late 1950s. After the Second World War, West Berlin served as a "showplace" of Western democracy and prosperity, a listening post for Western intelligence gathering, and a funnel through which news and propaganda from the West penetrated what British leader Winston Churchill had labeled the "iron curtain." Although East Germany had sealed its western frontiers, refugees could still pass from East to West Berlin. Each year, three hundred thousand East Germans defected to the West through Berlin, most of them young, well-educated professionals. On November 10, 1958, however, the unpredictable Khrushchev, who called West Berlin "a bone in his throat," threatened to give East Germany control of East Berlin and the air lanes into West Berlin. After the deadline he set, May 27, 1959, Western occupation authorities would have to deal with the Soviet-controlled East German government, in effect recognizing it, or face the possibility of another blockade.

Eisenhower refused to budge from his position on Berlin but sought a settlement. There was little hope of resolving the conflicting views on Berlin and German reunification, but the negotiations distracted attention from Khrushchev's deadline of May 27: it passed almost unnoticed. In September 1959, Khrushchev and Eisenhower agreed that the time was ripe for a summit meeting.

**Nikita Khrushchev**

The Soviet premier speaks on the problem of Berlin, 1959.

THE U-2 SUMMIT   The planned summit meeting blew up in Eisenhower's face, however. On Sunday morning, May 1, 1960, he learned that a Soviet rocket had brought down a U.S. spy plane (called the U-2) flying at 70,000 feet some 1,200 miles inside the Soviet border. Khrushchev, embarrassed by the ability of American spy planes to traverse the Soviet Union, sprang a trap on Eisenhower. At first, the Soviets announced only that the plane had been shot down. The U.S. government, not realizing that the Soviets had captured the downed pilot, tried to cover up the spying mission. The State Department issued a fabricated story that it was missing a weather plane over Turkey. Khrushchev then disclosed that the Soviets had veteran American pilot Francis Gary Powers "alive and kicking" and also had the photographs he had taken of Soviet military installations. On May 11, Eisenhower abandoned efforts to cover up the incident, acknowledging that "we will now just have to endure the storm." Rather than blame others, Eisenhower took personal responsibility for the aerial spying, explaining that such illegally obtained intelligence information was crucial to national security. At a testy summit meeting in Paris five days later, Khrushchev lambasted Eisenhower for forty-five minutes before walking out. The incident set back efforts between the two superpowers to reduce cold war tensions in Berlin and worldwide. Later, in 1962, Francis Gary Powers was exchanged for a captured Soviet spy.

CASTRO'S CUBA   Amid all of Eisenhower's crises in foreign affairs, the greatest embarrassment was **Fidel Castro**'s new Communist regime in Cuba, which came to power on January 1, 1959, after two years of guerrilla warfare against the U.S.-supported dictator. Americans assumed that Castro's revolution resulted from Soviet involvement, but Castro did not even acknowledge that he was a Communist until he and his supporters took control of Havana.

**Fidel Castro**

Castro (center) became Cuba's Communist premier in 1959, following three years of guerrilla warfare against the Batista regime. He planned a social and agrarian revolution and opposed foreign control of the Cuban economy.

He became a Communist because he was anti-American, not the reverse. To be sure, once in power, Castro readily embraced Soviet support, leading a CIA agent to predict that "We're going to take care of Castro just like we took care of Arbenz [in Guatemala]." The Soviets warned in response that any American intervention in Cuba would trigger a military response from them. One of Eisenhower's last acts as president, on January 3, 1961, was to suspend diplomatic relations with Castro's Cuba. The president also authorized the CIA to begin secretly training a force of Cuban refugees to oust Castro. But the final decision on the use of that anti-Castro invasion force would rest with the next president, John F. Kennedy.

## ASSESSING THE EISENHOWER PRESIDENCY

During President Eisenhower's second term, Congress added Alaska and Hawaii as the forty-ninth and fiftieth states (1959), while the nation experienced in 1958 the worst economic slump since the Great Depression.

Volatile issues such as civil rights, defense policy, and corrupt aides, including White House Chief of Staff Sherman Adams, Eisenhower's most trusted and influential adviser, compounded the administration's troubles. The president's desire to avoid contentious issues and maintain public goodwill at times led him to value harmony and public popularity over justice. By avoiding or postponing critical issues such as civil rights for all Americans, he unwittingly bequeathed even more explosive issues for his successors. One observer called the Eisenhower years "the time of the great postponement," during which the president left domestic and foreign policies "about where he found them in 1953."

Opinion of Eisenhower's presidency has improved with time, however. After all, the former general was the only twentieth-century president to preside over eight years of peace and prosperity. When he left office, his popularity rankings were as high as they were when he had entered office. He had ended the war in Korea, refused to intervene militarily in Indochina, and maintained the peace in the face of combustible global tensions. If Eisenhower failed to end the cold war and in fact institutionalized global confrontation, he also recognized the limits of America's power and applied it only to low-risk situations. He was a man of unusually shrewd judgment and firmness of purpose. Eisenhower understood the unintended consequences of war and the limits of military power better than other presidents. For the most part, he acted with poise, restraint, and intelligence in managing an increasingly complex cold war that he predicted would last for decades. If Eisenhower took few initiatives in addressing social and racial problems, he did sustain the major reforms of the New Deal. If he tolerated unemployment of as much as 7 percent, he saw to it that inflation remained minimal during his two terms. Even Adlai Stevenson, defeated twice by Eisenhower, admitted that Ike's victory in 1952 had been good for the nation. Eisenhower presided over a nation content with a leader whose essential virtue was prudence.

Eisenhower's January 17, 1961, televised farewell address to the American people focused on a topic never before addressed by a public official: the threat posed to government integrity by "an immense military establishment and a large arms industry." As a much-celebrated former general, Eisenhower highlighted—better than anyone else could have—the dangers of a large "military-industrial complex" exerting "unwarranted influence" in the halls of Congress and the White House. "The potential for the disastrous rise of misplaced power exists and will persist," he warned. Eisenhower confessed that his greatest disappointment as he prepared to leave the White House was that he could affirm only that "war has been avoided," not that "a lasting peace is in sight." His successors were not as successful.

## CHAPTER SUMMARY

- **Growth of U.S. Economy** High levels of government spending, begun before the war, continued during the postwar period. The GI Bill of Rights gave a boost to home buying and helped many veterans attend college and thereby enter the middle class. Unemployment was virtually nonexistent, and consumer demand for homes, cars, and household goods that had been unavailable during the war fueled the economy, as did buying on credit.

- **Conformity in American Society** After the Second World War, with the growth of suburbs, corporations, and advertising, society appeared highly uniform, yet pockets of poverty persisted, and minorities did not prosper to the extent that white Americans did. Although popular culture reflected the affluence of the white middle class, the art and literature of the period revealed an underlying alienation.

- **Eisenhower's Dynamic Conservatism** As president, Eisenhower expanded Social Security coverage and launched ambitious public works programs, such as the construction of the interstate highway system. He opposed massive government spending and large budget deficits, however, so he cut spending on an array of domestic programs and on national defense.

- **Civil Rights Movement** By the early 1950s, the NAACP was targeting state-mandated segregation in public schools. In the most significant case, *Brown v. Board of Education*, the Court nullified the "separate but equal" doctrine. Whereas white southerners defended their old way of life, rallying to a call for "Massive Resistance," proponents of desegregation sought to achieve integration through nonviolent means, as demonstrated in the Montgomery, Alabama, bus boycott and the desegregation of a public high school in Little Rock, Arkansas.

- **American Foreign Policy in the 1950s** Eisenhower continued the policy of containment to stem the spread of communism. His first major foreign-policy accomplishment in this respect was to end the fighting in Korea. To confront Soviet aggression, Eisenhower relied on nuclear deterrence, which allowed for reductions in conventional military forces and thus led to budgetary savings.

- **Communism in Southeast Asia** In Southeast Asia, Eisenhower believed that the French should regain control of Indochina so it could slow the spread of communism. But by 1957, after the defeat of the French and the division of the country in half, the Eisenhower administration had no option but to "sink or swim with the government of Ngo Dinh Diem" and the South Vietnamese.

## CHRONOLOGY

| | |
|---|---|
| 1944 | Congress passes the Servicemen's Readjustment Act (GI Bill of Rights) |
| 1952 | Ralph Ellison's *Invisible Man* is published |
| June 1953 | Ethel and Julius Rosenberg are executed |
| July 1953 | Armistice is reached in Korea |
| April–June 1954 | Army-McCarthy hearings are televised |
| 1954 | Supreme Court issues ruling in *Brown v. Board of Education of Topeka, Kansas* |
| July 1954 | Geneva Accords adopted |
| December 1955 | Montgomery, Alabama, bus boycott begins |
| 1956 | In Suez War, Israel, Britain, and France attack Egypt |
| 1956 | Hungarian revolt against the Warsaw Pact is quickly suppressed |
| 1957 | Federal troops ordered to protect students attempting to integrate Central High School in Little Rock, Arkansas |
| 1957 | Soviet Union launches *Sputnik 1* |
| 1957 | Jack Kerouac's *On the Road* is published |
| 1957 | Baby boom peaks |
| 1960 | U-2 incident reveals that the United States is flying spy planes over the Soviet Union |

## KEY TERMS & NAMES

# 31

## NEW FRONTIERS: POLITICS AND SOCIAL CHANGE IN THE 1960s

FOCUS QUESTIONS    (S)   wwnorton.com/studyspace

- What were the goals of John F. Kennedy's New Frontier program, and how successful was it?
- What was the aim of Lyndon B. Johnson's Great Society program, and how successful was it?
- What were the achievements of the civil rights movement by 1968?
- Why did the United States become increasingly involved in Vietnam?
- Why and how did Kennedy attempt to combat communism in Cuba?

For those pundits who considered the social and political climate of the fifties dull, the following decade would provide a striking contrast. The sixties were years of extraordinary social turbulence and insurgent liberalism in public affairs—as well as sudden tragedy and prolonged trauma. Many social ills that had been festering for decades suddenly forced their way onto the national agenda. At the same time, the deeply entrenched assumptions of the cold war directed against communism led the nation into the longest, most controversial, and least successful war in its history.

## THE NEW FRONTIER

KENNEDY VERSUS NIXON In 1960, there was little awareness of such dramatic change on the horizon. The presidential election of that year featured two candidates—Richard M. Nixon and John F. Kennedy—with very different personalities and backgrounds. Although better known than Kennedy because of his eight years as Eisenhower's vice president, Nixon had developed the reputation of a cunning chameleon, the "Tricky Dick" who concealed his duplicity behind a series of masks. "Nixon doesn't know who he is," Kennedy told an aide, "and so each time he makes a speech he has to decide which Nixon he is, and that will be very exhausting."

But Nixon could not be so easily dismissed. He possessed a shrewd intelligence and a compulsive love for combative politics. Born in suburban Los Angeles in 1913, he grew up in a working-class Quaker family that struggled to make ends meet. In 1946, having completed law school and a wartime stint in the navy, Nixon jumped into the political arena as a Republican and won election to Congress. Four years later he became the junior senator from California.

Nixon arrived in Washington eager to reverse the tide of New Deal liberalism. As a campaigner, he unleashed scurrilous personal attacks on his opponents, employing half-truths, lies, and rumors, and he shrewdly manipulated the growing anti-Communist hysteria. Yet Nixon became a respected member of Congress, and by 1950 he was the most requested Republican speaker in the country. The reward for his rapid rise to political stardom was the vice-presidential nomination in 1952, which led to successive terms as the partner of the popular Eisenhower and ensured his nomination for president in 1960.

**John F. Kennedy** lacked Nixon's political experience but boasted an abundance of assets, including a record of heroism in the Second World War, a glamorous wife and two adorable children, a bright, agile mind and a Harvard education, a rich, powerful Roman Catholic family, a handsome face, movie-star charisma, and a robust outlook. Yet the forty-three-year-old candidate had not distinguished himself in the House or the Senate. His political rise owed not so much to his abilities or his accomplishments as to the effective public relations campaign engineered by his ambitious father, Joseph Kennedy, a self-made tycoon.

During his campaign for the 1960 Democratic presidential nomination, the youthful Kennedy had shown that he had the energy and wit to match his grace and ambition, even though he suffered from lifelong health problems: Addison's disease (a debilitating disorder of the adrenal glands), recurrent blood disorders, venereal disease, chronic back pain, and fierce fevers. He took powerful prescription medicines daily, sometimes hourly. Like Franklin D. Roosevelt, he and his aides and family members masked his physical ailments—as well as his reckless sexual forays—from the public.

By the time of the Democratic Convention in 1960, the relentless Kennedy had traveled over 65,000 miles, visited 25 states, and made over 350 speeches.

In his acceptance speech, he featured the stirring, muscular rhetoric that would stamp the rest of his campaign and his presidency: "We stand today on the edge of a **New Frontier**—the frontier of unknown opportunities and perils—a frontier of unfulfilled hopes and threats." Kennedy and his staff fastened upon the frontier metaphor as the label for their domestic program because Americans had always been courageous adventurers, eager to conquer and exploit new frontiers. Kennedy promised to use his administration to "get the country moving again."

Three events shaped the presidential campaign that fall. First, as the only Catholic to run for the presidency since Alfred E. Smith in 1928, Kennedy strove to dispel the impression that his religion was a major political liability, especially among southern Protestants. In a speech before the Greater Houston Ministerial Association in 1960, he stressed that "the separation of church and state is absolute" and "no Catholic prelate would tell the President—should he be a Catholic—how to act and no Protestant minister should tell his parishioners for whom to vote." The religious question thereafter drew little public attention; Kennedy's candor had neutralized it.

Second, the 1960 election elevated the role of images over substance. Both campaigns hired sophisticated marketing specialists to shape the media coverage of the candidates. Television played a crucial role. Nixon violated one of the cardinal rules of politics when he agreed to debate his less prominent opponent on television. During the first of four debates, few significant policy differences surfaced, allowing viewers to shape their opinions more on matters of appearance and style. Some 70 million people watched this first-ever televised debate. They saw an obviously uncomfortable Nixon, still weak from a recent illness, perspiring heavily and looking pale, haggard, uneasy, and even sinister before the camera. Kennedy, on the other hand, appeared tanned and calm, projected a cool poise, and offered crisp answers that made him seem equal, if not superior, in his fitness for the nation's highest office. Kennedy's popularity immediately shot up in the polls. In the words of a bemused southern senator, Kennedy combined "the best qualities of Elvis Presley and Franklin D. Roosevelt."

Still, the momentum created by the first debate was not enough to ensure a Kennedy victory. The third key event in the campaign involved the deepening controversy over civil rights. Democratic strategists knew that in order to offset the loss of conservative white southern Democrats suspicious of Kennedy's Catholicism and strong civil rights positions, they had to increase the registration of minority voters and generate a high turnout among African Americans.

**Kennedy-Nixon debates**

John Kennedy's poise and precision in the debates with Richard Nixon impressed viewers and voters.

Perhaps the most crucial incident of the campaign occurred when Martin Luther King Jr. and some fifty civil rights demonstrators were arrested in Atlanta for "trespassing" in an all-white restaurant. Although the other demonstrators were soon released, King was sentenced to four months in prison, ostensibly because of an earlier traffic violation. Robert F. Kennedy, the candidate's younger brother and campaign manager, phoned the judge handling King's case, imploring him with the argument "that if he was a decent American, he would let King out of jail by sundown." King was soon released on bail, and the Kennedy campaign seized full advantage of the outcome, distributing some 2 million pamphlets in African American neighborhoods extolling Kennedy's efforts on behalf of Dr. King.

When the votes were counted, Kennedy and his running mate, Senator **Lyndon B. Johnson** of Texas, had won the closest presidential election since 1888. The winning margin was only 118,574 votes out of more than 68 million cast. Kennedy's wide lead in the electoral vote, 303 to 219, belied the close vote in several key states. Nixon had in fact carried more states than Kennedy, sweeping most of the West and holding four of the six southern states that Eisenhower had carried in 1956. Nixon claimed that he lost because "I spent too much time . . . on substance and too little time on

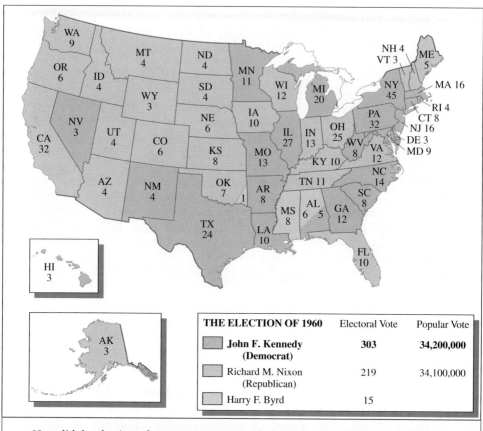

| THE ELECTION OF 1960 | Electoral Vote | Popular Vote |
|---|---|---|
| John F. Kennedy (Democrat) | **303** | **34,200,000** |
| Richard M. Nixon (Republican) | 219 | 34,100,000 |
| Harry F. Byrd | 15 | |

How did the election of 1960 represent a sea change in American presidential politics? What three events shaped the campaign? How did John F. Kennedy win the election in spite of winning fewer states than Richard M. Nixon?

appearance." Kennedy's majority was built on victories in southern New England, the populous mid-Atlantic states, and key states in the South where African American voters provided the critical margin of victory. Yet ominous rumblings of discontent appeared in the once-solid Democratic South, as all eight of Mississippi's electors and six of Alabama's eleven (as well as one elector from Oklahoma) defied the national ticket and voted for Virginia senator Harry F. Byrd, the arch segregationist.

A VIGOROUS NEW ADMINISTRATION  John F. Kennedy was the youngest person ever elected president, and he was determined to surround himself with the "best and the brightest" minds from across America, experts who would provide new ideas and fresh thinking—and inject a tough, pragmatic, and vigorous outlook into government affairs. Adlai E.

Stevenson was favored by liberal Democrats for the post of secretary of state, but Kennedy chose Dean Rusk, a career diplomat. Stevenson received the post of ambassador to the United Nations. Robert McNamara, one of the whiz kids who had reorganized the Ford Motor Company, was asked to bring his managerial magic to bear on the Department of Defense. C. Douglas Dillon, a Republican banker, was made secretary of the Treasury in an effort to reassure conservative business executives. When critics attacked the appointment of Kennedy's thirty-five-year-old brother Robert as attorney general, who had never practiced law, the president quipped, "I don't see what's wrong with giving Bobby a little experience before he goes into law practice." Harvard professor McGeorge Bundy, whom Kennedy called "the second smartest man I know," was made special assistant for national security affairs, lending additional credence to the impression that foreign policy would remain under tight White House control.

The inaugural ceremonies set the tone of elegance and youthful vigor that would come to be called the Kennedy style. In his lean, crisp address, President Kennedy dazzled listeners with uplifting rhetoric provided by talented speechwriters. He issued an idealistic call to action. "Let the word go forth from this time and place," he proclaimed. "Let every nation know, whether it wishes us well or ill, that we shall pay any price, bear any burden, meet any hardship, support any friend, oppose any foe, to assure the survival and success of liberty. And so, my fellow Americans: ask not what your country can do for you—ask what you can do for your country." Spines tingled; the glittering atmosphere and inspiring language of the inauguration seemed to herald an era of fresh promise, courageous action, and youthful energy.

THE KENNEDY RECORD   Despite his idealistic rhetoric, Kennedy called himself a realist or "an idealist without illusions," and he had a difficult time launching his New Frontier domestic program. Elected by a razor-thin margin, he did not enjoy a popular mandate. "Great innovations," Kennedy said, quoting Thomas Jefferson, "should not be forced on slender majorities." The new president preferred dealing with foreign policy rather than domestic issues. He struggled to shepherd legislation through a Congress controlled by conservative southern Democrats who repeatedly blocked his efforts to increase federal aid to education, provide health insurance for the aged, and create a department of urban affairs. When Kennedy finally followed the advice of his advisers in 1963 and proposed a drastic tax cut, Congress blocked that as well. During 1962, Kennedy admitted that his first year had been a "disaster": the social, political, and international "problems are more difficult than I imagined them to be. . . . It is much easier to make the speeches than it is to finally make the judgments."

Administration proposals did nevertheless win some notable victories in Congress. Legislators readily approved broad Alliance for Progress programs to help Latin America. They also endorsed the celebrated Peace Corps, created in 1961 to recruit idealistic volunteers who would provide educational and technical services abroad. Kennedy's greatest legislative accomplishment, however, may have been the Trade Expansion Act of 1962, which eventually led to tariff cuts averaging 35 percent on goods traded between the United States and the European Economic Community (the Common Market).

In the field of domestic social legislation, the Kennedy administration persuaded Congress to pass a Housing Act that earmarked nearly $5 billion for urban renewal over four years; an increase in the minimum wage and its application to more than 3 million additional workers; the Area Redevelopment Act of 1961, which provided nearly $400 million in loans and grants to "distressed areas"; an increase in Social Security benefits; and additional funds for sewage-treatment plants. Kennedy also won support for an accelerated space exploration program with the goal of landing astronauts on the moon before the end of the decade.

THE WARREN COURT   Under Chief Justice Earl Warren, the Supreme Court continued to be a decisive influence on domestic life during the sixties. In 1962, the Court ruled that a school prayer adopted by the New York State Board of Regents violated the constitutional prohibition against an established religion. In *Gideon v. Wainwright* (1963), the Court required that every felony defendant be provided a lawyer regardless of the defendant's ability to pay. In 1964 the Court ruled in *Escobedo v. Illinois* that a person accused of a crime must also be allowed to consult a lawyer before being interrogated by police. Two years later, in **Miranda v. Arizona**, the Warren Court issued perhaps its most bitterly criticized ruling when it ordered that an accused person in police custody be informed of certain basic rights: the right to remain silent; the right to know that anything said can be used against the individual in court; and the right to have a defense attorney present during interrogation. In addition, the Court established rules for police to follow in informing suspects of their legal rights before questioning could begin.

# EXPANSION OF THE CIVIL RIGHTS MOVEMENT

The most important development in domestic life during the sixties occurred in civil rights. Like Dwight D. Eisenhower, John F. Kennedy entered the White House reluctant to challenge conservative southern Democrats on the race issue. While committed to racial equality in theory, he balked at making civil rights a priority of his presidency because it was such an explosive issue, especially in the South. In fact, President Kennedy appointed segregationists as federal judges in the South as a gesture of appreciation for the role of southern Democrats in ensuring his narrow election victory. Neither he nor his brother Robert ("Bobby"), the president's closest adviser, embraced civil rights as a compelling cause that transcended political considerations. Both brothers had to be dragged unwillingly into active support for the civil rights movement. Despite a few dramatic gestures of support toward African American leaders, President Kennedy only belatedly grasped the moral and emotional significance of the most important reform movement of the decade. Like Franklin D. Roosevelt, he celebrated racial equality but did little to promote it. For the most part, he viewed the grassroots civil rights movement led by Martin Luther King Jr. as an irritant. (Jackie Kennedy dismissed King as a "phony.")

SIT-INS AND FREEDOM RIDES   After the Montgomery bus boycott of 1955–1956, King's philosophy of "militant nonviolence" inspired others to challenge the deeply entrenched patterns of racial segregation in the South. At the same time, lawsuits to desegregate the public schools got thousands of parents and young people involved. The momentum generated the first genuine mass movement in African American history when four well-dressed, polite black students enrolled at North Carolina A&T College sat down and ordered coffee and doughnuts at Woolworth's lunch counter in Greensboro, North Carolina, on February 1, 1960. The clerk refused to serve them because only whites could sit at the counter; blacks had to eat standing up or take their food outside. The Greensboro Four, as they were called, waited forty-five minutes and then returned the next day with two dozen more students. They returned every day thereafter for a week, patiently and quietly tolerating being jeered, cuffed, and spat upon by hooligans. By then, hundreds of rival protesters rallied outside. Meanwhile, the "sit-in" movement had spread to six more towns in the state, and within two months, similar sit-in demonstrations—involving blacks and whites, men and women, young and old—had occurred in fifty-four cities in thirteen states. By the end of July 1960, officials in Greensboro lifted the whites-only policy at the Woolworth's lunch counter. And the civil rights movement had found a new voice among courageous young activists and an effective new tactic: nonviolent direct action against segregation.

A few weeks later, in April 1960, some two hundred student activists, black and white, converged in Raleigh, North Carolina, to form the Student Nonviolent Coordinating Committee (SNCC). Their goal was to ratchet up the effort to dismantle segregation. The sit-ins, which began at restaurants,

**Sit-in at Woolworth's lunch counter, Greensboro, North Carolina**

Four of the protesters, students at North Carolina A&T College, were (from left) Joseph McNeil, Franklin McCain, Billy Smith, and Clarence Henderson.

were broadened to include "kneel-ins" at all-white churches and "wade-ins" at segregated public swimming pools. Most of the civil rights activists practiced King's concept of nonviolent interracial protest. They refused to retaliate, even when struck with clubs, poked with cattle prods, or subjected to vicious verbal abuse. The conservative white editor of the *Richmond News Leader* conceded his admiration for their courage:

> Here were the colored students, in coats, white shirts, ties, and one of them was reading Goethe, and one was taking notes from a biology text. And here, on the sidewalk, was a gang of white boys come to heckle, a ragtail rabble, slack-jawed, black-jacketed, grinning fit to kill, and some of them, God save the mark, were waving the proud and honored flag of the Southern States in the last war fought by gentlemen.

During the year after the Greensboro sit-ins, over 3,600 black and white activists spent time in jail. In many communities they were pelted with rocks, burned with cigarettes, and subjected to unending verbal abuse.

In 1961 leaders of the civil rights movement adopted a powerful new tactic directed at segregation in public transportation: buses and trains. Their larger goal was to force the Kennedy administration to engage the cause of civil rights in the Democratic South. On May 4, the New York–based Congress of Racial Equality (CORE), led by James Farmer, sent a courageous group of eighteen black and white activists, including three women, on two buses from Washington, D.C., through the Deep South. The **freedom riders**, as they were called, wanted to test a federal court ruling that had banned segregation on buses and trains and in terminals. Farmer warned Attorney General Robert F. Kennedy that the bus riders would encounter violence as they headed south.

The warning was needed, for on May 14, a mob of white racists in rural Alabama surrounded the Greyhound bus carrying white and black freedom riders. After throwing a firebomb into the bus, angry whites barricaded the bus's door. "Burn them alive," one of them yelled. "Fry the damned niggers." After the gas tank exploded, the riders were able to escape the burning bus, only to be attacked by whites using fists, pipes, and bats. The surly crowd also assaulted U.S. Justice Department observers. A few hours later, freedom riders on another bus, many of them SNCC members, were beaten with pipes, chains, and clubs after they entered whites-only waiting rooms at the bus terminal in Birmingham.

But the demonstrators persisted in the face of mob brutality and police indifference, and their brave efforts drew growing national attention. President Kennedy and his brother Bobby, however, were not inspired by the courageous freedom riders. They viewed the civil rights bus rides as unnecessarily provocative publicity stunts. The Kennedy brothers were "fed up with the Freedom Riders." Preoccupied with a crisis in Berlin, they ordered an aide to tell the civil rights leaders to "call it off." The freedom riders, whom the Kennedys dismissed as "publicity seekers" and whom white critics disparaged as "outside agitators," were in fact the vanguard of a civil rights movement determined to win over the hearts and minds of the American public. Finally, under pressure from Bobby Kennedy, the federal Interstate Commerce Commission (ICC) ordered in September 1961 that whites-only waiting areas in interstate transportation facilities be integrated.

The freedom rides were a turning point in the civil rights movement. Widespread media coverage showed the nation that the nonviolent protesters were prepared to die for their rights rather than continue to submit to the assault on their dignity. Future Congressman John L. Lewis, one of the original bus riders and the son of a sharecropper, recalled the benefits of being a freedom rider on buses and in jail cells: "We had moments there

**Freedom Riders**

Two activists are escorted by armed National Guardsmen on a bus to Jackson, Mississippi.

to learn, to teach each other the way of nonviolence, the way of love, the way of peace. The Freedom Ride created an unbelievable sense: Yes, we will make it. Yes, we will survive. And that nothing, but nothing, was going to stop this movement."

FEDERAL INTERVENTION
The Freedom Rides revealed that African Americans—especially young African Americans— were tired of waiting for the segregationist South to abide by federal laws and to align with American values. With each passing month, more southern blacks were willing to confront the deeply embedded racist political and social structure. In 1962, **James Meredith**, an African American student whose grandfather had been a slave, tried to enroll at the all-white University of Mississippi at Oxford ("Ole Miss"). Ross Barnett, the governor of Mississippi, who believed that God made "the Negro different to punish him," ignored a court order by refusing to allow Meredith to register for classes. Attorney General Robert F. Kennedy then dispatched federal marshals to enforce the law. When the marshals were assaulted by a white mob, federal troops (all white) intervened. The presence of soldiers ignited a night of rioting that left two deaths and dozens of injuries. But once the violence subsided, James Meredith was registered at Ole Miss a few days later.

In 1963, Martin Luther King Jr. defied the wishes of the Kennedy brothers by launching a series of demonstrations in Birmingham, Alabama, a state presided over by a governor—George Wallace—whose inauguration vow had been a pledge of "segregation now, segregation tomorrow, segregation forever!" King knew that a peaceful demonstration in Birmingham would likely provoke violence, but victory there would "break the back of segregation all over the nation." The Birmingham police commissioner, Eugene "Bull" Connor, served as the perfect foil for King's tactic of nonviolent civil disobedience. As King and other marchers demonstrated against the city's continuing segregationist practices, Connor's police used dogs, tear gas, electric cattle prods, and fire hoses on the protesters while millions of outraged Americans watched the confrontations on television.

King was arrested and jailed. While incarcerated, he wrote his now-famous "Letter from Birmingham City Jail," a stirring defense of the nonviolent strategy that became a classic document of the civil rights movement. "One who breaks an unjust law," he stressed, "must do so openly, lovingly, and with a willingness to accept the penalty." In his letter, King signaled a shift in his strategy for social change. Heretofore he had emphasized the need to educate southern whites about the injustice of segregation and other patterns of discrimination. Now he focused more on gaining federal enforcement of the law and new legislation by provoking racists to display their violent hatred in public. As King admitted in his letter, he sought through organized nonviolent protest to "create such a crisis and foster such a

**Birmingham, Alabama, May 1963**

Eugene "Bull" Connor's police unleash dogs on civil rights demonstrators.

tension that a community which has constantly refused to negotiate is forced to confront the issue." This concept of confrontational civil disobedience outraged J. Edgar Hoover, the powerful head of the FBI, who labeled King "the most dangerous Negro . . . in this nation." Hoover's hatred for King became an obsession. With Attorney General Kennedy's blessing, he ordered agents to follow King and to monitor his private telephone conversations. Hoover also had agents plant listening devices in King's motel rooms and circulate scandalous rumors to discredit him.

But King's actions and sacrifices prevailed when Birmingham officials finally agreed to end their segregationist practices. The sublime courage that King and many other grassroots protesters displayed helped mobilize national support for their integrationist objectives. (In 1964, King would be awarded the Nobel Peace Prize.) Nudged by his brother Robert, President Kennedy finally decided that enforcement of existing statutes was not enough; new legislation was needed to ensure civil rights for all. In 1963, he told the nation that racial discrimination "has no place in American life or law." He then endorsed an ambitious federal civil rights bill intended to end discrimination in public places, desegregate public schools, and protect African American voters. But southern Democrats quickly blocked the bill in Congress. As Kennedy told King, "This is a very serious fight. We're in this up to the neck. The worst trouble would be to lose the fight in Congress. . . . A good many programs I care about may go down the drain as a result of this [bill]—We may all go down the drain . . . so we are putting a lot on the line."

Throughout the Deep South, white traditionalists defied efforts at racial integration. In the fall of 1963, Alabama governor George Wallace dramatically stood in the doorway of a building at the University of Alabama to block the enrollment of African American students, but he stepped aside in the face of insistent federal marshals. That night, President Kennedy for the first time highlighted the *moral* issue facing the nation: "If an American, because his skin is black, cannot enjoy the full and free life which all of us want, then who among us would be content to have the color of his skin changed and stand in his place? Who among us would be content with the counsels of patience and delay?" Later the same night, an African American civil rights activist, Medgar Evers, was shot to death as he returned to his home in Jackson, Mississippi. Civil rights had become the nation's most acute social issue.

The civil rights movement gained great visibility and national support on August 28, 1963, when over two hundred thousand blacks and whites marched down the Mall in Washington, D.C., toward the Lincoln Memorial, singing "We Shall Overcome," "We Shall Never Turn Back," "Oh Freedom," and other defiant songs rooted in old spirituals. The **March on Washington** for Jobs and Freedom was the largest civil rights demonstration in history, and it garnered widespread media attention. Standing in front of Lincoln's famous statue, Martin Luther King Jr. delivered one of the century's most memorable speeches:

> I say to you today, my friends, that in spite of the difficulties and frustrations of the moment I still have a dream. It is a dream deeply rooted in the American dream.
>
> I have a dream that one day this nation will rise up and live out the true meaning of its creed: "We hold these truths to be self-evident; that all men are created equal."
>
> I have a dream that one day . . . the sons of former slaves and the sons of former slaveowners will be able to sit together at the table of brotherhood.

Such racial harmony had not yet arrived, however. Two weeks later, a bomb exploded in a Birmingham church, killing four black girls. Yet King's dream—shared and promoted by thousands of other activists—survived. The intransigence and violence that civil rights workers encountered won converts to their cause across the nation. Moreover, corporate and civic leaders

**"I Have a Dream," August 28, 1963**

Protesters in the March on Washington make their way to the Lincoln Memorial, where Martin Luther King Jr. delivered his now-famous speech.

in large southern cities promoted civil rights advances in large part because the continuing protests threatened economic development. Fast-growing Atlanta, for example, described itself as "the city too busy to hate."

## FOREIGN FRONTIERS

At the same time that the Kennedy administration was becoming increasingly embroiled in the civil rights movement, it was also wrestling with significant international issues. Kennedy had assumed the presidency at the peak of the cold war, and he fashioned himself a macho cold warrior. The cold war, he said, was a "struggle for supremacy between two conflicting ideologies: freedom under God versus ruthless, godless tyranny." Kennedy was determined to take the offensive against Soviet communism by accelerating the nuclear arms race and creating an elite army unit called the Special Forces (Green Berets) capable of dealing with communist insurgencies around the world. He and his aides believed that Dwight D. Eisenhower had not been aggressive enough with the Soviets. Where Eisenhower had been cautious and conciliatory, Kennedy was determined to be bold and confrontational. The undersecretary of state complained that the Kennedys and their top advisers were "looking for a chance to prove their muscle."

EARLY SETBACKS   John F. Kennedy's record in foreign relations, like that in domestic affairs, was mixed, but more spectacularly so. As a senator, he had blasted Eisenhower for allowing Fidel Castro to take over Cuba. Upon taking office, Kennedy learned that a secret CIA operation approved by President Eisenhower was training 1,500 anti-Castro Cubans in Guatemala for an invasion of their homeland at the same time that the CIA was working with Mafia crime bosses in the United States to arrange for the assassination of Castro. Based on their assumption that the president would authorize the use of U.S. military forces if the Cuban exiles ran into trouble, the Joint Chiefs of Staff assured the inexperienced Kennedy that the invasion plan (Operation Trinidad) was theoretically feasible; CIA analysts predicted that the invasion would inspire Cubans to rebel against Castro and his Communist regime.

In reality, the covert operation had little chance of succeeding and was an explicit violation of international law. Secretary of State Rusk urged the president to cancel the dubious operation, but Kennedy willfully ignored such advice and approved the ill-fated invasion. When the ragtag force, led by an American, landed at the Bay of Pigs on the southern shore of Cuba on April 17, 1961, it was brutally subdued in two days; more than 1,100 men were captured. Four U.S. pilots were killed. Kennedy refused desperate requests from the anti-Castro invaders for the U.S. military support they had been promised. A *New York Times* columnist lamented that Americans "looked like fools to our friends, rascals to our enemies, and incompetents to the rest." Kennedy called the bungled Bay of Pigs invasion a "colossal mistake." It was, he confessed to Richard Nixon, "the worst experience of my life. How could I have been so stupid?" The planners had underestimated Castro's popularity and his ability to react to the surprise attack. The invasion also suffered from poor communication, inaccurate maps, faulty equipment, and ineffective leadership. Former president Eisenhower characterized Kennedy's role in the botched invasion as a "Profile in Timidity and Indecision," a sarcastic reference to Kennedy's book *Profiles in Courage* (1956). Kennedy responded to the Bay of Pigs fiasco by firing the CIA director and the CIA officer who coordinated the invasion, but the incident greatly damaged the new president's international reputation.

Two months after the Bay of Pigs debacle, Kennedy met Soviet premier Nikita Khrushchev at a summit conference in Vienna. Kennedy resolved to show the blustering Soviet leader that he "could be as tough as he [Khrushchev] is." The volatile Khrushchev had decided after the Bay of Pigs disaster that young Kennedy was incompetent and could be intimidated. "This man is very inexperienced, even immature," Khrushchev told his interpreter. So he bullied and browbeat Kennedy and threatened to limit American access to Berlin, the divided city located one hundred miles within Communist East Germany. Kennedy was stunned by the Soviet leader's verbal assault. The browbeaten president told a journalist that Khrushchev "just beat the hell out of me."

Khrushchev described West Berlin as a "bone in his throat." Since 1945, some 2.8 million East Germans, a sixth of the Communist nation's population, had escaped to West Berlin. The flood of escapees, most of them under the age of forty-five, made a mockery of Communist claims that their ideological system provided a better life for Germans. The stream of exiles crossing over also sapped the strength of the floundering East German economy.

Upon his return home from the Vienna summit with Khrushchev, Kennedy demonstrated his resolve to protect West Berlin by calling up Army Reserve and National Guard units. The Soviets responded on August 13, 1961, by erecting the twenty-seven-mile-long Berlin Wall, which isolated U.S.-supported West Berlin and prevented all movement between the two parts of the city. Behind the concrete wall, topped with barbed wire, the Communists built minefields and watchtowers manned by soldiers with orders to shoot anyone trying to escape to the West. Never before had a wall

**The Berlin Wall**

Two West Berliners communicate with family members (visible in the open window on the upper right side of the apartment building) on the East Berlin side of the newly constructed Berlin Wall. The wall physically divided the city and served as a wedge between the United States and the Soviet Union.

been built around a city to keep people from leaving. The Berlin Wall demonstrated the Soviets' willingness to challenge American resolve in Europe, and it became another intractable barrier to improved relations between East and West. Kennedy told his aides that the Communist-constructed wall was "not a very nice solution, but the wall is a hell of a lot better than a war." In response to Khrushchev's blustering, Kennedy and Secretary of Defense McNamara embarked upon the most intense arms race in world history, increasing the number of nuclear missiles fivefold and growing the armed forces by three hundred thousand men.

THE CUBAN MISSILE CRISIS    A year later, in the fall of 1962, Khrushchev and the Soviets posed another challenge, this time only ninety miles off the coast of Florida. Khrushchev, who had brutally suppressed the Hungarian revolt in 1956, interpreted Kennedy's unwillingness to commit the forces necessary to overthrow Fidel Castro at the Bay of Pigs as a failure of will. So the Soviet leader decided to install missiles with nuclear warheads in Cuba, assuming that Kennedy would not act if the Americans discovered

what was going on. Khrushchev wanted to protect Cuba from another American-backed invasion, which Castro believed to be imminent, and to redress the strategic imbalance caused by the presence of U.S. missiles in Turkey aimed at the Soviet Union. Khrushchev relished the idea of throwing "a hedgehog at Uncle Sam's pants."

On October 14, 1962, U.S. intelligence analysts discovered evidence in photos taken by U-2 spy planes that Soviet missile sites were being constructed in Cuba. Kennedy was furious. While looking at the photos through a magnifying glass, his brother Robert, the attorney general, unleashed a string of expletives: "Oh s—t! s—t! s—t! Those sons of bitches Russians!" The president and his advisers decided that the forty Soviet missiles in Cuba represented a real threat to American security. Kennedy also worried that acquiescence to a Soviet military presence in Cuba would weaken the credibility of the American nuclear deterrent among Europeans and demoralize anti-Castro movements in Latin America. At the same time, the installation of Soviet missiles served Khrushchev's purpose of demonstrating his toughness to Chinese and Soviet critics of his earlier advocacy of peaceful coexistence. But he misjudged the American response.

From the beginning, Kennedy decided that the Soviet missiles had to be removed, even though the Soviet actions violated no law or treaty; the only

**The Cuban missile crisis**

Photographs taken from a U.S. surveillance plane on October 14, 1962, revealed both missile launchers and missile shelters near San Cristóbal, Cuba.

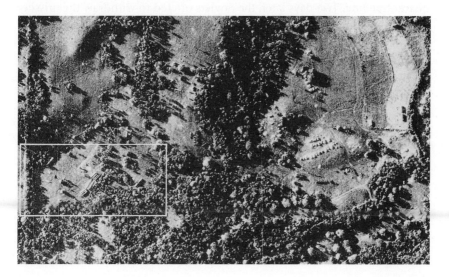

question was how. As the air force chief of staff told Kennedy, "You're in a pretty bad fix, Mr. President." In a grueling series of secret meetings, the Executive Committee of the National Security Council narrowed the options to a choice between a "surgical" air strike and a naval blockade of Cuba. President Kennedy wisely opted for a blockade, which was carefully disguised by the euphemism *quarantine,* since a blockade was technically an act of war. A blockade offered the advantage of forcing the Soviets to shoot first, if matters came to that, and left open the options of stronger action.

Thus, Monday, October 22, began one of the most perilous weeks in world history. That evening the president delivered a speech of extraordinary gravity to the American people, revealing that the Soviets were constructing missile sites in Cuba and that the U.S. Navy was establishing a quarantine of the island nation. He urged the Soviets to "move the world back from the abyss of destruction." The United States and the Soviet Union now headed toward their closest encounter with nuclear war. Both nations put their military forces on high alert. World financial markets collapsed, and Americans rushed to buy canned food and bottled water to use in case of a nuclear attack. The possibility of nuclear war was so real that White House aides ordered all wives of cabinet officers (all of whom were male) to leave Washington, D.C. Jacqueline Kennedy refused to leave the president, telling him, "I just want to be with you, and I want to die with you, and the children do, too—than live without you."

Tensions grew as Khrushchev charged that Kennedy had pushed humankind "toward the abyss of a world nuclear-missile war." Soviet ships, he declared, would ignore the quarantine. But on Wednesday, October 24, five Soviet ships, presumably with missiles aboard, stopped short of the quarantine line. Two days later, the Soviets offered to withdraw the missiles in return for a public pledge by the United States not to invade Cuba. Secretary of State Dean Rusk replied that the administration was interested in such a solution but stressed to a newscaster, "Remember, when you report this, [to say] that eyeball to eyeball, they [the Soviets] blinked first."

That evening, Kennedy received two messages from Khrushchev, the first repeating the original offer and the second demanding the removal of American missiles from Turkey. The two messages probably reflected divided counsels in the Kremlin. Ironically, Kennedy had already ordered removal of the outmoded missiles from Turkey, but he refused now to act under the gun. Instead, he followed his brother Robert's suggestion that he respond favorably to the first letter and ignore the second. On Sunday, October 28, Khrushchev agreed to remove the Soviet missiles from Cuba. The Chinese Communists as well as Soviet hard-liners were furious at Khrushchev for backing down. Within a year, the Soviet leader would be driven from power.

In the aftermath of the **Cuban missile crisis**, tensions between the United States and the Soviet Union subsided, relaxed in part by several symbolic steps: an agreement to sell the Soviet Union surplus American wheat, the installation of a "hot-line" telephone between Washington and Moscow to provide instant contact between the heads of government, and the removal of obsolete American missiles from Turkey, Italy, and Britain. On June 10, 1963, President Kennedy revealed that direct discussions with the Soviets would soon begin, and he called upon Americans to reexamine their attitudes toward peace, the Soviet Union, and the cold war. Those discussions resulted in a treaty with the Soviet Union and Britain to end nuclear weapons tests in the atmosphere, oceans, and outer space. The treaty, ratified in September 1963, was an important symbolic and substantive move toward détente (warmer relations). As Kennedy put it, "A journey of a thousand miles begins with one step."

KENNEDY AND VIETNAM   As tensions with the Soviet Union eased, a complex crisis was emerging in Southeast Asia. Events there were moving toward what would become the greatest American foreign-policy calamity of the century. During John F. Kennedy's "Thousand Days" as president, the turmoil of Indochina never preoccupied public attention for any extended period, but it dominated international diplomatic debates from the time the administration entered office.

The small landlocked kingdom of Laos, along with neighboring Cambodia to the south, had been declared neutral in the cold war by the Geneva Accords of 1954, but thereafter Laos had fallen into a complex struggle for power between the Communist Pathet Lao insurgents and the inept Royal Laotian Army. There matters stood when Eisenhower left office, and he told Kennedy that "you might have to go in there and fight it out." After a lengthy consideration of alternatives, Kennedy and his advisers decided to promote a neutral coalition government in Laos that would include Pathet Lao representatives yet prevent a Pathet Lao victory and would avoid U.S. military involvement. The Soviets, who were extending aid to the Pathet Lao, indicated a readiness to negotiate, and in 1961 talks began in Geneva. After more than a year of tangled negotiations, all parties agreed to a neutral coalition government. Kennedy told his aides, "If we have to fight in Southeast Asia, let's fight in Vietnam." American and Soviet aid to the opposing Laotian factions was supposed to end, but both countries in fact continued covert operations while North Vietnam kept open the Ho Chi Minh Trail through eastern Laos, which it used to supply its Viet Cong (VC) allies in South Vietnam.

**Ngo Dinh Diem**

The Vietnamese premier in 1962, celebrating the anniversary of Vietnam's independence from colonial rule.

The situation in South Vietnam worsened thereafter under the leadership of Premier Ngo Dinh Diem, a Catholic aristocrat. At the time, the problem was less the scattered Communist guerrilla attacks than Diem's failure to deliver promised social and economic reforms and his inability to rally popular support. His repressive tactics, directed not only against Communists but also against the Buddhist majority and other critics, played into the hands of his enemies. Kennedy continued to dispatch more military "advisers" in the hope of stabilizing the situation: when he took office, there had been two thousand U.S. troops in Vietnam; by the end of 1963, there were sixteen thousand, all of whom were classified as advisers rather than combatants.

By 1963, Kennedy was receiving sharply divergent reports from South Vietnam. U.S. military analysts expressed confidence in the Army of the Republic of Vietnam. On-site journalists, however, predicted civil turmoil as long as Diem remained in power. By midyear, growing Buddhist demonstrations against Diem ignited widespread discontent. The spectacle of Buddhist monks setting themselves on fire and killing themselves in protest against government tyranny stunned Americans. By the fall of 1963, the Kennedy administration had decided that the autocratic Diem had to go. On November 1 dissident generals seized the South Vietnamese government and murdered Diem. But the rebel generals provided no more political stability than had earlier regimes, and successive coups set the fragile country spinning from one military leader to another. South Vietnam had become a morass of corruption and violence.

KENNEDY'S ASSASSINATION    By the fall of 1963, President Kennedy had grown perplexed by the instability in Vietnam. In September, he declared of the South Vietnamese: "In the final analysis it's their war. They're the ones who have to win it or lose it. We can help them as advisers but they have to win it." The following month he announced the administration's intention to withdraw U.S. forces from South Vietnam by the end of 1965. What Kennedy would have done thereafter has remained a matter of endless controversy, endless because it is unanswerable, and unanswerable because on November 22, 1963, while riding in an open car through Dallas, Texas, Kennedy was shot in the neck and head by Lee Harvey Oswald. A twenty-four-year-old ex-marine drifter, Oswald had become so infatuated with communism that he had traveled to the Soviet Union and worked for twenty months in a failed effort to defect and become a Soviet citizen. After returning to the United States, he worked in the Texas School Book Depository, from which the shots were fired at Kennedy.

Oswald's motives remain unknown. Although a federal commission appointed by President Lyndon B. Johnson (LBJ) and headed by Chief Justice Earl Warren concluded that Oswald acted alone, debate still swirls around various conspiracy theories. Two days after the assassination, Jack Ruby, a Dallas nightclub owner dying of cancer, murdered Oswald as he was being transported to a court hearing in handcuffs. Film footage of both the assassination of Kennedy and the killing of Oswald ran repeatedly on television; the medium that had catapulted Kennedy's rise to the presidency now captured his death and the moving funeral at Arlington National Cemetery. Kennedy's assassination enshrined the young president in the public imagination as a martyred leader cut down in the prime of his life. His short-lived but drama-filled presidency had flamed up and out like a comet hitting the earth's atmosphere.

Over the years, the wave of sympathy for the murdered president and his family has led many people to exaggerate Kennedy's accomplishments and overlook his failings. His approval of the amateurish Bay of Pigs invasion and his grudging support of the civil rights movement punctured his martyred image. Although many of his loyal aides stressed that Kennedy would never have approved the massive escalation of American military involvement in Vietnam, the evidence is not clear on the subject. Finally, any assessment of Kennedy's presidency must take into account his reckless sexual behavior. On the night of his inauguration, in January 1961, after his wife Jacqueline had gone to sleep, the new president began the first in a series of brazen affairs in the White House, first with a prostitute, then a White House intern, and months later with Judith Campbell, the mistress of Sam Giancana, the Mafia boss in Chicago who was working with the CIA to assassinate Fidel Castro. Such boorish behavior with questionable people left the reckless president vulnerable to blackmail—or worse.

## Lyndon B. Johnson and the Great Society

Texan Lyndon B. Johnson took the presidential oath of office on board the plane that brought John F. Kennedy's body back to Washington from Dallas. Fifty-five years old, he had spent twenty-six years on the Washington scene and had served nearly a decade as the masterful Democratic leader in the Senate, where he had displayed the greatest gift for using power—coarse or delicate, blatant or subtle, cynical or maudlin—since Franklin Roosevelt. LBJ was a ruthless genius at backroom legislative maneuvering, blessed with a canny gift for compromise and manipulation not seen in the Congress since Henry Clay during the 1840s.

Johnson was one of America's most complex, conflicted, and compelling presidents. He brought to the White House a marked change of style from Kennedy. A self-made, self-centered man, tall and robust, who had worked

**Presidential assassination**

John F. Kennedy's vice president, Lyndon B. Johnson, takes the presidential oath aboard Air Force One before its return from Dallas with Jacqueline Kennedy (right), the presidential party, and the body of the assassinated president.

his way out of an impoverished rural Texas environment to become one of Washington's most powerful figures, Johnson had none of the Kennedy elegance. He was a bundle of conflicting elements: earthy, idealistic, domineering, insecure, gregarious, dishonest, cruel, visceral, and compassionate (the mutual hatred between him and Bobby Kennedy was toxic). His primary aide and press secretary called Johnson a Jekyll-and-Hyde personality. He could be "magnificent, inspiring" at one minute and an "insufferable bastard" the next. At times he could be an angel of compassion and a progressive statesman, and at other times he could display immense personal cruelty and breathtaking cynicism. Johnson was a creature of passion and excess. His ego was as huge as his ambition; he insisted on being the center of attention wherever he went. Like another southern president, Andrew Johnson, he harbored a sense of being the perpetual outsider despite his long experience with legislative power. And indeed he was so regarded by Kennedy insiders. He, in turn, "detested" the way Kennedy and his aides had ignored him as vice president.

Those who viewed Johnson as a stereotypical southern conservative failed to appreciate his long-standing admiration for Franklin D. Roosevelt, the depth of his concern for the poor, and his commitment to the cause of civil rights. "I'm going to be the best friend the Negro ever had," he told a member of the White House staff. In foreign affairs, however, he was, like Woodrow Wilson, a novice. Johnson wanted to be the greatest American president, the one who did the most good for the most people. And he would let nothing stand in his way. In the end, however, the grandiose Johnson promised far more than he could accomplish, raising false hopes and stoking fiery resentments.

POLITICS AND POVERTY  Lyndon Johnson was a chain smoker addicted to hard work and driven by a crushing ambition for greatness. Impatient and demanding, blessed and cursed with a staggering amount of energy, he required his staff to work day and night. He even conducted business with aides or visitors while using the bathroom. Domestic policy was Johnson's first priority. Amid the national grief after the assassination, as Americans were weeping in the streets and the world was on the edge of uncertainty, he knew that he would never again have such popular support. So he rushed to take advantage of the fleeting national unity provided by the tragedy in Dallas to launch programs that would have a transformational impact on American life. The logjam in Congress that had blocked John F. Kennedy's legislative efforts broke under Johnson's forceful leadership, and a torrent of legislation poured through. LBJ knew both the complex rules by which Congress operated and all of the key players—of both parties. He knew the right buttons to push to get things done—by hook or by crook.

Johnson put at the top of his agenda Kennedy's stalled measures for tax reductions and civil rights. In 1962, Kennedy had announced a then-unusual plan to jump-start the sluggish economy: a tax cut to stimulate consumer spending. Congressional Republicans opposed the idea because it would increase the federal budget deficit, and polls showed that public opinion was also skeptical. So Kennedy had postponed the proposed tax cut for a year. It was still bogged down in Congress when the president was assassinated, but Johnson shepherded it through. The Revenue Act of 1964 did provide a needed boost to the economy.

Likewise, the landmark Civil Rights Act that Kennedy had presented to Congress in 1963 became law in 1964 through Johnson's aggressive leadership and legislative savvy. It outlawed racial segregation in public facilities such as bus terminals, restaurants, theaters, and hotels. It also gave new powers to the federal government to bring lawsuits against organizations or businesses that violated constitutional rights, and it established the Equal Employment Opportunities Commission to ensure equal opportunities for people applying for jobs, regardless of race or gender. The civil rights bill passed the House in February 1964. In the Senate, however, southern legislators launched a filibuster that lasted two months. When worried aides warned the president of the risks of opposing the powerful Southern Democrats, Johnson replied: "Well, what the hell's the presidency for?" Johnson finally prevailed, and the bill became law on July 2. But the new president knew that it had come at a political price. On the night after signing the bill, Johnson told an aide that "we have just delivered the South to the Republican Party for a long time to come."

In addition to fulfilling Kennedy's major promises, Johnson launched an ambitious legislative program of his own. In his 1964 State of the Union address, he added to his must-do list a bold new idea that bore the Johnson brand: "This Administration today, here and now, declares unconditional war on poverty in America." The particulars of this "war on poverty" were to come later, the product of a task force that was at work before Johnson took office.

Americans had "rediscovered" poverty in 1962 when the social critic Michael Harrington published a powerful exposé titled *The Other America.* Harrington argued that more than 40 million people were mired in an invisible "culture of poverty" with a standard of living and way of life quite different from that envisioned in the American Dream. In such a culture of poverty, being poor was not simply a matter of low income; rather, prolonged

**The Civil Rights Act of 1964**

President Johnson reaches to shake hands with Dr. Martin Luther King Jr. after presenting the civil rights leader with one of the pens used to sign the Civil Rights Act of 1964.

poverty created a subculture whose residents were unlikely to escape from it. Poverty led to poor housing conditions, which in turn led to poor health, poor attendance at school or work, alcohol and drug abuse, unwanted pregnancies, single-parent families, and so on. Unlike the upwardly mobile immigrant poor at the beginning of the century, the modern poor lacked hope. Harrington revealed that poverty was much more extensive and more tenacious in the United States than people realized because much of it was hidden from view in isolated rural areas or inner-city slums often unseen by more prosperous Americans. He urged the United States to launch a "comprehensive assault on poverty."

President Kennedy had read Harrington's book and had asked his advisers in the fall of 1963, just before his assassination, to investigate the poverty problem and suggest solutions. Upon taking office as president, President Johnson announced that he wanted an anti-poverty package that was "big and bold, that would hit the nation with real impact." Money for the program would come from the tax revenues generated by corporate profits made possible by the tax reduction of 1964, which had led to one of the longest sustained economic booms in history.

The Johnson administration's war on poverty was embodied in an economic-opportunity bill passed in August 1964 that incorporated a wide range of programs designed to help the poor help themselves by providing a "hand up, not a hand out": a Job Corps for inner-city youths aged sixteen to twenty-one, a Head Start program for disadvantaged preschoolers, work-study programs for college students with financial need, grants to farmers and rural businesses, loans to employers willing to hire the chronically unemployed, the Volunteers in Service to America (a domestic Peace Corps), and the Community Action Program, which would allow the poor "maximum feasible participation" in directing neighborhood improvement programs designed for their benefit. Speaking at Ann Arbor, Michigan, in 1964, Johnson called for a "Great Society" resting on "abundance and liberty for all. The Great Society demands an end to poverty and racial injustice, to which we are fully committed in our time."

THE ELECTION OF 1964   Johnson's well-intentioned but hastily conceived war on poverty and his Great Society social programs provoked a Republican counterattack. Over the years, Republicans had come to fear that their party had fallen into the hands of an "eastern establishment" that had given in to the same internationalism and big-government policies that liberal Democrats promoted. Ever since 1940, so the theory went, the party had nominated "me-too" candidates who merely promised to run more efficiently the programs that Democrats designed. Offer the Republican voters "a choice, not an echo," they reasoned, and a true conservative majority would assert itself.

By 1960, Arizona senator Barry Goldwater, a millionaire department-store magnate, had emerged as the straight-talking leader of the Republican right. In his book *The Conscience of a Conservative* (1960), Goldwater proposed the abolition of the income tax and a drastic reduction in federal entitlement programs. Almost from the time of Kennedy's victory in 1960, a movement to draft Goldwater as president had begun, mobilizing right-wing activists to capture party caucuses and contest primaries. In 1964, they swept the all-important California primary, thereby enabling them to control the Republican Convention when it gathered in San Francisco. "I would remind you," Goldwater told the delegates, "that extremism in the defense of liberty is no vice." He later explained that his objective was "to reduce the size of government. Not to pass laws but repeal them."

Barry Goldwater later claimed in his memoirs that he had no chance to win the presidency in 1964: "I just wanted the conservatives to have a real voice in the country." His campaign certainly confirmed that prediction, for candidate Goldwater displayed a gift for frightening voters. He urged whole-sale bombing of North Vietnam and left the impression of being trigger-happy. He savaged Johnson's war on poverty and the entire New Deal tradition. At times he was foolishly candid. In Tennessee he proposed the sale of the Tennessee Valley Authority, a series of hydroelectric dams and recreational lakes; in St. Petersburg, Florida, a major retirement community, he questioned the value of Social Security. He also opposed the nuclear test ban and the 1964 Civil Rights Act. To Republican campaign buttons that claimed "In your heart, you know he's right," Democrats responded, "In your guts, you know he's nuts."

Johnson, on the other hand, portrayed himself as a responsible centrist. He chose as his running mate Hubert H. Humphrey of Minnesota, a prominent liberal senator who had long promoted civil rights. In contrast to Goldwater's bellicose rhetoric on Vietnam, Johnson pledged, "We are not about to send

**Barry Goldwater**

Many voters feared that the Republican presidential candidate in 1964, Senator Barry Goldwater, was trigger-happy. In this cartoon, Goldwater wields in one hand his book *The Conscience of a Conservative* and in the other a hydrogen bomb.

American boys nine or ten thousand miles from home to do what Asian boys ought to be doing for themselves."

The result was a landslide. Johnson polled 61 percent of the total vote; Goldwater carried only Arizona and five states in the Deep South, where race remained the salient issue. Vermont went Democratic for the first time ever in a presidential election. Johnson won the electoral vote by a whopping 486 to 52. In the Senate the Democrats increased their majority by two (68 to 32) and in the House by thirty-seven (295 to 140), but Goldwater's success in the Deep South continued that traditionally Democratic region's shift to the Republican party, whose conservative wing was riding a wave of grassroots momentum that would transform the landscape of American politics over the next half century. Goldwater's quixotic campaign failed to win the election, but it proved to be a turning point in the development of the national conservative movement. The Goldwater campaign inspired a young generation of conservative activists and the formation of conservative organizations, such as Young Americans for Freedom, that would eventually transform the dynamics of American politics.

LANDMARK LEGISLATION    Lyndon Johnson knew that the mandate provided by his lopsided victory could quickly erode; he shrewdly told his aides, "Every day I'm in office, I'm going to lose votes. I'm going to alienate somebody. . . . We've got to get this legislation fast. You've got to get it during my honeymoon." In 1965, Johnson flooded the new Congress with **Great Society** legislation that, he promised, would end poverty, revitalize decaying central cities, provide every young American with the chance to attend college, protect the health of the elderly, enhance the nation's cultural life, clean up the air and water, and make the highways safer and prettier.

The scope of Johnson's legislative program was unparalleled since Franklin D. Roosevelt's Hundred Days, in part because of the nation's humming prosperity. "This country," Johnson proclaimed, "is rich enough to do anything it has the guts to do and the vision to do and the will to do." Priority went to federal health insurance and aid to education, proposals that had languished since President Truman had proposed them in 1945. For twenty years, the steadfast opposition of the physicians making up the American Medical Association (AMA) had stalled a comprehensive national medical-insurance program. But now that Johnson had the votes, the AMA joined Republicans in supporting a bill providing medical insurance coverage for those over age sixty-five. The act that finally emerged went well beyond the original proposal. It created not just a Medicare program for the aged but also a Medicaid program of federal grants to states to help cover medical payments for the indigent. President Johnson signed the bill on July 30, 1965, in Independence, Missouri, with eighty-one-year-old Harry Truman looking on.

Five days after he submitted his Medicare program, Johnson sent to Congress a massive program of federal aid to elementary and secondary schools. Such proposals had been ignored since the forties, blocked alternately by issues of segregation and issues of separation of church and state. The **Civil Rights Act of 1964** had laid the first issue to rest, legally at least. Now Congress devised a means of extending aid to "poverty-impacted" school districts regardless of their public or religious character.

The momentum generated by these measures had already begun to carry others along, and that process continued through the following year. Before the Eighty-ninth Congress adjourned, it had established a record in the passage of landmark legislation unequaled since the time of the New Deal. Altogether, the tide of Great Society legislation had carried 435 bills through the Congress. Among them was the Appalachian Regional Development Act of 1966, which allocated $1 billion for programs in remote mountain areas that had long been pockets of desperate poverty. The Housing and Urban Development Act of 1965 provided for construction of 240,000 public-housing units and $3 billion for renewal of blighted urban areas. Funds for rent supplements for low-income families followed in 1966, and in that year a new Department of Housing and Urban Development appeared, headed by Robert C. Weaver, the first African American cabinet member. Lyndon Johnson had, in the words of one Washington reporter, "brought to harvest a generation's backlog of ideas and social legislation."

THE IMMIGRATION ACT    Little noticed in the stream of legislation flowing from Congress was a major new immigration bill that had originated in the Kennedy White House. President Johnson signed the Immigration and Nationality Services Act of 1965 in a ceremony held on Liberty Island in New York harbor. In his speech he stressed that the new law would redress the wrong done to those "from southern and eastern Europe" and the "developing continents" of Asia, Africa, and Latin America. It would do so by abolishing the discriminatory quotas based upon national origin that had governed immigration policy since the twenties. The new law treated all nationalities and races equally. In place of national quotas, it created hemispheric ceilings on visas issued: 170,000 for persons from outside the Western Hemisphere, 120,000 for persons from within. It also stipulated that no more than 20,000 people could come from any one country each year. The new act allowed the entry of immediate family members of American residents without limit. During the sixties, Asians and Latin Americans became the largest contingent of new Americans.

ASSESSING THE GREAT SOCIETY    Lyndon B. Johnson was an accidental president, brought to the White House by the assassination of John F. Kennedy. He knew as he took the oath of office that the nation was gripped in a mood of despair and uncertainty. As he told the nation in his first public address, the bereaving United States needed to "do away with uncertainty and doubt." Johnson was determined to convey vision and aspiration, courage, confidence, and compassion—as well as a demonstrated capacity to lead. Invoking Kennedy's own phrases, the new president said, "Let us begin. Let us continue." He understood that timidity in troubled times would not work. He sought to give the people a sense of forward movement and show them that he could overcome their fears of a divided America and create a "Great Society" whereby Americans would be "more concerned with the quality of their goals than the quantity of their goods."

**Great Society initiatives**

President Johnson listens to Tom Fletcher, a father of eight children, describe some of the economic problems in his hometown.

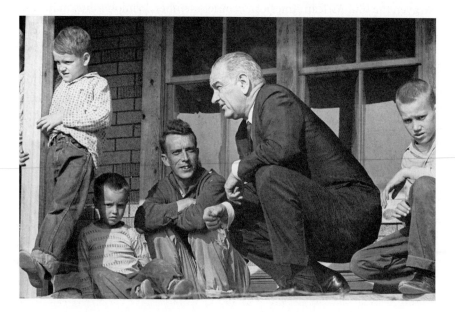

The Great Society failed to achieve its grandiose goals, but it did include several successes. The guarantee of civil rights and voting rights remains protected. Medicare and Medicaid have become two of the most appreciated (and expensive) government programs. As a result of Johnson's efforts, consumer rights now have federal advocates and protections. The Highway Safety Act and the National Traffic and Motor Vehicle Safety Act (both 1966) established safety standards for highway design and automobile manufacturers, and the scholarships provided for college students under the Higher Education Act (1965) were quite popular. Many of the Great Society initiatives aimed at improving the health, nutrition, and education of poor Americans, young and old, made some headway. So, too, did federal efforts to clean up air and water pollution.

Several of Johnson's most ambitious programs, however, were ill conceived, others were vastly underfunded, and many were mismanaged. As Joseph Califano, one of Johnson's senior aides, confessed: "Did we legislate too much? Were mistakes made? Plenty of them." Medicare, for example, removed incentives for hospitals to control costs, so medical bills skyrocketed. The Great Society helped reduce the number of people living in poverty, but it did so largely by providing federal welfare payments to individuals, not by finding people productive jobs. The war on poverty ended up being as disappointing as the war in Vietnam. Often funds appropriated for a program never made it through the tangled bureaucracy to the needy. Widely publicized cases of welfare fraud became a powerful weapon in the hands of those who were opposed to liberal social programs. By 1966, middle-class resentment over the cost and waste of the Great Society programs had generated a conservative backlash that fueled a Republican resurgence at the polls. By then, however, the Great Society had transformed public expectations of the power and role of the federal government—for good and for ill.

## FROM CIVIL RIGHTS TO BLACK POWER

During late 1963 and throughout 1964, the civil rights movement grew in scope, visibility, and power. But government-sanctioned racism remained entrenched in the Deep South. Blacks continued to be excluded from the political process. For example, in 1963 only 6.7 percent of Mississippi blacks were registered to vote, the lowest percentage in the nation. White officials in the South systematically kept African Americans from voting through a variety of means: charging them expensive poll taxes, forcing them to take difficult literacy tests, making the application process inconvenient, and intimidating them through the use of arson, beatings, and lynchings.

**FREEDOM SUMMER**   In early 1964, Harvard-educated Robert "Bob" Moses, a black New Yorker who served as field secretary of the Student Non-violent Coordinating Committee (SNCC) office in Mississippi, the nation's most rural and poorest state, decided it would take "an army" to penetrate the state's longstanding effort to deny voting rights to blacks. So he set about recruiting such an army of idealistic volunteers who would live with rural blacks, teach them in "freedom schools," and help people register to vote. Building upon the energy generated by the March on Washington, Moses recruited a thousand volunteers, most of them white college students, many of whom were Jewish, to participate in what came to be called "Freedom Summer." Mississippi's white leaders resented Moses's efforts. They prepared for "the nigger-communist invasion" by doubling the state police force and stockpiling tear gas, electric cattle prods, and shotguns. The prominent writer Eudora Welty reported from her hometown of Jackson that "this summer all hell is going to break loose."

**Robert "Bob" Moses**

Moses mobilized a thousand volunteer activists to educate and empower blacks across the South during his "Freedom Summer."

In mid-June, the volunteer activists converged at an Ohio college to learn about southern racial history, nonviolence, and the likely abuses they would suffer from white racists. On the final evening of the training session, Robert Moses pleaded with anyone who felt uncertain about their undertaking to go home; several of them did. The next day, the volunteers boarded buses and headed south, fanning across the rural state to hamlets named Harmony and

Holly Springs as well as cities such as Hattiesburg and Jackson. They lived with rural blacks (many of whom had never had a white person enter their home) and fanned out to teach children math, writing, and history and tutor blacks about the complicated process of voter registration.

Forty-six-year-old Fannie Lou Hamer was one of the local blacks who worked with the SNCC volunteers during Freedom Summer. The youngest of twenty children, she had spent most of her life working on local cotton plantations. Freedom Summer opened her eyes to new possibilities. Like so many other African Americans involved in the civil rights movement, she converted her deep Christian faith into a sword of redemption. During the summer of 1963, she led gatherings in freedom songs and excelled as a lay preacher. "God is not pleased with all the murdering and all the brutality and all the killing," she told one group. "God is not pleased that the Negro children in the state of Mississippi [are] suffering from malnutrition. God is not pleased that we have to go raggedy and work from ten to eleven hours for three lousy dollars."

In response to the activities of Freedom Summer, the Ku Klux Klan, local police, and other white racists assaulted and arrested the volunteers and murdered several of them. Hamer was brutally beaten by jail guards in Winona. Yet Freedom Summer was successful in refocusing the civil rights movement on political rights. The number of blacks registered to vote inched up.

CIVIL RIGHTS LEGISLATION    Early in 1965, Martin Luther King Jr. organized an effort to enroll the 3 million African Americans in the South who were not registered to vote. In Selma, Alabama, civil rights protesters began a march to Montgomery, the state capital, about forty miles away, only to be dispersed by five hundred state troopers. A federal judge agreed to allow the march to continue, and President Johnson provided troops for protection. By March 25, when the now twenty-five thousand demonstrators reached Montgomery, the original capital of the Confederacy, segregationists greeted them by flying Confederate flags. Undaunted by the hostile reception, King delivered a rousing address from the steps of the state capitol.

Several days earlier, President Johnson had urged Congress to "overcome the crippling legacy of bigotry and intolerance" by passing stronger laws protecting voting rights. He concluded by slowly intoning the words of the civil rights movement's hymn: "And we shall overcome." The resulting Voting Rights Act of 1965 ensured all citizens the right to vote. It authorized the attorney general to dispatch federal examiners to register voters. In states or counties where fewer than half the adults had voted in 1964, the act suspended literacy tests and other devices commonly used to defraud citizens of the vote. By the end of the year, some 250,000 African Americans were newly registered.

BLACK POWER    Amid this success, however, the civil rights movement began to fragment. On August 11, 1965, less than a week after the passage of the Voting Rights Act, Watts, the largest black ghetto in Los Angeles, exploded in a frenzy of rioting and looting. When the uprising ended, thirty-four were dead, almost four thousand rioters were in jail, and property damage exceeded $35 million. Chicago and Cleveland, along with forty other American cities, experienced similar race riots in the summer of 1966. The following summer, Newark and Detroit burst into flames. Between 1965 and 1968, there were nearly three hundred racial uprisings that shattered the peace of urban America and undermined Johnson's much-vaunted war on poverty.

In retrospect, it was predictable that the civil rights movement would shift its focus from the rural South to the plight of urban blacks nationwide. By the mid-sixties, about 70 percent of the nation's African Americans were living in metropolitan areas, most in central-city ghettos that the postwar prosperity had bypassed. At the same time, a disproportionate number of blacks were serving in an increasingly unpopular war in Vietnam. As those military veterans returned, they often grew disgruntled at what they came back to. "I had left one war and came back and got into another one," said Reginald "Malik" Edwards, a black Vietnam veteran. Once home, he enlisted in another war, this time fighting for the Black Panthers.

It seemed clear, in retrospect, that the nonviolent tactics that had worked in the South would not work as readily in large cities across the nation. "It may be," wrote a contributor to *Esquire* magazine, "that looting, rioting and burning . . . are really nothing more than radical forms of urban renewal, a response not only to the frustrations of the ghetto but the collapse of all ordinary modes of change, as if a body despairing of the indifference of doctors sought to rip a cancer out of itself." A special Commission on Civil Disorders noted that the urban upheavals of the mid-sixties were initiated by blacks themselves; whites, by contrast, had started earlier riots, which had then prompted black counterattacks. Now blacks visited violence and destruction upon themselves in an effort to destroy what they could not stomach and what civil rights legislation seemed unable to change. As a Gil Scott-Heron, a black musician, sang: "We are tired of praying and marching and thinking and learning/Brothers want to start cutting and shooting and stealing and burning."

By 1966, "black power" had become an imprecise but riveting rallying cry for young militants. When Stokely Carmichael, a twenty-five-year-old graduate of Howard University, became head of SNCC in 1966, he made the separatist philosophy of black power the official objective of the organization and ousted whites from the organization. "When you talk of black power," Carmichael shouted, "you talk of bringing this country to its knees, of building a movement that will smash everything Western civilization has created." H. Rap Brown, who succeeded Carmichael as head of SNCC in 1967, was even more outspoken and incendiary. He urged blacks to "get you some guns" and "kill the honkies." Carmichael, meanwhile, had moved on to the Black Panther party, a group of urban revolutionaries founded in Oakland, California, in 1966. Headed by Huey P. Newton, Bobby Seale, and Eldridge Cleaver, the provocative, armed Black Panthers initially terrified the public but eventually fragmented in spasms of violence.

MALCOLM X    The most articulate spokesman for black power was **Malcolm X** (formerly Malcolm Little, the X denoting his lost African surname). Born in 1925, tall and austere Malcolm had spent his childhood in Lansing, Michigan, where his family home was burned to the ground by white racists. His parents, Earl and Louise Little, were supporters of Marcus Garvey's controversial crusade for black nationalism. Earl frequently beat his wife and seven children, but he died violently when Malcolm was six, leaving the family in extreme poverty, dependent on local relief agencies for survival. When Malcolm was fourteen, his mother was confined to a mental hospital. He then moved to Boston to live with Ella, his older half sister, who was repeatedly arrested for minor crimes. Malcolm then took what he later called a "destructive detour." He quit school during ninth grade and began to display what would become a lifelong ability to reinvent himself. By age nineteen, known as Detroit Red, he had become a thief, drug dealer, gambler, and pimp. Between the ages of twenty and twenty-seven he was incarcerated in Massachusetts prisons, which ironically brought salvation.

While incarcerated, Malcolm developed a passion for reading and learning, enrolling in correspondence courses. "Where else but in a prison," he later wrote, "could I have attacked my ignorance by being able to study intensely sometimes as much as fifteen hours a day." He also had a spiritual awakening. Malcolm joined a small Chicago-based sect called the Nation of Islam (NOI), whose members were often called Black Muslims. The organization had little to do with Islam and everything to do with its domineering leader, Elijah Muhammad, and the cult-like devotion he required. Muhammad, a Georgian, characterized whites as "devils" and espoused black nationalism, racial pride, self-respect, and self-discipline. By 1953, a year after leaving prison, Malcolm X was a full-time NOI minister famous for his angry but electrifying speeches decrying white racism and black passivity, as well as his abilities as a grassroots community organizer. "We have a common oppressor, a common exploiter," he told black audiences. ". . . He's an enemy to all of us." Largely because of Malcolm's charisma as well as his confrontational language and threats of violence, the NOI grew from a few hundred members in 1952 to tens of thousands by 1960.

Malcolm X dismissed the mainstream civil rights leaders such as Martin Luther King Jr. as being "nothing but modern Uncle Toms" who "keep you and me in check, keep us under control, keep us passive and peaceful and nonviolent." He sought to appeal less to white America's moral conscience than to its fear of social revolution. While Dr. King's followers sang "We Shall Overcome," Malcolm X's supporters responded with "We Shall Overrun." His militant candor inspired thousands of blacks who had never identified with Martin Luther King's philosophy of non-violent civil disobedience. "Yes, I'm an extremist," Malcolm acknowledged in 1964. "The black race in the United States is in extremely bad shape. You show me a black man who isn't an extremist and I'll show you one who needs psychiatric attention."

**Malcolm X**

Malcolm X was the black power movement's most influential spokesman.

By March 1964, Malcolm had broken with Elijah Muhammad, toured Africa and the Middle East urging governments there to take the complaints of African Americans to the United Nations, embraced the Muslim faith, and founded an organization committed to the establishment of alliances between African Americans and the people of color around the world. More than most black leaders, Malcolm X experienced and expressed the turbulent emotions and frustrations of the African American poor and working class. After the publication of his acclaimed *Autobiography* in 1964, Malcolm became a symbol of the international human rights movement. But his conflict with Elijah Muhammad proved fatal; assassins representing a rival faction of Black Muslims gunned down 39-year-old Malcolm X in Manhattan while he was speaking at Harlem's Audubon Ballroom on February 21, 1965. With him went the most effective voice for urban black militancy since Marcus Garvey in the twenties. What made the assassination of Malcolm X especially tragic was that he had just months before begun to abandon his strident anti-white rhetoric and preach a biracial message of social change.

Although widely publicized and highly visible, the **black power movement** never attracted more than a small minority of mostly young African Americans. Only about 15 percent of American blacks labeled themselves separatists. The preponderant majority continued to identify with the philosophy of nonviolent, Christian-centered integration promoted by Martin Luther King Jr. and with organizations such as the NAACP. King dismissed black separatism and the promotion of violent social change by reminding his followers that "we can't win violently."

Despite its hyperbole, violence, and few adherents, the black power philosophy had two positive effects upon the civil rights movement. First, it motivated African Americans to take greater pride in their racial heritage. As Malcolm X often pointed out, prolonged slavery and institutionalized racism had eroded the self-esteem of many blacks. "The worst crime the white man has committed," he declared, "has been to teach us to hate ourselves." He and others helped blacks appreciate their African roots and their American accomplishments. In fact, it was Malcolm X who insisted that blacks call themselves African Americans as a symbol of pride in their roots and as a spur to learn more about their history as a people. As the popular singer James Brown urged, "Say it loud—I'm black and I'm proud."

Second, the assertiveness of black power advocates forced Martin Luther King and other mainstream black leaders and organizations to focus attention on the plight of poor inner-city blacks. Legal access to restaurants, schools, and other public accommodations, King pointed out, meant little to people mired in a degrading culture of urban poverty. They needed jobs and decent housing as much as they needed legal rights. To this end, King began to emphasize the economic plight of the black urban underclass. The time had come for radical measures "to provide jobs and income for the poor." Yet as King and others sought to heighten the war on poverty at home, the escalating conflict in Vietnam (LBJ called it "that bitch of a war") was consuming more and more of America's resources and energies.

## THE TRAGEDY OF VIETNAM

As racial violence erupted in America's cities, the war in Vietnam reached new levels of intensity and destruction. In November 1963, when President Kennedy was assassinated, there were sixteen thousand U.S. military "advisers" in South Vietnam. Lyndon B. Johnson inherited from Kennedy and Eisenhower a long-standing commitment to prevent a Communist takeover in Indochina as well as a reluctance on the part of American presidents to assume primary responsibility for fighting the Viet Cong (the Communist-led guerrillas in South Vietnam) and their North Vietnamese allies. Beginning with Harry S. Truman, one president after another had done just enough to avoid being charged with having "lost" Vietnam to communism. Johnson initially sought to do the same, fearing that any other course of action would undermine his political influence and jeopardize his Great Society programs in Congress. But this path took the United States deeper into an expanding military commitment in Southeast Asia. Early on, Johnson doubted that the poverty-stricken, peasant-based Vietnam was worth military involvement. In May 1964, he told his national security adviser, McGeorge Bundy, that he had spent a sleepless night worrying about Vietnam: "It looks to me like we are getting into another Korea. . . . I don't think we can fight them 10,000 miles away from home. . . . I don't think it's worth fighting for. And I don't think we can get out. It's just the biggest damned mess that I ever saw."

Yet Johnson's fear of appearing weak abroad was stronger than his misgivings and forebodings. By the end of 1965, there were 184,000 U.S. troops, well trained for the wrong war, in Vietnam; in 1966, there were 385,000; and by 1969, at the height of the American presence, 542,000. By the time the last troops left, in March 1973,

**"How Deep Do You Figure We'll Get Involved, Sir?"**

Although U.S. soldiers were first sent to Vietnam as noncombatant advisers, they soon found themselves involved in a quagmire of fighting.

some 58,000 Americans had died and another 300,000 had been wounded. The massive, prolonged war had cost taxpayers $150 billion and siphoned funding from many Great Society programs; it had produced 570,000 draft "dodgers" and 563,000 less-than-honorable military discharges, toppled Johnson's administration, and divided the nation as no event in history had since the Civil War.

ESCALATION  The official sanction for military "escalation" in Southeast Asia—a Defense Department term favored in the Vietnam era—was the **Tonkin Gulf resolution**, voted by Congress on August 7, 1964, after merely thirty minutes of discussion. On that day, Johnson told a national television audience that on August 2 and 4, North Vietnamese vessels had attacked two U.S. destroyers, the *Maddox* and the *C. Turner Joy,* in the Gulf of Tonkin, off the coast of North Vietnam. Johnson described the attack, called the Gulf of Tonkin incident, as unprovoked. In truth, the destroyers had been monitoring South Vietnamese attacks against two North Vietnamese islands—attacks planned by American advisers. The Tonkin Gulf resolution authorized the president to "take all necessary measures to repel any armed attack against the forces of the United States and to prevent further aggression." Only Senator Wayne Morse of Oregon and Senator Ernest Gruening of Alaska voted against the resolution, which Johnson thereafter interpreted as equivalent to a congressional declaration of war.

Soon after his landslide victory over Goldwater in November 1964, Johnson, while still plagued by private doubts, made the crucial decisions that committed the United States to a full-scale war in Vietnam for the next four years. On February 5, 1965, Viet Cong (VC) guerrillas killed 8 and wounded 126 Americans at Pleiku, in South Vietnam. More attacks later that week led Johnson to order Operation Rolling Thunder, the first sustained bombing of North Vietnam, which was intended to stop the flow of soldiers and supplies into the south. Six months later an extensive study concluded that the massive bombing was astonishingly ineffective; it had not slowed the supplies pouring down the Ho Chi Minh Trail from North Vietnam through Laos and into South Vietnam. Johnson's solution was to keep applying more pressure.

In March 1965, the new U.S. commander in Vietnam, General William C. Westmoreland, greeted the first installment of combat troops. By the summer, American forces were engaged in "search-and-destroy" operations throughout South Vietnam. As combat operations increased, so did casualties, announced each week on the nightly television news, along with the "body count" of alleged Viet Cong dead. "Westy's war," although fought with helicopter gunships,

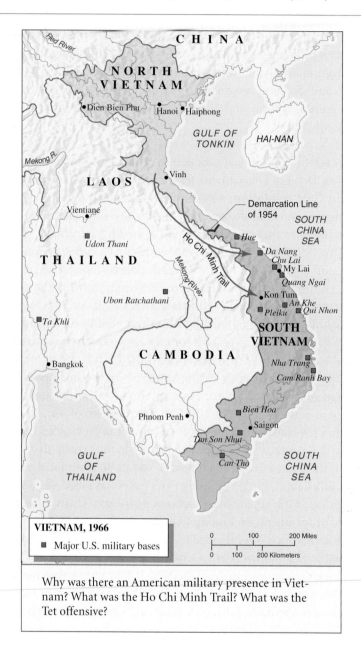

**VIETNAM, 1966**

■ Major U.S. military bases

0     100     200 Miles
0   100   200 Kilometers

Why was there an American military presence in Vietnam? What was the Ho Chi Minh Trail? What was the Tet offensive?

chemical defoliants, and napalm, became like the trench warfare of World War I—a war of attrition. "We will not be defeated," Johnson told the nation in April. "We will not grow tired. We will not withdraw." The containment doctrine would now face its greatest test.

THE CONTEXT FOR POLICY     President Johnson's decision to "Americanize" the Vietnam War, so ill-starred in retrospect, was consistent with the foreign-policy principles pursued by all presidents after the Second World War. The version of the theory intended to "contain" communism articulated in the Truman Doctrine, endorsed by Eisenhower throughout the fifties, and reaffirmed by Kennedy, pledged U.S. opposition to the advance of communism anywhere in the world. "Why are we in Vietnam?" Johnson asked rhetorically at Johns Hopkins University in 1965. "We are there because we have a promise to keep. . . . To leave Vietnam to its fate would shake the confidence of all these people in the value of American commitment." Secretary of State Dean Rusk frequently repeated this rationale, warning that the rest of Southeast Asia would fall "like dominoes" to communism if American forces withdrew from Vietnam. Military intervention was thus a logical culmination of the assumptions that were widely shared by the foreign-policy establishment and the leaders of both political parties since the early days of the cold war.

At the same time, Johnson and his advisers presumed that military involvement in Vietnam must not reach levels that would cause the Chinese or Soviets to intervene directly. And that meant, in effect, that a complete military victory was never possible. The goal of the United States was not to win the war in any traditional sense but to prevent the North Vietnamese and the Viet Cong from winning and, eventually, to force a negotiated settlement with the North Vietnamese. This meant that the United States would have to maintain a military presence as long as the enemy retained the will to fight.

As it turned out, American support for the war eroded faster than the will of the North Vietnamese leaders to tolerate devastating casualties and massive destruction. Systematic opposition to the war on college campuses began in 1965 with teach-ins at the University of Michigan. The following year, Senator J. William Fulbright of Arkansas, chairman of the Senate Foreign Relations Committee, began congressional investigations into American policy in Vietnam. George F. Kennan, the author of the containment doctrine in 1946-47, told Senator Fulbright's committee that the doctrine was appropriate for Europe but not for Southeast Asia. And a respected general testified that General Westmoreland's military strategy had no chance of achieving victory. By 1967, anti-war demonstrations were attracting massive support. Nightly television accounts of the fighting—Vietnam was the first war to receive extended television coverage and hence was dubbed the living-room war—called into question the official optimism. By May 1967, even Secretary of Defense Robert McNamara was wavering: "The picture of the world's greatest superpower killing or injuring 1,000 noncombatants a week, while trying to pound a tiny backward nation into submission on an issue whose merits are hotly disputed, is not a pretty one." Yet Johnson dismissed the anti-war protesters as "chickenshit."

In a war of political will, North Vietnam had the advantage. Johnson and his advisers grievously underestimated the tenacity of the North Vietnamese commitment to unify Vietnam and expel American forces. While the United States fought a limited war for limited objectives, the Vietnamese Communists fought an all-out war for their very survival. Just as General Westmoreland was assuring Johnson and the public that the war effort in early 1968 was on the verge of gaining the upper hand, the Communists organized widespread assaults that jolted American confidence and resolve.

THE TURNING POINT  On January 31, 1968, the first day of the Vietnamese New Year (Tet), the Viet Cong defied a holiday truce to launch ferocious assaults on American and South Vietnamese forces throughout South Vietnam. A squad of VC commandos besieged the U.S. embassy in Saigon; others attacked General Westmoreland's headquarters. VC units temporarily occupied the grounds of the U.S. embassy in Saigon, the capital of South Vietnam. After VC guerrillas took control of Hue, the ancient cultural capital of Vietnam, American forces launched a total effort to retake the historic city. As an army officer explained afterwards, "We had to destroy the city to save it."

General Westmoreland proclaimed the **Tet offensive** a major defeat for the Viet Cong, and most students of military strategy later agreed with him. While VC casualties were enormous, however, the impact of the surprise attacks on the American public was more telling. The scope and intensity of the offensive contradicted upbeat claims by U.S. commanders and LBJ that the war was going well. *Time* and *Newsweek* magazines soon ran anti-war editorials urging withdrawal. Even the conservative *Wall Street Journal* concluded after the Tet Offensive that "the whole Vietnam effort may be doomed." Polls showed that Johnson's popularity had declined to 35 percent. Civil rights leaders and social activists felt betrayed as they saw federal funds earmarked for the war on poverty gobbled up by the expanding war. In 1968, the United States was spending $322,000 on every Communist killed in Vietnam; the poverty programs at home received only $53 per person. As Martin Luther King Jr. pointed out, "the bombs in Vietnam explode at home—they destroy the hopes and possibilities for a decent America." He repeatedly pointed out that the amount being spent to kill each Vietnamese Communist was greater than the amount spent by the federal government on assisting an American living in poverty.

During 1968, a despondent President Johnson grew increasingly embittered and isolated. He suffered from depression and bouts of paranoia. It had at last become painfully evident to him that the Vietnam War was a never-ending stalemate that was fragmenting the nation and undermining the Great Society programs. Clark Clifford, Johnson's new secretary of defense, reported to the president that a task force of military and civilian leaders saw no prospect for a military victory. Robert F. Kennedy, now a senator from New York, was considering a run for the presidency in order to challenge Johnson's Vietnam policy. Senator Eugene McCarthy of Minnesota, a devout Catholic and a poet, had already decided to oppose Johnson in the Democratic primaries. With anti-war students rallying to his "Dump Johnson" candidacy, McCarthy polled a stunning 42 percent of the vote to Johnson's 48 percent in New Hampshire's March primary. It was a remarkable showing for a little-known senator. Each presidential primary now promised to become a referendum on Johnson's Vietnam policy. The war in Vietnam had become President Johnson's war; as more and more voters soured on the fighting, he saw his public support evaporate. In Wisconsin,

**The Tet offensive**

Many Vietnamese were driven from their homes during the bloody street battles of the 1968 Tet offensive. Here, following a lull in the fighting, civilians carrying a white flag approach U.S. Marines.

**Johnson and Vietnam**

The Vietnam War sapped the spirit of Lyndon B. Johnson, who decided not to run for reelection in 1968.

scene of the next Democratic primary, the president's political advisers forecast a humiliating defeat.

On March 31, Johnson made a dramatic decision. He appeared on national television to announce a limited halt to the bombing of North Vietnam and fresh initiatives for a negotiated cease-fire. Then he added a stunning postscript: "I shall not seek, and I will not accept, the nomination of my party for another term as your President." It was a humiliating end to a grandiose presidency. Although U.S. troops would remain in Vietnam for five more years and the casualties would continue, the quest for military victory had ended. Now the question was how the most powerful nation in the world could extricate itself from Vietnam with a minimum of damage to its prestige and its South Vietnamese allies.

## SIXTIES CRESCENDO

A TRAUMATIC YEAR    Change moved at a fearful pace throughout the sixties, but 1968 was the most turbulent and the most traumatic year of all. On April 4, only four days after Johnson's withdrawal from the presidential race, a white racist named James Earl Ray assassinated Martin Luther King Jr. in Memphis, Tennessee. King's death set off an outpouring of grief among whites and blacks and ignited riots in over sixty cities.

Two months later, on June 5, a young Jordanian named Sirhan Sirhan shot and killed forty-two-year-old Senator Robert F. Kennedy just after he had defeated Eugene McCarthy in the California Democratic primary. Political reporter David Halberstam of the *New York Times* thought back to the assassinations of John Kennedy and Malcolm X, then to the violent end of Martin Luther King, the most influential African American leader of the twentieth century, and then to Robert Kennedy, the heir to leadership of the Kennedy clan. "We could make a calendar of the decade," Halberstam wrote, "by marking where we were at the hours of those violent deaths."

CHICAGO AND MIAMI   In the summer of 1968, the social unrest roiling the nation morphed into political melodrama at the disruptive, divisive, and violent Democratic National Convention. In August, delegates gathered inside a Chicago convention hall to nominate Lyndon B. Johnson's faithful vice president, Hubert H. Humphrey. Outside, almost twenty thousand police officers and national guardsmen and a mob of television reporters stood watch over a gathering of eclectic protesters herded together miles away in a public park. Chicago's gruff Democratic mayor Richard J. Daley warned that he would not tolerate disruptions in his city. Nonetheless, riots broke out and were televised nationwide. As police used tear gas and billy clubs to pummel anti-war demonstrators, others chanted, "The whole world is watching." (See pages 1354–56 for further details.)

The Democratic party's liberal tradition was clearly in disarray, a fact that gave heart to the Republicans, who gathered in Miami Beach to nominate Richard Nixon. Only six years earlier, after he had lost the California gubernatorial race, Nixon had vowed never again to run for public office. But by 1968 he had changed his mind and had become a spokesman for the values of "middle America." Nixon and the Republicans offered a vision of stability and order that appealed to a majority of Americans—soon to be called the silent majority.

In 1968, George Wallace, the Democratic governor of Alabama who had made his reputation as an outspoken defender of segregation, ran on the American Independent party ticket. Wallace moderated his position on the race issue but appealed even more candidly than Nixon to voters' concerns about rioting anti-war protesters, the mushrooming welfare system, and the growth of the federal government. Wallace's reactionary candidacy generated considerable appeal outside his native South, especially among white working-class communities, where resentment of Johnson's Great Society liberalism flourished. Although never a possible winner, Wallace hoped to deny Humphrey or Nixon an electoral majority and thereby throw the choice into the House of Representatives, which would have provided an appropriate climax to a chaotic year.

NIXON AGAIN   It did not happen that way. Richard Nixon enjoyed an enormous lead in the polls, which narrowed as the election approached.

**The 1968 election**

Richard Nixon (left) and running mate Spiro Agnew (right).

Wallace's campaign was hurt by his outspoken running mate, retired air force general Curtis LeMay, who favored expanding the war in Vietnam and using nuclear weapons. In October 1968, Hubert Humphrey infuriated Johnson when he announced that, if elected, he would stop bombing North Vietnam "as an acceptable risk for peace."

Nixon and Governor Spiro Agnew of Maryland, his acid-tongued running mate, eked out a narrow victory of about 500,000 votes, a margin of about 1 percentage point. The electoral vote was more decisive, 301 to 191. George Wallace received 10 million votes, 13.5 percent of the total. It was the best showing by a third-party candidate since Robert M. La Follette ran on the Progressive party ticket in 1924. All but one of Wallace's 46 electoral votes were from the Deep South. Nixon swept all but four of the states west of the Mississippi. Humphrey's support came almost exclusively from the Northeast. Nixon's victory celebration was tempered by the fact that the Republicans did not gain control of the House or the Senate. He would be the first

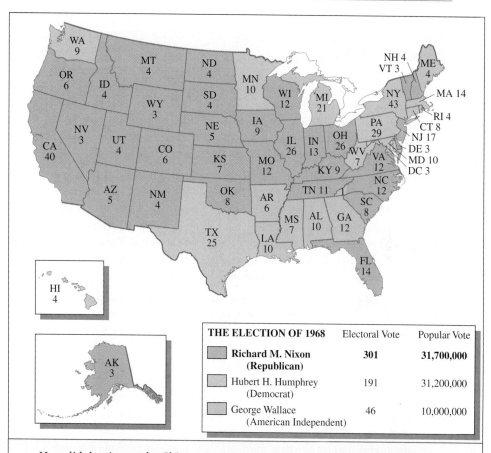

| THE ELECTION OF 1968 | Electoral Vote | Popular Vote |
|---|---|---|
| Richard M. Nixon (Republican) | 301 | 31,700,000 |
| Hubert H. Humphrey (Democrat) | 191 | 31,200,000 |
| George Wallace (American Independent) | 46 | 10,000,000 |

How did the riots at the Chicago Democratic Convention affect the 1968 presidential campaign? What does the electoral map reveal about the support base for each of the three major candidates? How was Nixon able to win enough electoral votes in such a close, three-way presidential race? What was Wallace's appeal to 10 million voters?

president since 1853 to assume office without his party controlling at least one house of Congress.

So at the end of a turbulent year, near the end of a traumatic decade, a nation on the verge of violent chaos looked to Richard Nixon to provide what he had promised in the campaign: "peace with honor" in Vietnam and a middle ground on which a majority of Americans, silent or otherwise, could come together.

*End of Chapter Review*

## CHAPTER SUMMARY

- **Kennedy's New Frontier**  President Kennedy promised "new frontiers" in domestic policy, but without a clear Democratic majority in Congress he was unable to increase federal aid to education, provide health insurance for the aged, create a cabinet-level department of urban affairs, or expand civil rights. He championed tariff cuts, however, and an expanded space program.

- **Johnson's Great Society**  President Johnson was committed to social reform, including civil rights. He forced the Civil Rights Act through Congress in 1964 and declared a "war" on poverty. Under the Great Society, welfare was expanded, Medicare and Medicaid were created, more grants for college students were established, and racial quotas for immigration were abolished. These programs were expensive and, coupled with the soaring costs of the war in Vietnam, necessitated tax increases, which were unpopular.

- **Civil Rights' Achievements**  By the sixties, significant numbers of African Americans and whites were staging nonviolent sit-ins. In 1961, "freedom riders" attempted to integrate buses, trains, and bus and train stations in the South. The high point of the early phase of the civil rights movement was the 1963 March on Washington for Jobs and Freedom, at which Martin Luther King Jr. delivered his famous "I Have a Dream" speech. In 1964, President Johnson signed the far-reaching Civil Rights Act. In 1965, King set in motion a massive drive to enroll the 3 million southern African Americans who were not registered to vote. Later that year, Johnson persuaded Congress to pass the Voting Rights Act. The legislation did little to ameliorate the poverty of inner-city blacks or stem the violence that swept northern cities in the hot summers of the late sixties. By 1968, nonviolent resistance had given way to the more militant black power movement.

- **Escalation in Vietnam**  The United States supported the government of South Vietnam even though it failed to deliver promised reforms, win the support of its citizens, or defeat the Communist insurgents, the Viet Cong. Kennedy increased America's commitment by sending 16,000 advisers, and Johnson went further, deploying combat troops. A turning point in the war was the Viet Cong's Tet offensive, which served to rally anti-war sentiment.

- **Communist Cuba**  In early 1961, Kennedy inherited a CIA plot to topple the regime of Fidel Castro, the premier of Cuba. Kennedy naïvely agreed to the plot, whereby some 1,500 anti-Castro Cubans landed at Cuba's Bay of Pigs. The plotters failed to inspire a revolution, and most were quickly captured. Kennedy's seeming weakness in the face of Soviet aggression led the Russian premier, Nikita Khrushchev, to believe that the Soviets could install ballistic missiles in Cuba without American opposition. In October 1962 in a tense standoff, Kennedy ordered a blockade of Cuba and succeeded in forcing Khrushchev to withdraw the missiles.

## CHRONOLOGY

| | |
|---|---|
| 1960 | Students in Greensboro, North Carolina, stage a sit-in to demand service at a "whites-only" lunch counter |
| 1961 | Bay of Pigs fiasco |
| 1961 | Soviets erect the Berlin Wall |
| October 1962 | Cuban missile crisis |
| August 1963 | March on Washington for Jobs and Freedom |
| November 1963 | John F. Kennedy is assassinated in Dallas, Texas |
| 1964 | Congress passes the Civil Rights Act |
| August 1964 | Congress passes the Tonkin Gulf resolution |
| 1965 | Malcolm X is assassinated by a rival group of black Muslims |
| 1965 | Riots break out in the African American community of Watts, California |
| January 1968 | Viet Cong stages the Tet offensive |
| April 1968 | Martin Luther King Jr. is assassinated |
| June 1968 | Robert Kennedy is assassinated |

## KEY TERMS & NAMES

John F. Kennedy p. 1301

New Frontier p. 1302

Lyndon B. Johnson p. 1303

*Miranda v. Arizona* p. 1306

freedom riders p. 1309

James Meredith p. 1310

March on Washington
p. 1312

Cuban missile crisis p. 1319

Great Society p. 1328

Civil Rights Act of 1964
p. 1329

Malcolm X p. 1335

black power movement
p. 1337

Tonkin Gulf resolution
p. 1339

Tet offensive p. 1342

# REBELLION AND REACTION: THE 1960s AND 1970s

## FOCUS QUESTIONS        wwnorton.com/studyspace

- What characterized the social rebellion and struggles for civil rights in the 1960s and 1970s?
- How did the war in Vietnam end?
- What was Watergate, and why did it lead to Nixon's resignation?
- Why did President Ford issue a pardon to Richard M. Nixon?
- What was "stagflation"?

As Richard M. Nixon entered the White House in early 1969, he took charge of a nation whose social fabric was in tatters. Everywhere, it seemed, conventional institutions and notions of authority were under attack. The traumatic events of 1968 were like a knife blade splitting past and future, then and now. They revealed how deeply divided society had become and how difficult a task Nixon faced in carrying out his pledge to restore social harmony. In the end, the stability he promised proved elusive. His controversial policies and his combative temperament heightened rather than reduced societal tensions. Ironically, many of the same forces that had enabled the complacent prosperity of the fifties—the baby boom, the cold war, and the burgeoning consumer culture—helped generate the social upheaval of the sixties and seventies. It was one of the most turbulent periods in American history—exciting, threatening, explosive, and transforming.

## THE ROOTS OF REBELLION

YOUTH REVOLT    By the early sixties, the baby boomers were maturing. Now young adults, they differed from their elders in that they had experienced neither economic depression nor a major war during their lifetimes. In record numbers they were attending colleges and universities: enrollment quadrupled between 1945 and 1970. Many universities had become gigantic institutions dependent upon huge research contracts from corporations and the federal government. As these "multiversities" grew larger and more bureaucratic, they unwittingly invited resistance from a generation of students wary of what President Dwight D. Eisenhower had labeled the military-industrial complex.

The Greensboro sit-ins in 1960 not only precipitated a decade of civil rights activism but also signaled an end to the complacency that had enveloped many college campuses and much of social life during the fifties. The sit-ins, marches, protests, ideals, and sacrifices associated with the civil rights movement inspired other groups—women, Native Americans, Hispanics, and gays—to demand justice, freedom, and equality as well.

During 1960–1961, white students joined African Americans in the sit-in movement. They and many others were also inspired by President John F. Kennedy's direct appeals to their youthful idealism. Thousands enrolled in the Peace Corps and VISTA (Volunteers in Service to America), while others continued to participate in civil rights demonstrations. But as criticism of escalating military involvement in Vietnam mounted, more and more young people grew disillusioned with the government. During the mid-sixties, a full-fledged youth revolt erupted across the nation. The youth revolt grew out of several impulses: to challenge authority; to change the world; and to indulge in pleasures of all sorts. As a popular song by Steppenwolf declared in 1968, "Like a true nature child/We were born, born to be wild/We have climbed so high/Never want to die." During the sixties and seventies, rebellious young people flowed into two distinct yet frequently overlapping movements: the New Left and the counterculture.

THE NEW LEFT    The explicitly political strain of the youth revolt originated when Tom Hayden and Al Haber, two University of Michigan students, formed Students for a Democratic Society (SDS) in 1960, an organization very much influenced by the tactics and ideals of the civil rights movement. In 1962, Hayden and Haber convened a meeting of sixty upstart activists at Port Huron, Michigan, all of whom shared a desire to remake the United States into a more democratic society. Hayden drafted for the group an impassioned manifesto that became known as the Port Huron Statement. It begins: "We are the people of this generation, bred in at least moderate comfort, housed in universities, looking uncomfortably to the world we inherit." Hayden then called for political reforms, racial equality, and workers' rights. Inspired by the example of African American activism in the South, Hayden declared that college students had the power to restore "participatory democracy" by wresting "control of the educational process from the administrative bureaucracy" and then forging links with other dissident movements. He and others adopted the term New Left to distinguish their efforts at grassroots democracy from those of the Old Left of the thirties, which had espoused an orthodox Marxism.

In the fall of 1964, students at the University of California at Berkeley took Hayden's program to heart. Several of them had returned to the campus after spending the summer working with the Student Nonviolent Coordinating Committee (SNCC) voter-registration project in Mississippi, where three volunteers had been killed, and nearly a thousand arrested. Their idealism and activism had been pricked by their participation in Freedom Summer, and they were eager to bring changes to campus life as they enrolled for the fall semester. When the UC Berkeley chancellor announced that political

**The free-speech movement**

Mario Savio, a founder of the free-speech movement, speaks at a rally at the University of California at Berkeley.

demonstrations would no longer be allowed on campus, several hundred students staged a sit-in. Thousands more joined in. After a tense thirty-two-hour standoff the administration relented. Student groups then formed the free-speech movement (FSM).

Led by Mario Savio, a philosophy major and compelling public speaker who had participated in Freedom Summer in Mississippi, the FSM initially protested on behalf of students' rights. But it quickly mounted a more general criticism of the university and what Savio called the "depersonalized, unresponsive bureaucracy" smothering American life. In 1964, Savio led hundreds of students into UC Berkeley's administration building and organized a sit-in. In the early-morning hours, six hundred policemen, dispatched by the governor, arrested the protesters. But their example lived on.

The goals and tactics of the FSM and SDS spread to colleges across the country. Issues large and small became the target of student protest: unpopular faculty tenure decisions, mandatory ROTC (Reserve Officers' Training Corps) programs, dress codes, curfews, and dormitory regulations.

Escalating U.S. military involvement in Vietnam soon changed the students' agenda. With the dramatic expansion of the war after 1965, millions of young men faced the grim prospect of being drafted to fight in an increasingly unpopular conflict. In fact, however, the Vietnam War, like virtually every other, was primarily a poor man's fight. Deferments enabled college students to postpone military service until they received their degree or reached the age of twenty-four; in 1965–1966, college students made up only 2 percent of all military inductees. In 1966, however, the Selective Service System made undergraduates eligible for the draft.

As the war dragged on and opposition mounted, 200,000 young men ignored their draft notices, and some 4,000 of them served prison sentences. Another 56,000 men qualified for conscientious objector status during the Vietnam War, compared with only 7,600 during the Korean conflict. Still others left the country altogether—several thousand fled to Canada or Sweden—to avoid military service. The most popular way to escape the draft was to flunk the physical examination. Whatever the preferred method, many students succeeded in avoiding military service. Of the 1,200 men in the Harvard senior class of 1970, only 56 served in the military, and just 2 of those went to Vietnam.

Still, the threat of being drafted generated widespread protests, on and off campuses. In the spring of 1967, 500,000 war protesters of all ages converged on New York City's Central Park, where the most popular chant was "Hey, hey, LBJ, how many kids did you kill today?" Dozens of young men ceremoniously burned their draft cards, thereby igniting the so-called resistance phase of the anti-war movement. Thereafter, a coalition of resistance groups around the country sponsored draft-card-burning rallies that led to numerous arrests. Meanwhile, some SDS leaders were growing even more militant. Inspired by the rhetoric and violence of black power spokesmen such as Stokely Carmichael, H. Rap Brown, and Huey P. Newton, Tom Hayden abandoned his earlier commitment to passive civil disobedience. Rap Brown told Hayden and other white radicals to "take up a gun and go shoot the enemy." As the SDS became more militant, it grew more centralized and authoritarian. Capitalist imperialism replaced university bureaucracy as the primary foe.

Throughout 1967 and 1968, the anti-war movement grew more volatile as inner-city ghettos were exploding in flames fanned by racial injustice. Frustration over deeply entrenched patterns of discrimination in employment and housing and staggering rates of joblessness among inner-city African American youths provoked chaotic violence in scores of urban ghettos. "There was a sense everywhere, in 1968," the journalist Garry Wills wrote, "that things were giving way. That man had not only lost control of his history, but might never regain it."

During the eventful spring of 1968—when Lyndon B. Johnson announced that he would not run for reelection and Martin Luther King Jr. was assassinated—campus unrest enveloped the country. Over two hundred major demonstrations took place. The turmoil reached a climax with the disruption of Columbia University in New York City, where Mark Rudd, the campus SDS leader, joined other student radicals in occupying the president's office and classroom buildings. They also kidnapped a dean—all in protest of the university's connection to a war research institute and Columbia's recent decision to displace an African American neighborhood in order to build a new gymnasium. Rudd explained that he and the other rebels were practicing "confrontation politics." During the next week, more buildings were occupied, faculty and administrative offices were ransacked, and classes were canceled. University officials finally called in the New York City police. In the process of arresting the protesters, officers injured innocent bystanders. Such excessive force outraged many unaligned students, who then staged a strike that shut down the university for the remainder of the semester. The riotous events at Columbia inspired similar clashes among students, administrators, and police at Harvard, Cornell, and San Francisco State.

At the 1968 Democratic National Convention in Chicago, the polarization of society reached a bizarre climax. Inside the tightly guarded convention hall, Democrats nominated Vice President Hubert H. Humphrey to succeed LBJ while on Chicago's streets the whole spectrum of antiwar dissenters gathered, from the earnest supporters of Senator Eugene McCarthy to the nihilistic Yippies, members of the new Youth International party. Abbie Hoffman,

**Students for a Democratic Society take over Columbia University**

Mark Rudd, leader of SDS at Columbia University, talking to representatives of the media during student protests of university policies, April 1968.

one of the Yippie leaders, explained that their "conception of revolution is that it's fun." The Yippies distributed a leaflet at the convention calling for the immediate legalization of marijuana as well as all psychedelic drugs, student-run schools, unregulated sex, and the abolition of money. They also hurled taunts, rocks, and urine-filled plastic bags at the police.

The outlandish behavior of the Yippies and the other demonstrators provoked an equally outlandish response by Chicago's Mayor Richard J. Daley and his army of city police. As a horrified television audience watched, many police officers went berserk, clubbing and gassing demonstrators as well as bystanders caught up in the melee. They also indiscriminately arrested protesters and bystanders. The chaotic spectacle lasted three days and seriously damaged Humphrey's candidacy. The televised Chicago riots also angered middle-class Americans, many of whom wondered: "Is America coming apart?" At the same time, the violence in Chicago fragmented the anti-war movement. Those groups committed to nonviolent protest, while castigating the reactionary policies of Mayor Daley and the police, felt betrayed by the actions of the Yippies and other anarchists.

In 1968, the SDS fractured into rival factions, the most extreme of which called itself the Weather Underground, a name derived from a lyric by the songwriter Bob Dylan: "You don't need a weather man to know which way

**Upheaval in Chicago**

The violence that accompanied the 1968 Democratic National Convention in Chicago seared the nation.

the wind blows." The Weathermen, said one of their leaders, were "against everything that's 'good and decent,' in honky America. We will burn and loot and destroy." These hardened young activists embarked on a campaign of violence and disruption, firebombing university buildings and killing innocent people—as well as several of their own by accident. Most of the Weathermen were arrested, and the rest went underground. By 1971, the New Left was dead as a political movement. In large measure it had committed suicide by abandoning the pacifist principles that had originally inspired participants and given the movement moral legitimacy. The larger anti-war movement also began to fade. There would be a new wave of student protests against the Nixon administration in 1970–1971, but thereafter campus unrest virtually disappeared as Nixon's decision to end the military draft defused the resistance movement.

If the social mood was changing during the early seventies, a large segment of the public continued the quest for social justice. The burgeoning environmental movement attested to the continuity of sixties idealism. A *New York Times* survey of college campuses in 1969 revealed that many students were refocusing their attention from protesting the war to protecting the environment. This new ecological awareness would blossom in the seventies into one of the most compelling items on the nation's social agenda.

THE COUNTERCULTURE   The numbing events of 1968 led other disaffected young activists to abandon politics in favor of **the counterculture**. Long hair on men and women, blue jeans, tie-dyed shirts, sandals, mind-altering drugs, rock music, and experimental living arrangements were more important than revolutionary ideology to the "hippies," the direct descendants of the Beats of the fifties. The countercultural hippies were primarily middle-class whites alienated by the Vietnam War, racism, political corruption, parental demands, runaway technology, and a crass corporate mentality that equated the good life with material goods. In their view a complacent materialism had settled over urban and suburban life. But the hippies were not attracted to organized political action or militant protests. Instead, they embraced the tactics promoted by the zany Harvard professor Timothy Leary: "Tune in, turn on, drop out."

For some, the counterculture entailed the embrace of Asian mysticism. For many, it meant the daily use of hallucinogenic drugs. Collective living in urban enclaves such as San Francisco's Haight-Ashbury district, New York's East Village, and Atlanta's Fourteenth Street was the rage for a time among hippies, until conditions grew so crowded, violent, and depressing that residents migrated elsewhere. Rural communes also attracted bourgeois rebels. During the sixties and early seventies, thousands of inexperienced romantics flocked to the countryside, eager to liberate themselves from parental and institutional restraints, live in harmony with nature, and coexist in an atmosphere of love and openness. The participants in the back-to-the-land movement, as it became known, were seeking a path to more authentic living that would deepen their sense of self while pursuing a simple life of self-sufficiency. They equated the good life with living close to nature and in conformity with its ecological imperatives and environmental limits.

Huge outdoor concerts were a popular source of community among the counterculture. The largest of these was the sprawling **Woodstock** Music and Art Fair ("Aquarian Exposition"). In mid-August 1969 some four hundred thousand young people converged on a six-hundred-acre farm near the tiny rural town of Bethel, New York. The promoters had not expected such a massive crowd; the hippie concertgoers created a fifty-mile traffic jam. For three days, the assembled flower children reveled in good music, rivers of mud, cheap marijuana, and casual sex. The *New York Times* predicted a "social catastrophe in the making," but instead there was remarkable cooperation among the citizens of "Woodstock Nation." Drug use was rampant, but there was little crime and virtually no violence. "Everyone swam nude in the lake," a journalist reported. The country had never "seen a society so free of repression." One young man, when asked why he had come to the festival, said, "there's gonna be a lot a ballin'." Another declared that "people are finally getting together." A sloping pasture provided a natural amphitheater for the open-air stage. The music was nonstop for three days and often magical. Among the many performers were the Grateful Dead; the Who; Jefferson Airplane; Blood, Sweat, and Tears; Richie Havens; Joan Baez; Arlo Guthrie; Janis Joplin; Crosby, Stills, Nash, and Young; Country Joe and the Fish; Sly and the Family Stone; Santana; and Jimi Hendrix.

But the carefree spirit of the Woodstock festival was short-lived. It did not produce the peaceful revolution its sponsors had promised. Just four months later, when other concert promoters tried to replicate the "Woodstock

**Woodstock**

The Woodstock music festival drew nearly half a million people to a farm in Bethel, New York. The concert was billed as three days of "peace, music, . . . and love."

Nation" experience at Altamont Speedway, forty miles east of San Francisco, the counterculture encountered the criminal culture. The Rolling Stones hired the Hells Angels motorcycle gang to provide "security" for their show. During the band's performance of "Under My Thumb," drunken white motorcyclists beat to death an eighteen-year-old African American man wielding a gun in front of the stage. Three other spectators were accidentally killed that night; much of the vitality and innocence of the counterculture died with them. After 1969, the hippie phenomenon began to wane as the counterculture had become counterproductive.

FEMINISM   The seductive ideal of liberation spawned during the sixties helped accelerate a powerful women's rights crusade. Like the New Left, the new feminism drew much of its inspiration and many of its tactics from the civil rights movement. Its aim was to challenge the conventional cult of female domesticity that had prevailed since the fifties.

Betty Friedan, a forty-two-year-old mother of three from Peoria, Illinois, led the mainstream of the women's movement. Her influential book, *The Feminine Mystique* (1963), helped launch the new phase of female protest on a national level. During the fifties, Friedan, a Smith College graduate, raised three children in a New York suburb. Still politically active but now socially domestic, she mothered her children, pampered her husband, "read *Vogue* under the hair dryer" in the beauty salon, and occasionally did some free-lance writing. In 1957 she conducted a poll of her fellow Smith alumnae and discovered that despite the prevailing rhetoric about the happy suburban housewife, many well-educated women were in fact miserable; they wanted much more out of life. This revelation led to more research, which culminated in the publication of *The Feminine Mystique*.

Women, Friedan wrote, had actually lost ground during the years after the Second World War, when many left wartime employment and settled down in suburbia as full-time wives and mothers. A propaganda campaign engineered by advertisers and women's magazines encouraged them to do so by creating the "feminine mystique" of blissful domesticity. Women, Friedan claimed, "were being duped into believing homemaking was their natural destiny." This notion that women were "gaily content in a world of bedroom, kitchen, sex, babies, and home" served to imprison them, however. In Friedan's view the middle-class home had become "a comfortable concentration camp" where women suffocated and stagnated in an atmosphere of mindless materialism, daytime television "soap operas," and neighborhood gossip.

*The Feminine Mystique*, an immediate best seller, inspired many affluent, well-educated women who felt trapped in their domestic doldrums. Moreover, Friedan discovered that there were far more women working outside the home than the pervasive "feminine mystique" suggested. Many of these working women were frustrated by the demands of holding "two full-time jobs instead of just one—underpaid clerical worker and unpaid housekeeper." Perhaps most important, Friedan helped to transform the feminist movement from the clear-cut demands of suffrage and equal pay to the less-defined but more fulfilling realm of empowerment—at home, in schools, in offices, and in politics.

**Betty Friedan**
Author of *The Feminine Mystique*.

In 1966, Friedan and other activists founded the National Organization for Women (NOW). NOW initially sought to end gender discrimination in the workplace and went on to spearhead efforts to legalize abortion and obtain federal and state support for child-care centers. The membership of NOW soared from one thousand in 1967 to forty thousand in 1974.

In the early seventies, members of Congress, the Supreme Court, and NOW advanced the cause of gender equality. Under Title IX of the Educational Amendments of 1972, colleges were required to institute "affirmative-action" programs to ensure equal opportunities for women in admissions and athletics. Also in 1972, Congress overwhelmingly approved an equal-rights amendment (ERA) to the federal constitution, which had been bottled up in a House committee since the twenties. In 1973, the Supreme Court, in *Roe v. Wade,* struck down state laws forbidding abortions during the first three months of pregnancy. Meanwhile, the all-male educational bastions, including Yale and Princeton, led a movement for coeducation that swept the country. "If the 1960s belonged to blacks," said one feminist, "the next ten years are ours." People began referring to the seventies as the "She Decade."

During the late sixties, a new wave of younger feminists emerged who challenged everything from women's economic, political, and legal status to the sexual double standards for men and women. The new generation of feminists was more militant than the older, more moderate generation that had established NOW. The goals of the women's liberation movement, said Susan Brownmiller, a self-described "radical feminist" who was also a veteran of the civil rights struggles, were to "go beyond a simple concept of equality. NOW's emphasis on legislative change left the radicals cold." She dismissed Friedan as "hopelessly bourgeois" in her preoccupation with conventional marriage and her rampant homophobia. Overthrowing the embedded structures and premises of centuries-old patriarchy, Brownmiller and others believed, required transforming every aspect of society: sexual relations, child rearing, entertainment, domestic duties, business, and the arts. Radical feminists formed provocative groups such as the Redstockings, WITCH (Women's International Terrorist Conspiracy from Hell), and the New York Radical Women.

Radical liberationists took direct action, such as picketing the 1968 Miss America Pageant, burning copies of *Playboy* and other men's magazines, tossing their bras into "freedom cans," and assaulting gender-based discrimination in all of its forms. For her part, Friedan warned young activists not to be seduced by the "bra-burning, anti-man" feminists who were pushing her aside. Whether young or old, conventional or radical, the women's movement focused on several basic issues: gender discrimination in the workplace, equal

### The "She Decade"

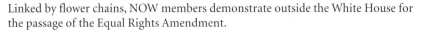

Linked by flower chains, NOW members demonstrate outside the White House for the passage of the Equal Rights Amendment.

pay for equal work, the availability of high-quality child care, and easier access to abortions. Women in growing numbers also began winning elected offices at the local, state, and national levels. In 1960, some 38 percent of women were working outside the home; by 1980, 52 percent were doing so.

By the end of the seventies, however, sharp disputes between moderate and radical feminists had fractured the women's movement in ways similar to the fragmentation experienced by civil rights organizations. The movement's failure to broaden its appeal much beyond the confines of the white middle class also caused reform efforts to stagnate. The ERA, which had once seemed a straightforward assertion of equal opportunity ("Equality of rights under the law shall not be denied or abridged by the United States or by any State on account of sex"), hit a roadblock in several state legislatures. By 1982 it had died, several states short of passage. And the very success of NOW's efforts to liberalize local and state abortion laws generated a powerful backlash, especially among Roman Catholics and fundamentalist Protestants, who mounted a potent "right-to-life" crusade against abortion that helped ignite the conservative political resurgence in the seventies and thereafter.

Yet the success of the women's movement endured long after the militant rhetoric had evaporated. A growing presence in the labor force brought women a greater share of economic and political influence. By 1976, over half the married women and nine out of ten female college graduates were employed outside the home, a development that one economist called "the single most outstanding phenomenon of this century." Women also enrolled in graduate and professional schools in record numbers. Between 1969 and 1973, the number of women in law schools quadrupled, and the number of female medical students doubled. Most career women, however, did not regard themselves as "feminists"; they took jobs because they and their families needed the money to achieve higher levels of material comfort. Whatever their motives, women were changing traditional gender roles and childbearing practices to accommodate the two-career family and the sexual revolution.

**THE SEXUAL REVOLUTION AND THE PILL**   The feminist movement coincided with the so-called sexual revolution, a much-discussed loosening of traditional restrictions on social behavior. Activists promoting more permissive sexual attitudes staged rallies, formed organizations, engaged in civil disobedience, filed suits against prevailing laws, and flouted social norms. The publicity given to the sexual revolution exaggerated its scope and depth, but the movement did help generate two major cultural changes: society became more tolerant of premarital sex, and women became more sexually active. Between 1960 and 1975, the number of college women engaging in sexual intercourse doubled, from 27 percent to 50 percent. Facilitating this change was a scientific breakthrough in contraception: the birth-control pill, first approved by the Food and Drug Administration in 1960.

The pill, as it came to be known, blocks ovulation by releasing synthetic hormones into a woman's body. Initially, birth-control pills were available only to married couples, but that restriction soon ended. Access to the pill gave women a much greater sense of sexual freedom than had any previous contraceptive device. No longer was sex necessarily tied to procreation. Although widespread use of the pill contributed to a rise in sexually transmitted diseases, many women (and men) viewed it as a godsend. "When the pill came out, it was a savior," recalled Eleanor Smeal, president of the Feminist Majority Foundation. "The whole country was waiting for it. I can't even describe to you how excited people were."

The pill quickly became the most popular birth-control method. In 1960 the U.S. birth rate was 3.6 children per woman. By 1970 it had plummeted to 2.5 children, and since 1980 it has remained slightly below 2. Eight out of ten women have taken birth-control pills at some time in their lives. Clare Boothe

**Birth control**

In an effort to spread the word about birth-control options, Planned Parenthood in 1967 displayed posters like this one in New York City buses.

Luce, a congresswoman, ambassador, journalist, and playwright, viewed the advent of the pill as a key element in the broader women's movement: "Modern woman is at last free as a man is free, to dispose of her own body, to earn her living, to pursue the improvement of her mind, to try a successful career."

HISPANIC RIGHTS   The activism that animated the student revolt, the civil rights movement, and the crusade for women's rights soon spread to various ethnic minority groups. *Hispanic,* a term used in the United States to refer to people who trace their ancestry to Spanish-speaking Latin America or Spain, came into increasing use after 1945 in conjunction with growing efforts to promote economic and social justice. (Although frequently used as a synonym for Hispanic, the term *Latino* technically refers only to people of Latin American descent.) The labor shortages during the Second World War had led defense industries to offer Hispanic Americans their first significant access to skilled-labor jobs. And as was the case with African Americans, service in the military during the war years helped to heighten an American identity among Hispanic Americans and excite their desire for equal rights and social opportunities.

But equality was elusive. After the Second World War, Hispanic Americans still faced widespread discrimination in hiring, housing, and education. Poverty was widespread. In 1960, for example, the median income of a Mexican American family was only 62 percent of the median income of a family in the general population. Hispanic American activists during the fifties and sixties mirrored the efforts of black civil rights leaders. They, too, denounced segregation, promoted efforts to improve the quality of public education, and struggled to increase Hispanic American political influence and economic opportunities.

Unlike their African American counterparts, however, Hispanic leaders faced an awkward dilemma: What should they do about the continuing stream of undocumented Mexicans flowing across the border? Many Mexican Americans argued that their hopes for economic advancement and social equality were put at risk by the daily influx of undocumented Mexican laborers willing to accept low-paying jobs. Mexican American leaders thus helped end the bracero program in 1964 (which trucked in contract day laborers from Mexico during harvest season) and in 1962 formed the United Farm Workers (UFW) to represent Mexican American migrant workers. The founder of the UFW was the charismatic **Cesar Chavez**. Born in 1927 in Yuma, Arizona, the son of Mexican immigrants, Chavez moved with his family to California in 1939. There they joined thousands of other migrant farmworkers moving from job to job, living in tents, cars, or ramshackle cabins. After serving in the navy during the Second World War and working as a migrant laborer, Chavez began a prolonged effort to organize migrant farm workers. His fledgling United Farm Workers association gained national attention in 1965 when it organized a strike against the corporate grape

**United Farm Workers**

Cesar Chavez (center) with organizers of the grape boycott. In 1968, Chavez ended a three-week fast by taking Communion and breaking bread with Senator Robert F. Kennedy.

growers in California's San Joaquin Valley. Chavez's energy and Catholic piety, his insistence upon nonviolent tactics and his reliance upon college-student volunteers, his skillful alliance with organized labor and religious groups—all combined to attract media interest and popular support.

Still, the grape strike itself brought no tangible gains. So Chavez organized a nationwide consumer boycott of grapes. In 1970, the grape strike and the consumer boycott brought twenty-six grape growers to the bargaining table. They signed formal contracts recognizing the UFW, and soon migrant workers throughout the West were benefiting from Chavez's strenuous efforts on their behalf. Wages increased, and working conditions improved. In 1975, the California state legislature passed a bill that required growers to bargain collectively with the elected representatives of the farm workers.

The chief strength of the Hispanic rights movement lay less in the duplication of civil rights strategies than in the rapid growth of the Hispanic American population. In 1960, Hispanics in the United States numbered slightly more than 3 million; by 1970 their numbers had increased to 9 million; and by 2012 they numbered well over 52 million, making them the nation's largest minority group. By 1980, aspiring presidential candidates were openly courting the Hispanic vote. The voting power of Hispanics and their concentration in states with key electoral votes has helped give the Hispanic point of view significant political clout.

NATIVE AMERICAN RIGHTS    American Indians—many of whom had begun calling themselves Native Americans—also emerged as a political force in the late sixties. Two conditions combined to make Indian rights a priority: first, many whites felt a persistent sense of guilt for the destructive policies of their ancestors toward a people who had, after all, been here first; second, the plight of the Native American minority was more desperate than that of any other group in the country. Indian unemployment was ten times the national rate, life expectancy was twenty years lower than the national average, and the suicide rate was a whopping hundred times higher than the rate for whites.

Although President Lyndon B. Johnson recognized the poverty of the Native Americans and attempted to funnel federal anti-poverty-program funds into reservations, militants within the Indian community grew impatient with the pace of change. They organized protests and demonstrations against local, state, and federal agencies. In 1963 two Chippewas (or Ojibwas) living in Minneapolis, George Mitchell and Dennis Banks, founded the **American Indian Movement (AIM)** to promote "red power." The leaders of AIM occupied Alcatraz Island in San Francisco Bay in 1969, claiming the site "by right of discovery." And in 1972, a sit-in at the Department of the Interior's

Bureau of Indian Affairs (BIA) in Washington, D.C., attracted national attention. The BIA was then—and still is—widely viewed as the worst-managed federal agency. Instead of finding creative ways to promote tribal autonomy and economic self-sufficiency, the BIA has served as a classic example of government inefficiency and paternalism gone awry.

In 1973, AIM led two hundred Sioux in the occupation of the tiny village of Wounded Knee, South Dakota, where the Seventh Cavalry massacred a Sioux village in 1890. Outraged by the light sentences given a group of local whites who had killed a Sioux in 1972, the organizers also sought to draw attention to the plight of the Indians living on the reservation there. Half of the families were dependent upon government welfare checks, alcoholism was rampant, and over 80 percent of the children had dropped out of school. After the militants took eleven hostages, federal marshals and FBI agents surrounded the encampment. For ten weeks the two sides engaged in a tense standoff. When AIM leaders tried to bring in food and supplies, a shoot-out resulted, with one Indian killed and another wounded. Soon thereafter the tense confrontation ended with a government promise to reexamine Indian treaty rights.

Indian protesters subsequently discovered a more effective tactic than direct action and sit-ins: they went into federal courts armed with copies of

**Wounded Knee**

Instigating a standoff with the FBI, members of AIM and local Oglala Sioux occupied the town of Wounded Knee, South Dakota, in March 1973 in an effort to focus attention on poverty and rampant alcoholism among Indians on reservations.

old treaties and demanded that those documents become the basis for restitution. In Alaska, Maine, South Carolina, and Massachusetts they won significant settlements that provided legal recognition of their tribal rights and financial compensation at levels that upgraded the standard of living on several reservations.

GAY RIGHTS   The liberationist impulses of the sixties also encouraged gays to organize and assert their right to equal treatment under the law. Throughout the Sixties, gay men and lesbians continued to be treated with disgust, cruelty, and violence. On Saturday night, June 28, 1969, New York City vice police raided the Stonewall Inn, a popular gay bar in the heart of Greenwich Village. The patrons bravely fought back, and the struggle spilled into the streets. Hundreds of other, mostly young gays and their supporters joined the fracas against the police. Raucous rioting lasted throughout the weekend. When it ended, gays had forged a new sense of solidarity and a new organization, the Gay Liberation Front. "Gay is good for all of us," proclaimed one of its members. "The artificial categories 'heterosexual' and 'homosexual' have been laid on us by a sexist society."

As news of the Stonewall riots spread across the country, the gay rights movement assumed national proportions. One of its main tactics was to encourage gays to "come out," to make public their sexual preferences. This was by no means an easy decision, for gays faced social ostracism, physical assault, exclusion from the military and civil service, and discrimination in the workplace. Yet despite the risks, thousands of gays did come out. By 1973, almost eight hundred gay organizations had been formed across the country, and every major city had a visible gay community and cultural life.

As was the case with the civil rights crusade and the women's movement, however, the campaign for gay rights soon suffered from internal divisions and a conservative backlash. Gay activists engaged in fractious disputes over tactics and objectives, and conservative moralists and Christian fundamentalists launched a nationwide counterattack. By the end of the seventies, the gay movement had lost its initial momentum and was struggling to salvage many of its hard-won gains.

## NIXON AND MIDDLE AMERICA

The social turmoil of the sixties—anti-war protesters, countercultural rebellions, liberationist movements, street violence—spawned a reactionary backlash that propelled **Richard M. Nixon**'s election victory in 1968. On many levels, he was an unlikely president with a peculiar personality. The hardworking son of poor, unloving parents, he grew up under difficult circumstances in southern California during the Great Depression. Painfully introverted, devoid of warmth or charm, he had few friends and admitted that he hated "pressing the flesh." Nixon was a loner all of his life who displayed violent mood swings punctuated by raging temper tantrums and anti-Semitic outbursts. His classmates in law school nicknamed him "Gloomy Gus." As a journalist pointed out, even Nixon's dog did not like being around him. Nixon nursed bitter grudges and took politics personally. He was a good hater who could be ruthless and vindictive in attacking his opponents. A leading Republican, Senator Robert A. Taft of Ohio, characterized young Congressman Nixon in the early fifties as a "little man in a big hurry" with "a mean and vindictive streak."

But Nixon also had extraordinary gifts: he was smart, shrewd, cunning, and doggedly determined to succeed in politics. As the 1968 campaign began, the former anti-Communist crusader now described himself as a "pragmatist" who was "a man for all factions" of the Republican party. He knew how to get things done, although he did not worry much about the ethics of his methods. He was nicknamed "Tricky Dick" for good reason. One of his aides admitted that "we did often lie, mislead, deceive, try to use [the media], and to con them." Throughout his long public career, Nixon displayed remarkable grit and resilience. As Henry Kissinger, Nixon's national security adviser, who later became secretary of state, acknowledged, "Can you imagine what this man would have been like if somebody had loved him?"

The new president selected men for his cabinet and White House staff who would carry out his orders with blind obedience. John Mitchell, the gruff attorney general who had been a senior partner in Nixon's New York law firm, was the new president's closest confidant. H. R. (Bob) Haldeman, an imperious former advertising executive, served as Nixon's chief of staff. As the short-tempered Haldeman explained, "Every President needs a son of a bitch, and I'm Nixon's. I'm his buffer, I'm his bastard." He was succeeded in 1973 by Colonel (later General) Alexander Haig, whom Nixon described as "the meanest, toughest, most ambitious son of a bitch I ever knew." John Ehrlichman, a Seattle attorney and college schoolmate of Haldeman's, served as chief domestic-policy adviser.

Nixon tapped as secretary of state his old friend William Rogers, who had served as attorney general under Dwight D. Eisenhower. But the president had no intention of making Rogers the nation's chief diplomat. Rogers's control over foreign policy was quickly preempted by Dr. **Henry Kissinger**, a distinguished German-born Harvard political scientist who served as national security adviser before becoming secretary of state in 1973. Kissinger came to dominate the Nixon administration's diplomatic planning and emerged as one of the most respected and internationally famous members of the White House staff. Kissinger's self-confidence was boundless; he did not suffer fools gladly. Nixon often had to mediate the tensions between Rogers and Kissinger, noting that Rogers considered Kissinger "Machiavellian, deceitful, egotistical, arrogant, and insulting," while Kissinger viewed Rogers as "vain, emotional, unable to keep a secret, and hopelessly dominated by the State Department bureaucracy." Teamwork and collegiality were rare in the Nixon administration.

NIXON'S SOUTHERN STRATEGY   Richard Nixon was no friend of the civil rights movement, the youth revolt, or the counterculture. He had been elected in 1968 as the representative of middle America, those middle-class citizens fed up with the liberal politics and radical culture of the sixties. Nixon explicitly appealed to the "silent majority" of predominantly white working-class and middle-class citizens determined to regain control of a society they feared was awash in permissiveness and anarchy. He promised voters that he would return "law and order" to a fractious nation riven with turmoil.

A major reason for Nixon's election victories in 1968 and 1972 was the effective "southern strategy" fashioned by his campaign staffers. Of all the nation's regions, the South had long been the most conservative. The majority of southern white voters were pious and patriotic, fervently anti-Communist, and skeptical of federal social welfare programs. For a century, the "Solid South" had steadfastly voted for Democrats in national elections. During the late sixties and seventies, however, a surging economy and wave of population growth transformed the so-called Sunbelt states in the South and the Southwest. The southern states had long been the nation's poorest and most backward-looking region, but that changed dramatically, in part because of the rapid expansion of air conditioning in the hot, humid sun-belt. By 1980, over 70 percent of southern homes were air-conditioned. "General Electric" said a journalist, "has proved a more devastating invader [of the South] than General [William T.] Sherman." The Sunbelt's warm climate, low cost of living, low taxes, conservative temperament, and promotion of economic development attracted waves of businesses to relocate to the region.

Between 1970 and 1990, the South's population grew by 40 percent, more than twice the national average. The New South promoted by Henry Grady in the 1880s finally arrived in the form of fast-growing and increasingly cosmopolitan cities such as Atlanta, Charlotte, Dallas, Houston, Miami, New

Orleans, and Richmond, all of which spawned affluent all-white suburbs that were enclaves of Christian conservatism. At the same time, retirees from across the nation migrated in large numbers to Florida, Texas, Arizona, and southern California. The Sunbelt states were attractive to migrants not only because of their mild climate and abundant natural resources; they also had the lowest rates of taxation and labor union participation as well as the highest rates of economic growth. In the seventies, southern "redneck" culture suddenly became chic, as people across the nation embraced NASCAR racing, cowboy boots, pickup trucks, and barbecue. As singer Charlie Daniels sang in 1974, "The South's Gonna Do It Again."

Since the Second World War, the South, in part because of the seniority of its long-serving Democratic senators and representatives, had been the great beneficiary of steadily increasing federal expenditures on the military and the aerospace industry. With each passing year, more and more northern businesses relocated to the southern states, leading journalists to label the nation's decaying industrial heartland—Michigan, New York, Ohio, Illinois, and Pennsylvania—the "rustbelt" in contrast to the booming states in the sunbelt. Journalists during the seventies excitedly described the "southernization of American life." The *New York Times* devoted a four-part series to the popularity of the sunbelt: "All day and through the lonely night, the moving vans push southward, the 14-wheeled boxcars of the highway, changing the demographic face of America." During the seventies, job growth in the South was seven times as great as that of New York and Pennsylvania. Rapid population growth brought the region more congressional seats and more electoral votes. Every president elected between 1964 and 2008 had roots in the sunbelt.

The sunbelt spearheaded the backlash against sixties radicalism. Merle Haggard, a country-and-western music star who was one of Nixon's favorite performers, captured the tone of the conservative backlash in a hit song titled "Okie from Muskogee." Haggard crooned: "I'm proud to be an Okie from Muskogee, a place where even squares can have a ball." Haggard's description of his Oklahoma town resonated with many listeners. "We don't smoke marijuana in Muskogee. We don't take our trips on LSD. We don't burn our draft cards down on Main Street. We like livin' right and bein' free." Like Haggard, his southern fans bristled at rising taxes, social welfare programs, and civil rights activism. So did many retirees. The alienation of many blue-collar whites from the liberalism of the Democratic party as well as the demographic changes transforming the sunbelt states created a welcome opportunity for the Republican party to exploit, which Richard Nixon seized.

Nixon and his aides forged a new conservative coalition that included two traditionally Democratic voting blocs: blue-collar ethnic voters in the North and white southerners. In the South, Nixon shrewdly played the race card: he assured southern conservatives that he would appoint pro-southern justices to the Supreme Court as part of a broader commitment to undermine federal enforcement of civil rights laws, including mandatory busing to achieve racially integrated schools and affirmative-action programs designed to give minorities priority in hiring decisions. Nixon also appealed to the economic concerns of middle-class southern whites by promising lower tax rates and less government regulation. Finally, Nixon specialized in hard-hitting, polarizing rhetoric, drawing vivid contrasts between the turmoil in the streets of Chicago during the 1968 Democratic nominating convention and the "law-and-order" theme of his own campaign.

Once in the White House, Nixon told an aide it was time to "get down to the nut-cutting." Conservatism was back, as the new president followed through on his campaign pledges to southern conservatives. He changed his personal residency from New York to Florida, appointed conservative Texas Democrat John Connally to his cabinet, and announced that it was time for the media and the cultural elite to "stop kicking the South around." In his 1972 reelection campaign, Nixon carried every southern state by whopping majorities. The transformation of the once "solid" Democratic South into the predominantly Republican South was the greatest realignment in American politics since Franklin D. Roosevelt's election in 1932.

President Nixon, like many of the people he appointed to his staff and cabinet, had a visceral personality. He hated the "liberal" media, expressed contempt for the civil rights movement, set out to dismantle LBJ's war on poverty programs, appointed no African Americans to his cabinet, and refused to meet with the Congressional Black Caucus. "We've had enough social programs: forced integration, education, housing," he told his chief of staff. "People don't want more [people] on welfare. They don't want to help the working poor, and our mood needs to be harder on this, not softer."

In 1970, Nixon launched a concerted effort to block congressional renewal of the Voting Rights Act of 1965 and to delay implementation of court orders requiring the desegregation of school districts in Mississippi. Sixty-five lawyers in the Justice Department signed a letter of protest against the administration's stance. The Democratic Congress then extended the Voting Rights Act over Nixon's veto. The Supreme Court, in the first decision made under the new chief justice, Warren Burger—a Nixon appointee—mandated the integration of the Mississippi public schools. In *Alexander v. Holmes County Board of Education* (1969), a unanimous Court ordered a quick end to segregation. During Nixon's first term and despite his wishes, more schools were desegregated than in all the Kennedy-Johnson years combined.

**Critics of integration**

Demonstrators at the Boston State House protest forced integration of the school system, May 1973.

Nixon also failed in his attempts to block desegregation efforts in urban areas. The Burger Court ruled unanimously in *Swann v. Charlotte-Mecklenburg Board of Education* (1971) that school systems must bus students out of their neighborhoods if necessary to achieve racially integrated schools. Protest over desegregation now began to erupt in the North, the Midwest, and the Southwest as white families in Boston, Denver, and other cities denounced the destruction of "the neighborhood school." Angry white parents in Pontiac, Michigan, firebombed school buses. Racial violence was no longer a southern issue.

Nixon asked the Democrat-controlled Congress to impose a moratorium on all busing orders by the federal courts. The House of Representatives, equally attuned to voter outrage at busing to achieve racial integration, went along. But a Senate filibuster blocked the president's anti-busing bill. Busing opponents won a limited victory when the Supreme Court ruled, in *Milliken v. Bradley* (1974), that desegregation plans in Detroit requiring the transfer of students from the inner city to the suburbs were unconstitutional. This landmark case, along with the *Regents of the University of California v. Bakke* (1978) decision, which restricted the use of college-admissions quotas to achieve racial balance, marked the transition of desegregation from an issue of simple justice to a more tangled thicket of conflicting group, individual, and states' rights.

To transfer greater responsibility from the federal government to the states, President Nixon in 1972 pushed through Congress a five-year revenue-sharing plan that would distribute $30 billion of federal revenues to the states for use as they saw fit. But Nixon was less an ideologue than a shrewd pragmatist. His domestic program was a hodgepodge of reactionary and progressive initiatives. Nixon juggled opposing positions in an effort to maintain public support. He was, said the journalist Tom Wicker, "at once liberal and conservative, generous and begrudging, cynical and idealistic, choleric and calm, resentful and forgiving." Nixon also had to deal with a stern political fact: the Democrats controlled both houses of Congress during his first term. Congress moved forward with significant new legislation which Nixon signed: the right of eighteen-year-olds to vote in national elections (1970) and in all elections under the Twenty-sixth Amendment (1971); increases in Social Security benefits indexed to the inflation rate and a rise in food-stamp funding; the Occupational Safety and Health Act (1970) to ensure safe workplaces; and the Federal Election Campaign Act (1971), which modified the rules of campaign finance to reduce the role of corporate financial donations.

ENVIRONMENTAL PROTECTION    Dramatic increases in the price of oil and gasoline during the seventies fueled a major energy crisis in the United States. People began to realize that natural resources were limited— and increasingly expensive. "Although it's positively un-American to think so," said one sociologist, "the environmental movement and energy shortage have forced us all to accept a sense of our limits, to lower our expectations, to seek prosperity through conservation rather than growth." The widespread recognition that America faced limits to economic growth spurred broad support for environmental protection in the seventies.

The realization that cities and industrial development were damaging the environment and altering the earth's ecology was not new. Rachel Carson's pathbreaking book *Silent Spring* (1962) had sounded the warning years earlier by graphically revealing how industries had been regularly dumping toxic chemicals and pesticides into waterways, doing incalculable ecological damage. More immediately, two dramatic environmental incidents in 1969 had captured public attention and prompted legislative action within the Democratic-controlled Congress. On January 28, 1969, an offshore oil-drilling platform near Santa Barbara, California ruptured. Within a ten-day period, some one hundred thousand barrels of crude oil spilled into the channel and onto the beaches of Santa Barbara County, fouling the coastline and killing thousands of

**Environmental awareness**

An Earth Day demonstration dramatizing the dangers of air pollution, April 1972.

sea birds and marine animals—porpoises, elephant seals, and sea lions. Six months later, in June, the Cuyahoga River in northeastern Ohio, near Cleveland, caught fire and burned for five days, its flames leaping fifty feet into the air. It was not the first time that the heavily polluted river, clogged with effluent from oil refineries, chemical plants, utilities, and factories, had ignited, but like the Santa Barbara oil spill, it became an important catalyst in the raising of environmental awareness. The public outrage at the fiery river and Pacific oil spill prompted numerous pieces of environmental legislation that created the legal and regulatory framework for the modern environmental movement.

Bowing to pressure from both parties, as well as to polls showing that 75 percent of voters supported stronger environmental protections, President Nixon told an aide to "keep me out of trouble on environmental issues." Ever the pragmatic politician, the president recognized that the public mood had shifted toward greater environmental protections. Nixon feared that if he vetoed legislative efforts to improve environmental quality, the Congress would overrule him, so he would not stand in the way. In late 1969 he reluctantly signed the amended Endangered Species Preservation Act and the National Environmental Policy Act. The latter became effective on January 1, 1970, the year that environmental groups established an annual Earth Day celebration. In 1970, Nixon by executive order created two new federal environmental agencies, the Environmental Protection Agency (EPA) and the National Oceanic and Atmospheric Administration (NOAA). That same year, he also signed the Clean Air Act to reduce air pollution on a national level. Two years, later, however, Nixon vetoed a new clean water act, only to see Congress override his effort. Nixon's support for the environmental movement, regardless of his motives, flabbergasted Republicans. Patrick Buchanan, one of Nixon's speechwriters, who later would run for president himself, said "the President is no longer a credible custodian of the conservative political tradition of the GOP."

ECONOMIC MALAISE   The major domestic development during the Nixon years was a floundering economy. Overheated by the accumulated expense of the Vietnam War, the annual inflation rate began to rise in 1967, when it was at 3 percent. By 1973, it was at 9 percent; a year later it was at 12 percent, and it remained in double digits for most of the seventies. The Dow Jones average of major industrial stocks fell by 36 percent between 1968 and 1970, its steepest decline in more than thirty years. Meanwhile unemployment, at a low of 3.3 percent when Nixon took office, climbed to 6 percent by the end of 1970 and threatened to keep rising. Somehow the economy was undergoing a recession and inflation at the same time. Economists coined the term **stagflation** to describe the unprecedented syndrome that defied the orthodox laws of economics. The unusual combination of a stagnant economy with inflationary prices befuddled experts. There were no easy answers, no certain solutions.

The economic malaise had at least three deep-rooted causes. First, the Johnson administration had financed both the Great Society social-welfare programs and the Vietnam War without a major tax increase, thereby generating larger federal deficits, a major expansion of the money supply, and price inflation. Second and more important, by the late sixties U.S. companies faced stiff competition in international markets from West Germany, Japan, and other emerging industrial powers. American technological and economic superiority was no longer unchallenged. Third, the post–World War II economy had depended heavily upon cheap sources of energy; no other nation was more dependent than the United States upon the automobile and the automobile industry, and no other nation was more wasteful in its use of fossil fuels in factories and homes.

Just as domestic petroleum reserves began to dwindle and dependence upon foreign sources of oil increased, the Organization of Petroleum

**Oil crisis, 1973**

The scarcity of oil was dealt with by the rationing of gasoline. Gas stations, such as this one in Colorado, closed on Sundays to conserve supplies.

Exporting Countries (OPEC) resolved to use its huge oil supplies as a political and economic weapon. In 1973, the United States sent massive aid to Israel after a devastating Syrian-Egyptian attack on Yom Kippur, the holiest day on the Jewish calendar. OPEC responded by announcing that it would not sell oil to nations supporting Israel and that it was raising its prices by 400 percent. Gasoline grew scarce, and prices soared. American motorists thereafter faced long lines at gas stations.

Another condition leading to stagflation was the flood of new workers—mainly baby boomers and women—entering the labor market. From 1965 to 1980, the workforce grew by 40 percent, almost 30 million workers, a number greater than the total labor force of France or West Germany. The number of new jobs could not keep up with the size of the workforce, leaving many unemployed. At the same time, worker productivity declined, further increasing inflation in the face of rising demand for goods and services.

Nixon responded erratically and ineffectively to stagflation, trying old remedies for a new problem. First he sought to reduce the federal deficit by raising taxes and cutting the budget. When the Democratic Congress refused to cooperate with that approach, he encouraged the Federal Reserve Board to reduce the nation's money supply by raising interest rates. The stock market immediately collapsed, and the economy plunged into the "Nixon recession."

A sense of desperation seized the White House as economic advisers struggled to respond to stagflation. In 1969, when asked about the possibility of imposing government restrictions on wages and prices, Nixon had been unequivocal: "Controls. Oh, my God, no! . . . We'll never go to controls." But in 1971 he reversed himself. He froze all wages and prices for ninety days. Still the economy floundered. By 1973, the wage and price guidelines were made voluntary and therefore ineffective.

## Nixon and Vietnam

Many among the "silent majority" of voters that Nixon courted shared his belief that Lyndon B. Johnson's Great Society programs were expensive failures. Such attitudes were highlighted in one of the period's most popular television shows, *All in the Family*, whose central character, Archie Bunker, was a lower-middle-class reactionary outraged by the permissiveness of modern society and the radicalism of young people. Large as the gap was between the "silent majority" and the youth revolt, both sides agreed that the Vietnam War remained the dominant event of the time. Until the war ended and all troops had returned home, the nation would find it difficult to achieve the equilibrium that President Nixon had promised.

GRADUAL WITHDRAWAL    Looking back on the Vietnam War, former secretary of state and national security adviser Henry Kissinger called it a "nightmare." In his view, "we should have never been there at all." When Nixon was inaugurated as president in January 1969, he inherited the nightmare; there were 530,000 U.S. troops in Vietnam. Nixon believed that "there's no way to win the war. But we can't say that, of course," because the United States needed to "keep some bargaining leverage" at the Paris negotiations with the North Vietnamese. During the 1968 presidential campaign, he had claimed to have a secret plan that would bring "peace with honor" in Vietnam. Nixon insisted that the United States could not simply "cut and run," leaving the 17 million South Vietnamese to a cruel fate under Communist tyranny. Yet he assured an aide that "I'm not going to end up like LBJ, holed up in the White House afraid to show my face on the street. I'm going to stop that war. Fast."

Peace, however, was long in coming and not very honorable. Nixon and Kissinger overestimated the ability of the Soviets to exert pressure on the North Vietnamese to sign a negotiated settlement, just as they misread their own ability to coerce the South Vietnamese government to sign an agreement. By the time a settlement was reached, in 1973, another twenty thousand Americans had died, the morale of the U.S. military had been shattered, millions of Asians had been killed or wounded, and fighting continued in Southeast Asia. In the end, Nixon's policy gained nothing the president could not have accomplished in 1969.

**The trauma of Vietnam**

Even as the Nixon administration began a phased withdrawal of U.S. troops from Vietnam, the war took a heavy toll on Vietnamese and Americans alike.

The new Vietnam policy implemented by Nixon and Kissinger moved along three fronts. First, U.S. negotiators in Paris demanded the withdrawal of Communist forces from South Vietnam and the preservation of the U.S.-backed regime of President Nguyen Van Thieu. The North Vietnamese and Viet Cong negotiators insisted on retaining a Communist military presence in the south and reunifying the Vietnamese people under a government dominated by the Communists. There was no common ground on which to come together. Hidden from public awareness and from America's South Vietnamese allies were secret meetings between Henry Kissinger, then Nixon's national security adviser, and the North Vietnamese.

On the second front, Nixon tried to quell domestic unrest stemming from the war. He labeled the anti-war movement a "brotherhood of the misguided, the mistaken, the well-meaning, and the malevolent." He sought to defuse the anti-war movement by reducing the number of U.S. troops in Vietnam, justifying the reduction as the natural result of "**Vietnamization**"— the equipping and training of South Vietnamese soldiers and pilots to assume the burden of combat in place of Americans. From a peak of 560,000 in 1969, U.S. combat forces were withdrawn at a steady pace that matched almost precisely the pace of the buildup from 1965 to 1969. By 1973, only 50,000 troops remained in Vietnam. In 1969, Nixon also established a draft lottery system that eliminated many inequities and clarified the likelihood of being drafted: only nineteen-year-olds with low lottery numbers would have to go—and in 1973 the president shrewdly did away with the draft altogether by creating an all-volunteer military.

On the third front, while reducing the number of U.S. combat troops, Nixon and Kissinger expanded the air war over Vietnam in hopes of persuading the North Vietnamese to come to terms. Heavy bombing of North Vietnam was part of what Nixon called his "madman theory." He wanted the North Vietnamese leaders to believe that he "might do *anything* to stop the war." In March 1969, the United States began a fourteen-month-long bombing campaign aimed at Communist forces that were using Cambodia as a sanctuary for raids into South Vietnam. Congress did not learn of those secret raids until 1970, although the total tonnage of bombs dropped was four times that dropped on Japan during the Second World War. Still, Hanoi's leaders did not flinch. Then, on April 30, 1970, Nixon announced what he called an "incursion" into "neutral" Cambodia by U.S. troops to "clean out" North Vietnamese military bases. Nixon knew that sending troops into Cambodia would ignite "absolute public hysteria." Several members of the National Security Council resigned in protest. Secretary of State William Rogers predicted that the Cambodian escalation "will make the [anti-war] students puke." Nixon told Kissinger, who strongly endorsed the decision to extend the fighting into Cambodia, "If this doesn't work, it'll be your ass, Henry."

DIVISIONS AT HOME    Strident public opposition to the Vietnam War and Nixon's slow withdrawal of combat forces from Vietnam had a devastating effect on the military's morale and reputation. "No one wants to be the last grunt to die in this lousy war," said one soldier. Between 1969 and 1971 there were 730 reported fragging incidents, efforts by troops to kill or injure their own officers, usually with fragmentation grenades. Drug abuse became a major problem in the armed forces. In 1971, four times as many troops were hospitalized for drug overdoses as for combat-related wounds.

Revelations of atrocities committed by U.S. soldiers in Vietnam caused even the staunchest supporters of the war to wince. Late in 1969, the shocking story of the **My Lai Massacre** broke in the press, plunging the country into two years of exposure to the gruesome tale of Lieutenant William Calley, who ordered the murder of 347 Vietnamese civilians in the village of My Lai in 1968. Twenty-five army officers were charged with complicity in the massacre and subsequent cover-up, but only Calley was convicted; Nixon later granted him parole.

The loudest public outcry against Nixon's Indochina policy occurred in the wake of the Cambodian "incursion." In the spring of 1970, hundreds of campuses across the country exploded in what the president of Columbia University called "the most disastrous month of May in the history of American higher education." Student protests led to the closing of hundreds of colleges and universities, and thousands of students were arrested. At Kent State University, the Ohio National Guard was called in to quell rioting, during which the building housing the campus ROTC (Reserve Officers' Training Corps) was burned down by anti-war protesters. The poorly trained guardsmen panicked and opened fire on the rock-throwing demonstrators, killing four student bystanders. Although an official investigation of the tragic deaths at **Kent State** condemned the "casual and indiscriminate shooting," polls indicated that the public supported the National Guard; students had "got what they were asking for." Eleven days after the Kent State tragedy, on May 15, Mississippi highway patrolmen riddled a dormitory at Jackson State College with bullets, killing two students. In New York City, anti-war demonstrators who gathered to protest the deaths at Kent State and the invasion of Cambodia were attacked by "hard-hat" construction workers, who forced the protesters to disperse and then marched on City Hall to raise the U.S. flag, which had been lowered to half staff in mourning for the Kent State victims.

The following year, in June, the *New York Times* began publishing excerpts from *The History of the U.S. Decision-Making Process of Vietnam Policy*, a secret Defense Department study commissioned by Robert McNamara before his resignation as in 1968 Lyndon Johnson's secretary of defense. The so-called **Pentagon Papers**, leaked to the press by a former Defense Department

**Kent State University**

National guardsmen shot and killed four student bystanders during anti-war demonstrations on the campus of Kent State University in Ohio.

official, Daniel Ellsberg, confirmed what many critics of the war had long suspected: Congress and the public had not received the full story on the Gulf of Tonkin incident of 1964, and contingency plans for American entry into the war were being drawn up while President Johnson was promising that combat troops would never be sent to Vietnam. Moreover, there was no plan for bringing the war to an end so long as the North Vietnamese persisted. Although the Pentagon Papers dealt with events only up to 1965, the Nixon administration blocked their publication, arguing that they endangered national security and that their publication would prolong the war. By a vote of 6 to 3, the Supreme Court ruled against the government. Newspapers throughout the country began publication of the controversial documents the next day.

Democracies, as Abraham Lincoln and Woodrow Wilson had realized, rarely can sustain long wars because long wars inevitably become unpopular wars. Responding to mounting public pressures, Congress in 1970 began to reclaim its authority to wage war. On December 31, 1970, Congress repealed the 1964 Gulf of Tonkin resolution that had given President Johnson a blank check to fight communism in Vietnam, but Nixon simply ignored the essentially symbolic legislative action.

# Nixon Triumphant

Because the Democrats controlled the Congress, President Nixon focused much of his effort on foreign policy, where presidential initiatives were less encumbered by the ceaseless squabbling and lobbying of interest groups. Nixon also personally preferred dealing in the international arena. In tandem with Henry Kissinger, with whom he enjoyed a love-hate relationship, he achieved several major breakthroughs. Nixon displayed his savvy and flexibility by making dramatic changes in U.S. relations with the major powers of the Communist world—China and the Soviet Union—changes that transformed the dynamics of the cold war.

By 1969, Nixon and Kissinger had come to envision a new multipolar world order replacing the conventional bipolar confrontation between the United States and the Soviet Union. Since 1945 the United States had lost its monopoly on nuclear weapons and its overwhelming economic dominance and geopolitical influence. The rapid rise of competing power centers in Europe, China, and Japan complicated international relations—the People's Republic of China (Communist China) had replaced the United States as the Soviet Union's most threatening competitor—but the competition between the two largest Communist nations also provided strategic opportunities for the United States, which Nixon and Kissinger seized. Their grand vision of the future world order focused on cultivating a partnership with Communist China, slowing the perennial arms race with the Soviet Union, and ending the war in Vietnam.

In early 1970, Nixon, eager to make his mark on history, announced a significant alteration in the containment doctrine that had guided U.S. foreign policy since the late 1940s. The United States, he stressed, could no longer be the world's policeman containing the expansion of communism: "America cannot—and will not—conceive *all* the plans, design *all* the programs, execute *all* the decisions, and undertake *all* the defense of the free nations of the world." In explaining what became known as the Nixon Doctrine, the president declared that "our *interests* must shape our *commitments,* rather than the other way around." The United States, he and Kissinger stressed, must become more selective in its commitments abroad, and America would begin to establish selected partnerships with Communist countries in areas of mutual interest.

CHINA   In 1971, Nixon, the crusading anti-Communist turned pragmatist, sent Henry Kissinger on a secret trip to Beijing to explore the possibility of U.S. recognition of Communist China. Since 1949, when Mao Zedong's

**The United States and China**

With President Richard M. Nixon's visit to China in 1972, the United States formally recognized China's Communist government. Here Nixon and Chinese premier Zhou Enlai drink a toast.

revolutionary movement established control in China, the United States had refused to recognize Communist China, preferring to regard Chiang Kai-shek's exiled regime on the island of Taiwan as the legitimate Chinese government. But now the time seemed ripe for a bold renewal of ties. Both the United States and Communist China were exhausted from prolonged wars (in Vietnam and clashes along the Sino-Soviet border) and intense domestic strife (anti-war protests in America, the Cultural Revolution in China). Both nations were eager to resist Soviet expansionism around the world.

During their secret discussions, Kissinger and Chinese leaders agreed that continuing confrontation made no sense for either nation. Seven months later, on February 21, 1972, stunned Americans watched on television as President Nixon drank toasts in Beijing with prime minister Zhou Enlai and Chairman Mao Zedong. In one simple but astonishing stroke, Nixon and Kissinger had ended two decades of diplomatic isolation of the People's Republic of China. The United States and China agreed to scientific and cultural exchanges, steps toward the resumption of trade, and the eventual reunification of Taiwan with the mainland. A year after the Nixon visit, "liaison offices" were established in Washington, D.C. and Beijing that served as unofficial embassies, and in 1979 diplomatic recognition was formalized. Richard Nixon had accomplished a diplomatic feat that his Democratic predecessors could not. Hard-line Republican conservatives were furious at Nixon's actions, but American corporations were eager to enter the huge Chinese market.

DÉTENTE    In truth, China welcomed the breakthrough in relations with the United States because its festering rivalry with the Soviet Union, with which it shares a long border, had become more threatening than its rivalry with the West. The Soviet leaders, troubled by the Sino-American agreements, were also eager to ease tensions with the United States. This was especially true now that they had, as a result of a huge arms buildup following the Cuban missile crisis, achieved virtual parity with the United States in nuclear weapons. Once again President Nixon surprised the world, announcing that he would visit Moscow in 1972 for discussions with Leonid Brezhnev, the Soviet premier. The high drama of the China visit was repeated in Moscow, with toasts and elegant dinners attended by world leaders who had previously regarded each other as incarnations of evil.

What became known as **détente** with the Soviets offered the promise of a more restrained competition between the two superpowers. Nixon and Brezhnev signed agreements reached at the Strategic Arms Limitation Talks (SALT), which negotiators had been working on since 1969. The SALT agreement did not end the arms race, but it did limit the number of missiles with nuclear warheads each nation could possess and prohibited the construction of antiballistic missile systems. In effect, the Soviets were allowed to retain a greater number of missiles with greater destructive power, while the United States retained a lead in the total number of warheads. No limitations were placed on new weapons systems, though each side agreed to work toward a permanent freeze on all nuclear weapons. The Moscow negotiations also produced new trade agreements, including an arrangement whereby the United States sold almost a quarter of its wheat crop to the Soviets at a favorable price. In sum, the Moscow summit revealed the dramatic easing of tensions between the two cold war superpowers. For Nixon and Kissinger, the agreements with China and the Soviet Union represented monumental changes in the global order that would have lasting consequences. Kissinger later boasted that the SALT agreement was his crowning achievement. Over time, the détente policy with the Soviet Union would help end the cold war by lowering Soviet hostility to Western influences penetrating their closed society, which slowly eroded Communist rule from the inside.

SHUTTLE DIPLOMACY    The Nixon-Kissinger initiatives in the Middle East were less dramatic and less conclusive than the agreements with China and the Soviet Union, but they did show that the United States at long last recognized the legitimacy of Arab interests in the region and its own dependence upon Middle Eastern oil, even though the Arab nations were adamantly opposed to the existence of Israel. In the Six-Day War of 1967, Israeli forces routed the armies of Egypt, Syria, and Jordan and seized territory from all three nations. Moreover, the number of Palestinian refugees, many of them homeless since the creation of Israel in 1948, increased after the 1967 Israeli victory.

The Middle East remained a tinderbox of tensions. On October 6, 1973, the Jewish holy day of Yom Kippur, Syria and Egypt attacked Israel, igniting what became the Yom Kippur War. It created the most dangerous confrontation between the United States and the Soviet Union since the Cuban missile crisis. President Nixon asked Henry Kissinger, now secretary of state, to keep the Soviets out of the Middle Eastern war. On October 20, Kissinger flew to Moscow to meet directly with Leonid Brezhnev just as "all hell had broken loose" in the White House with Nixon's firing of the attorney general and his staff for their unwillingness to cover up the Watergate mess. Kissinger deftly negotiated a cease-fire and exerted pressure to prevent Israel from taking additional Arab territory. He also promoted closer ties with Egypt and its president, Anwar el-Sadat, and more restrained support for Israel. In an attempt to broker a lasting settlement, Kissinger made numerous flights to the capitals of the Middle Eastern nations. His "shuttle diplomacy" won acclaim from all sides, but Kissinger failed to find a comprehensive formula for peace in the troubled region and ignored the Palestinian problem. He did, however, lay groundwork for the accord between Israel and Egypt in 1977.

### Henry Kissinger's "shuttle diplomacy"

President Anwar el-Sadat of Egypt and Secretary of State Henry Kissinger, during one of Kissinger's many visits to the Middle East, talk with reporters in an effort to bring peace.

WAR WITHOUT END    During 1972, the mounting social divisions at home and the approach of the presidential election influenced the stalled negotiations in Paris between the United States and representatives of North Vietnam. In the summer of 1972, Henry Kissinger again began meeting privately with the North Vietnamese negotiators, and he now dropped his insistence upon the removal of all North Vietnamese troops from the South before the withdrawal of the remaining U.S. troops. On October 26, only a week before the U.S. presidential election, Kissinger announced, "Peace is at hand." But this was a cynical ploy to win votes. Several days earlier, the Thieu regime in South Vietnam had rejected the Kissinger plan for a cease-fire, fearful that the presence of North Vietnamese troops in the south would virtually guarantee a Communist victory. The Paris peace talks broke off on December 16, and two days later the newly reelected Nixon ordered massive bombing of Hanoi and Haiphong, the two largest cities in North Vietnam. These so-called Christmas bombings and the simultaneous mining of North Vietnamese harbors aroused worldwide protest.

But the bombings also made the North Vietnamese more flexible at the negotiating table. The Christmas bombings stopped on December 29, and the talks in Paris soon resumed. On January 27, 1973, the United States, North and South Vietnam, and the Viet Cong signed an "agreement on ending the war and restoring peace in Vietnam." While Nixon and Kissinger claimed that the bombing had brought North Vietnam to its senses, in truth the North Vietnamese never altered their basic stance; they kept 150,000 troops in the South and remained committed to the reunification of Vietnam under one government. What had changed since the previous fall was the grudging willingness of South Vietnamese officials, who were never allowed to participate in the negotiations, to accept the agreement on the basis of Nixon's promise that the United States would respond "with full force" to any Communist violation of the agreement. Kissinger had little confidence that the treaty provisions would enable South Vietnam to survive on its own. He told a White House staffer, "If they're lucky, they can hold out for a year and a half."

THE ELECTION OF 1972    Nixon's foreign-policy achievements allowed him to stage the presidential campaign of 1972 as a triumphal procession. The main threat to his reelection came from Alabama's Democratic governor George Wallace, a populist segregationist who assailed the Washington political establishment, the "overeducated, ivory-tower folks with pointy heads" who wore "sissy britches." Wallace had the potential as a third-party candidate to deprive the Republicans of conservative southern votes and thereby throw the election to the Democrats or to the Democratic-controlled Congress. That threat ended, however, on May 15, 1972, when Wallace was shot by Arthur Bremer, a man eager to achieve a grisly brand of notoriety (he had earlier hoped to assassinate Nixon). Wallace survived but was left paralyzed below the waist, forcing him to withdraw from the campaign.

Meanwhile, the Democrats were further ensuring Nixon's victory by nominating Senator George McGovern of South Dakota, a steadfast anti-war liberal who proceeded to organize one of the most inept presidential campaigns in history. McGovern recognized that the old New Deal Democratic coalition of urban ethnic groups, organized labor, and southern white populists was fading so he tried to create a "new politics" coalition centered on minorities, women, and young, well-educated activists. However logical, it was an electoral disaster. In the 1972 election, Nixon won the greatest victory of any Republican presidential candidate in history, capturing 520 electoral votes to only 17 for McGovern. The popular vote was equally decisive: 46 million to 28 million, a proportion of the total vote (60.8 percent) that was second only to Lyndon B. Johnson's victory over Barry Goldwater in 1964. After his landslide victory, Nixon promised to complete his efforts at a conservative revolution. He planned to promote the "more conservative values and beliefs of the New Majority throughout the country and use my power to put some teeth in my new American Revolution."

But Nixon's easy victory and triumphant outlook would be short-lived. During the course of the presidential campaign, McGovern had complained about the numerous "dirty tricks" orchestrated by members of the Nixon administration during the campaign. The insecure Nixon, it turned out, had ordered aides to harass Democratic party leaders—by any means necessary. Attorney General Mitchell called the "dirty tricks" the "White House horrors." Nixon, for example, ordered illegal wiretaps on his opponents (as well as his aides), tried to coerce the Internal Revenue Service to intimidate Democrats, and told his chief of staff to break into the safe at the Brookings Institution, a Washington think tank with liberal ties. "Goddamnit," he told Bob Haldeman, "get in and get those files. Blow the safe and get it."

McGovern was especially disturbed by a curious incident on June 17, 1972, when five men were caught breaking into the Democratic National Committee headquarters in the Watergate apartment and office complex in Washington, D.C. The burglars were former CIA agents, one of whom, James W. McCord, worked for the Nixon campaign. They were caught installing eavesdropping devices ("bugs"). At the time, McGovern's shrill Watergate accusations seemed like sour grapes from a candidate running far behind in the polls. Nixon and his staff ignored the news of the break-in.

The president said that no one cares "when somebody bugs somebody else." Privately, however, he and his senior aides Bob Haldeman, John Dean, and John Ehrlichman began feverish efforts to cover up the Watergate break-in. The White House secretly provided legal assistance ("hush money") to the burglars to buy their silence and tried to keep the FBI out of the investigation. Nixon and his closest aides also discussed using the CIA to derail the Justice Department investigation of the Watergate burglary.

## WATERGATE

During the trial of the accused Watergate burglars in January 1973, the relentless prodding of federal Judge John J. Sirica led one of the accused to tell the full story of the Nixon administration's complicity in the **Watergate** episode. James W. McCord, security chief of the Committee to Re-Elect the President (CREEP), was the first in a long line of informers in a political melodrama that unfolded over two years, revealing the systematic efforts of Nixon and his aides to create an "imperial presidency" above the law. The scandal ended in the first presidential resignation in history, the conviction and imprisonment of twenty-five administration officials, including four cabinet members, and the most serious constitutional crisis since the impeachment trial of President Andrew Johnson in 1868.

UNCOVERING THE COVER-UP   The trail of evidence pursued first by Judge Sirica, a tough law-and-order Republican, then by a grand jury, and then by a Senate committee headed by Democrat Samuel J. Ervin Jr. of North Carolina led directly to the White House. Nixon was personally involved in the cover-up of the Watergate incident, using his presidential powers to discredit and block the investigation as well as coaching aides how to lie when questioned. And most alarming, as it turned out, the Watergate burglary was merely one small part of a larger pattern of corruption and criminality sanctioned by the Nixon White House.

For all of his abilities and accomplishments, Nixon was a chronically insecure person with a thirst for vengeance and a hair-trigger temper. The vicious partisanship of the sixties fueled his paranoia. As president, he began keeping lists of political enemies and launched secret efforts to embarrass and punish them. In 1970, after the *New York Times* had disclosed that secret American bombings in Cambodia had been going on for years, a furious Nixon ordered illegal telephone taps on several journalists and government employees suspected of leaking the story. The covert activity against the press and critics of Nixon's Vietnam policies increased in 1971, during the crisis generated by the publication of the classified Pentagon Papers, when a team of burglars under the direction of White House adviser John Ehrlichman broke into Daniel Ellsberg's psychiatrist's office in an effort to obtain damaging information on Ellsberg, the man who had given the Pentagon Papers to the press. By the spring of 1972, Ehrlichman was overseeing a team of "dirty tricksters" who performed various acts of sabotage against Democrats—for example, falsely accusing Senators Hubert H. Humphrey and Henry Jackson of sexual improprieties, forging press releases, setting off stink bombs at Democratic campaign events, and planting spies on the McGovern campaign plane. By the time of the Watergate break-in in June, the money to finance these pranks was being illegally collected through CREEP and had been placed under the control of the White House staff.

Nixon and his White House aides tried to cover-up the Watergate break-in. They secretly paid the burglars to keep quiet as they waited for trial. "They have to be paid," Nixon insisted. And he discussed pardoning them after they were convicted. Nixon aides also began destroying evidence not only of the Watergate break-in but other "dirty tricks" ordered by the White House. By January 1973, when the burglars were convicted, it appeared that the cover-up had worked, but in following months the conspiracy unraveled as various people, including John Dean, legal counsel to the president, began to cooperate with Senate investigators and later Justice Department prosecutors. At the same time, two reporters for the *Washington Post,* Carl Bernstein and Bob Woodward, relentlessly pursued the story and its money trail. It unraveled further in 1973 when L. Patrick Gray, acting director of the FBI, resigned after confessing that he had confiscated and destroyed several incriminating documents.

On April 30, Ehrlichman and Haldeman resigned (they would later serve time in prison, as would John Dean and former attorney general John Mitchell), together with Attorney General Richard Kleindienst. A few days later, the president nervously assured the public in a television address, "I am not a crook." Then John Dean, whom Nixon had dismissed because of his cooperation with prosecutors, testified to the Ervin committee in the Senate over the course of five riveting days, revealing that there had been a White House–orchestrated cover-up approved by the president. Nixon, meanwhile, refused to provide Senator Ervin's committee with documents it requested, citing "executive privilege" to protect national security. In another shocking disclosure, a White House aide told the Ervin committee that Nixon had installed a taping system in the Oval Office of the White House and that many of the conversations about the Watergate cover-up had been recorded.

That bombshell revelation set off a yearlong legal battle for the "Nixon tapes." Harvard law professor Archibald Cox, whom Nixon's new attorney general, Elliot Richardson, had appointed as special prosecutor to investigate the Watergate case, took the president to court in October 1973 to obtain the tapes. Nixon refused to release the recordings and ordered Cox fired. In what became known as the Saturday Night Massacre, on October 20 Attorney General Elliot Richardson and Deputy Attorney General William Ruckelshaus resigned rather than fire the special prosecutor. Solicitor General Robert Bork finally fired Cox. Nixon's dismissal of Cox ("that fucking Harvard professor") produced a firestorm of public indignation. Numerous newspaper and magazine editorials, as well as a growing chorus of legislators, called for the president to be impeached for obstructing justice. A Gallup poll revealed that Nixon's approval rating had plunged to 17 percent, the lowest level any president had ever experienced.

**The unraveling**

Fired Deputy Attorney General William Ruckelshaus discusses Watergate during an interview.

The firing of Cox failed to end Nixon's legal troubles. Cox's replacement as special prosecutor, Leon Jaworski, also took the president to court. In March 1974 the Watergate grand jury indicted John Ehrlichman, Bob Haldeman, and John Mitchell for obstruction of justice and named Nixon as an "unindicted co-conspirator." On April 30, Nixon, still refusing to turn over the actual Oval Office tapes, released 1,254 pages of transcribed recordings that he had edited himself, often substituting the phrase "expletive deleted" for the vulgar language and anti-Semitic rants he had frequently unleashed. At one point in the transcripts the president told his aides that they should have frequent memory lapses when testifying about the cover-up. The transcripts provoked widespread shock and revulsion as well as renewed demands for the president to resign. By the summer of 1974, Nixon was in full retreat, besieged on all fronts. He became alternately combative, melancholy, or petty. During White House visits, Henry Kissinger found the besieged president increasingly unstable and drinking heavily. Alcohol made Nixon even more surly and combative, and he drank a lot. After a meeting with Nixon, Senator Barry Goldwater reported that the president "jabbered incessantly, often incoherently." He seemed "to be cracking."

For months, the drama of Watergate transfixed Americans. Each day they watched the televised Ervin committee hearings as if they were daytime soap operas. On July 24, 1974, the Supreme Court ruled unanimously, in *United States v. Richard M. Nixon,* that the president must surrender *all* of the tape recordings. A few days later, the House Judiciary Committee voted to recommend three articles of impeachment: obstruction of justice through the payment of "hush money" to witnesses and the withholding of evidence, abuse of power through the use of federal agencies to deprive citizens of their constitutional rights, and defiance of Congress by withholding the tapes. But before the House of Representatives could meet to vote on impeachment, Nixon grudgingly handed over the complete set of White House tapes. Investigators then learned that sections of certain recordings were missing, including eighteen minutes of a key conversation in June 1972 during which Nixon first mentioned the Watergate burglary. The president's loyal secretary tried to accept blame for the erasure, claiming that she had accidentally pushed the wrong button, but technical experts later concluded that the missing segments had been intentionally deleted. The other transcripts, however, provided more than enough evidence of Nixon's involvement in the cover-up. At one point, the same president who had been the architect of détente with the Soviet Union and the recognition of Communist China had yelled at aides asking what they and others should say to Watergate investigators, "I don't give a shit what happens. I want you all to stonewall it, let them plead the Fifth Amendment, cover-up or anything else, if it'll save it, save the plan." In early August 1974, Barry Goldwater, the elder statesman of the Republican party, said that "Nixon should get his ass out of the White House—today."

On August 9, 1974, Richard Nixon resigned from office, the only president ever to do so. Crowds outside the White House chanted "Jail to the Chief!" In 1969, Nixon had begun his presidency hoping to heal America, to "bring people together." He left the presidency having deeply wounded the nation. The credibility gap between the presidency and the public that had developed under Lyndon B. Johnson had become a chasm under Nixon, as the Watergate revelations fueled a widespread cynicism about the integrity of politics and politicians. Nixon had earlier claimed that "virtue is not what lifts great leaders above others" and insisted that a president's actions could not be "illegal." He was wrong. The Watergate affair's clearest lesson was that not even a president is above the law.

THE EFFECTS OF WATER-
GATE Vice President Spiro
Agnew did not succeed Nixon
because he had been forced to
resign in October 1973 for having accepted bribes from contractors before and during his
term as vice president. The vice
president at the time of Nixon's
resignation was **Gerald Ford**,
the congenial former Michigan
congressman and House minority leader whom Nixon had
appointed, with the approval of
Congress, under the provisions
of the Twenty-fifth Amendment.

**Nixon's resignation**

Having resigned his office, Richard M. Nixon
waves farewell outside the White House on
August 9, 1974.

Ratified in 1967, the amendment provided for the appointment of a vice president when
the office became vacant. On
August 9, 1974, Gerald Ford was sworn in as the nation's first politically
appointed chief executive.

President Ford was a decent, honorable man who found himself in over his
head in the White House. A ponderous speaker with no charisma, he admitted
that he was a "Ford, not a Lincoln." Lyndon B. Johnson had been more brutal
in describing Ford, the former football star at the University of Michigan:
"Gerry Ford is a nice guy, but he played too much football with his helmet off."

Ford assumed the presidency by reassuring the nation that "our long
nightmare is over." But restoring national harmony was not so easy. Tensions
over racial and gender issues spawned ongoing battles in a variety of "culture
wars" that erupted over incendiary issues such as gay rights, affirmative
action, busing to achieve integrated schools, religious beliefs, and abortion.
Only a month after taking office, Ford reopened the wounds of Watergate by
issuing a "full, free, and absolute pardon" to a despondent Richard Nixon.
Many Americans, however, were not in a forgiving mood when it came to
Nixon's devious scheming. The announcement of Ford's pardon of Nixon
ignited a storm of controversy. The new president was grilled by a House
subcommittee wanting to know if he and Nixon had made a deal whereby
Nixon would resign and Ford would become president if Ford granted the
pardon. Ford steadfastly denied such charges and said that nothing was to be

gained by putting Nixon in prison, but the Nixon pardon hobbled Ford's presidency. His approval rating plummeted from 71 percent to 49 percent in one day, the steepest drop ever recorded. Even the president's press secretary resigned in protest. Ford was devastated by the "hostile reaction" to the pardon; he never recovered the public's confidence.

If there was a silver lining in the dark cloud of Watergate, it was the vigor and resilience of the institutions that had brought a rogue president to justice—the press, Congress, the courts, and an aroused public opinion. Congress responded to the Watergate revelations with several pieces of legislation designed to curb executive power. Already nervous about possible efforts to renew American military assistance to South Vietnam, the Democratic-led Congress passed the War Powers Act (1973), which requires a president to inform Congress within forty-eight hours if U.S. troops are deployed in combat abroad and to withdraw troops after sixty days unless Congress specifically approves their stay. In an effort to correct abuses in the use of campaign funds, Congress enacted legislation in 1974 that set new ceilings on political campaign contributions and expenditures. And in reaction to the Nixon claim of "executive privilege" as a means of withholding evidence, Congress strengthened the 1966 Freedom of Information Act to require prompt responses to requests for information from government files and to place on government agencies the burden of proof for classifying information as secret.

With Richard Nixon's resignation, the nation had weathered a profound constitutional crisis, but the aftershock of the Watergate episode produced a deep sense of disillusionment with the so-called imperial presidency. Apart from Nixon's illegal actions, the vulgar language he used in the White House and made public on the tape recordings stripped away the veil of majesty surrounding national leaders and left even the die-hard defenders of presidential authority shocked at the crudity and duplicity of Nixon and his subordinates. From prison, Bob Haldeman insisted that Nixon carried "greatness in him," but the former chief of staff admitted that the fallen president had a "dirty, mean, base side" and "a terrible temper." Nixon, he concluded, was a "coldly calculating, devious, [and] craftily manipulative" character who was "the weirdest man ever to live in the White House."

## AN UNELECTED PRESIDENT

During Richard Nixon's last year in office, the Watergate crisis so dominated national politics that major domestic and foreign problems received little executive attention. Stagflation, the perplexing combination of inflation and recession, worsened, as did the oil crisis. At the same time, Secretary of State Henry Kissinger, who assumed virtual control of foreign policy, watched helplessly as the South Vietnamese forces crumbled before North Vietnamese attacks, attempted with limited success to establish a framework for peace in the Middle East, and supported a CIA role in the overthrow of Salvador Allende Gossens, the popularly elected Marxist president of Chile, although neither Nixon nor Kissinger ever explained why a leftist government in Chile constituted a threat to the United States. Allende was subsequently murdered and replaced by General Augusto Pinochet Ugarte, a ruthless military dictator supposedly friendly to the United States.

**THE FORD YEARS**    As president, Gerald Ford soon adopted the posture he had developed as the minority leader in the House of Representatives: naysaying leader of the opposition who believed that the federal government exercised too much power. In his first fifteen months as president, Ford vetoed thirty-nine bills passed by the Democratic Congress, thereby outstripping Herbert Hoover's veto record in less than half the time. By resisting congressional pressure to reduce taxes and increase federal spending, he helped steer the struggling economy into the deepest recession since the Great Depression. Unemployment jumped to 9 percent in 1975, the annual rate of inflation had reached double digits, and the federal budget deficit hit a record the next year. Ford announced that inflation had become "Public Enemy No. 1," but he rejected bold actions such as implementing wage and price controls to curb inflation, preferring instead a timid public relations campaign, created by an advertising agency, featuring

**Gerald Ford**

Ford listens apprehensively to the rising rates of unemployment and inflation at an economic conference in 1974.

lapel buttons that simply read WIN, symbolizing the administration's publicity campaign to "Whip Inflation Now." The WIN buttons instead became a national joke and a popular symbol of Ford's ineffectiveness in the fight against stagflation. He himself admitted that it was a failed "gimmick." By 1975, when Ford delivered his State of the Union address, the president lamely admitted that "the state of the union is not good."

In foreign policy, Ford retained Henry Kissinger as secretary of state (while stripping him of his dual role of national security advisor) and attempted to continue Nixon's goals of stability in the Middle East, rapprochement with China, and détente with the Soviet Union. In addition, Kissinger's tireless Middle East diplomacy produced an important agreement: Israel promised to return to Egypt most of the Sinai territory captured in the 1967 War, and the two nations agreed to rely upon negotiations rather than force to settle future disagreements. These limited but significant achievements should have enhanced Ford's image, but they were drowned in the sea of criticism and carping that followed the collapse of South Vietnam to the Communists in May 1975.

THE COLLAPSE OF SOUTH VIETNAM    On March 29, 1973, the last U.S. combat troops left Vietnam. On that same day, almost six hundred American prisoners of war, most of them downed pilots, were released from Hanoi. Henry Kissinger was awarded the Nobel Peace Prize. Within months of the U.S. withdrawal, however, the cease-fire in Vietnam collapsed, the war between North and South resumed, and the Communist forces gained the upper hand. In Cambodia (renamed the Khmer Republic after it fell to the Communists and now called Kampuchea) and Laos, where fighting had been more sporadic, a Communist victory also seemed inevitable. In 1975, the North Vietnamese launched a full-scale invasion, and South Vietnamese president Thieu appealed to Washington for the promised U.S. assistance. Congress refused. The much-mentioned "peace with honor" had proved to be, in the words of one CIA official, only a "decent interval"—enough time for the United States to extricate itself from Vietnam before the collapse of the South Vietnamese government. On April 30, 1975, Americans watched on television as North Vietnamese tanks rolled into Saigon, soon to be renamed Ho Chi Minh City, and helicopters lifted the U.S. embassy officials to ships waiting offshore. In those desperate, chaotic final moments, terrified South Vietnamese fought to get on board the departing helicopters, for they knew that the Communists would be merciless victors.

The longest, most controversial, and least successful war in American history was finally over, leaving in its wake a bitter legacy. During the period of

U.S. involvement in the fighting, almost 2 million combatants and civilians were killed on both sides. North Vietnam absorbed incredible losses—some 600,000 soldiers and countless civilians killed. More than 58,000 Americans died in Vietnam, 300,000 were wounded, 2,500 were declared missing, almost 100,000 returned missing one or more limbs, and over 150,000 combat veterans suffered drug or alcohol addiction or severe psychological disorders. Most of the Vietnam veterans readjusted well to civilian life, but even they carried for years the stigma of a lost war.

The "loss" of the war and revelations of American atrocities such as those at My Lai eroded respect for the military so thoroughly that many young people came to regard military service as corrupting and ignoble. The Vietnam War, initially described as a crusade on behalf of democratic ideals, instead suggested that democracy was not easily transferable to third world regions that lacked any historical experience with representative government. Fought to show the world that the United States would be steadfast in containing the spread of communism, the war instead sapped the national

**Panic amid the withdrawal from Saigon**

Soldiers block people from climbing over the walls of the U.S. embassy in Saigon, South Vietnam, in 1975. South Vietnamese were seeking to flee before the Communist forces seized the city.

will and fragmented the national consensus that had governed foreign affairs since 1947. It also changed the balance of power in domestic politics. Not only did the war undermine Lyndon B. Johnson's presidency; it also created enduring fissures in the Democratic party. As anti-war senator and 1972 Democratic presidential candidate George S. McGovern said, "The Vietnam tragedy is at the root of the confusion and division of the Democratic party. It tore up our souls."

Not only had a decade of American effort in Vietnam proved futile, but the fall of Vietnam to communism also undermined the "domino theory" that had long undergirded America's containment doctrine. Instead of Vietnam toppling all of the other nations in the region, Communism proved not to be the monolithic force feared by American presidents since Truman. Within a year after taking control of the South, the Vietnamese Communists were at war with the Cambodian Communists, and in 1978 Vietnam would be fighting Communist China.

The Khmer Rouge, the Cambodian Communist movement, plunged that country into a colossal bloodbath. The maniacal Khmer Rouge leaders organized a genocidal campaign to destroy their opponents, killing almost a third of the total population. Meanwhile, the OPEC oil cartel was threatening another worldwide boycott, and various third world nations denounced the United States as a depraved and declining imperialist power. Ford lost his patience when he sent marines to rescue the crew of the American merchant ship *Mayaguez,* which had been captured by the Cambodian Communists. This vigorous move won popular acclaim until it was disclosed that the Cambodians had already agreed to release the captured Americans: the forty-one Americans killed in the operation had died for no purpose.

THE ELECTION OF 1976   Amid years of turmoil, both national parties were in disarray as they prepared for the 1976 presidential election. At the Republican Convention, Gerald Ford had to fend off a powerful challenge for the nomination from the darling of the conservative wing of the party, Ronald Reagan, a former two-term California governor and Hollywood actor. Nixon mistakenly told Ford that Reagan was "a lightweight and not someone to be considered seriously or feared." But Reagan's candidacy was hurt when Barry Goldwater endorsed Ford's candidacy. The fractured Democrats chose an obscure former naval officer and engineer turned peanut farmer who had served one term as governor of Georgia. James Earl (Jimmy) Carter Jr. represented the new moderate wing of the Democratic party. He was one of several Democratic southern governors who self-consciously sought to reorient their party away from runaway liberalism. Carter insisted that he was neither a liberal nor a conservative but a manager who would be adept at getting the "right thing" done in the "right ways." He capitalized on the post-Watergate cynicism by promising that he would "never tell a lie to the American people." Carter also trumpeted the advantages of his being a political "outsider" whose inexperience in Washington politics would be an asset to a nation still reeling from the Watergate debacle. Carter was certainly different from conventional candidates. Jaded political reporters covering the presidential campaign marveled at a Southern Baptist candidate who claimed to be "born again."

To the surprise of many pundits, the little-known Carter revived the New Deal voter coalition of southern whites, blacks, urban labor unionists, and ethnic groups to eke out a narrow win over Ford. Carter had 41 million votes to Ford's 39 million. A heavy turnout of African Americans in the South enabled Carter to sweep every state in the region except Virginia. Carter also benefited from the appeal of Walter F. Mondale, his liberal running mate and a favorite among northern blue-collar workers and the urban poor. Carter lost most of the trans-Mississippi West, but no Democratic candidate had made much headway there since Harry S. Truman in 1948. The significant story of the election was the low voter turnout. "Neither Ford nor Carter won as many votes as Mr. Nobody," said one reporter, commenting on the fact that almost half the eligible voters, apparently alienated by Watergate, the stagnant economy, and the two lackluster candidates, chose to sit out the election.

## CHAPTER SUMMARY

- **Rebellion and Reaction**  Civil rights activism was the catalyst for a heightened interest in social causes during the sixties, especially among the young. Students for a Democratic Society (SDS) launched the New Left. Other prominent causes of the era included the anti-war movement, the women's liberation movement, Native American rights, Hispanic rights, and gay rights. By 1970 a counterculture had emerged, featuring young people who used mind-altering drugs, lived on rural communes, and in other ways "dropped out" of the conventional world, which they viewed as corrupt.

- **End of the Vietnam War**  In 1968, Richard Nixon campaigned for the presidency pledging to secure a "peace with honor" in Vietnam, but years would pass before the war ended. His delays prompted an acceleration of anti-war protests. After the Kent State University shootings, the divisions between supporters and opponents of the war became especially contentious. The publication of the Pentagon Papers in 1971 and the heavy bombing of North Vietnam by the United States in December 1972 aroused intense worldwide protests. A month later North and South Vietnam agreed to end the war. The last U.S. troops left Vietnam in March 1973; two years later the government of South Vietnam collapsed, and the country was reunited under a Communist government.

- **Watergate**  In an incident in 1972, burglars were caught breaking into the Democratic campaign headquarters at the Watergate complex in Washington, D.C. Eventually the Committee to Re-Elect the President (CREEP) was implicated, and investigators began to probe the question of President Nixon's involvement. Nixon tried to block the judicial process, which led the public to call for the president to be impeached for obstruction of justice. In 1974, in *United States v. Richard M. Nixon,* the Supreme Court ruled that the president had to surrender the so-called Watergate tapes. Nixon resigned to avoid being impeached.

- **Middle East Crisis**  After the 1973 Yom Kippur War in the Middle East, the Organization of Petroleum Exporting Countries (OPEC) declined to sell oil to nations supporting Israel. President Carter brokered the Camp David Accords of 1978, which laid the groundwork for a peace treaty between Israel and Egypt.

## CHRONOLOGY

| | |
|---|---|
| 1960 | U.S. Food and Drug Administration approves the birth-control pill |
| 1963 | Betty Friedan's *The Feminine Mystique* is published |
| March 1969 | U.S. planes begin a fourteen-month-long bombing campaign aimed at Communist sanctuaries in Cambodia |
| 1971 | Ratification of the Twenty-sixth Amendment gives eighteen-year-olds the right to vote in all elections |
| 1972–74 | The Watergate scandal unfolds |
| January 1973 | In Paris, the United States, North and South Vietnam, and the Viet Cong agree to restore peace in Vietnam |
| 1973 | Congress passes the War Powers Act |
| April 1975 | Saigon falls to the North Vietnamese |

## KEY TERMS & NAMES

the counterculture  p. 1356

Woodstock  p. 1357

Cesar Chavez  p. 1364

American Indian Movement (AIM)  p. 1365

Richard M. Nixon  p. 1367

Henry Kissinger  p. 1368

stagflation  p. 1375

Vietnamization  p. 1378

My Lai Massacre  p. 1379

Kent State  p. 1379

Pentagon Papers  p. 1379

détente  p. 1383

Watergate  p. 1387

Gerald Ford  p. 1391

# 33

## A CONSERVATIVE
## REALIGNMENT: 1977–1990

FOCUS QUESTIONS    Ⓢ    wwnorton.com/studyspace

- What explains the rise of Ronald Reagan and Republican conservatism?
- What was the Iran-Contra affair, and what did it show about the nature of the executive branch of government, even after Watergate?
- What factors led to the end of the cold war?
- What characterized the economy and society in the eighties?
- What were the causes of the First Gulf War?

During the seventies, America began to lose its self-confidence. The failed Vietnam War, the sordid revelations of Watergate, and the explosion in oil prices, interest/mortgage rates, and inflation revealed the limits of American power, prosperity, and virtue. For a nation long accustomed to economic growth and spreading affluence, the frustrating persistence of stagflation undermined national optimism. At the same time, the growing environmental movement highlighted the damages imposed by runaway pollution and unregulated development on the nation's air, water, and other natural resources. In short, people during the seventies began downsizing their expectations of the American Dream. Out with the global interventionism required by the efforts to "contain" and "roll back" communism, in with the isolationism spawned by what became known as the Vietnam Syndrome—a reluctance to intervene militarily around the world. Out with gas-guzzling U.S.-produced Cadillacs, in with economical Toyotas made in Japan. Out with the "imperial presidency," in with honesty, transparency, humility at home, and hesitancy abroad.

## THE CARTER PRESIDENCY

James (Jimmy) Earl Carter Jr. won the very close election of 1976 for two primary reasons: he convinced voters that he was an incorruptible "outsider" who would restore integrity and honesty to the presidency in the aftermath of the Watergate scandal (his campaign slogan was "I'll never tell a lie"), and he represented a new generation of "moderate" southern Democratic leaders who were committed to fiscal responsibility rather than "big government." As he stressed in his 1977 inaugural address, "We have learned that 'more' is not necessarily 'better,' that even our great nation has limits." He did not heed his own remarks, however. Instead of focusing on a few top priorities, Carter tried to do too much too fast. He confessed in his diary that he found it "impossible" not to address "something I see needs to be done." In the end, his indiscriminate activism would be his undoing. Carter's inexperience in Washington politics often translated into incompetence, and his relentless moralizing depressed rather than excited the public mood. By the end of the decade, Carter's painful failure of leadership and his gloomy sermonizing would give way to Ronald Reagan's uplifting conservative crusade to restore American greatness.

**Jimmy Carter** suffered the fate of all presidents since John F. Kennedy: after an initial honeymoon, during which he displayed folksy charm by walking with his wife Rosalynn down Pennsylvania Avenue after his inauguration rather than riding in a limousine, his popularity waned as his political ineffectiveness soared. Like Gerald Ford before him, Carter faced vexing domestic problems and formidable international challenges. He was expected to cure the recession and reduce inflation at a time when all industrial economies were shaken by a shortage of oil and confidence.

**The Carter Administration**

President Jimmy Carter and his wife, Rosalynn, forgo the traditional limousine and walk down Pennsylvania Avenue after the inauguration, January 20, 1977.

Carter was also expected to restore American stature abroad, and lift the national spirit through a set of political institutions in which many people had lost faith. Meeting such expectations would be miraculous, but Carter, for all of his "almost arrogant self-confidence," was no miracle worker.

Still, during the first two years of his presidency, Carter enjoyed several successes. His administration included more African Americans and women than ever before. Carter fulfilled a controversial campaign pledge by offering amnesty to the thousands of young men who had fled the country rather than serve in Vietnam. He reorganized the executive branch and reduced government red tape by slowing the issuance of burdensome new regulations and creating two new cabinet-level agencies, the departments of Energy and Education. He also pushed through Congress several significant environmental initiatives, including more stringent regulations of strip coal mining, the creation of a $1.6 billion "Superfund" to clean up toxic chemical waste sites, and a proposal to protect over 100 million acres of Alaskan land from development.

But success was short-lived. As president, the bright, energetic Carter was his own worst enemy. By nature, he was a humorless technocrat rather than an inspiring leader, a compulsive micro-manager so fixated on details that he was unable to establish a compelling vision for the nation's future. Although he promised to make government "competent, economical, and efficient," he himself displayed none of those virtues. He tried to do everything at once rather than establish clear priorities. As a result, Carter got bogged down in minutiae and was unable to focus on strategic issues. He was so self-absorbed that he kept a detailed daily diary of everything he did, and he felt compelled to continue teaching a weekly Sunday Bible study class as president. He even insisted on scheduling who could play on the White House tennis court. At the same time, Carter's "born-again" religious faith translated into bouts of prolonged soul-searching that palsied his ability to make confident decisions. Although the sanctimonious Carter prayed for divine guidance as much as twenty-five times a day, he lacked steadiness of purpose. The West German chancellor once described the humorless Carter as "a man who never stopped searching his soul and tended repeatedly to change his mind." Jacqueline Kennedy, the widow of John F. Kennedy, described Carter as a "stiff, prissy little man."

As a self-defined "Washington outsider," Carter recruited most of his staff and many of his cabinet members from the people he had worked with in Georgia while serving as govenor. Joseph Lester (Jody) Powell Jr., the new press secretary, boasted to reporters that "this government is going to be run by people you've never heard of." The eccentric White House staffers and cabinet members who constituted what journalists called the "Georgia mafia," like the president, lacked experience and expertise at a national level. And it showed. Only too late did Carter acknowledge that he needed the wisdom of Washington insiders. In December 1977, the president admitted that he had not "learned yet" how to manage the political process. Thomas Phillip (Tip) O'Neill Jr., the veteran Democratic Speaker of the House, came to despise Carter's Georgia staffers. "They were all parochial," he said in frustration. "They were incompetent. They came in with a chip on their shoulder against the entrenched politicians. Washington to them was evil. They were going to change everything and didn't understand the rudiments of it."

Carter's political naïveté surfaced in the protracted debate over energy policy. He insisted that managing the energy crisis was the nation's (and his) greatest challenge. It constituted what he called the "moral equivalent of war," borrowing the phrase from the nineteenth-century philosopher William James. But Carter chose to keep Congress in the dark as he and a few close advisers developed his national energy program. Carter disliked stroking legislators or wheeling and dealing to get legislation passed. When he presented his energy bill to the Congress, it contained 113 separate initiatives. It was a miscellany, not a program, providing a little of everything and much of nothing. Tip O'Neill leafed through the five *volumes* making up the bill and groaned. Carter's energy package was also not well received in the Senate. As a result, the energy bill that the president signed in 1978 was a gutted version of the original, reflecting the power of special-interest lobbyists representing the oil, gas, and automotive industries. One Carter aide said that the bill looked like it had been "nibbled to death by ducks." The clumsy political maneuvers that plagued Carter and his inexperienced aides repeatedly frustrated the president's earnest efforts to remedy the energy crisis. Carter wrote later in his memoirs that his effort to galvanize the nation behind a comprehensive energy policy was like "chewing on a rock that lasted the whole four years." A journalist pointed out that the acronym for Carter's "moral equivalent of war" was, fittingly, "MEOW."

CARTER AND HUMAN RIGHTS   Several of Carter's early foreign-policy initiatives also got caught in political crossfires. Soon after his inauguration, Carter revived the idealistic spirit of Woodrow Wilson's internationalism when he vowed that "the soul of our foreign policy" should be the defense of human rights abroad. "Our commitment to human rights must be absolute." It was a noble goal, nobly stated. But as was true of Wilson's idealistic crusade, Carter's campaign for universal human rights abroad was wildly impractical and largely a failure. Over time, the gap between the idealistic goals and the actual achievements of Carter's foreign policy became a chasm. He decided to cut off aid to nations that chronically violated basic human rights. This human rights campaign aroused opposition from two sides, however: those who feared it sacrificed a detached appraisal of national interest for high-level moralizing, and those who believed that human rights were important but that the administration was applying the standard inconsistently to different nations.

Similarly, Carter's heroic negotiation of treaties to turn over control of the Panama Canal to the Panamanian government generated intense criticism. Although former Republican presidents Ford and Nixon, as well as Henry Kissinger, endorsed Carter's efforts, Ronald Reagan, knowing little about the history of America's involvement in Panama, claimed that the Canal Zone was sovereign American soil purchased "fair and square" during Theodore Roosevelt's administration. "We bought it, we paid for it, it's ours," he told cheering crowds, "and we're going to keep it."(In the congressional debate, one senator quipped, "We stole it fair and square, so why can't we keep it?") Carter argued that the limitations on U.S. influence in Latin America and the deep resentment of American colonialism in Panama left the United States with no other choice but to transfer the canal to Panama. The ten-mile wide, fifty-mile long Canal Zone would revert to Panama in stages, with completion of the process in 1999. The Senate ratified the treaties by a paper-thin margin (68 to 32, two votes more than the required two thirds), but conservatives lambasted Carter for surrendering American authority in a critical part of the world.

THE CAMP DAVID ACCORDS    Carter's crowning foreign-policy achievement, which even his most bitter critics applauded, was his brokering of a peace agreement between Israel and Egypt. In 1977, Egyptian president Anwar el-Sadat flew to Tel Aviv to speak to the Israeli parliament at the invitation of Israeli prime minister Menachem Begin. Sadat's bold act, and his accompanying announcement that Egypt was willing to recognize the legitimacy of the Israeli state, opened up diplomatic opportunities that Carter and Secretary of State Cyrus Vance quickly pursued.

In 1978, Carter invited Sadat and Begin to the presidential retreat at Camp David, in Maryland, for two weeks of difficult negotiations. The first part of the eventual agreement called for Israel to return all land in the Sinai in exchange for Egyptian recognition of Israel's sovereignty. This agreement, dubbed the **Camp David Accords**, was implemented in 1982, when the last Israeli settler vacated the peninsula. But the second part of the agreement,

**The Camp David Accords**

Egyptian president Anwar el-Sadat (left), Jimmy Carter (center), and Israeli prime minister Menachem Begin (right) at the announcement of the Camp David Accords, September 1978.

calling for Israel to negotiate with Sadat to resolve the Palestinian refugee dilemma, began to unravel soon after the Camp David summit.

By March 26, 1979, when Begin and Sadat returned to Washington to sign the formal treaty, Begin had already refused to block new Israeli settlements on the West Bank of the Jordan River, which Sadat had regarded as a prospective homeland for the Palestinians. In the wake of the Camp David Accords, most of the Arab nations condemned Sadat as a traitor. Islamic extremists assassinated him in 1981. Still, Carter and Vance's high-level diplomacy made an all-out war between Israel and the Arab world less likely.

MOUNTING TROUBLES  Carter's crowning failure, which even his most avid supporters acknowledged, was his mismanagement of the economy. In effect, he inherited a bad situation from President Ford and made it worse. Carter employed the same economic policies as Nixon and Ford to fight the mystery of stagflation, but he reversed the order of the federal "cure," preferring first to fight unemployment with a tax cut and increased government spending. Unemployment declined slightly, from 8 to 7 percent in 1977, but the annual inflation rate soared; at 5 percent when he took office, it reached 10 percent in 1978 and kept rising. During one month in 1980, it measured 18 percent. Stopping the runaway inflation preoccupied Carter's attention, but his efforts made little headway. Like previous presidents, Carter then reversed himself to fight the other side of the economic malaise: mushrooming federal budget deficits caused by the sagging economy. By midterm, he was delaying tax reductions and vetoing government spending programs that he had proposed in his first year. The result was the worst of both possible worlds: a deepened recession and inflation averaging between 12 and 13 percent per year.

The signing of a controversial new Strategic Arms Limitation Talks treaty with the Soviets (SALT II) put Carter's leadership to the test just as the mounting economic problems made him the subject of biting editorial cartoons nationwide. The new agreement placed a ceiling of 2,250 bombers and missiles on each side and set limits on the number of warheads and new weapons systems each power could assemble. But the proposed SALT II treaty became moot in 1979 when the Soviet army invaded Afghanistan to prop up the faltering Communist government there, which was being challenged by Muslim rebels. To protest the Soviet action, Carter immediately shelved SALT II, suspended grain shipments to the Soviet Union, and called for an international boycott of the 1980 Olympics, which were to be held that summer in Moscow.

IRAN   Then came the Iranian crisis, a yearlong cascade of unwelcome events that epitomized the inability of the United States to control world affairs and heightened public perceptions of Carter's weak leadership. The crisis began in 1979 with the fall of the shah of Iran, a dictatorial ruler whom Carter had supported in direct violation of his human rights policy. The revolutionaries who toppled the shah's government rallied around Ayatollah Ruhollah Khomeini, a fundamentalist Muslim religious leader who symbolized the orthodox Islamic values the shah had tried to replace with Western ways. Khomeini's hatred of the United States dated back to the CIA-sponsored overthrow of the government of Mohammed Mossadegh in 1953. Nor did it help the American image that the CIA had trained SAVAK, the shah's ruthless secret-police force. Late in 1979, Carter allowed the exiled shah to enter the United States to undergo emergency treatment for cancer. A few days later, on November 4, a frenzied mob of Iranian youths stormed the U.S. embassy in Tehran and seized the diplomats and staff. Khomeini endorsed the outrageous mob action and demanded the return of the shah along with all his wealth in exchange for the release of the fifty-two hostages still held captive.

Indignant Americans demanded a military response, but Carter's range of options was limited. He appealed to the United Nations, but Khomeini scoffed at UN requests for the release of the hostages. Carter then froze all Iranian assets in the United States and appealed to U.S. allies to join a trade embargo of Iran. The trade restrictions were only partially effective—even America's most loyal European allies did not want to lose their access to Iranian oil—so a frustrated and besieged Carter authorized a risky rescue attempt by commandos in 1980. Secretary of State Cyrus Vance resigned in protest against the secret mission and Carter's sharp turn toward a more hawkish foreign policy. The commando raid was aborted because of helicopter failures and ended with eight fatalities on April 25, 1980, when a helicopter collided with a transport plane in the desert. In hindsight, it was evident that the botched raid was poorly planned and badly executed,

**Tehran, 1979**

Iranian militants stormed the U.S. embassy in Tehran and held fifty-two Americans hostage for over a year. Here one of the hostages (face covered) is paraded before a camera.

hampered by inadequate preparation and training, poor communication, and cascading equipment failures, all of which led the U.S. military to create a Joint Special Operation Command to ensure that such problems did not occur again. Nightly television coverage of the taunting Iranian rebels burning American flags generated a near obsession with the falling fortunes of the United States and the fate of the hostages. The end came after 444 days, on January 20, 1981, when a feckless Carter released several billion dollars of Iranian assets to ransom the kidnapped hostages. By then however, Ronald Reagan had been elected president, and Carter was headed into retirement.

President Jimmy Carter and his embattled Democratic administration hobbled through 1979 and the onset of another presidential campaign season. The economy remained sluggish, double-digit annual inflation rates stymied spending, high prices and long waits angered drivers lined up at gas stations, and failed efforts to free the U.S. hostages in Iran combined to sour voters on the administration. Carter's tepid initiatives to slow inflation and his inability to persuade the nation to embrace his energy-conservation program revealed mortal flaws in his reading of the public mood and his understanding of legislative politics. That Democratic senator Edward M. Kennedy of Massachusetts, youngest brother of former President John Kennedy, chose to challenge Carter for the presidential nomination revealed how frustrated many Democrats were with their "outsider" president. In 1979, the inept Carter panicked, asking his entire cabinet to submit letters of resignation, five of which he accepted.

Carter's inability to galvanize national support for his efforts to deal with the energy crisis led him to cancel a televised address to the nation on July 5, 1979. He then secluded himself for two weeks at the presidential retreat near Camp David, Maryland, keeping the media at bay while he meditated and hosted leaders from all walks of life, asking them for advice. A southern governor told the president that "you are not leading this nation—you're just managing the government." Carter eventually concluded that a "crisis of spirit," a debilitating "malaise," was undermining the national will. On July 18, he gave a much-anticipated televised speech to an expectant nation. Some 100 million people watched as Carter delivered an unusual presidential address. He sounded more like a minister than a president when he warned that "this is not a message of happiness or reassurance, but it is the truth and it is a warning." Americans, he declared, had strayed from the ideals of the Founding Fathers: "In a nation that was proud of hard work, strong families, close-knit communities and our faith in God, too many of us now worship self-indulgence and consumption." He insisted, however, that "owning things and consuming things does not satisfy our longing for meaning." Carter's description of the state of the nation during the seventies may have been accurate, but his profoundly pessimistic solution was paralyzing rather than inspiring. He blamed the public rather than his presidency for the malaise he was describing. "All the legislation in the world can't fix what's wrong with America," the president concluded, for the nation was suffering from "a crisis of confidence."

The unique speech did not convince Congress or much of the public. A Phoenix, Arizona, newspaper editorial declared that "the nation did not tune in to Carter [last night] to hear a sermon. It wanted answers. It did not get them." By 1980, one of Carter's closest aides told the president that "leadership is the single biggest weakness in the public's perception of you. You are seen to be weak, providing no sense of direction, unsure yourself about where you want to lead the country." He was right.

While the lackluster Carter administration was foundering, conservative Republicans were forging an aggressive plan to win the White House in 1980 and assault runaway "liberalism" in Washington. Those plans centered on the popularity of plain-speaking **Ronald Reagan**, the Hollywood actor turned two-term California governor and prominent political commentator. Reagan was not a deep thinker, but he was a superb reader of the public mood, an unabashed patriot, and a committed champion of conservative principles. He was also charming and cheerful, a genial politician renowned for his folksy anecdotes and upbeat outlook. Where the self-righteous Carter denounced the evils of free-enterprise capitalism and scolded Americans to revive long-forgotten virtues of frugality and simplicity, a sunny Reagan promised a "revolution of ideas" that would reverse the tide of Democratic "New Deal liberalism" by unleashing free-enterprise capitalism, restoring national pride, and regaining international respect.

In contrast to Carter, Reagan insisted that there were "simple answers" to the complex problems facing the United States, but they were not easy answers. He pledged to increase military spending, dismantle the "bloated" federal bureaucracy, respect states' rights, reduce taxes and regulations, and in general shrink the role of the federal government. He also wanted to affirm old-time religious values by banning abortions and reinstituting prayer in public schools (he ended up doing neither). Reagan's appeal derived from his remarkable skill as a public speaker and his steadfast commitment to a few overarching ideas and simple themes. As a true believer and an able compromiser, he combined the fervor of a revolutionary with the pragmatism of a diplomat.

THE ELECTION OF 1980   Voters, including many long-time Democrats, applauded Reagan's cheery promises to shrink the federal government and restore prosperity. His "trickle-down," "supply-side" economic proposals, soon dubbed "**Reaganomics**" by supporters and "voodoo economics" by critics, argued that the stagflation of the seventies had resulted from excessive income taxes, which weakened incentives for individuals and businesses to increase productivity, save, and reinvest. The solution was to slash tax rates so as to boost economic growth by allowing affluent Americans to pay less taxes and thereby spend more money on consumer goods. For a long-suffering nation, it was an alluring economic panacea. Voters loved Reagan's simple solutions and upbeat personality. "Our optimism," he said during the campaign, "has once again been turned loose. And all of us recognize that these people [Jimmy Carter] who kept talking about the age of limits are really talking about their own limitations, not America's."

Reagan was a colorful campaigner who used humor to punctuate his themes. At one rally, for instance, he quipped: "A recession is when your neighbor loses his job. A depression is when you lose yours. A recovery is when Jimmy Carter loses his." Reagan scored with voters by repeatedly asking, "Are you better off than you were four years ago?" For his part, Carter portrayed Reagan as dangerously conservative, implying that his Republican opponent would roll back civil rights legislation and risk nuclear war against the Soviet Union. Voters, however, were more concerned with the stagnant economy. On election day, Reagan swept to a decisive victory, with 489 electoral votes to 49 for Carter, who carried only six states. The popular vote was 44 million (51 percent) for Reagan to Carter's 35 million (41 percent), with 7 percent going to John Anderson, a moderate Republican who bolted the party after the conservative Reagan's nomination and ran on an independent ticket. Flush with a sense of power and destiny, President-elect Reagan, the oldest president ever elected, headed toward Washington with an energetic blueprint for reorienting America.

But however optimistic Ronald Reagan was about America's future, the turbulent and often tragic events of the seventies—the Communist conquest of South Vietnam, the Watergate scandal and Nixon's resignation, the energy shortage and stagflation, the Iranian hostage episode—generated what Jimmy Carter labeled a "crisis of confidence" that had sapped America's energy. By 1980, U.S. power and prestige seemed to be on the decline, the economy remained in a shambles, and the social revolution launched in the sixties had sparked a backlash of resentment among middle America. With theatrical timing, Ronald Reagan emerged to tap the growing reservoir of public frustration and transform his political career into a crusade to

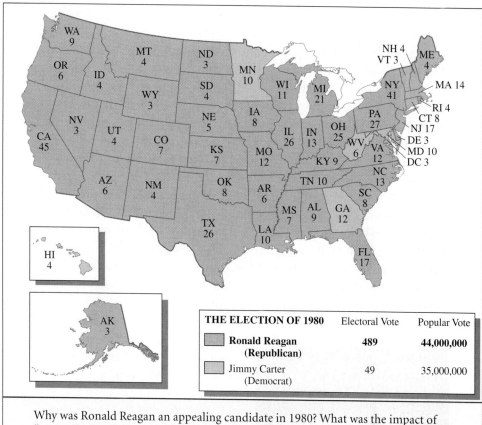

| THE ELECTION OF 1980 | Electoral Vote | Popular Vote |
|---|---|---|
| **Ronald Reagan (Republican)** | **489** | **44,000,000** |
| Jimmy Carter (Democrat) | 49 | 35,000,000 |

Why was Ronald Reagan an appealing candidate in 1980? What was the impact of "nonvoting"? Why was there so much voter apathy?

make America "stand tall again." He told his supporters that there was "a hunger in this land for a spiritual revival, a return to a belief in moral absolutes." The United States, he declared, remained the "greatest country in the world. We have the talent, we have the drive, we have the imagination. Now all we need is the leadership."

Reagan's ability to make the American people again believe in the greatness of their country won him two presidential elections, in 1980 and 1984, and ensured the victory of his anointed successor, Vice President George H. W. Bush, in 1988. Just how revolutionary the Reagan era was remains a subject of intense debate. What cannot be denied, however, is that Ronald Reagan's actions and beliefs set the tone for the decade's political and economic life.

## THE REAGAN REVOLUTION

THE MAKING OF A PRESIDENT   Born in the drab prairie town of Tampico, Illinois, in 1911, the son of an often-drunk shoe salesman and a devout, Bible-quoting mother, Ronald Reagan graduated from tiny Eureka College in 1932 during the depths of the Great Depression. He first worked as a radio sportscaster before starting a movie career in Hollywood in 1937. He appeared in thirty-one films before serving three years in the army during the Second World War, making training films. At that time, as he recalled, he was a Democrat, "a New Dealer to the core" who voted for Franklin D. Roosevelt four times. After the war, Reagan became president of the acting profession's union, the Screen Actors Guild (SAG). His leadership of SAG honed his negotiating skills and intensified his anti-communism as he fended off efforts to infiltrate the union. He learned "from firsthand experience how Communists used lies, deceit, violence, or any other tactic that suited them." Reagan had campaigned for Harry S. Truman in the 1948 presidential election, but during the fifties he decided that federal taxes were too high. In 1960 he campaigned as a Democrat for Richard Nixon,

**"The Great Communicator"**

Ronald Reagan in 1980, shortly before his election.

and two years later he joined the Republican party. Reagan achieved stardom in 1964 when he delivered a rousing speech on national television on behalf of Barry Goldwater's presidential candidacy.

Republican conservatives found in Ronald Reagan a new idol, whose appeal survived the defeat of Goldwater in 1964. Those who dismissed the former actor as a mental midget underrated his many virtues, including the importance of his years in front of a camera. Politics is a performing art, all the more so in an age of television, and few if any others in public life had Reagan's stage presence. Blessed with a baritone voice and a wealth of entertaining stories, he was a superb speaker who charmed audiences. Wealthy admirers convinced Reagan to run for governor of California in 1966, and he won by a landslide. As a two-term governor, Reagan displayed flexible practicality in working with Democrats in the state legislature.

THE RISE OF THE "NEW RIGHT"    By the eve of the 1980 election, Reagan had benefited from demographic developments that made his conservative vision of America a major asset. The 1980 census revealed that the proportion of the population over age sixty-five was soaring and moving from the Midwest and the Northeast to the sunbelt states of the South and the West. Fully 90 percent of the nation's total population growth during the eighties occurred in southern or western states. These population shifts forced a massive redistricting of the House of Representatives, with Florida, California, and Texas gaining seats and northern states such as New York losing them. The sunbelt states were attractive not only because of their mild climate; they also had the lowest tax rates in the nation, the highest rates of economic growth, and growing numbers of evangelical Christians and retirees. Such attributes also made the sunbelt states fertile ground for the Republican party. This dual development—an increase in the number of senior citizens and the steady relocation of a significant portion of the population to conservative regions of the country, where hostility to "big government" was deeply rooted—meant that demographics were carrying the United States toward Reagan's conservative political philosophy.

A related development during the seventies was a burgeoning tax revolt that swept across the nation as a result of the prolonged inflationary spiral. Inflation increased home values, which in turn brought a dramatic spike in property taxes. In California, Reagan's home state, voters organized a massive grassroots taxpayer revolt. Skyrocketing property taxes threatened to force many working-class people from their homes. The solution? Cut back on the size and cost of government to enable reductions in property taxes. In June 1978, tax rebels in California, with Reagan's support, succeeded in getting Proposition 13 on the state ballot. An overwhelming majority of voters—both Republicans and Democrats—approved the measure, which slashed property taxes by 57 percent and amended the state constitution to make raising taxes much more difficult. The tax revolt in California soon spread across the nation as other states passed measures similar to California. The *New York Times* compared the phenomenon to a "modern Boston Tea Party."

THE MORAL MAJORITY    The tax revolt fed into a national conservative resurgence that benefited from a massive revival of evangelical religion whose leaders sought to influence social and political change at the local and national levels. By the eighties, religious conservatism was no longer a local or provincial phenomenon. Catholic conservatives and Protestant evangelicals now owned television and radio stations, operated numerous schools and universities, and organized "mega-churches" in the sprawling suburbs, where they served as animating centers of social activity and spiritual life. A survey in 1977 revealed that more than 50 million Americans described themselves as "born-again Christians." And religious conservatives formed the strongest grassroots movement of the late twentieth century. During the seventies and eighties, they launched a cultural crusade against the forces of secularism and liberalism.

The Reverend Jerry Falwell's **Moral Majority** (later renamed the Liberty Alliance), formed in 1979, expressed the major political and social goals of the religious right wing: the economy should operate without "interference" by the government, which should be reduced in size; the Supreme Court decision in *Roe v. Wade* (1973) legalizing abortion should be reversed; Darwinian evolution should be replaced in school textbooks by the biblical story of creation; prayer should be allowed back in public schools; women should submit to their husbands; and Soviet communism should be opposed as a form of pagan totalitarianism. Falwell, the "televangelist" minister of a huge Baptist church in Lynchburg, Virginia, stressed that the Moral Majority was not a religious fellowship; it was a purely political organization open to conservatives of all faiths. "If you would like to know where I am politically," Falwell told reporters, "I am to the right of wherever you are. I thought [Barry] Goldwater was too liberal." The moralistic zeal and financial resources of the religious right made its adherents formidable opponents of liberal political candidates and programs. Falwell's Moral Majority recruited over 4 million members in eighteen states. Its base of support was in the South and was strongest among Baptists, but its appeal extended across the country. As Falwell declared, the Moral Majority was "pro-life, pro-family, pro-morality, and pro-American." But Falwell's cultural crusade also outraged many Americans. "Rarely has an organization set so many teeth on edge so rapidly," reported *Time* magazine. Democratic leader George S. McGovern called Falwell a "menace to the American political process."

A curiosity of the 1980 presidential campaign was that the religious right opposed Jimmy Carter, a self-professed "born-again" Baptist Sunday school teacher, and supported Ronald Reagan, a man who, like Dwight D. Eisenhower, rarely attended church. Reagan's divorce and remarriage, once an almost automatic disqualification for the presidency, raised little notice. Nor did the fact that as California's governor he had signed one of the most permissive abortion laws in the country. That Ronald Reagan became the messiah of the religious right was a tribute both to the force of social issues and to the candidate's political skills. Although famous for his personal piety, Carter lost the support of religious conservatives because he failed to promote their key social issues. He was not willing to ban abortions or restore daily prayers in public schools. His support for state ratification of the equal-rights amendment (ERA), passed by the Congress in 1972, also lost him votes among religious conservatives.

ANTI-FEMINIST BACKLASH    Another factor contributing to the conservative resurgence was a well-organized and well-financed backlash against the feminist movement. During the seventies, women who opposed the social goals of feminism formed counter organizations with names like Women Who Want to Be Women and Females Opposed to Equality. Spearheading those efforts was **Phyllis Schlafly**, a conservative Roman Catholic attorney and Republican activist from Alton, Illinois, who had played a key role in Barry Goldwater's 1964 presidential campaign. Schlafly led the successful campaign to keep the ERA amendment from being ratified by the required thirty-eight states. In the process, she became the galvanizing force behind a growing anti-feminist movement. Schlafly dismissed feminists as a "bunch of bitter women seeking a constitutional cure for their personal problems." Feminists, she claimed, were "anti-family, anti-children, and pro-abortion" fanatics who viewed the "home as a prison and the wife and mother as a slave." They were determined to "replace the image of woman as virtue and mother with the image of prostitute, swinger, and lesbian."

Schlafly's STOP (Stop Taking Our Privileges) ERA organization, founded in 1972, warned that the ERA would allow husbands to abandon wives without any financial support, force women into military service, and give gay "perverts" the right to marry. She and others also stressed that the sexual equality provided by the proposed amendment violated biblical teachings about women's God-given roles as nurturer and helpmate. By the late seventies, the effort to gain ratification of the ERA, although endorsed by First Lady Betty Ford, had failed, largely because no states in the conservative South and West ("Sunbelt") voted in favor of the amendment.

Many of Schlafly's supporters in the anti-ERA campaign also participated in the mushrooming anti-abortion, or "pro-life," movement. By 1980 more than a million legal abortions were occurring each year. To many

**Anti-abortion movement**

Anti-abortion demonstrators pass the Washington Monument on their way to the Capitol.

religious conservatives, this constituted infanticide. The National Right to Life Committee, supported by the National Conference of Catholic Bishops, boasted 11 million members representing most religious denominations. The intensity of the anti-abortion movement made it a powerful political force in its own right, and the Reagan campaign was quick to highlight its own support for traditional "family values," gender roles, and the "rights" of the unborn. Such combustible cultural issues helped persuade many northern Democrats—mostly working-class Catholics—to switch parties and support Reagan. White evangelicals alienated by the increasingly liberal social agenda of the Democratic party became a crucial element in Reagan's electoral strategy.

PROMOTING CONSERVATIVE IDEAS    Throughout the seventies, the business community also had become a source of conservative activism. In 1972, the leaders of the nation's largest corporations formed the Business Roundtable to promote business interests in Congress. Within a few years, many of those same corporations had formed political action committees (PACs) to distribute campaign contributions to pro-business political candidates. Corporate donations also helped spawn an array of conservative think tanks, such as the Heritage Foundation, founded in 1973 by the conservative business titan Joseph Coors. By 1980, the national conservative insurgency had coalesced into a powerful political force with substantial financial resources, carefully articulated ideas, and grassroots energy, all of which helped to fuel Ronald Reagan's presidential victory.

## REAGAN'S FIRST TERM

The American presidency is a drama of diversity. Presidents with very different personalities and temperaments have been successful in their own ways. Ronald Reagan was quite different from Jimmy Carter. Where Carter was a technocratic engineer by inclination and training, a compulsive micro-manager with an analytical mind who was unable to inspire his party or the public, Reagan was a principled pragmatist, a gracious, humble visionary, and a cheerful conservative uninterested in the details and complexities of issues but with a clear blueprint for what he wanted to accomplish. He was America's oldest president as well as the only one to have gone through a divorce. He was also a bundle of contradictions. A captivating speaker and genial conversationalist with a charming ability to work a crowd and dazzle a large audience, he was at heart a loner. A complex man who appeared simple, he trusted his instincts more than his advisers, and he delegated to staffers extraordinary freedom and responsibility (sometimes giving them too much authority). Reagan's opponents always underestimated him. True, the new president was not intellectually curious or especially knowledgeable about public policy (his devoted speechwriter once said Reagan's mind was "barren terrain"); he thought more anecdotally than analytically; he preferred hearing (or telling) a story than reading a book or a briefing paper. But he helped Americans believe in themselves again, and that was worth a lot more than being a know-it-all president. Reagan was neither brilliant nor sophisticated, but he was blessed with keen insight, reliable intuition, and far more energy than his critics admitted. And most of all he was sincere and down to earth. In 1980, a taxi driver explained that he voted for Reagan because "he's the only politician I can understand."

Reagan succeeded where Carter failed for three main reasons. First, he fastened with stubborn certitude on a few essential priorities (lower tax rates, a reduced federal government, increased military spending, and an aggressive anti-Soviet foreign policy); he knew what he wanted to accomplish and steadfastly pursued his primary goals with dogged consistency. In 1979, an aide had asked Reagan about his view of the cold war. Reagan replied that he was not interested in containing communism; he wanted to defeat it. His old-fashioned logic was quite simple: "We win. They lose." Second, unlike Carter, Reagan was adept at tactical compromises and legislative maneuvering with congressional leaders as well as foreign heads of state. James Wright, a seasoned Texas Democrat who served as the majority leader in the House of Representatives, said that he stood "in awe" of Reagan's "political skill. I am not sure that I have seen its equal." As a former union leader, Reagan was a masterful negotiator willing to modify his positions on some issues while sustaining his overarching goals. Reagan once told a journalist visiting the White House that "die-hard conservatives thought that if I couldn't get everything I asked for, I should jump off a cliff with the flag flying—go down in flames. No, if I can get 70 or 80 percent of what it is I am trying to get, yes I'll take that and then continue to try to get the rest in the future." Third, Reagan had the gift of inspiration. His infectious optimism inspired Americans with a sense of common purpose and a revived faith in the American spirit.

REAGANOMICS   As the nation's fortieth president, Ronald Reagan first had to survive an attempted assassination. On March 30, 1981, a young man eager for notoriety fired six shots at the president, one of which punctured a lung and lodged near his heart. The witty Reagan told doctors as they prepared for surgery: "Please tell me you're Republicans." Reagan's gritty response to the assassination and his injuries created an outpouring of public support.

Reagan inherited an America suffering from what Jimmy Carter had called a "crisis of confidence." The economy was in a shambles: the annual rate of inflation had reached 13 percent and unemployment hovered at 7.5 percent. At the same time, the cold war was heating up. The Soviet Union had just invaded Afghanistan. None of this fazed Reagan, however. He brought to Washington a cheerful conservative philosophy embodied in a simple message: "Government is not the solution to our problem," he insisted, "government is the problem." He credited President Calvin Coolidge's Treasury secretary, Andrew W. Mellon, with demonstrating in the twenties that by reducing taxes and easing government regulation of business, free-market capitalism would spur economic growth that would produce *more* government revenues, which in turn would help reduce the budget deficit. On August 1, 1981, the president signed the Economic Recovery Tax Act, which cut personal income taxes by

**Reaganomics**

Demonstrators in Ohio rail against the effects of Reaganomics, protesting an economics package that sacrificed funding in areas such as Social Security.

25 percent, lowered the maximum rate from 70 to 50 percent for 1982, and offered a broad array of other tax concessions.

BUDGET CUTS  David Stockman, Reagan's budget director, assumed responsibility for the president's efforts to reduce federal spending on various domestic programs. Liberal Democrats howled at Reagan's efforts to dismantle welfare programs. A year after taking office, Reagan explained in his diary that the "press is trying to paint me as trying to undo the New Deal. I remind them that I voted for FDR four times." But he added that he was determined "to undo the Great Society [launched by Lyndon Johnson]. It was LBJ's war on poverty that led us to our present mess." Despite intense rhetoric on both sides, the Reagan "cutbacks" in social programs were in fact reductions in the rate of growth that the Carter administration had approved. Overall federal spending for all social programs in 1982 was $53 billion *higher* than in 1980. But because that was $35 billion less than Carter wanted to spend, critics skewered Reagan for reducing the dollars spent for education and cultural programs, public housing, food stamps, and school lunches. Liberal groups cried foul. "The impact of the Reagan cuts on minority groups is likely to be severe," said a front-page story in the *Washington Post*. The

Democratic speaker of the house, Tip O'Neill, declared that the new president "has no concern, no regard, no care for the little man in America." Reagan responded that he remained committed to maintaining the "safety net" of government services for the "truly needy." Reagan was true to his word. Government subsidies to help poor people buy groceries ("food stamps") were cut only 4 percent from what the Carter administration had planned to spend, about $100 million out of a total budget of $11.4 billion.

David Stockman realized that the cuts in domestic spending had fallen far short of what would be needed to balance the budget in four years, as Reagan had promised. The president, he said, was "too kind, gentle, and sentimental" to make the necessary cuts. Massive increases in military spending complicated the situation. In the summer of 1981, Stockman warned Reagan and his top aides that "we're heading for a crash landing on the budget. We're facing potential deficit numbers so big that they could wreck the president's entire economic program."

Stockman was right. The soaring budget deficit, which triggered the worst economic recession since the thirties, was Reagan's greatest failure. Aides finally convinced the president that the government needed "revenue enhancements," a euphemism for tax increases. With Reagan's support, Congress passed a new tax bill in 1982 that would raise almost $100 billion, but the economic slump persisted through 1982, with unemployment standing at 10.4 percent. In early 1983, thirty states had double-digit rates of unemployment. By the summer of 1983, however, a major economic recovery was under way, in part because of increased government spending and lower interest rates and in part because of lower tax rates. But the federal deficits had grown ever larger, so much so that the president, who in 1980 had pledged to balance the federal budget by 1983, had in fact run up debts larger than those of all his predecessors combined. Yet Congress was in part responsible for the deficits. Legislators consistently approved budgets that were higher than those the president requested. Reagan was willing to tolerate growing budget deficits in part because he believed that they would force more responsible spending behavior in Congress and in part because he was so committed to increased military spending.

CONFLICTS OF INTEREST    The Reagan administration paralleled the Harding administration in finding itself embroiled in charges of conflict of interest, ethical misconduct, and actual criminal behavior. For example, Reagan showed an awful ignorance of and willful disdain about environmental issues. Public outcry forced the administrator of the Environmental

Protection Agency (EPA) to resign for granting favors to industrial polluters. Although some two hundred Reagan appointees were accused of unethical or illegal activities, the president himself remained untouched by any hint of impropriety. His personal charisma and aloof managerial style shielded him from the political fallout associated with the growing scandals and conflicts of interest involving his aides and cronies.

REAGAN'S ANTI-LIBERALISM   During Reagan's presidency, organized labor suffered severe setbacks, despite the fact that he himself had been a union leader. In 1981 Reagan fired members of the Professional Air Traffic Controllers Organization who had participated in an illegal strike intended to shut down air travel. Even more important, Reagan's smashing electoral victories in 1980 and 1984 broke the political power of the American Federation of Labor–Congress of Industrial Organizations (AFL-CIO), the powerful national confederation of labor unions that had traditionally supported Democratic candidates. His criticism of unions reflected a general trend in public opinion. Although record numbers of new jobs were created during the eighties, union membership steadily dropped. By 1987, unions represented only 17 percent of the nation's full-time workers, down from 24 percent in 1979.

Reagan also went on the offensive against feminism. Echoing Phyllis Schlafly, he opposed the ERA, abortion, and proposals to require equal pay for jobs of comparable worth. He did name Sandra Day O'Connor as the first woman Supreme Court justice, but critics labeled it a token gesture rather than a reflection of any genuine commitment to gender equality. Reagan also cut funds for civil rights enforcement and the Equal Employment Opportunity Commission, and he opposed renewal of the Voting Rights Act of 1965 before being overruled by Congress.

A MASSIVE DEFENSE BUILDUP   Reagan's conduct of foreign policy reflected his belief that trouble in the world stemmed mainly from Moscow, the capital of what he called the "evil empire." The Soviets, he charged, were "prepared to commit any crime, to lie, to cheat" and do anything necessary to promote world communism. Reagan had long believed that former Republican presidents Nixon and Ford—following the advice of Henry Kissinger—had been too soft on the Soviets. Kissinger's emphasis on détente, he said, had been a "one-way street" favoring the Soviets. To thwart the advance of Soviet communism, Reagan developed a strategy to exert constant economic and public pressure on the Soviets. He wanted to reduce the risk of nuclear war by convincing the Soviets they could not win such a conflict. To do so, he and Secretary of Defense Caspar Weinberger embarked upon a major buildup of nuclear and conventional weapons. Reagan also hoped that forcing the Soviets to spend much more on their own military budgets would bankrupt their economy and thereby implode the communist system. So in stark contrast to his efforts to cut back on government spending for social programs, Reagan gave the Pentagon a blank check, saying "spend what you need." To critics who complained about the enormous sums of money being spent on U.S. weapons systems, Reagan replied that "It will break the Soviets first." It did.

In 1983, Reagan escalated the nuclear arms race by authorizing the Defense Department to develop a controversial Strategic Defense Initiative (SDI) to construct a complex anti-missile defense system in outer space that would "intercept and destroy" Soviet missiles in flight. SDI was the most expensive defense system ever devised. Despite skepticism among the media, many scientists, and the secretaries of defense and state that such a "Star Wars" defense system could be built, the new program forced the Soviets to launch an expensive research and development effort of their own to keep

**Strategic Defense Initiative**

President Reagan addresses the nation on March 23, 1983, about the development of a space-age shield to intercept Soviet missiles.

pace. Over the course of Reagan's two presidential terms, defense spending totaled nearly $2 trillion.

Reagan's anti-Soviet strategy involved more than accelerated military spending. He borrowed the rhetoric of Harry S. Truman, John Foster Dulles, and John F. Kennedy to express American resolve in the face of "Communist aggression anywhere in the world." Détente deteriorated even further when the Soviets imposed martial law in Poland during the winter of 1981. The crackdown came after Polish workers, united under the banner of an independent union called Solidarity, challenged the Communist monopoly of power. As with the Soviet interventions in Hungary in 1956 and Czechoslovakia in 1968, the United States could not intervene in Poland. But Reagan forcefully protested the crackdown in Poland and imposed economic sanctions against Poland's Communist government. He also worked behind the scenes to support the Solidarity movement.

THE AMERICAS   Reagan's foremost international concern, however, was in Central America, where he detected the most serious Communist threat. The tiny nation of El Salvador, caught up since 1980 in a brutal struggle between Communist-supported revolutionaries and right-wing militants, received U.S. economic and military assistance. Critics argued that U.S. involvement ensured that the revolutionary forces would gain public support by capitalizing on "anti-Yankee" sentiment. Supporters countered that allowing a Communist victory in El Salvador would lead all of Central America to enter the Communist camp (a new "domino" theory). By 1984, however, the U.S.-backed government of President José Napoleón Duarte had brought a modicum of stability to El Salvador.

Even more troubling to Reagan was the situation in Nicaragua. The State Department claimed that the Cuban-sponsored Sandinista socialist government, which had seized power in 1979 after ousting a corrupt dictator, was sending Soviet and Cuban arms to leftist Salvadoran rebels. In response, the Reagan administration ordered the CIA to train and supply anti-Communist Nicaraguans, tagged **Contras** (short for counterrevolutionaries), who staged attacks on Sandinista bases from sanctuaries in Honduras. In supporting these "freedom fighters," Reagan sought not only to impede the traffic in arms to Salvadoran rebels but also to replace the Sandinistas with a democratic government.

Critics of Reagan's anti-Sandinista policy accused the Contras of being mostly right-wing fanatics who indiscriminately killed civilians as well as Sandinista soldiers. They also feared that the United States might eventually commit its own combat forces, thereby precipitating a Vietnam-like intervention.

**"Shhhh. It's Top Secret."**

A comment on the Reagan administration's covert operations in Nicaragua.

Reagan warned that if the Communists prevailed in Central America, "our credibility would collapse, our alliances would crumble, and the safety of our homeland would be jeopardized."

THE MIDDLE EAST    The Middle East remained a tinderbox of conflict during the eighties. No peaceable end seemed possible in the prolonged bloody Iran-Iraq War, entangled as it was with the passions of Islamic fundamentalism. In 1984, both sides began to attack tankers in the Persian Gulf, a major source of the world's oil. (The main international response was the sale of arms to both sides.) Nor was any settlement in sight in Afghanistan, where the Soviet occupation forces had bogged down as badly as the Americans had in Vietnam.

American presidents, both Democratic and Republican, continued to see Israel as the strongest and most reliable ally in the volatile region, all the while seeking to encourage moderate Arab groups. But the forces of moderation were dealt a blow during the mid-seventies when Lebanon, long an enclave of peace despite its ethnic complexity, collapsed into an anarchy of warring groups. The capital, Beirut, became a battleground for Sunni and

Shiite Muslims, the Druze, the Palestine Liberation Organization (PLO), Arab Christians, Syrian invaders cast as peacekeepers, and Israelis responding to PLO attacks across the border.

In 1982, Israeli forces pushed the PLO from southern Lebanon and then began shelling PLO strongholds in Beirut. Israeli troops moved into Beirut and looked the other way when Christian militiamen slaughtered Muslim women and children in Palestinian refugee camps. French, Italian, and U.S. forces then moved into Lebanon as "peacekeepers," but in such small numbers as to become targets themselves. Angry Muslims kept them constantly harassed. American warships and planes responded by shelling and bombing Muslim positions in the highlands behind Beirut, thereby increasing Muslim resentment. On October 23, 1983, an Islamic suicide bomber drove a truck laden with explosives into the U.S. Marine headquarters at the Beirut airport; the explosion left 241 Americans dead. In early 1984, Reagan announced that the marines would be "redeployed" to warships offshore. The Israeli forces pulled back to southern Lebanon, while the Syrians remained in eastern Lebanon. Bloody anarchy remained a way of life in a formerly peaceful country. The Reagan administration had blundered as badly in Lebanon as Carter had in Iran.

GRENADA    Fortune, as it happened, presented Reagan the chance for an easy triumph closer to home. On the tiny Caribbean island of Grenada, a former British colony and the smallest independent country in the Western Hemisphere, a leftist government had recruited Cuban workers to build a new airfield and signed military agreements with Communist countries. In 1983, an even more radical military council seized power. Appeals from the governments of neighboring island nations led Reagan to order 1,900 marines to invade Grenada, depose the new government, and evacuate a small group of American students enrolled in medical school. The UN General Assembly condemned the action, but it was popular among Grenadans and in the United States. Although a lopsided affair, the decisive action served notice to Latin American revolutionaries that Reagan might use military force elsewhere in the region.

## REAGAN'S SECOND TERM

By 1983, prosperity had returned, and Reagan's "supply-side" economic program was at last working as touted—except for growing budget deficits. Reagan's decision to remove government price controls on oil and natural gas as well as his efforts to pressure Saudi Arabia to increase oil production produced a decline in energy prices that helped to stimulate economic growth.

THE ELECTION OF 1984    By 1984, Reagan had restored strength and vitality to the White House and the nation. Reporters began to speak of the "Reagan Revolution." The economy surged with new energy. The slogan at the Republican Convention was "America is back and standing tall." By contrast, the nominee of the Democrats, former vice president Walter Mondale, struggled to mold a competing vision. Endorsed by the AFL-CIO, the National Organization for Women (NOW), and many prominent African Americans, Mondale was viewed as the candidate of liberal special interest groups. He set a precedent by choosing as his running mate New York representative Geraldine Ferraro, who was quickly placed on the defensive by the need to explain her spouse's complicated business dealings.

A fit of frankness in Mondale's acceptance speech further complicated his campaign. "Mr. Reagan will raise taxes, and so will I," he told the convention. "He won't tell you. I just did." Reagan responded by vowing never to approve a tax increase and by chiding Mondale for his commitment to tax increases. Reagan also repeated a theme he had used in his campaign against Jimmy Carter: the future according to Mondale and the Democrats was "dark and getting darker." His vision of America's future, however, was bright, buoyed by optimism and hope. Mondale never caught up. In the end, Reagan took 59 percent of the popular vote and lost only Minnesota and the District of Columbia.

DOMESTIC CHALLENGES    Buoyed by his overwhelming victory, Reagan called for "a Second American Revolution of hope and opportunity." He dared Democrats in Congress to raise taxes; his veto pen was ready: "Go ahead and make my day," he said in an echo of a popular line from a Clint Eastwood movie. Through much of 1985, the president drummed up support for a tax-simplification plan. After vigorous debate that ran nearly two years, Congress passed, and in 1986 the president signed, a comprehensive Tax Reform Act. The new measure reduced the number of federal tax brackets from fourteen to two and reduced rates from the maximum of 50 percent to 15 and 28 percent—the lowest since Calvin Coolidge was president.

THE IRAN-CONTRA AFFAIR    But Reagan's second term as president was not the triumph he and his supporters expected. During the fall of 1986, Democrats regained control of the Senate by 55 to 45. The Democrats picked up only 6 seats in the House, but they increased their already comfortable margin to 259 to 176. For his last two years as president, Reagan would face an opposition Congress.

What was worse, reports surfaced in late 1986 that the United States had been secretly selling arms to Iran in the hope of securing the release of American hostages held in Lebanon by extremist groups sympathetic to Iran. Such action contradicted Reagan's repeated insistence that his administration would never negotiate with terrorists. The disclosures angered America's allies as well as many Americans who vividly remembered the 1979 Iranian takeover of their country's embassy in Tehran.

There was even more to the sordid story. Over the next several months, revelations reminiscent of the Watergate affair disclosed a complicated series of covert activities carried out by administration officials. At the center of what came to be called the **Iran-Contra affair** was the much-decorated marine lieutenant colonel Oliver North. A swashbuckling aide to the National Security Council who specialized in counterterrorism, North, from the basement of the White House, had been secretly selling military supplies to Iran and using the money to subsidize the Contra rebels fighting in Nicaragua at a time when Congress had voted to ban such aid.

Oliver North's illegal activities, it turned out, had been approved by national security adviser Robert McFarlane; McFarlane's successor, Admiral John Poindexter; and CIA director William Casey. Both Secretary of State George Shultz and Secretary of Defense Caspar Weinberger criticized the arms sale to Iran, but their objections were ignored, and they were thereafter kept in the dark about what was going on. Later, on three occasions, Shultz threatened to resign over the continuing operation of the "pathetic" scheme. After information about the secret (and illegal) dealings surfaced in the press, McFarlane attempted suicide, Poindexter resigned, and North was fired. Casey, who denied any connection, left the CIA for health reasons and died shortly thereafter from a brain tumor.

Under increasing criticism, Reagan appointed both an independent counsel and a three-man commission, led by former Republican senator John Tower, to investigate the scandal. The Tower Commission issued a devastating report early in 1987 that placed much of the responsibility for the bungled Iran-Contra affair on Reagan's loose management style. During the spring and summer of 1987, a joint House-Senate investigating committee began holding hearings into the Iran-Contra affair. The televised sessions revealed a tangled web of inept financial and diplomatic transactions, the shredding of incriminating government documents, crass profiteering, and misguided patriotism.

**The Iran-Contra affair**

National security adviser Robert McFarlane (left) tells reporters about his resignation. Vice Admiral John Poindexter (far right) succeeds him in the post.

The investigations of the independent counsel led to six indictments in 1988. A Washington jury found Oliver North guilty of three relatively minor charges but innocent of nine more serious counts, apparently reflecting the jury's reasoning that he acted as an agent of higher-ups. His conviction was later overturned on appeal. Of those involved in the affair, only John Poindexter got a jail sentence—six months for his conviction on five felony counts of obstructing justice and lying to Congress.

TURMOIL IN CENTRAL AMERICA    The Iran-Contra affair showed the lengths to which members of the Reagan administration would go to support the rebels fighting the ruling Sandinistas in Nicaragua. Fearing heightened Soviet and U.S. involvement in Central America, neighboring countries during the mid-eighties pressed for a negotiated settlement to the unrest in Nicaragua. In 1988, Daniel Ortega, the Nicaraguan president, pledged to negotiate directly with the Contra rebels. In the spring of 1988, those negotiations produced a cease-fire agreement, ending nearly seven years of fighting in Nicaragua. Secretary of State George Shultz called the pact an "important step forward," but the settlement surprised and disappointed hard-liners within the Reagan administration, who saw in it a Contra surrender. The Contra leaders themselves, aware of the eroding support for their cause in the U.S. Congress, saw the truce as their only chance for tangible concessions such as amnesty for political prisoners, the return of the Contras from exile, and "unrestricted freedom of expression."

In neighboring El Salvador, meanwhile, the Reagan administration's attempt to shore up the centrist government of José Napoleón Duarte through economic and military aid suffered a setback when the far-right ARENA party scored an upset victory at the polls during the spring of 1988.

## THE CHANGING SOCIAL LANDSCAPE

During the eighties, profound changes transformed the tone and texture of American life. Women continued to enter the workforce in large numbers. In 1970, 38 percent of the workforce was male; by 1990 it was 45 percent. Women made their greatest gains in the skilled professions: medicine, dentistry, and law. The economy experienced a wrenching transformation in an effort to adapt to the shifting dynamics of an increasingly interconnected global marketplace. The nations that had been devastated by the Second World War—France, Germany, the Soviet Union, Japan, and China—by the eighties had developed formidable economies with higher levels of productivity than the United States. More and more American manufacturing companies shifted their production overseas, thereby accelerating the transition of the economy from its once-dominant industrial base to a more services-oriented economy. Driving all of these changes was the phenomenal impact of the computer revolution and the development of the Internet.

THE COMPUTER REVOLUTION The idea of a programmable machine that would rapidly perform mental tasks had been around since the eighteenth century, but it took the crisis of the Second World War to gather the intellectual and financial resources needed to create such a "computer." In 1946, a team of engineers at the University of Pennsylvania created ENIAC (electronic numerical integrator and computer), the first all-purpose, all-electronic digital computer.

The next major breakthrough was the invention in 1971 of the microprocessor—a tiny computer on a silicon chip. The functions that had once been performed by huge computers taking up an entire room could now be performed by a microchip circuit the size of a postage stamp. The

**The computer age**

Beginning with the cumbersome electronic numerical integrator and computer (ENIAC), pictured here in 1946, computer technology flourished, leading to the development of personal computers in the 1980s and the popularization of the Internet in the 1990s.

microchip made possible the personal computer. In 1975 an engineer named Ed Roberts developed the prototype of the so-called personal computer. The Altair 8800 was imperfect and cumbersome, with no display, no keyboard, and not enough memory to do anything useful. But its potential excited a Harvard sophomore named Bill Gates. He improved the software of the Altair 8800, dropped out of college, and formed a company called Microsoft to sell the new system. By 1977, Gates and others had helped transform the personal computer from a machine for hobbyists into a mass consumer product. The development of the Internet, electronic mail (e-mail), and cell-phone technology during the eighties and nineties allowed for instantaneous communication, thereby accelerating the globalization of the economy and dramatically increasing productivity in the workplace.

DEBT AND THE STOCK MARKET PLUNGE    In the late seventies, Jimmy Carter had urged Americans to lead simpler lives, cut back on conspicuous consumption, reduce energy use, and invest more time in faith and family. During the eighties, Ronald Reagan promoted very different behavior: he reduced tax rates so people would have more money to spend. Americans preferred Reagan's emphasis on prosperity rather than frugality, for it endorsed entrepreneurship as well as an increasingly consumption-oriented and hedonistic leisure culture. But Reagan succeeded too well in shifting the public mood back to the "more is more," "bigger is better" tradition of heedless consumerism. During the "Age of Reagan," marketers and advertisers celebrated instant gratification at the expense of the future. Michelob beer commercials began assuring Americans that "you can have it all," and many consumers went on a self-indulgent spending spree. The more they bought the more they wanted. In 1984, Hollywood producers launched a new TV show called *Lifestyles of the Rich and Famous* that exemplified the decade's runaway materialism. As the stock market soared, the number of multi-millionaires working on Wall Street and in the financial industry mushroomed. The money fever was contagious. Compulsive shoppers donned T-shirts proclaiming: "Born to Shop." By 1988, 110 million Americans had an average of seven credit cards each. In the hit movie *Wall Street* (1987), the high-flying land developer and corporate raider Gordon Gekko, played by actor Michael Douglas, announces that "greed . . . is good. Greed is right."

**Black Monday**

A frenzied trader calls for attention in the pit of the Chicago Board Options Exchange as the Dow Jones stock average loses over 500 points.

During the eighties, many Americans caught up in the materialism of the times began spending more money than they made. All kinds of debt—personal, corporate, and government—increased dramatically. Americans in the sixties had saved on average 10 percent of their income; in 1987 the figure was less than 4 percent. The federal debt more than tripled, from $908 billion in 1980 to $2.9 trillion at the end of the 1989 fiscal year. Then, on October 19, 1987, the bill collector suddenly arrived at the nation's doorstep. On that "Black Monday," the stock market experienced a tidal wave of selling reminiscent of the 1929 crash. The market plunge of 22.6 percent nearly doubled the record 12.8 percent fall on October 28, 1929. Wall Street's selling frenzy reverberated throughout the capitalist world, sending stock prices plummeting in Tokyo, London, Paris, and Toronto.

In the aftermath of the calamitous selling spree on Black Monday, fears of an impending recession led business leaders and economists to attack President Reagan for allowing such huge budget deficits. Within a few weeks, Reagan had agreed to work with Congress to develop a deficit-reduction package and for the first time indicated a willingness to include increased taxes in such a package. But the eventual compromise plan was so modest that it did little to restore investor confidence. As one Republican senator lamented, "There is a total lack of courage among those of us in the Congress to do what we all know has to be done."

## THE POOR, THE HOMELESS, AND THE VICTIMS OF AIDS

The eighties were years of vivid contrast. Despite unprecedented prosperity among the wealthiest Americans, there were growing numbers of underclass Americans bereft of hope: beggars in the streets and homeless people sleeping in doorways, in cardboard boxes, and on ventilation grates. Homelessness was the most acute social issue of the eighties. A variety of causes had led to a shortage of low-cost housing: the government had given up on building public housing; urban-renewal programs had demolished blighted areas but provided no housing for those they displaced; and owners had abandoned unprofitable buildings in poor neighborhoods or converted them into expensive condominiums, a process called gentrification. In addition, after new medications allowed for the deinstitutionalization of certain mentally ill patients, many of them ended up on the streets because the promised community mental-health services failed to materialize. Drug and alcohol abuse were rampant among the homeless, mostly unemployed single adults, a quarter of whom had spent time in mental institutions; some 40 percent had spent time in jail; a third

**AIDS Memorial Quilt**

Composed of more than 48,000 panels, the quilt commemorates those who have died of AIDS-related causes and continues to grow to this day.

were delusional. By the summer of 1988, the *New York Times* estimated, more than 45 percent of New York's adults constituted an underclass totally outside the labor force, because of a lack of skills, lack of motivation, drug abuse, and other problems.

Still another group of outcasts was composed of people suffering from a newly identified malady named AIDS (acquired immunodeficiency syndrome). At the beginning of the eighties, public health officials had reported that gay men and intravenous drug users were especially at risk for developing AIDS. People contracted the virus, HIV, by coming into contact with the blood or body fluids of an infected person. Those infected with the virus showed signs of extreme fatigue, developed a strange combination of infections, and soon died.

The Reagan administration showed little interest in AIDS in part because it was initially viewed as a "gay" disease. Patrick Buchanan, the conservative spokesman who served as Reagan's director of communications, said that homosexuals had "declared war on nature, and now nature is extracting an awful retribution." Buchanan and others convinced Reagan not to engage the **HIV/AIDS** issue.

By 2000, AIDS had claimed almost three hundred thousand American lives and was spreading among a larger segment of the population. Nearly 1 million Americans were carrying the deadly virus, and it had become the leading cause of death among men aged twenty-five to forty-four. The potential for the spread of HIV prompted the surgeon general to launch a controversial public-education program, which included encouraging "safe sex" through the use of condoms. With no prospect for a simple cure and with skyrocketing treatment costs, AIDS emerged as one of the nation's most intractable problems.

A HISTORIC TREATY   The most positive achievement at the end of Reagan's second term was a surprising arms-reduction agreement with the Soviet government. Under **Mikhail Gorbachev,** who came to power in 1985, the Soviets pursued renewed détente so that they could focus their energies and financial resources on pressing domestic problems. The logjam that had impeded arms negotiations suddenly broke in 1987, when Gorbachev announced that he was willing to consider mutually reducing nuclear weaponry. After nine months of strenuous negotiations, Reagan and Gor-bachev met amid much fanfare in Washington, D.C., on December 9, 1987, and signed a treaty to eliminate intermediate-range (300- to 3,000-mile) nuclear missiles. Gorbachev said that Reagan was "a serious man seeking serious reform. We are beginning to take down the barriers of the postwar era." How much of the credit for the treaty belonged to Reagan or to Gor-bachev remains a puzzle, but the result was profound.

The treaty marked the first time that the two nations had agreed to destroy a whole class of weapons systems. Under the terms of the treaty, the United States would destroy 859 missiles, and the Soviets would eliminate 1,752. Still, the reductions represented only 4 percent of the total nuclear-missile count on both sides. Arms-control advocates thus looked toward a second and more comprehensive treaty dealing with long-range strategic missiles.

Gorbachev's successful efforts to liberalize Soviet domestic life and improve East-West foreign relations cheered Americans. The Soviets sud-denly began stressing cooperation with the West in dealing with hot spots around the world. In the Middle East they urged the PLO to recognize Israel's right to exist and advocated a greater role for the United Nations in the volatile Persian Gulf. Perhaps the most dramatic symbol of a thawing cold

**Foreign relations**

A light moment at a meeting between U.S. president Ronald Reagan (left) and Soviet premier Mikhail Gorbachev (right).

war was the phased withdrawal of 115,000 Soviet troops from Afghanistan, which began in 1988, the final year of Reagan's presidency.

REAGAN'S LEGACY    Ronald Reagan was a transformational president. He restored the stature of the presidency and in the process transformed the tone and tenor of American political life. Politically, Reagan played the central role in accelerating the nation's shift toward conservatism and the Republican party. But he did not dismantle the welfare state; he fine-tuned it, in part because the Democrats controlled the House of Representatives throughout his presidency. Although Reagan had declared in 1981 his intention to "curb the size and influence of the federal establishment," the welfare state remained intact when he left office in early 1989. Neither the Social Security system nor Medicare had been dismantled or overhauled, nor had any other major welfare programs. And the federal agencies that Reagan had threatened to abolish, such as the Department of Education, not only survived but had seen their budgets grow. As Reagan acknowledged, a federal agency "is the nearest thing to eternal life we'll ever see on this earth." The federal budget as a percentage of economic output was higher when Reagan left office than when he had entered; the budget deficit when he retired was an all-time record, largely because of the massive increase in defense spending approved by Reagan. Moreover, he backed off his campaign promises directed at the religious right, such as reinstituting daily prayer in public schools and a ban on abortions.

What Ronald Reagan the genial conservative did accomplish was to end the prolonged period of economic "stagflation" and set in motion what economists called "The Great Expansion," an unprecedented twenty-year-long burst of productivity and prosperity. In the process, Reagan redefined the national political agenda and accelerated the grassroots conservative insurgency that had been developing for over twenty years. True, Reagan's pragmatic conservatism left the nation with a massive debt burden that would eventually cause major problems, and the prolonged prosperity served to widen the inequality gap between rich and poor, but the "Great Communicator" also renewed America's self-confidence and soaring sense of possibilities.

Reagan also helped end the cold war by negotiating the nuclear disarmament treaty and lighting the fuse of democratic freedom in Eastern Europe. In June 1987, he visited the Berlin Wall and in a dramatic speech called upon the Soviet Union to allow greater freedom within the Warsaw Pact countries under its control. "General Secretary Gorbachev, if you seek peace, if you seek prosperity for the Soviet Union and Eastern Europe, if you seek liberalization: Come here to this gate! Mr. Gorbachev, open this gate! Mr. Gorbachev, tear down this wall!" It was great theater and good politics. Through his policies and persistence, Reagan helped end communist control in East Germany, Hungary, Poland, and Czechoslovakia. By redirecting the thrust of both domestic and foreign policy during the eighties, Reagan put the fragmented Democratic party on the defensive and forced conventional New Deal "liberalism" into a panicked retreat. Reagan would cast a long shadow. He had fashioned the most consequential presidency since Franklin D. Roosevelt, the man he had voted for on four occasions.

THE ELECTION OF 1988 In 1988, eight Democratic presidential candidates engaged in a wild scramble for their party's nomination. As the primary season progressed, however, it soon became a two-man race between Massachusetts governor Michael Dukakis and Jesse Jackson, a charismatic African American civil rights activist who had been one of Martin Luther King Jr.'s chief lieutenants. Dukakis eventually won and managed a difficult reconciliation with the Jackson forces that left the Democrats unified and confident as the fall campaign began.

The Republicans nominated Reagan's two-term vice president, Texan **George H. W. Bush**, a government careerist who after a bumpy start had easily cast aside his rivals in the primaries. A veteran government official, having served as a Texas congressman, an envoy to China, an ambassador to the UN, and head of the CIA, Bush had none of Reagan's charisma or rhetorical skills. One Democrat described the wealthy Bush as a man born "with a silver foot in his mouth." Early polls showed Dukakis with a wide lead.

**The 1988 election**

George H. W. Bush (right) at the 1988 Republican National Convention with his newly chosen running mate, Dan Quayle, a senator from Indiana.

Yet Bush delivered a forceful address at the Republican nominating convention that sharply enhanced his stature. While pledging to continue the Reagan agenda, he also recognized that "things aren't perfect" in America. Bush was a centrist Republican who had never embraced the dogmatic assumptions of right-wing conservatism. He promised to use the White House to fight bigotry, illiteracy, and homelessness. Humane sympathies, he insisted, would guide his conservatism. "I want a kinder, gentler nation," Bush said in his acceptance speech. But the most memorable line in the speech was a defiant statement ruling out any tax increases as a means of dealing with the massive budget deficits created during the Reagan years. "The Congress will push me to raise taxes, and I'll say no, and they'll push, and I'll say no, and they'll push again. And I'll say to them: Read my lips. No new taxes."

In a not-so-kind-or-gentle campaign given over to mudslinging, Bush and his aides attacked Dukakis as a camouflaged liberal in the mold of George McGovern, Jimmy Carter, and Walter Mondale. In the end, Dukakis took only ten states plus the District of Columbia, with clusters of support in the Northeast, Midwest, and Northwest. Bush carried the rest, with a margin of about 54 percent to 46 percent in the popular vote and 426 to 111 in the Electoral College.

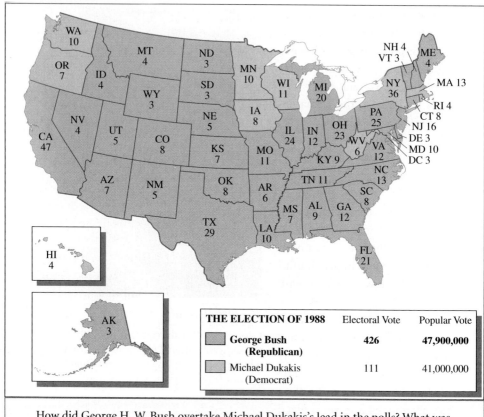

| THE ELECTION OF 1988 | Electoral Vote | Popular Vote |
|---|---|---|
| George Bush (Republican) | 426 | 47,900,000 |
| Michael Dukakis (Democrat) | 111 | 41,000,000 |

How did George H. W. Bush overtake Michael Dukakis's lead in the polls? What was the role of race and class in the election results?

Generally speaking, the more affluent and better-educated voters preferred the Republican ticket. While Dukakis won the urban areas, garnering 86 percent of the African American vote, Bush scored big in the suburbs and in rural areas, especially in the once-Democratic South, where his margin of support by white voters ranged from a low of 63 percent in Florida to a high of 80 percent in Mississippi. More significant was Bush's success among blue-collar workers: he captured 46 percent of these typically Democratic voters.

## THE BUSH ADMINISTRATION

George H. W. Bush viewed himself as a guardian president rather than an activist. He lacked Reagan's visionary outlook and seemed content to sustain Reagan's priorities. Bush was eager to avoid "stupid mistakes" and to find a way to get along with the Democratic majority in Congress. "We don't need to remake society," he announced. Bush therefore sought to consolidate the initiatives that Reagan had put in place rather than launch his own array of programs and policies.

DOMESTIC INITIATIVES   The biggest problem facing the Bush administration was the national debt, which stood at $2.6 trillion in 1989, nearly three times its 1980 level. Bush's pledge not to increase taxes (meaning mainly income taxes) and his insistence upon lowering capital-gains taxes—on profits from the sale of corporate stock and other property—made it more difficult to reduce the annual deficit or trim the long-term debt. Likewise, Bush was not willing to make substantial cutbacks in spending on defense, the federal bureaucracy, and welfare programs. As a result, by 1990 the country faced "a fiscal mess." During the summer of 1990, Bush agreed with Congressional Democrats "that both the size of the deficit problem and the need for a package that can be enacted" required budget cuts and "tax revenue increases," which he had sworn to avoid. The president's decision to support tax increases infuriated conservative organizations. They felt betrayed. The president of the Heritage Foundation, the leading conservative think tank in Washington, D.C., said that "our message" was being "sullied by a visionless White House pretending to be conservative." Bush's backsliding on taxes served to divide the conservative movement while unifying the Republican party (Reagan had unified both).

One of President Bush's few initiatives was a declaration of "war" on illegal drugs. During the eighties, cocaine addiction spread through sizable segments of society, luring not only the affluent but also those with little money to spare, who used the drug in its smokable form, known as crack. Bush vowed to make drug abuse his number-one domestic priority and appointed William J. Bennett, former education secretary, as "drug czar," or head of a new Office of National Drug Control Policy, with cabinet status but no department. Yet federal spending on programs intended to curb drug abuse rose only modestly. The message, on this as well as on education, housing, and other social problems, was that more of the burden should fall on state and local authorities.

THE DEMOCRACY MOVEMENT ABROAD   George H. W. Bush entered the White House with more foreign-policy experience than most presidents, and he found the spotlight of the world stage more congenial than wrestling with the intractable problems of the inner cities, drug abuse, and the deficit. Within two years of his inauguration, Bush would lead the United States into two wars. Throughout most of 1989, however, he merely had to sit back and observe the dissolution of one totalitarian or authoritarian regime after another around the world. For the first time in years, democracy was on the march in a sequence of mostly bloodless revolutions that surprised the world.

Although a grassroots democracy movement in communist China came to a tragic end in 1989 when government forces mounted a deadly assault on demonstrators in Beijing's Tiananmen Square, eastern Europe had an entirely different experience. With a rigid economic system failing to deliver the goods to the Soviet people, Mikhail Gorbachev responded with policies of *perestroika* (restructuring) and *glasnost* (openness), a loosening of centralized economic planning and censorship. His foreign policy sought rapprochement and trade with the West, and he aimed to relieve the Soviet economy of burdensome military costs.

Gorbachev also backed off from Soviet imperial ambitions. Early in 1989, Soviet troops left Afghanistan after spending nine years bogged down in civil war there. Gorbachev then repudiated the Brezhnev Doctrine, which had asserted the right of the Soviet Union to intervene in the internal affairs of other Communist countries. The days when Soviet tanks rolled through Warsaw and Prague were over, and hard-line leaders in the Eastern-bloc countries found themselves beset by demands for reform from their own people. With opposition strength building, the old regimes fell with surprisingly little bloodshed. Communist party rule ended first in Poland and Hungary, then in Czechoslovakia and Bulgaria. In Romania the year of peaceful revolution ended in a bloodbath when the people joined the army in a bloody uprising against the brutal dictator Nicolae Ceausescu. He and his wife were captured, tried, and then executed on Christmas Day.

The most spectacular event in the collapse of the Soviet Empire came on November 9, 1989, when Germans—using small tools and even their hands—tore down the chief symbol of the cold war, the Berlin Wall. The massive wall had long seemed impregnable and permanent, like the Cold War itself. With the barrier down, East Germans streamed across the border. As people celebrated in the streets, they were amazed, delighted, and moved to tears. With the borders to the West now fully open, the Communist government of East Germany collapsed, a freely elected government came to power, and on October 3, 1990, the five states of East Germany were united with West Germany. The unified German nation remained in NATO, and the Communist Warsaw Pact alliance was dissolved.

**Dissolution of the Soviet Empire**

West Germans hacking away at the Berlin Wall on November 11, 1989, two days after all crossings between East Germany and West Germany were opened.

The reform impulse that Gorbachev helped unleash in the Eastern-bloc countries careened out of control within the Soviet Union, however. Gorbachev proved unusually adept at political restructuring, yielding the Communist monopoly of government but building a new presidential system that gave him, if anything, increased powers. His political skills, though, did not extend to an antiquated economy that resisted change. The revival of ethnic allegiances added to the instability. Although Russia proper included slightly more than half the Soviet Union's population, it was only one of fifteen constituent republics, most of which began to seek autonomy, if not independence, from Russia.

Gorbachev's popularity shrank in the Soviet Union as it grew abroad. It especially eroded among the Communist hard-liners, who saw in his reforms the unraveling of their bureaucratic and political empire. Once the genie of freedom was released from the Communist lamp, however, it took on a momentum of its own. On August 18, 1991, political and military leaders tried to seize the reins of power in Russia. They accosted Gorbachev at his vacation retreat in the Crimea and demanded that he sign a decree

**Action against Gorbachev**

In August 1991, one day after Mikhail Gorbachev was placed under house arrest by Communists planning a coup, Russian president Boris Yeltsin (holding papers) makes a speech criticizing the plotters.

proclaiming a state of emergency and transferring his powers to them. He replied, "Go to hell," whereupon he was placed under house arrest.

The coup was doomed from the start, however. Poorly planned and clumsily implemented, it lacked effective coordination. The plotters failed to arrest popular leaders such as Boris Yeltsin, the president of the Russian republic; they neglected to close the airports or cut off telephone and television communications; and they were opposed by key elements of the military and KGB (the secret police). But most important, the plotters failed to recognize the strength of the democratic idealism unleashed by Gorbachev's reforms.

As the political drama unfolded in the Soviet Union, foreign leaders denounced the coup. On August 20, President Bush responded favorably to Yeltsin's request for support and persuaded other leaders to join him in refusing to recognize the legitimacy of the new Soviet government. The next day, word began to seep out that the plotters had given up and were fleeing. Several committed suicide, and a newly released Gorbachev ordered the others arrested. Yet things did not go back to the way they had been. Although

Gorbachev reclaimed the title of president of the Soviet Union, he was forced to resign as head of the Communist party and admit that he had made a grave mistake in appointing the men who had turned against him. Boris Yeltsin emerged as the most popular political figure in the country.

So what had begun as a reactionary coup turned into a powerful accelerant for stunning changes in the Soviet Union, or the "Soviet Disunion," as one wag termed it. Most of the fifteen republics proclaimed their independence, with the Baltic republics of Latvia, Lithuania, and Estonia regaining the status of independent nations. The Communist party apparatus was dismantled, prompting celebrating crowds to topple statues of Lenin and other Communist heroes.

A chastened Gorbachev could only acquiesce in the breakup of the Soviet Empire, whereas the systemic problems burdening the Soviet Union before the coup remained intractable. The economy was stagnant, food and coal shortages loomed on the horizon, and consumer goods remained scarce. The reformers had won, but they had yet to establish deep roots in a country with no democratic tradition. Leaping into the unknown, they faced years of hardship and uncertainty.

The aborted coup against Gorbachev also accelerated Soviet and American efforts to reduce their stockpiles of nuclear weapons. In late 1991, President Bush shocked the world by announcing that the United States would destroy all its tactical nuclear weapons on land and at sea in Europe and Asia, take its long-range bombers off twenty-four-hour-alert status, and initiate discussions with the Soviet Union for the purpose of instituting sharp cuts in missiles with multiple warheads. Bush explained that the prospect of a Soviet invasion of western Europe was "no longer a realistic threat," and this transformation provided an unprecedented opportunity for reducing the threat of nuclear holocaust. President Gorbachev responded by announcing reciprocal Soviet cutbacks.

PANAMA    The end of the cold war did not spell the end of international tensions and conflict, however. Indeed, before the end of 1989, U.S. troops were engaged in battle in Panama, where a petty tyrant provoked the first of America's military engagements under George H. W. Bush. In 1983, General Manuel Noriega had maneuvered himself into the position of leader of the Panamanian Defense Forces, which made him the de facto head of the government. Earlier, when Bush headed the CIA, Noriega, as chief of military intelligence, had developed a profitable business of supplying information on the region to the CIA. At the same time, he developed avenues in the region for drug smuggling and gunrunning, laundering the money from those activities through Panamanian banks. For a time, American intelligence analysts looked the other way, regarding Noriega as a useful contact, but eventually he became an embarrassment. In 1987 a rejected associate published charges of Noriega's drug activities and accused him further of rigged elections and political assassination.

In 1988, federal grand juries in Miami and Tampa indicted Noriega and fifteen others on drug smuggling charges. The next year the Panamanian president tried to fire Noriega, but the National Assembly ousted the president and named Noriega "maximum leader." The legislators then declared Panama "in a state of war" with the United States. The next day, December 16, 1989, a U.S. marine in Panama was killed. President Bush thereupon ordered an invasion of Panama with the purpose of capturing Noriega so that he might stand trial in the United States.

The twelve thousand U.S. military personnel already in Panama were quickly joined by twelve thousand more, and in the early morning of December 20 five military task forces struck at strategic targets in the country. Within hours, Noriega had surrendered. Twenty-three U.S. servicemen were killed in the action, and estimates of Panamanian casualties, including many civilians, were as high as four thousand. In April 1992, Noriega was convicted in the United States on eight counts of racketeering and drug distribution.

THE GULF WAR   Months after Panama had moved to the background of public attention, **Saddam Hussein**, dictator of Iraq, focused attention on the Middle East when his army suddenly invaded tiny Kuwait on August 2, 1990. Kuwait had raised its production of oil, contrary to agreements with the Organization of the Petroleum Exporting Countries (OPEC). The resulting drop in global oil prices offended the Iraqi regime, deep in debt and heavily dependent upon oil revenues. Saddam Hussein was surprised by the backlash his invasion of Kuwait caused. The UN Security Council unanimously condemned the invasion and demanded withdrawal. U.S. Secretary of State James A. Baker III and the Soviet foreign minister issued a joint statement of condemnation. On August 6 the Security Council endorsed Resolution 661, an embargo on trade with Iraq.

Bush condemned Iraq's "naked aggression" and dispatched planes and troops to Saudi Arabia on a "wholly defensive" mission: to protect Saudi Arabia. British forces soon joined in, as did Arab units from Egypt, Morocco, Syria, Oman, the United Arab Emirates, and Qatar. On August 22, Bush ordered the mobilization of American reserve forces for the operation, now dubbed **Operation Desert Shield**.

**The Gulf War**

U.S. soldiers adapt to desert conditions during Operation Desert Shield, December 1990.

A flurry of peace efforts sent diplomats scurrying, but without result. Iraq refused to yield. On January 12, Congress authorized the use of U.S. armed forces to "liberate" Kuwait. By January 1991, over thirty nations had joined Operation Desert Shield. Some nations sent only planes, warships, or support forces, but sixteen, including ten Islamic countries, committed ground forces. Desert Shield became **Operation Desert Storm** when the first allied cruise missiles began to hit Iraq on January 16.

Saddam Hussein, expecting an allied attack northward into Kuwait, concentrated his forces in that country. The Iraqis were outflanked when two hundred thousand allied troops, largely American, British, and French, turned up on the undefended Iraqi border with Saudi Arabia one hundred to two hundred miles to the west. The swift-moving allied ground assault began on February 24 and lasted only four days. Iraqi soldiers surrendered by the thousands.

On February 28, six weeks after the fighting began, President Bush called for a cease-fire, the Iraqis accepted, and the shooting ended. There were 137 American fatalities. The lowest estimate of Iraqi deaths, civilian and military, was 100,000. The coalition forces occupied about a fifth of Iraq, but Hussein's tyrannical regime remained intact. What came to be called the First Gulf War was thus a triumph without victory. Hussein had been defeated, but he was allowed to escape to foster more mischief. The consequences of the brief but intense First Gulf War, the "mother of all battles" in Saddam Hussein's words, would be played out in the future in ways that no one had predicted. Arabs humiliated by the American triumph over the Iraqis began plotting revenge that would spiral into a new war of terrorism.

## CULTURAL CONSERVATISM

Cultural conservatives helped elect Ronald Reagan and George Bush in the eighties, but they were disappointed with the results. Once in office, neither president had adequately addressed the moral agenda of the religious right, including a complete ban on abortions and the restoration of prayer in public schools. By the nineties, a new generation of young conservative activists, mostly political independents or Republicans and largely from the sunbelt states, had emerged as a major force in national affairs. They were more ideological, more libertarian, more partisan, more dogmatic, and more impatient than their predecessors. The new breed of cultural conservatives abhorred the excesses of social liberalism and the backsliding of RINOs (Republicans-in-Name-Only). They attacked affirmative-action programs designed to redress historic injustices committed against women and minorities. During the nineties, powerful groups inside and outside the Republican party mobilized to roll back government programs that gave preference to certain social groups. Prominent African American conservatives supported such efforts, arguing that racially based preferences were demeaning and condescending remedies for historical injustices.

THE RELIGIOUS RIGHT   Although quite diverse, cultural conservatives tended to be evangelical Christians or orthodox Catholics, and they joined together to exert increasing religious pressure on the political process. In 1989, the Virginia-based television evangelist Pat Robertson organized the Christian Coalition to replace Jerry Falwell's Moral Majority as the flagship organization of the resurgent religious right. The Christian Coalition chose the Republican party as the best vehicle for promoting its pro–school prayer, anti-abortion, and anti–gay rights positions. In addition to celebrating "traditional family values," it urged politicians to "radically downsize and delimit government." In many respects, the religious right took control of the political and social agendas in the nineties. As one journalist acknowledged in 1995, "the religious right is moving toward center stage in American secular life."

## CHAPTER SUMMARY

- **Rise of Conservatism** Ronald Reagan's charm, coupled with disillusionment over Jimmy Carter's presidency and the Republicans' call for a return to traditional values, won Reagan the presidency in 1980. The Republican insurgency, characterized by a cultural backlash against the feminist movement, was dominated by Christian evangelicals and people who wanted lower taxes and a smaller, less intrusive federal government.

- **Iran-Contra Scandal** During an Islamic revolution in Iran, enraged militants stormed the U.S. embassy in Tehran and seized American diplomats and staff members. In retaliation, President Carter froze all Iranian assets in the United States. Carter at last released several billion dollars in Iranian assets to ransom the hostages. The Iranians released the hostages—but not until Ronald Reagan was in office. Members of Reagan's administration secretly sold arms to Iran in the hopes of securing the release of American hostages held in Lebanon by extremists sympathetic to Iran. The deal contradicted the president's public claims that he would never deal with terrorists. Furthermore, profits from the arms sales were used to fund right-wing rebels in Nicaragua, known as Contras, despite Congress's having voted to ban any aid to the Contras. An independent commission appointed by the president determined that Reagan's loose management style was responsible for the illegal activities, and Reagan admitted that he had lied to the American people.

- **End of the Cold War** Toward the end of the century, democratic movements exploded in communist China, where they failed, and in Eastern Europe, where they largely succeeded. In the Soviet Union, Mikhail Gorbachev's steps to restructure the economy and promote more open policies led to demands for further reform. Communist party rule collapsed in the Soviet satellite states. In November 1989, the Berlin Wall was torn down, and a year later Germany was reunified. Russia itself survived a coup by hard-liners, and by 1991 the cold war had ended.

- **Reaganomics** Americans in the eighties experienced unprecedented prosperity, yet beggars and homeless people were visible in most cities. The prevailing mood was conservative, and AIDS was condemned as a "gay" disease. "Reaganomics" failed to reduce public spending, but the president nevertheless championed tax cuts for the rich. The result was massive public debt and the stock market collapse of 1987.

- **The Gulf War** Saddam Hussein of Iraq invaded Kuwait in 1990. The United Nations condemned Hussein's action and authorized the use of force to dislodge Iraq from Kuwait. Over thirty nations committed themselves to Operation Desert Shield. When Hussein did not withdraw, the allied forces launched Operation Desert Storm, and the Iraqis surrendered within six weeks.

# 34

## AMERICA IN A NEW MILLENNIUM

FOCUS QUESTIONS     Ⓢ   wwnorton.com/studyspace

- How did the demographics of the United States change between 1980 and 2010?
- What led to the Democratic resurgence of the early nineties and the surprising Republican landslide of 1994?
- What caused the surge and decline of the financial markets in the nineties and the early twenty-first century?
- What were the consequences of the rise of global terrorism in the early twenty-first century?
- In what ways was the 2008 presidential election historic?

The United States entered the final decade of the twentieth century triumphant. American vigilance in the cold war had contributed to the shocking collapse of the Soviet Union and the birth of democratic capitalism in eastern Europe. The United States was now the world's only superpower. Not since ancient Rome had one nation exercised such widespread influence, for good and for ill. By the mid-nineties, the American economy would become the marvel of the world as remarkable gains in productivity afforded by new technologies created the greatest period of prosperity in modern history. Yet no sooner did the century come to an end than America's sense of physical and material comfort was shattered by a horrifying terrorist assault that killed thousands, exacerbated the economic recession, and called into question conventional notions of national security and personal safety.

## AMERICA'S CHANGING MOSAIC

DEMOGRAPHIC SHIFTS   The nation's population had grown to over 309 million by 2010, and its racial and ethnic composition was rapidly changing. During the nineties, the foreign-born population increased by 57 percent, to 31 million, the largest ever, and far more than predicted. By 2010, the United States had more foreign-born and first-generation residents than ever before, and each year 1 million more immigrants arrived. Over 36 percent of Americans claimed African, Asian, Hispanic, or American Indian ancestry. Hispanics represented 16 percent of the total population, African Americans 11 percent, Asians about 4 percent, and American Indians almost 1 percent. The rate of increase among those four groups was twice as fast as it had been during the seventies. In 2005, Hispanics became the nation's largest minority group.

The primary cause of this dramatic change in the nation's ethnic mix was a surge of immigration. In 2000, the United States welcomed more than

**Illegal immigration**

Increasing numbers of Chinese risked their savings and their lives to gain entry to the United States. These illegal immigrants are trying to keep warm after being forced to swim ashore when the freighter carrying them to the United States ran aground near Rockaway Beach in New York City in June 1993.

twice as many immigrants as all other countries in the world combined. For the first time in the nation's history, the majority of immigrants came not from Europe but from other parts of the world: Asia, Latin America, and Africa. Among the legal immigrants, Mexicans made up the largest share, averaging over one hundred thousand a year. Many new immigrants compiled an astonishing record of achievement, yet their very success contributed to the resentment they encountered from other groups.

Other aspects of American life were also changing. The decline of the traditional family unit continued. In 2005, less than 65 percent of children lived with two parents, down from 85 percent in 1970. And more people were living alone than ever before, largely as a result of high divorce rates or a growing practice among young people of delaying marriage until well into their twenties. The number of single mothers increased 35 percent during the decade. The rate was much higher for African Americans: in 2000 fewer than 32 percent of black children lived with both parents, down from 67 percent in 1960.

Young African Americans in particular faced shrinking economic opportunities at the start of the twenty-first century. The urban poor more than others were victimized by high rates of crime and violence, with young black men suffering the most. In 2000, the leading cause of death among African American men between the ages of fifteen and twenty-four was homicide. Over 25 percent of African American men aged twenty to twenty-nine were in prison, on parole, or on probation, while only 4 percent were enrolled in college. And nearly 40 percent of African American men were functionally illiterate.

## BUSH TO CLINTON

The changing composition of American society would have a profound impact on politics. But during the last decade of the twentieth century, changing global dynamics held sway. For months after the First Gulf War in 1991, George H. W. Bush seemed unbeatable; his public approval rating soared to 91 percent. But the aftermath of Desert Storm was mixed, with Saddam Hussein's despotic grip on Iraq still intact. The Soviet Union meanwhile stumbled on to its surprising end. On December 25, 1991, the Soviet flag over the Kremlin was replaced by the flag of the Russian Federation. The cold war had ended with the dismemberment of the Soviet Union and its fifteen constituent republics. As a result, the United States had become the world's only dominant military power.

"Containment" of the Soviet Union, the bedrock of U.S. foreign policy for more than four decades, had become irrelevant. Bush struggled to interpret the fluid new international scene. He spoke of a "new world order" but never defined it. By his own admission he had trouble with "the vision thing." By the end of 1991, a listless Bush faced a strong challenge in the Republican primary from the feisty conservative commentator and former White House aide Patrick Buchanan, who adopted the slogan "America First" and called on Bush to "bring home the boys." As the euphoria of the Gulf War victory wore off, a popular bumper sticker reflected the growing public frustration with the economic policies of the Bush administration: "Saddam Hussein still has his job. What about you?"

RECESSION AND DOWNSIZING   For the Bush administration and for the nation, the most devastating development in the early nineties was a prolonged economic recession as the roller-coaster dynamic at the center of the capitalist system, continually counterbalancing periods of prosperity with periods of recession or depression, sent the economy plunging into the longest recession since the Great Depression. During 1991, 25 million workers—about 20 percent of the labor force—were unemployed at some point. The economy barely grew at all during the first three years of the Bush administration—the worst record since the end of the Second World War. Meanwhile, the federal budget deficit mushroomed by 57 percent, to $4.1 trillion. The euphoria over the allied victory in the Gulf War quickly gave way to surly anxiety generated by the depressed economy. At the end of 1991, *Time* magazine declared that "no one, not even George Bush" could deny "that the economy was sputtering." In addressing the recession, Bush tried a clumsy balancing act, on the one hand acknowledging that "people are hurting" while on the other telling Americans that "this is a good time to buy a car." By 1991, the public approval rating of his economic policy had plummeted to 18 percent.

REPUBLICAN TURMOIL   President Bush had already set a political trap for himself when he declared at the 1988 Republican Convention: "Read my lips. No new taxes." Fourteen months into his presidency, he decided that the federal budget deficit was a greater risk than violation of his no-new-taxes pledge. After intense negotiations with congressional Democrats, Bush announced that reducing the federal deficit required tax increases. His backsliding set off a revolt among House Republicans, but a bipartisan majority (with most Republicans still opposed) finally approved a tax increase, raising the top tax rate on personal income from 28 to 31 percent, disallowing certain deductions in the upper brackets, and raising various special taxes.

Such actions increased federal revenue but eroded Bush's political support among conservative Republicans.

At the 1992 Republican Convention, Patrick Buchanan, who had won about a third of the votes in the party's primaries, lambasted Bush for breaking his pledge not to raise taxes and for becoming the "biggest spender in American history." Buchanan claimed to be a crusader "for a Middle American revolution" that would halt illegal immigration and the gay rights movement. As the 1992 election unfolded, Bush's real problem was not Pat Buchanan and the conservative wing of the Republican party, however. What threatened his reelection was his own failed effort to jump-start the economy.

DEMOCRATIC RESURGENCE    In contrast to divisions among Republicans, the Democrats at their 1992 convention presented an image of centrist forces in control. For several years the Democratic Leadership Council, in which Arkansas governor **William Jefferson Clinton** figured prominently, had been pushing the party from the liberal left to the center of the political spectrum. Clinton strove to move the Democrats closer to the mainstream of political opinion by reinventing themselves as a socially liberal but pro-business, fiscally conservative party. He called for a "third way" positioned in between conservatism and liberalism, something he labeled "progressive centrism." Unlike the older generation of liberal Democrats led by Robert Kennedy, George McGovern, Jimmy Carter, Walter Mondale, and Michael Dukakis, Clinton was less confident that government could cure all ills.

Born in Hope, Arkansas, Bill Clinton grew to be a bright, ambitious young man who yearned to be a national political leader. To that end, he attended Georgetown University in Washington, D.C., won a Rhodes Scholarship to Oxford University, and then earned a law degree from Yale University, where he met his future wife, Hillary Rodham. Clinton returned to Arkansas and won election as the state's attorney general. By 1979, at age thirty-two, Bill Clinton was the youngest governor in the country. He served three more terms as Arkansas governor and in the process emerged as a dynamic young leader of the "New Democrats" committed to winning back the middle-class whites ("Reagan Democrats") who had voted Republican during the 1980s. Democratic politicians had grown so liberal, he argued, that they had alienated their key constituency, the "vital center." They needed to abandon their tired "tax-and-spend" policies and focus on sustaining prosperity at home and peace abroad.

A self-described moderate seeking the Democratic presidential nomination, Clinton promised to cut the defense budget, provide tax relief for the middle class, and create a massive economic aid package for the former republics of the Soviet Union to help them forge democratic societies. Witty, intelligent, and charismatic, with an in-depth knowledge of public policy, Clinton was adept at campaigning; he projected energy, youth, and optimism, reminding many political observers of John F. Kennedy. Clinton was also visibly compassionate (he could even weep on demand); he told struggling people that he could "feel your pain"—and he meant it.

But beneath the veneer of Clinton's charisma and his deep knowledge of public policy issues were several flaws. Self-absorbed and self-indulgent, he yearned to be loved. The *New York Times* explained that Clinton was "emotionally needy, indecisive, and undisciplined." He often courted popularity over principle. He was a political opportunist who had earned a well-deserved reputation for half-truths, exaggerations, and talking out of both sides of his mouth. Clinton was a policy "wonk" who relished the details and nuances of complex legislation. He was also very much a political animal. He made extensive use of polls to shape his stance on issues, pandered to special-interest groups, and flip-flopped on controversial subjects, leading critics to label him "Slick Willie." Even more enticing to the media were charges that Clinton was a chronic adulterer and that he had manipulated

**The 1992 presidential campaign**

Presidential candidate Bill Clinton and his running mate, Al Gore, brought youthful enthusiasm to the campaign trail.

the Reserve Officers' Training Corps (ROTC) program during the Vietnam War to avoid military service. Clinton's evasive denials of both allegations could not dispel a lingering distrust of his character.

Yet after a series of bruising party primaries, Clinton won the Democratic nomination in the summer of 1992. He chose Senator Albert "Al" Gore Jr. of Tennessee as his running mate. Gore described himself as a "raging moderate." So the Democratic candidates were two Southern Baptists from adjoining states. Flushed with their convention victory and sporting a ten-point lead over Bush in the polls, the Clinton-Gore team stressed economic issues to win over working-class voters. Clinton won the election with 370 electoral votes and about 43 percent of the vote; Bush received 168 electoral votes and 39 percent of the vote; and off-and-on independent candidate H. Ross Perot of Texas garnered 19 percent of the popular vote, more than any other third-party candidate since Theodore Roosevelt in 1912. A puckish billionaire, Perot found a large audience for his simplified explanations of national problems and his criticism of Reaganomics as "voodoo economics."

## DOMESTIC POLICY IN CLINTON'S FIRST TERM

Clinton's inexperience in international affairs and congressional maneuvering led to several missteps in his first year as president. Like George H. W. Bush before him, he reneged on several campaign promises. He abandoned his proposed middle-class tax cut in order to keep down the federal deficit. Then he dropped his promise to allow gays to serve in the armed forces after military commanders expressed strong opposition. Instead, he later announced an ambiguous new policy concerning gays in the military that came to be known as "don't ask, don't tell." In Clinton's first two weeks in office, his approval rating dropped 20 percent. But the true test for presidents is not how they begin but how fast they learn, how resilient they are, and where they end up.

THE ECONOMY   As a candidate, Clinton had pledged to reduce the federal deficit without damaging the economy or hurting the nation's most vulnerable people. To this end, on February 17 he proposed higher taxes for corporations and for individuals in higher tax brackets. He also called for an economic stimulus package for "investment" in public works (transportation, utilities, and the like) and "human capital" (education, skills, health, and welfare). The hotly contested bill finally passed by 218 to 216 in the House and 51 to 50 in the Senate, with Vice President Gore breaking the tie.

Equally contested was congressional approval of the **North American Free Trade Agreement (NAFTA)**, which the Bush administration had negotiated with Canada and Mexico. The debate revived old arguments on the tariff. Clinton stuck with his party's tradition of low tariffs and urged approval of NAFTA, which would make North America the largest free-trade area in the world, enabling the three

**NAFTA protesters**

Protesters going to a rally against NAFTA.

nations to trade with each other on equal footing. Opponents of the bill, such as gadfly Ross Perot and organized labor, favored tariff barriers that would discourage the importation of cheaper foreign products. Perot predicted that NAFTA would result in the "giant sucking sound" of American jobs being drawn to Mexico. Yet Clinton prevailed with solid Republican support while losing a sizable minority of Democrats, mostly from the South, where people feared that many textile mills would lose business to "cheap-labor" countries, as they did.

HEALTH-CARE REFORM    Clinton's major public-policy initiative was a federal health-care plan. "If I don't get health care," he declared, "I'll wish I didn't run for President." Government-subsidized health insurance was not a new idea. Other industrial countries had long ago started national health-insurance programs, Germany as early as 1883, Great Britain in 1911. Medicare, initiated in 1965, provided health insurance for people sixty-five and older, and Medicaid supported state medical assistance for the poor. Over the years, however, the cost of those programs had grown enormously, as had business spending on private health insurance. Sentiment for health-care reform spread as annual medical costs skyrocketed and some 39 million Americans went without medical insurance, most of them poor or unemployed. The Clinton administration argued that universal medical insurance would reduce the costs of health care to the nation as a whole.

President Clinton made a tactical error when he appointed his spouse, Hillary, to head up the task force created to design a federal health-care plan. She chose not to work with congressional leaders in drafting the proposal.

**Clinton's federal health-care plan**

President Bill Clinton holds up a proposed health security I.D. card while outlining his plan for health-care reform to Congress.

Instead, the final version, essentially designed by the Clintons, was presented to Congress with little consultation. The maddeningly complicated plan, dubbed "Hillarycare" by journalists, proposed to give access to health insurance to every citizen and legal immigrant. Under the proposal, people would no longer purchase health insurance through their employers. Instead, workers would be pooled into "regional health alliances" run by the states that would offer private insurance options. Employers would pay most of the premiums. Government would subsidize all or part of the payments for small businesses and the poor, the latter from funds that formerly went to Medicaid, and would collect a new "sin tax" on tobacco products and perhaps alcoholic beverages to pay for the program. The bill aroused opposition from Republicans and even moderate Democrats, as well as the pharmaceutical and insurance industries. By the summer of 1994, the Clinton health-insurance plan was doomed. Lacking the votes to stop a filibuster by Senate Republicans, the Democrats acknowledged defeat and gave up the fight for universal medical coverage.

## REPUBLICAN INSURGENCY

In 1994, Bill Clinton began to see his coveted presidency unravel. Unable to get either health-care reform or welfare-reform bills through the Democratic Congress and having failed to carry out his campaign pledge for middle-class tax relief, he and his party found themselves on the defensive. In the midterm elections of 1994, the Democrats suffered a humbling defeat. It was the first election since 1952 in which Republicans captured both houses of Congress at the same time.

THE CONTRACT WITH AMERICA   The Republican insurgency in Congress during the mid-nineties was led by a feisty, self-infatuated Georgian named Newton Leroy Gingrich. In early 1995, he became the first Republican Speaker of the House in forty-two years. Gingrich, a former history professor with a lust for controversy and an unruly ego (a journalist said that becoming Speaker of the House added thirty pounds to his girth and sixty pounds to his ego), was a superb tactician who had helped mobilize religious and social conservatives associated with the Christian Coalition. In 1995, he announced that "we are at the end of an era." Liberalism, he claimed, was dead, and the Democratic party was dying. The imperious Gingrich, ingenious yet undisciplined and erratic, viewed politics as a blood sport. He pledged to start a new reign of congressional Republican dominance that would dismantle the "corrupt liberal welfare state." He was aided in his efforts by newly elected Republican House members who promoted what Gingrich called with great fanfare the **Contract with America**. The ten-point contract outlined an anti-big-government program featuring less regulation of businesses, less environmental conservation, term limits for members of Congress, welfare reform, and a balanced-budget amendment. As one of the congressional Republicans explained, "We are ideologues. We have an agenda" to change America. Gingrich was blunter. He said that Republicans had not been "nasty" enough. That was about to change, as Gingrich launched an unrelenting assault on the Clinton administration and the Democratic party.

Yet the much-ballyhooed Contract with America quickly fizzled out. Triumph often undermines judgment, and the Republican revolution touted by Gingrich could not be sustained by the slim Republican majority in Congress. What is more, many of the seventy-three freshman Republican House members were dogmatists scornful of compromise. As legislative amateurs, they limited Gingrich's ability to maneuver. The Senate rejected many of the bills that had been passed in the House. Most of all, the Contract with America disintegrated because Newt Gingrich became such an unpopular figure, both in Congress and among the electorate. He was too ambitious, too abrasive, too polarizing. The cocky speaker repeatedly overplayed his hand. Republican senator Bob Dole said Gingrich was "a one-man band who rarely took advice."

Gingrich's clumsy bravado backfired. "No political figure in modern time," a journalist declared in 1996, "has done more to undermine the power of his message with the defects of his personality than the

**Newt Gingrich**

Gingrich discusses Congress's failure to strengthen the small business sector at a press conference.

disastrously voluble Speaker of the House." That same year, *U.S. News and World Report* labeled Gingrich the "most unpopular politician in America." In 1997, the House of Representatives censured Gingrich for an array of ethics violations, the first time in history that a Speaker of the House was disciplined for ethical wrongdoing. The following year, Republicans ousted Gingrich as Speaker of the House. The emerging lesson of politics in the 1990s was that Americans wanted elected federal officials to govern from the center rather than the extremes. As *Time* magazine noted in 1995, "Clinton and Gingrich— powerful yet indefinably immature—give off a bright, undisciplined energy, a vibration of adolescent recklessness."

LEGISLATIVE BREAKTHROUGH    In the late summer of 1996, Congress broke through its partisan gridlock and passed a flurry of legislation that President Clinton quickly signed, including bills increasing the minimum wage and broadening public access to health insurance. Most significant was a comprehensive welfare-reform measure that ended the federal government's open-ended guarantee of aid to the poor, a guarantee that had been in place since 1935. The Personal Responsibility and Work Opportunity Act of 1996 (PRWOA) was a centrist measure that illustrated Clinton's efforts to move the Democratic party away from the tired liberalism it had promoted since the 1930s. "The era of big government is over," Clinton proclaimed.

PRWOA abolished the Aid to Families with Dependent Children (AFDC) program and replaced it with the Temporary Assistance for Needy Families, which limited the duration of welfare payments to the unemployed to two years. Equally significant was that the PRWOA transferred administrative responsibility to the states, which were free to design their own aid programs funded by federal grants. The new bill also tightened restrictions on the issuance of federal food stamps, which enable poor people to purchase groceries at a discount. AFDC had long been criticized for providing financial incentives for poor women to have children and for discouraging women from joining the workforce. PRWOA also required that at least half of a state's welfare recipients have jobs or be enrolled in job-training programs by 2002. States failing to meet the deadline would have their federal funds cut.

The Republican-sponsored welfare-reform legislation passed the Senate by a vote of 74 to 24, and the Democratic president signed it into law on August 22, 1996, declaring that the new program "gives us a chance we haven't had before to break the cycle of dependency that has existed for millions and millions of our fellow citizens, exiling them from the world of work. It gives structure, meaning, and dignity to most of our lives." Others were not as excited by the new initiative. Liberals charged that Clinton was abandoning Democratic social principles in order to gain reelection amid the conservative public mood. Said one corporate executive, "Clinton is the most Republican Democrat in a long time."

The welfare-reform bill represented a turning point in modern politics. The war on poverty, launched by Lyndon B. Johnson in 1964 and broadened by Richard M. Nixon's expansion of the federal food-stamp program, had ended in defeat. Despite the massive amount of federal funds spent on various anti-poverty and social welfare programs, poverty was growing. Now, the federal government was turning over responsibility for several welfare programs to the states. And, despite criticism, the new approach seemed to work. Welfare recipients and poverty rates both declined during the late nineties, leading the editors of the left-leaning *The New Republic* to report that welfare reform had "worked much as its designers had hoped."

THE 1996 CAMPAIGN    After clinching the Republican presidential nomination in 1996, Senate majority leader Bob Dole resigned his seat in order to devote his attention to defeating Bill Clinton. As the 1996 presidential campaign unfolded, however, Clinton maintained a large lead in the polls. With an improving economy and no major foreign-policy crises to confront, cultural and personal issues again surged into prominence. Concern about Dole's age (seventy-three) and his acerbic personality, as well as rifts in the Republican party between economic conservatives and social conservatives over volatile issues such as abortion and gun control, hampered Dole's efforts to generate widespread support, especially among the growing number of independent voters.

**Bob Dole**

The Republican presidential candidate and former Senate majority leader on the campaign trail.

On November 5, 1996, the remarkably resilient Clinton won again, with an electoral vote of 379 to 159 and 49 percent of the popular vote. Clinton was the first Democratic presidential candidate to win an election while the Republicans controlled Congress. And he was the first Democratic president to win a second term since Franklin D. Roosevelt in 1936. Dole received only 41 percent of the popular vote, and third-party candidate Ross Perot got 8 percent. The Republicans lost eight seats in the House but retained an edge, 227 to 207, over the Democrats in the House; in the Senate, Republicans gained two seats for a 55–45 majority.

## THE CLINTON YEARS AT HOME

As the twentieth century came to a close, the United States benefited from a prolonged period of unprecedented prosperity. Buoyed by low inflation, high employment, declining federal budget deficits, dramatic improvements in industrial productivity and the sweeping globalization of economic life, business and industry witnessed record profits.

THE "NEW ECONOMY" By the end of the twentieth century, the "new economy" was centered on high-flying computer, software, telecommunications, and Internet firms. These "dot-com" enterprises had come to represent almost a third of stock-market values even though many of them were hollow-shelled companies fueled by the speculative mania. The result was a financial bubble that soon burst, but during the run-up in the 1990s investors gave little thought to a possible collapse. The robust economy set records in every area: low inflation, low unemployment, federal budget surpluses for the first time in modern history, and dizzying corporate profits and personal fortunes. People began to claim that the new economy defied the boom-and-bust cycles of the previous hundred years. Alan

Greenspan, the Federal Reserve Board chairman, foolishly suggested "that we have moved 'beyond history'"—into an economy that seemed only to grow. Only too late would people remember that human greed always breeds recklessness, leading to what Greenspan later called "irrational exuberance."

One major factor producing the economic boom of the nineties was the "peace dividend." The end of the cold war had enabled the U.S. government to reduce the proportion of the federal budget devoted to defense spending. Another major factor was the Clinton administration's 1993 initiative cutting taxes and reducing overall federal spending. But perhaps the single most important reason for the surge in prosperity was dramatic growth in per-worker productivity. New information technologies and high-tech production processes allowed for greater efficiency.

GLOBALIZATION    Another major feature of the "new economy" was globalization. Globe-spanning technologies shrank time and distance, enabling U.S.-based multinational companies to conduct a growing proportion of their business abroad as more and more nations lowered trade barriers such as tariffs and import fees. U.S. exports rose dramatically in the last two decades of the twentieth century. By the end of the century, the U.S. economy had become dependent on the global economy; foreign trade was central to American prosperity—and to American politics. By 2000, over a third of the production of American multinational companies was occurring abroad, compared with only 9 percent in 1980. Many U.S. manufacturing companies moved their production "offshore" to take advantage of lower labor costs and lax workplace regulations abroad, a controversial phenomenon often labeled "outsourcing." At the same time, many foreign manufacturers, such as Toyota, Honda, and BMW, built production facilities in the United States. The U.S. economy had become internationalized to such a profound extent that global concerns exercised an ever-increasing influence on domestic and foreign policies.

RACE INITIATIVES    After the triumphs of the civil rights movement in the sixties, the momentum for minority advancement had run out by the nineties—except for gains in college admissions and employment under the rubric of affirmative action. The conservative mood during the mid-nineties manifested itself in the Supreme Court. In 1995, the Court ruled against election districts redrawn to create African American or Latino majorities and narrowed federal affirmative-action programs intended to benefit minorities underrepresented In the workplace.

In one of those cases, *Adarand Constructors v. Peña* (1995), the Court assessed a program that gave some advantages to businesses owned by "disadvantaged" minorities. A Hispanic-owned firm had won a highway guardrail contract over a lower bid by a white-owned company that sued on the grounds of "reverse discrimination." Writing for the majority, Justice Sandra Day O'Connor said that such affirmative-action programs had to be "narrowly tailored" to serve a "compelling national interest." O'Connor did not define what the Court meant by a "compelling national interest," but the implication of her language was clear: the Court had come to share the growing public suspicion of the value and legality of such race-based benefit programs.

In 1996, two major steps were taken against affirmative action in college admissions. In *Hopwood v. Texas,* the U.S. Court of Appeals for the Fifth Circuit ruled that considering race to achieve a diverse student body at the University of Texas was "not a compelling interest under the Fourteenth Amendment." Later that year, the state of California passed Proposition 209, an initiative that ruled out race, sex, ethnicity, and national origin as criteria for preferring any group. These rulings gutted affirmative-action programs and reduced African American college enrollments, prompting second thoughts. In addition, the nation still had not addressed intractable problems that lay beyond civil rights—that is, chronic problems of adult illiteracy, poverty, unemployment, urban decay, and slums.

**THE SCANDAL MACHINE**   During his first term, President Clinton was dogged by allegations of improper involvement in the Whitewater Development Corporation. In 1978, while serving as governor of Arkansas, he had invested in a resort to be built in northern Arkansas. The project turned out to be a fraud and a failure, and the Clintons took a loss on their investment. In 1994, Kenneth Starr, a Republican, was appointed as independent counsel in an investigation of the Whitewater case. Starr did not uncover evidence that the Clintons were directly involved in the fraud, although several of their close associates had been caught in the web and convicted of various charges, some related to Whitewater and some not.

In the course of another investigation, a salacious scandal erupted when it was revealed that President Clinton had engaged in a prolonged sexual affair with a White House intern, Monica Lewinsky, a recent college graduate. Even more disturbing, he had pressed her to lie about their relationship under oath. Like Richard M. Nixon's handling of the Watergate incident, Clinton initially denied the charges, but the scandal would not disappear.

For the next thirteen months, "Monicagate" captured public attention and enlivened partisan debate about Clinton's presidency. In August 1998, Clinton agreed to appear before a grand jury convened to investigate the sexual allegations, thus becoming the first president in history to testify before a grand jury. On August 17, Clinton, a dogged fighter, self-pitying and defiant, recanted his earlier denials and acknowledged having had "inappropriate intimate physical contact" with Lewinsky. That evening the president delivered a four-minute nationally televised address in which he admitted an improper relationship with Lewinsky, but insisted that had done nothing illegal.

Public reaction to Clinton's remarkable about-face was mixed. A majority of Americans expressed sympathy for the president because of his public humiliation; they wanted the entire matter dropped. But Clinton's credibility had suffered a serious blow on account of his reckless lack of self-discipline and his efforts first to deny and then to cover up the scandal. Then, on September 9, 1998, the special prosecutor submitted to Congress a 445-page, sexually graphic report. The Starr Report found "substantial and creditable" evidence of presidential wrongdoing, prompting the House of Representatives on October 8 to begin a wide-ranging impeachment inquiry of the president. Thirty-one Democrats joined the Republicans in supporting the investigation. On December 19, 1998, William Jefferson Clinton became the second president to be impeached by the House of Representatives. The House officially approved two articles of impeachment, charging Clinton with lying under oath to a federal grand jury and obstructing justice. House Speaker Newt Gingrich led the effort to impeach the president over the Lewinsky scandal—even though he himself was secretly engaged in an adulterous affair with a congressional staffer.

The Senate trial of President Clinton began on January 7, 1999. Five weeks later, on February 12, Clinton was acquitted. Rejecting the first charge of perjury, 10 Republicans and all 45 Democrats voted "not guilty." On the charge of obstruction of justice, the Senate split 50–50 (which meant acquittal, since 67 votes were needed for conviction). In both instances, senators had a hard time interpreting Clinton's adultery and lies as constituting "high crimes and misdemeanors," the constitutional requirement for removal of a president from office. Clinton's supporters portrayed him as the victim of a puritanical special prosecutor and a partisan conspiracy run amok. His critics lambasted him as a lecherous man without honor or integrity. Both characterizations were accurate yet incomplete. Politically astute and well informed, Clinton had as much ability and potential as any president. Yet he

**Impeachment**

Representative Edward Pease, a member of the House Judiciary Committee, covers his face during the vote on the third of four articles of impeachment charging President Clinton with "high crimes and misdemeanors," December 1998.

was also shamelessly self-indulgent. The result was a scandalous presidency punctuated by dramatic achievements in welfare reform, economic growth, and foreign policy.

## FOREIGN-POLICY CHALLENGES

Like Woodrow Wilson, Lyndon Johnson, and Jimmy Carter before him, Bill Clinton was a Democratic president who came into office determined to focus on the nation's domestic problems only to find himself mired in foreign entanglements. Clinton continued the Bush administration's military intervention in Somalia, on the northeastern horn of Africa, where collapse of the government early in 1991 had left the country in anarchy, prey to tribal marauders. President Bush in 1992 had gained UN sanction for a military force led by American troops to relieve hunger and restore peace. The Somalian operation proved successful at its primary mission, but it never resolved the political anarchy that lay at the root of the population's starvation.

HAITI During its first term, the Clinton administration's most rewarding foreign-policy endeavor came in Haiti. The Caribbean island nation had emerged suddenly from a cycle of coups with a democratic election in 1990, which brought to the presidency a popular priest, Jean-Bertrand Aristide. When a Haitian army general ousted Aristide, the United States announced its intention to bring him back with the aid of the United Nations. With drawn-out negotiations leading nowhere, Clinton moved in July 1994 to get a UN resolution authorizing force as a last resort. At that juncture, former president Jimmy Carter asked permission to negotiate. He convinced the military leaders to quit by October 15. Aristide returned to Haiti and on March 31, 1995, the occupation was turned over to a UN force commanded by an American general.

THE MIDDLE EAST    President Clinton also continued George H. W. Bush's policy of sponsoring patient negotiations between the Arabs and the Israelis. A new development was the inclusion of the Palestinian Liberation Organization (PLO) in the negotiations. In 1993, secret talks between Israeli and Palestinian representatives in Oslo, Norway, resulted in a draft agreement between Israel and the PLO. This agreement provided for the restoration of Palestinian self-rule in the occupied Gaza Strip and in Jericho, on the West Bank, in an exchange of land for peace as provided in UN Security Council resolutions. A formal signing occurred at the White House on September 13, 1993. With President Clinton presiding, Israeli prime minister

**Clinton and the Middle East**

President Clinton presides as Israeli prime minister Yitzhak Rabin (left) and PLO leader Yasir Arafat (right) agree to a peace accord between Israel and the Palestinians, September 1993.

Yitzhak Rabin and PLO leader Yasir Arafat exchanged handshakes, and their foreign ministers signed the agreement.

The Middle East peace process suffered a terrible blow in early November 1995, however, when Prime Minister Rabin was assassinated by an Israeli zealot who resented Rabin's efforts to negotiate with the Palestinians. Some observers feared that the assassin had killed the peace process as well when seven months later conservative hard-liner Benjamin Netanyahu narrowly defeated the U.S.-backed Shimon Peres in the Israeli national elections. Yet in October 1998, Clinton brought Arafat, Netanyahu, and King Hussein of Jordan together at a conference in Maryland, where they reached an agreement. Under the Wye River Accord, Israel agreed to surrender land in return for security guarantees by the Palestinians.

**THE BALKANS**    Clinton's foreign policy also addressed the chaotic transition in eastern Europe from Soviet domination to independence. When combustible Yugoslavia imploded in 1991, fanatics and tyrants triggered ethnic conflict as four of its six republics seceded. Serb minorities, backed by the new republic of Serbia, stirred up civil wars in Croatia and Bosnia. In Bosnia especially, the war involved "**ethnic cleansing**"—driving Muslims from their homes and towns. Clinton sent food and medical supplies to besieged Bosnians and dispatched warplanes to retaliate for attacks on places designated "safe havens" by the United Nations.

In 1995, U.S. negotiators finally persuaded the foreign ministers of Croatia, Bosnia, and the Federal Republic of Yugoslavia to agree to a comprehensive peace plan. Bosnia would remain a single nation but would be divided into two states: a Muslim-Croat federation controlling 51 percent of the territory and a Bosnian-Serb republic controlling the remaining 49 percent. Basic human rights would be restored and free elections would be held to appoint a parliament and joint president. To enforce the agreement, sixty thousand NATO peacekeeping troops would be dispatched to Bosnia. A cease-fire went into effect in October 1995.

In 1998, the Balkan tinderbox flared up again, this time in the Yugoslav province of Kosovo, which had long been considered sacred ground by Christian Serbs. By 1989, however, over 90 percent of the 2 million Kosovars were ethnic Albanian Muslims. In that year, Yugoslav president Slobodan Milošević decided to reassert Serbian control over the province. He stripped Kosovo of its autonomy and established de facto martial law. When the Albanian Kosovars resisted and large numbers of Muslim men began to join the Kosovo Liberation Army, Serbian soldiers and state police ruthlessly burned Albanian villages, murdering men, raping women, and displacing hundreds of thousands of Muslim Kosovars.

On March 24, 1999, NATO, relying heavily upon U.S. military resources and leadership, launched air strikes against Yugoslavia. "Ending this tragedy is a moral imperative," explained President Clinton. After seventy-two days of unrelenting bombardment directed at Serbian military and civilian targets, Milošević sued for peace on NATO's terms, in part because his Russian allies had finally abandoned him. An agreement was reached on June 3, 1999. President Clinton pledged extensive U.S. aid in helping the Yugoslavs rebuild their war-torn economy.

THE CLINTON PRESIDENCY    Personality matters in presidential politics. Bill Clinton was a man of driving ambition and considerable talent. His charisma charmed people, and his rhetoric inspired them. His two terms included many successes. He presided over an unprecedented period of prolonged prosperity (115 consecutive months of economic growth and the lowest unemployment rate in thirty years), generated unheard-of federal budget surpluses, and passed a welfare-reform measure with support from both parties. In the process he salvaged liberalism from the dustbin and re-centered the Democratic party. Clinton also helped bring peace and stability to the Balkans, one of the most fractious and violent regions in all of Europe. Although less successful, his tireless efforts to mediate a lasting peace between Israel and the Palestinians displayed his courage and persistence.

Throughout his presidency, Clinton displayed a remarkable ability to manage crises and rebound from adversity. His resilience was extraordinary, in part because he was a master at spinning events and circumstances to his benefit. At times, however, his loyalty seemed focused on his ambition. His inflated self-confidence occasionally led to arrogant recklessness. He may have balanced the budget, but he also debased the presidency. He may have pushed through a dramatic reform of the welfare system, but his effort to bring health insurance to the uninsured was a clumsy failure. Clinton was less a great statesman than he was a great escape artist. He even survived his awful handling of the Monica Lewinsky scandal and his intensely partisan impeachment trial. In 2000, his last year in office, the smooth-talking Clinton enjoyed a public approval rating of 65 percent, the highest end-of-term rating since President Dwight D. Eisenhower. Yet Clinton's popularity was not deep enough to ensure the election of his vice president, Al Gore, as his successor.

## THE ELECTION OF 2000

The election of 2000 proved to be one of the closest and most controversial in history. The two major-party candidates for president, Vice President **Albert Gore Jr.**, the Democrat, and Texas governor **George W. Bush**,

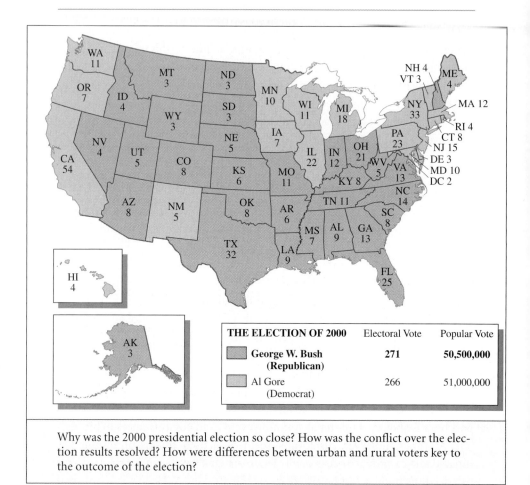

| THE ELECTION OF 2000 | Electoral Vote | Popular Vote |
|---|---|---|
| ■ George W. Bush (Republican) | 271 | 50,500,000 |
| □ Al Gore (Democrat) | 266 | 51,000,000 |

Why was the 2000 presidential election so close? How was the conflict over the election results resolved? How were differences between urban and rural voters key to the outcome of the election?

the son of the former Republican president, presented contrasting views on the role of the federal government, tax cuts, environmental policies, and the best way to preserve Social Security and Medicare. Gore, a Tennessee native and Harvard graduate whose father had been a senator, favored an active federal government that would subsidize prescription-medicine expenses for the elderly, and protect the environment. Bush, on the other hand, proposed a transfer of power from the federal government to the states, particularly in regard to environmental and educational policies. In international affairs, Bush questioned the need to maintain U.S. peacekeeping forces in Bosnia and the continuing expense of other global military commitments. He urged a more "humble" foreign policy, one that would end U.S. efforts to install democratic governments in undemocratic countries ("nation building") around the world.

The polarization of politics at the start of the twentieth century continued to spawn various third-party candidates at the extremes. Two independent candidates added zest to the 2000 presidential campaign: conservative columnist Patrick Buchanan and liberal activist Ralph Nader. Buchanan focused his campaign on criticism of NAFTA, while Nader lamented the corrupting effects of large corporate donations on the political process and the need for more robust efforts to protect the environment.

In the end, the election created high drama. The television networks initially reported that Gore had narrowly won the state of Florida and its decisive twenty-five electoral votes. Later in the evening, however, the networks reversed themselves, saying that Florida was too close to call. In the chaotic early-morning hours, the networks declared that Bush had been elected president. Gore called Bush to concede, only to issue a retraction a short time later when it appeared that the results in Florida remained a toss-up. The final tally in Florida showed Bush with a razor-thin lead, and state law required a recount. For the first time in 125 years, the results of a presidential election remained in doubt for weeks after the voting.

As a painstaking hand count of presidential ballots proceeded in Florida, supporters of Bush and Gore pursued legal maneuvers in the Florida courts

**The Florida recount**

A rally in Florida protesting the counting of ballots in the disputed 2000 presidential election.

and the U.S. Supreme Court; each side accused the other of trying to steal the election. The political drama remained stalemated for five weeks. At last, on December 12, 2000, a harshly divided Supreme Court halted the recounts in Florida. In the case known as *Bush v. Gore,* a bare 5–4 majority ruled that any new recount would clash with existing Florida law. Bush was declared the winner in Florida by only 537 votes. Although Gore had amassed a 540,000-vote lead nationwide, he lost in the Electoral College by two votes when he lost Florida. Although Al Gore "strongly disagreed" with the Supreme Court's decision, he asked voters to rally around President-elect Bush and move forward: "Partisan rancor must be put aside." It was not.

## COMPASSIONATE CONSERVATISM

George W. Bush arrived in the White House to confront a sputtering economy and a falling stock market. By the spring of 2000, many of the high-tech companies that had led the dizzying run-up on Wall Street during the nineties had collapsed. Greed fed by record profits and speculative excesses had led businesses and investors to take increasingly dangerous risks. Consumer confidence and capital investment plummeted with the falling stock market. By March 2001, the economy was in recession for the first time in over a decade. Yet neither the floundering economy nor the close political balance in Congress prevented President Bush from launching an ambitious legislative agenda. Confident that he could win over conservative Democrats, he promised to provide "an explosion of legislation" promoting his goal of "compassionate conservatism." The top item on Bush's wish list was a tax cut intended to stimulate the sagging economy. Bush signed it into law on June 7, 2001. By cutting taxes, however, federal revenue diminished, thus increasing the budget deficit. It also shifted more of the tax burden from the rich to the middle and working classes, and increased already high levels of income inequality.

NO CHILD LEFT BEHIND    In addition to tax reduction, one of President Bush's top priorities was to reform primary and secondary education. In late 2001, Congress passed a comprehensive education-improvement plan called **No Child Left Behind** that sought to improve educational quality by requiring states to set new learning standards and to develop standardized tests to ensure that all students were "proficient" at reading and math by 2014. It also mandated that all teachers be "highly qualified" in their subject area by 2005, allowed children in low-performing schools to transfer to other schools, and required states to submit annual standardized student test scores. A growing number of states criticized the program, claiming that it provided insufficient funds for remedial programs and that poor school districts, many of them in blighted inner cities or rural areas, would be especially hard-pressed to meet the new guidelines. The most common criticism, however, was that the federal program created a culture whereby teachers, feeling pressured to increase student performance, focused their classroom teaching on preparing students for the tests rather than fostering learning.

## GLOBAL TERRORISM

As had happened so often with presidents during the twentieth century, President Bush soon found himself distracted by global issues and foreign crises. With the implosion of the Soviet Union and the end of the cold war, world politics had grown less potent but more unstable during the nineties. Whereas competing ideologies such as capitalism and communism had earlier provided the fulcrum of foreign relations, issues of religion, ethnicity, and clashing cultural values now divided peoples. Islamic militants around the world especially resented what they viewed as the "imperial" globalization of U.S. culture and power. Multinational groups inspired by religious fanaticism and anti-American rage used high-tech terrorism to gain notoriety and exact vengeance. Well-financed and well-armed terrorists flourished in the cracks of fractured nations such as Sudan, Somalia, Pakistan, Yemen, and Afghanistan. Throughout the nineties, the United States fought a losing secret war against organized terrorism. The ineffectiveness of Western intelligence agencies in tracking the movements and intentions of militant extremists became tragically evident in the late summer of 2001.

9/11: A DAY OF INFAMY    At 8:45 A.M. on September 11, 2001, a commercial airliner hijacked by Islamic terrorists slammed into the north tower of the majestic World Trade Center in New York City. A second hijacked jumbo jet crashed into the south tower eighteen minutes later. The fuel-laden planes turned the majestic buildings into infernos, forcing desperate people who worked in the skyscrapers to jump to their deaths. The iconic twin towers, both 110 stories tall and occupied by thousands of employees, imploded from the intense heat. Surrounding buildings also collapsed. The southern end of Manhattan—ground zero—became a hellish scene of twisted steel, suffocating smoke, and wailing sirens.

While the catastrophic drama in New York City was unfolding, a third hijacked plane crashed into the Pentagon in Washington, D.C. A fourth airliner, probably headed for the White House, missed its mark when passengers—who had heard reports of the earlier hijackings via cell phones—assaulted the hijackers to prevent the plane from being used as a weapon. During the struggle in the cockpit, the plane went out of control and plummeted into the Pennsylvania countryside, killing all aboard.

The hijackings represented the worst terrorist assault in the nation's history. There were 266 passengers and crewmembers aboard the crashed jets. More than 100 civilians and military personnel were killed at the Pentagon. The death toll at the World Trade Center was over 2,700, with many firefighters, police officers, and rescue workers among the dead. Hundreds of those killed were foreign nationals working in the financial district; some eighty nations lost citizens in the attacks.

## 9/11

Smoke pours out of the north tower of the World Trade Center as the south tower bursts into flames after being struck by a second hijacked airplane. Both towers collapsed about an hour later.

The terrorist attacks of 9/11 created shock and chaos, grief and anger. People rushed to donate blood, food, and money. Volunteers clogged military-recruiting centers. For the first time in its history, NATO invoked Article 5 of its charter, which states that an attack on any member will be considered an attack on all members. The stunning terrorist assaults led the editors of the *New York Times* to observe that 9/11 was "one of those moments in which history splits, and we define the world as before and after."

Within hours of the hijackings, officials had identified the nineteen dead terrorists as members of al Qaeda (the Base), a well-financed worldwide network of Islamic extremists led by a wealthy Saudi renegade, **Osama bin Laden**. Years before, bin Laden had declared jihad (holy war) on the United States, Israel, and the Saudi monarchy. He believed that the United States, like the Soviet Union, was on the verge of collapse; all it needed was a spark to ignite its self-destruction. To that end, for several years he had been using remote bases in war-torn Afghanistan as terrorist training centers. Collaborating with bin Laden's terrorist network was Afghanistan's ruling Taliban, a coalition of ultraconservative Islamists that had emerged in the mid-nineties following the forced withdrawal of Soviet troops from Afghanistan. Taliban leaders provided bin Laden with a safe haven, enabling him to recruit Muslim militants and mobilize them into a global strike force. As many as twenty thousand recruits from twenty different countries circulated through Afghan training camps before joining secret jihadist cells around the world. Their goal was to engage in urban warfare, assassination, demolition, and sabotage, with the United States and Europe as the primary targets.

WAR ON TERRORISM   The **9/11** assault on the United States changed the course of modern life. The economy, already in decline, went into free fall. President Bush, who had never professed to know much about international relations or world affairs, was thrust onto center stage as commander in chief of a wounded nation eager for vengeance. The new president told the nation that the "deliberate and deadly attacks . . . were more than acts of terror. They were acts of war." The crisis gave the untested, happy-go-lucky Bush a profound sense of purpose. "I will not yield. I will not rest. I will not relent in waging this struggle for freedom and security."

The Bush administration mobilized America's allies to assault terrorism worldwide. The coalition demanded that Afghanistan's Taliban government surrender the al Qaeda terrorists or risk military attack. On October 7, 2001, after the Taliban refused to turn over bin Laden, the United States and its allies launched a ferocious military campaign—Operation Enduring Freedom—to punish terrorists or "those harboring terrorists." American and British cruise

**Operation Enduring Freedom**

Smoke rises from the Taliban village of Khanaqa, fifty-five miles from the Afghan capital Kabul, after a U.S. aircraft released bombs.

missiles and bombers destroyed Afghan military installations and al Qaeda training camps. On December 9, only two months after the U.S.-led military campaign in Afghanistan had begun, the Taliban regime collapsed. The war in Afghanistan then devolved into a high-stakes manhunt for the elusive Osama bin Laden and his international network of terrorists.

TERRORISM AT HOME    While the military campaign continued in Afghanistan, officials in Washington worried that terrorists might launch additional attacks in the United States with biological, chemical, or even nuclear weapons. To address the threat and to help restore public confidence, President Bush created a new federal agency, the Office of Homeland Security. Another new federal agency, the Transportation Security Administration, assumed responsibility for screening airline passengers for weapons and bombs. At the same time, President Bush and a supportive Congress created the USA Patriot Act, which gave government agencies the right to eavesdrop on confidential conversations between prison inmates and their lawyers and permitted suspected terrorists to be tried in secret military courts. Civil liberties groups voiced grave concerns that the measures jeopardized constitutional rights and protections. But the crisis atmosphere after 9/11 led most people to support these extraordinary steps.

**The Taliban**

A young woman shows her face in public for the first time in five years after Northern Alliance troops capture Kabul, the capital of Afghanistan, in November 2001. The strict sharia law enforced by the Taliban required that women be covered from head to foot.

THE BUSH DOCTRINE   In the fall of 2002, President Bush unveiled a new national security doctrine that marked a distinct shift from that of previous administrations. Containment and deterrence of communism had been the guiding strategic concepts of the cold war years. In the new unconventional war against terrorism, however, the cold war policies were outdated. Fanatics willing to act as suicide bombers would not be deterred or contained. The growing menace posed by "shadowy networks" of terrorist groups and unstable rogue nations with "weapons of mass destruction," President Bush declared, required a new doctrine of preemptive military action. "If we wait for threats to fully materialize," he explained, "we will have waited too long. In the world we have entered, the only path to safety is the path of action. And this nation will act."

A SECOND PERSIAN GULF WAR   During 2002 and 2003, Iraq emerged as the focus of the Bush administration's aggressive new policy of "preemptive" military action. In September 2002, President Bush urged the United Nations to confront the "grave and gathering danger" posed by Saddam Hussein's dictatorial regime and its supposed possession of biological and chemical weapons of mass destruction (WMDs). In November, the UN

**Bush's defense policy**

President George W. Bush addresses soldiers in July 2002 as part of an appeal to Congress to speed approval of increased defense spending after the 9/11 terrorist attacks.

Security Council passed Resolution 1441 ordering Iraq to disarm immediately or face "serious consequences."

On March 17, 2003, President Bush issued an ultimatum to Saddam Hussein: he and his sons must leave Iraq within forty-eight hours or face a U.S.-led invasion. Hussein refused. Two days later, on March 19, American and British forces, supported by other allies making up what Bush called the "coalition of the willing," attacked Iraq. Operation Iraqi Freedom involved a massive bombing campaign followed by a fast-moving invasion across the Iraqi desert from bases in Kuwait. Some 250,000 American soldiers, sailors, and marines were joined by 50,000 British troops as well as small contingents from other countries. On April 9, after three weeks of intense fighting amid sweltering heat and blinding sandstorms, allied forces occupied Baghdad, the capital of Iraq. Hussein's regime and his inept army collapsed and fled a week later. On May 1, 2003, President Bush exuberantly declared that the war was essentially over. "The battle of Iraq," he said, "is one victory in a war on terror that began on September 11, 2001, and still goes on."

The six-week war came at a cost of fewer than two hundred combat deaths among the three hundred thousand coalition troops. Over two thousand Iraqi soldiers were killed; civilian casualties numbered in the tens of thousands.

REBUILDING IRAQ    It proved far easier to win the brief war than to rebuild Iraq in America's image. The allies faced the daunting task of restoring order and installing a democratic government in a chaotic Iraq fractured by age-old religious feuds and ethnic tensions. Violence engulfed the war-torn country. Vengeful Islamic jihadists from around the world streamed in to wage a merciless campaign of terror and sabotage against the U.S.-led coalition forces and their Iraqi allies.

Defense Department analysts had greatly underestimated the difficulty and expense of occupying, pacifying, and reconstructing postwar Iraq. By the fall of 2003, President Bush admitted that substantial numbers of American troops (around 150,000) would remain in Iraq much longer than originally anticipated and that rebuilding the splintered nation would take years and cost almost a trillion dollars. Victory on the battlefields of Iraq did not bring peace to the Middle East. Militant Islamic groups seething with hatred for the United States remained a constant global threat. In addition, the destruction of Saddam Hussein's regime in Iraq made for a stronger, tyrannical Iran and the accelerating descent of Pakistan into sectarian violence.

**A continued presence in Iraq**

U.S. military police patrol the market in Abu Ghraib, on the outskirts of Baghdad.

The dispute over the legitimacy of the allied war on Iraq also strained relations between the Anglo-American alliance and France, Germany, and Russia, all of which had opposed the Iraq War.

Throughout 2003 and 2004, the Iraqi insurgency and its campaign of terror grew in scope and savagery. Suicide car bombings and roadside ambushes of U.S. military convoys wreaked havoc among Iraqi civilians and allied troops. Terrorists kidnapped foreign civilians and beheaded several of them in grisly rituals videotaped for the world to see. In the United States the euphoria of battlefield victory turned to dismay as the number of casualties and the expense of the occupation soared. In the face of mounting criticism, President Bush urged Americans to "stay the course," insisting that a democratic Iraq would bring stability to the volatile Middle East and thereby blunt the momentum of Islamic terrorism.

But the president's credibility suffered a sharp blow in January 2004 when administration officials admitted that no WMDs—the primary reason for launching the invasion—had been found in Iraq. The chief arms inspector told Congress that the intelligence reports about Hussein's supposed secret weapons were "almost all wrong." President Bush said that the absence of WMDs in Iraq left him with a "sickening feeling," for he knew that his primary justification for the assault on Iraq had been undermined. Furthermore, shocking photographs that surfaced in April 2004 showing American soldiers torturing and abusing Iraqi prisoners further eroded public confidence in Bush's handling of the war and its aftermath.

By September 2004, U.S. military deaths in Iraq had reached one thousand, and by the end of 2006 the number was nearly three thousand. Although Saddam Hussein had been captured in December 2003 and a new Iraqi government would hold its first democratic elections in January 2005, Iraq seemed less secure than ever to an anxious American public worried about the rising cost of an unending commitment in Iraq. The continuing guerrilla wars in Iraq and Afghanistan strained U.S. military resources and the federal budget.

THE ELECTION OF 2004 Growing public concern about the turmoil in Iraq complicated George W. Bush's campaign for a second presidential term. Throughout 2004, his approval rating plummeted. And in the new century the electorate had become deeply polarized. A toxic partisanship dominated political discourse and media commentary in the early years of the century. Democrats still fumed over the contested presidential election of 2000. When asked about the intensity of his critics, a combative President Bush declared the furor "a compliment. It means I'm willing to take a stand."

**The 2004 election**

President George W. Bush (center) and Democratic candidate Senator John Kerry (left) participate in the second presidential debate, a townhall-style exchange held at Washington University in St. Louis, Missouri.

One of his advisers explained it more bluntly: "He likes being hated. It lets him know he's doing the right thing."

The 2004 presidential campaign was punctuated by negative attacks by both campaigns as the two parties sought to galvanize their loyalists with strident rhetoric. The Democratic nominee, Senator John Kerry of Massachusetts, lambasted the Bush administration for misleading the nation about weapons of mass destruction in Iraq and for its inept handling of the reconstruction of postwar Iraq. Kerry also highlighted the record budget deficits occurring under the Republican administration. Bush countered that the tortuous efforts to create a democratic government in Iraq would enhance America's long-term security.

On election day, November 2, 2004, the exit polls suggested a Kerry victory, but in the end the election hinged on the crucial swing state of Ohio. No Republican had ever lost Ohio and still won the presidency. After an anxious night viewing returns from Ohio, Kerry conceded the election. "The outcome," he stressed, "should be decided by voters, not a protracted legal battle." By narrowly winning Ohio, Bush garnered 286 electoral votes to Kerry's 251. Yet in some respects the close election was not so close. Bush received

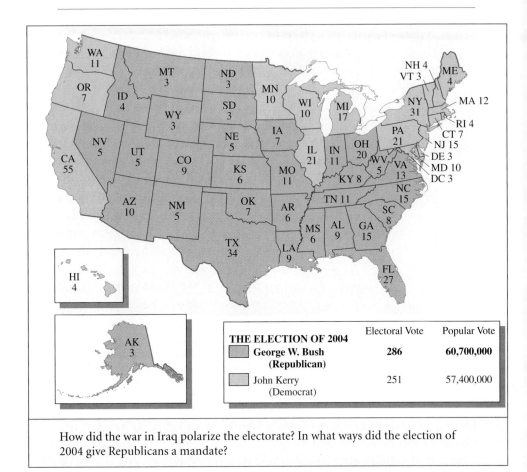

| THE ELECTION OF 2004 | Electoral Vote | Popular Vote |
|---|---|---|
| George W. Bush (Republican) | 286 | 60,700,000 |
| John Kerry (Democrat) | 251 | 57,400,000 |

How did the war in Iraq polarize the electorate? In what ways did the election of 2004 give Republicans a mandate?

3.5 million more votes nationwide than Kerry, and Republicans increased their control of both the House and the Senate. Trumpeting "the will of the people at my back," Bush pledged after his reelection to bring democracy and stability to Iraq, overhaul the tax code and eliminate the estate tax, revamp Social Security, trim the federal budget deficit, pass a major energy bill, and create many more jobs. "I earned capital in the campaign, political capital, and now I intend to spend it," he told reporters.

## SECOND-TERM BLUES

Yet like many modern presidents, George Bush stumbled in his second term. In 2005 he pushed through Congress an energy bill and a Central American Free Trade Act. But his effort to privatize Social Security retirement accounts, enabling individuals to invest their accumulated pension dollars themselves, went nowhere, and soaring budget deficits made many fiscal conservatives feel betrayed.

HURRICANE KATRINA    In 2005, President Bush's eroding public support suffered another blow, this time when a natural disaster turned into a political crisis. In late August, a killer hurricane named Katrina slammed into the Gulf coast, devastating large areas of Alabama, Mississippi, and Louisiana. In New Orleans, whole neighborhoods were under water, often up to the roofline. Nearly five hundred thousand city residents were displaced, most of them poor and many of them African American. Looting was so widespread that officials declared martial law; the streets were awash with soldiers and police. Katrina's awful wake left over a thousand people dead in three states and millions homeless and hopeless.

Local political officials and the Federal Emergency Management Agency (FEMA) were caught unprepared as the catastrophe unfolded. Disaster plans were incomplete; confusion and incompetence abounded. A wave of public outrage crashed against the Bush administration. In the face of blistering criticism, President Bush accepted responsibility for the balky federal response

**Katrina's aftermath**

Two men paddle through high water with wooden planks in a devastated New Orleans.

to the disaster and accepted the resignation of the FEMA director. Rebuilding the Gulf coast would take a long time and a lot of money.

A STALLED PRESIDENCY    George W. Bush bore the brunt of public indignation over the bungled federal response to the Katrina disaster. Thereafter, his second presidential term was beset by political problems, a sputtering economy, and growing public dissatisfaction with his performance and the continuing war in Iraq. Even his support among Republicans crumbled, and many social conservatives felt betrayed by his handling of their concerns. The editors of the *Economist*, an influential conservative newsmagazine, declared that Bush had become "the least popular re-elected president since Richard Nixon became embroiled in the Watergate fiasco." Soaring gasoline prices and the federal budget deficit fueled public frustration with the Bush administration. The president's efforts to reform the tax code, Social Security, and immigration laws languished during his second term, and the turmoil and violence in Iraq showed no signs of abating. Senator Chuck Hagel, a Nebraska Republican, declared in 2005 that "we're losing in Iraq."

VOTER REBELLION    In the November 2006 congressional elections, the Democrats capitalized on the public disapproval of the Bush administration to win control of the House of Representatives, the Senate, and a majority of governorships and state legislatures. The election results were so lopsided that for the first time in history the victorious party (the Democrats) did not lose a single incumbent or open congressional seat or governorship.

**House Speaker Nancy Pelosi**

At a news conference on Capitol Hill.

Former Texas Republican congressman Dick Armey said that "the Republican Revolution of 1994 officially ended" with the 2006 election. "It was a rout." George Bush admitted that the voters had given him and his party a "thumpin'" that would require a "new era of cooperation" with the victorious Democrats. As it turned out, however, the Bush White House and the Democratic Congress became mired in partisan gridlock. Stalemate trumped bipartisanship. The transformational election also included a significant milestone: Californian Nancy Pelosi, the leader of the Democrats in the House of Representatives, became the highest-ranking woman in the history of the U.S. Congress upon her election as House Speaker in January 2007.

THE "SURGE" IN IRAQ    The 2006 congressional elections were largely a referendum on the lack of progress in the Iraq War. Throughout the fall the violence and casualties in Iraq had spiraled upward. Bush eventually responded to declining public and political support for the Iraq War by creating the Iraq Study Group, a bipartisan task force whose final report recommended that the United States withdraw its combat forces from a "grave and deteriorating Iraq" by the spring of 2008.

President Bush disagreed with the findings of the Iraq Study Group and others, including key military leaders, who urged a phased withdrawal. On January 10, 2007, he announced that he was sending a "surge" of 20,000 (eventually 30,000) additional American troops to Iraq, bringing the total to almost 170,000. From a military perspective, **the "surge"** strategy succeeded. By the fall of 2008, the convulsive violence in Iraq had declined dramatically, and the U.S.-supported Iraqi government had grown in stature and confidence. But the financial expenses and human casualties of American involvement in Iraq continued to generate widespread criticism, and the "surge" failed to attain its political objectives. Iraqi political leaders had yet to build a stable, self-sustaining democracy. The U.S. general who masterminded the increase in troops admitted that the gains remained "fragile and reversible." In 2008, as the number of U.S. combat deaths in Iraq passed 4,000, President Bush acknowledged that the conflict was "longer and harder and more costly than we anticipated." During 2008, over 60 percent of Americans said that the war in Iraq had been a mistake.

ECONOMIC SHOCK    After the intense but brief 2001 recession, the American economy had begun another period of prolonged expansion. Prosperity was fueled primarily by a prolonged housing boom, ultra-low interest and mortgage rates, easy credit, and reckless consumer spending. Home values across the nation had risen at rates that were unprecedented—and, as it turned out, unsustainable. Between 1997 and 2006, home prices in the United States, especially in the sunbelt states, rose 85 percent, leading to a frenzy of irresponsible mortgage lending for new homes—and a debt-fueled consumer spending spree. Tens of millions of people bought houses that were more expensive than they could afford, refinanced their mortgages, or tapped home-equity loans to make discretionary purchases. The irrational confidence in soaring housing prices also led government regulatory agencies and mortgage lenders to ease credit restrictions so that more people could buy homes. Predatory lenders offered an array of so-called subprime loans with low initial "teaser" rates to homebuyers with weak credit ratings and a low annual income. Investment banks and brokerage firms exacerbated the housing bubble by buying and selling bundles of home mortgages and other complex financial instruments without understanding the risk.

Financial collapses typically follow real-estate bubbles, rising indebtedness, and prolonged budget deficits. The housing bubble burst in 2007, when home values and housing sales began a precipitous decline. During 2008, the loss of trillions of dollars in home-equity value set off a seismic shock across the economy. Record numbers of mortgage borrowers defaulted on their payments. Foreclosures soared, adding to the glut of homes for sale and further reducing home prices. Banks lost billions, first on shaky mortgages, then on most other categories of debt: credit cards, car loans, student loans, and an array of commercial mortgage-backed securities.

Capitalism depends on access to capital; short-term credit is the lifeblood of the economy. In 2008, however, the nation's credit supply froze up. Concerned about their own insolvency as well as their ability to gauge credit risks, banks essentially stopped lending—to the public and to each other. So people stopped buying; businesses stopped selling; industries slashed production, laid off workers, and postponed investment. The sudden contraction of consumer credit, corporate spending, and consumer purchases pushed the economy into a deepening recession in 2008. The scale and suddenness of the slump caught economic experts and business leaders by surprise. Some of the nation's most prestigious banks, investment firms, and insurance companies went belly-up. The price of food and gasoline spiked. Unemployment soared. "Almost all businesses are in a survival mode," said one economist, "and they're slashing payrolls and investments. We're in store for some big job losses." Indeed, some two million jobs disappeared in 2008.

The high-flying stock market, itself fed by artificially low interest rates, began to tremble in September 2008; during October the bottom fell out. The Dow Jones Industrial Average lost a third of its value. Panic set in amid the turmoil. By late fall of 2008, the United States was facing its greatest financial crisis since the Great Depression of the 1930s. What had begun as a decline in home prices had become a global economic meltdown—fed by the paralyzing fright of insecurity. No investment seemed safe. As people saw their home values plummet and their retirement savings accounts gutted, they were left confused, anxious, and angry. Even Alan Greenspan, the former chairman of the Federal Reserve Board, found himself in a state of "shocked disbelief" at the onset of what began to be called the Great Recession, which officially lasted from December 2007 to January 2009. But its effects would linger long thereafter. "The Age of Prosperity is over," announced the prominent Republican economist Arthur Laffer in 2008.

The economic crisis demanded decisive action. On October 3, 2008, after two weeks of contentious and often emotional congressional debate, President Bush signed into law a far-reaching historic bank bailout fund called the **Troubled Asset Relief Program (TARP)**. The TARP called for the Treasury Department to spend $700 billion to keep banks and other financial institutions from collapsing. "By coming together on this legislation, we have acted boldly to prevent the crisis on Wall Street from becoming a crisis in communities across our country," Bush said after the House voted 263 to 171 to pass the TARP bill. Despite such unprecedented government investment in the private financial sector, the economy still sputtered. In early October, stock markets around the world began to crash. Economists warned that the world was at risk of careening into a depression.

## A HISTORIC ELECTION

The economic crisis had potent political effects. As two preeminent economists noted, "In the eight years since George W. Bush took office, nearly every component of the U.S. economy has deteriorated." Budget deficits, trade deficits, and consumer debt had reached record levels, and the total expense of the American war in Iraq was projected to top $3 trillion. During President Bush's last year in office, just 29 percent of the voters "approved" of his leadership. And more than 80 percent said that the nation was headed in the "wrong direction." Even a prominent Republican strategist, Kevin Phillips, deemed Bush "perhaps the least competent president in modern history."

Bush's vulnerability excited Democrats about the possibility of regaining the White House in the 2008 election. Not only was the Bush presidency floundering, but the Republican party was in disarray, plagued by scandals, riven by factions, and lacking effective leadership. In 2004, the American electorate had been evenly divided by party identification: 43 percent for both the Democratic and the Republican parties. By 2008 the Democrats were leading the Republicans 50 percent to 35 percent.

The early front-runner for the Democratic nomination was New York senator **Hillary Rodham Clinton**, the highly visible spouse of ex-president Bill Clinton. Like her husband, she displayed an impressive command of policy issues and mobilized a well-funded campaign team. And as the first woman with a serious chance of gaining the presidency, she garnered widespread support among voters eager for female leadership. In the end,

**The Clinton campaign**

Democratic presidential hopeful Senator Hillary Rodham Clinton speaks at the Fort Worth Stockyards.

however, an overconfident Clinton was upset in the Democratic primaries and caucuses by little-known first-term senator **Barack Obama** of Illinois, an inspiring speaker who attracted huge crowds by promising a "politics of hope" and bolstering their desire for "change." While the Clinton campaign courted the powerful members of the party establishment, Obama mounted an innovative Internet-based campaign directed at grassroots voters, donors, and volunteers. In early June 2008, he gained enough delegates to secure the Democratic nomination.

Obama was the first African American presidential nominee of either party, the gifted biracial son of a white mother from Kansas and a black Kenyan father who left the household and returned to Africa when Barack was a toddler. The forty-seven-year-old Harvard Law School graduate and former professor, community organizer, and state legislator presented himself as a conciliator who could inspire and unite a diverse people and forge bipartisan collaborations. He promised to end "the petty grievances and false promises, the recriminations and worn-out dogmas that for too long have strangled our politics."

Obama exuded poise, confidence, and energy. By contrast, his Republican opponent, seventy-two-year-old Arizona senator John McCain, was the oldest presidential candidate in history. As a twenty-five-year veteran of Congress, a leading Republican senator, and a 2000 candidate for the Republican presidential nomination, he had developed a reputation as a bipartisan maverick willing to work with Democrats to achieve key legislative goals.

Concerns about McCain's support among Republican conservatives led him to select Alaska governor Sarah Palin as his running mate, the first woman on a Republican ticket. Although hardly known outside party circles, Palin held the promise of winning over religious conservatives nervous about McCain's ideological purity. She opposed abortion, gay marriage, and stem-cell research, and she endorsed the teaching of creationism in public schools. For his part, Barack Obama rejected calls to choose Hillary Clinton as his running mate. Instead, he selected seasoned Delaware senator Joseph Biden, in large part because of his knowledge of foreign policy and national security issues. Biden was chair of the Senate Foreign Relations Committee.

THE 2008 ELECTION   In the 2008 presidential campaign, Obama shrewdly capitalized on widespread dissatisfaction with the Republicans and centered his campaign on the echoing promise of "change." He

**The 2008 presidential debates**

Republican presidential candidate John McCain (left) and Democratic presidential candidate Barack Obama (right) focused on foreign policy, national security, and the financial crisis at the first of three presidential debates.

repeatedly linked McCain with the unpopular George W. Bush. Obama promised to end the war in Iraq and he denounced the prevailing Republican "economic philosophy that says we should give more and more to those with the most and hope that prosperity trickles down to everyone else." He described the 2008 financial meltdown as the "final verdict on this failed philosophy."

On November 4, 2008, Barack Obama made history by becoming the nation's first person of color elected president. "Change has come to America," he announced in his victory speech. His triumph was decisive and sweeping. The inspirational Obama won the popular vote by seven points: 53 percent to 46 percent. His margin in the electoral vote was even more impressive: 365 to 173. The president-elect won big among his core supporters—voters under age thirty, women, minorities, the very poor, and first-time voters. He collected 95 percent of the African American vote and 66 percent of voters aged eighteen to twenty-nine, and he won the increasingly important Hispanic vote. Obama also helped the Democrats win solid majorities in the House and Senate races.

**Election night rally**

President-elect Barack Obama, his wife Michelle, and two daughters, Sasha and Malia, wave to the crowd of supporters in Chicago's Grant Park.

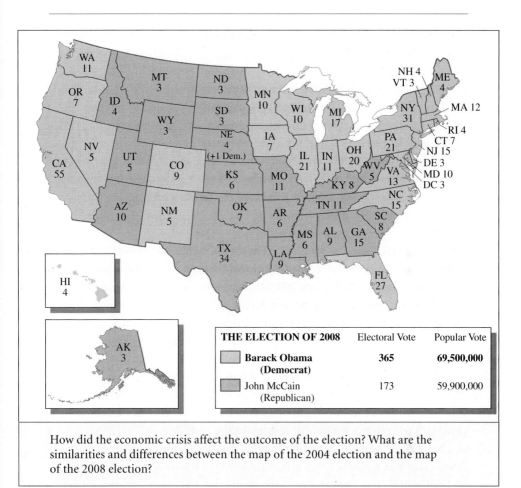

| THE ELECTION OF 2008 | Electoral Vote | Popular Vote |
|---|---|---|
| Barack Obama (Democrat) | 365 | 69,500,000 |
| John McCain (Republican) | 173 | 59,900,000 |

How did the economic crisis affect the outcome of the election? What are the similarities and differences between the map of the 2004 election and the map of the 2008 election?

Within days of his electoral victory, Barack Obama adopted a bipartisan approach in selecting his new cabinet members. He appointed Hillary Clinton secretary of state, renewed Republican Robert Gates as secretary of defense, selected retired general James Jones, who had campaigned for McCain, as his national security adviser, and appointed Eric Holder as the nation's first African American attorney general.

## OBAMA'S FIRST TERM

**THE FIRST HUNDRED DAYS**   On January 20, 2009, President Obama, calm and dispassionate, delivered his inaugural address in frigid weather amid daunting challenges. The United States was embroiled in two wars, in Iraq and Afghanistan. The economy was in shambles, unemployment was soaring, and the national debt was hemorrhaging. A supremely self-confident yet inexperienced Obama acted quickly—some said too quickly—to fulfill his campaign pledges. He wanted to be a transformative president, an agent of fundamental public policy changes. He pledged to overhaul unneeded government regulations, reform education, energy, environmental, and health-care policies, restructure the tax code, invigorate the economy, and recast U.S. foreign policy. In March, Obama froze the salaries of his senior staffers, mandated higher fuel-efficiency standards for automobiles, and increased the federal cigarette tax. Obama also eased restrictions on travel to Cuba that had been in place for nearly fifty years.

THE SLUGGISH ECONOMY   The new Obama administration's main challenge was to keep the deepening global recession from becoming a prolonged depression. During late 2008, the economy was shrinking at an annualized rate of nearly 9 percent and losing seven hundred thousand jobs a month—symptoms of a depression. Unemployment in early 2009 had passed 8 percent and was still rising. More than 5 million people had lost their jobs since 2007. The financial sector remained paralyzed. When Obama promised to act "boldly and wisely" to fulfill his campaign pledges and stimulate the stagnant economy, many progressive Democrats expected him to mimic Franklin D. Roosevelt in 1933 and launch an array of New Deal-like programs to help the needy and restore public confidence.

That did not happen. Most of Obama's financial advisers, as it turned out, came from the gigantic Wall Street investment banks like Goldman Sachs and Citigroup that were in part responsible for the greatest financial crisis since the Great Depression. In responding to that crisis, the new administration focused most of its efforts on helping shore up Wall Street—the very financial interests that had provoked the crisis. As *Time* magazine noted in 2010, Obama's advisers devised a recovery plan for the huge banks "that further enriched their cronies without doing much for the average Joe." The big banks and brokerage houses received lavish government bail-outs, while the working class and hard-pressed homeowners received much less help in the form of spending to provide debt relief or to stimulate the flagging economy. Yes, the massive infusion of federal money shored up the largest banks, but in a way that required taxpayers to assume all the risk for the reckless speculation the banks had engaged in that had triggered the crisis.

In mid-February, after a prolonged and often strident debate, Congress passed, and Obama signed, a $787-billion economic stimulus bill called the **American Recovery and Reinvestment Act**. It was the largest in history, but in the end not large enough to serve its purpose of restoring economic growth. The bill included cash distributions to the states, additional funds for food stamps, unemployment benefits, construction projects to renew the nation's infrastructure (roads, bridges, levees, government buildings, and the electricity grid), money for renewable-energy systems, and $212 billion in tax reductions for individuals and businesses. Yet the stimulus package was not robust enough to reverse the deepening recession. Moreover, congressional passage of the stimulus bill showed no evidence that Obama was successful in implementing a "bipartisan" presidency. Only three Senate Republicans voted for the bill. Not a single House Republican voted for it, and eleven House Democrats opposed it as well.

HEALTH CARE REFORM    Obama compounded his error in underestimating the depth and complexity of the recession by choosing to emphasize comprehensive health-care reform rather than concentrate on creating jobs and restoring prosperity. Obama explained that the nation's health-care system was so broken that it was "bankrupting families, bankrupting businesses, and bankrupting our government at the state and federal level." The president's goal was to streamline the nation's health-care system, make health insurance more affordable, and make health care accessible for everyone. Throughout 2009, White House staffers and congressional committees worked through a maze of complicated issues before presenting to the Congress the Patient Protection and Affordable Care Act (PPACA).

The ten-year-long, $940 billion proposal (a thousand pages long!), modeled after a Massachusetts health-care program enacted in 2006 under then–Republican governor Mitt Romney, included numerous provisions, the most controversial of which was the so-called individual mandate, which required that the uninsured must purchase an approved private insurance policy made available through state agencies or pay a tax penalty. Employers who did not offer health insurance would also have to pay higher taxes, and drug companies as well as manufacturers of medical devices would have to pay annual government fees. Everyone would pay higher Medicare payroll taxes to help fund the changes. The individual mandate was designed to ensure that all Americans had health insurance so as to reduce the skyrocketing costs of hospitals providing "charity care" for the 32 million uninsured Americans. But the idea of forcing people to buy health insurance flew in the face of the principle of individual freedom and personal responsibility. As a result, the health-care reform legislation became a highly partisan issue. Critics questioned not only the individual mandate but also the administration's projections that the new program would reduce federal expenditures over the long haul.

President Obama invested much of his time, energy, and political capital in shepherding the legislation through the Congress. In December 2009, the PPACA received Senate approval, with all Democrats and two Independents voting for, and all Republicans voting against. In March 2010, the House of Representatives narrowly approved the package, by a vote of 219–212, with 34 Democrats and all 178 Republicans voting against the bill. Obama signed PPACA into law on March 23, 2010. Its major provisions would be implemented over a four-year transition period.

REGULATING WALL STREET   The unprecedented meltdown of the nation's financial system beginning in 2008 prompted calls for overhauling the nation's financial regulatory system. On July 21, 2010, Obama signed the Wall Street Reform and Consumer Protection Act, also called Dodd–Frank after its two congressional sponsors. It was the most comprehensive overhaul of the financial system since the New Deal in the thirties. The 2,319-page law acknowledged the need to limit the amount of risk that Wall Street investment banks could take with their clients' money in order to generate revenue for the bank and huge bonuses for themselves. The Dodd-Frank bill also called for government agencies to exercise greater oversight over highly leverage and highly complex new financial instruments and protected consumers from unfair practices in loans and credit cards by establishing a new consumer financial-protection agency. While allowing the mega-banks to continue rather than be broken up, the Dodd-Frank legislation also empowered government regulators to dismantle any financial firms, not just banks, that were failing. At the signing ceremony in the Ronald Reagan Building in Washington, D.C., Obama claimed that the new bill would "lift our economy," give "certainty to everybody" about the legitimacy of financial transactions, and end "tax-funded bailouts [of big businesses]—period" because it would no longer allow corporations to become "too big to fail."

WARS IN IRAQ AND AFGHANISTAN   President Obama had more success in dealing with foreign affairs than in reviving the economy, in part because he appointed able people such as Hillary Clinton as secretary of state and Robert Gates as secretary of defense. Obama wanted to "change the trajectory of American foreign policy in a way that would end the war in Iraq, refocus on defeating our primary enemy, al Qaeda, strengthen our alliances and our leadership." His foremost concern was to rein in what he believed was the overextension of American power and prestige abroad. What journalists came to call the Obama Doctrine stressed that the United States could not afford to be the world's only policeman. As Obama explained, the

United States has limited "resources and capacity." It was imperative to adopt a multilateral approach to world crises so as to reduce America's investment in massive foreign commitments and interventions. Obama sought to mobilize collective action against tyranny and terrorism rather than continue to go it alone. And he was remarkably successful in doing so.

The Obama Doctrine grew out of the fact that the president inherited two enormously expensive wars, one in Iraq and the other in Afghanistan. On February 27, 2009, Obama announced that all U.S. combat troops would be withdrawn from Iraq by the end of 2011. Until then, a "transitional force" of thirty-five thousand to fifty thousand troops would assist Iraqi security forces, protect Americans, and fight terrorism. True to his word, the last U.S. troops left Iraq in December 2011. Their exit marked the end of a bitterly divisive war that had raged for nearly nine years and left Iraq shattered, with troubling questions lingering over whether the newly democratic Arab nation would be self-sustaining as well as a steadfast U.S. ally amid chronic sectarian clashes in a turbulent region. The U.S. intervention in Iraq had cost over four thousand

**Home from Iraq**

American troops returned from Iraq to more somber, humbler homecomings than the great fanfare that rounded off previous wars.

American lives, over one hundred thousand Iraqi lives, and $800 billion. Whether it was worth such an investment remained to be seen.

At the same time that he was reducing U.S. military involvement in Iraq, President Obama dispatched twenty-one thousand additional troops to Afghanistan, which he called "ground zero" in the continuing battle against global terrorism. The goal in Afghanistan was to "disrupt, dismantle, and defeat al Qaeda" at its Afghan base through a revitalized effort to assault the Taliban. When President Bush escalated U.S. military involvement in Afghanistan, the situation in the war-torn tribal land resembled the predicament the United States had found itself in during the Vietnam War: an indefensible border region harboring enemy sanctuaries; American reliance on a corrupt partner government; and the necessity of fighting a war of counterinsurgency—the most difficult type of conflict because there was no easy distinction between civilians and the insurgents. Yet by the summer of 2011, it appeared that the American strategy was working. President Obama announced that the "tide of war was receding" and that the United States had largely achieved its goals in Afghanistan, setting in motion a substantial withdrawal of U.S. forces beginning in 2011 and lasting until 2014. As was true in Iraq, Obama stressed that the Afghans must determine the future stability of Afghanistan. "We will not try to make Afghanistan a perfect place," he said. "We will not police its streets or patrol its mountains indefinitely. That is the responsibility of the Afghan government."

THE DEATH OF OSAMA BIN LADEN    At the same time that Obama was ending the U.S. role in Iraq and Afghanistan, he focused additional resources on counterterrorism, expanding the use of special operations forces and remote-controlled drones to assault the senior leaders of al Qaeda, almost all of whom operated out of Pakistan. The crowning achievement of Obama's efforts was the discovery, at long last, of Osama bin Laden's hideout. Ever since the attacks of 9/11, bin Laden had eluded an intense manhunt after crossing the Afghan border into Pakistan. His luck ran out in August 2011, however, when U.S. intelligence officials discovered bin Laden's sanctuary in a walled residential compound outside of Abbottabad, Pakistan. On May 1, 2011, President Obama authorized a daring night raid by a U.S. Navy SEAL team of two dozen specially trained commandos transported by helicopters from Afghanistan. After a brief firefight, caught on videotape and fed live by a satellite link to the White House situation room, the Navy SEAL team killed bin Laden and transported his body to an aircraft carrier in the Arabian Sea, where it was washed, wrapped in a white sheet, and dropped overboard. There were no American casualties. Ten years earlier, bin Laden had told a reporter that he "loves death. The Americans love life. I will engage them and fight. If I am to die, I would like to be killed by the bullet." The U.S. Special Forces assault team granted his wish. The news that the mastermind of global terrorism had been killed sparked worldwide celebrations. Violent Islamism no longer seemed inevitable or indomitable.

THE "ARAB AWAKENING"    The wars in Iraq and Afghanistan were simply the latest evidence of the massive investment that the United States had made in the stability of the Middle East and North Africa since the first Arab oil embargo in the 1970s. The security of Israel and ensuring American access to the region's vast oil reserves made the Middle East strategically important—and volatile. After 9/11, America's focus on the turbulent Middle East became an obsession. The invasions of Afghanistan in 2001 and Iraq in 2003 displaced and decimated al Qaeda and helped to prevent any more major attacks on U.S. soil. But the deepening involvement in the region also drained America's budget (costing well over a trillion dollars), created dissension at home, and emboldened enemies such as Iran and Syria to become even more aggressive in their provocations.

In late 2010 and early 2011, however, something remarkable and unexpected occurred: spontaneous democratic uprisings emerged throughout much of the Arab world, as long-oppressed peoples rose up against generations-old authoritarian regimes. The idealistic rebels demanded basic liberties such as meaningful voting rights, a credible judicial system, and freedom of the press. One by one, corrupt Arab tyrants were forced out of power by a new generation of young idealists inspired by democratic ideals and connected by social media on the Internet. They did not simply demand change; they embodied it, putting their lives on the line.

The **Arab Awakening** began in mid-December 2010 in Tunisia, on the coast of North Africa. Like much of the Arab world, Tunisia was a chronically poor nation suffering from high unemployment, runaway inflation, political corruption, and authoritarian rule. On December 17, Mohamed Bouazizi, a twenty-six-year-old street vendor distraught over rough police treatment, set himself on fire in a public square. His suicidal act was like a stone thrown into a pond whose ripples quickly spread outward. It sparked waves of pro-democracy demonstrations across Tunisia that forced the president, who had been in power for twenty-three years, to step down when his own security forces refused orders to shoot protesters. An interim government thereafter allowed democratic elections.

Rippling waves of unrest sparked by the Tunisian "Burning Man" soon rolled across Algeria, Bahrain, Jordan, Morocco, Egypt, Oman, Yemen, Libya, Saudi Arabia, and Syria. The people's insistence on exercising their basic

**Arab Awakening**

Thousands of protestors converge in Cairo's Tahrir Square to call for an end to Mubarak's rule.

rights as citizens, the marches and rallies in the streets and parks, and the sudden coming to voice of the voiceless were tangible signs of an old order crumbling. In Egypt, the Arab world's most populous country, several thousand protesters led by university students converged in the streets of teeming Cairo in late January, 2011. They demanded the end of the long rule of strongman President Hosni Moubarak, a staunch American ally who had treated his own people with contempt. The boldness of the youthful rebels was contagious. Within a few days, hundreds of thousands of demonstrators representing all walks of life converged on Tahrir Square, where many of them encamped for eighteen days, singing songs, holding candlelight vigils, and waving flags in the face of a brutal crackdown by security forces. Violence erupted when Moubarak's supporters attacked the protesters. The government tried to cut off access to social communications—mobile telephones, text-messaging, and the Internet—but its success was limited. Desperate to stay in power, Moubarak replaced his entire cabinet, but it was not enough to quell the anti-government movement. On February 11, 2011, Moubarak resigned, ceding control to the military leadership. On March 4, a civilian was appointed prime minister, and elections were promised within a year.

As the so-called Arab Awakening flared up in other parts of the region, some of the rebellions grew violent, some were brutally smashed (Syria), and some achieved substantial political changes. The remarkable uprisings heralded a new era in the history of the Middle East struggling to be born. Arabs had suddenly lost their fear—not just their fear of violent rulers, but also their fear that they were not capable of democratic government. By the millions, they demonstrated with their actions that they would no longer passively accept the old way of being governed.

LIBYA OUSTS GADDAFI    The pro-democracy turmoil in North Africa quickly spread to oil-rich Libya, long governed by the zany dictator Colonel Muammar Gaddafi, the Arab world's most violent despot. Anti-government demonstrations began on February 15, 2011, prompting Gaddafi to order Libyan soldiers and foreign mercenaries to suppress the rebellious "rats," first with rubber bullets, then with live ammunition, including artillery and war-planes. The soaring casualties spurred condemnations of Gaddafi's brutalities from around the world, including the United States. By the end of February, what began as a peaceful pro-democratic uprising had turned into a full-scale civil war in which the poorly organized, scantily armed rebels faced an entrenched regime willing to do anything to retain its stranglehold over the nation. On March 17, the UN Security Council authorized a no-fly zone over Libya designed to prevent Gaddafi's use of warplanes against the civilian rebels.

President Obama handled the Libyan uprising with patience and ingenu-ity. Eager to avoid the mistakes made in the Iraq War, he insisted on several conditions being met before involving U.S. forces in Libya. First, the pro-democratic rebel force needed to request American assistance. Second, any UN coalition must include Arab nations as well as the United States and its European allies. Third, the United States would commit warplanes and cruise missiles but not ground forces; it could not afford a third major war in the region. On March 19, those conditions were met. With the Arab League's support, France, the United States, and the United Kingdom intervened in Libya with a bombing campaign against pro-Gaddafi forces. One rebel leader called the Allied air strikes "a gift from God." For seven months, intense fighting raged back and forth across northern Libya. Slowly, the ragtag Libyan rebels gained confidence and coordination. What most observers believed was impossible—the overthrow of the Gaddafi regime—began to take hold. In late August, anti-Gaddafi forces, accompanied by television crews, captured the capital of Tripoli, scattering Gaddafi's government and marking the end of his forty-two-year dictatorship. On October 20, rebel fighters captured and killed Gaddafi in his hometown of Sirt.

The Obama administration believed that the root cause of Islamist terrorism was not religion but the absence of Arab democracy. Promoting democracy in the region represented a profound change in American policy. Since the end of the Second World War, U.S. leaders had tended to prize stability in the Arab nations, even if it meant propping up tyrants. Under President Obama, the United States did an about-face and supported the Arab Awakening's crusade for democratic change and human rights. Yet while the Arab Awakening had ensured that the political process in many countries would be more open and dynamic, it did not necessarily bring stability to the turbulent region. The Arab political stage had suddenly been repopulated with a new cast of characters acting out the first scene of an unfolding drama promoting pluralism and tolerance. "You have to understand," said a Syrian rebel, "that this is not a bunch of different revolutions. This is one big revolution for all the Arabs. It will not stop until it reaches everywhere."

THE TEA PARTY   At the same time that Arabs were rebelling against entrenched political elites, grassroots rebellions were occurring in the United States as well. No sooner was Obama sworn in than limited-government conservatives frustrated by his election began mobilizing to thwart any renewal of "tax-and-spend" liberalism. In January 2009, a New York stock trader named Graham Makohoniuk sent out an e-mail message urging people to send tea bags to the Senate and House of Representatives. He fastened on tea bags to symbolize the famous Boston Tea Party of 1773 during which outraged American colonists protested against British tax policies. The e-mail message "went viral" among anti-tax libertarians and conservatives across the nation. Within days, thousands of tea bags poured into congressional offices. Within weeks, the efforts of angry activists coalesced into a decentralized nationwide protest movement soon labeled "the **Tea Party**." It had neither a national headquarters nor an official governing body; nor was there a formal process for joining the grassroots movement. Within a year or so, there were about a thousand Tea Party groups spread across the fifty states. "The GOP is very worried," noted a political scientist. "It's very hard to deal with the Tea Party movement. It's like fighting guerrilla warfare with them."

The Tea Party is at once a mood, an attitude, and an ideology, an eruption of libertarians, mostly white, male, middle-class Republicans over the age of forty-five, boiling mad at a political system that they believe has grown dependent on spending their taxes. The overarching aim of the Tea Party is to transform the Republican party into a vehicle of conservative ideology and eliminate all those who resist the true faith. More immediately, the "tea parties" rallied against President Obama's health-care initiative and economic stimulus package, arguing that they verged on socialism in their efforts to bail out corporate America and distressed homeowners. On April 15, 2009, the Internal Revenue tax-filing deadline, Tea Party demonstrations occurred in 750 cities.

What began as a scattering of anti-tax protests crystallized into a powerful anti-government movement promoting fiscal conservatism at the local, state, and national levels. Like Ronald Reagan, the Tea Party saw government as the problem, not the solution. As candidates began to campaign for the 2010 congressional elections, the Tea Party mobilized to influence the results, not by forming a third political party but by trying to take over the leadership of the Republican party. Members of the Tea Party were as frustrated by the old-line

**The Tea Party Movement**

Tea Party supporters gather outside the New Hampshire Statehouse for a tax day rally.

Republican establishment (RINOs—Republicans in Name Only) as they were disgusted by liberal Democrats. As a Virginia Tea Party candidate claimed, "I don't think there'd be a Tea Party if the Republican Party had been a party of limited government in the first part of this decade." The Tea Party members were not seeking simply to rebuild the Republican party; they wanted to take over a "decaying" Republican party and restore its anti-tax focus. Democrats, including President Obama, initially dismissed the Tea Party as a fringe group of extremists, but the 2010 election results proved them wrong.

CONSERVATIVE RESURGENCE    Barack Obama had campaigned in 2008 on the promise of bringing dramatic change to the federal government. "Yes, we can" was his echoing campaign slogan. In the fall of 2010, however, many of the same voters who had embraced Obama's promises in 2008 now answered, "Oh, no you don't!" Democratic House and Senate candidates (as well a moderate Republicans), including many long-serving leaders, were defeated in droves as insurgent conservatives recaptured control of the House of Representatives (gaining sixty-three seats) and won a near majority in the Senate. Republicans also took control of both the governorships and the legislatures in twelve states; ten states were already Republican-controlled. It was the most lopsided midterm election since 1938. A humbled Obama,

who in a fit of hubris had earlier claimed that his first two years were comparable to the achievements of Abraham Lincoln, Franklin D. Roosevelt, and
Lyndon B. Johnson, called it a "shellacking" reminiscent of what Congressional Republicans had experienced in 2006. One of his aides was more apocalyptic: he called the election an "inflection point," suggesting that the rest of
the president's first term would be contentious; stalemate would trump
change as the new "Tea Party" Republicans strove to rebuke Obama at every
turn. Exit polls on election day showed widespread frustration about Obama's
handling of the slumping economy. Recovery and jobs growth remained elusive. Voters said that Obama and the Democrats had tried to do too much too
fast—bailing out huge banks and automobile companies, spending nearly a
trillion dollars on various pet projects designed to stimulate the flaccid economy, and reorganizing the national health-care system. Republican candidates were carried into office on a wave of discontent fomented by the Tea
Party movement that demanded ideological purity from its candidates.
"We've come to take our government back," declared one Republican congressional winner. Thereafter, Obama and the Republican-dominated Congress engaged in a strident sparring match, each side refusing to accommodate
the other as the incessant partisan bickering postponed meaningful action on
the languishing economy and the runaway federal budget deficit.

OCCUPY WALL STREET    The emergence of the Tea Party illustrated the
growing ideological extremism of twenty-first-century politics. On the left
wing of the political spectrum, the **Occupy Wall Street** (OWS) movement,
founded in the fall of 2011, represented the radical alternative to the Tea Party.
In the spring of 2011 Kalle Lasn, the founding editor of *Adbusters*, an anti-
consumerism magazine published in Vancouver, Canada, decided to promote a grassroots uprising against a capitalist system that was promoting
mindless materialism and growing economic and social inequality. What
America most needed, Lasn believed, was a focused conversation about
growing income inequality, diminishing opportunities for upward social
mobility, runaway corporate greed as well as the distorting impact of corporate donations to political campaigns, and economic fairness—all issues that
had been exacerbated by the government "bailouts" of huge banks and corporations weakened by the Great Recession. As the Pew Research Center
reported, the conflict between rich and poor had become "the greatest
source of tension in American society."

Lasn began circulating through his magazine and online networks a poster
showing a ballerina perched atop the famous "Charging Bull" sculpture on
Wall Street. The caption read: "What Is Our Demand? Occupy Wall Street.

Bring tent." The call to arms quickly circulated over the Internet, and another decentralized grassroots movement was born. Within a few days OWS had launched an anarchical website, OccupyWallSt.org, and moved the headquarters for the anti-capitalist uprising from Vancouver to New York City. Dozens, then hundreds, then thousands of people, mostly young adults, many of them unemployed, converged on Zuccotti Park in southern Manhattan in a kind of spontaneous democracy. They formed tent villages and gathered in groups to "occupy" Wall Street to protest corrupt banks and brokerage houses whose "fraudsters," they claimed, had caused the 2008 economic crash and forced the severe government cutbacks in social welfare programs. OWS charged that most of the nation's financiers at the heart of the Great Recession had not been prosecuted or even disciplined. The biggest banks were larger than ever, and huge bonuses were being paid to staff members.

The protesting "occupiers" drafted a "Declaration of the Occupation" that served as the manifesto of a decentralized movement dedicated to undermining the disproportionate political and economic power exercised by the Wall Street power brokers. OWS demanded that corporate donations to

## Occupy Wall Street

The grassroots movement expanded rapidly from rallies in Zuccotti Park, Manhattan, (left) into massive marches on financial districts nationwide. Right, thousands of protesters storm downtown Los Angeles.

political candidates cease and that elected officials focus on helping people rather than bailing out big business. Economic data showed that for decades the super-rich had been garnering a growing percentage of national wealth at the expense of the working and middle classes. In 1980, the richest one percent of Americans controlled ten percent of all personal income; by 2012, the top one percent amassed twenty-five percent of total income. And the people hurt most by the Great Recession were those at the bottom of the income scale. By 2010, there were 46.2 million Americans living below the U.S. poverty line, an all-time record. The OWS protesters were determined to reverse such economic and social trends. They described themselves as the voice of the 99 percent of Americans who were being victimized by the 1 percent of the wealthiest and most politically connected Americans. As one of the protesters proclaimed, "everyone can see that the [capitalist] system is deeply unjust and careening out of control. Unfettered greed has trashed the global economy. And it is trashing the natural world as well."

The OWS protesters excelled at creative disruption. They tried to shut down the New York Stock Exchange, held a sit-in at the nearby Brooklyn Bridge, and grappled with police. The vagueness ("We are our demands!") of a spontaneous grassroots "movement without demands" was initially a virtue, as the demonstrations attracted national media coverage. "We can't hold on to any authority," one organizer explained. "We don't want to." But soon thousands more alienated people showed up, many of whom brought their own agendas to the effort. A "horizontal" movement with organizers and facilitators but no leaders at times morphed into a chaotic mob punctuated by antic good cheer and zaniness (organizers dressed up as Wall Street executives, stuffed Monopoly "play" money in their mouths, etc.). At the same time, however, the anarchic energies of OWS began to spread like a virus across the nation. Similar efforts calling for a "government accountable to the people, freed up from corporate influence" emerged in cities around the globe; encampments of alienated activists sprang up in over a thousand towns and cities. On December 6, 2011, President Obama echoed the OWS movement when he deplored in a speech "the breathtaking greed of a few" and said that the effort to restore economic "fairness" was the "defining issue of our time." Although the OWS demonstrations receded after many cities ordered police to arrest the protesters and dismantle the ramshackle encampments, by the end of 2011 the OWS effort to spark a national conversation about growing income inequality had succeeded. As the *New York Times* announced, "The new progressive age has begun."

POLARIZED POLITICS   American politics has always been chaotic, combative, and fractious; its raucous energy is one of its strengths. But the

2010 election campaigns were spirited to the point of violence; polarizing partisan rhetoric had never been fiercer. Obama's pledge to be a bipartisan president fell victim to acidic battles between the two political parties. The increasingly dogmatic tone of American politics did not bode well for those hoping for bipartisan leadership cooperation. As a House Republican predicted in the aftermath of the 2010 elections, there would be "no compromise on stopping runaway spending, deficits, and debt. There will be no compromise on repealing Obamacare." The strident refusal to compromise became a point of honor for both parties—and created a nightmarish stalemate for the nation, as the dysfunctional political system harmed an already sick economy. The gulf between the two parties had become a chasm. "American politicians are intent," said the editors of *The Economist*, "not on improving the country's competitiveness, but on gouging each other's eyes out."

Ideological purity became the watchword of modern conservatism as libertarianism emerged as an appealing alternative to traditional conservatism. The libertarian wing of the conservative revolt was led by Texas Congressman Ron Paul, who not only disapproved of runaway federal spending on social programs but also on military defense. Paul disagreed with George W. Bush's decision to invade Iraq and upset religious conservatives by arguing that flashpoint cultural issues such as abortion and gay marriage should be addressed on a state-by-state basis, not by the federal government.

By 2011, the conservative insurgency led by the Tea Party focused on the record-breaking federal deficit and the tepid economic recovery (2011 home sales were the worst in history). The Tea Party faction in Congress theatrically began to practice a form of brinkmanship: they were willing to let the nation go bankrupt rather than raise the debt-ceiling limit. What Tea Party members hated most was the willingness of Republicans over the years to compromise with Democrats and thereby enable the federal government to keep growing and overspending its budgets. But if the Tea Party pushed too hard, it would fracture the Republican party. Some were not sure that was such a bad idea. "If the Republicans can't come through with their promises," a Rhode Island Tea Partier mused, "maybe the party needs to be blown up."

The politics of impasse stalemated American government during 2011 and 2012. Rather than work responsibly together to close the nation's gaping budget deficit, the two warring parties proved incapable of reaching a compromise; they instead opted for the easy way out by applying temporary patches that would expire after the November 2012 elections. Those patches created a fiscal "cliff" at the end of 2012, whereby the tax cuts created by George W. Bush would expire, as would a cut in payroll taxes. At the same time, a string of across-the-board federal budget cuts (called "sequesters") would also automatically occur unless Congress acted. Rather than bridge their differences during 2011–2012, both sides preferred to fight it out during the presidential election campaign in hopes that the voters would signal a clear message.

BOLD DECISIONS    In May 2012 President Obama jumped headfirst into the simmering cultural wars by courageously changing his longstanding position and announcing his support for the rights of gay couples to marry. That his statement came a day after the state of North Carolina legislature voted to ban all rights for gay couples illustrated how incendiary the issue was around the country. While asserting it was the "right" thing to do, Obama also knew that endorsing gay marriage had political ramifications. The gay community would play an energetic role in the 2012 presidential election, and the youth vote, the under-30 electorate who of all the voting-age cohorts supported gay marriage, would be equally crucial to Obama's reelection chances. No sooner had Obama made his pathbreaking announcement than polls showed that American voters split half and half on the charged issue, with Democrats and independent voters constituting the majority of such support.

The following month, in June 2012, Obama again stunned the nation by issuing an executive order (soon labeled the DREAM Act) allowing undocumented immigrants who were brought to the United States as children to remain in the country as citizens. His unanticipated decision thrilled Latino supporters who had lost heart over his failure to convince Congress to support a more comprehensive reform of immigration laws. The nation's changing demographics bolstered Obama's immigration initiatives. In 2005 Hispanics had become the largest minority group in the nation, surpassing African Americans. By 2012 the United States had more foreign-born and first-generation residents than ever before, and each year 1 million more immigrants arrived.

THE COURT RULES    No sooner had Obama pushed his controversial health care plan through Congress in 2010 than opponents—state governors, conservative organizations, businesses, and individual citizens, largely divided along party lines—began challenging the constitutionality of the Patient Protection and Affordable Care Act (PPACA), which Republicans labeled Obamacare. During the spring and summer of 2012, as the Supreme Court deliberated over the merits of the PPACA, most observers expected the conservative justices to declare Obama's most significant presidential achievement unconstitutional. But that did not happen. On June 28, 2012, the Court issued its much-awaited decision in a case titled *National Federation of Independent Business v. Sebelius*. The landmark 5-to-4 ruling surprised Court observers by declaring most of the new federal law constitutional. Even more surprising was that the deciding vote was cast by the chief justice, John G. Roberts, a philosophical conservative who had never before voted with the four "liberal" justices on the Court. Roberts upheld the PPACA's "individual mandate," requiring virtually every adult to buy private health insurance or else pay a tax, arguing that it was within the Congress's power to impose taxes as outlined in Article 1 of the Constitution. Because Congress had such authority, Justice Roberts declared, "it is not our role to forbid it, or to pass upon its wisdom or fairness." That would be up to the voters who elect the members of Congress. Many conservatives, including the four dissenting justices, felt betrayed by Roberts's unexpected ruling. The Court decision sent ripples through the 2012 presidential election campaign. The surprising verdict boosted Obama's reelection chances, leading the *New York Times* to predict that the ruling "may secure Obama's place in history." Republican candidate Mitt Romney, who as governor of Massachusetts had signed a similar health care bill only to repudiate it once he decided to run for president, promised to repeal the PPACA if elected.

As the November 2012 presidential election approached, it remained to be seen whether President Obama could shift the focus of voters from the sluggish economy to cultural politics and social issues. Mitt Romney won the Republican presidential nomination because he promised, as a former corporate executive, to accelerate economic growth. Romney sought to downplay volatile social issues, in part because of his inconsistent stances on hot-button topics such as abortion, gay marriage, and immigration reform. His shifting stances reflected a shift in the Republican strategy. Over the past forty years, their conservative positions on social issues were vote-getters; now they feared that too much moralizing by the religious right ran the risk of alienating the independent voters who continue to be the decisive factor in presidential elections. The question for Romney was whether the still-powerful religious right would allow him to sidestep tough social issues; the question for Obama was whether he could sidestep his failure to restore prosperity to an economy experiencing the slowest recession recovery since the 1930s.

*End of Chapter Review*

## CHAPTER SUMMARY

- **Changing Demographics**  From 1980 to 2010, the population of the United States grew by 25 percent to 306 million. The number of traditional family units continued to decline; the poverty rate was especially high among African Americans. A wave of immigrants caused Latinos to surpass African Americans as the nation's largest minority.

- **Divided Government**  The popularity of President George H. W. Bush waned after the Gulf War, an economic recession, and his decision to raise taxes. The election of William Jefferson Clinton in 1992 aroused Republican Speaker Newton Leroy Gingrich to craft his Contract with America to achieve the Republican landslide of 1994.

- **Economic Prosperity and Crises**  The United States benefited from a period of unprecedented prosperity during the 1990s, fueled by the dramatic effect of the new computer-based industries on the economy. The collapse of high-tech companies in 2000 betrayed the underlying insecurity of the market. Economic growth soon surged again primarily because of consumers' ability to borrow against the skyrocketing value of their home mortgages. In 2007, the country experienced an unparalleled crisis when the global financial markets collapsed under the weight of "toxic" financial securities.

- **Global Terrorism**  The 9/11 attacks led President George W. Bush to declare a war on terrorism and enunciate the Bush Doctrine. In 2002 the Bush administration shifted its focus to Saddam Hussein. The American-led Operation Iraqi Freedom succeeded in removing Hussein from power but was fully unprepared to establish order in a country that was soon wracked by sectarian violence. The American public became bitterly divided over the Iraq War.

- **2008 Presidential Election**  The 2008 presidential campaigns included the first major female candidate, Senator Hillary Clinton; an African American, Senator Barack Obama; and Senator John McCain, the oldest candidate in history. Obama won the popular vote and a landslide victory in the Electoral College, becoming the nation's first African American president. His victory was facilitated by the collapse of the economy, an unprecedented Internet- and grassroots-based campaign, and voters' weariness with President Bush and the Republican policies of the preceding eight years.

## CHRONOLOGY

| | |
|---|---|
| 1991 | Ethnic conflict explodes in Yugoslavia |
| 1995 | Republicans promote the Contract with America |
| 1996 | Congress passes the Personal Responsibility and Work Opportunity Act |
| 1998 | Kenneth Starr issues Whitewater report |
| 1998 | Bill Clinton brokers the Wye Mills Accord |
| 1999 | Bill Clinton is impeached and acquitted |
| 2000 | Supreme Court issues *Bush v. Gore* decision |
| September 11, 2001 | 9/11 attacks |
| 2003 | Iraq War begins with Operation Iraqi Freedom |
| 2005 | Hurricane Katrina |
| 2007 | Nancy Pelosi becomes the first female Speaker of the House of Representatives |
| 2008 | Global financial markets collapse |
| 2009 | Barack Obama becomes the nation's first African American president |
| 2011 | Occupy Wall Street movement begins |
| 2011 | U.S. troops return from Iraq |

## KEY TERMS & NAMES

# GLOSSARY

**36°30′** According to the Missouri Compromise, any part of the Louisiana Purchase north of this line (Missouri's southern border) was to be excluded from slavery.

**54th Massachusetts Regiment** After President Abraham Lincoln's Emancipation Proclamation, the Union army organized all black military units, which white officers led. The 54th Massachusetts Regiment was one of the first of such units to be organized.

**Abigail Adams (1744–1818)** As the wife of John Adams, she endured long periods of separation from him while he served in many political roles. During these times apart, she wrote often to her husband; and their correspondence has provided a detailed portrait of life during the Revolutionary War.

**abolition** In the early 1830s, the anti-slavery movement shifted its goal from the gradual end of slavery to the immediate end or abolition of slavery.

**John Adams (1735–1826)** He was a signer of the Declaration of Independence and a delegate to the First and Second Continental Congress. During the Revolutionary War, he worked as a diplomat in France and Holland and negotiated the peace treaty with Britain. After the Revolutionary War, he served as the minister to Britain as well as the vice president and the second president of the United States. As president, he passed the Alien and Sedition Acts and endured a stormy relationship with France, which included the XYZ affair.

**John Quincy Adams (1767–1848)** As secretary of state under President Monroe, he negotiated agreements to define the boundaries of the Oregon country and the Transcontinental Treaty. He urged President Monroe to issue the Monroe Doctrine, which incorporated Adams's views. As president, Adams envisioned an expanded federal government and a broader use of federal powers. Adams's nationalism and praise of European leaders caused a split in his party. Some Republicans suspected him of being a closet monarchist and left to form the Democrat party. In the presidential election of 1828, Andrew Jackson claimed that Adams had gained the presidency through a "corrupt bargain" with Henry Clay, which helped Jackson win the election.

**Samuel Adams (1722–1803)** A genius of revolutionary agitation, he believed that English Parliament had no right to legislate for the colonies. He organized the Sons of Liberty as well as protests in Boston against the British.

**Jane Addams (1860–1935)** As the leader of one of the best known settlement houses, she rejected the "do-goodism" spirit of religious reformers. Instead, she focused on solving the practical problems of the poor and tried to avoid the assumption that she and other social workers knew what was best for poor immigrants. She established child care for working mothers, health clinics, job training, and other social programs. She was also active in the peace movement and was awarded the Noble Peace Prize in 1931 for her work on its behalf.

**Agricultural Adjustment Act (1933)** New Deal legislation that established the Agricultural Adjustment Administration (AAA) to improve agricultural prices by limiting market supplies; declared unconstitutional in *United States v. Butler* (1936).

**Emilio Aguinaldo (1869?–1964)** He was a leader in Filipino struggle for independence. During the war of 1898, Commodore George Dewey brought Aguinaldo back to the Philippines from exile to help fight the Spanish. However, after the Spanish surrendered to Americans, America annexed the Philippines and Aguinaldo fought against the American military until he was captured in 1901.

**Alamo, Battle of the** Siege in the Texas War for Independence of 1836, in which the San Antonio mission fell to the Mexicans. Davy Crockett and Jim Bowie were among the courageous defenders.

**Alien and Sedition Acts (1798)** Four measures passed during the undeclared war with France that limited the freedoms of speech and press and restricted the liberty of noncitizens.

**American Colonization Society** An organization created in 1816 to address slavery and racial issues in the Old South. Proposed that slaves and freed blacks would be shipped to Africa.

**American Federation of Labor** Founded in 1881 as a federation of trade unions made up of skilled workers, the AFL under president Samuel Gompers successfully pushed for the eight-hour workday.

**American Indian Movement (AIM)** Fed up with the poor conditions on Indian reservations and the federal government's unwillingness to help, Native Americans founded the American Indian Movement (AIM) in 1963. In 1973, AIM led 200 Sioux in the occupation of Wounded Knee. After a ten-week standoff with the federal authorities, the government agreed to reexamine Indian treaty rights and the occupation ended.

**American Recovery and Reinvestment Act** Hoping to restart the weak economy, President Obama signed this $787-billion economic stimulus bill in February of 2009. The bill included cash distributions to states, funds for food stamps, unemployment benefits, construction projects to renew the nation's infrastructure, funds for renewable-energy systems, and tax reductions.

**American System** Program of internal improvements and protective tariffs promoted by Speaker of the House Henry Clay in his presidential campaign of 1824; his proposals formed the core of Whig ideology in the 1830s and 1840s.

**anaconda strategy** Union General Winfield Scott developed this three-pronged strategy to defeat the Confederacy. Like a snake strangling its prey, the Union army would crush its enemy through exerting pressure on Richmond, blockading Confederate ports, and dividing the South by invading its major waterways.

**Annapolis Convention** In 1786, all thirteen colonies were invited to a convention in Annapolis to discuss commercial problems, but only representatives from five states attended. However, the convention was not a complete failure because the delegates decided to have another convention in order to write the constitution.

**anti-Federalists** Forerunners of Thomas Jefferson's Democratic-Republican party; opposed the Constitution as a limitation on individual and states' rights, which led to the addition of a Bill of Rights to the document.

**Anti-Masonic party** This party grew out of popular hostility toward the Masonic fraternal order and entered the presidential election of 1832 as a third party. It was the first party to run as a third party in a presidential election as well as the first to hold a nomination convention and announce a party platform.

**Arab Awakening** A wave of spontaneous democratic uprisings that spread throughout the Arab world beginning in 2011, in which long-oppressed peoples demanded basic liberties from generations-old authoritarian regimes.

**Benedict Arnold (1741–1801)** A traitorous American commander who planned to sell out the American garrison at West Point to the British, but his plot was discovered before it could be executed and he joined the British army.

**Atlanta Compromise** Speech to the Cotton States and International Exposition in 1895 by educator Booker T. Washington, the leading black spokesman of the day; black scholar W. E. B. Du Bois gave the speech its derisive name and criticized Washington for encouraging blacks to accommodate segregation and disenfranchisement.

**Atlantic Charter** Issued August 12, 1941, following meetings in Newfoundland between President Franklin D. Roosevelt and British Prime Minister Winston Churchill, the charter signaled the allies' cooperation and stated their war aims.

**Crispus Attucks (1723–1770)** During the Boston Massacre, he was supposedly at the head of the crowd of hecklers who baited the British troops. He was killed when the British troops fired on the crowd.

**Stephen F. Austin (1793–1836)** He established the first colony of Americans in Texas, which eventually attracted 2,000 people.

**Axis powers** In the Second World War, the nations of Germany, Italy, and Japan.

**Aztec Empire** Mesoamerican people who were conquered by the Spanish under Hernando Cortés, 1519–1528.

**baby boom** Markedly higher birth rate in the years following the Second World War; led to the biggest demographic "bubble" in American history.

**Bacon's Rebellion** Unsuccessful 1676 revolt led by planter Nathaniel Bacon against Virginia governor William Berkeley's administration, because it had failed to protect settlers from Indian raids.

**Bank of the United States** Proposed by the first Secretary of the Treasury Alexander Hamilton, the bank opened in 1791 and operated until 1811 to issue a uniform currency, make business loans, and collect tax monies. The second Bank of the United States was chartered in 1816 but was not renewed by President Andrew Jackson twenty years later.

**barbary pirates** Plundering pirates off the Mediterranean coast of Africa; President Thomas Jefferson's refusal to pay them tribute to protect American ships sparked an undeclared naval war with North African nations, 1801–1805.

**Battle of the Bulge** On December 16, 1944, the German army launched a counter attack against the Allied forces, which pushed them back. However, the Allies were eventually able to recover and breakthrough the German lines. This defeat was a great blow to the Nazi's morale and their army's strength. The battle used up the last of Hitler's reserve units and opened a route into Germany's heartland.

**Bear Flag Republic** On June 14, 1846, a group of Americans in California captured Sonoma from the Mexican army and declared it the Republic of California whose flag featured a grizzly bear. In July, the commodore of the U.S. Pacific Fleet landed troops on California's shores and declared it part of the United States.

**Beats** A group of writers, artists, and musicians whose central concern was the discarding of organizational constraints and traditional conventions in favor of liberated forms of self expression. They came out of the bohemian underground in New York's Greenwich Village in the 1950s and included the writers Jack Kerouac, Allen Ginsberg, and William Burroughs. Their attitudes and lifestyles had a major influence on the youth of the 1960s.

**beatnik** A name referring to almost any young rebel who openly dissented from the middle-class life. The name itself stems from the Beats.

**Nicholas Biddle (1786–1844)** He was the president of the second Bank of the United States. In response to President Andrew Jackson's attacks on the bank, Biddle curtailed the bank's loans and exchanged its paper currency for gold and silver. He was hoping to provoke an economic crisis to prove the bank's importance. In response, state banks began printing paper without restraint and lent it to speculators, causing a binge in speculating and an enormous increase in debt.

**Bill of Rights** First ten amendments to the U.S. Constitution, adopted in 1791 to guarantee individual rights and to help secure ratification of the Constitution by the states.

**Osama bin Laden (1957–2011)** The Saudi-born leader of al Qaeda, whose members attacked America on September 11, 2001. Years before the attack, he had declared jihad (holy war) on the United States, Israel, and the Saudi monarchy. In Afghanistan, the Taliban leaders gave bin Laden a safe haven in exchange for aid in fighting the Northern Alliance, who were rebels opposed to the Taliban. After the 9/11 terrorist attacks, the United States asked the Taliban to turn over bin Laden. Following their refusal, America and a multinational coalition invaded Afghanistan and overthrew the Taliban. In May 2011, bin Laden was shot and killed by American special forces during a covert operation in Pakistan.

**black codes** Laws passed in southern states to restrict the rights of former slaves; to combat the codes, Congress passed the Civil Rights Act of 1866 and the Fourteenth Amendment and set up military governments in southern states that refused to ratify the amendment.

**black power movement** A more militant form of protest for civil rights that originated in urban communities, where nonviolent tactics were less effective than in the South. Black power encouraged African Americans to take pride in their racial heritage and forced black leaders and organizations to focus attention on the plight of poor inner-city blacks.

**James Gillepsie Blaine (1830–1893)** As a Republican congressman from Maine, he developed close ties with business leaders, which contributed to him losing the presidential election of 1884. He later opposed President Cleveland's efforts to reduce tariffs, which became a significant issue in the 1888 presidential election. Blaine served as secretary of state under President Benjamin Harrison and his flamboyant style often overshadowed the president.

**"bleeding" Kansas** Violence between pro- and antislavery settlers in the Kansas Territory, 1856.

*blitzkrieg* The German "lightening war" strategy used during the Second World War; the Germans invaded Poland, France, Russia, and other countries with fast-moving, well-coordinated attacks using aircraft, tanks, and other armored vehicles, followed by infantry.

**Bolsheviks** Under the leadership of Vladimir Lenin, this Marxist party led the November 1917 revolution against the newly formed provisional government in Russia. After seizing control, the Bolsheviks negotiated a peace treaty with Germany, the Treaty of Brest-Litovsk, and ended their participation in World War I.

**Bonus Expeditionary Force** Thousands of World War I veterans, who insisted on immediate payment of their bonus certificates, marched on Washington in 1932; violence ensued when President Herbert Hoover ordered their tent villages cleared.

**Daniel Boone (1734–1820)** He found and expanded a trail into Kentucky, which pioneers used to reach and settle the area.

**John Wilkes Booth (1838?–1865)** He assassinated President Abraham Lincoln at the Ford's Theater on April 14, 1865. He was pursued to Virginia and killed.

**Bourbons** In post–Civil War southern politics, the opponents of the Redeemers were called Bourbons. They were known for having forgotten nothing and learned nothing from the ordeal of the Civil War.

**Joseph Brant (1742?–1807)** He was the Mohawk leader who led the Iroquois against the Americans in the Revolutionary War.

**brinksmanship** Secretary of State John Foster Dulles believed that communism could be contained by bringing America to the brink of war with an aggressive communist nation. He believed that the aggressor would back down when confronted with the prospect of receiving a mass retaliation from a country with nuclear weapons.

**John Brown (1800–1859)** He was willing to use violence to further his antislavery beliefs. In 1856, a pro-slavery mob sacked the free-state town of Lawrence, Kansas. In response, John Brown went to the pro-slavery settlement of Pottawatomie, Kansas and hacked to death several people, which led to a guerrilla war in the Kansas territory. In 1859, he attempted to raid the federal arsenal at Harpers Ferry. He had hoped to use the stolen weapons to arm slaves, but he was captured and executed. His failed raid instilled panic throughout the South, and his execution turned him into a martyr for his cause.

***Brown v. Board of Education of Topeka, Kansas* (1954)** U.S. Supreme Court decision that struck down racial segregation in public education and declared "separate but equal" unconstitutional.

**William Jennings Bryan (1860–1925)** He delivered the pro-silver "cross of gold" speech at the 1896 Democratic Convention and won his party's nomination for president. Disappointed pro-gold Democrats chose to walk out of the convention and nominate their own candidate, which split the Democratic party and cost them the White House. Bryan's loss also crippled the Populist movement that had endorsed him.

**"Bull Moose" Progressive party** In the 1912 election, Theodore Roosevelt was unable to secure the Republican nomination for president. He left the Republican party and formed his own party of progressive Republicans, called the "Bull Moose" party. Roosevelt and Taft split the Republican vote, which allowed Democrat Woodrow Wilson to win.

**Bull Run, Battles of (First and Second Manassas)** First land engagement of the Civil War took place on July 21, 1861, at Manassas Junction, Virginia, at which surprised Union troops quickly retreated; one year later, on August 29–30, Confederates captured the federal supply depot and forced Union troops back to Washington.

**Martin Van Buren (1782–1862)** During President Jackson's first term, he served as secretary of state and minister to London. He often politically fought Vice President John C. Calhoun for the position of Jackson's successor. A rift between Jackson and Calhoun led to Van Buren becoming vice president during Jackson's second term. In 1836, Van Buren was elected president, and he inherited a financial crisis. He believed that the government should not continue to keep its deposits in state banks and set up an independent Treasury, which was approved by Congress after several years of political maneuvering.

**General John Burgoyne (1722–1792)** He was the commander of Britain's northern forces during the Revolutionary War. He and most of his troops surrendered to the Americans at the Battle of Saratoga.

**burned-over district** Area of western New York strongly influenced by the revivalist fervor of the Second Great Awakening; Disciples of Christ and Mormons are among the many sects that trace their roots to the phenomenon.

**Aaron Burr (1756–1836)** Even though he was Thomas Jefferson's vice president, he lost favor with Jefferson's supporters who were Republicans. He sought to work with the Federalists and run as their candidate for the governor of New York. Alexander Hamilton opposed Burr's candidacy and his stinging remarks on the subject led to Burr challenging him to duel in which Hamilton was killed.

**George H. W. Bush (1924–)** He had served as vice president during the Reagan administration and then won the presidential election of 1988. During his presidential campaign, Bush promised not to raise taxes. However, the federal deficit had become so big that he had to raise taxes. Bush chose to make fighting illegal drugs a priority. He created the Office of National Drug Control Policy, but it was only moderately successful in stopping drug use. In 1989, Bush ordered the invasion of Panama and the capture of Panamanian leader Manuel Noriega, who was wanted in America on drug charges. He was captured, tried, and convicted. In 1990, Saddam Hussein invaded Kuwait; and Bush sent the American military to Saudi Arabia on a defensive mission. He assembled a multinational force and launched Operation Desert Storm, which took Kuwait back from Saddam in 1991. The euphoria over the victory in Kuwait was short lived as the country slid into a recession. He lost the 1992 presidential election to Bill Clinton.

**George W. Bush (1946–)** In the 2000 presidential election, Texas governor George W. Bush ran as the Republican nominee against Democratic nominee Vice President Al Gore. The election ended in controversy over the final vote tally in Florida. Bush had slightly more votes, but a recount was required by state law. However, it was stopped by Supreme Court and Bush was declared president. After the September 11 terrorist attacks, he launched his "war on terrorism." President George W. Bush adapted the Bush Doctrine, which claimed the right to launch preemptive military attacks against enemies. The United States invaded Afghanistan and Iraq with unclear outcomes leaving the countries divided. In the summer of 2006, Hurricane Katrina struck the Gulf Coast and left destruction across several states and three-quarters of New Orleans flooded. Bush was attacked for the unpreparedness of the federal government to handle the disaster as well as his own slowness to react. In September 2008, the nation's economy nosedived as a credit crunch spiraled into a global economic meltdown. Bush signed into law the bank bailout fund called Troubled Asset Relief Program (TARP), but the economy did not improve.

**Bush v. Gore (2000)** The close 2000 presidential election came down to Florida's decisive twenty-five electoral votes. The final tally in Florida gave Bush a slight lead, but it was so small that a recount was required by state law. While the votes were being recounted, a legal battle was being waged to stop the recount. Finally, the case, *Bush v. Gore*, was present to the Supreme Court who ruled 5–4 to stop the recount and Bush was declared the winner.

**Bush Doctrine** Believing that America's enemies were now terrorist groups and unstable rogue nations, President George W. Bush adapted a foreign policy that claimed the right to launch preemptive military attacks against enemies.

**buying (stock) on margin** The investment practice of making a small down payment (the "margin") on a stock and borrowing the rest of money need for the purchase from a broker who held the stock as security against a down market. If the stock's value declined and the buyer failed to meet a margin call for more funds, the broker could sell the stock to cover his loan.

**John C. Calhoun (1782–1850)** He served in both the House of Representatives and the Senate for South Carolina before becoming secretary of war under President Monroe and then John Quincy Adams's vice president. He introduced the bill for the second national bank to Congress and led the minority of southerners who voted for the Tariff of 1816. However, he later chose to oppose tariffs. During his time as secretary of war under President Monroe, he authorized the use of federal troops against the Seminoles who were attacking settlers. As John Quincy Adams's vice president, he supported a new tariffs bill to win presidential candidate Andrew Jackson additional support. Jackson won the election, but the new tariffs bill passed and Calhoun had to explain why he had changed his opinion on tariffs.

**Camp David Accords** Peace agreement between Israeli Prime Minister Menachem Begin and Egyptian President Anwar Sadat, brokered by President Jimmy Carter in 1978.

**"Scarface" Al Capone (1899–1947)** He was the most successful gangster of the Prohibition era whose Chicago-based criminal empire included bootlegging, prostitution, and gambling.

**Andrew Carnegie (1835–1919)** He was a steel magnate who believed that the general public benefited from big business even if these companies employed harsh business practices. This philosophy became deeply ingrained in the conventional wisdom of some Americans. After retiring, he devoted himself to philanthropy in hopes of promoting social welfare and world peace.

**carpetbaggers** Northern emigrants who participated in the Republican governments of the reconstructed South.

**Jimmy Carter (1924–)** Jimmy Carter, an outsider to Washington, capitalized on the post-Watergate cynicism and won the 1976 presidential election. He created departments of Energy and Education and signed into law several environmental initiatives. However, his efforts to support the Panama Canal Treaties and his unwillingness to make deals with legislators caused other bills to be either gutted or stalled in Congress. Despite his efforts to improve the economy, the recession continued and inflation increased. In 1978, he successfully brokered a peace agreement between Israel and Egypt called the Camp David Accords. Then his administration was plagued with a series of crises. Fighting in the Middle East produced a fuel shortage in the United States. The Soviets invaded Afghanistan and Carter responded with the suspension of an arms-control treaty with the Soviets, the halting of grain shipments to the Soviet Union, and a call for a boycott of the Olympic Games in Moscow. In Iran, revolutionaries toppled the shah's government and seized the American embassy, taking hostage those inside. Carter struggled to get the hostages released and was unable to do so until after he lost the 1980 election to Ronald Reagan. He was awarded the Nobel Peace Prize in 2002 for his efforts to further peace and democratic elections around the world.

**Jacques Cartier (1491–1557)** He led the first French effort to colonize North America and explored the Gulf of St. Lawrence and reached as far as present day Montreal on the St. Lawrence River.

**Bartolomé de Las Casas (1484–1566)** A Catholic missionary who renounced the Spanish practice of coercively converting Indians and advocated the better treatment for them. In 1552, he wrote *A Brief Relation of the Destruction of the Indies*, which described the Spanish's cruel treatment of the Indians.

**Fidel Castro (1926–)** In 1959, his Communist regime came to power in Cuba after two years of guerrilla warfare against the dictator Fulgenico Batista. He enacted land redistribution programs and nationalized all foreign-owned property. The latter action as well as his political trials and summary executions damaged relations between Cuba and America. Castro was turned down when he asked for loans from the United States. However, he did receive aid from the Soviet Union.

**Carrie Chapman Catt (1859–1947)** She was a leader of a new generation of activists in the women's suffrage movement who carried on the work started by Elizabeth Cady Stanton and Susan B. Anthony.

**Cesar Chavez (1927–1993)** He founded the United Farm Workers (UFW) in 1962 and worked to organize migrant farm workers. In 1965, the UFW joined Filipino farm workers striking against corporate grape farmers in California's San Joaquin Valley. In 1970, the strike and a consumer boycott on grapes compelled the farmers to formally recognize the UFW. As the result of Chavez's efforts, wages and working conditions improved for migrant workers. In 1975, the California state legislature passed a bill that required growers to bargain collectively with representatives of the farm workers.

**Chinese Exclusion Act (1882)** The first federal law to restrict immigration on the basis of race and class. Passed in 1882, the act halted Chinese immigration for ten years, but it was periodically renewed and then indefinitely extended in 1902. Not until 1943 were the barriers to Chinese immigration finally removed.

**Church of Jesus Christ of Latter-day Saints / Mormons** Founded in 1830 by Joseph Smith, the sect was a product of the intense revivalism of the burned-over district of New York; Smith's successor Brigham Young led 15,000 followers to Utah in 1847 to escape persecution.

**Winston Churchill (1874–1965)** The British prime minister who led the country during the Second World War. Along with Roosevelt and Stalin, he helped shape the post-war world at the Yalta Conference. He also coined the term "iron curtain," which he used in his famous "The Sinews of Peace" speech.

**"city machines"** Local political party officials used these organizations to dispense patronage and favoritism amongst voters and businesses to ensure their loyal support to the political party.

**Civil Rights Act of 1957** First federal civil rights law since Reconstruction; established the Civil Rights Commission and the Civil Rights Division of the Department of Justice.

**Civil Rights Act of 1964** Outlawed discrimination in public accommodations and employment.

**Henry Clay (1777–1852)** In the first half of the nineteenth century, he was the foremost spokesman for the American system. As speaker of the House in the 1820s, he promoted economic nationalism, "market revolution," and the rapid development of western states and territories. He formulated the "second" Missouri Compromise, which denied the Missouri state legislature the power to exclude the rights of free blacks and mulattos. In the deadlocked presidential election of 1824, the House of Representatives decided the election. Clay supported John Quincy Adams, who won the presidency and appointed Clay to secretary of state. Andrew Jackson claimed that Clay had entered into a "corrupt bargain" with Adams for his own selfish gains.

**Hillary Rodham Clinton (1947–)** In the 2008 presidential election, Senator Hillary Clinton, the spouse of former President Bill Clinton, initially was the front-runner for the Democratic nomination, which made her the first woman with a serious chance to win the presidency. However, Senator Barack Obama's Internet-based and grassroots-orientated campaign garnered him enough delegates to win the nomination. After Obama became president, she was appointed secretary of state.

**William Jefferson Clinton (1946–)** The governor of Arkansas won the 1992 presidential election against President George H. W. Bush. In his first term, he pushed through Congress a tax increase, an economic stimulus package, the adoption of the North America Free Trade Agreement, welfare reform, a raise in the minimum wage, and improved public access to health insurance. However, he failed to institute major health-care reform, which had been one of his major goals. In 1996, Clinton defeated Republican presidential candidate

Bob Dole. Clinton was scrutinized for his investment in the fraudulent Whitewater Development Corporation, but no evidence was found of him being involved in any wrongdoing. In 1998, he was revealed to have had a sexual affair with a White House intern. Clinton had initially lied about the affair and tried to cover up it, which led to a vote in Congress on whether or not to begin an impeachment inquiry. The House of Representatives voted to impeach Clinton, but the Senate found him not guilty. Clinton's presidency faced several foreign policy challenges. In 1994, he used U.S. forces to restore Haiti's democratically elected president to power after he had been ousted during a coup. In 1995, the Clinton Administration negotiated the Dayton Accords, which stopped the ethnic strife in the former Yugoslavia and the Balkan region. Clinton sponsored peace talks between Arabs and Israelis, which culminated in Israeli Prime Minister Yitzhak Rabin and the Palestine Liberation Organization leader Yasir Arafat signing the Oslo Accords in 1993. This agreement provided for the restoration of Palestinian self-rule in specific areas in exchange for peace as provided in UN Security Council resolutions.

**Coercive Acts / Intolerable Acts (1774)** Four parliamentary measures in reaction to the Boston Tea Party that forced payment for the tea, disallowed colonial trials of British soldiers, forced their quartering in private homes, and set up a military government.

**coffin ships** Irish immigrants fleeing the potato famine had to endure a six-week journey across the Atlantic to reach America. During these voyages, thousands of passengers died of disease and starvation, which led to the ships being called "coffin ships."

**Christopher Columbus (1451–1506)** The Italian sailor who persuaded King Ferdinand and Queen Isabella of Spain to fund his expedition across the Atlantic to discover a new trade route to Asia. Instead of arriving at China or Japan, he reached the Bahamas in 1492.

**Committee on Public Information** During the First World War, this committee produced war propaganda that conveyed the Allies' war aims to Americans as well as attempted to weaken the enemy's morale.

**Committee to Re-elect the President (CREEP)** During Nixon's presidency, his administration engaged in a number of immoral acts, such as attempting to steal information and falsely accusing political appointments of sexual improprieties. These acts were funded by money illegally collected through CREEP.

**Thomas Paine's _Common Sense_** This pamphlet refocused the blame for the colonies' problems on King George III rather than on Parliament and advocated a declaration of independence, which few colonialists had considered prior to its appearance.

**Compromise of 1850** Complex compromise mediated by Senator Henry Clay that headed off southern secession over California statehood; to appease the South it included a stronger fugitive slave law and delayed determination of the slave status of the New Mexico and Utah territories.

**Compromise of 1877** Deal made by a special congressional commission on March 2, 1877, to resolve the disputed presidential election of 1876; Republican Rutherford B. Hayes, who had lost the popular vote, was declared the winner in exchange for the withdrawal of federal troops from the South, marking the end of Reconstruction.

**Conestoga wagons** These large horse-drawn wagons were used to carry people or heavy freight long distances, including from the East to the western frontier settlements.

*conquistadores* Spanish term for "conqueror," applied to European leaders of campaigns against indigenous peoples in central and southern America.

**consumer culture** In the post-World War II era, affluence seemed to be forever increasing in America. At the same time, there was a boom in construction as well as products and appliances for Americans to buy. As a result, shopping became a major recreational activity. Americans started spending more, saving less, and building more shopping centers.

**containment** U.S. strategy in the cold war that called for containing Soviet expansion; originally devised in 1947 by U.S. diplomat George F. Kennan.

**Continental army** Army authorized by the Continental Congress, 1775–1784, to fight the British; commanded by General George Washington.

**Contract with America** A ten-point document released by the Republican party during the 1994 Congressional election campaigns, which outlined a small-government program featuring less regulation of business, diminished environmental regulations, and other core values of the Republican revolution.

**Contras** The Reagan administration ordered the CIA to train and supply guerrilla bands of anti-Communist Nicaraguans called Contras. They were fighting the Sandinista government that had recently come to power in Nicaragua. The State Department believed that the Sandinista government was supplying the leftist Salvadoran rebels with Soviet and Cuban arms. A cease-fire agreement between the Contras and Sandinistas was signed in 1988.

**Calvin "Silent Cal" Coolidge (1872–1933)** After President Harding's death, his vice president, Calvin Coolidge, assumed the presidency. Coolidge believed that the nation's welfare was tied to the success of big business, and he worked to end government regulation of business and industry as well as reduce taxes. In particular, he focused on the nation's industrial development.

**Hernán Cortés (1485–1547)** The Spanish conquistador who conquered the Aztec Empire and set the precedent for other plundering conquistadores.

**General Charles Cornwallis (1738–1805)** He was in charge of British troops in the South during the Revolutionary War. His surrendering to George Washington at the Battle of Yorktown ended the Revolutionary War.

**Corps of Discovery** Meriwether Lewis and William Clark led this group of men on an expedition of the newly purchased Louisiana territory, which took them from Missouri to Oregon. As they traveled, they kept detailed journals and drew maps of the previously unexplored territory. Their reports attracted traders and trappers to the region and gave the United States a claim to the Oregon country by right of discovery and exploration.

**"corrupt bargain"** A vote in the House of Representatives decided the deadlocked presidential election of 1824 in favor of John Quincy Adams, who Speaker of the House Henry Clay had supported. Afterward, Adams appointed Clay secretary of state. Andrew Jackson charged Clay with having made a "corrupt bargain" with Adams that gave Adams the presidency and Clay a place in his administration. There was no evidence of such a deal, but it was widely believed.

**the counterculture** "Hippie" youth culture of the 1960s, which rejected the values of the dominant culture in favor of illicit drugs, communes, free sex, and rock music.

**court-packing plan** President Franklin D. Roosevelt's failed 1937 attempt to increase the number of U.S. Supreme Court justices from nine to fifteen in order to save his Second New Deal programs from constitutional challenges.

**covenant theory** A Puritan concept that believed true Christians could enter a voluntary union for the common worship of God. Taking the idea one step further, the union could also be used for the purposes of establishing governments.

**Coxey's Army** Jacob S. Coxey, a Populist, led this protest group that demanded the federal government provide the unemployed with meaningful employment. In 1894, Coxey's Army joined other protests groups in a march on Washington D.C. The combination of the march and the growing support of Populism scared many Americans.

**Crédit Mobilier scandal** Construction company guilt of massive overcharges for building the Union Pacific Railroad were exposed; high officials of the Ulysses S. Grant administration were implicated but never charged.

**George Creel (1876–1953)** He convinced President Woodrow Wilson that the best approach to influencing public opinion was through propaganda rather than censorship. As the executive head of the Committee on Public Information, he produced propaganda that conveyed the Allies' war aims.

**"Cross of Gold" Speech** In the 1896 election, the Democratic party split over the issue of whether to use gold or silver to back American currency. Significant to this division was the "Cross of Gold" speech that William Jennings Bryan delivered at the Democratic convention. This pro-silver speech was so well received that Bryan won the nomination to be their presidential candidate. Disappointed pro-gold Democrats chose to walk out of the convention and nominate their own candidate.

**Cuban missile crisis** Caused when the United States discovered Soviet offensive missile sites in Cuba in October 1962; the U.S.–Soviet confrontation was the cold war's closest brush with nuclear war.

**cult of domesticity** The belief that women should stay at home to manage the household, educate their children with strong moral values, and please their husbands.

**George A. Custer (1839–1876)** He was a reckless and glory-seeking Lieutenant Colonel of the U.S. Army who fought the Sioux Indians in the Great Sioux War. In 1876, he and his detachment of soldiers were entirely wiped out in the Battle of Little Bighorn.

**D-day** June 6, 1944, when an Allied amphibious assault landed on the Normandy coast and established a foothold in Europe from which Hitler's defenses could not recover.

**Jefferson Davis (1808–1889)** He was the president of the Confederacy during the Civil War. When the Confederacy's defeat seemed invitable in early 1865, he refused to surrender. Union forces captured him in May of that year.

**Eugene V. Debs (1855–1926)** He founded the American Railway Union, which he organized against the Pullman Palace Car Company during the Pullman strike. Later he organized the Social Democratic party, which eventually became the Socialist Party of America. In the 1912 presidential election, he ran as the Socialist party's candidate and received more than 900,000 votes.

**Declaratory Act** Following the repeal of the Stamp Act in 1766, Parliament passed this act which asserted Parliament's full power to make laws binding the colonies "in all cases whatsoever."

**deism** Enlightenment thought applied to religion; emphasized reason, morality, and natural law.

**détente** In the 1970s, the United States and Soviet Union began working together to achieve a more orderly and restrained competition between each other. Both countries signed an agreement to limit the number of Intercontinental Long Range Ballistic Missiles (ICBMs) that each country could possess and to not construct antiballistic missiles systems. They also signed new trade agreements.

**George Dewey (1837–1917)** On April 30, 1898, Commodore George Dewey's small U.S. naval squadron defeated the Spanish warships in Manila Bay in the Philippines. This quick victory aroused expansionist fever in the United States.

**John Dewey (1859–1952)** He is an important philosopher of pragmatism. However, he preferred to use the term *instrumentalism,* because he saw ideas as instruments of action.

**Ngo Dinh Diem (1901–1963)** Following the Geneva Accords, the French, with the support of America, forced the Vietnamese emperor to accept Dinh Diem as the new premier of South Vietnam. President Eisenhower sent advisors to train Diem's police and army. In return, the United States expected Diem to enact democratic reforms and distribute land to the peasants. Instead, he suppressed his political opponents, did little or no land distribution, and let corruption grow. In 1956, he refused to participate in elections to reunify Vietnam. Eventually, he ousted the emperor and declared himself president.

**Dorothea Lynde Dix (1802–1887)** She was an important figure in increasing the public's awareness of the plight of the mentally ill. After a two-year investigation of the treatment of the mentally ill in Massachusetts, she presented her findings and won the support of leading reformers. She eventually convinced twenty states to reform their treatment of the mentally ill.

**Dixiecrats** Deep South delegates who walked out of the 1948 Democratic National Convention in protest of the party's support for civil rights legislation and later formed the States' Rights (Dixiecrat) party, which nominated Strom Thurmond of South Carolina for president.

**dollar diplomacy** The Taft administration's policy of encouraging American bankers to aid debt-plagued governments in Haiti, Guatemala, Honduras, and Nicaragua.

**Donner party** Forty-seven surviving members of a group of migrants to California were forced to resort to cannibalism to survive a brutal winter trapped in the Sierra Nevadas, 1846–1847; highest death toll of any group traveling the Overland Trail.

**Stephen A. Douglas (1812–1861)** As a senator from Illinois, he authored the Kansas-Nebraska Act. Once passed, the act led to violence in Kansas between pro- and antislavery factions and damaged the Whig party. These damages prevented Senator Douglas from being chosen as the presidential candidate of his party. Running for senatorial reelection in 1858, he engaged Abraham Lincoln in a series of public debates about slavery in the territories. Even though Douglas won the election, the debates gave Lincoln a national reputation.

**Frederick Douglass (1818–1895)** He escaped from slavery and become an eloquent speaker and writer against slavery. In 1845, he published his autobiography entitled *Narrative of the Life of Frederick Douglass* and two years later he founded an abolitionist newspaper for blacks called the *North Star*.

**dot-coms** In the late 1990s, the stock market soared to new heights and defied the predictions of experts that the economy could not sustain such a performance. Much of the economic success was based on dot-com enterprises, which were firms specializing in computers, software, telecommunications, and the internet. However, many of the companies' stock market values were driven higher and higher by speculation instead of financial success. Eventually the stock market bubble burst.

***Dred Scott v. Sandford* (1857)** U.S. Supreme Court decision in which Chief Justice Roger B. Taney ruled that slaves could not sue for freedom and that Congress could not prohibit slavery in the territories, on the grounds that such a prohibition would violate the Fifth Amendment rights of slaveholders.

**W. E. B. Du Bois (1868–1963)** He criticized Booker T. Washington's views on civil rights as being accommodationist. He advocated "ceaseless agitation" for civil rights and the immediate end to segregation and an enforcement of laws to protect civil rights and equality. He promoted an education for African Americans that would nurture bold leaders who were willing to challenge discrimination in politics.

**John Foster Dulles (1888–1959)** As President Eisenhower's secretary of state, he institutionalized the policy of containment and introduced the strategy of deterrence. He believed in using brinkmanship to halt the spread of communism. He attempted to employ it in Indochina, which led to the United States' involvement in Vietnam.

**Dust Bowl** Great Plains counties where millions of tons of topsoil were blown away from parched farmland in the 1930s; massive migration of farm families followed.

**Peggy Eaton (1796–1879)** The wife of John Eaton, President Jackson's secretary of war, was the daughter of a tavern owner with an unsavory past. Supposedly her first husband had committed suicide after learning that she was having an affair with John Eaton. The wives of members of Jackson's cabinet snubbed her because of her lowly origins and past. The scandal that resulted was called the Eaton Affair.

**Jonathan Edwards (1703–1758)** New England Congregationalist minister, who began a religious revival in his Northampton church and was an important figure in the Great Awakening.

**election of 1912** The presidential election of 1912 featured four candidates: Wilson, Taft, Roosevelt, and Debs. Each candidate believed in the basic assumptions of progressive politics, but each had a different view on how progressive ideals should be implemented through policy. In the end, Taft and Roosevelt split the Republican party votes and Wilson emerged as the winner.

**Queen Elizabeth I of England (1533–1603)** The protestant daughter of Henry VIII, she was Queen of England from 1558–1603 and played a major role in the Protestant Reformation. During her long reign, the doctrines and services of the Church of England were defined and the Spanish Armada was defeated.

**General Dwight D. Eisenhower (1890–1969)** During the Second World War, he commanded the Allied Forces landing in Africa and was the supreme Allied commander as well as planner for Operation Overlord. In 1952, he was elected president on his popularity as a war hero and his promises to clean up Washington and find an honorable peace in the Korean War. His administration sought to cut the nation's domestic programs and budget, but he left the basic structure of the New Deal intact. In July of 1953, he announced the end of fighting in Korea. He appointed Earl Warren to the Supreme Court whose influence helped the court become an important force for social and political change. His secretary of state, John Foster Dulles, institutionalized the policies of containment and deterrence. Eisenhower supported the withdrawal of British forces from the Suez Canal and established the Eisenhower doctrine, which promised to aid any nation against aggression by a communist nation. Eisenhower preferred that state and local institutions to handle civil rights issues, and he refused to force states to comply with the Supreme Court's civil rights decisions. However, he did propose the legislation that became the Civil Rights Act of 1957.

**Ellis Island** Reception center in New York Harbor through which most European immigrants to America were processed from 1892 to 1954.

**Emancipation Proclamation (1863)** President Abraham Lincoln issued a preliminary proclamation on September 22, 1862, freeing the slaves in the Confederate states as of January 1, 1863, the date of the final proclamation.

**Ralph Waldo Emerson (1803–1882)** As a leader of the transcendentalist movement, he wrote poems, essays, and speeches that discussed the sacredness of nature, optimism, self-reliance, and the unlimited potential of the individual. He wanted to transcend the limitations of inherited conventions and rationalism to reach the inner recesses of the self.

***encomienda*** System under which officers of the Spanish conquistadores gained ownership of Indian land.

**Enlightenment** Revolution in thought begun in the seventeenth century that emphasized reason and science over the authority of traditional religion.

**enumerated goods** According to the Navigation Act, these particular goods, like tobacco or cotton, could only be shipped to England or other English colonies.

**Erie Canal** Most important and profitable of the barge canals of the 1820s and 1830s; stretched from Buffalo to Albany, New York, connecting the Great Lakes to the East Coast and making New York City the nation's largest port.

**ethnic cleansing** The act of killing an entire group of people in a region or country because of its ethnic background. After the collapse of the former Yugoslavia in 1991, Serbs in Bosnia attacked communities of Muslims, which led to intervention by the United Nations. In 1998, fighting broke out again in the Balkans between Serbia and Kosovo. Serbian police and military attacked, killed, raped, or forced Muslim Albanian Kosovars to leave their homes.

**Fair Employment Practices Commission** Created in 1941 by executive order, the FEPC sought to eliminate racial discrimination in jobs; it possessed little power but represented a step toward civil rights for African Americans.

**Farmers' Alliance** Two separate organizations (Northwestern and Southern) of the 1880s and 1890s that took the place of the Grange, worked for similar causes, and attracted landless, as well as landed, farmers to their membership.

**Federal Writers' Project** During the Great Depression, this project provided writers, such as Ralph Ellison, Richard Wright, and Saul Bellow, with work, which gave them a chance to develop as artists and be employed.

***The Federalist*** Collection of eighty-five essays that appeared in the New York press in 1787–1788 in support of the Constitution; written by Alexander Hamilton, James Madison, and John Jay but published under the pseudonym "Publius."

**Federalists** Proponents of a centralized federal system and the ratification of the Constitution. Most Federalists were relatively young, educated men who supported a broad interpretation of the Constitution whenever national interest dictated such flexibility. Notable Federalists included Alexander Hamilton and John Jay.

**Geraldine Ferraro (1935–)** In the 1984 presidential election, Democratic nominee, Walter Mondale, chose her as his running mate. As a member of the U.S. House of Representatives from New York, she was the first woman to be a vice-presidential nominee for a major political party. However, she was placed on the defensive because of her husband's complicated business dealings.

**Fifteenth Amendment** This amendment forbids states to deny any person the right to vote on grounds of "race, color or pervious condition of servitude." Former Confederate states were required to ratify this amendment before they could be readmitted to the Union.

**"final solution"** The Nazi party's systematic murder of some 6 million Jews along with more than a million other people including, but not limited to, gypsies, homosexuals, and handicap individuals.

**Food Administration** After America's entry into World War I, the economy of the home front needed to be reorganized to provide the most efficient means of conducting the war. The Food Administration was a part of this effort. Under the leadership of Herbert Hoover, the organization sought to increase agricultural production while reducing civilian consumption of foodstuffs.

**force bill** During the nullification crisis between President Andrew Jackson and South Carolina, Jackson asked Congress to pass this bill, which authorized him to use the army to force South Carolina to comply with federal law.

**Gerald Ford (1913–2006)** He was President Nixon's vice president and assumed the presidency after Nixon resigned. President Ford issued Nixon a pardon for any crimes related to the Watergate scandal. The American public's reaction was largely negative; and Ford never regained the public's confidence. He resisted congressional pressure to both reduce taxes and increase federal spending, which sent the American economy into the deepest recession since the Great Depression. Ford retained Kissinger as his secretary of state and continued Nixon's foreign policy goals, which included the signing of another arms-control agreement with the Soviet Union. He was heavily criticized following the collapse of South Vietnam.

**Fort Laramie Treaty (1851)** Restricted the Plains Indians from using the Overland Trail and permitted the building of government forts.

**Fort Necessity** After attacking a group of French soldiers, George Washington constructed and took shelter in this fort from vengeful French troops. Washington eventually surrendered to them after a day-long battle. This conflict was a significant event in igniting the French and Indian War.

**Fort Sumter** First battle of the Civil War, in which the federal fort in Charleston (South Carolina) Harbor was captured by the Confederates on April 14, 1861, after two days of shelling.

**"forty-niners"** Speculators who went to northern California following the discovery of gold in 1848; the first of several years of large-scale migration was 1849.

**Fourteen Points** President Woodrow Wilson's 1918 plan for peace after World War I; at the Versailles peace conference, however, he failed to incorporate all of the points into the treaty.

**Fourteenth Amendment (1868)** Guaranteed rights of citizenship to former slaves, in words similar to those of the Civil Rights Act of 1866.

**Franciscan Missions** In 1769, Franciscan missioners accompanied Spanish soldiers to California and over the next fifty years established a chain of missions from San Diego to San Francisco. At these missions, friars sought to convert Indians to Catholicism and make them members of the Spanish empire. The friars stripped the Indians of their native heritage and used soldiers to enforce their will.

**Benjamin Franklin (1706–1790)** A Boston-born American, who epitomized the Enlightenment for many Americans and Europeans, Franklin's wide range of interests led him to become a publisher, inventor, and statesman. As the latter, he contributed to the writing of the Declaration of Independence, served as the minister to France during the Revolutionary War, and was a delegate to the Constitutional Convention.

**Free-Soil party** Formed in 1848 to oppose slavery in the territory acquired in the Mexican War; nominated Martin Van Buren for president in 1848, but by 1854, most of the party's members had joined the Republican party.

**Freedmen's Bureau** Reconstruction agency established in 1865 to protect the legal rights of former slaves and to assist with their education, jobs, health care, and landowning.

**freedom riders** In 1961, the Congress of Racial Equality had this group of black and white demonstrators ride buses to test the federal court ruling that had banned segregation on buses and trains and in terminals. Despite being attacked, they never gave up. Their actions drew national attention and generated respect and support for their cause.

**Freeport Doctrine** Senator Stephen Douglas' method to reconcile the Dred Scott court ruling of 1857 with "popular sovereignty," of which he was a champion. Douglas believed that so long as residents of a given territory had the right to pass and uphold local laws, any Supreme Court ruling on slavery would be unenforceable and irrelevant.

**John C. Frémont "the Pathfinder" (1813–1890)** He was an explorer and surveyor who helped inspire Americans living in California to rebel against the Mexican government and declare independence.

**French and Indian War** Known in Europe as the Seven Years' War, the last (1755–1763) of four colonial wars fought between England and France for control of North America east of the Mississippi River.

**Sigmund Freud (1865–1939)** He was the founder of psychoanalysis, which suggested that human behavior was motivated by unconscious and irrational forces. By the 1920s, his ideas were being discussed more openly in America.

**Fugitive Slave Act of 1850** Gave federal government authority in cases involving runaway slaves; so much more punitive and prejudiced in favor of slaveholders than the 1793 Fugitive Slave Act had been that Harriet Beecher Stowe was inspired to write *Uncle Tom's Cabin* in protest; the new law was part of the Compromise of 1850, included to appease the South over the admission of California as a free state.

**fundamentalism** Anti-modernist Protestant movement started in the early twentieth century that proclaimed the literal truth of the Bible; the name came from *The Fundamentals,* published by conservative leaders.

**"gag rule"** In 1831, the House of Representatives adopted this rule, which prevented the discussion and presentation of any petitions for the abolition of slavery to the House. John Quincy Adams, who was elected to the House after his presidency ended, fought the rule on the grounds that it violated the First Amendment. In 1844, he succeeded in having it repealed.

**William Lloyd Garrison (1805–1879)** In 1831, he started the anti-slavery newspaper *Liberator* and helped start the New England Anti-Slavery Society. Two years later, he assisted Arthur and Lewis Tappan in the founding of the American Anti-Slavery Society. He and his followers believed that America had been thoroughly corrupted and needed a wide range of reforms. He embraced every major reform movement of the day: abolition, temperance, pacifism, and women's rights. He wanted to go beyond just freeing slaves and grant them equal social and legal rights.

**Marcus Garvey (1887–1940)** He was the leading spokesman for Negro Nationalism, which exalted blackness, black cultural expression, and black exclusiveness. He called upon African Americans to liberate themselves from the surrounding white culture and create their own businesses, cultural centers, and newspapers. He was also the founder of the Universal Negro Improvement Association.

**Citizen Genet (1763–1834)** As the ambassador to the United States from the new French Republic, he engaged American privateers to attack British ships and conspired with frontiersmen and land speculators to organize an attack on Spanish Florida and Louisiana. His actions and the French radicals excessive actions against their enemies in the new French Republic caused the French Revolution to lose support among Americans.

**Geneva Accords** In 1954, the Geneva Accords were signed, which ended French colonial rule in Indochina. The agreement created the independent nations of Laos and Cambodia and divided Vietnam along the 17th parallel until an election in 1956 would reunify the country.

**Gettysburg, Battle of** Fought in southern Pennsylvania, July 1–3, 1863; the Confederate defeat and the simultaneous loss at Vicksburg spelled the end of the South's chances in the Civil War.

**Ghost Dance movement** This spiritual and political movement came from a Paiute Indian named Wovoka (or Jack Wilson). He believed that a messiah would come and rescue the Indians and restore their lands. To hasten the arrival of the messiah, the Indians needed to take up a ceremonial dance at each new moon.

**Newt Gingrich (1943–)** He led the Republican insurgency in Congress in the mid 1990s through mobilizing religious and social conservatives. Along with other Republican congressmen, he created the Contract with America, which was a ten-point anti-big government program. However, the program fizzled out after many of its bills were not passed by Congress.

**Gilded Age** (1860–1896) An era of dramatic industrial and urban growth characterized by loose government oversight over corporations, which fostered unfettered capitalism and widespread political corruption.

***The Gilded Age*** Mark Twain and Charles Dudley Warner's 1873 novel, the title of which became the popular name for the period from the end of the Civil War to the turn of the century.

***glasnost*** Soviet leader Mikhail Gorbachev instituted this reform, which brought about a loosening of censorship.

**Glorious Revolution** In 1688, the Protestant Queen Mary and her husband, William of Orange, took the British throne from King James II in a bloodless coup. Afterward, Parliament greatly expanded its power and passed the Bill of Rights and the Act of Toleration, both of which would influence attitudes and events in the colonies.

**Barry Goldwater (1909–1998)** He was a leader of the Republican right whose book, *The Conscience of a Conservative*, was highly influential to that segment of the party. He proposed eliminating the income tax and overhauling Social Security. In 1964, he ran as the Republican presidential candidate and lost to President Johnson. He campaigned against Johnson's war on poverty, the tradition of New Deal, the nuclear test ban and the Civil Rights Act of 1964. He advocated the wholesale bombing of North Vietnam.

**Samuel Gompers (1850–1924)** He served as the president of the American Federation of Labor from its inception until his death. He focused on achieving concrete economic gains such as higher wages, shorter hours, and better working conditions.

**"good neighbor" policy** Proclaimed by President Franklin D. Roosevelt in his first inaugural address in 1933, it sought improved diplomatic relations between the United States and its Latin American neighbors.

**Mikhail Gorbachev (1931–)** In the late 1980s, Soviet leader Mikhail Gorbachev attempted to reform the Soviet Union through his programs of *perestroika* and *glasnost*. He pursued a renewal of détente with America and signed new arms-control agreements with President Reagan. Gorbachev chose not to involve the Soviet Union in the internal affairs of other Communist countries, which removed the threat of armed Soviet crackdowns on reformers and protesters in Eastern Europe. Gorbachev's decision allowed the velvet revolutions of Eastern Europe to occur without outside interference. Eventually the political, social, and economic upheaval he had unleashed would lead to the break-up of the Soviet Union.

**Albert Gore Jr. (1948–)** He served as a senator of Tennessee and then as President Clinton's vice president. In the 2000 presidential election, he was the Democratic candidate and campaigned on preserving Social Security, subsidizing prescription-medicine expenses for the elderly, and protecting the environment. His opponent was Governor George W. Bush, who promoted compassionate conservatism and the transferring of power from the federal government to the states. The election ended in controversy. The close election came down to Florida's electoral votes. The final tally in Florida gave Bush a slight lead, but it was so small that a recount was required by state law. While the votes were being recounted, a legal battle was being waged to stop the recount. Finally, the case, *Bush v. Gore*, was presented to the Supreme Court who ruled 5–4 to stop the recount and Bush was declared the winner.

**Jay Gould (1836–1892)** As one of the biggest railroad robber barons, he was infamous for buying rundown railroads, making cosmetic improvements and then reselling them for a profit. He used corporate funds for personal investments and to bribe politicians and judges.

**gradualism** This strategy for ending slavery involved promoting the banning of slavery in the new western territories and encouraging the release of slaves from slavery. Supporters of this method believed that it would bring about the gradual end of slavery.

**Granger movement** Political movement that grew out of the Patrons of Husbandry, an educational and social organization for farmers founded in 1867; the Grange had its greatest success in the Midwest of the 1870s, lobbying for government control of railroad and grain elevator rates and establishing farmers' cooperatives.

**Ulysses S. Grant (1822–1885)** After distinguishing himself in the western theater of the Civil War, he was appointed general in chief of the Union army in 1864. Afterward, he defeated General Robert E. Lee through a policy of aggressive attrition. He constantly attacked Lee's army until it was grind down. Lee surrendered to Grant on April 9th, 1865 at the Appomattox Court House. In 1868, he was elected President and his tenure suffered from scandals and fiscal problems including the debate on whether or not greenbacks, paper money, should be removed from circulation.

**Great Awakening** Fervent religious revival movement in the 1720s through the 1740s that was spread throughout the colonies by ministers like New England Congregationalist Jonathan Edwards and English revivalist George Whitefield.

**great migration** After World War II, rural southern blacks began moving to the urban North and Midwest in large numbers in search of better jobs, housing, and greater social equality. The massive influx of African American migrants overwhelmed the resources of urban governments and sparked racial conflicts. In order to cope with the new migrants and alleviate racial tension, cities constructed massive public-housing projects that segregated African Americans into overcrowded and poor neighborhoods.

**Great Compromise** (Connecticut Compromise) Mediated the differences between the New Jersey and Virginia delegations to the Constitutional Convention by providing for a bicameral legislature, the upper house of which would have equal representation and the lower house of which would be apportioned by population.

**Great Depression** Worst economic depression in American history; it was spurred by the stock market crash of 1929 and lasted until the Second World War.

**Great Sioux War** In 1874, Lieutenant Colonel Custard led an exploratory expedition into the Black Hills, which the United States government had promised to the Sioux Indians. Miners soon followed and the army did nothing to keep them out. Eventually, the army attacked the Sioux Indians and the fight against them lasted for fifteen months before the Sioux Indians were forced to give up their land and move onto a reservation.

**Great Society** Term coined by President Lyndon B. Johnson in his 1965 State of the Union address, in which he proposed legislation to address problems of voting rights, poverty, diseases, education, immigration, and the environment.

**Horace Greeley (1811–1872)** In reaction to Radical Reconstruction and corruption in President Ulysses S. Grant's administration, a group of Republicans broke from the party to form the Liberal Republicans. In 1872, the Liberal Republicans chose Horace Greeley as their presidential candidate who ran on a platform of favoring civil service reform and condemning the Republican's Reconstruction policy.

**greenbacks** Paper money issued during the Civil War. After the war ended, a debate emerged on whether or not to remove the paper currency from circulation and revert back to hard-money currency (gold coins). Opponents of hard-money feared that eliminating the greenbacks would shrink the money supply, which would lower crop prices and make it more difficult to repay long-term debts. President Ulysses S. Grant, as well as hard-currency advocates, believed that gold coins were morally preferable to paper currency.

**Greenback party** Formed in 1876 in reaction to economic depression, the party favored issuance of unsecured paper money to help farmers repay debts; the movement for free coinage of silver took the place of the greenback movement by the 1880s.

**General Nathanael Greene (1742–1786)** He was appointed by Congress to command the American army fighting in the South during the Revolutionary War. Using his patience and his skills of managing men, saving supplies, and avoiding needless risks, he waged a successful war of attrition against the British.

**Sarah Grimké (1792–1873)** and **Angelina Grimké (1805–1879)** These two sisters gave antislavery speeches to crowds of mixed gender that caused some people to condemn them for engaging in unfeminine activities. The sisters rejected this opinion and made the role of women in the anti-slavery movement a prominent issue. In 1840, William Lloyd Garrison convinced the Anti-Slavery Society to allow women equal participation in the organization. A group of members that did not agree with this decision left the Anti-Slavery Society to form the American and Foreign Anti-Slavery Society.

**Half-Way Covenant** Allowed baptized children of church members to be admitted to a "halfway" membership in the church and secure baptism for their own children in turn, but allowed them neither a vote in the church, nor communion.

**Alexander Hamilton (1755–1804)** His belief in a strong federal government led him to become a contributor to *The Federalist* and leader of the Federalists. As the first secretary of the Treasury, he laid the foundation for American capitalism through his creation of a federal budget, funded debt, a federal tax system, a national bank, a customs service, and a coast guard. His "Reports on Public Credit" and "Reports on Manufactures" outlined his vision for economic development and government finances in America. He died in a duel against Aaron Burr.

**Warren G. Harding (1865–1923)** In the 1920 presidential election, he was the Republican nominee who promised Americans a "return to normalcy," which would mean a return to conservative values and a turning away from President Wilson's internationalism. His message resonated with voters' conservative postwar mood; and he won the election. Once in office, Harding's administration dismantled many of the social and economic components of progressivism and pursued a pro-business agenda. Harding appointed four pro-business Supreme Court Justices and his administration cut taxes, increased tariffs and promoted a lenient attitude towards government regulation of corporations. However, he did speak out against racism and ended the exclusion of African Americans from federal positions. His administration did suffer from a series of scandals as the result of him appointing members of the Ohio gang to government positions.

**Harlem Renaissance** African American literary and artistic movement of the 1920s and 1930s centered in New York City's Harlem district; writers Langston Hughes, Jean Toomer, Zora Neale Hurston, and Countee Cullen were among those active in the movement.

**Hartford Convention** Meeting of New England Federalists on December 15, 1814, to protest the War of 1812; proposed seven constitutional amendments (limiting embargoes and changing requirements for officeholding, declaration of war, and admission of new states), but the war ended before Congress could respond.

**Patrick Henry (1736–1799)** He inspired the Virginia Resolves, which declared that Englishmen could only be taxed by their elected representatives. In March of 1775, he met with other colonial leaders to discuss the goals of the upcoming Continental Congress and famously declared "Give me liberty or give me death." During the ratification process of the U.S. Constitution, he became one of the leaders of the anti-federalists.

**Alger Hiss (1904–1996)** During the second Red Scare, Alger Hiss, who had served in several government departments, was accused of being a spy for the Soviet Union and was convicted of lying about espionage. The case was politically damaging to the Truman administration because the president called the charges against Hiss a "red herring." Richard Nixon, then a California congressman, used his persistent pursuit of the case and his anti-Communist rhetoric to raise his national profile and to win election to the Senate.

**Adolph Hitler "*Führer*" (1889–1945)** The leader of the Nazis who advocated a violent anti-Semitic, anti-Marxist, pan-German ideology. He started World War II in Europe and orchestrated the systematic murder of some 6 million Jews along with more than a million others.

**HIV/AIDS** Human Immunodeficiency Virus (HIV) is a virus that attacks the body's T-cells, which are necessary to help the immune system fight off infection and disease. Acquired Immunodeficiency Syndrome (AIDS) occurs after the HIV virus has destroyed the body's immune system. HIV is transferred when body fluids, such as blood or semen, which carry the virus, enter the body of an uninfected person. The virus appeared in America in the early 1980s. The Reagan administration was slow to respond to the "AIDS Epidemic," because effects of the virus were not fully understood and they deemed the spread of the disease as the result of immoral behavior.

**Homestead Act (1862)** Authorized Congress to grant 160 acres of public land to a western settler, who had only to live on the land for five years to establish title.

**Homestead steel strike** A violent labor conflict at the Homestead Steel Works near Pittsburgh, Pennsylvania, that occurred when its president, Henry Clay Frick, refused to renew the union contract with Amalgamated Association of Iron and Steel Workers. The strike, which began on June 29, 1892, culminated in an attempt on Frick's life and was swiftly put down by state militias. The strike marks one of the great setbacks in the emerging industrial-union movement.

**Herbert Hoover (1874–1964)** Prior to becoming president, Hoover served as the secretary of commerce in both the Harding and Coolidge administrations. During his tenure at the Commerce Department, he pursued new markets for business and encouraged business leaders to share information as part of the trade-association movement. The Great Depression hit while he was president. Hoover believed that the nation's business structure was sound and sought to revive the economy through boosting the nation's confidence. He also tried to restart the economy with government constructions projects, lower taxes and new federal loan programs, but nothing worked.

**House Un-American Activities Committee (HUAC)** Formed in 1938 to investigate subversives in the government; best-known investigations were of Hollywood notables and of former State Department official Alger Hiss, who was accused in 1948 of espionage and Communist party membership.

**Sam Houston (1793–1863)** During Texas's fight for independence from Mexico, Sam Houston was the commander in chief of the Texas forces, and he led the attack that captured General Antonio López de Santa Anna. After Texas gained its independence, he was name its first president.

**Jacob Riis' *How the Other Half Lives*** Jacob Riis was an early muckraking journalist who exposed the slum conditions in New York City in his book *How the Other Half Lives*.

**General William Howe (1729–1814)** As the commander of the British army in the Revolutionary War, he seized New York City from Washington's army, but failed to capture it. He missed several more opportunities to quickly end the rebellion, and he resigned his command after the British defeat at Saratoga.

**Saddam Hussein (1937–2006)** The former dictator of Iraq who became the head of state in 1979. In 1980, he invaded Iran and started the eight-year-long Iran-Iraq War. In 1990, he invaded Kuwait, which caused the Gulf War of 1991. In 2003, he was overthrown and captured when the United States invaded. He was sentenced to death by hanging in 2006.

**Anne Hutchinson (1591–1643)** The articulate, strong-willed, and intelligent wife of a prominent Boston merchant, who espoused her belief in direct divine revelation. She quarreled with Puritan leaders over her beliefs; and they banished her from the colony.

**impressment** The British navy used press-gangs to kidnap men in British and colonial ports who were then forced to serve in the British navy.

**"Indian New Deal"** This phrase refers to the reforms implemented for Native Americans during the New Deal era. John Collier, the commissioner of the Bureau of Indian Affairs (BIA), increased the access Native Americans had to relief programs and employed more Native Americans at the BIA. He worked to pass the Indian Reorganization Act. However, the version of the act passed by Congress was a much-diluted version of Collier's original proposal and did not greatly improve the lives of Native Americans.

**indentured servant** Settler who signed on for a temporary period of servitude to a master in exchange for passage to the New World; Virginia and Pennsylvania were largely peopled in the seventeenth and eighteenth centuries by English indentured servants.

**Indian Removal Act (1830)** Signed by President Andrew Jackson, the law permitted the negotiation of treaties to obtain the Indians' lands in exchange for their relocation to what became Oklahoma.

**Indochina** This area of Southeast Asian consists of Laos, Cambodia, and Vietnam and was once controlled by France as a colony. After the Viet Minh defeated the French, the Geneva Accords were signed, which ended French colonial rule. The agreement created the independent nations of Laos and Cambodia and divided Vietnam along the 17th parallel until an election would reunify the country. Fearing a communist take over, the United States government began intervening in the region during the Truman administration, which led to President Johnson's full-scale military involvement in Vietnam.

**industrial war** A new concept of war enabled by industrialization that developed from the early 1800s through the Atomic Age. New technologies, including automatic weaponry, forms of transportation like the railroad and airplane, and communication technologies such as the telegraph and telephone, enabled nations to equip large, mass-conscripted armies with chemical and automatic weapons to decimate opposing armies in a "total war."

**Industrial Workers of the World (IWW)** A radical union organized in Chicago in 1905, nicknamed the Wobblies; its opposition to World War I led to its destruction by the federal government under the Espionage Act.

**internationalists** Prior to the United States' entry in World War II, internationalists believed that America's national security depended on aiding Britain in its struggle against Germany.

**interstate highway system** In the late 1950s, construction began on a national network of interstate superhighways for the purpose of commerce and defense. The interstate highways would enable the rapid movement of military convoys and the evacuation of cities after a nuclear attack.

**Iranian Hostage Crisis** In 1979, a revolution in Iran placed the Ayatollah Ruhollah Khomeini, a fundamental religious leader, in power. In November 1979, revolutionaries seized the American embassy in Tehran and held those inside hostage. President Carter struggled to get the hostages. He tried pressuring Iran through appeals to the United Nations, freezing Iranian assets in the United States and imposing a trade embargo. During an aborted rescue operation, a helicopter collided with a transport plane and killed eight U.S. soldiers. Finally, Carter unfroze several billion dollars in Iranian assets, and the hostages were released after being held for 444 days; but not until Ronald Reagan had become president of the United States.

**Iran-Contra affair** Scandal of the second Reagan administration involving sale of arms to Iran in partial exchange for release of hostages in Lebanon and use of the arms money to aid the Contras in Nicaragua, which had been expressly forbidden by Congress.

**Irish Potato Famine** In 1845, an epidemic of potato rot brought a famine to rural Ireland that killed over 1 million peasants and instigated a huge increase in the number or Irish immigrating to America. By 1850, the Irish made up 43 percent of the foreign-born population in the United States; and in the 1850s, they made up over half the population of New York City and Boston.

**iron curtain** Term coined by Winston Churchill to describe the cold war divide between western Europe and the Soviet Union's Eastern European satellites.

**Iroquois League** An alliance of the Iroquois tribes that used their strength to force Europeans to work with them in the fur trade and to wage war across what is today eastern North America.

**Andrew Jackson (1767–1837)** As a major general in the Tennessee militia, he defeated the Creek Indians, invaded the panhandle of Spanish Florida and won the Battle of New Orleans. In 1818, his successful campaign against Spanish forces in Florida gave the

United States the upper hand in negotiating for Florida with Spain. As president, he vetoed bills for the federal funding of internal improvements and the re-chartering of the Second National Bank. When South Carolina nullified the Tariffs of 1828 and 1832, Jackson requested that Congress pass a "force bill" that would authorize him to use the army to compel the state to comply with the tariffs. He forced eastern Indians to move west of the Mississippi River so their lands could be used by white settlers. Groups of those who opposed Jackson come together to form a new political part called the Whigs.

**Jesse Jackson (1941–)** An African American civil rights activist who had been one of Martin Luther King Jr.'s chief lieutenants. He is most famous for founding the social justice organization the Rainbow Coalition. In 1988, he ran for the Democratic presidential nomination, which became a race primarily between him and Michael Dukakis. Dukakis won the nomination, but lost the election to Republican nominee Vice President George H. W. Bush.

**Thomas "Stonewall" Jackson (1824–1863)** He was a Confederate general who was known for his fearlessness in leading rapid marches, bold flanking movements, and furious assaults. He earned his nickname at the Battle of the First Bull Run for standing courageously against Union fire. During the battle of Chancellorsville, his own men accidently mortally wounded him.

**William James (1842–1910)** He was the founder of Pragmatism and one of the fathers of modern psychology. He believed that ideas gained their validity not from their inherent truth, but from their social consequences and practical application.

**Jay's Treaty** Treaty with Britain negotiated in 1794 by Chief Justice John Jay; Britain agreed to vacate forts in the Northwest Territories, and festering disagreements (border with Canada, prewar debts, shipping claims) would be settled by commission.

**Jazz Age** A term coined by F. Scott Fitzgerald to characterize the spirit of rebellion and spontaneity that spread among young Americans during the 1920s, epitomized by the emergence of jazz music and the popularity of carefree, improvisational dances, such as the Charleston and the Black Bottom.

**Thomas Jefferson (1743–1826)** He was a plantation owner, author, the drafter of the Declaration Independence, ambassador to France, leader of the Republican party, secretary of state, and the third president of the United States. As president, he purchased the Louisiana territory from France, withheld appointments made by President Adams leading to *Marybury v. Madison*, outlawed foreign slave trade, and was committed to a "wise and frugal" government.

**Jesuits** A religious order founded in 1540 by Ignatius Loyola. They sought to counter the spread of Protestantism during the Protestant Reformation and spread the Catholic faith through work as missionaries. Roughly 3,500 served in New Spain and New France.

**"Jim Crow" laws** In the New South, these laws mandated the separation of races in various public places that served as a way for the ruling whites to impose their will on all areas of black life.

**Andrew Johnson (1808–1875)** As President Abraham Lincoln's vice president, he was elevated to the presidency after Lincoln's assassination. In order to restore the Union after the

Civil War, he issued an amnesty proclamation and required former Confederate states to ratify the Thirteenth Amendment. He fought Radical Republicans in Congress over whether he or Congress had the authority to restore states rights to the former Confederate states. This fight weakened both his political and public support. In 1868, the Radical Republicans attempted to impeach Johnson but fell short on the required number of votes needed to remove him from office.

**Lyndon B. Johnson (1908–1973)** Former member of the United States House of Representatives and the former Majority Leader of the United States Senate, Vice President Lyndon Johnson, assumed the presidency after President Kennedy's assassination. He was able to push through Congress several pieces of Kennedy's legislation that had been stalled including the Civil Rights Act of 1964. He declared "war on poverty" and promoted his own social program called the Great Society, which sought to end poverty and racial injustice. In 1965, he signed the Immigration and Nationality Service Act, which abolished the discriminatory quotas system that had been the immigration policy since the 1920s. Johnson greatly increased America's role in Vietnam. By 1969, there were 542,000 U.S. troops fighting in Vietnam and a massive anti-war movement had developed in America. In 1968, Johnson announced that he would not run for re-election.

**Kansas-Nebraska Act (1854)** Law sponsored by Illinois senator Stephen A. Douglas to allow settlers in newly organized territories north of the Missouri border to decide the slavery issue for themselves; fury over the resulting nullification of the Missouri Compromise of 1820 led to violence in Kansas and to the formation of the Republican party.

**Florence Kelley (1859–1932)** As the head of the National Consumer's League, she led the crusade to promote state laws to regulate the number of working hours imposed on women who were wives and mothers.

**George F. Kennan (1904–2005)** While working as an American diplomat, he devised the strategy of containment, which called for the halting of Soviet expansion. It became America's choice strategy throughout the cold war.

**John F. Kennedy (1917–1963)** Elected president in 1960, he was interested in bringing new ideas to the White House. Despite the difficulties he had in getting his legislation through Congress, he did establish the Alliance for Progress programs to help Latin America, the Peace Corps, the Trade Expansion Act of 1962, and funding for urban renewal projects and the space program. He mistakenly proceeded with the Bay of Pigs invasion, but he successfully handled the Cuban missile crisis. In Indochina, his administration became increasingly involved in supporting local governments through aid, advisors, and covert operations. In 1963, he was assassinated by Lee Harvey Oswald in Dallas, Texas.

**Kent State** During the spring of 1970, students on college campuses across the country protested the expansion of the Vietnam War into Cambodia. At Kent State University, the National Guard attempted to quell the rioting students. The guardsmen panicked and shot at rock-throwing demonstrators. Four student bystanders were killed.

**Kentucky and Virginia Resolutions (1798–1799)** Passed in response to the Alien and Sedition Acts, the resolutions advanced the state-compact theory that held states could nullify an act of Congress if they deemed it unconstitutional.

**Francis Scott Key (1779–1843)** During the War of 1812, he watched British forces bombard Fort McHenry, but fail to take it. Seeing the American flag still flying over the fort at dawn inspired him to write "The Star-Spangled Banner," which became the American national anthem.

**Keynesian economics** A theory of economics developed by John Maynard Keynes. He argued that increased government spending, even if it increased the nation's deficit, during an economic downturn was necessary to reinvigorate a nation's economy. This view was held by Harry Hopkins and Harold Ickes who advised President Franklin Roosevelt during the Great Depression.

**Martin Luther King Jr. (1929–1968)** As an important leader of the civil rights movement, he urged people to use nonviolent civil disobedience to demand their rights and bring about change. He successfully led the Montgomery bus boycott. While in jail for his role in demonstrations, he wrote his famous "Letter from Birmingham City Jail," in which he defended his strategy of nonviolent protest. In 1963, he delivered his famous "I Have a Dream Speech" from the steps of the Lincoln Memorial as a part of the March on Washington. A year later, he was awarded the Nobel Peace Prize. In 1968, he was assassinated.

**King William's War (War of the League of Augsburg)** First (1689–1697) of four colonial wars between England and France.

**King Philip (?–1676)** or **Metacomet** The chief of the Wampanoages, who the colonists called King Philip. He resented English efforts to convert Indians to Christianity and waged a war against the English colonists in which he was killed.

**Henry Kissinger (1923–)** He served as the secretary of state and national security advisor in the Nixon administration. He negotiated with North Vietnam for an end to the Vietnam War. In 1973, an agreement was signed between America, North and South Vietnam, and the Viet Cong to end the war. The cease-fire did not last; and South Vietnam fell to North Vietnam. He helped organize Nixon's historic trips to China and the Soviet Union. In the Middle East, he negotiated a cease-fire between Israel and its neighbors following the Yom Kippur War and solidified Israel's promise to return to Egypt most of the land it had taken during the 1967 war.

**Knights of Labor** Founded in 1869, the first national union picked up many members after the disastrous 1877 railroad strike, but lasted under the leadership of Terence V. Powderly, only into the 1890s; supplanted by the American Federation of Labor.

**Know-Nothing party** Nativist, anti-Catholic third party organized in 1854 in reaction to large-scale German and Irish immigration; the party's only presidential candidate was Millard Fillmore in 1856.

**Ku Klux Klan** Organized in Pulaski, Tennessee, in 1866 to terrorize former slaves who voted and held political offices during Reconstruction; a revived organization in the 1910s and 1920s stressed white, Anglo-Saxon, fundamentalist Protestant supremacy; the Klan revived a third time to fight the civil rights movement of the 1950s and 1960s in the South.

**Marquis de Lafayette (1757–1834)** A wealthy French idealist excited by the American cause, he offered to serve in Washington's army for free in exchange for being named a major general. He overcame Washington's initial skepticism to become one of his most trusted aides.

**Land Ordinance of 1785** Directed surveying of the Northwest Territory into townships of thirty-six sections (square miles) each, the sale of the sixteenth section of which was to be used to finance public education.

**Bartolomé de Las Casas (1484–1566)** A Catholic missionary who renounced the Spanish practice of coercively converting Indians and advocated the better treatment for them. In 1552, he wrote *A Brief Relation of the Destruction of the Indies*, which described the Spanish's cruel treatment of the Indians.

**League of Nations** Organization of nations to mediate disputes and avoid war established after the First World War as part of the Treaty of Versailles; President Woodrow Wilson's "Fourteen Points" speech to Congress in 1918 proposed the formation of the league.

**Mary Elizabeth Lease (1850–1933)** She was a leader of the farm protest movement who advocated violence if change could not be obtained at the ballot box. She believed that the urban-industrial East was the enemy of the working class.

**Robert E. Lee (1807–1870)** Even though he had served in the United States Army for thirty years, he chose to fight on the side of the Confederacy and took command of the Army of North Virginia. Lee was excellent at using his field commanders; and his soldiers respected him. However, General Ulysses S. Grant eventually wore down his army, and Lee surrendered to Grant at the Appomattox Court House on April 9, 1865.

**Lend-Lease Act (1941)** Permitted the United States to lend or lease arms and other supplies to the Allies, signifying increasing likelihood of American involvement in the Second World War.

**Levittown** First low-cost, mass-produced development of suburban tract housing built by William Levitt on Long Island, New York, in 1947.

**Lexington and Concord, Battle of** The first shots fired in the Revolutionary War, on April 19, 1775, near Boston; approximately 100 Minutemen and 250 British soldiers were killed.

*Liberator* William Lloyd Garrison started this anti-slavery newspaper in 1831 in which he renounced gradualism and called for abolition.

**Queen Liliuokalani (1838–1917)** In 1891, she ascended to the throne of the Hawaiian royal family and tried to eliminate white control of the Hawaiian government. Two years later, Hawaii's white population revolted and seized power with the support of American marines.

**Abraham Lincoln (1809–1865)** His participation in the Lincoln-Douglas debates gave him a national reputation and he was nominated as the Republican party candidate for president in 1860. Shortly after he was elected president, southern states began succeeding from the Union and in April of 1861 he declared war on the succeeding states. On January 1, 1863, Lincoln signed the Emancipation Proclamation, which freed all slaves. At the end of the war, he favored a reconstruction strategy for the former Confederate states that did not radically alter southern social and economic life. However, before his plans could be finalized, John Wilkes Booth assassinated Lincoln at Ford's Theater on April 14, 1865.

**Lincoln-Douglas debates** Series of senatorial campaign debates in 1858 focusing on the issue of slavery in the territories; held in Illinois between Republican Abraham Lincoln, who made a national reputation for himself, and incumbent Democratic senator Stephen A. Douglas, who managed to hold onto his seat.

**John Locke (1632–1704)** An English philosopher whose ideas were influential during the Enlightenment. He argued in his *Essay on Human Understanding* (1690) that humanity is largely the product of the environment, the mind being a blank tablet, *tabula rasa*, on which experience is written.

**Henry Cabot Lodge (1850–1924)** He was the chairman of the Senate Foreign Relations Committee who favored limiting America's involvement in the League of Nations' covenant and sought to amend the Treaty of Versailles.

**de Lôme letter** Spanish ambassador Depuy de Lôme wrote a letter to a friend in Havana in which he described President McKinley as "weak" and a seeker of public admiration. This letter was stolen and published in the *New York Journal*, which increased the American public's dislike of Spain and moved the two countries closer to war.

**Lone Star Republic** After winning independence from Mexico, Texas became its own nation that was called the Lone Star Republic. In 1836, Texans drafted themselves a constitution, legalized slavery, banned free blacks, named Sam Houston president, and voted for the annexation to the United States. However, quarrels over adding a slave state and fears of instigating a war with Mexico delayed Texas's entrance into the Union until December 29, 1845.

**Huey P. Long (1893–1935)** He began his political career in Louisiana where he developed a reputation for being an unscrupulous reformer. As a U.S. senator, he became a critic of President Roosevelt's New Deal Plan and offered his alternative called the Share-the-Wealth program. He was assassinated in 1935.

**Lords Commissioners of Trade and Plantations (the Board of Trade)** William III created this organization in 1696 to investigate the enforcement of the Navigations Act, recommend ways to limit colonial manufactures, and encourage the production of raw materials in the colonies that were needed in Britain.

**Louisiana Purchase** President Thomas Jefferson's 1803 purchase from France of the important port of New Orleans and 828,000 square miles west of the Mississippi River to the Rocky Mountains; it more than doubled the territory of the United States at a cost of only $15 million.

**Lowell "girls"** Young female factory workers at the textile mills in Lowell, Massachusetts, which in the early 1820s provided its employees with prepared meals, dormitories, moral discipline, and educational opportunities.

**Lowell System** Lowell mills were the first to bring all the processes of spinning and weaving cloth together under one roof and have every aspect of the production mechanized. In addition, the Lowell mills were designed to be model factory communities that provided the young women employees with meals, a boardinghouse, moral discipline, and educational and cultural opportunities.

**Martin Luther (1483–1546)** A German monk who founded the Lutheran church. He protested abuses in the Catholic Church by posting his Ninety-five Theses, which began the Protestant Reformation.

**General Douglas MacArthur (1880–1964)** During World War II, he and Admiral Chester Nimitz dislodged the Japanese military from the Pacific Islands they had occupied. Following the war, he was in charge of the occupation of Japan. After North Korea invaded South Korea, Truman sent the U.S. military to defend South Korea under the command of MacArthur. Later in the war, Truman expressed his willingness to negotiate the restoration of prewar boundaries which MacArthur attempted to undermine. Truman fired MacArthur for his open insubordination.

**James Madison (1751–1836)** He participated in the Constitutional Convention during which he proposed the Virginia Plan. He believed in a strong federal government and was a leader of the Federalists and a contributor to *The Federalist*. However, he also presented to Congress the Bill of Rights and drafted the Virginia Resolutions. As the secretary of state, he withheld a commission for William Marbury, which led to the landmark *Marbury v. Madison* decision. During his presidency, he declared war on Britain in response to violations of American shipping rights, which started the War of 1812.

**Alfred Thayer Mahan's *The Influence of Sea Power Upon History, 1660–1783*** Alfred Thayer Mahan was an advocate for sea power and Western imperialism. In 1890, he published *The Influence of Sea Power Upon History, 1660–1783* in which he argued that a nation's greatness and prosperity comes from maritime power. He believed that America's "destiny" was to control the Caribbean, build the Panama Canal, and spread Western civilization across the Pacific.

**Malcolm X (1925–1964)** The most articulate spokesman for black power. Originally, the chief disciple of Elijah Muhammad, the black Muslim leader in the United States, Malcolm X broke away from him and founded his own organization committed to establishing relations between African Americans and the nonwhite peoples of the world. Near the end of his life, he began to preach a biracial message of social change. In 1964, he was assassinated by members of a rival group of black Muslims.

**Manchuria incident** The northeast region of Manchuria was an area contested between China and Russia. In 1931, the Japanese claimed that they needed to protect their extensive investments in the area and moved their army into Manchuria. They quickly conquered the region and set up their own puppet empire. China asked both the United States and the League of Nations for help and neither responded.

**Manifest Destiny** Imperialist phrase first used in 1845 to urge annexation of Texas; used thereafter to encourage American settlement of European colonial and Indian lands in the Great Plains and Far West.

**Horace Mann (1796–1859)** He believed the public school system was the best way to achieve social stability and equal opportunity. As a reformer of education, he sponsored a state board of education, the first state-supported "normal" school for training teachers, a state association for teachers, the minimum school year of six months, and led the drive for a statewide school system.

***Marbury v. Madison* (1803)** First U.S. Supreme Court decision to declare a federal law—the Judiciary Act of 1801—unconstitutional; President John Adams's "midnight appointment" of Federalist judges prompted the suit.

**March on Washington** Civil rights demonstration on August 28, 1963, where the Reverend Martin Luther King Jr. gave his "I Have a Dream" speech on the steps of the Lincoln Memorial.

**George C. Marshall (1880–1959)** As the chairman of the Joint Chiefs of Staff, he orchestrated the Allied victories over Germany and Japan in the Second World War. In 1947, he became President Truman's secretary of state and proposed the massive reconstruction program for western Europe called the Marshall Plan.

**Chief Justice John Marshall (1755–1835)** During his long tenure as chief justice of the supreme court (1801–1835), he established the foundations for American jurisprudence, the authority of the Supreme Court, and the constitutional supremacy of the national government over states.

**Marshall Plan** U.S. program for the reconstruction of post–Second World War Europe through massive aid to former enemy nations as well as allies; proposed by General George C. Marshall in 1947.

**massive resistance** In reaction to the *Brown v. Board of Education* decision of 1954, U.S. Senator Harry Byrd encouraged southern states to defy federally mandated school integration.

**massive retaliation** A doctrine of nuclear strategy in which the United States committed itself to retaliate with "massive retaliatory power" (nuclear weapons) in the event of an attack. Developed by Secretary of State John Foster Dulles during the Eisenhower administration to prevent communist aggression from the Soviet Union and China.

**Senator Joseph R. McCarthy (1908–1957)** In 1950, this senator became the shrewdest and most ruthless exploiter of America's anxiety of communism. He claimed that the United States government was full of Communists and led a witch hunt to find them, but he was never able to uncover a single communist agent.

**George B. McClellan (1826–1885)** In 1861, President Abraham Lincoln appointed him head of the Army of the Potomac and, later, general in chief of the U.S. Army. He built his army into well trained and powerful force. However, he often delayed taking action against the enemy even though Lincoln wanted him to attack. After failing to achieve a decisive victory against the Confederacy, Lincoln removed McClellan from command in 1862.

**Cyrus Hall McCormick (1809–1884)** In 1831, he invented a mechanical reaper to harvest wheat, which transformed the scale of agriculture. By hand a farmer could only harvest a half an acre a day, while the McCormick reaper allowed two people to harvest twelve acres of wheat a day.

**William McKinley (1843–1901)** As a congressman, he was responsible for the McKinley Tariff of 1890, which raised the duties on manufactured products to their highest level ever. Voters disliked the tariff and McKinley, as well as other Republicans, lost their seats in Congress the next election. However, he won the presidential election of 1896 and raised the tariffs again. In 1898, he annexed Hawaii and declared war on Spain. The war concluded with the Treaty of Paris, which gave America control over Puerto Rico, Guam, and the Philippines. Soon America was fighting Filipinos, who were seeking independence for their country. In 1901, McKinley was assassinated.

**Robert McNamara (1916–)** He was the secretary of defense for both President Kennedy and President Johnson and a supporter of America's involvement in Vietnam.

**McNary-Haugen Bill** Vetoed by President Calvin Coolidge in 1927 and 1928, the bill to aid farmers would have artificially raised agricultural prices by selling surpluses overseas for low prices and selling the reduced supply in the United States for higher prices.

**Andrew W. Mellon (1855–1937)** As President Harding's secretary of the Treasury, he sought to generate economic growth through reducing government spending and lowering taxes. However, he insisted that the tax reductions mainly go to the rich because he believed the wealthy would reinvest their money and spur economic growth. In order to bring greater efficiency and nonpartisanship to the government's budget process, he persuaded Congress to pass the Budget and Accounting Act of 1921, which created a new Bureau of the Budget and a General Accounting Office.

**mercantile system** A nationalistic program that assumed that the total amount of the world's gold and silver remained essentially fixed with only a nation's share of that wealth subject to change.

**James Meredith (1933–)** In 1962, the governor of Mississippi defied a Supreme Court ruling and refused to allow James Meredith, an African American, to enroll at the University of Mississippi. Federal marshals were sent to enforce the law which led to clashes between a white mob and the marshals. Federal troops intervened and two people were killed and many others were injured. A few days later, Meredith was able to register at the university.

**Merrimack (ship renamed the Virginia) and the Monitor** First engagement between ironclad ships; fought at Hampton Roads, Virginia, on March 9, 1862.

**Metacomet (?–1676) or King Philip** The chief of the Wampanoages, who the colonists called King Philip. He resented English efforts to convert Indians to Christianity and waged a war against the English colonists in which he was killed.

**militant nonviolence** After the success of the Montgomery bus boycott, people were inspired by Martin Luther King Jr.'s use of this nonviolent form of protest. Throughout the civil rights movement, demonstrators used this method of protest to challenge racial segregation in the South.

**Ho Chi Minh (1890–1969)** He was the Vietnamese communist resistance leader who drove the French and the United States out of Vietnam. After the Geneva Accords divided the region into four countries, he controlled North Vietnam, and ultimately became the leader of all of Vietnam at the conclusion of the Vietnam War.

**minstrelsy** A form of entertainment that was popular from the 1830s to the 1870s. The performances featured white performers who were made up as African Americans or blackface. They performed banjo and fiddle music, "shuffle" dances and lowbrow humor that reinforced racial stereotypes.

**Minutemen** Special units organized by the militia to be ready for quick mobilization.

***Miranda v. Arizona* (1966)** U.S. Supreme Court decision required police to advise persons in custody of their rights to legal counsel and against self-incrimination.

**Mississippi Plan** In 1890, Mississippi instituted policies that led to a near-total loss of voting rights for blacks and many poor whites. In order to vote, the state required that citizens pay all their taxes first, be literate, and have been residents of the state for two years and one year in an electoral district. Convicts were banned from voting. Seven other states followed this strategy of disenfranchisement.

**Missouri Compromise** Deal proposed by Kentucky senator Henry Clay to resolve the slave/free imbalance in Congress that would result from Missouri's admission as a slave state; in the compromise of March 20, 1820, Maine's admission as a free state offset Missouri, and slavery was prohibited in the remainder of the Louisiana Territory north of the southern border of Missouri.

**Model T Ford** Henry Ford developed this model of car so that it was affordable for everyone. Its success led to an increase in the production of automobiles which stimulated other related industries such steel, oil, and rubber. The mass use of automobiles increased the speed goods could be transported, encouraged urban sprawl, and sparked real estate booms in California and Florida.

**modernism** As both a mood and movement, modernism recognized that Western civilization had entered an era of change. Traditional ways of thinking and creating art were being rejected and replaced with new understandings and forms of expression.

**Molly Maguires** Secret organization of Irish coal miners that used violence to intimidate mine officials in the 1870s.

**Monroe Doctrine** President James Monroe's declaration to Congress on December 2, 1823, that the American continents would be thenceforth closed to colonization but that the United States would honor existing colonies of European nations.

**Montgomery bus boycott** Sparked by Rosa Parks's arrest on December 1, 1955, a successful year-long boycott protesting segregation on city buses; led by the Reverend Martin Luther King Jr.

**Moral Majority** Televangelist Jerry Falwell's political lobbying organization, the name of which became synonymous with the religious right—conservative evangelical Protestants who helped ensure President Ronald Reagan's 1980 victory.

**J. Pierpont Morgan (1837–1913)** As a powerful investment banker, he would acquire, reorganize, and consolidate companies into giant trusts. His biggest achievement was the consolidation of the steel industry into the United States Steel Corporation, which was the first billion-dollar corporation.

**James Monroe (1758–1831)** He served as secretary of state and war under President Madison and was elected president. As the latter, he signed the Transcontinental Treaty with

Spain which gave the United States Florida and expanded the Louisiana territory's western border to the Pacific coast. In 1823, he established the Monroe Doctrine. This foreign policy proclaimed the American continents were no longer open to colonization and America would be neutral in European affairs.

**Robert Morris (1734–1806)** He was the superintendent of finance for the Congress of the Confederation during the final years of the Revolutionary War. He envisioned a national finance plan of taxation and debt management, but the states did not approve the necessary amendments to the Articles of Confederation need to implement the plan.

**Samuel F. B. Morse (1791–1872)** In 1832, he invented the telegraph and revolutionized the speed of communication.

**mountain men** Inspired by the fur trade, these men left civilization to work as trappers and reverted to a primitive existence in the wilderness. They were the first whites to find routes through the Rocky Mountains, and they pioneered trails that settlers later used to reach the Oregon country and California in the 1840s.

**muckrakers** Writers who exposed corruption and abuses in politics, business, meat-packing, child labor, and more, primarily in the first decade of the twentieth century; their popular books and magazine articles spurred public interest in progressive reform.

**Mugwumps** Reform wing of the Republican party that supported Democrat Grover Cleveland for president in 1884 over Republican James G. Blaine, whose influence peddling had been revealed in the Mulligan letters of 1876.

**mulattoes** People of mixed racial ancestry, whose status in the Old South was somewhere between that of blacks and whites.

**Benito Mussolini "*Il Duce*" (1883–1945)** The Italian founder of the Fascist party who came to power in Italy in 1922 and allied himself with Adolf Hitler and the Axis powers during the Second World War.

**My Lai Massacre** In 1968, Lieutenant William Calley and his soldiers massacred 347 Vietnamese civilians in the village of My Lai. Twenty-five army officers were charged with complicity in the massacre and its cover-up but only Calley was convicted. Later, President Nixon granted him parole.

**North American Free Trade Agreement (NAFTA)** Approved in 1993, the North American Free Trade Agreement with Canada and Mexico allowed goods to travel across their borders free of tariffs; critics argued that American workers would lose their jobs to cheaper Mexican labor.

**National Industrial Recovery Act (1933)** Passed on the last of the Hundred Days; it created public-works jobs through the Federal Emergency Relief Administration and established a system of self-regulation for industry through the National Recovery Administration, which was ruled unconstitutional in 1935.

**National Recovery Administration** This organization's two goals were to stabilize business and generate purchasing power for consumers. The first goal was to be achieved through the implementation industry-wide codes that set wages and prices, which would reduce the chaotic competition. To provide consumers with purchasing power, the administration would provide jobs, define workplace standards, and raise wages.

**National Socialist German Workers' Party (Nazi)** Founded in the 1920s, this party gained control over Germany under the leadership of Adolf Hitler in 1933 and continued in power until Germany's defeat at the end of the Second World War. It advocated a violent anti-Semitic, anti-Marxist, pan-German ideology. The Nazi party systematically murdered some 6 million Jews along with more than a million others.

**nativism** Anti-immigrant and anti-Catholic feeling in the 1830s through the 1850s; the largest group was New York's Order of the Star-Spangled Banner, which expanded into the American, or Know-Nothing, party in 1854. In the 1920, there was a surge in nativism as Americans grew to fear immigrants who might be political radicals. In response, new strict immigration regulations were established.

**nativist** A native-born American who saw immigrants as a threat to his way of life and employment. During the 1880s, nativist groups worked to stop the flow of immigrates into the United States. Of these groups, the most successful was the American Protective Association who promoted government restrictions on immigration, tougher naturalization requirements, the teaching of English in schools and workplaces that refused to employ foreigners or Catholics.

**Navigation Acts** Passed by the English Parliament to control colonial trade and bolster the mercantile system, 1650–1775; enforcement of the acts led to growing resentment by colonists.

**new conservatism** The political philosophy of those who led the conservative insurgency of the early 1980s. This brand of conservatism was personified in Ronald Reagan who believed in less government, supply-side economics, and "family values."

**First New Deal** Franklin D. Roosevelt's campaign promise, in his speech to the Democratic National Convention of 1932, to combat the Great Depression with a "new deal for the American people;" the phrase became a catchword for his ambitious plan of economic programs.

**New France** The name used for the area of North America that was colonized by the French. Unlike Spanish or English colonies, New France had a small number of colonists, which forced them to initially seek good relations with the indigenous people they encountered.

**New Freedom** Democrat Woodrow Wilson's political slogan in the presidential campaign of 1912; Wilson wanted to improve the banking system, lower tariffs, and, by breaking up monopolies, give small businesses freedom to compete.

**New Frontier** John F. Kennedy's program, stymied by a Republican Congress and his abbreviated term; his successor Lyndon B. Johnson had greater success with many of the same concepts.

**New Jersey Plan** The delegations to the Constitutional Convention were divided between two plans on how to structure the government: New Jersey wanted one legislative body with equal representation for each state.

**New Nationalism** Platform of the Progressive party and slogan of former President Theodore Roosevelt in the presidential campaign of 1912; stressed government activism, including regulation of trusts, conservation, and recall of state court decisions that had nullified progressive programs.

**"New Negro"** In the 1920s, a slow and steady growth of black political influence occurred in northern cities where African Americans were freer to speak and act. This political activity created a spirit of protest that expressed itself culturally in the Harlem Renaissance and politically in "new Negro" nationalism.

**New Netherland** Dutch colony conquered by the English to become four new colonies New York, New Jersey, Pennsylvania, and Delaware.

**New South** *Atlanta Constitution* editor Henry W. Grady's 1886 term for the prosperous post–Civil War South: democratic, industrial, urban, and free of nostalgia for the defeated plantation South.

**William Randolph Hearst's *New York Journal*** In the late 1890s, the *New York Journal* and its rival, the *New York World*, printed sensationalism on the Cuban revolution as part of their heated competition for readership. The *New York Journal* printed a negative letter from the Spanish ambassador about President McKinley and inflammatory coverage of the sinking of the *Maine* in Havana Harbor. These two events roused the American public's outcry against Spain.

**Joseph Pulitzer's *New York World*** In the late 1890s, the *New York World* and its rival, *New York Journal*, printed sensationalism on the Cuban revolution as part of their heated competition for readership.

**Admiral Chester Nimitz (1885–1966)** During the Second World War, he was the commander of central Pacific. Along with General Douglas MacArthur, he dislodged the Japanese military from the Pacific Islands they had occupied.

**Nineteenth Amendment (1920)** Granted women the right to vote.

**Richard M. Nixon (1913–1994)** He first came to national prominence as a congressman involved in the investigation of Alger Hiss. Later he served as vice president during the Eisenhower administration. In 1960, he ran as the Republican nominee for president and lost to John Kennedy. In 1968, he ran and won the presidency against Democratic nominee Hubert Humphrey. During his campaign, he promised to bring about "peace with honor" in Vietnam. He told southern conservatives that he would slow the federal enforcement of civil rights laws and appoint pro-southern justices to the Supreme Court. After being elected, he fulfilled the latter promise attempted to keep the former. He opened talks with the North Vietnamese and began a program of Vietnamization of the war. He also bombed Cambodia. In 1973, America, North and South Vietnam, and the Viet Cong agreed to end the war and the United States withdrew. However, the cease-fire was broken, and the South Vietnam fell to North Vietnam. In 1970, Nixon changed U.S. foreign policy. He declared that the America was no longer the world's policemen and he would seek some partnerships with Communist countries. With his historic visit to China, he ended twenty years of diplomatically isolating China and he began taking steps towards cultural exchanges and trade. In 1972, Nixon travelled to Moscow and signed agreements with the Soviet Union on arms control and trade. That same year, Nixon was reelected, but the Watergate scandal erupted shortly after his victory. When his knowledge of the break-in and subsequent cover-up was revealed, Nixon resigned the presidency under threat of impeachment.

**No Child Left Behind** President George W. Bush's education reform plan that required states to set and meet learning standards for students and make sure that all students were "proficient" in reading and writing by 2014. States had to submit annual reports of students' standardized test scores. Teachers were required to be "proficient" in their subject area. Schools who failed to show progress would face sanctions. States criticized the lack of funding for remedial programs and noted that poor school districts would find it very difficult to meet the new guidelines.

**Lord North (1732–1792)** The first minister of King George III's cabinet whose efforts to subdue the colonies only brought them closer to revolution. He helped bring about the Tea Act of 1773, which led to the Boston Tea Party. In an effort to discipline Boston, he wrote, and Parliament passed, four acts that galvanized colonial resistance.

**North Atlantic Treaty Organization (NATO)** Defensive alliance founded in 1949 by ten western European nations, the United States, and Canada to deter Soviet expansion in Europe.

**Northwest Ordinance** Created the Northwest Territory (area north of the Ohio River and west of Pennsylvania), established conditions for self-government and statehood, included a Bill of Rights, and permanently prohibited slavery.

**nullification** Concept of invalidation of a federal law within the borders of a state; first expounded in the Kentucky and Virginia Resolutions (1798), cited by South Carolina in its Ordinance of Nullification (1832) of the Tariff of Abominations, used by southern states to explain their secession from the Union (1861), and cited again by southern states to oppose the *Brown v. Board of Education* decision (1954).

**Nuremberg trials** At the site of the annual Nazi party rallies, twenty-one major German offenders faced an international military tribunal for Nazi atrocities. After a ten-month trial, the court acquitted three and sentenced eleven to death, three to life imprisonment, and four to shorter terms.

**Barack Obama (1961–)** In the 2008 presidential election, Senator Barack Obama mounted an innovative Internet based and grassroots orientated campaign that garnered him enough delegates to win the Democratic nomination. As the nation's economy nosedived in the fall of 2008, Obama linked the Republican economic philosophy with the country's dismal financial state and promoted a message of "change" and "politics of hope," which resonated with voters. He decisively won the presidency and became America's first person of colored to be elected president.

**Occupy Wall Street** A grassroots movement protesting a capitalist system that fostered social and economic inequality. Begun in Zuccotti Park, New York City, during 2011, the movement spread rapidly across the nation, triggering a national conversation about income inequality and protests of the government's "bailouts" of the banks and corporations allegedly responsible for the Great Recession.

**Sandra Day O'Connor (1930–)** She was the first woman to serve on the Supreme Court of the United States and was appointed by President Reagan. Reagan's critics charged that her appointment was a token gesture and not a sign of any real commitment to gender equality.

**Ohio gang** In order to escape the pressures of the White House, President Harding met with a group of people, called the "Ohio gang," in a house on K Street in Washington D.C. Members of this gang were given low-level positions in the American government and they used their White House connection to "line their pockets" by granting government contracts without bidding, which led to a series of scandals, most notably the Teapot Dome Scandal.

**Frederick Law Olmsted (1822–1903)** In 1858, he constructed New York's Central Park, which led to a growth in the movement to create urban parks. He went on to design parks for Boston, Brooklyn, Chicago, Philadelphia, San Francisco, and many other cities.

**Opechancanough (?–1644)** The brother and successor of Powhatan who led his tribe in an attempt to repel the English settlers in Virginia in 1622.

**Open Door Policy** In hopes of protecting the Chinese market for U.S. exports, Secretary of State John Hay unilaterally announced in 1899 that Chinese trade would be open to all nations.

**Operation Desert Shield** After Saddam Hussein invaded Kuwait in 1990, President George H. W. Bush sent American military forces to Saudi Arabia on a strictly defensive mission. They were soon joined by a multinational coalition. When the coalition's mission changed to the retaking of Kuwait, the operation was renamed Desert Storm.

**Operation Desert Storm** Multinational allied force that defeated Iraq in the Gulf War of January 1991.

**Operation Overlord** The Allies' assault on Hitler's "Atlantic Wall," a seemingly impregnable series of fortifications and minefields along the French coastline that German forces had created using captive Europeans for laborers.

**J. Robert Oppenheimer (1904–1967)** He led the group of physicists at the laboratory in Los Alamos, New Mexico, who constructed the first atomic bomb.

**Oregon Country** The Convention of 1818 between Britain and the United States established the Oregon Country as being west of the crest of the Rocky Mountains and the two countries were to jointly occupy it. In 1824, the United States and Russia signed a treaty that established the line of 54°40′ as the southern boundary of Russia's territorial claim in North America. A similar agreement between Britain and Russia finally gave the Oregon Country clearly defined boarders, but it remained under joint British and American control.

**Oregon fever** Enthusiasm for emigration to the Oregon Country in the late 1830s and early 1840s.

**Osceola (1804?–1838)** He was the leader of the Seminole nation who resisted the federal Indian removal policy through a protracted guerilla war. In 1837, he was treacherously seized under a flag of truce and imprisoned at Fort Moultrie, where he was left to die.

**Overland (Oregon) Trails** Trail Route of wagon trains bearing settlers from Independence, Missouri, to the Oregon Country in the 1840s to 1860s.

**A. Mitchell Palmer (1872–1936)** As the attorney general, he played an active role in government's response to the Red Scare. After several bombings across America, including one at Palmer's home, he and other Americans became convinced that there was a well-organized Communist terror campaign at work. The federal government launched a campaign of raids, deportations, and collecting files on radical individuals.

**Panic of 1819** Financial collapse brought on by sharply falling cotton prices, declining demand for American exports, and reckless western land speculation.

**panning** A method of mining that used a large metal pan to sift gold dust and nuggets from riverbeds during the California gold rush of 1849.

**Rosa Parks (1913–2005)** In 1955, she refused to give up her seat to a white man on a city bus in Montgomery, Alabama, which a local ordinance required of blacks. She was arrested for disobeying the ordinance. In response, black community leaders organized the Montgomery bus boycott.

**paternalism** A moral position developed during the first half of the nineteenth century which claimed that slaves were deprived of liberty for their own "good." Such a rationalization was adopted by some slave owners to justify slavery.

**Alice Paul (1885–1977)** She was a leader of the women's suffrage movement and head of the Congressional Committee of National Women Suffrage Association. She instructed female suffrage activists to use more militant tactics, such as picketing state legislatures, chaining themselves to public buildings, inciting police to arrest them, and undertaking hunger strikes.

**Norman Vincent Peale (1898–1993)** He was a champion of the upbeat and feel-good theology that was popular in the 1950s religious revival. He advocated getting rid of any depressing or negative thoughts and replacing them with "faith, enthusiasm and joy," which would make an individual popular and well liked.

**"peculiar institution"** This term was used to describe slavery in America because slavery so fragrantly violated the principle of individual freedom that served as the basis for the Declaration of Independence.

**Pentagon Papers** Informal name for the Defense Department's secret history of the Vietnam conflict; leaked to the press by former official Daniel Ellsberg and published in the *New York Times* in 1971.

**Pequot War** Massacre in 1637 and subsequent dissolution of the Pequot Nation by Puritan settlers, who seized the Indians' lands.

**perestroika** Soviet leader Mikhail Gorbachev introduced these political and economic reforms, which included reconstructing the state bureaucracy, reducing the privileges of the political elite, and shifting from a centrally planned economy to a mixed economy.

**Commodore Matthew Perry (1794–1858)** In 1854, he negotiated the Treaty of Kanagawa, which was the first step in starting a political and commercial relationship between the United States and Japan.

**John J. Pershing (1860–1948)** After Pancho Villa had conducted several raids into Texas and New Mexico, President Woodrow Wilson sent troops under the command of General

John J. Pershing into Mexico to stop Villa. However, after a year of chasing Villa and not being able to catch him, they returned to the United States. During the First World War, Pershing commanded the first contingent of U.S. soldiers sent to Europe and advised the War Department to send additional American forces.

**"pet banks"** During President Andrew Jackson's fight with the national bank, Jackson resolved to remove all federal deposits from it. To comply with Jackson's demands, Secretary of Treasury Taney continued to draw on government's accounts in the national bank, but deposit all new federal receipts in state banks. The state banks that received these deposits were called "pet banks."

**Pilgrims** Puritan Separatists who broke completely with the Church of England and sailed to the New World aboard the *Mayflower*, founding Plymouth Colony on Cape Cod in 1620.

**Dien Bien Phu** The defining battle in the war between French colonialists and the Viet Minh. The Viet Minh's victory secured North Vietnam for Ho Chi Minh and was crucial in compelling the French to give up Indochina as a colony.

**Gifford Pinchot (1865–1946)** As the head of the Division of Forestry, he implemented a conservation policy that entailed the scientific management of natural resources to serve the public interest. His work helped start the conservation movement. In 1910, he exposed to the public the decision of Richard A. Ballinger's, President Taft's secretary of the interior, to open up previously protected land for commercial use. Pinchot was fired, but the damage to Taft's public image resulted in the loss of many pro-Taft candidates in 1910 congressional election.

**Elizabeth Lucas Pinckney (1722?–1793)** One of the most enterprising horticulturists in colonial America, she began managing her family's three plantations in South Carolina at the age of sixteen. She had tremendous success growing indigo, which led to many other plantations growing the crop as well.

**Pinckney's Treaty** Treaty with Spain negotiated by Thomas Pinckney in 1795; established United States boundaries at the Mississippi River and the 31st parallel and allowed open transportation on the Mississippi.

**Francisco Pizarro (1478?–1541)** In 1531, he lead his Spanish soldiers to Peru and conquered the Inca Empire.

**planters** In the antebellum South, the owner of a large farm worked by twenty or more slaves.

**political "machine"** A network of political activists and elected officials, usually controlled by a powerful "boss," that attempts to manipulate local politics

**James Knox Polk "Young Hickory" (1795–1849)** As president, his chief concern was the expansion of the United States. In 1846, his administration resolved the dispute with Britain over the Oregon Country border. Shortly, after taking office, Mexico broke off relations with the United States over the annexation of Texas. Polk declared war on Mexico and sought to subvert Mexican authority in California. The United States defeated Mexico; and the two nations signed the Treaty of Guadalupe Hidalgo in which Mexico gave up any claims on Texas north of the Rio Grande River and ceded New Mexico and California to the United States.

**Pontiac's Rebellion** The Peace Treaty of 1763 gave the British all French land east of the Mississippi River. This area included the territory of France's Indian allies who were not consulted about the transfer of their lands to British control. In an effort to recover their autonomy, Indians captured British forts around the Great Lakes and in the Ohio Valley as well as attacked settlements in Pennsylvania, Maryland, and Virginia.

**popular sovereignty** Allowed settlers in a disputed territory to decide the slavery issue for themselves.

**Populist/People's party** Political success of Farmers' Alliance candidates encouraged the formation in 1892 of the People's party (later renamed the Populist party); active until 1912, it advocated a variety of reform issues, including free coinage of silver, income tax, postal savings, regulation of railroads, and direct election of U.S. senators.

**Pottawatomie Massacre** In retaliation for the "sack of Lawrence," John Brown and his abolitionist cohorts hacked five men to death in the pro-slavery settlement of Pottawatomie, Kansas, on May 24, 1856, triggering a guerrilla war in the Kansas Territory that cost 200 settler lives.

**Chief Powhatan Wahunsonacock** He was called Powhatan by the English after the name of his tribe, and was the powerful, charismatic chief of numerous Algonquian-speaking towns in eastern Virginia representing over 10,000 Indians.

**pragmatism** William James founded this philosophy in the early 1900s. Pragmatists believed that ideas gained their validity not from their inherent truth, but from their social consequences and practical application.

**Proclamation of 1763** Royal directive issued after the French and Indian War prohibiting settlement, surveys, and land grants west of the Appalachian Mountains; although it was soon over-ridden by treaties, colonists continued to harbor resentment.

**proprietary colonies** A colony owned by an individual, rather than a joint-stock company.

***pueblos*** The Spanish term for the adobe cliff dwellings of the indigenous people of the southwestern United States.

**Pullman strike** Strike against the Pullman Palace Car Company in the company town of Pullman, Illinois, on May 11, 1894, by the American Railway Union under Eugene V. Debs; the strike was crushed by court injunctions and federal troops two months later.

**Puritans** English religious group that sought to purify the Church of England; founded the Massachusetts Bay Colony under John Winthrop in 1630.

**Quakers** George Fox founded the Quaker religion in 1647. They rejected the use of formal sacraments and ministry, refused to take oaths and embraced pacifism. Fleeing persecution, they settled and established the colony of Pennsylvania.

**Radical Republicans** Senators and congressmen who, strictly identifying the Civil War with the abolitionist cause, sought swift emancipation of the slaves, punishment of the rebels, and tight controls over the former Confederate states after the war.

**Raleigh's Roanoke Island Colony** English expedition of 117 settlers, including Virginia Dare, the first English child born in the New World; colony disappeared from Roanoke Island in the Outer Banks sometime between 1587 and 1590.

**A. Philip Randolph (1889–1979)** He was the head of the Brotherhood of Sleeping Car Porters who planned a march on Washington D.C. to demand an end to racial discrimination in the defense industries. To stop the march, Roosevelt administration negotiated an agreement with the Randolph group. The demonstration would be called off and an executive order would be issued that forbid discrimination in defense work and training programs and set up the Fair Employment Practices Committee.

**range wars** In the late 1800s, conflicting claims over land and water rights triggered violent disputes between farmers and ranchers in parts of the western United States.

**Ronald Reagan (1911–2004)** In 1980, the former actor and governor of California was elected president. In office, he reduced social spending, cut taxes, and increased defense spending. He was criticized for cutting important programs, such as housing and school lunches and increasing the federal deficit. By 1983, prosperity had returned to America and Reagan's economic reforms appeared to be working, but in October of 1987 the stock market crashed. Some blamed the federal debt, which had tripled in size since Reagan had taken office. In the early 1980s, HIV/AIDS cases were beginning to be reported in America, but the Reagan administration chose to do little about the growing epidemic. Reagan believed that most of the world's problems came from the Soviet Union, which he called the "evil empire." In response, he conducted a major arms build up. Then in 1987, he signed an arms-control treaty with the Soviet Union. He authorized covert CIA operations in Central America. In 1986, the Iran-Contra scandal came to light which revealed arms sales were being conducted with Iran in a partial exchange for the release of hostages in Lebanon. The arms money was being used to aid the Contras.

**Reaganomics** Popular name for President Ronald Reagan's philosophy of "supply side" economics, which combined tax cuts, less government spending, and a balanced budget with an unregulated marketplace.

**Reconstruction Finance Corporation (RFC)** Federal program established in 1932 under President Herbert Hoover to loan money to banks and other institutions to help them avert bankruptcy.

**First Red Scare** Fear among many Americans after the First World War of Communists in particular and noncitizens in general, a reaction to the Russian Revolution, mail bombs, strikes, and riots.

**redeemers** In post–Civil War southern politics, redeemers were supporters of postwar Democratic leaders who supposedly saved the South from Yankee domination and the constraints of a purely rural economy.

**Dr. Walter Reed (1851–1902)** His work on yellow fever in Cuba led to the discovery that the fever was carried by mosquitoes. This understanding helped develop more effective controls of the worldwide disease.

**Reform Darwinism** A social philosophy that challenged the ruthlessness of Social Darwinism by asserting that humans could actively shape the process of evolutionary social development through cooperation and innovation.

**Reformation** European religious movement that challenged the Catholic Church and resulted in the beginnings of Protestant Christianity. During this period, Catholics and Protestants persecuted, imprisoned, tortured, and killed each other in large numbers.

**reparations** As a part of the Treaty of Versailles, Germany was required to confess its responsibility for the First World War and make payments to the victors for the entire expense of the war. These two requirements created a deep bitterness among Germans.

**Alexander Hamilton's Report on Manufactures** First Secretary of the Treasury Alexander Hamilton's 1791 analysis that accurately foretold the future of American industry and proposed tariffs and subsidies to promote it.

**Republicans** First used during the early nineteenth century to describe supporters of a strict interpretation of the Constitution, which they believed would safeguard individual freedoms and states' rights from the threats posed by a strong central government. The idealist Republican vision of sustaing an agrarian-oriented union was developed largely by Thomas Jefferson.

**"return to normalcy"** In the 1920 presidential election, Republican nominee Warren G. Harding campaigned on the promise of a "return to normalcy," which would mean a return to conservative values and a turning away from President Wilson's internationalism.

**Paul Revere (1735–1818)** On the night of April 18, 1775, British soldiers marched towards Concord to arrest American Revolutionary leaders and seize their depot of supplies. Paul Revere famously rode through the night and raised the alarm about the approaching British troops.

**Roaring Twenties** In 1920s, urban America experienced an era of social and intellectual revolution. Young people experimented with new forms of recreation and sexuality as well as embraced jazz music. Leading young urban intellectuals expressed a disdain for old-fashioned rural and small-town values. The Eastern, urban cultural shift clashed with conservative and insular midwestern America, which increased the tensions between the two regions.

**Jackie Robinson (1919–1972)** In 1947, he became the first African American to play major league baseball. He won over fans and players and stimulated the integration of other professional sports.

**rock-and-roll music** Alan Freed, a disc jockey, noticed white teenagers were buying rhythm and blues records that had been only purchased by African Americans and Hispanic Americans. Freed began playing these records, but called them rock-and-roll records as a way to overcome the racial barrier. As the popularity of the music genre increased, it helped bridge the gap between "white" and "black" music.

**John D. Rockefeller (1839–1937)** In 1870, he founded the Standard Oil Company of Ohio, which was his first step in creating his vast oil empire. Eventually, he perfected the idea of a holding company: a company that controlled other companies by holding all or at least a majority of their stock. During his lifetime, he donated over $500 million in charitable contributions.

**Romanticism** Philosophical, literary, and artistic movement of the nineteenth century that was largely a reaction to the rationalism of the previous century; Romantics valued emotion, mysticism, and individualism.

**Eleanor Roosevelt (1884–1962)** She redefined the role of the presidential spouse and was the first woman to address a national political convention, write a nationally syndicated column and hold regular press conferences. She travelled throughout the nation to promote the New Deal, women's causes, organized labor, and meet with African American leaders. She was her husband's liaison to liberal groups and brought women activists and African American and labor leaders to the White House.

**Franklin Delano Roosevelt (1882–1945)** Elected during the Great Depression, Roosevelt sought to help struggling Americans through his New Deal programs that created employment and social programs, such as Social Security. Prior to American's entry into the Second World War, he supported Britain's fight against Germany through the lend-lease program. After the bombing of Pearl Harbor, he declared war on Japan and Germany and led the country through most of the Second World War before dying of cerebral hemorrhage. In 1945, he met with Winston Churchill and Joseph Stalin at the Yalta Conference to determine the shape of the post-war world.

**Theodore Roosevelt (1858–1919)** As the assistant secretary of the navy, he supported expansionism, American imperialism and war with Spain. He led the First Volunteer Cavalry, or Rough Riders, in Cuba during the war of 1898 and used the notoriety of this military campaign for political gain. As President McKinley's vice president, he succeeded McKinley after his assassination. His forceful foreign policy became known as "big stick diplomacy." Domestically, his policies on natural resources helped start the conversation movement. Unable to win the Republican nomination for president in 1912, he formed his own party of progressive Republicans called the "Bull Moose" party.

**Roosevelt Corollary to the Monroe Doctrine (1904)** President Theodore Roosevelt announced in what was essentially a corollary to the Monroe Doctrine that the United States could intervene militarily to prevent interference from European powers in the Western Hemisphere.

**Rough Riders** The First U.S. Volunteer Cavalry, led in battle in the Spanish-American War by Theodore Roosevelt; they were victorious in their only battle near Santiago, Cuba; and Roosevelt used the notoriety to aid his political career.

**Nicola Sacco (1891–1927)** In 1920, he and Bartolomeo Vanzetti were Italian immigrants who were arrested for stealing $16,000 and killing a paymaster and his guard. Their trial took place during a time of numerous bombings by anarchists and their judge was openly prejudicial. Many liberals and radicals believe that the conviction of Sacco and Vanzetti was based on their political ideas and ethnic origin rather than the evidence against them.

**"salutary neglect"** Edward Burke's description of Robert Walpole's relaxed policy towards the American colonies, which gave them greater independence in pursuing both their economic and political interests.

**Sandinista** Cuban-sponsored government that came to power in Nicaragua after toppling a corrupt dictator. The State Department believed that the Sandinistas were supplying the leftist Salvadoran rebels with Cuban and Soviet arms. In response, the Reagan administration ordered the CIA to train and supply guerrilla bands of anti-Communist Nicaraguans called Contras. A cease-fire agreement between the Contras and Sandinistas was signed in 1988.

**Margaret Sanger (1883–1966)** As a birth-control activist, she worked to distribute birth control information to working-class women and opened the nation's first family-planning clinic in 1916. She organized the American Birth Control League, which eventually changed its name to Planned Parenthood.

**General Antonio López de Santa Anna (1794–1876)** In 1834, he seized political power in Mexico and became a dictator. In 1835, Texans rebelled against him and he led his army to Texas to crush their rebellion. He captured the missionary called the Alamo and killed all of its defenders, which inspired Texans to continue to resistance and Americans to volunteer to fight for Texas. The Texans captured Santa Anna during a surprise attack and he bought his freedom by signing a treaty recognizing Texas's independence.

**Saratoga, Battle of** Major defeat of British general John Burgoyne and more than 5,000 British troops at Saratoga, New York, on October 17, 1777.

**scalawags** White southern Republicans—some former Unionists—who served in Reconstruction governments.

**Phyllis Schlafly (1924–)** A right-wing Republican activist who spearheaded the anti-feminism movement. She believed feminist were "anti-family, anti-children, and pro-abortion." She worked against the equal-rights amendment for women and civil rights protection for gays.

**Winfield Scott (1786–1866)** During the Mexican War, he was the American general who captured Mexico City, which ended the war. Using his popularity from his military success, he ran as a Whig party candidate for President.

**Sears, Roebuck and Company** By the end of the nineteenth century, this company dominated the mail-order industry and helped create a truly national market. Its mail-order catalog and low prices allowed people living in rural areas and small towns to buy products that were previously too expensive or available only to city dwellers.

**secession** Shortly after President Abraham Lincoln was elected, southern states began dissolving their ties with the United States because they believed Lincoln and the Republican party were a threat to slavery.

**second Bank of the United States** In 1816, the second Bank of the United States was established in order to bring stability to the national economy, serve as the depository for national funds, and provide the government with the means of floating loans and transferring money across the country.

**Second Great Awakening** Religious revival movement of the early decades of the nineteenth century, in reaction to the growth of secularism and rationalist religion; began the predominance of the Baptist and Methodist churches.

**Second New Deal** To rescue his New Deal program form judicial and political challenges, President Roosevelt launched a second phase of the New Deal in 1935. He was able to convince Congress to pass key pieces of legislation including the National Labor Relations act and Social Security Act. Roosevelt called the latter the New Deal's "supreme achievement" and pensioners started receiving monthly checks in 1940.

**Seneca Falls Convention** First women's rights meeting and the genesis of the women's suffrage movement; held in July 1848 in a church in Seneca Falls, New York, by Elizabeth Cady Stanton and Lucretia Coffin Mott.

**"separate but equal"** Principle underlying legal racial segregation, which was upheld in *Plessy v. Ferguson* (1896) and struck down in *Brown v. Board of Education* (1954).

**separation of powers** The powers of government are split between three separate branches (executive, legislative, and judicial) who check and balance each other.

**September 11** On September 11, 2001, Islamic terrorists, who were members of al Qaeda terrorist organization, hijacked four commercial airliners. Two were flown into the World Trade Center and a third into the Pentagon. A fourth plane was brought down in Shanksville, Pennsylvania, when its passengers attacked the cockpit. In response, President George W. Bush launched his "war on terrorism." His administration assembled an international coalition to fight terrorism, and they invaded Afghanistan after the country's government would not turn over al Qaeda's leader, Osama bin Laden. However, bin Laden evaded capture. Fearful of new attacks, Bush created the Office of Homeland Security and the Transportation Security Administration. Bush and Congress passed the U.S.A. Patriot Act, which allowed government agencies to try suspected terrorists in secret military courts and eavesdrop on confidential conversations.

**settlement houses** Product of the late nineteenth-century movement to offer a broad array of social services in urban immigrant neighborhoods; Chicago's Hull House was one of hundreds of settlement houses that operated by the early twentieth century.

**Shakers** Founded by Mother Ann Lee Stanley in England, the United Society of Believers in Christ's Second Appearing settled in Watervliet, New York, in 1774 and subsequently established eighteen additional communes in the Northeast, Indiana, and Kentucky.

**sharecropping** Type of farm tenancy that developed after the Civil War in which landless workers—often former slaves—farmed land in exchange for farm supplies and a share of the crop; differed from tenancy in that the terms were generally less favorable.

**Share-the-Wealth program** Huey Long, a critic of President Roosevelt, offered this program as an alternative to the New Deal. The program proposed to confiscate large personal fortunes, which would be used to guarantee every poor family a cash grant of $5,000 and every worker an annual income of $2,500. Under this program, Long promised to provide pensions, reduce working hours, pay veterans' bonuses, and ensures a college education to every qualified student.

**Shays's Rebellion** Massachusetts farmer Daniel Shays and 1,200 compatriots, seeking debt relief through issuance of paper currency and lower taxes, stormed the federal arsenal at Springfield in the winter of 1787 but were quickly repulsed.

**William T. Sherman's "March to the Sea"** Union General William T. Sherman believed that there was a connection between the South's economy, morale, and ability to wage war. During his March through Georgia, he wanted to demoralize the civilian populace and destroy the resources they needed to fight. His army seized food and livestock that the Confederate Army might have used as well as wrecked railroads and mills and burned plantations.

**Sixteenth Amendment (1913)** Legalized the federal income tax.

**Alfred E. Smith (1873–1944)** In the 1928 presidential election, he won the Democratic nomination, but failed to win the presidency. Rural voters distrusted him for being Catholic and the son of Irish immigrants as well as his anti-Prohibition stance.

**Captain John Smith (1580–1631)** A swashbuckling soldier of fortune with rare powers of leadership and self-promotion, he was appointed to the resident council to manage Jamestown.

**Joseph Smith (1805–1844)** In 1823, he claimed that the Angel Moroni showed him the location of several gold tablets on which the Book of Mormon was written. Using the Book of Mormon as his gospel, he founded the Church of Jesus Christ of Latter-day Saints, or Mormons. Joseph and his followers upset non-Mormons living near them so they began looking for a refuge from persecution. In 1839, they settled in Commerce, Illinois, which they renamed Nauvoo. In 1844, Joseph and his brother were arrested and jailed for ordering the destruction of a newspaper that opposed them. While in jail, an anti-Mormon mob stormed the jail and killed both of them.

**social Darwinism** Application of Charles Darwin's theory of natural selection to society; used the concept of the "survival of the fittest" to justify class distinctions and to explain poverty.

**social gospel** Preached by liberal Protestant clergymen in the late nineteenth and early twentieth centuries; advocated the application of Christian principles to social problems generated by industrialization.

**social justice** An important part of the Progressive's agenda, social justice sought to solve social problems through reform and regulation. Methods used to bring about social justice ranged from the founding of charities to the legislation of a ban on child labor.

**Sons of Liberty** Organized by Samuel Adams, they were colonialists with a militant view against the British government's control of the colonies.

**Hernando de Soto (1500?–1542)** A conquistador who explored the west coast of Florida, western North Carolina, and along the Arkansas river from 1539 till his death in 1542.

**Southern Christian Leadership Conference (SCLC)** Civil rights organization founded in 1957 by the Reverend Martin Luther King Jr. and other civil rights leaders.

**"southern strategy"** This strategy was a major reason for Richard Nixon's victory in the 1968 presidential election. To gain support in the South, Nixon assured southern conservatives that he would slow the federal enforcement of civil rights laws and appoint pro-southern justices to the Supreme Court. As president, Nixon fulfilled these promises.

**Spanish flu** Unprecedentedly lethal influenza epidemic of 1918 that killed more than 22 million people worldwide.

**Herbert Spencer (1820–1903)** As the first major proponent of social Darwinism, he argued that human society and institutions are subject to the process of natural selection and that society naturally evolves for the better. Therefore, he was against any form of government interference with the evolution of society, like business regulations, because it would help the "unfit" to survive.

**spirituals** Songs, often encoded, which enslaved peoples used to express their frustration at being kept in bondage and forged their own sense of hope and community.

**spoils system** The term—meaning the filling of federal government jobs with persons loyal to the party of the president—originated in Andrew Jackson's first term; the system was replaced in the Progressive Era by civil service.

**stagflation** During the Nixon administration, the economy experienced inflation and a recession at the same time, which is syndrome that defies the orthodox laws of economics. Economists named this phenomenon "stagflation."

**Joseph Stalin (1879–1953)** The Bolshevik leader who succeeded Lenin as the leader of the Soviet Union in 1924 and ruled the country until his death. During his totalitarian rule of the Soviet Union, he used purges and a system of forced labor camps to maintain control over the country. During the Yalta Conference, he claimed vast areas of Eastern Europe for Soviet domination. After the end of the Second World War, the alliance between the Soviet Union and the Western powers altered into the tension of the cold war and Stalin erected the "iron curtain" between Eastern and Western Europe.

**Stalwarts** Conservative Republican party faction during the presidency of Rutherford B. Hayes, 1877–1881; led by Senator Roscoe B. Conkling of New York, Stalwarts opposed civil service reform and favored a third term for President Ulysses S. Grant.

**Stamp Act Congress** Twenty-seven delegates from nine of the colonies met from October 7 to 25, 1765 and wrote a Declaration of the Rights and Grievances of the Colonies, a petition to the King and a petition to Parliament for the repeal of the Stamp Act.

**Standard Oil Company of Ohio** John D. Rockefeller found this company in 1870, which grew to monopolize 90 to 95 percent of all the oil refineries in the country. It was also a "vertical monopoly" in that the company controlled all aspects of production and the services it needed to conduct business. For example, Standard Oil produced their own oil barrels and cans as well as owned their own pipelines, railroad tank cars, and oil-storage facilities.

**Elizabeth Cady Stanton (1815–1902)** She was a prominent reformer and advocate for the rights of women, and she helped organize the Seneca Falls Convention to discuss women's rights. The convention was the first of its kind and produced the Declaration of Sentiments, which proclaimed the equality of men and women.

**staple crop, or cash crop** A profitable market crop, such as cotton or tobacco.

**Thaddeus Stevens (1792–1868)** As one of the leaders of the Radical Republicans, he argued that the former Confederate states should be viewed as conquered provinces, which were subject to the demands of the conquerors. He believed that all of southern society needed to be changed, and he supported the abolition of slavery and racial equality.

**Adlai E. Stevenson (1900–1965)** In the 1952 and 1956 presidential elections, he was the Democratic nominee who lost to Dwight Eisenhower. He was also the U.S. Ambassador to the United Nations and is remembered for his famous speech in 1962 before the UN Security Council that unequivocally demonstrated that the Soviet Union had built nuclear missile bases in Cuba.

**Strategic Defense Initiative ("Star Wars")** Defense Department's plan during the Reagan administration to build a system to destroy incoming missiles in space.

**Levi Strauss (1829–1902)** A Jewish tailor who followed miners to California during the gold rush and began making durable work pants that were later dubbed blue jeans or Levi's.

**Students for a Democratic Society (SDS)** Major organization of the New Left, founded at the University of Michigan in 1960 by Tom Hayden and Al Haber.

**suburbia** The postwar era witnessed a mass migration to the suburbs. As the population in cities areas grew, people began to spread further out within the urban areas, which created new suburban communities. By 1970 more people lived in the suburbs (76 million) than in central cities (64 million).

**Sunbelt** The label for an arc that stretched from the Carolinas to California. During the postwar era, much of the urban population growth occurred in this area.

**the "surge"** In early 2007, President Bush decided he would send a "surge" of new troops to Iraq and implement a new strategy. U.S. forces would shift their focus from offensive operations to the protection of Iraqi civilians from attacks by terrorist insurgents and sectarian militias. While the "surge" reduced the violence in Iraq, Iraqi leaders were still unable to develop a self-sustaining democracy.

**Taliban** A coalition of ultraconservative Islamists who rose to power in Afghanistan after the Soviets withdrew. The Taliban leaders gave Osama bin Laden a safe haven in their country in exchange for aid in fighting the Northern Alliance, who were rebels opposed to the Taliban. After September 11 terrorist attacks, the United States asked the Taliban to turn over bin Laden. After they refused, America invaded Afghanistan, but bin Laden evaded capture.

**Tammany Hall** The "city machine" used by "Boss" Tweed to dominate politics in New York City until his arrest in 1871.

**Tariff of 1816** First true protective tariff, intended strictly to protect American goods against foreign competition.

**Tariff of 1832** This tariff act reduced the duties on many items, but the tariffs on cloth and iron remained high. South Carolina nullified it along with the tariff of 1828. President Andrew Jackson sent federal troops to the state and asked Congress to grant him the authority to enforce the tariffs. Henry Clay presented a plan of gradually reducing the tariffs until 1842, which Congress passed and ended the crisis.

**Troubled Asset Relief Program (TARP)** In 2008 President George W. Bush signed into law the bank bailout fund called Troubled Asset Relief Program (TARP), which required the Treasury Department to spend $700 billion to keep banks and other financial institutions from collapsing.

**Zachary Taylor (1784–1850)** During the Mexican War, he scored two quick victories against Mexico, which made him very popular in America. President Polk chose him as the commander in charge of the war. However, after he was not put in charge of the campaign to capture Mexico City, he chose to return home. Later he used his popularity from his military victories to be elected the president as a member of the Whig party.

**Taylorism** In his book *The Principles of Scientific Management*, Frederick W. Taylor explained a management system that claimed to be able to reduce waste through the scientific analysis of the labor process. This system called Taylorism, promised to find the optimum technique for the average worker and establish detailed performance standards for each job classification.

**Tea Party** A decentralized, nationwide movement of limited-government conservatives that emerged during the early twenty-first century. Its members sent thousands of tea bags into congressional offices to draw a parallel between President Obama's "tax-and-spend" liberalism and the British tax policies that led to the famous Boston Tea Party of 1773.

**Teapot Dome** Harding administration scandal in which Secretary of the Interior Albert B. Fall profited from secret leasing to private oil companies of government oil reserves at Teapot Dome, Wyoming, and Elk Hills, California.

**Tecumseh (1768–1813)** He was a leader of the Shawnee tribe who tried to unite all Indians into a confederation that could defend their hunting grounds. He believed that no land cessions could be made without the consent of all the tribes since they held the land in common. His beliefs and leadership made him seem dangerous to the American government and they waged war on him and his tribe. He was killed at the Battle of the Thames.

**Tejanos** Texas settlers of Spanish or Mexican descent.

**Teller Amendment** On April 20, 1898, a joint resolution of Congress declared Cuba independent and demanded the withdrawal of Spanish forces. The Teller amendment was added to this resolution, and it declaimed any designs the United States had on Cuban territory.

**Tenochtitlán** The capital city of the Aztec Empire. The city was built on marshy islands on the western side of Lake Tetzcoco, which is the site of present-day Mexico City.

**Tet offensive** Surprise attack by the Viet Cong and North Vietnamese during the Vietnamese New Year of 1968; turned American public opinion strongly against the war in Vietnam.

**Thirteenth Amendment** This amendment to the U.S. Constitution freed all slaves in the United States. After the Civil War ended, the former confederate states were required to ratify this amendment before they could be readmitted to the Union.

**Gulf of Tonkin incident** On August 2 and 4 of 1964, North Vietnamese vessels attacked two American destroyers in Gulf of Tonkin off the coast of North Vietnam. President Johnson described the attacks as unprovoked. In reality, the U.S. ships were monitoring South Vietnamese attacks on North Vietnamese islands that America advisors had planned. The incident spurred the Tonkin Gulf resolution.

**Tonkin Gulf resolution (1964)** Passed by Congress in reaction to supposedly unprovoked attacks on American warships off the coast of North Vietnam; it gave the president unlimited authority to defend U.S. forces and members of SEATO.

**Tories** Term used by Patriots to refer to Loyalists, or colonists who supported the Crown after the Declaration of Independence.

**Trail of Tears** Cherokees' own term for their forced march, 1838–1839, from the southern Appalachians to Indian lands (later Oklahoma); of 15,000 forced to march, 4,000 died on the way.

**Transcendentalism** Philosophy of a small group of mid-nineteenth-century New England writers and thinkers, including Ralph Waldo Emerson, Henry David Thoreau, and Margaret Fuller; they stressed "plain living and high thinking."

**Transcontinental railroad** First line across the continent from Omaha, Nebraska, to Sacramento, California, established in 1869 with the linkage of the Union Pacific and Central Pacific railroads at Promontory, Utah.

**triangular trade** Means by which exports to one country or colony provided the means for imports from another country or colony. For example, merchants from colonial New England shipped rum to West Africa and used it to barter for slaves who were then taken to the West Indies. The slaves were sold or traded for materials that the ships brought back to New England including molasses which is need to make rum.

**Treaty of Ghent** The signing of this treaty in 1814 ended the War of 1812 without solving any of the disputes between Britain and the United States.

**Harry S. Truman (1884–1972)** As President Roosevelt's vice president, he succeeded him after his death near the end of the Second World War. After the war, Truman wrestled with the inflation of both prices and wages, and his attempts to bring them both under control led to clashes with organized labor and Republicans. He did work with Congress to pass the National Security Act, which made the Joint Chiefs of Staff a permanent position and created the National Military Establishment and the Central Intelligence Agency. He banned racial discrimination in the hiring of federal employees and ended racial segregation in the armed forces. In foreign affairs, he established the Truman Doctrine to contain communism and the Marshall Plan to rebuild Europe. After North Korea invaded South Korea, Truman sent the U.S. military to defend South Korea under the command of General Douglas MacArthur. Later in the war, Truman expressed his willingness to negotiate the restoration of prewar boundaries which MacArthur attempted to undermine. Truman fired MacArthur for his open insubordination.

**Truman Doctrine** President Harry S. Truman's program of post–Second World War aid to European countries—particularly Greece and Turkey—in danger of being undermined by communism.

**Sojourner Truth (1797?–1883)** She was born into slavery, but New York State freed her in 1827. She spent the 1840s and 1850s travelling across the country and speaking to audiences about her experiences as slave and asking them to support abolition and women's rights.

**Harriet Tubman (1820–1913)** She was born a slave, but escaped to the North. Then she returned to the South nineteen times and guided 300 slaves to freedom.

**Frederick Jackson Turner** An influential historian who authored the "Frontier Thesis" in 1893, arguing that the existence of an alluring frontier and the experience of persistent westward expansion informed the nation's democratic politics, unfettered economy, and rugged individualism.

**Nat Turner (1800–1831)** He was the leader of the only slave revolt to get past the planning stages. In August of 1831, the revolt began with the slaves killing the members of Turner's master's household. Then they attacked other neighboring farmhouses and recruited more slaves until the militia crushed the revolt. At least fifty-five whites were killed during the uprising and seventeen slaves were hanged afterwards.

**Tuskegee Airmen** During the Second World War, African Americans in the armed forces usually served in segregated units. African American pilots were trained at a separate flight school in Tuskegee, Alabama, and were known as Tuskegee Airmen.

**Mark Twain (1835–1910)** Born Samuel Langhorne Clemens in Missouri, he became a popular humorous writer and lecturer and established himself as one of the great American authors. Like other authors of the local-color movement, his stories expressed the nostalgia people had for rural culture and old folkways as America became increasingly urban. His two greatest books, *The Adventures of Tom Sawyer* and *The Adventures of Huckleberry Finn*, drew heavily on his childhood in Missouri.

**"Boss" Tweed (1823–1878)** An infamous political boss in New York City, Tweed used his "city machine," the Tammany Hall ring, to rule, plunder and sometimes improve the city's government. His political domination of New York City ended with his arrest in 1871 and conviction in 1873.

**Twenty-first Amendment (1933)** Repealed prohibition on the manufacture, sale, and transportation of alcoholic beverages, effectively nullifying the Eighteenth Amendment.

**Underground Railroad** Operating in the decades before the Civil War, the "railroad" was a clandestine system of routes and safehouses through which slaves were led to freedom in the North.

**Unitarianism** Late eighteenth-century liberal offshoot of the New England Congregationalist church; Unitarianism professed the oneness of God and the goodness of rational man.

**United Nations Security Council** A major agency within the United Nations which remains in permanent session and has the responsibility of maintaining international peace and security. Originally, it consisted of five permanent members, (United States, Soviet Union, Britain, France, and the Republic of China), and six members elected to two-year terms. After 1965, the number of rotating members was increased to ten. In 1971, the Republic of China was replaced with the People's Republic of China and the Soviet Union was replaced by the Russian Federation in 1991.

**Unterseeboot (or U-boat)** A military submarine operated by the German government in the First World War, used to attack enemy merchant ships in war zone waters. The sinking of the ocean liner *Lusitania* by a German submarine caused a public outcry in America, which contributed to the demands to expand the United States' military.

**Utopian communities** These communities flourished during the Jacksonian era and were attempts to create the ideal community. They were social experiments conducted in relative isolation, so they had little impact on the world outside of their communities. In most cases, the communities quickly ran out of steam and ended.

**Cornelius Vanderbilt (1794–1877)** In the 1860s, he consolidated several separate railroad companies into one vast entity, New York Central Railroad.

**Bartolomeo Vanzetti (1888–1927)** In 1920, he and Nicola Sacco were Italian immigrants who were arrested for stealing $16,000 and killing a paymaster and his guard. Their trial took place during a time of numerous bombings by anarchists and their judge was openly prejudicial. Many liberals and radicals believe that the conviction of Sacco and Vanzetti was based on their political ideas and ethnic origin rather than the evidence against them.

**Amerigo Vespucci (1455–1512)** Italian explorer who reached the New World in 1499 and was the first to suggest that South America was a new continent. Afterward, European map-makers used a variant of his first name, America, to label the New World.

**Viet Cong** In 1956, these guerrilla forces began attacking South Vietnam's government and in 1960 the resistance groups coalesced as the National Liberation Front.

**Vietnamization** President Nixon's policy of equipping and training the South Vietnamese so that they could assume ground combat operations in the place of American soldiers. Nixon hoped that a reduction in U.S. forces in Vietnam would defuse the anti-war movement.

**Vikings** Norse people from Scandinavia who sailed to Newfoundland about A.D. 1001.

**Francisco Pancho Villa (1877–1923)** While the leader of one of the competing factions in the Mexican civil war, he provoked the United States into intervening. He hoped attacking the United States would help him build a reputation as an opponent of the United States, which would increase his popularity and discredit Mexican President Carranza.

**Virginia Company** A joint stock enterprise that King James I chartered in 1606. The company was to spread Christianity in the New World as well as find ways to make a profit in it.

**Virginia Plan** The delegations to the Constitutional Convention were divided between two plans on how to structure the government: Virginia called for a strong central government and a two-house legislature apportioned by population.

**George Wallace (1919–1998)** An outspoken defender of segregation. As the governor of Alabama, he once attempted to block African American students from enrolling at the University of Alabama. He ran as the presidential candidate for the American Independent party in 1968. He appealed to voters who were concerned about rioting anti-war protestors, the welfare system, and the growth of the federal government.

**war hawks** In 1811, congressional members from the southern and western districts who clamored for a war to seize Canada and Florida were dubbed "war hawks."

**Warren Court** The U.S. Supreme Court under Chief Justice Earl Warren, 1953–1969, decided such landmark cases as *Brown v. Board of Education* (school desegregation), *Baker v. Carr* (legislative redistricting), and *Gideon v. Wainwright* and *Miranda v. Arizona* (rights of criminal defendants).

**Booker T. Washington (1856–1915)** He founded a leading college for African Americans in Tuskegee, Alabama, and become the foremost black educator in America by the 1890s. He believed that the African American community should establish an economic base for its advancement before striving for social equality. His critics charged that his philosophy sacrificed educational and civil rights for dubious social acceptance and economic opportunities.

**George Washington (1732–1799)** In 1775, the Continental Congress named him the commander in chief of the Continental Army. He had previously served as an officer in the French and Indian War, but had never commanded a large unit. Initially, his army was poorly supplied and inexperienced, which led to repeated defeats. Washington realized that he could only defeat the British through wearing them down, and he implemented a strategy of evasion and selective confrontations. Gradually, the army developed into an effective force and, with the aid of the French, defeated the British. In 1787, he was the presiding officer over the Constitutional Convention, but participated little in the debates. In 1789, the Electoral College chose Washington to be the nation's first president. He assembled a cabinet of brilliant minds, which included Thomas Jefferson, James Madison, and Alexander Hamilton. Together, they would lay the foundations of American government and capitalism. Washington faced the nation's first foreign and domestic crises. In 1793, the British and French were at war. Washington chose to keep America neutral in the conflict even though France and the United States had signed a treaty of alliance. A year later, the Whiskey Rebellion erupted in Pennsylvania, and Washington sent militiamen to suppress the rebels. After two terms in office, Washington chose to step down; and the power of the presidency was peacefully passed to John Adams.

**Watergate** Washington office and apartment complex that lent its name to the 1972–1974 scandal of the Nixon administration; when his knowledge of the break-in at the Watergate and subsequent cover-up was revealed, Nixon resigned the presidency under threat of impeachment.

**Daniel Webster (1782–1852)** As a representative from New Hampshire, he led the New Federalists in opposition to the moving of the second national bank from Boston to Philadelphia. Later, he served as representative and a senator for Massachusetts and emerged as a champion of a stronger national government. He also switched from opposing to supporting tariffs because New England had built up its manufactures with the understanding tariffs would protect them from foreign competitors.

**Webster-Ashburton Treaty** Settlement in 1842 of U.S.–Canadian border disputes in Maine, New York, Vermont, and in the Wisconsin Territory (now northern Minnesota).

**Webster-Hayne debate** U.S. Senate debate of January 1830 between Daniel Webster of Massachusetts and Robert Hayne of South Carolina over nullification and states' rights.

**Ida B. Wells (1862–1931)** After being denied a seat on a railroad car because she was black, she became the first African American to file a suit against such discrimination. As a journalist, she criticized Jim Crow laws, demanded that blacks have their voting rights restored and crusaded against lynching. In 1909, she helped found the National Association for the Advancement of Colored People (NAACP).

**western front** The military front that stretched from the English Channel through Belgium and France to the Alps during the First World War.

**Whig party** Founded in 1834 to unite factions opposed to President Andrew Jackson, the party favored federal responsibility for internal improvements; the party ceased to exist by the late 1850s, when party members divided over the slavery issue.

**Whigs** Another name for revolutionary Patriots.

**Whiskey Rebellion** Violent protest by western Pennsylvania farmers against the federal excise tax on corn whiskey, 1794.

**Eli Whitney (1765–1825)** He invented the cotton gin which could separate cotton from its seeds. One machine operator could separate fifty times more cotton than worker could by hand, which led to an increase in cotton production and prices. These increases gave planters a new profitable use for slavery and a lucrative slave trade emerged from the coastal South to the Southwest.

**George Whitefield (1714–1770)** A true catalyst of the Great Awakening, he sought to reignite religious fervor in the American congregations. During his tour of the American Colonies in 1739, he gave spellbinding sermons and preached the notion of "new birth"—a sudden, emotional moment of conversion and salvation.

**Wilderness Road** Originally an Indian path through the Cumberland Gap, it was used by over 300,000 settlers who migrated westward to Kentucky in the last quarter of the eighteenth century.

**Roger Williams (1603–1683)** Puritan who believed that the purity of the church required a complete separation between church and state and freedom from coercion in matters of faith. In 1636, he established the town of Providence, the first permanent settlement in Rhode Island and the first to allow religious freedom in America.

**Wendell L. Willkie (1892–1944)** In the 1940 presidential election, he was the Republican nominee who ran against President Roosevelt. He supported aid to the Allies and criticized the New Deal programs. Voters looked at the increasingly dangerous world situation and chose to keep President Roosevelt in office for a third term.

**Wilmot Proviso** Proposal to prohibit slavery in any land acquired in the Mexican War, but southern senators, led by John C. Calhoun of South Carolina, defeated the measure in 1846 and 1847.

**Woodrow Wilson (1856–1924)** In the 1912 presidential election, Woodrow Wilson ran under the slogan of New Freedom, which promised to improve of the banking system, lower tariffs, and break up monopolies. He sought to deliver on these promises through passage of the Underwood-Simmons Tariff, the Federal Reserve Act of 1913, and new antitrust laws. Though he was weak on implementing social change and showed a little interest in the plight of African Americans, he did eventually support some labor reform. At the beginning of the First World War, Wilson kept America neutral, but provided the Allies with credit for purchases of supplies. However, the sinking of U.S. merchant ships and the news of Germany encouraging Mexico to attack America caused Wilson to ask Congress to declare war on Germany. Following the war, Wilson supported the entry of America into the League of Nations and the ratification of the Treaty of Versailles; but Congress would not approve the entry or ratification.

**John Winthrop** Puritan leader and Governor of the Massachusetts Bay Colony who resolved to use the colony as a refuge for persecuted Puritans and as an instrument of building a "wilderness Zion" in America.

**Women Accepted for Voluntary Emergency Services (WAVES)** During the Second World War, the increased demand for labor shook up old prejudices about gender roles in workplace and in the military. Nearly 200,000 women served in the Women's Army Corps or its naval equivalent, Women Accepted for Volunteer Emergency Service (WAVES).

**Women's Army Corps (WAC)** During the Second World War, the increased demand for labor shook up old prejudices about gender roles in workplace and in the military. Nearly 200,000 women served in the Women's Army Corps or its naval equivalent, Women Accepted for Volunteer Emergency Service (WAVES).

**Woodstock** In 1969, roughly a half a million young people converged on a farm near Bethel, New York, for a three-day music festival that was an expression of the flower children's free spirit.

**Wounded Knee, Battle of** Last incident of the Indians Wars took place in 1890 in the Dakota Territory, where the U.S. Cavalry killed over 200 Sioux men, women, and children who were in the process of surrender.

**XYZ affair** French foreign minister Tallyrand's three anonymous agents demanded payments to stop French plundering of American ships in 1797; refusal to pay the bribe led to two years of sea war with France (1798–1800).

**Yalta Conference** Meeting of Franklin D. Roosevelt, Winston Churchill, and Joseph Stalin at a Crimean resort to discuss the postwar world on February 4–11, 1945; Soviet leader Joseph Stalin claimed large areas in eastern Europe for Soviet domination.

**yellow journalism** A type of journalism, epitomized in the 1890s by the newspaper empires of William Randolph Hearst and Joseph Pulitzer, that intentionally manipulates public opinion through sensational headlines about both real and invented events.

**yeomen** Small landowners (the majority of white families in the South) who farmed their own land and usually did not own slaves.

**surrender at Yorktown** Last battle of the Revolutionary War; General Lord Charles Cornwallis along with over 7,000 British troops surrendered at Yorktown, Virginia, on October 17, 1781.

**Brigham Young (1801–1877)** Following Joseph Smith's death, he became the leader of the Mormons and promised Illinois officials that the Mormons would leave the state. In 1846, he led the Mormons to Utah and settled near the Salt Lake. After the United States gained Utah as part of the Treaty of Guadalupe Hidalgo, he became the governor of the territory and kept the Mormons virtually independent of federal authority.

**youth culture** The youth of the 1950s had more money and free time than any previous generation which allowed a distinct youth culture to emerge. A market emerged for products and activities that were specifically for young people such as transistor radios, rock records, *Seventeen* magazine, and Pat Boone movies.

# APPENDIX

APPENDIX

# THE DECLARATION OF INDEPENDENCE (1776)

WHEN IN THE COURSE OF HUMAN EVENTS, it becomes necessary for one people to dissolve the political bands which have connected them with another, and to assume the Powers of the earth, the separate and equal station to which the Laws of Nature and of Nature's God entitle them, a decent respect to the opinions of mankind requires that they should declare the causes which impel them to the separation.

We hold these truths to be self-evident, that all men are created equal, that they are endowed by their Creator with certain unalienable rights, that among these are Life, Liberty, and the pursuit of Happiness. That to secure these rights, Governments are instituted among Men, deriving their just powers from the consent of the governed. That whenever any Form of Government becomes destructive of these ends, it is the Right of the People to alter or to abolish it, and to institute new Government, laying its foundation on such principles and organizing its powers in such form, as to them shall seem most likely to effect their Safety and Happiness. Prudence, indeed, will dictate that Governments long established should not be changed for light and transient causes; and accordingly all experience hath shown, that mankind are more disposed to suffer, while evils are sufferable, than to right themselves by abolishing the forms to which they are accustomed. But when a long train of abuses and usurpations, pursuing invariably the same Object evinces a design to reduce them under absolute Despotism, it is their right, it is their duty, to throw off such Government, and to provide new Guards for their future security.—Such has been the patient sufferance of these Colonies; and such is now the necessity which constrains them to alter their former Systems of Government. The history of the present King of Great Britain is a history of repeated injuries and usurpations, all having in direct object the establishment of an absolute Tyranny over these States. To prove this, let Facts be submitted to a candid world.

He has refused his Assent to Laws, the most wholesome and necessary for the public good.

He has forbidden his Governors to pass Laws of immediate and pressing importance, unless suspended in their operation till his Assent should be obtained; and when so suspended, he has utterly neglected to attend to them.

He has refused to pass other Laws for the accommodation of large districts of people, unless those people would relinquish the right of Representation in the Legislature, a right inestimable to them and formidable to tyrants only.

He has called together legislative bodies at places unusual, uncomfortable, and distant from the depository of their public Records, for the sole purpose of fatiguing them into compliance with his measures.

He has dissolved Representative Houses repeatedly, for opposing with manly firmness his invasions on the rights of the people.

He has refused for a long time, after such dissolutions, to cause others to be elected; whereby the Legislative powers, incapable of Annihilation, have returned to the People at large for their exercise; the State remaining in the mean time exposed to all dangers of invasion from without, and convulsions within.

He has endeavoured to prevent the population of these States; for that purpose obstructing the Laws of Naturalization of Foreigners; refusing to pass others to encourage their migrations hither, and raising the conditions of new Appropriations of Lands.

He has obstructed the Administration of Justice, by refusing his Assent to Laws for establishing Judiciary powers.

He has made Judges dependent on his Will alone, for the tenure of their offices, and the amount and payment of their salaries.

He has erected a multitude of New Offices, and sent hither swarms of Officers to harass our People, and eat out their substance.

He has kept among us, in times of peace, Standing Armies without the Consent of our legislatures.

He has affected to render the Military independent of and superior to the Civil Power.

He has combined with others to subject us to a jurisdiction foreign to our constitution, and unacknowledged by our laws; giving his Assent to their Acts of pretended Legislation:

For quartering large bodies of armed troops among us:

For protecting them, by a mock Trial, from Punishment for any Murders which they should commit on the Inhabitants of these States:

For cutting off our Trade with all parts of the world:

For imposing taxes on us without our Consent:

For depriving us of many cases, of the benefits of Trial by jury:

For transporting us beyond Seas to be tried for pretended offences:

For abolishing the free System of English Laws in a neighbouring Province, establishing therein an Arbitrary government, and enlarging its

Boundaries so as to render it at once an example and fit instrument for introducing the same absolute rule into these Colonies:

For taking away our Charters, abolishing our most valuable Laws, and altering fundamentally the Forms of our Governments:

For suspending our own Legislatures, and declaring themselves in vested with Power to legislate for us in all cases whatsoever.

He has abdicated Government here, by declaring us out of his Protection and waging War against us.

He has plundered our seas, ravaged our Coasts, burnt our towns, and destroyed the lives of our people.

He is at this time transporting large armies of foreign mercenaries to compleat the works of death, desolation, and tyranny, already begun with circumstances of Cruelty & perfidy scarcely paralleled in the most barbarous ages, and totally unworthy the Head of a civilized nation.

He has constrained our fellow Citizens taken Captive on the high Seas to bear Arms against their Country, to become the executioners of their friends and Brethren, or to fall themselves by their Hands.

He has excited domestic insurrections amongst us, and has endeavoured to bring on the inhabitants of our frontiers, the merciless Indian Savages, whose known rule of warfare, is an undistinguished destruction of all ages, sexes, and conditions.

In every stage of these Oppressions We have Petitioned for Redress in the most humble terms: Our repeated Petitions have been answered only by repeated injury. A Prince, whose character is thus marked by every act which may define a Tyrant, is unfit to be the ruler of a free people.

Nor have We been wanting in attention to our British brethren. We have warned them from time to time of attempts by their legislature to extend an unwarrantable jurisdiction over us. We have reminded them of the circumstances of our emigration and settlement here. We have appealed to their native justice and magnanimity, and we have conjured them by the ties of our common kindred to disavow these usurpations, which, would inevitably interrupt our connections and correspondence. They too must have been deaf to the voice of justice and of consanguinity. We must, therefore, acquiesce in the necessity, which denounces our Separation, and hold them, as we hold the rest of mankind, Enemies in War, in Peace Friends.

WE, THEREFORE, the Representatives of the UNITED STATES OF AMERICA, in General Congress, Assembled, appealing to the Supreme Judge of the world for the rectitude of our intentions, do, in the Name, and by Authority of the good People of these Colonies, solemnly publish and declare, That these United Colonies are, and of Right ought to be FREE AND INDEPENDENT STATES; that they are Absolved from all Allegiance to the

British Crown, and that all political connection between them and the State of Great Britain, is and ought to be totally dissolved; and that as Free and Independent States, they have full Power to levy War, conclude Peace, contract Alliances, establish Commerce, and to do all other Acts and Things which Independent States may of right do. And for the support of this Declaration, with a firm reliance on the Protection of Divine Providence, we mutually pledge to each other our Lives, our Fortunes, and our sacred Honor.

The foregoing Declaration was, by order of Congress, engrossed, and signed by the following members:

*John Hancock*

**NEW HAMPSHIRE**
*Josiah Bartlett*
*William Whipple*
*Matthew Thornton*

**MASSACHUSETTS BAY**
*Samuel Adams*
*John Adams*
*Robert Treat Paine*
*Elbridge Gerry*

**RHODE ISLAND**
*Stephen Hopkins*
*William Ellery*

**CONNECTICUT**
*Roger Sherman*
*Samuel Huntington*
*William Williams*
*Oliver Wolcott*

**NEW YORK**
*William Floyd*
*Philip Livingston*
*Francis Lewis*
*Lewis Morris*

**NEW JERSEY**
*Richard Stockton*
*John Witherspoon*
*Francis Hopkinson*
*John Hart*
*Abraham Clark*

**PENNSYLVANIA**
*Robert Morris*
*Benjamin Rush*
*Benjamin Franklin*
*John Morton*
*George Clymer*
*James Smith*
*George Taylor*
*James Wilson*
*George Ross*

**DELAWARE**
*Caesar Rodney*
*George Read*
*Thomas M'Kean*

**MARYLAND**
*Samuel Chase*
*William Paca*
*Thomas Stone*
*Charles Carroll, of
Carrollton*

**VIRGINIA**
*George Wythe*
*Richard Henry Lee*
*Thomas Jefferson*
*Benjamin Harrison*
*Thomas Nelson, Jr.*
*Francis Lightfoot Lee*
*Carter Braxton*

**NORTH CAROLINA**
*William Hooper*
*Joseph Hewes*
*John Penn*

**SOUTH CAROLINA**
*Edward Rutledge*
*Thomas Heyward, Jr.*
*Thomas Lynch, Jr.*
*Arthur Middleton*

**GEORGIA**
*Button Gwinnett*
*Lyman Hall*
*George Walton*

*Resolved,* that copies of the declaration be sent to the several assemblies, conventions, and committees, or councils of safety, and to the several commanding officers of the continental troops; that it be proclaimed in each of the united states, at the head of the army.

# ARTICLES OF CONFEDERATION (1778)

To all to whom these Presents shall come, we the undersigned Delegates of the States affixed to our Names send greeting.

Whereas the Delegates of the United States of America in Congress assembled did on the fifteenth day of November in the Year of our Lord One Thousand Seven Hundred and Seventy-seven, and in the Second Year of the Independence of America agree to certain articles of Confederation and perpetual Union between the States of Newhampshire, Massachusetts-bay, Rhodeisland and Providence Plantations, Connecticut, New York, New Jersey, Pennsylvania, Delaware, Maryland, Virginia, North-Carolina, South-Carolina and Georgia in the Words following, viz.

Articles of Confederation and perpetual Union between the States of Newhampshire, Massachusetts-bay, Rhodeisland and Providence Plantations, Connecticut, New-York, New-Jersey, Pennsylvania, Delaware, Maryland, Virginia, North-Carolina, South-Carolina and Georgia.

ARTICLE I. The stile of this confederacy shall be "The United States of America."

ARTICLE II. Each State retains its sovereignty, freedom and independence, and every power, jurisdiction and right, which is not by this confederation expressly delegated to the United States, in Congress assembled.

ARTICLE III. The said States hereby severally enter into a firm league of friendship with each other, for their common defence, the security of their liberties, and their mutual and general welfare, binding themselves to assist each other, against all force offered to, or attacks made upon them, or any of them, on account of religion, sovereignty, trade or any other pretence whatever.

ARTICLE IV. The better to secure and perpetuate mutual friendship and inter-course among the people of the different States in this Union, the free inhab-itants of each of these States, paupers, vagabonds and fugitives from justice excepted, shall be entitled to all privileges and immunities of free citizens in the several States; and the people of each State shall have free ingress and regress to and from any other State, and shall enjoy therein all the privileges of trade and commerce, subject to the same duties, impositions and restric-tions as the inhabitants thereof respectively, provided that such restrictions shall not extend so far as to prevent the removal of property imported into any State, to any other State of which the owner is an inhabitant; provided also that no imposition, duties or restriction shall be laid by any State, on the property of the United States, or either of them.

If any person guilty of, or charged with treason, felony, or other high mis-demeanor in any State, shall flee from justice, and be found in any of the United States, he shall upon demand of the Governor or Executive power, of the State from which he fled, be delivered up and removed to the State having jurisdiction of his offence.

Full faith and credit shall be given in each of these States to the records, acts and judicial proceedings of the courts and magistrates of every other State.

ARTICLE V. For the more convenient management of the general interests of the United States, delegates shall be annually appointed in such manner as the legislature of each State shall direct, to meet in Congress on the first Monday in November, in every year, with a power reserved to each State, to recall its delegates, or any of them, at any time within the year, and to send others in their stead, for the remainder of the year.

No State shall be represented in Congress by less than two, nor by more than seven members; and no person shall be capable of being a delegate for more than three years in any term of six years; nor shall any person, being a delegate, be capable of holding any office under the United States, for which he, or another for his benefit receives any salary, fees or emolument of any kind.

Each State shall maintain its own delegates in a meeting of the States, and while they act as members of the committee of the States.

In determining questions in the United States, in Congress assembled, each State shall have one vote.

Freedom of speech and debate in Congress shall not be impeached or questioned in any court, or place out of Congress, and the members of Con-gress shall be protected in their persons from arrests and imprisonments, during the time of their going to and from, and attendance on Congress, except for treason, felony, or breach of the peace.

ARTICLE VI. No State without the consent of the United States in Congress assembled, shall send any embassy to, or receive any embassy from, or enter into any conference, agreement, alliance or treaty with any king, prince or state; nor shall any person holding any office of profit or trust under the United States, or any of them, accept of any present, emolument, office or title of any kind whatever from any king, prince or foreign state; nor shall the United States in Congress assembled, or any of them, grant any title of nobility.

No two or more States shall enter into any treaty, confederation or alliance whatever between them, without the consent of the United States in Congress assembled, specifying accurately the purposes for which the same is to be entered into, and how long it shall continue.

No State shall lay any imposts or duties, which may interfere with any stipulations in treaties, entered into by the United States in Congress assembled, with any king, prince or state, in pursuance of any treaties already proposed by Congress, to the courts of France and Spain.

No vessels of war shall be kept up in time of peace by any State, except such number only, as shall be deemed necessary by the United States in Congress assembled, for the defence of such State, or its trade; nor shall any body of forces be kept up by any State, in time of peace, except such number only, as in the judgment of the United States, in Congress assembled, shall be deemed requisite to garrison the forts necessary for the defence of such State; but every State shall always keep up a well regulated and disciplined militia, sufficiently armed and accoutred, and shall provide and constantly have ready for use, in public stores, a due number of field pieces and tents, and a proper quantity of arms, ammunition and camp equipage.

No State shall engage in any war without the consent of the United States in Congress assembled, unless such State be actually invaded by enemies, or shall have received certain advice of a resolution being formed by some nation of Indians to invade such State, and the danger is so imminent as not to admit of a delay, till the United States in Congress assembled can be consulted: nor shall any State grant commissions to any ships or vessels of war, nor letters of marque or reprisal, except it be after a declaration of war by the United States in Congress assembled, and then only against the kingdom or state and the subjects thereof, against which war has been so declared, and under such regulations as shall be established by the United States in Congress assembled, unless such State be infested by pirates, in which case vessels of war may be fitted out for that occasion, and kept so long as the danger shall continue, or until the United States in Congress assembled shall determine otherwise.

ARTICLE VII. When land-forces are raised by any State of the common defence, all officers of or under the rank of colonel, shall be appointed by the Legislature of each State respectively by whom such forces shall be raised, or in such manner as such State shall direct, and all vacancies shall be filled up by the State which first made the appointment.

ARTICLE VIII. All charges of war, and all other expenses that shall be incurred for the common defence or general welfare, and allowed by the United States in Congress assembled, shall be defrayed out of a common treasury, which shall be supplied by the several States, in proportion to the value of all land within each State, granted to or surveyed for any person, as such land and the buildings and improvements thereon shall be estimated according to such mode as the United States in Congress assembled, shall from time to time direct and appoint.

The taxes for paying that proportion shall be laid and levied by the authority and direction of the Legislatures of the several States within the time agreed upon by the United States in Congress assembled.

ARTICLE IX. The United States in Congress assembled, shall have the sole and exclusive right and power of determining on peace and war, except in the cases mentioned in the sixth article—of sending and receiving ambassadors—entering into treaties and alliances, provided that no treaty of commerce shall be made whereby the legislative power of the respective States shall be restrained from imposing such imposts and duties on foreigners, as their own people are subjected to, or from prohibiting the exportation or importation of and species of goods or commodities whatsoever—of establishing rules for deciding in all cases, what captures on land or water shall be legal, and in what manner prizes taken by land or naval forces in the service of the United States shall be divided or appropriated—of granting letters of marque and reprisal in times of peace—appointing courts for the trial of piracies and felonies committed on the high seas and establishing courts for receiving and determining finally appeals in all cases of captures, provided that no member of Congress shall be appointed a judge of any of the said courts.

The United States in Congress assembled shall also be the last resort on appeal in all disputes and differences now subsisting or that hereafter may arise between two or more States concerning boundary, jurisdiction or any other cause whatever; which authority shall always be exercised in the manner following. Whenever the legislative or executive authority or lawful agent of any State in controversy with another shall present a petition to Congress, stating the matter in question and praying for a hearing, notice thereof shall be given by order of Congress to the legislative or executive authority of the other State in controversy, and a day assigned for the appearance of the parties by their lawful agents, who shall then be directed to appoint by joint consent, commissioners or judges to constitute a court for hearing and determining the matter in question: but if they cannot agree, Congress shall name three persons out of each of the United States, and from the list of such persons each party shall alternately strike out one, the petitioners beginning, until the number shall be reduced to thirteen; and from that number not less than seven, nor more than nine names as Congress shall direct, shall in the presence of Congress be drawn out by lot, and the persons whose names shall be so drawn or any five of them, shall be commissioners or judges, to hear and finally determine the controversy, so always as a major part of the judges who shall hear the cause shall agree in the determination: and if either party shall neglect to attend at the day appointed, without reasons, which Congress shall judge sufficient, or being present shall refuse to strike, the Congress shall proceed to nominate three persons out of each State, and the Secretary of Congress shall strike in behalf of such party absent or refusing; and the judgment and sentence of the court to be appointed, in the manner before prescribed, shall be final and conclusive; and if any of the parties shall refuse to submit to the authority of such court, or to appear or defend their claim or cause, the court shall nevertheless proceed to pronounce sentence, or judgment, which shall in like manner be final and decisive, the judgment or sentence and other proceedings being in either case transmitted to Congress, and lodged among the acts of Congress for the security of the parties concerned: provided that every commissioner, before he sits in judgment, shall take an oath to be administered by one of the judges of the supreme or superior court of the State where the case shall be tried, "well and truly to hear and determine the matter in question, according to the best of his judgment, without favour, affection or hope of reward:" provided also that no State shall be deprived of territory for the benefit of the United States.

All controversies concerning the private right of soil claimed under different grants of two or more States, whose jurisdiction as they may respect such lands, and the states which passed such grants are adjusted, the said grants or either of them being at the same time claimed to have originated antecedent to such settlement of jurisdiction, shall on the petition of either party to the Congress of the United States, be finally determined as near as may be in the same manner as is before prescribed for deciding disputes respecting territorial jurisdiction between different States.

The United States in Congress assembled shall also have the sole and exclusive right and power of regulating the alloy and value of coin struck by their own authority, or by that of the respective States—fixing the standard of weights and measures throughout the United States—regulating the trade and managing all affairs with the Indians, not members of any of the States, provided that the legislative right of any State within its own limits be not infringed or violated—establishing and regulating post-offices from one State to another, throughout all of the United States, and exacting such postage on the papers passing thro' the same as may be requisite to defray the expenses of the said office—appointing all officers of the land forces, in the service of the United States, excepting regimental officers—appointing all the officers of the naval forces, and commissioning all officers whatever in the service of the United States—making rules for the government and regulation of the said land and naval forces, and directing their operations.

The United States in Congress assembled shall have authority to appoint a committee, to sit in the recess of Congress, to be denominated "a Committee of the States," and to consist of one delegate from each State; and to appoint such other committees and civil officers as may be necessary for managing the general affairs of the United States under their direction—to appoint one of their number to preside, provided that no person be allowed to serve in the office of president more than one year in any term of three years; to ascertain the necessary sums of money to be raised for the service of the United States, and to appropriate and apply the same for defraying the public expenses—to borrow money, or emit bills on the credit of the United States, transmitting every half year to the respective States an account of the sums of money so borrowed or emitted,—to build and equip a navy—to agree upon the number of land forces, and to make requisitions from each State for its quota, in proportion to the number of white inhabitants in such State; which requisition shall be binding, and thereupon the Legislature of each State shall appoint the regimental officers, raise the men and cloath, arm and equip them in a soldier like manner, at the expense of the United States; and the officers and men so cloathed, armed and equipped shall march to the place appointed, and within the time agreed on by the United States in Congress assembled: but if the United States in Congress assembled shall, on consideration of circumstances judge proper that any State should not raise men, or should raise a smaller number of men than the quota thereof, such extra number shall be raised, officered, cloathed, armed and equipped in the same manner as the quota of such State, unless the legislature of such State shall judge that such extra number cannot be safely spared out of the same, in which case they shall raise officer, cloath, arm and equip as many of such extra number as they judge can be safely spared. And the officers and men so cloathed, armed and equipped, shall march to the place appointed, and within the time agreed on by the United States in Congress assembled.

The United States in Congress assembled shall never engage in a war, nor grant letters of marque and reprisal in time of peace, nor enter into any treaties or alliances, nor coin money, nor regulate the value thereof, nor ascertain the sums and expenses necessary for the defence and welfare of the United States, or any of them, nor emit bills, nor borrow money on the credit of the United States, nor appropriate money, nor agree upon the number of vessels to be built or purchased, or the number of land or sea forces to be raised, nor appoint a commander in chief of the army or navy, unless nine States assent to the same: nor shall a question on any other point, except for adjourning from day to day be determined, unless by the votes of a majority of the United States in Congress assembled.

The Congress of the United States shall have power to adjourn to any time within the year, and to any place within the United States, so that no period of adjournment be for a longer duration than the space of six months, and shall publish the journal of their proceedings monthly, except such parts thereof relating to treaties, alliances or military operations, as in their judgment require secrecy; and the yeas and nays of the delegates of each State on any question shall be entered on the Journal, when it is desired by any delegate; and the delegates of a State, or any of them, at his or their request shall be furnished with a transcript of the said journal, except such parts as are above excepted, to lay before the Legislatures of the several States.

ARTICLE X. The committee of the States, or any nine of them, shall be authorized to execute, in the recess of Congress, such of the powers of Congress as the United States in Congress assembled, by the consent of nine States, shall from time to time think expedient to vest them with; provided that no power be delegated to the said committee, for the exercise of which, by the articles of confederation, the voice of nine States in the Congress of the United States assembled is requisite.

ARTICLE XI. Canada acceding to this confederation, and joining in the measures of the United States, shall be admitted into, and entitled to all the advantages of this Union: but no other colony shall be admitted into the same, unless such admission be agreed to by nine States.

ARTICLE XII. All bills of credit emitted, monies borrowed and debts contracted by, or under the authority of Congress, before the assembling of the United States, in pursuance of the present confederation, shall be deemed and considered as a charge against the United States, for payment and satisfaction whereof the said United States, and the public faith are hereby solemnly pledged.

ARTICLE XIII. Every State shall abide by the determinations of the United States in Congress assembled, on all questions which by this confederation are submitted to them. And the articles of this confederation shall be inviolably observed by every State, and the Union shall be perpetual; nor shall any alteration at any time hereafter be made in any of them; unless such alteration be agreed to in a Congress of the United States, and be afterwards confirmed by the Legislatures of every State.

And whereas it has pleased the Great Governor of the world to incline the hearts of the Legislatures we respectively represent in Congress, to approve of, and to authorize us to ratify the said articles of confederation and perpetual union. Know ye that we the undersigned delegates, by virtue of the power and authority to us given for that purpose, do by these presents, in the name and in behalf of our respective constituents, fully and entirely ratify and confirm each and every of the said articles of confederation and perpetual union, and all and singular the matters and things therein contained: and we do further solemnly plight and engage the faith of our respective constituents, that they shall abide by the determinations of the United States in Congress assembled, on all questions, which by the said confederation are submitted to them. And that the articles thereof shall be inviolably observed by the States we respectively represent, and that the Union shall be perpetual.

In witness thereof we have hereunto set our hands in Congress. Done at Philadelphia in the State of Pennsylvania the ninth day of July in the year of our Lord one thousand seven hundred and seventy-eight, and in the third year of the independence of America.

# THE CONSTITUTION OF THE UNITED STATES (1787)

WE THE PEOPLE OF THE UNITED STATES, in order to form a more perfect Union, establish Justice, insure domestic Tranquility, provide for the common defence, promote the general Welfare, and secure the Blessings of Liberty to ourselves and our Posterity, do ordain and establish this Constitution for the United States of America.

## ARTICLE. I.

*Section. 1.* All legislative Powers herein granted shall be vested in a Congress of the United States, which shall consist of a Senate and House of Representatives.

*Section. 2.* The House of Representatives shall be composed of Members chosen every second Year by the People of the several States, and the Electors in each State shall have the Qualifications requisite for Electors of the most numerous Branch of the State Legislature.

No Person shall be a Representative who shall not have attained to the Age of twenty five Years, and been seven Years a Citizen of the United States, and who shall not, when elected, be an Inhabitant of that State in which he shall be chosen.

Representatives and direct Taxes shall be apportioned among the several States which may be included within this Union, according to their respective Numbers, which shall be determined by adding to the whole Number of free Persons, including those bound to Service for a Term of Years, and excluding Indians not taxed, three fifths of all other Persons. The actual Enumeration shall be made within three Years after the first Meeting of the Congress of the United States, and within every subsequent Term of ten Years, in such

Manner as they shall by Law direct. The Number of Representatives shall not exceed one for every thirty Thousand, but each State shall have at Least one Representative; and until such enumeration shall be made, the State of New Hampshire shall be entitled to chuse three, Massachusetts eight, Rhode-Island and Providence Plantations one, Connecticut five, New-York six, New Jersey four, Pennsylvania eight, Delaware one, Maryland six, Virginia ten, North Carolina five, South Carolina five, and Georgia three.

When vacancies happen in the Representation from any state, the Executive Authority thereof shall issue Writs of Election to fill such Vacancies.

The House of Representatives shall chuse their Speaker and other Officers; and shall have the sole Power of Impeachment.

*Section. 3.* The Senate of the United States shall be composed of two Senators from each State, chosen by the legislature thereof, for six Years; and each Senator shall have one Vote.

Immediately after they shall be assembled in Consequence of the first Election, they shall be divided as equally as may be into three Classes. The Seats of the Senators of the first Class shall be vacated at the Expiration of the second Year, of the second Class at the Expiration of the fourth Year, and of the third Class at the Expiration of the sixth Year, so that one third maybe chosen every second Year; and if Vacancies happen by Resignation, or otherwise, during the Recess of the Legislature of any State, the Executive thereof may make temporary Appointments until the next Meeting of the Legislature, which shall then fill such Vacancies.

No Person shall be a Senator who shall not have attained to the Age of thirty Years, and been nine Years a Citizen of the United States, and who shall not, when elected, be an Inhabitant of that State for which he shall be chosen.

The Vice President of the United States shall be President of the Senate, but shall have no Vote, unless they be equally divided.

The Senate shall chuse their other Officers, and also a President pro tempore, in the Absence of the Vice President, or when he shall exercise the Office of President of the United States.

The Senate shall have the sole Power to try all Impeachments. When sitting for that Purpose, they shall be on Oath or Affirmation. When the President of the United States is tried, the Chief Justice shall preside: And no Person shall be convicted without the Concurrence of two thirds of the Members present.

Judgment in Cases of Impeachment shall not extend further than to removal from Office, and disqualification to hold and enjoy any Office of honor, Trust or Profit under the United States: but the Party convicted shall nevertheless be liable and subject to Indictment, Trial, Judgment and Punishment, according to Law.

*Section. 4.* The Times, Places and Manner of holding Elections for Senators and Representatives, shall be prescribed in each State by the Legislature thereof; but the Congress may at any time by Law make or alter such Regulations, except as to the Places of chusing Senators.

The Congress shall assemble at least once in every Year, and such Meeting shall be on the first Monday in December, unless they shall by Law appoint a different Day.

*Section. 5.* Each House shall be the Judge of the Elections, Returns and Qualifications of its own Members, and a Majority of each shall constitute a Quorum to do Business; but a smaller Number may adjourn from day to day, and may be authorized to compel the Attendance of absent Members, in such Manner, and under such Penalties as each House may provide.

Each House may determine the Rules of its Proceedings, punish its Members for disorderly Behaviour, and, with the Concurrence of two thirds, expel a Member.

Each House shall keep a Journal of its Proceedings, and from time to time publish the same, excepting such Parts as may in their Judgment require Secrecy; and the Yeas and Nays of the Members of either House on any question shall, at the Desire of one fifth of those Present, be entered on the Journal.

Neither House, during the Session of Congress, shall, without the Consent of the other, adjourn for more than three days, not to any other Place than that in which the two Houses shall be sitting.

*Section. 6.* The Senators and Representatives shall receive a Compensation for their Services, to be ascertained by Law, and paid out of the Treasury of the United States. They shall in all Cases, except Treason, Felony and Breach of the Peace, be privileged from Arrest during their Attendance at the Session of their respective Houses, and in going to and returning from the same; and for any Speech or Debate in either House, they shall not be questioned in any other Place.

No Senator or Representative shall, during the Time for which he was elected, be appointed to any civil Office under the Authority of the United States, which shall have been created, or the Emoluments whereof shall have been encreased during such time; and no Person holding any Office under the United States, shall be a Member of either House during his Continuance in Office.

*Section. 7.* All Bills for raising Revenue shall originate in the House of Representatives; but the Senate may propose or concur with Amendments as on other Bills.

Every Bill which shall have passed the House of Representatives and the Senate shall, before it become a Law, be presented to the President of the United States; If he approve he shall sign it, but if not he shall return it, with his Objections to that House in which it shall have originated, who shall enter the Objections at large on their Journal, and proceed to reconsider it. If after such Reconsideration two thirds of that House shall agree to pass the Bill, it shall be sent, together with the Objections, to the other House, by which it shall likewise be reconsidered, and if approved by two thirds of that House, it shall become a Law. But in all such Cases the Votes of both Houses shall be determined by yeas and Nays, and the Names of the Persons voting for and against the Bill shall be entered on the Journal of each House respectively. If any Bill shall not be returned by the President within ten Days (Sundays excepted) after it shall have been presented to him, the Same shall be a Law, in like Manner as if he had signed it, unless the Congress by their Adjournment prevent its Return, in which Case it shall not be a Law.

Every Order, Resolution, or Vote to which the Concurrence of the Senate and House of Representatives may be necessary (except on a question of Adjournment) shall be presented to the President of the United States; and before the Same shall take Effect, shall be approved by him, or being disapproved by him, shall be repassed by two thirds of the Senate and House of Representatives, according to the Rules and Limitations prescribed in the Case of a Bill.

*Section. 8.* The Congress shall have Power To lay and collect Taxes, Duties, Imposts and Excises, to pay the Debts and provide for the common Defence and general Welfare of the United States; but all Duties, Imposts and Excises shall be uniform throughout the United States;

To borrow Money on the credit of the United States;

To regulate Commerce with foreign Nations, and among the several States, and with the Indian Tribes;

To establish an uniform Rule of Naturalization, and uniform Laws on the subject of Bankruptcies throughout the United States;

To coin Money, regulate the Value thereof, and of foreign Coin, and fix the Standard of Weights and Measures;

To provide for the Punishment of counterfeiting the Securities and current Coin of the United States;

To establish Post Offices and Post Roads;

To promote the Progress of Science and useful Arts, by securing for limited Times to Authors and Inventors the exclusive Right to their respective Writings and Discoveries;

To constitute Tribunals inferior to the supreme Court;

To define and punish Piracies and Felonies committed on the high Seas, and Offences against the Law of Nations;

To declare War, grant Letters of Marque and Reprisal, and make Rules concerning Captures on land and Water;

To raise and support Armies, but no Appropriation of Money to that Use shall be for a longer Term than two Years;

To provide and maintain a Navy;

To make Rules for the Government and Regulation of the land and naval Forces;

To provide for calling forth the Militia to execute the Laws of the Union, suppress Insurrections and repel Invasions;

To provide for organizing, arming, and disciplining, the Militia, and for governing such Part of them as may be employed in the Service of the United States, reserving to the States respectively, the Appointment of the Officers, and the Authority of training the Militia according to the discipline prescribed by Congress.

To exercise exclusive Legislation in all Cases whatsoever, over such District (not exceeding ten Miles square) as may, by Cession of Particular States, and the Acceptance of Congress, become the Seat of the Government of the United States, and to exercise like Authority over all Places purchased by the Consent of the Legislature of the State in which the Same shall be, for the Erection of Forts, Magazines, Arsenals, dock-Yards, and other needful Buildings;—And

To make all Laws which shall be necessary and proper for carrying into Execution the foregoing Powers, and all other Powers vested by this Constitution in the Government of the United States, or in any Department or Officer thereof.

*Section. 9.* The Migration or Importation of such Persons as any of the States now existing shall think proper to admit, shall not be prohibited by the Congress prior to the Year one thousand eight hundred and eight, but a Tax or duty may be imposed on such Importation, not exceeding ten dollars for each Person.

The Privilege of the Writ of Habeas Corpus shall not be suspended, unless when in Cases of Rebellion or Invasion the public Safety may require it.

No Bill of Attainder or ex post facto Law shall be passed.

No Capitation, or other direct, Tax shall be laid, unless in Proportion to the Census or Enumeration herein before directed to be taken.

No Tax or Duty shall be laid on Articles exported from any State.

No Preference shall be given by any Regulation of Commerce or Revenue to the Ports of one State over those of another: nor shall Vessels bound to, or from, one State, be obliged to enter, clear, or pay Duties in another.

No Money shall be drawn from the Treasury, but in Consequence of Appropriations made by Law; and a regular Statement and Account of the Receipts and Expenditures of all public Money shall be published from time to time.

No Title of Nobility shall be granted by the United States: And no Person holding any Office of Profit or trust under them, shall, without the Consent of the Congress, accept of any present, Emolument, Office, or Title, of any kind whatever, from any King, Prince, or foreign State.

*Section 10.* No State shall enter into any Treaty, Alliance, or Confederation; grant Letters of Marque and Reprisal; coin Money; emit Bills of Credit; make any Thing but gold and silver Coin a Tender in Payment of Debts; pass any Bill of Attainder, ex post facto Law, or Law impairing the Obligation of Contracts, or grant any Title of Nobility.

No State shall, without the Consent of the Congress, lay any Imposts or Duties on Imports or Exports, except what may be absolutely necessary for executing its inspection Laws: and the net Produce of all Duties and Imposts, laid by any State on Imports or Exports, shall be for the Use of the Treasury of the United States; and all such Laws shall be subject to the Revision and Controul of the Congress.

No State shall, without the Consent of Congress, lay any Duty of Tonnage, keep Troops, or Ships of War in time of Peace, enter into any Agreement or Compact with another State, or with a foreign Power, or engage in War, unless actually invaded, or in such imminent Danger as will not admit of delay.

# ARTICLE. II.

*Section. 1.* The executive Power shall be vested in a President of the United States of America. He shall hold his Office during the term of four Years, and, together with the Vice President, chosen for the same Term, be elected, as follows:

Each State shall appoint, in such Manner as the Legislature thereof may direct, a Number of Electors, equal to the whole Number of Senators and Representatives to which the State may be entitled in the Congress: but no Senator or Representative, or Person holding an Office of Trust or Profit under the United States, shall be appointed an Elector.

The Electors shall meet in their respective States, and vote by Ballot for two Persons, of whom one at least shall not be an Inhabitant of the same State with themselves. And they shall make a List of all the Persons voted for, and of the Number of Votes for each; which List they shall sign and certify, and transmit sealed to the Seat of the Government of the United States, directed to the President of the Senate. The President of the Senate shall, in the Presence of the Senate and House of Representatives, open all the Certificates, and the Votes shall then be counted. The Person having the greatest Number of Votes shall be the President, if such Number be a Majority of the whole Number of Electors appointed; and if there be more than one who have such Majority, and have an equal Number of Votes, then the House of Representatives shall immediately chuse by Ballot one of them for President; and if no Person have a Majority, then from the five highest on the List the said House shall in like Manner chuse the President. But in chusing the President, the Votes shall be taken by States, the Representation from each State having one Vote; A quorum for this Purpose shall consist of a Member or Members from two thirds of the States, and a Majority of all the States shall be necessary to a Choice. In every Case, after the Choice of the President, the Person having the greatest Number of Votes of the Electors shall be the Vice President. But if there should remain two or more who have equal Votes, the Senate shall chuse from them by Ballot the Vice President.

The Congress may determine the Time of chusing the Electors, and the Day on which they shall give their Votes; which Day shall be the same throughout the United States.

No Person except a natural born Citizen, or a Citizen of the United States, at the time of the Adoption of this Constitution, shall be eligible to the Office of President; neither shall any Person be eligible to that Office who shall not have attained to the Age of thirty five Years, and been fourteen Years a Resident within the United States.

In Case of the Removal of the President from Office, or of his Death, Resignation, or Inability to discharge the Powers and Duties of the said Office, the Same shall devolve on the Vice President, and the Congress may by Law provide for the Case of Removal, Death, Resignation or Inability, both of the President and Vice President, declaring what Officer shall then act as President, and such Officer shall act accordingly, until the Disability be removed, or a President shall be elected.

The President shall, at stated Times, receive for his Services, a Compensation, which shall neither be encreased or diminished during the Period for which he shall have been elected, and he shall not receive within that Period any other Emolument from the United States, or any of them.

Before he enters on the Execution of his Office, he shall take the following Oath or Affirmation:—"I do solemnly swear (or affirm) that I will faithfully execute the Office of President of the United States, and will to the best of my Ability, preserve, protect and defend the Constitution of the United States."

*Section. 2.* The President shall be Commander in Chief of the Army and Navy of the United States, and of the Militia of the several States, when called into the actual Service of the United States; he may require the Opinion, in writing, of the principal Officer in each of the executive Departments, upon any Subject relating to the Duties of their respective Offices, and he shall have Power to grant Reprieves and Pardons for Offences against the United States, except in Cases of Impeachment.

He shall have Power, by and with the Advice and Consent of the Senate, to make Treaties, provided two thirds of the Senators present concur; and he shall nominate, and by and with the Advice and Consent of the Senate, shall appoint Ambassadors, other public Ministers and Consuls, Judges of the supreme Court, and all other Officers of the United States, whose Appointments are not herein otherwise provided for, and which shall be established by Law; but the Congress may by Law vest the Appointment of such inferior Officers, as they think proper, in the President alone, in the Courts of Law, or in the Heads of Departments.

The President shall have Power to fill up all Vacancies that may happen during the Recess of the Senate, by granting Commissions which shall expire at the End of their next Session.

*Section. 3.* He shall from time to time give to the Congress Information of the State of the Union, and recommend to their Consideration such Measures as he shall judge necessary and expedient; he may, on extraordinary Occasions, convene both Houses, or either of them, and in Case of Disagreement between them, with Respect to the Time of Adjournment, he may adjourn them to such Time as he shall think proper; he shall receive Ambassadors and other public Ministers; he shall take Care that the Laws be faithfully executed, and shall Commission all the Officers of the United States.

*Section. 4.* The President, Vice President and all civil Officers of the United States, shall be removed from Office on Impeachment for, and Conviction of, Treason, Bribery, or other high Crimes and Misdemeanors.

# ARTICLE. III.

*Section. 1.* The judicial Power of the United States, shall be vested in one supreme Court, and in such inferior Courts as the Congress may from time to time ordain and establish. The Judges, both of the supreme and inferior Courts, shall hold their Offices during good Behavior, and shall, at stated Times, receive for their Services, a Compensation, which shall not be diminished during their Continuance in Office.

*Section. 2.* The judicial Power shall extend to all Cases, in Law and Equity, arising under this Constitution, the Laws of the United States, and Treaties made, or which shall be made, under their Authority;—to all Cases affecting Ambassadors, other public Ministers and Consuls;—to all Cases of admiralty and maritime Jurisdiction;—the Controversies to which the United States shall be a Party;—to Controversies between two or more States;—between a State and Citizens of another State;—between Citizens of different States;—between Citizens of the same State claiming Lands under Grants of different States, and between a State, or the Citizens thereof, and foreign States, Citizens or Subjects.

In all cases affecting Ambassadors, other public Ministers and Consuls, and those in which a State shall be Party, the supreme Court shall have original Jurisdiction. In all the other Cases before mentioned, the supreme Court shall have appellate Jurisdiction, both as to Law and Fact, with such Exceptions, and under such Regulations as the Congress shall make.

The Trial of all Crimes, except in Cases of Impeachment, shall be by Jury; and such Trial shall be held in the State where the said Crimes shall have been committed; but when not committed within any State, the Trial shall be at such Place or Places as the Congress may by Law have directed.

*Section. 3.* Treason against the United States, shall consist only in levying War against them, or in adhering to their Enemies, giving them Aid and Comfort. No Person shall be convicted of Treason unless on the Testimony of two Witnesses to the same overt Act, or on Confession in open Court.

The Congress shall have Power to declare the Punishment of Treason, but no Attainder of Treason shall work Corruption of Blood, or Forfeiture except during the Life of the Person attainted.

# ARTICLE. IV.

*Section. 1.* Full Faith and Credit shall be given in each State to the public Acts, Records, and judicial Proceedings of every other State. And the Congress may by general Laws prescribe the Manner in which such Acts, Records and Proceedings shall be proved, and the Effect thereof.

*Section. 2.* The Citizens of each State shall be entitled to all Privileges and Immunities of Citizens in the several States.

A Person charged in any State with Treason, Felony, or other Crime, who shall flee from Justice, and be found in another State, shall on Demand of the executive Authority of the State from which he fled, be delivered up, to be removed to the State having Jurisdiction of the Crime.

No Person held to Service or Labour in one State, under the Laws thereof, escaping into another, shall, in Consequence of any Law or Regulation therein, be discharged from such Service or Labour, but shall be delivered up on Claim of the Party to whom such Service or Labour may be due.

*Section. 3.* New States may be admitted by the Congress into this Union; but no new State shall be formed or erected within the Jurisdiction of any other State; nor any State be formed by the Junction of two or more States, or Parts of States, without the consent of the Legislatures of the States concerned as well as of the Congress.

The Congress shall have Power to dispose of and make all needful Rules and Regulations respecting the Territory or other Property belonging to the United States; and nothing in this Constitution shall be so construed as to Prejudice any Claims of the United States, or of any particular States.

*Section. 4.* The United States shall guarantee to every State in this Union a Republican Form of Government, and shall protect each of them against Invasion; and on Application of the Legislature, or of the Executive (when the Legislature cannot be convened) against domestic Violence.

# ARTICLE. V.

The Congress, whenever two thirds of both Houses shall deem it necessary, shall propose Amendments to this Constitution, or, on the Application of the

Legislatures of two thirds of the several States, shall call a Convention for proposing Amendments, which, in either Case, shall be valid to all Intents and Purposes, as Part of this Constitution, when ratified by the Legislatures of three fourths of the several States, or by Conventions in three fourths thereof, as the one or the other Mode of Ratification may be proposed by the Congress; Provided that no Amendment which may be made prior to the Year One thousand eight hundred and eight shall in any Manner affect the first and fourth Clauses in the Ninth Section of the first Article; and that no State, without its Consent, shall be deprived of its equal Suffrage in the Senate.

## ARTICLE. VI.

All Debts contracted and Engagements entered into, before the Adoption of this Constitution, shall be as valid against the United States under this Constitution, as under the Confederation.

This Constitution, and the Laws of the United States which shall be made in Pursuance thereof; and all Treaties made, or which shall be made, under the Authority of the United States, shall be the supreme Law of the Land; and the Judges in every State shall be bound thereby, any Thing in the Constitution or Laws of any State to the Contrary notwithstanding.

The Senators and Representatives before mentioned, and the Members of the several State Legislatures, and all executive and judicial Officers, both of the United States and of the several States, shall be bound by Oath or Affirmation, to support this Constitution; but no religious Test shall ever be required as a Qualification to any Office or public Trust under the United States.

## ARTICLE. VII.

The Ratification of the Conventions of nine States, shall be sufficient for the Establishment of this Constitution between the States so ratifying the Same.

Done in Convention by the Unanimous Consent of the States present the Seventeenth Day of September in the Year of our Lord one thousand seven hundred and Eighty seven and of the Independence of the United States of America the Twelfth. In witness thereof We have hereunto subscribed our Names,

Go. WASHINGTON—Presdt.
and deputy from Virginia.

| New Hampshire | { John Langdon | | Delaware | { Geo: Read |
| | Nicholas Gilman | | | Gunning Bedford jun |
| | | | | John Dickinson |
| Massachusetts | { Nathaniel Gorham | | | Richard Bassett |
| | Rufus King | | | Jaco: Broom |
| | | | | |
| Connecticut | { W^m Sam^l Johnson | | Maryland | { James McHenry |
| | Roger Sherman | | | Dan of St Tho^s Jenifer |
| New York: ... | Alexander Hamilton | | | Dan^l Carroll |
| | | | Virginia | { John Blair— |
| New Jersey | { Wil: Livingston | | | James Madison Jr. |
| | David A. Brearley. | | North Carolina | { W^m Blount |
| | W^m Paterson. | | | Rich^d Dobbs Spaight. |
| | Jona: Dayton | | | Hu Williamson |
| Pennsylvania | { B Franklin | | South Carolina | { J. Rutledge |
| | Thomas Mifflin | | | Charles Cotesworth |
| | Rob^t Morris | | | Pinckney |
| | Geo. Clymer | | | Charles Pinckney |
| | Tho^s FitzSimons | | | Pierce Butler. |
| | Jared Ingersoll | | Georgia | { William Few |
| | James Wilson | | | Abr Baldwin |
| | Gouv Morris | | | |

# AMENDMENTS TO THE CONSTITUTION

ARTICLES IN ADDITION TO, and Amendment of the Constitution of the United States of America, proposed by Congress, and ratified by the Legislatures of the several States, pursuant to the fifth Article of the original Constitution.

## AMENDMENT I.

Congress shall make no law respecting an establishment of religion, or prohibiting the free exercise thereof; or abridging the freedom of speech, or of the press; or the right of the people peaceably to assemble, and to petition the Government for a redress of grievances.

## AMENDMENT II.

A well regulated Militia, being necessary to the security of a free State, the right of the people to keep and bear Arms, shall not be infringed.

## AMENDMENT III.

No Soldier shall, in time of peace be quartered in any house, without the consent of the Owner, nor in time of war, but in a manner to be prescribed by law.

## AMENDMENT IV.

The right of the people to be secure in their persons, houses, papers, and effects, against unreasonable searches and seizures, shall not be violated, and no Warrants shall issue, but upon probable cause, supported by Oath or affirmation, and particularly describing the place to be searched, and the persons or things to be seized.

## Amendment V.

No person shall be held to answer for a capital, or otherwise infamous crime, unless on a presentment or indictment of a Grand Jury, except in cases arising in the land or naval forces, or in the Militia, when in actual service in time of War or public danger; nor shall any person be subject for the same offence to be twice put in jeopardy of life or limb; nor shall be compelled in any criminal case to be a witness against himself, nor be deprived of life, liberty, or property, without due process of law; nor shall private property be taken for public use, without just compensation.

## Amendment VI.

In all criminal prosecutions, the accused shall enjoy the right to a speedy and public trial, by an impartial jury of the State and district wherein the crime shall have been committed, which district shall have been previously ascertained by law, and to be informed of the nature and cause of the accusation; to be confronted with the witnesses against him; to have compulsory process for obtaining witnesses in his favor, and to have the Assistance of Counsel for his defence.

## Amendment VII.

In Suits at common law, where the value in controversy shall exceed twenty dollars, the right of trial by jury shall be preserved, and no fact tried by a jury, shall be otherwise re-examined in any Court of the United States, than according to the rules of the common law.

## Amendment VIII.

Excessive bail shall not be required, nor excessive fines imposed, nor cruel and unusual punishments inflicted.

## AMENDMENT IX.

The enumeration in the Constitution, of certain rights, shall not be construed to deny or disparage others retained by the people.

## AMENDMENT X.

The powers not delegated to the United States by the Constitution, nor prohibited by it to the States, are reserved to the States respectively, or to the people. [The first ten amendments went into effect December 15, 1791.]

## AMENDMENT XI.

The Judicial power of the United States shall not be construed to extend to any suit in law or equity, commenced or prosecuted against one of the United States by Citizens of another State, or by Citizens or Subjects of any Foreign State. [January 8, 1798.]

## AMENDMENT XII.

The Electors shall meet in their respective states, and vote by ballot for President and Vice-President, one of whom, at least, shall not be an inhabitant of the same state with themselves; they shall name in their ballots the person voted for as President, and in distinct ballots the person voted for as Vice-President, and they shall make distinct lists of all persons voted for as President, and of all persons voted for as Vice President, and of the number of votes for each, which lists they shall sign and certify, and transmit sealed to the seat of the government of the United States, directed to the President of the Senate;—The President of the Senate shall, in the presence of the Senate and House of Representatives, open all the certificates and the votes shall then be counted;—The person having the greatest number of votes for President, shall be the President, if such number be a majority of the whole number of Electors appointed; and if no person have such majority, then from the persons having the highest numbers not exceeding three on the list of those voted for as President, the House of Representatives shall choose immediately, by ballot, the President. But in choosing the President, the votes shall be taken by states, the representation from each state having one vote; a quorum for this purpose shall consist of a member or members from two-thirds of the states, and a majority of all the states shall be necessary to a choice. And if the House of Representatives shall not choose a President whenever the right of choice shall devolve upon them, before the fourth day of March next following, then the Vice-President shall act as President, as in the case of the death or other constitutional disability of the President.— The person having the greatest number of votes as Vice-President, shall be the Vice-President, if such number be a majority of the whole number of Electors appointed, and if no person have a majority, then from the two highest numbers on the list, the Senate shall choose the Vice-President; a quorum for the purpose shall consist of two-thirds of the whole number of Senators, and a majority of the whole number shall be necessary to a choice. But no person constitutionally ineligible to the office of President shall be eligible to that of Vice-President of the United States. [September 25, 1804.]

# AMENDMENT XIII.

*Section 1*. Neither slavery nor involuntary servitude, except as a punishment for crime whereof the party shall have been duly convicted, shall exist within the United States, or any place subject to their jurisdiction.

*Section 2*. Congress shall have power to enforce this article by appropriate legislation. [December 18, 1865.]

# AMENDMENT XIV.

*Section 1*. All persons born or naturalized in the United States, and subject to the jurisdiction thereof, are citizens of the United States and of the State wherein they reside. No State shall make or enforce any law which shall abridge the privileges or immunities of citizens of the United States; nor shall any State deprive any person of life, liberty, or property, without due process of law; nor deny to any person within its jurisdiction the equal protection of the laws.

*Section 2*. Representatives shall be apportioned among the several States according to their respective numbers, counting the whole number of persons in each State, excluding Indians not taxed. But when the right to vote at any election for the choice of electors for President and Vice President of the United States, Representatives in Congress, the Executive and Judicial officers of a State, or the members of the Legislature thereof, is denied to any of the male inhabitants of such State, being twenty-one years of age, and citizens of the United States, or in any way abridged, except for participation in rebellion, or other crime, the basis of representation therein shall be reduced in the proportion which the number of such male citizens shall bear to the whole number of male citizens twenty-one years of age in such State.

*Section 3.* No person shall be a Senator or Representative in Congress, or elector of President and Vice President, or hold any office, civil or military, under the United States, or under any State, who, having previously taken an oath, as a member of Congress, or as an officer of the United States, or as a member of any State legislature, or as an executive or judicial officer of any State, to support the Constitution of the United States, shall have engaged in insurrection or rebellion against the same, or given aid or comfort to the enemies thereof. But Congress may by a vote of two-thirds of each House, remove such disability.

*Section 4.* The validity of the public debt of the United States, authorized by law, including debts incurred for payment of pensions and bounties for services in suppressing insurrection or rebellion, shall not be questioned. But neither the United States nor any State shall assume or pay any debt or obligation incurred in aid of insurrection or rebellion against the United States, or any claim for the loss or emancipation of any slave; but all such debts, obligations and claims shall be held illegal and void.

*Section 5.* The Congress shall have power to enforce, by appropriate legislation, the provisions of this article. [July 28, 1868.]

# AMENDMENT XV.

*Section 1.* The right of citizens of the United States to vote shall not be denied or abridged by the United States or by any State on account of race, color, or previous condition of servitude—

*Section 2.* The Congress shall have power to enforce this article by appropriate legislation.—[March 30, 1870.]

# AMENDMENT XVI.

The Congress shall have power to lay and collect taxes on incomes, from whatever source derived, without apportionment among the several

States, and without regard to any census or enumeration. [February 25, 1913.]

## Amendment XVII.

The Senate of the United States shall be composed of two senators from each State, elected by the people thereof, for six years; and each Senator shall have one vote. The electors in each State shall have the qualifications requisite for electors of the most numerous branch of the State legislature.

When vacancies happen in the representation of any State in the Senate, the executive authority of such State shall issue writs of election to fill such vacancies: *Provided,* That the legislature of any State may empower the executive thereof to make temporary appointments until the people fill the vacancies by election as the legislature may direct.

This amendment shall not be so construed as to affect the election or term of any senator chosen before it becomes valid as part of the Constitution. [May 31, 1913.]

## Amendment XVIII.

After one year from the ratification of this article, the manufacture, sale, or transportation of intoxicating liquors within, the importation thereof into, or the exportation thereof from the United States and all territory subject to the jurisdiction thereof for beverage purposes is hereby prohibited.

The Congress and the several States shall have concurrent power to enforce this article by appropriate legislation.

This article shall be inoperative unless it shall have been ratified as an amendment to the Constitution by the legislatures of the several States, as provided in the Constitution, within seven years from the date of the submission thereof to the States by Congress. [January 29, 1919.]

## Amendment XIX.

The right of citizens of the United States to vote shall not be denied or abridged by the United States or by any State on account of sex.

The Congress shall have power by appropriate legislation to enforce the provisions of this article. [August 26, 1920.]

## Amendment XX.

*Section 1.* The terms of the President and Vice-President shall end at noon on the twentieth day of January, and the terms of Senators and Representatives at noon on the third day of January, of the years in which such terms would have ended if this article had not been ratified; and the terms of their successors shall then begin.

*Section 2.* The Congress shall assemble at least once in every year, and such meeting shall begin at noon on the third day of January, unless they shall by law appoint a different day.

*Section 3.* If, at the time fixed for the beginning of the term of the President, the President-elect shall have died, the Vice-President-elect shall become President. If a President shall not have been chosen before the time fixed for the beginning of his term, or if the President-elect shall have failed to qualify, then the Vice-President-elect shall act as President until a President shall have qualified; and the Congress may by law provide for the case wherein neither a President-elect nor a Vice-President-elect shall have qualified, declaring who shall then act as President, or the manner in which one who is to act shall be selected, and such person shall act accordingly until a President or Vice-President shall have qualified.

*Section 4.* The Congress may by law provide for the case of the death of any of the persons from whom the House of Representatives may choose a President whenever the right of choice shall have devolved upon them, and for the case of the death of any of the persons from whom the Senate may choose a Vice-President whenever the right of choice shall have devolved upon them.

*Section 5.* Sections 1 and 2 shall take effect on the 15th day of October following the ratification of this article.

*Section 6.* This article shall be inoperative unless it shall have been ratified as an amendment to the Constitution by the legislatures of three-fourths of the several States within seven years from the date of its submission. [February 6, 1933.]

# AMENDMENT XXI.

*Section 1.* The eighteenth article of amendment to the Constitution of the United States is hereby repealed.

*Section 2.* The transportation or importation into any State, Territory or possession of the United States for delivery or use therein of intoxicating liquors, in violation of the laws thereof, is hereby prohibited.

*Section 3.* This article shall be inoperative unless it shall have been ratified as an amendment to the Constitution by convention in the several States, as provided in the Constitution, within seven years from the date of the submission thereof to the States by the Congress. [December 5, 1933.]

# AMENDMENT XXII.

*Section 1.* No person shall be elected to the office of the President more than twice, and no person who has held the office of President, or acted as President, for more than two years of a term to which some other person was elected President shall be elected to the office of the President more than once. But this Article shall not apply to any person holding the office of President when this Article was proposed by the Congress, and shall not prevent any person who may be holding the office of President, or acting as President, during the term within which this Article becomes operative from holding the office of President or acting as President during the remainder of such term.

*Section 2.* This article shall be inoperative unless it shall have been ratified as an amendment to the Constitution by the legislatures of three-fourths of the several states within seven years from the date of its submission to the States by the Congress. [February 27, 1951.]

# AMENDMENT XXIII.

*Section 1.* The District constituting the seat of government of the United States shall appoint in such manner as the Congress may direct:

A number of electors of President and Vice-President equal to the whole number of Senators and Representatives in Congress to which the District would be entitled if it were a State, but in no event more than the least populous State; they shall be in addition to those appointed by the States, but they shall be considered, for the purposes of the election of President and Vice-President, to be electors appointed by a State; and they shall meet in the District and perform such duties as provided by the twelfth article of amendment.

*Section 2.* The Congress shall have the power to enforce this article by appropriate legislation. [March 29, 1961.]

# AMENDMENT XXIV.

*Section 1.* The right of citizens of the United States to vote in any primary or other election for President or Vice President, for electors for President or Vice President, or for Senator or Representative in Congress, shall not be denied or abridged by the United States or any State by reason of failure to pay any poll tax or other tax.

*Section 2.* The Congress shall have power to enforce this article by appropriate legislation. [January 23, 1964.]

# AMENDMENT XXV.

*Section 1.* In case of the removal of the President from office or of his death or resignation, the Vice President shall become President.

*Section 2.* Whenever there is a vacancy in the office of Vice President, the President shall nominate a Vice President who shall take office upon confirmation by a majority vote of both Houses of Congress.

*Section 3.* Whenever the President transmits to the President pro tempore of the Senate and the Speaker of the House of Representatives his written declaration that he is unable to discharge the powers and duties of his office, and until he transmits to them a written declaration to the contrary, such powers and duties shall be discharged by the Vice President as Acting President.

*Section 4.* Whenever the Vice President and a majority of either the principal officers of the executive departments or of such other body as Congress may by law provide, transmit to the President pro tempore of the Senate and the Speaker of the House of Representatives their written declaration that the President is unable to discharge the powers and duties of his office, the Vice President shall immediately assume the powers and duties of the office as Acting President.

Thereafter, when the President transmits to the President pro tempore of the Senate and the Speaker of the House of Representatives his written declaration that no inability exists, he shall resume the powers and duties of his office unless the Vice President and a majority of either the principal officers of the executive departments or of such other body as Congress may by law provide, transmit within four days to the President pro tempore of the Senate and the Speaker of the House of Representatives their written declaration that the President is unable to discharge the powers and duties of his office. Thereupon Congress shall decide the issue, assembling within forty-eight hours for that purpose if not in session. If the Congress, within twenty-one days after receipt of the latter written declaration, or, if Congress is not in session, within twenty-one days after Congress is required to assemble, determines by two-thirds vote of both Houses that the President is unable to discharge the powers and duties of his office, the Vice President shall continue to discharge the same as Acting President; otherwise, the President shall resume the powers and duties of his office. [February 10, 1967.]

## AMENDMENT XXVI.

*Section 1.* The right of citizens of the United States, who are eighteen years of age or older, to vote shall not be denied or abridged by the United States or by any State on account of age.

*Section 2.* The Congress shall have power to enforce this article by appropriate legislation [June 30, 1971.]

## AMENDMENT XXVII.

No law, varying the compensation for the services of the Senators and Representatives shall take effect, until an election of Representatives shall have intervened. [May 8, 1992.]

## PRESIDENTIAL ELECTIONS

| Year | Number of States | Candidates | Parties | Popular Vote | % of Popular Vote | Electoral Vote | % Voter Participation |
|---|---|---|---|---|---|---|---|
| 1789 | 11 | **GEORGE WASHINGTON** | No party designations | | | 69 | |
| | | John Adams | | | | 34 | |
| | | Other candidates | | | | 35 | |
| 1792 | 15 | **GEORGE WASHINGTON** | No party designations | | | 132 | |
| | | John Adams | | | | 77 | |
| | | George Clinton | | | | 50 | |
| | | Other candidates | | | | 5 | |
| 1796 | 16 | **JOHN ADAMS** | Federalist | | | 71 | |
| | | Thomas Jefferson | Democratic-Republican | | | 68 | |
| | | Thomas Pinckney | Federalist | | | 59 | |
| | | Aaron Burr | Democratic-Republican | | | 30 | |
| | | Other candidates | | | | 48 | |
| 1800 | 16 | **THOMAS JEFFERSON** | Democratic-Republican | | | 73 | |
| | | Aaron Burr | Democratic-Republican | | | 73 | |
| | | John Adams | Federalist | | | 65 | |
| | | Charles C. Pinckney | Federalist | | | 64 | |
| | | John Jay | Federalist | | | 1 | |
| 1804 | 17 | **THOMAS JEFFERSON** | Democratic-Republican | | | 162 | |
| | | Charles C. Pinckney | Federalist | | | 14 | |

| Year | Number of States | Candidates | Parties | Popular Vote | % of Popular Vote | Electoral Vote | % Voter Participation |
|---|---|---|---|---|---|---|---|
| 1808 | 17 | JAMES MADISON | Democratic-Republican | | | 122 | |
| | | Charles C. Pinckney | Federalist | | | 47 | |
| | | George Clinton | Democratic-Republican | | | 6 | |
| 1812 | 18 | JAMES MADISON | Democratic-Republican | | | 128 | |
| | | DeWitt Clinton | Federalist | | | 89 | |
| 1816 | 19 | JAMES MONROE | Democratic-Republican | | | 183 | |
| | | Rufus King | Federalist | | | 34 | |
| 1820 | 24 | JAMES MONROE | Democratic-Republican | | | 231 | |
| | | John Quincy Adams | Independent | | | 1 | |
| 1824 | 24 | JOHN QUINCY ADAMS | Democratic-Republican | 108,740 | 30.5 | 84 | 26.9 |
| | | Andrew Jackson | Democratic-Republican | 153,544 | 43.1 | 99 | |
| | | Henry Clay | Democratic-Republican | 47,136 | 13.2 | 37 | |
| | | William H. Crawford | Democratic-Republican | 46,618 | 13.1 | 41 | |
| 1828 | 24 | ANDREW JACKSON | Democratic | 647,286 | 56.0 | 178 | 57.6 |
| | | John Quincy Adams | National-Republican | 508,064 | 44.0 | 83 | |

| Year | Number of States | Candidates | Parties | Popular Vote | % of Popular Vote | Electoral Vote | % Voter Participation |
|---|---|---|---|---|---|---|---|
| 1832 | 24 | **ANDREW JACKSON** | Democratic | 688,242 | 54.5 | 219 | 55.4 |
| | | Henry Clay | National-Republican | 473,462 | 37.5 | 49 | |
| | | William Wirt | Anti-Masonic | 101,051 | 8.0 | 7 | |
| | | John Floyd | Democratic | | | 11 | |
| 1836 | 26 | **MARTIN VAN BUREN** | Democratic | 765,483 | 50.9 | 170 | 57.8 |
| | | William H. Harrison | Whig | | | 73 | |
| | | Hugh L. White | Whig | 739,795 | 49.1 | 26 | |
| | | Daniel Webster | Whig | | | 14 | |
| | | W. P. Mangum | Whig | | | 11 | |
| 1840 | 26 | **WILLIAM H. HARRISON** | Whig | 1,274,624 | 53.1 | 234 | 80.2 |
| | | Martin Van Buren | Democratic | 1,127,781 | 46.9 | 60 | |
| 1844 | 26 | **JAMES K. POLK** | Democratic | 1,338,464 | 49.6 | 170 | 78.9 |
| | | Henry Clay | Whig | 1,300,097 | 48.1 | 105 | |
| | | James G. Birney | Liberty | 62,300 | 2.3 | | |
| 1848 | 30 | **ZACHARY TAYLOR** | Whig | 1,360,967 | 47.4 | 163 | 72.7 |
| | | Lewis Cass | Democratic | 1,222,342 | 42.5 | 127 | |
| | | Martin Van Buren | Free Soil | 291,263 | 10.1 | | |
| 1852 | 31 | **FRANKLIN PIERCE** | Democratic | 1,601,117 | 50.9 | 254 | 69.6 |
| | | Winfield Scott | Whig | 1,385,453 | 44.1 | 42 | |
| | | John P. Hale | Free Soil | 155,825 | 5.0 | | |
| 1856 | 31 | **JAMES BUCHANAN** | Democratic | 1,832,955 | 45.3 | 174 | 78.9 |
| | | John C. Frémont | Republican | 1,339,932 | 33.1 | 114 | |
| | | Millard Fillmore | American | 871,731 | 21.6 | 8 | |

| Year | No. | Candidate | Party | Popular Vote | % | Electoral Vote | % Participation |
|---|---|---|---|---|---|---|---|
| 1860 | 33 | **ABRAHAM LINCOLN** | Republican | 1,865,593 | 39.8 | 180 | 81.2 |
| | | Stephen A. Douglas | Democratic | 1,382,713 | 29.5 | 12 | |
| | | John C. Breckinridge | Democratic | 848,356 | 18.1 | 72 | |
| | | John Bell | Constitutional Union | 592,906 | 12.6 | 39 | |
| 1864 | 36 | **ABRAHAM LINCOLN** | Republican | 2,206,938 | 55.0 | 212 | 73.8 |
| | | George B. McClellan | Democratic | 1,803,787 | 45.0 | 21 | |
| 1868 | 37 | **ULYSSES S. GRANT** | Republican | 3,013,421 | 52.7 | 214 | 78.1 |
| | | Horatio Seymour | Democratic | 2,706,829 | 47.3 | 80 | |
| 1872 | 37 | **ULYSSES S. GRANT** | Republican | 3,596,745 | 55.6 | 286 | 71.3 |
| | | Horace Greeley | Democratic | 2,843,446 | 43.9 | 66 | |
| 1876 | 38 | Rutherford B. Hayes | Republican | 4,036,572 | 48.0 | 185 | 81.8 |
| | | Samuel J. Tilden | Democratic | 4,284,020 | 51.0 | 184 | |
| 1880 | 38 | **JAMES A. GARFIELD** | Republican | 4,453,295 | 48.5 | 214 | 79.4 |
| | | Winfield S. Hancock | Democratic | 4,414,082 | 48.1 | 155 | |
| | | James B. Weaver | Greenback-Labor | 308,578 | 3.4 | | |
| 1884 | 38 | **GROVER CLEVELAND** | Democratic | 4,879,507 | 48.5 | 219 | 77.5 |
| | | James G. Blaine | Republican | 4,850,293 | 48.2 | 182 | |
| | | Benjamin F. Butler | Greenback-Labor | 175,370 | 1.8 | | |
| | | John P. St. John | Prohibition | 150,369 | 1.5 | | |
| 1888 | 38 | **BENJAMIN HARRISON** | Republican | 5,477,129 | 47.9 | 233 | 79.3 |
| | | Grover Cleveland | Democratic | 5,537,857 | 48.6 | 168 | |
| | | Clinton B. Fisk | Prohibition | 249,506 | 2.2 | | |
| | | Anson J. Streeter | Union Labor | 146,935 | 1.3 | | |

| Year | Number of States | Candidates | Parties | Popular Vote | % of Popular Vote | Electoral Vote | % Voter Participation |
|---|---|---|---|---|---|---|---|
| 1892 | 44 | **GROVER CLEVELAND** | Democratic | 5,555,426 | 46.1 | 277 | 74.7 |
|  |  | Benjamin Harrison | Republican | 5,182,690 | 43.0 | 145 |  |
|  |  | James B. Weaver | People's | 1,029,846 | 8.5 | 22 |  |
|  |  | John Bidwell | Prohibition | 264,133 | 2.2 |  |  |
| 1896 | 45 | **WILLIAM MCKINLEY** | Republican | 7,102,246 | 51.1 | 271 | 79.3 |
|  |  | William J. Bryan | Democratic | 6,492,559 | 47.7 | 176 |  |
| 1900 | 45 | **WILLIAM MCKINLEY** | Republican | 7,218,491 | 51.7 | 292 | 73.2 |
|  |  | William J. Bryan | Democratic; Populist | 6,356,734 | 45.5 | 155 |  |
|  |  | John C. Wooley | Prohibition | 208,914 | 1.5 |  |  |
| 1904 | 45 | **THEODORE ROOSEVELT** | Republican | 7,628,461 | 57.4 | 336 | 65.2 |
|  |  | Alton B. Parker | Democratic | 5,084,223 | 37.6 | 140 |  |
|  |  | Eugene V. Debs | Socialist | 402,283 | 3.0 |  |  |
|  |  | Silas C. Swallow | Prohibition | 258,536 | 1.9 |  |  |
| 1908 | 46 | **WILLIAM H. TAFT** | Republican | 7,675,320 | 51.6 | 321 | 65.4 |
|  |  | William J. Bryan | Democratic | 6,412,294 | 43.1 | 162 |  |
|  |  | Eugene V. Debs | Socialist | 420,793 | 2.8 |  |  |
|  |  | Eugene W. Chafin | Prohibition | 253,840 | 1.7 |  |  |
| 1912 | 48 | **WOODROW WILSON** | Democratic | 6,296,547 | 41.9 | 435 | 58.8 |
|  |  | Theodore Roosevelt | Progressive | 4,118,571 | 27.4 | 88 |  |
|  |  | William H. Taft | Republican | 3,486,720 | 23.2 | 8 |  |
|  |  | Eugene V. Debs | Socialist | 900,672 | 6.0 |  |  |
|  |  | Eugene W. Chafin | Prohibition | 206,275 | 1.4 |  |  |

| Year | Number of States | Candidates | Parties | Popular Vote | % of Popular Vote | Electoral Vote | % Voter Participation |
|---|---|---|---|---|---|---|---|
| 1916 | 48 | **WOODROW WILSON** | Democratic | 9,127,695 | 49.4 | 277 | 61.6 |
| | | Charles E. Hughes | Republican | 8,533,507 | 46.2 | 254 | |
| | | A. L. Benson | Socialist | 585,113 | 3.2 | | |
| | | J. Frank Hanly | Prohibition | 220,506 | 1.2 | | |
| 1920 | 48 | **WARREN G. HARDING** | Republican | 16,143,407 | 60.4 | 404 | 49.2 |
| | | James M. Cox | Democratic | 9,130,328 | 34.2 | 127 | |
| | | Eugene V. Debs | Socialist | 919,799 | 3.4 | | |
| | | P. P. Christensen | Farmer-Labor | 265,411 | 1.0 | | |
| 1924 | 48 | **CALVIN COOLIDGE** | Republican | 15,718,211 | 54.0 | 382 | 48.9 |
| | | John W. Davis | Democratic | 8,385,283 | 28.8 | 136 | |
| | | Robert M. La Follette | Progressive | 4,831,289 | 16.6 | 13 | |
| 1928 | 48 | **HERBERT C. HOOVER** | Republican | 21,391,993 | 58.2 | 444 | 56.9 |
| | | Alfred E. Smith | Democratic | 15,016,169 | 40.9 | 87 | |
| 1932 | 48 | **FRANKLIN D. ROOSEVELT** | Democratic | 22,809,638 | 57.4 | 472 | 56.9 |
| | | Herbert C. Hoover | Republican | 15,758,901 | 39.7 | 59 | |
| | | Norman Thomas | Socialist | 881,951 | 2.2 | | |
| 1936 | 48 | **FRANKLIN D. ROOSEVELT** | Democratic | 27,752,869 | 60.8 | 523 | 61.0 |
| | | Alfred M. Landon | Republican | 16,674,665 | 36.5 | 8 | |
| | | William Lemke | Union | 882,479 | 1.9 | | |
| 1940 | 48 | **FRANKLIN D. ROOSEVELT** | Democratic | 27,307,819 | 54.8 | 449 | 62.5 |
| | | Wendell L. Willkie | Republican | 22,321,018 | 44.8 | 82 | |
| 1944 | 48 | **FRANKLIN D. ROOSEVELT** | Democratic | 25,606,585 | 53.5 | 432 | 55.9 |
| | | Thomas E. Dewey | Republican | 22,014,745 | 46.0 | 99 | |

| Year | Number of States | Candidates | Parties | Popular Vote | % of Popular Vote | Electoral Vote | % Voter Participation |
|---|---|---|---|---|---|---|---|
| 1948 | 48 | **HARRY S. TRUMAN** | Democratic | 24,179,345 | 49.6 | 303 | 53.0 |
| | | Thomas E. Dewey | Republican | 21,991,291 | 45.1 | 189 | |
| | | J. Strom Thurmond | States' Rights | 1,176,125 | 2.4 | 39 | |
| | | Henry A. Wallace | Progressive | 1,157,326 | 2.4 | | |
| 1952 | 48 | **DWIGHT D. EISENHOWER** | Republican | 33,936,234 | 55.1 | 442 | 63.3 |
| | | Adlai E. Stevenson | Democratic | 27,314,992 | 44.4 | 89 | |
| 1956 | 48 | **DWIGHT D. EISENHOWER** | Republican | 35,590,472 | 57.6 | 457 | 60.6 |
| | | Adlai E. Stevenson | Democratic | 26,022,752 | 42.1 | 73 | |
| 1960 | 50 | **JOHN F. KENNEDY** | Democratic | 34,226,731 | 49.7 | 303 | 62.8 |
| | | Richard M. Nixon | Republican | 34,108,157 | 49.5 | 219 | |
| 1964 | 50 | **LYNDON B. JOHNSON** | Democratic | 43,129,566 | 61.1 | 486 | 61.9 |
| | | Barry M. Goldwater | Republican | 27,178,188 | 38.5 | 52 | |
| 1968 | 50 | **RICHARD M. NIXON** | Republican | 31,785,480 | 43.4 | 301 | 60.9 |
| | | Hubert H. Humphrey | Democratic | 31,275,166 | 42.7 | 191 | |
| | | George C. Wallace | American Independent | 9,906,473 | 13.5 | 46 | |
| 1972 | 50 | **RICHARD M. NIXON** | Republican | 47,169,911 | 60.7 | 520 | 55.2 |
| | | George S. McGovern | Democratic | 29,170,383 | 37.5 | 17 | |
| | | John G. Schmitz | American | 1,099,482 | 1.4 | | |

| Year | Number of States | Candidates | Parties | Popular Vote | % of Popular Vote | Electoral Vote | % Voter Participation |
|---|---|---|---|---|---|---|---|
| 1976 | 50 | **JIMMY CARTER**<br>Gerald R. Ford | Democratic<br>Republican | 40,830,763<br>39,147,793 | 50.1<br>48.0 | 297<br>240 | 53.5 |
| 1980 | 50 | **RONALD REAGAN**<br>Jimmy Carter<br>John B. Anderson<br>Ed Clark | Republican<br>Democratic<br>Independent<br>Libertarian | 43,901,812<br>35,483,820<br>5,719,437<br>921,188 | 50.7<br>41.0<br>6.6<br>1.1 | 489<br>49 | 52.6 |
| 1984 | 50 | **RONALD REAGAN**<br>Walter F. Mondale | Republican<br>Democratic | 54,451,521<br>37,565,334 | 58.8<br>40.6 | 525<br>13 | 53.1 |
| 1988 | 50 | **GEORGE H. W. BUSH**<br>Michael Dukakis | Republican<br>Democratic | 47,917,341<br>41,013,030 | 53.4<br>45.6 | 426<br>111 | 50.1 |
| 1992 | 50 | **BILL CLINTON**<br>George H. W. Bush<br>H. Ross Perot | Democratic<br>Republican<br>Independent | 44,908,254<br>39,102,343<br>19,741,065 | 43.0<br>37.4<br>18.9 | 370<br>168 | 55.0 |
| 1996 | 50 | **BILL CLINTON**<br>Bob Dole<br>H. Ross Perot | Democratic<br>Republican<br>Independent | 47,401,185<br>39,197,469<br>8,085,295 | 49.0<br>41.0<br>8.0 | 379<br>159 | 49.0 |
| 2000 | 50 | **GEORGE W. BUSH**<br>Al Gore<br>Ralph Nader | Republican<br>Democrat<br>Green | 50,455,156<br>50,997,335<br>2,882,897 | 47.9<br>48.4<br>2.7 | 271<br>266 | 50.4 |
| 2004 | 50 | **GEORGE W. BUSH**<br>John F. Kerry | Republican<br>Democrat | 62,040,610<br>59,028,444 | 50.7<br>48.3 | 286<br>251 | 60.7 |
| 2008 | 50 | **BARACK OBAMA**<br>John McCain | Democrat<br>Republican | 69,456,897<br>59,934,814 | 52.92%<br>45.66% | 365<br>173 | 63.0 |

Candidates receiving less than 1 percent of the popular vote have been omitted. Thus the percentage of popular vote given for any election year may not total 100 percent.

Before the passage of the Twelfth Amendment in 1804, the electoral college voted for two presidential candidates; the runner-up became vice president.

## ADMISSION OF STATES

| Order of Admission | State | Date of Admission | Order of Admission | State | Date of Admission |
|---|---|---|---|---|---|
| 1 | Delaware | December 7, 1787 | 26 | Michigan | January 26, 1837 |
| 2 | Pennsylvania | December 12, 1787 | 27 | Florida | March 3, 1845 |
| 3 | New Jersey | December 18, 1787 | 28 | Texas | December 29, 1845 |
| 4 | Georgia | January 2, 1788 | 29 | Iowa | December 28, 1846 |
| 5 | Connecticut | January 9, 1788 | 30 | Wisconsin | May 29, 1848 |
| 6 | Massachusetts | February 7, 1788 | 31 | California | September 9, 1850 |
| 7 | Maryland | April 28, 1788 | 32 | Minnesota | May 11, 1858 |
| 8 | South Carolina | May 23, 1788 | 33 | Oregon | February 14, 1859 |
| 9 | New Hampshire | June 21, 1788 | 34 | Kansas | January 29, 1861 |
| 10 | Virginia | June 25, 1788 | 35 | West Virginia | June 30, 1863 |
| 11 | New York | July 26, 1788 | 36 | Nevada | October 31, 1864 |
| 12 | North Carolina | November 21, 1789 | 37 | Nebraska | March 1, 1867 |
| 13 | Rhode Island | May 29, 1790 | 38 | Colorado | August 1, 1876 |
| 14 | Vermont | March 4, 1791 | 39 | North Dakota | November 2, 1889 |
| 15 | Kentucky | June 1, 1792 | 40 | South Dakota | November 2, 1889 |
| 16 | Tennessee | June 1, 1796 | 41 | Montana | November 8, 1889 |
| 17 | Ohio | March 1, 1803 | 42 | Washington | November 11, 1889 |
| 18 | Louisiana | April 30, 1812 | 43 | Idaho | July 3, 1890 |
| 19 | Indiana | December 11, 1816 | 44 | Wyoming | July 10, 1890 |
| 20 | Mississippi | December 10, 1817 | 45 | Utah | January 4, 1896 |
| 21 | Illinois | December 3, 1818 | 46 | Oklahoma | November 16, 1907 |
| 22 | Alabama | December 14, 1819 | 47 | New Mexico | January 6, 1912 |
| 23 | Maine | March 15, 1820 | 48 | Arizona | February 14, 1912 |
| 24 | Missouri | August 10, 1821 | 49 | Alaska | January 3, 1959 |
| 25 | Arkansas | June 15, 1836 | 50 | Hawaii | August 21, 1959 |

## POPULATION OF THE UNITED STATES

| Year | Number of States | Population | % Increase | Population per Square Mile |
|------|------------------|------------|------------|----------------------------|
| 1790 | 13 | 3,929,214 | | 4.5 |
| 1800 | 16 | 5,308,483 | 35.1 | 6.1 |
| 1810 | 17 | 7,239,881 | 36.4 | 4.3 |
| 1820 | 23 | 9,638,453 | 33.1 | 5.5 |
| 1830 | 24 | 12,866,020 | 33.5 | 7.4 |
| 1840 | 26 | 17,069,453 | 32.7 | 9.8 |
| 1850 | 31 | 23,191,876 | 35.9 | 7.9 |
| 1860 | 33 | 31,443,321 | 35.6 | 10.6 |
| 1870 | 37 | 39,818,449 | 26.6 | 13.4 |
| 1880 | 38 | 50,155,783 | 26.0 | 16.9 |
| 1890 | 44 | 62,947,714 | 25.5 | 21.1 |
| 1900 | 45 | 75,994,575 | 20.7 | 25.6 |
| 1910 | 46 | 91,972,266 | 21.0 | 31.0 |
| 1920 | 48 | 105,710,620 | 14.9 | 35.6 |
| 1930 | 48 | 122,775,046 | 16.1 | 41.2 |
| 1940 | 48 | 131,669,275 | 7.2 | 44.2 |
| 1950 | 48 | 150,697,361 | 14.5 | 50.7 |
| 1960 | 50 | 179,323,175 | 19.0 | 50.6 |
| 1970 | 50 | 203,235,298 | 13.3 | 57.5 |
| 1980 | 50 | 226,504,825 | 11.4 | 64.0 |
| 1985 | 50 | 237,839,000 | 5.0 | 67.2 |
| 1990 | 50 | 250,122,000 | 5.2 | 70.6 |
| 1995 | 50 | 263,411,707 | 5.3 | 74.4 |
| 2000 | 50 | 281,421,906 | 6.8 | 77.0 |
| 2005 | 50 | 296,410,404 | 5.3 | 77.9 |
| 2010 | 50 | 308,745,538 | 9.7 | 87.4 |

## IMMIGRATION TO THE UNITED STATES, FISCAL YEARS 1820–2011

| Year | Number | Year | Number | Year | Number | Year | Number |
|---|---|---|---|---|---|---|---|
| 1820–1989 | 55,457,531 | 1871–80 | 2,812,191 | 1921–30 | 4,107,209 | 1971–80 | 4,493,314 |
| 1820 | 8,385 | 1871 | 321,350 | 1921 | 805,228 | 1971 | 370,478 |
| 1821–30 | 143,439 | 1872 | 404,806 | 1922 | 309,556 | 1972 | 384,685 |
| 1821 | 9,127 | 1873 | 459,803 | 1923 | 522,919 | 1973 | 400,063 |
| 1822 | 6,911 | 1874 | 313,339 | 1924 | 706,896 | 1974 | 394,861 |
| 1823 | 6,354 | 1875 | 227,498 | 1925 | 294,314 | 1975 | 386,914 |
| 1824 | 7,912 | 1876 | 169,986 | 1926 | 304,488 | 1976 | 398,613 |
| 1825 | 10,199 | 1877 | 141,857 | 1927 | 335,175 | 1976 | 103,676 |
| 1826 | 10,837 | 1878 | 138,469 | 1928 | 307,255 | 1977 | 462,315 |
| 1827 | 18,875 | 1879 | 177,826 | 1929 | 279,678 | 1978 | 601,442 |
| 1828 | 27,382 | 1880 | 457,257 | 1930 | 241,700 | 1979 | 460,348 |
| 1829 | 22,520 | 1881–90 | 5,246,613 | 1931–40 | 528,431 | 1980 | 530,639 |
| 1830 | 23,322 | 1881 | 669,431 | 1931 | 97,139 | 1981–90 | 7,338,062 |
| 1831–40 | 599,125 | 1882 | 788,992 | 1932 | 35,576 | 1981 | 596,600 |
| 1831 | 22,633 | 1883 | 603,322 | 1933 | 23,068 | 1982 | 594,131 |
| 1832 | 60,482 | 1884 | 518,592 | 1934 | 29,470 | 1983 | 559,763 |
| 1833 | 58,640 | 1885 | 395,346 | 1935 | 34,956 | 1984 | 543,903 |
| 1834 | 65,365 | 1886 | 334,203 | 1936 | 36,329 | 1985 | 570,009 |
| 1835 | 45,374 | 1887 | 490,109 | 1937 | 50,244 | 1986 | 601,708 |
| 1836 | 76,242 | 1888 | 546,889 | 1938 | 67,895 | 1987 | 601,516 |
| 1837 | 79,340 | 1889 | 444,427 | 1939 | 82,998 | 1988 | 643,025 |
| 1838 | 38,914 | 1890 | 455,302 | 1940 | 70,756 | 1989 | 1,090,924 |
| 1839 | 68,069 | 1891–1900 | 3,687,564 | 1941–50 | 1,035,039 | 1990 | 1,536,483 |
| 1840 | 84,066 | 1891 | 560,319 | 1941 | 51,776 | 1991–2000 | 9,090,857 |
| 1841–50 | 1,713,251 | 1892 | 579,663 | 1942 | 28,781 | 1991 | 1,827,167 |
| 1841 | 80,289 | 1893 | 439,730 | 1943 | 23,725 | 1992 | 973,977 |
| 1842 | 104,565 | 1894 | 285,631 | 1944 | 28,551 | 1993 | 904,292 |
| | | 1895 | 258,536 | 1945 | 38,119 | 1994 | 804,416 |
| | | 1896 | 343,267 | 1946 | 108,721 | | |

| Year | Number | Year | Number | Year | Number | Year | Number |
| --- | --- | --- | --- | --- | --- | --- | --- |
| 1843 | 52,496 | 1897 | 230,832 | 1947 | 147,292 | 1995 | 720,461 |
| 1844 | 78,615 | 1898 | 229,299 | 1948 | 170,570 | 1996 | 915,900 |
| 1845 | 114,371 | 1899 | 311,715 | 1949 | 188,317 | 1997 | 798,378 |
| 1846 | 154,416 | 1900 | 448,572 | 1950 | 249,187 | 1998 | 660,477 |
| 1847 | 234,968 | | | | | 1999 | 644,787 |
| 1848 | 226,527 | **1901–10** | **8,795,386** | **1951–60** | **2,515,479** | 2000 | 841,002 |
| 1849 | 297,024 | 1901 | 487,918 | 1951 | 205,717 | **2001–10** | **10,501,053** |
| 1850 | 369,980 | 1902 | 648,743 | 1952 | 265,520 | 2001 | 1,058,902 |
| | | 1903 | 857,046 | 1953 | 170,434 | 2002 | 1,059,356 |
| **1851–60** | **2,598,214** | 1904 | 812,870 | 1954 | 208,177 | 2003 | 705,827 |
| 1851 | 379,466 | 1905 | 1,026,499 | 1955 | 237,790 | 2004 | 957,883 |
| 1852 | 371,603 | 1906 | 1,100,735 | 1956 | 321,625 | 2005 | 1,122,373 |
| 1853 | 368,645 | 1907 | 1,285,349 | 1957 | 326,867 | 2006 | 1,266,129 |
| 1854 | 427,833 | 1908 | 782,870 | 1958 | 253,265 | 2007 | 1,052,415 |
| 1855 | 200,877 | 1909 | 751,786 | 1959 | 260,686 | 2008 | 1,107,126 |
| 1856 | 200,436 | 1910 | 1,041,570 | 1960 | 265,398 | 2009 | 1,130,818 |
| 1857 | 251,306 | | | | | 2010 | 1,042,625 |
| 1858 | 123,126 | **1911–20** | **5,735,811** | **1961–70** | **3,321,677** | 2011 | 1,062,040 |
| 1859 | 121,282 | 1911 | 878,587 | 1961 | 271,344 | | |
| 1860 | 153,640 | 1912 | 838,172 | 1962 | 283,763 | | |
| | | 1913 | 1,197,892 | 1963 | 306,260 | | |
| **1861–70** | **2,314,824** | 1914 | 1,218,480 | 1964 | 292,248 | | |
| 1861 | 91,918 | 1915 | 326,700 | 1965 | 296,697 | | |
| 1862 | 91,985 | 1916 | 298,826 | 1966 | 323,040 | | |
| 1863 | 176,282 | 1917 | 295,403 | 1967 | 361,972 | | |
| 1864 | 193,418 | 1918 | 110,618 | 1968 | 454,448 | | |
| 1865 | 248,120 | 1919 | 141,132 | 1969 | 358,579 | | |
| 1866 | 318,568 | 1920 | 430,001 | 1970 | 373,326 | | |
| 1867 | 315,722 | | | | | | |
| 1868 | 138,840 | | | | | | |
| 1869 | 352,768 | | | | | | |
| 1870 | 387,203 | | | | | | |

Source: U.S. Department of Homeland Security.

## IMMIGRATION BY REGION AND SELECTED COUNTRY OF LAST RESIDENCE, FISCAL YEARS 1820–2011

| Region and country of last residence | 1820 to 1829 | 1830 to 1839 | 1840 to 1849 | 1850 to 1859 | 1860 to 1869 | 1870 to 1879 | 1880 to 1889 | 1890 to 1899 |
|---|---|---|---|---|---|---|---|---|
| Total | 128,502 | 538,381 | 1,427,337 | 2,814,554 | 2,081,261 | 2,742,137 | 5,248,568 | 3,694,294 |
| Europe | 99,272 | 422,771 | 1,369,259 | 2,619,680 | 1,877,726 | 2,251,878 | 4,638,677 | 3,576,411 |
| Austria-Hungary | — | — | — | — | 3,375 | 60,127 | 314,787 | 534,059 |
| Austria | — | — | — | — | 2,700 | 54,529 | 204,805 | 268,218 |
| Hungary | — | — | — | — | 483 | 5,598 | 109,982 | 203,350 |
| Belgium | 28 | 20 | 3,996 | 5,765 | 5,785 | 6,991 | 18,738 | 19,642 |
| Bulgaria | — | — | — | — | — | — | — | 52 |
| Czechoslovakia | — | — | — | — | — | — | — | — |
| Denmark | 173 | 927 | 671 | 3,227 | 13,553 | 29,278 | 85,342 | 56,671 |
| Finland | — | — | — | — | — | — | — | — |
| France | 7,694 | 39,330 | 75,300 | 81,778 | 35,938 | 71,901 | 48,193 | 35,616 |
| Germany | 5,753 | 124,726 | 385,434 | 976,072 | 723,734 | 751,769 | 1,445,181 | 579,072 |
| Greece | 17 | 49 | 17 | 32 | 51 | 209 | 1,807 | 12,732 |
| Ireland | 51,617 | 170,672 | 656,145 | 1,029,486 | 427,419 | 422,264 | 674,061 | 405,710 |
| Italy | 430 | 2,225 | 1,476 | 8,643 | 9,853 | 46,296 | 267,660 | 603,761 |
| Netherlands | 1,105 | 1,377 | 7,624 | 11,122 | 8,387 | 14,267 | 52,715 | 29,349 |
| Norway-Sweden | 91 | 1,149 | 12,389 | 22,202 | 82,937 | 178,823 | 586,441 | 334,058 |
| Norway | — | — | — | — | 16,068 | 88,644 | 185,111 | 96,810 |
| Sweden | — | — | — | — | 24,224 | 90,179 | 401,330 | 237,248 |
| Poland | 19 | 366 | 105 | 1,087 | 1,886 | 11,016 | 42,910 | 107,793 |
| Portugal | 177 | 820 | 196 | 1,299 | 2,083 | 13,971 | 15,186 | 25,874 |
| Romania | — | — | — | — | — | — | 5,842 | 6,808 |
| Russia | 86 | 280 | 520 | 423 | 1,670 | 35,177 | 182,698 | 450,101 |
| Spain | 2,595 | 2,010 | 1,916 | 8,795 | 6,966 | 5,540 | 3,995 | 9,189 |
| Switzerland | 3,148 | 4,430 | 4,819 | 24,423 | 21,124 | 25,212 | 81,151 | 37,020 |
| United Kingdom | 26,336 | 74,350 | 218,572 | 445,322 | 532,956 | 578,447 | 810,900 | 328,759 |
| Yugoslavia | — | — | — | — | — | — | — | — |
| Other Europe | 3 | 40 | 79 | 4 | 9 | 590 | 1,070 | 145 |

| | | | | | | | | |
|---|---|---|---|---|---|---|---|---|
| Asia | 34 | 55 | 121 | 36,080 | 54,408 | 134,128 | 71,151 | 61,285 |
| China | 3 | 8 | 32 | 35,933 | 54,028 | 133,139 | 65,797 | 15,268 |
| Hong Kong | — | 38 | 33 | 42 | 50 | 166 | 247 | 102 |
| India | 9 | — | — | — | — | — | — | 102 |
| Iran | — | — | — | — | — | — | — | — |
| Israel | — | — | — | — | — | — | — | — |
| Japan | — | — | — | — | 138 | 193 | 1,583 | 13,998 |
| Jordan | — | — | — | — | — | — | — | — |
| Korea | — | — | — | — | — | — | — | — |
| Philippines | — | — | — | — | — | — | — | — |
| Syria | — | — | — | — | — | — | — | — |
| Taiwan | — | — | — | — | — | — | — | — |
| Turkey | 19 | 8 | 45 | 94 | 129 | 382 | 2,478 | 27,510 |
| Vietnam | — | — | — | — | — | — | — | — |
| Other Asia | 3 | 1 | 11 | 11 | 63 | 248 | 1,046 | 4,407 |
| America | 9,655 | 31,905 | 50,516 | 84,145 | 130,292 | 345,010 | 524,826 | 37,350 |
| Canada and Newfoundland | 2,297 | 11,875 | 34,285 | 64,171 | 117,978 | 324,310 | 492,865 | 3,098 |
| Mexico | 3,835 | 7,187 | 3,069 | 3,446 | 1,957 | 5,133 | 2,405 | 734 |
| Caribbean | 3,061 | 11,792 | 11,803 | 12,447 | 8,751 | 14,285 | 27,323 | 31,480 |
| Cuba | — | — | — | — | — | — | — | — |
| Dominican Republic | — | — | — | — | — | — | — | — |
| Haiti | — | — | — | — | — | — | — | — |
| Jamaica | — | — | — | — | — | — | — | — |
| Other Caribbean | 3,061 | 11,792 | 11,803 | 12,447 | 8,751 | 14,285 | 27,323 | 31,480 |
| Central America | 57 | 94 | 297 | 512 | 70 | 173 | 279 | 649 |
| Belize | — | — | — | — | — | — | — | — |
| Costa Rica | — | — | — | — | — | — | — | — |
| El Salvador | — | — | — | — | — | — | — | — |
| Guatemala | — | — | — | — | — | — | — | — |
| Honduras | — | — | — | — | — | — | — | — |
| Nicaragua | — | — | — | — | — | — | — | — |
| Panama | — | — | — | — | — | — | — | — |
| Other Central America | 57 | 94 | 297 | 512 | 70 | 173 | 279 | 649 |
| South America | 405 | 957 | 1,062 | 3,569 | 1,536 | 1,109 | 1,954 | 1,389 |
| Argentina | — | — | — | — | — | — | — | — |
| Bolivia | — | — | — | — | — | — | — | — |

| Region and country of last residence | 1820 to 1829 | 1830 to 1839 | 1840 to 1849 | 1850 to 1859 | 1860 to 1869 | 1870 to 1879 | 1880 to 1889 | 1890 to 1899 |
|---|---|---|---|---|---|---|---|---|
| Brazil | — | — | — | — | — | — | — | — |
| Chile | — | — | — | — | — | — | — | — |
| Colombia | — | — | — | — | — | — | — | — |
| Ecuador | — | — | — | — | — | — | — | — |
| Guyana | — | — | — | — | — | — | — | — |
| Paraguay | — | — | — | — | — | — | — | — |
| Peru | — | — | — | — | — | — | — | — |
| Suriname | — | — | — | — | — | — | — | — |
| Uruguay | — | — | — | — | — | — | — | — |
| Venezuela | — | — | — | — | — | — | — | — |
| Other South America | 405 | 957 | 1,062 | 3,569 | 1,536 | 1,109 | 1,954 | 1,389 |
| Other America | 15 | 50 | 61 | 84 | 407 | 371 | 763 | 432 |
| Africa | | | | | | | | |
| Egypt | — | — | — | — | 4 | 29 | 145 | 51 |
| Ethiopia | — | — | — | — | — | — | — | — |
| Liberia | 1 | 8 | 5 | 7 | 43 | 52 | 21 | 9 |
| Morocco | — | — | — | — | — | — | — | — |
| South Africa | — | — | — | — | 35 | 48 | 23 | 9 |
| Other Africa | 14 | 42 | 56 | 77 | 325 | 242 | 574 | 363 |
| Oceania | — | — | — | — | — | 9,996 | 12,361 | 4,704 |
| Australia | 3 | 7 | 14 | 166 | 187 | 8,930 | 7,250 | 3,098 |
| New Zealand | 2 | 1 | 2 | 15 | — | 39 | 21 | 12 |
| Other Oceania | 1 | 6 | 12 | 151 | 187 | 1,027 | 5,090 | 1,534 |
| Not Specified | 19,523 | 83,593 | 7,366 | 74,399 | 18,241 | 754 | 790 | 14,112 |

| | | | | | | | | |
|---|--:|--:|--:|--:|--:|--:|--:|--:|
| Total | 8,202,388 | 6,347,380 | 4,295,510 | 699,375 | 856,608 | 2,499,268 | 3,213,749 | 6,244,379 |
| Europe | 7,572,569 | 4,985,411 | 2,560,340 | 444,399 | 472,524 | 1,404,973 | 1,133,443 | 668,866 |
| Austria-Hungary | 2,001,376 | 1,154,727 | 60,891 | 12,531 | 13,574 | 113,015 | 27,590 | 20,437 |
| Austria | 532,416 | 589,174 | 31,392 | 5,307 | 8,393 | 81,354 | 17,571 | 15,374 |
| Hungary | 685,567 | 565,553 | 29,499 | 7,224 | 5,181 | 31,661 | 10,019 | 5,063 |
| Belgium | 37,429 | 32,574 | 21,511 | 4,013 | 12,473 | 18,885 | 9,647 | 7,028 |
| Bulgaria | 34,651 | 27,180 | 2,824 | 1,062 | 449 | 97 | 598 | 1,124 |
| Czechoslovakia | — | — | 101,182 | 17,757 | 8,475 | 1,624 | 2,758 | 5,678 |
| Denmark | 61,227 | 45,830 | 34,406 | 3,470 | 4,549 | 10,918 | 9,797 | 4,847 |
| Finland | — | — | 16,922 | 2,438 | 2,230 | 4,923 | 4,310 | 2,569 |
| France | 67,735 | 60,335 | 54,842 | 13,761 | 36,954 | 50,113 | 46,975 | 32,066 |
| Germany | 328,722 | 174,227 | 386,634 | 119,107 | 119,506 | 576,905 | 209,616 | 85,752 |
| Greece | 145,402 | 198,108 | 60,774 | 10,599 | 8,605 | 45,153 | 74,173 | 37,729 |
| Ireland | 344,940 | 166,445 | 202,854 | 28,195 | 15,701 | 47,189 | 37,788 | 22,210 |
| Italy | 1,930,475 | 1,229,916 | 528,133 | 85,053 | 50,509 | 184,576 | 200,111 | 55,562 |
| Netherlands | 42,463 | 46,065 | 29,397 | 7,791 | 13,877 | 46,703 | 37,918 | 11,234 |
| Norway-Sweden | 426,981 | 192,445 | 170,329 | 13,452 | 17,326 | 44,224 | 36,150 | 13,941 |
| Norway | 182,542 | 79,488 | 70,327 | 6,901 | 8,326 | 22,806 | 17,371 | 3,835 |
| Sweden | 244,439 | 112,957 | 100,002 | 6,551 | 9,000 | 21,418 | 18,779 | 10,106 |
| Poland | — | — | 223,316 | 25,555 | 7,577 | 6,465 | 55,742 | 63,483 |
| Portugal | 65,154 | 82,489 | 44,829 | 3,518 | 6,765 | 13,928 | 70,568 | 42,685 |
| Romania | 57,322 | 13,566 | 67,810 | 5,264 | 1,254 | 914 | 2,339 | 24,753 |
| Russia | 1,501,301 | 1,106,998 | 61,604 | 2,463 | 605 | 453 | 2,329 | 33,311 |
| Spain | 24,818 | 53,262 | 47,109 | 3,669 | 2,774 | 6,880 | 40,793 | 22,783 |
| Switzerland | 32,541 | 22,839 | 31,772 | 5,990 | 9,904 | 17,577 | 19,193 | 8,316 |
| United Kingdom | 469,518 | 371,878 | 341,552 | 61,813 | 131,794 | 195,709 | 220,213 | 153,644 |
| Yugoslavia | — | — | 49,215 | 6,920 | 2,039 | 6,966 | 17,990 | 16,267 |
| Other Europe | 514 | 6,527 | 22,434 | 9,978 | 5,584 | 11,756 | 6,845 | 3,447 |
| Asia | 299,836 | 269,736 | 126,740 | 19,231 | 34,532 | 135,844 | 358,605 | 2,391,356 |
| China | 19,884 | 20,916 | 30,648 | 5,874 | 16,072 | 8,836 | 14,060 | 170,897 |
| Hong Kong | — | — | — | — | — | 13,781 | 67,047 | 112,132 |
| India | 3,026 | 3,478 | 2,076 | 554 | 1,692 | 1,850 | 18,638 | 231,649 |
| Iran | — | — | 208 | 198 | 1,144 | 3,195 | 9,059 | 98,141 |
| Israel | — | — | — | — | 98 | 21,376 | 30,911 | 43,669 |

| Region and country of last residence | 1900 to 1909 | 1910 to 1919 | 1920 to 1929 | 1930 to 1939 | 1940 to 1949 | 1950 to 1959 | 1960 to 1969 | 1980 to 1989 |
|---|---|---|---|---|---|---|---|---|
| Japan | 139,712 | 77,125 | 42,057 | 2,683 | 1,557 | 40,651 | 40,956 | 44,150 |
| Jordan | — | — | — | — | — | 4,899 | 9,230 | 28,928 |
| Korea | — | — | — | — | 83 | 4,845 | 27,048 | 322,708 |
| Philippines | — | — | — | 391 | 4,099 | 17,245 | 70,660 | 502,056 |
| Syria | — | — | 5,307 | 2,188 | 1,179 | 1,091 | 2,432 | 14,534 |
| Taiwan | — | — | — | — | — | 721 | 15,657 | 119,051 |
| Turkey | 127,999 | 160,717 | 40,450 | 1,327 | 754 | 2,980 | 9,464 | 19,208 |
| Vietnam | — | — | — | — | — | 290 | 2,949 | 200,632 |
| Other Asia | 9,215 | 7,500 | 5,994 | 6,016 | 7,854 | 14,084 | 40,494 | 483,601 |
| America | 277,809 | 1,070,539 | 1,591,278 | 230,319 | 328,435 | 921,610 | 1,674,172 | 2,695,329 |
| Canada and Newfoundland | 123,067 | 708,715 | 949,286 | 162,703 | 160,911 | 353,169 | 433,128 | 156,313 |
| Mexico | 31,188 | 185,334 | 498,945 | 32,709 | 56,158 | 273,847 | 441,824 | 1,009,586 |
| Caribbean | 100,960 | 120,860 | 83,482 | 18,052 | 46,194 | 115,661 | 427,235 | 790,109 |
| Cuba | — | — | 12,769 | 10,641 | 25,976 | 73,221 | 202,030 | 132,552 |
| Dominican Republic | — | — | — | 1,026 | 4,802 | 10,219 | 83,552 | 221,552 |
| Haiti | — | — | — | 156 | 823 | 3,787 | 28,992 | 121,406 |
| Jamaica | — | — | — | — | — | 7,397 | 62,218 | 193,374 |
| Other Caribbean | 100,960 | 120,860 | 70,713 | 6,229 | 14,593 | 21,037 | 50,443 | 120,725 |
| Central America | 7,341 | 15,692 | 16,511 | 6,840 | 20,135 | 40,201 | 98,560 | 339,376 |
| Belize | 77 | 40 | 285 | 193 | 433 | 1,133 | 4,185 | 14,964 |
| Costa Rica | — | — | — | 431 | 1,965 | 4,044 | 17,975 | 25,017 |
| El Salvador | — | — | — | 597 | 4,885 | 5,094 | 14,405 | 137,418 |
| Guatemala | — | — | — | 423 | 1,303 | 4,197 | 14,357 | 58,847 |
| Honduras | — | — | — | 679 | 1,874 | 5,320 | 15,078 | 39,071 |
| Nicaragua | — | — | — | 405 | 4,393 | 7,812 | 10,383 | 31,102 |
| Panama | — | — | — | 1,452 | 5,282 | 12,601 | 22,177 | 32,957 |
| Other Central America | 7,264 | 15,652 | 16,226 | 2,660 | — | — | — | — |

| | | | | | | | | |
|---|---|---|---|---|---|---|---|---|
| South America | 15,253 | 39,938 | 43,025 | 9,990 | 19,662 | 78,418 | 250,754 | 399,862 |
| Argentina | — | — | — | 1,067 | 3,108 | 16,346 | 49,384 | 23,442 |
| Bolivia | — | — | — | 50 | 893 | 2,759 | 6,205 | 9,798 |
| Brazil | — | — | 4,627 | 1,468 | 3,653 | 11,547 | 29,238 | 22,944 |
| Chile | — | — | — | 347 | 1,320 | 4,669 | 12,384 | 19,749 |
| Colombia | — | — | — | 1,027 | 3,454 | 15,567 | 68,371 | 105,494 |
| Ecuador | — | — | — | 244 | 2,207 | 8,574 | 34,107 | 48,015 |
| Guyana | — | — | — | 131 | 596 | 1,131 | 4,546 | 85,886 |
| Paraguay | — | — | — | 33 | 85 | 576 | 1,249 | 3,518 |
| Peru | — | — | — | 321 | 1,273 | 5,980 | 19,783 | 49,958 |
| Suriname | — | — | — | 25 | 130 | 299 | 612 | 1,357 |
| Uruguay | — | — | — | 112 | 754 | 1,026 | 4,089 | 7,235 |
| Venezuela | — | — | — | 1,155 | 2,182 | 9,927 | 20,758 | 22,405 |
| Other South America | 15,253 | 39,938 | 38,398 | 4,010 | 7 | 17 | 28 | 61 |
| Other America | 6,326 | 8,867 | 29 | 25 | 25,375 | 60,314 | 22,671 | 83 |
| Africa | — | — | 6,362 | 2,120 | 6,720 | 13,016 | 23,780 | 141,990 |
| Egypt | — | — | 1,063 | 781 | 1,613 | 1,996 | 5,581 | 26,744 |
| Ethiopia | — | — | — | 10 | 28 | 302 | 804 | 12,927 |
| Liberia | — | — | — | 35 | 37 | 289 | 841 | 6,420 |
| Morocco | — | — | — | 73 | 879 | 2,703 | 2,880 | 3,471 |
| South Africa | 6,326 | 8,867 | 5,299 | 312 | 1,022 | 2,278 | 4,360 | 15,505 |
| Other Africa | 12,355 | 12,339 | 9,860 | 909 | 3,141 | 5,448 | 9,314 | 76,923 |
| Oceania | 11,191 | 11,280 | 8,404 | 3,306 | 14,262 | 11,353 | 23,630 | 41,432 |
| Australia | — | — | 935 | 2,260 | 11,201 | 8,275 | 14,986 | 16,901 |
| New Zealand | 1,164 | 1,059 | 521 | 790 | 2,351 | 1,799 | 3,775 | 6,129 |
| Other Oceania | 33,493 | 488 | 930 | 256 | 710 | 1,279 | 4,869 | 18,402 |
| Not Specified | | | | — | 135 | 12,472 | 119 | 305,406 |

| Region and country of last residence | 1990 to 1999 | 2000 to 2009 | 2010 | 2011 |
|---|---|---|---|---|
| Total | 9,775,398 | 10,299,430 | 1,042,625 | 1,062,040 |
| Europe | 1,348,612 | 1,349,609 | 95,429 | 90,712 |
| Austria-Hungary | 27,529 | 33,929 | 4,325 | 4,703 |
| Austria | 18,234 | 21,151 | 3,319 | 3,654 |
| Hungary | 9,295 | 12,778 | 1,006 | 1,049 |
| Belgium | 7,077 | 8,157 | 732 | 700 |
| Bulgaria | 16,948 | 40,003 | 2,465 | 2,549 |
| Czechoslovakia | 8,970 | 18,691 | 1,510 | 1,374 |
| Denmark | 6,189 | 6,049 | 545 | 473 |
| Finland | 3,970 | 3,970 | 414 | 398 |
| France | 35,945 | 45,637 | 4,339 | 3,967 |
| Germany | 92,207 | 122,373 | 7,929 | 7,072 |
| Greece | 25,403 | 16,841 | 966 | 1,196 |
| Ireland | 65,384 | 15,642 | 1,610 | 1,533 |
| Italy | 75,992 | 28,329 | 2,956 | 2,670 |
| Netherlands | 13,345 | 17,351 | 1,520 | 1,258 |
| Norway-Sweden | 17,825 | 19,382 | 1,662 | 1,530 |
| Norway | 5,211 | 4,599 | 363 | 405 |
| Sweden | 12,614 | 14,783 | 1,299 | 1,125 |
| Poland | 172,249 | 117,921 | 7,391 | 6,634 |
| Portugal | 25,497 | 11,479 | 759 | 878 |
| Romania | 48,136 | 52,154 | 3,735 | 3,679 |
| Russia | 433,427 | 167,152 | 7,502 | 8,548 |
| Spain | 18,443 | 17,695 | 2,040 | 2,319 |
| Switzerland | 11,768 | 12,173 | 868 | 861 |
| United Kingdom | 156,182 | 171,979 | 14,781 | 13,443 |
| Yugoslavia | 57,039 | 131,831 | 4,772 | 4,611 |
| Other Europe | 29,087 | 290,871 | 22,608 | 20,316 |

| | | | | |
|---|---|---|---|---|
| Asia | 2,859,899 | 3,470,835 | 410,209 | 438,580 |
| China | 342,058 | 591,711 | 67,634 | 83,603 |
| Hong Kong | 116,894 | 57,583 | 3,263 | 3,149 |
| India | 352,528 | 590,464 | 66,185 | 66,331 |
| Iran | 76,899 | 76,755 | 9,078 | 9,015 |
| Israel | 41,340 | 54,081 | 5,172 | 4,389 |
| Japan | 66,582 | 84,552 | 7,100 | 6,751 |
| Jordan | 42,755 | 53,550 | 9,327 | 8,211 |
| Korea | 179,770 | 209,758 | 22,022 | 22,748 |
| Philippines | 534,338 | 545,463 | 56,399 | 55,251 |
| Syria | 22,906 | 30,807 | 7,424 | 7,983 |
| Taiwan | 132,647 | 92,657 | 6,785 | 6,206 |
| Turkey | 38,687 | 48,394 | 7,435 | 9,040 |
| Vietnam | 275,379 | 289,616 | 30,065 | 33,486 |
| Other Asia | 637,116 | 745,444 | 112,320 | 122,417 |
| America | 5,137,743 | 4,441,529 | 426,981 | 423,277 |
| Canada and Newfoundland | 194,788 | 236,349 | 19,491 | 19,506 |
| Mexico | 2,757,418 | 1,704,166 | 138,717 | 142,823 |
| Caribbean | 1,004,687 | 1,053,357 | 139,389 | 133,012 |
| Cuba | 159,037 | 271,742 | 33,372 | 36,261 |
| Dominican Republic | 359,818 | 291,492 | 53,890 | 46,036 |
| Haiti | 177,446 | 203,827 | 22,336 | 21,802 |
| Jamaica | 177,143 | 172,523 | 19,439 | 19,298 |
| Other Caribbean | 181,243 | 113,773 | 10,352 | 9,615 |
| Central America | 610,189 | 591,130 | 43,597 | 43,249 |
| Belize | 12,600 | 9,682 | 997 | 933 |
| Costa Rica | 17,054 | 21,571 | 2,306 | 2,230 |
| El Salvador | 273,017 | 251,237 | 18,547 | 18,477 |
| Guatemala | 126,043 | 156,992 | 10,263 | 10,795 |
| Honduras | 72,880 | 63,513 | 6,381 | 6,053 |

| Region and country of last residence | 1990 to 1999 | 2000 to 2009 | 2010 | 2011 |
|---|---|---|---|---|
| Nicaragua | 80,446 | 70,015 | 3,476 | 3,314 |
| Panama | 28,149 | 18,120 | 1,627 | 1,447 |
| Other Central America | — | | | - |
| South America | 570,624 | 856,508 | 85,783 | 84,687 |
| Argentina | 30,065 | 47,955 | 4,312 | 4,335 |
| Bolivia | 18,111 | 21,921 | 2,211 | 2,113 |
| Brazil | 50,744 | 115,404 | 12,057 | 11,643 |
| Chile | 18,200 | 19,792 | 1,940 | 1,854 |
| Colombia | 137,985 | 236,570 | 21,861 | 22,130 |
| Ecuador | 81,358 | 107,977 | 11,463 | 11,068 |
| Guyana | 74,407 | 70,373 | 6,441 | 6,288 |
| Paraguay | 6,082 | 4,623 | 449 | 501 |
| Peru | 110,117 | 137,614 | 14,063 | 13,836 |
| Suriname | 2,285 | 2,363 | 202 | 167 |
| Uruguay | 6,062 | 9,827 | 1,286 | 1,521 |
| Venezuela | 35,180 | 82,087 | 9,497 | 9,229 |
| Other South America | 28 | 2 | 1 | 2 |
| Other America | 37 | 19 | 4 | - |
| Africa | 346,416 | 759,734 | 98,246 | 97,429 |
| Egypt | 44,604 | 81,564 | 9,822 | 9,096 |
| Ethiopia | 40,097 | 87,207 | 13,853 | 13,985 |
| Liberia | 13,587 | 23,316 | 2,924 | 3,117 |
| Morocco | 15,768 | 40,844 | 4,847 | 4,249 |
| South Africa | 21,964 | 32,221 | 2,705 | 2,754 |
| Other Africa | 210,396 | 494,582 | 64,095 | 64,228 |
| Oceania | 56,800 | 65,793 | 5,946 | 5,825 |
| Australia | 24,288 | 32,728 | 3,077 | 3,062 |
| New Zealand | 8,600 | 12,495 | 1,046 | 1,006 |
| Other Oceania | 23,912 | 20,570 | 1,823 | 1,757 |
| Not Specified | 25,928 | 211,930 | 5,814 | 6,217 |

— Represents zero or not available.

## PRESIDENTS, VICE PRESIDENTS,
## AND SECRETARIES OF STATE

| | President | Vice President | Secretary of State |
|---|---|---|---|
| 1. | George Washington, Federalist 1789 | John Adams, Federalist 1789 | Thomas Jefferson 1789 Edmund Randolph 1794 Timothy Pickering 1795 |
| 2. | John Adams, Federalist 1797 | Thomas Jefferson, Dem.-Rep. 1797 | Timothy Pickering 1797 John Marshall 1800 |
| 3. | Thomas Jefferson, Dem.-Rep. 1801 | Aaron Burr, Dem.-Rep. 1801 George Clinton, Dem.-Rep. 1805 | James Madison 1801 |
| 4. | James Madison, Dem.-Rep. 1809 | George Clinton, Dem.-Rep. 1809 Elbridge Gerry, Dem.-Rep. 1813 | Robert Smith 1809 James Monroe 1811 |
| 5. | James Monroe, Dem.-Rep. 1817 | Daniel D. Tompkins, Dem.-Rep. 1817 | John Q. Adams 1817 |
| 6. | John Quincy Adams, Dem.-Rep. 1825 | John C. Calhoun, Dem.-Rep. 1825 | Henry Clay 1825 |
| 7. | Andrew Jackson, Democratic 1829 | John C. Calhoun, Democratic 1829 Martin Van Buren, Democratic 1833 | Martin Van Buren 1829 Edward Livingston 1831 Louis McLane 1833 John Forsyth 1834 |
| 8. | Martin Van Buren, Democratic 1837 | Richard M. Johnson, Democratic 1837 | John Forsyth 1837 |
| 9. | William H. Harrison, Whig 1841 | John Tyler, Whig 1841 | Daniel Webster 1841 |

| | President | Vice President | Secretary of State |
|---|---|---|---|
| 10. | John Tyler, Whig and Democratic 1841 | None | Daniel Webster 1841<br>Hugh S. Legaré 1843<br>Abel P. Upshur 1843<br>John C. Calhoun 1844 |
| 11. | James K. Polk, Democratic 1845 | George M. Dallas, Democratic 1845 | James Buchanan 1845 |
| 12. | Zachary Taylor, Whig 1849 | Millard Fillmore, Whig 1848 | John M. Clayton 1849 |
| 13. | Millard Fillmore, Whig 1850 | None | Daniel Webster 1850<br>Edward Everett 1852 |
| 14. | Franklin Pierce, Democratic 1853 | William R. King, Democratic 1853 | William L. Marcy 1853 |
| 15. | James Buchanan, Democratic 1857 | John C. Breckinridge, Democratic 1857 | Lewis Cass 1857<br>Jeremiah S. Black 1860 |
| 16. | Abraham Lincoln, Republican 1861 | Hannibal Hamlin, Republican 1861<br>Andrew Johnson, Unionist 1865 | William H. Seward 1861 |
| 17. | Andrew Johnson, Unionist 1865 | None | William H. Seward 1865 |
| 18. | Ulysses S. Grant, Republican 1869 | Schuyler Colfax, Republican 1869<br>Henry Wilson, Republican 1873 | Elihu B. Washburne 1869<br>Hamilton Fish 1869 |
| 19. | Rutherford B. Hayes, Republican 1877 | William A. Wheeler, Republican 1877 | William M. Evarts 1877 |

| | President | Vice President | Secretary of State |
|---|---|---|---|
| 20. | James A. Garfield, Republican 1881 | Chester A. Arthur, Republican 1881 | James G. Blaine 1881 |
| 21. | Chester A. Arthur, Republican 1881 | None | Frederick T. Frelinghuysen 1881 |
| 22. | Grover Cleveland, Democratic 1885 | Thomas A. Hendricks, Democratic 1885 | Thomas F. Bayard 1885 |
| 23. | Benjamin Harrison, Republican 1889 | Levi P. Morton, Republican 1889 | James G. Blaine 1889<br>John W. Foster 1892 |
| 24. | Grover Cleveland, Democratic 1893 | Adlai E. Stevenson, Democratic 1893 | Walter Q. Gresham 1893<br>Richard Olney 1895 |
| 25. | William McKinley, Republican 1897 | Garret A. Hobart, Republican 1897<br>Theodore Roosevelt, Republican 1901 | John Sherman 1897<br>William R. Day 1898<br>John Hay 1898 |
| 26. | Theodore Roosevelt, Republican 1901 | Charles Fairbanks, Republican 1905 | John Hay 1901<br>Elihu Root 1905<br>Robert Bacon 1909 |
| 27. | William H. Taft, Republican 1909 | James S. Sherman, Republican 1909 | Philander C. Knox 1909 |
| 28. | Woodrow Wilson, Democratic 1913 | Thomas R. Marshall, Democratic 1913 | William J. Bryan 1913<br>Robert Lansing 1915<br>Bainbridge Colby 1920 |
| 29. | Warren G. Harding, Republican 1921 | Calvin Coolidge, Republican 1921 | Charles E. Hughes 1921 |
| 30. | Calvin Coolidge, Republican 1923 | Charles G. Dawes, Republican 1925 | Charles E. Hughes 1923<br>Frank B. Kellogg 1925 |

| | President | Vice President | Secretary of State |
|---|---|---|---|
| 31. | Herbert Hoover, Republican 1929 | Charles Curtis, Republican 1929 | Henry L. Stimson 1929 |
| 32. | Franklin D. Roosevelt, Democratic 1933 | John Nance Garner, Democratic 1933 Henry A. Wallace, Democratic 1941 Harry S. Truman, Democratic 1945 | Cordell Hull 1933 Edward R. Stettinius, Jr. 1944 |
| 33. | Harry S. Truman, Democratic 1945 | Alben W. Barkley, Democratic 1949 | Edward R. Stettinius, Jr. 1945 James F. Byrnes 1945 George C. Marshall 1947 Dean G. Acheson 1949 |
| 34. | Dwight D. Eisenhower, Republican 1953 | Richard M. Nixon, Republican 1953 | John F. Dulles 1953 Christian A. Herter 1959 |
| 35. | John F. Kennedy, Democratic 1961 | Lyndon B. Johnson, Democratic 1961 | Dean Rusk 1961 |
| 36. | Lyndon B. Johnson, Democratic 1963 | Hubert H. Humphrey, Democratic 1965 | Dean Rusk 1963 |
| 37. | Richard M. Nixon, Republican 1969 | Spiro T. Agnew, Republican 1969 Gerald R. Ford, Republican 1973 | William P. Rogers 1969 Henry Kissinger 1973 |
| 38. | Gerald R. Ford, Republican 1974 | Nelson Rockefeller, Republican 1974 | Henry Kissinger 1974 |
| 39. | Jimmy Carter, Democratic 1977 | Walter Mondale, Democratic 1977 | Cyrus Vance 1977 Edmund Muskie 1980 |

|  | *President* | *Vice President* | *Secretary of State* |
|---|---|---|---|
| 40. | Ronald Reagan, Republican 1981 | George H. W. Bush, Republican 1981 | Alexander Haig 1981<br>George Schultz 1982 |
| 41. | George H. W. Bush, Republican 1989 | J. Danforth Quayle, Republican 1989 | James A. Baker 1989<br>Lawrence Eagleburger 1992 |
| 42. | William J. Clinton, Democratic 1993 | Albert Gore, Jr., Democratic 1993 | Warren Christopher 1993<br>Madeleine Albright 1997 |
| 43. | George W. Bush, Republican 2001 | Richard B. Cheney, Republican 2001 | Colin L. Powell 2001<br>Condoleezza Rice 2005 |
| 44. | Barack Obama, Democratic 2009 | Joseph R. Biden, Democratic 2009 | Hillary Rodham Clinton 2009 |

# FURTHER READINGS

## CHAPTER 17

The most comprehensive treatment of Reconstruction is Eric Foner's *Reconstruction: America's Unfinished Revolution, 1863–1877* (1988). On Andrew Johnson, see Hans L. Trefousse's *Andrew Johnson: A Biography* (1989) and David D. Stewart's *Impeached: The Trial of Andrew Johnson and the Fight for Lincoln's Legacy* (2009). An excellent brief biography of Grant is Josiah Bunting III's *Ulysses S. Grant* (2004).

Scholars have been sympathetic to the aims and motives of the Radical Republicans. See, for instance, Herman Belz's *Reconstructing the Union: Theory and Policy during the Civil War* (1969) and Richard Nelson Current's *Those Terrible Carpetbaggers: A Reinterpretation* (1988). The ideology of the Radicals is explored in Michael Les Benedict's *A Compromise of Principle: Congressional Republicans and Reconstruction, 1863–1869* (1974). On the black political leaders, see Phillip Dray's *Capitol Men: The Epic Story of Reconstruction through the Lives of the First Black Congressmen* (2008).

The intransigence of southern white attitudes is examined in Michael Perman's *Reunion without Compromise: The South and Reconstruction, 1865–1868* (1973) and Dan T. Carter's *When the War Was Over: The Failure of Self-Reconstruction in the South, 1865–1867* (1985). Allen W. Trelease's *White Terror: The Ku Klux Klan Conspiracy and Southern Reconstruction* (1971) covers the various organizations that practiced vigilante tactics. On the massacre of African Americans, see Charles Lane's *The Day Freedom Died: The Colfax Massacre, the Supreme Court, and the Betrayal of Reconstruction* (2008). The difficulties former slaves had in adjusting to the new labor system are documented in James L. Roark's *Masters without Slaves: Southern Planters in the Civil War and Reconstruction* (1977). Books on southern politics during Reconstruction include Michael Perman's *The Road to Redemption: Southern Politics, 1869–1879* (1984), Terry L. Seip's *The South Returns to Congress: Men, Economic Measures, and Intersectional Relationships, 1868–1879* (1983), and Mark W. Summers's *Railroads, Reconstruction, and the Gospel of Prosperity: Aid under the Radical Republicans, 1865–1877* (1984).

Numerous works study the freed blacks' experience in the South. Start with Leon F. Litwack's *Been in the Storm So Long: The Aftermath of Slavery* (1979). Joel Williamson's *After Slavery: The Negro in South Carolina during Reconstruction, 1861–1877* (1965) argues that South Carolina blacks took an active role in pursuing their political and economic rights. The Freedmen's Bureau is explored in William S. McFeely's *Yankee Stepfather: General O. O. Howard and the Freedmen* (1968). The situation of freed slave women is discussed in Jacqueline Jones's *Labor of Love, Labor of Sorrow: Black Women, Work and the Family, from Slavery to the Present* (1985).

The politics of corruption outside the South is depicted in William S. McFeely's *Grant: A Biography* (1981). The political maneuvers of the election of 1876 and the resultant crisis and compromise are explained in Michael Holt's *By One Vote: The Disputed Presidential Election of 1876* (2008).

# CHAPTER 18

For masterly syntheses of post–Civil War industrial development, see Walter Licht's *Industrializing America: The Nineteenth Century* (1995) and Maury Klein's *The Genesis of Industrial America, 1870–1920* (2007). On the growth of railroads, see Richard White's *Railroaded: The Transcontinentals and the Making of Modern America* (2011) and Albro Martin's *Railroad Triumphant: The Growth, Rejection, and Rebirth of a Vital American Force* (1992).

On entrepreneurship in the iron and steel sector, see Thomas J. Misa's *A Nation of Steel: The Making of Modern America, 1865–1925* (1995). The best biographies of the leading business tycoons are Ron Chernow's *Titan: The Life of John D. Rockefeller, Sr.* (1998), David Nasaw's *Andrew Carnegie* (2006), and Jean Strouse's *Morgan: American Financier* (1999). Nathan Rosenberg's *Technology and American Economic Growth* (1972) documents the growth of invention during the period.

For an overview of the struggle of workers to organize unions, see Philip Bray's *There Is Power in a Union: The Epic Story of Labor in America* (2010). On the 1877 railroad strike, see David O. Stowell's *Streets, Railroad, and the Great Strike of 1877* (1999). For the role of women in the changing workplace, see Alice Kessler-Harris's *Out to Work: A History of Wage-Earning Women in the United States* (1982) and Susan E. Kennedy's *If All We Did Was to Weep at Home: A History of White Working-Class Women in American* (1979). On Mother Jones, see Elliott J. Gorn's *Mother Jones: The Most Dangerous Woman in America* (2001). To trace the rise of socialism among organized workers, see Nick Salvatore's *Eugene V. Debs: Citizen and Socialist* (1982). The key strikes are discussed in Paul Arvich's *The Haymarket Tragedy* (1984) and Paul Krause's *The Battle for Homestead, 1880–1892: Politics, Culture, and Steel* (1992).

# CHAPTER 19

The classic study of the emergence of the New South remains C. Vann Woodward's *Origins of the New South, 1877–1913* (1951). A more recent treatment of southern society after the end of Reconstruction is Edward L. Ayers's *Southern Crossing: A History of the American South, 1877–1906* (1995). A thorough survey of industrialization in the South is James C. Cobb's *Industrialization and Southern Society, 1877–1984* (1984).

C. Vann Woodward's *The Strange Career of Jim Crow,* commemorative ed. (2002), remains the standard on southern race relations. Some of Woodward's points are challenged in Howard N. Rabinowitz's *Race Relations in the Urban South, 1865–1890* (1978). Leon F. Litwack's *Trouble in Mind: Black Southerners in the Age of Jim Crow* (1998) treats the rise of legal segregation, while Michael Perman's *Struggle for Mastery: Disfranchisement in the South, 1888–1908* (2001) surveys efforts to keep African Americans from voting. An award-winning study of white women and the race issue is Glenda Elizabeth Gilmore's *Gender and Jim Crow: Women and the Politics of White Supremacy in North Carolina, 1896–1920* (1996). On W. E. B. Du Bois, see David Levering Lewis's *W. E. B. Du Bois: Biography of a Race, 1868–1919* (1993). On Booker T. Washing-ton, see Robert J. Norrell's *Up from History: The Life of Booker T. Washington* (2009).

For stimulating reinterpretations of the frontier and the development of the West, see William Cronon's *Nature's Metropolis: Chicago and the Great West* (1991), Patricia Nelson Limer-ick's *The Legacy of Conquest: The Unbroken Past of the American West* (1987), Richard White's *"It's Your Misfortune and None of My Own": A New History of the American West* (1991), and Walter Nugent's *Into the West: The Story of Its People* (1999). An excellent overview is James M. McPher-son's *Into the West: From Reconstruction to the Final Days of the American Frontier* (2006).

The role of African Americans in western settlement is the focus of William Loren Katz's *The Black West: A Documentary and Pictorial History of the African American Role in the West-ward Expansion of the United States,* rev. ed. (2005), and Nell Irvin Painter's *Exodusters: Black Migration to Kansas after Reconstruction* (1977). The best account of the conflicts between Indians and whites is Robert M. Utley's *The Indian Frontier of the American West, 1846–1890* (1984). On the Battle of the Little Bighorn, see Nathaniel Philbrick's *The Last Stand: Custer, Sitting Bull, and the Battle of the Little Bighorn* (2010). On Crazy Horse, see Thomas Powers's *The Killing of Crazy Horse* (2010). For a presentation of the Native American side of the story, see Peter Nabokov's *Native American Testimony: A Chronicle of Indian-White Relations from Prophecy to the Present, 1492–2000,* rev. ed. (1999). On the demise of the buffalo herds, see Andrew C. Isenberg's *The Destruction of the Bison: An Environmental History, 1750–1920* (2000).

## CHAPTER 20

For a survey of urbanization, see David R. Goldfield's *Urban America: A History,* 2nd ed. (1989). Gunther Barth discusses the emergence of a new urban culture in *City People: The Rise of Modern City Culture in Nineteenth-Century America* (1980). John Bodnar offers a synthesis of the urban immigrant experience in *The Transplanted: A History of Immigrants in Urban America* (1985). See also Roger Daniels's *Guarding the Golden Door: American Immigration Policy and Immigrants since 1882* (2004). Walter Nugent's *Crossings: The Great Transatlantic Migrations, 1870–1914* (1992) provides a wealth of demographic information and insight. Efforts to stop Chi-nese immigration are described in Erika Lee's *At America's Gates: Chinese Immigration during the Exclusion Era* (2003).

On urban environments and sanitary reforms, see Martin V. Melosi's *The Sanitary City: Urban Infrastructure in America from Colonial Times to the Present* (2000), Joel A. Tarr's *The Search for the Ultimate Sink: Urban Pollution in Historical Perspective* (1996), and Suellen Hoy's *Chasing Dirt: The American Pursuit of Cleanliness* (1995).

For the growth of urban leisure and sports, see Roy Rosenzweig's *Eight Hours for What We Will: Workers and Leisure in an Industrial City, 1870–1920* (1983) and Steven A. Riess's *City Games: The Evolution of American Urban Society and the Rise of Sports* (1989). Saloon culture is examined in Madelon Powers's *Faces along the Bar: Lore and Order in the Workingman's Saloon, 1870–1920* (1998).

On the impact of the theory of evolution, see Barry Werth's *Banquet at Delmonico's: Great Minds, the Gilded Age, and the Triumph of Evolution in America* (2009). On the rise of realism in thought and the arts during the second half of the nineteenth century, see David E. Shi's *Facing Facts: Realism in American Thought and Culture, 1850–1920* (1995). Pragmatism is the focus of Louis Menand's *The Metaphysical Club: A Story of Ideas in America* (2001).

# CHAPTER 21

Two good overviews of the Gilded Age are Sean Cashman's *America in the Gilded Age: From the Death of Lincoln to the Rise of Theodore Roosevelt* (1984) and Mark Summers's *The Gilded Age or, The Hazard of New Functions* (1996). Nell Irvin Painter's *Standing at Armageddon: The United States, 1877–1919* (1987) focuses on the experience of the working class. For a stimulating overview of the political, social, and economic trends during the Gilded Age, see Jack Beatty's *Age of Betrayal: The Triumph of Money in America, 1865–1900* (2007). On the development of city rings and bosses, see Kenneth D. Ackerman's *Boss Tweed: The Rise and Fall of the Corrupt Pol Who Conceived the Soul of Modern New York* (2005). Excellent presidential biographies include Hans L. Trefousse's *Rutherford B. Hayes* (2002), Zachary Karabell's *Chester Alan Arthur* (2004), Henry F. Graff's *Grover Cleveland* (2002), and Kevin Phillips's *William McKinley* (2003). On the political culture of the Gilded Age, see Charles Calhoun's *Minority Victory: Gilded Age Politics and the Front Porch Campaign of 1888* (2008).

Scholars have also examined various Gilded Age issues and interest groups. Gerald W. McFarland's *Mugwumps, Morals, and Politics, 1884–1920* (1975) examines the issue of reforming government service. Tom E. Terrill's *The Tariff, Politics, and American Foreign Policy, 1874–1901* (1973) lends clarity to that complex issue. The finances of the Gilded Age are covered in Walter T. K. Nugent's *Money and American Society, 1865–1880* (1968).

A balanced account of Populism is Charles Postel's *The Populist Vision* (2007). The election of 1896 is the focus of R. Hal Williams's *Realigning America: McKinley, Bryan, and the Remarkable Election of 1896* (2010). On the role of religion in the agrarian protest movements, see Joe Creech's *Righteous Indignation: Religion and the Populist Revolution* (2006). The best biography of Bryan is Michael Kazin's *A Godly Hero: The Life of William Jennings Bryan* (2006). For an innovative of the politics and culture of the Gilded Age, see Jackson Lears, *Rebirth of a Nation: The Making of Modern America, 1877–1920* (2009).

# CHAPTER 22

An excellent survey of the diplomacy of the era is Charles S. Campbell's *The Transformation of American Foreign Relations, 1865–1900* (1976). For background on the events of the 1890s, see David Healy's *U.S. Expansionism: The Imperialist Urge in the 1890s* (1970). The dispute over American policy in Hawaii is covered in Thomas J. Osborne's *"Empire Can Wait": American Opposition to Hawaiian Annexation, 1893–1898* (1981).

Ivan Musicant's *Empire by Default: The Spanish-American War and the Dawn of the American Century* (1998) is the most comprehensive volume on the conflict. A colorful treatment of the powerful men promoting war is Evan Thomas's *The War Lovers: Roosevelt, Lodge, Mahan, and the Rush to Empire, 1898* (2010). For the war's aftermath in the Philippines, see Stuart Creighton Miller's *"Benevolent Assimilation": The American Conquest of the Philippines, 1899–1903* (1982). Robert L. Beisner's *Twelve against Empire: The Anti-Imperialists, 1898–1900* (1968) handles the debate over annexation. On the Philippine-American War, see David J. Silbey's *A War of Frontier and Empire: The Philippine-American War, 1899–1902* (2007).

A good introduction to American interest in China is Michael H. Hunt's *The Making of a Special Relationship: The United States and China to 1914* (1983). Kenton J. Clymer's *John Hay: The Gentleman as Diplomat* (1975) examines the role of this key secretary of state in forming policy.

For U.S. policy in the Caribbean and Central America, see Walter LaFeber's *Inevitable Revolutions: The United States in Central America*, 2nd ed. (1993). David McCullough's *The Path between the Seas: The Creation of the Panama Canal, 1870–1914* (1977) presents an admiring account of how the United States secured the Panama Canal. A more sober assessment is Julie Greene's *The Canal Builders: Making America's Empire at the Panama Canal* (2009).

## CHAPTER 23

Splendid analyses of progressivism can be found in John Whiteclay Chambers II's *The Tyranny of Change: America in the Progressive Era, 1890–1920*, rev. ed. (2000), John M. Cooper's *Pivotal Decades: The United States, 1900–1920* (1990), Steven J. Diner's *A Very Different Age: Americans of the Progressive Era* (1997), Maureen A. Flanagan's *America Reformed: Progressives and Progressivisms, 1890–1920* (2006), Michael McGerr's *A Fierce Discontent: The Rise and Fall of the Progressive Movement in America* (2003), and David Traxel's *Crusader Nation: The United States in Peace and the Great War, 1898–1920* (2006). On Ida Tarbell and the muckrakers, see Steve Weinberg's *Taking on the Trust: The Epic Battle of Ida Tarbell and John D. Rockefeller* (2008). The evolution of government policy toward business is examined in Martin J. Sklar's *The Corporate Reconstruction of American Capitalism, 1890–1916: The Market, the Law, and Politics* (1988). Mina Carson's *Settlement Folk: Social Thought and the American Settlement Movement, 1885–1930* (1990) and Jack M. Holl's *Juvenile Reform in the Progressive Era: William R. George and the Junior Republic Movement* (1971) examine the social problems in the cities. Robert Kanigel's *The One Best Way: Frederick Winslow Taylor and the Enigma of Efficiency* (1997) highlights the role of efficiency in the Progressive Era.

An excellent study of the role of women in progressivism's emphasis on social justice is Kathryn Kish Sklar's *Florence Kelley and the Nation's Work: The Rise of Women's Political Culture, 1830–1900* (1995). On the tragic fire at the Triangle Shirtwaist Company, see David Von Drehle's *Triangle: The Fire That Changed America* (2003). Eleanor Flexner and Ellen Fitzpatrick's *Century of Struggle: The Woman's Rights Movement in the United States*, enl. ed. (1996), surveys the condition of women in the late nineteenth century. The best study of the settlement house movement is Jean Bethke Elshtain's *Jane Addams and the Dream of American Democracy: A Life* (2002).

On Theodore Roosevelt and the conservation movement, see Douglas Brinkley's *The Wilderness Warrior: Theodore Roosevelt and the Crusade for America* (2009). The pivotal election of 1912 is covered in James Chace's *1912: Wilson, Roosevelt, Taft, and Debs—The Election That Changed the Country* (2004) and Sidney M. Milkis's *TR, the Progressive Party, and the Transformation of Democracy* (2009). Excellent biographies include Kathleen Dalton's *Theodore Roosevelt: A Strenuous Life* (2002) and H. W. Brands's *Woodrow Wilson* (2003). For banking developments, see Allan H. Meltzer's *A History of the Federal Reserve*, vol. 1, *1913–1951* (2003). The racial blind spot of Progressivism is assessed in David W. Southern's *The Progressive Era and Race: Reform and Reaction, 1900–1917* (2006).

## CHAPTER 24

A lucid overview of international events in the early twentieth century is Robert H. Ferrell's *Woodrow Wilson and World War I, 1917–1921* (1985). For a vivid account of U.S. intervention in Mexico, see Frederick Katz's *The Life and Times of Pancho Villa* (1999). On Wilson's stance toward war, see Robert W. Tucker's *Woodrow Wilson and the Great War: Reconsidering America's Neutrality, 1914–1917* (2007). An excellent biography is John Milton Cooper Jr.'s *Woodrow Wilson: A Biography* (2010).

For the European experience in the First World War, see Adam Hochschild's *To End All Wars: A Story of Loyalty and Rebellion, 1914–1918* (2011). Edward M. Coffman's *The War to End All Wars: The American Military Experience in World War I* (1968) is a detailed presentation of America's military involvement. See also Gary Mead's *The Doughboys: America and the First World War* (2000). For a survey of the impact of the war on the home front, see Meirion Harries and Susie Harries's *The Last Days of Innocence: America at War, 1917–1918* (1997). Maurine Weiner Greenwald's *Women, War, and Work: The Impact of World War I on Women Workers in the United States* (1980) discusses the role of women. Ronald Schaffer's *America in the Great War: The Rise of the War Welfare State* (1991) shows the effect of war mobilization on business organization. Richard Polenberg's *Fighting Faiths: The Abrams Case, the Supreme Court, and Free Speech* (1987) examines the prosecution of a case under the 1918 Sedition Act. See also Ernest Freeberg's *Democracy's Prisoner: Eugene V. Debs, the Great War, and the Right to Dissent* (2009).

How American diplomacy fared in the making of peace has received considerable attention. Thomas J. Knock interrelates domestic affairs and foreign relations in his explanation of Wilson's peacemaking in *To End All Wars: Woodrow Wilson and the Quest for a New World Order* (1992). See also John Milton Cooper Jr.'s *Breaking the Heart of the World: Woodrow Wilson and the Fight for the League of Nations* (2002).

The problems of the immediate postwar years are chronicled by a number of historians. The best overview is Ann Hagedorn's *Savage Peace: Hope and Fear in America, 1919* (2007). On the Spanish flu, see John M. Barry's *The Great Influenza: The Epic Story of the Deadliest Plague in History* (2004). Labor tensions are examined in David E. Brody's *Labor in Crisis: The Steel Strike of 1919* (1965) and Francis Russell's *A City in Terror: Calvin Coolidge and the 1919 Boston Police Strike* (1975). On racial strife, see Jan Voogd's *Race Riots and Resistance: The Red Summer of 1919* (2008). The fear of Communists is analyzed in Robert K. Murray's *Red Scare: A Study in National Hysteria, 1919–1920* (1955).

## CHAPTER 25

For a lively survey of the social and cultural changes during the interwar period, start with William E. Leuchtenburg's *The Perils of Prosperity, 1914–32,* 2nd ed. (1993). Even more comprehensive s Michael E. Parrish's *Anxious Decades: America in Prosperity and Depression, 1920–1941* (1992). The best introduction to the culture of the twenties remains Roderick Nash's *The Nervous Generation: American Thought, 1917–1930* (1990). See also Lynn Dumenil's *The Modern Temper: American Culture and Society in the 1920s* (1995).

John Higham's *Strangers in the Land: Patterns of American Nativism, 1860–1925,* 2nd ed. (2002) details the story of immigration restriction. The controversial Sacco and Vanzetti case is the focus of Moshik Temkin's *The Sacco-Vanzetti Affair: America on Trial* (2009). For analysis of the revival of Klan activity, see Thomas R. Pegram's *One Hundred Percent American: The Rebirth and Decline of the Ku Klux Klan in the 1920s* (2011). The best analysis of the Scopes trial is Edward J. Larson's *Summer for the Gods: The Scopes Trial and America's Continuing Debate over Science and Religion* (1997). On Prohibition, see Daniel Okrent's *Last Call: The Rise and Fall of Prohibition* (2011).

Woman suffrage is treated in Sara Hunter Graham's *Woman Suffrage and the New Democracy* (1996) and Kristi Anderson's *After Suffrage: Women in Partisan and Electoral Politics before the New Deal* (1996). The best study of the birth-control movement is Ellen Chesler's *Woman of Valor: Margaret Sanger and the Birth Control Movement in America* (1992). See Charles Flint Kellogg's *NAACP: A History of the National Association for the Advancement of Colored People* (1967) for his analysis of the pioneering court cases against racial discrimination. Nathan Irvin Huggins's *Harlem Renaissance* (1971) assesses the cultural impact of the Great Migration on New York City. The emergence of jazz is ably documented in Burton W. Peretti's *The Creation of Jazz: Music, Race, and Culture in Urban America* (1992). On the African American migration from the South, see James N. Gregory's *The Southern Diaspora: How the Great Migrations of Black and White Southerners Transformed America* (2005).

Scientific breakthroughs are analyzed in Manjit Kumar's *Quantum: Einstein, Bohr, and the Great Debate about the Nature of Reality* (2010). The best overview of cultural modernism in Europe is Peter Gay's *Modernism: The Lure of Heresy from Baudelaire to Beckett and Beyond* (2009). See also Stephen Kern's *The Culture of Time and Space, 1880–1918* (2003). A compelling biography the champion of modernist verse is David Moody's *Ezra Pount: Poet* (2007). On southern modernism, see Daniel Joseph Singal's *The War Within: From Victorian to Modernist Thought in the South, 1919–1945* (1982). Stanley Coben's *Rebellion against Victorianism: The Impetus for Cultural Change in 1920s America* (1991) surveys the appeal of modernism among writers, artists, and intellectuals.

## CHAPTER 26

A fine synthesis of events immediately following the First World War is Ellis W. Hawley's *The Great War and the Search for a Modern Order: A History of the American People and Their Institutions, 1917–1933*, 2nd ed. (1992). On the election of 1920, see David Pietrusza, *1920: The Year of the Six Presidents* (2006).

On Harding, see Robert K. Murray's *The Harding Era: Warren G. Harding and His Administration* (1969). On Coolidge, see Robert H. Ferrell's *The Presidency of Calvin Coolidge* (1998). On Hoover, see Martin L. Fausold's *The Presidency of Herbert C. Hoover* (1985). The Democratic candidate for president in 1928 is explored in Robert A. Slayton's *Empire Statesman: The Rise and Redemption of Al Smith* (2001). The influential secretary of the Treasury during the twenties is ably analyzed in David Cannadine's *Mellon: An American Life* (2006).

On the stock-market crash in 1929 see Maury Klein's *Rainbow's End: The Crash of 1929* (2000). Overviews of the depressed economy are found in Charles P. Kindleberger's *The World in Depression, 1929–1939*, rev. and enlarged ed. (1986) and Peter Fearon's *War, Prosperity, and Depression: The U.S. Economy, 1917–1945* (1987). John A. Garraty's *The Great Depression: An Inquiry into the Causes, Course, and Consequences of the Worldwide Depression of the Nineteen-Thirties* (1986) describes how people survived the Depression. On the removal of the Bonus Army, see Paul Dickson and Thomas B. Allen's *The Bonus Army: An American Epic* (2004).

## CHAPTER 27

A comprehensive overview of the New Deal is David M. Kennedy's *Freedom from Fear: The American People in Depression and War, 1929–1945* (1999). A lively biography of Franklin D. Roosevelt is H. W. Brands's *Traitor to His Class: The Privileged Life and Radical Presidency of Franklin Delano Roosevelt* (2009). The Roosevelt marriage is well described in Hazel Rowley's

*Franklin and Eleanor: An Extraordinary Marriage* (2011). On the first woman cabinet member, see Kirstin Downey's *The Woman behind the New Deal: The Life of Frances Perkins* (2009). The busy first year of the New Deal is ably detailed in Anthony J. Badger's *FDR: The First Hundred Days* (2008). Perhaps the most successful of the early New Deal programs is the focus of Neil M. Maher's *Nature's New Deal: The Civilian Conservation Corps and the Roots of the American Environmental Movement* (2008). On the political opponents of the New Deal, see Alan Brinkley's *Voices of Protest: Huey Long, Father Coughlin, and the Great Depression* (1982). Roosevelt's battle with the Supreme Court is detailed in Jeff Shesol's *Supreme Power: Franklin Roosevelt vs. The Supreme Court* (2010). The actual effects of the New Deal on the economy are detailed in Elliot A. Rosen's *Roosevelt, the Great Depression, and the Economics of Recovery* (2005).

A critical assessment of Roosevelt and the New Deal is Amity Schlaes's *The Forgotten Man* (2007). James N. Gregory's *American Exodus: The Dust Bowl Migration and Okie Culture in California* (1989) describes the migratory movement. On the environmental and human causes of the dust bowl, see Donald Worster, *Dust Bowl: The Southern Plains in the 1930s* (1979). On cultural life during the thirties, see Morris Dickstein's *Dancing in the Dark: A Cultural History of the Great Depression* (2009).

The best overview of diplomacy between the world wars remains Selig Adler's *The Uncertain Giant, 1921–1941: American Foreign Policy between the Wars* (1965). Robert Dallek's *Franklin D. Roosevelt and American Foreign Policy, 1932–1945* (1979) provides a judicious assessment of Roosevelt's foreign-policy initiatives during the thirties.

A noteworthy study is Waldo Heinrichs's *Threshold of War: Franklin D. Roosevelt and American Entry into World War II* (1988). See also David Reynolds's *From Munich to Pearl Harbor: Roosevelt's America and the Origins of the Second World War* (2001). On the surprise attack on Pearl Harbor, see Gordon W. Prange's *Pearl Harbor: The Verdict of History* (1986). Japan's perspective is described in Akira Iriye's *The Origins of the Second World War in Asia and the Pacific* (1987).

# CHAPTER 28

For sweeping surveys of the Second World War, consult Anthony Roberts's *The Storm of War: A New History of the Second World War* (2011) and Max Hastings's *The World at War, 1939–1945* (2011), while Charles B. MacDonald's *The Mighty Endeavor: The American War in Europe* (1986) concentrates on U.S. involvement. Roosevelt's wartime leadership is analyzed in Eric Larrabee's *Commander in Chief: Franklin Delano Roosevelt, His Lieutenants, and Their War* (1987).

Books on specific European campaigns include Anthony Beevor's *D-Day: The Battle for Normandy* (2010) and Charles B. MacDonald's *A Time for Trumpets: The Untold Story of the Battle of the Bulge* (1985). On the Allied commander, see Carlo D'Este's *Eisenhower: A Soldier's Life* (2002).

For the war in the Far East, see John Costello's *The Pacific War, 1941–1945* (1981), Ronald H. Spector's *Eagle against the Sun: The American War with Japan* (1985), John W. Dower's award-winning *War without Mercy: Race and Power in the Pacific War* (1986), and Dan van der Vat's *The Pacific Campaign: The U.S.-Japanese Naval War, 1941–1945* (1991).

An excellent overview of the war's effects on the home front is Michael C. C. Adams's *The Best War Ever: America and World War II* (1994). On economic effects, see Harold G. Vatter's *The U.S. Economy in World War II* (1985). Susan M. Hartmann's *The Home Front and Beyond:*

*American Women in the 1940s* (1982) treats the new working environment for women. Kenneth D. Rose tells the story of problems on the home front in *Myth and the Greatest Generation: A Social History of Americans in World War II* (2008). Neil A. Wynn looks at the participation of blacks in *The Afro-American and the Second World War* (1976). A more focused study of black airmen is J. Todd Moye's *Freedom Flyers: The Tuskegee Airmen of World War II* (2010). The story of the oppression of Japanese Americans is told in Greg Robinson's A Tragedy for Democracy: Japanese Confinement in North America (2009). On the development of the atomic bomb, see Jim Baggott's *The First War of Physics: The Secret History of the Atomic Bomb* (2010).

A sound introduction to U.S. diplomacy during the conflict can be found in Gaddis Smith's *American Diplomacy during the Second World War, 1941–1945* (1965). To understand the role that Roosevelt played in policy making, consult Warren F. Kimball's *The Juggler: Franklin Roosevelt as Wartime Statesman* (1991). The most important wartime summit is assessed in S. M. Plokhy's *Yalta: The Price of Peace* (2010). The issues and events that led to the deployment of atomic weapons are addressed in Martin J. Sherwin's *A World Destroyed: The Atomic Bomb and the Grand Alliance* (1975).

## CHAPTER 29

The cold war remains a hotly debated topic. The traditional interpretation is best reflected in John Lewis Gaddis's *The Cold War: A New History* (2005). Both superpowers, Gaddis argues, were responsible for causing the cold war, but the Soviet Union was more culpable. The revisionist perspective is represented by Gar Alperovitz's *Atomic Diplomacy: Hiroshima and Potsdam: The Use of the Atomic Bomb and the American Confrontation with Soviet Power,* 2nd ed. (1994). Alperovitz places primary responsibility for the conflict on the United States. Also see H. W. Brands's *The Devil We Knew: Americans and the Cold War* (1993) and Melvyn P. Leffler's *For the Soul of Mankind: The United States, the Soviet Union, and the Cold War* (2007). On the architect of the containment strategy, see John L. Gaddis, *George F. Kennan: An American Life* (2011).

Arnold A. Offner indicts Truman for clumsy statesmanship in *Another Such Victory: President Truman and the Cold War, 1945–1953* (2002). For a positive assessment of Truman's leadership, see Alonzo L. Hamby's *Beyond the New Deal: Harry S. Truman and American Liberalism* (1973) and Robert Dallek's *The Lost Peace: Leadership in a Time of Horror and Hope, 1945–1953* (2010). The domestic policies of the Fair Deal are treated in William C. Berman's *The Politics of Civil Rights in the Truman Administration* (1970), Richard M. Dalfiume's *Desegregation of the U.S. Armed Forces: Fighting on Two Fronts, 1939–1953* (1969), and Maeva Marcus's *Truman and the Steel Seizure Case: The Limits of Presidential Power* (1977). The most comprehensive biography of Truman is David McCullough's *Truman* (1992).

For an introduction to the tensions in Asia, see Akira Iriye's *The Cold War in Asia: A Historical Introduction* (1974). For the Korean conflict, see Callum A. MacDonald's *Korea: The War before Vietnam* (1986) and Max Hasting's *The Korean War* (1987).

The anti-Communist syndrome is surveyed in David Caute's *The Great Fear: The Anti-Communist Purge under Truman and Eisenhower* (1978). Arthur Herman's *Joseph McCarthy: Reexamining the Life and Legacy of America's Most Hated Senator* (2000) covers McCarthy himself. For a well-documented account of how the cold war was sustained by superpatriotism, intolerance, and suspicion, see Stephen J. Whitfield's *The Culture of the Cold War,* 2nd ed. (1996).

## CHAPTER 30

Two excellent overviews of social and cultural trends in the postwar era are William H. Chafe's *The Unfinished Journey: America since World War II*, 6th ed. (2006) and William E. Leuchtenburg's *A Troubled Feast: America since 1945*, rev. ed. (1979). For insights into the cultural life of the fifties, see Jeffrey Hart's *When the Going Was Good! American Life in the Fifties* (1982) and David Halberstam's *The Fifties* (1993).

The baby boom generation and its impact are vividly described in Paul C. Light's *Baby Boomers* (1988). The emergence of the television industry is discussed in Erik Barnouw's *Tube of Plenty: The Evolution of American Television*, 2nd rev. ed. (1990), and Ella Taylor's *Prime-Time Families: Television Culture in Postwar America* (1989).

A comprehensive account of the process of suburban development is Kenneth T. Jackson's *Crabgrass Frontier: The Suburbanization of the United States* (1985). Equally good is Tom Martinson's *American Dreamscape: The Pursuit of Happiness in Postwar Suburbia* (2000).

The middle-class ideal of family life in the fifties is examined in Elaine Tyler May's *Homeward Bound: American Families in the Cold War Era*, rev. ed. (2008). Thorough accounts of women's issues are found in Wini Breines's *Young, White, and Miserable: Growing Up Female in the Fifties* (1992). For an overview of the resurgence of religion in the fifties, see George M. Marsden's *Religion and American Culture*, 2nd ed. (2000).

A lively discussion of movies of the fifties can be found in Peter Biskind's *Seeing Is Believing: How Hollywood Taught Us to Stop Worrying and Love the Fifties* (1983). The origins and growth of rock and roll are surveyed in Carl Belz's *The Story of Rock*, 2nd ed. (1972). Thoughtful interpretive surveys of postwar literature include Josephine Hendin's *Vulnerable People: A View of American Fiction since 1945* (1978) and Malcolm Bradbury's *The Modern American Novel* (1983). The colorful Beats are brought to life in Steven Watson's *The Birth of the Beat Generation: Visionaries, Rebels, and Hipsters, 1944–1960* (1995).

Scholarship on the Eisenhower years is extensive. A carefully balanced overview of the period is Chester J. Pach Jr. and Elmo Richardson's *The Presidency of Dwight D. Eisenhower*, rev. ed. (1991). For the manner in which Eisenhower conducted foreign policy, see Robert A. Divine's *Eisenhower and the Cold War* (1981). Tom Wicker deems Eisenhower a better person than a president in *Dwight D. Eisenhower* (2002).

The best overview of American foreign policy since 1945 is Stephen E. Ambrose and Douglas G. Brinkley's *Rise to Globalism: American Foreign Policy since 1938*, 9th ed. (2011). For the buildup of U.S. involvement in Indochina, consult Lloyd C. Gardner's *Approaching Vietnam: From World War II through Dienbienphu, 1941–1954* (1988) and David L. Anderson's *Trapped by Success: The Eisenhower Administration and Vietnam, 1953–61* (1991). How the Eisenhower Doctrine came to be implemented is traced in Stephen E. Ambrose and Douglas G. Brinkley's *Rise to Globalism: American Foreign Policy since 1938*, 8th ed. (1997). The cold war strategy of the Eisenhower administration is the focus of Chris Tudda's *The Truth Is Our Weapon: The Rhetorical Diplomacy of Dwight D. Eisenhower and John Foster Dulles* (2006).

The impact of the Supreme Court during the fifties is the focus of Archibald Cox's *The Warren Court: Constitutional Decision as an Instrument of Reform* (1968). A masterly study of the important Warren Court decision on school desegregation is James T. Patterson's *Brown v. Board of Education: A Civil Rights Milestone and Its Troubled Legacy* (2001).

For the story of the early years of the civil rights movement, see Taylor Branch's *Parting the Waters: America in the King Years, 1954–1963* (1988), Robert Weisbrot's *Freedom Bound: A History of America's Civil Rights Movement* (1990), and David A. Nicholas's *A Matter of Justice: Eisenhower and the Beginning of the Civil Rights Revolution* (2007).

## CHAPTER 31

A dispassionate analysis of John F. Kennedy's life is Thomas C. Reeves's *A Question of Character: A Life of John F. Kennedy* (1991). The 1960 campaign is detailed in Gary A. Donaldson's *The First Modern Campaign: Kennedy, Nixon, and the Election of 1960* (2007). The best study of the Kennedy administration's domestic policies is Irving Bernstein's *Promises Kept: John F. Kennedy's New Frontier* (1991). For details on the still swirling conspiracy theories about the assassination, see David W. Belin's *Final Disclosure: The Full Truth about the Assassination of President Kennedy* (1988).

The most comprehensive biography of Lyndon B. Johnson is Robert Dallek's two-volume work, *Lone Star Rising: Lyndon Johnson and His Times, 1908–1960* (1991) and *Flawed Giant: Lyndon Johnson and His Times, 1961–1973* (1998). On the Johnson administration, see Vaughn Davis Bornet's *The Presidency of Lyndon B. Johnson* (1984).

Among the works that interpret liberal social policy during the sixties, John E. Schwarz's *America's Hidden Success: A Reassessment of Twenty Years of Public Policy* (1983) offers a glowing endorsement of Democratic programs. For a contrasting perspective, see Charles Murray's *Losing Ground: American Social Policy, 1950–1980*, rev. ed. (1994).

On foreign policy, see *Kennedy's Quest for Victory: American Foreign Policy, 1961–1963* (1989), edited by Thomas G. Paterson. To learn more about Kennedy's problems in Cuba, see Mark J. White's *Missiles in Cuba: Kennedy, Khrushchev, Castro and the 1962 Crisis* (1997). See also Aleksandr Fursenko and Timothy Naftali's *"One Hell of a Gamble": Khrushchev, Castro and Kennedy, 1958–1964* (1997).

American involvement in Vietnam has received voluminous treatment from all political perspectives. For an excellent overview, see Larry Berman's *Planning a Tragedy: The Americanization of the War in Vietnam* (1983) and *Lyndon Johnson's War: The Road to Stalemate in Vietnam* (1989), as well as Stanley Karnow's *Vietnam: A History*, 2nd rev. ed. (1997). An analysis of policy making concerning the Vietnam War is David M. Barrett's *Uncertain Warriors: Lyndon Johnson and His Vietnam Advisors* (1993). A fine account of the military involvement is Robert D. Schulzinger's *A Time for War: The United States and Vietnam, 1941–1975* (1997). On the legacy of the Vietnam War, see Arnold R. Isaacs's *Vietnam Shadows: The War, Its Ghosts, and Its Legacy* (1997).

Many scholars have dealt with various aspects of the civil rights movement and race relations in the sixties. See especially Carl M. Brauer's *John F. Kennedy and the Second Reconstruction* (1977), David J. Garrow's *Bearing the Cross: Martin Luther King, Jr., and the Southern Christian Leadership Conference* (1986), and Adam Fairclough's *To Redeem the Soul of America: The Southern Christian Leadership Conference and Martin Luther King, Jr.* (1987). William H. Chafe's *Civilities and Civil Rights: Greensboro, North Carolina, and the Black Struggle for Freedom* (1980) details the original sit-ins. An award-winning study of racial and economic inequality in a representative American city is Thomas J. Sugrue's *The Origins of the Urban Crisis: Race and Inequality in Postwar Detroit* (1996).

## CHAPTER 32

An engaging overview of the cultural trends of the sixties is Maurice Isserman and Michael Kazin's *America Divided: The Civil War of the 1960s*, 3rd ed. (2007). The New Left is assessed in Irwin Unger's *The Movement: A History of the American New Left, 1959–1972* (1974). On the Students for a Democratic Society, see Kirkpatrick Sale's *SDS* (1973) and Allen J. Matusow's *The*

*Unraveling of America: A History of Liberalism in the 1960s* (1984). Also useful is Todd Gitlin's *The Sixties: Years of Hope, Days of Rage*, rev. ed. (1993).

Two influential assessments of the counterculture by sympathetic commentators are Theodore Roszak's *The Making of a Counter-culture: Reflections on the Technocratic Society and Its Youthful Opposition* (1969) and Charles A. Reich's *The Greening of America: How the Youth Revolution Is Trying to Make America Livable* (1970). A good scholarly analysis that takes the hippies seriously is Timothy Miller's *The Hippies and American Values* (1991).

The best study of the women's liberation movement is Ruth Rosen's *The World Split Open: How the Modern Women's Movement Changed America*, rev. ed. (2006). The organizing efforts of Cesar Chavez are detailed in Ronald B. Taylor's *Chavez and the Farm Workers* (1975). The struggles of Native Americans for recognition and power are sympathetically described in Stan Steiner's *The New Indians* (1968).

The best overview of the seventies and eighties is James T. Patterson's *Restless Giant: The United States from Watergate to Bush v. Gore* (2005). On Nixon, see Melvin Small's thorough analysis in *The Presidency of Richard Nixon* (1999). A good slim biography is Elizabeth Drew's *Richard M. Nixon* (2007). For an overview of the Watergate scandal, see Stanley I. Kutler's *The Wars of Watergate: The Last Crisis of Richard Nixon* (1990). For the way the Republicans handled foreign affairs, consult Tad Szulc's *The Illusion of Peace: Foreign Policy in the Nixon Years* (1978).

The Communist takeover of Vietnam and the end of American involvement there are traced in Larry Berman's *No Peace, No Honor: Nixon, Kissinger, and Betrayal in Vietnam* (2001). William Shawcross's *Sideshow: Kissinger, Nixon and the Destruction of Cambodia*, rev. ed. (2002), deals with the broadening of the war, while Larry Berman's *Planning a Tragedy: The Americanization of the War in Vietnam* (1982) assesses the final impact of U.S. involvement. The most comprehensive treatment of the anti-war movement is Tom Wells's *The War Within: America's Battle over Vietnam* (1994).

A comprehensive treatment of the Ford administration is contained in John Robert Greene's *The Presidency of Gerald R. Ford* (1995). The best overview of the Carter administration is Burton I. Kaufman's *The Presidency of James Earl Carter, Jr.*, 2nd rev. ed. (2006). A work more sympathetic to the Carter administration is John Dumbrell's *The Carter Presidency: A Re-evaluation*, 2nd ed. (1995). Gaddis Smith's *Morality, Reason, and Power: American Diplomacy in the Carter Years* (1986) provides an overview. Background on how the Middle East came to dominate much of American policy is found in William B. Quandt's *Decade of Decisions: American Policy toward the Arab-Israeli Conflict, 1967–1976* (1977).

# CHAPTER 33

Two brief accounts of Reagan's presidency are David Mervin's *Ronald Reagan and the American Presidency* (1990) and Michael Schaller's *Reckoning with Reagan: America and Its President in the 1980s* (1992). More substantial biographies are John Patrick Diggins's *Ronald Reagan: Fate, Freedom, and the Making of History* (2007) and Richard Reeves's *President Reagan: The Triumph of Imagination* (2005). The best political analysis is Robert M. Collins's *Transforming America: Politics and Culture during the Reagan Years* (2007). An excellent analysis of the 1980 election is Andrew E. Busch's *Reagan's Victory: The Presidential Election of 1980 and the Rise of the Right* (2005). A more comprehensive summary of the Reagan years is Sean Wilentz's *The Age of Reagan: A History, 1974–2008* (2008).

The story of the rise of modern conservatism is well told in Patrick Allitt's *The Conservatives: Ideas and Personalities throughout American History* (2009) and Michael Schaller's *Right Turn: American Life in the Reagan-Bush Era, 1980–1992* (2007).

On Reaganomics, see David A. Stockman's *The Triumph of Politics: Why the Reagan Revolution Failed* (1986) and Robert Lekachman's *Greed Is Not Enough: Reaganomics* (1982). On the issue of arms control, see Strobe Talbott's *Deadly Gambits: The Reagan Administration and the Stalemate in Nuclear Arms Control* (1984).

For Reagan's foreign policy in Central America, see James Chace's *Endless War: How We Got Involved in Central America—and What Can Be Done* (1984) and Walter LaFeber's *Inevitable Revolutions: The United States in Central America*, 2nd ed. (1993). Insider views of Reagan's foreign policy are offered in Alexander M. Haig Jr.'s *Caveat: Realism, Reagan, and Foreign Policy* (1984) and Caspar W. Weinberger's *Fighting for Peace: Seven Critical Years in the Pentagon* (1990).

On Reagan's second term, see Jane Mayer and Doyle McManus's *Landslide: The Unmaking of the President, 1984–1988* (1988). For a masterly work on the Iran-Contra affair, see Theodore Draper's *A Very Thin Line: The Iran Contra Affairs* (1991). Several collections of essays include varying assessments of the Reagan years. Among these are *The Reagan Revolution?* (1988), edited by B. B. Kymlicka and Jean V. Matthews; *The Reagan Presidency: An Incomplete Revolution?* (1990), edited by Dilys M. Hill, Raymond A. Moore, and Phil Williams, and *Looking Back on the Reagan Presidency* (1990), edited by Larry Berman.

On the 1988 campaign, see Jack W. Germond and Jules Witcover's *Whose Broad Stripes and Bright Stars? The Trivial Pursuit of the Presidency, 1988* (1989) and Sidney Blumenthal's *Pledging Allegiance: The Last Campaign of the Cold War* (1990). For a social history of the decade, see John Ehrman's *The Eighties: America in the Age of Reagan* (2005).

## CHAPTER 34

Analysis of the Clinton years can be found in Joe Klein's *The Natural: The Misunderstood Presidency of Bill Clinton* (2002). Clinton's impeachment is assessed in Richard A. Posner's *An Affair of State: The Investigation, Impeachment, and Trial of President Clinton* (1999).

On changing demographic trends, see Sam Roberts's *Who We Are Now: The Changing Face of America in the Twenty-First Century* (2004). On social and cultural life in the nineties, see Haynes Johnson's *The Best of Times: America in the Clinton Years* (2001). Economic and technological changes are assessed in Daniel T. Rogers's *Age of Fracture* (2011). The onset and growth of the AIDS epidemic are traced in *And the Band Played On: Politics, People, and the AIDS Epidemic*, 20th anniversary ed. (2007), by Randy Shilts.

Aspects of fundamentalist and apocalyptic movements are the subject of Paul Boyer's *When Time Shall Be No More: Prophecy Belief in Modern American Culture* (1992), George M. Marsden's *Understanding Fundamentalism and Evangelicalism*, new ed. (2006), and Ralph E. Reed's *Politically Incorrect: The Emerging Faith Factor in American Politics* (1994).

On the invention of the computer and the Internet, see Paul E. Ceruzzi's *A History of Modern Computing*, 2nd ed. (2003), and Janet Abbate's *Inventing the Internet* (1999). The booming economy of the nineties is well analyzed in Joseph E. Stiglitz's *The Roaring Nineties: A New History of the World's Most Prosperous Decade* (2003). On the rising stress within the workplace, see Jill Andresky Fraser's *White-Collar Sweatshop: The Deterioration of Work and Its Rewards in Corporate America* (2001). Aspects of corporate restructuring and downsizing are the subjects of Bennett Harrison's *Lean and Mean: The Changing Landscape of Corporate Power in the Age of Flexibility* (1994).

For further treatment of the end of the cold war, see Michael R. Beschloss and Strobe Talbott's *At the Highest Levels: The Inside Story of the End of the Cold War* (1993) and Richard Crockatt's *The Fifty Years War: The United States and the Soviet Union in World Politics, 1941–1991* (1995). On the Persian Gulf conflict, see Lester H. Brune's *America and the Iraqi Crisis, 1990–1992: Origins and Aftermath* (1993). On the transformation of American foreign policy, see James Mann's *Rise of the Vulcans: The History of Bush's War Cabinet* (2004), Claes G. Ryn's *America the Virtuous: The Crisis of Democracy and the Quest for Empire* (2003), and Stephen M. Walt's *Taming American Power: The Global Response to U.S. Primacy* (2005).

The disputed 2000 presidential election is the focus of Jeffrey Toobin's *Too Close to Call: The Thirty-Six-Day Battle to Decide the 2000 Election* (2001). On the Bush presidency, see *The Presidency of George W. Bush: A First Historical Assessment,* edited by Julian E. Zelizer (2010). On the 9/11 attacks and their aftermath, see *The Age of Terror: America and the World after September 11,* edited by Strobe Talbott and Nayan Chanda (2001).

For a devastating account of the Bush administration by a White House insider, see Scott McClellan's *What Happened: Inside the Bush White House and Washington's Culture of Deception* (2008). On the historic 2008 election, see Michael Nelson's *The Elections of 2008* (2009). An excellent early interpretation of the nation's first African American president is Pete Souza's *The Rise of Barack Obama* (2010).

The Tea Party movement is assessed in Theda Skocpol and Vanessa Williamson's *The Tea Party and the Remaking of Republican Conservatism* (2012) and Elizabeth Price Foley's *The Tea Party: Three Principles* (2012).

# CREDITS

CHAPTER 17: **p. 704**: Library of Congress; **p. 706**: Library of Congress; **p. 709**: Corbis; **p. 711**: Library of Congress; **p. 714**: Bettmann/Corbis; **p. 715**: Library of Congress; **p. 717**: Library of Congress; **p. 722**: National Archives; **p. 725**: Granger Collection; **p. 727**: Bettmann/Corbis; **p. 728**: Library of Congress; **p. 731**: Library of Congress; **p. 732**: Library of Congress; **p. 735**: Library of Congress; **p. 737**: Library of Congress; **p. 740**: Granger Collection; **p. 741**: Library of Congress.

CHAPTER 18: **p. 747**: Granger Collection; **p. 748**: Granger Collection; **p. 751**: Library of Congress; **p. 756**: Bettmann/Corbis; **p. 757**: Union Pacific Museum; **p. 759**: Collection of the New-York Historical Society; **p. 760**: National Archives; **p. 761**: Granger Collection; **p. 762**: Warder Collection; **p. 763**: American Petroleum Institute Historical Photo Collection; **p. 764**: Carnegie Library of Pittsburgh; **p. 765**: Keystone-Mast Collection; **p. 766**: National Portrait Gallery, Smithsonian Institution/Art Resource, NY; **p. 767**: Carnegie Library of Pittsburgh; **p. 768**: Granger Collection; **p. 770**: Bettmann/Corbis; **p. 773**: Granger Collection; **p. 775**: T.V. Powderly Photographic Collection, The American Catholic History Research Center University Archives, The Catholic University of America, Washington, D.C; **p. 777**: F&A Archive/The Art Archive at Art Resource, NY; **p. 779**: Bettmann/Corbis; **p. 782**: Library of Congress; **p. 784**: Bettmann/Corbis; **p. 785**: Walter P. Reuther Library, Wayne State University.

CHAPTER 19: **p. 790**: Library of Congress; **p. 794**: Granger Collection; **p. 797**: Granger Collection; **p. 799**: Kansas State Historical Society; **p. 801**: Bettmann/Corbis; **p. 807**: Warder Collection; **p. 808**: SPC Plateau Nez Perce NAA 4876 00942000, Smithsonian Institution National Anthropological Archives; **p. 811**: Bettmann/Corbis; **p. 812**: National Archives; **p. 814**: Corbis; **p. 816**: Western Historical Collections University of Oklahoma Library.

CHAPTER 20: **p. 820**: Library of Congress; **p. 824**: The Art Archive / Culver Pictures/Art Resource; **p. 827**: Bettmann/Corbis; **p. 827**: The Bryon Collection, Museum of the City of New York; **p. 829**: William Williams Papers, Manuscripts and Archives Division, The New York Public Library, Astor, Lenox and Tilden Foundations; **p. 832**: The Denver Public Library, Western History Collection; **p. 833**: Bettmann/Corbis; **p. 836**: Brown Brothers; **p. 837**: Old York Library/Avery Library, Columbia University; **p. 838**: Library of Congress; **p. 840**: Bettmann/Corbis; **p. 842**: Special Collections, Vassar College Libraries; **p. 843**: Bettmann/Corbis; **p. 844**: National Library of Medicine; **p. 845**: John Carter Brown Library.

CHAPTER 21: **p. 848**: Library of Congress; **p. 850**: Library of Congress; **p. 854**: Library of Congress; **p. 857**: Warder Collection; **p. 859**: Warder Collection; **p. 860**: Bettmann/Corbis; **p. 861**: Warder Collection; **p. 862**: Bettmann/Corbis; **p. 864**: Library of Congress; **p. 867**: Wooten Studios; **p. 869**: Kansas State Historical Society; **p. 871**: Nebraska State Historical Society; **p. 872**: Library of Congress; **p. 875**: Library of Congress; **p. 882**: Granger Collection; **p. 883**: Photograph Courtesy of the

New Hanover County Public Library; **p. 885**: Special Collections, University of Chicago Library; **p. 886**: Library of Congress; **p. 887**: Warder Collection.

**CHAPTER 22: p. 893**: Library of Congress; **p. 895**: Library of Congress; **p. 897**: Bettmann/Corbis; **p. 901**: Bettmann/Corbis; **p. 902**: Adoc-photos/Art Resource, NY; **p. 903**: Hawaii State Archives; **p. 905**: Library of Congress; **p. 906**: Bettmann/Corbis; **p. 914**: National Archives; **p. 915**: Corporal George J. Vennage c/o Ohio State University Rare Books and Manuscripts Library; **p. 918**: Library of Congress; **p. 920**: Granger Collection; **p. 921**: Bettmann/Corbis; **p. 924**: Granger Collection; **p. 925**: Bettmann/Corbis; **p. 927**: Bettmann/Corbis.

**CHAPTER 23: p. 932**: Library of Congress; **p. 938**: University of Illinois at Chicago; **p. 939**: Granger Collection; **p. 943**: Granger Collection; **p. 946**: Library of Congress; **p. 947**: Corbis; **p. 948**: Bettmann/Corbis; **p. 952 (top)**: Collection of the New-York Historical Society; (**bottom**): Library of Congress; **p. 954**: Bettmann/Corbis; **p. 955**: Library of Congress; **p. 956**: Bettmann/Corbis; **p. 957**: Bettmann/Corbis; **p. 958**: Library of Congress; **p. 961**: Library of Congress; **p. 962**: Library of Congress; **p. 964**: Warder Collection; **p. 968**: Warder Collection; **p. 971**: Corbis; **p. 974**: Granger Collection.

**CHAPTER 24: p. 980**: Library of Congress; **p. 983**: Bettmann/Corbis; **p. 985**: Alamy; **p. 986**: Granger Collection; **p. 987**: Warder Collection; **p. 990**: The *New York Times*; **p. 991**: Rollin Kirby; **p. 993**: Bettmann/Corbis; **p. 996**: Bettmann/Corbis; **p. 998**: Bettmann/Corbis; **p. 1000**: Everett Collection; **p. 1002**: Bettmann/Corbis; **p. 1004**: National Archives; **p. 1006**: Warder Collection; **p. 1009**: Mary Evans Picture Library; **p. 1010**: Courtesy of the "Ding" Darling Wildlife Society; **p. 1016**: Bettmann/Corbis; **p. 1018**: Chicago History Museum.

**CHAPTER 25: p. 1022**: Bettmann/Corbis; **p. 1025**: Bettmann/Corbis; **p. 1027**: Bettmann/Corbis; **p. 1030**: Bettmann/Corbis; **p. 1033**: Bettmann/Corbis; **p. 1035**: Bettmann/Corbis; **p. 1038**: NYPL Digital; **p. 1040**: Art © Heirs of Aaron Douglas/Licensed by VAGA, New York, NY *Into Bondage*, 1936 (oil on canvas), Douglas, Aaron (1899–1979) / Corcoran Gallery of Art, Washington D.C., USA / Museum Purchase and partial gift of Thurlow Evans Tibbs, Jr. The Evans-Tibbs Collection/Bridgeman Art Library; **p. 1041**: Ramsey Archive; **p. 1042**: AP Photo; **p. 1043**: Library of Congress; **p. 1045**: Bettmann/Corbis; **p. 1046**: Bettmann/Corbis; **p. 1048**: From the Collections of The Henry Ford Museum; **p. 1051**: Warder Collection; **p. 1053**: Brown Brothers; **p. 1056**: Image copyright © The Metropolitan Museum of Art / Art Resource, NY. © 2012 Estate of Pablo Picasso/Artists Rights Society (ARS), New York.

**CHAPTER 26: p. 1060**: Bettmann/Corbis; **p. 1063**: Corbis; **p. 1067**: AP Photo; **p. 1070**: *The Washington Post*. Reprinted with permission; **p. 1072**: Hulton Archive/Getty Images; **p. 1076**: Gehl Company/Corbis; **p. 1077**: Bettmann/Corbis; **p. 1079**: David J. & Janice L. Frent Collection/Corbis; **p. 1080**: Herbert Hoover Presidential Library; **p. 1083**: AP Photo; **p. 1087**: Granger Collection; **p. 1088**: Bettmann/Corbis; **p. 1092**: *New York Daily News*; **p. 1094**: AP Photo.

**CHAPTER 27: p. 1100**: Bettmann/Corbis; **p. 1103**: National Archives; **p. 1104**: Bettmann/Corbis; **p. 1108**: Library of Congress; **p. 1109**: Bettmann/Corbis; **p. 1111**: National Archives; **p. 1112**: Library of Congress; **p. 1115**: Library of Congress; **p. 1116**: Bettmann/Corbis; **p. 1119**: Bettmann/Corbis; **p. 1121**: Hulton Archives/Getty Images; **p. 1122**: Bettmann/Corbis; **p. 1124**: Bettmann/Corbis; **p. 1126**: Robert Holmes/Corbis; **p. 1127**: Library of Congress; **p. 1130**: Corbis; **p. 1132**: 1936, *The Washington Post*; **p. 1134**: Bettmann/Corbis; **p. 1138**: Bettmann/Corbis.

**CHAPTER 28: p. 1142**: Bettmann/Corbis; **p. 1145**: National Archives; **p. 1147**: Imperial War Museum, London; **p. 1150**: 1938, *The Washington Post*; **p. 1154**: British Information Services; **p. 1155**: Granger Collection; **p. 1156**: Bettmann/Corbis; **p. 1162**: Library of Congress; **p. 1164**: Warder Collection; **p. 1167**: Swim Ink LLC/Corbis; **p. 1168**: Granger Collection; **p. 1169**: Library of

Congress; **p. 1171**: AP Photo; **p. 1172**: National Archives; **p. 1174**: Bettmann/Corbis; **p. 1175**: Russell Lee/Getty Images; **p. 1181**: AP Photo; **p. 1182**: Eisenhower Presidential Library; **p. 1184**: National Archives; **p. 1188**: National Archives; **p. 1190**: Hulton Archives/Getty Images; **p. 1191**: National Archives; **p. 1194**: National Archives; **p. 1195**: National Archives; **p. 1198**: Bettmann/Corbis; **p. 1199**: Hulton Archives/Getty Images.

CHAPTER 29: **p. 1205**: Bill Eppridge/Getty Images; **p. 1207**: Peter Turnley/Corbis; **p. 1209**: Bettmann/Corbis; **p. 1211**: University of Louisville; **p. 1214 (left)**: Collections of the New York Public Library, Astor, Lenox and Tilden Foundations; **(right)**: Granger Collection; **p. 1217**: Herman Landshoff; **p. 1221**: Library of Congress; **p. 1223**: Hartford Courant; **p. 1227**: Hy Peskin/Getty Images; **p. 1228**: 1948, *The Washington Post*; **p. 1229**: Bettmann/Corbis; **p. 1230 (top)**: AP Photo; **(bottom)**: Bettmann/Corbis; **p. 1237**: Bettmann/Corbis; **p. 1239**: Bettmann/Corbis; **p. 1240**: Yale Joel/Getty Images.

CHAPTER 30: **p. 1246**: Hulton Archives/Getty Images; **p. 1249**: Time & Life Pictures/Getty Images; **p. 1251**: William Joseph O'Keefe Collection, Veterans History Project, Library of Congress; **p. 1253**: AP Photo; **p. 1254**: Hulton Archives/Getty Images; **p. 1256**: Library of Congress; **p. 1259**: Image copyright © The Metropolitan Museum of Art / Art Resource, NY; **p. 1260**: Fogg Art Museum, Harvard University; **p. 1262**: William Gottlieb/Corbis; **p. 1263**: Bernard Gotfryd /Getty Images; **p. 1264**: Time & Life Pictures/Getty Images; **p. 1266**: Hulton Archives/Getty Images; **p. 1267**: AP Photo; **p. 1269**: Library of Congress; **p. 1274**: AP Photo; **p. 1275**: University of Louisville; **p. 1277**: Granger Collection; **p. 1279**: Charles Moore/Black Star; **p. 1281**: Bettmann/Corbis; **p. 1284**: Herb Block Foundation; **p. 1286**: AP Photo; **p. 1288**: AP Photo; **p. 1293**: Detroit News; **p. 1295**: AP Photo; **p. 1296**: AP Photo.

CHAPTER 31: **p. 1300**: Bettmann/Corbis; **p. 1303**: Time & Life Pictures/Getty Images; **p. 1308**: John G. Moebes/Corbis; **p. 1310**: Time & Life Pictures/Getty Images; **p. 1311**: AP Photo; **p. 1313**: Hulton Archives/Getty Images; **p. 1316**: Bettmann/Corbis; **p. 1317**: National Archives; **p. 1320**: Hulton Archives/Getty Images; **p. 1322**: National Archives; **p. 1325**: AP Photo; **p. 1327**: Cartoon by Victor (Vicky) Weisz, The New Statesman; **p. 1330**: Bettmann/Corbis; **p. 1332**: George Ballis/Take Stock Photos; **p. 1336**: Bettmann/Corbis; **p. 1338**: © 1963, *The Star-Ledger*, All rights reserved, Reprinted with permission; **p. 1343**: Bettmann/Corbis; **p. 1344**: Jack Kightlinger, LBJ Library and Museum; **p. 1346**: Bettmann/Corbis.

CHAPTER 32: **p. 1350**: Bettmann/Corbis; **p. 1352**: Ted Streshinsky/Corbis; **p. 1355**: AP Photo; **p. 1356**: © Roger Malloch/Magnum Photos; **p. 1358**: John Dominis/Getty Images; **p. 1359**: Warder Collection; **p. 1361**: Bettmann/Corbis; **p. 1363**: H. William Tetlow/Getty Images; **p. 1365**: AP Photo; **p. 1366**: Bettmann/Corbis; **p. 1372**: Bettmann/Corbis; **p. 1374**: AP Photo; **p. 1375**: Bettmann/Corbis; **p. 1377**: National Archives; **p. 1380**: Howard Ruffner/Time & Life Pictures/Getty Images; **p. 1382**: John Dominis/Getty Images; **p. 1384**: AP Photo; **p. 1389**: AP Photo; **p. 1391**: AP Photo; **p. 1394**: Dirck Halstead/Time Life Pictures/Getty Images; **p. 1395**: Nik Wheeler/Corbis.

CHAPTER 33: **p. 1400**: Robert Maass/Corbis; **p. 1401**: National Archives; **p. 1405**: AP Photo; **p. 1408**: Kaveh Kazemi/Corbis; **p. 1412**: Bettmann/Corbis; **p. 1416**: Bettmann/Corbis; **p. 1418**: Wally McNamee/Corbis; **p. 1422**: Bettmann/Corbis; **p. 1424**: Los Angeles Times Syndicate; **p. 1428**: Bettmann/Corbis; **p. 1431**: Library of Congress; **p. 1432**: Bettmann/Corbis; **p. 1434**: Mark Thiesson © 1992 The NAMES Project; **p. 1435**: AP Photo; **p. 1437**: Black Star Stock Photo; **p. 1441**: Woodfin Camp; **p. 1442**: AP Photo; **p. 1445**: Bettmann/Corbis.

CHAPTER 34: **p. 1450**: Smiley N. Pool/Dallas Morning News/Corbis; **p. 1451**: AP Photo; **p. 1455**: Chris Wilkins/Getty Images; **p. 1457**: AP Photo; **p. 1458**: AP Photo; **p. 1460**: Richard Ellis/AFP/Getty Images; **p. 1462**: AP Photo; **p. 1466**: AP Photo; **p. 1467**: AP Photo; **p. 1471**: Najlah Feanny/Corbis;

# INDEX

Page numbers in *italics* refer to illustrations.